Dance Upon the Shore

DANCE UPON THE SHORE

The National Library of Poetry

Richard Schaub, Editor

Dance Upon the Shore

Library of Congress
Cataloging in Publication Data

ISBN 1-57553-404-5

Manufactured in The United States of America by
Watermark Press
One Poetry Plaza
Owings Mills, MD 21117.

Editor's Note

The freedom of motion is apparent in the natural world. The bubbling crest of an ocean wave folds in on itself until it rests comfortably in the pull of the tide. A gentle breeze carries a soft mist languidly up the coast kissing the glass panes of a beachfront cottage, beading silent drops on its smooth surfaces. A sail breathes with the wind while the vessel's sharp rudder cuts the frothy sea with a seamless incision. Motion in nature is the spark of a poet's intention. In order to accurately represent the beauty of the natural world, a poet must be aware of the infinite complexities the natural world offers.

The search for new forms of expression and creative artistry is a daily struggle for writers. In order to slip a subtle nuance into his or her writing, a poet must be able to accurately reflect the "true nature of things" as well as to show us what we may otherwise have been incapable of seeing. Perhaps the most liberating form of creative motion is the dance. Dancing is an ancient ritual of motion that embodies the ideal of what a poet hopes to achieve in the poem: freedom from inhibitions and beauty in movement. Like poetry, the art of dancing has evolved through a strong tradition which helps to further shape the development of the form. Many artists find it difficult to freely express themselves under the shadow of such a strong tradition. One of the great innovators in modern dance who managed to break from the established order was Isadora Duncan (1878-1927) who struggled all of her life to carve her niche in the somewhat conservative world of dance. Despite very critical opposition to her bold dancing style, Duncan's grace and agility inspired President Theodore Roosevelt to comment "Isadora Duncan seems to me as innocent as a child dancing through the garden in the morning sunshine and picking the beautiful flowers of her fantasy."

While she perhaps did not receive in her lifetime the credit she deserved for her creativity, Isadora Duncan is now highly regarded as a leading and inspirational precursor to modern dance. As is the case with many artists, Duncan's vision far exceeded the established ideals of her contemporaries.

While motion is often the spark of a poet's intention, creativity is the fuel that will ignite into a bright burst of originality. Heidi Bloem's excellent depiction of the complex relationship between a mental patient and a health-care worker clearly shines with a life of its own. In "Treatment" (page 1) we see both the striking similarities and sharp contrasts of these memorable characters. With clear and lucid imagery, Bloem describes the medication of the patient in relation to the patient's own chemically balanced mental state.

> *Yellow, chalky pills make lolling circles in white paper cups,*
> *like Weebles wobbling (but they don't fall down) on a tray*
> *precariously balanced.*

The poet does a wonderful job of pulling together these two characters by reflecting the inherent nature of the "patient" existing in the health-care giver. The persona (the health-care worker) often speaks in a very simple and repetitious tone that at times has a haunting, and yet soothing sound to it. In the first stanza, the persona sounds almost child-like in his or her description:

> *Up the hall, down the hall, I look for Ted;*
> *three stocking hats, four-day beard, one trench coat, and a face with*
> *a map of Schizophrenia's long, scenic vacation etched in grooves and lines.*

The last few lines of the poem not only directly correlate the persona and "Ted" through the disturbing rantings of the persona, but they also reveal the mission that both parties undertake. While Ted struggles with schizophrenia, the persona struggles with trying to help Ted work through his illness.

> *In an unspoken pact, we perform the rite that helps keep the voices at bay.*
> *Later, he may vomit and his mouth will feel like burning sand, but to*
> *keep the voices quiet we will try, we will try, every day, he and I.*

It is easy to see that while Ted is struggling with the voices of his disordered mind, the persona is attempting to quiet the disturbed voice of Ted. Bloem does a marvelous job forging unforgettable imagery in this work. With careful articulation the poet paints the haunting landscapes that create the basis for Ted's illness.

> *Ted's out back, smoking his relief, pulling the nicotine and tar in*
> *hard, get it there, get it there, it burns but it's oh so nice, it*
> *makes you forget the crawling, the eyes, the wires.*

While "Treatment" does indeed portray a rather disquieting vision of the mind of a mentally ill person, it does so without being overly sympathetic, or condescending in its pity. This has the advantage of revealing both the persona and Ted as ordinary humans struggling with a common but conquerable problem. Thus Bloem removes a portion of the fear from the situation and replaces it with human empathy and understanding. Because of Heidi Bloem's in-depth and multi-dimensional character study in the creation of her poem "Treatment," she has been awarded the Grand Prize in the contest held in association with the anthology *Dance Upon the Shore*.

Priya Narasimhan's eloquent work "waxing" (page 298) also reveals a great deal about the processes of the mind and how these processes help shape an individual's mental state. With incredible detail, the poet explains the intricate process of how a philosophical viewpoint is formed (or in this case, not formed) from the ashes of older ones. Narasimhan's eye for detail is photographic in its clarity. The poet manages to conjure surreal and fantastic imagery that is both exceptional and sharp. The first stanza reveals the pain and difficulty of attaining mental growth in a world where nothing is certain. This is evident in the poet's unique description of the persona's dilemma, being unable to shape permanent truths due to the existence of constant, perpetual change.

> *stretching the skin between my bones*
> *cleaning the spaces inside my heart*
> *dabbing at tears not yet fallen*
> *i find a way to flatten out meanings*

The poet further reveals the inconsistencies of permanent truths by displaying, through a clever metaphor, the cycle of constant change. That is, every broken truth is created from a new thought process that in effect rips the shrouds that "blanket" truths. However, every new truth is then also torn, leaving the persona in a state of permanent change.

> *thoughts that tried*
> *so hard to try*
> *rip like dusty linen sheets*
> *that blanket my truths*
> *leaving them stark and raw;*
> *the breaking of thoughts*
> *seems to tear at them too.*

This prompts the rather ominous question which ends the poem revealing that change is escapable, as well as a catalyst for mental growth.

> *is this what it is to grow*
> *out of myself?*

"Waxing" addresses in a very philosophical way the function of change in our lives. "Father's Smile," (page 196) by Dan Truong, deals with change in a much less abstract and more concrete way. The persona describes his aging father and the rather costly price he has paid for a life of constant work.

> *His fingerprints were stolen from him as he lay wasted*
> *tired from sand papering his hands against dishes and floors*
>
> *He smiles sheepishly, like a fool to his king*

Truong's sharp and carefully constructed images work together to create a lasting and somewhat disturbing portrait of a shell of a man who has given the best years of his life to his occupation.

> *Situated by the pale yellow light*
> *a raisin wrinkled-faced man*
> *warmed by the soft beams from the muddy brown lamp*
> *is caught in a solemn rapture*
> *as he stares into a familiar empty wall*

Truong creates a visually arresting work of art with an excellent economy of language showing the poet's skill as a wordsmith. Brevity in poetry is a gift left to the truly skilled. Just as a picture is worth a thousand words, so too is excellent verse worth more than its weight in vowels and consonants. Ann Robbins short (only eight lines) but compact poem "Octet: Dylan Thomas" (page 344) is a poem that shows that excellence in poetry is not reserved for the verbose.

> *What servant god has carved the naked howl,*
> *Curved root through leaf to sculpt a verbing ram?*
> *What tongue and fork with break have made this jowl*
> *The breather of the drunken anagram?*
> *In flooding dram, what nerved the seed and pinned*
> *The verb into the wounds, made waking scars?*
> *He's not mute to mock the living wind*
> *That shock has cast a curtain round the stars.*

Taking its pretext from the song "Ole Mulholland," by rock-singer Frank Black, Margaret Phillips' poem "Frank Black's Got It Right" (page 131) presents an interesting and captivating look at the rural areas of Los Angeles.

> *there's a stretch of road i know*
> *it can be found in the backyard of Los Angeles*
> *lapping at the dusty feet of desert mountains*
> *and frank whirls me over asphalt, sunsplit and leaking,*

Phillip's close attention to colorful details makes this poem visually stunning. As the persona soaks in the scenery of the desert landscape, the reader also absorbs the full scope and breadth of the view.

> *nights spent up on the fire roads above old mulholland gazing down*
> *and out across the bowl of the city thrown slantways by too much love*
> *i have realized the singular beauty of the cold desert dark.*

The will to create art is propelled by the forces of nature. Much like the ocean's ever-crashing waves and the dancing wind that carries the sea gulls to the lapping shores, a writer is inspired by the beauty of existence. I would like to congratulate all of you on your creative success and wish you good luck in all of your future endeavors.

I would also like to direct your attention to the following poems which have merited special recognition: "Feeling Mortality" (page 121) by Joyce Erickson, "The Lawnmower" (page 345) by Debra Smith, "Ozymandias II" (page 224) by Jason Kelley, "Cape May In March" (page 497) by Jean MacKay, "The Surf" (page 69) by John De Lao, "Renders" (page 523) by Danny Barrious, "Nestor Of The Park" (page 530) by Bart Rippl, and "Dear Scott, I Am Foundering" (page 140) by Christopher Silva. All of these poems are worthy of a careful reading.

Once again I would like to thank all of you for your many submissions and I would also like to congratulate you on helping to create this fine anthology. I hope you enjoy reading the many excellent works in *Dance Upon the Shore* and I wish you the best of luck in all your creative pursuits.

Richard Schaub,
Editor

Acknowledgments

The publication of **Dance Upon the Shore** is a culmination of the efforts of many individuals. Judges, editors, assistant editors, customer service representatives, graphic artists, layout artists, office administrators, data entry, and the mail-room staff have all brought their respective talents to bear on this project. The editors are **grateful** for the contributions of these fine people.

Howard Ely, Managing Editor

Winners of the North American Open Poetry Contest

Grand Prize Winner

Heidi Bloem / Des Moines, IA

Second Prize Winners

Davis, John / Savannah, GA

Joyce Erickson / Thousand Oaks, CA

L. A Grant / Torrance, CA

Julie Holiday / Golf Shores, AL

Priya Narasimhan / Flemington, NJ

Margaret Phillips / Louisville, KY

Ann Robbins / Ypsilanti, MI

Debra Smith / Churchville, NY

Dan Truong / Davis, CA

Anne Williams / Lawrenceville, NJ

Third Prize Winners

Judy Aslesen-Rekela / Minneapolis, MN

Danny Barrious / Modesto, CA

Helen Beeson / Aptos, CA

Micah Bingaman / Rialto, CA

Stuart Byrne / Winnetka, CA

Alison Carley / Elmont, NY

Carl Carlson / Stockton, CA

Carson Cistulli / Milton, MA

James Clark / Maryville, MO

White Cloud / Rochester Hills, MI

Meredith Cochran / Binghamton, NY

Brian Collette / Wilkesboro, NC

Darren Davey / Fairborn, OH

Kathryn Davis / Highstown, NJ

John De Lao / Brooklyn, NY

Robert Eastman / Pelham, AL

Timothy Erskine Jr / Battle Creek, MI

Amy Floretta / Saint Louis, MO

Christa Gahlman-Kongslie / Oxford, WI

Jonathan Glynn / New York, NY

Marie Guidice / Lebanon, NJ

Charles Hackett / Babylon, NY

Lisa Hilliker / Trenton, MI

Sandra Hudgins Oklahoma City, OK

Blaine Hummel / Austin, TX

Rebecca Ischida / Saint Paul, MN

Alice Johnson / Pompano Beach, FL

Jason Kelley / Briarcliff Manor, NY

Jason Kemppainen / Melpitas, CA

Beth Krumholz / Reading, PA

Vincent LaCalamita / Coral Springs, FL

Dale Lawhon / Newberg, OR

Larry Laws / North Liberty, IA

Jean MacKay / Wilton, NH

Tara Mahady / Manchester, NH

Chris Martin / Los Angeles, CA

Jennifer Martin / New York, NY

Christopher Mason / Brentwood, TN

Nicky Melton / Wooton, KY

G.A. Prewitt / Tulsa, OK

Susan Printup / Eden Prarie, MN

Connie Pursell / Laguna Niguel, CA

Elam Raymond / Honolulu, HI

Marylin Reed Beaverton, OR

Bart Rippl / Westlake, OH

Dawn Rogers / Rensselaer, IN

L. Gwen Ruthven / Walsenburg, CO

Esther Ryder / New Bedford, MA

Heather Schmaedeke / Homewood, IL

Mae Seon / Williamsville, NY

Luann Sessions / Boulder, CO

Yioula Sigounas / Greenville, NC

Christopher Silva / Rocky Point, NY

Ruth Smith / Norristown, PA

William Stone / Elk Grove, CA

Dave Swanson / Deerfield, IL

Kimberly Treiber / Morgantown, NC

Geneva Truesdale / Warrensburg, NY

Vernon Warner / Clifton, NC

Congratulations also to all semi-finalists.

Grand Prize Winner

Treatment

Yellow, chalky pills make lolling circles in white paper cups,
  like Weebles wobbling (but they don't fall down) on a tray
  precariously balanced.
Up the hall, down the hall, I look for Ted; three stocking hats,
  four-day beard, one trench coat, and a face with a map of
  Schizophrenia's long, scenic vacation etched in grooves and lines.

Ted's out back, smoking his relief, pulling the nicotine and tar in hard,
  get it there, get it there, it burns but it's oh so nice, it
  makes you forget the crawling, the eyes, the wires.
He knows I do not understand but he humors me,
  even manages a smile.
It's time for Communion.

The bread is the bitter powder, all neat and sweet
  in its little machine-manufactured disc, and the wine is water
  (tastes like pennies) in a sterile, disposable paper goblet.
In an unspoken pact, we perform the rite
  that helps keep the voices at bay.
Later, he may vomit and his mouth will feel like burning sand,
  but to keep the voices quiet we will try, we will try,
  every day, he and I.
  Heidi J. Bloem

Complexity Of Love

Love is a very conflicting word,
It will lead you to think there is a utopia,
And some times it even becomes absurd,
When you know the word love is a phobia.

Take love apart and it becomes incredible,
It leaves a mark that is indelible,
If all of the meanings of "Love" were true,
Life would not be the prevailing stew.

Time in itself is a burden to bear,
But the time will come to analyze love,
Therefore be tolerant with a listening ear,
Then all of the fingers will fit into the glove,
Be like a dove - give into love.

Joseph S. Weekes

God Sent You My Way

Tricia, my special granddaughter
God sent you my way
I thought I would be in your life every day
but fate has not given us that pleasure
so I keep my love for you in my heart
that's my treasure

When I think of you
I see eloquent style
a tender heart so sensitive to others
reaching out an extra mile

Tricia, meticulous in everything you do
there is no other person
that could fit into your shoes
I know you will always be my special
grandchild, Tricia

God sent you my way

Patricia A. Bradford

Accomplishment

For 12 long years mother and house wife,
Don't get me wrong I've enjoyed my life.

Married at 16, never finished school,
Leave your shoes at the door has been the rule.

Our firstborn Amanda has already reached 10,
A thriving young artist just around the bend!

Ryan's the middle he's usually forgot,
Stunning blue eyes, attention he's sought.

The baby Cody, yes, the spoiled one,
A strength "A" student, not to be undone.

I love being their mom, but there is more on my mind.
I've never had a job, what will I find?

Real estate school it is, educations a must,
10 hour days, the homework's a bust.

I did make it through and it does feel good.
It is just a start, but I have with stood!

It's been an accomplishment I've done on my own,
I'm smart and intelligent this I have shown.

Real estate, school, mother and house wife,
Don't get me wrong I'm enjoying my life!

Sarah Cummins

My Endless Love

Another night slowly closes in, and I feel so lonely.
I can't believe we're through you said it would last forever.
You were my first true love and you'll be the last.
My heart aches for your lovin' baby please come
back to me you're all I know. I need you in my life don't
be so cruel. I have to feel your arms holding me once again.
True love never dies. From now till eternity I
will be waiting for your return.

Michele Masi

Gems Of The Mind

Deeply buried in ancient memory,
Are the finest of diamonds and pearls you'll ever see.
Washed by a lifetime of tears!
And viewed through the patina of years,
Their shine doth ever last and glow,
As moonlight on new fallen snow!
Glistening and gleaming within our sight,
A million facets of purest beauty bright!
With a glow that illuminates the darkest night,
And turns deepest gloom into ecstasy's light!
Muse not wherein to set these stone,
For in lustre and beauty they stand alone!
Thus keep them unset and strictly your own!
As no amount for their loss could atone!

Jesse D. Peay Jr.

Every Day

Every day the dove flies
Into the darkness and the light
Sometimes knowing the difference between them
Other times too rapt to care

Yet he flies on and does not see
The angel crowning his precious head
And the fires he sets with the tips of his wings
He is blind to all things except his mission

He has keep his promises, He has keep his vow

However the dove's heart and mind are still thirsty
The spirit inside him is not yet quenched
He hunts for the things that will give him peace
He does not know he already has them

No one has told him, no one has shown him

So every day the dove flies on
Still ignoring the differences between the darkness and light
Too immersed in his mission to see the truth
That what he is longing for he already has

Heather May Culton

Friend Of Mine

This friend of mine is identifiable in my life.
This friend of mine is locatable and available in my life.
To be close to this friend of mine, I must be obeyable.
This friend of mine has never let me down.
This friend of mine is approachable, dependable, and reliable.
I honor and glorify this friend of mine.
This friend of mine is Jesus. Oh what a wonderful child.

Rita Marks

In Loving Memory...(1996)

The essence of your gentle love
Still shines on us from up above.
The mother that we used to know
Still fills our hearts and makes them glow.

We think of you each waking day
And still recall your loving ways.
Your smile is just a memory now,
That helps us through the day somehow.

Some nights you come to us in dreams,
And in our sleeping minds it seems
That years and death just fall away
And we are children lost in play.

Little sisters, little brothers,
With our living, loving mother.
But always, morning brings us back
To sense our loss and face the facts.

The mother that we loved is gone,
But still our love for you lives on.
And though the years will come and go,
We'll always feel your loving glow.

Elizabeth Zerbst

Words Spoken In Anger

Unprotected;
Words selected;

Used in anger;
A verbal danger;

Causing, internal damage;
From, that verbal rampage!

A penetrating and saturating;
Agonizing and criticizing;

Kind, of physical and mental abuse;
From extended, verbal use!

Disrupting, one's mental and physical state;
With words, that continue, to aggravate;

Leaving a person, un-mentally sound;
Depressed and suicidal bound!

It doesn't matter, old or young'
The lashing we get, from a vicious tongue;

Penetrating, undetected, without a trace;
Coming, from an angry face!

Cutting and piercing, clear down to the core;
Leaving one devastated, and not wanting, to live any more!

Robert E. Filip

Manhattan Morning

The chilled wind tugs the covers off the night
    With sly, thin fingers while the midtown sleeps,
A cheap, metallic love-song moans its plight
    From village shadows where the wastrel weeps.
The skyline shoulders through the Chelsea mists
    Its lullaby-line penciled in the haze;
When Wall Street wakes to shake its golden fists
    The Bowery spins its web of wasted days.

The toilers read the headlines, scan the sky
    And hurry through the crowded dust-blown street,
And on the East Side frightened statesmen cry
    That nothing's left but conflict or defeat.

Yet, in an hour Peace might gain its sway
    In Central Park when children start to play.

Charles J. Hackett

Conquer The Weeds

Don't plant weeds in your garden.
Sow the good seeds.
You know that they are for pardon;
Everything else will be weeds.

A cross word spoken,
Means a heart that is broken.
A degrading slur, a false accusation,
What ever will cause a media sensation.

Something you don't know to be true
Turns into gossip for more than a few.
Jealousy, cruelty, resentment, hate —
They control your fate.

At one time my garden was congested, sin infested.
There wasn't any room for beauty, nor tranquility.
My garden bore no fruit, just weeds.

When everything was lost, and there wasn't much to live for,
I was brought to my knees, in more ways than one.
On bended knee, I talked with the Lord.

Then one day the Son shone, and the Light came into my life,
His Love redeemed me, and my garden flourished with good seed.

Alyce Trimm Williams

Ezekiels' Encounter

An unusual dust cloud arose across the desert,
From its midst came four strange creatures.
Though man-like their faces were as lion, ox, and eagle.

One spoke to me, I said I was a captive priest.
I inquired as to their faces, he did answer
Yet most was beyond my ability to comprehend.

Their wings, when employed, carried them up
Creating noise and casting a bluish light.
It was extremely frightful to see them so high.

More startling was the approach of a throne
Like structure bearing yet another living
Creature having the same likeness as the others.

Fire and lightning was about all of them, also
The appearance of a wheel within a wheel.
Frightened, I feel prostate in worship!

What next occurred is vague for I was
Apparently lifted away and eventually returned.
For seven days I contemplated my deliverance.

This occurrence is inscribed for posterity.

D. Rodger Long

The Red Rose

Two sweethearts hiking over the mountain trails
hand in hand, sharing their wonderful
silent moments together.
Skiing down the mountain slopes
with laughter and excitement.
At night a warm glowing fireplace
sharing tender moments together.
Then suddenly He was gone forever!
She walked through the mountains
seeking; tears gently falling, a heart
full of sadness; looking up
to the heaven for answers, suddenly
a red rose gently swirling in the snow
fell at her feet. She knelt slowly
and reached out and gently held it close to her heart.
Her face radiant with a smile
That lit up the heavens, there
was hope for true love again.

Gertrude M. Yeager

Precious Moments

Looking through the eyes of a child, their voices sound
so sweet and mild. Running, laughing, and carefree playing,
As young bodies in motion are constantly swaying.
They have an anonymous effect on people that is profound,
It is like a new toy that has just been wound. As each
new day arises, children are sent as packages of joy filled
with surprises. Like a sunshine that brightens a day,
Their smiles can touch our hearts in a sweet way.
Almost unconscious in their innocent minds, it's like a
familiar face that always reminds. Without knowing,
like a weed, they're quickly growing.
Reflecting upon those childhood days, holding on to precious
moments in a different phase. We've changed our ways
and grown so much, the memories still stand like a statue
we first started out, one moment in time when there
was no doubt. It is a memory that seems like
yesterday, as we recall, we can proudly say,
"This was our childhood, a place where our small
feet once stood."

Doris Renee Parsons

A Blossoming World

A blossoming world of exquisite color
Meets my eye this month of May.
A sense of rapture floods my being
As I enjoy this grand array.

The yellow mustard covering the hills
Is a bright and glorious sight.
Its tiny seed is a symbol of faith
To give us spiritual light.

The ice plant spreads its blanket of pink
All over the canyon walls,
And daisies beautifully decorate
The spaces in our malls.

We can thank our Maker for such gifts
By sharing happiness, joy and cheer.
Perhaps that is the reason the flowers come,
And could that be our purpose here?

Catherine Platt

Our Tears

Sometimes when our hearts are heavy
    Words just seem to cease,
Remember Jesus knows our heartache
    When to Him our tears release.

Tears speak to the heart of Jesus
    He reads every thought in our mind,
So don't criticize that person who cries
    Don't judge them or be unkind.

Tears bring washing and cleansing
    Some wash away grief and pain,
It's refreshment to many who hurt dear friend
    Deep peace they will surely gain.

Tears also tell of joy and gladness
    Of gratitude hard to express,
We want to praise and thank the Lord
    Now these tears He does caress.

So if you feel like crying
    And feel it's the only way,
Release those tears to Jesus
    No matter what others may say.

Joyce E. Shafer

Heaven

If my mother is in heaven
    she has her cigarettes

If my mother is in heaven
    she has her percolated coffee and her daily crossword

When my mother was smoking her brand,
    sipping her brew, and solving her puzzle,
    she was always in heaven...

Eva Charney

Fifty Years is a Long Time to Love

Fifty years is a long time to love,
it must be a blessing from the Lord above.
They have been together through war and peace,
their love for each other will never cease.
I remember the times when I was a child
the first grandson—and I was kind of wild.
They always did something to show that they care,
they were always together, and always there.
They are still the same as they get up in age
and today we will turn yet another page.
In this book of life that is not yet complete,
we know twenty-five more is not an impossible feat.
This bond that they have was made forever,
their love for each other you could never sever.
I'm glad they have a marriage for life—
they are the perfect model for a husband and wife.
But most all, what I wanted to say
was congratulations on such a wonderful day.

Shannon Bannister

Alluring

The magnificence in beauty bursting on the
scene, extolling ecstasy with in my soul, when I
behold in quiet joy this lady clothed in majestic
red with her the artistic friend, in pink array, we
give ourselves to a birth of misty tears as our sight
takes in this lovely scene that God created in his
marvelous way to show his excellence as we go
our way with wonder on display.

T. R. Woodward

Melissa

A wicker basket, a flower bouquet
Sat on an oak bench beside the brick way.
The lure was too great for me to pass by,
Pausing, I saw a small note tucked inside.

Lines penned in grief, an outpouring of love
For one quickly called to heaven above,
Revealing the hurt, words cannot express,
The loss of a child, a cheek to caress.

My mind strolled the lane of memories past,
To storytime angels and questions I asked.
Do they play games, do big people things,
How good must I be to earn myself wings?

"You see it's like this," my mother replied,
"Angels are people, much like you and I.
Their favorite game is "Pinning The Wings"
On those God has called, who make His heart sing".

I cried a few tears I hoped wouldn't show,
Thinking of mom who always did know,
When through them I saw a sight never seen,
An angel with wings in Paradise Green.

Ernest Hodson

Faces In The Clouds

Who belongs to the faces in the clouds?
Pictures of those who have gone above?
Peeking down to others looking up
For a glimpse of God's heaven?
A cherub face, a whiskered one,
A boy breathing a breath of white chill,
A father with burrowed brow?
For all my looking, they are fading now.
No, wait! There is a mother's sweet smile.
Someday will my face be in the clouds?
God's beautiful canvas in the sky.
Each day different than the one before.
If I fail to look today, for the beauty
In His sky, it is my loss forever more.
Peace for me as I watch
The changing faces in the clouds.

Diana J. Weigel

Sonnet II

As creeping winter comes on snowbound feet
And lost in ice and fog the roads are closed,
Then freezing streams run sluggish, slow and deep.
Life seems grounded, bound in deep repose.
My feelings seem to hibernate and sleep,
While in and out of dreams is interposed
The thought of you; it's woven true and deep.
I find myself wrapped up; in love enclosed.
The darkness that is coming soon with night
Will bring a cold that freezes to the marrow
And will deny all knowledge of the light.
So while there's time today, let's beg or borrow
From all we know of love and one another
To lay in stores of joy, and warmth, and summer.

Sandra S. Hudgins

Mary And I

Being in the hospital on my anniversary wasn't what I planned.
I am sure giving birth to her first baby in a stable,
    Mary too - didn't completely understand.
There always seems to be many unanswered questions -
    how come and why.
However, several of the apostles didn't understand why
    Jesus had to die.

He died to save sinners like you and me;
    We can now be free.

Death on the cross seems to be such a cruel one;
Satan has now been defeated and the victory is won!
Love was the reason He died on that tree.
It is an unconditional love for you and me.

Sometimes there aren't answers right now, for questions
    that are important to you and me.
Maybe not now, but on the other side of eternity.

In our busy lives we want an answer now, if not yesterday.
But, we must remember our timetable is not God's, when we pray.
I am thankful for answered prayer and the blessings God sends
    to me each day.

Virginia Rhodes

Brother Joe

His grip was a little tighter.
His smile was a little brighter.
If you needed a little "cash", you'd go to Brother Joe.
When the chips were down, you'd go to Brother Joe.
When father was about to retire, who ran the "show," Brother Joe.
When the fields needed plowed,
    who made the tractor go Brother Joe.
When Aunt Maggie's car wouldn't go, who would she call,
    nephew, our Brother Joe.
When a friend was in trouble, who would come on the double,
    Brother Joe.
If there's a heaven I guess you know, there you'll find
    Brother Joe!

Genevieve Molloy

The Land That I Know

I see the land - the land that I know
The vision is with me wherever I go.
Each stone, each hill, each valley and plain
They are part of my being - a section of my brain.
I walked there and worked there and grew some each day
Until suddenly college lured me away.
That has been many years and many lands ago,
But there will always be some part of me to show
The love of this land, the land that I know.
I see the skies - skies of brightest hues
They are the reddest or reds and the bluest of blues.
There are nothing but fence posts to block the view
And even those are very few.
I see the corps all planted in a row
Waiting for sunshine and rain to grow.
Sometimes there are hailstorms that wipe them out,
But other times they flourish and the farmers shout.
They hurry and harvest the golden grain each year,
So there will be food aplenty for all people far and near.

Nina Spearman Reese

Moon Light's Haze

Sitting in the moon light's haze,
the night sounds are tranquil and put me in a daze.
My thoughts ponder over work from today,
but my free spirit side only wants to play!
The waves are calm as they break the shore,
how I wish I could stay — just a little while more.
The coolness of the night begins to embrace me,
that tell tale sign it's time to leave the sea.
As I leave the moon light's haze.
I package my thoughts and continue to move on in my daze.

Cindy Tumilty

Decorating A Home, Wisely With Love

A home may have some flowers,
a sofa here a chair there.
    A statue of an 18 point buck hanging
on a wall captured in a frame for all to see.
    But what really makes a home are the
people that you see there.
    How they care and share those touching
moments. How they hold your hand in grieving moments.
How their hearts become one when another
is lost or hurting.
    Decorating a home can be rewarding if
you choose your pictures wisely.
    My picture for you is my ever
loving heart in a frame, hanging high
for all to see.

Joyce Lynn Higgs

A Rebel And His Flag

A handsome young man was driving his truck
Was shot by a cowardly criminal's gun
A Kentucky man who ran out of luck
One Saturday evening on route 41

He'd smile when he spoke of his baby twins
And he had good reason to cheerfully brag
He loved his wife, parents and friends
And Westerman sure loved the old rebel flag

One cold winter day they lowered him under
And in the far distance the rumble of thunder
An old man said, "It just ain't right
To shoot a young man on sight

Just because he was flying a rebel flag
Then drive away and to others brag
Some need to read their history books
They need to read and take a good long look"

The mourners came in from the east and west
Across the valley's hills, and crags
And many gathered to lay him to rest
They were proudly flying the old rebel flag.

Eva Byrnes

Grandmother's House

We once had all these cousins now they have become so few,
we all love one another as brothers and sisters do.
T'was at Grandmother's house where we would always meet
Fried chicken, home made ice cream are the memories that we keep.
It was always on a Sunday to Grandma's house we'd go
we would play our own made up games, sometimes friend or foe.
Many years have long since passed since those delightful days,
we've lived many miles apart and changed in many ways.

Those of us who are left behind get together still and
we remember Grandma's house and we always will.

Betty G. Bruce

Face Of Death

The Face of Death stares back at me, and smirks.
It knows what I ask of it, yet it does not grant me my wish.
It is no fault of Death, for it is his duty to take lives,
The blame falls upon me, it knowing I am not ready.

I have grown tired of the pain of life
And I fear the torture of life will leave a lifeless shell.
And Death will have nothing to take
I know that the pain will never stop.

So now I stand face to face with myself, blade in hand
Now is the time to perform the task Death cannot.
Now is the time for my pain to end.
So why do I hesitate?

A mere slash of the wrists
And my last minutes of pain will be my last minutes of joy.
To see the life blood run through my hands
And know that I am finally free of the pain.

Yet why do I hesitate?
With so much to look forward to.
Why don't I complete the final act?
I look up and see Death smirk once again.

Mark Flissinger

Trials And Tribulations

Carpe Diem....seize the day!
As each day passes by, you see and
experience a variety of things. There doesn't
seem to be enough time in the day, to
accomplish, conquer, and proceed.
But, fear of the unknown leads to,
too many unanswered questions. Failure
is not an evil to avoid, but a lesson to
help you succeed. Remember: in life
there are no guarantees.
Your decisions determine your fate,
Your destiny awaits... So don't let a
day pass you by. Life may be short
and complex, but don't despair.
It can be filled with passion and
delight, only if you,

Carpe Diem... Seize the day!
Victoria L. Fischer

Deer Hunters Abomination

Standin' here, gettin' cold;
Feel like I'm extremely old.
I know my toes have now turned pink
And the creek beside me really stinks!
Hidin' in the big tall grass
Ain't seen nothin', just freezin' my ass!
If the sun would shine, it would give off heat;
I'm hungry now and man I want to eat.
I wish I had a car right here
Cuz I'm sick of waitin' for a blasted deer.

Elizabeth Wilson

Minister Said!!!

This will not change next year!!
Contentedly grazing in their field
Sheep, and Donkey taken for Nativity
By truck, No more to see their field.

The Donkey's leg was cut to bone.
Then must stand depicting the scene.
With Sheep together in the cold,
When prowling dogs did roam.

The farm Animals alone in the city
Wild dogs did savage two sheep.
The Donkey bolted from the scene.
Being hit by car, no one seen.

When found and help did arrive,
The two sheep, and Donkey did cry.
All so hurt were put to sleep
Such careless wasted life these Animal's reaped.

The Church above all is supposed to teach
In Christmas Nativity love to all who seek.
The caring for the Babe and Animals,
This was deplorable for all, and each.

Ruth Yson Hadfield

A Child's Love

Look thru the eyes of a child and you see God everywhere,
The things that cross their little minds that only He can hear.
There's beauty all around in the innocence of their smile,
For He's in their little hearts and is with them all the while.
So when you get down hearted just put a smile upon your face,
With all the loving memories of a child's love we cannot erase.

Marty Rae Royer

Hope

When ever I'm over-burdened,
  Discouraged: my health poor, too...
I stop, and say to myself:
  "There is someone worse off than you."

I don't need to look very far
  To see someone lonely and blue...
The sightless the crippled, the homeless,
  The desperate incurable, too,

When I have stiffness and painful limbs
  And wish it would go away...
I soon see someone who has no legs...
  As I journey from day to day.

But if I have faith in God,
  And know that He cares about me...
I need only to put faith to practice,
  Then I plead on bended knee!

For I know that I am His child,
  As I am, to my earthly father..
Who loves me so much, He'd give up his life
  Just as would my earthly mother!

  Faye W. Guercio

For Daniel On His Seventh Birthday

Once there was a mighty train
He had a song
He sang, "Choo-ooo Choo-oooo".

And to the woods
And to the hills
And to the valleys wide and deep
He gave his song
While he rolled along
For a secret he did keep.

He loved his valleys, woods and hills
When he passed them every day
And in his song
So loud and long
They learned his secret too,
In locomotive language
"Choo-oooo choo-oooo" means, "I Love You".

I hope you will remember this
Each time you hear his song
And know we both are singing
And both will love you long.

  Becky McCarley

Today

Today I'll make the best of life
When trouble comes my way.
When all I see is toil and strife
With no light to brighten the day.
I'll forget the hurts of yesterday
And set some reachable goals,
With a hopeful heart
I'll gear my thoughts to lighten my soul.

Just for today I'll look for rainbows,
I'll gather flowers along the way.
I'll look for beauty in every place.
I'll let the light shine on my face,
I'll stand the tests of time,
Sadness I'll try to erase.
When the twilight begins to fade,
I'll know I did my best
When my eyes shall close in rest.

  Dorothy Kuxhausen

A Facade

Vacation time for the husband's job
Wife will miss work for sick baby
Husband would lose respect
Defend her rights and stand in a bog
She will leave you a bit hazy
Those who help themselves will direct
Liberation, equal rights, a facade
Sensitivity and defensiveness makes one crazy
Proclamation, not responsibility, do they expect
The assertive or the aggressive, which is the cog
A man's world is the cop-out for the lazy
The real story, lack of coping from the inept
Lack of sharing is an excuse for this mob
Inability at depth, ability at control is the Daisy
The only feeling at this game is regret

  Carl Casteel

Mighty Niagara

It's one of the mightiest of all nature's giants
Although it has been harnessed by science,

It keeps on flowing in the fresh misty air
And continues to run with sparkling glare,

The Niagara river flowing over the falls
Its roaring never stills, its voice always calls,

See it over and over, a sight to see and adore
No matter how many times, it's never a bore,

Above Niagara appears a beautiful rainbow
Glistening with multi colors that glow,

It touches gentle Lake Ontario below
Where its green waters continue to flow,

Old Niagara with its mighty power
Rushes its way beyond the Observation Tower,

The boat ride below should not be missed,
A wonderful experience on the "Maid of the Mist",

Whether the weather is cold, or if it is hot
Niagara Falls is the place to tie the knot,

Sooner or later, every one discovers
Historical Niagara is for lovers.

  Frank Pellegrino

How To Induce A Person To Jump Off A Cliff

Bread does strange things to the gallows
ruining the view with bristling silt
the efficient flower the everlasting twist
three fingers in your gorgeous blonde hair
catches fire in the evening
forcefully unzipping the ghost son
speared on devilish suspicions
is a family game
hot water in the horse's mouth
droll and kicking the children's toys
roars and rushes to suckle
but the black thrill gets votes
pimps for torn chrysanthemums
in the folds of an August coat
and bites anything within reason
as you recognize
the position of the ice
still and vagrant
fisted in loaves

  Jerry Trimmell

Our Grandsons

Grandsons! Yes! We have three.
All a joy to their grandma and me!
Ages vary from high to low,
And all three you'd like to know.
Number one grandson, our marine with appeal,
Holds more loyalty to the corps than he'll ever reveal.
Devoted son, husband and father, I must say.
Why, this? He was reared that way!
Number two grandson, he's on his way
To be quite outstanding some future day.
He'll have his good times and bad times, too.
But, with family support, he'll see them thru.
Number three grandson, quite new to this world of stress,
As the saying goes: "Plays it day by day!"
With parent guidance he'll attain wisdom and happiness,
Spreading love along the way.

John W. Kauffman

Some Sure Signs Of Spring

You start to think it's spring,
 When birds chirp and tulips bloom,
You're bitten by the cleaning bug,
 To make your home sparkle room by room.

You scrub the walls and clean the rugs,
 And pile up trash galore,
The garbage collector thinks you're moving,
 But there's no "For Sale" sign on your door.

Your shovel is replaced by a lawn mower,
 Gone, too, scarfs, gloves and boots,
You reorganize your closets,
 and start dreaming of T-shirts and shorts.

You've seen the Easter Bunny,
 The TV season comes to an end,
March Madness bounced right by you,
 April 15th's just around the bend.

You turned your clock forward,
 And lost a little "zzz"s,
But you really know it's spring,
 When your car turns green and you start to sneeze!!!

Karen DeLuca Katchmeric

Where Only Angels Fly

There was a boy named Andy that all the angels knew,
And when He walked upon this Earth he looked like me and you.

His life on Earth was very short
But he didn't live in vain,
His living spirits with us now,
To help us ease our pain.

Come, be with us Andy
Help us learn to pray,
Help us all to understand
We'll be with you some day.

Come and tell us Andy
Help us understand,
That life and death upon the earth
Is just a part of Jesus Plan.

Tell all of us that live on Earth
Why we should read the Book,
The one that meant so much to you,
when you met Jesus by the brook.

Help us all to find the light before our time to die,
And join you in that Magic place, where only angels fly.

Daniel J. Snook

Learning To Cope

The Forty Niners must have wondered,
As they crossed the Dust Bowl Plains,
How they could make a living
And if it a ever rains.

They wondered if they could continue
Or how they could even want to stay,
But they learned to use the things they had
And were too poor to move away.

They learned to hunt and eat the buffalo
Ate wild berries and game they found.
And if the winds didn't blow
They grew things in the ground.

Sometimes we get so overwhelmed,
and we feel we have been put on the shelf,
But we, for sure, are going no where
Just feeling sorry for ourself.

On cold and dreary mornings
When we can't get it all together
We need to pause and pray for strength,
And not just blame it all on the weather.

Willie Lou Shirley

All Things Are Known

I made a promise to God the day you were born.
To love and Protect you from any world scorn.
For all children are precious and not meant to be torn.

When ready for slumberland at the end of the day.
It's my duty to see you're safely snuggled away.
I gladly kneel by your bed and together we pray.

Your little arms try to hug me so tight.
You squeeze the breath out of me with all of your might.
Forever Blessed - For I know what I am doing is right.

You once asked a question, "Will we ever be apart?"
I replied, "God has known of my promise right from the start."
"Together we will remain as His Plan says is our part."

My Child be free of those worries, there's nothing to fear.
No harm can come upon us nor ever get near.
For He sees the Love between us is ever so Dear.

May all children be loved as I so love my own.
Between Heaven and Earth there is only a zone.
Nothing can be hidden - For All Things Are Known.

Irene Perry Unger

A Cover Of White

A cover of white; a beautiful sight;
The snowflakes are falling so free.
Six inches more is what is in store
That requires some shoveling, you see.

Can't the snow fall down and cover the groun'
And leave the roads and the sidewalks be?
Of course that's not right to restrict the flight
Of a snowflake to grass blade or tree.

So a shovel you get, and it's a sure bet,
That your back muscles and mind won't agree.
But when it's all done and you have had your "fun,"
You can retire to the kitchen for tea.

Stanley T. Gray

Self Evaluation

Oft enjoyed, learned conversation
Evolves into excellent observation;
Thus my satisfying declaration.
Thoughtful effort beats perspiration.

I've searched far and wandered wide,
Tightly bound ideas, deep inside.
They wouldn't express, hard as I tried.
Talking to myself, quickly, I hied.

Nice to know just whom to blame,
Falling behind; part of the game;
Opportunities, lost, after they came,
Progress dampened, dimmed, like burnt out flame.

Tried expressing to my others,
Showed plans to sister, father, brother.
From them I heard nothing but "ah, rather".
Ideas, progressive, successfully smothered.

Generated plans I now keep to myself;
Stored, like canned goods on a shelf.
Great thoughts, in silence, tiptoe like elves
Seeking a home, fine tuned to themselves.

Israel Baron

Immortality

Grieve not for me when I am gone,
For grieving turns the heart to stone,
And leaves no tenderness to care
For those who live in deep despair.

Mourn not for me when I am gone,
For mourning keeps you all alone,
And takes the purpose from your life,
Replacing it with painful strife.

Weep not for me when I am gone,
For weeping makes the day grow long,
And fills the sleepless night with fears
That linger past the flood of tears.

Cry not for me when I am gone,
For crying stills the lovely song
That emanates from voices, sweet,
And thrills the soul with joy, complete.

Remember me when I am gone
With hearts serene, steadfast, and strong;
Let my love live in memory,
And give me immortality.

Gladys Harmon Birmingham

Mountain Sunset

The beautiful sunset over the mountain peaks,
So perfect to my love and me.
But as we sat close, hand in hand.
A lonely man sat close by, not a word did he speak.

His face so lonely and painful to see,
As he wiped away a tear
He stared into space, and acted as if he
Was seeking a dear ones face.

He then rose quickly with a wave of his hand.
As if to say, a sad final good-bye.
His face was so sad, I wished I had
A word to comfort as he did cry.

I felt compassion, as this man I observed
He had said good-bye to his love without words,
Had she really died or just gone away?
I don't know but his sadness touched my heart til this day

Eloise Callin

Beauty Is Forever

The whole of nature is a symphony;
Pleasant sights and sounds and aromas one can perceive;
The universe reflects pure harmony;
A miraculous cosmos the Infinite did conceive.
A multicolored ribbon across the sky,
The rolling waves as lofty as they seem,
The dazzling snow that opens the stolid eye
Are the will and handiwork of the Supreme.
The fragrance of the flowers and new-mown grass,
The splendor of green valleys cloaked with trees,
Sweet melodies of whispering winds that pass:
The perceptive and the unobservant they please.
  The beauties of this world, old but unworn,
  Await the generations yet unborn.

John B. Calhoun Jr.

My Friend

Nearly five years ago, a lady I chanced to meet
At the time never to guess she'd be so sweet.
With hammer, saw, and the love of toil
We became neighbors on adjoining soil

We've become good friends I can say with pride
In four years of living side by side.
True friends a really hard to find,
They are not always faithful and kind.

We have shared good times it's true...
Dear friend it's a pleasure...
Being a neighbor to you.

Nadine M. Bushong

A Point In Time And The Beauty Of P.S. 209

  It's in happy little Spanish eyes,
staring at a very large order of fries.
  It's in little round Asian faces,
questioning the complexity of shoe laces.
  It's in European voices,
seeking out American choices.
  It's in two little white eyes contrasting with an African
    complexion,
wondering about a video projection.
  It's in little hands that have traveled from Calcutta,
to hold, in our lunchroom, their curry with bread and butter.
  It's when you have the joy to see,
six gentile boys playing dreidle with glee.
  It's in the matzos and the pastas,
  It's in the smell of exotic dishes,
that fulfill the tastes of a thousand different wishes.
  It's when you find a thousand years of history and culture;
when you look into a child's eyes to see the future.
  Such was a time,
of beauty, at P.S. 209.

Joel H. Finkel

Days That Intertwine

Tomorrow is unknown mostly a worry
Today is precious for it is happening
Yesterday is a memory only a picture in our minds
They are all intertwined
Rotating till they become one's life
We pull something from each of them
Yesterday's memories to console or remind
Today to live the moment
Tomorrow to wait for with either worry or dreams
... In our hearts

Theresa K. Allgood

Nikwasi "The Center"

The old town center of Nikwasi
was built on the banks of the Little Tennessee

Natives came from all around
to celebrate at the sacred mound

The Green Corn Festival was held each year
to thank the Great Spirit for his goodness and care

They extinguished all the fires and gathered the corn
and set out for the festival to see the mound reborn

The men filled their baskets with soil from the field
and emptied the earth on the sides of the hill

A new fire was made in a great offering
to replenish all the fires for the year following

Old men rubbed sticks together and prayed for the tire
till the Great Spirit sent it when they began to fire

A big bonfire was built to roast the food
and feasting began under the pale new moon

The groundhog dance and the pheasant dance too
were a part of the ritual of the seven day do

This is how renewal of the social order came to be
in the Sacred Town of the Middle Cherokee

Lois Deal Bressler

Birth, The Precursor To Death

To be born, is to predestine death;
for birth and death
become different sides to the same coin.

I lament the passing of my father, mother and brother;
yet, here am I with warm breath
an extension of their being; and as
homage to their preordained death.

My husband of 48 years - loved and honored
to him I must consign a tomb.
Here, he may know Grace; and,
rest the peace of his mother's womb.

My children mourn, for they have not learned
to perceive death as perpetuation of self;
therefore, by their lack of understanding,
life invalidates itself.

There is a darkness in death
not yet fully know - but
through the resurrection - a new light is shown.
Rooted deep within the footsteps of our Savior
seeds of understanding are nurtured and grown.

Elva B. D'Antoni

Animals

Animals are a great part of creation.
They are beautiful, cute, fascinating,
And provide terms to describe a situation.

Badger: to annoy persistently or harass.
Ape: to copy closely, clumsily, or crass.
Horse: to move by brute force.
Wolf: to eat greedily from any source.
Squirrel: to store up for future use.
Cat: to search for a sexual mate but no abuse.
Dog: to fail to do best or track like a hound.
Beaver: to work energetically all around.
Hawk: to sell by calling out on the street.
Cow: to intimidate with threats to beat.
Fox: to trick or outwit by anything said.
Sheep: a timid person easily scared or led.

Jo-Ann B. Segall

And Heart Obeys

Sweet oboe's sound in placid days,
there's flowered ground — and heart obeys —
— Soon envelopes sweet and true,
a tranquil trust — a love renewed.

Sweet flow of gown — her young of face,
she'll be your own — and heart obeys.
June develops — sweet and true,
a tranquil trust — a love renewed.

Sweet small of town the sun's displays,
the singing sound — and heart obeys.
We'll develop — sweet and true,
a tranquil trust — a love renewed.

It's still so fond — in elder days
the love grows on — and heart obeys.
Full developed — tried and true,
a tranquil trust — a love renewed.

Sweet oboe's sound — in placid days,
there's flowered ground — and heart obeys.
Soon envelopes — sweet and true,
a tranquil trust — a love renewed.

Mark W. Haggerty

"Au Revoir"...Sun

The sun rises in the cool morning air
To charge black edge of night as if a dare.
His lady's colors brandished in the sky...
For lavender, turquoise and pink... To die!
The first cheering yellow glow brings the dew.
Flower faces sparkle as washed anew.
Sunbeams flush dark corners of night in flight
Sundials mark "noon-light" victor in the fight.
The sun having captured our waking hours
Then wains to rest... sends brief tearful showers...
Musters one last victorious display...
Her colors set... His "Au Revoir" to say.

Marjorie Foster Fleming

Christmas Memories Keep

Jingle bells and fun filled sleigh rides
    mistletoe and loving kisses
Christmas carollers joyfully singing
    all a part of one's Yuletide wishes.

Building a smiling snowman in the front yard
    buying and decorating a Christmas tree
Selecting a thoughtful gift for loved ones
    provides memories for future reveries.

Writing heartfelt notes in Christmas cards
    sent to family and loving friends
Recalling memories cherished
    of times long past that love transcends.

Twinkling lights around the neighborhood
    reflecting soft colors in fluffy snow
Creating that kindred Christmas spirit
    filling our hearts and souls with a special glow.

Yes, it is the Yuletide season once again
    a time for friends and family gatherings
Providing nostalgia for memories keep
    the building blocks of love and friendships everlasting.

William Henry Jones

Untitled

I've often heard you say
"The best has never come my way."
Have you been kissed by the sun,
the moon, and your lover?
Held the hands of your parents
as they guided you to cover?
Heard the "Thank you"
of people you've fed and clothed?
Seen a boy's smile
That's beautiful to behold!
Never say, "The best has escaped my way."
Your "Better" is "Best"
Because of your good deeds each day!

Margaret R. Youngren

Forever My Friend

In this lifetime no one has shown me better.
Mistakes are disregarded just as
each sun rises anew.
Your gift of laughter and good
times is an adventure to the soul.
I have traveled the dim path and
discovered a lighted trail.
Here you have shown me a river
that flows with freewill.
Now, my entertaining friend, I
wish you well, for I will love
and hold you confined to my heart forever.

Michelle Maylum

The Mother's Circle (Argentina)

Old women walking and walking around.
Old women, gray women, making no sound.
The children they had, the young that they bore
Are living and breathing and walking no more,
But the mothers still walk and some grandmothers, too
Holding their photos for all to view.
They're picketing God! With their sad, dry eyes
Imploring his justice to fall from the skies,
And they're walking and walking around and around,
And the breaking of hearts is the only sound.

Betty Balanoff

Never To Be

An idea is conceived,
Attaches snugly to my mind.
Will I nurture you, watch you grow,
Or will you travel the path as others before?
As I stand at hell's gate
Consumed with flames of doubt,
Excuses decide your fate.
Swiftly I bury you ever so deep
In the dark hole of my pathetic soul.

Barbara Dyson

Little Boy Lost

See the child on the street
He has money for something to eat
  But he has something else on his mind
Something in a straight white line
  He'll be lucky to reach seventeen
Growing up on the streets can make a boy mean
  He falls between society's rules
He won't make it in life without the right tools
  He's parents don't know or they just don't care
Without our help he won't have a prayer

Glenna L. Dudley

Build A Castle On A Rock

A silver castle on the sand
Tunnels and bridges it did stand
Magnificent arches and towers grand
A gleaming vision upon the land.

The breaking waves one quiet night
Gently kissed the beach so light
When moon above shone silver bright
The shining castle was a sight.

A wayward wind came from the blue
Sang its song in notes so new
Gathered clouds across the heaven they flew
Restless waters rose and grew.

Evil touched the shifting wall
Tumbling arches and towers did fall
Surges washed a sweeping haul
Nothing left of one so tall.

Shifting sand moves to a rhyme
Solid rocks endure the clime
Unfriendly sea no more sublime
Rocks or sand-and a question of time.

Carol Pfankuchen

The Quest

I feel so puny, insignificant, and incomplete,
As I behold with awe the wonderment of nature,
As I contemplate in astonishment its mysteries and beauty,
I recognize that I belong; I am part of what is.

My ignorance enhances this suffering, and yearning;
Yet the compulsion within, pushes me on.
Ever seeking to identify with some mystical force,
Wanting to be complete, to find total realization.

Ever wary to discern this universal mystery,
Positive energy flows from my soul,
To replace an empty and ineffectual life
Fulfilling this yearning of eternal hope.

Let me create an exhilarating feeling,
As humility and compassion replace self-esteem,
Give me the gratification of being able to understand humanity,
That I may find comfort and fulfillment.

Leaving me imperfect until I conform,
Until I find my place in this scheme of things,
My pursuit for knowledge must endure
As my fortitude commends this Quest.

George Dandrade

Untitled

Yesterday one of Sara's little friends came to the door

With a broken voice I had to tell her
Sara doesn't live here anymore

Sara said "I love you Daddy, but Mommy can't stay"

They packed up their things and moved far away

Now I walk through the house without the echo
of her voice to hear

Where only in my dreams can I find her near

Only to realize and wake up in tears

I have a swing in the backyard and a little
cash register where she use to play store

A toy box filled with her toys that once cluttered the floor

Sara my little girl doesn't live here anymore

Gregory Sturgill

A Picture Of Peace

Coming upon an art show where "Pictures of Peace"
  was the theme,
It seemed like all the paintings were quiet and serene.
But in one angry storm clouds rolled in a canvas sky.
Trees bowed, as if in homage, as the God of the storm passed by.
Lightning's jagged signature slashed across the scene.
The picture that stood before me was anything but serene.
Then I looked more closely; there in a great rock's crease,
A tiny bird sang a paean of praise to his Maker,
  the Author Of Peace.
It was plain to see the message portrayed:
"True Peace does not depend
On outward circumstances but on conditions from within."
Looking at that little bird, a thought to me occurred,
The tiny bird was in the storm but the storm was not in the bird.
I learned a lesson from that bird and came to understand,
Amidst life's storm we still can be at peace with
God and man.

LaVey Adams Alexander

Feeding Time

Feeding time at our house,
  is quite a sight to see.
It's my time to be a star,
  all eyes are searching for me.
Burros are braying - horses are neighing,
  cats are scampering about,
The rooster is trying to round up his flock,
  so no one will be left out,
Rabbits start bouncing around in their cages,
  it's their favorite part of the day.
The dogs are all barking - can't make up their minds,
  if they want to eat, or to play.
The old horse is waiting for her special food,
  she nickers to me soft and low.
Retired - her riding days over,
  she's taking things easy and slow.
Finally I'm finished, chores are all done,
  love glows from the eyes that meet mine.
We don't have to go out for excitement or fun,
  that's at our house, at feeding time.

Barbara Sparks Yearling

Moonlit Showers On Life's Pathway

Aimlessly wondering what to do each vanishing day
trekking nomadically through life's eternal pathway

A breathtaking full moon another phenomenal sight
astonishing moonbeams prancing radiantly all night

Glitter, twinkle, and sparkle, shining chiaroscately bright
what a preeminently time fantasizing til daylight

Emphatically it can't be that way at all
cloudbursts have moved in with ravishing rain starting to fall

We can't have everything with peaches and cream
and just conciliatory sailing down life's stream

Storm clouds will motivate and be active awhile
for when they dissipate we'll have a refulgent smile

That's an au courant life to have beautiful flowers
after refulgent revitalization of moonlit showers

Gilbert Hedges

Gifts In Season

Crispy air skips to an enchanted moon
  a fullness in bounty to harvest soon.
From growth and green, life seems to fade
  into a restful beauty creation made.

Equinox in decay with sleepy head,
  winter its solstice soon covers the bed.
September growth breathes a final sigh
  out quickened by October with active reply.

Pulpy fruits, brown nuts now clutter the ground
  migrations in flight, honk directions in sound.
Frosty cold and silence conquers the dew,
  flowers in havoc wilts to a few.

Melancholy the days, bewitched the nights,
  "Jack" in his fantasy flings colors in fright.
Dawn in newness, mirror drenches of gold,
  aesthetics profound, beauteous presence behold.

Sunset then night leaving day after dawn
  softly and silently falls white on the lawn.
Purity captures gold, leaving the magic of night
  to the whiteness of snow, his gift, our delight.

Francis W. Huff

Nature's Way

You cannot have peace without order.
It is the law of nature; that tall
things be done decently and in order.
It would be nice if everyone found their
niche and embraced it.
Many of us are like small preschool
children, not well disciplined.
We want to run around and do, do, do
everything, without care or reason.
The enemy cleverly excites this child in
us, and drives it into a frenzy with honey
drugs and flattery.
Propaganda makes chaos, and pushes
nd pushes and pushes....
until it comes to shove; then it
attrition wins; and puts the masses
into a teachable frame of mind.
But, not without tragedies and many
causalities, as nature can be harsh.

Ray O'Neal

Full Circle

God said, "Thirty years shall thou have good."
It was a joyful life acquiring knowledge, enjoying
The spouse and children. And then it was time for me to go.
I begged God for some time more.

God said, "Eighteen years shall thou be responsible."
It was a donkey's life shouldering the burden
Of my family. And then it was time for me to go.
I begged God for some time more.

God said, "Twelve years shall thou be pushed."
It was an old dog's life being kicked around
By the children. And then it was time for me to go.
I begged God for some time more.

God said, "Ten years shall thou act the fool."
It was a monkey's life making funny faces
For the grandchildren. Then I knew it was time for me to go.
I asked God wherefore?

God said, "A child to being a child hast thou come."
It was in humour and appreciation I saluted
My Master. A full circle had I had to go.
I asked God no more.

Meera Prakash

Oh What A Plan

"Born of a woman", of One it was said
   ...Revealing His seed was not from a man
Though Divine in genre, His cast instead
   Was lower than angels...Oh what a plan!

God gave up His only begotten Son
   To sojourn the path predestined above
Indeed His death sowed seeds of adoption
   By which believers He rescues in love

Oh what a plan where a mother's love will
   Rescue the life of her child through giving
Predestined for this are souls to fulfill
   What God has prepared within this calling

Though not of their seed, adoptive parents
   Show love in their deeds instead of their genes
And thereby children receive acceptance
   Within these divine misunderstood means

What precious mothers...Love's custodians!
   Their ultimate sacrifice has begun
Heaven's gentle exchange of guardians...
   Much like our Father...Who gave up His Son

   Bob G. Martinez

Have We Forgotten About Victory Gardens?

For many millennium man has depended upon his private garden.
He ate luxuriously from such a dependable private source.
But this mass production era has people depending upon others
For their immediate dietary needs as a matter of course.

Have people forgotten the importance of private gardens,
Those luscious products nature produces so abundantly
With little expense other then simple, loving attendance
Which provides a close comradeship with abundance at once?

A great man always pays constant attention
To the needs of the family he provides for.
The spouse in her house obligingly cooperates with acknowledgment
Of responsibility toward the fulfillment of a well-planned store.

The spouse accepts the vegetables, melons and strawberries,
Preparing them for meals and for storing, like freezing.
Can anyone think of a dietary habit more merrily
Enjoyable then from one's very own garden in the free breeze?

Why has man forgotten the need for emergency food supplies?
Misfortune keeps knocking at the door of the unthinking, unwary,
Who haven't laid up emergency provisions in case
An unusual occurrence develops and springs a catastrophe!

   Theodore R. Reich

I Wondered

I sat in my garden and felt a gentle breeze,
And I wondered if it carried any joy your way;
Suddenly there was a gentle rain,
And I wondered if it would nurture any flowers in your path;
I sat alone and the night fell silently,
And I wondered if it would bring any peace to you;
One day the wind began to stir,
And I wondered if it would carry any of your cares away;
One night the sky was clear, ablaze with stars,
And I wondered if your eyes would always shine as they do now;
At dawn the sun rose in all its glory,
But, I wondered if it had ever seen your smile.
I suddenly realized my fields were almost barren,
But, that they would bloom forever if I were to have the
love of Karon.

   George H. Klavitter

The Lady Rides (For Stephanie)

Watching her gives me joy
Even though she isn't wearing a dress or a bow
And a ribbon in her hair.
Understated style, a bit of a tomboy, but a lady inside
Rides with the best of them
Jumping the doubles, like a bird, so graceful she flies
Then pedaling hard to be the first across the finish line.
Smart and competitive, a beautiful young lady
with a soft light in her eyes.
Even though she isn't wearing a dress or a bow
And a ribbon in her hair, I love her just the same.
A bit of a tomboy, but a lady inside
She shines... and when someone asks
"Who's daughter is that?" I'm proud to say "She's mine".
And the lady rides.

   Ruth Yates

The Sun Will Come Again

Dark clouds fill the sky hiding the sun
Like a king hides his kingdom in the fold of his rode.
Life itself seem to scatter in fear of the winds mighty roar
Rain dances on my window, and lighting flashes its mystical
   light into my eyes.
Like a knight imprisoning me in my own home.
Sadness becomes a house guest, only to stay for eternity.
Finally the storm leaves as if to run in fear.
The sun warms the land and seems to awaken life.
New flowers bloom, and leaves from the tree cast a green tint
   all around me.
The air is clean, and birds sing softly above me
And I find myself surrounded by new life
And become overwhelmed with compassion for the sight I hold.

   Stacy L. Keller

The Child Inside!

There is a child inside
she puts the sparkle in my eye
And keeps me alive.

She is the spontaneous one.
Wanting to pull away when things get rough
Leaving stops at none.
Wanting attention and love.

Wanting to be successful,
I put the child aside.
Stress heightens and she lashes,
"I'm here," relief sets in.

I guess I will never loose the child inside
she is what makes me who I am.
Both responsible and a child,
Not fully grown, having a life
that she once never had.

   Jennifer Bennett

The Unseen

There are children on the corners of the streets
Who will never have the chance to defeat.
Even though they are children of this land
We fend to not offer them a helping hand.
We know the way our future must grow
So how can we leave these children alone?
Naturally, every child can offer something
So why do we look at them as nothing?
Does it take good hygiene and fancy clothes
For a child to be recognized and to belong?
No matter what they look like or what they wear
They still have a mind that thinks and feels;
And a life to bare...

   Teresa G. Whitaker

Storm Coming!

All day the stillness held me
Listless in its thrall
Wandering an alien land.
And as anticipation filled the air,
Restless for change, fear held my hand.

An ominous leaden sky meld with a leaden sea
Robbing the world of light.
Gulls tumbled low from sky to sea,
And sea to sky, crying
Alarm in aimless flight.

Then, on a sigh, the winds arrived
To course the streets,
The beach, the dark'ning sky
Lashing the waves, a Fury on the sea
Dervish in the sands
Muting the gull's cry.

Splinters of fire pierced the clouds
Great peals of thunder echoed their own refrain
Resounding far down that storm-filled
Sky, to herald a torrent of windswept rain.

Selene Smith

Daddy's Got A Sweetheart

Daddy's got a sweetheart but, mind you, nothing's wrong!
Mother doesn't sigh or start; in fact, she hums a song.

Now, who's that pretty lady who stole his heart away?
Has she a past that's shady? Or, is she young and gay?

Daddy surely is in love and doesn't care who knows it.
Isn't he the foolish cove to shamelessly show it.

She's pretty as a picture; dances so divinely.
He's rooted like a fixture; behaves so supinely.

This little shy and coy minx twirls him 'round her finger.
What harm, he thinks, can there be if he cares to linger.

She leads him a merry chase. His tongue hangs out a mile.
He doesn't think his motive base if he can make her smile.

Yes! Daddy's got a girlfriend who's loyal, warm and true.
I guess his ways will never mend for daughters are too few.

Humphrey J. Darling

Last Day, First Day

Mournful winds make the only sounds on the carnage
that was the earth. They rustle like ghostly brooms
to sweep the skeletal ashes into senseless heaps,
then swirl them willy-nilly into darkened crannies.
No trace remains of fingers or of buttons pushed
in man's final act of hate for man; desolate,
barren one-story cities overlook
incinerated wastelands in the global fire;
a mash of poison cinders in a soup of toxic air -
corrupt, defiled by faceless warhead couriers -
mushrooms which do not discriminate the continents
nonchalantly glaze the charred destruction.

Perhaps, in time, inquisitive forms from the deep
will venture forth upon the isotopic crust,
evolve, and start anew a complex dereliction;
or maybe He will shake His head in awe,
consider jealousy the lost endeavors,
and try again to make it work somewhere...
...like promising Europa.

Gordon Dean Schlundt

Just Like A Yo-Yo

Buried within the depths of life, a little
Mysterious, and vulnerable wrapper en-snare the soul.
It has its moments to rise and fall
Without unseen propulsion for its actions.
And unlike a yo-yo which needs
Mechanical charge for its action,
The soul needs neither thought nor touch
To have it rise and fall.
It dips to the depths of the ocean without an anchor
Then floats with ecstatic joy like a pendulum,
As though released from bondage.

Why does the soul play this mysterious game?
One moment life fades like a dying plant
Then revival eschewed by a drink of water.
Why! Why does the soul wrap itself
In the form of a Yo-Yo?
Are there lessons to be learned.
From this mysterious Soul?

Then, perhaps each of us will claim understanding
Within ourselves, through its mysterious actions.

Joan E. Gettry

His Hand Upon Me

That night I slumbered restlessly when darkness engulfed me.
My thoughts were murky from anxiety and fear.
The darkness across my soul was like a lock and key.
A risky medical procedure I was to undergo, and I was
Trembling from apprehension as time grew near.
I prayed, "Lord, please be with me and keep me safe."

The nurse touched me gently and her smile I could see;
The doctor's dexterity was confident and reassuring.
My disquiet began to diminish as they talked to me.
I felt the heavy burden of my distress lifting.
The Lord placed his hands upon me; thus, bringing healing.

Resting in the recovery area, the doctor and nurse came
To me and told me that the procedure went well.
Comfort and assistance were given to me dispelling my fear.
I was awe-inspired, because the Lord almighty approached
Small and insignificant me where I dwell.
In my heart and upon my lips are praises and thanksgiving,
Because He came near.
His kindness, care, and healing touch I will constantly
Call to mind.

Joanne Marie Lake

My Plea

When it's dark gray, and in the gloom,
It sure is a contrast from flowers in bloom!

It has an effect on your mood,
Making you feel depressed,
Making you feel rude,
I feel tired to the point of obsessed.

Where is the sun?
With it will come fun!
I just want to play and run!

Instead of feeling so bad,
Lift my spirit!
So I'm not so sad!
with my plea, hear it!

Paula Patterson-Stevenson

Flooding

Sad tears are flooding our eyes and soul.
Church bells are ringing in mournful toll.
Raging waters are rising o'er the land
People are rushing to fill bags with sand.

Bridges are floating on chocolate brown seas
The pilings below are being buffeted with debris
Houses are sliding down mud strewn hills
Roadbeds are sinking through their man-made fills.

Wildlife is clinging to wind battered trees.
A dog's mournful howl is heard in the breeze.
Cattle are lying in their watery grave
People are trying very hard to be brave.

Mankind keeps trying to tame her.
But Mother Nature is giving her answer.
No man made levees can hold her in sway
When her cleansing flooding comes in to play

June Serviss

Repair?   Reconstruction?

In all the History of civilization
Downfall has come to many a nation
From 'the Cookie' crumbling on itself,
Beginning with Excess love of Self!
This leads to greed and blindness to Need!
Then Respect is soon lost in a Society
That had had a more kindly propriety!
No greater gift can a nation lose
Than that of good values and common sense!
The Scheme is devoid of Light
When 'Rights' count for more than 'Right'!
The Times have become so very tense,
Trust has gone by the way...
To ever restore the balance
Calls for Patience and many to pray
For Hope to improve each passing day!..
That hearts will be changed
To a more kindly, truthful way,
That the twice-baked 'Cookie' will be less deranged!

Virginia Pease Ewersen

Wondering

A young man wondering,
As his mind wanders many places,
Confusion, memories, pain, laughter,
His imagination, what-ifs, and could-have-beens.

It's the mind of every man,
The thoughts at night all alone,
Whether he has made the right choices,
And chosen the right paths.

He sees himself in many roles,
As a father, a son, a husband, a child.
Never keeping one separate from the others,
But each distinct in its own way.

It's the nights spent wondering,
The hours of sleepless thought,
That fuel this man to action,
His goals, his fears, his life.

For as this man drifts off to sleep,
As he prays for yet another day.
He regrets, smiles, cries and knows,
A life spent wondering only, is a life wasted.

Richard Maltsbarger

Books

Books can be serious, mysterious, and frank.
But when it comes to the cowdog Hank,
Books are funny and silly in rank.

Books may be melancholy, sorrowful, and sad.
But even then, they're not all bad.
Because books may have a happy part to make it really glad.

Books can be false, fiction, and fake.
But when they are, you may laugh and shake,
Because you may think, they've made a mistake!

Books, there are so many out there.
Brand new ones, and old ones, to love and share,
But the fire, in the car, or just anywhere.

Jessie Lynne Hughes

We All Melt Differently

It is no fresh revelation to aver
    that each one of us is a unique snow flake
But it may be such to tellingly infer
    we all melt quite differently - for God's sake.

When happily surprised, don't we dissolve to mush?
    But each expresses same, individually
When victorious, don't we oft glory and gush?
    But each winner's reaction differs in degree.

When publicly flustered, don't many flush and blush?
    Some redden in the cheeks, others in the neck
When romantically touched, don't we feel a rush?
    The reaction: amorous - or to run like heck!

When love's lost or sorrow stays and pain persists
    the snowflake floods into a puddle of tears
God assures cures and ordains when grief desists
He, who made us melt differently, from fears or cheers.

Norman R. Nelsen

Untitled

Strike! Strike!
Hear those pins rattle and shake!
All the pins from alley cleared
For the hook on the ball so did take
That even my opponent stood and cheered!

Miss! Miss!
That lousy five pin stands there still
To flaunt its easy charm, there by!
Had it been the ten pin still
They would say, you're gutter shy!

Split! Split!
Oh! Oh! Right on the nose so true
And left the seven-ten to try.
Take one, the crowd counsels you,
Not me, I'll give it the old college try!

Bowl! Bowl!
Those splits and misses still irk you,
With most of us are exasperating,
But in later games when you follow thru
Spares and strikes are very scintillating.

Edward P. Yackel

My Childhood House

They tore down my childhood house today.
    I stood and watched the wrecker
Smash in my bedroom window,
    Then swing back and crack the front door
In half.
    They tore down my childhood house today,
But they could not touch my memories.

Kathy Devers

It's You

I was wondering why we don't stay in touch.
I miss the talking and laughing we shared so much.
I still get lost in memories of you and me.
You're always in my thoughts that's plain to see.
Days turn into weeks we keep each other out of site
It just doesn't seem quite right.
Even being apart we will always have
   that special bond that makes us one
I know you must at times think about
    All the we've done
    All the love - and lots laughs of fun.
To think and wonder why it has
   to be like this.
I'm sure you know "it's you"
   that I really do miss.
     William Copley

To My Love

To the love of my life
   The great joy of your wife.
To the laughs and the tears
   and the sharing of some fears.
To the one I adore
   for all you are and more.
You are my guardian, my keeper
with each breath my love grows deeper.
For the one I share my dreams with —
   I give you my heart, my body, my mind.
With your actions please be kind.
I will do for you as you wish me to do;
   To show you how much I truly love you.
     Julie Murphy

My Beloved Father

My dearest father so much I love.
I have to say to him, "goodbye".
His tears are falling from his face
while I am preparing to immigrate.
My father says he doesn't mind.
If only John Kennedy were still alive!
He trusted and liked John Kennedy a lot,
but now he says he is afraid for my safety.
Don't worry father, I'll be OK.
I say once more, "goodbye".
I wasn't thinking that this was the last time
that I would see my father alive.
He passed away while I was living in the USA.
I blame and criticize the communist regime!
I was forced to flee
from the pressure of police brutality.
I miss my father dearly,
He is, at last, free.
My beloved father, please rest in peace.
     Pal Imeri

Life's Circle

Said the little boy, "Sometimes I drop my spoon".
Said the little old man, "I do too".
The little boy whispered, "I wet my pants".
"I do that too", laughed the little old man.

Said the little boy, "I often cry".
The little old man nodded, "So do I".
"But worst of all", said the little boy,
"It seems grown-ups don't pay attention to me".

And he felt the warmth of a wrinkled old hand.
"I know what you mean", said the little old man.
     Patricia A. Crabtree

Fallin' Love

A tear falls from my hollow eyes
onto my shattered heart
that beats in pieces on the rocks below
as people just turn and glare at me.

One picks up a jagged piece.
Thrusts it deep within my soul.
The others laugh heartily
as only blackness pours out onto the ground.

I weep, for no one will help me
gather the pieces of my puzzle.
They only shrug their shoulders,
look at me in disgust, and walk away.

Why can't peace reign?
Why can't love stay and make the glue stick?
A feather duster brushes my lips,
and takes away the wrinkles and the gray.
     Becky Compson

School Bus

Kindergarten: The wheels of the bus turn
A child sits up front
Obviously crying
Having been called the runt.

Elementary: She rides the bus but everyday
She gets closer to the back
She's grown tall and strong
Not taking any slack.

Junior High: She sits in back
But the bus comes to a stop
Next time the bus arrives
She's moved back to the top.

High School: Back to the old ways
Getting older everyday
Striving further back
Until the bus just pulls away.

Future: The bus just drives by
Not opening its doors
A new girl sits up front
"She" rides the bus no more.
     Tamara Hegedus

A Great Life Recipe

Oh no! Life is not a bowl full of cherries
as some people like to say.
Life is mostly full of worries but
we can chase those worries away;
They may visit, but they won't stay!

You may rid some days of worries,
and others will soon roll into town.
If we stay strong willed and be alert
no kind of worries can keep us down.
A happy outlook will stop our worries
from staying around.

Life is a journey from the day we are born.
There will be days to laugh and days to mourn.
Sometimes we will feel sad and so forlorn.
Great love for life helps weather the storm
Then we will be happy from the time we were born.

Read a good book or hum a happy song
to cheer the heart from thought or wrong.
Then sweet memories soon come rolling along.
You will feel much better with the worries all gone.
     Joie L. Bullock

The Beast

He was thought to have come from water or air
But He came from somewhere much closer than there
Only one understood the place to which He binds
For everyone owns Him, He dwells in our minds
Some people feel He is something you can kill
But just controlling Him takes more than sheer will
If you let Him take over, fear and instinct are increased
For everyone must learn to conquer their Beast

Melanie Brosig

Quiet Moment

Her small frame lay motionless against me,
Except for the slightly detectable rising and falling
Of her small torso as she breathes.
Her breath a hot wind brushing across my bosom.

I run my fingers through her fine hair,
Feeling each strand as I go.
Brushing my fingers across her ruddy cheek,
I embrace her face in my mind.

Slowly I rub my hand
Methodically up and down her back.
Unconsciously I wrap my arms around her
Squeezing her tight.

Bending to place a tender kiss
Upon her soft angelic brow
I whisper a word of thanksgiving
For this precious miracle I hold.

Laurel Alyson Farb

Bright Morning

Early in the morning, when a new day arrives
Darkness has pulled its drapes and
    presents the sun
Birds awake and thrill the hills with song
All signs celebrate, the day which
    has just begun
Leaves, inhale, shiver and wave to
    their neighbors
Dew races to slake the thirst of grass
    and flowers
Spiders working through the night enjoys
    the call to the bar
The sun warms the earth and the
    life it empowers

Joanne Caruso

Lamplight

Darkness falls on rain soaked streets,
As strangers hurry past without care.
I walk down those sleeping streets
And feeling a presence, I turn and look,
    But no one is there.

A single lamp lights the way,
But I have no where to go, no prayer to say.
The night's eyes follow my journey.
And uneasily I glance back,
    But no one is there.

I live my life in darkness,
With no one to guide me through.
I walk alone down silent streets
Not bothering to look back anymore,
    Because no one is there.

Jessica Gagliardi

The Burdens We Carry

If life could be so simple, so free, so clean, so gay
Then we would all be happy folk with each passing day.
But life brings us happiness sometimes the sorrow creeps in
Then we are tested for our strength, to see if we can win.
Life goes on and time erases all the pain we feel...
Even though we think we can't go on; God give us the "will!"

God only know just how much burdens we can bear,
He puts us to a 'Special' test, to see how we fare.
He knows within his heart that we are children of worth,
that's why he gave his only son for us to live on earth.
And now he's giving you a chance to show how strong you are
For he will not forsaken you nor take you away too far.

So, lift your head up high to God and say a little prayer
For he will hear your every word, because he's always there!
And when the times get rugged, the road seem long and so
fall upon your knees and pray; he'll show you which way to go.
God is always by your side as well as being your 'best' friend
and he will be beside you always through thick and thin!

Elsie M. Jackson

If It Does Not Fit...

I hate the way you practice your trade
This phony honesty, this tell it all
'You have the right to know'
What if you need to put your life in order

I hate the way you practice your trade
Painting this scary picture
Not leaving out any possible wrong
Just in case it turns sour, your hands are washed
the steam is off.

I hate the way you practice your trade
Underlining the negatives
Instead of encouragement and building confidence
You tell them they may die
If they live you saved them

I hate the way you practice your trade
You know who you are
Why can't you help people believe in their strength
You still be needed not to worry
And the credit you'll get will be true glory.

Eva A. Schiff

Nature's Message

Listen when it's silent, listen carefully.
Look when nothing's there, you may hear
And see nature out there talking to you,
Making sounds only nature can
Above the noise of people near.
Above the pounding and machines.
Although close we don't often hear. Listen
when it's silent. Look when nothing's there.

That buzzing is from an insect. That sound
comes from a quail. A rabbit just ran
across that log. See the white of his tail?
That flash of light was lightning streaking
through the sky. That rumbling was a thunder roll.
It wasn't a truck going by.

Nature's color in wonderful shades,
Displaying hues of tranquility.
A glimmer of red, a touch of blue.
Look! There is so much to see.
When the cares of the day cause concern,
Listen! Observe! Nature's talking to you.

Carol Helmkay

Somewhere In A War On Planet Earth

It was raining and cold
. . . A bleak winter day
But the pilots
. . . Dropped their bombs anyway
Papa . . . papa . . . I heard him call
. . . Just before I saw him fall
He rose and staggered toward me
. . . As if to hide
One arm outstretched
. . . One dangling by his side
Blood spurted softly out of each ear
. . . And from his mouth came moans of fear
His wild eyes looked toward me with pleading terror
. . . And if I could correct this horrendous error
I knelt with him there in the rain and mud
. . . And watched him choke on the gurgling blood
His face grew pale . . . his eyes rolled back
. . . His body jerked . . . and then grew slack
I screamed and cursed in wild despair
. . . As he died in my arms . . . my son so fair

Norman Edgmon

My Haven

There is a place that I call home
free from worry a peacefulness,
for Serenity is there
a blessed quiet, which all our souls need
our thoughts become other worldly
a sigh is given, a prayer is spoken
we are as one, a unity of spirit prevails
a coming together

Hosannah in the highest...

A choir whose songs are uplifting
noble words to help us on our way
The blessings are many
    and as we stand to say goodbye
    there's a smile for a stranger
a handshake freely given, a neighbor to say hello to
and the business of life begins
    But we take with us a happiness of knowing it can be again
Once we enter its door and choose a quite place
to sit once more and meditate
    with him...

Joan Collins Kleist

No Food

Love is the food we all hunger for, only
Some of us will never admit our need for it.
As a result, we have a supposedly civilized
World, that is willing to kill without thought
Of compassion or of consequence.

I wonder just when it was that someone's life
Became so unimportant? 'Even life inside the womb'...

Love is the food we all hunger for, only
Some of us can never show it.
As a result, we have supposedly civilized
World that can watch people starve and
Little babies and children die without
Batting an eye.

Love is the food we all hunger for,
Yet some of us can't give. If only King
Solomon were here today and through his
Wisdom; maybe he could decide which
Babies should live by deciding who at
First, was fit to be a mother!

Shirley D. Ladson

In Bethlehem

Nested in hay, a baby sleeps.
Wearily the young peasant woman
Leans on her husband's shoulder,
Glad for his gentle strength,
As they settle to rest in stable hay.
The patient donkey drowses
After his long journey;
While cattle meditatively watch
Pondering what they've seen.
But there will be no quiet rest
For here come sturdy shepherds
'Though 'tis but the middle of the night.
Alert, anxious, excited, they come
For this night is strange, so different-
There's that star, dazzling bright,
Angel voices, wondrous promises,
They came to know, to worship.

The baby wakes
And smiles.

Audrey C. Hague

The Ultimate Emotion

There are those who believe,
Love cannot be explained,
For if this is true,
There is no wrong way.
Listen, and I shall explain.
From the inside middle there lies a soul;
And a heart, without being torn;
From this middle part-heart
Builds a raging burst of energy;
That releases every emotion within you
And bleeds through your body
Like a warm spell.
Such a sensation is a piece of art,
Given only by the Love Goddess.
This feeling, unlike most, is intense.
This is — The Ultimate Emotion!
So treat it like gold, don't let it go,
Then when you're in love,
You'll be the one who knows
That love is explain only by — The one in love.

Loretta Twardesky

One More Chance

One more chance
To say, "I love you"
One last chance
To say goodbye

You are gone
But not forgotten
I will remember everything

One more chance
To do the things we did
One last chance for fun

Everything we've done are memories
All those times, I took for granted
Thinking you'd be here forever

One more chance to feel your love
One last chance to hear your laugh

Saying goodbye is the hardest of all
As the realization hits me that you are not here

One more chance to see your smile
One last chance to say goodbye

Just one more chance...

Misti McCanna

Why Did Grandpa Have To Die

Why did grandpa have to die?
To help hold the baby angels in his hand.
To help the little ones in the promised land.
To help with the angels' wings.
And many more things.

Why did grandpa have to die?
To help dust the moon beams.
To help polish the rainbow until it gleams.
To help light the stars each night.
To help keep the sun so bright.

Why did grandpa have to die?
To chase the clouds away.
To help change the night into day.
To help with worms and fishing poles.
To help comfort the lost souls.

Why did grandpa have to die?
To find the path we must take.
To guide us in our decisions we must make.
To greet us when we see him again.
To be there for his family and friends.

Michelle Braden

Our Happy New Year

I say to every one a Merry Happy New Year
Every one knows that this is a annual event
This is the time for your cheer and joy
Every one now seems to be very bold and happy

Most every one wants to show their great joy
This is one of the great times of the whole year
All the people realize this is their great time
Their spirit is indeed full of great joy and love

The new year will be our very great thrill
Every one now is indeed ready for the affair
With good health and great pride is a joy
So be ready for your great smashing new year

The new year can be a very great and good affair
It will make feel a pleasure to be filled with joy
Just as a musical show will say with great love
Be ready for all the great events and be sincere

Charles Vallo

Aries

I miss my poodle, Aries was black
I'll never get that feeling back
'Cause I won't give my heart again
for six long years I've felt the pain.

Protective and loyal for fifteen years
no dog had ever been so dear;
my Aries gave me pleasure and pride
so loving and always close to my side.

He had his time of being contrary,
a royal pain, sometimes was my Aries,
but just like children, you love them forever,
they contribute to life, even after it's over.

No one gives unconditionally
the love dogs give to us so free
he trusted me until the end
did I do right? Will my heart mend?

When holidays come, I miss him the most.
Aries loved turkey - of that I can boast.
So sweet and loving he used to be,
we were so close, my Aries and me.

Helena Stein Collins

Humility

Lord, slow me down, when I go ahead of you
And tread on petals meant only for angel's feet,
And light my way with the glow of holy fire,
That I may always follow the path where we may meet.

Lord, take my hand and guide me through the waters
That crash around me, and make me fear and tremble.
Oh let me see with eyes of unfeigned faith
The joys you place before me, that make me truly humble.

Lord, take my heart and fill it with your love.
That I may see all others as you do,
And hide me behind your cross of sacrifice
Until my will becomes one with you.

Beatrice Northcutt

Fallin' Love

A tear falls from my hollow eyes
onto my shattered heart
that beats in pieces on the rocks below
as people just turn and glare at me.

One picks up a jagged piece.
Thrusts it deep within my soul.
The others laugh heartily
as only blackness pours out onto the ground.

I weep, for no one will help me
gather the pieces of my puzzle.
They only shrug their shoulders,
look at me in disgust, and walk away.

Why can't peace reign?
Why can't love stay and make the glue stick?
A feather duster brushes my lips,
and takes away the wrinkles and the gray.

Becky Compson

Homesick For Heaven

He sits very quiet in the very first row
Alone in the church, he hangs his head low.
He covers his face, holding back the tears
Without being asked, the Lord then appears
"Tell me son, what makes you cry?"
The Lord asked the man and he then replied,
"I want to go to Heaven, but it seems a hard road
And this burden I carry becomes a heavy load.
Please take me now, I'm ready to leave
I've suffered enough, please give me peace."
The Lord then answered, "I know this pain
I felt it once, so you would be saved.
I promised you that I would go
And prepare a place for you in my home
But it's not ready, it's not yet time
For your job's not finished and neither is mine."

Mary Henry

Halloween

On all Hallow's Eve when the moon turns round,
Creatures of night arise from the ground.
Ghosts and demons arise from their graves,
They come out to eat you, make you their slaves

Go down to the pond when the moon is full,
What you will see shall go untol'.
Goblins of darkness will swallow you whole,
And the next thing you know you're stuck on a pole.

Climb into your bed at the midnight hour,
What you shall hear is not the shower.
Zombies and monsters look thru a screen
And then screech "Boo It's Halloween!"

Kyle Jarrett

Like Any Other Fugitive

Like any other fugitive I spurn the traveled roads.
I shun responsibility, and popular abodes.
I see my mortal enemy behind each rock and tree.
Paranoia's catching on, I swear they follow me.
I'm a fugitive from love without a home address,
A fugitive from love a love that couldn't care less.

I stop for food and coffee; more often for a drink.
I slide beside my silent friend and side by side we think.
I thought that you loved me. I thought that you were true.
But you were only using me, if I had only knew...

Love is the most dangerous game,
They talk all sweet, and yet, so vain,
They tease you, leave you, it's always the same.
The whole damn play's driving me insane

Now it's me and the silver centipede who runs along my right.
He moves ahead, endlessly, faster in his flight.
On to the end of the rainbow, on to my pot of gold.
On to the end of this very earth until I grow old.

I'm a fugitive from love without a home address,
A fugitive from love - a love that couldn't care less.

Robert E. Wall Jr.

A Challenge

Did you know, we are having another contest?
All right lets have it and do our best.
You write me we'll give 'em a good poem, to-boot,
Realizing we must put forth a good bit of time,
Ending our poem too soon wouldn't be worth a dime,
Anyhow we'll give it our very best shot,
Knowing our effort might put us in the winning pot,
On we go, full steam ahead, do not shirk a bit,
Now that we've started we must not quit,
The end is in sight, glory be, could it be?
Heavenly days, I can already faintly see,
Everything is coming together, now give it a shove,
Let's give it a little more, it will fit like a glove.
All aboard now, two more stations to pass,
Now we have achieved our best laid plan,
Do you know, we have written about, day break on the Land?

Edgar P. Boslaugh

Innocence Abused

She entered life, shining eyes aglow
Her pain to come, she couldn't know.
She loved her parents, thought them good
But they didn't treat her like they should.

Burns and breaks, she suffered all
Slaps and shoves, was this her call?
Still she loved them, yet, didn't know why
Cowering in the corner she continued to cry.

Daily punishment, most certainly, strife
Why, dear God, did they give her life?
She did not know how she would fair
At the hands of her parents, her own nightmare.

She prayed at night, forgiving the abuse
But deep inside, she knew there was no use.
She wasn't convinced, and thought she might die
A good, quiet girl, she wondered why.

After so much pain, she now rests in peace
Was she, a mere child, only here on lease?
Now she soars with the angels, wearing a smile
But alas, how long before it's another child?

Deborah Xanthakis

Holocaust

There is an unseen holocaust,
Flying up above,
The worst thing to happen,
So far away from love.
Their little hands and fingers,
And little feet and toes,
Right down to their little ears,
And tiny little nose.
The mothers need a taste of their own medicine,
It's a child, not a choice,
But unfortunately there is no man,
With a strong enough voice.
If only people would listen,
That either unborn or born,
It's still a human being,
All their thoughts are forlorn.
There is an unseen holocaust,
And people's minds are in a state of contortion,
Because this unseen holocaust,
Is unfortunately ABORTION.

Christine Rees

The Journey From Pain

It was the desperate loneliness that I still recall,
as if no one was listening, and no one could hear...
the cry for help coming from deep within my soul.
The memory of that time can still draw a tear.

It was time when I chose to walk alone,
slowly drowning amidst the despair and the strife.
Not knowing it was my disbelief, a lack of faith...
that kept God's light from shining on my life

...And I remember believing how it must be true
that a loving God would not allow so much pain.
Until I walked a garden and began to understand,
to bloom a flower needs both sun and the rain.

It was the desperate loneliness that I still recall,
and the realization now is so very clear...
that the pain and the hurt were part of the growth...
and I had to be there, before I could get here.

Stephen P. Maxson

Old Charlie Rocking Chair

Old Charlie Rocking Chair aged and worn,
Awaited in the attic a new life to be born.
Treasure of antiques standing idle and retired,
Mellowing in seclusion, hope nearly expired.

With an air of expectancy something was in store!
Charlie could sense it even on the third floor.
He was moved downstairs to a spacious room;
Dusted and polished again life would bloom.

All chairs in the house were being collected,
And placed in rows, many people were expected.
A fabulous fashion show was soon to start;
Charlie was so proud to be doing his part.

Then the guests arrived, the show was underway;
The fates smiled on Charlie, this was his day.
From the still of the attic with all hopes fading,
To now soft music with new fashions parading.

A huge portly lady representing the press,
Rocked back on Charlie, the show a success.
Then a shrill scream as she sprawled in the aisle!
Old Charlie Rocking Chair had omit collapsed in style.

C. C. Anderson

Love Is Sovereign

Love is a har-mon-iously complex so-na-ta for two
an e-labo-rate cer-e-mo-ni-ous-ly feast, a banquet
a spir-i-tu-al-ized- rebirth of pu-ri-fi-ca-tion, a baptism
a splendorous gran-dil-ol-quence multi-plex of emotions
a spon-ta-ne-ous quaking of the soul and spirit, with a
peaceful manifold of sen-sa-tions

Love is a rhyth-mi-cal-ly succession of sweet sounds, a melody
a monarch reigning over a glo-ri-ous empire,a su-preme power
a pre-cious gem, pre-em-i-nent-ly flow-less, trans-par-ent, a diamond
A sym-pho-ny of vi-o-lins strummed, by be-nev-o-lence of love
A gift of he heart, your innermost being, a red ruby

Love is bril-liant can-des-cent light glow-ting, an-chored
on the top of a great mountain, that sit in the midst of the deep blue sea,
and paints beautifully colored pictures, and ex-ot-ic de-signs
on all the creatures in the deep
love is a stat-ue of lib-er-ty, for all the world to see,
love is the ab-so-lute sov-er-eign-ty

Belle Buckley

A Wild King

Tempest desert wind, a wild king on the march.
A whip in the hand of a conqueror,
beating a land into a kingdom,
life imprisoned by his verdict.
Desert dragon breath, a wild kings tormenting voice,
Fire baked earth pottery, blazing in dazzlement.
A blistered land, gnarled and twisted.
Sunrise and sunset painting his destiny.
Scorched desert riverbed, a wild kings unquenchable thirst.
Lost lakes waiting for centuries.
A land of vanished dreams and memories,
only a mirage for hope.

Desert thunder desire, a wild kings privacy intruded.
A moment of heavenly conquest.
A little drink to last for years.
A chamber of flowers, a queens gown.
Howling, hissing and screeching, a wild kings selfish cry
Little room for queens, scales and thorns his crown.
Dust, sand and eternal sun his royal robes.
Beauty from waste and destruction his only honor.

Robert Price

My Cross

From all eternity God's wisdom could see
My cross from His inmost heart...
As a greeting to show His love for me,
And the grace that I'd do my part.

With His all-knowing eyes and his mind so divine,
He has tested with justice so wise,
It was warmed in His arms,
    weighed in hands, oh so kind,
To make sure it would be just my size.

With the blessings of His most holy name,
He anointed it with His grace...
And along with it His consolation came,
As He took one last glance at my face.

He knew just much courage
    He would on me bestow,
As His alms of all-merciful love...
And He gave me the light and the faith to know,
That my cross was His gift from above!

Patricia A. Sibley

January Chill

A cold snap that cast a pall on the Godless world,
A screen door loose bangs loudly in the raging wind
The wreath long trashed, the razor needles fine curled
Mock the Christmas and New Year that blast their way in.
Alone, I have two monthly and painful curses,
The absent spouse, and the red stain of promises not kept.
My father's seventy-fifth longs for eloquent verses.
A barren womb lies empty, expectant, and unspent.
A screen door loose bangs loudly in the raging wind,
A pulsing drumbeat of broken, sacred vows.
This casket for a womb, cannot conceive even in sin.
The husband returns; the winds continue to howl.
A cold snap did cast a pall on the Godless world,
Spring will come, and he will let loose his pearl.

Anne Faynberg

It Hurt So Bad

It hurt so bad
I feel so bad
Now I'm mad
The pain in my heart feels so bad
This pain makes me sad
My life sometimes makes me mad
Don't let my smile fool you nor my
Body language or my sweetness
Even though I may speak like every things okay
That's because I have faith and I know
God will come through for me and if you're
going through something,
The same God that comes through for me
Will come through for you also "but you have to believe"

Rhonda E. Lloyd

Why Poetry?

Why do we write poetry you ask?
Now you've given me an enjoyable task
telling a story and making it rhyme
words fill my thoughts all the time
without poems there'd be no songs
we'd really miss those sing-a-longs
expressing emotions - messages from the heart
putting it together is fun once you start
to tell about the babbling brooks
or expressing how the scenery looks
to bring back memories we hold dear
or just some foolishness pleasing to the ear
Some poems can sooth the mind
While others a happy spot may find
praising God for all we've been given
to let him know we're thankful to be livin'
the beauty that surrounds our life
or the help words can be in times of strife
happy or fun - religious or nostalgic
having poetry is really fantastic

Peggy A. Wolford

The Lovers Rendezvous

Hearts throbs, on route to their spot.
Greetings so intense, it's hot, hot, hot.
Lovers touch deep inside, its the desire to be,
In the kiss you can see.
The union so bold,
As lovers immerse in each other soul.
Knowing the world that each other must face,
Holding loving memories, in what seem like an endless brace.
Rendezvous precious moments, as they depart,
With love contentment in their hearts.

Michelle Griffith

The Key Of Christmas

Where was the peace the angels brought?
Where was the star the wisemen sought?
The star was dimmed by the clouds of smoke that covered the sky
And seemed to choke the brilliance of its radiant light
That once glowed brightly each Christmas night.
The peace has come after years of war when a key of hatred
Had locked the door, it did then and has before.
Forever destroy this key of hate and let people live in
A blessed state of peace with all his fellowmen, let us keep
Faith and then we can look to the Lord for a helping hand.
And forge a key of peace on earth and polish it brightly for
All its worth, it will weigh as gold.
And will shine in the heavens as the star of old shone down
With its radiance bright on that first Christmas Eve that
Holy night, the key of peace will unlock the door to love
And hope as it has before, it will shine brightly as before
The war, each Christmas night men will delight
As they gaze at the heavens of christmas night.
And so let us with the angels sing,
"Praises to God, our Maker and king!"

Anita Carlson

The Players

We are the chosen actors in a dimensional play.
Stories unwind before us to be told another day.
Memories remain behind the mind, good and bad combined,
To torment or produce pleasure, whichever desire inclined.
Audience applauding, enjoying just to gaze.
What is to come next, they wonder,
Or is it just writings on a page.
Dance while the rhythm takes the soul,
to planes of spiritual stage.
Laughter echoes from within,
Soothing sounds of violent rage.
Players follow instinct planted from a seed.
To grow and flourish with a thought,
Is quite unique indeed.
Others will learn from our mistakes,
Or follow in our shoes.
We only have time to practice,
There is nothing else to lose.

Connie Mae Miller

The Oldest Living Child In History

In parks and yards I watch the children play
And listen to the music of their caravan
That lightens all the burdens of their day
With chords that were as sweet when I began.

In parks and yards I know what children feel,
They never see beyond what they behold,
Tomorrow does not seem to be so real,
Till children look at me and say, "He's old!"

In parks and yards I am a sad old fool.
On my park bench I sit and think of me.
I never learned the truths they taught in school;
But life, that teacher taught them vividly.

In parks and yards I watch the sun go down
And yawn beneath the feeble evening lights,
Who peep when earth puts on her evening gown,
And all I dare to say are fond good nights.

Old fools like me grow tired from time's decay.
Life's treasure was that childhood filled with glee,
And you may find me there again someday,
The oldest living child in history.

Russell Phillips

Sonnet Shop

Of well stocked rhymes in fourteen lines; iambic pentameter.
I chose several two line stanzas to form a couplet.
Precisely placed I grab the Villanelle and Ballad.
Next to shelves of four line stanza names,
Were tantalizing strains of fine quatrains.
Marked two for one, made the rubai valid.
These sonnet products I collect without regret.
I took the only octave left, though it was bent a centimeter.

Items checked, the bill is met, I delight in resolution.
My eye then caught the pattern of a bright Rondeau-
A last selection thought the clerk remaining in position,
Who bagged the latest items of my last decision.
A discount on a book of sonnets - to see me through,
Then I select the sestet last to make my sound conclusion.

Marylin Matthews Reed

Beauty

Take pride in what you do
Let it show the beauty of you

Take a look at the earth
Its glorious beauty shines forth with birth
The flowers in the season of their bloom
The insects that keep them groomed

The waters that form a fall
Trees that grow short and tall
The waves that come to the beach
The fishes that swim sea deep

All together the beauty of love
Given so graciously from the one above
Let your beauty be a display
Start with others by what you say

Dee Rivers

My Grandma Memories Of Her Death

My grandma always had a open heart
and a great big smile.
When you stopped by she would sit
and talk.
No matter how busy she always rested
awhile.
Or go outside and take a walk.
One day I woke up and everything was fine
Then I received a call about my Grandma.
and it just blew my mind.
It was my Mom to tell me she was gone.
The doctors tried and tried but it just was her time.
I'm really trying to be strong.
It was just two years but it doesn't
seem that long.
The pain is there, but I know she is fine.
The angels have her and are playing her song.
Someday it might not hurt, but it will be fine.
Until then I'll just keep her memory in my mind.

Shari Goldstein

A Dewdrop For Jay

A drew drop forms on the early morning grass;
it is saying: I will not stay, for I am
passing in due time, and your mission is to
remain and grow, in love, and be sublime.
For what is life, if not a fiery hell, but,
rather a time for sharing, in love, and a time
to dwell on things profound, yet make us well.
So little dewdrop don't despair, your sojourn
is brief but sublimely rare -
for only those who see and understand and care.

Richard Belsky

Winding Paths to Happiness

Is there a shepherd of words,
By any chance a guard of thoughts?
Wisdom is not merchandise on which to bet,
Nor for showing around in a fancy fair.
Who could claim without making of oneself a fool
To be the owner of someone else's mind, spirit or soul?

Leading paths to happiness
Are often engulfed by waves of sadness.
Like a twinkling light reflecting on ice,
Therefore seen as countless devices,
Whereas the source remains secret;
Joy springs from life's multiple facets.

I'd like for you to be bold, beloved daughter,
Not to mourn so long for a silent sorrow.
Very soon will resonate vibrations of laughter
When love will shine anew like a beaming rainbow.

Anything that really matters and moves
Adds a scent of wisdom to our most humble move.
Sorrow will transmute into the richest array
When you will give it way to flow away.

Dominique Aguessy

Grieving

I sit alone late of an evening
Unable to sleep 'cause inside I'm grieving
Thinking of one so far away
Who is disappearing a little each day
I'll call her and hear that dear voice
She is cheerful and my heart will rejoice
Perhaps it is only my imagination
Suddenly the conversation causes consternation
As it is full of disjointed thoughts
Like a manuscript covered with so many blots
She'll close abruptly thinking she has called me
So I turn and hang up the phone sadly
It is so hard for me to comprehend
As I see her slowly going 'round the bend
Realizing her spirit will soon be out of sight
And I sit here and grieve in the night

Joan M. Baker

To Walk Away

Lifting the baby in her arms,
And taking her second son's hand,
She leaned forward and knocked
    on the heavy brown door of the shelter.

Why are they taking so long?
Why so slow? Please come,
It was hard to walk away.
Her strength and courage were gone.

"Hello", a soft voice spoke.
"Come in, my dear. Come out
    of the cold.
Here, let me take the child."

"We have a warm fire,
And food is on the table".
The kind lady smiled and
    led the way.

It was working. She had done it.
At last, she had walked away
    from the hell-filled house.
"An angel". She kissed the baby's face.

Jettie M. McWilliams

Fourth Of July

The scene was of a picture book picnic
on the Fourth of July
Friends, family and those we just met
came together for an occasion
I'll never forget
Fun and games, food and song, fireworks and noise
As the day went on
From daylight to dark
or as we say dust to dawn
It was a wonderful day
and I wanted it to go on and on and on
The closeness and the wonderful times shared by all
It makes you remember back
When you were so very small
How simple it was and how
much fun
Why can't those days come back
When the family was number #1

Sharlene Gagnon

Any Moment...I Am Waiting!

The shuffle of a sturdy stride,
approaches through the darkened hall
there is no one, no one at all

Any moment...I am waiting!

The scent is pungent, sweat and salt,
the heightened senses, an excited call
there is no one, no one at all

Any moment...I am waiting!

The faintest silhouette black as oil,
glides across an empty wall
there is no one, no one at all

Any moment...I am waiting!

What is it, has me so aroused?
The scent, the sound, the sight, the call
there is no one, no one at all.

But any moment...

Bill Hoeppner

Shadow Dancer

I've danced with my shadow many times,
But mostly through the pain,
One step to the left, a step to the right,
I used to dance all morning,
But, now not even at night,
It's not that I don't want to,
I'd love to dance again,
With cancer it's impossible to do,
I have a favor to ask of you,
If you could, please,
Take my shadow by the hand, and I'll give a little squeeze,
Dance with my shadow when I am gone,
It doesn't take very long,
When you dance with my shadow,
There's no need to cry,
I've done it all when I danced through my pain,
I'll leave when my final dance is over, with you that is,
You won't need to look for me,
You will see my hand in your dreams, clutched in yours,
Just wait; I'll see you in heaven.
                Sincerely, Your Shadow Dancer

Michelle Basinger

With Eyes Full Of Pale Lust

Some desire our magnificent love and
the sacred pleasure which we devour,
but soon will come the enormous ache,
Perhaps it will caress the morning angel.

The breeze that pierced through another sad dream
seeps like honey through a thousand familiar embraces.

Come, let's dance like drunken stars,
be my prisoner and death will not know
the starving blaze,
but only the taste of sugar-sweet naked air.

But with this,
I ask you,
would it be ridiculously hard
    to clutch my flower,
melt my ice,
and celebrate this evening with me?

Sunni L. Sheets

At The Feet Of Jesus

Dedicated to my Children, David, Heather and Holly
An angel appeared to the mother to be,
    a son she would have on Christmas eve.
No mention of all the pain she'd sown.
Only that her son would be someone we'd all know.

The love of her life, a son named Jesus,
Whom would become a savior for us,
Many people would learn to believe in and trust.
He came from God above to show us, love one another we must.

Little did Mary know the suffering her son would bestow,
Mary loved him like only a mother could know.
She would endure each pain and suffering as his life went on
    the way we would all be shown.
For the depth of a mothers love can never really be understood,
For even today no son can ever really have known.

A mother can never really let go, even Mary begged with God so.
At Calvary Mary knelt that day,
    her son was not the only one who would bleed.
A cry from her lips would also lowly be heard,
    just let it be over from you God I need.

At the feet of Jesus she was all along as her son hung on that
    dogwood tree,
That wondrous day, she showed the strength of a mothers
    bond for all the world to see.
To give to us a life in eternity.

Shirley J. Bierly

Winter's Flight

Black, gray and downy white
juxtaposed against a south winter's sky so blue
reflect nature's rhythmatic flight.

Outstretched wings construct a perfect V
as inner instincts beckon them back
to winter's home near a snowy jubilee.

Mother nature has guided her children home
where old man winter scatters glistening frost
on morning wings that she calls her own.

But when glistening frost turns into dew
mother nature's children will again take flight
in search of a north winter's sky so blue.

C. Kay Bassett

In The Beginning "Our Creator"

When we watch the sky at sunset,
Or when we gaze at the clouds so high,
As we look at the vastness without end,
We think of our Creator as He fashioned the sky.

As we reach the top of a mountain,
Or watch the power of the waves and tides,
In awe we are filled with wonders,
At the beauty our Creator provides.

The heavens send the rain, wind and snow,
Which men with all knowledge and skill,
Cannot control what our Creator sends,
He rules the universe, and forever will.

The floods, earthquakes and hurricanes come,
Causing destruction and havoc to men,
Helpless to stop our Creator's power,
Bringing to all, acknowledgement of Him.

Patricia Taylor

Seasons Greetings

Decorating the trees and putting up the lights,
Christmas time is full of beautiful sights.
Snow is falling upon the ground,
Making not even a little sound.
Santa and his reindeer flying overhead,
To deliver presents for those who are in bed.
The next morning when we all awake,
We'll find many presents for all to take.
Everyone is shouting out with glee,
Hope your Christmas is merry!

At Christmas people tend to overlook,
What is stated in that Bible book.
What does Christmas really mean?
What past people have really seen.
It's not about the presents that you get upon that day,
Nor Santa and his reindeer flying in his sleigh.
Jesus was born for all to see,
How much God loves you and me.
So this Christmas don't overlook,
Why we have Christmas and what's in that book!

Ashley Annette Bauman

"Happy Faces"

Why is it that December and January
so much happiness seems to send.
Then around February and March
that happiness seems to end.
Why can't Christmas and New Years
be the same all year through,
To see all those happy faces
in a dream that can come true.
You see we all have our ups and downs.
This you must understand.
But you as a loving person
could reach out with a helping hand.
Let someone know you love them,
and you'll be there in their time of need.
Then they could put on a happy face
and you also for your good deed.
So take time to understand what I'm saying,
'Cause what I say is true.
Just remember that day may come along
When that person who needs someone is you.

Anne Quetel

Is It I?

In all the world is there only one?
Was the pattern destroyed when it was done?
Very carefully I've tried to preserve
This mortal being who gets on my nerves!

Contemptible - arrogant - detestable too!
All of these adjectives well describe who?
Not very flattering - wouldn't you say?
Can't change a loser there's just no way!

Is this perhaps a description of me?
Oh dear Lord - please don't let it be!
I do match that description on bad days -
But only on some - not always!

Helene Treadway

Twilight

Twilight brings the evening sounds,
I hear the footsteps of my love.
He comes along the path,
Out of the woods he came.

I see the clouds painted pink,
As the golden sun doth go to rest,
And my love comes walking,
Out of the fields, he comes.

Clouds float overhead,
And birds settle down to rest,
And look, there comes my love,
Up from the valley and through the woods.

There comes my love,
With eyes so clear and blue,
Like the water clear,
And the heavens blue.

In the evening so quiet,
My love comes to me
With a beautiful smile,
Out of the woods he came to me!

Nadine Moonje Pleil

Frustration

We live in a crisis
Our lives are full of pain.

We get thru one crisis,
but what do we gain?

Our life is full of turmoil, one
thing after another.

One problem solved and another one appears.
It just makes you want to sit and let out the tears.

But the tears don't help, just a release,
Sort of like a short term lease.

Pamela Powell

Through My Window

Through my window are wonderful things.
Little green elves and horses with wings.
If you go through my window,
Where will you be?
A place of enchantment
And blue salty seas.
Where wizards fly and rule the sky,
Where dwarfs dwell with magic spells.
This place where my life should be
Is my imagination that's full
of adventures and glee.

Sarah Hammond

Nothing More

As I look up into the sky, I see no stars, no moon,
just blue

When I look out into the street, I see no people, no
movement, just cars

I stare to the ground, I see no life, no warmth, just dirt
I then stare at me; I peer into myself, and I see no
heart, no soul, just flesh

While wondering who or what I am, I feel my
surroundings

I listen to the sounds of nothing

My soul is calling out for someone, anyone to hear me
but I am nothing

I belong to no one, so no one hears my cry

I have become a shell

My heart was once as strong as a whale

My life was once a meaningful one

Now I am left with nothing more than cold, hard, and
desperate flesh

Dominique L. Hill

Needing You

As I walk along the beach
  I take a look at the past,
Wondering where the years went
  Or why they never last.

"What have I done? What will I do?"
"What will life be like, living without you?"

You were there to guide me
  to help me sort my mind,
Even with the little things
  you always took the time.

I guess the time had come,
  when someone else needed you too.
Why does this happen? Only God can make it true.

Now you are gone, forever
  I can't "Wish" you back,
This is called death
  and no one can change these facts.

So no matter where you are keep looking over me,
Cause now I feel blind needing your eyes to see.

Tina M. Bowser

Untitled

There is always right from wrong
No matter what the reason,
It is not the same old song,
Not the black or white, or Indian or Croation - Lebanon
There is always right from wrong,
Like child abuse - just no excuse
There is always right from wrong;
Let's not blame it on the seasons
or the welted burnt out lawns
With crosses, chains that do us harm-
There is always right from wrong;
Not Republican or Democrat
Or even independent "Spats"
Without we all should be.
The truth you see, my friends,
Lies deep within us all -
Can't we all just get along
There is always right from wrong.

Nathan K. Sanders

Treasure The Memories

Even though we are far away
the miles don't diminish the love

Since we cherish our special connection
which was blessed from up above

As each day passes, I stop and think
of the years that have gone by

I will always treasure the memories
and all the beauty that has touched
our lives

You are my soul inspiration
teaching me guidance and hope

Love and understanding with
smiles to cope

With deepest sincerity for all
you do and say

May our rewards always show us
the happiness in a giving way.

Marla Aweau Britten

Great Ship

Great ship where are you headed?
Great ship with your sails so high
Soaring like eagles toward the sky
Sails waving like the dreams of time
Great ship where are you headed?
Your arms are towers that shout to the stars
Like a child, your head looks toward the land of peace and joy
Great ship where are you headed?
Land that awaits you is the land of freedom for all men
The water that you float upon are the many sorrows of time
The waves are like cold hearts that wait upon the river's shore
Is the God that awaited you, the God from whom Freedom flow?
Great ship where are you headed?

Johnnie Mae Queen

I Can Remember...

I can remember the summers, the long drive there.
the love that would be waiting,
with arms full of care.
hamburgers frying,
old dog on the rug,
hands wet from dishwater,
but you still got a hug.

I can remember getting hurt, and she'd ask, "are
you okay?" Then kiss the hurt, call you squirt, and
send you on your way.

Even when she was in poor health,
she'd worry of others instead of herself.

Then pain and the suffering, the thought of her
death, in spite of that, she still had fight left.

She held onto life as long as she could,
living it to the fullest as we knew she would.

We all received the chance, to make with her peace,
to hear her words to put our souls at ease.
To my Grandma, we give thanks for the memories
we have, the good ones, the bad ones, the happy and sad...

Opaljean Rogers

Of Love And Hate

Each brought on by an emotion
With out a conscious notion.
Sometimes both lingers with the energy of a mountain,
But can be drained like a fountain.
Sometimes confused, and many times misused.
Some say it's shy, and some as the reason why,
some will live for it, and some will kill for it.
Some have many, and some have few,
but for some it never knew.
Some will lie for it,a nd some will die for it,
but there's never a reason why for it.
Because of it there are no laws against it.

Billy E. Harris

"The Dream"

Yesterday I had a dream, a soft-spoken whisper in my ear.
I know it was felt throughout the atmosphere.

The dream was short, but ever so real. It gladdened me with
so much appeal. It told me to "Believe in Me", and everything
my eyes could see.

Then for one moment I felt a quake, could this have been all a
mistake? For, all in one second, the dream was alive, the
whisper in my ear...oh, it felt ever so near.

Quickly I laid down to sleep, for forever it will be my "Dream
to keep"!

Helen Loftus

Nature's Cry

Put yourself in her shoes, and set yourself aside,
By laws of the land, will man ever abide?

We swim in her waters, and bathe in her sun,
Only to destroy it with things we have done.

Wise men at work, with their inventions so great,
They never stopped to think, and now it's too late.

You ask me what you did, where you went wrong,
Look in your lives the problem was there all along.

The waters aren't safe, for drink or for play,
What will you do, have you nothing to say?

Stop and listen for a moment, before you hurriedly rush by,
Can't you hear in the wind, the soft pleading cry?

It is not a child, or even a man,
It is the cry of the nature, you don't understand.

So when you look in the mirror, before starting your day,
Please remember it's not only your life you're throwing away.

Heather Denise Hagen

Unfinished Anthem To Fall Never-Ending

Love is alive on a gray, fall day.
Mist is the air, while the sun is away.
Feeling no sorrow, my heart beats gay.
This is my joy, encouraging my stay.

Feeling the breeze as it penetrates my skin,
chills me inside as if it were sin.
What to surmise, to make of my grin?
As fall was before so be it Again!

Some colors yet blooming while other trees bare,
bring from me an unquenchable, uncontrollable stare.
How I love these days as a child's first fair.
Glad to see nature and hope Forever . . .
it's there.

Scott A. Bowser

I Am Me

I am me
can't you see
a little girl
that's me.
Please don't look at me with sorrow
because there is always tomorrow.
I am different but so are you
if you look in your heart you will see it is true.
People say I am handicapped, but I am still a child.
When you look at me see the child, I am me.

Caroline A. Clapper

Before The World Began

Before the world began,
life was known to man.
In our pre-existent state,
We (spirits then), eagerly
and anxiously awaited our journey
to a home called Earth,
where we could receive a body
of flesh and blood at our birth.

Our First Estate became perfect then,
giving us the form, we call man.
Both Body and Spirit, combined as one;
Our soul, our Entity.

We knew before we came to Earth,
We face adversity;
Even temptations, joy sorrow—
Opposition of all kinds

We were given the right to choose
the path we would follow.
The long and winding road to Exaltation—
or endless torment.

Naomi J. Hall

Hope's Flames Burn Brilliant

Hope's flames burn brilliant
in this day and age of darkness,
time is getting shorter and bleak,
but Jesus gives strength to the weak,
His flame burns brightly;
bright with hope on our starless skies nightly.

Hope's flames burn brilliant
to the sound of good news of the gospel of our savior;
come now lets reason together,
in season and out of season,
so that we may prosper in all kinds of weather.

Hope's flames burn brilliant
in God's perfect time
casting away our vain imaginations
for Father's perfect day, for: this Son's bride.
Victorious champions we are on our trek,
the pearly gates of heaven we shall see,
in God's perfect day we will be,
what the Holy Spirit intended for us to be.

Joe Hendrickson

Steadfast Love

The stars shine brightly in the sky as does
His love for you and I. He loves us deeply
As we know no matter which way we go. His love
Is all forgiving you see as he loves forever
You and me. I have fallen many times but he has
Forgiven me time after time. I get stronger as
I plod along as I know he loves whether I am
Weak or strong...

Gordon M. Morse

A Christian's Journey

Cast the infinite light upon this pilgrim's lonely face,
Guide me along my venture with inspirational grace.
Faithless hours tempt me and test me all about,
While intellectual thoughts weigh my mind with doubt.
Render to me the serenity that I surely hope to find,
With divine tranquility which is host to peace of mind.
Set my course of philosophy on that which you do aspire,
Manifest your glory to me when I begin to tire.
Bless me with reassurance as I take this perilous trip,
When the waters become turbulent deliver this sinking ship.
Grant me your benevolent wisdom and show me where to go,
And as I travel through my journey compel my mind to grow.
Humble me in my pride and exalt me in my shame,
Give to me forgiveness when my heart is filled with blame.
Instruct me in the way of life and how I ought to live,
Furnish my soul with charity and show me how to give.
Impel me with the motivation that I'll always have a friend,
Who'll lead me to the destination that never has an end.

Robert Calhoun

Heaven Can Wait

Bodies die, but the souls fly high
Much speculation, but no certain "Why"
Are they confined in a certain border
Or roam about without order
Segregated black, white, yellow, or red
Does it matter now that they're dead
Young and bold
Share space with weak and old
Do they finally see the light
Or like humans continue to find petty reasons to fight
Perhaps they join to celebrate "All Souls Day"
Instead of the usual "my way"
Endless possibilities occur to me
Varied as the imagination can see
One by one we fly away
The secret "Calendar of Life" knows the day
No one knows the answer why
We may one day fly with the clouds in the sky
Until then relax and enjoy life - Heaven can wait
The mystery to be solved on a blind day and date.

Grace Pascocello

E-Toast @ Aught Rising

Boot to the flatlands,
windows on the new cybergrooved frontier
Past clans on lining the 'Net,
blackspace,
the intermanic pragmatic panic
Digsig the lockouts and leave the hulks posing—the imagined
Tron
It's the homebase friendlies closing, zooming the infobhan
Real time changeover, highend if not style
The new files

That techno dislocation venting Nasty Nineties kung-fu,
Its accrued malaise, the electronic town meeting milieu
Left to construe
the open-ended antithetical
silicon venues: and
neoLuddities brainboxing Prozac

RAM on,
mindjets splaying the skywriters' tradeoffs
Uncertainty scanning the interactive consumer paradigm
Rooms full of more stuff—the same routine
Never enough

Dave Swanson

December Poem

Would that I were a great tree flowering,
One which men wanted to raise...
Alone, and over lesser limbs towering,
But never needful of plaudits or praise.

Questions, while blowing in the wind,
This tree would silently ponder.
What for, this company for others,
Yet nothing for him save wonder?

Is there no honor or balm for the branch
Which shoulders the righteous within its grasp?
Bowed down and heavy laden,
My tree of Truth is all but craven.

Mary Joyner Henry

Love's Melody

Love plucked at my heart strings, calling me away,
Sense and reason took their wings, and would not stay.
Voices of emotion, filled my ears, and veiled my eyes,
Awakening the empty years, showing me paradise.
Love plucked at my heart strings, and played a melody,
That in my wild imaginings, was played alone for me.
But love was only playing games, with my romantic heart,
Reality released the chains, tearing me apart.
But sometimes, I recall again, the music of those years,
Moving me to swift rebellion, and my heart to tears!

Brenda Orndorf

The Happy Child And The Judge

"Happiness is," the story-book said,
"to jump on the leaves." How he laughed as I read!
Our grandson and I set out for the park and
we jumped on the leaves until it grew dark.

The leaves, rust and scarlet and gold on the ground
in moveable mounds went swirling around.
How carefree our hearts, full of innocent joy:
The doting grandmother: The three year old boy!

Next morn, it was dawn when he came to our bed,
his baby curls humid, his cheeks warm and red,
(Oh, bless Dr. Denton's for thick padded feet,
snug flannel pajamas with buttoned drop-seat)

"Move over, grandpa," the child pleaded `The Court'
who burrowed down deeper mind snores and a snort.
Like a young billy-goat our boy vaulted the spread,
then, stood straight peering down at his folks in the bed.

I turned back the cover, there was just the right space
for a small boy to crawl in...how shining his face!
But before settling in with a leap and a nudge,
he said, "Happiness is - I jump on the Judge!"

Tigelia Cisco DiGiovanna

Summer Medley

Tall, green grass laden with dew
Bends beneath the whirring mower
And bees with stomachs filled with nectar
Suddenly take flight and head for home.

Grasshoppers cavort across the yard
As children scurry to capture them
And snails creep along the walk
Where roses release their heavy perfume.

Twilight falls on a summer evening
As crickets chirp their well-known song
And tiny lights blink off and on
As lightning bugs dance upon the lawn.

Sybil W. Nelms

If I Could

If I could live my life again,
I would graduate as valedictorian.
I'd travel through the universe,
Run the Boston marathon and come in first,
And ride the rapid rivers to quench my thirst.
I'd be the master of PhD's,
Then play short stop for the Yankees.
Writing stories might be fun,
And for an hour I might be a nun.
I'd swoosh on skies through snow, then bask in the sun.
Then I'd go fishing and roller blading,
Find a stream and do some wading,
And win the presidency without too much persuading.
The forest would set my soul at ease,
I'd fish all the rivers and swing by my knees
From the vines and branches growing on trees.
I'd live in a small house with a pet,
A dog named Petey who loved to get wet.
We would run to the ocean and sail far away,
But we would always return home where we are today.

Pat Reed

Desire

Why do I love her so? Where
When she is gone do my thoughts go?
To the dark mists around the waterfall of her hair,
To her brows like the touch of a finger
To linger around her smiling eyes, wide
And brimming, her mouth like a red camellia floated
On milk, her tongue - ah! her tongue
Living like another lover inside,
Her lips unpouted
Loving while the world is young.

Or to her neck, like the stroke of an artist's brush
Above the flush
Of her breasts, drifting like a fall of snow;
Or to that gate where all happinesses are,
Where I have been and have not been, not seen,
To speak of which I do not dare.

O my dear me, my sweet,
My love flows toward you. Run to it with swift feet.

Charles Shute

Flux

Time turns again as the night splits then cracks
    to hatch the garish familiar orb, morning star, sun
Jolting the world awake, prying with the early songs
    from feathery birds
Clamoring to the exhaust of industry belching smoke
Whine of electric razors and monotonous drip of
    coffee makers
Lost, blind in the opaque day now ready to break
Fit to bust the seams by noon
Previous velvet night calm, cool lust, convoluted
    in the thrashing
Overthrown reign of beauteous night and all the
    jeweled crown of peace
Jewels, stars laden with wishes and dreams of lost souls
Souls taken prisoner in the coup
Destined to change hands, the power
    ever inconstant fluctuation
Preying on the minds and nerves of too many nervous people
Already dancing too close to the edge
Looking for a reason to give in

Heather M. Schmaedeke

Total Strangers

I can't believe it's me sitting here looking at you and seeking a
    stranger
I remember when looking at you made my heart beat like a drum
Now standing besides you I don't feel any different
Than someone who has never touched my life at all
Once you were my soul my total existence
Once the sound of your voice could make me weep
Now I look at you and I don't even feel anger
I just wonder how wrong I have been
I saw the world in you- the center of my being
You were my heartbeat, the blood in my veins
Now you are like the wind
Who just swept through the mountain
Showing no trace, only empty space
It hasn't even been a year and we are total strangers
I cannot even remember the good times we had
All the feelings we shared and we did share many
Are washed out from my mind - How can it be
Could it have been true love that died so suddenly
Was the hurt too big to leave the memories alive
Can I be fooling myself or protecting from hurt
but burying the past so soon Am I?
    Hana Parker

The Assassin

A fanatic mad with rage and hate,
  lies with cradled gun in wait.
Crouched behind a pile of books,
  then peering down the sights he looks.

Waiting with the sights aimed high,
  to deal out death from out the sky.
Down below the crowd all cheer's,
  in one brief moment turns to tears.

Three shots have left the assassin's gun,
  the foul deed murder; has been done.
Now a man lies cold and still,
  throughout the world we feel the chill.

And wonder why this man so great,
  In the Rotunda; lies in state.
Then they start to take his stock,
  And know his loss the States will rock.

But we've learned from J.F.K.
  In every cloud there is a ray.
And we'll take a lead from him,
  his leadership will never dim.
    Gerry Driver

City Of Angels

No stars may be seen when the view is so gray
The smog and pollution severing the veins
The skyscraper filled sky an added terrain
The noisy street lights, the traffic is a pain
It even cracks the brain

The crime festered streets are east out of the way
The baby blue colors a platinum parade
The poshy convertibles belonging to Barbi and Ken
Are safe behind gates

The silly professors in their ivory tents
Just like the city laying in waste

Fermenting ideas like algae they spread
Not fit for the rim of the very dust bin
    Jacqueline Lopez

Paternal Biography

Daddies always have pens
in their pockets, jelly on their fingers,
coffee stains on white
table cloths, and loving eyes.
Always the one to call when car troubles arise,
when kleenexes, or bad jokes are needed.

Overdrawn check-mender,
ex-boyfriend-dog-sender.
("Tell him to make out with this!") Growl, growl, growl.

Fount of wisdom, gulf of giddiness,
fearful temper, mismatched clothes.
Twinkling eyes, all a-mischief,
balding forehead, Irish nose.

Love of the land, taste for adventure.
Greatest friend, cherished mentor.
    Christina J. Hare

Dreamers

Mysteriously you came,
So alone, so wanting love,
Yet too frightened to accept it.

Once you let us take you in,
You became our companion,
Our lover.
Constantly with us,
Healing the breach an indiscretion had forged.

Years of happiness we shared
Before evil struck you.
So wanting to remain,
You struggled to cling to life.

One day you cuddled close,
Fell asleep in my arms,
Never again to awaken.

Now my beloved also sleeps.
Dream together my dears.
    William G. Wolfgang

The Astronomer's Dream

He waited, patiently, almost endlessly,
Until the sky began to turn pink and gray,
He walked alone to his place on the hill,
And lay on a blanket until the end of day.

He closed his eyes until dusk and darkened,
And the fiery sun had faded from his view,
Opening them slowly to gaze at the moon,
Pale and silvery against the midnight blue.

No tools for measuring distance or speed,
No laboratory walls to confine his sight,
The weight of his day lifted from his chest,
And his soul danced amid sweet star light.

And the moon watched him watching her,
Like a lover he had known sometime ago,
He watched, enchanted by her presence,
As the soft morning winds began to blow.

His rapture had now turned bittersweet,
As the skies lightened to pink and grey,
Then the astronomer arose from the hill,
And like the moon, he quietly faded away.
    Lisa Gray

Life

Life is like a river,
Some times it's nice, calm and everything is right.
The sun will rise every morning and set every night,
Promising us a new day but it is as uncertain for
what is to come in the new day as we are.

Then the clouds get dark and things begin to change.
Little ripples begin to appear in the water,
Just a little challenge . . .
But then the ripples get bigger and Bigger
and we begin to scream!

I know as long as the Lord is watching over me,
and the sun is sure to rise once again,
As long as my sweet heart is by my side,
holding my hand with our hearts filled with the Lord's
most precious gift,
I can make it though any storm, fear, or uncertainty
whatever life may throw my way because I've got true love
Inside of my heart, the most precious gift . . .

Crystal McKain

Walking In A West Michigan Orchard

In late afternoon winds ceased
to sweep, to streak the sky white.
Tumbling from their wild whirling
dance, tattered leaves rustled
under new fallen snow where she walked
among apple trees crinkling autumn

Underfoot. In an orchard stripped
of its fruit she recalled climbing
trees, mom's salt shaker in hand, to read
books and eat mouthwatering green apples.
Soon Golden Delicious promises tempted
her, Jonathan's provided an honest

Sweet gentle nature, but she found delight
in the bright red/green MacIntosh, firm
flesh bursting with crisp tart taste,
a treat to eat curled in a cozy chair,
or better yet, savored with cinnamon
and sugar inside rich buttery crust.

Susanna Mason Defever

Suspension

Where did your dreams go, and where are you?
The absence of influx contrives boredom
Constance remains-
The ongoing cycle of death in not living
The conformist rests easy
Prospects of indolence hinder imagination
Imagination has no place here
Existing is to accept, losing all inquiry
Surviving becomes the label of self-worth
Must one reside in this locus?
Our apprehension of the future
Delivers us into the hands of hope
Accused of ambition, however,
presents a suitable scapegoat.
Our journey thus, entails oceans-
Dangers of scorn and hate await around every corner.
If our choosing is the idea lacking the action,
then our hypocrisy should not be tolerated.
Regardless, we are forever suspended within its grasp.

Holly Sharlow

Poetry In Motion

The opening of your eyes to see a beautiful day
The Thanking of God in every way
To notice each twig on top of each tree
To notice each animal and even a bee
The shake of a hand
The smile on someone's face
The words "Thank You" when you have kept the pace
A few minutes of silence after a hard days work
The fresh smell of coffee about to perk
A glass of cold water to quench your thirst
A fine cooked meal to eat, till you burst
The loving family all safe and sound
The petting of our protective old hound
The friends we holler and ha too
The fun we laugh and play through
A kiss and love from our little lady
And one from our grown baby
Checking and knowing everyone's sleeping fine
Then Thanking God one more time

Jean L. Murphy

Windchimes

Favorite songs, hopeful dreams, soft whispers fill the air.
Falling stars, drifting water, street lights everywhere.
Writing poems, dancing freely, seeing friends for a long time.
Skating fast, family's love, canal's hills are hard to climb.
Sledding race, ice skating, snowy crystals in the breeze.
Fireworks, sunsets, laughing on your knees.
Snowflakes fall, time goes on, friends met along the way.
Wildlife, bike riding, sun rises to start the day.
Watching movies, flying kites, and my favorite color blue.
Basketball, wheat fields, and things that I must do.
Colorado's mountains, skiing fast, watching clouds pass by.
Airplane rides, sandy beaches, smelling fresh apple pie.
Stuffed toys, playing games, seeing and remembering things.
Just sitting and listening as the windchime sings.

Sarah Schneider

Untitled

Creeping through the savannah, I came upon a banana,
"Fancy that!" said I, gazing towards the sky.
It could not be from a tree,
for there is none in sight.
And then, a scream with such might, I jumped from sheer fright!
A gorilla, I did see, staring straight at me!

I ran and I ran, as fast as any man can,
But not fast enough, cause with a big huff,
that gorilla, you see, was on top of me.
"Oh! Lordy!" Cried I, as I prepared to die.
But, the gorilla, you see, had plans not for me,
for he grabbed the banana,
and headed across the savannah!

John Tabor

The Dreams Of Life

Life is what we live from day to day, as
broken dreams, and promises slowly pass
our way. Never to be seen or talked about
again, but deeply missed in your heart
like a childhood friend. I thank God for
dreams, and promises, and each day in which
we live, because we as people have a lot
to give.

Paul A. Fields

My Day

This morning I awoke at dawn's early light
And saw through my window a beautiful sight!
The bright rays of the sun beaming over the hill
Sent a silent message, "Peace, be still".

I took a moment to silently pray
and thank God for creating this brand new day.
And I noticed as the day went along
I had more courage and felt very strong.

This evening as my day's work was done
I paused to glance at the setting sun.
Vivid colors of every shade and hue
Splashed against a background of blue.

I was totally mesmerized
By the artwork of God painted across the skies.
And again I whispered a prayer
and knew that He would always be there.

Barbara Lusk

Zodiac

Pisces, a sign of the water
Yet a sign of every element
Water, lapping against the earth, eroding
the past, carrying the bad times with its
current
Water, when left, evaporates into air, lonely
and transparent
Water extinguishes fire, mediator of all anger
Pisces, a sign of the water
Yet, a sign of Earth, Air, and Fire
A sign of the sun, moon, and stars.
A sign of the water.

Lauren Fabrizio

Thinking Of My Sister

Even in this final decade rushing.
Millennium two, Anno Domini.
My soul's inner joy, little Sis, at home,
Lives a day's drive beyond great Sol's diving.
Would my life been less far destined to change?!
Less apt to separate heart's need from base,
Desire. Woman within whom love can't age,
Would nearer be. Alas! I miss her face.
Girl whom I adore holds legacy,
With one stout arm, balancing telephone,
Receiver in free hand complaining, though,
Through laughter, in her arms, babe lies smiling.
Two fairer, mother and daughter, to me,
Than wave crests lit by sunbeams upon the sea.

Gregor Southard

Free And Make Them

Free the animals.
Make them like the land.
Free just one person in this world.
Free a pebble in the sand.

Free the world of sin that it might survive.
Free the dead in their graves.
Make them once again alive.
Free the rich for they are really poor.
Free the unknown and make it for sure.

But most of all free the people like me.
"Open up our minds and let us see
What's real and what's costly
And judge what's real between imaginary."

Kathryn Reynolds

My Guiding Light

Dedicated to my parents
Over the years I have looked to you to grant my wishes
both big and small;
It seems to me that you succeeded in granting them all.

You were always there when I needed you to be;
You made me feel that I was the only one, just me.

But as I grew older I guess you thought that I didn't need
you anymore;
I need you now just as much as I did before.

Faced with a future in a world filled with uncertainty and
despair;
I need the support and advice of someone like you who has
already been there.

You are my most precious, faithful guiding light;
Only second to the one above which shines ever so bright.

I know time has brought many changes to your life, too;
But always remember, just as you were always there for
me, I will always be there for you.

Beulah H. Davis

Graduation

A milestone accomplished
Memories gathered only for reflecting
Friends gained, friends lost
The intelligence, learning, and wisdom
set upon us as a challenge
Accounts, stories; things better left
unsaid, silent, forgotten
The fondest of years so unwilling to let go
Yet what lies ahead makes the past unattainable
Fall out of the nest, spread your wings
strive, seek, find
Such costly teaching, but given
freely because of love, patience, and growth
too late, too old
a character built
Enter vastness, reach out to the
Unfamiliar
View your own profile
Glance back and miss the
"memories that are only made to fade"

Britta Flemmer

Ghosts

We were the ghosts who walk at night
Another land, another day, another life
Out of time, out of place, out of sight

Jungle like a womb, darkened eyes in flight
Artist assassins creating a still life
We were the ghosts who walk at night

Years gone by, still blinking in the light
Dreaming soft, so not to wake my wife
Out of time, out of place, out of sight

Our past and passions wrapped up tight
Mold and blood and winking knife
We were the ghosts who walk at night

Wrapped in bandages of time, we're all right
Nicely tucked in an everyday life
Out of time, out of place, out of sight

Just an old man, walking past your streetlight
Miles and years from Asian strife
We were the ghosts who walk at night
Out of time, out of place, out of sight

Russ Mann

Farewells

Good-byes echo through the yesterdays and all of our
    tomorrows,
Emptiness filled with memory and sorrows.
All of the pleasures won and known add to the pain,
Vacuum contrasts the fulfillment of love, without which
    wounds
Of absence pale to minor irritation.
How is pain hidden, behind the fear of bleak unknowns?
To well forth and fill empty distances with waves of
    loneliness...
Absence with love; Emptiness of receding memory...
Replaced or erased by time and another, or not, ever,
Joined, forever in ashes and dust.

    Bruce D. Tefft

Images

What you think you see
Or, what you thought you saw
May only be images in your mind.
Then, again, you really saw
What you saw and
May never see again in time.
How you prove reality or
How you understand it
Is whatever you have pictured or
Remember in the distance
When you are finally asked to recall the images...
The ones you really saw
  or
Did you see at all?

    Marjorie Jean Hall

Depression

A love that once was yours has gone away.
This emptiness inside of you is real.
A giant void that haunts you everyday.
Your skin so numb that you no longer feel.

A hurt so strong, your heart begins to crack.
One tear rolls slowly down your face again.
Your stomach gnarling, echoing the black.
Ten screams of anguish, now your head extends.

Cruel bitterness disguised beneath your smile.
He sneers and holds his fist as if to kill.
Your veins pump blood like water in the Nile.
Each breath you take is now beyond your will.

This substance your abuse will never go.
Your attitude hurts everyone you know.

    Brian Rice

The Green Horn

My father came from Ireland with talk
of Banshee. The black and tan and
Leprechauns with pots of gold for me

He once owned a Shillelagh that gave
certain powers could turn a tuff of
shamrocks into a glade of flowers.

He told of St. Patrick how he drove the
snakes away and a wistful glint
came to his pale blue eyes for
all he had to say.

For true some of his tales my
mothers could not condone, but
what to expect for me an Irishmen
that's kissed the Blarney Stone.

    Alice Reynolds

Death

An essence of stillness not known
Eerie quietness not enjoyed during life
All pain has quietly disappeared
A walk of unbounded softness awaits

Looking for that place of total happiness
Is there such a level
From our dreams we connect the possibilities
A second beginning to come forward

Total lost is rampant
We scramble for protection
Is afterlife a mirror image of the living
Please not now do we need further anguish

    Denis P. DuBois

He Is Looking For You And Me

Some say my God is dead
But that is not true.
For I have seen him,
When the day is new
There he is in all his splendor
With all colors of the rainbow
Looking for you and me!

I see God walking through the trees
For he is moving he is the breeze
For all the leaves are swaying
With his words of love and life
As he passes through all time and eternity
Looking for you and me!

And when the night grows dark and black
He hangs his moon for light
Open his windows of heaven
To let his stars shine out
And as we kneel to pray
He softly knock at our hearts
Looking for you and me!

    Marion Darling

This Child

This child is but an angel upon a heartless earth
Surrounded by evil since the moment of birth
A vessel of innocence so scared and unsure
That this disease called loneliness may not have a cure.
He closes his eyes and tries to shut out
The cries of anger and hatred the world tends to shout.
He walks through life and gets by the best that he can
As his innocence slowly dies and this child becomes a man.

    Kimberly Smeltzer

The Bonds Of Time

Just two people, their whole lives spent;
Trying to love and tie the ends,
But there are times in trying they fail to see,
Just how sacred that love can be.
It flows like a river and comes from within,
Love can't be bought or put aside
Because it always exists within ones mind.
When one is loved, the other loves,
It's a mutual agreement,
A kind of trust.
So give me your love as I give you mine
And our bonds will be strong,
Until the end of time.

    Julie C. Grubbs

Jacarandas

In early February on the lower slopes
With nights quite cool but winter on the wing
Soft evening rains awake the buds
Of Jacaranda trees and gently bring
Puffs of lavender to dot the mountainside
Like smoke signals heralding an early spring.

Within the greening of the trees
In every forest, stand, and grove,
Majestic sentinels here and there
Midst all this emerald treasure trove,
The Jacarandas grace the shade
With smoky lilac, lavender, and mauve.

Later when the blooms are full
And fresh-washed trees with rains are blessed,
This canopy of luminous hyacinth o'erhead
And underneath, a carpet of sunlit amethyst
Make magic of this moment, this enchanted hour of
Wondrous Jacarandas at their best.

James E. Morgan

Sea Gulls

You birds are miraculous, little creatures,
I salute you all,
You sit upon a piling imperturbably
As I listen to the sea gulls' call
Speaking sparingly to me,
Then you turn away and fly on out to sea.

As I meander through the haunts you choose,
I seek to know the mystique of your mind,
You love the sky and water, and a piling for a perch
And have the cares of humans' earth behind.

Sometimes you accept a little crumbled bread,
But, you're really self-sufficient,
To look at you, no one would guess that you are so efficient
I'm watching you and wondering
When you will return,
Your freedom is the greatest prize you've earned.

June Whitelock

Birth Of Creation

"I" am the first being that came
    from the void
"I" did create another being from
    the void and he is known as
    the six-pointed star the star of heaven

We are only two of a kind in the whole universe

There is no existing direction
That leads to the void and that
Means that void does not exist

Earth was created in a existing
Dimension and there for you can
Not go to the void except one person and "I"
The void is not a concept in your way
Of thinking because it is empty and
There is absolutely nothing in the void

The void has no dimension, no light, no
Darkness, no air, no space, and no color

"I" love to create things into being
    Because of my origin. "I" am known as the God of creation and
My name is "I"

John M. Tapia

Mind's Empty Room

The old man is long gone who
toiled so hard to foil Mistress spider.
He would start each day
with oil and rag, sweat and heat
'till even tide when all stood in shiny array.

Tear steals down a long dry cheek
as memory's smells and sights assail
and fragile heart breaks anew.
Echoes of metal ring thru the air,
smoke round echoes entwine
and fill mind's empty room
with warmth of love
and strength of roughened hand.

Mistress spider spins her web
masking over once again
smell and sound and sight
but ne'er erasing love that lives there still.
And none come to admire her work
or destroy its delicate pattern.

Janiece Maloney

Life Within

The names of people are simplified,
It's not the name, it's the heart inside,
A good name isn't the important part,
God looks only what is in the heart,

Laughter is a face of the unwise,
Like a fool without a purpose,
The wise is full of the Lords Wisdom,
Which finds their way to Eternal life,

Pride is the venture of Satins world,
Doing the evil things of fools,
Turning life into a total death,
Where hell has no meaning,

Under the sun in which we live,
Is life that only God can give,
A life in which God can give or take,
Any given time or place,

Margie Schooley

Just Passing Through

In Remembrance of Mrs. Hazel Ruth Rarick
As I wake-up every morn....
And ponder what to do...
I'm reminded of my parents adage...
That "We're all just passing through"...

So as I spring up from my bed...
And begin to revel in the day...
I look at life thru "Rose Colored" glasses...
Then toss my cares away...

That's not to say I never worry...
About the future or days gone past...
For my message is to tell you, simply...
"You have to make the good-times last!"...

For we are but mere mortals here...
Thee chosen few from birth...
Whom God has sent from up above...
To do his work on Earth...

So, looking back in retrospect...
We must strive to make life sublime...
As we are just but beings here...
Living on borrowed time...

Sherri Ann Rarick

"A Prisoner's Memory Of His Daughter"

Twin diamonds sparkle in her eyes
    within their pools of ebony depth.
A smile that tells naught of lies
    where dreamy innocence is kept.

Her miniature fingers search the world
    for all new and vivid things,
    they brush back the flowing locks;
    her movements seem to sing.

Laughter spills like streaming kindness,
    enchanting to my soul.
Her heart; worlds without distress,
    as of newly fallen snow.

She can pull me from my sorrow
    and wash me in her bliss.
She helps me see tomorrow,
    for she is why it does exist.

How I miss those diamond fires,
    the smile that makes a day,
    simple laughter of life's desire;
    my precious Desirae.

Alan A. Avila

The Dragon's Tear

When you see the knight in shining armor,
You know he's not some weak old farmer.

The brave, bold knight, will be finished by day.
That horrible dragon, he will have slain.

As he prances off on his horse to the valley,
He shall miss his dear wife Sally.

As the knight meets the dragon eye to eye,
He knows that he must either fight or die.

As the battle continues to grow stronger,
The knight hopes it doesn't last any longer.

When he seen the dragon shed a tear.
He knew that he had nothing more to fear.

He didn't have the heart to complete his task,
He got on his horse and rode home behind the mask.

From the day foreword, he didn't tell a soul,
He didn't want them to think of him as a fool.

Heather Bush

New Frontiers

Do not get depressed easily
    my dear child
You don't know what it's like
    to fight without a shield
Sometimes we do keep on wondering
    about what life has to offer
If it offers sunshine and springtime
    why do we always see people suffer
I have flown over the Pacific
    thinking that I have won the battle
Not until I laid down to rest
    and found out it is a continuous struggle
Life is not always fair
    things do not turn out to be splendor
I know that you are tired
    you should not be ready to surrender
With faith hope and love
    we need constantly encourage each other
Let us set up our sail
    we have new frontiers to conquer.

Shirley Chang Juan

Mothers And Fathers

Mothers and fathers seem to be alike,
Mothers love giving hugs and kisses.
Fathers like playing games.
Mothers are very serious.
Fathers are funny and fun.
Mothers bake cakes and pies.
Fathers cook steak and chicken.
Mothers are tellers of stories.
Fathers are tellers of funny tales.
But mothers and fathers are mostly people to love.

Kristen Devers

Patt

In life there are many, whom you will meet,
but none like my cousin, so genuine and sweet.
Her spirit is angelic, but elegant is she,
nothing's phoney, or fake, just plain quality.
If ever you're blessed, to enter her home,
she'll show you kindness, which you've never known.
She'll roll out the carpet, but pink it will be,
for the color of love, is just what you'll see.
She'll wine you and dine you, and fill you with treats,
rich in her kindness, there is no deceit.
She has helped many, who were saddened with grief,
and some, who's lives had no belief.
Especially the child, who's life wasn't long,
She showed him a rainbow, putting love in his song.
Such passion she gives, to all she surrounds,
for in giving, there's joy and comfort renowned.
Her life has been filled, with much sorrow and pain,
as loved ones God took, without any refrain.
Oh, how I love this dear Cousin of mine,
for she has been touched, by God's love, so divine.

Sherel Warwood

The Radioactive, Nudist Dust Bunnies
That Live Under My Bed

Big, small, medium balls of stuff you find under a bed,
Glowing so bright,
No need for a night light.
I don't mind their presence much,
But why won't they put their clothes on?

Silent and still,
It's like they are not real.
They tumble and roll only when the vacuum comes near.

Somehow, someway,
They just appeared there one day.

They are like pets,
Except you don't have to feed them,
Or walk them,
Or pet them,
Or take care of them.

I watch them every now and then,
They just sit there.
I talk to them every now and then,
They just sit there.
Did I kill them?

Sarah Mathias

Born Anew

The leaf is born after frost — a baby new

The tree has died — a man is lost
What other way is the world to be,
Than to lose a life and honour them.

Joyce Glittenberg

35

My Phyllis

Life is time I'm passing thru, often failing in things I
should do. Like expressing the inspiration, of my love for you.

Not really knowing, my very own fate, this I must tell you,
before it's too late.

My life's greatest blessings, with you I find, comes from the
heart, body, soul, and mind.

You're not only their mother, my lover, wife, and best
friend, you're my pot of gold, at the rainbows end.

William Bender

My Grandparents And Me

We went to McDonald's my Grandparents and me;
I slept over your house, you and me;
I tried to sleep, but I was so excited;
I heard fireworks, and we listened,
just my Grandparents and me.
We shared our waffles, just us together;
I didn't want to leave, but I had to say good-bye;
Grandma said "You'll be back again",
we'll have great adventure's when it's just
my Grandparents and me.

Lauren E. Randall

Aim For The Stars

But, remember to shoot higher
Set your heart, and soul, and eyes
On the man with all the power
Who is way beyond the moon.

It has been said for over two thousand years
That he is coming soon
No ocean could hold the shedding of tears
That has been cried out to him.

Calling on his mercy and grace
To feel his loving touch
Of his holy spirit up on their face
Oh, what peace and joy.

The comfort we feel
And we know in our hearts
That he is real
The one beyond the stars.

Ruth Clark

Pull Up A Chair

Pull up a chair and leave it there
in some out of the way corner will do;
if would should turn to could
I'd be there with you!

Even if just look and see
your face of brimming smile
would be a precious gift to me
and sustain my heart awhile!

Time seems too short to the very young
and too long as we grow old
to share all the joy's, I'd have sung
and the love I'd have you hold!
Distance seems to grow us father apart
as if we exist only, in words written or spoken
and I pen a poem from a longing heart
and seems a worthless token.

I pen this not to know you care,
but that you know, I do!
Pull up a chair and leave it there
and pretend I'm there with you!

Dahni

Blank Waltz

Fair sky
Who's white silk gown whispers against the floor
Pearls woven and lost within trellises of
Ivory curls.
She dances
A blank waltz that spirals in torrents of chill
Fold after fold of fabric sweeping the polished earth
As lace teases the barren arms of the oak and elm.
And deaf I remain to the music of this dance
All but the sharpest violins pierce the rhythm
With high hints of wind.
She takes another ghostly step
In succession of motions that leave the earth
Lost in the flurry of chalky skirts.
The music dwindles
And the hem of her gown swirls a last time
To fade with tones of snowing glory
Dissipate into oblivious horizon.

Julia Barrett

Love Again

When I wake up in the morning
  I won't feel any pain
I'm in your arms
  Feeling our love again

We were apart
  because of lies and deceit
We've found our way home
  to a love that's so sweet

Running my fingers through your dreadlocks
  and feeling your heartbeat against mine
Where nothing exists but you and me
  and I want it this way for all time

We've talked things out
  and eased the strain
We are back where we belong
  Together - feeling our love again.

Dinah Gourdet

Eyes Of A Child

Children's innocence, pure of heart,
  Born of tenderness, blessed from the start.
Eyes of a child so eager to learn,
  Waiting and watching at every turn.

They are the future generations,
  Filled with hope and expectations.
Brought with fondness so endearing,
  With hopes and dreams ever nearing.

They see with love's sweet embrace,
  Kindness shines upon their face.
Wishing for the world to know,
  With laughter's echo set aglow.

When they look with open eyes,
  They then begin to realize.
Their world is such an open place,
  To grow and trust without disgrace.

So when the children look to us,
  For answers we choose to discuss.
With them we can often see,
  Through their eyes, their true destiny.

Austin Forrest

Recollecting Dreams

Remembering, and cherishing the things we have done, and will do.
Recollecting, and reflecting each of my many dreams....for you!
Spending a lifetime, if that's what it take in order to see
Everything we are, and all I know we can truly be.

Loving you as if your heart was joined with mine
Looking back with ever so sweet, not bitter emotions
Withstanding not one regret - tell me if this can be done.

Trying to find myself - when lost in your eyes
Catching my breath - when enchanted by your smile.

You are the reason for I am strong!
You are the reason for I am weak!

Finding the truth in love, how very hard for one to do
believing you are good for me, the one thing that reigns true.

Tania A. Gonzalez

An Angel's Voice

I lie in a field of daisies,
Thinking about you.
Wishing that you were here with me.
Knowing how much I care about you.
I close my eyes and smell the breeze,
It feels good against my face.
I hold your picture near my heart,
I whisper softly to the breeze,
"I love him with all my heart".
When I call your name,
It seems that I hear an angel's voice.
She whispers to the breeze,
And the sun smiles.
The most important thing to me right now,
Is the fact ...
    that I love you!

Emily Smart

Children Of The Darkest Night

Night after night they roam the streets.
In the alley they sometimes meet.
They rape and kill without fear.
Imagine the pain their victims bear.

They never had a place to call home.
To support their habits they'll walk to Rome,
Searching for a fix and a needle to share,
For survival they really don't care.

Deprived of knowledge and future goals,
They're prone to jail and death row.
Who will save their souls in time,
From the evil that possessed their minds?

Can the government make a drastic change,
To co-operate positively and re-arrange?
If they challenge the problem the right way,
Many lives may-be spared this very day.

Eileen Williams

You Sweet Thing

Your eyes are as beautiful as plums
Your lips are as sweet as watermelon wine
Your face is like a cherry
Your body is like a ripe peach
And that's why I love you so,
For you are my sweet thing.

Dennis R. Rose

Seasons Symmetry

Rose petals reflect their rev'rent beauty
Like sunshine upon the plains
Summer's music abounds
In its magical sounds
To the beat of the drumming rains.

Leaves fall like colored confetti
As the wind gusts blow them down
Pure azure-blue skies
Just somehow belies
That Autumn now is winter bound.

Blue icicles cast their silvery spell
Upon Winter's pristine scene
Whirling flakes of snow
Create a warm afterglow
When all around is serene.

The seasons have ended their show
Like puppets on Nature's strings
Green'ry bursting forth
And birds flying north
Signal anew the arrival of Spring.

Doris Kohler-Shockley

The Lost Souls

Have you ever wondered why people are so blue
They keep to themselves not knowing what to do
It's not that they don't have a heart or don't care
It's because they lost something that kept faith inside
They lost their souls and now they have nothing inside
An emptiness of where it was
But now what can they do
people say there's a place lost souls go
To a certain place where faith and happiness is always there
This place might be true but then maybe not, you never know
People who are down and blue believe there is such a place
And hope to find it someday
    For you see you don't know what it's like to be without a soul
so you can not judge them
Like I said those people no longer believe anything good
will happen to them
    But they can think about what would happen if they got
their souls back
    And the emptiness was filled with joy and belief.

Karissa Pauli

Clouds

Cloud moving across the blue sky
You are free and soft
With no care
The wind blowing you in different directions
The sun always hiding the warmth of the sun
You sometimes bring rain and tell the weather
You come in different shapes and colors
Does each one tell your emotions
Cloud you are - Just like me
I drift from place to place with no care
And no one runs my life but me
Cloud you never tell lies
And are always above me
Cloud you are just like me
Each one tells your emotions
Cloud you are the gateway to heaven
What's my emotion today
Look at the clouds
Just look at the clouds baby

Marie Hilley

My Son, My Son

God gave me a Boy
  And he fit me to a "T";
The biggest little reason was
  He was God's gift to "Me".

As he was a young boy
  And just starting to grow,
He played all types of sports
  With dreams of being a Pro.

Kids don't always listen
  To what parents have to say;
But you can bet they watch our lives...
  The way we live day by day.

As I watched him grow and mature,
  Oh, the things I have learned
As I see him start to accomplish
  All the things for which I have yearned!

No Father could ever expect more Pleasure
  From a boy he gave his name, after the fun
That I have already in my life received
  From my adopted Son!

    Arnold Eugene Bradley

The Time Still Goes On

I think of what we have done,
but the time still goes on,
I look to the past wondering
if I could change it,
but the time still goes on,
I look to the future to see
what we could have done,
but the time still goes on,
I wonder if I could ever make the time stop,
so you wouldn't be gone,
but the time still goes on.

    Shandi Dukes

The King Of Soap And The Queen Of Shampoo

I want to tell you a story, that I remember well.
About when I was just a kid, "I used to smell!"

Since I didn't take a bath,
I was itchy and had fleas
And everyone I ever met
yelled, "Get Away From Me!"

But my story doesn't end here,
For there is always hope.
Because my life was turned around,
When I met the King of Soap.

He introduced me to the tub,
where he scrubbed and scrubbed and scrubbed.
I was soon sparkling clean, except for my hair
Which, I thought, was kind of unfair.

I said to the King, "Now what do I do?"
He said to me, "Meet the Queen of Shampoo!"
It wasn't long, before she was done,
"Now wasn't that fun!"

The moral of this story is, "Keep clean!"
so you can have fun, with King and Queen!

    Joshua D. Vories

The Wilting Ways Of Us

I seek the natural feeling,
I float in my own thoughts.

She strives for attention,
I'm the voice in your head.

You killed all the innocent flowers,
Everything is in beauty.

We can run across the water,
The tree and the moon will never go away.

I am a dream flier,
My world is a rainbow.

The wires are turning into beasts,
I'm a lion, I'm a sun, I fly and I run.

It is missing life,
What is so illustrious about a telephone wire?

We would be expert tree hoppers,
The sky is a friend.

I will go ride a giant beautiful butterfly,
I once watched a flower grow.

Love is the simple act of being yourself,
Seek sanctuary in your soul!

    Ann Myres

Live Life

Live life looking for a rainbow.
There is always one there to behold.
To others, always a kindness show.
One must never be afraid to grow old.

Live life searching for some sunshine.
Every day has some there waiting.
It may be in the color of a good wine,
Just waiting for your lips tasting.

When time has pasted, and we look back,
We will smile at all the happiness found,
And in fact
Every day of our lives with beauty was bound.

    Judy Beschoner

Little Rascal

Little rascal went to dog heaven
Where he is happy and at peace
Up there in beautiful dog heaven
Roaming free, without a leash

He loves it there in dog heaven
Where the sun is warm and bright
As he romps around on the fresh green grass
He makes such a pretty sight

Little rascal gave us much pleasure
Through the years that he was here
And as we took him to his maker
We wiped away another tear

Little Rascal will be missed
Though he is better off in the end
Up there in beautiful dog heaven
Playing with a little dog friend

    Charlotte C. O'Dell

Denial's Playground

Drops of water locked in ice...
Savory crystal's brittle cold.
Hearts that weather spring-time meltings,
bid ado memories new and old.

More profound: Confused members....
Longing embers: Stick's decay.
Wooded hills replete yet senile.
Wash the warmth forever 'way.

Blinded sights of past and present,
hiding from the radiant Son....
As abandoned houses: Archaic titles,
His tethered frame and name we shun.

Liquid anguish over covered meadows,
puddles ignorance at my feet;
and advance to chambers bought by many....
For now denial's the task to reap!

Donna M. M. Yount

Desire To Play God

Once I asked the Farroh. "Why proclaimed God?
Just a particle of dust and that's all you are.
Someday you will fall and get lost in the past.
You are a man after all, like any one on Earth.
You eat like a man, you drink like a man.
All your needs are like those of a man."
"Why! But you never stopped me." The Farroh smiled.
"You bow down before me. And I get the thrill.
I push you down more, you go down on you knees.
I push you further down and you kiss the ground.
And, by God! That's what makes me feel like God."
"But that is not fair." I protested with fear.
"Ah! What nonsense is fair!" The Farroh frowned.
"There is a God in every man, however you deny.
You are a God for those whomever you command.
All you need is power, power over human being.
The more power you get the more drunk you are.
It's too intoxicating for you and me to digest.
Once you get the power, with no limits and bonds.
You won't be what you are, you too will play God."

Nazir Uddin Khan

Summer Time

Summer is here as you can see,
All the lilies are dancing with glee,
Roses are proudly putting on their show,
Daisies are nodding and just seem to glow.

The trees now are all fully dressed,
The birds are plentiful and squirrels are stressed,
To get the bird feed, they do their thing,
And they like to chatter while the birds sing,

There are flowers here and flowers there,
They bloom and their aroma fills the air.
In July and August there is a beautiful surprise,
Naked lady, pink lady from the earth they rise,

As summer ends, Mums are ready to paint the town,
To usher in fall there are signs all abound.
Yes we cherish flowers to their last bloom,
For we know just ahead is Winter's dull gloom.

As summer fades and fall sets in,
We look forward to colored leaves with a grin.
Can hardly wait to plant tulips and daffodils too,
Then again in the spring there will be life anew.

Lillian McAllister

Just How Much

It seems to me, you're always there
I know that's just, the way you care.
No matter what, no matter who,
You'll lend a hand, you always do

Even all that I have done, you've always been
the only one, to come to me, arms
open wide, you were here right by my side

"Thank you" isn't near enough, 'cause
sometimes it got pretty rough

Then you became my dearest friend,
straight through, until the very end

When you put your hand in mine,
Somehow I knew, that I'd be fine
My health and mind I must maintain,
So from the bad, I must refrain
Maybe this will help you see
Just how much you mean to me

I thank you Mom and love you so,
But "just how much," you'll never know

Debra L. Scheller

The Gift

What can I give you, the little boy said
I've cleaned my room, and I've made my bed.
The dogs been fed, my homework's most done
But something is wrong, cause I really had fun
I want you to know, that my love is sincere
But I have no money and christmas is here
What can you give me the mother did say
Taking his hand, as she knelt down to pray
My prayers were answered, the day you were sent
Straight out of heaven, my heart was content
What can you give me son have no fear
You give me a gift, every day of the year
When I see the love, that shines in your eyes
As you kiss me good night, or say your good byes
No greater gift could I ask of you
Than to be a good boy, in things that you do
There are so many things, that money can't buy
But I'd give a million, for the love in your eyes
So what can you give me like diamonds galore
You gave me the world, when you walked in the door.

Clara R. Deas

March On

Behold the beauty of the brothers
boarding the bus, for the cause.

The vehicle that transported them to the March
once again, played a symbolic role in our history.

Their eagerness, questioned by some,
made their quest necessary
to show the world their unity.

The brothers couldn't wait
to exhale their atoned message
with their families, and in their neighborhoods.

Bless the free mind to see
the need for change,
1 million strong, rejoicing in song
their spirit won't be broken.

Sheila K. Robinson

Regret

Your laughter suddenly faded,
my tears now gently fallen,
day after day my empty life continues
the only thing that could ever fill it up is gone.

Your heartbeat taken,
while mine still beats.
I'm still here,
Stuck with a harsh pain so deep.

I had taken what I had for granted,
I never knew what it was
I've just realized what I had,
Now it's gone.

Frances Peirce

Veil Of Memory

Oh tears of pain to God they cry.
And, only He knows why.
Of burning flesh and hollow faces
Where are the traces...

Folded in Gods hands
We cannot condescend to Him, our reasons for apathy
and the absence of humanity.

Each cry, each prayer, each grain of fear, each tear
are counted by angles and carried all to Him.
And, each of these souls are His.

Upon the moment of death
All pain, violence, anger and sickness are taken away.
This must be the release of the soul.
To unveil all of our existence
and bring remembrance of our journey into one.

Only then will we learn way we suffer
and the lessons to be learned along our way.

Our spirits, ourselves, in completion.
A gift of God.
And a quieter death.

Diane James

Jaded Eyes

Void
Empty of substance
Dead to emotion
Lifeless

Living just to escape
The pain is too great
Restless
Alone in groups
Frightened to be alone

Desolate were his dreams
Dark were his eyes
Faded from all of his lies
Somewhere inside he cries
Somewhere within he dies

Death becomes an option
Afraid of dying
Afraid of trying to change

Thoughts scurry for a moment then a peace ensues
Now unconscious to all of his fear
Until tomorrow when it will be right here

Michael O'Shea

My Guy

With one split second, and a blink of an eye,
His features go together, as the days goes by.

His face is not oval, round in fact.
His hair is brown, blond if not that.

His eyes are brown, and freckles too,
But I love him dearly, I do, I do.

He's tall and muscular, not thin or fat.
He screams and yells, at one little voice,
It's my friend Lauren, as you can see,
She gets on his nerves, so easily.

She's a pain in the butt, he always would say,
Why can't she leave me alone, for one single day.

He loves to dance, he's good at that.
He can do the hula, he can do the dance,
He may not have the rhythm, but he still has his pants.

He uses all his might, when he tries to fight.
When he uses his fist, he ends up doing the twist.
And just by this, he misses my kiss.

My guy will never die, his soul is with me, at my side.
I love him now, I'll love him then, I'll love him forever, Amen.

Valarie Lynn Sabo

For Khan

At the wreckage of another day
As the night beats you with the fists of love
When your tears fall as hollow as your heart
When you think that they'll never understand you
When you feel you are solitary in your desolation
And your only hopes are hopeless . . .
Think of me.
Whether crying on your sleeve or screaming in a dream
Holding on to nothing tight
And crippled from a lost embrace . . .
We weep upon our damaged wings.
We are the same.

Amy Graham

Love Letters To Napoleon

Though rocks may fall in front of me.
To my right a stream bubbles with life and hope.
In that stream, stones sit, unmoving, steadfast.
I see a rope descending from heaven, it is tied around
the mouth of a white horse. I fear no evil.
He shakes his head to unbound himself.
I walk up a white stair way, professing
the goodness of the Lord and how he saved me.
I will bless the Lord with all my heart,
my soul and strength. I asked God to send Napoleon
in truth and righteousness. He has honored my request.
In my heartbeats a steady drum. It tells of
salvation to come. Jesus, Jesus in my home
Jesus, Jesus I am not alone. Jesus, Jesus
in you I am free. Jesus, Jesus abide in me.
Jesus, Jesus all through the night. Jesus,
Jesus it will be all right. Jesus, Jesus
Oh Lord. Jesus, Jesus keep me from harm.
Jesus, Jesus, all through day. Jesus, Jesus,
it will be okay.

Josette A. Smith

Untitled

My eyes dance and my heart flutters
  as you stand in front of me.
Your body is a sanctuary and I am the
  life it breathes.
Water thunders down your shoulders
  touching them and streaming down.
And here I am. I become yours. You
  become mine.
My fingers dance. My breathing staggers
your body becomes my place of being.
Where I touch you and you shiver.
And you taste me like a child longing for
  a popsicle on a hot day.
Hold me close like something you'll cling to
  for life.
Because now you are my sanctuary and I am
  what I breathes.
Become mine and I'll become yours.
and we'll become one.

Liz Justafson

The Tree

The tree grows straight and tall;
It branches out to cover all.
The branches represent all life around;
The base, it is held by the ground.
The happiness is found in its leaves;
They cycle and eventually leave the tree.
Jehovah God has put rings inside to show
How our life together really doth grow.
With roots spreading far and wide
To hold the family's love inside,
The branches grow stronger through the years,
And, of course, the trees is watered by tears;
Whether they come from eyes or oceans,
It makes the tree grow by emotions.
This results in a deep-seated love,
Which can only come to us from above.
As we bond ourselves throughout our life,
We find the joy of being husband and wife.
May we continue together as we grow old;
May our tree be considered a God-given mold.

John M. Bodley

When Comes A Horseman

From the distance,
a mirage like figure is seen.
The heart jumps at the instance.
What should this courier mean?
Sometimes with the earnestness of speed.
Occasionally the trot of shadow.
Could be a letter of goodness and need,
or news that turns the blood shallow.
Only one item comes to mind,
what this messenger will bring.
When comes a horseman, the world is left behind.
It matters not should a visit come in winter or in spring.

James Trammel

A Journey Of The Mind

A child like thought of fun and games, distorted now
by demented illusion. Once peaceful like the calm sea
at sunrise, changes as quickly as a storm. Thoughts
once peaceful and serene, now of death and misery
whatever happened to those great dreams of success
now memories of what should have been or could
have been. Rocky shores, now turned to sand, like
the journey of the mind that never ends...

Christopher Melendez

This Doll's Life

I am a doll waiting for a glance, a sign, a call.
Well, here I am sitting in the corner on a chair,
just waiting for someone to have a care.
Touch my hand and then I shall come to life as
I sing, laugh, and dance as you watch with every
delightful glance.
Or would you rather leave me there to stay,
as you go out and play? Can you sense it?
You can't see the solemn expression on my
delicate, soft, hand-crafted face, because
it comes and goes without a trace.
In my heart, I was waiting from the very
start, when no one wanted to bring me to life.
Loneliness was like a stab in the heart, like a
knife, piercing through my very soul. My life didn't
seem whole. But now my eyes were full of love, and
I was too. Because you stayed and you didn't make
this doll's life a bore. Now, as I move happily to and
fro, I'll never forget how precious life is, and how I love it so.

Siji Kollappallil

Give Respect

A woman for all times
Mother, sister, wife, friend

A woman to understand
Strong, determined, provider, defender.

A woman to know
Loving, forgiving, caring unceasing

A woman...one woman
Supporting, encouraging, rebuking, endearing.

Not any woman...this woman
Mother of one
Mother of many
Mother of all
Mother of mothers

You woman
Mother, sister, wife, friend.

Stephen Allistair Yearwood

Stillness Of Night

When we are in the stillness of night,
We can look to God for he is the light.
In the stillness of the night is joy divine,
To know that Jesus is really mine,
When the cares of life are more than we can bear
We can reach out to someone who really care
When the battle is raging within our soul,
We can look to God he can make us whole.
There is peace in the storm that rages,
Because Jesus is the rock of ages.
The solid rock, he doth stand,
He's right there to hold us by the hand.
When Satan comes along, and tells you what to do,
Point your finger at him, and say you're through,
Tormenting soon there will cause them go astray.
Someday soon there will be a pay day.
Please listen to what I have to say,
Put that prayer in your heart today,
May God bless you along the way,
And bring you to a brighter day.

Billie Jean Higgins

A Man, A Woman

A man, a woman, a new life they found.
A love they felt, stronger than life, they were bound,
Feelings of ease, feelings so just at last a friend,
No other messages, only true love to send.
Being with each other, each day, each way always.
Our life together, a special love with no complicated delays.
To spend our days, until time shall run out,
No other for me, no others for you, partners without a doubt.
"A man a woman" enjoying all of life's pleasure,
Knowing at last, love for us not being able to measure.
To be as one, and yet live as two, with feelings very divine.
And shout our feelings, express our love, never to decline,
Then a glorious day, at a happy glorious time,
The happiest ever, you and I shall soar and climb.
"A man a woman" in love, never to know where it had started.
Songs of love, act's of love offered from my happy heart.
A yesterday, a today and always inspired from above.
"A man a woman" a new life a wonderful new love,
Eternity together you and I in a most happy place,
Our life before us, nothing but the past to erase!

Ronald G. Spinelli

Missing

Long dead and
Long forgotten
We walk across the railroad tracks
Underneath the stars
The house is burning behind us
Heat pushing us forward
And I refuse to wake up
The roses died in a circle
I will never let you go
The most obvious sacrilege
Like spitting on your grave
So I fall to the ground
Dirt clenched in my fists
And smeared on my face
And children whispered to me in the night
"It is better to have nothing"
They said
"It is better to have nothing"

Melanie Hemphill

Trapped

I'm trapped.
I don't know what to do.
I'm surrounded by a world.
A world full of hate.
A world full of violence.
A world full of uncaring, selfish, dangerous minds.
I go to sleep and dream.
I dream about peace.
Happiness.
Love and hope.
I don't want to wake up.
But I do.
No matter how much I try.
I always wake up.
I wake up to reality. To hate. To violence.
To danger and selfishness.
How am I supposed to live like this?
Afraid to wake up.
Afraid to face the world.
Afraid to live.

Jackie Wochos

The Miracle Of Flying

Come watch with me
And listen to the hum:
Of the motors of the airplanes
As they pass one by one.
Their lights shining on the wings
Blinking as they pass by:
Heading for their destinations
High up in the sky.
Hardly do you see a day go by
When there before your eyes:
You see the vapor trails of the jets
Streaking across the skies.
At times the planes are just a little speck
You can hardly see them at all:
Then they vanish behind a cloud
And your spirit begins to fall.
It's a miracle of God
To see them in the air;
So high and heavy and you wonder
How can they stay up there!

Delphia Foell

Golf

Things that are challenging in golf.
    Makes you want to play the house.
The weather plays important part.
    Makes you want to get really smart.
Like selecting clubs for distance yardages
    and to the green.
    Makes you tell that you have to be on the beam.
When you try to hit all the fairways and not
    the rough and waterponds
    Makes you feel that your game is not on
When you are on the green to put. Makes you feel it was tough.
When you play in tournaments.
    Makes you feel like you're ornament
Most of all we want to be like a pro.
    But you just can't get all your shots to go.
Even a pro has his ups and down. Has you know.
But remember he does it for a living.
    So he can't afford to be kidding.
So put all this together
    it's just a game to play each other

Frederick Bacon

The Wave

Yeah, I rode the wave. I rode the wave to the
edge and back. It started as nothing but it is
nothing. Before I knew though, it had me. I
fought to stay afloat, but it took me. It took me
places so desolate, so barren I hope never to return
there. From the darkest of seas forbidden, to
the doldrums of despair, I drifted. I drifted
for an eternity until I washed ashore. The
wave abated and it left me as it had found me. Alone.
But it never really leaves. The wave is always
there. It's hidden around the corner, lurking in the
deepest, darkest recesses of every soul. Waiting,
Deny its existence and that's the denial of life
itself. The wave is the paradox proclaimed and reality.
Sure, I ride the wave. I ride the wave to the
farthest reaches of the continuum. I ride it past
the sign posts of logic and reason to a place
where time and matter converge and meld as one.

C. F. Winner

The Golden Age

Life is a pyramid of Ages
Each year pre-empting the last.
The Golden Age is the pinnacle
Of many years that's past.
Are you shuffling down a corridor among strangers?
Are you lying in bed not caring or asking why??
Are you confused and mixed up in your thinking?
Is your interest only of days gone by?
Do you feel you are a burden to your loved ones?
Does your heart yearn to understand the times?
Questions always questions —with no answers,
No explanations, no considerations, no time??
Where — Oh Where is the Golden Age promised??
Where we bask in merits of the past??
This time of honor and recognition —
Obviously it has turned to brass —.

Mildred C. Sprouse

I Am Music

I am music, I am here to make you happy.
Though sometimes I can make you sad.
I can make you go faster when your timing is too slow
I can make you go very slow if your timing is too fast.
        Because I am music
I was there with you at your baptism
I did perform for you when you were crying in your cradle
Oh, I did perform for you on your sixteenth birthday.
Oh, here comes your graduation, the sound I make for you
        Because I am music
I was there with you at the marriage altar
I spend some hours with you at your reception
I make your body move with emotional feelings
You and your spouse were spinning around like a merry go round
        Because I am music
I serve one as I serve all people
I serve in the Church on the Sabbath day
I serve in the club twenty four hours per day
I serve for every tribe and nation, I serve I serve.
        Because I am music.

Gladstone C. Walters

Now That I Have Met You

Meeting you has given me a
Special feeling, that I never new existed.
You are so many things to me,
Your my best friend,
You are someone who I can depend on,
You are my strong hold.
Your the part of my life that makes me complete.
A chemistry change has taken place within me.
Without you life would have no meaning.
The world might just as we'll come to an end.
For that is how much love, I have for you.

Victoria Richichi

Heavy Heart

Heavy heart is troubled with sorrow and shame.
He is bitter and hides the pain
grief is his weakness and distress
But nothing out weighs his emptiness
He's learned that despair is a burden
a heavyweight

But so is love when it accompanies hate.
Heavy heart is grounded with wounded wings
sadness is the only song he sings
Heavy heart is on troubled road and
comes on with his heavy load.

Rachel Hughes

Harriet Tubman

In Dorchester County there was a baby,
Her name was Harriet, and she was born into slavery.

Put to work as a young field hand,
Harriet ended up marrying an older man.

His name was John Tubman, and that name she did take,
Then the day came when she had to make her break.

Leaving her husband behind,
Harriet escaped in 1949.

It was the slaves, that Harriet showed,
The safe passage through the underground railroad.

Tho' scared and frightened, some tried to turn away,
But Harriet Tubman convinced them that they must obey.

There were more than 300 slaves to win freedom
Because Harriet Tubman was a wonderful leadman.

After the Civil War, Harriet settled in,
And continued to work for the Negro Freedman.

Her good deeds were many, her bravery we've seen,
But Harriet died on March of 1913.

A house in her memory was given her name,
A refuge for blacks is what it became.

Kim LaMoureaux

Creek

The river that runs past my house is really a creek;
Its thin body winding in and out of
the rock bed maze covering the bottom of this
indentation in the tall marshy grass,
infested with dragon flies and mosquitoes,
who buzz, buzz, buzz from blade to blade,
landing only as long as is needed to take off again,
never slowing down, always busy, busy, busy
epileptic in their movements, the seizures
last till death do they part and I only wish
your willingness towards me was as constant
as the rush, rush, rush and the step, stop, skip
of my river, my misery, my creek.

Preeti Rachel Davidson

The Wind

Wind, quit hiding, I know that you're there.
    I can feel you running through my hair.
I see the leaves move as if by an invisible hand,
    I know it's your work as you blow across the land.
The flowers nod there head in fear, as you go by,
    While you go blowing along I hear you sigh.
Are you getting tired and you have miles to go?
    You can't stop now, you make our cheeks glow.
Scraps of paper flutter by me as I stand here.
    I know you're blowing fast, but I have no fear.
Rather you blow gentle or as fast as a jet,
    I want you to know I am glad that we met.
But come out of hiding so I can see,
    Just how nice a cool breeze you can be.
I always want your loving gentle side,
    It gives us a peace that we can abide.
Hey! Where in the world did you go?
    The grass stopped swaying to and fro,
The leaves don't move, the flowers have no fear,
    You just said hello, and then you disappear.

Dorothy Hennige

Untitled

I walk through evil everyday
I wish all the bad people would go away

Control, anger, unreleased stress
Sure makes this workplace a mess

Silence abides
Shadowed glances on the sly

When one enters this sanctimonious den
One is never treated as a friend

Self doubt is implanted, anti-confident seeds are sown
She-Wolves making their territory known

Lacking self esteem to an excess
Stifling creativity at its best

Kathryn Ann Montalbano

Mama's Pocket Book

Tattered brown leather and worn out straps
Overstuffed pockets under zippered flaps
Many loose threads and a broken brass hook
It's Mama's pocket book.

It carried lots of little stuff and kiddie things
No silver, no gold, no glittering diamond rings
A diaper or two has been carried in there
Six of us where placed by God in her loving care
Brushes, barrettes, and ribbons for sister and me
Millions of band-aids for the newly boo-booed knee
Chunks of string, odds and ends, batteries for toy cars
Something green four brothers swore came from Mars
Eleven macaroni necklaces and a dried yellow daffodil
A wallet full of pictures and an overdue electric bill
A checkbook with an almost always zero balance
But you'd never know it, home was better than any palace.

So what if it's tattered and worn, a yuky brown
Worn on her shoulder near her heart like a queen's crown
More love inside than you can imagine, just take a look
Inside Mama's pocket book.

Deborah Ann Dahlmann

Is It You?

"Is it you?" I say, being filled with alarm,
knowing you've come back to do me more harm.
"Where the hell have you been?" you shout — lunging at me
And I'm tasting the blood and I'm holding my knee

Where you've punched me and kicked me a thousand times
and you've cut me and beat me and yelled that I'm lying
and you've yanked me and broke me and pulled out my hair
yelling "I wouldn't do this if I didn't care

'Cause I love you and love makes me do this to you!"
Dare I think — this ain't love — knowing I've been a fool.
And my hatred of you I am nursing quite well
keeping it hidden from all of this Hell.

My love is cold ashes for him who would bruise me.
Breaking his plans to tear me, to use me.
Leaving it all — a breath of fresh air
Don't give a damn, 'cause he never cared.

You don't treat the one that you love like a dog
Taking my sex like you was a hog.
I can't account for the demons in you.
I've walked out of your life — still faithful and true.

Cheryl J. Thompson

War Cookies

I have witnessed
   too many casualties to mention,
Due to wandering thoughts
   stealing needed attention.
The cease fire of Christmas '67
   was all so absurd,
As rifling sounds of conflict
   were everywhere to be heard.
No holiday sounds,
   no holiday sights,
Just Mom's cookies
   of which we quietly shared bites.
I learned quickly
   to chase thoughts of loved ones away,
Keeping my feelings in check
   so my mind wouldn't stray.
A habit-forming, troubling trend,
   following me sadly through many a year's end.
Now I work hard at sharing my thoughts and feelings,
   and venture out of myself for much long-needed healing.

George F. MacNamee

Alone Here

Here I sit, beer in hand; cigarette in another.
   The crescent moon, napping on its side in
a bed of universe; and she's in a bungalow,
   across the path.

A still night it is; an occasional note in one
   ear, out the other.
Engulfed in time; it is only energy that releases
   my mind.

A shot of rye, may do right by me. It's all too
   easy, to misunderstand all I see; the flow
must be stopped, before I proceed.

Nothing unchanged; the earth continues rolling
   eastward, towards a new day; and she sleeps
in a bungalow, across the path.

Bruce Rabin

Butterfly

So dainty in the wind
Using all of your energies to bend
A delicate thing you are
Going hither and afar
Your camouflage colouring the drab blue sky
You are flying, fly my butterfly

Your structure so unique
So fragile and yet not weak
Climbing to reach your goal
Soaring beyond obstacles no more
Let not fear or problems stand in your way
For none can compare or defeat you I say

I have seen you in action
A sight 'Oh so grand!'
You deserve so much more than the harmonious stand
I wish I could give to your every need
To help you in flight and watch you succeed
But no, you are fine and doing well indeed
So, continue your flight to higher skies
Even without me you are flying, fly my butterfly

Derwinn Green

Terrible Thoughts

She was my missing link, as beautiful as
a sun setting between a pair of purple mountains.
My love for her was like a healing wound, growing
stronger every day. When she left, my life
seemed to be over.
What a terrible thought.

Or did I want it to be over?
An easy way to ease the pain that pounded my
insides. Who would care, I was a nobody.
No one would miss me.
What a terrible thought.

One question, how would I do it. Like in the
seat belt commercials, but without one; with a
gun, one bullet was all I needed, or should I
dangle from a rope tied to the tree of life?
What a terrible thought.

I couldn't believe it, she was lying there with a knife
through her heart. She put it there herself. The one that
left me with so much pain leaves me with even more.
What a terrible thought.

Timothy J. Murray

"Small Town" Sounds Before Sunrise

"Swish" — paper delivery — on concrete.
"Soft-drone" — small plane — flying low
    over rice fields.
"Crowing-practice" young rooster-struts.
"Sassy" — blue jay — chatters and scolds.
"Spitting" — sprinkles — soothing — thirsty grass.
"Easy-talk and light laughter" walkers
    passing by.
"Rushing" — roller blades — on dusty pavement.
"Hissing" — street cleaner — brushes along gutter.
"Click-clacking — "train rolls along tracks on the levee.
"Moaning" — trucks — on distant highways.
"Tingle-dingle" — chimes dance in breeze.
"Patter" — welcome — rain falls lightly.
"Sharpening-claws" — Percy, on wooden deck.
Then - "peaceful-silence" — the
Almighty listening to unspoken prayers . . .

Joan Stoddard Haak

Shannon

Unempty any longer Tracing past a pacing gale
My solid fortress friend fell failed
I fought the thought or faring fonder
Shapes or sizes. Vices vary wary
What Becomes my ponder
I'm jaded Jostled Far-cry faded
Fossiled Within wise remains
Seething Breathing Broken grins
On weary wrists my skin spreads thin
With firm framed fists my reach begins
Steady Upright Tribal stance
Fear of cage With grace I rage
I court your rhythmic dance
Foster me My child like dreams on
Spite Of wild fight like freedoms
Enlighten me Don't frighten me
I never sight you slighting me
In fantasy I fancy me
Fair to you to feign for me?
Pretend a friend for me?

Marie Dean Kenyon

The Cemetery

Trees out in the open, ducks into the creek.
Turtles by the creek shore, graves for all you see.
Someone caught a dragonfly, colors green and blue.
Maybe a few months old, or maybe just brand new.
We just saw a Great Heron, sitting on a root.
Probably just resting, knowing not a clue.
Big tall redwoods, protecting all the graves.
Grow here with his brothers, for many nights and days.
We saw some poison oak, colors red and green.
But go by the shape, 'cause the color's not as it seems.
Frederick Law Olmstead, worked hard on this place.
Worked on many parks, but this one had good taste.

Dominic Hunter

A Gift From God

One day this couple was seeking a gift —
a gift of life. God provided this gift to the
couple. The couple watched this gift
grow before their eyes; after several months it was time —
time to reveal this gift. A gift from God — what was it?
Life, a new life for them to share. Life
grew and grew wrapping and unwrapping
many gifts along the way. One day Life
was gone. Where did Life go? God
needed Life back and so the couple wrapped Life
into a beautiful box with many flowers and bows
and they gave their gift to God. Once again it was time
— time to reveal this gift — what was it —
Life . . .

A Gift From God!!!
Bertha M. Kilpatrick

Wolves

Their life is not easy, it's hard to survive.
They kill for food only, just staying alive.

The proud parent's puppies, cuddled warm in the den,
Completely unaware of the danger they're in.

The sad mournful howling haunts all through the night
As they gaze at the moon like a saucer so bright.

Their thick fur protects them from wind and from cold,
And hunger, it drives them, both young and the old.

They set out to hunt now, to prey on the weak,
And weed out the sick ones, it's them that they seek.

"To live, to live, just to live" is their cry.
They're needed here with us, so don't let them die.

Angela Hornsby

Draw Me Near To You Lord

When I'm drifting out in the
World alone, draw me near to you.
When I'm lost and scared and far from home,
Draw me near to you.
Help me stay on course with you,
And guide me near your throne,
Keep me safe from danger, Lord,
'Till I reach my heavenly home.

When all seems dark and dreary Lord,
Draw me near to you,
When the way is step and scary Lord,
Keep me close to you.
When all around is dark and gray, and
The foes grow stronger everyday
Help me on my heavenly way,
Lord keep me close to you.

Wilma Darlene McDonald

Tears

Confinement pain can cause some tears,
As her child grows larger day by day.
An expectant mom in awe and fears,
Asks good health when she kneels to pray.

Then came the day for the baby's birth,
Great pain and tears as she bears a boy.
Their cuddling days are filled with mirth,
Then school brings on proud tears of joy.

The years that pass make man from boy,
Then copious tears for her soldiers son.
He's home at last and she weeps with joy,
Now her times for tears are surely done.

Good days go by and the years march on,
Her auburn hair turned white with time.
Then the saddest of days, my Mom is gone,
And the tears that flow are only mine.

Royal L. Nicholas

Sunset

Glowing ball of orange,
disappearing out of sight.
Breathtaking beauty...
fading into night.

Only to be replaced, by moon and stars....
to dream and wish upon from afar.

Until the clouds are kissed once more...
by the shimmering pastels,
seen before.

Mountaintops,
touched with illuminating gold...
Nature's greatest gift,
Ever to behold!

Melody Dawn Mull

Melissa And Candace

Melissa and Candace are two special friends,
Always together, their love never ends.
They share a friendship, a friendship of love,
As close and sweet as a small white dove.

Together they are, together as one,
Their love for each other is never undone.
They never argue, they never fight,
For when they are together they see the light.

The light that brings them through each day,
The light that always brightens their way.
Together forever they float through the trees,
Two flowers petals flowing in the breeze.

Melissa Kelly

So Much It Hurts

I am filled and torn between joy and sorrow;
Somebody throw me a knife so that I might pry it apart.
Afraid to say I love you, afraid to show you I care,
If you saw who I be and don't like what you see,
then off you will go, far away from me.
So I hold my love back,
and as pressure it builds.
Painful indeed, I weep in my sleep,
walk alone on the streets,
despising myself for being such a creep.
No one could tell me, we were not meant to be,
when it was you I love only, and you I will keep.

Kevin Crane

Am I

Why am I here?
I need to know.
Why did God choose me?
I don't understand.

Am I suppose to go through pain in my teenage years,
Then understand why when I am an adult?
Am I suppose to write for others,
Or just for myself?
Am I suppose to learn about life now,
Then understand it but don't?
Am I suppose to be careful in life,
Or just take it easy?
Am I suppose to accomplish everything I've dreamed of,
Then think about the memories when I prepare to die?

Why am I here?
I don't understand.
Why did God choose me?
I need to know.

Jennifer Cunningham

Resurrection

A heart broken, twisted, torn, in utter despair.
A joy ended, bended, crushed beyond repair.
A light gone out with a whimper, not a shout.
A voice muted; a sound silenced,
Finished, no doubt.

A vibrant soul turned to ashes.
A spirit that soared, crashes.
A heap of what used to be whole,
Now gone down to defeat.
A loss of the most precious, youthful,
Heart that no longer beats
A steady rhythm in a crisis.

A spirit slowly rises; a phoenix longs to soar.
A true friend found and treasured.
A love for God to great to be measured.
A lost hope renewed, restored.

A final look at a painful past,
Too long profound;
Now it's gone; at last.

Laura L. Burns

Even Me

I find this so amazing
Thou who set the stars ablazing
Would look down to earth and see
and care for infinitesimal me.
To commune or not, the choice is mine
To be in a place where there is no time
The choice for my journey is settled then
I need only prepare and anticipate when
I choose to sail among the stars
Where angels play their golden guitars
I'd like to slide down the milky way
Where all the little children play
I'd like to look down on the world from above
And see a place of peace and love
My home will be the whole universe
And you'll care for me as you did at first
I may wish to rest on a silvery cloud
And with my verse praise you aloud
For it's still so amazing you see
That you can care for infinitesimal me.

Mildred Hyatt McLoud

Like A Child

Like a child I look at the world.
With the eyes of a little girl.
Sun shining and the sky a perfect blue.
Perfect blooms and perfect smells too.
The hopes and dreams fill my face.
Tomorrow is a brand new place.
The tree that lost it leaves, that Fall day.
Will grow greener and stronger on that Springs day.
Like a child I have to grow,
That mustard seed I must sow.
I have to pray for a better Day,
When everyone can say what they need to say.
I'm not your enemy and you're not mine,
Why is this happening time after time.
Why is your heart so hard to find,
Filled with bitterness has clouded your mind.
Like a child I still have hopes and dreams,
Loving each other isn't as hard as it seems.
If we all step together and take God's hand,
Be more like a child and help our land.

Lorei Jones

Lust Takes Love Gives

The lustful head of sin did raise its head
To snare all that was within.

The boundaries of love is clear,
To tread outside brings dread and tears.

It robs your very state, it promises but
Really only takes.

It causes shame and embarrasses your heart
To think you were fooled with such an old art.

If bonds are not broken, love will be true
It will be warm and always waiting for you.

It will fulfill and always be giving,
With growth that is promised and blessed by
Reserved living.

Lynnell B. Fitzwilliams

Journey

We breathe on the edge of the earth,
separated by a sea of weeping grass.
Disguised by the moon,
    as a blue tigers tongue,
stars moving inches from my dark face
    fireflies vanish,
        than reappear,
Covered by a mysterious dome,
    light poking pinholes in the canvas sky.
My body becomes immersed in tears,
    as the serpent lurks in the sea,
frightened by the serpent with no eyes,
we cling to the edge,
    and we laugh at the dog,
and we leave in search
    for one more journey...

Christopher B. Robinson

Spaceman

I met a man from Mars who was going to the races
He said he came down to earth cause, he ran out of spaces.

Pauline M. King

Lost Love

A young girl looks out over the water and cries.
She lost her true love.
The world around her seems to have fallen apart,
    and she wants to just die.
She is left just standing looking out over the water,
    trying to decide what she did wrong.
The more she thinks the harder she cries.
Life seems to have no more meaning.
All she wants to do is to be by herself and cry.
As the sun starts to fall the girl grows weary.
She wants to go home but she knows she cannot.
So she waits till morning and then she thinks,
    today is a new day.

Frances Belvin

Hope For Tomorrow

Hope for tomorrow, joy for today,
Your heart may be burdened, your soul may stray.
'Cause I'm not weak, I only pray for the meek,
I only pray for the meek.
I'll send you someone who'll see it your way,
I'll try to show you what's inside of me.
We only bring hope for tomorrow, joy for today,
Your heart may be burdened, your soul may stray.

Clarence Palacio

The Old Sourdough

It was 40 below with the snow coming down,
The old sourdough knew he had to reach the next town.
On the huskies ran with tails waving high,
For if they stopped on the trail their master would die.

As he mushed on towards Nome,
The old sourdough dreamed of his home.
Of his wife waiting there with a pot of warm tea,
He would soon be back by the Bering sea.

He sang about the lordly moose,
Deer and caribou,
The deep piled snow and cold crisp air,
He loved the north, his home is there,

He dreamed of his trips to deliver the mail
As he mushed his dog team over the trail,
He dreamed of Nola—his eskimo wife,
And his search for gold was the dream of his life.

Morning Star

Mother And Joshua

Joshua is born with vigor and life.
A life soon filled with love and strife.
Joshua cries.
Mother sighs.
Mother frets.
But no regrets.
Does Joshua want held its perhaps pain.
Mother soon knows. Its a repeating refrain.
Joshua plays.
Mothers stays.
Mother smiles.
Its all worthwhile.
Hiding from mom is so much fun.
Its always a game when Josh can run.
As Josh grows.
What does life hold.
Mother will be there.
Even when old.

Donna Carner

God's Gift

Children are God's gift to us
Pure unconditional love and trust
To love to nurture to embrace
To capture as they fall from grace
To preserve the light that shines within
To rid the soul of original sin
To answer when the little one's call
Extend a hand before they fall
The power to preserve what the future will bring
If only to hear the songs they sing
When life confronts you and judgement is made
How many souls can you say you've save
Born out of love defying lust
The children are God's gift to us.

Jacqueline A. Bryson

As The Sun Goes Down

As the sun goes down at the end of
the day I wonder if I will get to see
the flowers that grow in the meadows,
the horses that run free in the wilderness.
As days go by I wonder if the sun
will ever shine again, will the sun shine
on that lonesome valley before I wake.
As the sun goes down, I sit and
wait to see how many stars come out,
and I still wonder, will there ever be
a time of peace, as the sun goes down.

Jennifer Thames

Confusion

Running around,
a million different places to go.
Each one a bad decision.
Confusion rules my body.

I feel no love and
I feel no hate.
The pain and frustration
has blinded me to all feelings except pain.
Confusion rules my mind.

Worshipping the Gods
of my choice, I am lost between
religions and beliefs.
Confusion rules my soul.

Death is filling my days.
Am I next?
Is there any reason that
I shouldn't be?
Confusion takes hold
and slowly starts to kill me.

Jon Carlson

Stranger

His voice is like none I've ever heard before.
Charming and almost hypnotic. I could stand to
listen to him talk for hours and never once
utter a single word. I notice something new
about him all the time. I know absolutely
nothing about him yet I feel I have seen his
soul. Given the chance, I would pour my heart
out to him. Or maybe just sit and watch him.
I could do that for hours too.

Amelia Leyenberger

To My Saeth

As night and day come and go,
  I wonder if he'll ever know,
That the love that lies within my heart,
  Is there in hopes we'll never part.

The times spent together,
  The nights on the phone,
I cherish them all,
  Cause, they're our own.

I love his eyes,
  Those wonderful brown eyes.
I love his lips,
  So perfect to kiss.
I love the way he talks.
  I love the way he walks.
He's everything I dreamed he would be.
  He's perfect - to me.

Tonight, as I say my prayers,
  I will also thank my lucky stars.
For, I wonder how I could ever deserve,
  My sweetheart, my love... my Saeth Gronberg.

Wendy Michelle Saure

Untitled

How many times will I slice my wrist
before I finally learn life is a great thing
How many times must I fail in my life
before I finally succeed
How many times will I regret things
before I learn to accept the things I did.

How many times must I leave
the good guy for a bad guy
How many times more
will it be before I will get a disease
How many times will I get hurt
before I finally learn to be smart

How many times will I hurt the people
that care for me before they forget about me
How many times will they tell me stuff for my
own good before I finally decide to listen
How many times will they cry for me
before I will wake up
The answer is all in my heart.

Kristina Olivarez

A Dream By The Fire

The sun's rays play with the midnight sky,
The fire is arms reach way up high
But why am I here all alone
Sitting by the fire wondering why
I have often looked for the
  right one but never succeeded
My days for hope shall never end
For I know we shall be together again.
Then maybe I wouldn't be sitting alone.
To escape the heartache
  I shall silently enjoy the fires dance.
The midnights snow covered
  stars bring silent hopes and dreams.
Two young lovers in love
  shall never know what it means.
For me I do understand
  the fires dance, the snow
  covered stars, and the mysterious
midnight skies.

Shannon Bullard

Pardon My Insanity

And the evil, better terrors
Peek down from their knotted twig
Into my small name - nothing
Into my small heart - rushing

Thank God, at least, for the broken mirrors
To stop the reminiscing of something big
With, "Wouldn't it be lovely" disappearing
And our listening ears - wait for hearing

But then here we are left
With bodies who's eyes are deaf
Traveling that short road to somewhere
Knowing soon we'll be getting nowhere

This insanely empty with which to fill
This cruelty light with which we'll kill

Miles Duke

Who Am I?

In my cocoon safe and sound,
Grow fat, sassy, healthy and round.
All noises and racket are muted,
To my quiet world I'm suited.
I breath not yet, your world not seen,
I slumber still, fear not any being.
Wish that I could go on and on, the same,
I must come out and you name a name.
I come into your world without defenses,
Come into it screaming, with no pretenses.
Like a tiny vagabond, all alone,
Mercy, Mercy, give I a home.
For I be only a part of you,
Think bad me not, I want to live too.
Who am I?

Kate Durden

The Rising Sun And The Fallen Man

As the sun rises this morn
I see the clouds coming through
I met you as the clouds
came into my life
When I wanted the days to end
you told me there was more than just clouds
you gave me the light of day
straight into my heart
I only wish I had met you at the break of dawn
now it's a quarter till nine
and the days not over yet
I'm only glad
you didn't let me end it too soon

Elliott Ferguson

Country Christians

It was just a small country church
Out a long winding road.
But its members could be heard praying
and sharing many heavy load.
Enter ye heavy laden. God will give ye rest
Spirit filled Christians sing and tell of love so blest.
A crown of eternal life we don't deserve
yet Christ wore a crown of thorns - our soul to preserve.
A child like faith — Yet a faith so strong
with the love of God and faith in him —
he will never steer us wrong.

Linda Hastings

Love To Mom

It's the sweet smell of the roses
that bring your memory to mind.
It's the beauty of the honeysuckle
blooming on the vine.
Many years and many tears have
all slipped away.
But, now that I look back on things
I ain't got but one thing to say.
Thank you for all I learned and all
that you taught me.
It was for my own benefit and
now I begin to see.
All the good things that I've done
and all good ones to come.
I have you to thank, oh gee mom you're
number one, in my heart you're number one.

Love you
Ray Williams

Amazing Grace

When my life was dark and dreary
    When my feet had gone astray,
Jesus said, "Come follow me,
    And I'll show you the Way."

I fell down on my knees,
    And said, "Lord help me please."
He came down from above
    To show me His precious love.

I said, "Thank You, oh so much,
    I can never praise You enough
For saving a sinner like me
    When You died on calvary."

He said, "For you My life I gave,
    And through this you are saved;
For this you can't repay
    But give your life today.

A living sacrifice you'll be, and through you all will see
The God who lives in you in everything you do.

Feed My stubborn sheep, my Words you must always keep.
Your reward is heaven fair, a robe and crown you'll surely wear.

Twila Evonne Yeatts

Creation's Symphony

Stars gleam from ebon skies,
As sleeping earth below it lies;
While the moon, on silver feet,
Treads silently down each dark street.
Frost glistens 'neath her silver gaze,
As its gilded patterns glaze
Each tiny twig and window pane
Which dwells in winter's vast domain.
The winter wind whining 'mongst the trees
Is cousin to a summer breeze;
But his tongue's too sharp for summer air,
And he whines, for it seems to him unfair
That he's not able to do as he please
And warm the world as a summer breeze.
But a wise old wind blew from the West
And scolded him for his thoughtlessness:
"Why do you complain?" she asked.
"God assigned you to complete this task;
So go about it cheerfully,
For you're part of creation's symphony!"

Alyssa A. Newton

Untitled

In the world of magic . . .
There is nothing of love.
Magic comes from hate,
It binds us with its blackness.

In the world of magic . . .
Not a single person cares.
Magic takes from us,
All emotions that are good.

In the world of magic . . .
People fight and war with one another.
Magic makes us selfish.
It makes us take from others to satisfy ourselves.

In the world of magic . . .
There is a fire that burns forever.
It never ends.
That eternal flame of hatred.

In the world of magic . . .
We care nothing about the things around us.
We let things wither and die,
Thinking ourselves to be immortal although we are not.

Pamela S. Adkins

There Is A Life After Pain

After so much pain it's been
hard the sustain. After so much
misfortune and vain. If there's
something I know now that I
didn't know then, there is a
life after pain. But life goes
on and you get through the
rain, and now you too realize
there is a life after pain.
You cut off all of your unnecessary
things and people too.
All they have done is brought
you down in everything you do.
So now I have someone in my life who can understand me.
He's shown me so much love. So
much I'd never thought I'd see.
We have respect, trust, honesty and love.
Everyday and every night I thank my heavenly father above.
He's help my life to very much sustain
and through God he has shown me there is a life after pain.

Charnice D. Reaves

A Man's Love

As I look out at the vast Northern sea, my soul clings to the
  marrow in my bones.
Already missing the soft warm love of my family.
The very nerve endings under my flesh throb, from the
  bitter cold that has dried my skin.
The ice on my face prevents that final kiss I so desire,
  so I must settle for a hug to warm my soul
As I depart to enter the rugged ole ship I call my job,
  I'm reminded that only a man among men could perform
  such a task.
I would shed a tear of sorrow, but it would show a weakness,
  I'm no man for that.
But I am only a man that loves dearly, so I will shed that tear,
  Whether it freezes or not, my families love will warm my
  very soul.
Till I embrace them again.

James M. Farnam Sr.

Life As It Is!

Life is a big hill with a white house on top
with five different windows symbolizing five
different ways we look at perspectives
The double doors for freedom.
The moon by your side for night
The sun big and bright to guide you for day
The brick wall for being trapped at the ways you look at things.
The never ending winding road for leading yourself
  in the same direction
Sleep for dreams that take us to another world or place
Thunder, lightning, and rain for making us think of
what nightmares really are.
The sea for lost souls trying to get to heaven
And the world drowning in its own path.
Is this life as it is?

Caitlyn Thiem

Sundown

The Sunset spins its self-consuming fires
in ceasing lights and shadows,
thrown from its center unseen,
unknown, untouched,
by human eyes whose lives and desires require
the lessening,
deepening,
darkening of light
to rest at last in silence,
and slumber soft through skies' new dance
of pure, pale, cold,
slight, bright, light
which governs and rules over the night.

Wendi Giezentanner

Out My Window

A rainbow shines bright,
  under the rays of the sunlight.

A leaf slowly falls to the ground,
  without a sound.

A bird lands on the top of a tree,
  but what does she not see?

She sees the world from her point of view,
  too bad she can't see it from ours to.

The last golden ray of sun,
  and I know the day is done.

The curtain slowly falls,
  and who knows what's behind these walls.

Tammy Racette

Memories

Jesus all my memories center around you.
You're all I think about and know your love is true.
No matter what tribulation I been through,
Jesus, I remember you always are the one
Who helped me through.
I love you Jesus Christ and you know my
Love for you is strong and true.

Remember our love will grow as the rings
On a tree in the redwood forest to the end
Of all time, my whole life through with you.

Catherine D. Feathers

Reunion Upon the Rainbow

I read of a place called the Rainbow Bridge
And the lush meadow which lies at its base,
And of the promise that there, once again,
I would gaze at your hauntingly beautiful face.

And feel once more the love that we shared
And the warmth of the kiss from your tongue,
And see how the meadow has magically healed,
And made you once again young.

I cried yet again for the distance and time
that remain between me and that place,
For each day that goes by without you at my side,
Seems such a terrible waste!

I yearn for the day when the journey I'll take
To that place where I'll find you still waiting,
And together again we'll cross over the bridge,
For in my mind there is no debating:

That it matters not where we go from that point
Just so long as we travel together;
For heaven, I know, will be locked in our hearts,
And there shall remain, forever . . .

Franci Sparks

Life And Love

I stroll along a lonely lane,
I hear a mourning dove,
I see a doe with her fawn,
Here there's life and love.

I hike along a country creek,
Wending through the wood.
I see shiners shimmer, trout at play,
All life with love is good.

I see my wife in our living room,
Our baby at her breast.
In the shadowy glow of the fire place,
Life and love are best.

I sit and watch the evening news,
Angry men brandish guns, and shove.
With cursing lips, and blazing eyes,
They express their life, ...but love?

There's a sudden rush of searing heat.
Instantly, viewing from above,
I see a cindered earth, a mushroom cloud,
Man's greed, hatred and mistrust, destroys all life and love.

John A. Coghill

A Moment

It was, in time, a simple space
your flowing movement, timeless face
as all the background blurred and faded
there you stood, in contrast, clearly stated.

Your suit outline degrees of geometry
your loving eyes my soul can see
A look from you penetrates each part
through my eyes, my head, my chest, my heart.

The world falls still beyond each sense
my receptors flooded, it's so intense
this brain can barely comprehend
the vastness of the love you send.

I am awash like tides on sand
will, waves of love you touch my hand
in that instant I am transported
"Back to the world", my mind's reported
my soul unlocked and given away
In that moment's look - on that glorious day.

Mary Schuh

You've Been There...

One of you has always been there,
Whenever I've been upset.
To cheer me up when I was down
Or encourage me to forget.

You've been there on those terribly rough days,
That come more often than few.
To tell me everything would be all right
And that I'd make it through.

You've been there on those special occasions,
That mean so much to me.
To show me how much I mean to you,
which sometimes I find hard to believe.

You've been there on the happy times,
When we laughed until we cried.
Sometimes from our silly jokes,
That gave us such joy inside.

But our time together is winding down,
Soon our lives will take different paths,
But the memories of our times together,
In our hearts forever lasts.

Melissa Slavicz

The Missing Piece

As I'm running through the trees, I weep silently . . .
Searching for something I can not find
and if I did — I couldn't see . . .
I'm puzzled by this madness, feeling all alone . . .
not knowing what I'm searching for — it seems to be unknown.
A steady pain grips at my chest — I fall down to my knees . . .
I'm fighting with something inside of me —
Something that needs to be freed
I search my soul for the missing piece
I've been looking for all along . . .
I realize I have to know what's missing,
before I know it's gone.
I get up to run and search all around.
When yet my puzzle piece has not yet been found.
Not knowing what I'm looking for —
the tears are blinding my view
then I realized this piece was my heart —
and it had always been with you.

Heather Bishop

Good-Bye

I will never forgive myself, seeing him
lying there so still. He should be
up moving around,
but he's not. The viewing was hard,
but not going to the funeral was
the hardest. I went to the nursery with
my nephew so I didn't have to say good-bye.
Later at his grave, seeing the dark brown
coffin with white and peach roses on top;
being lifted into the ground made me
think of how he is never coming back.

Now at night I cry myself
to sleep thinking of all the memories.

I wish I had taken the
chance to say Good-Bye.

Shantel Christensen

Memories

It seems I used to try my hardest
To think to myself as this great artist.

My scribbles proved that wasn't so
So I had to let that idea go.

Then I decided poetry was for me
Anybody could rhyme lines, you see.

I soon realized you had to spell
Words correctly for thoughts to jell.

Now needlework seems to be the best
They think I'm working while I rest.

While pretty colors go through my hands
I think of home and foreign lands.

But what really never leaves my heart
Are people I've known from the very start.

Family and friends and houses and barns
Up in the cities and down on the farms.

I'm on a roll and could go on and on
But you'd know for sure my mind is gone.

So please don't cross off this old girl
Much love to you all from your old Aunt Pearl.

Pearl K. Allen

Great Grandpa

Great Grandpa lies in a hospital
bed, dressed in his striped, open backed
hospital issued pajamas, reminiscing about
days gone by.

About days when he would sit in his
comfortable chair and watch the legend,
John Wayne, ride about on his
rarely used T.V. screen.

Or, when he would sit out on the front porch
chewing and spitting tobacco, while telling
one of his all famous political stories, about those
darn old Democrats.

Then it hit him-
The Stroke!

It took away most everything, even his speech-
but we still have memories of the old days,
when his laughter would fill our ears,
as we sat in the swing
and watched the fire flies.

Eric Verdoorn

A Typical Day

I look out the window and what do I see,
nothing much but a bunch of trees. The
sky light blue that we abuse, the sun so strong
you can't stare at it for long. The air so sweet
of morning due, and me on my feet raring to go.
I ride to school every day on my bike all the way.
The class is over and I walk away always afraid of
being late, but by then I'm ready to go home to
lay on my bed and talk on the phone, but now
it's time to go to bed so I say good night and that's

Dalia Gracia

Lost Soul Crying

Sitting alone in the dark trying to find a light
a broken heart keeps on an endless fight
desperate in search of everlasting love
closing his eyes he prays for a dove
someone to care for someone to hold
a girl he can run to when the world is cold
never wanting perfection, just a pretty smile
a good personality to laugh with him a while
"am I asking too much" he often wonders
for he has met nice ones in very small numbers
what do they want, what to they need
could it be that they're all full of greed
true it takes money to live a good life
does this mean a man just buys his wife
love can't be bought with the price of a gift
the flowers and jewelry just give it a lift
financial security something everyone hopes for
his dream is loving girl behind the door
as he lays down in bed his broken heart dying
he says to himself "my lost souls is crying"

Zachary McCarty

Remember

Send me flowers when I say goodbye
and send me a tear if you miss me and cry.
Place importance on the love I gave
Think of me at night with only memories to have and save.
My companion my pal, my lover my friend.
Send your love when it feels right.
Give me your fire while it still burns bright,
and don't forget what has been from now until our end.

Jason Maxwell

Shadows of Love

Arising out of ashes grown cold,
White hot passions sear my soul.
Breathlessly, shamelessly I reach for you.
Your lips so warm, your scent so dear.
Yet tears fill my eyes, my heart swells with
love so great and pain so near, because
I know, the embers soon grow cold, leaving
me an empty soul. I have loved you.

Glenda M. Stephens

If You Dare

If you dare to open up your mind
and confront the things you fear,
to stand still, believe and trust yourself
and allow your soul to hear;

If you dare to seize the moments run
and let your mind be free,
to touch the sky, the ground below
and all you dare to see.

If you try to see the face of God
and let your heart be touched,
to know the Glory that gave you life,
when yourself, you did not trust.

If you challenge yourself to know the truth
that time will not undo,
to accept it, and then move on
and to thine own self be true;

Then God's great gift he gave to all
that in life we may not fear,
the blood that washed is yours to have
Ah! But only if you dare.

Nicola Harvey, Jr.

Rape

As my heart was racing,
all the memories of him I was erasing.
He said that he loved me, so why won't he stop?
He said that he respected me, why is he taking off my top?
I feel his body getting closer to mine,
I wish I could feel like him, perfectly fine.
What is he doing? Why is he doing this?
To think it all started with one sweet kiss.
He takes off his jeans and mine too
While holding me down he whispers I love you.
I feel his hands and body over mine like I'm a toy
I can't believe he's only a boy.
I try to yell, scream, and shout,
But all I can do is pout.
I finally get away, but it's too late
He did it to me already, now all I feel is hate.

Elizabeth Westergaard

Our Love

For Bob Blackmer, 1991
Sharing with my wonderful one
As under moon and shining sun
Yours is heavenly, pure delight
Mine weakens not when out of sight.

Wild like a roller coaster ride
Both thrill and fear the year provide
On yonder horizon love's silhouette
N'er stronger bond has been known yet.

Spark undying in both doth lie
Each other's company comfort's sigh.
Side by the other at call of moon
Blessed rest and peace, dawn comes too soon.

Morning sweet bid each to the other
None to consider, save the other
Vow life and love each feels a must
Side by the other till call to dust.

Ann Huskisson Blackmer

Or Else

She gave me an ultimatum...marry her or stop wasting
her time. I told her it's been fun, but I'd miss her.
A week later she called me. She said she was holding
a gun to her head. She couldn't live without me.
I heard the clunk clunk clunk of the gun against
the phone while she spoke. She's there and I'm here.
I told her there was nothing I could do. If she wants
to do it, I'm better off without her anyway.

Chad Vandergriff

Me

This is me, proud and free, but sometimes I'm
not me.
Sometimes I'm cool and sometimes I'm a
clumsy fool.
I like to read, I like to write and sometimes I
feel fright, late at night.
I like Spelling and math and taking a bath.
But most of all, I love my parents because they
made me, me.

Bradley Yates

Untitled

Emotions, endless waves - feelings erupt and die
Confusion, order in the universe
To follow my heart, but where will it lead?
Stability and passion - two opposite worlds.
Jupiter, enormous, beautiful - no life
Pluto, distant small
Takes its time
Makes a complete circle, not in this lifetime
Make a wish upon a star
Hoping, anticipating the ball of dust will make it all come true
Why? How?
Dust shines so brilliantly in the sky yet not on the ground
Pressure, internal, external, keeps everything bottled up
which path to choose, not like a planet stuck in or bit,
not like meteors falling, shooting so freely from the sky
They aren't free, predictable
Same place, same time the pressure releases
Common fate, burn, crash, die, just to sparkle for
a moment.
 Then it all repeats.

Christa Amoriello

Dreams Of Bliss Revival

As I stand in the January sun of Alabama
I recall my childhood on the snow covered plains
Did happiness wash away with the silt
 in the strong summer rains

Does happiness drift through our heart
 like the snow across a meadow
Does it disappear from our minds
 like a breeze through an open window

When happiness returns, can we hold it
 in the corner of our hearts and minds
Will it build with great force
 til it nearly explodes from within

Does happiness really exist at all
Or, does our heart tell our mind
 to bend to the whim of warm winds
Perhaps it's there to make our heart fall

Gentle is the happiness of a newborn child
Like sunlight on a face on a warm spring day
Oh, to recapture the happiness
 that once ran wild!

Jeffrey P. Schacherer

Black History

Black History,
only celebrated one month of the year
yet they expect us to smile and cheer.

You claim were equal but that's not true
the color of my skin matters to you.

You don't see me for who I am
you see what has been taught upon this land.

You say black is dark destitute of light
you say that black is gloomy and out of sight.

Black I am and proud to be
in the end I shall be free.

Black and proud I do stand
a black face upon the land.

Tawauna Teneyek-Williams

Silence

The silencing night attacks its victims,
Preying on all,
But only conquering those who are weak and frail.
With a cold bust of snow,
The weak fall upon the icy white ground.
Loosing all strength,
They are unable to lift their freezing bodies from the snow,
They know that they will die.
But some feel as though they will survive,
Living through the silencing night.
This false sense of security eases their pain,
Laying in the snow,
They begin to feel warm, and want to go to sleep.
One by one, their lives fade away,
Not caring if they ever wake to return to their frozen bodies.
They lay in the bitter snow.
Never again will these lost souls see a warm summer day,
But they will live forever in eternal silence.

Pat O'Connor

The Paths We Cross

Martha was so small and frail,
Just like a fragile dove.

So full of smiles strained through the pain,
And still so full of love.

What life dealt her accepted.
Though somewhat she denied.

She was going to beat this thing,
If only with her pride.

Her illness though she mentioned, but
Never by its name,

She spoke of positively, though it took
Its toll the same.

Though our paths crossed but briefly,
I will be grateful to my end,

That in my life I had the chance to have
Martha as my friend.

Now that she has passed on to what we're
All destined for,

I believe God answered, to her first knock
At his door.

Shirley A. Fultz

Love Springs Eternal

How good it is to stand out there
And watch the birds glide through the air,
And know as long as there's a bird's sweet song
That things can never be so terribly wrong.

There may be wars, there may be strife,
But yet there's happiness in life;
For just as sure as there are stars above,
With each new spring, there blooms new love.

Such is the case with us, my dear;
For like the spring, I'll want you near.

Alberta Miller

My Hero

My hero, My hero, My hero I see! He's coming just to save me!
Bullies have fear for the hero is here.
My hero, My hero, My hero I see. Oop's! He's just passed me.
But wait, There's hope, My hero is nice, which means he'll come
back and save my life!
My hero, My hero, My hero I see! Wow! Cool! My hero is me!

E. J. Henricks

Dreams

I often wonder why people dream.
  Maybe it is so we won't get bored.
Or it is because we can't fall asleep.
  Some of us can't get to sleep
Because some of us are scared of the dark:
  And some want to read stories...
I guess I know now why people dream!

Kirsten F. Tarillion

The Relativity Of Pain

I'd die a thousand torturing deaths
To keep alive your sweet blossomed breath
I'd suffer a thousand throat searing screams
To keep alive your glistening dreams
I'd rend a thousand heart wrenching cries
To keep alive your lightning filled eyes

There's a thousand things I'd say or do
To make this life better for you

I'd travel to hell a million soul burning trips
To run my tongue along your rose budded lips
I'd climb a million mountains, one by one
To have a taste of your honey-dripped tongue
I'd work a million years without a day of rest
To immerse my head in the warmth of your breast

There's a million things I'd say or do
To have my life entwined with you

But I don't think I could draw another breath
For the blinding pain that I've felt since your death

Christopher M. Soloway

My Life

Yes, it is true my parents have gotten a divorce,
And there was a lot of pain and force.
I was sad and depressed for many years.
I didn't see life through anything but tears.
They were pulling and tugging me I like a rope,
I thought just one more moment and I would be broke.
If anything my life was pretty bad,
The fighting, arguing, and lies made me very sad.
Why, why were they doing this to me?
All of this confusion just made me want to flee.
At school my grades were slowly slipping.
But at home I had a very helpful sibling.
But gradually my life has gotten better.
And my grades have at least raised one letter.
I also had a lot of help from one certain friend.
And having her there made all my troubles end.
There is still a lot of tension between my Mom and Dad.
But all it does now is make me mad.
Even though I've had a lot of strife,
I've had a pretty wonderful life.

Crystal Rallo

EVIL

Full of innocence, happiness, peace, calm and dreams,
we never suspected that EVIL was lurking, watching...
and had plans for us in his schemes.
I ask myself why us, a thousand times, I am still in disbelief,
but in the end JUSTICE won out, much to our relief.
He can not hurt us now, he is just a bad memory,
he will get out some day, but he will never be free.
We are all okay, we have learned a great deal,
someone up there heard me pray to have time to heal.
Our eyes are open, we do not take anything for granted,
Thank you God, for the things that really mattered.

Jolene Dennis Martin

Once I Had A Dream

Once I had a dream that,
I would be a princess.
Once I had a dream that,
I would be a millionaire.
Once I had a dream that,
I would have a family; a husband, a girl and a boy.
Once I dreamt all these
dreams would come true.
You're the one who left me.
You're the only one to blame.
I loved you, but you're the one,
that made the change.
I thought countless thoughts.
And I believed you when you said you cared.
You said "I love you" every night.
I planned my life with you and began to feel my love build.

...but I only had a dream.

Lyle-Anne Pelles

Fear In The Loop

Old woman pushes a rusty shopping cart of gold
Kid plays a beat on trash cans I'm told
Guitar case wide open to catch a few coins
Street music rises above the city noise
Puppeteer sets up shop
Against a painted brick wall
Rich people peer a minute, then stop
On their way to the shopping malls
Toss him a dollar; he has nothing to eat
Find her a bed; she has nowhere to sleep
Society people hastily stroll by
Fists clutching purses held captive by suspicious eyes
An aura of fear blankets the block
As merchants and passers-by check their locks
There must be a way
We can close the distance between us
Somehow, we can all camouflage as one
Why not share with the deserving just
And abandon this ritual run?

Terri Tiernan Maguire

Wandering Wonder

I wonder why the crime rate has to be so high;
Children killing children, for what ever reason, why?

I wonder why the elderly no longer receive respect;
And for those who are less fortunate, we choose to forget,

I wonder why love is no longer ever lasting;
Why we rather choose drugs than praying and fasting,

I wonder why God gave His only begotten Son;
For one day His job with us will be over and done,

Sometimes I wonder why life can't be a bed of roses;
But then life would be boring, full of Z's and dozes.

Lillita Bridgeforth

Collapse

Carefully, quickly she crosses the path
Purposely, painfully forgetting the wrath.
Quietly quivering, she closes her eyes
to shadow the coldness, to banish the lies.
No warmth of truth, no visible light
to vanish the darkness, to regain the sight.
So softly, silent she whispers a sound
Lifeless fading falling to the ground.

Lisa Kallio

The Power Of Love

This is the sweetest day of the year,
When we remember those about whom we care,
We give candy, flowers, gifts, and such,
We bring miles of smiles, we can't do too much.

I love it all and I'm sure you do too,
It's fun all these special things we do,
But, for me, there's a gift, O Lord, I pray,
This is what I'd like for Valentine's day.

Create in me a clean heart, O God,
Please be with me wherever I trod,
And renew a right spirit within me,
For I surrender myself to thee.

It's not only a day for sweethearts, you see,
Don't take for granted what love could be,
It's a powerful gift we get from above,
Practice it daily - the Power Of Love!

Teresa Taylor

Untitled

Don't let my ribs be a cage for my heart
From which my feelings could never depart
I don't want to live like a bird in a cage
Showing no feelings — not even rage
I want my heart to waft like a tune
I don't want to live inside a cocoon
Surrounded by bars and covered at night
With no one to understand my plight
I want to be free as a bird on high
Not having to suppress a single sigh
I want this heart to be able to sing
As though this life I slowly wing
My heart wants to let all people know
The feeling I oft times cannot show
Love, hatred and sin or even sorrow
For I would be caught in an endless tomorrow
Don't let my ribs be a cage for my heart
From which my feelings could never depart

Cynthia Worley

The Night The Stars Cried

As I wished upon the lonely star,
It winked at me, listening from afar.
I asked the star to protect her,
But it could only see, not effect her.

"Where is she now, can you see?"
"Yes, she's home, just turning the key."
"Is she okay?", I wondered aloud.
"She's crying...", it said, it's voice no longer loud.

"What can I do?", I asked feeling bleak.
"Call her, but hurry, we're all getting weak."
"We're dying up here!", cried another star.
All of them dimmed, in a sky as dark as tar.

Some stars cried in pain, others just cried.
To home, I rushed, no help to be denied.
I dialed her number, fingers trembling.
She answered, "Hello?", on the very first ring.

"What's wrong?", I asked, hoping to help her.
"I've been lonely,", she said, "but now I'm better."
The stars were bright, shiny once more.
And none of them cried, none, evermore.

Paul L. Williams

Heart and Soul

When you look at me . . .
Your eyes dark and heavy with desire
All control is gone.
Thoughts of loving you fill my head.

You take my mind away.

When the softness of your hands reach out to me . . .
I can't resist.
So sweetly you smile
As your fingertips caress my face.

You take my heart away.

When I feel your lips . . .
Pressed gently against mine
Kissing me with longing and passion
Like lovers do —

You take my breath away.

When you hold me in your arms . . .
I loose myself.
Our worlds collide
And time stands still —

You take my soul away.

Becky W. Crowe

Cocoon

My youth had escaped me
As the caterpillar has spun its cocoon
I've graduated
As the butterfly graces the sky
Flashlight tag and grasping at lighting bugs
Are all but distant memories
As my future holds no boundaries
My yesterdays are fond, free spirits
Remaining captured in my heart eternally

Valorie Hirsch

An Unforgiving Thing

Born months before his time on earth
A perfect little mind was shattered at birth
He lives in a world of his own making
I love him so much my heart is breaking
He just rocks and sings, rocks and sings.
    Autism such an unforgiving Thing!
He doesn't know of puppies and such.
How can he know I love him so much
The little boy locked inside
Doesn't really want to hide.
He just rocks and sings, rocks and sings.
    Autism such an Unforgiving Thing!
I will search until I find the key
That will provide the secret of me,
To heal his shattered precious mind
Then my little boy I'll find.
He just rocks and sings, rocks and sings
    Autism such an Unforgiving Thing!

Diana Hone

A Portrait Of Mother

Gentle Mother with silver hair
Sits sleeping in her rocking chair.
Little Bandit on her lap,
Both adrift on the Sea of Knap.
Precious Mother with silver hair
Where have you journeyed while dreaming there?

Ruth Johns

Like Any Other Fugitive

Like any other fugitive I spurn the traveled roads.
I shun responsibility, and popular abodes.
I see my mortal enemy behind each rock and tree.
Paranoia's catching on, I swear they follow me.
I'm a fugitive from love without a home address,
A fugitive from love a love that couldn't care less.

I stop for food and coffee; more often for a drink.
I slide beside my silent friend and side by side we think.
I thought that you loved me. I thought that you were true.
But you were only using me, if I had only knew...

Love is the most dangerous game,
They talk all sweet, and yet, so vain,
They tease you, leave you, it's always the same.
The whole damn play's driving me insane

Now it's me and the silver centipede who runs along my right.
He moves ahead, endlessly, faster in his flight.
On to the end of the rainbow, on to my pot of gold.
On to the end of this very earth until I grow old.

I'm a fugitive from love without a home address,
A fugitive from love - a love that couldn't care less.

Robert E. Wall Jr.

Dusk

At dusk when the sun is sinking low.
And the yellow moon is about to glow.
I sit outside and look up at the sky.
And watch the beautiful white clouds floating by.
The sun is sinking low.
And the moon is rising high.
And it is almost time for day to say good-bye.

Jane Larson

A Prayer For Us

Dear Lord have I failed to thank you today
For this angel of love you sent my way?

Don't let me forget how precious she is
Or how all the moments she fills with such bliss.

May I be ever mindful of this joy she brings
To have her to love me makes my heart sing.

May I honor and cherish her all of my days
As she loves me despite my often strange ways.

While we bask in thy love, please bind us together
To walk hand in hand for ever and ever.

Jim Lyons

Loving You

Inside a sweet dream, I surround myself with you:
Your voice is the wind that blows gently through my hair,
and your eyes are the sun that burns into my deepest
dreams and caresses my fears.
I think of your hands as the falling summer rain,
that covers my body softly and leaves me
needing more of your love.
The sound of your voice makes me want to love you,
and when I look into your eyes,
I no longer have to wonder what heaven looks like.
To be with you,
I have found a paradise
and will always be wondering how I would
sleep without dreaming of you.

Holly M. Dolan

No Way Out

Paradise
Just one swallow and she's there
the world around her distant
fear and worries disappear
gone, for now.

Skipping through fields of fresh flowers
their scents permeate each nostril
Heavenly; she feels like an angel
flying above the world contentedly

This land so deceitful
so fake
Everything deteriorating
The flowers seemed so fresh
now wilting in their own despair
Her wings snap
Plummeting towards the ground
Frightened, she pleads with a stranger
"I must leave, how do I get back?"
"No way out," he answers
No way out.

Brendan D. Carty

Foolish Heart

Do not look upon me with such adoring eyes
For I am the Devil in disguise
Discard not my flaws
For they exist deep inside

If I laugh at your jokes or reward you with a smile
Think not I love you
You insolent child

My curtains have been drawn
The last lantern out
My house is now cold
No one's about

The ashes of love which once burned so deep
No longer stir
Yet I still keep

There will never be another...

From the pain I could not recover
Never again shall I see the bright light of day
Alone in my grave
Trapped
Till my dying day

M. Amanda Galicia

Poem For Erik

Two years have passed filled with love.
Two bodies flitting together like a hand and glove.
I've fallen in love time and time again.
Only to have it ruin and end.
Mistakes were made by both us two,
But I'm the one feeling lonely and blue.
Forever my love will be given to you,
But who will yours be given to?
Sitting here I pray each day,
Trying ever so hard to get you to stay.
Erik, my love, I just want you to know,
You're the one I love, so please be so.

Amy Peterson

Drinking From The Saucer

I have never made a fortune, and
I'll never make one now! But it really
doesn't matter, cause I'm happy anyhow!

As I go along my journey, I'm reaping
better than I've sowed! I'm drinking from
the saucer, cause my cup has overflowed!

I don't have a lot of riches - and
sometimes the going rough! But while I've
got friends who love me I think I'm
rich enough!

I will thank God for the Blessings that
his mercy has bestowed, I'm now drinking
From the saucer, cause my cup has overflowed

If God gives me strength and courage
when the way grows steeps and rough. I'll
not ask for other Blessings - for I'm already
Blessed enough.

May I never be too busy to help bear another
load. Then I'll be drinking from the saucer
cause my cup has overflowed!

Ronnie Kennedy

Life's Concerto

Life is a merry tune
You hum all day long.
As bright as a sunny day in June,
It bursts into a song.

Life is a melody you hear from a distance.
As distinct as a cricket
It fades by persistence.

Life is a symphony.
You succumb to its spell.
As distorted as a meiosis,
It leads to the pits of hell.

Life is a sonata. You perceive its theme
As clear as a crystal brook,
It flows gently into the mainstream.

Life is a descant. You choose the course
If mastered by evil's whim,
It cannot find its source.

Life is a symphony. You seek its reprise
If conducted by the composer,
Its reposal is love's never-ending ties.

Kathleen S. Coley

The Bum

There he stood in front of the store,
My eyes met his with a fright.
His face was tan and his eyes were gleaming
Like stars in the black of the night.

His hair was real long and he was kind of scary,
So I hurried on into the store.
While inside, I heard them talking,
About the bum in front of the door.

One young man said, "I work for my check,"
Another said, "I don't give money out to the poor."
I thought to myself how God loved this man
The bum in front of the door.

I prayed, "Dear God, let this man know
The free gift you gave in your Son".
It's the gift of salvation for you and me,
And, yes, for even the bum.

Thomas J. Keller

A Psalm Of Praise For Gentle Silence

Praise you Lord, God in silence dwells
Who in this world of noise and clamor
Reign with peace and joy
O'er the wild and wanton space
A quiet, gentle sound.

Thou art the king of silent, gentle thought.
Amidst a weak and restless man,
So lost in worldly din,
We hear your sweet and loving voice,
A quiet, gentle sound.

Our hearts are yearning, Almighty God
To be clothed in quiet pleasure
To hear your voice and feel your glory
To know your awesome presence
In quiet, gentle sound.

We see your gentle streams of glory
With the earth in full surrender
Melt our hearts - your earthly home
To know the rapture of Your love,
Oh Lord of quiet, gentle sound.

Carolyn G. Bundash

I Felt The Future Today

Life has been so full and so busy
Not much time - to open — this heart of mine.
But something happened today — years I've
—known you — heard the good, and the bad
Never once thinking - our paths would one
day cross but as I think it over I
felt the future today.
Pasts cannot feel tomorrow yet we
always remember good times and bad.
So many write of the past and cannot
see beyond tomorrow, but your look,
feel, and touch made me see the future today
For a while I dropped the loneliness and felt
the joy I dropped the fear. And felt my
heart swell with new pride.
I smiled thru my eyes and felt no shame
For thoughts that came all the way to my soul.
A need came up from way down deep inside.
To be there in the future with you,
Give me your love, the future awaits.

Darlene Shuwe Bennett

A Rainbow

A rainbow came down from the
sky one day

After a down pour of rain in the
month of May

It was colorful as it could be
Just so everyone would surely see.

The colors were yellow, red and blue
and there were also many others shaded hues

It didn't stay long and it faded fast
It was here and then it was part of the past.

I will watch for it again someday, for this
beautiful sight to behold

When the rain comes down and the sun
comes out and we will look for that
pot of gold.

Florence M. Schrider

Woodfruit

This Almond, this tapered elegance
Tastefully fine in it's hardshelled excellence

Pink Pistachio, uniquely green
Its surprising delicacy not yet seen

Savory Peanuts roasted brown
Enjoyed by both kings and clowns

This Cashew curved with pride
With sturdy wood for its hide

This Pecan, this divine
With vari-colored rinds.

This Walnut, so desired
Cracks by the fireside

This Hazelnut which summer brings
Grows in the rain; the rainbow sings

The Chestnut traditional
We pleasurably salute,
Its estimable cousins woodenly repute
To be delightfully delectable
As is all of nature's

Mary Louise Mann

My Window

As I look upon my windowsill, I see a
small delicate kitten lying fast asleep, tired
from watching a gay little bluebird, singing
happily upon the branches of the lemon
tree. As I look at the tree, it looks like
it has no worries, so it spreads itself out.
Through the bare spots in the tree, you
could see spots of gazing light peeking
through the leaves, as if they were lost.
I look upon the ivy I planted last year,
growing with the love I gave it to grow.
It grew a lot, spreading across my bamboo
fence, it shows me that I have a green
thumb and a loving heart.

Amanda Jennie Conatser

Hope

Are we that different you and me?
Friends you say, that can never be.

You judge me for the way I dress.
This dose not make me like you less.

Designer clothes, are not on my back.
I don't care if they're bought from a clearance rack.

The shoes I wear may not be new.
At the big race, I kept up with you.

Just once I wish you would ask me to play.
Instead you tell me go away.

I lie awake each night in my bed.
Thinking of the day, and the mean things you said.

I dry the final tear and drift off to sleep.
Wounds that can not be seen are ones so deep.

When my dreams set in, a friend I find,
A friend for me...one so kind.

I wonder what you would do, if you knew,
The face of that friend was,...you.

Darlene Sweet

Alone

"Alone" we descend, wherefrom, who can tell?
Alone we go back, summoned by His calling bell!
Who sends us, when, to where and why?
Who calls back, when and where to, to tell "Good-bye".

Alone we come down all the way to this mother earth,
To play, laugh or cry, work and occupy a small berth;
Affluence is the thing that attracts company or friends,
If you don't have it, you don't find many to depend!

Sharing pleasure is but natural, alone no one can rejoice,
But pains, you suffer alone, you have no other choice;
The most dear and near ones, do not share your pains,
It is you, alone live with it, world is only after gain!

I have this to say, though, have faith, love and compassion,
In God and all His creation, this is no place for passion;
The only hope for every one is, own faith to which you hold,
In weather foul or fair, hold to it until death comes to fold!

World could be selfish, but not He, is all love and kind,
Never He deserts any one, who have Him all the time in mind;
Holding to Him in heart, you don't need anything else to own,
In time of need, He keeps you company, you will not walk
"Alone!"

Malamal S. Nair

A Mother's Card Game

You are born into a game of chance
God deals you the cards of life

Some will reveal great happiness,
Others will cut you like a knife.

He may deal you a new grandson,
Or a card that takes a son you love.

You've always been my wild card,
Dealt to me by the Almighty above.

You taught me to respect my elders,
Women were to be loved and cherished

Without your love and guidance,
I surely would have perished

Thank's for the life you've given me,
You always showed me the correct way.

I hope you're holding a Royal Flush,
And may you have a happy Mother's Day!

David R. Wooderson

Swamp Talk

Deep in the Okefenoke, hidden in the moss,
There's a snake or a 'gator, just waiting for a frog!
It's dark during the day, even darker at night!
I know what he's thinking, I'll just have a bite!
The snake, he is swift, and the 'gator is strong.
No sleep for me, not even a yawn!
The snake, he is listening to hear my frog song.
He'll listen and taste and slither along!
So if at eye level, should I see a light,
It's not a moon beam reflection that stirs in the night!
No 'possum, or man, or even a deer,
Creeps like this predator, that's ever so near!
I look good as a meal, and I think I know why!
He knows what he's looking at, eyeball to eye!
Hop away quickly, swim away fast!
I'd make a good meal, a good meal at last!
So if you should find that you are a frog,
Stay out of the swamps! Stay away from the bog!
Be ever wary, in the thick fog!
'Cause you know he's a snake, and he knows you're a frog!

Connie Nordhus

Forgive And Forget

I forgive you if you do the same,
people after awhile should want to change
I hope we can forget who was the blame;
for life is to short to hate without shame.

We are here today and could be gone tomorrow,
thy only thing left-over would be pain and sorrow.

If I'm still here to live in this world and
remember the times we shared

When all was said and done, and no longer fun
The hurt would come shining through causing
me to hate you.

It was hard to forgive and nerve-racking to forget.

But I'm glad we did before one of us split.

Lois Hurrigan

One Cool Summer Night Dream

On the cool summer night when good met evil
The sky burst into flames,
Lives were lost
Hearts were broken
And feelings were never the same.
The screams from hell drowned out songs from heaven
A baby was born still,
The sun turned black
The stars turned fast
And all who were healthy turned ill.
Then angels sparked the mountains and demons arose the wind
Blood shed filled the sea,
Darkness robbed the light
Poison killed the oxygen
And locks were left without keys
On the cool summer night when saints met sinners
I was left to tell,
The earth split open
The clouds gave way
As good bowed its head to evil.

Leanna Lynn Whetstone

Dandelion Fluff

i have learned that nothing
can be something, if the something

once was nothing. i watched
a cyclone spin inside out

and heard the sound of thought.
it tumbled out of the grasp of

my reaching mind and distanced
itself out of my sight.

when i looked beyond the glare of overcast
skies, i found fleeting glimpses

of something undefined and it
tumbles still so gracefully

out of my reaching
mind. in between the

nothing and the something, i've found
dandelion fluff floating through a winter

air. but that could not be.
but that could not be.
and that glimpse said to me:
"thought is free."

Christa Gahlman-Kongslie

Delusion

This is something wonderful to hold
in the heart for all eternity.
The way in which the body is tenderly worshipped
by the lover is totally overwhelming.
The low husky voice expresses undying love for only one,
love for me.
He Loves Me!
My heart leaps in my chest as I fervently
although hopelessly hold his body to mine.
The entirety of my life is his now.
We are wholly one together.

Melinda M. Feist

Truth

Trust encrusted with lies.
Honesty choked to its core.
Faithfulness lost in the absence of love.
Reality and fantasy dance together,
swaying the fruits of righteousness.

Swagging tongues always speak falsehood.
The quiet one talks to truth,
it flows from the eyes of an honest soul.

Dark is the shroud of those who wear the cloak of deceit.
Long and weighed is its substance.
Prolonged anguish is their sanctuary.
Immortality alone in their multitudes.

Sweet is the essence and purity of truth!
Light and fragrant the odor!
Delicate and kind are its bounties.
Endless wealth of peace for those who recite its legacy!
Truth begets truth...honesty always follows.

Deborah L. Chacon

Open Eyes

I feel the world of hate
As I stare off at the stars so late.
Can I be living a needless fate.
I talk to myself softly, trying to
Rectify the whole situation. As I lay awake.
I try to fight my mind. Keep myself quiet
And occupied.   Trying to rise above the upside
Down frown I've learned to fake.
I guess it's my feelings, got to be I guess.
It's the place at which my soul stays.
I know sometimes I reach a blank
Where I'm at a free loaded state.
And sometimes it keeps me sane through
This endless body drain. Round and round
It goes, to a darker place I suppose.
I fell it inside, hush now mind no one
   Needs to cry.

John A. Kuchar III

Death

It has always been something so mysterious,
Like the theory of life itself.
Like a bottomless pit of emptiness,
Or the depth of a soul's own self.
It is always something sudden,
Like a horrible nightmare come true.
Like a flash of light in the darkness,
It's like something out of the blue.
You'll never see it coming,
You'll never see it go.
It's like an inscrutable secret
That no one on this earth will ever know.

Yasmin Perez

To The Discouraged

Do not listen to me with your ears,
but with your heart.
Do not listen to me with an opinionated, pessimistic mind,
but with an open one.
Reject the turmoil that is wrong.
Do not let your peers deteriorate your life,
though it may seem hopeless.
Rejoice, and be thankful for what you have,
though what you have may be little.
Express your hopes and dreams,
and people will respect you.
See through appearances,
and nothing shall deceive you.
Do not give up on hope,
and hope will not give up on you.

Amielyn Farnbach

Your Love

Your eyes are like the stars above,
shinning bright with love.

Your love is like the bright sun,
when we're together we're as one.

Your love is like the moon in the night,
shinning oh so bright.

Your love is like a bird in the sky,
when we're together we'll fly high.

Your love is like rainbow,
full of color and glow.

Your love is like a tear,
full of moister but no fear.

Your love is like a grain of sand,
together forever we will stand.

Your love is like the milky way,
life without you there's just no way.

Your love is like an eagle soaring,
when we're together our love is never boring.

Tracie Lynn Dempsey

The Lives Of Bums

He sludged along past a fish and chips shop
In moldy clothes
Tightly knit in his own cocoon
Leaving the dust of gray fields behind

A scavenger looking through windows
The sea worms squirming
In the pigments in his stomach

He emptied his last bit of java
Into his cottony face plastered with earth
Closing the two webs that covered his eyes
And pulling invisible rip cords as he stretched

Rain drops dimple the rainbow oil
In the black asphalt puddle
And wet the fibers on his skull

He inhales fragrances from the frictions
Then takes a spit bath and the blue turns to darkness
Comets chart their way around ghosts

He didn't choose who he was
He wasn't present during his conception
Only by proxy

L. A. Grant

Musings On Life

What are the things for which I aspire?
What is my heartfelt greatest desire?
    I want to be a Christian, Lord, sincere and true.
I want to value nothing more in life than you.

    I believe your promises from beginning to end,
I know you have forgiven me for all my sins.
    The doubts I have are concerning me,
Have I been as sincere as a christian as I could be?

    Lord, I'm sorry and I know I'm forgiven,
I know you've prepared me a place in heaven
    But I want to bring glory and honor to you
By witnessing to others, by the things that I do.

    With the temptations of life I could not cope,
Without faith in Jesus I would have no hope,
    But thanks to your word and the privilege of prayer,
I know I am constantly in your loving care.

    So help me, Lord, from day to day,
To live in a loving unselfish way,
    And help me, Lord, a truly Christ like person to be
So my living example will lead others to Thee.

    Dorothy McCoy

My Friend From The Past

We were brought together as friends and only time would ever say
It's in the eyes, it's in the touch, it's just that I've found
    I loved you so very much.
We could only be friends-I was promised to another...
but, as souls go-that's what brought us together.
So many boundaries-to many paths, where will life take us
friend from the past. Find me, take me, I'm already yours.
Where two lost souls waiting, forever wanting are we,
will we be, soul mates till the end?
It's in my eyes, in my touch, can't you feel it?
I love you so much. Why did you leave? Why did
you let me go? Only if you thought you deserved me so.
Forever wanting to try-longing to feel.
That friend from the past that made my life feel so real.
No one will ever know the way that I feel...
It's in the eyes, it's in my touch, it's that I
still love you so very much.

    Debbie Jarvie

The Angels Sing

The angels sing to the man above
A song of love

The angels sing to a newborn child
A song of joy

The angels sing to the death of a loved one
A song of peace

The angels sing to the hurried
A song of patience

The angels sing at life's cruelties
A song of kindness

The angels sing to the greedy
A song of generosity

The angels sing to the lost
A song of faithfulness

The angels sing to the proud
A song of meekness

The angels sing to the selfish
A song of self control

So open your hearts and listen....to the angels sing

    Angela Gray

You Are Meant For Me

You loved me once before, we can always try again.
You touched me in a way, that I'll always understand.
Every time I see you, chills run up my spine.
You treated me like a princess, which I really didn't mind.
I think of all the memories, that we have shared through time.
We had something special, that I took for granted,
And regret that our relationship ever ended.
I trust you more than anyone,
And I'm sure that you can see,
How much I really love you,
And how much I really care.
I sorted out my feelings,
And I finally figured out,
That I want you by my side,
Till the end of time.

    Stephanie Honorowski

Love Me Not Possessively But Freely

I'm sitting here almost in tears, although it's only
been months it seem like years. Years we've been together
seems like I've known you forever thing's seem to go
wrong because I might have conceived, but if I haven't
you'll probably be relieved the bad part about it is that
I love you so much I don't know what to do I'll only want
to be with you, I know you and I didn't what this to happen
But how do you end something that didn't really begin.
You are a big part of me, any fool can see that you and I
were meant to be every relationship has up and downs
and some days we both have walk around with frowns.
It takes separation to bring appreciation I'm sorry we're
in this situation, I'm missing your touch and it's because
I love you miss you so much I never meant to hurt you,
Just love and cherish the things you do, you are very
special to me. Having you close to me makes me feel
safe and warm and so free, if I've hurt you
please forgive me and love me not possessively but freely.

    Martha Gipson

Comforts In Christ

Christ is our savior we must not forget,
He will take care of your problems, you don't have to fret
You must include him in all your plans,
If in heaven someday you want you hold his nail scared hand.
Jesus suffered pain as he died on a tree,
He willingly done this for you and for me.
We can never deserve such a wonderful gift,
But if we are faithful he will give us a lift,
To his heavenly home on high,
When we come to the river of death, and cross to the other side.

    Raymond R. Westbrook

Look Beyond

To look at the world with open eyes
To look at the world with an open heart
This is the way to see the earth and the sky
But do we really see all this and more
Or is so much hidden behind our walls
When we see that the end of our travels is near
Do we stop, look or fear
Not if we look over our walls and above
Not if we have really known love.

    Elinior Farrelly

The Long Walk

As I walk on through the wind and snow,
I think, why do I always walk alone.

I think why must it have to be,
That I have nobody who will walk with me.

I walk my path and leave a trail,
For all who follow cold and frail.

The man nobody wants to hear,
A cry that goes in no one's ear.

A foot that never leaves the trail,
A soul that never does betrayal.

I go about from mountains to sea,
To walk alone is my destiny.

Ryan Edmunds

Peace Of Mind

Your body is a precious shell
Containing your inner works
It acts as your cover
Your protector

Your minds thoughts have no barriers
Imagination stems further than your reach
For the preservation of the body
Is sought through peace of mind...

Warren L. Foster

The Devil And The Chain

If it's the devil I'll have to be
Then no man will pick up a chain for me
Shield himself from the rain or even ease the pain
Feel the wind blow or place his eyes upon the new fallen snow
You'll even have to take a side of your own
Because along this road theirs no way home
Finding excuses is no way to get their
Then loosing your way back because nobody dares
Remembering any works that have been read
Or noticing anything but the nod of a head
Hoping for tomorrow new frame of mind
Because that's what it takes to keep you in line
Then if theirs no man who will pick up a chain for me
Then after all that's been said I'll always be free

Billy Jack Williamson

I'm Still In Love With You

Tomorrow is dead
She only loved an end.
To let us be led
I need my wings to mend.
If by chance you'll be some slave,
I'll always know the hate.
She died young in a handmade grave
What moves some to lie in wait?
I'm on my knees
Your magic speaks such.
I deny what she sees,
I know far too much.
For what you want, I'll never know the cost.
In a dream you came to,
Bringing shame to the ones who lost
Still, my mantra remains to be true,
I'm still in love with you.

Abigail Taylor

In The Silence

From the cries of the loons, to the rustling of
the trees. There is a silence in the North Woods.
It's not the silence of a deer frozen still from
fright, or the silence of fine dew dripping from
the crisp morning leaves.
It's the silence of her glistening eyes, and
her soft velvety touch, its the silence of her
warming smile.
It's a silence the North Woods will never
hear again. It's a silence I will never forget.
Even though I must leave these North Woods
with the silence behind, its comfort to know
I can go into any woods and listen to the silence
and she will always be there, in the silence,
she will always be with me!

Gail Vallone

No Man's Land

Somewhere between a breath and a song,
Something between a man and a women,
Somehow in a place near yet far,
The life diminishes, quietly holding hope.

No music to be played,
Not a person to share a dance,
Vacant is this house, hollow are its walls,
Life diminishes quietly holding hope.

White becomes the darkness,
A ghost drifts across the plain,
The room begins to fade away,
Quietly holding hope.

Deaf is now the jester,
No one comes here anymore,
Blindness is the God we seek.
Holding hope.

The letters reads "I did my best",
A used up shell is put to rest,
A God now wills the final test,
Hope.

Robert W. Whitehead Jr.

The Forest Tree

In majesty stands so straight and true;
Wrapped in a cloak of green it stretches high
Above the lesser growth and seems to touch
The flying clouds that shield a sky of blue.

For centuries the animals and birds
Did make a home and always sheltered there.
And native man when roaming land so free
Would worship nature 'neath the forest tree.

But modern man, who has but one desire
To gratify his life with scarce a thought,
Has come to use his mighty power to wrest
From slow-built nature all he can acquire.

So steely spikes on whirling blades attack
The mighty tree that took so long to grow.
With powerful cuts and smoothing planes it comes
To be a set of standard planks laid low.

Yet man has skills which often can amaze;
And those same planks may later on be joined
As one great beam that holds a vaulted span
To roof a monumental house of praise.

William Babb

I Love The Way You Are...

I can't find the words to tell you what I'm feeling
or how much I care,
I can only tell you that I love you
and show you by my actions during the times that we share.
You mean so much to me,
and why I can't explain;
is it your eyes or maybe your smile?

Well, it's really a combination of a lot of things...

I love the way you walk and the authority in your stride,
I love the way you hold me and keep me warm at night.
I love that you love God and that he walks right by your side.
I love the way you love me and make every thing feel right.

Brenda Rudelich

Out There

In her own world,
She sees her family young and put together.
Even though confused at times.
She soon finds her way back.

She lives far away,
But we still need her and she needs us.
Together we form a team,
To work out problems of our lives.

Her house is quiet and old,
But it has bursts of sunlight in it.
The furniture look unique and fragile,
Though when you sit down, you feel comfort.

When we visit,
We take a new tour each time,
Through a world that we don't
Completely understand,
We know she's there, somewhere,
Just like us.

Melissa Kanuk

Melody

To the woman I truly love
Deep in my heart, there is a memory,
There is a name, the memory and the name,
Is a melody that is sung and heard each day.
As my heart beats, as the birds sing,
As the cool breeze whispers through the trees.
In the night you can see the melody as
The stars dance under the mystic glow of the moon.
The Melody is of happiness, warmth and
Love, sung by angels, to the Lord,
Who has created the melody of happiness,
Warmth and love.
To Melody the woman I truly love!

Andrew H. DeMilt

Hate Is

An evil which helps to make men fight
To enhance their beliefs to write their right
The victims being all mortal souls
Whose bodies then cast into cavernous holes
Then why do we hate a soul you ask
It's one man's idea and the foot soldier's task
To carry out 'Hate' so 'twill spread like disease
Through millions of lives for only one to appease
As 'Hate' ain't innate yet escapes no birth
But takes just few years for it to unearth
So listen, take heed e'er following my plight
I'd 'Hate' to think you could be right

Wes LeFevre

A Tribute To The Lord Jesus Christ

With people yelling and laughing at Him,
With spitting and madness, the love was so dim.
Jesus still loved them whether they were bad or good.
Mary was crying, she'd help if she could.
They put thorns on His head with blood running down.
Then the people yelled "There is your crown!"
He carried a cross up a big hill,
In His eyes tears would fill.
He hung on the cross, in His hands were nails.
It was worse than any jails.
He hung on the cross 'till He was dead,
With nails in His hands and thorns in His head.
He rose from His tomb still loving everyone,
He went to Heaven as God's loving Son.

Melodie Roberts

Take The Time

Touch my hand and allow me to guide you.
Smile at me and I will make you laugh.
Believe in me and life sweat will be in all tomorrows,
No price I ask you to pay in me,
Then you will see the beauty around you
    and others same as you, before had
        found me
Life sweeter, tomorrow's brighter, and all
    you will have if you just
        accept me.

Yoina Palameira Wilson

Never Again

I am cold, I am helpless
I gave you my heart, my life.
And what did you do? You took and
stabbed a knife right through my heart.
My soul is gone. You sick bastard.
The hurt I feel gives you strength,
a strength I wish never do endure.
I will always live in you, your mind, your heart.
But I am over you and will remain above you.
My cries will haunt you, wake you at night,
I feel no remorse, not for you.
I may have died but my heart will never bleed.
I will return because I am strong.
My soul is eternal and will live forever.
You can stab me or hurt me but I am
bigger than you. You can't hurt me anymore.
Not with words nor emotions
I am stale, I feel no more. Good-bye.

Rebecca R. Kral

What It Seems

A thought is not a thought until you think about it.
An effort is not made until you make it.
A life is not lived until well lived.
You are not loved until you love.

Your thoughts are not heard, but they are spoken.
And it will be that way until the spell is broken.
The world is not seen the way it is,
We need to look at it the way we see it.

Cuz nothing ever seems what it seems to be.
When you've dreamt upon a dream.
You can't make a difference until you start.
Though you can always be loved by a young ones heart.

Tiffany E. Box

What Do I Do?

Something inside wants to hold on,
but something tells me to let go.

If I hold on it could be for the better.
I would be happier and a relationship
    would be too.

If I let go, something tragic or bad
might happen, and it would be my fault.

So should I stay and hope for better,
or go and hope that nothing bad happens?

I don't know what to do!
Do you?

Why should you know, you can't see what I see.
Just let me be!

We'll see.

Maybe I should just stay put,
and see what comes to me.

June 5, 1996
Christen Lemen

Moth To Butterfly

You feel helpless and slightly exposed.
Your feelings right out there when you use to be closed.

Yes closed up, shut off, not a sign of your tears, and God
forbid you expressed you had fears.

Slowly tentatively wings unfold, scared to stretch
too far, not too bold.

Fret not my love, for you've come out of your cocoon,
and now all that's left is the butterfly here soon,

Like a fresh, new flower on a warm spring day,
you'll start off slowly, and then soar away.

Your beauty and love springing forth from your
soul, the people will talk . . . the story told.

Of this man so sweet, heart made of gold, we
are graced with his presence in this world so cold.

My love for you grows each day, like
a moth to a butterfly.

Michelle Lehner

Untitled

I see an Angel not far away
He came to me as if to say.
The glow of his halo, warmth of his soul
He makes me feel that I'm never alone.
He guides me up towards the sky
The clouds so white, sun so bright.
He comes to show me wonderful things
All the heavens and joy it brings.
Up through Heavens gate, just knock on the door
You'll feel more love than you've ever felt before.
Family and friends all waiting for you
Love in their faces, "Heavens not ready for you".
Leaving my family with the angel hand in hand.
I'll never forget the memories we've had.
The Angel left me in the same place
Where he had seen my crying face.
"Goodbye", he said, some day we'll meet again.
Into the clouds, right back to Heaven.

Alexandra Tamame

I Love You

I Love You now, I'll love You forever
Time will change, but I will never.
Time will come for us to part
but time will never change my heart.
I do believe the Lord above
picked you out for me to love.
He picked you out from all the rest
because he knew I'd love you the best.
I had a heart and it was true
because now its gone from me to you.
When I die and go afar
I'll carve your name on a golden star.
So all the angels there can see
just how much you mean to me.
And if your not there on judgement day
I'll know you went the other way.
So, I'll give the angels back their wings,
Their golden harps, and all those things.
And just to show my love is true,
I'll go to hell to be with you!

Chris Schuler

To My Father On Father's Day

From you I learned to work
And from responsibilities never to shirk.
The bright way on life I look.
Did I learn that from a book?
I learned that by year and by day
In the things you do and say.
You taught me my God to love,
To others be gentle as a dove,
You showed me in him to trust,
In worldly things not to lust.
When hard times knock us about,
You taught me to stand up and be stout.
I saw how deeply you loved my mother
And now for me my wife there is no other.
For all of these things so true
I simple say "Thank You"
I will sum all these words up as such
That's to say "I love you very much"

Cecil Lessly

The Mask

We wear the mask that grins and lies,
It hides our cheeks and shades our eyes.
This debt we pay to human guile,
With torn and bleeding hearts we smile.
With the truth not far behind,
When the truth comes the mask moans and whines.
Soon those lies will disappear,
Then we will have nothing to fear.
But for now the mask exists,
And it does not desist.
But with this mask on our face,
It gives Satan the power to chase.
And when Satan decides to chase,
He will wipe out the entire human race.
Then demons will have the world, by sword,
Not for long because here comes the Lord.
And when he comes we will fight Satan,
Because we're through with Satan's hate'n.
And after we defeat Satan's army,
We can all live in peace and harmony.

Ryan William Karl Stafford Hampson

Children In The Crossfire

Children in the crossfire,
Do you hear their broken cries?
The children of the crossfire,
Do you see their bitter eyes?
They are all grown up,
Never young.
Children in the crossfire,
Do you hear their hopeless sighs?
They are dead with no chance to be alive.
Why are there children in the crossfire?
Do they dare learn to dream,
Or will their dreams be crushed?
They don't want to see their hopes,
Scattered like the dust.
Often we see them on the news,
They are plastic on our screens.
We won't see what's really going on.
We won't hear their bitter screams.
Why are children in the crossfire?

RoseMarie Walsh-Lyons

Untitled

I have not the strength to think deep thoughts
Or to ponder the why's of life.
If I tuck all of my cares and troubles away,
I need only to struggle with today.
I'm passing through my twilight years
On the way to my last sunset.
In thinking back to the long ago and up to the
   present time,
Life is made of memories and my memories are mine.

Alice Schulz

Miracles

Miracles happen, they happen to you
Miracles happen, they happen to be new
Miracles are joys, joys to me and you
Miracles are joys, joys for us to pursue
Miracles are fun, fun when they are true
Miracles are fun, especially fun to you
   Miracles, miracles, miracles
Like a baby born, flowers grown, love grown old
   The sight of two people together again
   Is a miracle only to them at hand
   Miracles are fun, especially fun to you
   Miracles are fun, fun when they are true
   Miracles are joys, joys for us to pursue
   Miracles are joys, joys to me and you
   Miracles happen, they happen to be new
   Miracles happen, they happen to you

Kristin Ostrom

Madness In My Minds Eye

Precocious precognition depriving injunction
Gluttonous rages eating inner glory
Gnostic evil, fierce fiction preventing reality
Relinquish religion, psychotic mind, immobile flesh
Illusions, Illusions delirium fusion
Disfunctioning conscience causing confusion
Illusions, Illusions, vision Lucifers home
Illusions, Illusions, devilish union
Satan has taken thy soul

Fernando Linn

Sunsets

The sun sets as the waves tumble at your shivering feet.
I, the Beholder, see that you are at the end.
"What end?" you ask. The end of childhood and onto the
Off ramp to a whole new world. You see it before
You, but think your windshield is dirty. You step
Out of your car of life. As you take the step you are
Engulfed with the realization that you are not a child anymore.
You look at the unforgiving sky,
And the sun dims and the moon captures your
Thoughts as you tumble into the next point of
Your life....adulthood.

Alicia Koontz

Did You Or Do You

   Do you ever wonder why, The Sun, The Moon,
And the stars, are so far away?

   Did you pass someone along the way today and
Gave them a friendly smile or perhaps say hello?

   Did you ever wish that you could turn
Back the hands of times, so that you could start anew?

   Do you remember all the times you felt like
Crying, but somehow you keep on trying?

   Do you ever stop and say, what can I do
To help someone along their way?

   Do you know that it's time to get in a
Hurry and do it now?

   Do you know that it's late in the evening
And the sun is going down?

   Did you remember this morning to bow down
On your Knees And Say, "Lord I Thank You For This Brand
New Day?"

Ruby Lois Tyson

Not So Green

The green of the earth is not always so green:
   Its beauty on the surface seems equivocally fine,
With purposes pure, and lush valleys divine,
   Cradling rivers which rush into pleasures unseen,
Twisting and bending 'round rocks and trees;
   The roar of persuasion determines their course.
With purposes pure these rivers won't freeze
   If all are flowing with burning white force.
So headlong down passion's current we're pulled,
   Twisting and spinning and bobbing for air,
loving the torture which green valleys can bear;
   We swim undaunted, like salmon - and equally as fooled;
When thrust to the surface our thoughts become clean,
   And we see our own rivers and valleys are not so green.

James Halatin

Untitled

Last night I walked alone
through a peaceful maze of loving creatures.
I, a young girl lost in a fast life,
found simplicity on a trail of God's light.
I feel happiness warms my body and softness covers my heart,
it's from the essence of flourishing wild flowers of yellows,
purples and whites.
The roar of crickets and chirps of birds don't even seem loud.
As I walk further into my dream of happiness
I see the light is not always bright
but my mind will always hold the memory
and my heart always feel the warmth
but yet, I walk alone.

Tina Hargrove

Your Whisper

Will he tell you you're the only one
that his love has just begun
then will he hold you
while you whisper my name

Does he tell you that he needs you
and that he'll never leave you
then does he hear you
when you whisper my name

Does he say he'll be a friend
that he'll always understand
but can you tell him that when you close your eyes
you whisper my name

When you make love does it cut so deep
that hell could not repeat
the pain that still remains
when he holds you and you whisper my name

Try not to let the pain get you down
I'm not ashamed, just proud
to know where you want to be
just close your eyes and whisper to me

Greg Althammer

The River

Now in the Whirlwind of Life
I see all I have done, What I have been
And maybe I don't like it.
All I needed was what I had,
But now all I want is what I haven't.

The One Disturbing Question Remains,
To make me toss and turn.
Should I jump into the river and
Become a mindless, gutless member of society?

At the Last Second I Let Out a Scream.
Its desperate, distraught.
Questioning my every move.
Will it be approved or outcasted?
I have, for so long tried,
Tried to stay on the bank.
But now, amidst my struggle,
I realize its too late,
My one goal has been stripped from me.
Its too late,
I've Fallen In, And I Can't Swim.

Chad Scheer

Alex's Grandma

Alex's Grandma makes toys for good
    little girls and boys!
They eat their food, sleep all night,
    and they are very bright.
Alex's grandma bought Alex some new clothes;
    But first she counted all his toes!
There are eight little ones and two big ones.
    This was lots of fun!
When will Alex come to Grandma's again?
    To get toys form the toy bin?
Grandma has no car and can't go very far but
    Maybe, she can go to the mail box
And send an invitation to him.
    Is the red truck coming or will
They come in a van?
    Anyway they can is the best plan.

Betty V. Sherman Riviere
Peoria, Ill

Lord, When I Grow Old, May I Remember

Other people may be busy even though I'm not.
Not to expect people to entertain me all of the time.
Keep my clothes neat, clean and up to date.
If my home gets too large move into something smaller
So it is easier for me and my family.
Hire a cleaning lady if I'm not able to keep home clean
Have meals on wheels if I find it hard to cook for one
If I have any money may I never act like a pauper.
May I keeps conversation on todays topics, not to repeat
Do not be afraid to throw things away I do not need
If I can't go as much as I like use the phone.
Do simple exercise, it is good for mind and body.
Do not have people running around buying my
Products at my prices.
Remember I can't go back, look forward.
I maybe lonely sometimes but God is my
Best friend and he will never leave me.

Miriam Baer

To My Son Michael

My heart has been shattered
Broken pieces never to be found
Those pieces went with you when,
You were heaven bound.

The night you died
There was a teardrop in the corner of your eye
I left it there so God would see
He took you far to soon from me.

My grief for you runs so deep
Many nights I cannot sleep
Knowing you will never walk thru the door
Knowing I'll never see you anymore.

My only son with crystal blue eyes
I miss your bright shining smiles
You will always have my heart and my love
I think you will know as you look
    down from heaven above.

Laurie Richardson

While You Are Away

While you are away
Know that I will think of you everyday
I will wonder if you are alright
If you are sleeping at night
I will wonder if you can handle the weather
And long for the day that we'll be together
When you look up at the sky at night
And see the biggest star that is shining bright
Remember that I will be looking at that same star
Then it won't seem like I'm that far
As I look at that star each night
I will say a prayer for you
To keep you safe in all that you do
One last thing before I go
Know that I do love you so
Keep safe, my love
And know that you will be watched from above
A part of you will also be in my heart
That way we will never really be apart

Angie Naquin

Victory

Who is the enemy and what is their number?
Can the faceless horde ever be counted?
Against such a number can I ever be victorious?
Maybe the best strategy is to count them as they go by.

John M. Wood

What Is Needed?

Given time I will proceed
Given love I will indeed
Take one away and I may die
Try to change and it may be a lie
Follow one's heart for it may be
The best reminder to live a life with alacrity
Own myself and not the one beside
For my next day has yet to reside
I must ask myself these 2 questions
Only then will I understand my cogitations
Can I feel it in my blood; in my vein?
Does it flow into the sea like the rain?
I can never ask to rewrite a day
Or ponder on what is that may
Just accept the life of both I need
Given together will then I succeed.

Trung Dao

Grocery Store Dilemma

Pushing my cart down the grocery store aisle...
Amid the canned soups, I stopped for awhile...
There was Potato, Tomato, and Bacon 'N Bean,
Onion and celery...all kinds quite supreme!

There was Chunky, and Beef-Broths, all types and all kinds...
But the soup that I want....
Is the one I Can't Find!

Sharon Robertson

Have You Heard

Echoes like heartbeats
Thunder in silence
Reminiscent of unspoken words.
Yet a heart-wrenching cry
Or the slightest of sighs,
Inevitably emerge unheard.
We hear the wind as it whispers
Through the trees,
The waves as they caress the shore
Yet the troubled heart who's been knocking
Waits unnoticed at the door.
While dreaming of the future
Entangled in our pasts,
Distracted by the moment
Distress is left to pass.
Not the most thunderous of cries
Nor the resounding tear in anothers' eye
Will ever a single heart christen...
Until love and faith encompass our hearts
Wakening ears which will infinitely listen.

Tanya M. Spencer

The Greatest Miracle Of All

How precious it is to know,
That the Lord Jesus came to earth long ago.

As it is foretold, he was born like you and me,
But out of a virgin's womb, he was sent to set us free.

He lived his life to the fullest,
Doing miracles great and small.
The greatest one, though, is when he told God the Father,
He would die to save, not one, but for all.

So on that cross he shed his blood and bore our shame,
And with that, it caused him much pain.

So now in this life, through all our troubles and our woe,
Have faith, love and live for Jesus, for in our passing, it
is Him, and heaven and forever happiness he shall bestow.

Rebekah Alice Ciardi

The Rose Of God —— An Easter Promise

Of all of the beautiful flowers
That God in his kindness made,
The rose is the symbol of his love
Everlasting, never to fade.

The thorns are the crown
Which set upon his son's head.
The petals are the drops of blood crimson red.

The stem is the spear which did pierce his side.
It is also the cross upon which
Our precious savior died.

The leaves are the father's hands
Into which Jesus did commit his soul — for our soul.
His life he did forfeit.

And so each spring the rose blooms anew.
To remind us of the promise of everlasting life—
A gift from Christ to you.

This rose is a symbol of our friendship.
Never to be torn apart.
To you it is but a flower,
To me it is my heart.

Susan M. Smith-Hinds

Self Pity

When I'm weary and things close in,
I think of nails driven into skin.

When I'm lonely and I feel lost,
I think of dragging a heavy cross.

When I'm upset and anger storms,
I think of a crown made out of thorns.

And when someone my trust betrays,
I think of the kiss that Judas gave.

When from some task my back feels sprain,
I think of hanging on a cross in pain.

When I'm sure I deserve much more,
I think of blood flowing from every pore.

When I'm filled with doubt and fear,
I think of a sponge at the end of a spear.

And when to the end of the rope I've come,
I think of Mary at the Cross of Her Son.

Marie McCormick

Mystery

The pale moonlight
Casting reflections onto the blue water,
Cascading into beautiful spectrums,
Light against the red background,
Silhouetting the sea gulls.
Their voices, an echo of the past,
Drifting upon desolate beaches.
Reflections dance in my eyes,
The future revealed in my hands.
The wind rises on the sand covered beach,
dormant are the ivory shells basking in lavender light.
Wishing it would last,
The sun slowly rises above the sea.
Another night is gone.
Mystery still remains untold.

Stacey Smith

Jesus, The Holy One

Shining bright as the morning sun —
Glowing until the day is done,
Christ's sweet love will show the way
That we should follow every day.
Dear Jesus, the Holy One.

Gleaming clear as the crystal sea
While waves are rushing full and free,
The power of God's word can make us strong
And fill our hearts with love and song
For Jesus, the Holy One.

Majestic and great as the mountains high —
Reaching as if to touch the sky,
So is God's wondrous and glorious plan
Created to benefit woman and man
Through Jesus, the Holy One.

Patricia L. Traeger

John

I see so many moods
    from the gaze in your eyes
I feel the vibration
    from your silent sighs
There is no need to be verbal
    I certainly understand
Just walk beside me
    as we walk hand in hand
Breath deeply my love
    borrow my strength
Together we will travel
    the road we must take
Because I believe in everything you do
    I know that our wishes will all come true
I know sometimes it's hard to comprehend
    the s**t in life never seems to end
Together babe we can make it right
    the end of the rainbow can be ours tonight
Our love grows in so many ways
    I hope that it lasts til our dying days!

Cyndi I. Mood

A Lilly Of The Valley

Her laughter, was like a beautiful rainbow;
Her touch, like the sun rising in the morning;
Her advice an ever flowing stream saying everything will be O.K;
Her smile, like the flickering star's in heaven.
A a mother-in-law, she was a dream come true.

Joan Wager

Excuses, Excuses

In their eyes the tears did fill.
In their hearts it was the Lord they feared.
Time ran out and the darkness came about.
The ground below is now their home.
For in this place there is no day.
It is time for them to state their claim.
"I didn't have time," one replies.
The other just sighs.
The third turns his head away,
He knows where he'll stay.
Down under is where they'll slumber.

April Fortner

An Addict's Song

I am not glorifying
I am not moralizing
I am not qualifying
I am testifying
To use is to lose
I use to say, get high till I die,but that's a lie.
I never saw a man cry until I saw a man die.
There is no hope if you use dope.
Because where there is life there's hope.
To get high is to die, that's no lie.
To pick up is to give up.
Do one day at a time, don't put your life on the line.
For your life you'll find it's worth more than two dimes.
You'll find the key to life is abstinence.
All you do is use your common sense.
My brothers and sisters one day you'll see
How happy and serene you'll be.
In the fullness of recovery.

Jai Jai Sims

Give Me Your Hand

Give me your hand
Let me take you beyond this page of poetry
Allow me to show you this beautiful land
Give me your hand
Prove to me that you are my man
Let me see whether or not you understand
Give me your hand
Come with me into a world where only love exists
You will realize it is my everlasting kiss
That you won't be able to resist
Give me your hand
Would you follow me anywhere?
Time with you is magical, can't you see I care?
Give me your hand
Will you trust me with your heart?
Can our life together now start?
Give me your hand
Come along, your heart is the only thing you need to bring
It's a place where I will be queen, and you will be king
Give me your hand

Amanda Altman

Travel Across The Globe

I started in Spain sad but true.
But then went to France because I was blue.
Then to Great Britain to see the queen.
But left for Japan because she was mean.
Then to India to see what they make.
But then I left for Jamaica to sit in the sun and bake.
Then to hawaii to sit on the shore.
But left for Cuba because it was a bore.
Then to Alaska to use a phone.
But decided just to come home.

Michael K. Greene

Friendship

We are so close we hold secrets of the
past, our relationship was growing fast,
for now our lives are filled with
sorrow, who knows what will bring tomorrow.
We are different, that I know
I never tried to let it show,
but whatever happens, whatever does
I'll be your friend always, forever till the end.

Wendy A. Nelson

Signs Of Life

Waves crash onto the shore
Wind whips the sand around and around
Blue turns to black as the night comes to life
Moonlight ripples in the water
Stars turn to diamonds on the sea
Somewhere out there dolphins play
While fish swim and kelp sways

The planet rotates and night is gone
Wind whistles across the dunes
Black turns to blue as the day comes to stay
Moonlight hides behind the sun
Stars magically disappear
Somewhere the dolphins still play
While the fish swim and kelp sways

Let's protect our planet, not just for you and me
But for the sun, moon, and stars
As well as Gods creatures on land and sea

Anna Baucom

Tic Tac Toe

Oh Hi Mommy do you want to play a game of tic tac toe?
Okay! You can be the X,
And I'll be the O.
Put down the rows
And I'll put down the O
Then together we'll play the game of tic tac toe.
Ugh! I hate the game of tic tac toe.
You won three games in a row.
I don't want to play!
We could play any other day!
So that's my reason any way
For not wanting to play
I'm to sleepy...
So I'll watch the...
What the
Adventures of Pete and Pete
I'm a goner
I've gone to sleep
You won't see a wink or hear a peep....
Zzzzz I'm asleep

Chloe.Mourai Whitaker

The Surf

The orchestra of sea shells,
You can hear their songs from afar.
When she stretches the skin from her back over the canyons...
An odyssey of space.
From locks of hair to locks of sky,
To summer's day embrace.
The cedars grace the hills,
the sunflower's demise...
The structures,
Blossoms/mills,
Tear it down for light.
Taste the night in drops,
And the waking gaps between scattered dreams.
I need you to call upon the night,
And to burn the day,
And kiss its charred remains.
I need you to serve as an orchard.
I need you to serve as my skin.

John De Lao

What Choice?

Which would you rather be,
A mountain or a valley?

Which would you rather be,
A dragon or unicorn?

Some may wonder why it matters,
And some may not care about these choices.
To some these choices have to do with their dreams
Of life, love, and happiness.

To those that wonder why does it matter,
To those afraid to show their emotions,
What about the choice of Love with Death or
    Hate with Life?

What many may not know is that Life with Hate
    is Death
And Love with Death is really Life!

Love can never die, and Hate kill us all!
The choice is just ours. What do you choose?

Susan E. Callahan

Butterfly Sky

Today as I gaze into October's clear sky,
    Hundreds of thousands of monarchs I see fly;
These beautiful creatures will soon be so few,
    In this cloudless sky so endless blue.

The timetable schedule of this predestined flight
    Began months ago on a warm spring night,
Where eggs deposited before the milkweeds first bloom
    Fluttered brownish red wings as they left the cocoon.

Heeding nature's strong call they were soon northward bound
    To seek out the fragrance of the first flower found.
Then in beauty and grace their lifetime was spent
    completing the task for which they were sent.

A return journey of death now to a home never seen,
    To the resting place of parents in the deep piney green;
Flying tirelessly higher they seem to effortlessly soar
    Not knowing their tenure here soon will be o'er.

Man fits the same pattern during his life,
    For time is so short, the time of his strife.
Life is so relative as confirmed by our work,
    Both the monarch and man return to the earth.

Troy E. Gibson

What It Is, Is Winter

Here it is, another brand new year;
January 1997 came quietly and is now here.
This is a place for summers, humid and hot
And winters that are mild, but maybe not.

Sometimes mother nature is heard is heard loud and clear;
You never know what kind of weather will appear.
For awhile we've had a blast of cold air with sleet;
Only the young think slipping and sliding is neat.

Schools closed and their energy levels high;
So what if more frozen rain falls from the sky?
Sleds are out, and kids racing down hills
On their very own ice rinks with chills and thrills.

Now going to work is another story to tell;
Many call bosses, they aren't feeling well.
Others try to go and it's nightmare time in the city;
Slick overpasses, brooking nervous drivers, it's not pretty.

Once in a while we too shiver and shake
But braving blizzards we couldn't take.
Soon the harsh cold days move out and spring will arrive,
As the sun warms soil and man, to renew, to be alive.

Deanna Holman

Golf

The game of golf is fun.
It takes lots of practice and skill.

To master is a challenge.
You need an iron will.

What club? How to swing?
Can be very confusing.

Who's to say if you're
Winning or losing.

The feeling you get when
you hit that one good shot,

Will keep you returning
until that one, becomes a lot.

And so with practice and patience
the days go on,
Gradually improving your game.

If a miracle happens, and you're good enough,
Someone will remember your name.

Linda S. Tarpley

Life Today

This life today-though only borrowed
  The here the now
    Not seeing tomorrow
a whisper of days many
  and more not yet remembered
I'm awakened to my truth
    My experience now rendered.

This life today
  Understand it is not mine
  To stray from this path means journey in mind
  Alas oh yesterday
  What memories you bring
  There is hope for tomorrow
    therefor today I believe

The thrill is seeking
  what I don't understand
The pleasure is finding
  that I could not demand

It is surreal this day and its meaning
  because my life today doesn't stop beginning.

Dwayne Weber

My Friend

When life deals you some unexpected blows;
That is when you talk to someone who knows.
Let me introduce you to my Friend; because
on Him you can truly depend.
For He said; He would be there from the beginning
until the end.
There is no problem too big or too small;
Just give it to Him; He will handle it all.
I know, because He's my Friend.
When your so-called friends turn and walk away;
Turn to Him, He will lighten and brighten up your day.
You see, I know, because He's my friend.
When life seems all uphill; and you've lost your will.
Don't give up, because my Friend is there ready to care
for you and He's willing to see you through.
He's just and someone you can trust; I know because
He's my Friend and His name is Jesus.

Teena P. Alston

For You

I would search for a diamond in a house of mirrors
drown the sahara in a single tear
at the end of the world I will show no fear
as long as you promise to be near

Of all the birds that have ever flown
I will carve their image on a single stone
and when the wind begins to moan
I'll paint a rainbow where it's flown

The endless race I will gladly run
the endless cloth will be happily spun
invisible nets catch the rays of the sun
for when these tasks are finally done

If you were to cast them all aside
and proclaim you are dissatisfied

I will pick the pieces off the floor
and immediately start for the door

To begin again once more

Amber Herrick

It Could Happen To You

With all of my heart I cannot truly believe
That you could have possibly really cared for me

Watching before me the love I adore
It was so obvious that I've meant nothing more

Always be kind in what you respond to this
So to let it be known the love you might miss

With my own eyes you have made me see
There was truly nothing in your heart for me

Maybe someday the tables might turn
Then you may know the lessons I've learned

Love, honor and cherish what one has been handed
Some never knows when love may have landed

Until this day I may have never known
One things for sure I've really been shown
Always be loving, honest and true
For one never knows
It could happen
To you

Sharon A. Baisden

My Beautiful Angel

When I first bought you Angel
You were bucking and rearing
The meanest personality you ever did see
When we walked past you, your ears went flat
Oh my beautiful Angel!

During the second month of owning you
Your temper did get better
Your ears did not go flat
And you came more willing to listen
Oh my beautiful Angel!

The third month of owning you, your temper was sweeter
Your ears were up straight
Your coat began to shine like copper
Everyone was starting to like you
Oh my beautiful Angel!

Up to now you have started to trust me
You've shown me that by not putting up a fight outside
I'm not going to hurt you, or break your trust
For that trust has made us a better team
Oh my beautiful Angel!

Margaret Anne Hayden

The Runaway Train

I find myself moving like a runaway train.
Just me alone on the tracks, nobody there to stop me.
I feel free to do as I want, when I want, when I want,
No care in the world. My mind begins to flow
emptily as I see myself moving steadily down the
track. At first it seems fun cause there is no
particular destination in sight, no one I have to
answer to, just me in command. For the first
time I am alone and it feels good as I continue
to gain speed, roaring thru open space, hoping this
will never end. I find myself not giving a damn
about the world, knowing that right now the world
can give a damn about me. At 95 to 100 mph. I
steadily feel the wind as it coolly calms me on
hot days. At night the stars seems peaceful as I
realize it's me and no one else. I begin to feel
a sense of authority, take charge, knowing I'm
in command. Answering to no one it's all about me.

Lolita Newman

Demon In My View

From the first sight that I took view
I contemplated if it were true

As the sun 'round me grew higher,
I grew older
The heart that sustained me stored blood far colder
An endless thirst and a raging hunger
Shook me with their deafening thunder
My own beliefs authenticity, I would often wonder

I walked a lonely road, totally self-paved,
While others questioned if my soul
Was worth being saved

As the sun 'round me grew higher,
My eyes filled with tears
Each one shed is a testament to the misery and the fears
The fire I so wanted, now burns and sears

At where that sun stands, in the sky,
Clouds collect and light is blocked form shining through
All that I now see
Is a demon in my view

Jon David

Take Them In Your Heart

Speak to my heart,
Speak not to my ears.
Look at yourself in your mind,
Look not in any mirrors.

Let your mind listen,
Let your heart talk,
Let your legs carry you
As you go for a walk.

See with your heart,
See not with your eyes.
Love with your heart,
Love not with your voice.

Feel with your heart,
Feel not with your hands.
Don't just look at the world,
Look at the lands.

Place your thoughts in your heart,
Place not in your words.
Look and love all things, place them in your heart.

Love and understand for, tomorrow's a start.

Joshua Davis

Roses

I saw a row of Roses
And I thought of you
I laid me down in a field of grass
To sleep and dream of you
Seeing you lay next to me
I give you for Roses

White: For the purity in your soul
Pink: For the sweetness is your kiss
Yellow: For the friend I have found in you and
Red: For the heart that you may break

The sun sets upon my skin
I awake
With the memory of your kiss upon my lips and
Your Roses placed upon my heart.

Delilah Garcia

Goodbye

As I look back to yesterday,
The days you and I would play.
I see how close we used to be,
Back when it was you and me.
I remember your magically charming style,
Your handsome face and loving smile.
Your beautiful eyes and gorgeous hair,
Your soft lips that said, "I care!"
I remember your eyes looking into mine,
Letting me know everything was fine.
I loved you and all your ways,
You always left me in a daze.
Over these many years,
I have cried and dried my tears.
I try to forget, I really try,
But I still remember you said, "Goodbye!"

Rhonda G. Collins

Can We Really See?

We see with our eyes open
The blind see with their
    Hands,
    Nose,
    Mouth, and
    Ears
Some can see objects,
Some can't
We take for granted what we have
Take a day and see what the blind see
    Nothing
Sit and listen to the sounds, the
    Noise, the
    Air, the
    Birds, and the
    Sea
Take a deep breath into yourself and remember,
Can we really see?
Be thankful you can see.

Stacie D. Davis

The Rebirth Of Spring

With spring comes fresh new green things,
And new hope soars like a bird on wings.
There is a special peace and beauty on earth,
Which is felt with its glorious rebirth.

A wonderful closeness to God above,
Is strongly felt as spring shows us His love.
For the beauty of spring unfolding each hour,
Reminds us of God's love, peace, and eternal power.

Linda D. Cate

The Little Hallowe'eners

It's a spooky time at Hallowe'en;
If you've ever seen one, you know what I mean!
There's cats and goblins and ghosts galore;
You never know what to expect any more!
There's painted windows and painted faces;
But not much that looks like the human races.
A devil, a skeleton, a witch on a broom;
You might even see a man from the moon!
You may think you can tell a boy from a girl;
But with all of the garb, your head's in a whirl!
There are short ones and tall ones and fat and slim;
You can't tell if one is a her or a him!
They've a bag for your treats, or a trick up their sleeve;
But with all the false faces, they never could sneeze!
From door to door, and from house to house;
They'd sure scare away a cat or a mouse!
So homeward they bounce, all shouting and roaring;
But before many hours, they're fast asleep snoring.

Gladys C. Paddock

Undying Soul

In your heart I am waiting for you to see,
To look long and look hard for me,
You are my friend I'll love you always,
I rest in your soul staring, my love stays,
Waiting for you to see my soul glowing like the sun,
I see that sunset through your eyes loved one,
I hear the birds through your ears, my darling,
And if you look inside yourself; in your heart is my being,
Even as I am gone from this mortal life,
I will see you have no strife,
And with your love I will live and love, my dear,
Even though your eyes can not see me and your ears don't hear,
Your soul will always touch mine and I live,
In your heart you will feel the love I give,
And with your everlasting, loving soul you will know,
I will be here and I will never let you go!

Michelle C. Price

Written Pictures

Poetry flows from his mind to his quill,
About all the things in his heart.
Things which made time stand still,
Things of which we are a part.

His words travel some unseen beams,
To find their way to his pad.
Sometimes they are happy, it seems,
At other times, so sad.

Painted pictures can fade as time goes by,
But the words written along the way,
Will be there long after we die,
And can be read day by day.

His words painted a picture of flowers,
In a field with the woman he loves.
He showed us a man who cowers,
At the slightest sound of doves.

It seems the poetry has run dry,
No new pictures are being written.
There has to be a reason why
The words are there, unwritten.

Regina Wesselman

Confused

What do you do when
The same things go through you mind
Time and time again?
It seems like there is no answer
Yet I can't give up 'till I find one!
There is no end in sight.
I feel as if I'm lost in a storm
Without a guiding light.
Should I or shouldn't I?
I don't know, and neither does anyone else.
Who do you turn to for answers
To the unsolved problems inside of you?

Amy Mansker

Nature's Touch

I look out to the horizon
To see the yellow diamond Fall.
Its color spread across my body like a blanket.
I can feel the warmth of nature
When it cradles me.
As I sit I can see the colors fade.
My blanket starts to fall
And the cool air nips at my body.
I am sad to see my blanket go.
But I know it will be back again tomorrow.

Cheryl M. Evans

The Secret Of Eternity

Blessed is the summit
on which the mysterious oak lies,
the secret of eternity
is said to rustle through the branches of this tree.

Never a man hath crossed the summit
and lived to tell the stories of the soft winds,
but I have lived on the outskirts of this summit
for a fortnight,
and my fire gleams on what is to be
my eternal fate.

Riddled by the complexity of something far greater,
I retire to what is now my chosen life,
and wipe away all tears of past grievances
for the morrow will bring eternal peace.

William K. Gresh

Ode To A Rose

Rose, you are ever admired so,
Your petals, like silk, when you begin to grow.
We wait with anticipation for Spring,
To see the immense beauty you bring.

You stand on the ground with your arms stretched high,
To show your grace, as the people walk by.
Pink, yellow, white or red,
Are the colors you bloom, when you have been fed.

Thou fragrance so sweet, fresh and clean,
As the water in a forest of a nearby stream.
You are solely unique, no others will do,
By your gratifying elegance and fragility in you.

Sharon A. Delloso

Martin Luther King Jr. Through My Eyes...

Why did we March?
Why did we meet the fireman's hose?
Why were we beat with the policeman's night stick?
Why did we have to die?

In the 60's was when he came
Came in peace crying March, let's March,
We must March for human rights

The 60's was when we made our move
No more back doors
No more back rows
He cried vote, let's vote, we must vote

With churches bombed, houses bombed
Lives were given
Jails doors closing, school doors opening
Are we winning?

With the March on washington and the civil rights act
He had a dream that; "Times, they are a changing"
With a sniper's bullet, the world crying
He knew we had to die

Tondeleria T. Tull

Sonnet

A raven haired princess
with a heart stopping smile.
Your beauty makes me senseless
And my emotions are on trial.
For your name, I know not.
How many others have been drawn to you?
Is it your love they have sought?
Were their intentions pure and true?
If you could be placed among the stars
Your beauty would touch the hearts of one and all.
The joys you feel are not just yours but ours
For seeing you makes me walk when I used to crawl
And it truly is a shame,
That the word for beauty is not your name.

Steven Waite

I Carry You With Me

Your party was grand, I had a great time
To see lots of friends, Is always a fun time
   When I finally left, And started to drive back
   A feeling came over me, Which I cannot describe exact

Breathing normally became, A nostalgic look
To a long lost path, In my memory nook
   The scent of your cologne, Which came from a hug
   Was surrounding my head, and smelled like love

I carried you with me, All the way home
Emotions out-crying, For all that I've known
   No matter how tired, You seemed to have been
   Always with a smile, You let everyone in

There is no deterrent, To your spirit, your life
And you have with you forever, A beautiful wife
   When I returned home, You were still there
   In every aroma, That filled the air

When you are no longer with me, skin to skin
You will always be remembered, And make me smile within.

Julie Ann Sprutte

Killing

I loved you, with all my heart.
We were the best of friends,
And had been for years.

I was the most important person,
In your life, you were in mine.
But our importance, was our difference.

You loved drugs,
And I loved sports.
I told you I didn't care,
What you did, but I lied.

I saw what you were to blind to see.
I saw you killing yourself.
I saw you killing me.

Everybody has faults in there life.
It takes a special person,
To look past them, that was me.

Always lying, and covering up for you.
I knew it would catch up to you. I just didn't know when

But now you're gone. And I'm all alone.
Everyone says love hurts, but your love killed.

K. C. Gray

Carrie's Promise Land

There is a strong winters chill
And frost on the window sill
Carrie reaches for her bottle of pills
Soon the clouds will start to lay
A little more whiskey is all it will take
The photo album flashes through her mind
Of all the family she's buried in the days behind
What has happened to all her holiday cheer
Oh you mean the family past out from eggnog and beer
A tear slides down her cheek
Her thoughts have been the same all this week
Of the baby she lost a years ago
How she would have loved it so
Then the dad made his final stand
With a razor blade in his hand
What has happened to Carrie's promise land.

Rick Gardner

God's DJ

Keith is in God's loving arms,
In Heaven he will forever be.
Never again to experience the pain and hurt
Of the world we live,
But to feel eternally loved and care-free.

We will keep him alive in our memories,
And love him all the same.
He will forever be in our hearts,
This will never change.

His pictures will never be tucked away,
We will hold them close to our hearts,
Because with love as pure as ours,
We will never be apart.

Though we continue to live our lives,
We will always treasure his name
For someday we will meet again,
And forever together remain.

Emily Lamb

Miss Statue Of Liberty

Miss Statue of Liberty are you proud of what you see.
Our children are crying and feeling alone.
To many bruised faces and broken bones.
Parents are trying and falling short.
What happened to community love and support.
Companies are taking over the family farms.
Give the land back to whom it really belongs.
Bring our jobs back from overseas.
Our people made them not machinery.
Were hungry and homeless don't turn your eyes away.
Tell me are you proud of America today.

Deborah L. Hogan

Missing In Action

Morning time was laughter but the feeling is not that good
Every single soldier knew and understood
Daylight hours are empty as the morning fades away
For every ounce of energy one more soul was saved

The government said we'd win and the communist would fall
If you don't fight to win why should anyone recall
A commitment to a country whose intentions were to stall
Pile up the money and profit from the call

Now the time just passes by now the time just let's them die
In a land so far away in a land so far away a land we never saved

Some mothers and some fathers are still waiting for the call
It never seems to happen as the names just appear upon the wall
We don't have to wonder why the pain won't go away
As empty wooden boxes serve as markers for the graves
Of a man a man such as he for a man a man much like me

Rollin Stoner

Christ Jesus My Lord

Creator of
History and He
Reigns on high.
It's so good to know the
Savior bye and bye!
Times with Jesus are so grand,

Just try Him out to understand.
Eternal life
Sounds mighty fine;
Until then, I'll let my life
Shine.

My only hope in life, is Jesus my Lord.
You know, He saved me; and, boy, I'm shor'!

Love from the Father, forgives
Our sin and shame. The
Redeemer that
Died, has taken away my blame.

Katina Brodie

"Immutabilis"

When I close these mortal eyes
I see, within, a different universe; another world.
I see the swirling, incandescent mists that are our lives.
Their essence, just behind our words, lies curled.
They meet and merge, separate, and meet again.
Ever changing, yet still the same.

Within this seamless Circle of our lives,
Destiny? It matters not.
All misunderstandings we survive.
For whatever is to be our lot,
In front, behind, below, above,
We remain, knowing always, only...Love.

Clare Livingston

To My Mother

I thought that you had gone away and left me all alone,
With saddened heart and an empty life so forlorn.
But, I see you in the summer breeze as it blows around my head.
I see you in the evening star as I hop into my bed.
I see you in the early morn, your smile was like the sun.
I see you in the afternoon, when daily tasks are done.
I see you in the sunset, with all its golden hue.
I see you in the early eye, your tears were like the dew.
All things that are beautiful will always me there will never be
    another you.
But you have gone on head, and now I understand
That you are waiting there for me and holding out your hand.

Mabel Ganung

The Man Under The Bridge

Didn't the lines in the man's face tell the story?
Betrayed, it's sad, now and forever.
Placed beneath others by his own will.
Worthless to all is the contagious feeling that confines
Him to his place of rest.
Death in its feeling of happiness is more the friend to Mr.
Mr. What? Does a name have any importance
In the serenity of this man?
Is it you? Is it your friend?
What all powerful feeling breaks the will we are born with?
To live beneath a bridge severs the already broken will.
Spoken more clearly than words are the intricate lines of
Sorrow in the man's face.
The lines in the man's face tell the story.

Dan Moore

Thank You Lord - I'm Blind

I thank you Lord, for all the sights
I saw before this loss,
I felt the leaves of beautiful flowers,
And picked those of my choice.

I saw the sunrise, big and bright,
Appearing from behind the clouds,
Looking so strong and steadfast,
As it smiled down at the crowds.

I looked at the innocence in a baby's face,
While listening to a newborn cry.
Oh! Lord, You've given me much to love,
So, I have to ask you why?

Why do I cry when it turns to evening,
Cause I haven't seen all day?

Margaret F. Davis

Friends

Friends are there to lend you a hand.
Friends are there to help you as much as they can.
Friends never ever put you down.
Friends never turn smiles into frowns.

Friends are there when you need them the most
Through thick and thin, coast to coast.
Caring and sharing all the love.
They never ever push or shove.

You have fallen once then again.
They are there to pick you up and take a little spin.
Friendships mean more then just being there.
Friendships mean more then just stopping to care.

Friends should love you always and forever.
They should always be there through whatever.
Never break plans with you
Even if they are blue.

Becky Lynn Beasley

The Silence

In the Silence there are no words,
Only thoughts.
Thoughts of a most unbelievable capacity.
Ideas of great importance waiting to be voiced.
Visions on a new and altogether greater scale.
And dreams...
It is a land of near catastrophes
Upstaged by brilliant performances.
A place of beautiful friendships,
And that one perfect love.
It's where things always turn out for the best.
In the Silence I am protected by an utopian world.
Nothing can hurt me here...
Except the silence.

Christopher L. England

Skeleton Key

A gold key opens you to your house
A silver key opens you to your car
but the skeleton key opens you to the world

The skeleton key has no color
or it can have every color
It has no shape
but it can fit any lock
the skeleton key opens the door to
heaven and hell
love and pain
but some never see what's on the other side

Not everyone owns this key
only the one's who know
the door that is unlocked by
the skeleton key

Kimberly J. Platt

The End

Today is the last day.
The end of eternity
This dawn is the beginning of the end.
The last sunrise, the last sunset,
Savor it, you'll never see it again.

Now we think of all we've done,
And wish our lives had been more fun.
We take a stroll down mem'ry lane.
But only have our selves to blame.
Don't sit there crying in your bed
As all your thoughts soar through your head.
Just do what you feel is right
No consequences after tonight.

We've always said there is tomorrow,
But now I know it's true.
This day will be the last day,
And I want to be with you.

Mary Springel

Sunshine Love

Can you believe the sun,
Promising you the power to run,
Can you believe the day that it brings,
Promising you a thousand beautiful things.
Can you believe its warm whispering wind,
Promising you I have a warm wonderful friend.
If yes
Then as the sun shines down from above,
Let me shine into your heart and warm it with love.

Beverlee Keathley

Searching...

Channel searching, a daily habit I have become
accustomed to. Every channel, all those half-hour shows,
sappy sickos who all have those three things we strive to
achieve. Their petty little problems never encounter the
daily confrontation reality creates.
As I glance to my wall I stare at the posters
cluttering the disastrous room. Mostly they contain famous
faces staring into oblivion with fictitious eyes persuading
my inquisitiveness to wonder how their lives really are.
Who are the phantoms behind the masks?
Turning my head, rejecting thoughts of
amazement and curiosity, I see a play of colors leap out at
me. Immediately I notice the peace, a symbol written and
imprinted continuously in an ironic display of patterns.
Accompanying the chaotic dark, a bright love illuminates as
the neighbor. Both working together, originally made to
create the ultimate destiny we spend our lives searching
for, yet as I look at my wall...
...it is missing.

Amanda Beth

First Light

They sit in their blinds
in the early morning
just before it is light
calling to ducks flying high
trying to coax them
to fly into their decoys.
The air is full of excitement
as the ducks fly lower
and are faintly silhouetted
against the sky as it grows lighter.
Soon the shooting horn sounds.
The air is full of far off gunshots.
A flock of ducks circle above their heads.
He calls and they start coming lower
and lower and lower.
The last thing heard
is the whistling of the wind
running through the ducks wings
before the shots
and two ducks fall.

Dustin Kuehn

Alexandria

Your absence reminds me of a motherless child —
Crying all alone with no one at all.
I miss you.
I wish we had known each other.
My mother seems to be just like you,
There's something unique about her that says,
"I'll always be here for you."
It isn't her — it's something else,
I believe it's you.
I see pictures of you and wonder,
"What are you like?"
Are you like Mom?"
"Do we look alike? Act alike?"
Most of all,
"If you knew me, would you like me?"
I wish I knew.
I feel that I've spoken to you —
And that you've heard me . . . have you?
I am a part of you, I feel you with me —
Are you? . . . I think you are.

Kristen A. Ratigan

Memories

You clutched a rag doll —
Bright ribbons bedecked your dark curls.
The clackety-clack of old high-heeled shoes filled the air.
Dress-up togs tossed here and yon —
Playing "Queen for a Day"!
So many questions — a never ending chain of "whys".
Broken crayons, spilt milk,
Smudges of flour on a "turned-up-nose"!
Pennies clutched in a tight little fist,
For a "nilla" ice-cream cone.
Chasing lightning bugs on a warm summer eve —
Tiny bouquets of flowers "for you, Mommy"!
Chubby arms embrace,
As I kiss a moist brow
and sing a soft lullaby.
Music, laughter, tears —
Never to be forgotten joys.
Memories — so precious to every Mother.
Seems only yesterday —
You were my little girl!

Clara Faye Lankford

She Is My Fair Lady

When I need something done,
She is always ready, that's my hon.
If I misplace a book,
She drops everything to hunt and look.
She puts food upon my tray,
That keeps me healthy everyday.
If I lose my pills around,
She'll search and search till they are found.
Even when we are on the run,
She makes life a lot of fun.

When others have a problem on any day,
She suggests let's stop and pray.
There's beauty in her soul,
I've seen it shine in many a goal.
I feel her deep love flow,
That keeps my heart aglow.
God has blessed us with a good long life,
Which I owe in part to my wonderful wife.
This is my story of love,
To God be the glory flowing down from above.

Richard D. Cornelius

Till I Let Jesus Into My Life

There was a time I had no peace of mind
Till I let Jesus into my life
He put a light in my heart to shine
So that I would have a better life
And I wouldn't have to seek and not find.

When I found peace in my mind,
There was a song in my heart to sing,
And I never have to seek to find
I always hear the glory bells ring,
They are always in my heart and mind.

I have never known such glory divine,
That a person could have such a happy life
And love that would always be mine
Until I let Jesus into my life
A love I nevermore have to seek to find.

Vickie R. Hanes

Darkness Of Spite

Twice in a row I've seen the light
Then comes the darkness-only out of spite
A darkness so thick only thunder and lightening would
    dare to strike
The finder of the souls is in the back of my mind
If only I could think to at least save mine
The face in the mirror touches eyes just like gold
A shimmering brightness is so dear yet too bold
A whisper in the hallway as I listen to hear
Will not constrain but 'tis out of fear
What breaks the wind, a spear in my heart
What washes blood, the song of a lark
Yonder I notice the speech I just gave
On a cold old stone-underneath it, a grave
The cold chills through my veins like ice
The tree above runs wild through the night
False fight, false fate frightens her mate
And yonder waits for the wind to break

Maria C. Guevara

In Memory Of Grandmama

She was born in a small town deep in the South
she worked very hard to feed every mouth
she was very understanding and always gave a hand
took care of her family better than the average man

That dear old lady meant the world to me
cause she was just as sweet as sweet could be
the day has come and she's finally gone
but the memory of mama still lingers on

So here's a word from me to you
I know it's hard what you're going through
so try to be strong and don't feel so sad
cause my grandma had God in the bag

She lived her life and she served him well
just by being around her anyone could tell
my God has come and taken her home
but you know my grandmama is not alone

You know that mama wouldn't want the tears
cause she served our Lord throughout the years
she held on and she finished the race
now she'll see our saviour face to face.

Barbara Borden

Old Age

You will come to be
at about age eighty-three.
When that time is near,
it maybe hard for you to hear.
And when it comes to your sight,
daylight might seem like night.
You may have trouble on the stairs
just remember its easier in pairs.
You may take a nap
not knowing your great-grand child
    is sitting on your lap.
People may say you are old,
Why? Because that is what they are told.
Year after year on your day
they will say happy birthday.
You are only as old as you feel
just show them how you walk up a hill.
Let them know old age is great
even though you can't stand straight.

Danielle Renae Stillitano

Midpoint

As I sit here, alone in the dark
I reflect on the way it all used to be.
Was it all supposed to end like this
With me alone in the darkness of the day?
Flashes of my former self appear before my eyes
Behold, the past laid out like a map
Tracing the journey that has been my years
Forming as I go along
Into the future without a clue.
Of images that will soon be memories
A collection in a box in the corner of my mind
Growing old, musty, and soon forgotten.
An old, worn out toy
Abandoned by a child in the snow
Left to disappear into oblivion.

Madhavi Katikaneni

Untitled

A bird in flight or a horse running free
That is what I wish to be,
Free from all worries, free from all feelings,
This is how I wish to be,
Being able to take flight or run free,
worry and pain is all I see and feel,
So grant me the spirit of a running horse
or a bird in flight and
I will race with the wind
Till there is no end in sight.

Christine A. Moyes

Loneliness

Loneliness is not a feeling of the heart,
it is a feeling of the soul.
It is having plenty of love,
with no one to give it to or share with.
A heart aching for love and compassion,
searching but never finding.
Like finding one tiny star among millions,
never to find the same one again.
One tiny raindrop...falling with a million other,
drying up before feeding the rose, which needed it so badly.
Like a beautiful song being played,
with no one around to hear.
Like a beautiful poem written for all,
but not found because no one is looking.
Like a beautiful memory locked inside a heart,
for the feeling it might be lost.

Kristine Ballinger

Page Sixty-Nine

"I'm getting too old for this,"
she says slyly with a mad giggle in her soul
and a tear in her eye
her blood running down her wrists
down her bloody fists..., "to old for this"
Hanging clothes on a line, to dry
Skid Row, that's where she is
with a needle in her vein
death to numb her pain
"Mirror, mirror on the wall,
if I stretch you out
will you make me tall?"

Rachel A. McMullen

He's Gone

As they lower him into the ground
    Hearts fall.
You have empty feelings inside, missing him
    Love shows.
Long dry tears down the family's face
    Missing Love.
As someone sings Amazing Grace
    As he's lowered
Only the memories stay in
    Love goes out
Only remember the last words
    He's gone.

Jami T. Lynn Salsbery

Comfort Zone

Comfort zone
give a doggie a bone
so he can have a comfort zone,
little candy sits by the phone
that's her comfort zone.
Pete eats his ice cream cone
that's his comfort zone.
Me, I don't know my comfort zone
so, may I take a loan?
A loan to take your bone, your phone,
and your ice cream cone?
Just so I can have a zone.
A zone where I am alone.
Just my feelings and me
So I don't have to lock them up with a key.
Just a comfort zone
Where I can feel company, but am still alone.

John Paul Lisciandro

Untitled

When life's adventures start to stall
And dreams begin to fade,
We turn our hearts to treasures past
And picnics in the shade.
To days when gentle breezes blew
And spring rains filled the air.
To nights when stars would light the skies
For children everywhere.
These treasured times return again
When quiet nights abound.
The memories once we thought were lost
Are yearning to be found.

Jeff Hoover

A Christmas Night In Winnipeg

Hurry Daddy . . . Hurry
If my stockings not up Santa won't leave anything
Knowing looks from his older siblings . . . a glare from me.
Please don't disillusion the young ones . . . please
The service was beautiful but I have so much to do
And, already, it is Christmas Day
Excited children to tuck into bed
Christmas bread to be made. God give me strength
It is 40° below zero and we are 40 miles from home
Mummy . . . is that the star of Bethlehem?
A star hovers over a lamp post . . . over every lamp post
An optical illusion on this frigid night
A small voice whispers . . . Mummy . . . baby Jesus is everywhere
Suddenly we are quiet
My heart fills with joy
Love
Peace

Naomi Menard

The Mirror, Memories And Me

What will I say that has not been said?
What might I write that has not been read?
By someone living or dead.

I have only to give my point of view and pray
you see what I do. If blessed with your point
to view, I pray the same for me as you.

As a little girl, my three brothers gave to me a
gift that meant the world. No view to me
has ever been clearer than what I read a
back that mirror "To know me is to love me."

Time and memories are all we share. I ask
but for forgiveness, yes I dare. For we all die
and die alone. All I need is pardon from
those I've done wrong.

Wicked hate do as you will. Love will soon
make its kill. Oh, let us stand on the Rock
of Faith in love, with peace of a dove,
And after dead, may we live to hear our
names in The Book of Life read. Amen.

Lisa E. Locklier

Moments

There are moments when we sit and ponder,
    or maybe just let our mind wander;
    of the paths that we need to go,
    and of the things we reap and sow.

There are moments that stay forever in our hearts,
    and other times moments may drift apart;
    but the moments that we hold so dear,
    are never lost, so we need not fear.

Some moments we feel should not be,
    and may often ask, "Oh why me?"
    those maybe the moments we choose not to share,
    but find comfort in knowing someone is there
There are moments I know that will come to mind,
    when we all wish we could turn back the time;
    but that privilege belong not to man
    so this we must do while we have a chance.
Of moments that tend to make you smile,
Grab hold, grab hold! No man knows the extent of his miles.

Amelia Weldon

A Christmas Dream

There is a day more precious than most.
A day to sing great praise to the heavenly host.
I'm only too sad it comes but once a year.
It's a day of good tiding, great love and good cheer.

For the day of Christmas is the day of Christ's birth.
And because of this day we have peace here on earth.
It comes in December, a cold time indeed.
But fills the heart with a warmth we all need.

For the love in your heart you feel on this day.
Is worth more than money any king could pay.
Love is a gift from heaven above,
But is often forgotten and taken lightly of.
So try and imagine this world every day.
If we kept the spirit of Christmas along our way.
It would heal all wounds and settle our past.
And give us a peace that would forever last.

Don Mathis

Remembrance

Across the shiny meadows,
Through the pine-filled woods,
Spread across the ocean,
Lies me glorious sister.

The strong silk of her hair glistened as she ran.
The fulfillment of her heart gave away the
stern, beautiful face.

Her strong, sleek body always beat me when
we raced.

So I ask myself to this day,
"Why? Why did she have to leave me?"

Anna Pattison

For The Animal Lover In You

The little girl —
    wants a kitty,
        her name is Arlene . . .
Someone to talk to, to hold, to share with,
To giggle with, perhaps even to love . . .

The woman wants —
    A kat,
        Her name is Arlene . . .
Someone to talk to, to hold, to share with,
To laugh with, perhaps even to love . . .

I have a friend,
    Her name is Arlene . . .
I am her lover, soul-mate, and special guide;
    My name is — Kit-Kat . . .
Perhaps, I'm what she's been
    Questing towards?! . . .
        Maybe, just may-be.

(No dogs — please)

Mel Boyd

Cool Boy And Valley Girl

A cool boy. A valley girl.
Dancing in the streets. Taking on the world.
Her brilliant eyes of iris green, her attitude so
cute and mean.
His arrogance is hard to hide, but he knows
that she holds his pride.
A perfect day, the sun was cold, but he had
her to tease and hold.
The freezing night turned warm again as she
lay quiet next to him.
He wished for nothing but his new friend
and she wished this night would never end.

Brandon S. Maroon

Ode To Saturday Nite

Oh, that there must be
Better days for me
Wondering when I can go back to work
I feel like such a jerk
Went out and got skunked
And fell down drunk.
I broke my ankle
Now I have to tango
With my wife who had a fit.
Reading St. Peter I find love and a quiet spirit
Sober now and a better man for it.

Randy Boone

The River

Time passes as the clouds move across the sky.
It is true what they say about the river;
The same stream will never pass your foot again.
The things of today, may not be there tomorrow;
No matter how much you love it,
No matter how hard you hold on.
Cherish every moment as precious,
For they may never come again.
Some things were never meant to be.

The tears, the smiles, every emotion, I remember.
There is no use in asking why,
God wills it, and the Lord knows best.
The pain I feel now, the questions that I have,
The Lord will answer in His time.
Who am I to complain?
These things I believe with my whole heart,
But I will always remember the river.

Alan Wang

A Friend

A girl, a boy, two people together,
A shoulder for support when times are rough,
An ear to listen, being forever,
A person for comfort when times are tough.
Honesty, trusting, special acquaintance,
Some joking, laughing, having a good time,
Some advise, opinions, it all makes sense,
I'm lucky to have your friendship as mine.
Through good times and bad, I know you'll be there,
Though miles apart we'll always be close,
With a smile, a hug, a tear we'll share,
You're special to me because you matter the most.
You're great and kind and will always be true,
Thanks for always being there, I Love You.

Michelle Libich

Open Up

There's a prison in my mind
With all the memories locked behind
Sometimes I wonder what's behind the door
The things I can't remember anymore
The pain was deep, it hurt so bad
I fear the sorrow of being sad
Sad about the past I cannot change
Yet to remember brings me pain

They say to bring it out, to open up, unlock the door
And I won't have to live with pain anymore
They say there's a child inside my soul
Who never grew up while I grew old
She's hiding back, behind the door
As I remember I've done before
Come out my child, come out and play.
Together we'll make a better day.
We'll unlock the door and set ourselves free
For within a prison is no place to be.

Sharon L. Wolf

Never

We may Never see the day we dream of,
The day we long for.
We may Never feel what we want to feel,
Be where we want to be,
Love who we want to love.
We will always want more, need more.
Never have everything right.
But we must learn to Never let it get us down.
Learn to Never stop our dreaming, feeling, wanting, loving.
Never!!

Scott Longo

When I Found You

All of my life I've been searching for a love that was true.
I'm always seeming to end up with the wrong ones.
    That's when I found you.

When you came along I knew it was true love.
It was like I was the hand and you were the glove.

You are my partner, I am your lover.
To me I can see there is no other.
Special times are shared by two
I knew all of this when I found you.

Felisa Smalley

Imagine

Alone and depressed,
isolated from everybody,
death is toying with my mind,
darkness gathers around me,
my mind starts to drift,
remembering a place I haven't been since I was a kid,
a place where good and bad don't exist,
it's a place where you're run free from any hurt,
a place where you don't have to worry about anything,
it's like this place is your kingdom and you can do what
you want and what you feel like,
this wondrous place is your imagination,
the only true place people can call their own.

Nicholas Galetti

Oh Precious Dove

Oh precious dove help me,
Please take me away.
Relieve me of my burdens,
Anything I will pay.
The world's weight is on my shoulders,
Cutting through my flesh.
Shredding me to pieces,
Smothering me to death.
The weight I can't bear any longer,
How long must I suffer on?
Each problem is a tear added to mine eyes,
Lift me up with your wings of love.
Go seek your creator quickly,
Report that his servant is distraught.
In desperation I reach for his hand,
Yet in the circle of worldly things am I caught.
So fly quickly to heaven my precious dove,
For Jesus is my only Hope.
I want to be rescued from this angry world,
I desire to be with my Lord.

Pam Schroer

Sarah

Welcome my child and see your new world
With eyes that are hazel or brown or blue
Is your hair dark or blond or mayhap its red
Will it be curly or straight or just slightly bent
Will you be tall or be short or somewhere between
Have I given you even one important gene
Will you live in this realm of earth time and sky
Or travel in space and watch stars floating by
What are you like my new little child
Will the path that you follow be calm or be wild
Whatever you do or do not do
Whatever you are or are not
You'll always be loved by all whom you touch
And cherished for each gene you've been given

Norma R. Hebel

Now

For hours nothing happened.
I sat and watched.
Then in a crystalline moment, something stirred.
A petal turned; a dew drop fell,
A bud opened; fragrance arose.
Something changed forever.
A bud no longer, now a rose.

For a time nothing happened,
I kept careful notes.
Then in a crystalline moment, something awoke.
A thread split; a dew drop fell,
A cocoon opened, beauty flew out.
Something changed forever.
A caterpillar no longer, now a Monarch.

For a time nothing happened.
Roses withered, butterflies flew.
Then in a crystalline moment, someone cried.
A heart opened; a tear drop fell; feeling flowed.
Something changed forever.
An attraction no longer; now a passion, now a love.

Danielle Schultz

Time

This thing called time;
We cannot grasp it in our hands.
Here for now and then it's gone,
Like a beach with drifting sands.

You hear, "Where did time go?"
Or "Time sure does fly."
Sometimes it moves very slow,
Then it disappears like clouds in the sky.

Most of all time is here for love.
Your children come to you in time.
They know your love as soft as wings of a dove.
Then they leave when you're in your prime.

You think it seems like yesterday,
When they were small.
Again old time has stolen away;
They grew straight and tall.

If we're to know this thing called time;
We would say it's a worldly measure,
With no reason or rhyme,
A small whisper in an eternal treasure.

S. Wesselmann

Peril

As he rowed, the waves lapped the side,
And the fine mist sparkled on his skin.
The current was pulling with the changing tide,
And he knew, soon it would win.

The jagged rocks leaped up at him,
Their dangerous peril laid in his wake.
His fate, as he used his might, looked grim,
Would these pinnacles, his life, take?

The very essence of defeat!
His life, in flashes before him.
Despair, as his body raced with a beat.
For him, what were his chances - dim?

The sea in its mighty haste to hug the shore,
Took with it - life and evermore,
The rocks, like an altar, a body bore,
To breathe, to walk, to talk - nevermore.

Valerie A. McGrady

What I See

I see men and women in blue
I see people trying to help others
But do the people ever think
What their efforts cost

Some can't sleep because of what they see
Some do almost anything not to remember
Some may drink or look for other comforts
And yes, some can't make it and take their life

What I see when I look at my husband
Is a man of honor, a man who cares
What I see in some of our friends in blue
Is people who care a lot for not much pay

But what I see when there is an officer down
Is quick response, with maximum effort
And when one dies and leaves us alone
I see love, sadness, and a badge of honor.

Carolyn Kay McNeely

Poem On A Winter Day

Today is Sunday, silent and snowy
Wintry white and five degrees.

Soft footprints trace from the shed out back
To the step where I place a meal and warm milk
For two feral kittens, well trained by their mom,
Thus refusing my care
In every way but this.

Last summer I set out food, and chatted at them
As they condescended to eat,
While watching me from the cautious corners
Of their golden eyes.

Now bundled up, I chatter from the designated distance
So they won't race back to the shed's poor safety,
Leaving their meal for the even less lucky,
And themselves hungry.

When winds storm, rains pour, snows blow, or I must be away,
I worry - while they, dependent, yet uncompromising,
Trusting, yet fearing,
Refuse to accept more care.

Sally W. Lowry

Molly

Molly, Oh! Sweet Molly,
just like sweet wine,
I wish you could be mine,
lets lay it on the line!

She dances in the wind,
like a sweet smelling flower,
she is the fantasy,
making her impression every hour.

The memory of her still burns bright,
her hazel eyes shine like a gleaming light,
When she talks I am in a daze,
she lights up my heart like a powerful blaze.

In a land of desire,
Molly is the queen,
something mystically special,
she is the core of the dream.

Molly, Sweet Molly,
I am glad you are mine,
we are one soul,
so sweet, so divine, so fine!

Aaron Holcomb

Reflections

Reflections are real not just a thought
You see them everyday outside of your heart

Whether your looking in the mirror
Or looking in the pond

It is a image of the things that you look upon

Even when looking at yourself
Your looking at reflections

I look at a picture each and everyday

The thought of my daughter
Leads my mind astray

I see her in my dream
I see her in my thoughts

A reflection of me she's definitely got

As the mother of my daughter
I'm sure you can see

The resemblance in her is reflecting from me

Even thought we're not together
We will never be apart

Cause the reflections of our daughter
Will stay in each of our hearts
Derrick Cain

Don't Talk To Strangers

My daddy waved at people, everywhere he went
He said no one's a stranger, they're just someone you ain't met.
I'd love to show my children the world my daddy showed me
A world that doesn't lock its mind for security.

He'd say to me "that old man has a story to tell".
And I'd climb up on his lap to hear some story about a well.
But I must tell my daughter, that it's not safe to be
Listening to a story on a strange man's knee.

And I tell her:
Don't you talk to strangers for it could be your bitter end
Don't you talk to anyone who says they're mommy's friend
And don't you let your daddy tell you that you mommy's dead
And when you go to sleep and rest your weary head
Scream if any stranger gets into your bed
And don't you talk to strangers
Trena O'Neal Ford

Myself

If I could write down all the thoughts and feelings I have inside
to make them clear and not to hide,
The pen I hold would fly across the pages to bring the past
where I am now and tomorrow a day behind.
Those words on paper, not just to fill a line but could brighten
someone's day down through time.
I am not one of schooling to make them all rhyme nor can I tell
a story that fits the times.
In myself, I try to live for my savior in my heart and mind
to do as he asks and make use of time and take only what I need
and always try to answer another's plea.
If I could only write what I have inside to let it come
to the surface, not to hide I know God is the answer. Someday
when it's time he give me all the words I need to finish
every rhyme. God Bless you Jesus for helping me through all
the hard times by holding me forever in your arms.
Dora L. Williams

Sweet Torture

You have a divine beauty and a sense of grace.
From your soft blue eyes, to the smile on your face.
Those curls that are hidden in that long blond hair.
Keeps taunting me, saying touch me if you dare.
Those sweet lips that seem to quench my thirst.
And the feel of your skin, that makes me want to burst.
Your heart and soul so vibrant, so pure.
To your words that are so passionately sure.
You've ripped out the heart that was beating in my chest.
You flaunt it in front of me, not letting me rest.
My thoughts of you keep me dancing around.
All the while my feet never even touch the ground.
I don't know why I want such torture, such despair.
All I know is you leaving is what I couldn't bare.
So take what you want from me, it's all for you.
I'll just pick up the pieces later, that's all I can do.
George A. Oltmans

Magic

Magic is like a dream,
you don't always remember what happened
and what will happen next.
You may believe something is real or not, a illusion or a vision.
Magic is also like life.
Things don't turn out as you planned,
and things appear and disappeared.
You always need someone to help you with a tricks
and to depend on.
Thru life, things remain a puzzle and a mystery.
But in life you can't saw someone in
half and get away with it.
Belinda Karpf

I Am

I am the breath of life that gives the infant its first cry
I am the strength that sends the treetops soaring to the sky
I am the spirit of the eagle, fiercely wild and free
I am the driving urge that prods the rivers to the sea
In your times of stress I am your calm serenity
When you are confused I am blessed clarity
In our calm and sweet oasis I refresh your soul
When brokenly you to me call I come to make you whole
I am the everlasting one, your well that won't run dry
You are my precious, precious child, the apple of my eye.
H. Elizabeth Morris

To Amber, Love Daddy

Baby so tiny, baby so dear
Innocent child, you have nothing to fear
My little miracle, Daddy is here
Baby so small yet strongest of heart,
I fell in love with you right from the start.
I have no pity to offer your ear
I'm awed by your strength,
little wonder, so dear . . .
don't be afraid, don't shed a tear
Amber Leigh, sweetheart,
Daddy is here
Child so special,
Little lady so grand
God has sent us an angel
graced by His own hand.
So, if you are frightened
or think nobody cares,
remember my princess,
Daddy will always be there.
Victor Jay Ford

Peace

Peace....A state of mind,
  Can it truly exist for all of mankind?
  Wars come and go, strife all around;
   Hunger, discontent, prejudice abounds.

Peace...Just a word in hope expressed,
   While all around people live in distress!
   Searched for by many midst hardship and strife,
   Some never find peace in what we call life.

Peace....Accepting God's will, in Him confide;
   This is the answer when all else has been tried.
   No more seeking, no more distrust;
   The shackles are lifted, loving others a must.

Peace...An innermost feeling, a serene state of mind;
   A calmness of knowing God's plan for mankind.
   True peace is received when one finds the Son.
   Then and only then, is the quest for Peace won!

   Karen LaMar

The Rebel

He stands on the outskirts of town,
Wanting to be let in.
But no one lets him join the fun,
No one understands him.

It would take only one person,
To open their heart to him.
Then he could change his ways,
And become a real man.

Instead of the rebel he's always been,
The bully in the streets.
But only I can see,
What he really needs.

He needs someone to hold him,
To tell him that he's loved.
Someone to spend his nights with,
A woman he can love.

I am that woman,
Thought I seem gentle as a dove.
I've been captured by the warmth in his smile,
And he already has my love.

   Brandy N. White

Shoebox

Among the sun-stained lilies
and velvet trees,
at cotton-ball clouds.

And as they pass,
making shapes and faces,
he watches them - dangling,
suspended by some unseen wires
in the pale blue sky of his candle-wax world.

And as his thoughts begin
to clutter the air around him,
he sends them all away -
to water the weeds and crabgrass
of some other shoebox playground.

And as the day passes,
the clouds turn dark and disappear.

And as the lemon-seed sun
falls behind the cardboard hillside, he forgets it.

And so he sits, tired and alone,
in the dark blue of the drunken twilight -
falling asleep.... And thinking of her.

   Corey Miller

Did Anyone Listen

Sunny day, beautiful sky;
Smiles on people's faces.
We look back and time has passed us by,
Leaving you looking for some trace.

Some trace of what it was or what it used to be;
For, you look up now, and what do you see?
Crime, violence, at an all time high,
Has no one taken time to wonder why?

Where does it lead to?
In which direction is it going?
Trying to do all that you can do...
Hoping to have a decent showing.

A showing of what you believe, a showing of you, yourself;
Need not attempt to live for someone else.
For, the world outside can be oh, so cold,
As we strive in search of our own pot of gold.

   James Edward Gray

Summer Day

It was one summer night,
The air was nice and cool,
The trees were swaying,
With the midnight breeze.
I was watching the stars, shine so bright.

I found myself at peace,
Because the moon and stars,
Sparkle in the night
Made me realize how the moon
And stars sparkle so bright in the night.

I was watching the light of the
Moon on my pool.
But, then the light was beginning to
Fade away, because the night turned
Into dawn, so it became a new day.

It was one summer day, when the
Sun was looking through the trees,
To see what was going on with the
New day. While I was just standing outside
To see all the birds, and living animals roaming around.

   Anne-Marie Ribeiro

"Still"

You are gone
but I still feel the pain
caused by you everyday
your words they stung
as if hit by your fist
it's hard to understand
Why you're still missed
when we fought and you made me cry.
I still forgave you after every little sigh
but that will no longer happen
for I have somewhere to go
someone I can turn to
and let my true feelings show
the scars you left upon me
are slowly fading away
yet I still think of you everyday
you are no longer here
and I no longer there
but yes it's true
I still do care

   Jennifer Chapman

Simian Dream

Never die a happy man before looking at the world
Through its universal prism. Consider this palace your
garden of death, spinning past the eyes of Atlas.
Have you ever danced with the fear of traveling across
pain? It waltzes slowly with ease and moves gracefully, like
a young, champion matador.

This vast garden, this world of imaginary evolution,
Smiles at our humanity from its position of infinity. Just
consider yourself lost in the race for complication. Have
you ever glared the snake in his deadly eye, a piercing
demon, beast of pain. I licked his poison and my name was
inscribed on the Valley, where I ride upon his scales.

I keep expecting this pavilion to take its flight, soft and
agile like the pinnal's of night. Now we assemble together
to discover something, this mass of world we know falling
upon us like a deadly car crash. Have we even reached
completion? Or has life completely overtaken what
it has naturally received? This is the simian dream.

Timothy Joseph Erskine Jr.

Autumn Wind

The darkened midnight sky was gently
illuminated by the iridescent glow of a
descending crescent moon.
Nocturnal beasts scurry and rustle through
The multi-colored foliage that covered the
forest floor.
High in the trees, the hissing of a lonely
Autumn wind brings despair on ones faith
An owl the size of a small wolf, pears down
At fleeing rodents as they catch a glimpse
of her emerald like eyes.
Young fruit bats dart in and out of the
Twisted vines that run wild, through the fog
engulfed pumpkin patches.
Lonely is the autumn wind that entices your
very soul, the summer comes to a shrieking halt.
Reality is back with a vengeance all emptiness
Is felt . . . From the Autumn Wind.

John P. Shea

Untitled

What does your stamp say?
Edmund White MD? F.S. Fitzgerald?
Mary Cassatt? Maria Rilke?
Abigail Thernstrom; Diane Ravitch?
Timothy Ferris? D. J. Boorstin?
Lance Morrow; David Van Biema?
Have I not heard of Mr. Ely?
I have heard of Demosthenes (but not before Dr. S.
Freud.) Walter Bagehot (not before Marshall McLuhan).
Marshall Blucher was before our Gen. Marshall of
the Plan (c) '46. Elvis the King was not Jack Weber Or
W.J. Lederer's The Ugly American (c) '70.
Ayn Rand (The Virtue of Selfishness; Atlas Shrugged;
and The Fountainhead) probably had read Henry
James; probably knew investor Mr. Warren Buffet,
and architect F.L. Wright; yet not architects
Pei; Salvadori; and Koolhaus.
C or Cd is what Parliament commands to have
printed. Some of us are Bob's friends and others
of us are friends of Bill. Correct Time...?

Ralph R. Weber

Go To Jesus

Are you tired, feeling weary,
find yourself often a little teary?
Go To Jesus . . .
Are you hurting, crushed with despair,
nobody knows or seems to care?
Go to Jesus . . .
Are you restless, feeling really stressed out,
Life's full of worries, cares and doubts?
Go to Jesus . . .
Are you afraid, full of torment and fear,
darkness and hopelessness always so near?
Go To Jesus . . .
Go To Jesus and pour out your heart.
Go To Jesus and get a fresh start.
Go To Jesus where grace abounds.
Joy is flowing and peace is found.
Go To Jesus . . .

Becky Cowley

Rose Colored Glasses

Things always appear a little out of focus
At this time of the night.
Why is it more so now?
The clouds are moving in
To cover the red sun
The hour is growing late
The sky dark
The night chilled.
I think at times that I can clear it all away
By picking up a piece of tissue
And wiping off my glasses.
Maybe the rose will start showing
Like it used to when I was younger...
...But when I was younger I had few friends
And I knew few things...
I wasn't concerned about others around me
And I felt empty...
...What good is it to have rose colored glasses...
...And nothing to look at.

Beverly Cameron

Some Men

Want their women
To be like cigarettes
In a case
Just so many — all slender and trim
Waiting in a row
To be selected — set aflame — and discarded.

More fastidious men
Prefer women
Like cigars these are more expensive
Look better and last longer
If the brand is good
They aren't given away.

Nice men treat women like pipes
And become more attached to them
As older they grow.
When the flame is burnt out
They still look after them
Knock them gently but lovingly
And care for them always
No man shares his pipe.

Clarence Reed Gum

Black Roses

One day I loved.
One day Love loved me.
One day was enough
One day was bloody.

One day I cried.
One day Love left me.
One day it died.
One day it pricked me.

I slept in the black roses.
On each jagged thorn.
I knelt in the black roses.
And the love was gone.

One day I prayed.
One day Love hit me.
One day it stayed.
One day it spit on me.

One day I fell.
One day Love killed me.
One day was Hell.
One day Love buried me - in the black roses.

Joshua Lazarus Carreiro

A Letter To All My Black Men

My brothers look at me and tell me what you see
I carried you for nine months and this is the thanks I get
You beat me, raped me, and called me b*tch
I had your kids cause I love you so much
All you did was cheat
That's why I put your stuff on the streets
This is a letter to all my black men
I stood by your side when times got rough
Watched a million of you march in D.C.
As you pledged to be a better father, husband, and brother
And never to harm one who looks like you
I will stand by you side till the end of time
Pick you up when the world knocks you down
This is a letter to all my black men
So listen up cause I won't say it again
I'll be your strong independent black woman
Your shoulder when you need me to
Never argue and never fight
I guess what I'm trying to say
Is that I love you unconditionally.

Tamika K. Hall

A Minuscule Message

We received our recent postcard, with its words so minuscule.
We found our magnifying glass — 'twas not the proper tool!

We crawled up thru the attic, and found our microscope
We still had trouble reading it. We thought there was no hope!

Then a neighbor told us of a man in a distant town
"He writes upon the head of a pin." We decided to track him down.

We made a special trip there, sixty-two miles away.
To find this man of talent, took us all the day.

His hacienda we finally found, but he spoke only Spanish.
We thought our trip was all in vain. Our hopes began to vanish!

Our Spanish handbook we luckily found in the mapcase of our car,
With halting, stuttering mumbled words, we began our verbal spar.

We finally did get thru to him! We thrust your card in sight!
"I can't read this!", he shouted, "Fine print I only write!"

Robert H. Perrine

Saying Goodbye

I feel so sad inside for I know I must say goodbye,
You have always been there for me.
But I was too selfish, I couldn't see.
I made you sad, I made you cry,
You must still feel the hurt inside.
I never meant to hurt you.
I never meant to cause you pain,
For you meant the world to me.
You were the one person who believed in me.
All I have ever wanted was you to be my friend,
I didn't mean to turn you against me.
I know I must let go of the friendship that could never be.
For I can't stand to see the tears fall from your eyes.
And the sadness I brought into your life,
My friend it's time to say goodbye.

Ruth Kelley

One Last Time

Whispers is all I want to hear at night
telling me that you're alright
That you are safe and in the sky
and that you're sorry you didn't say bye
It happened so fast and you had to go
but don't forget that I love you so
come to me once through water fall and stream
tell me you love me and that it's a dream
you're really not gone you're here with me
and you will be here for all eternity
but it won't happen cause it's not true
you really are gone and I miss you
whisper me at night and tell me you know
tell me to move on and just let go
please hear my prayers give me a sign
come to me just one last time

AnnMarie Alicea

Time

How far back in the endless ages do we go?
Oh well, we may never know.

The sand in the hour glass sure flows fast;
While we treasure sweet moments and things that will last,

Some of us grow old without a lot of trouble,
While some of us get trampled and lost in the stubble.

Oh the beauty of a sunrise in our land,
A life well lived is a sunset grand.

One thing we hope for sure,
A life in the heavens we will procure.

Grant eternity with he who reigns sublime,
Surely we will find all the answers when it's time.

Harold E. Owenby

Distance

I seem distant,
Though I am near,
Hiding inside life's greatest fear.
Like a warm summer day,
Or a cold winter's night,
What is the cause of this terrible fright?
Who knows, who knows?
Is it cause the wind blows?
Or because of the rain?
What is the cause of this terrible pain?
What is the pain,
That I speak of?
Is it because of my lost love?

Christina Scara

Reflection

In the dark of day I slip away
And feel sorry for myself
I think of all the things that didn't go my way
and all the things that turned to gray
and then I'd say
"Why me...why I...who did I anger
for such mistreatment?
Did I tell a lie?
Did I say a word so offensive
to upset the tide?
What must I do to set things straight?
How do I correct these mistakes?"
And as these words whisper through my mind
I see the light come up from behind,
ever so clear, ever so bright,
it is my realization that has brought the light.
"Is that all," I say...
"to find the things I've done wrong today
and to sincerely want to correct them?"

Kimberly M. James

Love

It's like a flower in the spring
or a freshly cut, diamond ring
it's like a rain drop on your nose
or the way moist grass feels between your toes
it's like a heart on Valentines Day
how it feels
it's not hard to say
it's like a roller coaster as you reach the top
and that kind of feeling is hard to stop
it's like a star on a gloomy night
your heart starts to pound
when the feeling is right
I believe love is the only thing real
because no one can change the way we feel

Kathy Lee

Untitled

The righteous wrong, acts so strong,
to condemn one for their beliefs.
A venomous song, with words pronged
death would be, but a relief.
A malevolent abode, for those who loathe,
Apathy for a man based on race.
A scapegoat mold, His ancestors told,
No place for disgrace.
It is written in word, most definitely been heard,
Can we be a victim of fate.
The poison is the cure, we fly south like a bird,
there'll be no-one left to hate.

Christopher Robin Karecki

The Gift

A gift is known to be of
material things.
But the best gift of all, is
the gift from the King of Kings.
Well, of course the gift is Salvation,
for there is nothing better
across the nation.
The gift of Salvation is only
one way for if you don't
have it, "Hell" is the price you pay.

So make it clear!
Make it strong!
Jesus is the way you belong!

Anna Alicia Snodgrass

Inhuman Revelation

The light of the fiery moon
burned deep into the sea
The charred mountains
were as ghostly giants
against the blood red sky
The earth smouldered in the spattered din
like the remains of a dying fire
In the distance skeletons of trees
reached longingly towards the heavens
no song of bird
nor laughter of child could be heard
The waves crashing to the shore
seemed like thunder in the deadly silence
Then, the rain began to fall
to drown the cracked, barren fields
The scorching sun rose
but in the west
and faintly,
a rainbow appeared over the horizon

Irene Van Stockum

Untitled

The world once followed its normal course,
But was pushed away by an unknown force.
The starlight's shine is as bright as the sun,
And the moon sets high upon the horizon.
As the world becomes what we want not to be,
The sane are locked up and the insane set free!
So much it takes for this world to turn,
So much teaching for one thing to learn.
As the world turns 'round before our eyes,
We remember how once we had day and night skies.
Now the moon's the same as the stars and sun,
And no darkness conveys neither light from above.
Both yet neither are always within,
Full of our love and full of our sins,
Full of our rights and full of our wrongs,
Full of our talks and all of our songs.
Step one foot in Hell and never return,
What we thought we knew, we'll have to re-learn,
Just one question before I'm slain,
Would you be free, or locked in chains?

Christina Kay King

A Silent Cry

Come and listen, give it a try
can you hear a little girl's silent cry?
Lost and alone
With no place to call her home
No one is there to show her care
No one to with which she may share
All the hurt and pain she holds inside
in great amounts, rushing in like the tide
As each day goes by, she struggles to cope
As sadness fills her heart, she has lost all hope
She knows not what it means to be loved
but longs for a gentle touch, as if held like a dove
Have you ever wondered why?
Quite possibly you have never heard
her silent cry
She is always very mild and meek
Gone unobserved as one small tear
Falls silently from her cheek

Penny A. Houim

Dogs

Black, white, yellow or brown, you'll
find a dog in your town. Ugly, pretty,
short, or tall, what can be better than
your own dog?

Here they are, here to stay, they love
you every day. Hug, kiss, snuggle, and love,
curl in your lap, nice and snug.

Barking up, barking down, barking all
around the town. Over here, over there,
barking, barking everywhere.

They are thin, they are fat, they love
to chase cats. Chase the cat day
and night they will get in a fight.

Scratch his tail, scratch her head,
scratch them in their doggy bed.
They run fast, they run slow, let them
loose and there they go!

Devon Davis

My Haven

There is something in the park
    That is native to my soul
Where the kids are calling
    And swing sets are a coat
There is something there of me —
    Something peaceful, calm, remote.

There is something of me written
    On the old graffitied slides
From the hollow iron trash cans
    Something of my childhood calls
Days spent among the swings
    When I wanted to be free
From the outer world's intrusions —
    When needed time to be.

The park sees me rarely
    Now that I am nearly grown
I know longer have the time
    To seek a place to be alone
Yet when outer pressures crowd me, when I need to be away,
    There stirs something in the park, half remembered, in my heart.

Jessica David

Touch Of The Rain

John Quincy Lockwood 1/13/74 - 9/22/93
Wake to the moment
Live life to the fullest
Don't look back
And don't say goodbye
For the time we have is but an instant
Gone with the passing of the wind
Gone with the passing of time
Why must we hate
And why must we hurt
Why must we cry tears of pain
And why must one die to feel the touch of the rain
Now you are free to roam
Free of your pain
Left behind you
Tears from the ones who love you
Emptiness and the rain

Traci Zeigler

By Way Of The Stars

Lying awake in the cold winter's night
Guided by stars and loves pure white light
She sails through the clouds blocking the view
With plans and dreams to soon start anew
Light - hearted and awed, for her troubles would cease
Happy and calm for soon her soul would find peace
Alone in her room she rose with the morning
Her dark troubled soul gave out a warning
She'd promised herself away in the night
Guided by stars and a dreamer's soft light
To go with the wind and soar like a star
A happier life she knew was not far,
So before all she stood, prepared for her day
Past dreams, like the stars, had guided her way.

Iris Moulton

Female To Female

She grasps the rope with calloused hands
Coils it with quite strength in her stance
Confident of her skill the situation demands.

The heifer bellars, crashes against the gate
We watch the angry bovine stop and hesitate
As the loop settles we see the bloody water break.

We feel her confusion - hear her quiet moan
We seek to comfort her in our own low tones
Giving our assurances she is not alone.

We two women watch her heaving girth
One experienced at the pain of giving birth
Realization striking the other to its actual worth.

Deanna Dickinson McCall

The Loon

Thrice thrust upon my sleep
of which I hear a lonely cry.
Thrice times do I keep
darkness masked upon mine eye.
What pains thee more,
The bitter touch of Autumn's end
or memories upon thy sore,
where gentle rains shalt never mend?
Thrice more the dreary call I hear
piercing as my dreams do talk.
Thrice thrust upon thy slumber ear,
my dreams, through desolate sands do walk.
Upon the evenings lonesome moon
I see what in darkness calls...The Loon.

Shane Sullivan

Exposed

Naked I lay in the prairie today
watching the straw grass blow
the only thing real that I can feel is
your memory touching my soul.
The wind whipped by and I thought that I could
feel your body on mine
but it was only the breeze, coming in to tease
wishful thoughts I have in mind.
The southwest wind plays and bends
the grass and the tall pine trees
and through my mind's eye, I capture the sight
of your face smiling at me.
In the prairie high, where it's hot and dry
and the sun can bake your thoughts
the only thing real that I can feel is
the path where our hearts walked.

Kim Ross

Fields Of Gold

The air so sweet, so soft
blowing through the tree tops,
as I sit there listening
to the song you make.
Wishing there were clouds,
so I could watch them play;

Instead I ran through the Fields of Gold
laughing with joy
as I rolled in the daisies by the sea side.
Rolling to the ground
right before the cliffs of death,
seeing the water at the horizon
jump with excitement.
Thinking of people in my life,
hoping they love me
as I do love them.

Candi Little

Bird A Prey

Whoot, whoot the tree owl would say
in hours silence besides the little lake
The fields which grow almost by night
and a stillness stayed
The waters in the wind would ripple swiftly
and change, the fish would no longer bite
as seasons passed.
While the tractor lay bore
beneath the bordering sky
A gazebo doth appear its
red wood turning withered
so, I thought I still could hear,
the whoots of my feathered friend
who soaked in sunlight yet lost its life
beside that quiet lake.

Edmund Walker Goddard

The Soul

It is dark, but there is light
It is small, but at its greatest height
It races, but yet it burns
For your love it yearns

It bleeds, but it heals
It has no senses, but it feels
It goes fast, it goes slow
It's always yelling "Keep me here" or "let me go"

The Soul is a wonderful thing
It sometimes takes you under its wing
It will burn, but it shall learn
And for your love it will always yearn

Chad Laurence

Desperate Mother

The heat too hot - the day too long
Gotta keep working - no food at home
Cotton stalks scratching - the pain is real
Load getting heavy - Lord on my knees I kneel
Bread is what I need, some milk and maybe honey
Children still waiting - sure need this money
Gotta keep working - must move steadfast
This day will pass - This too will pass -
Quite now! I hear the wind...
I feel the breeze in the air
Is it possible Lord you heard my prayer
Finally sunset - now I got me some money
Faster T'ward home now - got bread, milk and honey

Elizabeth J. Curry

Eternal Night

On the day, I will know,
I will tell you, I will show.
  The sun will flame,
Burning up in the sky,
But when the day comes,
Do not ask why.
  The stars will drop,
When the sun goes down,
Hitting the sea,
Then they may drown.
  The clouds will turn,
Black and grey with hate,
That is when I will state:
Here is the day,
When the sky flames with no light,
This is the day, where it is eternal night.
  Then you will look at me,
With a frown of disgust,
I never lost hope,
But who can I trust?

Jessica Engle

Shall We Meet Again

One day, the time will come
And you and I will meet again
Yes, there may be silence, but
the silence will be content
No, we may not be the same people,
but we will know each other still the same
what has become of me has become of you, and you of I
Once we were strangers, then we were more than
friends, and
now something words cannot explain
Whatever happens in our lives, whether we travel
the same road or not, remember the friendship you
gained along the way
Fear not, for I will always be there whether in the flesh
or in the mind
You have a piece of my heart and that will never change

Katherine Smoak

Time

There once was a creature made of crystal
She lived on a comet that had nowhere to go
She lived in a forest of frost
That dated back to the invention of water
Her house she'd been building
As long as she could remember
From gems that would drift into her reach
She would sometimes sit in her tower for ages
And; with her eyes, feel the distances of space

There once was a creature on expedition
Wondering seeking
With everywhere to go
He came upon a comet
A pretty little place
Touched his ship down for a snapshot or two
He came upon a sculpture
In a tower made of ice
Of a beautiful woman staring at the stars
He took a picture and left, never knowing,
To her eyes, he was only a flash

Chris Sundberg

The Most Precious Gift

Life is the most precious gift that anyone can give,
Everyone has the God-given gift to live.
We should not abuse it, and we should not want
    to lose it

We should live it to the fullest
Take it easy day by day
For we never know when God is going to take it away

I know that sometimes we are driven into a world
    of total dismay,
And wonder about what we did to deserve it
But we must learn to accept those such things, for we must
    learn to accept the things that cannot change
For it is beyond our power

But whenever we feel this way, just turn to God and pray
He will then make things okay
So that we can move on
    as we approach another day
    Natalia Peralta

Little Girl Of Yesterday

Can you remember where the lilacs grow,
And you first played out in the snow,
    Oh! Little girl of yesterday.

Can you recall in days of yore,
Those golden years that were before,
    Oh! Young girl of yesterday.

Do you feel the love that lingers still,
In both our hearts - and always will,
    Oh! Young lady of yesterday.

If you know this now - remember it well,
For we have seen you grow - for quite a spell,
    Oh! Lovely woman of today.

All grown up for the world to see,
But to us - you will always be —
    Our little girl of yesterday!
    Emmi Pomerleau

What's The Difference?

Life — going toward the light
bright and warm — confident of my future
so little — I need you
first step
first word — need a dress for the prom
out on my own — living dreams
touched my heart
knowing your love

Life — going toward the light
blinding, cold and I'm very scared
so little — I need you
first fall — skin my knee
tears fall un-noticed
silent thoughts, no words spoken
that same old dress again
out on my own frightened and all alone
seeing someone else's dreams
the pain the heart feels
not knowing your love
That's the difference . . .
    Kathy Marie Lord

My Uncle Sam

I've got an uncle and his name is Sam
The best darn uncle to have around.
Some people likes him because he chief
Most people like him because his pockets are deep.
We all run to greet him like half grown pups
Wagging our tails and our paws cupped up.
He's a little like santa and santa a lot like him
Every bodies wondering whats in it for them.

He's the only rich uncle I've got around
I treat him like royalty when he comes to towns.
With these words of few; the world can see
Want to say thanks for what he has done for me.
Here's looking at you through his bubbling brew
Thanking you a million and cheers to you.
I will sign off; close up like a clam
A feather for his hat for my uncle Sam.
    Silas S. Owens

The Piper

A strange peculiar shadow
Piping an enchanting tune
Dancing across a midnight valley
We'll be there to follow you soon

Piper your tune is the song of the living
Your music an enchanting spell
All of those listening will follow
And where they are going no one can tell

Piper you give the world its hopes
You give the dreamers their dreams
You stand on the edge of the world
Your flute your working peace

A strange peculiar shadow
Piping your enchanting song
Piper the world is listening
And we shall greet you ere long
    Carol Clark

Sandpipers

Sandpipers exert a special fascination.
Perhaps it is their fragile spun-glass legs
That unbelievably support plump feathered boats of bodies
Skimming them so smoothly over sand.
The birds might just as easily be floating
    on a placid pool
Against a dark tumultuous backdrop
Crests of booming water dashing on the shore.
These come centimeters short of crushing
    winged animated mites
Whose chief subsistence, precious pabulum,
The bounteous ocean spills with roaring chuckles
    Upon the golden stage
    Of his miniature
        Corps de ballet
    Esther F. Ryder

The Morning Song

If one is to have a good day, let it begin with song,
It gives one a soothing good feeling, like being far out at sea;
So peaceful the music sounds when there is no fear, or wrong.
When sailing so gracefully on a ship, such beauty is she,
In tranquility, that confounds all the powers that be.

When it is time, for this old body, to return to the dust,
We will hear His call, and board the old gospel ship, and up we fly;
Being judged by the great righteous one, and found to be just.
We sail over Jordan to Heaven, our new home in the sky,
And sing the new morning song, We Will Never Die!
    John D. Richie

My Sentiment

I often think about how things are put together,
I think about the pattern everything rhymes in
That will be my Sentiment
My Sentiments turn into ideas of opinion and sometimes
 of my knowledge.

This cluster . . . not of ignorance produces an idea,
Repetitiously transforms to a series . . . not of simplicity,
A large complex question . . . most expected,
It clings to my conscience, dancing,
Is it a violent answer?

This large unanswered question will dwell in my mind until
 it is answered, or commonly until it is one small series
 of its kind.

Someday this unanswered question might just be the key to
 my existence.
What is the answer? . . . What is the question?

 Terry Stewart

The Night Before

There are no bombs, no lifeless bodies,
or sounds of guns, no cries, no screams, no
mounting anger. Because this is the Night Before
No need to run, and scream, and cry.
No need to fight or reason to die.
No little children hiding in fear.
No haunting stories passed down through years.
No time to run or reason to fight.
Because this is still the peaceful night.
Despite this night when men are sane.
Deep inside they're full of pain.
Tonight they hide their pain deep inside,
and sleep in peace with natural pride.
None are sure of tomorrow's fight.
But they get their rest on this peaceful night.
No one wants to fight this war,
but it's too late now the night before.

 John Jackson

Mother And Son Valentine Poem

Silent is the soul that quietly floats within,
A caring voice speaks on the outside befriends;
A few months go by the none is the wiser,
Then five exposes the movements of the piper.

As the days progress the new life expands,
One day his being will bring awe to the land;
The mother talks softly to the unborn child,
She knows the coming birth will not be mild.

A closeness is formed and two hearts beat as one,
She awaits the arrival of her unborn son;
As the years drift by there is much sorrow and pain,
With persistence and wisdom they both conquered their own shame.

God has given them both a unique blessing of love,
May it go on forever as gentle as a dove.

 Terry M. Riggle

"Carl"

Angels roam this precious earth,
You were one,
A mother knows at birth.
God sent you from up above,
A son to be so proud of.
The special child,
So meek and mild,
To help his fellowman,
This was Gods plan.
Devoted husband, father, and brother,
Friend to all others.
You gave advice knowing it could hurt,
To that person you would give your shirt.
Taking that chance praying for the best,
Just to help that person was your quest.
On this earth you have done your chore,
So God has taken you to suffer no more.
The memory of Carl forever in my mind,
Will change my life and help man kind.

 Holly Lynn Ramsey

Love

On a Winter's night, it dawned on me,
 that love was fate, fate for me.
When she said to me, I love thee,
My heart sailed away, to the island's sea.
The spider's there, entangled me, like she would soon, do to me.
With the rope hung, the crowd gathered,
 so she sung with me about to shatter.
The knot was tied, with strength of love,
 so soon we cried, for our emotional trove.
We were pleased, but nothing was said,
 far above the trees, our souls were not at all dead.
The physical meant nothing, the other was everything,
separately we were nothing, together we were everything.
My mind and body separated, I could not live without her
 Together once again, we said the words,
 I'll love you again, we saw the bird.
The everlasting Phoenix, oh grateful Phoenix,
 oh please, give us the castings of death.
But on that winter's night, it had dawned on me,
 that love was fate, just fate for me.

 John V. Chmielowiec

The Intelligent Kingdom

He only kills for food
He is curious but knows his limits
He doesn't attempt to change the world
He simply lives with the planet God granted him
He is humane
He is sane

He is not jealous or greedy or vile
He shows compassion
He is harmless
He is necessary to the system

He is being destroyed
He is mutilated millions of times a day
Abused and used
Refused a choice.

He is animal
And he deserves this earth

 Daniell Valenti

Our Love's Understanding

You must remember dear
Our lives are past but here
We learn and live again
An met and loved again.
We understand the problems
And know how we can change
But only God, will tell us
What we will do today

Nancy B. Jensen

To My Valentine

"A rose is a rose"
Yet no man get knows
The mind of woman,
Not since time began!
I know one's warm love
Gentle as a turtle-dove,
Her name is plain Jane
My own Chatelaine;
In her fond embrace
I orbit in space,
Return then from heights
Of ecstatic delights
Eager to fly again!
Be my Valentine forever!

John N. Blow

The Cat And The Bird

Home at the top of the stairs
Looking way down stairs
Staring at the window sill
And sitting very still.

It is a bird with bright and
colorful feathers,
Sitting there due to bad weather

As the still cat moved sneakingly,
The bird without a clue stood eagerly,
Soon the bird almost flew away.

But, then...!
In a flash, the bird was in the
cat's claws,
Eaten by a cat without a pause.,
And one who then licks,
And Kicks it paws.

Cynthia C. Myers

Untitled

Amidst my joys and sorrows
My dreams and hopes
I have every now and then
Tasted the nectar of peace
Making my joy to shine

Life's currents flow ceaselessly
Amidst the sun and stars
From day after day
Carrying the smile of existence
To many shores known and unknown

Waves rise and falls
Flowers bloom and fade
Life grows through births and death
My heart yearns today for its place
At the feet of the endless

Romi Mallik

In Twenty Lines Or Less

I have read in so many papers
and there are so many requests
that, "poets submit their poems."
In "twenty lines or less.?"

The loves, the joys we have known
in which we have been so blessed
can one really gaze on the heart of man
in "twenty lines or less."?

To tell of all the sorrows known
of all partings pain and trees
can one see all those tears that fall
in "twenty lines or less.?"

I fast approach that twenty you, stress
and I really must confess duress, unless
have I my point to you expressed
in "twenty lines.....not less."?

Edwin P. Spivey

Song Of Romance

As the birds sing, I sing, too;
A special love song, I sing to you.

Melodies of love divine,
I am yours and you are mine.

As we sit here, perched on this branch,
May we give our love a chance.

Come, let us fly high into the sky!
Let us share our romantic cry!

As the eagles soar high in the air,
I'm so glad we are a loving pair.

We're so high we fly with ease,
Darling, you're the one I aim to please.

There's a plane, let's fly above it;
Over cloud nine, I really love it!

Now I see the tops of the trees!
Let us glide amongst all of these;
Until we land softly on a branch,
Thank you, Darling, for sweet romance!

Al Thomas

Be My Brother Be My Sister

In the struggle to have real freedom
With understanding, respect, and love
In the struggle to have real peace
With life being maintained on earth

In the struggle to have justice
With laws that apply to all people
In the struggle to maintain honesty
As to be applied to all relationships

Be my brother be my sister

In the struggle to teach children
Give them love and positive morale
Be like clouds creating electricity
Lightning speed morals to be heavenly

Be my sister be my brother

Like gravity helps to balance earth
Let us work together to have harmony
Like earth turns to confirm its life
Let us always replace night with light

Be my sister be my brother
With a desire to show love

Larry Curtiss Davis

Rubber Band Survival

Trifling with a rubber band.
Stretching, snapping, plucking,
and strumming it.
Unaware of the articles value.

Insight into the commodity,
gained at a flying school.
Revealed through a demonstration,
in packing, a safety parachute.

Parachute lines spread across
the floor, folding begins.
Placing systematically at each
gather, a rubber band.

Rip cord pulled! Each rubber
band, designed to slip off, one
by one, regulating the tension,
opening the chute.

A rubber band survival, holding
life in the balance.
Similar to life, delicate,
fragile, and complex.

Pat Bordner

Passing Of A Loved One

Did you ever make a wish
You knew couldn't come true
But made it anyway
It meant so much to you.

A moment of happiness
From out of the past
You wanted to keep forever
But it didn't last.

A loyal friend
To whom you could go
With a song of joy
Or a tale of woe.

You always knew
Deep in your heart
That sometime in the future
You would have to part.

Twenty-two years have passed
That were long and lonely
And now I sit alone
Thinking of you only.

Mary Elizabeth Chapman

No Guessing

If you could succeed,
  in fulfilling a dream,
let not your efforts,
  ever lose their steam.

You must think positive,
  be creative too,
rise above failure,
in all that you do.

As long as you live,
  you can solve your problems,
by thinking logically,
  which destroys mental goblins.

As you rise above failure,
  count each blessing,
the awards received,
  which bear no guessing.

Luke N. Baxter

Mountains

The mountains tall majestic peaks
Gray granite towering above the trees
Dressed in a cloak of snowy white
To pierce the blue of morning light
Each vying for its place with God
Standing strong and naked in the air
No trees can grow or anything
Pink in the early morning light
Turns to a lavender gray
As morning slowly turns to day
The winds whip up a lacy vale
From snow that lay on hill and dale.

Keith John Nichol

Majestic Heartguest

My life is neither up nor down
or fixedly in between.
The mountain from the mole hill
climb and I am on the beam!

No case for upmanship do I display.
Nor do I miss a scene but
growing from the Spark Divine
into a well lit fire.

I'm burning with a joy supreme
Counter clock, clockwise still
anytime you think.

My time has come forever...
My computers are in sync...

I am gathering violets and daisies with
my thoughts and dreaming of roses mild.

The master of the universe resides
within my heart. My child,
And all the things He promised
me are about to start.

C. Wagner

Your Life

The life you live
Is up to you.
It can be wonderful;
It can be lonely too.

Think of others;
Bless them each day.
To do this will bring
Much happiness your way.

Walk to your window;
View the sky above;
Thank your Lord
For His wonderful love.

Virginia B. Brainard

Everyone Dies In Denmark Tonight

Rages turmoil throughout the streets
Screams echo through the night
Searing us to the core
Yet too many walk away
And pretend they cannot hear
Blood is streaming through the streets
Staining all it touches
Making us wince and cry
But so many turn away
Pretending they can't see
Before long, it'll consume us all
Until everyone dies in Denmark tonight

Lenora Popa

Untitled

You are my love
I feel you were sent from above
To open my mind
and be peaceful and kind
to come along
and give me a song
to sing in my heart
till we grow far apart
and the song fades away
it just does not stay
you said "forever we shall be"
you said you would always love me
I thought your heart was pure and true
It was something I thought I knew
But you weren't sent from above
you aren't my love

Sherry L. Olson

Snow Flakes

Winter is a delightful time
Snowflakes fall from heaven afar
Cold and dampness fill the air
Flakes in the image of a star

Look closely at the fancy shapes
Such a brilliant shade of white
Some cling to trees or drop to ground
Others fade right out of sight

Sometimes they all mass together
And pile up on a busy street
Drivers nerves all stray from steady
Walkers are destined for cold wet feet

Always when the snowflakes fall
There is a quiet, silent hush
Then the feeling turns to anger
When the flakes all turn to slush

Roads end up dirty or slick with ice
Trees drooping from massive weight
That changes from the next snow fall
And gladness overcomes all hate

Carl F. Stratton

Graveyard Visit

Dew is sparkling in the sun
And bird song is so sweet;
The sky is blue above me
And grass green at my feet.

My hands are full of flowers,
Their spring colors bright,
As I kneel upon the earth
To place them all just right.

My tears are flowing freely now
And fall on your resting place;
My great sorrow in losing you
Has marked anguish on my face.

It's only your earthly house
Sleeping now beneath the sod;
Your soul has made the journey
To your eternal home with God.

My grief was fleeing quickly
And within my heart a prayer;
I'll wait with happy memories
Until I will join you there.

Betty Daniel Pack

To C.E.

Sing to me!
Your voice I want to hear.
Convince me that it's all real:
The fire in your loving eyes,
The sensation of your touch,
The sweetness of your lips,
The longing, the desire...
The magic of this moment
May it never disappear.
And if it is a dream,
Your song will help it persevere.
Sing to me!

Tatiana D. Sypko

Crustworthy?

If life were a loaf of bread
Would we find the grain of truth?
If life were oil painted red
Would pink be the stain of youth?

If life were a deck of cards
Would everyone follow suit?
If life were left to the bards
Would we harken to the lute?

If life were a common cold
Would it be an easy catch?
If life were pregermined mold
Would it make us want to retch?

If life were National Trust
Would Savings be all a loan?
If life were a bag of dust
Would the vacuum hold its own?

If life were what was just said
Would the words remain uncouth?
If life were a loaf of bread
Would we find the grain of truth?

Floyd David Caplow

And The Wind Whispers Rainbows On Me

A kiss to the wind
as the suns set red.
Embrace the darkness
that looms overhead.
The light of a thousand souls
watches over me.
Into the night
my spirit runs, runs free.
To sleep in dreams
of yesterdays past.
While tomorrow's future
slips away so fast.
Look beyond the eyes in the mirror
watching you.
Look into your heart
for the answers true.

Ron E. Shelton

Untitled

Soldiers can rise above their Sergeant
and his sensitive powers

Because you has another road to Power
which carries him farther

"All spirit do obey Perfect Souls"

Lord Von Feister III

Untitled

Jesus, you taught me about your church
To go, listen and pray
To receive the holy Eucharist
Which is you in every way.

You shed your blood for me
and brought a new life for me to see.
Still of ups and downs
But of better things to be.

Now I'm alone
With you as my guide
You'll give me the direction
With your arms open wide.

I say to you Lord
I desire to love someone
what's in God's will
That's what will be done.

Marygrace Esposito

Winter's Blight Of Soul

As the tree limbs lay drooped
   As if some burden to bare,
Carrying a load
   That they did not ask to share,
Strive in their strength
   To hold their own,
Knowing that now
   Most of their sap is gone.
Laid heavy with ice
   From winter's wintery storm
Wondering what scars
   Will have to be worn.

Winter's blight, in its pure form,
   Reminds me of the heavy burdens
That, at times, lay on
   Man's very heart, soul and mind.
At times not asked for,
   A caused moment in time,
Rides on the inner strength
   That also wears with time.

Winona Hamm

Out Of The Darkness

Our eyes are wonderful things,
Because of the light it brings.

One morning, instead of sight,
My right eye was black as night.

I was in terror, screaming..
"Please God, let me be dreaming."

My eye examination,
Was only aggravation.

My retina was detached
And it would have to be patched.

Laser surgery for me,
Was the only way to see.

Once again, I can see light
and it makes my future bright.

Joseph M. Snyder

Lonely Shadow

Shadows hold no fear
for me,
I have seen them dancing about
on twinkle toes,
or vivid rows and rows
of quiet repose,
Stretching out and reaching out
to me . . .

Two shadows entwined and roaming
with me,
I have felt their desire,
The empty space of their hearts
yearning to glow like the evening star,
Glowing all the brighter
for me . . .

For I don't go chasing after dreams,
And I am not a shadow chaser,
Only one silhouette remains . . .
Lonely shadow bending inward
bending in to find a friend.

Carolyn Gresham Cook

Enclosure

Square the grass
   and circle the moon.
Harness the stone
   to trouble the breeze.

Pipe the reeds
   for love song's gurgle.
As by the languid eye
   rests the curve.

Lace the thoughts
   'til wooded hills.
Howl her silence
   in scarlet streaks.

Stroke the pallid
   noonday hour.
Whilst feasting on
   time's fossil bones.

Came the laughter
   from reflection.
Dew and salty tear...
   Swallows in the air.

Kathryn J. Davis

Life In The Old Lane

Life in the old lane,
has uglied my face.
Time, stolen my beauty,
from every place.

While gazing in the mirror,
how terrifying! Is this me?
I see barrels of fat,
where my waist use to be.

Life in the old lane,
age taking its claim.
The rewards given,
only wrinkles and pain.

Life in the old lane,
attacks, twists and bend.
Shouts, victory! Victory!
When life has ended.

Hazel Morris

Winter's Pause

Let me not, O Heavenly Father,
Only is summer sing, when
Skies shine bright and rivers flow.
Let me today find delight
In winter walks and gentle snow.
May I feel the caress of
Soft flakes upon my cheek
And see the clouds play leap-frog
Down valleys, still and deep.

Sometimes I wonder as
Seasons so swiftly fly;
Does God wrap in beauty
Distant hills in purple haze
And light the stars of heaven
That we, his errant children,
Might pause to thank and praise,
And contemplate the blessings
He showers all our days?

Alice Dommer Berg

The Sea Of Life

I feel the surge of life around
Me flowing like an ocean wave
The ocean lifts me slowly to its crest
Then let me slide down to my grave
The universal light we share
gives each a torch which different goal
In some the flame consumes the flesh
In others dreams may sear the soul
However weak the sparks we hold
They're falling somewhere on the sea
What part they play we'll never guess
In life's un-ending mystery
Reincarnation might reveal
Some clues from flotsam on the sea
But final charts are held by God
Aboard His ship, "Eternity!"

Leland Embert Andrews

Sunset

We should have walked into the sunset
Hand in hand
Until we both had met
A new and foreign land
Where we could put aside
All burdens dragged for years
Where both of us could hide
In freedom from all fears.

Your shadow just passed by
In sunset all alone
I thought I recognized
Your face, your voice, its tone
Why I am left behind
No sense in this I find
Why couldn't we two be
Together in eternity?

Karin Dovring

Untitled

Frostbitten ol' man
   sittin' on a steam vent
eatin' cookies
   Thunderbird drippin'
on his Goodwill shoes

Charles Bernard Rodning

A Letter From Key West
907 Whitehead Street

Dearest Mr. Hemingway,
Not odd that I should write this day,
From this place you loved, Key West.
A favorite place of Harry and Bess,
Where the "Little White House" stands,
Decisions made by that true man.
Where sunshine beams in skies of blue,
And green waves wisp, some Emerald, too.
Where Navy bands did once parade,
While Acacia trees provide the shade.
Where long and gentle sunsets reach,
Toward water blue and combs the beach,
And starfish lie and sun themselves,
Along the coral ocean shelves.
Ernest, seems, not much does change,
The cats and garden withstood the rains,
I hope this letter finds you free,
To come again to visit me,
Respectfully,
   Your "Old Man of the Sea".

Jack DeYoung

The Laser

In that tiny inner world
Hidden from all mortal eyes,
Where the atoms plot their goal
To absorb and energize,
There enters in a stream of light,
Rousing all the tiny things
That migrate between the tiers,
Propelled as if by mighty wings.
In this charged, excited state,
Atoms do their tenants cast
Swift into the outer orbits,
Only to reel them in as fast.
All the host of quickened beings
Join the dance of rapture bright,
Striving with their radiant souls
To form their own peculiar light.
Then this light as if inspired,
Enamored of its own reflection,
Intensifies with wild abandon
And casts a beam with fixed direction.

Henry M. Ditman

Slash

I have a dog living in my house
With the fitting name of 'Slash'.
He has an alligator mouth
And a set of teeth to match.

If he decided to crash a party,
No one could dare refuse him;
For he is of such formidable size,
It would be foolish to abuse him.

Yet, 'Slash' is a very gentle dog;
For, when standing to his full length,
And placing his paws on my shoulders,
He doesn't shove me with all his
   strength.

He loves to play "Catch" with any limb
That he, sometimes, chances to see;
But it wouldn't be very surprising
To see "Slash" bring me the entire tree.

Jack A. Feldman

Thought's

A thought is a picture in the mind,
Although no one can see your thoughts,
They are there for you to find
And build something from the mind.

Some unknown inventive thing,
Even a piece of unwritten writing
That others admire and read each day
Or even a song for you to sing.

A thought can be very positive
And impress upon your mind,
But as you think, what is a thought?
It maybe something for you to find.

Edison, making the first light bulb,
As a thought first in his mind,
Placed there for a good reason,
Was an invention for him to find.

He brought forth the thought that came,
And it made honor for him, in his day
Lighting the whole world from thought,
He did it, in many important ways.

Eileen Corey Norwood

Senryu Secular Miscellanea Five

Pachinko Mom:
   Pachinko jinglings
   So cheer a young mom to leave
   Her baby in cart.

Fear in aging:
   Aged men count down
   Remainders as decreasing
   In lives and savings.

Politician's songs:
   Politicians sing
   Sweet fake songs before voting
   Facts after winning.

Puppy in spleen:
   Even a pup bites back
   His fond madam's fragrant shin
   When his paw is squished.

Pesky squirrel:
   A pesky squirrel
   Fell off my rigged bird feeder
   While stretching four legs.

Esaku Kondo

The Birds Were Happy

A cheery "Hello" to you
so the birds said to me
they seemed to be so happy
and contented
as they were sitting in a tree

When I looked at them in a tree
and wondered why they were so happy
they don't worry about nothing
like you and me

So we should take lessons
from the birds that come here
they come every year
and they don't have no fear,

They then flew in the tree
and returned to their nests
They were so happy and gay
as they did their best

Dolores Mahan

Untitled

Life is complex with its
   pain and relief,
In the midst of our happiness
We're visited with grief.
A deliberate balance to keep
   us in tow,
reassures us thought joy will
   pass
So to will our woe.

Patti Sires

Romance

The passion from my heart will
forever last;
And I walk in the darkness and
am afraid to let you know,
I love you and never want to let
you go.

Can you hear me;
Sweet lover of mine?
Hear my joy, my sorrow, my pain,
that I can not hide.

Do you feel the way I feel,
Oh man of my dreams?
Do you know my heart ache;
when I see you with another?
Can you stop this pain
that's deep inside of me?

Will you hold me again and will
this be forever?

Christia Upton

Firefly

Firefly, where are you flying
   In the sky so dark and blue?
Do you know where you are going?
   May I come along with you?

Can we ride through the night-time?
   Can we see what there's to see?
It's these times when I'm so lonesome.
   Won't you please come back to me?

Where do you go when it is raining?
   Do you hide under the leaves?
What do you when the wind is blowing?
   Are you too weak for the breeze?

Oh, I envy you my firefly
   To be flying and be free.
To be lighting up the darkness
   So our paths are clear to see.

Firely, where are you flying
   In the sky so dark and blue?
Do you know where you are going?
   May I come along with you?

Lisa Y. Eskin

Lazareth Jones

I face the wind and accept its fury
Forbidden, forgiven, forlorn
A strange man offered his hand
Ragged, tattered and torn.
Kind eyes did smile
Alas for a while
Until his soul became unborn.

Steven L. Craig

Calm After The Storm

Thank you Lord,
  For stormy weather that makes
Us seek the calm together
  Thank thee for written word
And wonderful song that speaks
  Of life forever.
I've searched the world
  Found no release tried man's way
Found no peace but in searching
  The scriptures, I found
An open door that lifted me
  From the valley floor.
The message of eternal life
  We shall not all sleep-
But we will be changed
  Through life with God,
We're re-arranged in truth
  And grace we will not stop-
There's Victory!!
  On the mountain top.

Callie M. Moss

Mom's Eulogy

(Pauline Hoffman)
With a heart filled with love
She taught us right from wrong
Always gave us what she could
That helped to make us strong

Nothing was there that she had
To lighten the cross she had to bear
Twelve of us she raised full grown
On what little bit was there

When we were sick or we were hurt
Right by our bed she stayed
The silent vigil of our Mother
All the while she wept and prayed

Thank you "Lord" for giving us
The greatest Mother that could be
Take her into "Your" sacred house
For now she belongs with "Thee"

Francis Hoffman

Forefathers

They sailed across the ocean
Searching to be free
Leaving home and family;
Searching to be free.

Some were Lords and Ladies
Other common thieves
Each had a glorious vision;
Searching to be free.

No fame or fortune called them
From the lands from which they came
Only visions of a future;
Searching to be free.

They faced the hardships bravely
They formed a country free
Leaving us a legacy,
While searching to be free.

We call them our forefathers
We praise the work they've done
Let's continue with their mission,
Let's keep our country free.

Joyce A. Daniels

(Friendship)

Friends of yesterday
and the promises that were
forever in yesterday's past,
where the autumn leaves had fallen
on the memories that once were
carved on a Red Wood Tree,
where friendships were shared
and thoughts were forever
remembered in yesterday's past,
where honesty and trust was
always there in the autumn leaves
that had fallen from the branches
of the Red Wood Tree, where
virtue was precious
in yesterday's past.

Paul Holland

Something About A Sunrise

There's "Something About A Sunrise"
That makes the heart feel warm
Just like a soft gentle breeze
After midnight's raging storm

There's "Something About A Sunrise"
When the black of night is gone
And all the darkness that you felt
Flees with the break of dawn

There's "Something About A Sunrise"
As it shines across the skies
When you see the beauty of a Hand
That fills the heart with, why's

There's "Something About A Sunrise"
That fills the heart with fears
As they wonder what will happen
Before the night appears

There's "Something About A Sunrise"
They come and then they go
Yes, There's "Something About A
Sunrise"
That no man seems to know

Bob Lang

Stop The Violent

It's killing the young and the old
they are being dead in the street
why can't we just meet
and be friend not enemy
and love one another like we can
turn to Jesus he will show us the way
Violent will knock you off your feet
stop carry guns in the street
just be sweet and you will see
how love can really be
you and me no more blue no more
tear, you will be here not over there
this is for all to hear
stop the violent and show that we care
stop stop stop the violent every where

Rachel Elizabeth Neal

Visions Of The Future

An unknown world lies ahead . . .
We are uncovering secrets
Allowing new questions to arise
What lies ahead . . .
Only time will tell
. . . An unknown world lies ahead

Josh Haskins

Island Portrait

Rows on rows of spruce trees
Dot the island,
Rising verdant
From the sheer gray rock
To which they cling tenaciously.
Here and there a hungry osprey
  hovers;
Clasping its food in talons
  sharp and keen.
A clear-cut figure
Stands against the misty curtain
  of fog
For just a moment until it
  slowly fades
And melts into the mist.

Mildred N. Thayer

Untitled

I sent a poem to you
  I didn't win a prize
However, it was published
  Now in black and white it lies...

You told me it was wonderful
  You made me feel so grand;
Then among a thousand other
  grains upon the land
I finally found My shining golden
  little grain of sand.

Dorothy Allen Nicholson

Sleep

Come the sunrise, my peaceful sleeps
Ends
The dawning of a new day
another day filled with
Pain
At mid-day, my heart and head
both ache
I need the night.
Sundown — I'm almost there
The only peace I know is while
Sleeping
Except for the dreams
that haunt me
Please
I need peaceful slumber.

Denice Peterson

Searching

Throughout our life we're searching
For something we don't know
It might be wealth or happiness
But it helps us as we grow
Progress seems slow going
We have our upsets too
But if we keep our goal in mind
It will help to see us through
Peace of mind we have it
For we never thought we could
Although we never found our goal
We were searching as we should
The moral of this story
Is searching you must go
And if your life is a happy one
Well that something...now you know.

Barbara A. Reed

Indian Summer

Indian summer crept in last night.
The clear blue sky, a starry sight.
Nature's air so crisp and cold,
Trees all dressed in scarlet and gold.
Trembling leaves fall to the ground,
Wafting freely with out a sound.
Smoky haze, o'er rolling hills,
Ghostly outlines of sky and rills.
Fields all covered with tan and brown,
New fallen snow their winter's crown.
Harvest time of ripened fields,
Bounteous harvest that nature yields.
Corn-sentinels standing tall,
Frosty pumpkins, snow covered all,.
A final flash of red-orange sky,
Bold wintry clouds, way up high.
Indian Summer, we cannot hold,
'Tis end of summer, so we're told.

Edna Leonard

The Heart Of Home

The heart of home is the Mother
Making it happy and secure,
With her wisdom and her courage
And a life that is good and pure.

The patient way she listens,
Then her council with a smile;
Giving hope and that encouragement,
Which makes life become worthwhile.

Her gracious and loyal manners,
Her love for the best in life,
Her triumph over heartbreak,
Makes her a champion over strife.

God's plan from the beginning
Established the family order;
A Righteous Man to be the Head,
But the Heart of the Home is the Mother.

With tender love, he'll guide and lead,
Showing the right way for all to go,
While she supports and sheds the light,
That binds the home, to make it glow.

Therlow R. Leach

A Greeting Card And A Flower

A greeting card and a flower
With the holidays.
Coming ever so close

And you are at as loss
For words
All you need is a greeting card
And an envelope to close

To be in tune with
The holiday spirits

So don't be a loner
In the crowd
Get on board
The merry go round

With a greeting card
In your pocket
And a flower
In your hand
Is all the message
You will need
To win her hand

John J. Chironno

Thoughts Of Doing Good

Thoughts from the head
About doing this or that
May never get done.
But if they do, it could be
For the wrong reason.

Thoughts from the heart
About doing this or that
May always get done
For the right reason.

Floyd W. Danley

The Flute Player

Kokapelli, your music haunts me,
your flute, whistles to my heart.
I am drawn to the canyon's edge
and made to feel as if I were a part,
of that ancient, mysterious place,
that I seek through the music I hear,
oft times wondering, why I can't see you
if the melody is oh so near.
Come, deeper into the canyon,
find what makes your heart free,
am I alone in this music,
are you playing it just for me?
You are the casanova of the canyons,
this I cannot refute...
for I fell in love with the music
that comes from your magical flute.

Sandra E. Beguhn

Beach At Night

I have found a way to fly
Jump where there is nowhere to jump
Turn away when there is no room to move
Forget all that was taught
Never look back
There is no going back
Just let go — and soar
Fly like the wind
Move like the tide
I am not the same person
I have become one who has travelled
To unknown realms
Where I know not what goes on
I have moved along this new road
I owe this way to you
It was you who showed me the way
The moon is in my eyes
And so now is this one
Only in my eyes, only in my mind
The once reality, slowly dies.

Virginia Anne Bautista

The Meaning Of Love

Now, I know what love means
But to discover the meaning
I had to have a broken heart
At love, I learned not to play
But by the time I found this out
Your love for me, you let die
So I found out, much too late
How much love really meant

Howard A. Deaton

A World For Two

Love is this sharing

A world for two,
Awake,
Or sleeping,
Together renewed each moment,
Infinite in proof,
Truth's diurnal presence
Of word, smile, touch,
Equal need,
And equal giving,
Ambiance of nurturing desire,
Feast of mind,
Remembered music,
Beloved books,
Names,
Tremulous with beauty,
And haunting sensuality
Of intimate joy

Love is this sharing.

Bill C. West

Why Can't We

If I offer my hand
will you extend yours?
If we should meet
Just nod or show a smile
you see we are
bellow travelers
on this planet
for such a short while
Lets forget past hurts
Suspicion - distrust and
violent trends
so again I ask
Why can't we be
Just friends?

Ellen F. Krummel

The Apple

When somebody is too afraid to admit
he has something important to say,
the inhibiting factors
which cause him not to
speak define the nature
of modern alienation.

Between steel bars, the
death row patient is
ready to fly, but the
time never seems appropriate.

Launching into a kinetic
daydream, other-worldly
creatures
from an even
darker dream ruin
his sense of
finality.

And as the grass grows green
under the trees,
he plucks off a ripe apple and seethes

Mike McNair

Thunder

People who fight can only hear
   the thunder!
People who can get along can
   chase the thunder away!

Nelva Kimberly Grossnickle

In The Countryside

A hike in the countryside
on any day or time,
makes me feel like a kid again
when I was in my prime.

The scenery relaxes me
it brings a smile to my face,
to see the detailed beauty
of this magical place.

From a cow I hear a moo
and from a horse I hear a neigh,
it's like they're saying "hello" to me
as I head on my way.

I look up into the sky
the clouds are a joy to see,
I imagine they are angels
looking over me.

Being in the countryside
puts a sparkle on my face,
to see the breathtaking beauty
of this far and spread out place.

Martin H. Degener

USA Women - All The Way

Here they stand
Side by side,
Nobody here
Along for the ride.
Seven together
They stole the show,
Each one wearing
The Olympian glow.

Six are okay
 one is in pain
But she grabbed
The glory today.
No more shadow
For this young lady
 only moxie
And tenacity.

So proudly they stand
 heart in hand,
Around each neck
They hold the gold.

Barbara L. Scott

Freedom

I'll never have the chance
To live the real you
Day into Night into Day
Eating into all I have
Knowing what I knew
Escape possession - I stay.

Face into the mirror
For thirty missing smiles
Losing too much sleep at night
Face lost in the mirror
Days splashed against the wall
So tired, surrender the fight.

Your lead, followed, led the way
A rainbow path - you said.
Freedom is in your head
Chained to my bed alone
With you, someone might see
There's someone who wishes me dead.

Marcia K. Roberts

Life Is But A Day That Ends

I
The dawn
Wakes the sleeping world,
Rousing the forlorn to new life
With more strength
To plod through the toils of the day,
While the burdens they carry
Weakens.

II
Sunset
Marks the close of day
And signals out the milestones passed
On the road
Of life's journey, long and weary
With all its travels ending
In death.

III
Then we'll shed this life
With all its earthly strife
For a hope to live forever
With the God of love
In His eternal home above.

Rufus W. Johnson

In Loving Memory Of Bob Craven

Someone whose love we all have shared
Has passed from us to the great beyond
Our thoughts and prayers
Fly with him to heaven.
His laughter and wisdom
We've come to treasure
Is something that most people
Can't even measure.
His soul is shared by one and all.
So as we mourn
Our tears of sorrow
His heart is still with us
And will be for all the tomorrows.

Linda Streng

Interlude In E-Flat Minor

And there was an intersection,
And the winds were passing by.
I was standing in reflection
In the middle of July.

In the middle of the summer
Under red-green blinking guide
Life had turned into a bummer;
I had something to decide.

And there was the path behind me,
But I did know where it led;
And I feared to take so blindly
The unknown way ahead.

I was standing in a doubt
At the cross-roads of my life;
I was getting tired out
Of this useless bitter strife...

Sounds of music, children's laughter
Reached me from somewhere afar;
And I made a step. And after —
Up on high I've seen a star.

Alexander Celebrowski

Color Between The Lines

One never knows
How deeply entwined
Our lives may be
If we color between the lines

The generations of past
A gray area of times
They were not permitted
To color between the lines

If we stay above
All the strife
How can we learn
And experience life

Painting the color
Only on a straight line
one may never learn
The true concept of time

Each generation has its limits
We are a product of times
We may now, indeed
Color between the lines.

Rose E. Hollingsworth

Little Boy Red

I love the way you look at me,
the way you smile and tilt your head,
the tenderness of your caress,
I love you, my little boy Red.

Even though you're always kind,
you are a pixie in disguise;
you always smile, you never cry;
you bring excitement to my mind.

Is it the red hair that you wear,
is it the twinkle in your eyes,
is it the way you show you love me;
or it is the fire in my heart.

My little boy Red, I love you,
'til the sky meets the sea;
that's how long our love will be,
I love you, my little boy Red.

Gina Daidone

The Letter

My dear friend, my star, my love,
I'll open window for two doves,
And let them go to fly away,
And bring the world my letter pray.

My pray to you, my pray to me,
My pray for all who lives on earth.
Let love be in the hearts my dream,
Let love will blossom like a rose.

And love will sing you like a bird,
If heart you open for her song.
She'll teach you all the best in world,
With love you never be alone.

But never let your love be sad,
Please never let your love to cry,
For love like rose can simply die
When windy rain her lonely friend.

Oksana Julia Orlenko

Sometimes Perfection

We drove
    the two of us
a bit on edge
    with each other
and with the rain.

Skies cleared
    to an earth
showered fresh
    and skies
powdered blue.

A double rainbow
    perfect in formation
extended before us
    and swallowed the earth
north to south.

Colors were vivid
    and absolute.
For a minute or two
    our souls enraptured
we viewed perfection.

Darlene Cree Johnson

Christmas For Children

A rousing welcome and triumphant cheer,
"Christmas,"
Will soon be here.
A treasure in all its glory,
Faith, love and worship
Reveal the story.
Heartfelt love is
Extended to all,
For donations and volunteered efforts,
None too small.

But, the perfect part of the season,
Is love of our children
No higher power of reason.
Christmas day all over the nation,
The greatest day of innovation.
It's God we must thank
For the children we share,
With "Worship and Trust."
Our hearts, forever, will be there.

Del Meader

Time

Why is it so that we blame time
When we have been delayed?
For without time where would we be
If time had only stayed?

Time shan't wait for any man
Says his tics and tocs,
For man can't even capture time
By turning back his clocks.

Shouldn't we cherish all our time
For promised time is taled,
And any man who has lost his time
His sure result is failed.

Looking back so long ago
Time then came to pass,
Now looking forward many years
Time doesn't have to last.

It is time we've looked on time
And valued what it's worth,
For without time there is no life
And therefore there's no birth.

Cherrile J. O'Garro

Endless Search

The hand that I long to hold,
The eyes that I long to behold,
The face that I long to caress,
The body that I long to undress,
The lips that I long to connect with,
The heart that I long to share with.

Where are you my sweet love,
    Where are you?

Andrew Turnbull

Little Green Frog

This is the story about a little
    green frog
Who hatched from an egg to
    become a pollywog
He absorbed his great tail one
    day for his dinner
Then hoped onto a lilly pad a
    great deal thinner.
He's so proud of the many warts
    on his skin
As are piglets the hair on their
    chinny chin chins
He stays awake chirping songs
    all through the night
Drooping lids o'er popped eyes
    make a comical sight.
When his tongue flecks out to catch
    any bug in flight
His rubber faced grin is every
    child's delight.

Mary Estright de Minico

Masterpiece

Some things are hard to see;
For instance, the exact moment in time
That we have come to be
So, we use our hearts to feel
And our minds to comprehend
And, a clear painting is portrayed
Within the depths of our souls
A masterpiece
A precious, yet boldly strong friendship
That can recognize no beginning
And see no end.

Anita V. Gangadin

Ageless

Aged,
Care-worn faces
With sunken
Filmy eyes;
Beseeching you for kindness,
For gentleness - of touch.
Reaching out
With gnarled, sand-paper hands
To grasp - your hand.
Seeking the touch
Of humankind,
Seeking ageless love
Of human being for human being.

Edith M. Bowen-Wilcox

Broken Window

The windows broke
who threw the brick?
Glass shattered
Like the family mattered
It was just a joke

The glass is split
like mom and dad is
Where did it go wrong?
Family is gone
like the broken window

The pain we felt
When the glass fell
The blood from the cuts
Fall like our tears
but the cut's to deep to cry

All we heard was crash
Who was that?
it was a slap
Who let in dad?
It was the window smashing

Jeremy McNeil

Summersaults
And Backward Flips

The moral
of a story,
makes that
story be,
that's what leaves
the story's
impression, on me!
When, it's sad
then, so, am, I,
sometimes I
might even cry,
if, it's, boring
and kind of dry,
I hurriedly,
pass it by!
When it's, happy
the funny type of quips,
I feel like
doin' summersaults
and backward flips!

John Search

Concealment

The radiant sun
Shines in my eyes, closing them
Wishing I not see.

Kristina Allende

"Hear The God's Laughing"

We mortals live
such complex lies,
of vanity and self importance.
If we only knew,
what is really true.
We would be so disappointed.

How the God's must laugh,
How they must cry.
At such fools as you, and
Especially I!

Penny James

Untitled

Day or night
Ocean or sea
Up above
And lower than me
Questions, answers
Who know's why
Who know's anything
Maybe everything's a lie
Fact to me
But false to you
Opinions vary
Which is true
Life is short
Life is fun
But no remote
For anyone
Questions answers
Who even cares
Just go with life
And all will be fair.

Elena Berzon

The Cookies

I went to get a cookie.
I opened up the box.
I really wanted cookies,
Not tuna fish or lox.
Inside, to my displeasure,
Were beetles, worms and dust.
A thriving bug community,
My cookies were a bust.

I threw them in the garbage.
I cursed and blamed myself
For leaving them too long a time
Upon the cookie shelf.
I guess I won't have cookies;
I let them get too old.
I'll have a piece of cheese instead.
Oh, Heavens! Fuzzy mold!

Judith Weintraub

The Transformation

Watch the metamorphosis,
that our body's undergo;
when your every touch makes me tingle,
while my touch makes your love grow.
As our breathes become heavy,
and our voices become low,
and as you prepare to enter,
a place where no other man will go;
You slowly proceed to touch,
The very essence of my being;
our eyes closed tightly shut,
I hope you can see what I am seeing.
And as I feel you thrust,
into the center of my universe
it feels like a balloon just burst
as your juice quenches my thirst.
and while I feel you inside,
your movements are gentle yet abrupt;
I feel how in and out you glide,
as I wrap my legs around you and erupt.

Na'Tiki C. Patterson

Eternity

A space within a space, within a space
    the world turns over and in,
    solid mass is empty,
    yet space is full, so full.

An eye within an eye, within an eye.
    The wheels go on and on.
    We look but do not see
    and touch without response.

A world within a world, within a world
    goes through and in and on.
    I am space yet I am full.
    I am all eternity.

Ruth Craig

My Own Place

Once there was a place for me,
deep away upon a tree,
up so high, near that blue sky,
fingernails of beauty green,
view so pleasant to be seen,
bond with birds that live so near,
grateful thoughts, feeling no fear,
watching the world move below,
all of those things seem so slow,
breezy winds begin to soothe,
close my eyes, feeling the groove,
my own place to get away,
though soon I will have to move,
for if I could I would stay.

Scott Allan Taube

The Miracle Of You

    You brought new meaning to
my life... Understanding...
A direction in life...
    Each day... To learn
more about you... To be
told... "How fortunate I am"
To love.... The miracle of you...
    Each day... New meaning...
To the depths of your being...
Of caring... Understanding...
Loving... In my experience
Of loving you...
    In life... Together...
You will always know... My
depth of love... In loving you...
    I've been blessed... With
the miracle of you...

Billy L. Angevine

We're Moving

We're moving
From north to south,
Sold our home,
Don't have one now.

We're moving.
No home in sight.
God will help
With Jesus' might.

Ruth Copechal

"Years Ago"

It seems like years and years ago,
But it was only yesterday;
Now you're just a memory,
You have left and gone away.
I wish my heart was pure again;
So that you could quench its thirst;
I wish I could go back in time;
Than you would be my first.
I wish my soul could sing a song;
With words to set you free;
And to show the world before I die;
How very much you mean to me.

Elaine Mary Boyle

Happy Anniversary My Love

We have now been,
    married for five years.
Through the joy of birth,
    and parental fears.

I feel as though,
    we make a good team.
Sure hope the rest of our,
    years make you gleam.

I love you more now,
    than from the start.
And pray each night,
    that we'll never part.

So Happy Anniversary,
    my dear.
Now let's get started,
    on our sixth year.

Denise Birch

Air Force People

These people,
coming from afar,
will reach the stars.
Their futures look good.
Working,
Together as they should.
These people, of a special source,
are the ones of the U.S. Air Force.

Karen Morris

A Covenant Of Love

As we say these vows together
May our love last forever
With these rings I do wed thee
Pledging our love and our trust
These rings are but a symbol
A symbol of a contract
A contract God calls a covenant
A covenant of love

If our love should ever fail us
And strife should come between us
Let us always remember
This contract we made together
This contract God calls a covenant
A covenant of love

As we grow old together
Going through those gates of Pearl
Let us always remember
This contract that keeps us together
This contract God calls a covenant
A covenant of love

Charles Patterson

Well, Fudd

Her morals were spoon-fed
From a can labeled passive
Her thoughts through an IV
She wants life instead
Stands by her window
Or so she's been told
As far as the world knows
She's about two months old

So, carry me someone
I'm too lazy for feet
When the world waits behind
Then the world I shall meet
And if he was a rock
Then I am a boulder
As I stand here brooding
With grief on my shoulders

In one hand, Identity
Then in the other her mind
She's spent all eternity
Chasing dreams blind.

Kelly Queener

Pleading

We thank you Lord Jesus
every single day
let us sing this prayer
we are completely yours.
we cover your path
with roses and tulips
and beautiful music
fill the words of Love.
We adore you Lord
with the faith you give us
and the precious peace
that keeps us olive.
O Lord we adore you
please give us good health
in our minds and our body
fill our hearts with light.
You the only God
Please rein in our hearts
We adore you Lord
Please make us alive.

Fausto A. Velez

Shadows Of The Night

Two lovers meet in secret
in the shadows of the night
to share a desire
that's burning deep inside
the grass of green
beneath their feet
will be their bed tonight
and the moon
up in the heavens
will be their only light
no words are ever spoken
they both know that it's right
and when the passions over
in the heat of the night
they both lye in silence
each soul satisfied
knowing they'll be lovers
again in the night.

Linda Clark

The Volunteer

He picked up the phone
one cold, blistery night
and on the other line
he was told to bring a good light.

High and low
they searched all around.
There was a little girl
who needed to be found.

As everyone searched
they wished it was a dream.
Down by the creek
someone let out a scream.

Their blood ran cold
as they found the first clue.
Some ripped up clothes
and one bloody shoe.

The test came back
leaving no stone unturned.
The parents finally knew
their girl will never be returned.

David Westerman

Life's Garden

Look at the lovely flowers.
They grow one by one in a row;
The yellow, green and blue,
The red on pink - like a bow.

All delightful, little flowers,
Growing in my garden bed;
How much I love to look at them,

Especially the bow-like pink and red.
Beholding my flower garden,
Reminds me of God above,
Who made each one of us different,
And showered on us - His love.

For flowers are like people,
Emerging in different color and shape.
Alone, they are "just ordinary",
But together, an elegant bouquet make.

Ruth Gambino

Fear Not The Storm

When the dark clouds roll in
and God darkens the day;
He's letting you know
He'll guide your way;
When you see the lightening
mixed with the shower.
He's letting you see
his magnificent power;
The thunder's his voice
To let you hear;
He's there to protect you
so have no fear;
When you feel the wind
which you cannot see;
He's whispering,
"I'm with you for eternity".

Wanda Hughes

Jesus Loves You

You're very special to Jesus
He knows you by your name,
Each hair on your head He's counted
For your sins He took the blame.

He walks with you each day
Watches over you at night,
Listens to every word you pray
Intercedes to make things right.

Oh, what blessings you encounter
When you let Him be your guide,
Pray to follow as He leads you
And don't ever leave His side.

You may not think it possible
To have a love as this,
But all you need to do is ask
He has so much to give.

You'll never be alone
So this is what you do,
Just picture Jesus sitting
There, right next to you.

Verona Duchrow

Too Close

The walls keep moving inward,
A bit each day,
Choking me,
Suffocating me!

No where to go,
No where to run,
Caught in a web,
Unable to get out.

Nobody can see
How much it's hurting me -
I want to get out,
And have fun for once!

These damned walls are too close,
And I wish with all my heart,
That I could break them down,
And be free!

Dawn Roof

Santa Ana Winds

You can sit and stare at the sky
And wonder if it ever ends
You can sit alone at night
And listen to the crying wind

Santa Ana Winds are blowing
And it's making me blue
Santa Ana Winds are blowing
But what can I do

And if I could change the tide
Then I could change the moon
If I could change the weather
Then I would be changing you

Santa Ana Winds are blowing
And it's bringing me rain
Santa Ana Winds are blowing
And I'll never be the same

Another night, another wind
Another day, another one ends
I want to hold you but I'll pretend
I long to feel Santa Ana Winds

Jeffrey Ray Boyd

Guardian Angel

All people have a Guardian Angel.
Some see them,
Some don't.
Some have wings.
My Guardian Angel is a man.
He states he's dead.
A being of darkness.
Yet he sheds light.
How can this be?
I don't know, but he's mine.
And a guardian to so many more.

Goodnight ... And dead keep.

Terry Jackson

Senses Of Spring

I see the brook running
with the melting snow.
I feel a gentle breeze that
in the air doth blow.
I hear the frogs croaking and
the sparrow's song sweet
I taste may halls that fall on
my bare feet.
I smell honey suckles that are
like rare perfume.
I feel God's presence and
sing a happy tune.
There's something in this
season that sparks a melody
causing me to rejoice in
the things my senses let me see!

Renee Wascom

Unconditional Love

It cannot be bought
It cannot be sold
It comes to use free
And can never grow old.

It cannot be borrowed
It cannot be earned
It is never deserved
This we must learn.

Our hearts must be open
And willing to hold
A gift without limits
And graces untold.

It comes to us pure
On the wings of a dove
This blessing from God
Unconditional love.

C. J. Sexton

A Fledgling Diplomat

He dreamt of world peace
   as a man of youth
He worked for justice
   and human rights.

He dreamed the world saved
   as a man of middle age
And promoted by serene language
   a safer place to stay.

He saw the world in chaos
   as a wizened man of age
And dreamt of fledgling diplomats
   dreaming of world peace.

David Greeley

The Essence Of My Poetry

Would that some prodigious rare perfume
eloquently blended by this hand,
become an exquisitely packaged
gift to open and savor.
It's fragrance born of prudent measure.

No flowers bloom within my garden.
Nor pregnant seeds upon one daisy.
To coax and nurture into fields of.
To pluck then press between these pages.
Denied of excellence's ecstasy.
Doomed by my own mediocrity.

Know this . . .
I wanted to will you CHANEL's equal,
and not this soon forgotten scent.
Many paint yet few originate.
And many poems are written.

Alice Clay Johnson

Untitled

That scholarly novelist Drabble
Claimed sex was meant merely for rabble,
   Observing that she
   Remained fancy free
And much preferred games such as
Scrabble.

Armand E. Singer

A Grandma's Love

Seldom Heard
I love you both -
Seeing so little of the-
The children's children-
Loving far afar!
The needs so seldom known
The slow time of waiting -
So fast the growing in age:
The picture's! Unshared!
Happy just to receive that much!!
Oh the faces!
Wanting more than their is!!
The priceless love!!
A grandpa's lost-
The high cost of travel - yet forgotten-
40's should be free to children!!—Free!

P. Vivian Cote

Untitled

Please be kind, gentle, and warm,
For I am very fragile.

Please be patient and understanding,
For I am sometimes slow.

Please encourage me with kind words,
For I feel I am such a burden.

Please lend me a strong hand,
For I am sometimes weak.

Please forgive me if I struggle,
For I am very confused.

Please help me through the day,
For I depend completely on you.

Please see me as yourself,
For someday you will be Me.

Myshell L. Brown

Lost Soul

It was a cold and lonely autumn night
And I was out - on an endless flight.

I was searchin' for my lost soul
and flyin' - without a goal

There's no angel in sight
Through my cold and endless flight

Val Morey

Philosophy

I sit and think, thinking of things
I hope my hopes, dream my dreams
of what I want, what I don't
of what I lack, what I won't

I think of love, of whom loves me
of life, youth, the elderly

I think of what may never be
a happy world society

Is everybody else like me,
Confused, concerned for family

I think of God, his thinking of things
his hope of hopes, dream of dreams
I think God is concerned, like me
but not confused, eternally.

Dennis Stephens

Confused

Do we live just to die or
do we become angels
grow wings
and fly
Is all that we've achieved over
and done or
is there life beyond the sun
Is there a God or
is God just a gesture
Do we stay in the ground or
do we walk through the green pasture
Are we living or
are we dead or
are we an illusion in
somebodies head
I can't make sense of this,
can you or
are you willing to admit that
you've confusion too.

Michelle Eichenberger

Earth

Earth is our planet,
It is where I live.

Earth is beautiful,
Earth is clean.

I like Earth,
It's my planet.

I keep it clean,
So I can breath.

Why don't we all tackle it,
recycle it, and reuse it.

Jorge O. Ortega

You Taught Me How To Love Again

You taught me how to love again
When the world is full of distrust
You seemed to know just what to say
To make my weary heart whole again
I have never known the gentleness
Of the way you take me in your arms.
And crease and smooth the distrust
and loneliness away.
You taught me how to love again
By just being yourself
Letting me trust in you showing
Me all the wonders of a newfound world.
Never to be afraid of the unknown
Your gentle touch and loving heart
Has taught me how to love all over again

Carolyn Edgerley

alone

alone
i sit here
listening to the silence
which fills the room
while telltale tears course down my face

alone
i wait here
in deep despair
i wait and watch for you

alone
i lie here
tossing and turning
worrying my way through the dark hours

alone
and lonely
assailed by the sound
the sad sound of silence
which fills my life
as i wait in vain for you

Glenn Bowen

Ghost

Can you feel these chains
Tight around your hands?
You've become enslaved to pride
    In all your efforts
    to be a man

Can you feel my presence
In the air you breath?
You struggle to survive; to live
    There is no one
    you can believe

Can you see my reflection
When you look into the mirror?
A chilling gaze to haunt your soul
    I've become
    all of your fears

Can you hear my voice
When you close your eyes to sleep?
I've made myself your nightmare
    So pray the Lord
    your soul to keep.

Tirzah Truesdell

My Love Which I Have Obtained

I have felt a strong
passionate love come across me.

Come share this passionate
love with me, if you only
knew how I felt when you
where there, next to me, oh
how I wanted to share my love
with you.

Day and day I pray and pray and
wish that you would say that
we are meant to be.

Night and night how I want
to hold you tight close to me
forever.

Sarah A. Gonzales

The First Time

There is always a first time,
The first day,
The first smile,
The first tooth
The first step,
The first birthday,
There is always a first time,
The first school day,
The first crush,
The first kiss,
The first date,
The first dance,
The first orchid.
There is always a first time.
The first prom'.
The first diamond
The first wedding vow,
The first husband
The first child,
There is always a first time.

Mattie M. Stewart

My Angel Christine

It hurts the way you left me,
My soul just wants to cry.
A part of me now missing,
No chance to say goodbye.
My love for you is endless,
My angel you will be.
And when I'm with your children,
Please share my life with me.
Your hugs are gone forever,
I wish it wasn't true.
Some things we take for granted,
Like never losing you.
And now your home is heaven,
A child of God you are.
At night I'll search Orion,
That's where I'll find your star.

Robert K. Bailey

Funny how it seems

Funny how it always seems,
I'm left alone with all my dreams,
and though my dreams are very few,
funny how they're all of you.

Kristine Iacopelli

Big Talk

You picture me, I have no doubt,
Forlorn and desolate without
The pleasure of your company.
It's plain you don't know much of me!
My head is neither bowed nor bloody,
I challenge you, or anybody
To prove I've ever shed one tear,
Or sighed one sigh for you, My Dear.
So, when in some far distant city,
You think of me with pallid pity,
Don't fancy I am prostrated
Upon my wan and sleepless bed.
This is the more authentic pose:
My thumb adjacent to my nose!

Paula L. Clayton

Cold Wind

Awaken by the blowing wind
I sat on the side of the bed
I was fully awake by the smell
of freshly brewed coffee

With coffee cup in hand and gazing
out my window enjoying the frozen snow
I saw a big brown leaf blowing
across the yard

While I sip my coffee I see a squirrel
oh! I see two of them they are running
and playing with each other
High up in a tree on a limb far
away from the neighbors cat

Although it's cold blowing snow
outside. The sun wants to shine through
this warms my heart and I do not
feel alone on this cold winter day

Aletha J. Hart

Our World

From round the world they come
Those who hope
Those who dare
    Leaving behind
The force of predatory
    power and greed
To a land where fortune
    is for all
And helping hands reach out
So dreams become reality and
Hope prevails
To believe, to know
There is a share for everyone of
The goodness in life
Reach out, let courage
Strengthen the resolve
To come to our world
Where every man is supreme.

Josephine Giambalvo

The Letter

Go little bird, fly far and wide;
Take my thoughts, they're
Tucked inside.
To my loved one, fond
Affection bring.
Help my heart, to soar, like spring.

Claire V. Chow

Tides Of Love

The tide is splashing against the shore,
I know I could love no other more.
The wind comes strong across the sea,
I can feel your eyes upon me.
The sand below sparkles like gold,
inside, it's your heart I long to hold.
The sun is shining high and bright,
being near you makes everything right.
Now it's time to leave the beach,
my vow of love I'll never breach.

Laura Lee

My Smile

Not every smile is a smile
for the greetings of the day

My smile is a smile that
Means so much more
My smile is to ensure that
Your day is not a bore

My smile is from there which
You can't break apart
Yes my smile is from there,
The place known as the heart

My smile is wide,
Bright and deep
My smile is one, when received,
You will undoubtedly keep

Samuel Rhodes

Sky

Sky, sky, how I love the sky.
When I'm sitting on the swing I say,
"Sky, sky, I love you sky! I love
the way you move. I love the color.
I love the clouds." Sky, sky I
love the sky.

Jessica Castro

The Song Of A Happy Man

This rhyme will tell of an honest man,
Who built his home on a hill,
And should you wish to travel there,
You'd see it standing still.

The house was small with little room,
For the large piano inside,
But there he played his old-time tunes,
To please his lovely bride.

He worked from dawn to dusk each day,
With a hammer in his hand,
And as he worked he sang a song,
The song of a happy man!

He built his homes for common folk,
Whom he knew could never pay,
And many of those who live there now,
Still owe him - to this day!

He told his truths, and sang his songs,
And always did things his way,
This happy man, who lived on a hill,
My grandfather — what more to say!

Jim Grand

Sports Today

Anytime someone gets beat
  They stand on two feet
And make excuses, all do,
  Saying they will come through.

It was this or that
  A faulty ball or bat,
They have got to reorganize
  They are full of lies.

Owners bow their heads and sigh
  They want to fire the coach,
They can tell you just why
  They lost crawling like a cockroach.

Excuses, excuses, that's all they know
  They grab their caps and go,
Why can't they just admit
  Their opponent was better fit?

Charles A. Felker

Beginnings

Enlightened heart,
  Impromptu start,
Anticipating good endings,
  Singing a song,
  In search so long,
Great love for new beginnings.

  Starting so bold,
  Becoming old,
Seeking for happy endings,
  Pursuits await,
  Failures abate,
A quest of fine beginnings.

  Rough roads ahead,
  The heart, Godspeed,
Expectations of great endings,
  Hoping the best,
  To greet success,
Due to joyous beginnings.

  New sights, behold,
  Of fortunes untold,
From unexpected endings,
  Loving the path,
  Finished at last,
The results of new beginnings.

Annie Mae Flakes

Waiting For

As I look across the room,
gazing into your eyes.
I know there is a person,
I would like to get to know.
But as I dream on,
I know it can't be so.
For how can you feel that way,
for a heart that isn't that strong.

I live for a day to come,
for you to think of me.
A lonely soul,
that can't be free.
A heart that would rather die,
than laugh and cry.
And a love for you,
that's warm and free.

Paula Cary

Sailing

Sailing behind a cloud
On Caribbean seas
To catch that cloud
On this bright day
Would be sure rest
From the bright sun shining, sun
I thirst for the cloud,
Although water everywhere
To catch that cloud
On this sea of Caribbean
Blue and green,
Would be refreshing
Refreshing as a cool stream

L. Brady Steward

My Personal Angel

Without a sound
Her candles glowed,
As she looked down
So, beautiful.

With her radiant glow,
I felt her words
This, I want you to know
Everything is, O.K.

Europhia was the energy
That wrapped my soul.
As, if it were meant to be,
From her illuminate glow.

Only I could see,
My very own personal Angel.
She was there for me
Astronomically.

Renee A. McNabb

The Dream: Ode To Martin Luther King Jr.

This man had a dream
That we could all walk someday
Hand in hand

Believing people could
Become, color blind, one day
And reach that promised land

Let's always remember
The dream this man had
And never let it die
Trying to finalize
His dream forever
And keep his, flame alive...

But work still needs to be done
To progress and go forward
Because there, is still, a problem

Ignorant people still exist
And apathy, won't protect us
So we, must stand up now!!!

Robert James Verador

Untitled

Now you're gone.
Rooms full of empty
Joyous echoes of life.
Nothing but time,
Send no flowers - I'll be fine.

Patty N. Morris

My Angel

I saw my guardian angel
today. She was all dressed
in white and her hair was
glistening in the sunlight and
the rays of light was shining
all around her. And her smile
was as warm as the sun. Her
eyes were glimmering like bright
stars shining through to all of
our hearts.

Tammy Flanigan

Smiles Smells Sights Sounds

You want to, but you won't
She won't smile so you can't.
You don't know so you begin
Think, think
Oh how pretty
Don't think, don't think
Falling while crickets chirp
Damn if you do, damned if you don't
Damn if you don't, damned if you do
And whales cry as she frowns
So another day dies,
It's no real matter
The siren scream.

Carl D. Schultz

Untitled

I followed the dog, so I could see,
Where he would hide the bone from me.
Oh! Lots of dirt and rock to hide,
his bone he carried here with pride.
He worked so hard for hours on in,
not knowing I was watching him,
At last he's done, and tired you see
and proud he hide this bone from me.
But as I walk away I say!
"Cats hate bones anyway!"

Louise McManis

People

When people are forsaken,
they fight with all these might.
When people learn to trust,
the fighter beats them down.
When people learn to hate,
the beaten pleads for mercy.
When people learn to love,
they are shielded for the world.

Veronica L. Cooney

Release

All at once, the skis respond
to spirit!

The mountain of fear melts.
The snow glistens - the hill beckons.
A swallow within the breast
is freed, and soars
Before the skier
saying, "Follow, follow."

Martha Jackson Newhard

If I Ever Leave...

Who will be Daddy's girl
If I ever leave,
The one to which all lost souls go
Their burdens to relieve.
Who will be the daughter
To stand behind her Mom,
If at any moment
The prominent time shall come.
Who will show affection
To a brother full of joy,
Because deep inside his heart
He's merely just a boy.
Who will be there in times
When all is bright and gay,
Or at the darkest moments
When the sky turns a shade of gray.
If I shall ever go
I'll always keep with me,
A chest of sacred memories
Pray save my heart the key!

Kristen Maynard

My Wish

I wish I were a tree,
able to blow free in the breeze,
to whisper in the wind
and tell secrets no one interprets.

Mary C. Geiman

New Beginning

Elope with a fantasy
Enter the unreal.
Discover new ways
Where everyone can feel.
Approach the unexpected
with complicated words.
Develop new ideas
with chemicals for cures.
Listen to the future,
advance beyond the past.
Make a new beginning
with something that will last.

Karlee Markovich

Sunset

I treasure your love,
    all the days that I needed you,
You were there to hold me close
    with loving arms and a caring touch.
At night I wish you were here
    in my arms and close to my body
    with a love that will always
    be strong and true.
We have the kind of love
    people only dream of.

Colleen F. DesMarais

Dawn

Fairy tracings laced with dew drops
Silver threads among the gold
Silky petals of a flower
slowly start to unfold
A tiny creature suddenly appears
to glide on an invisible thread
The fairy tracings seem much larger
as the spider continues on her web.

June Kappen

Untitled

The love of my life,
The apple of my eye,
Is so far from me
That often I cry.
My heart often aches
For the things far away.
The time when I'll hold you,
I long for that day.
But for now I must suffer
Through the time in between,
Waiting for my loved one,
My happiness, my queen.
In years to come
We'll be happily married,
But that doesn't seem
To keep my sorrows buried.
When that time comes
We'll have forgotten these hurts.
We'll be filled with joy,
We'll be as free as the birds.

Aaron Collins

Friends

Friends will be friends
Until the end.

Friends will always
have a hand to lend.

Friends will be there
when there's a broken
Heart to mend.

Friends will be friends
until the end.

Beth Brady

A Star

At night I see a little light,
a light so very very bright.
The light's not near but very far,
in fact I think it is a star.

Clare Greene

Seasons

When the wintry winds are blowing
And the skies are dark and gray
My memories drift towards summertime
To bright and balmy days.

To soft meadows filled with flowers
And rich scents of perfume
that seem to be unfolding
With each and every bloom.

As sunrise gives away to sunset
In the distant fields beyond
Daylight gives way to darkness
As "Mother Nature" waves her wand.

Beneath the silvery moonlight
There's young lovers strolling by
Embracing all the beauty
Of the peaceful summer skies.

They're holding onto every moment
For summer ends too soon
Yielding once again, my friend
To the cold and wintry moon.

Concetta Carter

Marriage

Marriage is a sacred vow
between a man and woman
Love is a sign of marriage
Always being there for one another
knowing that you can trust the other
marriage is not just a piece of paper
A lifelong commitment, eternity
forsaking all others for as long as you
Both shall live

Jennifer M. Cain

Sweet Words Of Love

Sweet words of love surround me,
And echo through this room.
Though distance can't erase them,
They ended all to soon.

My fingers trace your nearness,
Caress the black pen lines.
Some day we'll be together,
For in my heart you're mine.

But time shifts oh so slowly,
Like tiny grains of sand,
Through the hour glass of memories,
I hold here in my hand.

Raegan Martin

Coming To The End

The walls are closing in,
Or are they falling down?
The sky is rather dim,
A peculiar shade of brown.
The trees are bending over,
Very unusual for the month of May.
If we wait any longer,
Will there be another day?
The seas are churning with madness,
Washing away the sandy shores.
Animals, weary with sadness,
Don't know what's in store.
The earth is opening wide,
Splitting straight through the center.
How hard everyone could have tried,
Just to make the world seem better.

Michelle Grau

Confined

Hideous,
    odors rank,
      sank.
Diseases
    seen,
      unseen...
What could be
    worse?
Coffins curse,
    carriaged
      hearse
    a soul
      confined!

Christine L. Brand

Shadowing

She peered through the window
Window with so much anger
Anger of her own
Her own heart was to explode
Explode with anger
Anger of people
People who care no more
More than anything
Anything of feeling
Feeling pain, anger
anger of herself
Herself gone
Gone into the mist
Mist of paradise.

Alesia Sargent

The Many Legged Spider

Contemplating . . .
The cracks in the cement
Listening . . .
To the ground below
Breathing breathing breathing
Feeling . . .
The breeze from above
Blowing . . .
Across the face
That belongs to
My blind and hidden soul
Knowing . . . what the many legged
Spider is doing to me
Sucking . . .
My life's spark away
Wondering . . .
Only one simple question
Left to ask.
Will there be enough time
Left for play?

Toby S. Snoddy

To Hurt To Cry

You are my husband
I am your wife.
As we vowed to each other
To be together for life.

For richer and for poorer
For good times and bad.
But all the good is gone
What is left is sad.

A circle of endless love
That was suppose to never end.
But our circle is broken
To you, I'm not even a friend.

Until death do we part
Between now and forever.
That would be a dream
But how do we start.

Our time together is gone
Our love somehow died.
We need a divorce
Not to live a lie.
To hurt to cry.

Vickie Lewis

My First Love

My first love has come and gone;
but in my memory lives on and on.
The sweet kiss, the gentle touch,
the face of one I love so much.

When loneliness in my heart appears
and my face is filled with falling tears
all of a sudden; out of the blue;
comes your face and memory of you.

As times goes on day by day
and I go on my lonely way;
I thank God for his part
in putting and keeping you in my heart.

Helen Urda Smith

Isn't Death (Life) A Funny Thing

Way out in the pasture
Where the green grass grows high
An old man lay down
And decided to die
He could've lived
Could've lived had he tried
But he just didn't feel like it
And for him no one cried
But poor little Jimmy
So full of life
So full of spunk
Was killed yesterday
When his mother drove drunk
Just last week he reached seven years
And for him my friends
We all cried rivers of tears

Christopher McLaren

Moon Watchers

Suddenly, a murmur low
    Drifted through the galaxy,
"The Eagle is cleared for go,
    Hurry, hurry, come and see".

Jason left his Golden Fleece,
    Whistled up a hoary crew,
Marco, Chris, Henry and Leif,
    All mighty heroes who knew,

The doubts, the fears, stars that call,
    Men like Neil, Buzz, and Michael,
To stand tall and bet it all.
    Listen! A radio's cackle,

"Houston, Tranquility Base here".
    Did someone hear that ghostly cheer?

Ezell Kimsey

Some One I Love

Some one who is a teacher
Some one who is a leader
Some one who cares
Some one will always be there
Some one I love
Some one I am proud of
Some one like me
Some one I am going to be
Some one I really love
And the good land up above.

Dorothy L. Heidelberg

Night

Liquid with silver glints,
Blackness and flowing hints
Endless and dark,
like the shadow of a bird on wing.
Crawling with eloquent grace
With a light touch of eyelet lace
Threaded with luminous rain,
Frozen in the black terrain
Then ending in brilliant burst
and illumination now has the sky immersed

Nicole Mallette

The Least Of These

Go to the least of these,
to those who have not heard.
Tell them that I love them
and teach them from my word.

Go to the least of these,
those the world has cast away.
Tell them that I love them
and that Jesus is the way.

Go to the least of these,
the poor, the crippled, the blind.
Tell them that I love them
and don't want them left behind.

Go to the least of these,
the wounded and sad of heart.
Tell them that I love them,
and want them to play a part.

Go to the least of these,
those remaining true to me
Tell them that I love them
and to shine for all to see!

Dawn E. Vories

Gleeson

Agave and mesquite crowd
the crumbling stone walls of
an old miner's shack.
Cattle range where once
a city of adobe stood.
Rusty tin roofs and
earth-brown walls pay
homage to the dead while
the old saloon still lingers
remembering the days
when this was the
Mother-Lode.

William Staatz

Mother Earth

Shining down sun
water rippling through a valley
calm stream bound for larger waters
grass shining with morning dew
soft green carpet fresh with life
trees speaking with the wind
graceful swaying motions for all to see
deep blue sky a colorful delight
bringing changes from snow to rain
deer running through a field of flowers
horses grazing in a pasture
remember a time long gone by
all creatures lived in equal balance
shine down sun, power of life

Jeremy Daniel McCarty

Just For A Ride

I packed up all my laundry
Put it on my back
It's funny how you can carry
Your life is some ole sack
My shoes seem kind of old
But their is something on my feet
I still have my blue jacket
That I guess I'll always keep
Wonder who I'll meet today
Thumbing for a ride
Maybe someone special
It's a nice day outside
Yes I have a future
And someday I will see
Just where I belong
And where I need to be
Why is it too much asking'
As a car pulls at my side
Would it be too much trouble
If I could have a ride?

Jesse Steve Wallace Sr.

The Generation Gap

We have a teen-age daughter
The sweetest thing you've ever seen
Although she's just a teen to some
To us she is a queen

She helps me much around the house
Like taking care of sis and brother
The thing I like about her most
Is the way she calls me mother

She's learning how to sew a little
And how to mend a sweater
And she can cook a real good meal
For any kind of weather

She thinks quite differently than us
In music and in clothes
I know the reason for this is
She is young and we are old

We must not try to change her way
She goes through many stages
Again I think the reason is
The difference is our ages

Earline Caldwell

Like A Rose

Sometimes she's so lonely.
She's scared she's going to be
shattered. Crushed like a rose in
the hand of a man.
   A teardrop rolls down the
petals from her crying eyes, as
she lets it fall she looks around.
   There's no sign of him,
and don't know when there
will be. She must stay strong
for her babies, and she always will.
   Like arose her touch is
soft and gentle. Until you break
her and reach the thorns. She's
   Like a Rose.

Maggie Price

My Precious Gift Of Love

I knew one day the time would come
when we would say good-bye,
And in my head, I understood,
but, my heart kept asking why?

I know there's a place to go to
where pain and sorrow lives no more,
And I know he will let you in
when you get to his front door.

I do not want to let you go
for here is where I want you to be,
But, when the time has come around
only he can set you free.

Golden gates, running streams
and, sun will fill your days,
You need not be afraid no more
for he will show you the way.

And in the night, before I sleep
I pray that up above,
That you'll receive this gift I give
My Precious Gift Of Love.

Patty Marchuk

Autumn

Autumn is, as children know
A parade of color before the snow.
White frost, brown leaves
Spooky look of naked trees.
Halloween with eerie sights
Black cats, starlit nights.
Water puddles tipped with ice
Capture moonlight as a prize.
Silence of an empty park
Warmth of home after dark.
Jack-O-Lanterns all aglow
Casting shadows to and fro.
Beggars knock in disguise
Scary faces, merry eyes.
Palms outstretched for the loot
Hand it over, off they scoot.
Moving on into the night
With such joy, sheer delight.
Then, like a spectre, autumn's gone

Just the memories linger on.

Richard Howell

Thirst

There was a sunrise!
My north-view window
Showed a rosy glow
Of what must been
A madness in the east.

Held prisoner by a typewriter,
A mortgage and
Tomorrow's dinner table,
I sat, my parched eyes yearning
To drink this wine of morning,
Knowing there was a sunrise!

Doris Jackson Wittig

Hands

The newborn's hands curl tight around,
Pull into reach a life new-found,
And slowly they extend their reach,
With help of hands that mold and teach,
So as the potter molds his clay,
The hands of life shape each new day,
They act to slowly fill life's page,
Through soft caress and fist of rage,
Still clutching life with grip so tight,
It stains each straining knuckle white,
The hands that wave at passing years,
That grasp old hopes and calm new fears,
Well marked by rings to stake our claim,
Yet strangers to us all the same,
When life's long battles no more engage,
The stiffened wrinkled hands of age,
Their vise-like grip on life release,
Lie folded in eternal peace.

Michelle A. Carrier-Migliozzi

Husband

You,
are the special person in my life;
I love you for who you are,
and not what you expect from me.
You guide me through life-
with love, faith, and understanding.
You have picked me up when I was down.
And...
made me strong when you
were not around.
You,
took care of me in time of need;
And...
I respect you for everything.
You cherished my daughter like your own,
So..
Baby,
sit down and relax...
now you are home!

Kathleen Herrera

Untitled

I called out loud
But no one heard
this little lost lamb
away from the herd.

I was lost far from home
Nowhere to turn no where to go.
But living in sin and the worldly pride
Wondering when I might die.

But just as I thought that I was there
deaths door step and not a pray.

God picked me up and sat me back down
on his holy rock on his firm ground.

The moral of the story
you're wondering why.

What ever you do.
What ever you try.

When the deep pit of sin
is almost nigh.

You can always count on
the unchanging hand from high.

Mandy J. Adkins

Good Bye

Although the time has passed us by
It's always made me think
That if we were together more
will our love begin to shrink
The space is big, the time is far
The relationship grows dry
So if I let this go on any longer
I believe I'm going to cry
I want to tell you this in a way
That will not make you sad
Don't get me wrong, I did enjoy
The good times that we had
This isn't working out, I know this now
We cannot make this tie
Our separate ways is best we go
So it's time to say "Good Bye"

Frances Harrell

The Stage

The hot spot lights are shining bright
The play is not over to my delight
The audience claps and smiles and cheers
But now the end is almost here.

I move upstage and center, then left
I'm supposed to act like I'm upset
But up on stage, all eyes on me
All I really am is happy.

Now it's over, the curtains close
I'm really glad I guess it shows
Everyone was great not one mistake
But now it is getting late

The cast says good-bye the end is here
Now everybody disappears
The performance is over and it was great
Until next time all we can do is wait.

Thelma Medina

Monster!

Crazed machine.
Teeth shiny
and razor sharp.
Devours
little children,
With an earth-shaking
Gulp!
No other students know
exactly what it's for.
It just sits
in the corner
of the quiet classroom,
slyly smiling
at our fear.

When will it strike next?
The creaky screech it makes,
when it opens
its jaws.
Look out-
Here it comes!

Laura Bagwell

What I Stand For

I stand for peace
and more happiness
that's what I stand for

I stand for love
and doing your best
that's what I stand for

I stand for joy
and good friendliness
that's what I stand for

I stand for God
and his righteousness
that's what I stand for

Steven Searls

Dragon Of Fire

Dragon of fire
Has no light
Dragon of fire
Can never be bright

What happened to the life he knew
Is it lost-we'll never know
Is it dark or is it night

He spared the light
Dragon of fire
I miss your soul

Stephen R. D. Kain

more than nothing

i am one with the earth
i came from the earth
a collection of things
that were then molded to form me
and i want to return to the earth
to be spread
out over all
and around everything
to give back what i merely borrowed
to disassemble the creation
and give back the parts
then move on to a new objective
and have a new destination
and reason
then maybe borrow some new materials,
maybe from some place else,
and make something new.

Julia Cokelet

Blue Moon

She stands alone all alone
For what seems like eternity
She's tossed away like a dream
And they continue with gaiety

Who is she, who is she
Many people have asked
She is a girl of solitude
Who always wears a mask

Inside she cries and whimpers
Sounds normally from the lips
She has but one thing
A blue moon friendship

When can she take off her mask
She's tried of this colored moon
She she throws away her hint of nothing
And prays for something soon.

Jamie Clover

Heaven Come To Earth

To see your eyes gaze upon mine
Moves me as the moon moves the seas

To touch your hand
Is as great to me as all

Your smile and feminine warmth
Overpower me beyond description

Your scent so sweet and subtle
To love you is a blessing

For you to love me is
Heaven come to earth

Robert P. Buccella

The Love I Fell Into

You make me feel
Like never before
The touch of your hands
Are never a bore

Your sweet gentle kisses
The look in your eyes
The love I fell into
Was all a surprise

Your soft touch
Caressing my body
The words "I love you"
Whispered softly

I feel very special
In everything you do
'Cause the love I fell into
Was with you

Elizabeth Mock

What Is Love

Love is something you get from God
When you are born in the world God shows
You love through your parents and God
Shows your parents how to love you
And how to love others in life
God shows us His love though
What we do for each other and
What other people do for God is
Full of love even when we do
Wrong he still loves us very
Much God had given us for our
Sins and God give us this
Land and sea to share with
The world God is love through
Our eyes we se people doing
Wrong and though our eyes we
See people doing good God
Is here with us very day and night

Victoria L. Pegler

Best Friends

Someone who laughs, someone who plays,
Someone who likes you for all the days.
They can be caring, they can be kind,
They always have an open mind.
They comfort you when you're sad,
And run with you when you're glad.
All of the words and phrases above,
Yes they all describe a best friends love.

Carrie O'Grady

When My Lord Returns

The Lord will come and make his stand
All across this fearless land.
He'll take us high upon a cloud
As Gabriel blows his trumpet loud.
Then the dead in Christ will rise
Singing praises throughout the skies.
And on that day you will see
That God has won the victory.
So open your heart and let him in
He'll wash away your every sin.
His words are true and powers strong
Just trust in him
You'll never go wrong.
For when we meet on his Celestial Shore
We will all be happy forever more.

Carla Horton

The Dandelion

I picked a faded dandelion
And blew it in the air
Its tiny little parachutes
Went floating everywhere.

They caught the wind
And danced awhile
Bending to and fro
In splendid ballerina style.

Finally as the wind grew still
They floated back to earth
And bedded in the dark warm soil
To start their new rebirth.

When next the summer comes
And dandelions are everywhere
I'll pick another faded flower
And blew it in the air.

Janet L. Niehaus

Coming Into

I've been distant you see
Looking out at things
From deep inside of me
Solace; my thought brings
Numb of life and love
Until at last I found
In the heavens above
My emotions unbound
Everything once again new
Delusions come and go
But I try to stick to what's true
What I am is what I know
Answers don't come easily
I torture myself by this
Tickle the mind pleasingly
Create my special bliss
Words burst from dry lips
It feels like honey drops
When conversation drips
And the twisted thinking stops

Andrew Rockman

Mesmerized Truth

The time has come
and it always will,
Maybe we'll meet again.
Some day sometime,
Just remember...
Let all the memories
soak in.

Carolyn Y. Redman-Barr

From A Soldier To A Fallen Soldier

May the Stars that cover
your heart, the Field of
Blue on which they are
placed, and the Stripes of
Red and White which
surround your body lead
you ever into victory in
the face of thine enemy.
As you march in the
Lord's army stand tall
brave soldier for the
battle is near. Fear not for
the Lord is at your side
for all eternity.

Michael T. Germain

In A Drought Year

Caught through the pines
By thirsty eyes
Clouds
Racing running turning
White wooly wooly
Sheep gamboling
In the heavens
Quite unconcerned
About making
Rain
And me?
Gardener to my soul
Momentarily content
To sip slowly
This remarkable
Celestial
Cocktail

Betty Grower

Death - A Sad Thing?

What is death? Really!
Does death have to be sad?
Death and sadness, a combination,
One taken by most people. Usually!
Death does not have to be sad,
Perhaps a time of peace and be glad.
I believe death is an image,
The way we see it, good or bad.
A loved-one is going to die,
She is badly suffering in pain.
Should she die and go to heaven,
She will never feel pain again.
So, is that a reason to be sad,
For that, we should be happy.
To force one to live by a machine,
This is only selfish and cruelty.
I ask the question again,
What is it that you think?
Why must it always be, or is it,
Death "A sad thing?"

Rebecca L. Buzek

That Blue Flower I Saw Yesterday

That blue flower I saw yesterday
was as blue as the Atlantic Sea.
It had a twinkle that shined
brighter than ever seen. I looked
for more of these wonderful
flowers, I looked and looked all
the next day, but I did not
see that twinkle I saw yesterday.

Allie Garavaglia

Do This Do That

Hop, hop, hop
Like a frog
Bark, bark, bark
Like a dog
Meow, meow, meow
Like a cat
Why can't we all be like that?

Fall, fall, fall
Like a leaf
Grow, grow, grow
Like a plant
Walk, walk, walk
Like an ant
Why can't we all be like that?

I know why certainly
Why would I want to be a bee?
No, no, no, no sirree!
You are you and I am me
Never, never will that change
Yes sirree ain't that strange?

Lauren Castellaw

Fallen Heroes

Dedicated to Robert E. Carey, Cpl.
Korean War, 1930-1993, beloved gran
The war ends a tragic ending
Fallen heroes lie at your feet
Fallen heroes die for a cause
The cause: To save a country
The heroes becomes heroes only in death

Fallen from grace to glory
They fell to save a country
They fell for a billion people
Nothing to do with them
Pack them in a shed not
The heroes belong not in a shed

Bury them well
Bury them with respect
Honor the dead who died for a cause
Burn them not

Jennifer Rushforth

In the Twinkling of an Angel's Eye

From deep in my soul,
in the depths of its glow,
a love beyond mortal thought.

The song that it sings,
is not reasoning,
but a language concealed or forgot.

Like the wind it doth move,
through the smallest of groove,
in the twinkling of an angel's eye.

And with the passage of time,
this love will be mine,
for her love is the tie that binds.

There are many who wish
they had her great gift:
a love beyond mortal expression.

The force that it is,
and the power that it gives,
is not an earthly possession.

Stephen Valley

My Special Angel

This is about my special angel.
The one sent to me from above.
The one I knew down in my heart,
that I was meant to love.
The one who brings me happiness
and fills my heart with smiles,
the one I'll walk with hand in hand
through the rest of my life's miles.
The one who always highlights my days
and makes the sun shine bright,
the one who cuddles up with me
each and every night.
The one who takes good care of me,
when I'm sick or well,
my one and only true love
my special angel April Dell.

William C. Smith

Self Preservation

State of mind
  is the
Clarity of perceiving
the fantasy of life
that makes one explore
learning and failing to naivete
knowing to always rise
to fall
but to rise
again

Tenley M. Jones

The C Train

Through a dark passage we fill
As the outside screams by
Though I remain still
An unsettling feeling subsides

No faces read of a name
No inside sounds to be sung
In a world where everyone looks the same
Nobody knowing anyone

I hide the look of ignorance
To run I fight the temptation
Avoiding such a performance
As I await my destination

Elaine Ruggieri

Death

The darkness of death swept over him
as he mumbled soft words
to the family weeping for him.
His eyes staring at the heavens above.

He looked like a little child
intrigued by a magical toy
that kept him mesmerized,
as if he was in a trance.

As he lay there
the family wandered what to do.
And later when his body was hauled off,
they flinched at the sound of him
being dropped into the ocean.

Rebecca Reischman

Ascension

How far must I climb
On mountains of wearisome height?
Paths of rocky, raisFd ground
Seem long when known without delight.

The staff I used to lean upon
Was carved from ancient, twisted wood.
But cast down at God's command,
He transformed it into something good.

How far will I see
From peaks of transitory joy?
Keen awareness turns to thought;
Time dims what it cannot destroy.

The glass that sharpened distant sight
Likewise darkened much from view.
Until God touched the inner eye,
I had no faith in something true.

Anne M. Mickel

Karla The Kitty From The City

Karla the kitty,
Did not like the city.

Without a sound,
She moved out of town.

She came to a house,
Occupied by a mouse.

Go away, said the mouse,
Stay away from my house.

Over there is a flat,
Just made for a cat.

Karla went on her way,
To find a place to stay.

She found a house,
Not far from the mouse.

Here they gave her some milk,
And a red pillow of silk.

A little girl asked her to stay,
There you will find her to this day.

Sharon Lewis

Written

Sitting,
Standing,
Hoping,
Wishing,
That you'll find love.

Wanting,
Waiting,
That someday you'll be ok.

Living ,
Dieing,
Trying,
To hold on, but still letting go.

Still sitting,
Still standing,
Still hoping,
Still wishing,
But love hasn't found you yet.

Laura Eller

Grandma

My grandma is a child, she's short
of stature and can beat me in golf.
My grandma is geometry, she can always
get out of tough situations.

When she joins us at the dinner
table it's like inviting a baby bird
to the dinner table. My grandma is
a puppy dog, she's always ready to
try something different.

My grandma smells like a ripe
orange waiting for fall from a
tree. Grandma grandma come
out and play I hate it when you're away.

Jonathan Genetelli

Danna's Thread

Cast down into the place where it all began.
Where morals exist in blurring streams,
I walked to the edge of the cliff
Called sanity, and leaped into the
Spirals of loneliness and hate.
I landed and found myself without
Morals where it all began. Looking
Out, I stopped to see forever not
wanting to see my sin. I followed
Many battles I fought, pain
in my left hand looking for
love in my right extended out
Accepting peace as I plummet.
Now in the cold, empty valley
of loneliness I seek warmth
In the dark folds of his
Robe. But once again, I am
Alone... Where it all began.

Steven R. Newton II

Untitled

I am just a pollywag...
Swimi'n in the big blue sea...
Thought I'd 'come a great big frog...
Now I see I am here to bee...

I thought that I would get a life...
Just drop a hook and get a bite...
Instead a gots two kids and a wife...
And no life even insight...

I think a drink would do me good...
Let me free to ponder...
But I really don't think I could...
With out going on a bender...

Well Fauesa is on line two...
And I really got to poo...
So fairwell from strongville land...
Cause now I am going to disneyland...

God I need a real life...

Rellim Divad

The Theft

I stole the smell of lilac trees
As I walked to work today.
Wrapped them up in memories
And stored them tight away.

When the winter's wind grows cold,
And snow is piled up high,
The memory of those lilac trees
Will make the winter fly!

Ona Shepherd

Friendship

A friendship is a
very special thing. It's
special because when
you have a friend you
someone to talk to in
class, and to tell your
problems to. Also you can
laugh with a friend and
have a sleep over. A friendship
doesn't just have to be with
one friend, it can be with
twenty friends. Also in a
friendship you can call each
other and write notes back
and forth.
A friendship is very special
to have!

Melissa Schulz

I'm Leaving

Maybe it's time to leave here.
I don't like what I see.

Maybe it's time to leave here.
Please listen to my plea.

Maybe it's time to leave here.
I really don't like the lies.

Maybe it's time to leave here.
All I seem to do is cry.

Maybe it's time to leave here.
So I'll just say good-bye.

Jacqueline A. Bizzozero

Synchronicity

I lay heavenward
under the stern hatch
rocking rhythmically
in the peace of the
embryonic swell,
when the whisper touch
of tepid raindrops
slowly, symmetrically
fell
on my face
like an eternal braille
reaching out
for communication
through the blindness
of sleep.

Marie Eleana Guidice

Longing

A love you want
but can't have,
You yearn for it
but you never get it.

You tell that person
how you feel,
They ignore you
and turn you away.

Finally you find
the love that you've been wanting,
And that particular person
finally stops pushing you away.

Ashley M. Nelson

Crucify

Why is this vulture perched so heavy?
Bearing down, game for my soul
Claw-clenched heart in her eyes
Well Jesus never took my hand;
Never knelt down to give the warmth
Of his blanket of forgiveness.
Always apathetic to the nails that
Crucify me
As if I were the cross he bore
The scarlet letter on his shroud.
So I stand before this mirror
And see him in me
The nails, the cross, the letter.
The thorns that prick my thoughts,
And the apathetic mirror that
Crucifies me.

Corey V. Seymour

Daughter

My daughter is a blessed gift
sent to me from God above,
so I can give her all my love.

Although at times she goes adrift,
I pray I'm there to give her
a lift in time of need.

She knows not how I love her so.
and I just can't stand to let her go.
But I know she must grow.

A woman now some may say.
But I still see my child of yesterday.
She played for years, I'd dry her tears,
and wipe away all her fears.

But now appears she needs me not, but
I have not forgot my daughter when
she was just a tot.

Teresa Bolton

Light

Clear you open a new day
and fill with color the world.

You illuminate with unique
brightness and make happy all
the hearts.

You show white, blue, green and
brown. You enlarge truths and
cover sorrows.

You stand out in the dark
like an intense ray of Spring.

For you, awaken the living and
for you, sigh those gone.

You are intense, pure, truthful.
Also, real, like a fresh morning.

You warm up the spirit of those
who dream you.
Natural or not, you always
clarify confusions,
You are high, like grandiose,
goddess of the day.

Esteban F. Hernandez

Robbed Of Your Love

I awoke one morning about three
Your side of the bed was cold,
I couldn't get up or move my head
I was numb from head to toe
I've been robbed of your love.

This thief wasn't after my money
She stole what my eyes couldn't see,
A heart that beat with love,
When you body lay close to me.
I've been robbed of your love.

You cheated on a true love
Laughed at a bleeding heart,
Now I'm paying for stolen love
the one with the broken heart,
I've been robbed of your love

We haven't heard a word from you
The Children still cry for their Dad,
Wish you were here to tell them
What happened to what we had;
I've been robbed of your love.

Nancy O. Warden

Anchor's Aweigh

We cannot direct the wind,
But we can adjust the sails.
We cannot change the weather,
But seek shelter when it hails.
When we are away from shore
With danger all around,
We make the best of what we have;
We're sure of where we're bound.

Fear may come and fear may go-
It neither warns nor asks.
But confidence and compromise
Shall overcome that mask.
About our own abilities,
We have no limits there.
It matters not what's right or wrong
Or even what is fair!
What matters most, I say to you
Without pretense or rancor,
In time, we must get off our butts,
And finally weigh that anchor!

Steven Blumenfeld

Coming Out Of The Dark

Coming out of the dark,
Where I have roamed for many years...
Into the light of life,
Where I can release all my fears.

Coming out of the dark,
From that path I've had to follow...
Learning by suffering,
From things I've found hard to swallow.

Coming out of the dark,
To that puzzling junction in life...
But unlike the others,
I know which path will hold no strife.

Coming out of the dark,
Following a soft voice calling...
I walk toward this voice,
Now no longer scared of falling.

Rebecca A. Davis

In Memory Of My Mother

My mother lies in a garden
Attended by those unaware
She really lives in my heart
The house of her soul lay there

A refuge was this house
For the light that shined with in
Was the soul that reached out to God
And was lighted for her by him

In remembrance of my mother
I will seek her God in truth
Oh! God help me to find that torch
That will light this darkened booth

The light that shined so deep within
Is the light that comes from God
And only they who seek him
Will find this gift of love

Dorothy L. Fish

Time

Tick.
The ever ebbing
tide of life
that rolls along
the ocean shore
will whisper
in a weary ear
that he won't
live forever more.

Like a fluttering butterfly
on a gloomy spring day
will flit to you
then sweep away

The clock is calling
Hear it tick
It's time to go
Please,
let it be quick.
Tock.

Donna D. Wajda

The Color Mud

It's cross country at the Bend
    rain and mud for days on end

One team piles up with a thud
    then gets up the color mud

Mud sprays up my whole backside
    run right on to keep my stride

Rain on the head and shoulders too
    splash that runner why not two?

Stuff the mud clothes in a bag
    drive home as the wipers wag

It's cross country in the rain
    (here my story starts to gain)

Mom and Maytag won on slow
    stuff the shoes and bake on low

It's cross country at the Bend
    rain and has got to end...

Cathy Harrison

illusion

i cry
i don't know why
i have fear
no reasons appear
i give up
and fill a cup
with tears of confusion
then i have an illusion
of how life could be
if i could only see
how precious each moment is
even with all its
pain and sorrow
we must remember there is always
tomorrow

Patricia Ann Taft

Fish

My fish is big and scary,
But some say he is small.
His home looks very dirty,
Until you clean it all.
He sleeps all night.
He swims all day.
When my dad comes in,
He swims away.
Whenever my fish sees me or my mom,
He gets very happy.
And then I usually feed him,
And he takes a little nappy.

David Grzedzinski

One Bridge Too Far

Helping hands hang by hopeless
Headlight eyes look on blind
Sherwood band robbed of Robin
Sculpted screams melt undefined

Someone else will be the hero
911 has heard the calls
The calvary their horses mounted
The forest blocks one tree that falls

One voice aloud is all that's needed
All scared to scale one flimsy fence
One voice above can propel people
Number safety shows no defense

One for all all of one
What we are is where we are
One is God and we are one
Just don't go one bridge to far

Richard Borge

Saved

The emptiness so deep inside,
I tried to run I tried to hide
to fill this void, I couldn't see,
I thought I knew, thought I was free,
Almost lost hope, with it my soul,
Loud voice persuasive, was from below,
I closed my ears, opened my eyes,
I looked above, saw clear blue skies,
Then to my knees, in desperate need,
I prayed to God, to please save me,
Through his son, his sacrifice,
my burden lifted, freed from my vice,
Jesus my savior, now I know
within fulfillment, with spiritual growth.

John Turner

Loneliness

Living in the present
Dreaming of the past
Loneliness engulfs me
How long will I last?

Hearing your laughter
Remembering your smile
Holding onto memories
never to defile

Alone with my sorrow
Will I ever love again?
If only I could forget
what we may have been

Erica Lynn De Rycke

Windows To Your Soul

Through friendly eyes
I clearly see,
your thoughts and feelings
revealed to me.

Dancing it mischief;
how can it be?
For now they're filled with
innocent glee.

Honesty plays a key role
in your eyes;
making it impossible
for a fib to get by.

While deep in thought,
they look so intent;
but when excitement moves in
they jump and skip.

Gazing into your eyes,
it's plain to see,
a tender loving heart
staring back at me.

Ranae Gonzales

Your Words Have Worth

Musician sings, sounds his songs
His thoughts, his heart, his soul.

Poet pens his innermost
With words that sway and flow.

Author writes descriptive verse
on paper black and white
With sights and sounds his tale we read
and story does take flight.

Now my brother, sister, friend
Set down your thoughtful mind.
You too have something for us all
Preserve it for all time.

Your words have worth
Opinions value
Heartbeat without price.
I'll be here with loves ear listen
Share your precious lines.

Dave Toms

Love Is Blind

Was it there all along?
I felt it I'm sure, but
I never knew!

Cynthia Smith

My Lost Love

I wonder if the time has come
    for you to come and find me.
If your heart has felt the passion
    mine has.
Or if this year it will bring the
    one like we had together.
But now my wishes have to
    stop!
You will disappear and bring
    me sadness.
One day maybe, I will find
    my love so true.

Kristin Marie Huffman

Untitled

I, with the rain
I am
Adrift
In my world
Pain and pleasure, engulfed
Me, I am
You are not
Life
We all share
But destiny
Has chosen one
Some
And others not
Like fallen leaves
Or this lamb on your plate
The wind will blow
The earth will turn
And the rain Will fall.

Ines Pacheco

Wish

I could kiss your lips all night long
Those lips that are far beyond
Perfection
I could gaze into your beautiful eyes
For days upon end
Those eyes that are far more beautiful
Than the stars
Themselves
I could caress your skin
Smooth as silk
For as long as the chills
Run up your spine
And I could love you
For all eternity
Even though you will
Never be
Mine

Chris Spagnola

Fabulous Chocolate
Covered Strawberries

Incredibly tasty, sweet, luscious,
Amazingly appetizing, yummy, delicious,
Stunningly soft, polished and smooth,
Superbly divine, sweet,
A seed in each groove,
Radically red, covered in brown,
Small and plump,
Green leaves on the crown

Daniel Gordon

For All, I Share

I wake up in the morning,
happy for the day.

This joy I spread to all,
All I come in contact with
This wonderful day.

To everyone, I share
my love of the sun
and the stars
and the clouds,
the trees, the flowers,
snow, rain, wind,
people, animals,
  All.
Everything I see,
Everything I do,
I share.

For if I don't share,
I shall go sour
with each hour
that passes by.

Andrea Gossert

Them

They seem to know everything
But they know nothing
They are all around me
Can't they go away
He causes problems
She doesn't understand
They get in the way
Should I bother to stay
I never know what to do
Who cares
They don't
He doesn't care and doesn't know
They never will know
What it's like to live in my world
My world is pain, happiness, confusion
I don't know what to do with them
Tell me
Then they will understand
And I won't.

Molly Callahan

Faith In Plastic

I'm hungry.
Very, very hungry.
And I'm stupid
for wearing blue suede shoes
on a rainy, bloody day.
For not understanding
yes and no
when I mean them the most
or the least.

I have asthma.
I'm coughing up glue
and my inhaler doesn't work
but I don't tell anyone.
Must have faith in plastic.
Must drink bad coffee.
Drive cool cars.
Believe in bad guys
and good guys.
Must be young, blushing,
forever.

Liana Allday

Broken Down

For my entire life
my emotions have been pushed around
I have been kicked with dirt
while I was lying on the ground

My self esteem has been beaten
then shoved in my face
it seems I am always,
being put in my place

Always being made,
to feel down and out
but I can't seem to figure
what it's all about

Really tired of this life
and the way I'm made to feel
I need to be given a break
to allow my wounds to heal

One wonders why I can't escape
and set my myself free
it makes it difficult
when the one doing it is me.

Bill Nulph

Do You Care?

I say, "I love you."
You don't say a word
I say, "I need you"
You don't notice
I say the simplest things to you,
To show you I care
But, you never answer me
No matter what I say or do.
It's like I'm talking to myself
But, I ask you, "Are you there?
Do you love me?
Do you care?
I've always wondered,
"Where have you gone to?"
As I've walked threw life.
But, when I look back
I see you there
But, something is wrong.
I don't know
I guess I'll never know if you cared.

Leigh Ann Davis

My Father

He walks the dust earth,
breathing in her soul.
His skin, baked-bronze,
scorched by the noonday sun.
His face, marked by her strength.

He remains proud, confident;
Owning a good name.
Though his stature immense,
intimidating many,
his heart abides
gentle as a new born kitten.

He does not cry.
A veil conceals the anguish
for his wife,
buried in the cold ground!
Waiting for him.

To people,
he is just a man.
An ordinary man.
To me, he is more; He is my Father.

Lisa P. Brown

Be My Valentine

Be my Valentine my love.
For you are like a bird,
Who flew into my heart.
I have seen the world
In a different life
Through your eyes.
A life full of love and joy.
The love and joy,
To share with others.
You have trusted me
With your thoughts and deepest secret,
Which will always be kept
Deep in my heart.
For you are the first one,
Who ever stolen my heart away.
For this I thank you my love.
For you have given me something special.
You have given me your heart.
This mean so much to me.
For this, you'll always be my Valentine.

Albertina Mendes

Long Lonely Nights

The night is dark
The cold wind does blow
The chill to the bone
As it snows and snows

The stars have no brightness
The moon has no glow
As only a night time
Of sadness does show

The lights how they flicker
As each candle burns
And the log's on the fire
Are ready to turn

Where are you tonight?
I look out to the dark
But the darkness just looks back
And has no remark

So the long night goes on
More darker than 'ere'
And my lonely heart knows
Not the secret it bares....

Barbara Lang

I'll Always Remember You

He did not complain of his maladies
But quietly always did hope for remedies

When the remedy did not come
And his body eventually did succumb

Family and friends a short while crying
Know now that his spirit is flying

And even though you are not here
I can still hold you close and dear

For right from the start
I have held you, here, in my heart

Cheryl A. Fedak

Life Is Ever So Fleeting

The child is born
The candle lit

The child starts aging
The candle diminishing

The teeth start growing
Then there's walking

School is here
So very soon

The adolescent years
Oh how cool

Then college arrives
for just awhile

An adult now
A family to raise

Grandchildren to love
What a joy

The hair turns silver
The steps feeble

Still a book to write
A poet no doubt

Life is over
Before we know it

The child has made full circle
The candle goes out.

Life is ever so fleeting.
June N. Hamlett

Diamante

Home
tranquil, safe
loving, helping, protecting
family, furnishings, streets, strangers
hating, harming, disregarding
chaotic, precarious
world

Barbara Watkins

Lament

Oh the night the endless night
No sleep, no sleep for me
The words, the thoughts,
Come on pour out
Pour out like rain
Rain from the heavens
Gray —
Like the gray days of autumn
Cold—
Like the cold days of winter
So gray and cold
A match for my soul
The swollen rivers, no mystery to me
Swollen from my tears
As my soul flows to the sea
The emptiness that is left,
The void,
The void that can't be filled
A part of me is gone.

Janis Ortman

The Place Where The Berries Grow

The rising sun beckons us along a sand-dune trail
For we are going berryin', I and my little blue pail.
I hum as I pick my way along a path that I well know,
that leads to the hills of purple and blue....
the place where the berries grow.

I zig-zag through a stand of pine; their needles cloak the ground
where foot-fall, tip-toe soft, is free of sound.
hiding in the shadows the nosey, noisy crow
says he knows I'm on my way...
to the place where the berries grow.

Beyond the woods the purple hills rise to meet the sky,
and grey gulls circle overhead while a small snake wriggles by.
From the top I look around; there, far below,
is the ocean too, all purple and blue....
like the place where the berries grow.

As berries fill my pail I dream of banquets for a queen;
hot biscuits and clover honey, wild blueb'ries and cream.
All too soon, my pail replete, shows me it's time to go,
so I bid goodbye to the blue hills and sky....
and the place where the berries grow.

Connie Hess

Dear God

Dear God, there is a lot to me you don't know,
I don't cook, clean, or sew.
I don't go to church every week,
and sometimes I'm a little meek.
I don't get all A's,
and I don't pray on most days,
but, Dear God, when I did you didn't see,
and if you were wondering that is how you lost me.
Yes, sometimes I sin,
and no, I can't remember everywhere I've been,
but I do know right from wrong,
and that there is nowhere in my heart you belong.
Dear God, if you were wondering why,
it's because you take the innocent,
and leave us to watch them die.
So, Dear God, as you sit on your throne,
and pretend you are the reason this little world has grown,
Dear God, remember, I don't care, and never will,
because you take the praise, and leave us with the bill.

Christy Lynn Stewart

Citybird

The bird is dead
That's that
As for the cat
Felix was well fed
The songbird never dreamed this descendant of the lion
had killing in his head
mistook the cat for a pet, pussyfoot, fat
chaser of string, never a rat
This citybird should have known, instead
it ventured down from its catbird's seat
into the backyard on Main
What a catastrophe!
Who is mewing now and licking its feet
some things never change
Tweetledee

Lee Harris

Once Upon A Lovely Time

Once upon a lovely time, the trees were made of forests.
When the unicorns flew by, the angels sang a chorus.
The birds were made of many colors, like green, red and blue.
Their singing sounds like a flute, they sang as they flew.
The animals had lovely coats, they always cleaned their fur.
The cats were very nice creatures, you could tell, they always purred.
These creatures were very kind, they never harmed a thing.
Whenever you want to see one, you only have to sing,
"Once upon a lovely time, the trees were made of forests.
When the unicorns flew by, the angels sang a chorus".

Jennifer Kreutzer

One On One

Disgust, disgust, and more disgust,
dear Lord, can bring to the best Christian mind
a bit of discouragement, from any number of us.

It appears while keeping faith, and doing what's right to do,
at times, seems blessed rewards, are far and few.

Could just up my hands high,
let the tears stream upon the cheek,
leading to an outright cry.

Probably would have the need for usage of extra tissue,
however, the same disgust would still be an issue.

But, instead of a good boo-hoo,
dear Lord, I'll have a one on one with you.

I'm asking dear Lord, have patience. Give me a moment to pray.
Just feeling a bit let down, a sort of feel sorry for self day.

Please forgive me for complaining.
Whatever the disgust felt, it's all known by you.
No need for explaining.
Let me lay aside all thoughts that annoy.
With your loving arms ever stretched,
there is always much love and joy.

Elvera Story

A Woman For All Seasons

You are a woman for all seasons.
A gift of God's grace can be but one of many reasons.
In winter the snow drapes your soft shoulders like a royal gown.
Because of your reign the entire universe is erased of any frown.
In the spring a robin makes her nest upon your head,
And nature adorns your angelic face with a necklace of fresh
flowers and leaves to signify new life has begun.
In the summer not just the air but hearts as well are warmed
by the sweet embrace of your loving arms.
The golden brown color of your hair matches the leaves blowing
in the breeze fall of a crisp New England fall to a tee.
All the good things you do are worth remembering.
Maybe a wonder women you're not, but you are a wonderful woman.
And perhaps that's even harder to be.
You are a woman for all seasons it is plain to see.
So when the passing seasons become at least a century
make a list of all those who have loved you.
And a long list I'm sure it will be.
I hope - No, I pray that the name at the top of that list will be me.

Michael Wishon

The Beauty Of The Monarch

Small, meek, and harmless,
as tender as a flower bud, as magical as a first snow.
Their soft feet so tender, their wings flutter with the wind.
Such color, beauty, grace.
The butterfly does not possess this, this possesses the butterfly.
A tiny dot it sometimes seems to be, a tiny dot facing the everlasting
sky, the everlasting universe.

Maggie Klein

Ponder

Suffocation is how it's been.
No place for salvation except
from within. Mind starts to
wander. I feel a need to shout.
What have the decisions,
really been about? What to seek?
I just don't have a clue. My
mind swollen with thoughts, of
what I need to do. Rid me of
this organized chaos! Help me
find the way. For happiness is
all I seek, in my future days....CWB

Craig Babino

The Book Of John; Chapter 95: Verse 96

Johns are all the same, you see.
Wholesome, intelligent me.

Johns tap your soul.
They steal your key.
Unlock the secrets, open the mind, the soul, the body.
Then shut the door on what we could be.

Johns are all the same you see.
Painted up, whorish, flagrant me.

Johns tap your soul.
Paying dollars for the key.
Unburden the secrets, open the mind, the soul, the body;
of their own decree.
Then shut the door on what we might as well be, leaving the money,
    leaving the key.

No John is different to me.
They are all the same, you see?

Barbara Seefahrt

God's Loveletter To Mankind The Holy Bible

Of all the books ever written — none can compare to the Bible
And all of it is true — in all its words — there is no Libel
God created everything and describes it in his word to us
He had a plan for all creation — there were no feather's and no fuss
But lucifer rebelled and said, "I shall be like God".
And so God banished him from heaven
    and now lucifer tempts man on this sod
Now God's plan for man was that he should
    have dominion on this world,
But satan foiled plan-A and thus God's plan-B was unfurled
God's intent was that, through the church, his wisdom should
    be made known
Though man, in his own knowledge, from God's wisdom has flown
God loved us still, and on the cross provided us — his righteousness
But man, in his forgetfulness
Remembers not what Christ did for him on the cross
Man still wants to be his own boss
Even though Christ said, "If you love me - keep my commandments".
And don't attempt to walk the fence
But give your life to Christ and make him king
For then joy and peace he will bring and one day at his feet,
    our crowns we will fling
Then new songs of praise for him — all his saved will sing.

Dean Crist

Born Free

Don't grieve for me, for now I'm born free;
I'm falling the path God laid out for me, I'm born free;
I took his hand when I heard him call, why! I'm born free
I turned my back and left it all because I was born free.

I could not stay another day that way, I was born free
To laugh, to love to work, or play, I was born free.
Tasks left undone must stay that day, why! I was born free.
I found that place at the close of the day, I was born free.

If my parting has left a void. Because I was born free.
Then fill it with remembered joy, I was born free.
A friendship shared, a laugh, a kiss, why, I was born free.
Ah yes, these things, I too, will miss and why, I was born free.

Be not the burdened with the times of sorrow. I was born free.
I wish you a sunshine of tomorrow, you were born free.
My life has been full, I savored so much. I was born free.
Good friends, good times, a loved one has touched, I was born free.

Perhaps my time seemed all too brief, because I was born free.
Don't lengthened it now with your undue grief. Why! I was born free.
Lift up your hearts then share this with me. I was born free.
God wanted me right now, he has set me free, why, I was born free.

Anthony Vincent DiGiannurio

Permission Not Granted

Malicious words acts designed to hurt today we abolish we
implore new self esteem a protective polish, permission granted
Realizing anew, you can't hurt unless permission is given to you
hurtful words and attitudes from others we will circumvent,
just don't give consent decide ugliness will not be received,
mental anguish relieved simply, permission not granted
Acts unacknowledged in our minds will soon die on the proverbial vine
Permission granted to hurt destroy admitting they do tend to annoy
can't change people petty and mean we can use our self esteem
don't give consent to be hurt by it. Permission not granted

Jeanette H. Jefferson

The Sunshine Of A Smile

Sunshine like you is free, it warms the cockles bold;
It brings a lift to the spirit, a gift of life foretold,
It's pleasant rays a guideline, a way to inner grace;
It's pleasant warmth a highway, to bring a smile upon your face.
The inner human spirit, shows us that you care;
A breech of human dignity makes us all beware.
A frown means an umbrella, a tear upon the eye;
To change a frown, from upside down, you really have to try.
A smile is something very special, it comes from deep within;
To get one out, from inside out you'll have a happy grin.
Forget your troubles, just be happy, some have been known to say;
Forgetting troubles is a problem, the tears get in the way.
But try to find a happy thought, they rescue and are true blue;
For happy thoughts are blessings, and are life savers for me and you.
A smile cannot be turned on like a faucet, or make you fly like Peter Pan;
For fairy dust can't do it, and it doesn't come inside a can.
Don't force yourself to do it, 'twould be a mortal sin;
Just let yourself connect it, and let your smile begin!

Shirley Allen

Promise

The wind blows cold this eve'.
Summers fragrance, rose and lilac are now but memory.
Life appears to sleep in this vague fog that covers every substance
within reach of her white misty folds.
A glimmer of light passes through the storm cloud,
    penetrates the haze, embraces the Earth.
The tempest entices and teases her way on through, creating a promise.

The Rainbow.

Donna J. Gallardo

Looking Through My Soul

I look at myself in the mirror
And I see a girl
A mere girl, no one special, plain and simple
Struggling to grow up
Trying to be noticed. Wanting to be notice
To be beautiful, to be remembered
But, I'm not
I wonder how many spears of loneliness it will take
   to make me wince in pain
No matter how many arrows strike my heart
I will survive. I will go on
No matter how many bullets of humiliation pierce my soul
The sun will rise the next day. My wounds will heal,
   and I will go on
Even though I'm just a girl, I know I can be more.
I know I will be more
There will always be tomorrow
Now, I look at myself again
This time, I look through my soul
I see a noticed, beautiful, remembered girl
Me
I don't need a mirror to see who I really am
For I see myself through my soul

   Dipa Joshi

The H Words

Helen, the face that launched a thousand ships
Homer, the poet of the wine-dark sea
Heraclitus, the philosopher who said
   you can never step into the same river twice
Hippocrates, the author of the physician's oath
Heracles, the genius who did twelve miraculous labors
Hadrian, the Roman emperor who loved Greece
Hera, the wife of Zeus, the queen of the Gods,
   the goddess of women and marriage
Herodotus, the Father of History
Hero, a priestess beloved of leander,
   who swam the Hellespont every night to be with her
Hellespont, the strait named for Helle, who drowned in it
Helicon, a mountain group, the home of the Muses
Hades, the home of the dead, beneath the earth
Hippolyta, the queen of the Amazons
Why does Greece attract all these "H" words?
Well, of course, Greece calls herself "Hellas"!

   Barbara R. DuBois

If I Were An Angel

If I were an Angel I would caress and kiss the air that surrounds you.
I would follow your footsteps, gather them in my arms,
   and imprint them inside my heart.
In the dark, we would fly away.

If I were an Angel I would crown you Master of the sky, hand
you a cloud to float upon and slowly glide you to glimpse the
sun as you pass you'll see it smile. Looming somewhere near
the rainbow proudly enhances; its colors illuminating your face.
The wind whispers and silently stands still taking notice
   of your exceptional grace.
Joyously the rain ceases for the moment to give birth to a
   special lily bearing your name, announcing it Peace.

If I were an Angel I would command you the authority to rule
the bolts of thunder, you would wander way out yonder where
stars would dance in celebration. I would lend you a pair of
wings to fly into eternity where you would sight God upon his
golden throne and bestow your soul. In light of it all, it seems a
wondrous bliss to rest in heaven for even a moment.

In this dream, promises I have made as I awake I realize I cannot
keep for I am earth-bonded absent the powers of an angel.
Panos, be it known, if I were an angel, truth would be this dream.

   Barbara Annalisa Kelalis

Rodman Suspended

Rodman, Rodman,
Tisk, tisk, tisk.
Bad language on TV,
In front of kids.
You got suspended,
For acting like a punk.
Now you pay the price,
In great big bucks.
You know and I know,
You shouldn't have lost.
But most of all,
You made a bad call.
People can't believe it,
You're so bad.
You should know better,
Because you're a dad.
You're a role model,
To kids in this country.
How could you make such a scene?
Straighten up, stand tall, behave yourself,
   and stop acting so mean.

   Dax Fredrick Spanogle

A True Story

"There is a shout of voices across this nation
To stop child protective service and social services from
tearing families recklessly apart without proper investigations!"

"This happened to me as a mother
due to the lies and frauds of another to make a long story short
I have since found out I am declared dead in a court!"

"This is a true story of a man who did not have to die
of numerous child abuses that would not have happened
if C.P.S. social workers sheriffs and D.A.S. would
have listened and acted to uncover the lie!"

"People in county government cover up and corruption
   wish I would just go away"
"Paper work presented to the grand jury was torn up and
hidden by the Merced county D.A. of the truth while I was still
Albert Sanchez Gonzales legal wife another woman took over my life!"

"A very close and personal friendship by this couple with a deputy
sherif of Merced County has been shown that's how my first
husband and this woman kept the frands and lies from being known!"

"With pen in hand this mother-grandmother-nurse and army vet
began to write to the house and senate and even the President
of her plight and has vowed for truth and justice to never give
up the fight!"

   Donna J. Crowder

"Awakening"

Sometimes when I look in the mirror, I see myself as someone else.
I see a man who has lived his life to the fullest, without regret or
Remorse. Then I picture the reality of the struggle.
I see a young man on a sailboat with a broken sail, being tossed in
The fury of the storm, ragged, though still alive
   he searched for the Calm.
Not knowing where He'll end up and not sure of the purpose,
He's like a fish at sea looking for its next meal, knowing that the
   shark is always close-by waiting for the next victim!
The young man, who has lost touch with himself and the world in so
Many ways, hopes that someday he will wake up, someday he will.

   Donald E. Lake

Tower Abyss

The claws and fingers curl, one to each and sheathed in red
the umber firelight brittle and flecked with silver-grey
Banshee howls of silence, screaming the night with sympathies cries
resting stone and silence on the balustrade, thick eyes of night
seeping sound and black
running veins of stillness

The sheath of nightmare sooth, dreamer to the dream and
cloaked in
moon silver leaves cool and speak of breeze, flutter the walls
midnight sings in the garden siren of morning
lying cold on the cobblestones, beads of ice and blue
sway of time and black
running veins of stillness

Kimberly Treiber

Daddy

Daddy,
I miss you!
I wish you were here
To walk me down the aisle
My special day - no one else is worthy
But miles steal the privilege away from you.
I'm sorry.

Daddy,
I wish you were here
I made it... a degree
I know you're proud of me
You would have come if you could
Again, miles keep you from the pleasure of seeing my accomplishment
I wish...

Daddy,
I wish you could be here
Fragmented visits are not enough...
My children on your lap are only in my dreams
They don't know the tenderness - who you are
Memories of Grandpa are only pieces of what I know
if only...

Daddy,
I wish you could be here
Coming home is not the same.
Your chair is empty
Your fruit trees yield fruit and the elderly miss your gift of their refreshment
The kitchen doesn't swirl with the smells of your on going cuisine. Oh, how I miss you!
I love you Daddy!!!

Birdie Harms

Maturity, What Are You?

Maturity, you are the final touch that adorns life.
Maturity, you are the last decor put on our perspective toward life.
Maturity, you are acceptance of situation and adaptation
  to circumstance.
Maturity, you are the beautiful element that embellishes
  life just as a knife carves exquisitely wood.
Maturity, you are refined wisdom.
Maturity, you are like the gardener who beautifies and
  brings harmony to nature's many wonders.
Maturity, in spite of the balance and harmony you provide
  man, you are a rare commodity.
Maturity, the decor of life, final intelligence of mankind,
  splendid navigator of life; these are the beautiful things
  you are.

Nehla Zikria

On Silver Wings

My friend, you came into this world riding on silver wings.
As you are transported to the heavens above,
we your brothers in arms, are asking the almighty,
to induct you into his heavenly armies,
as you arrive on silver wings.

You have earned the privilege of joining his ranks,
when in your youth you wanted to be a soldier,
and protect our great country, further earning your ride on silver wings.
When you arrived home you could not forget
your buddies left on the battlefield.

You were decorated for bravery under fire,
You served with honor and courage
therefore earning your ride on silver wings.
When you came home, you did not want
to talk about your war experiences,
but you found other comrades who helped you to adjust.

We your comrades, will surely miss you, so when you get to
your destination in the heavens above, will you please ask
the Lords, angels to consider our qualifications, as U.S. Veterans,
as we too would like to ride home on silver wings.

So as we prepare to say goodbye for now,
Let us render you a last salute, as you ride home on silver wings.
The rifles, have fired in your honor,
Announcing your arrival into the heavens above riding on silver wings.

Julio Y. Martinez

Solitude

While fallen in the dark abyss that hunts a human mind,
Engulfed by utter loneliness, with dismal gloom entwined,
Where, morbidly, lies hopeless doom as futile to elude,
I watched the candle's flick'ring flame and cursed the solitude.

In seeking to dispel the curse my vast seclusion wrought,
Supposing some abandoned verse might sway my somber thought,
I happened upon forsaken lines - somehow left unpursued,
A work called only "Nothingness" - subtitled "Solitude."

Had solemn depth befallen me to vex my very soul,
Or, was some mystery to be of virtue to extol?
I waited in the shad'wy night to learn what truth ensued,
And took up pen, intent to write the henceforth, "Solitude."

When presently, my spirit rose as though power endued,
Alert was I - afraid to doze, amid such hoisted mood.
There came each word as if a bough, by wand'ring though accrued;
Creation, like a mighty oak - its roots in solitude.

Although that blackened night wore late, I durst not close my eyes,
Rememb'ring my excited state first came in morbid guise.
Then, marv'ling at such strange events, I hastened to conclude:
That awesome heights shall be reached hence, from depth - of solitude.

Stephen Paul Schulz

Jeanne

Eyes - just full of sweetness, brown hair with some gray;
Heart as big as all outdoors - Wait! There's lots I want to say.

Jeanne is my sister. I am proud of this.
She's sweet as vanilla pudding and bright as the day is.

She's quick to catch on to things; except for jokes - oh me!
It's so much fun to watch her when - she's laughing, he, he, he!!

Jeanne is retiring now, she's looked forward to this day.
She has worked hard all her life, and now it's time to play!

I pray that she enjoys her life, oh Lord, and I thank Thee,
For blessing me with this sister to love, yes, for my sister - Jeanne!

Peggy Bone

No One There

Oh, I hate the days of hurting when my life seems so unfair;
When I think I'm going crazy and it's just too much to bear;
When my heart is full of anguish and it hurts too much to care;
It would be of such great comfort just to know that someone's there.

When my days are full of trouble and my sun is going down;
When my flowers are all dying and my world is turning brown;
When my ears refuse to register the laughter of the clown;
It's as though I'm in an ocean and I fear I'll surely drown.

How I wish some caring person would reach out with a hand,
To pull me from the water and help me cross the sand.
To pick me up if I should fall, to lean on as I stand;
To help me make it through the painful times unplanned.

Like a cool and soothing washcloth to a pounding, hurting head
Or to wander in the desert and to find a riverbed.
As I turn to look around and find my world so full of dread;
I would feel a little better if there was a watershed.

But my life is just a pathway that I wander solitaire;
And the thorns along the edges, deep they cut me everywhere.
So I look around for comfort from my troubles and my care.
How I wish there was an answer! But there is no one there.

Karen M. Johnson

A Letter From My Dog In Heaven

I'm sending you this little note to ask you not to grieve for me
I'm thankful that the strength was summoned
Up to finally set me free

So stop your crying, dry your eyes, as I tell you of paradise

My journey here was peaceful and oh what a wondrous sight
My cataracts had disappeared, I saw a brilliant light

Then suddenly I found myself right at the pearly gate
Would you believe, there was a line, good grief I had to wait

St. Peter, then, did call to me "it's your turn, scampy come"
Then, miracle of miracles I found that I could run

Full speed ahead, no stopping me, and what's the first thing that
    I see?
A little birdie greeting me

"Hey scamp, what took you so darned long? We figured something
    had gone wrong
According to our calendar you're five days overdue
Well never mind, come on, we have a feast prepared for you"

I'm happy here, it's heavenly, it really is the place to be
I run for mile after mile, so when you think of me just smile!

Celia Risoli

Another Day Has Past

Here alone, I sit in my cell, as if I was the last,
I've no idea, of the time, but I know another day has past.

Forcibly separated from my family, and those I love the most,
My enigma, and circumstances, are read in the daily post.

I'm out of touch with nature, and deemed an outcast of society,
By the mere nature, of my dilemma, I should suffer great anxiety.

It is unfortunate, for me, to be subject to live like this,
My body and soul sinks beneath me, I feel no spiritual bliss.

My family, friends and even my church, are having some doubt,
By saying, this man, is beyond himself, and lacks intelligent clout.

Quite frankly I'm seeing once again, my reflection in the glass,
It seems as though, history repeats itself, and "Another Day has Past."

Wilkie L. Sanders Sr.

Death

Life was the one thing I feared most, even more than Death herself.
I would accept death wherever I could meet it.
I searched, but no one would accept the offer.
I tried suicide.
My attempt failed; not once, but several times.
However, I did not give up.
Day after day, night after night, I was persistent.
Finally I gave up; I became sleepy.
But, it was no sooner than the moment that I closed my eyes,
that I met death.

Darkness surrounded me; that was until Death had opened the door.
Rays of light struck my eyes, like lightning striking a beam of metal.
Death had entered the room.
I sensed her presence.
I had an image of her: young and beautiful.
Questions filled my thoughts.
I searched for answers; none.
She called my name. I reached out.
She led me into the light.
Now I knew I would never be seen again.

Sumit Sahdev

How Can You Help

  Wish be this, it's not my time.   Wish be that, it's not my time.
In spot I start to cry. In my corner I whither and die. Time
consumes me when I maul. When you touch me with your
thoughts I quiver. I the taker, you the giver. How can you help
me fix my mind? How can you help me become my own kind?
How can you help this land I save? How can you help this
dream I crave? I sit and stare at this empty blank room. As I
stare my thoughts come to bloom. A barrage of nothingness is
fired at me. The occurrence of this has left me unable to see.
My wisdom is the sailor that keeps my mind afloat.
My feelings are the shark which to whom makes me gloat.
I'm sinking into the magic sand. I don't know if I should take a
stand. How can you help my perspective on life?
How can you help me concur my strife?
Look in my eyes deep, and watch the clouds change with time.
Look in my eyes deep, and watch me get high. Once again
you've seen the end. Once again you've killed my friend.
Your weapon is guilt, it could concur my soul. It could take my
feelings and use them to dole. How can you help me fix my
mind? How can you help me become my own kind?
How can you help me heal my health? How can you help me
find myself?

Jessie Hunter

Committed Iranian

She came from a Deadly Land....Tehran, Iran...
    Far A Way.
A land where Terror
Mounted Swiftly Everyday...
A people united In
    Fear...
Their Screams stifled
    Deep Inside...
No Music, No dances, only the leader prances
women in veil's...robes of black...
looking down...if they disobey, death will follow.
    This is the way...
No Hope...fear to breathe... To speak....
    Do as they say, everyday.
    Committed Iranian, scurrying about like mice, doomed to a life
of misery...invisible chains, but bound none-the-less, like all the rest...
    A life of Hell...No place to hide...
    Committed Iranian blown away...

Gloria J. Marshall

Can't Find My Way Through The Night

Cloudy dark skies, conceals the moon-lit night.
Can't find my way, through the night.

A hollow red light plays upon her hair,
  her moving body kisses the sultry air.
Couples dance in strange arrangement,
  in wait of the sun's earthly judgement.

Movement from across the room; darkness conceals the light.
Can't find my way, in the night.

Drifting breath of air, rising up to meet the angel's flight.
  a girl with gold in her hair, quietly sitting over there.
With her eyes, passionately she signals, come here.
A moment to explore, a gentle flit of her hair,
  a scent of perfume in the air.
Darkness conceals the light.

Dances is the fire of fear.
Streets outside roam, those go who dare.
Can't find my way, through the night.

In a cemetery not far away, walk through
  the tombs of another day.
In time, let the wild horses carry you away,
  to be marooned in the wilderness, the sacred forest.
Like children with freedom we will play,
  and in this earthly shallow place to lay,
Will come again some other day.
Can't find my way, in the night.

Stuart L. Spanier

A Higher Purpose

I talked to God the other day, He said I should go to Green Bay
To bring together this great team, and now fulfilled-a lifelong dream

With Jesus guiding every move, there's not much left He has to prove
All colors come together here, this sure has been a glorious year

A higher purpose was His goal, not just to win the Super Bowl
But to show people, everywhere, that folks in Green Bay, truly, care

If people take the time to pray, and thank our Savior every day
Then love of neighbor would be "In," no matter what - No matter when

Great athletes come - Great athletes go, but God's forever, this I know
He wants for us to understand, each other, all across this land

An athletes gift is not his own, it's from our Lord, it's just a loan
It disappears when we get old, so don't act cocky - don't act bold

I have been blessed by God above,
He's filled with joy - He's filled with Love
So may I tell each one of you,
  it's from my heart-these words come true

This Super Sunday has been great, what can I say - it's truly fate
When players triumph as a team, fulfilled from God, a lifelong dream

Darrell Ree

Echoes Of Memories

That wooden structure 'way out back, the end of a path so worn
Still echoes precious memories of a time when hardships were borne.
Come rain or shine, or come what may, that little path we trod.
Its security and comfort there, kinda brought me closer to God.

Sometimes great plans were formed right there,
  so quiet with time to think
With solitude and close to Nature, problems solved without a blink.
Sometimes my mind can't help but go just wandering astray.
Those times simple, quiet and pure, no clutter of today.

If you turned back the page of time - some happiness - some wrath
One of the peaceful, calming thoughts would be at the end of that path.

Mabel T. Moss

Pascal

Where is Pascal?
I have asked many for his name,
Some say he went to the sun, others forgot his face,
Suddenly he is not to those he was.

Distant shores captured our footsteps,
As we ralied to the threshold of the future.
Through clouds of cobalt blue satin,
We found the past of our fathers.
Diving into rivers of burning rocks,
Could not cleanse our souls of matted hair.

There on an isolated beach in Mozambique, where only seasons go,
We became intoxicated with scents of beautiful wild flowers
And tasted the pungency of exotic spices,
that forever lingered in the memories of our tongues.

Whispering into my sleepy ears,
He said he would no longer be,
But I was haunted by the lullaby of sighs
And did not notice as he walked into the dawn of shredded sorrows.
Weary of the chilled embrace of endless nights,
I await his sweet smell and wonder will his return ever smile.

Vincent Anthony Zeccola

I Said I Was Fine

I was hurt, I was mad, I never listened to my Dad
When he said I didn't know what love was, I couldn't grow
Couldn't grow with a man who always put me down
Couldn't grow with a man who acted like a clown
In front of other people who never really knew, the hurt, the pain I felt -
They didn't have a clue!
It was facade, you see, that he put on for the community.
And all the while I was dying inside -
  not saying anything because of my pride.

And now I want to scream and shout to let them know
  what he's all about.
I would always defend him, protect him, you see afraid, perhaps of
  the blame put on me
The blame of a good marriage now going bad -
  the blame of young love -
  oh, it's so sad

Should I have given it one more try?
I was exhausted, no tears to cry
For my tears were dried up over crying in vain
For a marriage I wanted that gave so much pain.

I felt so alone so much of the time
But no one knew — I said I was fine.

Sue Lambert

Erik's Tribute

Death will come to all of us but why to someone so young?
Who's life had just begun? So unfair to the ones who cared,
  the little boy hoping everyone will remember the love and
    memories shared.
He wouldn't have wanted the tears, he has no fears.
He knows he's going to a place of no pain,
  a place of eternal light where there is no night.
Playing games with all the little children,
  running and laughing without ever worrying if he will hurt again.
Watching over us, whether he be a star in the sky,
  the rainbow above us or an eternal angel who taught us how
    to live and never to take for granted the life we live.
Cry no more he has found peace,
  he will live in our hearts as loving memories.

Heather Petrie

Fear

In the distance I see a loom of light,
Though all around me is the darkness of night.
What's in the distance which is shining so bright,
Is it the lights of a city, or campfires burning at a large campsite?

I am too far away so I cannot see,
I am miles from shore, way out to sea.
Surely there are people there, but will they welcome me,
Or take me as a prisoner and tie me to a tree?

How dark and quiet it is out here,
What will I find there as I get near,
Will there be voices that I will hear,
Will I be greeted by an uproarious cheer?

Right now the sea is quiet and calm,
Yet in my mind I keep repeating the 23rd Psalm,
For fear that at any moment I'll explode like a bomb,
Oh how I hope His Words will cause me to become calm.

I hear my heart beating rapid and loud,
It is darker still, as the moon drifts behind a cloud.
Is it something supernatural, or what my imagination has allowed?
How I wish I were not alone, rather with a very large crowd!

Frederick A. Mochel

Re-Cycled

The leaves are all out in polyethylene bags
Lining the street today
Like people who wait for a parade to go by
Dressed in their clothes so gay.

As they wait they talk among themselves you know.
Leaves have lots to say:
"How's about that wind?" "Sure needed that rain."
"Watch that game on Saturday?"
"Hey, Charlie!
The wife says some of our kind are going to the dump this year."
"Boy, howdy! Times sure have changed. Re-cycle. Whooee!"
"Mulch. Hey! I wanna be mulch. I wanna be mulch. I wanna be..."
"Settle down Junior and stop that bouncin'.
You're gonna bust your bag hoppin' up and down."

Trucks and shovels will be along soon
Light snow's starting to fall
Retired soldiers to the old folks home
Responding to Winter's call.

"Mama, what's it like to be Re-cycled?"
"Hush, child. Don't fret. Mama's here."

Deborah Haas

Delancy Street - During The Depression
(On The Lower Eastside)

It's a cold wintry day and everyone is hustling and bustling on
their way as they start their day. The merchants are hanging
their signs on their pushcarts to tell you the bargains of the day.
There's so much noise it's so very hard to hear the horses saying
Neigh! Neigh! As they protect their pushcart if anyone dares to
steal a thing or two today! Children are playing ball against
the wall as you hear all their pennies start to sing as each one
is hit with a very special ring. Who will win today? As they play
to win some pennies to buy a piece of fruit or something warm to
drink. Just think, these children enjoy a game or two, when if the
winner, it would bring a reward that comes so rarely each day.
Mother's are rushing to get their bargains of the day so they
can be on their hurried way. It's a friendly street as you stop to
greet all the neighbors you meet. How's by you?, is the question
most asked and the answer/always is. Some food a little heat in
our apartment and this is the best way to say! Thank goodness
nothing worse should come our way. How would I describe
Delancy street?. Oh, my! I'd have to say I can't imagine a more
charming way to start my day. So by the way I'll see you tomorrow!

Esther Kogan

Genocide In Heaven

Sacrifice of the innocent, Sacrifice of the lambs;
Surgical genocide, chemical genocide whatever form the
   circumstances command.
Lives are shattered and left in disarray; lives ebb slowly,
   to expire and then man has to pay.

Money has become their God, money their goal to attain-

Legal intimidation, the populations helpless resignation;
over stimulation, manipulation; controlling all is easy to instate.

No voice for their protection, least any desire insurrection
   or justice for the victim who suffers more than is escapeable-

No, no ethics here; the oath they quote is quite clear; morals
   for the subjectors do not exist; they harm you more when you resist.

Sacrifice of the innocent, sacrifice of the lambs-

A twisted soul committed such acts five decades and eight years past.
In a foreign land, God's children endured humiliation,
   degradation, near annihilation in a blazing bath.

The same insanity is among us, dear God who is there to defend us,
   from the sacrilege of soul and body-
Have they abandoned the spiritual maker?
Who are these offenders that have elected themselves
   the unholy takers?
God is aware that his lambs suffer in silence;
   they are heard and will be vindicated
   before the unholy have all eradicated

Dorinha E. Morandi

In The Eyes Of A Slave

I'm a black man strong and proud
This white world I'm living in can do me no harm

The white man thinks he can own a black
But he has another thing coming thinking like that

He thinks he is stronger and smarter than I
But only I can see the truth that lies

He is blinded by all the things he sees
The riches the gold and even me

But when are they without a queen
To stand and see the good in thee

Does he not see the riches in life
Jesus the King, Your wife, your queen, the love ones who are there
they all give you love and care

But just wait and see
The blacks will rise with dignity

And all they can do is stare
Because there is nothing they can do that we will care

I'm a black man strong and proud
Don't forget where you came from when we rise out loud

Treva Patton

My Friend

If butterflies could sing, oh what a song they'd sing.
To lift the minds and hearts of everything.
Fireflies who light up the sky parading their beauty far and wide,
But cannot match the style of your eyes your soul.
Door full of wonders to be explored, your friendship,
I cherish more and more. Life's journeys quest now stretching
Out across infinities breast.

Michael Thomas

119

This Feeling

There is a feeling inside me that no one else knows of -
  it's an unusual feeling like no other in many ways
It makes me smile in gratefulness and seems to pierce my heart
  like a sharpened dagger...all at once
Its familiar happiness and gruesome heartbreak...in perfect sync

It's like a dramatic symphony with black-tainted instruments
  that plays on and shows no signs of ending
It teases and torments every sense of hope my soul contains
It's a peaceful ballad with acoustic melodies and a gothic tune filled
  with heart - wrenching chords all in the most natural harmony

It seems to flow through my veins like cool and soft running water...
  yet it burns with primitive fire, raging and multiplying throughout
  every vacant and hollow corner in my mind...
  an odd sensation of comforting terror it excites me in the worst way.
It gives me a reason to live, yet it kills me

This feeling controls my every thought...my every move,
  and seems to consume me,
I can neither create it nor conquer it...
I can only surrender, and I have.
It was like selling my soul to this strange feeling which grows
  inside of me as each day goes by.
I despise it, but it feeds me and nurtures me

This feeling has no name or simple definition, not that I have
  discovered yet.
It has followed me all my life and has been with me
  like an abusive lover you love so dearly but hate severely...
  at the same time.
It's almost like a presence heaven and hell, euphoria andpain...
  in one distinct being - it's the strangest addiction you could
  imagine it's the beginning of the end of my life,
  and the end of the beginning...in the same moment and if I ever
  chose to escape it, I would never be the same

The feeling tortures me and traps me, and leaves me in agonizing awe
Nevertheless, it hurts. And even worse...it's real

  Holly Gollnick

The Truth Yet To Know

Are we to die yet in vein?
To uphold the names of our enemies slain?
People of nations who rise and fall;
Cries of echoed sorrow, from the graves they call.
Calling for the truth to eyes unseen;
Must make right, for the soul's unclean.
Laying in rest until the day they are called;
Ascend unto Heaven before the Great White Hall.
Leadeth to our Lord, who shall judge the dead;
Fear not my fallen brothers, rest thine heads.
For truth shall be unveiled to eyes that are blind;
Who thought nothing of killing, leaving conscience behind.

The selfish and greedy, who choose thy own path;
  have not even an inkling of the coming wrath.
People turn from God, to seek their own pleasure;
Having no thought of consequence, to abide in earthly treasures.
Hiding behind walls of idolatry and lust; giving into the
Devil's needs with him the soul will rust!

People who've strayed from God cannot hear his voice;
looking for other ways, in turn making a selfish choice.
The just shall be rewarded, into Heaven they will go;
  may God have mercy on the foolish,
  for the truth that's yet to know.

  David H. Tafel

Autumn

Autumn, golden autumn, the best days of the year,
When grains begin to ripen, and harvest time draws near.

Now golden stooks stand on the hill, and also in the vale,
Soon down each row, stook racks will go,
Bringing in the sheaves to flail.

With the rising sun, the surly hum of threshers can be heard,
And men begin, with happy grins, the golden sheaves to hurl.

From dawn to dark they toe the mark, and thus from day to day,
After supper's done, with all its fun, they're glad to "hit the hay."

Now you can see why I like to be in the harvest fields so dear,
Of course there's work, which you cannot shirk,
But there's this throughout the year.

I get a thrill from the goodwill which is with a threshing crew,
And if I miss a time like this, there'll be good reason to.

  Hillmen M. Holm

I Never Thought

Never thought that I could feel this way not at my age
Not after the life that I've been though never thought I could love
again but than I have never met anyone like you
What makes you touch my heart in such a way
That the armor I've built begs to be cracked open
Is it the need in me that responds to the need in you
Or it's the sincerity in you that holds my soul wide open
Thank you for letting me feel again for no matter what happens
in the end I didn't want to become an empty shell
And knowing you, made me see.
That there are others who felt just like me
If someone told me even a short month ago
That I could fall like a rock I would have thought they're crazy
But what is happening to me is completely amazing
Finally someone understands the rhythm of my mind
Someone who can feel the waves of my emotions
Even if the practical sides of our life are still in commotion
I feel so alive and free of all the absurd things
That have enslaved my mind afraid to feel any emotions
Now the dam is open and they can fill an ocean

  Hana Parker

Serving Thee

  How best can I serve thee, my love? Shall I weave
for thee a carpet of stars - a luminous path from
earth to the nearest golden galaxy?

  Or shall I create for thee a planetary playground
with purple and orange daffodils, African violets and pansies,
a Prussian blue sky with streaks of Matisson pink,
an ultramarine, transparent, calm sea with soft, azure
apples - silky yellow, sunbaked sandy beaches extending
as far as the eye can see, the palms flexing in the
cool, mellow wind; a star studded sky of silvery white
twinkling luminaries - thy bidding is but my creation, my liege.

Prepare will I for the a spiritual bed of
serene cumulus clouds with a coverlet of sunbeams by
day and moonbeams by night - for you to ascend to at will to
ponder your fear - reaching postulates. And upon thy bed,
oh great sage, I have placed a pillow of stars, and nearby
a lamp of moonlight, - a quill of quartz for thy nightly writings.

  Oh, yes, how best can I serve thee, my Lord
They wish being both blessed purpose and pleasure to me.

  Louise Albagli

Weep Not For Me

Weep not for me;
  we have shared joy, laughter and sunshine;
  we have know pain and sorrow, grief and tragedy.
Memories of special moments. Weep not for me

Send me no flowers, send me no flowers.
I cannot smell their sweet scented fragrance.
Send me no flowers, I cannot gaze upon their beauty.

Sing me no phrases of glory,
  leave me with no compliments of how kind I was, of how I cared.
For they may fall upon deaf ears.
I cannot hear how you loved me.
I cannot hear of our cherished friendship.

Weep not for me,
Weep with me in times of sadness, happiness and hope.

Send me flowers, while they can be enjoyed,
so that I may know their beauty and sincerity.

Sing my phrases now, so I can appreciate them.
Compliment me when I can be grateful, while I can enjoy your
friendship.

Deaf ears cannot hear. Expired eyes cannot see.
A dying heart cannot smile, it cannot love.

Weep not for me when I am gone in death I can never know.

   Samuel C. Miles

"Dad"

When I was just a child;
I sat upon your knee;
You were always there;
To hold and comfort me.
You saw me through the bad times;
When things were not so great;
You showed us love and kindness;
There was never room for hate.
You held us close beside you;
That night our mother died;
But I know you loved her "Daddy";
I know you must have cried.
I was a child of barely three;
Too young to know her yet;
But I remember that awful tragedy; that no-one can forget.
You kept us, safe and happy, being a mother and a dad;
And I remember all those years, and the good times that we've had.
Now, we've gone our separate ways; but I'll love you "Dad" forever;
That's one thing that time won't change;
And the days we shared together.

   Elaine Mary Boyle

Don't Fear

I fear not when I close my eyes for each day is a gift not a prize
So in the morning don't cry when I don't open my eyes my
physical and earthly body have gone but my soul lives on
Don't fear!

No moaning and tears then the un-answerable question why?
For those who have known me my heart will always live through
so don't fear!

I'll walk through the light my soul in hand I've just gone
home to my "Fathers Land" and my soul lives on
So you see I'll always be with you think happy thoughts as
the day's go on and on so does life - Don't Fear!

   Maderia C. Mack

Feeling Mortality

Drums of primal childhood vibrate across a tangle of memories.
Ear to ear a message pounds usurping an infinite mix of words.
A hundred piercing spears with again the pain of father's command.
"Stop that crying, stop now!" Quivering ceases, stammering stops.
In youthful obedience one stands subjugated by tribal ritual.
Healing by decree, like a voodoo cure caps a smoldering volcano.

A lifetime later the voice within rings without, "stop that crying!"
Poison of yesterday's darts lingers in a residue of the past.
If only that phrase could be a panacea, a poultice to draw the fester.
Must one submit to reality as a boiling thirst overflows?
Surging, seeking, I hurdle chasms to cascade words unwritten.
Stage "why not" visions in yearning fantasy.
Ooze through closed books to view vignettes unread.
Melt heart strings sent sizzling with melodies unsung.
Explore palette for hues never prismed in rainbow's arch.
Then, a viscous change solidifies as "never shall" belches forth.
Ultimately, must one acquiesce - will tears cease - will heart heal?
I fear maverick blood broods eternal in my brain.
I cannot prostrate my nature even while turning to stone.
But I would if I could to quiet this seeking, weeping, childish soul.

   Joyce Erickson

A Mother's Thoughts

I treasure the child that you are
Curious, smart, and unafraid, knowing the limits
Is what you must learn and learning is your job and play.

I'm doing my best to teach you all you must know
before you move beyond my reach I'll do all I can to help you grow.

I'm not doing this to prepare you for the world
  at my feet but for your world you must be
prepared so you can be all that you can be and so the
  light ahead can shine brighter than the sun above.

It's my job to teach you love, trust, patience, kindness,
  and understanding but also understand
    my sons everyone is not to be trusted for not all
people are what they seem to be. Your quest for knowledge
  will change the world and make it a better place.

I'm doing my best to let you know that you are truly
  loved and I'm teaching you all that
    I can so that you can take your place in this world.

   Keatha Poullard

The Great City Of Pompeii

A day emerges, a populous fills the square,
They carry out their business, seemingly without care.
A mother leads her child, a lazy dog hides in the shade,
Two lovers walk whispering, engrossed and unafraid.
Wealthy merchants conduct their business,
  the market is animated and full of life,
Children start out for school, a kiss from a loving husband to his wife.
Today this great Metropolis, its grandeur will be its last,
Its illustrious days behind it, just a memory from its past.
The inexhaustible Mount Vesuvius, a God within their eyes,
An unassuming and heedless body ignores its groans and sighs.
An eruption so swift and powerful, forever consumed within their fear,
No time to run to safety, no time to shed a tear.
Laying dormant but not forgotten, shrouded and waiting for the day,
When unearthed, is reborn the legend, the great City of Pompeii.

   Cynthia M. Diehl

Home

Place upon a crowded beach, by the Creator's loving hand
Near a vast ocean, rests a single grain of sand.
Settled upon this green and blue earth, an entire human race
Appearing from above as little specks on a colorful round face.

From one handful of her rich humus topsoil, can be found
More living organisms than ever walked an acre of ground.
One drop of water from a pond nearby
Is home to thousands of plants and animals, not seen by naked eye.

More cells can be found in one human mind
Than number all the stars known to mankind.
Light from these distant stars, we know
Was sent our direction over 10, 000 years ago.

When we look to the universe far beyond neighbor Mars,
We are as a single drop of precious water in a vast ocean of stars.
What is written here, that we have discussed
—Thousand of years from now will only be dust.

Bob Greenwood Jr.

A Sailor Remembers

In the waking hour of dawn, there stands a lonely figure of
A man whose shadow stretches out to the sea.

He waits there patiently, listening as if the waves were
Calling out to him. He bends down to touch the water but in
Its coolness, he draws back his hand.

He remembers a time in his youth when he once sailed the sea,
He saw it as something to be conquered but quickly, he realized,
That his thoughts were misguided, as the sea nearly swallowed Him up.

He sailed on many voyages carrying cargo to and fro. He sailed
For days at a time, even months before descending upon dry land.
In the ports, many would come out to greet the crew, so he was
Never alone.

Now, he stands and watches the sea
  as the waves draw closer to the shore.
He holds out his hands as if to catch the waves as they
Come in, the sea is his friend from days gone by, he smiles and
Then walks away. A sailor will always remember his friend the sea!

Cassandra Satberry

No Amount Of Pleasure, Is Worth This Amount Of Pain!

With each passing day,
tears are no longer a sign of disappointment,
they just fall without reason.

Reality becomes fiction,
as you begin to live out your worst nightmares.

No! I refuse to live that nightmare:
Facing furious parents; disappointed friends
  and astonished co-workers

I would rather...
I don't want to be judged by one mistake.
Don't want to be the topic of today's gossip.
Don't want to hear whispers....

"Oh, what a shame, she was such an intelligent girl
and look what she went and did to herself."

"Didn't they learn from us?" shouts a relative and close friend.

No! I can't and refuse to live like that!
Don't want my whole life to be based upon one foolish mistake.

So, cast judgment upon me now, as I - as we lay...
As we lay peacefully in an endless sleep.

Christine Moreira

Liquid

Liquid words engaging over cloudless visions.
Rooms with walls so smoldering.
Caked and filled up with anguish,
And I can't buy.
Floating and spinning.
Sentences overcome passengers
  and their taxi-coated drivers cruise.
No intentions except contentment,
And I can't stand.
Wanting comes game pieces.
Silver-tapped skies carrying his fear,
And I can't cry.
Electric flashes red coated green.
Time running away with my hand.
Tongue wrapped around that tree of life,
And I can't crawl.
Flesh stained on my brow. Night before torn from it's pages.
Tears surfacing the later hope,
And I can't see.
Smells circumference these words.
After all it's just rattling noise, vibrating.
And I can't breathe.

Dawn M. Rogers

The Beauty All Around Us

If I could describe nature's beauty,
I would think of no words to use,
  For our minds cannot comprehend it, without being confused.
I could only tell you of the sight I see as the sun sets in the west,
  As its golden wings touch the mountains highest crest.
Or when I look down upon the misty mountain stream,
  And see a fisherman casting for a dream.
As I watch the waves constantly crash on the snow-white sands,
  And it brings to mind winter's first snowflake, melting in my hand.
When I notice a flock of birds
riding the never-ending sea of air,
  I feel I could not imagine the sky
  without them, for that would leave it so bare.
Not to mention the feeling I possess
when I notice the first rose of spring,
  Its sensational beauty makes me burst
  into a song that only my heart can sing.
God created mother nature for us to always admire,
  And her memory will never stop burning
  inside us like an eternal fire.

Cheyenne Barnard

To Haunt Another Living Soul

The screaming voices.
The nightmares echoing into the night sky.
People pulling me in all directions.
Where is the silence?
Why won't the voices stop?
Why won't the nightmares go away?
Leave me alone, please!
Just leave me in silence.
What have I done?
Why won't you stop?
The crying voices of children.
The phantom figures and faces of the people of the past.
Why can't they leave me in peace?
I Cannot Stand It!!
I am going insane.
Shut Up! Shut Up!
My body can't take this anymore.
The stress is too great to bare for one heart, one mine, and one soul.
I shall join the voices soon, to haunt another living soul.
For this plague has conquered me at last.

Luane M. Tatro

Their Eyes Speak Their Words

Do you listen to the words that echo through the eyes of your children
Children may not understand...but if you listen, their eyes will
    speak their words

When their surroundings are peaceful
    and their home filled with laughter
Their eyes will speak of their comfort and joy thereafter

When there is no one at home and they enter silence....
When they are left to feed and to clothe themselves...
When there is no one to tuck them in at night...
Their eyes will speak of their fright

Their eyes speak their tears
Their eyes speak their fears
        Debra Pitta

Only Friends

I'm writing you this letter, I hope you get it today.
When you told me I was hurt, but now I am okay.
It's a sad story how our secret love ends.
Now you tell me you can't see me, now we're only friends.
Is it possible for a friend to care?
And when it comes to feelings is it possible for a friend to share?

Lips together, mind's apart.
When you touched my hands you also touched my heart.
So, I ask for your forgiveness as my letter ends.
Now I'm okay, and now we're only friends.
        Shelley Cornett

Try

As you stand upon that distant shore and reach up for a star,
Do you ever feel it slipping away? Does it ever seem too far?
Just hold on tight to your dreams, never let those wishes die,
When all the odds are down on you, the only thing to do is try.
Such is the case when it comes to love
    and that special someone you know,
Even when you are down on your luck, don't let your feeling go.
Your doubts and worries may be high
    and you may wonder day and night,
but if you do not try again, then when will it be right?
Find the one who holds the key, the one that unlocks your heart,
Let them know just how you feel, it can be a good place to start.
Don't look for love, it's a waste of time, don't search for it anymore,
For one day you may find a love come knocking on your door.
Love is a chance some people take, others may not feel the same,
    and if you wind up with a broken heart,
    you have only yourself to blame.
You should never start what you cannot end
    even though you don't know what's in store,
But when you find your one true love,
You'll know what the waiting was for.
So when you stand upon that distant shore and reach up to the sky,
Know in your heart it's not too far and all you must do is try!!!
        Brandy Harville

In Search Of It

I know not when I came to be but outside myself a world to see.
I took my ruck, packed my kit, and set out bold in search of it
I sailed the sea, I tramped the lands, tried myself at many hands.
Lives are born, likes expire, some by fate, some by fire.
No time to pause, no time to sit, too busy still in search of it.
Through summer's fire, through winter's chill, of this race I've
    had my fill.
Now's the time I think to quit, I've truly had the best of it.
        Jarrell Dennis Ogle

If The Angels Flew Away

If the angels took just one day off from this earth
it would surely be a pity.
There would be such a severe jolt of a power failure
that there would be a blackout in all of the major cities.

Just imagine if there would be no warm sound of a babbling brook
and no one to save you from the attempts of a perilous crook.

There would be no voice of conscience to tell you right from wrong
and there would be no sweet sound of music
when you would want to hear a song.

There would be no real laughter left upon this earth
and we might start to get frightened of our very worth.

What if warmth and human compassion were ripped
suddenly away from the atmosphere
You may find yourselves on your knees with something real to fear.

Just imagine how it would feel to be in a world that had no love
You might start to think it might all be
a warning from someone higher up above.

If there ever came a day that the angels flew away
I don't think that I would ever want to face another day.
        Eileen Sullivan Longauer

Giving Thanks At Thanksgiving A Tribute To My Mom

I came to you an 8-lb. malleable mass you lovingly called your "turkey"
You set about to mold me into the person you thought I ought to be
On this anniversary of my birth I give thanks for all your lessons
and for the grace of God in giving you the task of rearing me

You taught me that the ultimate sin is to knowingly hurt others
That integrity makes no room for theft or lies
That a girl should always strive to be a lady
It was always hard to hide transgression from your eyes

You had a word of wisdom to handle each occasion
You said a word of praise for the reaching of each goal
You offered love in many different packages
I still feel the warmth of your presence within my soul

The role of mother fit you better than anyone I have ever known
And I'm glad I had that realization while you were living,
not only after you were gone
        Mary Emma Ireland Bird

Conformity, Dream

How precious and magnificent each one is with originality and
splendor, isn't it disheartening to feel entrapped today with
the latest sophisticated sensor?
The innocence of youth, the freedom of spirit,
all too quickly consumed by expected conformity!
Wouldn't this short version of life, with open
honesty and integrity be assured tranquility?

To dream is to go beyond reality to another
place without conformity, without restriction or control.
It's a place where faith is beyond limitation,
where pure love may flourish, where absolution may enter the soul!
It may be where the most important question is answered,
or where the darkness leads us back to this existence.
Slipping in and out of dream state, knowing, feeling, or forgetting,
or another frightening night, due to the dream's persistence!

The hope God provides is around us, each and every
day or night, in all so many ways, wouldn't you and I be better,
trying unforeseen faith at times when the spirit may say?

Anarchy would reign, be it not for conformity, please use the
Golden Rule and the 10 Commandments as human's hopeful unity!
God, Jesus, and Holy Spirit, may we be inspired by dreams and
perceptions, worship and praise Thee, Absolute Three, always to be!!!
        Daniel T. Hyser

Untitled

If I could give you just one thing tonight,
I'd give you the moon.

I'd give you its completeness to make you whole.
I'd give you its fullness to satisfy you.

I'd give you its width to broaden your perspective,
    and its depth to probe.
I'd give you its brightness to cheer you,
    and its position to free you.

I'd give you its function to occupy you,
    and as for the man in the moon,
Picture me instead, to color your world.

And when the moon starts to fade, I'd give you its dimness
So I could overpower you with my emotions
    which now burn like the blazing sun — the moon's counterpart.

They always did say that opposites attract.
    Gabrielle A. Sprauve

For Nana, At Easter

This Easter I would like to share what's in my heart today,
To honor you for all you've done and He who led the way;
You helped me with my child needs and offered friendship too,
You were an angel sent by God and I, I pray, to you;

    We shared the happy and the sad
    The music played through good and bad
    We were content with life we had
    With Grandmom, Grandpop and with Dad;

The times we spent together, on Bridge Street all alone,
Were some of the most cherished my life had ever known;
But life is not a static thing, it's always fresh and new,
To mold and make and shape us from our Father's point of view;

    The jobs He gives can sometimes sting
    As Easter proves and angels sing
    So we may have a gift to bring
    To Him our Lord and Heavenly King;

We've done our best to serve Him, you and I, in special ways,
And for our gift we're blessed with love for each and all our days;
Please know I'll always love you and hold you in my heart,
For only one can fill the place where Mother's love departs.
    Sheree L. Birkbeck

21 Years

You've been married 21 years some filled with laughter
    and some with tears,
21 years is a long time to be together
    but I hope you'll stay that way forever.
Happy, glad, mad or sad
It don't matter you're are still in love's and that's why
I thank the Lord above.

I know there are bad times and things are on your minds
    and I wish I could help you through
    but sometimes there is nothing I can do.
When time gets you down and you think there is no love to be found
Just come to me and love is what you will see.

You'll have done so many things for me don't you see
Like buy me food and things I need
    and see I get an education to succeed.
When I'm sick and don't feel like I should you'll treat me very good
But even when I'm well you'll treat me swell.

If something was to hurt you bad I would be very sad
Crippled or not I still love you a whole lot
Remember I will always love you until I fall
But even when I'm dead you will still be in my heart and head.
    Jennifer Kay Tucker

Oak Tree

I sit under the big oak wondering. Wondering of what?
Just sitting there why? For what?
To think of the world and its worries.

No, to dream of what will happen as the years slowly go by.
The years pass, but still I sit there wondering under the big oak,
    my protector.

Centuries go by, but still I sit there wondering.
My protector soothes my worries and sorrows forever.

My protector stands by my side giving me advice,
    along the path to the kingdom of God.
I will sit under my protector forever, never leaving his side.
I will follow the path he has sat down before me.

When I have sorrows, he will cleanse them from my soul.
When I do a sin he will forgive me and take me back
    and teach me good from wrong.

I worry of what will come of life,
    but as long as my protector is at my side
I will have no worries of my future.
My protector teaches me to care, forgive, and love.
He teaches me many more things so I can teach others.

One day I might be that great oak tree.
I will stand by a person's side and lead them down the great
    path to the kingdom of God.
I will forgive their sins and cleanse their soul
    of sins and sorrows.
    Jamie Kathryn Heil

Ardent Love

Way deep down in my heart and soul,
There is a stranger waiting to explode.
Just let me be free! Just let me be me!
    she cries, for this ardent love!
I can't no longer hide.

She will hold you in her arms and entice you with her charms.
She will whisper in your ear, how she wants you oh... So near.

Just let me be free! Just let me be me!
    she cries, for this ardent love! I can't no longer hide.

She yearns to feel your tender touch
    rubbing down into her back.
And with her burning of your finger tips.

Oh.. My sweet love she cries.
Just take me up above the sky,
    don't you see that I can't hide this ardent love I have inside!

She embraced him with all the passion
    she was feeling, and they made love
Until her heart was screaming.
Way deep down in my heart and soul
    the stranger finally did explode.
She was free yes indeed but it was
    no stranger it was just me.
    Madeline Donohue

Sleep

The man of good sleep is here tonight, standing by my bed.
He has a bag of dreams held softly in his hand.
As he sprinkles the soft dreams on me, his golden nightcap glows,
for he enjoys giving people dreams.
With a turn of his silvery nightgown, he steps to the door.
My little brother's crying turns him back,
    and he draws from his hat a packet.
He opens it above my brother and out comes peaceful sleep.
He turns to leave and does.
    Joshua A. Smith

Wife Of My Life

Of life and love, and unicorn giggles, they call her my "wife,"
  but her I call my "life."
She, a goddess to this heart of mine,
  tis she who sings the sweetest of love songs for me
  to hear 'tis her eyes I see deep in my sleep.
And 'tis the touch of her sweet lips I do dream of.

Upon a shiny, still night, I unfurled the sails of my mind,
  and cast them away to sail the star studded sky.
It was a night of moonbeam delight, for when I opened up my eyes,
  it was her this wife of mine,
  who had boarded that dream of mine.

A smile, a smile, it touches my eyes and thaws this heart of mine.
She is the kiss of the moon, and the song I sing.
'Tis her and no one else, who stirs my feelings so I might fly.
So, if life is love, who might be more of my life than she, my wife?

And now, on this sea of life, I this human you see,
  has found a quiet harbor in the love she does give.
And, in this harbor we have made I, this man you see,
  shall love the goddess who is my wife.
Yet, these words matter not,
  for these feelings are my sight to this night made for love.

  Dale Consley

His Rose

I believe when I was born God saw me as a rose.
God saw everything that happen to His rose. He saw
the sexual abuse, the beating but most of all He saw the hurt inside
God still saw me as His Rose. Even thou His Rose was hurting inside.
I still showed love to others.
I put a smile on my face. Plus, I showed others that I caved.
His Rose needed a lot of water and sun to keep me growing.
God gave me special people in my life.
That helped me to grow.
God did see His Rose Fade away until it almost died.
God used those special people to help me grow inside.
God will see His Rose go through some hard times.
God will always looked down at me as His Rose.

  Charlene Coleman

Why

I do not understand
  why people do not care about pollution.
  Why people let some people or animals, die.
  Why they consider money more important than life,
But most of all I do not understand
  how they can get rid of a pet,
  and just leave it somewhere to fend for itself.
  How people could care less about a missing child,
  Why people are cruel to children and animals.
  And how they can walk past someone, or something hurt.

But most of all I understand
  how people can appreciate nature.
  Care when a child's toy is stolen.
  Listen when someone needs help.
  People who care enough to raise an injured or stray animal.
  And the need to keep hope, faith, trust, and love alive in us all.

  Sharon Stutz

Despair For Me

Cast into the corner of damnation. Faced with my own realization.
Uncertain of my choices. Confronted by my fears.
No-one seems to care the least bit how I feel.
Time is but a bearer, compassion but a wall,
  and my dreams just a reminder of my own living hell.

  Tracy Alan Goodson

Eyes

The heart that once pumped strong and steady
Now prepared for donor awaiting and ready,
The kidneys that once perfectly purified,
Transplanted to save the life that would have died.

DNA testing to answer the rhymes to crimes that were unsolvable
Nearing the new millennium, these current years are most incredible.

The world on a fast track of the information age,
Remote control selectors, Nintendo, Microsoft are the rage.

E-mail, faxes, silicon microchips, CD rom in cyberspace,
Accurate genetic testing, liposuction, radiation cause my mind to race.
Dealing with maximum human ingenuity, we must don the special
headgear for virtual reality.

Electronically stored x-ray, chemotherapy, ultrasound,
Anti-cellulie, autoimmune disorders, these terms abound.
The words swirl through my brain, like an elusive butterfly,
Causing my mental machinery to breakdown and cry.

All this advanced technology aids us, we know this is true.
Just don't leave this old body stranded, quaking among the residue.

  Gail D. Miller

Oh What A Mother!

Mother why do you care so deeply?
Why do you care for so many?
Why doesn't the valley confound you?
Why don't the obstacles overwhelm you?
Why Mother don't you give up?
Mother where did you get this love?
This never ending love - was it from your mother or father?
Mother said, "child this love only comes from Jesus Christ. He is
  higher than the highest mountain, lower than the lowest valley.
He is everywhere, knows everything, and is all powerful. He is
  a friend that surrendered his life for you. Child, silver and gold
  have I none, but such as I have, I give you Jesus."
Mother will forever be my example, fearless,
  woman of stamina, determination, and guts.
I understand now Mother it was your Jesus, who is now my Jesus
  drawing me to be just like Him -
Just like you Mother!

  Lena C. Staton

A Lovely Bouquet

Children are like flowers, blooming during April showers.
Like flowers, children develop from a seed.
They evolve into a bud and burst open into beautiful creatures.
Like flowers, children are defenseless and helpless.

Like flowers, children are of different sizes and colors.
Like flowers, children have different needs and wants.
Like flowers, children need to be loved, consoled and pampered.
Children needs to be taught respect for life and their surroundings.

Like flowers, children greets with open arms and bright smiles.
Like flowers, each child has it's own wonderful fragrance.
Like flowers, children should be chosen with great care.
So when they bloom they will be loved and adored.

Like flowers, children must be watered,
  cultivated and kept free from harm.
So they will stand tall, stand firm, for all the world to behold.
We must give children the same love and affection that we give flowers.
Then will their bright smiles light the pathway to a brighter future.

God has given us these precious gifts, only for a season.
Therefore teach the children and train them well.
Like flowers, children are innocent and trusting.
Unlike flowers, children are the world's greatest asset.

  Leola Johnson

125

Love Is Not Alternative

A peace supreme in ours.
Never to be spoken to those who know not of love,
or to those who wish not to hear.
Nor to those who see with their eyes and not with their hearts,
for they are in the bondage of their own ignorance.

Learning to follow ones' own true path begins with a sip from
the "cup of sorrow". Too bitter for most, they quickly retreat
with blinders intact; to their own pleasures in hypocritical
darkness. It is their own selfish cravings of conditioned
sweetness which prevents them from discovering the joy found
beyond what first tastes prevent them from discovering the
vision of ones' true self.

The moment flesh come to flesh is also truly a blessed union of
fields. Creating a dwelling where physical presence ceases to
exist, liberating our higher selves from the maddening darkness
of the majority and a conscience awareness take us beyond
what is and what is not, with the Infinite Form.

Valerie K. E. Jochum

Kissed By The Wind

One clear, beautiful Autumn eve I stepped out of my car
suddenly it hit me like a heavenly touch from above
I stood still and listened quietly
as the cool crisp breeze wrapped me ever so gently in its touch
Astonished that something so cold could make me feel
so warm and tingly inside

As the wind swept softly across my face I was reminded
of your sweet gentle kiss, slowly but steadily
the wind carefully wrapped around me
the way you would tenderly caress me in your loving embrace
I stood, motionless, smiling caught in this magical moment

I felt the wind brush my cheek slightly, as you have so many times
with a kind touch from your tender hand, when we would say
good night for the evening
As the wind ceased, I shook my head in amazement
Saddened for a moment as I thought of days of old, but then
I looked up, smiled and whispered
I Miss You too My Love

Yvette Norman

A Birthday Poem

H - Is for the happiness that I hope you experience for the rest of
  your life.
A - Is for the awareness of your happiness so you can enjoy it.
P - Is for the presents you may receive on your special day.
P - Is for your perspective on different opinions to teach me to
  listen to both sides of the story.
Y - Is for the yelling that taught me right from wrong.

B - Is for the bravery you've always had.
I - Is for believing I always innocent before proven guilty.
R - Is for reminding me of all my great qualities.
T - Is for the trust you've always had for me.
H - Is for the great sense of humor that made you laugh at my jokes.
D - Is for the very rare dumbness that you had.
A - Is for helping me with my arithmetic.
Y - Is for yearning for my happiness.

M - Is for the motherly love you always showed me.
O - Is for opening many doors of my life.
T - Is for helping triumph in my dreams.
H - Is for hearing my opinion and considering that it might be true.
E - Is for buying cheap essentials to get me most of the stuff
  I've ever wanted.
R - Is for the respect that you have always showed me.

Daniel Ray Price

Memories Suite, 1.The Box

My Love, she keeps a box of memories like the corners of her mind;
  misty, smoky memories of what she left behind.

Pictures of faces, lovers she knew
  and movie tickets torn in two,
  candles from a table set for two,
  photos with her eyes sparkling blue,

My Love, she keeps a box of memories,
  like the shadows of yesterday,
melancholy memories gathered and stored away.

Old love poems tied in ribbon ends
  from college sweethearts and high school friends,
  love letters and a man's class ring,
  and all the tears her past can bring.

She keeps close her box of memories, like the traces of her past,
  fondly remembered memories hidden far beneath her mask.
Memories she ties in ribbons and bows,
  as if her fairy tale has come to a close.

Eric M. Miller

My God Means So Much To Me

My God means so much to me
He guides my path to teach me what I ought to be
I cannot keep track of the countless times you have lifted up my soul
You have given me strength to teach me to be bold
You are there when struggles arrive in my life
How you have shown me to keep my head upright
In my life just to reach a goal my heart would grip with fear
I would sit in self-pity and there comes that drop of tear

My God means so much to me
He guides my path to teach me what I ought to be
The Spirit says: Seek first his kingdom and his righteousness
and all these things will be given to you as well
These very words comes from the mouth of the Lord so how can I fail

Whenever my spirit is low and my heart began to go astray
My Lord encourages me to kneel to my knees to pray
For me to sustain my life and be able to cope
I lean dearly on the Lord because he is my only hope

Oh yes! My God means so much to me
He always guides my path to teach me what I ought to be

Amen

Doris J. Massey

For My Friend, My Sister And My Other Mother

For Lila Jean With All My Love - Anne
There are so many things to tell you before we say good-bye.
But it happened I could not find in me the courage that's needed to try.
You are my friend, I know that's true for all that we have shared.
You've always been there when I needed you to let me know you cared.
You've shown me things throughout the years
  that have a special place.
My memories of you are stored inside a heart-shaped vase.
We share our secrets, laughs and fears as sisters normally do.
Who'd ever thought I would be so lucky to have a "sis" like you.
You're truthful, you're open,you're courageous and wise.
That's how
I've always viewed your reflection in my eyes.
I love to call you my "other mother" for reasons clear to me.
I'm proud to have people see you standing next to me.
I'd like to leave you thinking of the things that I've said here.
My friend, my sister and my "other mother"...
I hold you all so dear.

Anne Wright

Untitled

A moment for silence, time to ease my pain.
Personal affirmations, my psychological reign.
Reflections and infection of mental violence,
Distant glimpses, nothing but flashbacks,
This one for instance... A confinement to four corners,
Eyes cold for not to be told. Infections night, jackets of white.
Collision of time, calm nurturing mind.
Imbedded in my bottomless hole. Life without light, my eternal soul.
On this life, picture this, as the blood on my mental knife.
A jacket of confinement punctures my skin,
Locked down, I've confessed my sin.
Simple grins, immoral sin, life or death, lose or win.
A gracious blessing from a desperate cry.
My pulse flattens, no time for that, we all die.
Immature death, my four corners is where my soul rests.
My jacket snow white, light and darkness battle for night.
Completion of my mental relation, lifeless body lay deep for
eternal incubation. My mind infested, nothing but dead.
Images of life, my wooden cocoon, now I lay down the bed.
I apologize for my unholy beings,
Just wanted to taste death and reside in the sky's ceilings.

Wes J. Johnson

Hidden Faith

There was a time I could not find my innocence.
My love was distorted, disoriented, disillusioned.
I tried so hard to get the affection; desperate, despairing,
   all were disinterested.
So sad to have emotions so strong!
Swirling above me so strong with voice!
Time goes by, still I am here waiting.
Me, suppressed of wanting life,
Me, depressed because of the intensity,
Me, molested into submission, me so very young,
Me, didn't want to go on. Now, my children need me.
My health is hard to keep.
My needs are neglected, my home I don't have.
My mind is adrift with aggression.
My mother said I was selfish! Ramble on...
Some say happiness is what you make it.
I've tried the pain, sometimes excruciating.
Working in the fields growing up, blisters on my hands going to school.
We made it to the city, but nothing changed.
I was hoping, well I was just hoping . . .

Sandi Sue Rodriguez

The Raven

Blackbird, raven, are you free? Are you happy in your tree?
Do you fly alone and blue when the sun shines, dark on you?
When you're shimmering wings expand
   does it frighten birds and man?
Are they threatened by your flight? Do you wonder if it's right?
Don't you wonder if it's fair? Can you settle anywhere?
Are you free to just explore boundless sky or ocean floor?
Does the cardinal on her nest cover up her reddened breast
With a nervous fluttery wing when you lift your head and sing?
Does she want to calm you down
   when she sees you fly around?
While they try to settle you are you dying through and through?
Are you lonely for a friend: someone who could understand
You're not different, strange, or weird,
   and nicer than you first appeared?
Blackbird, are you ever free when you're flying...black like me?

Tanica Willis Campbell

Hope

To stand on the rim of nature and behold our wondrous land,
   is to compare the moment we are with eons of sea and sand.
The peak of the highest mountain, the deep of the ocean floor
Have been there from creation and will be, for time evermore.
There are prophets of doom and destruction, and weapons men
   have contrived to destroy all that God gave us,
   when tomorrow comes, will we survive?
Look then for hope to the mountains so undisturbed by it all,
   are the seasons constant as always,
   do the rivers still flow and fall on their journey to the sea,
   is the rainbow a sign for you and me?
While the sunshines, flowers bloom, friendships grow,
   we are awed by love, and understanding, kindness,
   and respect are part of the life we see, lets do our best,
   dream our dreams, never contemplating mortality.

Jessie Robertson Maxwell

A Moment At The Dock

I am watching the sunset, as the dock makes my seat
The weather is so perfect, over the calm water hangs my feet
The sun is a soft orange, the sky is pure and clear
I'm thinking about you, and how your love is so sincere

The water creates a mirror, which reflects life above
The view is so beautiful, as if touched by your love
The marsh is bright green, the birds are flying around
It's so calm and quiet, that even my blink protrudes a sound

The sun is now light red, and is slipping behind a cloud
And I can think of nothing other, than the love that we have vowed
To the left it drizzles rain, but here remains dry
The rain is from the angels, they feel our pain and cry

I would give up my own soul, if that could bring you here to me
I painfully miss you, and love you more than you or I could ever see
The sun has laid to rest, and gone beyond the dome
And now it's getting dark, so I must travel home

David L. Barefield Jr.

"Love"

Love - The only word with no meaning, Why? Because it has so many.
Love - The only word that contradicts itself, Why?
Because it hurts terribly.
Love - The one word of unity and bond, Why?
Because in its absence,
   it makes the heart grow fond.
Love - A strong word, Why? Because it makes Man weak.
Love - A word of divinity and holiness, Why?
Because it was created
   by God and it is the only word in which He speaks.

Marilyn Pena

Untitled

In January the snow falls down
In February hearts filled with love and care are flying everywhere
In March you dress in green and wait for leprechauns to be seen
In April colors fill the air and bunnies are hopping everywhere.
In May the sun shines as golden as gold.
In June different colored flowers come out to be set in hold.
In July brightly colored fireworks come out and everyone shouts.
In August we have to go back to school but it can be really cool.
In September it starts to rain leaves.
In October it's Halloween, everyone dresses
   in the costumes and screams!
In November we have a big feast.
In December while the snow falls down,
   two best friends sit by the fire.

Jessica Bowman

A Beacon Of Light

I stand tall with water at my feet, with God's fury all around me.
Pounding, thrusting, beaten on and shaken;
I'm still here one light not mistaken.
Never forgotten, never alone, winter, summer, rain or snow.
They come for miles just to see me show,
That beacon of light that sailor's foretold.
Stories of truth not imagination,
Heard miles and miles up and down this great nation.
I'm as old as this ground as strong as the spirit of the sea;
I've seen men come and go making history.
A monument to the seagulls and eagles flying high;
One faith; one trust; one tide. I only talk at night in a cloak of
fog; I even reach out and put my cape over the cod.
I protect and serve my fellow man,
Keep him safe from the mist to land.
For a light shining inward; a man of soul;
To attack his voice to speak out loud; land ho!
Rescued from the spirit of the dark to man's light;
A sailor's warning, a sailor's delight.
If not this beacon of life what am I?

Pamela King

Or Not to Be

This unending morning funeral, a farce from start to end
before the body's cold, it will happen once again

The newest heir the target, knows no danger to his life
tries to play off paranoia, fails to realize his own strife

For once the killing's started, who's to say that it should die
even those in greatest danger, deafly scoff at those who try

They believe they're in no danger, "benefactor will protect"
"he will not let hem hurt me, will not leave his children wrecked"

He has many times before, and will many times again
and as they drop like flies, he will blame it all on sin

Blindly follow him forever, as he spits into their face
still they worship at his feet, and glorify his saving grace

They beg for his forgiveness, when they know they have done wrong
when they come to his attention, suddenly they're up and gone

You may ask just who this is, or who can this idol be
be it spirit or emotion, institution, or all three

Must decide this for yourself, listen to whose beck and call
For each person it is different, but must you have one at all

David Palangi

And Me?

The lurid lasciviousness of their lives
                renders reasonability and rationality
at the behest of the doer
                                and the doer...
Knows not whether,   rationally or sane
she might again   or   maybe   lose?
So in the rain of life the plains of spice are rather nice
                and yet who's to say
That you or I may have the pleasure of the secret nectars
Or be banished forever to torments unnamed.
Oh fame where art thou when I am drained and much pain drives
Every strain of sound, rendering my mind a shattered nard
eclipsed
Then shall I be...eternity!

Gary A. Smith

Life Alone

Life is but a journey, some times better spent alone,
To walk by yourself down that dark and lonely road.
For when two people get together one's heart will surely die,
When in the end they find out it was all but a lie.
For the road in life that we must travel,
Is sometime found to be so narrow.
And the feelings we have down deep,
Are not made for anyone else to keep.
And when you cry, you cry alone,
Because there is no one else at home.
Some times love is thought to be boughten,
Only to find out it is soon forgotten.
And sometimes two people that should not have been one,
End up having a delicate new born.
And through the years and the screams and the fights.
That grown baby now sees only one parent in sight.
And through the divorce and the separation,
Many things are said and done in desperation.
Words that cannot be broken, now have been outright spoken,
Feelings that cannot be forgiven, some how come up as the
anger has
risen.

Jason Cundiff

He Runs With The Antelopes

Cool evening winds have lain upon dull scenes of
Sunday. Tides of leaves have danced on the parks's path.
He sits, he watches, He listens he sits...in the face of an
Abandoned carousel with silence for music. But in this man's mind
He sees more, children's euphoric laughter, hypnotic tunes from the
Carousel and the soft melody from the pupils of her
Cerulean eyes. She only smiled when they kissed, but the angels
Teach her how to smile now.
He weeps...he stares..at the box that has lain on his lap.
He thinks of her, her giggles...burn, her eyes...burn
The carousel..burn, children burn
His mind races, his body shivers like antelopes rummaging
Through the remains of him.
He is left with ashes.
He sits...he waits..
He thinks of her...
Smiles...youth has enclosed
Him...holds his box
He sits...closes his eyes, he thought of her..
He sits .. Sits .. So very still.

Melanie J. Patterson

The Ditch

It's the month of May and the weather is warm
And my lawn is growing like crazy
I should get the mower out and cut the thick grass
But some times I just feel so darn lazy

You see I have hay fever, my eyes itch, my nose runs and I sneeze
In fact it is pure misery
It is no fun to do yardwork when you suffer like that all day
But the grass has to be cut before it reaches the top of my knee

When I'm on the riding mower there's not much to it
It's hardly any work at all
But when it comes down to pushing there's one part I hate the most
That's why I let it get so tall

That one certain part, it's out by the road
It's long and wide and has a deep pitch
Down in it can be water or even a beer can
It is what we call The Ditch

It's the part I hate the most and I wouldn't have to do it
If only I were rich
I would then pay the neighbor kid to do it
Because on a hot day it can be a Son Of A B***h

Steven Pingatore

Death Put On A Quiet Cold Show

Childhood love that was meant to be,
Born for each other, the delight of the day,
Let's make every moment count,
When possible, cherish, appreciate parents,
Procrastinate not what can be done today,
The time, none the day unknown to us,
The caring, protective hands and warm loveliness,
Never there to be found, the home is blanket cold,
Death puts on cold quiet show, the rays of the sun no longer bright,

Things changed though nothing new,
   deep within my heart is restless sight,
New awareness suddenly stunned me, empty echo quiet home,
Is constant reminder they are gone, harsh reality the order of the day,
Strength, love of live time no more,
Together love and unity shun, together the light was extinguished,
To console the distressed heart, both quietly depart without good-bye,
Taking kindly, gracefully, the counsel of yester-years,
Lives well lived touched every soul, let's not vex or whine,
Broken dreams, and bonds will strive for peace and happiness,
Let not the darkest moment blind our faith,
Rest in perfect peace till we meet and part no more.

Juliana A. Opara

Death

To be dying is a scary experience.
To die alone is a pure Hell-Nobody should have to.
While I lie here in this bed, gasping for every breath,
I feel my feet become very cold and the feeling goes up my body.
I can't get warm.
My eyes are half open and half closed
I haven't got the strength to close to them, so all I see is black.
Instead, I can see in my room nobody is there.
Occasionally, someone will walk by
or only step in to see if I'm breathing.
I am.
I can hear everything. Still.
But nobody knows this. Nobody cares.
It's scary as Hell to be dying here and alone.
Nobody knows that unless they've been here.
Usually they don't live to tell it.
If someone did, they'd say "Someone sit with me."
I don't want to die alone.

Jeni Riley

Treasure

As a pirate who unearths the priceless treasure
   he undeservedly attains . . .
While on the sight of his glimmering golden treasure
Is doused by his bounty of the object of his pleasure
And doused is the destitute flame within
Treasure as recompense for the love and hate of him
Poverty stricken days are over, privation gone away
Infinite wealth, delightful dreams begin and end each day
Any hearts desire his glimmering gold can provide
Too perfect his treasure his awe he can not hide
A pedestal higher than the height of his skull ridden mast
And on his treasure sublime expectation is cast
Not out of obligation or rightful debit due
But out of his perception of what his gold can do

So please forgive me because I believe you do no wrong
I don't understand you're mortal and sing a human song
Precious treasure, you are so much more
   that this pirate ever dreamed of disappointing
   this unworthy soul is the one thing you can't do, love.
My love for my treasure will each forever grow
So forgive me cause I love you more than you can know

Ricky Scatterday

Jesus, Our Friend

We have a friend in Thee, a friend we cannot see
Who gave us life and blessed us with a soul.
Who has loved for everyone, all great things He has done
He is loving, He is holy, He is bold.
He is Thy precious Son, all great things He has done
He is the only One with life completely whole.

Let us kneel and pray, our King will lead the way
Until that day we are all called home.

He is blessed for all creation, our waters, lands and nations
And the power to make our lives secure and whole
We cannot see Him but, we know He is everywhere
For all great things He has done.

We bow our heads in prayer, we hang our heads in shame
He was crucified in pain, a sinful nation didn't seem to care
He was crucified by evil men, to save our souls from all our sins
He arose to be our Lord and King.

Let us kneel and pray, our King will lead the way
Until that day we are all called home.

Let us stand and sing, glory bells will ring
We love you for the great things you have done we love our
Lord, our hearts He has won he will always be Thy begotten Son.

Ernest E. Winchel

A Nurse

A nurse is one who cares and shares her knowledge with the sick.
Who gives her all to those in need.
A smile, a touch, a disease to heed.

A newborn babe, a sight to see. A sick child upon her knee.
A teenager in distress, can sometimes cause a family mess.
A helping hand to calm the pain.
To return to all the stakes they claim.

A young adult so very ill, no cure found with just a pill.
The machines, the tubes, the pain they feel.
Are just a few of life's less appeal.

An older person with memory lost, with fragile bones and body.
The family recalls the days gone by, when things were really jolly.

A nursing career, not for all. Such memories to recall.
The sad, the glad, the pain to ease.
The different shifts are not a breeze.
Personal satisfaction, a reward so great.
And may we meet again at Heaven's gait.

To the many patients, I have cared for.
The privilege has been all mine.
A minute of my life, I wouldn't change, for a different step in time.

Mary Barela

The Tie That Binds

Marriage is an institute, built on love and trust
And to go into this institute, honesty is a must.
To unite in holy matrimony, is till death do we part
To give one's self another, is to give with one's whole heart.

Blessed is this union, in which we become as one
Standing united side by side, until our days are done.
As we live our lives together, through thick and thin
Our love for one another will go on and never end.

Always know that I am here, to lend a helping hand
And in those times of pain and strife, I'll be there to understand.
Life is not always perfect, so know I'm always here
To give my love and support to the one I hold so dear.

As this day is witnessed, by the ones we love
May this union always be blessed, by almighty God above.
I believe in your love, for it is a rare find
And the belief in this love, will be the tie that binds.

Donna Dixon

129

A Prayer For My Father

Dear God, watch over my father.
Dear God, keep him close to me. Let him know I
vision his past and understand his world that shaped him
To be a reflection of all the truths my God in heaven is.

Let him know he walks in your presence, that he emanates
your light which draws many spirits to him.

Let him know dear God, that I sit silently from afar and feel
so much love and admiration tears fall from my eyes.

Let him know that when he feels pain, so do I and that my love
For the world exists because of the love he so unselfishly gives to me.

Thank you my Father in Heaven...
Thank you for my father.

Lynn L. Chernek

To Start '94 - '95 School Year

Dear God, I pray
That you will help me this day
To teach each child and help them learn in some kind of way.

Dear God, I pray
That you will give me a compassionate heart
To clear my head of all that I have heard,
So that I can give each one a new start.
Let me think only of them, not knowing if they have a color to
   their skin,
Not caring if they were at the head of the class or at the end,
But let it only matter what I can help them achieve.
While I have them the mine months with me,
Let this August of 94 be the beginning of a
Blessed school year of for me.

Susie L. Davis

Show Me The Way

You counted the cost,
   And found my spiritual value in need of growth.
You guided my vision toward God,
   When my eyes no longer beheld Him.
You gently breathed upon me God's grace,
   When my nose no longer smelled the sweetness of His Word.
You turned my speech to give Honor to God,
   When my tongue no longer spoke of Him.
You reminded me of Christ's crucifixion,
   When my head was held so high - that I could not see God.
You straightened out my relationship with God,
   When my back slouched with unconcern for His will in my life.
You read of Christ's spike-driven wrists,
   When my hands no longer worked for God.
You provided a mental picture of Christ's
   agonizing hour in Gethsemane,
   When my knees would not bend in prayer.
You showed me the way to God thru Jesus Christ His Son,
   When my feet refused to follow God the Father.
You counted the cost,
   And won a deeper friendship.

Jamie J. Smith

A Very Special Friend

You are someone I can talk to; Whom no one can replace.
You are someone I can laugh with; 'Till tears run down my face.

You are someone I can turn to; When I need a helping hand.
You are someone I can count on; To always understand.

You are someone I can sit with; And not say a word.
You are someone I can trust, To keep each confidence you've heard.

You are someone I think more of; as each day comes to an end.
I'm a very lucky person; Because you're "A Very Special Friend"

Serena Sherriff

Challenger's Last Seven

It was early in the day, when the
crew sat down together;
The morning was so nice, the Cape had
good weather;

A send off meal was served, as many times before:
We all watched as those seven, made
their exit out the door.

Their faces were all smiles, their Challenger stood just ahead:
They were ready for the flight to space, none of it did they
dread;

A countdown was begun, as the seconds faded away!
This was to be their moment for space, for one her first day!

As the shuttle began its journey, everything was still go:
Then came the command a "throttle up" Challengers
flight was aglow!

It happened in an instant, we can't even comprehend:
What had gone wrong with this mission?
Seven lives had met their end.

They left this earth in a ball of fire,
that's all we'll ever see.
They are now with their Father in Heaven.
May they rest and forever be.

Don Greenway

My Mother And Renewer

Lasting revolutions turn the years still lasting
and always being renewed by mother, a revolutionary beauty.

She creates night flight with chilling unforgetfullness-
re-energizing the earth's cells and smoothing wrinkles, protecting
her young perennial seeds.

She is an energy serum. In photons she revitalizes.
Two daughters receive light.
My sisters and I share her cyclical and concentrated radiance.

Everything about mother minimizes imperfections of all sorts
and she leaves indelible imprints sweetly painted on my skin forever.

Lisa A. Barker

The Man Of Sorrows

Do you see Him on the cross? Do you see a man betrayed?
Do you see His Holy Mother, distressed and so dismayed?
What made this Man to suffer so and caused His wounds so deep?
What caused Him so much anguish and made His Mother weep?

Do you see the "Man of Sorrows", bleeding, scourged, forlorn?
Rejected, cursed, blasphemed, defiled, with a crown of thorn?
Why, what evil has He done, what could His offense be?
You say He claimed to be a King, but He died for you and me.

See His Holy Mother who stands silent in the rain,
Is there none to comfort her or help to ease her pain?
But there is Mary Magdalene and yes, beloved John,
"There's your Mother, there's your son", and His life is gone.

Then the sky was darkened and became as black as night,
Mighty rolls of thunder and lightning, flashing bright,
The temple veil was torn in two and dead saints walked around,
And the "Man of Sorrows" bows His head, His blood upon the ground.

But wait! What is this glorious sight! The stone is rolled away!
Who is this young man dressed in white? What has he to say?
"Do not fear- come and see! Your Jesus is not dead!
Look! The tomb is empty! He has risen as He said!"

Dorothy Kordiak

The Zone

The Zone was where the bus went, its passengers sought knowledge.
Their ages young, their minds abound with thirst and their hearts
    full of trust and joy.
That zone was many years ago.

The Zone was where they went to be safe and free from drugs.
Their ages were still young, their minds most impressionable and their
    hearts full of caution.
That zone was not too long ago.

The Zone was where they went to be free from drugs
and safe from weapons.
Their ages were so very young, their minds filled of confusion
    and their hearts desensitized.
That zone was yesterday.

The Zone is where the bus goes, it brings the parents near.
Their children will be safe and free from harm.
Their ages will always be young,
    but their thirst for knowledge will cease,
    their hearts will beat no more.

That Zone is today.

   Darrilyn Di Nardo

Granmas' Reflection

Gran-ma! Oh Gran-ma! Gran-ma don't you hear me call?
I am Six years old you know, and I am getting tall...leest
    That's what you said, the other night, just before telling me it
    was time for bed!

I am Thirsty Gran-ma! Yes! I'd like a glass
    of milk . . . and some of your cookies too?
I like the stories you read, Gran-ma! Only
    I wish, they weren't so few!
Every little boy, should ask God how to get
    a Gran-ma, just like you! Then that
    little boy would know love, without
    boundries very deep and very true!
My uncle bought a shirt for me that says:
    "When the going gets tough...the tough
    go to Gran-mas", I know that's right,
    especially, when I get ready to say my prayers at night!
You're kind and gentle, yet firm, and strong
    and no matter how much fuss, I make, we
Two, still get along! You remind me of some
one! I am not sure who...maybe it's my
Ma-Ma, for some reason, she's a lot like you!

   Ronald J. Kasher

Outside

I'm on the outside looking in
Always striving for dreams that seem to be eternally locked within
Living in a reality that's supposedly sane
Dealing with hurt, guilt, and pain
Time being an ongoing illusion
Incomprehensible for me - am I insane?
I'm on the outside looking in
Looking at my life or someone that I supposedly am
Reaching for life's line
Height always being my nature's unkind
Riding on a carriage whose destinations unsure
Tears being my hearts only cure
Someone once said, "I have a dream.."
A dream that could have only possibly been a hallucination
I'm on the outside looking in
Yes! That's me!
Searching for the passage way that will help me find my way within
To the real me!

   Susanne M. Balla

Manic

Let me tell you about a place of deep darkness
    and desolation, full of desperation.
No one goes there now, it is forever lost in the flow of sadness.
The plants do not flourish there
    and the animals are under-nourished.

When you hear a sound, it is not joyful, it is a whimper.
Here things tend to lose their tempers easily.
Only anger thrives in this dark realm of reality.
Enter if you dare.

Beware of the monster that awaits.
It will seek you out and hunt you down as soon
    as you pass through the gates.
It devours all, nothing will be left of you.
This place has no pity.

Long ago love was cast out.
Now nothing lasts, not even memories of loves of the past.
Feel the pain all round, enjoy the rain, the only sound
    of this land of desolation.

It is my heart, tortured and abused, hear it cry, feel my pain,
    watch me slowly die and fade away into oblivion.

   Jennifer L. Greenwell

Frank Black's Got It Right

there's a stretch of road i know
it can be found in the backyard of Los Angeles
lapping at the dusty feet of desert mountains
and frank whirls me over asphalt sunsplit and leaking
licking our bare toes in brief tastes
and frank stomps his feet and claps his hands cries out
"ole, ole, for mulholland"
and well, I can't help but agree
"hooray, hooray the ants are crawling"
right across my toes and on down the road
single file and undisturbed in the thick afternoon heat
while the city swarms and breeds and plots ten miles behind
all around me swim the dust motes carrying specks of sunshine
straight up my nose and into my head
exploding the magic of this highway, oh, how it speaks to me
and frank whispers again and again on mulholland how it can scream
nights spent up on the fire roads above old mulholland gazing down
and out across the bowl of the city thrown slantways by too
much love i have realized the singular beauty of the cold desert dark.

   Margaret Phillips

The Assassination

One man saving another, you seldom see,
for only the assassinator to his victims life, holds the key.
Blonde hair, black hair, whose here, whose there,
which man is which? The evilness in ones eyes
will turn on a switch.

He's here, he's there, they both try to stay undercover,
But in his mind, somehow they will find each other.
One by one, he carefully studied each one of his chaps,
for only one wrong clue will break the assassinator's back.

Questions, Questions, Questions are winding channels in his mind,
Hoping someday, the assassinator he will find.
The assassinator finds people who want enemies killed,
for only the assassinator out of this, gets a thrill.

Pictures on papers of one more man down,
sends a hopeful face into a twisted frown.
One more friend of his, says every where, he's dead,
leaves one more raging thought stuck in his head.

But now the role is switched, the good guy has won,
for someone payed him to kill the assassinator,
justice has been done.

   Sarah Strickland

To Shelby

You are my Grandchild, how I Love You so.
The day you were born, the a joy I received you will never know.
You were beautiful, kicking and crying with red, beautiful red hair.
Kicking and crying with skin so fair.
You are the very best of your Mommy and Daddy.
You are loving and kind with a sense of humor, mischief all mixed in.
When we dance and sing together,
I know your heart is in the song you sing.
Even though your song has no words,
    your eyes tell me all I need to know.
In the years to come our love will grow and grow.
When you say "rocky" with blanket in hand,
There is nothing more important or anything as grand.
You are treasure to me, more precious than gold,
A treasure not to just look at, but one to hug and hold.
Your arms are tiny and loving, yet able to hold on strong.
You are sure you want to hold me, of that I am not wrong.
As your Grandma we can always have a special bond,
    one of caring and trusting.
You see I will always be in the background if you need a special friend.
Grandmas can do that and I will be there to my end.
You see, on the day you were born, I was already a Mother.
On the day you were born, you made me Grand.

    Linda Hoppe

All For Friendship

Last night I stayed up late listening to songs on the radio.
They were just a sad reminder that soon you will go.
What's going to happen to me when you leave?
What will I go through, how much will I grieve?
Will playing volleyball still be the same?
Will my faith remain strong or fade like a dying flame?
When I have problems, who will I turn to?
When you are gone, how much will I miss you?
How many tears will I cry?
How much apart of me is going to die?
How close I've gotten and my feelings I just can't show.
Mem'ries are sweet but I still can't let go.
A true friend would do anything for a friend,
Even lay down her life and stay faithful 'till the end.
If this means suffering the pain and swallowing the selfish pleas,
Then I will go through it and pray you fulfill your dreams.
I only wish the best for you
Even though it will be hard for me.
I will bear it all for friendship
And I will pray for you unfailingly.

    Stephanie Clarke

Pre-Dawn

An alteration in my subconscious mind stifles me awake.
I see a world stranded in darkness, as ancient light graces my eyes.
The stars that are wished to have all been wished upon before,
a standard fix in a world that is not so sure.
Coincidental beginnings give way to destined ends.
The dream of freedom from the regrets of sleep
    arouses my ambition to search for something new.
A perilous journey that I have longed for.
    An idea forgotten yesterday is matched with an epiphany
        of unprecedented heights conquering a mind where curiosity
            overpowers logic.

Each day I wander through unknown lands opening new doors
    and on the way finding things that were never meant to be found,
        and things I never wanted to find.
Still I move on, oddly attracted to the direction I am facing,
    as if I know it's the right one,
        as if I know I am.

    Jason J. Kemppainen

Mesmerize

The children rode the streets of dark suede
    and they came upon a man with an umbrella in his hand
        pointed to the heavens To The Stars
        to keep them from falling down upon his head
And his smile Mesmerized
    while the night went on in that land beyond stars above,
Above the children loved it, the night, the light, the flight, and death

I am a nymph or a woodland sprite with love and danger in my blood
I dance with the deer and cheer to the moon To The Moon
I float on kindred lusts of magic
    and we call the creatures from their secret lairs Mesmerizing
While the light goes on in our land beyond the moon above,
Above
We all dance here, the night, the light, the flight, and death

The men own the biggest phallic guns
    ready to fire, ready to expire tilt them to God To The Sky
    we kill for our holy nation, and keep our false elation
Mesmerize while the night goes on forever,
    in that land burning to the sky, above,
Above and the men died
    love the night, the light, the flight, and death

    Shawn Carroll

What Is A Tree

Is a tree simply a shady plant that relieves us
    from the scorching summer heat?
Or is it a cruel punishment from God that litters
    the ground with leaves?
Is a tree like a mother that nurtures her children with her fruit?
Or is it like a baby brother that does things that make you sick?
Is a tree an emotionless object that spends its time withering away?
Or is it a sensitive being that sheds sweet tears when pricked?
Is a tree some mysterious creation from God put here
    to battle all of mankind?
Or is it simply whatever everyone thinks it is; a tree.

    Brian Everett Staton

The Wound

Three years later and the wound so carefully tended has been
Ripped open once again; a gaping hole of oh, too much pain.
No, not by you, perish that thought.
All that is left of you is sweet memories:

Childhood Summers and "pink bellies,"
Winters and "flying saucer" rides down never-ending hills.
High School — parties, crushes, problems.
Almost adults — laughter, mutual friends,
    a wild ride in a streak of red.
Adults —
Strangers, yet still connected by an invisible bond called love.

This to me is you and always will be.
Not sad memories,
    but good times that we thought somehow would never end.
You and I loved each other with a love born of pride
In each other's achievements and dreams.

No, it was another who brought back this pain.
She who thought she should be able to tell me
How I should be handling your death to this day!
Oh, she is "coping" so well, she who has
Ripped the scab off the wound and left it gaping and bleeding.

How dare she tell me how to feel!

    Marilyn N. Corazza

132

Being Adopted

The others gave the egg, but it was you who provided the shell.
The others gave me life, but it's you who watches me grow.
The others pointed out the sun, but it's you
   who showed me the rainbow.
The others prayed for help, but it's you who answered their prayers.
The others hand bad luck, but it's yours that turned around.
The others made the gift, but it's you who gets to keep it.
The others gave me knowledge, but it's you who teaches me to use it.
The others gave me legs, but it's you who saw my first steps.
The others hoped for the best and it was the best we both received.
The others gave me blue eyes, but it's you who opens them.
The others brought me into the world, but with you it's the world I see.
The others wonder, but it's the wonder you know so well.
The others gave me feelings, but it's who lets me feel them.
The others gave me sweet, little lips,
   but it's you who receives the kisses.
The other saw me first, but it's you who sees me now.
The others can only imagine and it's me that lets my imagination run.
The others will always be in my thoughts,
   but it's your presence that fills mine.
The others have the answers, but it's me who has the questions.
We all live under the same sky,
   but our horizons are completely different.
The other need not fear because I couldn't be happier here.

   Rachel Moore

Children

Yesterday, I heard a man remark that he "was not born yesterday."
I believe that we were all born yesterday, for,
   we are all as needy as an infant and as independent as a toddler.
We all have our faults, as any three year old does,
   and we all want the freedom of a four year old.
We can all relate to a five year old, in the way that we take pride
   in even the simplest of things, and at six we first learn the rules of life.
We are strong like a seven year old, in the sense that we can wave
   good-bye in the morning and run off to that unknown world
   with only one thought,
"What will I do today?"
We can be like an eight year old,
   becoming truly independent for the first time.
We are all like nine year olds, when we find faults with others
   and start to judge them by ways that are unexplainable.
We are like ten year olds when we become persistent and trustworthy.

And, therefore, we are all like children, repeatedly learning and
   discovering, needing love and support,
   and wanting things to turn out the way they were planned.

   Bernadette O'Keefe

Tomorrow

I want to see you tomorrow I can't see you today
I want to see you tomorrow please don't go away

Tomorrow I'll call your house I hope that you'll be there
Tomorrow I'll call your house please don't go anywhere

I long to see your smiling face I long to feel your loving embrace
I want to leave here right now and come over to your place

Talking to you on the phone isn't enough for me
I've got to be beside you to make myself happy

Tonight I have to work I can't come to your room
I sit here all alone, full of sadness and gloom

But I'll see you tomorrow I say this matter of fact
I promise to see you tomorrow, and every day after that.

   Josh Price

My Mother

You've shown me things I never dreamt to see.
How one person's mind is barred, yet another flies free.
You've shown me that though the earth is filled with darkness
   and sorrow, one can find peace, joy, love
   and hope in another tomorrow.
Our love has grown through the years to bind us,
   with an unbreakable friendship and lasting understanding.
A few foolish words said in hate and fear, could never tear
   what is forever intertwined mother and daughter.
You've taught me so much and I have given back so little.
You are the mother sparrow who taught her young to fly,
   and I the naive fledgling who could have never succeeded
   without help and encouragement.
Though I now grow older and slowly apart,
   thank you dear, loving mother you shall always
   remain forever deep within my heart.

   Diana Louise Stanley

Until Someday Comes

I saw an old man today-he walked with a limp
   and wore a hat with a ball on the top which did not cover his ears —
   but that's okay because winter is already gone,
   maybe he just missed it and is making up for lost time —
I hope you wear a hat like that someday

Remember the clothes you used to wear?
The ones too dated, and everyone made comments on —
   the ones you wore before I entered your life?
I hope you wear those clothes again someday

You know when some people get old —
Their mind tends to fade, so they need someone
   to depend on and look after them
I hope someday your mind fades

Sometimes when you get old, you start talking to yourself,
Grandma says that's okay though,
   just so long as you don't start answering
I hope someday you start talking to yourself,
   so that I can be the one to answer

Sometimes when you get old —
You wake up to find your friends are gone
   and your family has moved away —
And all that you have left is God and your wife
   to give all of your love and attention to
I hope someday you wake up and are all alone

But until someday comes —
I promise to love you, answer you, look after you, dress you,
   and make sure you bundle up for winters that have already
   come and gone

   Lauri Bradley

On This Cold Winter Day

It's amazing what the eyes can see, on a cold winter day.
As I stood outside on my porch, starring upward at the grayish sky,
   that had appeared before my eyes.
The day was wet and cold, and ice overhanging
   from trees and poles. I noticed a bird sitting on an
   electrical line, with his feathers fluff.
Then the bird flew away, maybe to his or her nest,
   where it would be warm.
   It was as the weather man predicted for this cold winter day.
He said in the surrounding area would be ice and no snow.
Then the wind blew through the trees and the ice cycles
   making a crackling sound, that I never heard before.
I'll always remember what my eyes had seen
   and my ears had heard, on this cold winter day.

   Linda S. Everett

Venerate Nostalgia

Toward captured pictures, seemingly traced
Over distant occurrences in succession
Dubbed; are temporal stored listening's
Prior accounts, compiled in chaste density
Viral fluency sways; over timid retentions

Acquired teachings pierced by plagues and lascivious hungers
Coated thick: the languid heating of the sun
Cumulative exertions clouding the nightly grounds
Embodied fixtures, candy glazed: Trivial minds' thought
Shower flush, the unscrupulous placement of side-rails and steps

Joyously rein unwonted true beliefs;
    consistent imbalances now stamped
Flared up in vibrant essence:
Lost embers, of clear-sighted drawings
Inevitably, hung with synaptic hooks; each frame inscribed
Perpetual recorded files, thumbed through for principle
Arranged in syntactical order; natural breviary sense for direction

Glowing, through hardships and crisp turmoil, bimembral souls' rebirth
Ripened by the burning light; reminiscent curves of beauty
Continually driven by bunged foundations; culpatory esprit remains
Elusive views, respectfully and unconditionally, elative veneration
Unformed films, aesthetically prepared for nostalgia.

Micah Kenneth Bingaman

In The Stillness Of Time . . .

Majestic red rock mountains ablaze with the color of God's
    paintbrush . . . magnificent . . . indescribable . . . wondrous!
Water has carved its signature in beautiful manuscript
    across the face of the rock.
Windblown etchings tease our imaginations . . . Santa Claus . . .
    soldiers . . . a watchful angel . . .
    images that leap out simultaneously when two hearts
    share the beauty of the world and the magic of friendship.

Discovering cool, dark caves . . . a bit eery . . . but fun.
Black lava rocks covered with fuzzy green moss . . . we giggle.
Sitting on giant turtle shells we see a tree
    growing out of the dry red rock . . . alone . . . yet determined . . .
    finding freedom at last.

Time stands still. The clouds part . . . the sun warms our faces.
A lone hawk floats effortlessly by . . . hold this moment . . . forever.
Peacefulness overflows . . . connecting one soul to another . . .
    to the splendor of the world . . . to this lovely gift from God.

Daylight becomes twilight. Kissed by the sun, the thin
    wispy clouds turn pink . . . peach . . . orange. Reverence is felt.

In the stillness of time, God's paintbrush colors our world
    with beauty, plays a symphony upon the strings of our souls,
    and opens our hearts to the precious gift of friendship.

Nancy Hoskins

In Wait

The rain trickles down the window going in it own direction, it turns
a way you do not want it to go. You know you have made it a path
to follow with your finger, yet it's like it doesn't care what you
have done. The rain continues down the pain seeming to be
more chaotic in every turn it takes. Your hand trembles to make
a new path for it to follow, in swift moments of haste you work.
But again, and again the water goes on, in its own way. The
ground below the window awaits the inevitable splash that will
surely come. But instead as sure as you thought it would, it
doesn't happen, instead the rain gathers on the seal, it waits in
anxious movements, but for what, you don't know what for.
You only know that the rain in your heart hurts, the slumber of
the night is so inviting, when it comes, it, in golfs you like a
protective glove. Once again the rain trickles down, but only
now it's from you and in the silence of the night, you cry, you
hurt, and you wait for the night to pass, for once again it will start.

Cindy Jackson

The Great Exchange

Christmas! It was the beginning of an earth shaking change.
My father's choice. Me in you, and You in me.
I come to change the world, not as a king or some one great, No!
But as a mere Babe, like you. Yet so different.
For it was my life, from the beginning to be a ransom.
I was like you, associating with you, in every way, yet
    full of power to do for you, what you could not do for yourself.
So that all who would believe in me, and my life's work, trust in
Me to do it well, even unto Death;
    which was "Great Price" of the ransom.
These who would believe and trust, would not perish,
    but have ever lasting life.
This was my father's choice, and I consented.
I was willing to do it all, for the Hope that was in Me,
    for the Glory that would follow.
My pleasure was to do my Father's will, to rescue his creation
His children who were doomed to Hell's destruction.
My Father's Great Exchange, to all who were willing to exchange
their life for mine, so for a moment I could visit Hell,
and lead the captives free, for I would pay the ransom needed,
my very life, there was no other way.
Christmas the beginning of the "Great Exchange".

Eleanor L. Christensen

Smiling Lady

Seems only yesterday when I was four I reached to rap upon a door.
A little girl lived within, I came to make her my small friend.

The door was opened I recall by a pretty lady with a smile for all.
Her hair was dark and wavy too, her eyes were of the brightest blue.

She invited me into her home that day,
for with her little girl I had come to play.

Her little girl was also four, and when she entered through the door,
I found her to be quite like me, with short bobbed hair as I could see.

We played for a while and then I had to leave,
Because my grandmother didn't know my whereabouts I do believe.
Before I left her home that day and ran back up the street,
Her mother reached into her tree and gave me figs to eat.

As years flew by and I grew fast, the memories seemed to always last,
Of a smiling lady so very kind, who had left her memory
    in my small mind.

How was I to know in years to be, I would marry her brother,
    and then to see,
That smiling lady that was so kind, I still had her memory in my mind.

Lois M. Goree

You Were There

With love from all your children, we just want you to know
We're all here to say thank you for helping us to grow
You were there when we fell down to kiss away the pain
To pick us up and dust us off and start us over again

You were there,

When we did wrong you corrected us, but with tender love and care
When we needed praise for doing good, you were always there
You were doctor, teacher, preacher, counselor, and friend
You advised us on our walk through life with love without end

Yes you were there

You taught us to love each other; to strive for what is right
To live one day at a time and don't give up the fight
There are things that you taught us that words cannot express
So we're here to say we love you and mother your the best

You were there, yes you were there!!!

Walt Smith

When Is Our Love

When the sun rises, that's your smile.
When the cool breeze sweeps over the calm water, that is your kiss.
When the sweet aroma of the summer honeysuckle flows,
    that's your touch.
When the bee in flight returns to that same honeysuckle, that is me.

With the gentleness of delicate hands, and the rhythm of upbeat music,
    those are your vibrations.
And for me to bask in the presence of your countenance
    makes me elated
A special place, and the perfect time always brings to mind
The glorious day you fell in love with me.
Your words are often silent, or soft spoken, but the evidence of you
    being there tells the tale.

When we feel our hearts beating
    there is an urge to press closer together.
When the powerful winds blow like ships passing windward
The excitement is almost unbearable.
As my eyes close, my toes curl, and my lips moisten I think I can't
    handle the vigorous trembling.
As our breathe quickens, the volcano erupts and suddenly quiets down
    with golden passion, that's our love.

When the warmth of the summer nights blankets that place, we lay in
    each other's arms and dream, yet;
Never invading each other's space.

Libby Hogan-Hornbuckle

Life's Desire

This is not something we can wish for or easily acquire.
It's something we must earn to truly deserve.
It's what we all most desire.

It can happen in a mere moment,
    with something as simple as a touch, a sigh.
But if it's not nurtured it will wither with longing and
    in the end it will surely die.

At first, it's like reaching for the moon, wishing upon a star,
    seeing the rise of our glorious sun.
It's a sensation only we can imagine in our hearts.
It's all things wonderful together as one.

It's someone's feelings, dreams and wants
    we hold in the palm of our hand.
It's as unique as a snowflake or each individual grain of sand.

It can be as fragile as a rose petal blowing in the wind or as
    strong as a raging storm.
This is something our entire being needs.
This is why we are here. Why we are born.

All this is love. It's not just feelings or thoughts.
It's in our actions and what we say.
It's how we treat someone.
It's something we should endlessly give from day to day.

Karen Nutt

Springtime Here At Last

A sense of excitement quickly settles in
Springtime fever is just about to begin
Coming are those warm evening nights and clear sky blue days
Joyful sounds of nature and families out to play
New friends to be made in camps and recreation parks
Anticipation of catching fire flies from early evening way into the dark
Pleasant thoughts of picnics and mile high ice cream cones to start
The leaves and flowers blossoming leaving behind the winters cold
Thoughts of joy and wondrous things beginning to unfold
Here's to cutting grass and trimming trees only if we're told
Joining ball teams and setting out on other adventures for those
    who might be bold
Here's to Winters thankful past
Here's to Springtime finally here for all at last

Robert Charles Steinmeyer

The Storm

Twas a bright and sunny summer day,
    Out on the old farm.
The old house in all of its splendor,
    gave a glorious look of charm
The birds were flitting from tree to tree,
    with a joyous note of song.
The quiet and peace of the country side,
    seemed as if nothing could go wrong
But lo! In the distance was a rumble
    and the wind was rising high,
The bright skies began to shadow,
    the dark clouds came rolling by
The storm in all of its fury,
    beat down upon the old house.
It seemed, as if it was a moment,
    when all was quiet as a mouse.
Once again the sun was shining,
    and the blue sky was so clear.
The wet meadows were glistening,
    like a dew drop or a tear
The old farm house was still standing,
    even though the wind was high.
The birds continued their singing,
    for the STORM had passed by.

LaHoma F. Butler

This Old House

There's no more tall roof to shelter my pain,
    the house is for sale and I'm left in the rain.
I've no coat nor umbrella, they're all packed away.
They're in some box with my stability in decay.
The fireplace inside has logs still warm
    and I shiver to imagine the coming storm.

Now the rooms and I are alone, our walls bare,
    to the storm that's a comin' from somewhere out "there."
But my back turns against the wind now
    and if I keep walking, I'll get "there" somehow;
    to another roof to shelter my pain,
    another here where tears are not so plain.

Cynthia McCoy

My Special Star

I saw a star in heaven, And wished that it were mine.
I'd clasp it safely in my hands, And watch it brightly shine.

I'd gaze upon its beauty, And wonder at its birth.
And why it looks so brightly clear, When it's so far from earth.

I wonder if it led them, The wise men from afar.
To Bethlehem's manger where did lay, The infant Christ our Lord.

I'd dream about the future. I'd close my eyes real tight.
And make a wish for happiness, And love for all mankind

I'd make a wish for peace on earth, All friends on earth we'd be,
And know this wish would become true, If we'd wish it to be.

If every star were wished on, And our wishes all came true.
I know my special star would hold, A wish of Peace for You.

Shirley Woodlock

A New Love Is Shining Brightly Through

Sometimes I wonder what should I do or say if I'm not in love with you
anymore someday anyway. Atop the snow covered mountains and hills
I see blankets of white crystal clear sparkling snowflakes everywhere.
As I hear and see you sit there and cry I would love to hold you close
and kiss you tears away, and tell you your pain won't be here another
day. 'Oh to kiss your tears away, and hear your fears and sorrows
to feel your sadness and pain, for you to feel my love surround you
and for you to whisper my name.

'But I know you don't care about my pain, and now I feel no more that
I'm to blame now I know I can go on and live without you in my life.'
I watched the raindrops fall yesterday with a dark black cloudy sky,
and then suddenly through the raindrops in the sky a bright sunshine
appeared above with a beautiful multicolored rainbow shining largely
in the late afternoon sky.

'Oh and with this colorful rainbow in the light blue sky I feel a
new feeling of love come alive, and I'm sure I've gotten completely
over you, and a new love is shining brightly through.' Now that I'm
completely out of love with you I know what to feel say and do. The
rainbow I saw and chanced was so colorful it seemed that the green was
for jealousy, the yellow for confused, the pink for pretty and red for
love now the blue of the rainbow was for sadness over losing you.
Now I feel a new love is shining brightly through...

Audrey Meilhammer

The Holidays Again?

Sweet memories of the old and new seem visible to you...day dreams of
good times and bad seem to be aimed at you...you are fired-up! Hey,
where is that pretty smile?

Throw away the knife; bad thoughts and open the window to let the
sunshine upon you...staple your pretty lips; leave out the immortal
sin/guilt within...let the pretty smile come out instead!

Thrust your arms into the glory of kindness and respect for one another
manifest a self-confidence in "you.." bite down on that bone called
commitment and serve everyone the same taste...

Dedicate our living souls to the love one's who have departed the
"here and now..." paste joy to the endless love to serve our families
squeeze the compassion from the new roots replenished from the old
and new tragedies in our present lives, "for our father who are in
heaven...! Love you!

George V. Guy Sr.

Special Thoughts Of You

My heart is often carried away, when my thoughts are of you.
My life is filled with happiness and love, and it's from the things you do.

Life is nothing but heartache and pain, but you make that go away.
The way that your love makes me feel, turns darkness into gray.

Like it's been said, life's sad but true, but you turn my life around.
I never knew love could feel like this, but from you it was quickly found.

You're the best thing that's ever happened to me,
  and I'll never tell you goodbye.
I want to be with you now and always, and that I won't deny.

I can't explain exactly how I feel, because words can hardly define
The love that's combined between two hearts, especially yours and mine.

Please tell me you'll always be in my life, I promise to always be true.
Because I have never wanted anything more, than I want to be with you.

Mary Conner

A Shadow

A shadow passes by my heart,
Sometimes is close, sometimes is far,
One voice, One verse of poem, One song,
Flows through my nervous system like blood,
A shadow makes me realize my loneliness,
It fills emptiness and sadness in my heart,
I want to see her,
Get to know her,
I Want to feel her,
A shadow in my fantasy is very close to me,
In reality is very far,
I listen to her footstep,
Turn my face around,
Try to make an eye contact,
I forget my self, I lose my conscious.

Sanjeeu Kataria

Silent Footsteps

These footsteps were once alive with fresh,
fresh snow, now they are only memories of a time
long ago, someday perhaps these footsteps will
be trod upon once again, but until that time
the snow will come and the snow will go, but
until that very time they will be Silent
Footsteps in the snow.

Anthony P. Salt

Sonnet I

The night reached down and seduced my soul
and took her for his own,
He slit her throat and spilled her blood
into the waters of the Rhone,
But oh! Her beautiful eyes he stole
and cast into the skies,
To protect my bloodless, eyeless soul
from society's silent lies.
He finished my soul by taking her skin
and draping it on the valleys and hills,
and gave her voice to the wandering wind
to fill my heart with shrieks and shrills!
So now my soul belongs to the night
and fuels mother nature's eternal light.

Stephen Jones

Here's to 1997

Here's to 1997
when I will study my hardest;
when I will do my best; and
when I will get excellent grades.

Here's to 1997
when I will spend my money wisely;
when I will save my money; and
when I will buy my nike jacket.

Here's to 1997
when I will be more friendly;
when I will be nicer to others; and
when I will gain more friends.

Here's to 1997, an interesting year ahead
of me.

Janelle Ulep Taburaza

Someone

Have you ever met someone, who left a deep impression in your life,
Someone who was there, to listen to your tales of joy, sorrow or strife,
Have you ever shared secrets with someone, you never thought you would tell,
Someone knowing all your faults, yet on judging you did not dwell,
Have you ever looked into someone's eyes, and saw compassion there,
Someone so special, without their presence, a tiny spot in your heart would have been bare,
Have you ever shared laughter with someone, who had wit and was so very kind,
Someone who had the ability, to ease the troubles of your mind,
Have you ever met someone, who showed strength and character in their face,
Someone with ageless beauty, not even time itself could ever erase,
Have you ever stopped and pondered, having never met someone special at all,
Someone who was there for you, all you needed was to give them a call,
We have been blessed to know someone special, in which all of these qualities can be seen,
God crossed our paths with someone special, our very unique, sweet
    Sister Marie Kathleen

Cecelia M. Zimmerman

View Of The New Millennium From Not So Young Winter Comfort

It now is all white and snowing, for this grand season has come around again,
In this prison with restlessness growing, this is one of so few things
Bringing me peace, just a touch of tranquility to ease within.
I see the individual snowflakes floating, then lying gently down,
Without sound tenderly covering, seeming as a blanket to keep one safe
    and warm surround -
Pray tell me how can something so white be so cold,
Is not this beauty bright, this as I am told is pure light...
Such glory revealed in heaven, truly through and through then is this
Not warmth beyond sight of which we live in -
And is not the smallest speck of light, within suffocating darkness thick,
A glimmering hope which is the white hot fire, shining forth from this cold dark pit...
If this is light, then gloom must raise, let me see it;
if this white left alone is pure, unblemished truth, let me be it;
Most assuredly if this blanket of beauty is warmth,
His unfailing love, conceal me in it...
Then so rain down this glory and all consuming awesome brightness,
As His righteousness, let this cover never end...

Keith Everett Gregg

A Familiar Place . . .

Upon the grounds of a familiar place I lie and face the sky. I gaze
    with wonder and awe upon the fiery firmament and conglomeration of
    misty vapors that fill the dark spectrum above. My world begins to
    dance... to sway... and move. Away is put all baser matter and the
    doors of my mind are opened wide as well as the windows of my soul.
    I am here.

About me, the pines and oaks try to conceal their faint sighs and
    they whisper sonnets of enduring patience that hold unutterable
    content. They laugh as the hand of wind bends their backs.
    They are the breath of the rock. They are the eyes of the earth.
    I understand them.

Above me, the Moon wanes ever so slowly and bathes the Earth in her
    blue light. It is from the great Sunlord that she receives her
    radiance and is able to cast it upon all that behold. Her love
    falls down through the dark sky and around the clouds to find its
    way at last to my very spirit where it washes the storehouses of
    my soul. The River of Hercules was not as great as her gentle
    silver fingers. She sees only me.
    I know her.

Below me, I feel the immensity of the cool earth. Far below resides
    the beating heart of molten rock and avenues of hot springs rushing
    through tiny fissures. "From whence comes thy life Great Mother
    Earth ... for it is from your flesh that I was born and it is to
    you that I shall return my life in time". She dances with my Lady
    Moon who pulls and tugs at her waters and my own blood coursing my
    veins. She clothes herself with velvet fields and delicate ivy.
    The lotus springs from her bosom and the forest girds her waist.
    She crowns herself with fire and with ice. She touches herself
    with the perfumes of morning dew and the incense of evening rain.
    I desire her.

H. Kirk Jones

He

He treated everyone equal,
there are two after him,
kind of like his sequel.
He was unlike any other,
some what like an older brother.
He guided people through stuff,
through the smooth and rough.
And would do anything
you wanted him to do.
He was the greatest...
and in my eyes he still is.

Christina L. Benjamin

Key To My Heart

I had closed the door upon my heart
and would let no one come in
I had trusted and I'd been hurt,
But it would never happen again.
I had locked the door, and thrown the key,
As hard and as far as I could.
Love would never enter there again;
my heart was closed for good,
Then you came into my life,
and you made me change my mind.
Just when I thought that tiny key
was impossible to find.
That's when you held out your hand
And showed me I was wrong.
Inside it was the key to my heart,
You'd had it all along.

Ruth Bailey

I Am One Of A Kind

I am one of a kind
I wonder what others think of me
I hear only ringing in my ears
I see people whisper as I cross their path
I want to know what they say
I am one of a kind
I pretend that I am someone different
I feel only pain
I touch not a soul with my words
I worry whether or not...
I am what others want me to be
I cry when people's backs are turned
I am one of a kind
I understand why people are the way they are
I say not a word since no one listens
I dream of starting over again and...
I am sorry if I am not perfect

Jennifer Walker

Darkness

I will be tired, worn and weak
when darkness sets upon my eyes
Take me to a seat by a riverside
for I will not sigh nor will I cry
I can hear the fish play in the bubbling streams
I can smell the river and everything that's green
My mind paints beautiful dreams
It is too bad the picture
I can only see
But when night falls on the sky
Take my hand and guide me home
I will not know darkness has come again

Keith P. Norris

I Was A Western Man

I was a Western Man, he said, with a far away look in his eyes
I've traveled this land from mountain to plain and slept under western skies.

I rode hard and worked hard and had very little to say
No man had a word against me, I always earned my pay.

Sometimes I'd hire out for a cattle drive, those times I remember best
We all worked hard from dawn to dusk, then it was time to rest.

Someone would pull out a mouth harp and the song was always sad
About going home to loved ones and a girl he'd never had.

We would sit round the fire drinking coffee and each one had a tale
We talked about the horse that couldn't be rode or spending the night in jail.

The fire would burn down to embers. The night around us was dark.
Away in the hills a wolf would howl or a hungry coyote would bark.

Next day we'd be back in the saddle to drive the herd to the rails.
Day after day the sun would beat down as we followed the well known trails.

We might ride in the driving rain for days plodding in mud and slime
Then ride harder than ever when the rain quit, trying to make up time.

The life I lived was a hard one, but I never will regret it.
God has certainly done me a favor not letting me forget it.

I pray that in His great wisdom, when my time comes to die
That God will find a place for me on a round up in the sky.

   Jo Ann Berry

She Was The Pearl Of Heaven

She sat alone hurting no one,
A thing of wonder and beauty and beauty for generations to marvel at.
Being the very essence of life, we were not satisfied to just let her be,
Man felt compelled to tamper with her, and play with her.
This wasn't enough.

Unprovoked, man began to beat on her, dig at her,
Scarring her face of beauty with their bare hands.
Using tools of destruction, they tried to change her and mold her,
Into what they wanted her to be.

Sad and horrified, she can do nothing but endure the pain, helplessly.
Once a beautiful pearl that only the heaven's could create, she slowly dies,
She gave of herself in complete, unselfishness.

Now, with the very fibers that kept her alive being ripped apart by man, she suffocates.
While the very spirit of her soul is being drained by man,
She drifts into eternity.

Sadly our children's children may never see her beauty
For then may not even be around.
This once beautiful pearl has gone by many names, I call her earth!

   Brad Scarborough

The Battles Of Bull Run

It was an hour before the war that day, it was very easy to describe I'd say.
Flowers and grass were everywhere, and butterflies fluttered in my hair.
An hour later it began, the soldiers marched and then they ran.
The sounds you could hear for miles around. Whoosh! Boom!
As men hit the ground.
There was blood as far as the eye could see, and bodies laying there so lifelessly.
I could not stand the sight at all, the sight of men once so tall.
The North has stopped firing, the north is retreating and fleeing.
Yeah! The south has won. Hey!
We could call it the Battle of Bull Run!
The North was sad that day, for they lost brothers and cousins on the way.
Another war happened one year later, the North had it again in their favor.
The battle field was scarred from the earlier fight, The North thought
   they could win, they just might.
The fight happened pretty much the same way, as the North fought
   the South again that hot but cold day.
The South won again, hooray! We fought for our independence they say.
And that is the story of two days now done, the days that they call
The Battles of Bull Run.

   Ty Ehrlich

Strangers

I talked to Angels from the coast.
I walked with strangers that were friends.
I held the ones you hurt the most.
Heard mama whispering in the wind.
I cried for you.
Said good-bye to you.
I lied for you, when they asked me
where you'd been.

Times wasted,
Still, nothing matters.
You see?
All I think and feel has been shattered.
Doesn't matter my friend, to me.

...And, it hurts sometimes...
to be all alone.
Yes, it hurts sometimes...
when your mind is not your own.
Fall from pride...
Live, love, and hope.

Know it's all a lie.
Search for answers, they never come.

   Todd Austin Callicotte

A Blinded Love

I am dark, I am deep
I am weak when I weep
I am quiet, not even a peep.

Why, o why must we meet?

Your body may be sleek
I can sense the heat
Your smell may be sweet
You may cause me to weep.

Why, o why must we meet?

Your mystery causes my sleepless nights;
In the morning I see birds in flight.
I am without the sense or use of sight
I wonder if this love is right;
If not, I will take flight.

Why, o why must we meet?

   Bobby Hadfield

My Father's Legacy

To all of you who have gathered here
To say your last farewell
Believe me friends and have no fear
For I am doing well

The times we laughed, the times we shared
I hold deep in my heart
And though I walk this earth no more
My soul will never part

I'm with you in this time of stress
Of this you need not fear
For I am watching over you
My loved ones bring me here

So put your sorrows and tears aside
Be strong and gather together
And if you should do this little I ask
I will live on forever.

   Debbie Gunn

Nervous Breakdown

Spring came chaotic with color.
The azaleas bloomed in wild abandon.
The trees born new leaves and the bumble bees were busy
with nature. The calendar said it was April.
Blithely my mind cracked one day.
Why in spring when everything was new, why did my mind
go away? I saw but did not care to feel.
The institutional walls carefully kept the secret
of why, on this April day my mind suddenly went away.
Summer crept in by hot and humid inches; storms were violent
in the purple sky. I lazed in the pool and wondered "Why?"
Routines pressed on with the paganistic ritual of exploring
the id, the reservoir of the libido.
It was brutal but therapeutic I was carefully told.
Summer waned and autumn entered in a blaze style
but it didn't really matter with my mind gone away.
October arrived - sere and barren.
It was time to depart - alone, afraid and broken.
October 3rd was the fateful day my mind came back so they say.

Virginia L. Hall

All The Lovely Memories

I asked that you return to me
to a place we shared in time.

A place where sunlight shimmered on water
and the air was fragrant with pine.

I asked for chandeliers and wine
to see that lazy smile light your face
and to see blue eyes cool with intelligence
and warm with feeling.

I asked that you return to me.
And you do - each day, each season
through all the lovely memories.

Kaye M. Evans

Stars

Stars of wonder,
Stars to light,
Watching for the little ones, all through the night,
As the darkness falls, the shadows of the
moon disappears.
In the morning, they hide in the
blankets of the clouds as the
sunlight appears.

Sushmeet Singh

Love Hiccupped

I had you, I loved you, I love you still.
I could not keep you. I gave you up against my will.

We met on a time flash, our worlds coming together;
flashing on by forever and ever.

It was a cruel mistake. We were not meant to be.
Our worlds stopped in error, never intending a "we."

A hic-cup in timing, we should not have met.
We did and that's something I'll never regret.

I may never again have you. You've slipped from my grasp.
You'll remain in my mind till I breathe my last.

I need you, I want you, I forever shall.
Could this wrong be righted? Only time will tell.

Judith M. Dunlap

The Wall

A little girl is crying she's all alone...
her daddy left her, there's no one home.
She stands up tall, (she can handle it all)
And slowly, slowly she's building a wall.
Dark time tears are in her eyes. No one can
see them she has a great disguise.
Slowly she lay down to sleep, and the tears of
fear roll down her cheek.
Silent fears within her mind, she keeps blaming
herself, she's one of a kind.
No one can put her mind to a halt. She keeps
on saying it's all her fault.
Never coming to reality of it all, she marries a man
and recaptures it all.
Slowly, slowly she's building a wall.

Dina Braun

Dear Sister Candice On The Last Day Of 1996

Alas this year will soon be gone
Behind closed doors; how we carried on...
Giggling, talking 'bout band and John.

Our helicopter ride at the mall
Soared so high even I felt tall...
Then landed close o'er roof and wall.

Thomas and I cheered in the stands
Proudly watching your marching band
With Mom and Dad who clapped their hands.

Full of play and of plots
I watched you chase Chip, the dog with spots.
His quick stop - uh-oh! Down you plop.

I cherish all the talks we had,
Some alone, some joined by Mom, Dad,
Virginia, and Greg, always glad.

To yourself and God be true.
In this new year, I pray for you...
And thank God for what He will do.

With Love, Rebecca Newbaker

The Contract

Mommy said I'd be safe
But she lied
Daddy said everything would be okay
But he lied too

Mommy said she knew what was best
But she lied
Daddy said he knew what was right
But he lied too

Mommy said I could only trust her
But she lied
Daddy said he would always protect me
But he lied too

Mommy said I was her little baby
But she lied
Daddy said he loved me
But he lied too

I said to Mommy and Daddy that I'd stay with them forever
But I lied
When they came to take me away I said I'd comeback
But I lied about that too

Stene't Contrades

Sixtieth Wedding Anniversary

Since time began, 'twas always true
Boy meets girl, and then ensue
Two souls entwined forever, and you
Captured my heart.

We've worked, we've loved, and played
Through it all our love has stayed,
All problems solved because we prayed
To never part.

At times we laughed, at times we cried,
I'm your groom, you're still my bride
Together yet, because we tried,
Not cause we're smart.

Though time has passed, our love is strong,
When hearts are true, what can go wrong?
And, sixty years is not that long,
'Tis but the start!

J. M. Blazer

To My Baby

My thoughts are overwhelmed with you as you grow inside me
I do not fully understand the miracle that is you
You are so small now and people will say
I am not a mother yet, but I feel like I am
I want to protect you at all costs
And make you as healthy as possible,
live every day for you and love you to no end.
If ever a baby was wanted, it is you, my little one
I have imagined you a million times
And no dream could describe how wonderful you actually feel
I am scared
You are the greatest gift I have ever received and
I hope I am what you need in a mother
I give you a promise
I will always love you
Nothing in this world will ever change the way I feel
My love is unconditional and
You need ever question it
For it will always be there
Love, Mom

Kimberly P. Iuvara

Amazing Minds. . . Boggling

Minds are their own places;
Many which have different faces.

Minds set their own limits,
And do what you permit it.

Minds can go anywhere,
Without even a care.

Minds can do and say,
thoughts which can cause you to run away.

Minds can be strictly of business,
Even some of short-sidedness.

Minds are able to become unbalance,
Some even grow into silence.

Minds can be very strange;
If filled with guilt and pain.

Minds can be evil, minds can be kind;
It's up to you to make up your mind.

Do you own which mind is you?

Deborah Ann Lockerby

The Race

You have a husband, Dad, brother or son
that loves to race
It's a drive that's in their blood, whether they win or lose
you can see that special look on their face.

It's a passion within them
their love to complete
They'll go to their limit
whatever the feat.

Most people don't understand
they say it's costly, dangerous and a kids game
Who gives us the right to criticize or to blame?

The smile, the proud look on the face of the racer when
he's number one across that finish line
You can see it was worth all the work, all the money,
all the sweat and all the time.

The Race...

It's their sport, their way to relax and have fun
Others just need to understand, give their support, and be
proud of their husband, Dad, brother or son.
It's their race!

Rhonda Stark

Dear Scott, I Am Foundering

A foundation for a house must
be but built otherwise the
pillars all fall down,
    like the dominoes that Mabel played
    with before she grew up and became
    bored at night and started fights
    with her husband Dale.

Dale was frail, Scott.,
    and he ended up embalming
    at Magoo's bar downtown.

    The pool table bumper there is scarred
by Dale's fingernails, significant of
his losses both monetary and mental.

I beat him in billiards last Friday,
adding more money towards my savings that will
    hopefully let me escape.

    But certainty is a suit not well worn on me,
and traditional design tells me that
    I am foundering here, Scott,
and wondering how the hell you got out.

Christopher Silva

Song Of The Sea

There have been men from years long ago.
That have felt a vengeful lady's blow.
Ask any man young or old,
About a beautiful lady and
the treasures she holds.
You'll hear many of them with stories to tell,
How they lost their hearts and was under her spell.
Many say she holds vast fortune and gold,
But she's wicked and cruel and her blood is ice cold.
The lady is calm and moves with such grace,
But she has devoured ships and men without a trace.
You'll hear her songs when out to sea and a dead sailors
mournful plea,
Under the night sky and the
pounding waves as he meets
the fair lady in a watery grave.

Lorri Eve Willey

Our Blanket Of Love

As I sit by the window this cold and winter
night. Thoughts of you keep dancing before my sight.
Remembering the love and passion we
shared our very first night.
I knew without a doubt that you were and
always will be my Mr. Right.
Our time was short and sweet but I never
though our beginning would end so soon.
Thoughts of you invade my mind both
day and night.
As I sit by the window this cold and winter
night with only our blanket of love to keep
warm as thoughts of you keep dancing before my sight.

Shantelle M. Mason

Glimpse

Could it be dear souls departed
that I have seen a glimpse of the truth
Life in its circular perfection
realized in days of youth

Oh how we long for the new, the strange
How we shape our lives in the face of change
All the while we are what we are
searching for dreams in lands afar

But paradise is here and now
and moments are wasted wondering how
it has come to be that we are all here
living for joy in an ignorant fear

Of myths and rules and the great unknown
look in your self and you will be shown
The path of the spirit on which we sail
and the part you play in this beautiful tale

Samuel Houston Gray

Violet

Violet is the color of when you give away your heart to love.
Violet is a happy tear in the corner of your eye.
Violet is the moon dancing with the stars among the last rays of the sun.
Violet is the sensation of a lover's kiss.
Violet is peace in knowing you are cared for.
Violet is seeing a baby walk for the first time.
Violet is the love in a friend's eyes.
Violet is like a walk on a new spring evening.
Violet is coming to accept yourself for who you are.
Violet is how others like to know you.
Violet is care when you hurt.
Violet is liking yourself.

Lisa Bless

Why...

Seventeen and finally free, I ran
not knowing where I was going or what I was running from, I ran
my journey took me to far away places
where dreams often come true
but I found no answers to the unspoken questions inside me
and my dreams were left unfulfilled
I searched everywhere and in everyone but myself
and finally, at full speed, I fell
I fell into a hole deep enough to drown within
and drown, I did, for awhile
lying there I began to see this was where I was running to
I needed a new beginning and when you hit the bottom
you can only start over or give up
it was here I discovered, heart and soul, who I was
it was a far cry from who I pretended to be
with courage and passion I run still
but I have already reached my destination

Stacy J. Wilde

Never Knew

There was this man I never knew,
he left this world when I was two.
He always had a lot to say,
the grandchildren he loved to praise.
He was good at love,
he gave it freely.
This little girl I always knew
never had much to receive,
but this man I never knew
changed that fact very quickly.
He held me tight and said quietly,
"Little girl, you're loved and I'll never leave you."
The greatest man I never knew,
left that very night,
his promise remained the same
he stayed right in my heart.
He was my inspiration
to become the person I am.
The greatest man I never knew
was my beloved grandfather.

Sausley R. Behrens

Perhaps God Only Sleeps

We are crawled about, in and upon!
We are a jungle: Our physiologies, our physiognomies,
our homes, our habitats...all jungle!
Internally and externally we are a forage field and forest.
We are stalking grounds for predation of fearsome,
weird, exotic beasts of horn, fang and claw!

In exponential numbers such is shown us by our biologists
and microbiologists: They tell us of vast armies,
invisible and insatiable, engaged in consumerism
not unlike ourselves, some violent, some benign.
Zoologist say "Food Chain", physicists say "Energy Exchange."

Ah...but the poet, the philosophic and visual conceptualist,
artists and aesthetes and mystic minds
can see it all as a vast, nay, an infinity of the surreal
or a chaotic phantasmagoria....a Nightmare!

Perhaps one best take solace from the east,
from whence the dancing Shiva signals: "Fear not,
it's only a dream," only a dream from which,
with God, with Brahman, we shall Awaken!

Ben Read

Untitled

You ask; "What do I love?"
I shall answer; "I love that which is her."
Then you ask;
    "Why do you love her?"
And I shall answer:
    "I love her because she is life itself."
And you will ask;
    'Why do you love life?'
And my answer will be;
    "Because she is there and I love her."

Then you will nod your head and say;
    "I understand."
But you don't.
And as you walk away, shaking your head.
You will be saying to yourself;
    "Poor soul, I feel sorry for him."
But no, friend.
It is I who should feel sorrow for you.
For of your knowledge of love I can only say.
    "Poor soul, he has never known life."

Anthony Bricca

141

Silence

Complete utter silence
What a change from before
Just a couple of hours ago a parade went by
Footsteps - footsteps
then came the loud pounding and.
Scraping, pounding so loved, it brought
back the feeling of once a young child
so scared, he could hear his own
heartbeat pounding pounding
like a drum of a band that is heard
repeatively over any other instrument
pound pound and...
Scraping, scraping
as if finger nails were being thrashed
across a chalk board in a rage of madness
but, soon it all came back
a cold dark aura filled my place
and a musky smell soon took over
the smell of a cold damp basement crippled
and I lay at rest for the power now decides my destination.

C. Guadagnino

Wonder Of Wonders

The greatest of all the wonders I see,
Is the wonder of Jesus dying for me.
Though I was a sinner, foul and unclean,
Headed for nowhere he came between.
Satan no longer my life can sway;
Since I met Jesus, there dawns a new day.

A day of Salvation, a day for my praise;
Tell others of Jesus miraculous ways.
How he saves men; any race, color, creed.
How he ever cares and supplies every need.
Yes, wonder of wonders, Jesus paid my way,
May I praise and thank Him everyday.

And even with death I'll continue to sing
Of the unending love of my precious King.
Yes, there through the ages, eternity's years;
I'll know no sorrows, there'll be no tears.
Because God in his mercy gave his only son
To die in my place, the victory is won.

Joyce A. Wyre

Eternal, Vernal Renewal

I walked out one morning, the day was brand-new.
I sensed a live presence, my dog felt it, too.

The tiny wild flowers have come into bloom,
To say, "It is spring! We dispel winter's gloom!"

The rain falls upon them, they sparkle with light,
Then fold in the evening, to sleep through the night.

They burst forth each morning, to vibrantly show
That life is worth living, how e'er soon we go.

When next I walked out, all the flowers were gone,
Like mem'ries of loved ones, their beauty lives on.

They all will come back again, one year from now.
We know this is true, and we even know how!

Their seeds never die, only rest for a time;
As man, and all creatures win respite sublime.

The flowers remain here on earth, to inspire
The faith of all those who take thought to inquire

If we should be mournful for those gone away -
No! Flowers bring joy when they welcome the day;

And we, like the flowers, will rise, every one,
Some splendid, clear morning, with God's glorious sun!

George Cornelius

My Emotion Of Love

Closer I come to my heart's own right.
And as I am ready to claim my gold,
The fool still shines through.
But magic of power and incandescent light
Will shine through my tryings.
Resistance cannot overcome any magic,
Of such mutant power.
And as you try, I fall deeper
  n'deeper
   n'deeper
    n'deeper
     n'deeper
      n'deeper
       n'deeper
        n'deeper
In love with your heart.

Jennifer R. Ingersoll-Cazier

What I'd Like

I'd like to hold you every night,
sharing most cherished and treasured dreams;
and make you smile the most brilliant smile,
with the intensity of a million sunbeams.

To kiss your lips of woven silk,
stare deep into your eyes;
which are two of the brightest shining stars,
stolen from the skies.

Escape with you to an enchanted forest,
a meadow surrounded by trees.
and lay with you to watch the clouds,
wisp by in the summers breeze.

To feel your hand entwined with mine,
offering strength and security;
to spend my life devoted, so true,
and love you for all eternity.

Gerri R. Hatfield

The Future Is Now

She stands in the mist of silver rains
Another drop - Another falls,
The tears, the more cumbersome of the downpour.
The wind holds the sound of a crying child...
A hollow echo of agony.
"Save us," it weakly whispers and
Then is lost in the dust of the Thunder.

Dry throats, dry eyes, dry minds.
This desert, a drying oasis in Hell.
The Black Storm brews...
Cleansing the land with its filth and intangible debris.
Her river runs red,
And God is a passing memory in the cold heart of man,
A Holy Hostage of his logic.

T. Riegner

Misunderstood

Misunderstood, such as I am,
guys think I'm a flirt for the way that I look.
My eyes so intense, I pierce there souls,
That they squirm their way into a big fat hole.
The intensity of my eyes I can not help,
But a hot iron prod can do just as well,
For praying to God surely won't help.

Desiree Flynn

H e

His breath is like the wind, beneath
The wings of a dove,
That soar above the earth, who is he?
The almighty God above,
He never sleep or slumber, no matter how it my seem,
He's always there to guide you, whether
through mountain, valleys, or small streams,
So trust in him always
He has never failed anyone yet
Come, now don't be a skeptic, try him
And see what you will get,
Everlasting life is a guarantee
His promises are true,
They are found from Genesis to Revelation,
And I'm sure they applies to you,
So give him your hand now,
He is reaching out to you, one day at a time,
he will see you through,
I gave him my life, will not you do the same?
There is nothing to loose, only heaven to gain.

Alice Hall

Love What Is It?

Love is a warm and tender feeling,
   like a soft and cuddly animal.
Love is holding hands while walking together.
It's knowing how the other feels
   without a word being spoken.
Love is a kind word, a soft, kiss, a warm embrace.
Love is sharing each other's joys and sorrows;
   each other's pain and pleasure.
It's knowing when the other needs to be held
   or a shoulder to cry on.
Love makes you see things differently,
   through each other's eyes.
It's discovering everyday things around you that
   you take for granted, in a new light.
Love is enjoying a golden sunset at the end
   of a beautiful day.
It's gazing at the stars in the sky and
   in each other's eyes,
Love....is life itself.

Sonja R. Reaves

Wonderful Bells

The bells at Christmas ring all over the world
Their ring is clear and sweet,
Their message clear and simple
Come, celebrate this day.
God sent his son in the form of a man
Many long years ago,
He came that we might learn to live
The decent honest way.
His years of growing up were of the humble kind,
In the eyes of other people
He was the carpenters son.
But God he had a purpose for him
So he installed him with wisdom,
And knowledge that overflowed.
His days upon this earth were few
But such a message he had, that he died for me and you.
So great was this man that we celebrate his birthday to day
Come join us the bells are saying,
Learn to live, laugh and love the christian way.

Phyllis Young

Monday

Ever have one of those days?
you know the one.
You can't find a thing to wear.
You spill coffee on your white work shirt.
Your hair won't behave.
Your rent is past due.
Every bill imaginable is due.
The baby gets sick
You have a migraine as big as tears
Next door's radio is blaring
Boss needs to be surgically removed from your back
Traffic is packed to Egypt and back
Oh, forgot mom's birthday! (It was yesterday!)
Trash bag busted open on the kitchen door
Dog decided to personalize the new carpet
Playing beat the bank, and the bank wins.
Some bozo cuts you off in traffic
Almost forgot kids at soccer practice
And it's only Monday

Kris Constantine

Our World

   We are in world filled with hatred
and love. We are in a world filled with
Health and Disease. We have the rich,
the poor and the mid-class of people.
   Everyone wants peace, health, and love,
but no one wants to work for it.
A world filled with racism, hate, and
disease is going to die. A world filled with
love, peace, and health will live for a long while.
   But in our world we have it all. The
peace, the love, the hate, the disease,
and the health. As long as we're living,
we're still dying. We are killing each
other off with the hate, racism, and
disease. But we are keeping each other
alive with the love and peace.
   But until we choose the one we want,
we will never, truly be alive.

Mary K. L. Darden

Broken Song

   So many tears
in that lonely temple she calls a heart
so many fears
not knowing now this journey for love is only the start

Confusion over rules her brain
her cries creep around in times
her body over flows with pain
she's had her share of hard luck binds

And now comes a time
where her life feels the lowest
the alone feeling sets in her mind
a man in which she was the closest
is now an endless memory in a world of lost time

Answerless questions kept deep inside
her source of wisdom is gone
and no one there to confide
her "magical" life . . . a broken song

Tanya R. Bruno

Infected

Rage is what they all feel.
Drugs is what makes the pain heal.
Blood boiling while their hearts
race, brings them back to a familiar place.
Lies lurk within the walls which
shelter them from the bluest skies.
These walls melt slowly, enraged
in furry.
They must get more drugs in a hurry
As they walk we turn our backs,
only to let them dwell in their tracks.
Society is in denial, but as we
wait we see them fall.
Upon their return to these melting
walls, their children run through the
halls.
Over again, they're infected with
rage, and over again our love is restrained.

Nicole Chase

Crayon Box

I'm sitting in my crayon box, surrounded by the sun,
Fingers touch me lightly, but I'm not the pretty one.
All my friends are clouds, lined with silver glow
Or little purple flowers that stand in perfect row.
I was used before, but only to be tried,
Now I'm all alone, now I'm locked inside.
I'm sitting in my crayon box and I'm never coming out;
I'm just the ugly color that no one cares about.

Angela Michelle Gassert

An Acre Of Heart

After a day's work, I walk out my back door,
and look down the yard, as I've done times before.
I gaze over the fence, and along the grass,
to a yard that's much bigger, and has lots of class.
That's neighbor Ed's place, a warm hearted man,
who ought to be home, in about five or ten.
But I won't see his face, around there today,
with that big old smile, you could see far away.
He had an attack, and then did depart,
from what I suspect, was an acre of heart.
He gave of it freely, to everyone he knew,
to children, to strangers, and animals too.
He must of had it in boxes, piled high on a shelf,
but then in the end, he ran out for himself.
All you who received it, from seeds he had sown,
then it's richer and wiser, that your heart has grown.

"Goodbye old kabayo, old strawberry roan"

Gerald Mowka

Don't Know Why

I Don't know why my life turned out this way.
Or why I have to live it day by day.
Don't know why my life is filled with sorrow.
Sometime I wish their was never a 'morrow.
Don't know why my life is in such a rut.
Every time I try to stand someone kicks me in the butt.
Don't know why the sky is so grey,
Maybe I will just sleep all day.
Don't know why or where my life has gone so wrong.
Oh well, maybe this poem will make a nice song.
This is the end of what I have to say.
Well, maybe tomorrow will be a better day.
But I don't know why.

Matthew R. Gilkeson

Is Anyone Going To Take My Hand

Is anyone going to take my hand,
and save me from this darkened land?
Pull me up from the pain,
and let what love I have left try to remain.
Give me a new world and name,
and say things are going to change.
Say the dark empty box will be forever gone,
and the bright rising sun will always be turned on.
Say the lonely night, which is all my days,
will be forgotten through a "forgotten haze."
Hopefully this "forgotten haze" will be only a short phase,
and when it is gone my self-esteem will raise.
Raise so high that I will not have the yearning
to commit suicide, or die, and burn in hell
enternally and fry.
I thought you could save me, and lend me your
hand, but all you did was leave me in the
end.

Kelly Ashby

Passing On

Fates unraveled and destiny sealed,
on the marrow the truth revealed.
The clash of time from whence life came
death to march for souls to claim.
Freedom thus buried with a burdened soul,
youth now catches the overflow.
Life retraced with winds of time, with
whirling winds thou does ask why.
Finally at rest no witness to bare, the cost so
heavy the price unfair.
One last plea thou lips must pass a fight for
freedom as life clash with death.
Fates unraveled and destiny sealed,
on the marrow the truth revealed.

Carrie

Whenever You're Blue

Whenever you're blue
You may feel like you don't know what to do.
Go to our God in prayer.
Thank the Lord for each new day.
Ask him to give you strength.
So that you can get through the day O.K.
Don't give up because
Of better days ahead.
Instead of crying or being sad.
Keep busy more often too.
You're never alone
Our precious Lord is always watching over you.
Always guiding you through each new day.
Always knowing everything will be O.K.

Joan Donnelly

To Give America

And so to freedom's land they came,
all different, no two are the same,
ambition, and bright ideas fill their heads,
first work, then hoard, and last will come their beds,

For they have reached a place that God has blessed,
in such a way that all can build a nest,
but in your building remember to be true
to give America just as she gave you.

Keith A. Norgriff

Untitled

I woke up with a new sun in my window,
An endless sky on a new horizon,
There's something new in everything that's old,
A fallen leaf from a dying tree,
I see the canvas behind your painted thoughts,
I see the air in the words you breathe,
Human nature has no meaning,
An empty thought behind a bloodshot eye,
Sadness is driven by a petty thing,
Hatred hides behind a closed door,
The glitter in the eyes of an innocent child,
Quickly lost through growing old,
Life has gone on forever,
Forever is a time that is short lived,
There's a flaw in everyone's perception,
It's the only one there is,
A soul is lost, a new soul is created,
This is everything, this is nothing.

Carl A. T. Carlson

Trust?

My trust was once completely shattered;
it left my heart feeling bruised and battered.

No longer willing to let anyone inside,
deep within myself I chose to hide.

In loving no one, no pain could follow,
but the feeling inside is mostly hollow.

Now I have come to realize,
you have to love to be alive.

And though I'm still not a trusting soul,
I am finally closer to reaching my goal:

Trust completely those who are deserving;
leave those behind who cause only hurting.

Kimberly Woodruff

Untitled

As we go to our garden
   With the rising sun
And the work in the garden
   Has only begun.

We glance at the buds
   As the petals unfold
Oh Lord we thank thee
   For the rose

The rose that blooms
   With such fragrant grace
No other flower could
   Ever take its place.

As we drink in the splendor much as red wine
We are unaware of the passing of time.

But what is time but something that goes.
Oh Lord we thank thee for the rose.

In the late evening as the sun sinks low
We store the shovel the rake and the hoe

Then we look at our garden as the soft wind blows
Oh Lord we thank thee for the rose.

Jerry W. Perry

Empty Fireplace

The fireplace is dark and foreboding
by its warmth I'll not be nurtured.
Stygian and lifeless, each matching spire
is like the gates of hell
without the fire
or even a soul to be tortured.

Winter's ebony shroud is everywhere
its icy daggers spike the air
but the scintilla within is diminished.
Only ashes remain
of embers aflame
that never will be replenished.

The fire in my soul has gone
from passion's flame to somber anguish,
the winter night grows colder.
I sit and ruminate till dawn
as all alone I languish
and the barren ashes smolder.

Carl Hans Culbertson

Paradox, Change And Acceptance

Mourners there beside the engraved box of
the loved one that had and gave good times.

Doctors announced it as a boy, mother crying,
father gleaming, having brought a life to this world.

They cried, knowing it was best that it had been
a quick, painless death, knowing he was somewhere.

The baby, barely opening its eyes, cried and screamed
not knowing what was happening, only to breathe of relief.

Jeffrey Rittberg

Maturing

As a child, I grew up in happiness
With love, caring, and tenderness.
As a teen, I began to see
That everything wasn't just for me.
As a young adult, I did marry.
I learned responsibilities adults carry.
As I matured and had children of my own;
I tried to impart the same love I was shown.
Then as a mother, I came to know
The happiness and heartache a child can bestow.
At my middle years, I learned that life
Can sometimes give you pain and strife.
As a senior citizen, I found the treasure
Of grandchildren to give life much pleasure.

Betty S. Berry

To The Black Crow

If tears could talk they'd rival history
   and connect the holes in time

If tears could sing they'd pierce a rock
   and calm the fiercest storm

If tears could teach there'd be no dark
   no questions left in hunger

If tears could talk there'd be no need
   to slap a face in anger

For I have shown in front of folk
   the treasures of my soul

And now I weep away from them
   Embraced within my home

Maria Hansen

War

A saddening, terrible, and tragic thing
That into this dear world that we did bring

Men dying for a cause they think right
Anger and violence clouding their sight

Lives crashing down hundreds after the other
War even makes brother hate brother

Why kill each other to prove different views?
To all this madness, give me some clues

Many still can hear the crashes
Most cannot heal the gashes

All of the lives that are lost
Families left behind to pay the cost

Total destruction of country side
Now very peaceful where soldiers have died

Row upon row of the white crosses
Always reminding us of the losses

War is nothing but a useless waste
Ugly in color and bitter in taste

A saddening, terrible, and tragic thing
That into this dear world that we did bring.

Connie Dominick

A Time For Everything

There's a time to live; a time to die
A time to be happy. A time to cry.
There's a time to love; a time to care
A time when God will always be there.

There's a time for you; a time for me,
A time that I can't wait to see.
There's a time to talk; a time to pray
A time to trust God in every way.

There's a time to say no; a time to say yes,
A time when we shall all be blessed.
There's a time to sing; a time to praise
A time when all God's angels raise.

There's a time to hope; a time to learn,
A time to let your own light burn.
There's a time to preach; a time to grow
A time to let God's kindness show.

There's a time to go to heaven;
That time is near.
Let's hope that God
Will soon be here.

Rebecca Kesler

As Time Flows...

The skys are blue
Blue over the rolling, grassy plains of our life.
Life is fresh, new
Nair' a cloud nor dust to blow.
The days roll swiftly on a breeze
The land becomes aged, and wise;
The clouds begin to build.
Shifting, swelling the blackening clouds are beginning to gather.
Grasses sway with a changing wind...
The rain pours down,
The trees bend, twist;
Shaking, splitting, shifting.

The storm is over...
We see the land is changed-flowers sprout;
A white glow encompasses the scene...

Kyle Edmonds

Falling In Love

My wings had been cut I could no longer fly.
My heart had been broken and I didn't know why.
I tried to run but unfortunately I could not hide.
From the pain I suffered from deep down inside.
I was a butterfly in a cocoon waiting to be free.
Wishing and hoping to have my life back and
begging someone to love me.
Then I saw you, your smile so wide, your eyes so bright.
Hoping to fall in love but yet scared that I might.
You press your lips on mine and hold me so tight.
I long to be with you morning through night.
My eyes begin to sparkle as I feel what I
feel inside.
And I know in my heart my love for you
will never die.
My heart mends itself as the sun comes up
in the sky.
Now once again I can fly.

Katherine Perkins

Nash's Cool Pool

Splash, Splash. Look at Nash
as he plays in the summer pool.

The weather is hot. But Nash is not
the water has made him cool.

As time went by. There was a sigh.
Little Nash was having real fun.

What a way to spend the day
and just get out of the sun.

But the fun was stopped.
When his mom got hot

For Nash could see her steam.
Son you have splashed. You have splashed.
So don't think your mom is mean.

But then the weather is hot.
And even when it's not.

Please do me this favor.
The pool that you use. Whenever you chose.
Should be ours and not the neighbor's.

Thomas J. Ervin

Is This Freedom?

Someone decides whether you have the right looks
and color for the job.

Someone tells you how much your intelligence
is worth.

Someone tells you what time to arrive
at work.

Someone tells you what time to go to lunch, and
how much time to take

Someone watches you when you go to the restroom,
and checks to see how much time you spend in there.

Someone passes by in a sneaky way to see if
you are working or goofing off.

Someone tries to tell you how many times to get
sick in a year.

Someone tells you when to go on vacation.

Someone tells you what time to go home at
the end of the day.

Is this freedom?

Jacqueline Alfred

Dreams

Let me out, let my heart run free with joy,
Let the sun shine on my face so I can feel
the warmth,
Let my feet touch the ocean and the waves
wash over them,
Let me stand in a field of roses and smell
their sweet scent in the air,
Let my spirit of being me reach to new
heights of understanding and never
stop learning,
and most of all, let my dreams be filled
with wonderful places I have never seen
but only in my dreams.
Robin D. McBride

Untitled

From a marble sky comes a chorus of razor-winged angles,
like the inevitable frenzy that follows a cannibalistic feeding.

"All of it...All of it...Do you see me yet in focus."
"Tilt the lens...yes, like that"

Caught in heaven's burning light.
So cold my bones shatter.
So high the air is to thin to breathe.

With that picture perfect vision just before you begin to fall,
I see my dirt fall first.

My black glue, my finishing touches,
all drift like paper burnt all the way down.

Oh, that sweetness impossible to fake.
It's so surprising.
Sublime
Leann M. Faber

And Ever

The sun creeps hollow through the grass; her sigh
Is gently carried by the wind aloft.
Her liquid light has seared the eternal sky
And the rays drip through the wound, streaming, soft.
Injured sky veils his bride in morning mist
To avenge the sweet anguish her beauty causes him.
But the crystals dissolved into tears when she kissed
them. And sky forgives; sun shines; memories dim.
Yet, summer afternoons are brief. They soon remember
Past wrongs; anger builds; storms are unfurled.
The sun is sacrificed to night like a burning ember,
A petal of the Fire-God's flower, that awes the world.
Envious sky, close heaven's portal.
Days depart swiftly. Love is immortal.

Yioula Sigounas

Mystical Night

A wolf's howl tares through the silence of the
misty night world like the shattering of glass.
The moon rise over a winter horizon.
The misty air like sparkling water sprayed from heaven.
And the moon and his glow look as if they
are plastered to the sky with glue.
As the hearth is aglow, fireside a family gathers,
Laughter is present in the many hearts
A sight not to be seen, for there is no more.
Helaina Chiofolo

The Poet And The Public

The poet wasn't needing, wasn't wanting,
didn't care. If the public wasn't
bleeding then the public thought it fair.

The poet wasn't starving, wasn't lonely, wasn't sad.
That the public didn't find a use for anything he had.

So the poet didn't cry out, didn't die form
selfish cuts. Then the public had a meeting,
banged a gavel, said "You're nuts."

So the poet wasn't talking, wasn't laughing,
thought it fair. If the public wasn't needing,
wasn't wanting, didn't care.

Then the poet finally fell upon his most
timely verse. And the public thought of ways
to end this most untimely curse.

So the poet he was bleeding, he was starving
in the square. And the public they were
laughing. They were talking everywhere.

But the poet found his destiny in all
that he had penned. And the public they
were fawning. Asking "Aren't you a friend."
Edward Holman

When You Went Away

It's a shame what happened that day
when you fell asleep and went away.
The day you left me my heart won't mend
but I know some day I will see you again.
If I were a bird I'd fly so high
and see my special angel far away in the sky.
But until that day I see you again,
I'll think of you in a special way
today, tomorrow and everyday.
I love you mom but I can't forget that awful day
when you fell asleep and went away.
Christina Jo Horn

Wind Chimes

In the still of evening, a symphony of wind breathes
on two silver dancers swinging from their joined hands.
They glimmer as the full moon watches their hollow,
lonely bodies briefly touch, resonating a somber tune.
They fret while the melody continues, wanting to embrace;
their life is an endless pursuit, twisting and swaying
to grasp each other, shimmering and ringing
in the quiet, moonlit night.
James D. Ortiz

The Shade Of Jade

Bloods first taste, Sweet and Good.
Perchance bitterness arises. Harsh and misunderstood.
The first step on the long journey are where the victims wait.
After the bloody marriage of destiny and fate.
The road belongs to the hunter, the killer. He knows.
He chooses, hand selects. He watches as we grow.

As sweet as birth. As new as each day.
To seduce, then torture. To recreate to play.
To be a hunter; to be a victim.
Understanding and indecision.

Nothing scared, nothing holy can charm change.
Change can't save us. It's been arranged.
It can't save any of us from the dark memories we've made.
And the hunter will remain in the shade of jade.
Jondelle Edgerton

Horses In The Pasture

Horses in the pasture
   They frisk about and play
Always running faster and faster
   They are running around all day

They only stop to eat the grass
   Then they run around again
They run and run they run real fast
   But they can't run in the rain

They wait until the rain stops
   Then they run around some more
They run and then they take some hops
   Then they go right through the barn door
    Briena Dunkel

The Awakening

Today the scales were dropped from my eyes
I saw things like never before.
My world was viewed without hope, nor lies
and wisdom turned into a whore.
Stripped of all my naivety and innocence,
I stared in wide-eyed awe.
The air of beings was much to dense
they raped me and beat me raw.
A scream of terror uncurled from my lips,
but not a sound had been made.
The scream was last in the cracking of whips
as the beings invited their friends out to play.
Heaped into a ball on the floor,
I prayed for this not to be true.
My hand reached up to open another door,
while my blood was that of a witches brew.
Too weak to move, I allowed myself to be drowned.
Then, a feeling of stillness rushed through me
a peace of apathy had been found.
    Amber Towers

The Magic

When we walk the sands of time it,
stopped for just a moment in our
presence.
And in that moment of time we new
that this was magic, for time stopped
and the earth was still.
All else was gone from our realm but
the two of us.
And I thank God for bringing us
together, because of you I lived a
life in the magic of us.
I thank you for coming into my life,
when I needed you and I will always
have love in my heart for you, for now
and all time, I will live in the magic of
the moment.
    Terry L. Martin

Stars

As I look in the depths of the darkest night,
I know the stars will keep me from fright.
The small diamonds glisten and gleam,
As they guide me through a peaceful dream.
The constellations that they make is my dream
   going through my head.
And as I wake up in my bed, the glowing sun
   shines in my room,
I remember the dream that the stars led me
   through
    Megan Minkow

Mother's Cedar Chest

There's nothing much within the chest,
Just a blanket; fresh and clean.
But what a story this chest could tell,
if it could relate what it has seen.
It was purchased by a loving mom and a very proud, proud dad.
For a sweet young girl, who would one day
   be some fellow's loving wife.
It was filled with care, with treasures
   laid aside for that fine day.
Cloths, laces, spreads, and dreams and hopes
   collected along the way.
It served her through her marriage and
   passed into her daughter's hands.
It took a terrible beating at the grand children's playful hands.
And now it's a toy for the great-grandchild
who uses it and pretends.
About a future yet unknown, but filling with happy plans.
Oh yes, there is one treasure within this dear old chest.
It's the flag that draped the coffin of the man who loved great
   grandma best.
    Julia Kennan

Untitled

There stands a tree all alone, in a desert unknown
Without a friend, without love,
   the tree was fading like a dying dove
The tree was different in a peculiar way,
   its peaches were grown on every fifth day
There was a mystical power, only the peaches would devour
You wouldn't know, for the tree had a unfamiliar glow
Visible to only those,
   who accept the way we are chose
Admire us from within,
   not if we're fat or thin
We are all humans living with each other,
   why is it so hard to love one another
We're here for a reason,
   discover yourself and celebrate the season
For a time will come when our purpose is done,
   away we will sail into God's mail
At last we rest without worry or distress,
   with the hand of God in His Heavenly nest
    Nichole Wilde

Sharing

Love is pain until it's shared.
A beautiful day is still difficult to enjoy all by myself,
A lady is not.
A beautiful lady is a delight to admire.
The moon and the stars were meant for couples,
Alone the darkness is frightening.

An Angel once told me that I was a beautiful person.
I miss her still,
For she was a very big part of that beauty she saw in me.
If it were not for the sun, we would never see the moon,
And mistletoe is a parasite.

The more beauty I see,
The more I long for that very special someone to share it with.
How can life be so empty,
When it takes only one person to fill it???
Why do I thirst,
For that which has threatened my life most?

Is love an addiction???
    Larry Totoro

North By Northwest

The lines that separate, the lines that
divide. I can't decide which way, left
or right. No particular place of choice,
maybe I'll follow your voice. I'm such
a tourist to his, there's nothing that
I want to miss, like a kiss. Understand
that I don't understand, please help me if you can.
The lines that connect, the lines that curve.
There is so much more for me to learn. Please
don't talk to me in signs, the words I need
are hard enough to find. And the grey clouds
watch us as we go. I caught a drop of rain
in my back pocket and it felt like home. Little
drops of rain on our heads, but we didn't
haste. There is too much scenery that we would waste.

Thomas J. Talkington

Golden Memories

Oh golden anniversary, how sweet the memory
Of moments too precious to share.
Fifty years have passed by, together — you and I;
Just look at the loved ones who care!

In sickness or health, in poverty or wealth,
We traveled through laughter and tears;
To have and to hold, of more value than gold
Is the love that we've had through the years.

With happy hearts beating, it's well worth repeating
The vows that we made long ago;
The joy that we knew when we first said "I do",
Forever lingers in soft afterglow.

This moment remember, it's just past September
And our lives are filled to the brim;
May the angels above bring us God's holy love;
We couldn't have made it without Him.

Elaine Hadley

Thinkin

I'm thinkin . . . 'bout life
About how it goes so fast
How the summers fly by
When your young and having fun

I'm thinkin . . . about relationships
And about how people take advantage of them
And how they throw them away
Until they are ready to settle down again

I'm thinkin . . . 'bout my friends
And how they are screwing up their lives
By trying to grow up too fast
Because they think they are invincible

I'm thinking about how many parents think that
They do not need to talk to their kids about drugs or sex
Thinkin about how many ignorant people
Contract the HIV virus daily

I am thinkin . . . about how this life goes so fast . . .
About how I can make the most of it . . .
Because before you know it . . .
This life is over . . .

Mike Hicks

A Bout With Authority

I don't remember exactly when my little authority
problem came about . . .

It must have been severe for my parents
to always shout . . .

Thinking I had the world in the palm of my hand,
with no remorse or cares . . .

My little authority problem soon became
a lot bigger as I would go through
my adolescent years . . .

I somehow got through those troubled times
with my head still intact . . .

It wasn't until adulthood when I
understood the wisdom that I lack . . .

I could not wait to test my new found philosophy with my kids
who sometimes rebel and show authority . . .

It only goes to show that my life has made a full circle,
for my kids are just like me . . .

Dave Dodge

November Sky

Under the chilly gray November sky,
We sit looking at each other,
Feeling the cool crisp breeze blow around us.
We pull each other closer,
Hoping that by doing so
We will create enough passion to produce heat.
Under the chilly gray November sky,
I feel the warmth of his breath on my neck
He feels the warmth of my tender touch.
He whispers softly to me,
As the snow begins to fall.
Again we pull each other closer
Holding on for dear life,
Scared that if we let go to what we started,
Then it will be lost forever.

Under the chilly gray November sky,
I can't help but to think of you
And wonder where you are tonight.

Jennifer K. Costello

Love Water's

Love flows like a river
moving sometime against your will
the wind is her compass
moving you any which way she like

When strong tides push you over stoney
ground, that doesn't mean it's over for you,
love is moving you through unsure streams,
to blue and cleared waters assuring smoother
sailing ahead

Even when you feel you've road her biggest
wave, and the calm has all but sat in,
then comes another and often time bigger
wave, and life's guard surfing where you
never been

Cause when love splashes you're not prepared
it flows so uncontrolled
it's sometime right and sometimes it's wrong,
but the sweetest due is the joy awaken
in you, that comes and causes no one else harm

Anita Brooks

Just Living

On a trail of joys, no shoes about my feet.
Just the way I like it, just the blue sky and me.

Sailing on the sea, no land for a hundred days.
Just the way I like it, just the seagulls and me.

Flying through the air, no safe haven to rest.
Just the way I like it, just the warm sun upon my wings.

Gliding under the sea, no air to breathe.
Just the way I like it, just the bottom feeders and me.

Crawling across the desert, a camel on my back.
Just the way I like it, just the hot sand underneath.

Floating in outer space, no atmosphere to cling.
Just the way I like it, just the stars and me.

Smoking down the highway, no cops to see.
Just the way I like it, just the bike and me.

All alone in my mind, no noise to distract.
Just the way I like it, just adventure for me.

Walking through life alone, no friends or lovers to see.
Just the way some like it, but not me.

Gabe Hernandez

In Memory Of Grandma

The strong embrace with every hello
    The rough hands crocheting
That quick smile for every child
    The soulful eyes, always praying

Heartfelt passion for all pets
    The love for family radiated from you
Flowers in spring, sightings of deer with the snow
    These memories of my grandma are but just a few

As time passes, I will recall more
    When my heart isn't so heavy, I shall smile with the thoughts
I will speak proudly of my grandma, as I always have before
    But there shall forever be a void in my heart

For I shall miss you in my life
    I'll continue to cherish the memories so dear
Taking comfort today that you are in heaven with Pappap and God
    And yet, I still feel you so near.

Linda Henderson

A Foster Child We Have

A whirlwind they come
anticipation at a high.
Measuring up their surroundings and welcome
like a stray they have drifted by.

A honeymoon does then begin
when only good and grateful stand tall.
Until the comfort sets in
now the world owes them all.

The system, the system, the system they ride.
Blame on their parents Not.
Blood is thicker and love abides.
Abuse and neglect have long since forgot.

No respect for those who care.
Our feelings hurt-they feel no pain.
As loving folks we only dare
take in another's child again.

Donna Klein

Michele's First Love

When I first saw him he was clowning around
with his friends. I stood in a distance
looking at him, enjoying his friends.
He looked up at me, his eyes met mine, I
wanted him to say something to me, but I
didn't want him to stop playing with his
friends, because he attracts my attention.
He seems to have something special
about his eyes they were saying something.
They were telling me how he felt on
the inside. He was happy but yet sad at
the same time. He came to were I
was standing, he ask me my name
I told him Michele. He asked me for
my phone number I pretended I didn't
hear him. He walked me to my class.
He asked a second time I gave my
number to him. This must be love.

Michele Miller

Broken Heart

Sitting in the dark all night
With tears on my face, I cried
When a true lover has changed
What can I do is right?

Thinking about the past we shared?
My heart now is in despaired
When a true lover has changed
The picture of us, I will tear

Sitting all alone at night
With tears on my face, I cried
When a true lover has changed
What can I do is right?

Missing the kiss he sealed?
Oh! Very sad I feel
When a true has changed
I wish I wash killed

Sitting in the dark all night with tears on my face, I cried
When a true lover has changed what can I do is right?

Hoping he'll come back someday? Oh! How long can I wait?
When a true lover has changed "Death!!!" is all I can say

Hang Nguyen

Abyss

The colors blend as in a painting
The children sit there patiently waiting
Among them lies a soul so dark
A soul with room only for hate in his heart
He thrives on the bad thoughts
Of others around him
'Till he takes them over, completely surrounds them
People wonder why hate shows
It's because they allow it to grow
Secretly within us all lives a piece of hatred
Enough to take us all it can't be negotiated
He sits there waiting in the midst of darkness
The people don't know it but they are his accomplices
Helping to feed his hunger
Of death and destruction nothing but plunder
His voice is loud louder than thunder
And if you don't watch out he'll take you under
To a place so deep
You'd wish you were asleep
But you're not and your soul he'll always keep

Ruth Rodriguez

To My Parents

The most priceless parents in the world, you see,
Belong to me!
The things they deal with,
the things they do.
Why do they put up with so much,
I ask you?
The trouble I cause,
The things I do.
They deserve better, I assure you!
Maybe someday I'll get it together,
And make my parents proud!
Then they'll be glad they were with me in each endeavor,
Even the ones they shroud!

David Stevens

He's More Than Stained Glass And Steeples

There is a man that heals the sick,
Opens blind eyes, and ministers so quick.
Deaf and Dumb he has touched, walked on water,
Oh there's so much.

More than Stained Glass and Steeples,
He's here to touch his people.
Many look to it as a Religion,
But he came so we could be forgiven.

The Alpha and Omega, The beginning and the End.
Look to him for the answer and your life will he mend.
He's the lily of the Valley, the bright & Morning Star,
THE I AM THAT I AM, He even holds tomorrow.

Yes, he's more than Stained Glass & Steeples,
And he's more than a Ritual for his people.
Look up, lift your hands, and praise his name,
Through it all he'll take you and you'll never be the same.

He's the precious Lamb of God, the greatest of them all,
The one I put my trust in, on his name I call.
Not four walls does he live, but much greater than you see,
He wants to touch a hurting world,
He wants to touch even me.

So don't put him in a box, cause you won't get blessed
Open up your heart, and he'll do the rest. Through
all the programs and ceremonies lets please don't
miss, The true work of God and that HE IS.

Kim Jackson

Thoughts On Getting To Know Plants

I sit quietly a bit, inwardly centered and open,
and allow the plant to evoke sensations within me.
It dances around me, through me, in me.
I feel its substance in my being, my body. I am inside it.
The plant then sits quietly in the middle
and I dance around it. I move around it,
feeling its form with my eyes and my hands.

My dance is centered around, is formed by the plant's form,
(directed by it?) I am outside it.
The plant being rises and we dance together . . .
The movement we make is the gesture of the plant,
the particular species. The steps we take relate to all plants.
I am one with it, neither inside or outside,
or both inside and outside at once.

The music . . . what is the music:
sun, earth, warmth, air, ether?
How is the music different for each particular plant?
Who is, or was, the dance teacher?
Who taught this plant its particular steps?

James Robert Chapman

The Doll

My doll is made of porcelain,
a face the shape of a crescent moon.
Her eyes shine of glittering glass,
with lips the shape of a silver spoon.

The look of tight, dark, brunette curls,
a painted face, she's a real young girl.
Tall height, a gorgeous dress,
totally dazzling, her name is Meg.

My doll walks and talks,
she's durable, and lovable.
A real original masterpiece,
she reminds me of my sisters niece.

There she stands on my shelf,
sometimes I think and can't help.
I see the light glint in her eyes,
I can almost hear her cry.

My doll gives me such happiness,
if I did not have her, what would I miss.
She is one of a kind,
one I was very lucky to find.

Jeannie LaForgia

Dreamer Of Horses

What can I say that hasn't been said
How do you measure their beauty?
Of the countless stories that have been read
They have such power and a sense of duty

Respect them and they return it
They can be your friend or foe
If they could speak they'd show their wit
As seen on the faces of some I know

I used to love them from afar
Now I have many of my own
Always wish upon a star
Even after you are grown

If running free or in a stable
Enjoy them if you can
They run like the wind and are able
To be part of this ever changing land

Louise Kursave

Reflections On Precarious Solitude

I fall out of time once again
as the wind beats-beats-beats on my back.
The spirit-wind fills my lungs
within the vacuum of my intangible body
Transparent and empty I sit
sighing beneath the inky black
membrane above my dry and straining eyes;
Just as my mind pierces through
the night like the razor blade of
the lighthouse, I am such an
empathic pillar (among the seas
of animals in cloth and steel which
find themselves mewling in their cages
of earth and mortar), like the rocks
before me: which let themselves
be beaten-beaten-beaten into
humble submission until all that
is left of their universe is
white, malleable silent, sand.

Shaun Michael Gilligan

Fear

What are you afraid of?
Are your fears so great that you respect your fear and
let it take control of your life?
Should a person give in to their fear?
Or should a person be like a wild wolf and hunt their fear away?
Fear can come in different forms
Fear can come in the form of commitment, responsibility,
security
and conscious
Fear is what you make of it
If a person doesn't deal and take control of their fear it can
take control your life
Fear then can be a sword cutting and cutting at your soul
leaving
it to bleed

Chris Taylor

Your's Very Sincerely

Listen to the silence, can you hear the song
Far out in the starshine, when the nights are long?

Listen to the silence, can you hear the Word
Deep within the cooing of the white dove bird?

Listen to the silence, can you hear the bell
In every drop of water in the deep heart's well?

Listen to the silence, can you hear the sound,
Laying in the morning on the dew soaked ground?

Listen to the silence, can you hear the pipe,
In the sweetness of the apple that the sun's made ripe?

Listen to the silence, can you hear the tune
In the perfect perfume of a rose in bloom?

Listen to the silence, can you hear it free
Slowly breathing beauty in the greening of a tree?

Listen to the silence, can you hear it ring
In the purpling dusk, when nightingales sing?

Listen to the silence, can you daily die
His love the wings to lift your soul on high?

Listen in the silence to His melody divine
"Lo I'm always with you, I have made you mine."

Jeremy G. C. Bradford

The Last Memories

Far east of the land,
Where people scattered,
   away from their sacred mountains,
they protect their own.
Our people, our land,
   our warriors,
   our fighters,
our stories, our prayers and songs
that last a lifetime.
The past as gone with the wind.
   To us, the memories are not forgotten.
   Our elders hold the key
before us,
   willing to teach and
past their knowledge onto us.
   Yet . . .,
   many have forgotten . . .

Darlene Webb

Bodies And Souls

Hair matted with the sweat of love
bodies glistening, moving in the rhythm of life
two souls searching for each other
in the darkness of night
begging to have their humanness validated
and their love shared
with the sweetness of fulfillment
slumber comes

Sue Eckert

Inspired By The Book Of Bob

On a day like the throaty rasp of a Bob Dylan lyric,
Quagmired in musings born of bleak,
I heard a harmonica wail to the jerky
Thrum of an arrhythmic bass.

While contemplating the bluesy
Bustle of grey misgivings
And sultry sensibilities, a
Spider sobbed out for form but found
Instead only the plaintive queries of a
Thousand bygone balladeers.

Connie Pursell

Nature

As the wisping wind comes through the air.
The quiet stream is too precious to bare
You can sit there all day without a care
The birds chirp up in the oak tree
The mountains go as far as you can see
Nature sits there untouched
But someday this is the place
I would like to be.

Nick Saenz

I Bid The World A Goodnight

I close my eyes, think a thought.
As I drift off
I bid the world a goodnight,
to the day
I give a silent goodbye.
In my mind tomorrow awaits
Tomorrow - the wonderful excuse
   for what wasn't done today.
A small splash of dream paint drops in my head,
As the sandman taps at my skull.
This is my mind's time - to do what it likes.
I have no control.
I close my eyes,
Think a thought.
As I drift off
I bid the world a goodnight.

Cassandra Leone

Forever Love

"I Love You" was the last thing he said
Those words repeated over in her head
She hears his voice among the wind
And wishes he was back again
Everytime those winds blow her way
She thinks back to that very day
When he asked her for her hand
And the day he was taken from this land
Then she thinks of her time to say good-bye
And be reunited again with him in the sky

Danielle Champine

Dumped

Sugar and spice, with everything nice,
comes together to form feminine life.
This infiltration brings society alive...and the world's
never the same.
Heart and soul, won't let go.
Crippled when I am alone.
Inspiration seems so slow, when someone speaks your name.
World is not the same.
Not how I planned to be but what can you do?
I am alive...empty heart, black sky.
Hello I'm doing fine at
the bottom.
Love and hate, plenty inside.
They stand together at no surprise.
Manipulate to control your mind,
    but she dare not take the blame.
She crushes me like she crushes you.
Did not want this to be, but what can you do?
Red star, black sky.
Hello I'm doing fine at
the bottom.

Dearl Tucker

Spinning Chair

Sitting in a spinning chair,
Face to face with a stare.
The words so strong to keep in mind,
For so deep in love they'd think we were blind.

You taught me how to live some time ago,
I learned from you, you may not know.
I hurt you so much, I made you cry.
I broke a peace of your heart with every lie.

Now when we talk it's not the same,
It wasn't your fault, I was to blame.
I want you back with all my heart,
I never thought we'd ever part.

I try to live day by day,
Finding someone to show me the way.
Week after week, as I start to feel pure,
For to have someone to love is always the cure.

Now that I'm over my stress, feeling so new,
I thought I should say, I miss and love you.
While face to face with a stare.
Seeing you in that spinning chair.

Dan Swilley

Just Work, Bobo

These hands on these keys
    are at work.
Other hands gripping hard tools
    thrusting in the dirt.
Saws pulled and pushed,
    levers, wheels and minds
at work. What would we do
    without this use?
Who'd carry the mail?
    Change the oil?
What else is there to do?
    How would we know joy?
I need your work
    And offer mine in trade.
We fancy other ways but
    it's all work:
The dancer whirling in the lavender light,
The actor, frame by frame thirty to a second,
The clown encircled by smiles are all at work.
Seems fair - thanks, Bobo, after all: I smiled too.

Alex Baker

Pener The Ostrich

Pener looking like a Queen.
Her head held high so lean and keen.
Picking at my buttons, at my buttons as always she
Was never mean.

With a sparkle in her eye she would do her dance,
As always the Lady could prance.

As precious as she was the Lady went into a trance.

With her head held so low Pener was telling me she had to go.
Now we knew she had done her best as always, she was laid to rest.

Frank Bray

The Love Of God Christmas

C - is for Christ - He died so we would not fall;
H - is for the Heirs he made of us all;
R - is for the Righteous who will reign above;
I - is for the Intercessions He makes with His love;
S - is for His Sacrifice where we can be pardoned;
T - is for His Tears He shed in The Garden;
M - is for His loving Mercy He pours on us all;
A - is for the Agony He withstood in the Hall;
S - is for our Sins which only He can forgive.

William V. Burdges

Missing You

Here I sit in the dark with my thoughts of you, and my
heart is so blue. I'm missing you. Where is the laughter we
once shard, the love, the smiles, and the tears. There not
lost in the years there here in my heart and in my thoughts
of you, oh how I'm missing you. There's a place in my
heart that's so very near to you a place that no one can
touch but you. There's a place in my life that's empty for
you a place no one can fill but you. I'm missing you.

Janet McCrory

Untitled

Why make things that are meant to last
When one push and it is all destroyed in a blast
When that giant skyscraper comes falling down
Will that giant skyscraper make a sound
When that giant skyscraper hits the ground
Will there be lots of people standing around
Or will they all have picked up left that town
Did they get out of the city real fast
And are we doomed to repeat the sins of the past
Why don't we get our own to last

Tim Henry

Golf Artistry

Alone.
Metal, wood and surlyn:
Tools of artistry; tools to humble.
Cool blue overhead.
Mocking green underfoot
For those who miss the precision of the craftsman.
Arrow straight:
Artistry in flight.
Air hangs heavy as the second surlyn lands.
The chip is clean; pin high.
Metal guides the surlyn along the soft, fast green;
Distance, accuracy
The only obstacles to the completed sculpture.
As it reaches its ultimate reward,
Artistry in motion.

Virginia E. Martin

That Morning

I wake up one morning, nothing is the same.
Windows aren't broken, I feel no more pain.

The sky is lit up, like a firefly at night.
No longer is anything wrong, wrongs are all right.

Shadow in the corner, no longer seem dull.
Birds are all flying, even the gull.

Words that are written,
are all in a dream.

Words that are written,
are now what they mean.

I wake up one morning, everything is the same.
Windows are broken, again I feel pain.

The sky is all dark, like a brown bat in flight.
Everything is wrong, no longer is anything right.

Shadows in the corner, are once again dull.
Birds have stopped flying, even the gull.

Words that are written,
are no longer a dream.

Words that are written,
are what I do men.

Kati Sydejko

If Anybody Cares

If anybody cares, I'm tired and bored too
It's getting really late and there's nothing I can do
If anybody cares my life has no point
I'm too bad to sit and study and too good to smoke a joint
If anybody cares my boyfriend's gone for good
He left me here crying just like they said he would
If anybody cares I don't now what to say
My life is almost worthless I'm told every day
If anybody cares I'll tell you how I feel
As far as I'm concerned it's time for one last meal
If anybody cares I want to go away
Though I'm yet to find a place where I'm welcome to stay
If anybody cares I need to get some sleep
Late at night I lay down and all I do is weep
If anybody cares I need to have some fun
The battles fought in my mind are sadly never won
If anybody cares I'm sick of your dirty stare
I guess it doesn't matter unless you really care

Diana Gonzalez

Falling In Love With A Friend

Sometimes when I look at
you it hits me "I was right."
Lord only knows I tried to deny
it with all of my might.
Honestly I want to be friends.
But deep down in my heart it's not
true. Whenever I'm around you, or
standing right by your side, I'll die
if I look into your beautiful eyes.
When older people watch us,
and see us stand together. They see
the way I look at you. Their eyes and
hearts, tell me "This'll last forever."
I didn't want to believe it, no one could
prove it. That a friendship wrecking
plague could come between us two.

This plague was brought on by me,
no blame is given to you.
It hurts me to say, but you really need to know,
that I've fallen in love with you.

Bethany Vilate Faulkner

Truth

I didn't think I could live with the truth, but I am.
I have to.
It eats away at me, but I keep it inside.
You always remind me that this is my fault.
You won't let me feel, but I am human.

There are times when I don't know what I should feel.
Betrayal, longing, no.
Hate, yes.
Then who?
Should I hate her, did she betray a friend?
Should I hate you, did you forget?
Should I hate myself, did I cause you to leave?

Maybe I already do.
That's why I have to live with the truth.
This will always remain with me.
I'll keep it inside, but I won't let it keep me from you.

Rachael Severson

Untitled

How can I adequately explain
A child waking up to the dream like haze of summer,
Mother setting out his clothes,
The warmth is welcome upon skin
In the normally cool house.
The sound of grass hoppers humming in the distance,
Singing their song of summer,
And through the brightened window
A child's world of play.
The sun lights the world for another day,
Outside the window a perfect picture,
The tall grass with apple trees on the hill side,
The fragrant smell of apple blossoms wafting through the
window...

Michael D. Bartholomew

Beautee Is Unique

Beetle eyes
Leer at me, gleaming in the sunlight.
Green ribbon streams its tail.
Eel mimicks ribbon.
Eeriness elongates both.
Eerie be us all.
Seek the wind to float upon;
Free thy life, flee thy world.
Breeze jets hair in fine imaginative lines
Seemingly stretching my mind;
Peeking eyes grasp peak awareness.
Peers are awed into confusion.
Redeem your dreams in awaken state,
Unsheet ghosts to play.
Beetle flies away.

Jeff Prusia

The "Ol' Corn Hole"

My husband told me he loved me
at the "Ol' Corn Hole"
A place in Montana where you sit and soak
to rid yourself of corn's on the feet
Why he was so romantic in this spot, I will never know
But it is nearly 50 years now married to my Joe
He had just returned from England and a B-17 base
I was just plain lucky to meet him, in any case
Together we raised two wonderful boys
All these year's together made our life full of joys
I could never have chosen a man with a better soul
Than my Joe who first kissed me at the "Ol' Corn Hole"

Janice Harlick

Dear Son

Inspired by Greg Davis and Kevin Kona
I may sit today and reflect about the day you were born.
I may smile warmly to myself, while tears feel my eyes.
For, I can not be with you today, as we are far apart.

This was not my plan, the day you laid in my
arms for the very first time.
The feelings of love so strong, so overwhelming.
I was part of you, you were part of me
It was the proudest day of my life!

Your little hand reached and grabbed my finger,
What a grip you had...I would give you only the best.
I would enjoy, being a Daddy, I loved you so!

Now to realize we are apart only by miles, is what I must do.
And find comfort in knowing some things are forever.
The pride I still feel when I hear you say "Daddy".
The grip you still have holding on strong to my heart.
And that through love and guidance, I still hold you.

I give you the best, I give you me.
I enjoy being a Daddy, I love you so!

Forever, Your Daddy, Greg Davis

Poetry Behind Bars

I am an artist in the truest form,
  Tho' my colors are not cool or warm.
I paint my pictures with words of life,
  Of joys, happiness, hardships and strife.
I have no beginning and I have no end;
  Call me Alpha or Omega, or just call me Friend.
My words are sometimes soft and sometimes hard,
  But there's no reason to be on guard.
You can see my music and hear my colors,
  if you can read between the lines.
You can find the past, present, or the future,
  if you can read between the signs.
Your soul is the mirror of my mind, because
Behind these bars I'm emotionally blind.
I reach out with my pen to touch your eyes,
  With truth and humility, but never with lies.
Why deceive yourself or deceive even me?
I would ask you for nothing, and I charge you no fee.

Dominick Vincent Malachi

Lady - The Bug

lady you aren't as pretty in
your red dress anymore
and you haven't made me smile
in years.
And lady what are your damn spots for?
Have they kept track of your soft spoken tears?
you walk too slowly lady
you can never keep my pace,
and lady you will never know
the secret of my winning race.
it's so easy to walk on you lady,
i love to weaken your self,
fly lady fly
as i throw you from this sloven shelf.
you stained my foot today lady,
as i crushed you with my skin,
oh lady you sure know how
to make this tough boy grin;
change the color of you dress lady
you don't look good in red.

Gina LoSauro

The Road To My Emotions

I'm walking a long, cold road,
Carpeted with thorns that tear at my innocence
And tenderness.
A road that leads to loss and heart break.
A road I must face alone, time after time,
With out companionship or relief.
The pain I try to side step always hurts the most.
And the fear I try to avoid,
Knocks me down and laughs in my face.
Sometimes the path turns,
And reveals happiness, sunshine, and peacefulness.
But then I realize that it's too good to be true.
The sun burns out,
And the evil shadows swallow me,
And grip me,
Until I am forced to surrender,
To the darkness of my emotions.

Tanya Graham

Winter's Snow

The snow falls softly and cold
As we slumber in the warmth of our covers
Each snow flake different from the other
Falling side by side
Covering, where it falls,
A thin dusting of crystal white
Layer upon layer
Until the dust becomes one
A thick blanket
Of contradiction
So cold up above
Sealing in the heat below
Preserving the secrets within
Preparing to rise again
When the warm rains come
As we wake from sleep
To live another day
Refreshed and renewed
All traces of slumber
Washed away

Spring Rain
Deborah J. Slaughter

Twilight

Who are you?
What are you?
That's taking control of our
  lives!
You are turning us against
  each other,
And we treat each other as
  spies.
What happen to our beautiful people?
All lost in a jungle of fear,
At times looking over our shoulders,
But believes me, more times, no one is there.
Paranoid and scared is our get high,
But we know not what we do, or,
  who we fear.
That is why I ask this great question!
  Who are you?
  What are you?
And tell me, why are you here?

Judy Herrera

The Meaning Of Life

As I walk through the woods,
I watch and amaze as the animals behave in their natural ways
I wonder how and why everything under the earth and sky
work together in a delicate balance.
In nature it's true under the sky so blue,
that also by you even we have a special place on this earth,
even before our birth.
God knew what was in store for me and you.
To only be true to the people so few that have a special meaning.
A true and special place in our hearts.
We shall never be torn apart.
To be kind and open to anyone who may want and need our love.
Is this why we are placed on this delicate earth?
I believe so . . . Ever since our birth.

Krista Hedrick

Offering Of Me

Heard you calling from a distance, many years ago.
Although I met with much resistance,
your love for me still shows.
With ignorance and pride,
I walked a crooked path.
You were always by my side,
and gently brought me back.
You opened up my blind eyes,
and helped me to see again.
And when I strayed or stumbled,
a helping hand you'd lend.
I have taken from you my whole life,
And not once did you complain.
And even when temptation won,
Your love remained the same.
I used you when convenient,
Placing you upon a shelf.
Took you down when you were needed, only to reap your wealth.
I come to you now, I am down on bended knees.
I raise my hands to heaven, with an offering of me.

Corey Scott Kurth

Like Breathing

Love is like the air, with it you breathe comfortably without
problems, but without it you will surely die.

Love is needed to be able to survive because without it you
feel as if you have no purpose in life.

The love of your parents gives you strength.

The love of your children protects you and gives you a proudness
of accomplishment, and it makes you feel beautiful and happy to
be alive.

The love of your spouse your soul mate that is your rock.
the love which sustains you in life and gives you the security
you need.

Like breathing love is sequential to live, without either
life has no meaning.

Awilda Gonzalez

The Storm

As chaos breaks the light
An ionized crash splits open the night
The air fills with a vaporous zest
As the tempest glides in from the west
Watery spirits scatter down
Cascading wildly as they touch ground
A force roars through with an ominous howl
Touching each blade and leaf afoul

Christopher A. Williams

Snows Comin'

The easterly winds ain't comin' my way,
the west winds come without warmth today.
As Ottomans marching, she blasts her way,
dial for help, please dial today.
It may be sweaty Rhodesla's way,
but mystic crystals are here today.
Tress toss their leaves over my way,
and riccochet twigs throughout the day,
I feel like a popsicle, not melting away,
I hears a little whisper of wind today.
Whom do you want that you whisper my way?
An oman of luck, or to freeze my day?
He utters to me, "boo", me your way,
I'll kiss you with snow your entire day.
I see lopped eared bunnies away,
a tidal wave of birds leave today.
Zilch is left this autumn, my way,
and tints of a new leaf blossom today.
Ain't goin' outside, cold goin' my way,
'cause pelts of snow are comin' today.

Sheila Sterling Shots

Sonnet Appassionata My Beloved, Mick

O passion of my sensuous throbbing heart,
In surging waves of love I come to rest
Upon your soft warm breast and burning breath;
A song of love, of yearning to impart
Erotic appassionata, in excelsi blessed:
Vibrating strings of harmony thou art,
Melodic chords of passion never rests,
The restless spirit challenges the heart.

An innuendo glance, and kiss is blown,
Emotions quiver for the tender touch,
And pulsing, gripping fingers seal the fate.
On flights of fantasy my passion lives
Engraved in heart, concealed forevermore
In death, until my restless spirit parts.

Margaret M. Joy

A Special Friend

I feel very special to have someone as
special as you. To see you in my life opens
many doors there that keep you close to
my heart. I feel a very warm feeling of
friendship that draws me closer to you.
Even if I am close to you or far away from
you there are many thoughts that roam
within my mind of what we can learn from
one another as each day, and each night
continue to pass among our path.
I feel so close to you even when I am far
from you and as each day continues to come
and go I come closer to you. I know that
this friendship will continue to flourish
and we will always know that in the
future there will be many opportunities
to be just as close as we want to be. This is
a very special friend that holds a very
special place within my heart.

Samuel Flores

Into The World

Sometimes I feel I have it
Nothing can rattle me, upset me, or break me
Then I go into the world

At times I feel I'm the molder of my destiny
The intellect, the athlete, the artist
Then I go into the world

Then at times I feel I can love and be loved
I can say hello to my fellow man
I can give advice to those who have lost their way
Then I go into the world

Then at times I know I can make a difference
Nothing can break my spirit
then I go into the world

I call out to God and say arm me with
Serenity, wisdom and courage
let faith be my shield
And strength my sword to slay fear and doubt
Then truly do I know I can go into the world
James Gillard

Untitled

So, with my entire heart,
with my entire soul,
I managed to go ahead and buy you this thing.
So here is this ring.
I love you so much.
And just as this diamond will last forever,
just as long will we be together.
It is worthless to me without you wearing it.
You are worth so much more to me.
It cannot love
as I love.
It cannot feel
as I feel.
For I love with a love that is more than love,
and I feel with feelings much stronger than this diamond.
Without this ring on your tiny finger,
it has no purpose, no shine.
Forever you live in heart of mine,
just as I hope forever will this ring live on hand of yours.
Nothing, nobody means more to me than you.
Erik

1st Love - My Ideal My Ideal

Out of the darkest of many dark nights
The heavy rain ceased, and tiny raindrops fell.
But an awakening light shown for me this night
As I thought of the one I loved so well.

Like a Heavenly vision he descended into my mind
Sounds of heavenly music, like angels wings,
Flapping in the breeze.
It was the vision of my Ideal - My Ideal My Ideal like an echo

So if you watch a rainbow in the sky
And wonder why you didn't try,
To harness a star in years gone by,
And never let it fly. Don't cry.

For better things, angels wings, birds that sing
Bells that ring, will awake you
Yes, he was truly out of this world, so
Wonderfully kind and true

And his heart of gold shines out like a light
His faith in God is real
He was My Ideal - My Ideal - My Ideal
1st love
Ruth Precie

What's A Poem?

What's a poem my dear Son?
A poem is a mere string of words.
So why don't you write one?
I don't have the flair of words.
Is that your only problem with
poetry, the problem of wordsmith?

Sometimes I have words but not the feeling.
So poetry is only words and feeling?
Yes, and the ability to string the words in a certain way.
Then poetry is more than words and feeling is what you say?
Yes, and some dubious thing they call the Muse.
Muse! Is that the idea of the poem by any means?

No, it's a feeling, a mood, or eccentricism,
that strings the words so beautifully,
We call the lines a poem, rather pitifully,
When the words rhyme with the idea,
And the idea rhymes in the ear,
to call up the image of a thoughtful Sage,
whose words your thoughts engage and presage.
Frank Frimpong

Waiting For You

In the silence of the frozen still
In heart, in mind, your image fills
Like the beauty of the waterfall
The cascading rush quenches all
The fears and pains and aching soul
While the dream resides in waiting's cold
And patience slumbers for a living touch
To awake the fire in a whispered hush
Yet time flows like a frozen sea
As destiny gazes into eternity
Life goes on in muted chill
and hope yet send its beacon still
And all the while I stand alone
When will wondering become a home
And all the while I wait for you
And when time will make this journey new
Aron Strong

We Must Trust Him

The road looks so dark and dreary.
The way looks so long and weary;
But surely it will be worth it all,
When we hear our Dear Masters call.
There is a rainbow that shines behind our darkest hour.
We know, God knows what we are needing most.
He does know what is best.
He is the one who has it all in control.
Oh, help us to simply trust.
He knows how much we need the rain,
The darkness and the pain.
If everyday was always bright,
If everything always seemed just right,
How could we our heavenly home gain?
We must trust Him hour by hour day by day.
We must trust Him with each minute.
We must trust Him when we know not what each day holds in it.
We must trust Him when the day is dark.
We must trust Him when we know not how, to face another day.
Oh God, help us, give us thy strength, show us the way.
Katie Schmucker

A Shoulder To Cry On

Sometimes we all need
A shoulder to cry on.
Someone who listens
With a sympathetic ear,
To all our troubles and problems,
Someone who really cares.
Pain is often easier to bear
When we don't hold it all inside.
Instead we can tell a close friend without fear,
Who will listen without judgement.
Someone who gives us
A shoulder to cry on,
Someone to help wipe away the tears.
Sometimes we all need
A shoulder to cry on.
Someone who listens,
Someone who cares.
You're there to give me
A shoulder to cry on.
You help me feel better, and you always care.

Nancy L. Ruggiers

The Wedding

The mood is soft, as the sun fades away;
My loved one I shall marry today.

Too long we have been alone, we two.
Then we found each other; our love is true.

What are the thoughts that we hold dear?
Happiness, commitment, year after year...

Wanting for each other a dream life without pain;
But knowing together, we will dance in the rain!

Whatever may be ahead in our unfolding roles,
May God bless us from our heads down to our soles.

Now the march forward begins on a note,
And with a big lump in our throats—

So together, here we stand!
And "life's just begun" as we join hands.

Mary Cale

Magic Shadows

She stands silently before me,
    shadows of a candle's light dancing around her.
I can feel her warmth,
    so I know she's there.
I can see her soft features,
    her hair, smooth as night.
I can taste the sweetness
    of her unselfish kiss.
I can sense her wisdom
    and her passion for life.

Her love is inside of me,
    though she doesn't need it to be.
Her dreams humble me,
    feeding from my own.
She thinks not of my pain,
    neither do I.
She thinks not of my love,
    it would unease her.
She knows not what I have given, she is not really here.
It is only me, the shadows, and a love no longer to be shared-

Dan Harvie

Forgotten

No worries.
Backyard football and crick tag.
Warm dew on bare feet in the morning,
Cold dew on bare feet at night.
No bills.
No taxes.
"Let's go play in the orchard,"
"No...A castle in the sandbox."
Fear was late for dinner,
Hatred was taking a bath.
Its all changed now.
Responsibility.
Dependence.
I can never go back.
Only remember as I care for the little me in my arms.

David Bohman

Religion

Under storming skies, on hardened stone
    we started to build an altar,
    a monument to ourselves.

To bandage wounds inflicted by lovers
    past and make new scars.

With teeth and nails and words.
    We shattered and ripped and smashed
    and comforted.

We learned cynicism and some magic
    and we met elves and talked
    with wizards and found God,
    then gave him away.

We crushed those who didn't understand;
    we eliminated the other.
    And became mind readers and children
    and parents and students and scholars.
    And priests and artists and masters.

Whitney Calvert

I Swear, I Swear

The fragrance of the air,
    from the spring flower bed,
smells like your hair,
    when I kissed thy forehead

The freshness of the water,
    in the summer creek,
speaks of the (love) treasure,
    in thy heart, so meek.

The warmth of the fire,
    on a cold winter night,
makes me desire,
    to hold you tight.

The beauty of the sky,
    with an autumn rainbow,
is in thy eye,
    girdled with eyebrow.

Autumn, Winter, Spring or Summer.
    Sky, fire, air, water upon, I swear.
You are my flower, you are my lover.
    I will be yours for ever, I swear, I swear.

Shankar Raneru

Looking Out The Eyes Of A Child

They fall like raindrops.
With drugs, crime, and society's problems
   they can't make it.
So they fall.

When will it stop raining?
Carl Bates II

Wisdom Cries Out In The Darkness And Light Brings In A New Sky

As the new born baby cries out in the night,
for her bottle or her Mother's breast.
Or a wandering man in the desert in plight,
searching for that certain rest.
When a prisoner sits in a dark lonely cell with no hope,
after given a Bible he suddenly starts to learn how to cope,
As every human hears the Lord knocking at his heart,
but always the devil comes to make the Lord's word depart.
Wisdom cries out in the darkness.
As the sun rises to start the day anew,
and the darkness by no means can comprehend.
Or how the course of time is almost through,
and those who have done right will cause their time to extend.
When a certain young lady meets a special guy,
whenever their together she receives a natural high.
God freely gives eternal life,
to all those who will believe on His Son Jesus Christ.
Jesus is the light that brings in a new sky!

Tracy Paul Williams

Love And Hate

If love is a dream, than I hope not to wake
If love is confusion then let my mind shake
If love is the sun, then let it burn on
And if love is God, let him rule long
If love is a fairy tale, do let me see.
And if Love is a person, please let it be me.
If hate is a fire, then give me a pool.
If hate is a trick, I hope I'll out fool.
If hate is a rhythm, then I'll break the beat.
And if hate is a hunger, I just won't eat
If hate is a story, I'll close the book.
And if Hate is a vision, I just won't look.
If Hate is a power, I'm stronger than he
And if hate is a person, I pray it isn't me.

Tracy Onyskin

The Cloud Of Loneliness

There are times in life that you are just all alone.
It doesn't matter how many people are around you
The loneliness just seeps in way down to the bone.
And no matter how hard you try to get through
All the gloom and grayness, you find that there's no way
To evade the cloud that threatens torrents of rain drops
To be released from swollen eyes, once blue, now gray.
The sadness just hangs there and defeats all your hopes.
It's like a huge blanket of woolen thread
Causing burning sores in your heart and head.
You can't escape the turmoil you're in.
Loneliness can cause such despair and pain
That the will to live can flee and give way
To a desire for relief, a searching to gain
New direction for life, or lack of, you might say.
You hold on to that thin thread of a chance
That life might get better in the days ahead.
But as you look in the mirror and take a long glance,
You decide that it's best to just go back to bed.

Donna Christenberry

Lost

Now I stand in the cold wind
waiting for my life to end
scared, alone and so, so, lost
like a flower killed in a frost
my regrets tear me apart
ripping out my soul, ripping out my heart
God I cry for your appeal
does not anyone understand what it is that I feel?
Mistake, mistake, break after break
My heart has had all it can take
I regret this and I regret that,
as I fell into this mental trap
stealing my strength and all my pride
I wish you could see me from the inside
see how I'm sinking, sinking down
everyday, falling to the ground
I can't find God in my heart
please don't let me depart
so I'll try, cry and cry
God, I don't want to die, I don't want to die...

David W. Hitchcock

Memories

   As you look through your photo albums, you think of the
years that have gone by.
Your heart is filled with happiness as you begin to cry.
You recall all those fun times you had.
And how your parents loved you even when you did bad,
The memories you can never forget and there were times that
you had regrets.
You minded your p's and q's and made your parents proud, and
now you move on to a different life ready for excitement and strife.
You appreciate your parents very much, and you can't tell them
thank you enough.
There were things in the past you wish you could take back,
and how a lot of times your world seemed black.
They always said I love you no matter what you would do.
There is not enough words to tell them thank you for all they
do for you.
So put a smile on your face and let them know that they will
always have a place.

Keturah Ruth Wendlandt

First Woman

My shoe's blood-stained tip, what
I have left of her

First woman I saw die,
big lady with belly pain

Take this pill,
swallow this cup
it'll make your stomach
settle

Then, as your eyes recede
code calls scream and the knife men
split you sternum to pubic bone

Your warmth they said you had so much of
puddles out leaving you
so cold.

Adam P. Klausner

Strong Love

I never knew love could
be so strong,
between two people
for this long.
I know this relationship
has had many pauses
but I think as long as we
work them out instead of
throwing them in the closet.
This marriage will last forever,
cause deep down we know it
will get a whole lot better
as long as we never pull
the string that connects our
hearts together at the seam.
Our love for each other will
Never fade away,
cause there is always a brighter new day.
So till this day I never knew love
could be this strong till the day I married you.

Jessica Anderson

Reality

Prone, hugging the earth he lies.
Deliberately with solemn joy he puffs,
The dandelions dainty fluff becomes airborne.

Delicate, graceful it soars
Soft white beauty against blue sky
Breath taking in sweep simplicity

The momentary flash of beauty gone
Absent mindedly he reaches forth
To pluck to taste
And finds the stalk of stark reality
bitter.

Agnes P. Hunter

Black On White

I am who I am, and you are who you are;
And I do not care nor care to know how far
Nor how much you think you are better than me
For I know I am great and I have my own destiny.

I plan for the future and do not live in the past
Like those in the "hay days" who could not last.
Lasting a long time, if I can, is my plan;
Either with or without anyone's help, I still know I can

Do as I wish, when I wish, and how I like;
Because I knowing where I'm going in life is my right.
No one can get me down or put me aside
Because I hold my head up higher than an ocean tide.

I can do anything I put my mind to do,
And even if I have to, I'll even surpass you.
Then you'll look surprised to find it is me
That has outlived your torment and proven our equality.

Aaron Jermaine Griffen

Life Goes On!

The world turns and the sun burns.
Nature blooms and people are doomed.
People say good bye and people die.
Then we turn and say hi and a baby is alive,
and now I say good bye and for the people that die.
May they rest in peace.

Matthew Denning

Silent Killer

Who is the silent killer that haunts his dreams,
as it carries out its evil schemes?
And why does it have to be,
that he must suffer so endlessly?
He must endure the silent stares,
of people who choose not to care.
He was unfairly convicted of a crime,
and now he lives on borrowed time.
His old life was stolen by a heartless thief,
when he was infected with HIV.
Any infection can easily turn deadly,
because his immune system is no longer ready.
His eyes are a reflection of the pain inside,
that his hollow cheeks and dark eyes will not hide.
I do not understand why Aids had to be,
a part of his life's plans and dreams.
This man is a good person and did nothing wrong,
but now he is inevitably forced to be strong.
I don't know what to do, but I will be a friend,
a true friend - right up to the ultimate end.

Christina Bull

Winds Of Life

Butterflies dancing on the winds of life.
You and I on a journey as two hearts unite.

Moved along by the streams of love,
As they cut a deep path thru the psyche.
Remembrance of struggles to return,
Memories of a distant past,
Following the chords of love to find you, at last.

Held in the heart as a feeling,
Imprinted in the mind as a concept...Love.

Grand canyons etched across the landscape of our Souls.
The badge of timeless honor, a tribute untold,
Of endless trips from etheric to the physical world so cold.

To dance like the butterfly on the unseen rivers of time.
To find joy, as you share your life with mine.
To find beauty in existence, dancing all the while.
To find our love once again,
To touch your heart and see your smile.

Linda Duquesne

Poetry Contest

I really don't know what I'm doing
Nor really do I seem to care
If only I can find my way to Heaven
Because my father dear is there.

With tears I see how he would help me
A timid, sky, and lonely child
My thoughts and actions didn't seen to function
But he did seem to understand and smiled.

So why not go to him with all my troubles
With knots in shoe strings or forsaken friend.
My undeveloped brain it could not muster,
Or understand or comprehend.

So now since he has gone and I am older
I have another Father here below
Who said that He will not forsake me
Until the time is set for me to go.

Iva Troyer

Heavenly Fate

For the one we knew and all so dearly loved,
has been freed from the pain and sent up above.

She's struggled through the pain, and now laid to rest,
we'll miss her all so greatly, and hope it's for the best.

Through the years she's been there and taken care of us all.
and taking the responsibility, that all just seemed so small.

Although she was a lady, made of brittle bone,
she always kept the smile on, with a heart of golden stone.

It was Grandma's family, friends, and will to strive,
that kept her in our presence, kept her alive.

In the past few months, we've all hoped and prayed,
we'd wonder and dream that she would stay.

And after all her pain and her dreadful wait,
we hope the best is for her and her oncoming fate.

Misty Polen

Beautiful

Throughout the sky among the stars
shake these feelings
So shattered and torn.
You're beautiful — so beautiful
Of all that you mean to me
You're beautiful — so beautiful
That's what you are to me.

Upon the breath, from which I breathe
a delicate embrace to know you're with me
to love, is a fault so wrong to appear
to question without answer the feelings disappear

It pains me to know that you are still there
laughing with the song of the strong and the fair

I want you to love me
as I so, love you
I want you to need me
Just as I need you
I want you to hold me and never let go
Beautiful, so beautiful
That's what you are to me

Baylee Marie Rayhorn

Prayer

all my life i've been told to pray for myself
the world and my family
although i prayed — it was not true
i prayed not for salvation — but for tradition
my faith was unborn — i never questioned
just believed — i didn't think — just trusted
tragedy came and i thought
i questioned
why us why her
she doesn't deserve it
then like the sun, the answer dawned on me.
it was to teach that out of tragedy comes greatness.
She did deserve it.
She deserved to be great — now she is.
now I reflect — questioning all —
thinking always — faith was born — all
has reason — nothing is irrelevant
my tragedy has occurred
I will be great
now I pray.

Benjamin Maldonado III

The Final Curtain Call

Night nestles against the earth
in a subtle blending of sky and ground.
Thousands of tiny night lights
sparkle across the land
like a mirror image of the stars in heaven.

If one should zero in,
myriad dramas unfold
like thousands of tiny stage plays
on a theater-in-the-round.
There is no beginning and no end
until the final curtain call.

Marieta McMillen

Life Is Like A Flower

Life is like a flower, the budding of a rose,
It has a lovely fragrance as it unfolds.

Life is like a flower, the blooming
everywhere, in sun and rain it
restrains and needs so little care.

Life is like a flower, as its blooms
unfold, and loses its fragrance
as it becomes old,
For then the storm clouds gather, and hides
its beauty rays,
Life is like a flower, its roots forever stay.

Though the storms are many, the clouds
will role away, and beyond the shadow
it blooms a new to stay.

Jaunita Hicks

It's Not Hard To Be Easy

It's easy to say life is unfair...
It's easy to say no one cares.
You can be easily led astray...
You can easily think there's no other way.
It's easy to say no, sometimes it's easy to let go.
It can become quite easy to lie...
It can become quite easy to die.
It's easy to cheat...
It's easy to beat.
It can be easy to love someone...
It can be easy to hate no one.
It's easy to cry, when you don't know why.
It's easy to laugh and shout...
It's easy to have no doubt.
    It's not hard to be easy, because
no matter how hard you think
life is...it becomes easy.

Novalea S. Wilde

Untitled

The joy of music is everywhere
Music is a melody of tunes
The tunes create a sense of a temporary world
They can move people to do crazy things
The tempo cause faster or slower actions in people
Music can create new life into things
If a person looks real hard he cannot find it
But it a person can feel the tunes he will find it
After he discovers it; the feeling is pleasant
Or the feeling can be unpleasant
The joy of music will always be in the air
Whether pleasant or unpleasant

Jeffrey Myers

In Your Eyes

I see myself in your eyes
someone who cares, but never pry's.

I see visions of hope and dreams,
I see grace and love beyond all means.

In your eyes I see charm,
I see a person who could never bring harm.

I see myself from day to day,
showing faith through prayer and grace.

I see a strong and vital person giving, caring, and
showing her strength.

In your eyes I'm happy and gay strictly for
business with little time to play.

In your eyes is a woman beyond all others
working toiling, but never complaining, and that
special person I see is your perfect me.

Karenann Dulaney

My Dream

We live in a world where we struggle since birth,
And we're expected to spread all this love on the earth.
And most people believe that God's on their side,
Our lives have become an amusement park ride.

We search the world over for this thing "inner peace",
And we find people killing - seems never to cease.
You must lock your doors, there are criminals stealing,
We must understand or we can't start the healing.

We're teaching our children that it's alright to base,
What we think of others on color or race.
The results of these acts cause suspicion and fear,
And those who would listen have turned a deaf ear.

Will the world end tomorrow? I can't foretell that,
Our lives are a huge maze, and we are the rats.
And only the Lord knows which way we're headed
We hope that it's heaven, not a place that is dreaded.

We do have the power to change what is wrong,
If we reach out our arms, and sing happy songs.
My dream is to give love, with me it will start,
'Cause I've opened my eyes and put love in my heart.

Rick Chaikin

Summer's End

I look out, expecting summer, expecting to see
The red hot sun shimmering for me.
A late-blooming cosmos, dressed in pink,
Pretends that Summer is on the brink.
Holding tightly to her Beauty
Days squandered carelessly doing her Duty.
But bone-chill wind and leaden skies
Are heralding Summer's sure demise.

I thought Summer would always stay;
I would forever be young and gay.
Childhood dreams I would pursue
And life would grant me all my due.
I played and worked and did my part
But Summer is leaving—it has no heart.
Nostalgia cannot recall
The certainty of approaching Fall.

Still, the memories we share
The Autumn rain cannot lay bare.
My love for you will last, my friend,
Far beyond the Summer's end.

Carol L. Sekara

Mourning Journey

In Memory of Maria Louisa Guzman Hesse
It may come quick or slow
No one will ever know
It may be painful or fast
for the undead it will always last
Memories which will never fade.
Will eat at you until your day
When you too will only be a memory
You'll make a journey to a new place
Leaving behind the rest
In search of the best
As people mourn and cry
They don't realize you better off in the sky.
So as we say our last goodbye.
We sit and wonder why?
Why did you have to die
That's a question we'll never have an answer for
Until we make our own journey towards, the lightened door
Where you'll meet again and wait for the rest
As your soul is blessed and your body is put to rest
After completing God's test.

Ely Hesse

Destiny Unchanged

Abstract thought He lives first hand
The unknowing genius, the "New World Man"

He is angry and Love
Feels the passion of tenderness and hate
Wants to flutter like the dove
Or like the eagle, for the kill fly straight

He perceives the world around him
Through the kaleidoscope of his youth
He understands the patterns
But does not yet know the truth

A quote from a song strikes a resonant tone
He now knows he belongs He is no longer alone

No longer the lone target of misery, or of grief
He recognizes his destiny as a leader, as a chief

That quote from that song connects the future and the past
The marathon has begun and he now has a chance to last

With the knowledge of his destiny He lays his kaleidoscope aside
No longer burdened with the patterns of his youth
Into his future heart, body, mind and soul are free to ride

Thanks to Alex, Geddy and Neil

Andrew P. Rebmann

Autumn Season

The sun rising, far above your head.
Falls on the fields of, greens, browns, yellows, and reds.
There's no other season as beautiful as this.
To come out in the morning and see
what the sun has kissed.
To walk among the trees and bushes,
with colors array.
Means that mother nature, has shown
her finest display.
To walk through the woods, I need
no other reason.
It's beautiful as always, in the
Autumn Season.

Leo J. Wonsewith

If I Was A Tree..

If I was a tree,
Oh the sights that I could see.
I could see a little bird taking flight,
From a terrific height.
I could see airplanes soaring high,
Up in the big, blue, sky.
I could see squirrels being born,
While their fathers are gathering acorns.
But what I like most of all,
Is when the season turns to fall.
For this is when my view's the best,
And I can see all the rest.
Lindsey Beirne

The Lady In The Light

There she is the lady in the light
Walking the shore on a moon lit night
Her radiance and beauty is clear and bright
As graceful as a dove in the midst of flight

Her eyes are as blue as the summer sky
So vibrant with colour made never to cry
Eyes so perfect that indeed do reveal
Magnificent for certain, Le Beau Ideal

Her hair flows free with the whims of the breeze
As natural and divine as the oceans and seas
With color so brown and a hint of gold
A tale of better has never been told

Her skin is like ivory, as soft as light
The mere sight of which keeps dreams a flight
Her hands and face hold the light of the moon
As she walks along the dark lagoon

The fragrance she keeps is a sweet as a flower
Flowing through the air with an enchanting power
A smell so strong I'm forced to weep
And fall eternally into an amorous sleep
Eric J. Meer

Her Hands

In younger days, we thought it fine;
To hold her hands so was sublime!

As adults then, we still held hands,
And looked ahead, for life so grand.

As years went on, we planned it through,
An thought it best, the thing to do!

Her father placed her hand in mine,
And said, "She's yours 'til the end of time."

Too soon it came; the end of time,
God came; and took her hand from mine.
Andrew F. Vario

Gone

I wish, I wish, I wish my wishes came true
Because then I would wish for nothing,
My love, but you
I dream, I dream, I dream my dreams came true
Because then, my love, I would dream nothing
But of you
I look, I look, yet I do not see, for all my wishes and
Dreams have done nothing but drifted out to sea
Andrea Perrino

Yesterdays Roses

Yesterdays roses are withered and dry
A symbol of a love, that will never die
I still smell their fragrance, so sweet and compelling
I want to remember that story, they are telling
You signed the card, with a hand bold and true
It said to my darling, I'll always love you
I felt very special, because I know that you care
This bond between us, will always be there
Oceans and continents can't keep us apart
Because I have you so close, right here in my heart
What ever the time, what ever the day
Our love will flourish, in every way
After all, I will always have, yesterdays roses
June Ann Johnson

The Wait

Waiting alone in my quiet niche.
The darkness lies like serpent coiled
Ready to strike me down.
New ideas swirl to the front.
Met by subtle contradictions,
They vaporize into a logical mist.
My restless quill dances on the page
Leaving cryptic signs to betray the time wasted.
Impossible to gather or understand,
The letters gain size and shape.
Quietly, they struggle to find her their way
Into the real world of images and ideas
Only to be silenced on reality's edge.

Now, I must try to reach my muse
Feel her warmth flood my mind.
Touch the fleeting fabric of dreams
Enter the world of the magical rhyme.
Only here, can I find my meaning.
Hopes and fears come into their own.
Only here, can I find what I seek
Before my thoughts leave me cold and alone.
William R. Stone

Midnight Stroll

As it walks along the beach on its silvery hooves,
It makes no sound as it silently moves.

Its coat shines like silver as it walks by the ocean;
Power and grace are in its every motion.

It takes in a deep breath and then lets it out
As the cold salty air tingles its velvety snout.

Water splashes its feet as it trots along
While the waves crash on the beach, creating a song.

As the moon rises higher, a new feature appears;
An ivory horn on its forehead, between its two ears.

The horn spirals upwards toward the night sky,
And it shimmers like a pearl as it silently glides by.

Every hair on its body is the purest of white;
Yet it seems to glow silver in the pale moonlight.

Now the moon starts to set, and the sun starts to rise
As the last stars twinkle in its deep blue eyes.

It turns and begins to head into the forest
As the birds start to sing their morning chorus.
Megan A. Ruess

163

To My Friend Eileen On Her Three Score Years And Ten

My sources tell me, that you have reached,
An age when many, feel they're beached,
When joints creek more,
And backs are sore,
And Life declines, as strength is leached.

Some older folks may empathize,
As cataracts may cloud our eyes.
So many things appear afoot,
I have to laugh, some things are moot,
It's all our part to realize.

The lot we had, I see was blessed,
For times gone by, we did our best,
Those times are past, our oats, to "sow,"
The script says "patch," to get more go,
And play some cards, less near our chest.

This age of three score years and ten,
Adjusts my thinking, towards all men,
The gray cells left, I do believe,
May help another to achieve,
A life well made, might not have been

Paul A. Faeth

Mother

To the woman who holds a special in my heart
No matter how far away we are, somehow we never part.

I'll always be your little man, and if you ever need me,
in your heart is where I am.

Now when my time comes to pass away, I hope that on this
earth is where you stay

I couldn't stand to lose you first, because of all tragedies,
that would be the worst.

To take your place, there is no other,
You're my one and only dear Mother.

James R. F. Ellison Jr.

Remember Always

If someone dies and goes away
There is not a lot that you can say
To those of us whose left behind
With broken hearts and lonesome minds.

But we must remember as we cry
That they are up where the angels fly
Where they can be most anything
Throughout summer, winter and spring.

They can be the wind that blows around your face
Or the sun that shines all over the place.
They also could be the rain or the snow
And even trees in the forest that grow.,

So when we mourn for the ones we miss
Maybe we should try and remember this
They have not died and gone away
They are still near us everyday.

With the winds that blow and that sun that shines
And all the memories in our minds
We keep them with us everyday
It is only their bodies that have gone away.

Beverly Mae Nielsen

I Waited For You On The Shores Of Adriatic

I waited for you on the shores of Adriatic.
Seeing the waves that swell with eagerness.
Adriatic had changed its blue color into gray,
and the sky wasn't blue anymore, it was red.

I waited for you with my view across it.
I loved Adriatic as much as I could, but...
I couldn't suffer anymore,
and one day I escaped from my land leaving Adriatic behind.

The dogs were behind me the day I left Adriatic.
The followed me all the way across it.
They wanted to punish and bury me alive,
and I finally went in the foreign doors.

I suffered not seeing Adriatic anymore.
Not seeing my sky anymore and forgetting all the faces
there, even though I forget my mother.
Leaving her to die in the darkest of places.

One day death came to me,
and I closed my eyes forever - but
Adriatic was unforgettable in a letter.

Margarita Bango

The Way It's Goes

Life is like a game with so many tricks,
fouling and messing with my heart.
Why does life have to be so hard?
I have always wondered why.
   At times I just want to break down
but same how I always press on.
Thinking it'll get better, which it always
does but one of this days I am gonna
break and not care what the future
holds for me. It may not be the
smartest idea but what else am I
suppose to think at the times I want
to end. Yeah, my life has good points
at times but beware even good things
can hurt you, so be careful.
   I always wonder what is gonna happen
in the future, who really knows. I guess
that's the reason I seem to push on.
Everything's full of surprise and challenge,
life may not go your way all the time
but hey that's the way it goes!

Danielle Stevens

After Dark

After dark, when the moon and stars appear and
push the clouds away
After dark, when the bats and nights creatures
come out and play
After dark, when all the families are snuggled up in
their beds fast asleep
After dark, when the cows in the barn, and in the
pasture lies the sheep
After dark, and after the bats and owls come back
from their fly
After dark, and after the sun comes up and shines
brightly in the sky
After dark, and after the sun comes up and melts
the beautiful dew away
After dark, and after the sun comes up, the birds
chirp on the branches as they sway
After dark, when the sun comes up, it's time for
dinner at the break of day
After dark, when the moon and stars appear and
push the clouds away

Kim Warner

The Bird Sings

The bird sings an old woman sighs.
The man on the bench begins to cry.
His life is gone he has nowhere to stay,
his children don't care they've all gone away.
He had hopes, he had dreams,
he thought it was beautiful and the bird sings.

Lisa Leemheer

Love

In my eyes love is a river,
Still flowing far from home,
Love is a tiger,
Free for-ever more to roam.

If love is a flower,
It's spring time in my soul,
But winter is coming.
My heart is getting cold.

No longer will I hear your name,
And in my heart there's a dying flame,
I'm sorry I must leave,
To you I'd love to cleave.

The burden of sadness in my life,
I wish we were old and you could be my wife
Onward he to Michigan,
But believe me I will come again,

To get the one who's dear to me,
Your sweet face again I'll see.

Ron Young

"Whole Again"

I look into your velvety green eyes
They reflect your soul
Your effervescent personality illuminates the room
A man as sweet as candy
As refreshing as a swim on a sweltering day
My best friend
My loving friend
No man is an island
To feel like a puzzle missing one piece
What's a deck of cards without the aces?
What's a chocolate chip cake without the chips?
Your presence makes my surroundings complete
You fill the void in my heart
Constantly on my mind
Just thinking about you makes me smile
Some say there is no such thing as a perfect guy
I don't think so
I've found my knight in shining armor
Please be mine forever!

Hinda Kaplan

A Portrait

God painted a portrait late last night,
A portrait so beautiful white,
Brushing the ground with new fallen snow,
Oh, how it sparkled and glistened and glowed!

Then he decorated the trees with 'cicles of ice.
How they shine—ever so nice.

Taking the most misty gray,
He painted the sky in a winter's way,
Finishing his portrait of a winter's day.

Annette Alexander

My Mask

I wear a mask of invisible lace
To hide the tears upon my face.
To hide the scars of years gone by,
To laugh when I need to cry.
No one knows my true identity,
But only the outside of me.
This mask is only happy and free,
If someone just would only see
There's a person inside who cries out in fear,
Who dreads the coming of another year.
But no one hears my silent cries
And my hidden tears no one dries.
And so my life is all a show
Until the curtain only I will know.
How much I long for someone to cry to
Instead of hide beneath my mask and lie to.

Brittney Lee Nichols

The Journey Home

When is enough, enough?
When our restless hearts
seek to fill the emptiness
with trinkets of tarnished gold,
We hope this time that it's the real thing.

We thrash about, gasping for air,
Writhing in desperation,
waiting to be connected,
to belong, to matter.

Suddenly, in all our fury,
you call, "Come here, my love."
"Let me replace your weary ache,
with serenity and peace."

We curl our finger around the
Mystery of Being who
has finally brought us back
to our true selves,

We have come home!
Home to the cosmos
And Creator. Amen . . .

Sister Joanne Picciurro, F.S.P.

Obscured Vision

Oh night, your darkness holds a spell,
that blots the light and binds the soul as well.
You've got me so that I don't want to flee
from this dark curse of love and ecstasy.

Oh, night, dark night, you whisper so quietly to me.
You sooth my soul and fold me lovingly.
You've flooded my mind and blindly lead me on
from what is right to what doesn't seem so wrong!

I feel you standing, oh, so close to me
and as we move, you hold me tenderly.
Though words unsaid, there're still outspoken, ummm,
we've found a semblance of a love that has to be.

Dark, dark, night, don't ever flee from me
'Cause in the day, this feeling ceases to be;
if this is not true, I do not know this thing
that mystifies my soul and set my heart aflame.

Now, witchful, mist, your cunning ways are clear.
I know the truth. Of you I have no fear.
At last it's day. The focus is unstrained.
I know that love and lust are not the same.

Lillian Warren Lazenberry

The Chill

an utterance unheard
between us sped
forward and back
as i set the milkshake
down, unfinished

i glanced again
and wondered when,
what special turn he'd taken
or decision made
that fostered those conditions

his shoes were worn
his clothes ill-kept
but he was real; inside,
a work of Art,
a genuine Human Being

had he been a stray dog or cat
i could have adopted him
without question but not a stray Human Being
for what would Ganymede, the cupbearer, say
or the Nymph of Callisto

Mignon Tedesco

Experience Is...

It's not until we fall, can we clearly see
Just what is really meant to be.

Like a hound dog taking a ride
And leans too far over the side
And he slips and falls and lands
On the pavement, stunned —
And there he sits all out done.
Wondering, what just happened to me?

He opened his eyes and he did see,
He wasn't as careful as he should have been
To keep from falling on his shins.

Gaydell M. Bradley

Perfect

In a world full of such perfect hate,
there is only one thing that can be done.

She would have to live her dreams,
her dreams of the past where such
hate was not yet heard of.

A dream where people of all distinctness
lived in harmony and love

Such places found only in books and reveries

It had long been a hope of hers...
To go into that world and bring enough
pieces back to her present, that she could one
day reach beyond the limits of others,
to teach what she had found

What this new found knowledge would bring
to such a people was unknown,
but there was one thing she did know.

She knew that if the war in her brothers'
hearts died, then that could be enough...
Enough to one day live in a dream.

A dream only she could have, a dream full of such perfectness.

Rebekah Zoe Coyne

Whipping Whirl

The sky is filled with haze
and shallowness,
The nights are long
and the days never last
stranded from long lasting memories
roads of life that go on never
seem to fade,
hard ship that never goes away
no sympathy for those alive,
trying people always being judged
not knowing the simple things,
that never seem to be enough
the joys of love
but much sorrow in life,
The laughter of children but
in there own little world
The mountains they hold are nation only to crumble,
the sea of courage that keeps on going
with the motion of anger that's
In us all.

Denise M. Brown

Waiting

A seed falls.
A child is conceived.
And the mother waits and loves.
And God sees and knows.
And the seed sprouts and grows.

The child is born.
And the mother waits and loves
for the child to feel, to walk, to speak,
to learn, to laugh, to love, to share.
And the tree grows and waits.
And God sees and knows.

And the mother's heart fills with precious moments:
each smile, each tear, each touch.
And the tree grows and waits. And the mother waits and loves.
And God sees and knows.

No lightning strike. No stunted growth.
Both tree and child grow straight and true.
And God sees and knows. And the mother waits and loves.

And God smiles. And the tree falls.
And the mother waits.

Jean E. Wynne

Lament To A Love Lost

Oh to be in old Ireland, and being lost in her fresh meadows
Especially in the summer, beneath the dancing swallows
   And have beside me my maiden fair,
    With skin so soft and silken hair
There a kiss I would beg to borrow,
A favor she may return tomorrow
We'd skip down the lanes by the bogs and streams
   Sharing together our thoughts and dreams
Watching the sun-set on the western shore
And we promised to stay for evermore evermore...

But my love my love I could not stay
And with heavy heart sailed for Americae
Promises made were promises broken
And words that had meaning are now unspoken
Even though I am not a native son
I fight for old glory I carry the gun
I dream of you on that western shore
With treasured thoughts in my memories store
And bid I'll return with the dancing swallows
To stay with my love for evermore evermore...

Damien Cotter

Dad's Sonnet

Long about the end of December
The bitter cold sets in;
Entirely different from November,
This cold calls all debts in:
The wood that didn't get cut,
The windows that were not calked,
The door that won't quite shut,
The car that suddenly balked.
But—the stars are never so close;
Moonshadows play tag on steel ice;
Naked branches rasp—the wind blows,
Creatures huddle, from men to mice.
Thoughts stir, ashen embers come to life:
Dad, thanks for letting me grow without strife.

Elmer L. Butler

Two Seasons

The leaves are orange, the leaves are red.
When they change colors,
They're dying or dead.
When the leaves are on the ground,
Under our feet
They make a crunching sound.
It's starting to snow sleet hail and rain.
That means fall is over
And winter is coming in Maine.
The winter is cold.
The ground is covered with snow.
Anyone that goes outside is bold!
It's getting colder and colder each day.
That means we stay inside,
And have fun in every way.

Tasha Overmyer

The Gift Of The Shell

One day, long ago, as I walked along the beach,
I saw this shell there in the sand.
I picked it up and looked at it.
I felt its texture in my hand.

My fingers touched its surface.
I looked at its lovely design.
What once had belonged to the sea,
The tide had now made mine.

Somehow, as I stood in the vastness
Of the sea and the sky and the sun,
I was reminded of all God's creations
And the wonderful things He has done.

Holding the shell there in my hand,
Gave my heart and my soul such a lift,
I winged a prayer of thank you to God
For giving me such a wonderful gift.

Jean L. Brodmann

Untitled

A thought a dream an inspiration
Questions and answers
Look at the graceful dancers
watching the sunset and sunrise
the sadness of goodbyes
the howling of the wolfs
when the rain comes down
beautiful ladies in white satin gowns
soft comforting hands that we can hold tight
A twinkle of a star in the mid of night
There's a world full of poems which haven't been written
It's up to us to find where they're hidden

Ashlee Burris

The Old Tree

The branches on the old tree are bare,
Winter arrived early this year with a
lot of fanfare.
Covered with ice, sleet and snow
she is the beautiful queen of the winter ice show.
She stands proudly in the cold,
holding two bird feeders which are both very old.
Many beautiful birds visit her each day,
such as the Titmouse, Tree Sparrow, Cardinal and Blue Jay.
Their brilliant colors on her icy old limbs,
look as if she is adorned with precious gems.
She loves her group of special friends,
and is thankful they are with her till each days end.

Geraldine Mitchell

The Forgotten Rose

The beggar child cried pitifully,
her body broke, and bent,
no one cared for where she came
nor sorrowed when she went.
Her eye's could have been beautiful,
had they not been swollen red,
so sad that filth should dare to hide,
the gold that crowned her head.
She could have been a beauty a rose without a thorn.
But she was picked before her bloom
her petals ripped and torn,
she once had been cared for in a loving home,
but fates blind intervention left the child alone.
What's to become of this fruitless charity?
No place for a child but the cold and uncaring streets.
Three days ago a week at the most, the child dosed her eye's
She had no will to open them this angel in disguise!
So if passing threw a cemetery, holding an unbloomed rose,
lay it on baby Janes small grave.
It's fitting I suppose?

Nicky Melton

The Power Of The Night

In the midst of the moonlight,
the energy within the night,
lurks in us, without a fright.

The sounds of cars, barking of dogs,
leaves rustling, and consequences a fussing.

Gimme guts, gimme glory,
gimme power to fulfill this story.

Endless reward and the longing to remain astray,
but, within this world we must stay.

For it is the night which lacks light a bright.
For it is the night that keeps us out of sight.

Warmth from the energy of the soul
removes the chill of the wind, it is energy wool.
That is why we are nearly never cool.

So we run, and we leap away,
For a while...hidden we must stay.
So quietly we wait to make our get away.

Juliana Feldmeier

I'll Get It Done

I have the paints, marble and clay,
Ideas galore and eager to play,
The years fly by - I'm seventy-five,
Must hurry, must hurry while still alive,
No time to waste - it's so much fun,
I must make haste - I'll get it done!

Eugenia Chuan

A Strange Melody

A strange melody flowed through the wind,
And it crept into my head,
Like a haunting memory
Of some ancient past

Melting into the thought
Of a deserted road,
Leading me into a dream,
Hypnotized by the glimmer of an orange colored moon,
Seen only though my eyes.

Standing alone in the dark,
Like a silhouette in the midnight sky,
Looking down at us
As we look up at them,
Lost in some foreign land
Far beyond the edges of time,
But just barely touching the horizon,
I found the greatest secret
As it was thrown away,
And blew a kiss to the moon,
As I fell into you.

Candice Lindsay Jones

Untitled

When you look in my eyes - I see a spark
but too quickly would you turn away - that the light would stay

You held my hand - you kissed my lips
when I was cold - you held me warm
when I needed your love - you caressed me sweeter than sweet
you loved me deeper than deep

Romeo and Juliet - John Smith and Pocahontas
their story-sounds familiar - ours is similar
so parallel to history - a true tragedy

Cinderella and her prince charming - Beauty and the Beast
their story-seems familiar - ours could be similar
so close to fantasy - a dream that could come true

Hold my hand - kiss my lips
I'm cold - so hold me warm
I need your love - so caress me sweet
love me deep

I want you to love me - like the way I love you
make love to me - and complete this dream
of ever-ending fantasy

Thu Ha

A Love Poem

A poem I have write
For I love you more than a little bit.
You have passed another year,
Another year to keep you near.
Another year to love,
My little Dove.
Another year of work hassle.
Another year of building our dream castle.
Another year of sick cars and good health
But not much wealth.
Another fear of finding more of the treasure I married
With your talents so varied.
Another year to say, "I love you
And I'm glad of you there are so few."
Another year of more each day.
Without you I'd probably be a stray.
Another year to sing, "I love you" from the housetop
For I cannot stop.
Another year of blue eyes and soft skin
That didn't come from any cosmetic bin.

Trafford Huteson

Pond

As I look upon the pond of life,
I wonder how much I have accomplished,
I feel as if I can go no further,
But the pond of life is big,
There are people in my life I don't understand will I ever?
The pond of life doesn't have all the answers,
To my questions.
Will I ever find the answer?
I don't understand what I am here for
I know the meaning of part of life
but what does the rest mean?

Danielle Clokey

I Pray For You!

Poor! That's what I am!
   But have no time for useless tears.
Your words jumbling . . . stumbling . . . smoothing
   out at the end of your grin.
I'm aware of that familiar deceitful, nervousness odor
   seeping out of your skin.
Your practiced eye to eye hollow smile . . . pitiful stare.

How can you still wonder?
Twist and mangle the facts!
Avoid obvious looks at my skin, my hair, my back.

Why am I awake while you still sleepwalk my pain
   . . . stepping through my birthdays . . . again and again.

When? . . . Why? Didn't my God make you care?
   If you could ever kneel and pray with me your heart would
      hear my cries of unanswered prayers that my soul has
         bled for you to hear for hundreds of years.

Pamela P. Terrell

Still Counting The Years

Fifty years ago today
You promised each other, come what may,
To share a love that never ends
To meet head on whatever life sends.

That life you shared sometimes brought tears
More often laughter filled the years.
He only lives now in your heart
But you are never far apart.

He holds the ribbons from your hair
He loves with a love that is so rare.
A love that goes beyond tomorrow
A love that heals the deepest sorrow.

He uses your arms to hold his loved ones
Grandchildren, in-laws, daughters and sons.
He uses their arms to hold you tight
Until you meet again in the Light.

Mary Starbuck

An Inconceivable Love

They say we could never work;
for our age within us would always lurk
and wonder if there is really another
you could love more than your mother.
You say your words of love can never be expressed.
Is that why you simply say, "We are blessed"?
Within ourselves, we have everlasting fuel
that will carry us through every yearly Yule;
fore no one on this planet could ever understand
that there has been greater love since the beginning of man.

Angela G. Kissel

Silence

I need someone to break the silence.
I feel it pushing me closer, closer,
over the edge.
nowhere left for me to hide.
thoughts disappear,
hope has died.
I am alone,
stalked by my memories,
falling now
only to redeem
this broken measure,
a hidden treasure.
hear my screams,
screams of silence.
I will not live, I refuse to.
I refuse to live with this perpetual nightmare,
refuse to live with this burden, this hole.
see me fall, in the crevasse,
now I am safe, nothing can hurt me here.
I need someone to break the silence.

Amanda Harper

The New Mothers Of The World

Oh, what has happened, to the mothers of now days?
What happened to their instinct, of their children to raise?
One throwing a child out the window pane,
Another drown her two, have they gone insane?

While another leaves hers out in the cold to die,
The world looks on, with only the question, why?
Has their instinct to love and nourish the little ones gone?
Have they lost site of what's right and what's wrong?

What ever happened, to the mothers like old?
That threated their children as if they were gold?
Is the new generation missing what they had?
In this world of chaos, have the mothers gone mad?

Wake up all you new mother's of the world,
Look what you're doing to the little boys and girls.
Get a rip on your life, do what you've been put here to do,
Devote your life to your children, there's still hope for you.

Lawanda Crook

Our Forgotten God

It makes me sad, when I think.
How our land has forgotten thee.

We were founded on God's love and care.
Always knowing help will soon be there.

But, somehow on our growing way —
All his love and caring seemed to go away.

Nothing but bitterness and hate.
Makes our lovely land grow with weight.

With greed and violence all around.
Soon our land's strong hold, will,
no longer be found.

Oh! If we could turn back to God.
Before His love and protection,
no longer will be on our sod.

Donna Bell

Homeless

I was once a professor, who taught a brilliant class
But now I hold a cup out to strangers as they pass
I was once a lawyer who never lost a case
But now I barter for food ashamed to show my face
I often sit and wonder why people pass me by
with their gazes always falling on the ground or to the sky
Sometimes I get angry that others have so much
But reality and myself are remotely out of touch
The days have grown so long and the nights so alone
And I remember a time when I used to have a home
My house is now un underpass, a boxcar, or a street
My only means of travel is by my own two feet
It's sad that I am overlooked and seemingly no one cares
But humankind's most difficult lesson is learning to share
Somehow it isn't quite acceptable because I seem so crude
To offer me your help, your home, or your food
Though vanity and fashion block my existence from your mind
Don't be vain enough to think there might not come a time
When you quite unexpectedly find yourself my roommate
And I will welcome you without malice or debate

Melinda Jones

Time Dreamer

Memories of time passes, into a phase,
Hovered over the mountains, into the haze.
That lingers, for miles and days.
They come to us, in many ways.

Beyond the shadow of myth.
Reaches out over a cliff.
Wanting answers of some kind,
As the wind blows through my mind,

The vapors of a life time.
Can't compare, to the wind that, blows through my mind.
The silence, in the dark,
Give's feelings of softness, to my heart

Beautiful thought of far away.
Feeds my spirits, while I'm here today.
An appetite for life, has gone to stay.
Never to return to say, it was just yesterday.

Willard Hufford

Little Bobby

He was only a tiny little rose bud,
Not long upon this earth,
We knew he had no chance to live,
From the minute of his birth.

God sent down an angle,
In the form of a little boy,
Even though he wasn't with us long,
God gave us a touch of great joy.

He's up in heaven with Jesus today,
And some times it seems we can hear him say,
Mommy, and Daddy I love you,
And I know that you love me too.

He's walking with Jesus on streets of pure gold,
We know our baby will never grow old,
Son please listen to what we say,
Daddy and mommy will be with you some day.

Thank you God for our little boy,
His memory will always live on,
He's walking with Jesus hand in hand,
Up there in heaven on Gods golden sand.

Jackie Mizelle

My Folks

My folks might never measure up
To what some say is great.
We never had much money
And a bill could have been late.

But I look back now after all these years
And I know down in my heart.
We had the best of everything
And our folks just didn't part.

No matter what mistakes we made
And God knows we made a few.
Mother and Dad were always there
To help us see it through.

We always felt they loved us
And would help us in every way.
To make the best of what we had
As we lived from day to day.

We build our lives on hope and strength
And faith in God above.
Each day always bring something new
But it works with family love.

Karen Snell

Sasha

To awaken from sleep with clouded eyes,
Fear filled heart and realize,
Sasha is gone I know not where,
Can she not see how deeply we are.
The mind is numb, chilled with fear,
for Sasha my child, to hold her near,
I'd give my heart, and both my arms,
If she were hear, and safe from harm.
Sasha my child wherever you may be,
Hear my prayers, listen to me.
God, please send Sasha home safely to me,
To brush back her hair and kiss her cheek,
A mother's love comes straight from the heart,
There is no end, only continuous start.
Sasha my darling come home to me,
What was a prayer, is now a plea.
Darling, I love you...

Lora M. Prat

Memories That Last...Or Stay In The Past

The tears that fell from her eyes
were as a souvenir from the past
Even though young she felt very wise
For it is through tears that memories last

Holding them back would hurt even more
Each drop illustrating a unique work of art
painting the picture that would restore
each moment buried deep in her heart

She knew not any other thing
but to sit down and write
It was the only way she could sing
for in pen and paper she found delight

But she also knew she could look to the sky above
and find the only true caring One
who would no matter what, give her love
the Holiest Being, who sent His Son

Only one thought came to her mind
to the world she would become blind
And never again would she open the door of her heart
nor would her feelings break apart...

Sylvia Ybarra

Untitled

The dreams rain down upon us we run.

We fill our glasses with forgiveness
Tip them to this night.
The world hard, we find this by living
So simple is this line
So real are the days spent
Swimming in the confusion

Have you found hope.
Far from where I dreamt
I would be on those days of long lost summer nights
In the comfort of not knowing

We fill our glasses with forgiveness
Tip them to the night
Trying to find
Those long lost summer nights

Bryan Newman

Loneliness

The moon arises on a cloudy, stormy night.
The lightning flashes; not a single star in sight.

Still, it climbs higher, its muffled, waning light
Sends a chill up my spine and exaggerates my fright.

The wind sends out a moaning scream encased in woeful gloom.
It bats the trees in apparent protest of the rising moon.
A piercing crack now stills the storm and a broken branch
tumbles down.
It lies prostrate in the glowing light and seems to shiver
on the ground.
A distant thunder torments the broken tree.
Never could a soul be frightened more; especially me.
Nothing can calm my racing heart.
It seems my spirit will depart!
The storm is leaving; it's heading west,
And I am left with my loneliness.

Nikki Bacchus

A Dream Of Peace

Thirty-Four years ago my hero had a dream of peace.
He would do anything to have civil rights.
He spoke to the public and gave a good fight.
Someone killed him they had the smallest heart,
And if I were to see him I'd run as fast as a dart,
Far away so I couldn't see his face.
Someone killed my hero because of his race.
I know I shouldn't hate,
But the murderer is an exception.
Why did he have to kill one of peace's possessions?
Martin Luther King is the hero in my soul.
I will never bury his dreams deep in a hole.
Today his dreams are coming closer to reality.
And I will try to take them farther,
because I love Martin Luther King,
as much as my father.

Jennifer Van Roekel

Butterfly

Beneath the petals of my daisies
Utterly oblivious to my gaze
Taking freely of the nectar
Thrilling all my summer days
Ever flitting from flower to flower
Releasing warmth at every stop
Fearing neither bee nor hornet
Landing lightly without a plop
You, butterfly, nectar giver, draw nearer and fill my empty cup.

Alice M. Hamilton

Star Dust

As you gaze up in the sky,
Don't you often wonder why,
Stars do shine and never fade,
In this present day and age.

An angel treads and showers light
From star-lit beams throughout the night.
The light of love to all proclaims,
This heart decries all pain and shame.

We find our love forever more
Entwined with stars that shine and soar.
The realm of God like dawn appears,
And joyfully sends His message clear.

Stars may come and stars may go
As we search and want to know,
Herein lies our hidden goal
For journeys far that reach our soul.

Charlotte B. Abell

Untitled

Cancerous cognition bears sensecent mind
Thirty odd years before my time
  Solo Alone
  I bemoan
Reclusive friends with callow ears defeat my
Pleas for integration as trepidation trips up faces
Their time is not dear
Isolated Segregated The staring mirror
Yoked to hope
Fantasizing of intellectual connection with eager peer
Alas
Quietus nears Faith abjures
No companion nor peer
Just the staring mirror in neatly dressed veneer
Bereft of comrades cronies and peers
Yet, as the void draws near through synaptic snapping
I hear "I am here"
An old pal appears
One who's shared my journeys been amused by my fears
One I've ignored for years

Dale Emil Lawhon

Time's Regret

And if tomorrow never comes
  I hope you know just how I felt
  And how my love for you did grow
  Where words need never be spoken.
And if a morning should ever come
  Where my eyes would never see
  With only thoughts of your beauty
  Would my mind's eye not be blind.
And if night should ever pass
  Where I should never hear
  Memories of your laughter
  Would sing songs in my heart.
And if morning never comes
  And another breath I'll never take
  Fragrances of you, shall I take with me
  On a journey I'll traverse alone.
But all I can leave with you
  Is the knowledge of my love
  A fond memory of times gone by
  And my regret that life is too short.

Jamie Sasha Dousa

Goals In Life

What are your goals in life?
Well I'm going to be a writer
That's my goal for life.

Writing poetry is my life
That is what I do best.
I write what comes to mind
or from within myself.

Goals in life can be easy if
you're determined enough.
Goals I have for life are planned
out for me.

Goals in life are something you
have to pursue.
Goals in life are something you
have to reach for.

My goals are to be the best poetry writer.
I will get there because I've planned my true goal.
I have my goals that I wanna do for life.

That's exactly what I'm going to do,
Achieve my goals in life.

Brandi Simmons

July

My heart is pounding!
  My temperature's rising!
My skin is sweating
  and my mouth is drying out!
The smell of passion fills the air
  and dreams of the future fill my head!
Never before has so much love passed between two lips.
With each kiss I hear wedding bells.
  With each touch I envision our children.
    With each long stare I could cry out in joy.

  And
  then
  the
    tears
    fall . . .

  I realize it's only a memory.
I am always longing for your return, or so it seems,
But until then you own my heart, my mind, and my dreams.

Patrick A. Waddell

Untitled

As I climb and climb on the ladder of life I realize that my
destination is a mystery but I try to do good where I've done
bad. Yet always trying to mend the heart of hurt souls. Yes I
will climb until I can climb no more and when I stop I will
know my time has come and another person will climb on the
latter of life.

"The latter of life."

Life is a giant maze, you never know where you will end,
maybe you'll come to a dead end for when you face this
problem you must fight from becoming one
who gives up, so always try new ways
that might lead you to the
path of happiness.

"The twists and turns of life."

Tim Damroth

Midnight

As I look out of my window up at the
wonders, it's as if the sky were painted
with a touch of love.

I feel the tears in my eyes for I know soon
I will be leaving the peaceful night to walk
in the kingdom of stars, someday.

I hear the melody of the night, the
tenderness of the stars and my life starts
streaming down my face.

Misty Brewer

The Grand Canyon Of Arizona

What can I say that has not been said,
Or write but that someone somewhere has read,
Of this Canyon whose walls are but echoes of time,
Of the dim distant past, from where centuries climb
To our present few years; and how can I tell
Of the silence, the beauty, the wonders that dwell
Here in this light and shadow filled space —
From the sky, where the clouds and silent winds race
To the depth of the Canyon where torturous floor
Was carved by the river and is filled with its roar!
I can do only what others have done,
And take, when I go, a bit of the sun
That brightens this canyon, I'll carry away
A bit of the silence - remember the way
'Neath the cliffs the towering temples are placed,
And the trails on the rim where twisted trees lace their branches
These things I'll keep in my heart.

Oliva Slyter

Anxiety

I talked to you today on the phone, a whispering
cry I've never known. A fragile little voice
should never be alone.

You said to me, "pick me up"! For only I could.
You said to me, "pick me up"! If only I would.

In your desperate plea I cried inside, knowing
it just couldn't be, I asked you to be strong,
the time would surely come. I know this is wrong.

But daddy, "my heart beats to see you"!
"I love you son"! My heart is torn knowing I'll
have to wait another day.

Finally I said, "you are in my mind all
the time and no matter if we are together or
apart it's all the same. "I love you with all
my soul, just one more day and I'll hold you,
together we'll play and share the happiest feeling
of being together again"!

The phone went silent, I cried aloud . . .

Steven James

Family

To have a family so dear and true
You wonder, "what did I do?"

To have a love so near your heart
You wonder, "where did it start?"

To have a home so nice and new,
You wonder, "how can it be true?"

To have a family so loving and gay
You wonder, "what more could you want anyway?"

Tami Dyman

Can This Time I Trust In You?

Could this time be for real?
    I'm not sure just how to feel.
You left me once — my heart despair,
    How can I be sure, this time you care?

You say at first, I stole your heart;
    All you did was tear mine apart.
Can this time I trust in you —
    That to me, you will be true?

Is it worth it, to take a chance?
    Can your heart meet my demands?
All I want, is someone to love;
    The perfect romance I've dreamed of.

You can be that man for me,
    If in your own heart, you've found peace —
But for now, this friendship is true,
    The one, found again, with me and you.

So take it slow, take time to find,
    The perfect romance, that's one of a kind.
Who knows what lies for you ahead —
    You could fall in love with your dear friend.

Misty B. Ackerman

The Journey

Time spent in discussion by two
Placed side by side
Gliding on a sea of air

Philosophical in nature
Destiny in thought, or chance

Drinking a black drink
Energizes the mind, stimulates reflection
Breaking boredom so to accelerate time

We talk

Chance or destiny, spirit or simple existence
We exchange ideas
And try to create consistency
out of abstract reason

Funny, as it seems, all that's concluded
Is, that we live

John Sosnowsky (Sozra)

Desires

I was sitting underneath the almost full moon,
with a chill in the air hinting of fall,
engulfing me, caressing me, going inside of me.
My attention is captured by the dancing flames,
over the wood they glide carelessly, begging me to join.
I kindly decline, and move closer, so warm, so joyful.
Again persuasively invited, my acceptance greeted warmly.
As they lead me to their stage, overpowering feelings hit me.
Lust, selfishness, and greed.
Only then, I realize, I have left my world of innocence.
Behind, a pool of tepid water waving, beckoning me to return.
I dare to daze upon my dancing comrades once again.
A confession arises. They are scorching me, turning me to ash.
I turn to run towards my redemption, the water, but fall short,
only fingertips entering the water ending the burning pain.
After I give my acknowledgements to the water, I sit.
Watching the flames with a new found hatred.
I realize even if my desires burnt me black,
they would never go deep enough to sear my soul.
My Soul Is What I Am.

Dana Smothers

How Many Miles To Heaven

"How many miles to Heaven?" I heard my little boy say.
How many miles to heaven? I'm going there today.

As he lay upon his pillow so fragile and so weak;
I held his hand and listened, as he tried so hard to speak.

I'm going home to Heaven, but mommy please don't cry.
I can hear my Savior calling, and I'm not afraid to die.

The angels are coming to take me, to my heavenly home above
so take comfort in this message,
Our heavenly father sends his love.

Lean closer please dear Mommy, let me look upon your face
I know we'll meet again someday, when God calls you from
this place.

I must go now Mommy, the angels are drawing near,
To take me on a journey, so far away from here.

I held his hand so tightly, as he smiled his last goodbye
When all life had left his body, I bowed my head and cried.

Now every time I miss him, I remember his last words;
As his eyes gazed up toward heaven, here's the last thing
that I heard.

How many miles to heaven? I'm going there today.
But please don't cry dear Mommy, we'll meet again,
In heaven, some day.

Donna J. Herod

Flowing Secretly

Sharing my dreams and sorrows with you
Just simply longing and feeling blue.
I hear your voice and feel your presence
Like a desert, my heart feels so desolate.

I am with you now more than ever
And I am told your guidance remains forever.
Afraid I am not, whisper the way
For I will be with you some day.

Laughter, tears whatever it may be
Loving and missing you costs nothing; it's free!
Stay with me forever for I am in need
After all it is you, my angel who leads.

Strength, I have inherited from you father
And sometimes problems can be a bother.
But I can simply and proudly say
You always seem to pave the way.

Kaye Tullos

Alone

If I close my eyes real tight, I can almost feel
   and imagine that I am back in my old home town,
Back in a time and place where I felt safe and
   none of these feelings existed.

Back in the house where I grew most of my years.
Back before college.
Back before my innocence was so gruesomely stolen from me.
And way back before my best friend Kristi moved away.

But as I stand here facing out to the world
   from my dorm room window,
I open my eyes with tears streaming down my face
   and see that I am the one who is truly alone.

Oh how I wish one solitary wish not to be
   Alone.

Jennifer L. Komm

Black Mother

I look in your eyes I can see your soul
for it tells me you been down a long road.
I look at your face for it makes me
proud of my race
I look at your hands for it tells me
you done a lot of work on this land
I see your tears running down your
face for it tells me the years have been hard.
I feel your love for it tells me your are
one of God's sweet doves from heaven above
for all these things I see that makes
me happy and proud of you and happy
I have a mother like you.
For you are smart, thoughtful, beautiful
special caring, and loving
for you are a black mother.

Rachal Johnson

How To End The Day

The sky is purple, blue and pink. These are the colors of the
sunset. A peaceful breeze comes through. Peaceful sounds.
Things that God created just for you, so you can rest from your
tiresome day, and think about God in every great way. Pray
to God to thank him for his beauty. You look at the stars under
the moonlight and say: God you're wonderful.

Shalonda Rawls

We Thank You God For Everything

Dear God as I watched the morning break
I look at all the things you did make,
The dew on the grass, the birds in the trees,
The flowers in bloom, the air we breathe.

The sun in the morning, the dawns first light
The heavens, the sky, and the moon at night.
The trees in autumn, as they shed their leaves,
You made all of this for us to see.

A baby, a mother's touch, a father's hearty hug,
A handshake, a smile, a kiss in the name of love.
Your clouds caress the sky like a tender kiss,
Dear God we thank you for all of this.

To leave your mark on this earthly world
Love every man, woman, boy and girl.
Be thankful for all he's given to you,
Give some of it back when your time is due.

Love animals and all people, including yourself
May God bless you and keep you in good health.
No treasure can measure, all that you bring,
Dear God in heaven we thank you for everything.

Donald Ray Gross

Untitled

As the warm wet winds blow atop my
   mountain
The warm waters flow within.

The winds slide down the winding trail
   til they reach the forest below

They stop, flow up, then back, til it touches
   the canyons
The river roars, then slowly runs down the
   waterfall
A calm comes, the waves continue til sleep
   takes us.

Cathy M. Ali-Bocas

Christmas Is Coming

Christmas is coming so let's "deck the halls".
After that we can all fight our way through the malls.
Christmas is jolly, so let's get the holly,
And hope we haven't forgotten anything, by golly!
My reason right now to make light of the season,
Is I've got everything ready (in my mind) is the reason.
But wait a minute....
We're looking for Christmas to be more this year,
Than tinsel and holly and outward cheer.
But holding on to our traditions has become very dear down
    through the years,
With the baking, buying, bills,
    hurry and hassle coming out of our ears.
But Jesus looks at us and says with His tears,
"It's Me, I'm the one you're doing it for.
Spend time with Me and I'll open the door,
To joy and delight and a stillness in the hectic stress of this
Christmas madness.
I offer you the gifts of My love and peace in a world filled
with emptiness and sadness.
Come to Me, put Me first, and then you'll be blest.
Put Me first and I'll help you handle all of the rest."

Christmas is coming so let's "deck the halls".
But let's first prepare our hearts for Him when He calls.

Bonnie Marnell Trostad

My Birthday Poem To My Mother

Another year has gone by...
Don't know whether to laugh or cry

The birthday dinner...cake and pie
All those candles could light the sky

In come the presents...pretty paper and bows
Then comes the time that only Mom knows

While I have the spotlight...it's my time to shine
Mom's eyes seem to gaze as if gone back in time...
back to that precious "figure of nine"

Back to the day, the hour, the minute...
wondering if she could even bear one more

The nine months of waiting
for the one she'll adore

It's your daughter, her eyes, her hair,
her fingers and toes

Yes, we all know why this celebration really glows...
My Mother

Nanci Matthews

A Little Boy

A little boy, not long ago;
a little boy who loved and played;
whose eyes sparkled and shone;
and when then grew..., to be a man.

A little boy who seldom grew tired;
who grew amazed at every thing.
A little boy who grew ever inspired;
and then he grew..., to be a man.

A little boy that would swing and slide;
a little boy who would ride his dog.
He was a little man at his Daddy's side!
And then he grew..., to be a man.

I received a card the other day;
my little boy's name was there inside;
a wedding invitation from a young lady.
But then he grew..., to be a man.

Glenn Bennett

I Pray It Is Not Tomorrow

Like a whisper in the night dear God;
To your door will come someday.
With her face radiant as a star.
A sweet old lady will come to stay.

Be merciful with her, I beg you!
She has been mine all these years,
Knowing she is at your side,
I will not cry so many tears.

What will I do without her?
Forever I will miss her sweet voice.
I want her to stay with me,
But I know I have no choice.

The day she is gone from my life,
The rest of my days will be in sorrow.
Dear God, soon she will knock on your door.
I just pray it is not tomorrow!

Maria H. Gutierrez

Familiar Strangers

I'm lost in a world of Familiar Strangers,
I live day to day.
I treat people the way they treat me.
If I'm loved, it's returned.
I owe no one favors, and expect none in return;
I've loved and lost, I've gambled, yet won nothing;
I've competed, and never entered the game.
I've even felt sorrow, and never understood the reason why.

It's said you can feel lost in a room full of strangers.
I know what is meant,
for I feel lost in a world of Familiar Strangers.

People I've known, yet never knew,
Lovers I've loved, yet never felt their warmth.
People who are friends, but we share no common bond.
For, I'm lost in a world of Familiar Strangers;
Yes, I'm lost in this world I call home.

Lawrence T. Ritenour

Unforgettable Roses

The roses of spring let the air smell sweet.
Their wonderful fragrance makes any garden complete.
With a hot summer breeze, the temperature will soar.
Some flowers wilt and bloom no more.
Autumn winds have the leaves flying.
Then fall to the ground like tears when you're crying.
Winter snow gives the roses a rest.
And when spring comes again, they can smell their best.
Each season roses have a different touch and smell.
With different shades of color, but I really can't tell.
My roses I see with only my hands.
My sight may be gone, but see them, I can.
Cause my mind can't forget the beauty of a rose.
I only see them with my hands, but I can't fool my nose.

Dianna Murphy Cox

Target

They persist to change my world and are waiting
to watch me flounder, and
When I do, they blurt out in laughter and prejudice.
For I am a target of endless and hateful chants
that have no other use but to degrade my morale.
So, day by day, my emotions become more inert.

It is my peers who treat me immorally,
but they are cretins for doing so.
For it is sad, because I have no one elses
shoulder to lean on but my own.

David Andrew Bartley

You Really Don't Care

You say you still care
Even though you weren't there
At the time I needed you most
You disappeared like a ghost
You were nowhere to be found
I haven't heard a word from you,
not a peep, not a sound
The message just isn't clear to me
That it's with me you want to be
You're always too busy for me
But I'm always suppose to be there
for you to see
Well I won't always be around for you
When you decide you need someone to talk to
When I need you you're never there
So how can you say you still care
The message you're sending is you don't
care at all
When you don't come to see me or when you
don't even call

Tina Marie Hollis

Experimental Pizza

I'm making a pizza with everything on it,
With taco shells, and pastry gels
Tight packed sardines dipped in ice-cream
Tomato sauce and chicken fat gloss
Parmesan cheese and snow so cold that it'll make your
teeth freeze.
Goldfish crackers and beefstick snackers
Chocolate chips and potato chips
A few grapefruits and some turnip roots
A whip-cream wisp and apple crisp.
A turkey that still goes gobble gobble and tall corn stalks
that wave and wobble.
Bits of beef and bits of pork, and fragments of a champagne cork.
A casserole-that's a bit of a hassle-and a gold wheat tassel.
Raspberry jello and squash that's yellow
Apricot pits and pineapple bits.
And for flavor, add sugar and spice.
In and out of the oven it comes. Now that it's done.
Do you want a slice?

Christine Heckmann

Mirage

Come away with me, for a journey is at hand.
Open your mind, trust me with your heart
as our spirits soar freely among the clouds,
gliding on currents to faraway places
deep within our imaginations.

Sail away with me on the trade winds to the south,
to a land of exotic riches and rain forest teeming with life.
Warm days spent in nature's splendor in the sand,
cool nights tasting the sweet moisture of our passion.
Our bodies imprint left untouched for eternity.

Swim away with me to an enticing, hidden cove
sheltered by fragrant orchids and lush ferns moistened with dew.
Let us whisper secrets deep from within our souls,
sharing our whims and desires, baring our frailties
as the warm waters swirl around and consume us.

Run away with me and partake of my essence,
take hold of my passion and encase me in your love.
Lie with me, devour me, fill the emptiness inside of me.
Pacify me and erase the fears I have contrived.
Rescue me from a barren existence without you.

Susan E. Tobin

A Thing Called Cancer

Cancer is the most horrible thing one can have
    something no one can control,
It can take away everything we have
    including our highest goals.

Things won't be the same anymore
    one's put in a different situation,
That breaks down a person's mental frame
    and ruins the precious family tradition!

A woman, she loses her hair
    the most glamorous part of all,
A man, he loses his pride and self esteem
    to this thing called cancer.

One is sick for many days, months, and even years
    then wakes up one morning and say why go on,
The 'miracle' drug, 'chemotherapy', couldn't budge
    a single part, of this thing called cancer!

The needle marks, the medicine, and all the pills
    how much more can one body take?
It hurts within, so much, in so many ways
    one wonders, why won't God take it away?

Jerry D. Davis

Remember

Remember when those times had eyes?
Everything that happened we saw so clear.
Never knowing where it could leave us,
But now it has all disappeared.
Remember when those nights kept secrets?
Only us two told things never once spoken.
Capturing the looks you gave me inside,
How could you leave my heart so broken?
Can you think back to our time together?
Or do those moments not exists?
Not knowing it wouldn't be forever,
But only hoping those times are missed?
Can you remember our time?
Try to imagine what we had so long before,
When I was yours and you were mine.
Changes are made and we all move on,
Forgetting the word...forever.
Letting you go was never easy to do.
Do you remember?

Amy Fitzgibbons

Black Ghost

Not black enough, not white enough
Much too skinny, not wide enough
Not rich enough, not right enough
What am I? Perfect in whose eyes? The black ghost.

I can't take no more of this life
So full of turmoil and strife
God, all I asked for is someone who'll love
Not to be taken advantage of
What have I been given instead?
22 men that don't understand exactly where I've been
Who probably wouldn't give a damn if I were alive or dead.

How much longer must I give my heart to another
To be hurt — one step forward and two steps back
Let me express myself: I am not your mother
And yes, although my skin is light, I Am Black!

God what happened when you created me?
Mom says I didn't want to come out of her womb
Maybe that's because I knew before its time
I would end up in a tomb.
Is this my destiny? — Black Ghost Please — Let Me Be — Free!

Anastasia Garbutt

Vignette

I am just a child
A golden star glows upon my sleeve
I eat a cookie that tastes of bitter almonds

The train yard is filled with silent box cars
The former occupants no longer speak
Everyone is cord wood since the winter is so cold

Mommy's face has turned blue
And has another eye between her closed two
It cries red tears

God is walking through the snow

Strange creatures from a dark fairy tale
walk upon their hind legs
and speak
        Michele Cobb

A New Day

As I stood; staring dreamily at the setting sun
I observed a miraculous transformation;
the vibrant, gold luster of the sun
(resembling that of ancient forgotten Egyptian treasures)
    was lost.
A dull, heavy black blotted the sphere's surface
and spread like a rampaging plague across the mass.

As the last drops of radiant light touched me,
penetrating deep into my body, mind, and soul;
A feeling, a sense of release and immense warmth took hold.
Then I stood; like a omniscient statue gazing
towards a bleak tarnished future.
No longer seeing the powerful star,
but noticing darkness sweep the land
While a chorus of dread cries quickly bellowed from the earth's core,
Echoing in my consciousness.

Apprehension fell over me then,
As I contemplated what,
the next day would bring.
        Cathy Sutfin

The Dance Of Stones

On the windswept plain the kestrels' call
announces soon dark night will fall.
The moon glows black, the stars only light
the dance of stones brings power and might.
Our fires flare, the smokes waft high
we turn the dance, all life must die.
Cool mist creeps low, and death comes to all
we must live life, before we fall.
Our lives snuffed out, like the fire's flame
live for now, enjoy life's game.
Turn the dance, life undenied
leave no piece of life untried.
Hate and love, joy and strife
all are parts, the mystery of life.
We all are born, we all must die
listen again as the kestrels cry.
The darkness lifts, the sun dawns bright
the dance of stones halts, and waits for the night.
        Chael Mizell

Rookie Season

There I was at first base
Wondering if I was in the right place
Next pitch was hit in my face
I caught the ball and threw it to first base
The throw was wild
What a disgrace
        Joey P. Gyengo

Eight Year Old Request

Mother may I plant a garden?
Cindy, what do you wish to plant?
Tomatoes - big red tomatoes.
Sometime later Cindy would say "Today I take my tomatoes,
to the fair, to display."

Now she will display the red red first prize ribbon,
and a big smile on her happy face.
        Doris Norman

Conscience

Sense of right and wrong,
with each life's purpose meant.
Some of peace and love,
others with grief and strife.
Many years may come and go.
With wrong you'll surely bear,
conscience have no creed are race.
It follows you everywhere.
Being right there is no guilt.
Where no shadows of evil fall.
Only trust in each and everyday.
And you can count them all,
put all the past behind you,
yesterday's failures you cannot change.
Many years may come and go,
make them all rightfully count each day.
To give up and quit to wrongful ways.
Your conscience and guilt will always know,
who gave up and failed,
there's always another rightful day.
        Donald Chester

Savior Lost

Can a Lion talk tonight?
To hold Her close, to ease Her fright?
Can His claws strike through the air,
and clear the memories lingering there?
Can His eyes penetrate Her soul
to ease Her pain, to make Her bold?
Will it be enough to save
the Little Child from the rage?
Huddling small against the blows,
Needing him where none can go

A Symbol Of Strength, The Epitome Of Hope
Without Courage Now, You Lend No Rope.
Staring Up The Stony Well, Hearing Words Her Glory Fell.

Once burning bright with desire
the lion's eyes begin to tire.
Tin man finally got his heart,
the wizard still fulfilled his part
but the lion with the chance to heal
lacked the courage to make her real...
        Lindsey S. McKeen

Over Weasel Stone Wall

Over weasel stone wall there is a magnificent sight
a field of flowers stretches to the sea
but it is never night there
nor day
for it is always sunset
and in the sea
the dolphins play in the pink and purple light
        Jeremiah Wagner

Black Earth

Black earth with exotic perfumes,
Magic you perform.
Deep within your depth of darkness,
Life's miracles are born.
   Mothered within your breast
And moist with the tears of dew,
Tenderly from the pods beneath your crust
Is life and hope anew.
   You are washed with your own elements.
They are drawn from you to the sky.
To give and to take, ever is your desire,
And to reproduce is your cry.
   Up from your depth you gave.
And out of your giving came man,
Came love, came laughter and hope,
Came as much as time and sand.
   Black earth, pregnant with your life.
Mother earth, forsake not our cry!
Deep within your bosom keep us,
Hold us tenderly, when we die.

   Cecil Louisa Propst

Black Roses

   How could I start to tell the world
my true feelings when I don't even know
what they are?
   All I know is everyday I got a red rose
from you then somewhere out of the blue
they became black.
   Whatever happened to what we had?
Where did it all go?
   Some way we got through all our problems
and I started to get a red rose again, but
then they somehow became black again.
   Once again we worked through our
differences and once again I started to get
a red rose and somehow they became
black, but the one difference was
it was the last time I was going
to take your beatings.
   Now the only roses I'll be getting
from you is what you give me on
my grave the day I die! Red or Black.

   Jenifer Tenwilleger

Mistaken Identity

One day while downtown shopping.
And passing by this store
I saw a woman staring
That I thought I'd seen before.

She was on the plumpish side
With slightly messy hair,
I thought, "She needs to diet,
And a trip to the barber's chair."

She frowned at me, I frowned at her
We both must think the same
"She's much older than I," I thought
"Now, what can be her name?"

All these thoughts flashed through my mind
As I was drawing nearer
And then I knew the awful truth
I was looking in a mirror!

   Jane Osborne

A Mother's Love

A mother's love is like a diamond
it last forever. No matter what we
as children may do rather we brought
Joy or Pain her love for us never changed.
For when she had to punish one of us
her love got even stronger. When she
had a restless night because one of us
were sick her love for us seemed to make us
better so remember a mother's love is
forever. Even if she's gone above to be with
the maker of us all her love is present
in all we do. So cherish that wonderful
jewel. A Mother's love

   Patricia Vines-Scales

Untitled

Somewhere along the border of Mexico and Heaven
I sat on God's patio and we shared a cup of sunshine
and talked of many ethereal things
and even though He didn't have to do this thing
He took pity on my meek, inquisitive brain
and this He told me then- and I listened since He is who He is
the beauty of this- of life itself- is that it ends
and you're all gonna die
there will never be we or them or they forever
but there will always be I
and the funny thing is
all this came from His
two compassionate perfect eyes

   Stephen Koch

Lil' Black Girl

Lil' black girl, are you not a princess?
With your kinky black hair,
And your soulful brownness.

Something of old forgotten queens
Lies within the beauty you hold.
Your eyes seem to sparkle
With hope-filled dreams
And anticipation for a heritage unique and bold.

Lil black girl, you'll have people envy you
Because you hold so much knowledge.
They'll try to put you down and hurt you
Because your dream is to go to college.

Soon you'll have sleek, wide, thick hips
Inherited from the Great Queens,
And your sweet, full, honeyed lips
Will hum African's once sung melodies.

Lil black girl, you are a princess
Born from a strong black race
You are truly unique with your regal blackness
So be proud of your smooth brown face.

   Sabrina R. Dortch

Loneliness

I sit alone in a dark corner,
I wait and listen for daylight to come,
My stomach grumbles with the excruciating pain of hungriness,
I have no one to turn to and no where to go,
I make each day as best as it can be,
But the best will never be good enough for me,
I cry at night and ask God why,
And I still wait for His answer,
Will I find out why He did this to me,
Or should I blame myself for all that has happened?

   Lauren Lauer

A Precious Gift From God

I am a small child that doesn't know a thing.
I have two lovely parents to care for me.
I am a precious gift from God above.
I feel the warmth my parents give to me.
Like the warmth of the sun on my face.
I can hear them whisper in my ear.
We love you very much.
You're a precious gift from God to us.
It's such a joy to have you here.
To hear you laugh, to hear you cry.
It's hard for me to say a word.
So all I do is hug you tight.
That's my way of saying I love you too.
You're a precious gift from God to me.
I hear them whisper in the air.
Thank you God so very much.
We love this child, so keep it safe.
There's a bond of love between us all.
Which keeps us one in him.

Mary Riley

Amber's Glow

In Loving Memory of Amber Robey
who lost her life on January 5, 1997.
The candle has always burned brilliantly,
Spreading her light to whomever she knows,
Willing to give help where ever needed.

The candle rarely raged out of control,
Being so joyful and sweet,
She was beloved and admired.

The candle was exceptionally bright,
Having many successes,
Which would lead to a promising future.

The candle was very beautiful,
So tall and slender,
With her long flowing blonde tresses.

The candle's glow was blown out forever,
We will miss her greatly,
But she still beams radiantly inside us always.

Christen Carroll

World Within

Rocking, walking, with fixed absent stares;
Standing, sleeping, on worn couch or torn chairs.

Pacing, pacing, across dirty floors and rooms;
Smelling, coughing, from smoke and foul fumes.

Smells and yells and blood-dripped walls;
Stripped beds and bodies - shared and exposed to all.

Talking, playing, but no sense to be made;
Of words and reasons why they are here today.

Cold, curt nurses locked in a stall;
Laughing, talking, oblivious to all.

Family visitors few or none;
One doctor on duty, not to be seen, but with all to be done.

Day's shadows cross the sky;
Lights on, lights out, wards locked, but why?

Loud crying, low sighing;
With few caring if they are living or dying.

Dixie M. Troy

Pain

When I close my eyes
I can't sleep
All I do is think
I try to think about good things
But I don't
All I think about is the bad
As I lie awake, thinking of the bad things
I can't help but cry
As I take a tear on my finger
Instead of the salty water, it is blood
I cry blood because of the pain inside, eating me away
People don't know there is so much pain inside of me
Pain which is hard to explain
The pain is like there is no one to care about me
I don't know if there is a person who truly cares
I've gone most of my life with this pain
I don't know how much longer I can go on living like this
With all this pain.

Jesse Kealiher

Untitled

In the distance, on a hill there's a tree.
It stands tall and strong, but alone.
Barren from the winter's wrath and fury,
an empty shell devoid of any signs of life:
strong and majestic besides, it is there.
Many branches that reach for the sky and more;
its past lays on the ground with the dead leaves.
They were all once green and vibrant, but
everything passes in the journey through time.
As the years pass it still stands tall,
good and bad, season after season, always.
No drams or wishes it just is there.
In the wind it sways and sometimes;
it can be heard crying in the night.
In the spring it starts new, then,
in the fall it dies again.
Life then death, year after year after year.
In the distance, on a hill there's a tree.
It has no dreams or wishes, it is alone.
It is an everyday sight, it's just a tree.

Matthew J. DelCoco

A Thing About Squares

"And...no wreaths please."
I said to the back of the blonde head
The curls bouncing across the room
I assumed toward the special Christmas section

My mom wanted garland, my aunt wanted poinsettias
My grandma wanted walnuts
She cracked them till her hands turned blue

But my uncle had an odd wish a sort of minus request
With all the Christmas plants and toys
He had asked for there to be no wreaths
Dead, alive, plastic, wood, painted, or plain
No one reacted strangely
Even I just smiled and noted it on my list
He just had a thing about squares, and round made him
Nervous, like how he preferred hot to cold
Or suspenders to belts.

The smile, grey eyes and
Nose belonging to the blonde head returned
"What did you say before?" asked the blonde's pursed lips
Smiling to myself I repeated "No wreaths please."

Julie M. Holiday

Who Is God?

Sometimes I wonder if there is a God
but if there is a God
is it wrong to wonder?

And if there is a God,
why is there a God?
Is he the one who creates the sound of thunder

And if there is such a God
where did he come from?
Who is his parents I wonder

What is his house like, this God?
To us, would his house be odd?
And what is it like down under?

Is hell a place the opposite of God?
Or is it the home of the ex-lover?
I don't think I'll ever know,
I'll just wonder.

Amber Pelch

Making Rivers

I won't cry in front of him...
I won't cry in front of them.
I won't cry in front of myself.

Each time I cry I lose something.
'Though weeping doesn't make me stronger...
It doesn't make me weaker...
My tear just seem to add to my confusion.

I have learned so much...
Needed so little...cried so loud -...fell so far and hit so hard.
Have I loved too much...
Or maybe not enough?
I talk too long...
Or do I just feel too much?

So I am not going to cry anymore.
That's a lie:
I say that one minute, I make rivers the next.
I make rivers...
That is why I cry in front of him...
In front of them...
In front of myself.

Elata Chenault

Fall

I can't wait til summer,
My days will be spent in the pool,
But then it gets too hot,
And I wish the days were cool.

Soon some plants and flowers,
Begin to wither and die,
Leaves here and there,
And I start to wonder why.

I take my kitty outside,
Where is the sun?
My kitty plays and frolics like this day is her last one.
"Cassie" I ask, "where has the warm weather gone?"
"Meow" she answers as she frolics along.

It's gone I see,
Summer's no longer here to play,
Fall I see,
Is playing here today.

Erin L. Wilkinson

My Baby Boy Wonder...

I remember the moment of feeling you grow.
A feeling so strong only a mother would know.
As time went on, and I felt you explore
The wonder, the joy, the amazement and more,
Of knowing I had a life inside to be
Someone so small, so cute, and dependent on me
When the day arrived and I felt you were near
I felt only excitement, love and so little fear
Then you arrived so precious and so new
I kissed your face and said "I love you".
I counted your fingers and tickled your toes
I caressed your angel hair and kissed your nose
Held you oh so tight, and close to your ear
I said thanks for my bundle and to God I said prayer
Oh! Thank you Lord for my boy wonder so true
I couldn't have done the hard work without the blessings from you.

Joy M. Adams

The Eyes Of A Child

Grammy sat in her rocker in the same old way,
When Annie brought up her book, a present this Christmas day.
Silently she gave it to the woman, who said,
"No my child this book can't be read."

The little ones' eyes formed two large tears,
"Don't cry, with your eyes you can see crystal clear.
In everyone you see only the true and good,
See the innocence in a person, no adult ever could."

"Experience everything, my girl, that's what they're for,
You will experience earth's goodness, your spirits will soar.
View the mountains and taste the sea,
Everything's fresh, new and waiting for thee."

"But these eyes will not last forever, girl,
In time you will lose this beautiful world.
It will all be dull and stale,
With a boredom that can make you wail."

"This leather bound book will bring a gift true,
It will open new worlds and insights to you.
Experiences and ideas will come to thee,
And with new child's eyes will you finally see."

Anjuli White

Untitled

From out of nowhere, like an angel she came,
I'd heard of her beauty, but not of her name.
Many men saw her, and fell to her feet,
But still she stared on, perfect and sweet.
No one man had her, but many she had,
She kept each one happy, for with her they were glad.
I at first fell for this playful disguise,
Until one day I caught a strange shine in her eyes.
It was a shine of love, beyond all measure,
A hidden beauty, an unseen treasure.
A love that knew friendship, and summers of gladness,
A love that knew pain, and a heart that knew sadness.
And I was lost into those beautiful eyes,
Until I felt the pain of a thousand goodbyes.
My only desire was to cradle her fears,
To comfort her pain and soak up her tears.
But then she came to my side, and gave me a grin,
"With my pain comes my strength, don't worry my friend."
She taught me a love that went past goodbye,
I miss you Bonnie. I have to go. (sigh)

Jason Stillman

Missing You

Each day that passes by
Is one day closer to you by my side
I miss you more and more each day
Because in my heart you'll always stay
You're on my mind day through night,
I think of your smile and it's a wonderful sight,
You make me happy as can be
And in return you will see,
You can't go wrong with loving me
Whatever happens down the road
Good and bad it's nice to know
Every day I've spent with you
Proves that love is real and true
I hope you're in my life forever
leave your side I will never
I love you more than words can say
If you ever have doubts come what may
This poem should prove it day to day.

Dena Telfair

Time

Self conscience state of subconsciousness,
Holding us back from the future.
Were looking ahead from the past.

Time...

Clocks ticking my life away.
Awaken to another day of blinded certainly,
that everything will go my way.

Dreams and nightmares,
those endless subconscious stares.
Nothing in my mind but another meaningless rhyme,
and there's only time to consider.

Negative reasoning vs. positive wanting,
It seems no patience is present,
Because patience takes time.
No time to dine or sip on cheap wine.
Accepting the shivers down my spine
As my spirit weeps out a sigh.
Always a slave until the grave,
to his burden called time.

Matt J. Fakult

Used To Be A Gypsy

For every chapter of your life
there's always a road that leads you home
for what could have been said
can never be written again
as I run out of blames the same
but if I could turn the hourglass upside down
if I could turn the clock on a backwards path
I would walk out onto that field
surrounded by stories of trees
only to see the light ring
between the page and the page mark
so I walk past the past
and I continue to follow the road
moving days seem so far behind me
one thing that you never told me
there's a last time for everything
people said our relationship was
longer than most marriages last
we will never escape the past

Nicholas Tindell

A Family

I lie in my room and think where
could you possibly be, but know one knows
where you could be. I wish I could just
see you and know everything will be alright
just being in your presence just once more
I would give anything to be held and
loved and be part of the family you have
created sense I've been gone. To see
everyone grow as well as they see me grow.
To be close like family's should, to make
a mistake and not be condemned.
To show your true side and be loved
just cause you're you and to have
you there when I go through my struggles
each day. Until I find you I
will be in my room and think all about you.

Rose Burton-Hampton

Laugh, Love, Cry

Her laughter and smile have brightened our day
They are gone now, but this is life's cruel way.
I realize, now, I took for granted
The days I passed her by.
The memories are now planted
We laugh, we love, we cry.

Life goes on, indifferent as it seems
Though in our minds and pictures
Her radiance still beams.
We know she's kept in loving hands
Our thoughts will never die.
In our hearts, there she stands
While we laugh, we love, we cry.

Star in the heavens, shines and beams
She'll always be with us
In thoughts and prayers and dreams.
I know we'll eventually be reunited
Soon all the tears will dry,
While your prayers are being recited,
Remember to laugh, to love, to cry.

Deedra Lokken

We Talk Of Many Things

We talk of many things: Of
Rabbits and Streetcars, of
Romans and Old Men, of
Blessings and Deliverance, of
The Dead and the Naked, of
Black Elk, under the Kentucky Coffee Tree.

We talk of Tantalus and
Wherewithal and
A raft on the Mississippi. And
Gatsby and a displaced Yankee, and
A far-off African Mountain.

Outside: Teams win,
   Players strike,
   Debts climb,
   Skies fall,
   Bombers bomb,
   Leaders lie.
   People die.

But inside:
We talk of many things.

James R. Clark

Sleepless Moment

Sleep, she could no longer fake
for the bright light keeps her wide awake.
It's well past midnight, according to the clock,
and out yonder the full moon beckons, as if to mock.

The night is whisper silent and deep within a sleep,
as she relinquishes her warm bed, and takes a spirited leap.
Enthusiastically hasty, she stubs her right great toe,
astonished she yelps out at that unforeseen foe.

But awstruck by the power of glinting vibrant rays,
she limps toward the window in a twinge and painful daze.
A flood of radiant beams are shining upon a carpet of snow,
while the temperature has dropped, down ever so low.

The wintery landscape crystalline pure and silvery white,
is exhilarating and fantastic on this moonlit night.
Across the street the rushing river is steaming
waving watery ripples are reflectively gleaming.

As behind her the ticking clock staccatos on,
a reminder that this night soon rebounds a new dawn.
Reluctantly, back to a cold bed she must fly,
appeased by this sleepless moment, she heaves a happy sigh.

Dagmar Bissinger

Gentle Hue

To witness darkness
as an everyday occurrence,
one learns to shy away
from the light.
But when presented with a gift,
out of love or envy, a gift of a candle,
this creature of darkness slowly learns
that lights offers warmth.
And soon more candles are added
until a gentle hue engulfs the creature
and this being begins to sing songs of hope.
Only when the darkness storms in
and dreadfully extinguishes each candle
can the creature turn to the embers
and gently coax them to life.
Soon, hopefully, the darkness ebbs away
until calming shades reappear,
and the shadows are chased away
by one who learned to love the brightness
of the day once more.

Terry Lynn Murphy

Empty

Today someone special has gone away
my smile only a mask
covering my tears
hiding the loss
A feeling you won't come back
is closing in on my fears

Your absence has gone through me
like a thread through
the eye of a needle
Everything I do I stitched with its color.

My light has gone out
I'm not beaming anymore
All the diamonds in this world
can't make me shine
Pretty clothes on the outside
can't make me feel beautiful on the inside.

I need a polish, a warm embrace
to put a smile back on my face
Feels so empty inside
I need to be filled up with love I need a hug.

April Jean Crook

The Voice Of The Sea

The mighty dolphin,
The voice of the sea,
Their world is magic,
Their life, so carefree.

When man is out in the ocean,
Faced with an alarming sight,
The dolphin comes to the rescue,
Relieving all of man's fright.

But man never seems to return the favor,
Never treating the dolphin as a friend,
Never rescuing a dolphin in need,
Never bringing their fear to an end.

And the fishing nets continue to drag them in,
As the dolphin struggles to get out,
Their once beautiful voice of the sea
Has turned into a harsh shout.

Please stop this horrible treatment,
And let the life of the dolphin ring,
Let their souls live on forever,
Let their voices forever sing.

Jessica Kemling

My Daughter, My Joy

"I want my mommy" is music to my ears,
as she allows only me to dry her salty tears;
A gift from heaven with which I was blessed,
the intense bond that's formed, I would never have guessed.

My precious, sweet babe, my daughter, my joy,
my frilly ballerina, my tomboy;
Spending time together, we laugh and we play,
learning more about each other day after day.

So many of my mannerisms and personality traits,
appear in her as time goes on - I can hardly wait;
To see her as a woman, so mature and all grown up,
and other days I wish that I could make time stop.

And keep her as my little girl, forever by my side,
from hurt and disappointment I want to help her hide;
I believe in her as much as she believes in me,
I'll always be there for her, because I'm her mom, you see.

Kelley S. Levis

Mystery In The Rain

Why does love in a relationship slowly drain
Hidden tear drops in the rain

Children crying in the park
Their parents fighting in the dark
They vowed their love, but still there's pain
Hidden tear drops in the rain

The children grow, but can no longer cry
Their parents ask each other why
As older children they learn to hide the pain
Hidden tear drops in the rain.

The children have families, as time goes by
And as parents they fight, but know not why
They all grow tense from the strain
Hidden tear drops in the rain

The next generation cries in the park
Because their parents fight in the dark
Children learning to vow their love and hide their pain
So the coming generation bear the strain
mysteries in the rain

Jim Clancy

181

My Amazing God Poem

My amazing God is a person who loves me
so high up above the clouds and the trees a person
who looks after me. When I'm down and out and
I have no way out my God is always there to help
me out. Through strength and courage and even
fear when I need my God he is always near.
When my Gods angels come about the churches
will sing Glory hallelujah they will sing it out.
When I think of how fun it is to me to have
someone who cares about me.

Yolonda Dunnington

Grievance

Step across my threshold...a backwards thrust.
Memories suppressed...leaving scars to erupt.
Blinding white storm shrouded the earth as
    though masked.
The calm of silence...desolation in a flash.
Pure driven sweet playland, deceiving indeed.
Bitter cold carries ill and snatches newly
    delivered dreams.
This day is marked...etched deeply in my soul.
Stealer of my sleep...devastating my world
    as I unfold.
Descent of my darkest dawn begins my mourn.
For on this day I flowered the earth to bury
    my born.
Hell...would be splendid if the two were collate.
Endless suffering...should not be a mother's fate.

Shawn R. Clark

Sand-drifts

I stroll through life amongst grains of sand,
As my soul obeys the rhythms of where I stray.
Walls grow tall ever around me,
Favored moments drift away.

I yearn to harbor beyond the sand
To meadows loved and clear,
Yet the hills determine to surround me
With sand-drifts mortals cannot bear.

Still on and more I journey,
Intense with dreams anew,
To be lost in mist and ivy,
And swallowed by the dew.

With increased pace I hasten
Towards a shadow I long to see,
Leaping above the san drifts
To a fancy that shall never be.

Ralph P. Cappello

Bared

   A tree stands firm amidst a forest.
It lies alee to the wind and to the rain.
Birds live in this forest too,
They nest in the limbs and sing from the branches,
But no bird sings from the rough oak.
A rare and beautiful bird soars through
The forest and luck rests her on his branches.
The wind blows, the tree shakes, and the bird flies away
The tree is no longer shielded from the wind,
And the wind howls, breaking branches and shaking the tree.
It was her smile.

Bryan Richard Shanaver

'Tis Halloween

Look at the sky, 'tis midnight
The witches on their brooms
Flying so high in the moonlight
Nibbling on poison mushrooms

Look! One's black hat fell to the earth
Her grey, stringy hair is flying
The other witches are laughing with mirth
But poor old Maggie is crying

Say! Maybe we can help her out
Run - go fetch daddy's top hat
Kick it around and beat it about
Make the brim real wide and flat

Sail it to her through the air
Aim it for her broom handle
Oh! She sees, just look at her stare!
She caught it on the toe of her sandal!

A wreath of smiles breaks her weathered face
That must be a thousand years old
As every wrinkle falls into place
We forget scary things we've been told.

Nelline P. Ross

Winter Storm

   Late at night, in bed, cozy, comfortable
feeling deliciously warm and heavily blanketed.
   My head turns toward the window, what
absolute delight, a blizzard I shout.
   I am spellbound by the elements as
they control the outside world. The wind
howls with an eerie wail as if some
strange grotesque creature were in agony
and torment. Delicate symmetrical flakes,
transformed into projectiles crash against
the window pane, making scratch like sounds.
   Below my bedroom window, down in the
street, nature's frenzy is witnessed with equal
amazement. The groaning, sputtering and
clunking of the snow plow as it feebly
challenges its obstacle, but never defeating it.
   The plows heavy metal blade makes
muffled sounds as it scrapes the surface
of the smothering snow. Then, without fanfare,
it is swallowed up in the night.

Arnold Grell

Silence

Release me from this burden of pain
Crawling, clawing from the pit of desperation
It feeds on my body from within
Drinking from my veins the sorrow and fear
This beast is my master my lover
Unto death the last breath I expel
Silence
Warm my soul my light my love
Peace and tranquility in my grasp
Opening my eyes myself beneath
Safety from the pain and suffering
Free from my shackles the bindings removed
Comfort my soul my wounds healed
Take my hand to hold with yours
To walk along together this path of freedom
To life to love to forever away
Silence

Angela Harmon

Seasoned Greetings

These are holiday wishes from me to you,
and I'm hoping them to all be true:

As you travel through the year 1997,
May you feel like you are in seventh heaven!

I wish you an abundance of love,
and many blessings from our great God above,

Then there's joy and peace of heart,
May nothing you encounter tear you apart.

Great health is a must throughout the year,
with test results that make you and your doctor cheer!

An abundance of friends who are always around,
to share in all of life's ups and downs.

And this should come as no surprise,
so much laughter that it brings tears to your eyes!

But I also send my heartfelt thanks to you, too,
for the gift of friendship and the gift of you!

I have learned something from you, each and everyone,
I wouldn't trade it for dollars, not even a million and one.

For I now know that cancer cannot touch our soul,
it cannot break our spirit; We will remain whole!!!!!

Suzie Garvey

To All The Unheard People!!!

Some knew him from a glance,
others knew him from his little prance.

Not many knew him for his true feelings,
they just knew of those so called "Drug Dealings".

He was a true man inside,
but all his feelings he had to hide.

When he was young he was a shy boy,
off alone playing with his special toy.

He cared about the true things in life:
friends, family, and having a wife.

If he hadn't thought of his feelings
as something to hide,
Maybe to this day,
he wouldn't have died.

Elayne Harrison

Waiting

I'm eagerly waiting and watching to see,
What purpose and direction God has for me.

I've drifted through life many years with no clue,
Not knowing there's something He wants me to do.

But finally, I've realized, my life's no mistake,
There is a small difference He wants me to make.

Just how, or just when, is still quite unclear,
But I'm eagerly waiting and wanting to hear.

To others still drifting, still waiting to know,
In just which direction your life will go,

Remember to praise Him, remember to pray,
For His will to be done, for strength to obey.

There is a purpose for you and for me,
Someday He'll show us, someday we'll see.

Then we'll earn our way to great Heaven's gate,
But until He says "now", we'll just have to wait.

Connie R. Holthaus

My Dying Rose

Withering away from a once passionate red
It dies, it dies, in a sorrowful despair
Its once glorious beauty is now gloriously dead
Its rotting stench now runs within the air
Why did I ever pick this blasted rose
It has brought me less joy and more pain
Yet it was I, yes I, whose gruesome fate imposed
When I plucked it from its spot in the rain

I can't say I'm sad to see the rose go
But nothing in this world lasts forever so the say
Everything that lives soon must die you know
And newer things take the deads place the next day
So die my dying rose, once so red, die
I say to you good riddance and a bitter sweet goodbye

Terrence Wells

Life

When life's doors have been bound by sadness and sorrow
One must live for today and just pray for tomorrow
For life's hinged on love and love is the way
To nourish each moment with laughter and play
When so many we've known so few that are left
The friends and our families passed on like a theft
Thou tragic some times of our past we have seen
Tomorrows the future the light in our dreams
And together the love, the laughter and light
Will enlighten our days for which we must fight
As for sadness I swear and sorrow I say
Let's just pray for tomorrow and live for today

Tracy Dean Smith

My Best Friend

I have a friend.
She is living of course.

Her name is Rose.
She doesn't have a nose . . . (or head, or feet.)

But, she lives right next door and loves to chat.
She always loves a great big snack!!

She is small, but will get big.
She is my friend.

She does not argue. She is never mean.
She is always seen.

She loves to eat all the time.
She is quiet and fine.

She likes it when it's hot.
She has her own cool spot.

Who can my friend be?
Well she is a Rosebud tree!!

Sara Ann Gaines

God's Little Creatures

Where do all of God's little creatures go
When the sun goes down and the moon begins to glow?
Do they hide in the tall grasses over the hill?
Or do they sleep in the trees so still?
When daybreak comes again they clatter and sing,
Their voices have a wonderfully sweet ring,
I thank God each day for all his little's creatures,
Who make my days into "special features"

Wade M. Terrebonne

My Purple Blanket

I try to go on with my life
   concentrate on something else
     put you out of my mind
       escape from your grasp
  but, as soon as you're gone
    you're back in my thoughts again.

Photo-flashes of you and me all alone under infinity.
Feeling perfect all the while but,
   when it ends you're without your smile.
We both are.
Underneath my purple blanket we both feel judged.
Judged by who knows who.
Our feelings get smothered and so do we.
There seems to be no way out but, there has to be.
There's always a way.
I've always found a way to find a way.
And with you as my motive it should come easily.

    Gina M. Cassesse

More Than A Friend

As I sit thinking of her my eyes begin to tear,
It's because I hold her so, so dear.
I remember the times we've had both up close and afar,
She'll always be my brightest shining star,
To me she's the perfect one, perfect for me,
Then I think to myself, "Well, we'll see."
Her hair is blonde like perfectly spun gold,
She'll always be beautiful even when she's old.
Eyes are blue as deep as the ocean,
When I look into them it quiets my commotion.
Sometimes I think she doesn't know truly how I feel,
And I think maybe she will if I go to her and kneel.
She's my friend, the best one I've got,
Maybe that's why I put her on the spot.
For now I'll see what the future will hold,
But without her I know it will be long, dark, and cold.

    Sean K. Hamilton

Alone, Alone

With no one to share your day
Brings many a sleepless night
Waking up as never being a couple
Means a time to curse the light
Walking in the streets eyeing their smile
Brings you a hurt, dews your sight
Not knowing what comes tomorrow
Makes this day a little less bright
Watching the pairs, and being alone
No one to hold, it's so not right

Alone alone tis so wrong to be so
So hard to change, try as you might
Along with every imagined hope
As your pulse reaches a new height
Comes the ever saddening truth
Maybe someday life will be all right
But until this time comes to be
And you've fought the lonely fight
Wake up content at being alone
Till your heart is no longer tight

    Jeremiah J. Mahoney IV

Solitude At The Old Mill Pond

   Deep in the woods there is this old mill pond
something of a tribute to the past. In this picturesque
natural setting it is serene surrounded by woods.
   At night there is quiet and stillness, the silence is
broken only in the early morning when it comes alive with
the native wild animals and waterfowl, animals such as
beaver, fox, squirrels, rabbits.
   Sometimes a deer will come through the woods going
to the mill pond for a drink.
   The trees in the woods are in the variety of birch, alter,
pine, aspen and sycamore. In this abundance of natures
surrounding can be found waterfowl such as cranes, ducks, swans
and on occasion an otter may slide into the pond for a swim.
   Then with surprising quickness the woods and mill pond
become silent, as dusk comes across the woods and mill
pond, then again, there is silence and stillness in the
woods and on the pond, and then there is complete solitude.

    Neil E. Roddy

The Day Racing Lost Scotty

In nineteen ninety six on the seventeenth day
of the big race month, the month of May
a tragic event occurred on the track
a life was taken that can't be brought back
the life that passed on had the number one spot
most people know that that man's name was Scott
at twelve seventeen in turn number two
his tire blew, there was nothing he could do
smashing the wall and hitting his head
thirty three minutes later he was pronounced dead
as the statement was read silence hit the stands
eyes filled with tears and were covered by hands
black clouds filled the sky while the sun shined on
no one wanted to believe that Scott Brayton was gone
Scotty was known for wearing a smile
which he wore every year on those five hundred miles
the racing world has lost a great friend
who enjoyed what he did until the very end
our memories of Brayton will remain everyday
as we know Scott is watching over our speedway

    Chris Cook

Father

Father, with rage I stare at your face,
Which has a feeble cover.
Sometimes I want to cry out
That your enemy is not here
But, in fact, looking back from the mirror.

I do not know what you wish of me
And I cannot read minds.
You stay locked in your self-perfected world
Where you expect your bidding done,
But not saying what; guessing games are not fun.

A chilly air blows through me on the hottest day of July.
A single shiver severs my spine,
Freezing my body until at last
I have changed; I cannot move,
And with each of your cold gusts, more of myself removed.

When this thing is finally through,
I'll leave you far behind.
Lonely and afraid I'll go,
Holding my head up high
And promising myself I will not cry.

    Stacey R. Maves

Gardens

Hummingbirds visited my garden today,
Drank of nectar and flew away.
They'll be back as they have before,
To sample the throats of flowers galore.

Butterflies also visit my yard,
To bring them back, I work hard.
They know what flowers they like best,
So I plant them most and some I test.

What kind of garden is best of all?
The kind that blooms from spring till fall.
All colors of the rainbow can be found,
They grow and bloom in the richest ground.

Some like specialty gardens, not like mine,
I plant and change and mark the time.
Mine's like a quilt of patchwork made,
Some in the sun and some in the shade.

Tall and short, strong and fine,
I like them all because they're mine.
I like to share with others who grow,
Because soon enough it will all be snow.

John E. Hall

Self Appointed Messiah

In the beginning there was wood and ores
People lived in hell with their chores.
A man dreamt of God and religion
We live in fear of death and Armageddon.

I'll never leave your side no matter how much you run!

Jesus grew up in a trade as a carpenter
His father was born unto earth as a philosopher.
Society was an anabolic competition.
This grew into a self-destructive condition.

I'll never leave your side no matter how much you yell!

Hidden meanings, secrets joys, constructing the devils' crosses
A boy grown into a man knowing no loses.
An ancient mariner hated and seen no veils
Later to die a death with holes and nails.

I'll never leave your side no matter how much you beg!

Stopped to ask whose life do you guide
No apologies it's death without a mind.
Try to find an emotion without self devotion
Is it a game of understanding or a way around evolution?

I'll never leave your side even if there was a way!

Daniel Lyle Petersen

The Silent Scream

A silent scream, a muffled cry
the sounds of a soul too tortured to die
the sounds that begin from so deep within
the sounds of a soul that haunts most men,
men in darkness, men in light,
will hear the sounds and tremble with fright
afraid to scream, afraid to cry,
they live in darkness afraid to die
afraid of the darkness, afraid of the light,
they muffle their cries and sob thru the night

When light comes and darkness flees
the sounds of the soul are put at ease
the silent scream, the muffled cry,
the sounds of a soul too tortured to die.

C. Miller-Grant

For The Man I Loved, Yet Never Had

Their is a young man whom I
wanted to be mine for a very long time
we've had our share of good times, and
bad ones too, but that never stopped my
love for him.
   He could never understand the
feelings I have for him. I love him for
his sensitivity, loyalty, and just because
he is beautiful all together.
   When were not together I feel
like my life has ended and my heart
has stopped. He is my every thought. Being
without him is very painful, and suffocating
I often find myself crying, and praying
to just be with him one day for a
few hours to show him my love as
we make love under the stars. Someday
I hope to share my heart and soul
with him, for him to love too.

Katrina Ahern

Life As Roses

Each moment somewhere in the world
            there is a new rosebud
blooming
               within the same moment
     you hear a newborn cry.

Slowly the rosebud will open
        petal by petal
just as life   will unfold
         many few experiences
            that will become memories.

Once the rose has opened   to its fullest
     life is then complete.
As each petal falls
     gracefully   to the ground,
life slowly dwindles
          away to inexistence.
The fallen petals   as do the faded memories
    become rich ingredients
for the future roses
            of our world.

Debbie Perkins

Allen

An unsettled dream of a past spirit is calling,
Speaking of an unknown place I've never been,
Anticipated uncertainty awaiting,
A journey paying homage to my kin.

To see through the eyes and heart not mine,
Will comfort, yet cause me pain.
Though mountains stand majestically tall,
Ashes of you are all that remain.

We never have reunited,
The way it could have been.
Time has taken you from me,
All but the memories within.

May the wind forever carry your spirit,
O'er the mountains and sky above.
Soon I will be with you always,
In my westward passage of love.

Robyn Leigh Zach

185

Planet Earth

Thank you, God, for allowing us to spend
Some time on your planet earth.
We aren't the best, or the worst,
Or the least, or the first.

We love to listen to the breeze,
Blowing through the fields and trees.
The murmur of the howling wind,
Tells me that it is my friend.
To see the tall and swaying grass,
Reminds me that I cannot surpass.
The breeze where ere I go
It's always there to blow and blow,
And it's been that way since the first birth.

Moriel L. Hill

Snow Angel

As a child; how could I know
That making angels in the snow

Would change with time from youthful fun;
To lasting images of earthly mourn

Walking on new fallen snow;
Memories carry me to not long ago

On a euphoric, magic carpet ride;
mother and child by my side

To dreams we shared; plans we made
Then, shaken to reality; the images fade

The crunching snow awakens me;
On the white, velvet blanket I see

The tiny stone; then icicle tears
Cover this face; leathered by years

I lay down a rose; find my way home
Embrace your momma by the fire alone

But never alone; for we both know
You live in our hearts; our fallen angel...
In the snow

As a child; how could I know

Curt Belford

A Secret Love

Wal boys, yu've asked me a tough one,
        But I reckon I should tell yu true,
Ol'Dave does hev a secret sweetheart,
        Of which yu red-eyed kiyotes never knew.
Her eyes are the blue prairie skies,
        Thet sparkle with the evenin' stars,
An' it's a safe bet thet where she is,
        This waddie's heart ain't never thet far.

Her hair is the golden, long grass,
        Her lips are the red prairie sunset,
Her whisper is the cool, gentle wind,
        An' she's the purtiest thing I ever met.
Her caress is the warmth of the campf'ar,
        Her perfume is the scent of the sage,
Her laughter is the tricklin' crick,
        An' I've loved her from a very young age.

Her hug is the encompassin' horizon,
        Her spirit makes my heart feel as free,
As the tumbleweed an' the mustang bands,
        An' with the mawnin' dew she kisses me.
Now boys, I see yur all misty-eyed,
        But I'm afraid yu don't understand,
She ain't no human female wonder,
        She's this wide open, beautiful land!

David D. Oaks

My Flower

God planted the splendid seed,
Precisely in the center of my young mind,
It soon germinated into beautiful dreams
So I could recognize the love I wanted to find

In my sleep, we drove through the countryside,
The wind blowing through our hair,
Although you were flourishing at my side
I still knew not who was there.

Try as I might, I could not see your face
But there was no question about your beauty,
Beauty inside and out, endless beauty, peace and grace,
Yes, so much beauty - infinite, flower - like beauty.

In later, painful, lonely years,
I would hold you in my waking mind's eye,
The softness of your petals brought tears.
The sweet smell of you made me cry.

Then suddenly over the ocean our eyes met,
Yes, the flower in my mind was you
I knew that there could be love and happiness yet,
With my flower, life could be pure, perfect, and true..

Craig N. Carter

A Life To Tend

We need not be belittled, dragged or punched.
Women were not placed on earth for this
But to share a love that was meant for two
The pain she bears at child birth, "Is that not enough?

A man may go from women to women
Not knowing or caring who might be hurt
Thinking he will never be caught
Taking chances at someone's cost, not knowing the odds.

Man complain about a ball and chain
A yet say "A women's place is to obey!"
She had a life, why bear more pain?
There's a life to tend. So pack your bags be on your way!

A woman is strong and can conquer all
She believed, love was created for two
Wipe those tears, leave him crying wolf!
You have a life to tend

Ask God to take your hand
With him you can be strong, you have done no wrong
Man have Love all confused
But you don't have to be the one to loose.

Consuelo V. Aguilar

Screams Of Silence

As I sat there
in the quiet noise,
amidst the cobwebs and shadows of my mind,

Those memories of you
washed over me like a flood of tears.

In that blinding darkness
I saw the truth woven like the spider's web.
I will realize that you are truly gone
how much you hurt me,
the pain which you caused.

But with that I wonder
and ask those demons which haunt me,

Why do I wish
to have that back?

Is it that for which we once shared?
Or that those shadows haunt my nights,
to remind me of the emptiness.

Matthew Kachura

Someday

Someday I'll wake up in the morning
turn my head and you'll be there
with that sunlit sparkle in your eyes
and the sunlight dancing in your hair.
But for now I wake up lonely
but for my dreams, that's all I have.
Someday we will walk the beach together
hand in hand as lovers do, the waves
splashing to our love songs, that were
made for me and you. But for now I walk
that beach alone, and sing our songs unto myself
Someday our love will be the mountains
and the green grass, and the wild flowers
For our love is an eternity
it's not just days and hours
But for now our love must be alone
this is my cross to bare, it is not there
for each of us, for alone we cannot share.
Someday I'll wake up in the morning
turn my head and you'll be there.

John Wayne Adkins

Untitled

As the cold takes the thought of her out of my mind
I let them go, I don't hold I let them go
I don't need the pain of the past so I let it go,
by the cold I let the cold take her from
my mind I let her go to let her go is to let
my self go free, free that is what I mean
free to see what life can be so I let go by the
cold my heart grows silent by letting the cold
to succeed in its task to help me let her go
and to let me be free.

Gary Lee Rogers

I Miss You

I can't feel your tender touch
Which I urn for so much.
Your warm breath lying upon my neck,
There is no way this feeling can be wrecked.
You made me feel so loved,
As if you were sent from above.
I only wish this love would last,
But we both know what is lying in our past:
Two broken hearts,
Too many empty parts.
Fate brought us together,
Hoping it would be forever.
Now we are pulled apart forever,
Knowing we will never be together.

Michelle Ware

I'll Love You Forever If I Want To

For just one touch I would give you all of my heart
For just one look I would give you all of my love
For just one kiss I would give my soul
For just one word I would give my world
For just one smile I would give my being
All of this I would gladly say good-bye to if you would
be mine until the End-Of-Time.

Trena Gaye Locke Strickland

My Collection

My Collection was started
many years ago.
From the beginning with two people,
that did not even know.

My Collection is filled
with many Precious Moments.
But unlike the purchased figurines,
my Collection comes from gathered events.

It has grown quite large
as you can see,
and I will never know
where the end will be.

Although through time the pieces
have received some chips and cracks,
and I have even had one precious piece
that has shattered in fact.

But with each treasured addition that joins us together,
my Collection will always be with me forever.

My Collection is of Love and that is my family, you see
and there is nothing in this world that means more to me!

Lisa Schaefbauer

When Men Had Wings

When men had wings,
and could fly freely through the sky,
and touch heaven, and hear new born angels cry;

Like magnificent birds,
they would light up the sky,
and their songs of glory, made God cry;

And from his tears the golden fields did grow,
So all men could know the passion and beauty,
that from his glory does grow;

When men could fly,
no wars, no hate, no death was there to fear,
for at God's hand, man was always near;

When men could fly,
there hearts were filled with love, not hate
So fly young angels, and sing your praise,
of when men could fly in Golden days.

Charles W. Strickland

Twenty Odd Years

For twenty odd years it was her fate
to be wed to a cold and heartless mate.

The love in her heart which she yearned to share
was not accepted, for he just did not care.

For sake of the children, she held back the tears
and endured the pain for twenty odd years.

Never gaining his love for which she prayed
she filed the papers to end the charade.

To her surprise, she soon found another
with love in his heart for her to discover.

She now knows it was a great Divine plan...
twenty odd years to earn her perfect man.

JoAnne Keaton

The Song Of My Heart

I do thank God the Lord above,
Created the man whom I love;
Who shares my joys and dreams in life,
A man who's glad to have me for a wife.

He's always there in time of sorrow;
And cheers me up for a better tomorrow;
He does everything to make me laugh,
All these fourteen years and a half.

The days will go and pass,
I know for sure our love will last;
As we grow old and look no younger,
Our hearts will stay meek and stronger.

O Lord, our Father in heaven,
There are countless things you've given;
I wake up in the morning feeling blessed,
Throughout the day till night's rest.

No words of mine will reciprocate,
All the things I highly appreciate;
To write this poem is just a start,
For me to express the song of my heart.

Imelda G. Yago-Koppes

Remembrance

Your hands flow artfully across the
crevices of God's created clay, forming it
into a piece of art to your liking.
Your lips filled with the sweetest
juices that glides like the ocean
shone on the beach sand, ready to
create a mixture with mine - oh
so divine.
I listen. As your voice enters the night
air in soft whispers; tickling and chilling
each cell of my body.
In fear; I fear the volcano that will
soon erupt - exploding, covering all
mountains and lands.
I remember the way we made love.

Stephanie A. Edwards

Wailing For Those Words

That night you kissed me I felt on your tender lips those
words I have been wailing for,
those words that now touch me dearly but I feared so long ago.
I long to hear those words whispered from your mouth,
I lie in bed at night dreaming of those words.
It's those words that make life strong,
it's the words I love you that makes our love last long.

Carrie Sitzman

Love

Love is just like a glass sphere,
Love can shed many tears.
Love is when two people feel for each other,
When you are in love you want to
be near each other.

Love is such a delicate thing,
Just imagine how much joy love can bring.

Love is one thing that we all must share,
Love its more than a glare.
Love is there when you really need it,
Love is there if you just believe it.

Enika Levy

Just Look Inside

Don't judge this book by its cover,
I look in and found you.

Look into my eyes,
tell me what you see!

Do you feel my pain and
how you feel towards me?

Can you feel my pain
just like I do?

Look into my heart,
do you feel my pain just like I do?

Just give me a chance and I'll prove it to you,
there's so much I can do.

Look into my eyes,
tell me what you see!

Don't judge this book by its cover,
I looked in and found you.

Kelli Taylor

Love Thy Neighbor

I have often looked into the eyes of another,
And seen deep within their soul, penetrating their cover.

For the eyes are the windows of the very soul;
A kind of spiritual type of port-hole.

When souls touch each other and spirits entwine,
Then my problems are his and his troubles are mine.

To feel loneliness, fear, or even to care,
About my fellow-man, while receiving his glassy-eyed stare.

If only I could feel just what you are feeling,
Maybe our relationship would be more appealing.

For when one man walks in another man's shoes,
He may then realize why his soul is so bruised.

And until we can learn to feel as one,
Our relationship will be over, before it's begun.

Kenneth Sikorsky

A Tribute To Mother

On December 27, 1996, another milestone will pass;
May you receive many blessings, but not your last.

Eighty-five years of Seasons untold —
Writing a book as memories unfold.

A time for everything, to everything a time
A time to every purpose, and not always a rhyme.

To everything a Season to break down and to build up,
A time to plant, and a time to fill your cup.

A time to be born, and a time to dance,
A time to embrace, and a time to take a chance.

A time to laugh, a time to speak,
A time to cast away, and a time to keep.

A time to weep, and a time to heal,
A time to mend, and a time to build.

A time to love, and a time to hate,
A time for creative expressions — that can't wait.

Making time to work with your hands,
Mending, sewing, cooking, and meeting demands.

So enjoy your blessings, as you so deserve
Upon this "Great Land" share your wisdom and verve.

Barbara McDonald-Wathen

A Lone Wolf

A lone wolf afraid of all who came near
He runs when they come but they catch him
He fights but does not win
He cries for help but none will listen
I cry out, isn't he something like me

A lone wolf he trusts no one
He has seen the worst of man his body is held captive
But his mind remains free he is forever alone
I fear for him I have seen through his eyes
I cry out again, isn't he something like me

He fights everyday his body is tortured
But his mind remains forever free
He is unbreakable
He escapes he is free
But they may come again he is fearful
I cry out once again, isn't he something like me

Courtney Stefka

Eyes

We see the world through eyes of glass,
But know not what we see.
We go through life at speeds of time,
but know not where we go.

We see the world through eyes of ice,
But we feel not the cold of ice.
We head in life towards one bright light,
But know not what it is.

We see the world through eyes of fire,
Yet we are cold inside.
We feel the warmth of others,
But feel no warmth inside.

Josh Zike

1996 Eastern Conference Semi-Finals Bulls Vs. Orlando

Today I was watching the game
It's really great-never the same
Bulls and Orlando goin' strong
The next 7 games are goin' to be long
A 3 pointer at half-court by
Anfernee Hardaway
He's on Orlando to stay
Michael Jordan is still the best
He's better than all the rest
Dennis Rodman and his multi-color hair
When it's rebound time he's always there
Well, gotta go, Horace Grant has the ball
Why are all these guys so tall?

Susan M. Markovich

Orbes

The earth and heavens, drawn from chaos' spring
From liquid void where only spirits move,
Became divided by horizon's ring;
A world for man and one for gods. But Jove,
Like Vulcan forging iron to repair
A broken chain, shaped truth and living light
Into a link, a sun whose brilliant glare
Was foreseen in the witness to the night.
Apollo, dawning on our world, inclined
To break the dark horizon of our hearts
And came that, set and risen, he might bind
Together the horizon severed parts.
Praise Jove who forged the wedding band and sent
The Way to heal our world's most worldly bent.

Donald VanderKolk

Untitled

I have an unquenchable thirst for something that's beyond me
How can I make it mine?
How long will it take?
Will I suffer like this forever?
Never quite reaching my destination . . .
I stumble onto nothing
As my heart pours itself into the ground
What use it to a body that deserted it long ago?
So now it leave me, as everything else does
That never really enters my life to begin with
Does it really belong with me anyway?
Or does it just pretend?
Why?
Why don't I ever know what happens . . .
After boy meets girl?
The movie always ends
Before it begins
And my life is an endless stream of credits
Due to those who have carelessly entered and exited
My life.

Ashley S. Wells

Mannequin

Mannequin's is all they are.
Can't they see?
Can't they hear?
Can't they feel it around them,
the intense pain of depression?
What are they, blind?
Can't they see
the loneliness caused by lack of attention?
What are they, blind?
Can't they hear
the fighting between friends because of trust
No they are not blind
They can see it, hear it and feel it.
But they don't bother to stop walking away from us.
They're just mannequin's who call us bad kids,
but never stop to ask, "Why"?

Jessica Carter

My Mom

My mom is generous.
My mom is kind.
My mom will be there all the time.
My mom is pretty.
My mom is nice.
What would I do without her good advice?
If it wasn't for her where would I be?
I learn everything from her great personality.
If my mom was not my mom how could I survive,
I couldn't, she is the one that brightens up my life.
Everything she says and everything she does
pleases me so much.
She will reach for my hand and pull me up.
That is my mom and I love her so much!

Lacey Mason

Winter

As the clouds build on a cold November day, and all
the flowers wilt away. The birds songs leave the sky, and
all of the butterflies seem to die. A dark cover is pulled
down, and all good things seem to drown. Who has fun on
a day like this? When the world seems to fall into a great
abyss. It is damp and cold, and the wind seems so bold to
break through this icy mold. This does no good. It seems
nothing could, but still I stay until the sun's first ray.

Donna A. Reed

Christmas Angel!

Mom! You laid me to rest on Christmas Day. A lot of
tears were shed, but shed no more tears. Think of me
as an angel flying over your head. The tears which
now burn on your cheek may impart the deep
thoughts that dwell in the silence of your heart,
A little sister I left behind, her bright eyes will be
imaged in thy stream — Yes! They will meet the wave
I gaze on now. Mine cannot witness, even in a dream.
That happy wave repass me in its flow. Bright be
the place of thy soul. Wipe the tear from your cheek ever so slow.
The step-Dad, I left behind on a snowy December, don't
weep no more tears, because I am one of God's members.
God took me by the hand and lead me to Heaven, I'm
the Angel flying over your head. To everyone that knew
me and loved me, don't forget me, but put me to rest,
I'm in a better place.

Lisa Tackett

Untitled

It was late afternoon, early evening he was fearing the meeting
For it was a date the kind most hate

Blind

He had heard many a story which made him worry
Is this the act of cupid or just plain stupid

He was in a bind

He went to her house feeling like a louse
She looked lovely he felt lucky

The situation was one of a kind

They went to dinner his wallet got thinner
They went to a dance but all they did was prance

And she left him behind

Did they have a good time to him it was prime
To her we do not know for conversation was slow

Her answer is left undefined

Is there a chance for a second date one can only speculate
For now they go their separate ways and toward future days

Thus this paper has been lined

Justin Schleibaum Jr.

Cries Of The Caged Dragon Children

Dethroned child emperor could not prevent
the golden dragon from sorrowful lament
over her children ruled by bitter despair.

And haunted by blood baths of Tienanmen Square
splattered with grotesque remains
of annihilated youths demanding change.

The Great Wall that blocked invaders could not stop foes within,
especially cruel dictators calling freedom a sin,
who instruct young children from a sick curriculum.

To watch brain tissue of prisoners fly during execution,
setting an example for terrified eyes to follow
as they choke on their tears in tight Mandarin collars.

A sadistic empire brutally reigns,
the nervous people walking cautiously in invisible chains
until their last gasping breaths,

With their art and literature condemned to cultural death;
creative ideas are subject to guilt,
shredding hopes into pieces like delicate silk.

Amanda Rose Taulbee

Stop The Violence

Stoping the violence, and bringing the peace.
Trying to get along, and let the love increase.
Opened arms, we all should have.
People together, we all smile and laugh.

Together as one, is how it should be.
Hand guns and knifes, all the insanity.
Eternal - safer world for you and me.

Violence all over, what happened to the world?
Innocents dieing, little boys and girls.
Open your eyes, and maybe you'll see,
Life could be better for you and me.
Enough I had, fed up for shore.
Never thinking, will we endure.
Certainly we can make it, if given a chance.
Everyone should try, lets stop the violence.

Sean Porter

Ian

His beautiful brown eyes, about which I dream.
His skin so soft, his hair so clean.
His outside's sexy, his inside's groovy,
Like the kind of man you'd see in a movie.

I love him and he says he likes me too.
I wonder if what he says is true?
The way he acts-so calm, so cool.
It makes me want to drown myself in my swimming pool.

He also says he loves that whore,
The girl who all of them adore.
He tells me that he like me best,
I wonder if he says that to all the rest?

The girl he likes, she is so blind,
She doesn't even have a mind.
She's in love with a slack,
He could never love her back.

She'll love him 'til her dying day,
Knowing he won't love her she'll say she's gay.
The guy I want, won't want her then.
And all to myself I will have him.

Cari Stubler

Silent Speaking Soul

Sweet silent soul, singing in the summer rain
Drifting upon a cloud of luminescent light, feeling no pain

The days pass by, another morning sun
Majestic twilight shows the night has begun

Entranced within the midnight sky, a star set to fly
Living in Utopia's bliss, my silent soul shall laugh and cry

Soft vibrant music are the silent words, my tongue speaketh not
For the purring place of peace is a space inside that time forgot

Alive alas, along a narrow bed of nails
The silent soul sees the light that hails

Flowing beyond the illusion of fear, the eagle soars above
I've seen me in my dreams become the Universal Dove

Love passeth threw a window, unto the soul of the ship
Gathering from the eternal sea brings knowledge for my trip

Ever-present, here and now, dancing in the light
I've experienced fear to overcome the fright

I am a river, running wild with compassion's passion and joy
A child of light receiving a brand new toy

Oh, I thank you, silent speaking soul
For it is your love that has made me whole...

Jason Coviello

Get Away

Get away from me.
I don't need you or your pseudo-sympathy.
Leave me alone and let me die.
Come near and I'll hit you in the eye.

Cut me open to apply the salt.
Everyone knows that I'm at fault.
Oh, make it ache. Please make it burn.
My pain is none of your concern.

Rinse me off with chlorine bleach.
Grab whatever sharp object is within your reach.
Tear me apart 'til your heart's desire.
Slice me, dice me, throw me in the fire.

Your job is over and now you're through.
It's time for me to do it to you.
If you object, I'm sorry to say:
Please, please, please just get away.

Johnnell S. LaFreniere

Untitled

Our numbers used to be great,
Now disease is our fate.
Once we were young and green,
Now there is brown to be seen.
Animals are around used to abound,
Now there are none for I'm on the ground.
Squirrels used to run on me with great speed,
Now they left for I cannot produce a seed.
Yesterday when the winds blew with such force,
I could stand strong and tall with no remorse.
Tomorrow when the winds beat at my side,
I fear I will take that mighty slide.
When great numbers fall this way,
Can you imagine all that disarray?
Why! Where great animals used to play,
The wolf will find easy to slay.
What great sadness I will feel,
When this is all that fate has to deal.
My young could have had a chance,
If I could of had a paper dance.

Brenda Breed

Country Visions

As she sipped her coffee and gazed out the window,
Oh, how she wished to see the flutter of a sparrow.
But blacktop and concrete laid beside
was too much for even the morning fog to hide.
So with a smile she lifted her gaze
to the golden sun filtering through the haze.
She closed her eyes and now she could see
spring flowers and a busy little bee.
In her minds eye she watched the flight of a blue bird,
listened to children's laughter and words to be heard.
Her eyes traveled over her garden to be hoed,
the lush and green lawn freshly mowed.
A fluffy tailed squirrel scampers up a tree,
while a Robin dives for a worm only he can see.
Out in the street the honking of a horn
brings back reality and leaves her forlorn.
With a silly grin she realizes, no reason to be sore,
tomorrow I may visit the country again and vision all the more.

Debra Lynn Quick

Loving, Wise And Free

They start out as babies, begin to grow,
Innocent and vulnerable yearning to know.

Family and friends have love to share,
Lets wipe out the sadness, show them we care.

Parents are responsible for what children are taught,
Give them an adventure to be sought.

Spoil them with discipline to show you're there,
Teach them in life to always play fair.

Good times and bad times go hand in hand,
Lots of hugs and kisses should be law of the land.

Children are a gift, we should all appreciate,
Take care in a child, help guide their fate.

Children learn a lot from what they see,
Help them become loving, wise and free.

Michele Petroski

Colored Stones

I remember playing alone,
wondering when papa's coming home.
We went to see him today,
I brought him a stone colored in grey.

For grey is the way that I feel, knowing your sittin' in jail,
I hope you won't be in there long.
So you can help me color my stones.

I remember watching other children play,
With bikes and trains and big ol' airplanes,
And wondering why I had none of my own,
But how I loved to paint and color stones.

Dessell Lawson

Gone Is The Rustle Of Angel Wings

Gone is the rustle of angel wings.
  The golden hour of God is past.
    How with the crush and clutter of things
      Can the promise of Christmas last?

We can because we have seen the Christ,
  Keep walking with him every day.
    We can be wise like wise men of old
      And then go back another way.

Like shepherds went back to their silent skies,
  Returning to their dying fires,
    We can tend our sheep more faithfully,
      Still dreaming of angelic choirs.

We can sing and laugh and love and lift
  And hold this lovely world more dear
    And still hear the whirring of angel wings,
      The hour of God is always near!

Rex H. Knowles

The Soul of Destiny

To see is to envision the path you must follow,
Life leads you to the destiny you long for.
Only if the heart believes, the mind can do it,
One is true to their soul.
As you envision the path your soul must follow,
Life leads you to your destiny.

Laura A. Shiltz

Untitled

I've climbed mountains high, seen
valleys low, gazed out at the ocean blue.
  I've seen a small flower grow from a
stone to be kissed by the morning dew.
  I've seen lighting crack, heard
thunder roll, high winds that whipped the sea.
  But nothing ever turned my head,
   until you smiled at me.

  I've been around the world so many
times. I've seen all the far off lands.
  I've seen every star up in the sky,
that shines by God's command.
  I've heard every note the robins
sing, and they all were clear and true.
  But I know the day my life began
was the day that I met you.

Gaylon Buck

Love....

How does one know he's in love?
Should you wait for a sign from up above?
Or simply feel the warmth inside
That doesn't cool when laughter subsides

Should one feel happy, mad or sad?
Should one feel angry, lonely or glad?
The answer seems to be so complicated
It almost seems as you would have to be sophisticated

Can you tell me your point of view
Of how you felt when love came to you
Or will I have to keep on asking day by day
How will I know if love comes my way?

Maybe it won't, maybe it will
But just in case I'll always be still
It maybe in the morning, it maybe at night
Who knows, it maybe in plain day light

But I know one thing for sure
The answer to the question is no blur
It doesn't matter if you're close or far apart
For the real answer lies within the heart

Martha Y. Garcia

The Desecration Of Sanity

  As the sun goes down, nighttime shrouds around...
thus beginning the dreaded nightmare.
None of us can see it but it is there. No one can hide from
it for it is there. There is more than one of them they
hide everywhere. Behind the bush, beneath the sewer. They're
secretly plotting to plan their war. They hide from the day,
but bask in the night. They love to feed off your deepest,
darkest fright. Nothing can stop them, no good deed or
prayer. Nothing you can do will make them spare you.
You're as ignorant as prey as they come up from behind.
You don't even know they're there until they're in your mind.
They don't want your life, no, not in the least. They find
your fear to their appetite, just like a glorious feast.
They tease and they taunt, till you scream in horror. You
already know you won't see tomorrow. They rip and they slice,
in a perverse sort of way, at your soul, till you have
released your hopes of the promise of day. You have no hope,
not even a prayer, so when they come for you, just succumb
to their hellish nightmare.

Craig Dieck

Untitled

In the distance, I remember you.
The impression you made on my life still lingers on.
Why you had to leave is still an unresolved mystery to me.
But that doesn't matter, because the fact remains you are gone.

My anger, frustration, and sadness,
Continue to cling to me like a heavy burden.
Each emotion surfacing at the most unexpected moments.
The reality of it forcing me to cope with your death.

The years pass and somehow you follow.
Still, I'm left with the need to keep you close to my heart.
Closing my eyes I can still see you sharing a part of my dreams.
That gives me the strength to carry on without you in my life.

But perseverance will reward me.
When the time draws neigh, I know I will see you again!
No longer will your smile, your eyes, and your voice be a memory.
Peace will then soothe my soul when we're reunited in Heaven.

The moment will come, but not right now.
I am consoled just knowing our paths will cross again.
But my destiny must first be fulfilled before my life's complete.
And until then I will hold your memory close to my heart.

Heide Zuckschwerdt

Untitled

Their eyes are black, their hands are red.
Their skin is pale, their feet of lead.
They are stuck, with stains they bled.
Down...down...the lost and dead

Their clothes are worn, their lives are lead.
Islands roaming, inside their heads
Feeling sick from what they said
Down...down...the lost and dead.

Their world will die, with life they wed.
Their faces fallen, below their heads.
They are hidden, but still naked.
Down...down...the lost and dead.

Their life is two, they can't pick one.
They go with words, but have no fun.
They express a grin, but smiles will shed.
We're looking down.
We're lost and dead.

Nate Rustemeyer

Memories

The lights dim.
The music dies.
Another life has gone by.
A family weeps for their loss.
Someone special has left their lives
Forever.

But never shall they forget the memories.
For memories are our way into the past,
To recreate the good ol' times.
Memories are more precious than any jewel or stone.
And no one can steal your memories from you.

The key to life is to live for the future,
And to never forget the past.
For as they say, history repeats itself.
And the good ol' times may be relived once again.
Because one day you shall become a parent,
And then a grandparent.
And then after you are gone,
Your grandchildren will be the ones
Who must remember.

Shelly Ramdial

Forever

I want to be with you forever.
It will be an adventure I am willing to endeavor.
I want to wake up everyday to see your beautiful green eyes.
To hear your voice that sends me high.
I hope we never lose the romance.
I hope across the land of passion we dance.
You and me forever, is written in the heavens and clouds.
Knowing your mine makes me proud.
I love you with all my heart.
Whoever made the move to put us together was smart.

Tracey Kaderka

Dance Of Life

Hold me close in this dance of life,
this dance of being with You;
Gentle touch, whispering against my heart,
carving the bowl of my being;

Drawing down spirals within circles,
delicate feathered dreams
stilling my fears;

Whirling, twisting, dancing leaves of light
tinkling in the wind,
Sacred Dance of Life;

Gossamer webs,
sighing into the night,
gently drawing me,
calling me within;

Dreams, visions of wholeness
on this Sacred Ground,
glowing embers of the Eternal One;
Breath whispering love into being,
what is into what will be.

Marilyn Brown

Agony, Misery And Me

Some say don't complain, it's not so bad
I realize I shouldn't feel sad
Guilt and Agony and Misery and Me
The only one who can change my life is me
Exhaustion and guilt and Agony and Misery and Me
People say things will get better
Hatred and exhaustion and guilt and Agony and Misery and Me
If I could find a little piece of happiness,
there would be no more hatred and exhaustion
and guilt and agony and misery.
There would be just me.

Laura Olson

Rajah

Rajah is my very best friend,
He makes me laugh with his grin.

Rajah is special to me,
He's a little dog you should see.

He's a bunch of faithful fur,
But, I tell you he's not a cur.

Rajah is a Lahsa Apso; he's my little man,
And, when he was a puppy he fit in my hand.

Rajah is my very best friend,
And, I will love him to the end.

Miranda Lee Klick

I Have Nothing To Do

Nothing to do but sit and cry,
nothing left but an alibi.
Nothing to do but look at the sky,
and watch dark clouds passing by.
Nothing to do but think of the past,
nothing left that could or would last.
Nothing to do but ask why,
even thought the answer makes me cry.
Nothing to do with this emptiness,
maybe reality has given me a test.
Nothing to do with the feelings I hold,
my world like everything will soon fold.
Nothing to do but my ways I must mend,
because very soon my world will come to an end.

I have nothing to do.

Stacy M. Cole

On The Sound

Gentle rain sprinkles the quiet Sound.
An egret passes to the right,
extending its long neck
as it struts across the impressionable sand.

A family of ducks with their bills in the water
look for the day's provisions.

One solitary shape stands out,
White, tall, and noble
among the dark forms.

Vessels are anchored, sails down,
Stately and motionless, they point heavenward.
A mist blankets the water with tranquility
and hazy outlines are sketched in the distance.

Land birds herald their pleasant songs for so few to hear.
Not a wasted moment.

Amy Diamond

One Knight

One Knight came to a lonely town,
Seeking a place to settle down.
He searched all through the empty place,
He found many a caring and friendly face.
A damsel he heard, though not in distress.
To her castle he decided to press.
Through the darkness he swiftly rode.
When he drew near a brilliance from the castle showed.
The brilliance was the maiden's beauty beyond compare,
Her face, her lips, her eyes, her hair.
He knew he found that which he sought,
A precious thing that could never be bought.
This Knight no longer searches anymore,
He has found what he was looking for.
The Knight is me, the damsel you.
I speak with a heart that's pure and true
I'm unsure of exactly what will be,
But, I am sure I always want you here with me.

Pacer Jay Rumbaugh

Like An Eagle

We as Christian should be like the eagle,
with the claws of eagles to hang onto His Word,
the strength of eagles to endure hardships and
problems of the day,
The wings of eagles to fly above our circumstances,
the eyes of eagles to see dangers and spiritual things
as the Lord reveals them to us,
the beaks of eagles to tear down the stronghold
of the enemy.

Alan F. Palmer

Strategy

He stared at me and tried my thoughts to guess.
  There was a thick and solid still between
  His eyes and mine. A stimulating scene
Lay on the board. A prolonged game of chess

Began to tire our heavy eyes. Unless
  We should retire, I felt, he'd claim my queen.
  Fatigue o'er came me. A move unforeseen
Could lose my game. I began to acquiesce

To sleep, so I suggested we retire.
He soon agreed, for such was his desire.
  I slept; and knew I'd make my game improve.

My sleep would win my game for me. You see?
That early sleep was my own strategy.
  I'd be well rested, then make my best move.

Chris Sandstrom

Journey We Call Life

As we travel through the journey we call life
and enter adulthood,
the scenes of childhood remain in our mind;
As we unlace our hearts and our bodies get taller;
As we grow and change, the leaves still blow in the wind,
and every spring the flowers still bloom.
And the secrets are still untold,
and our favorite color is still purple;
And our shadow still remains behind us at all times.
But we have not yet come to an epiphany to
the compelling journey we call life.
We remain illiterate to the wonders of life,
and unfortunately, we get older, and get fuzzy, and collapse,
leaving the earth with still no strategy to
clarify the journey we call life.
And the plants still grow, and the leaves still blow in the wind,
and every spring the flowers bloom.
And we are just left with the view of the journey we call life.

Marcia James

Sonnet Of The Dreamer

Dreams as soft as the whispering winds blow,
As glistening as the sun set in blue.
Only the simplest dreamer could know,
Pure happiness follows his wish come true.

Ever so beloved as the mourning dove,
That sings the sweet essence of harmony.
A song that only the listeners love,
As the leaves in the breeze accompany.

And the ecstasy of the day remains,
Because the dreamer still silently dreams.
Serenity and peacefulness shall claim,
When everything is as good as it seems.

When the purest of gold resides in love
Only then will your dreams be heard above.

Shauna Lock

War Is A Bore

War is a bore, no more than the limits of its core.
Children dying, people lying on the floor.
Helplessly in pain as the other side will gain.
Why war, is that the only reason of the entire army corps.
Why war, I ask myself as I read the newspaper or watch the news.
As I try to turn the dial,
it seems as nothing else is worth the trial.
How bad, how sad, who needs a war.
And that's why I say war is a bore.

Dana Risteska

Black Hour

How deep can you push a knife into your heart,
and still go on?
The pain that is felt is like a whisper in the darkness.
Hearts cry for that gentle hand to catch the tears
that wash them away.
They ask for a voice that held the secrets of life they
should have led.
They find themselves trying to help the sun break through
to stop the downfall of rain.
The nightmare finally dies.
The battles are lost.
But the blood is still shed.
Hoping on another day.
that fear will surrender its embrace.
So that the Black Hour will fall.
But their hands are still hidden in blood
of dead still in armor.
They wrap their fears in a package of lies.
Shadows on the deathbed cry for strength.
The nightmare has not ended, it has just begun.

Johanna Holtan

Faces

I heard them first . . .
A constant clip-clop, clip-clop
My grip tightened around my spear
Lord, forgive me for what I am about to do . . .
A rider was exposed in the haze
His was the face of the enemy
The face of death
Eyes ablaze with fiery wrath, he charged
Clash!
A potent sound . . .
Metal against bone
The sound that drove hardened men insane
The face of death, on the ground, dying
The fire in his eyes extinguished with the dying of his breath
There was the face that would plague me
The face that was different
The face that was dead
By my hand . . .

Dan Otto

On First Encountering A Temperate Fall

Summer's searing heat and humid air
Now seem a fast vanishing fear.
Convection currents no longer rise
Like simmering waves from torrid pavements bare.

Oh! What welcome change appears?
Changes of flora excite the senses.
Behold nature's glorious tapestry
Varied but vivid shades and tints of
Green, yellow, brown, magenta.

Forest floors and shady glens golden shrouds wear
Enhanced by glimmering shafts of light thro yon canopy.
But soon the welcome vista's gone.
Alas! So soon? How sad!

Chilly winds wind amock
Nature's pruning saws at work
Weak, dry, broken branches forced byes utter
Bare, sturdy, stately frames remain.
Alas! How drab!

Will other beauties soon be here?

Ripton Bailey

Neglecting To Drown

Today the house was busy.
Beavers in the mudroom,
riding the dryer for free.
The milk expired a day ago.
Grandma is fatter than
last year at this time.
Her birth certificates expire soon.

The judge is sending me to
Austin, Texas. Says,
"You got to ride a bike, boy."
I am answering the phone everyday now.
Not even 900-numbers are good enough.

Little Alyssandra came over.
Brought a sign. Says,
"Welcome to the World of
Carbonated Beverages."
I hang it over Grandma. She smiled today.
I hope she eats her birthday cake.

Carson Cistulli

Hope No More

The stranger who knocks at my door today
is just another traveller and will go
his own way, tomorrow. The glimmer of hope
that lights up my house tonight
will die with me tomorrow, unsatisfied.

The candles I burn at the dinner table,
the bows that dance on the violin strings
will tire themselves in another some hours.
The candles will drip themselves to a flicker
and the strings will refuse to sing . . .

And in the morning when I open my eyes,
the stranger that shared my bed last night
will have mysteriously dissolved
into the mists of the night!

I might, just as well, not open the door
and let the wanderer seek another haunt.
I might as well just blow out the candles,
erase all my poems and climb once more
into my bed, all alone . . .

Anant Kumar

Unforgotten

When you were born you made me smile.
Like the heavens above, you had that glow
With the softness around you who would ever know.
that when you turned six the angels would come
to take you away from the people who loved you day to day.
With your last gasp of breath and a tear in your eye,
You struggled to say your last good-bye.
Retina Blastoma took you from me, and all the
world new, that it would be.
The hardship you felt and the pain you went through,
You covered it up and hoped no one knew.
You lived through your life without a care
You laughed at the site when you lost your hair
With a smile on your face and the pain in your heart
You always knew some day we would part
But my son now you know that is not so
For you're closer to me now than you'll ever know.
For when I look up I will always see.
The smile on your face like the heavens above
and that glow all around spreading your love.

Wendy J. Longen

Quiet Roses

Quiet roses, bleeding, falling in the autumn rain
Smile sweetly, hold you close, and swallow all the pain
If you must believe in something love, please don't believe in me
The sun may burn, but water cures, and blinded eyes can see
Set the hook and tow the line, and hope that someone's there
Walk a mile and walk for days, and find a place to care
If there's a road that I have missed, please help me find a way
But if you can't it's just as well, I'll breathe some other day
Above me all the skies so black, the light is shining through
Cold hand running down my back, I can only reach for you
The little things you gave me now lay broken on the floor
Quiet dreams and love, and I have never wanted more
If hope is real, sometimes my soul is only made for you
Waterfalls and dreams still falling, make the morning new
If there's a place where no one drowns then maybe I can live
You know that I've already lost much more than I can give
Turn your face up to the sky and sing a lonely song
You're not alone, I swear, I've been there with you all along
And though I've tried I just can't think of another thing to say
So close your eyes and fold your hands and pass the time away

Vincent Aldrich

Memories Of A Friend

Time may be able to mend many things;
　Yet it seems grief invariably remains.
She helped with my problems and dried my tears,
　Held my hand, alleviated my fears.
She never lamented her fate or plight,
　But just labored on from morning to night,
　Doing all of her work from day to day.
She did things in quite a usual way.
I never heard complaints about her life;
　She knew on Earth there was a lot of strife.
One morning her soul was quickly taken.
My heart shattered; she did not awaken.
She was loving, pleasant, and never cold;
　And I was only twenty-three years old.
I often dwell on things she used to say;
　Time still has not taken my grief away.
Night after night as I lie in bed,
　I think of my friend and honor the dead.

Tamara Forsyth

Grayness

The shadows envelope me
(The shadows creep under your bed at night)
A fight rages on within me
(They creep along your wall; along your ceiling)
The battle climaxes as my spirit's trampled
(They see you sleeping; they see you defenseless)
I rise from ashes just like the mighty Phoenix
(They look inside you and see the heart of a sheep)
In all my glory I vanquish the shadows
(They destroy you for all the evils you haven't committed)
It is only in my glory that I realize I haven't won
(For all the times you've looked the other way)
For in destroying these shadows they have corrupted me
(For all the times you haven't helped a person in need)
We will always be one in our sin
(For all the times you haven't risked your life)
There darkness has consumed me
(For all the times you haven't died saving someone)
My light is fused with them
(For the good life you think you've lived)

Andrew R. Proto

London On Two Quid A Day

mice living on electrified tracks
burrowing in the tunnels racing
through the city's undercurrent
stench of sewage from unwashed
sin lies in the nose of the
business man laying 10p in their
hands

animals learn to live by instinct
perceiving safety from the elements
nesting in the stomach of the snake
alcoholics — prostitutes — drug addicts —
musicians — artists — mothers — children —
their squeaks explode King's Cross
station.

Amber L. Weigand-Buckley

Father's Smile

Situated by the pale yellow light
a raisin wrinkled faced man
warmed by the soft beams from the old muddy brown lamp
is caught in a solemn rapture
as he stares into a familiar empty wall

The sharp wrinkles buried within his stale face
whisper soft silent secrets
a scowl so fixed and firmed
he learned to cry with a laugh
he kept his stomach full
full with work

Heavy black craters around the sullen eyes
grafted, battered, beaten

Rub, rub...scrub...scrap scrabble scrub
thumbs worn down to a nub
the hand cracked and broken
like an old muddied caked pair of torn gloves

His fingerprints were stolen from him as he lay wasted
tired from sand papering his hands against dishes and floors

He smiles sheepishly, like a fool to his king

Dan Truong

Untitled

Powder, dust blown in through clouds.
Dilatory, held back flow of white rain.

Brought for rest, allay the chaos bedded on ground.
Soft gentle illness, smooth as peach skin, as
white as acumen from hardened hearts.

Drawn in your albino flesh, leaving fresh body
streaking white.

Irritatingly procrastinating over through flesh.
Five fingers, sense the apathy for pain you
can't whisper from off weakened lips.

Breaths of silent emotion, caressing the heart.
As tears run over the gape of my mouth.

Scared of death, by the procure of a warm hand

His prodigy, sank hate out to take soul.
From staunch, leaks vibration from within a lamenting heart.

I see death. I fear death. No more will I
struggle to remove the hand that holds death
close between me and my soul.

I have death in mind, to pacify the pang
of my body, while I forego this panicked energy.

Rebecca Celeste Ischida

Sores Of Wars

Once upon a time I saw, a life fluttering ever so.
It fluttered like a butterfly,
But on the ground not in flight. Its eyes stared at me.
I heard its pleas; yet, it didn't speak.

Though its screams echoed in my head,
And I caught the sores the body wore,
I couldn't extend a helping hand.

Swollen knees and sore feet,
Held only by flesh and bones, struggled to get up once more;
Wobbling underneath their frame,
Home to scores of sycophant.

Steps were taken going nowhere.
And though no tears showed,
A mother's love no longer was. Her sprawled body,
Feet from him, stricken down by guns of wars.

Aghast people ran about, heedless of the little boy
Staring at faces in the crowd.

Dressed in pity, I viewed the tube
Displaying visions of the war. I watched it all unable to help.
Then I saw him trip and fall, fluttering forever more.

Maria A. Ortiz

The Stygian Reality

A denatured corpse lay in the emptiness of time,
Feasted upon by the hearts of humanity.
An eternal cry of horrid pain echoed...,
As I approached with awe.

Once a proud warrior,
Lush with vitality.
The Guardian of dreams,
Now laid under my feet.

The mother of life, the mother of death,
Lived to nurture and to caress.
Without pity, without mercy,
Born to die under you and I.

Life among death,
I too submerged myself to a feasting.
A drop of blood teared from within,
Begging mercy for my soul.

Kenny Lu

Wedding Day

A lifetime of love awaits you
In the start of your new life
Your love is made strong with a three-fold cord
In your union as husband and wife

Your Heavenly Father has blessed you
With a love for all to see
A love so intense, a love so pure
Meant to last for eternity

Your many friends and family
Have gathered to witness this day
They wish you years of marital bliss
For your happiness they constantly pray

Cling lovingly to one another
Rely on your God above
Let nothing come between you
And he will strengthen your love

So let this day and this moment
Forever be dear to your hearts
For what our God has joined together
Must never be torn apart

Andrea R. Thomas

Ghost Of The Rain The Storm

The wind was howling,
and the rain pouring down.
Just out of nowhere,
A stranger appeared in town.
His clothes were all ragged,
and No shoes on his feet.
He walked up to the bar,
And he took himself A seat.
Everyone Stared And To their surprise,
he had a Face Full of scars,
and he had four eyes.
Everyone there tried to sneak through the door,
and to this about five of them fell to the floor.
The few that fell dead, he didn't shoot hit or touch,
by just a wave of his finger, he killed this much.
All the time he was there, he never said a word,
and as he got up to leave, Not a sound was heard.
At the bar where he sat, he left a tag on chain,
Which the bartender read, "Ghost of the Rain."

Jerry H. Pullam

If I Should Go

If I should go before you go
Place my life upon white snow
Find a place where sun is sweet
Upon my stone quote Emerson
Sing songs of praise to God above
Know with you I leave my love
Your hearts may break
Mine's broken too
Walk through the trees
I'll walk with you
Your tears left there upon the ground
Each stain becomes sweet flowers around
My love I'll bring in ways you've known
Be still my loves. Take heart, live on
Upon damp sand my footprints clear
Whispers from breezes
You know I am here
Birds know — Listen! Her song sings clear
Kitty's soft eyes glisten
Creatures know I'm near

Ann Alyssa-Elise Williams

Glory

Lifeless vessels, freed of souls
Rot in an open grave on a wintry plain
Of death for all the brave.
Blood seeping through the hard, rocky snow
Leaves a crimson island
Of fallen friend and foe.
Bitter, bitting wind, the earth's own hateful breath,
Screeches to the world
Its calls of putrid death.
Scattered about the gory scene
Are the heroes of the day,
Corpses on the ground,
Dead in fields now they lay,
Sacrificed to war, the long and pointless fight,
The God who has no care
For neither wrong nor right.
Endless slaughter, on they fight
Through eternal sleep.
The nightmare is reality, yet closed minds do we keep.

Nick DaSilva

Forever Yours

Your touch is gone . . . my heart forlorns

The wind has blown away
The sky has darkened gray
My heart turned black
My soul cries so deep . . .
For you . . .

I walked into the abyss
For which I lay
I crawled for love
And then I died

In that death I stay
Until your image fades away
There is merely darkness . . .

And that, is where I stay
For my love, you are no longer near

Brian Gregory

zoe

she stands in the doorway
slowly she takes a drag from her
            camel (straight)
she looks into her cup of coffee
watching — as the
 warm steam rises — as the
 sweet crema swirls
she blows the
            camel (straight)
smoke into her cup of coffee
the cup of coffee falls — hitting the floor
   shattering
tossing the coffee
  (an) artist on the floor.
she bends over
crushing her camel (straight)
into the artwork
pushing her camel (straight)
 into the leaded-drink: singing her work

Jeff Wright

Secrets

Shhh. I can barely hear them whisper.
The tension is growing crispier.

The rumors are starting to grow.
Where did the color in her eyes go?

Why does she run?
What has she done?

I walk carelessly down the hall.
I'm waiting for that long anticipated phone call.

Everyday her face looks a little more strained.
She acts like she's so ashamed.

The phone will ring for me soon.
My heart is playing a forbidden tune.

No more can I lie.
I know I'm going to die.

I cannot stand it any longer! Goodbye.

Jennifer Erickson

The Great I Am

I have always been, and will always be
I came for you, and not for Me
But you can only be, in Me.

I have purchased you, with My life and blood
Even drug My name through mud
That you might have life, eternally.

For I am the great I Am
And I love you, with all I Am
I am your sacrificial Lamb.

The road is a narrow one
But through Me it has all been done
Open your heart, accept the Son.

For I have always been, and will always be
I came for you, and not for Me
But you can only be, in Me.
Jan Boughey

The World Arrives, Reluctantly

The Sun glows on lazy mornings
past glassy convex lenses,
burning slabs of concrete,
as warm tightened muscle flexes.

Living purple courses
on a microcosm express,
which super-sensitive follicles
endure with no duress.

Lazy heat fingers the air,
when a static voice begins to tear;
Sturdy marrow! Sinews! To the pace!
Snuffed out candle-like, now to join the race!

Pounding down external, middle, inner ear,
encoding to electrostatic cords,
'til lightning sense is made of it
at sad cerebral switchboards.

Thus the cold bites in,
and the world arrives, reluctantly,
questioning the veracity
of all that left with my security.
Aaron Benjamin McKissen

In A Land Without Sunshine

In the ground one day was planted a seed,
Spawned a Drake of Suffering, causing people to plead:
'What can stop it? Who will dare?'
In a land without sunshine,
Whispered the Maiden, 'Why should I care?'

Men lusted, women despised,
Children and elders laughed at her eyes,
'How strange she is! She doesn't belong!'
In a land without sunshine,
Begged the Maiden, 'Take heed of my song?'

The Dragon of old, soared high overhead,
Baring sharp fangs, snarling words of dread:
'What fools you are! Suffer your fate!'
In a land without sunshine,
Decided the Maiden, 'Who deserves such hate?'

A flash of her blade, a fire in her eyes,
The Maiden slew the Wyrm, thrown from the sky.
'Without praise she fought. Our pain she relieved.'
In a land without sunshine,
The sun shines upon one who believed.
Anthony Halat

Growing

Just a few days ago it seems,
Elated, amazed we first saw you —

A tiny bundle, with tiny hands
Eyes closed, sleeping soundly.
Completely helpless in mother's arms.
A proud day, Dad was so strong.
You depended on them so,
How very gentle was their touch though.

But how quickly time has passed
Helpless? Oh no — not at all.
Eyes closed? — not very long.
Tiny hands still, but how busy they are
pulling, pushing and reaching so far.
Mom's arms may hold you but soon you are down
Squirming, jumping and turning around.

Walking soon? How can this be?
That tiny baby is growing you see.
Charlotte B. Wood

Seasons

I think when I've come to this life's end,
I'd like to come back
as the wind.

It came to me on a cold wintery day,
as snow fell down
it came to play.

It tossed and twirled the snow around
and blew it all along the ground.

It tossed and twirled the snow around
and blew it all along the ground.

I'd never thought of it as a living thing,
but on a hot summers day,
oh what a joy I'd bring.

And in the fall my main delight,
would be to clear the trees
of their leaves at night.

While in the spring I'd travel places I've never been
and gather seeds and plant again.

I think I'd like to come back, as the wind.
Bill Lee

Maternal Woman

Maternal woman, where are you?
In search for the perfect happiness.
Your heart is broken, and your mind has wandered.
The illusions are many which break up your view.

Your soul is guilty from the abundance of sins.
The looks around you, you feel are strange.
The sun seems farther, and farther away.
Walk out of the dark, away from the dusky dens.

You think of how you live, your life is forbidden.
You've made wrong choices, and opened closed doors.
You've walked slanted pathways, and fallen on murky floors.
Little did you know, you've already been forgiven.

Explore the light, and discover your hidden hue.
Mend your heart, and gather your mind.
You soon will find the perfect happiness.
Maternal woman, where are you?
Toby Martisius

See The Lady We Call America

I saw her from afar; there she was standing,
  bakin' in the hot, hot, sun.

I watched the sweat rollin' down her brow,
  but looked at the smile upon her face instead.

Do you have a moment to sign this please? If not,
  I'll be here when you leave.

This is a lady standing in the sun for our rights to be
  counted for one by one.

If you pass her by she will still say with a smile, you
  have a nice day and I'll see you in awhile.

But stop and think for all the rights you have here in
  this land we call America.
And it all could end with the wrong man's vote.

So please stop and see the Lady so she can count your vote.
For who for all our rights here in America
Please Register to Vote.

  Rain F. Barrett

Confused In One's Own Rite

The fortune in disguise
The man behind the boat
War between the goats
Fire on the horizon
The magistrate's sin
With a world at war
And a golden door
The nights pass with their legions of stars
Taut lines of frustration
Fear for the unknown
Power in an amorphous form
Rock the night away
No, just let the blood flow away
From the punctured vein
The ruptured heart
Where there is no return
Or release from the horrors
Entrapment at a table
Lost generations flow through the mind
Yet I shall be happy, in a grain of sand.

  Brian Hendrickson

Remove The Thorn From Your Heart

Don't let the memory of hurt and pain taunt you
Forget the past that comes to haunt you
Others may rather seek revenge
Like an open wound that never mends

Your future depends on the choices you make
Only you decide the path to take
With patience the wound will close and heal
Removing the anger that you feel

Forgiveness will set you free like the wind
Continuing on without an end
Lift up your head and reach for the sky
Raising your spirit and soaring high

Will your heart be filled with love or hate
You have the power to choose your fate
Loosen the straps of hate that bind you
Let go of the feelings that confine you

Search within yourself and you will find
That if you want some peace of mind
Forgiveness is the way to start
To remove the thorn from your heart

  Alena M. Bennett

Quarter After (Midnight)

My memories are sealed in wax,
spilled from the candles which light my way
They cast-their amber spell, over all the ghosts who live
in shadows of my past.
Heat breathes life onto the faces in my heart.
The Wax spills quick like water, translucent as tears —
(I cry for you)
Pure white (the angel's wing) one cannot see behind,
only through.
There-(they sleep) Green eyes-grey skies, rainy days,
coffee houses, sad hours, and (exhausted) city streets.
Words, feelings, faces, forever dormant in their waxy shell.
The punk noise in the backdrop of my mind, sounds like angels.
Pulsing snow, fire of the soul, like those damn candles
doomed to burn for eternity. The cold blood in my veins.
The (extinguished) flames of my heart, leap and reach for the
darkness somewhere above, cloaked in black velvet night
wax encased tears drifting down. Just for a silent
melancholy moment, time stops, all is still, you are mine
And everything is beautiful.

  Channyne Thompson

Help!

The memories of my mind are still formulating
And I feel they are tearing and mutilating
Sooner I'm going to find release and spill or
Later I will start to get destructive and kill
The memories of my mind are ready to dwindle

My brain is starting to decay
And nothing I think is okay
You tell me I'm at peace
But others say I'm delirious
They think my problems are just hilarious

Nothing I do is right
I feel you think I should be perfect
When I need you, you can't understand it
With your support it will help me through it!

  Lauren M. Zelman

The Gates Of The Chosen

Follow the puffs of ivory,
The untouchable blanket of indigo.
Follow the never ending hills of green,
The path trodden by few before you.
Follow all of these things until you come to
The last of ivory, indigo and green,
And there, at the end of the path,
Turn your head to the mighty heavens,
And lift up your hands.
For when you open your eyes,
If you are one of the chosen,
You will see a key of pure gold, kissed by the God's.
This is the key that opens the gates to the kingdom of
Magic, Power and a touch of immortality.
Then thank of God's for you have been given a gift
Many only dream of.
A dream of passing through the gates,
Walking through the doors of the hollow hills,
And tasted the sweet flavor of the other world.

  Lauren Fedders

This Day

I found out today,
But, I didn't know what to say.

This couldn't be happening to me.
Then I found myself lost in what could be.

I laid here in silence,
Listening to your heart beat with mine.
And for a moment I was lost in time.

I couldn't believe a part of him was with me in you.
I struggled with the right thing to do.

God made this choice for you and I.
God made me say good-bye.

On this day I fell in love with him
Because of you.
My boy, my son
What have I done?

Forgive me, I'm sorry,
I couldn't cry.
Inside I just wanted to die.

A part of my soul was taken away,
This day.

Christine Adkins

Leave Her To Heaven

Do not cry for me now, for I am with you always.
Do not cry for me tomorrow, for I will always be there.
God has given me life beyond what eyes can see.
God has given me his love and set my soul free.
He said to me "My child take my hand and do not fear,
for with faith and believing I will guide you here".
My pain is now gone, and I suffer no more.
God has given me his grace, and love evermore.
My strength I've regained, and my tears have all dried
Do not cry for me now, because I've not died.
If peace and everlasting love are what you hope to achieve,
you must believe in God, his Love and Glory and what
you cannot see.

Crystal Dawn Gearhart

Here Lies The Land

Listen to the whispers that cry for mercy and grace
Look at the rays of hope that brightly glare
Along a path that stretches far beyond a place
Following the Morning Star to get there

A brilliant touch has answered
A love great and divine
The prayer the Lord has heard
In His fortress one can find

Hearts are filled with sweet laughter
Joys unfold among the way
To grasps Christ's sacrifice now and after
In every moment of a passing day.

Carried unto a crystal stream that is flowing
Many rushing currents roar
A King of majesty who is all knowing
Before His presence come and adore

Across a vast field of flowers, many gentle winds blow
Over mountains on eagle wings to freely soar high above
As soft rains begin to fall, fruit begin to grow
Here lies the land within the arms of God's unfailing love

Eddie Ruiz

Unretractable

He gazed at me
His eyes had a voice
They shivered my soul
No words spoken.

Seconds before, consumed with life
Now, statued in the earth below
Sinking into darkness
Suffocating in silence.

Like a colt revolver, sleeping in a dresser drawer
It waited peacefully for its deadly call
It shot through my mouth, searing my lips
Ripping into his soul, stealing my breath, crippling his eyes
Cold silence.

Chin to chest, my eyes couldn't reach his
His calmness frightening, his wound everlasting
My soul crying, my eyes dying
His silence stifling.

His wound remains agape, protected by a shield
Reflecting deceiving colors, tarnished, warn, tired
Forever impenetrable...Never words spoken.

John David Szymczyk

Vision Of Youth

Will I ever chase raging tides at bay?
Along shores where sand meets the deep blue sea
Such radiance shines there since break of day
Where I remain alone with my thoughts free
With soul pursuit of virtue beauty thrives
As this moment of inner strength reveals
No fear or rage will touch spiritual strives
And the human spirit shines not conceals
These are days for all humans to console
When life remains as unknown and fragile
All are but parts of one stupendous whole
So much being unique in God's own style
No where else I find the word and the truth
Only with love in my vision of youth

A. M. Fudurich

An Inner Voice

Heart is racing, tears are falling,
pain that's coming, voice that's calling.

Daddy stop, Daddy won't. Mommy
please, Daddy don't.

I hear the cry, I hear the screams.
I see the hurt, I dream the dreams.

Daddy's coming fear covers the face.
Daddy's home the face leaves without a trace.

Now I watch tears run hurried,
the dirt now covers my child buried.

I heard the screams, seen the eyes wild.
Nightmares same I did not protect my child.

Now there's a new seed to be carried.
I will not live to see this child buried.

The new inner voice told me to go, or
I would never see him grow.

I walked, I ran with my new inner
voice. Not of fear, but of choice.

Now my seed old, married, I did not
live to see him buried.

Chaconda Scott

Sandstones And Stained Glass

Sandstones and Stained Glass, we ask ourselves why are
they so precious? Then we remember how they show their
beauty. This is how I look at you. You are strong as a
rock with some rough edges and yet when I look through
your Stained Glass heart and soul I see a man that is
gentle and sweet.
When I'm with you I feel like a whole woman and that
makes life worth living for. Someday the right wave
will come too wash away this wall that blocks us. So
as long as we have the sun shining through our hearts
and the wind blowing we will hold onto all the
Sandstones we can find.

Doris Straka

The Last Flight

There were thunderous rumblings in the west.
Roaring jet engines engaged in a conquest.
Like pins in line across the alley,
Planes, in formation, flew over the valley.

My eyes were focused in a steady gaze
As a plane exploded through the haze.
A blinding flash lit up the sky;
Heavenly fire balls bid good bye.

The debris came down in a rush.
Mangled bodies return to dust;
Spirits were herald to their reward.
The crew is in the care of the Lord.

Elton English

Bended Knees

On bended knees he came to me, with love and promises
for all eternity.

On bended knees he reached for his child and promised
to always love. With a father's pride he held his hand to
guide his child through life.

On bended knees, beside my bed, his strength he gave to me.
Years of love and friendship he never wavered from me.

On bended knees I wept for the man who always loved me.
Headstone cold, flowers upon his grave, on bended knees I pray.

A simple man of the greatest heights, my love on bended
knees.

Deloris B. Mathes

How To Raze, How To Crumble

A non-committal tide crawls onto
   shore toting along dying strands
Of algae and unsuspecting fish.

Claw-bound crabs struggle along
   unforgiving sand pursuing taunting
Treasure, an open armed mistress.

   Mountain ranges raise relentlessly
against pressing sky, rebelling
   Against gravity's unwanted claims.

   Natural towers lacking languages to
disperse are instead cursed to grow
   Without notice, raised in isolation.

Meaningless men walk unsteadily through
   metaphorical traffic, and unlike Ulysses,
Seek the Sirens who mete out heartache.

Condemned to mediocrity, these men
   imagine heroes in their own hearts in
An effort to cover residing cowardice.

Timothy Smith

Wendy Lee

Wendy,
is,
A bubbling shout of laughter,
High spirited air, red - gold hair,
combed casually wild.
I look, unbidden, at this amazing grandchild.
Her hurts well hidden,
That glorious laughter,
peals, and rattles a rafter.
She's an ex-cop, wife and mother,
With all the duties that come after.
This woman-child will laugh at everything,
and never count the cost.
I listen, awhile, and smile.
Remembering the laughter that I have lost.
To me, now and forever after,
Wendy Lee is Laughter.

Lillian B. Belflower

A Love Poem For My Lord

When there was no one to hear my cries
You Did

When there was no one to hold me
You Did

When there was no one to embrace me
You Did

When there was no one to understand me
You Did

When there was no one to guide me
You Did

When there was no one to love me
You Did

When there was inner turmoil you brought me peace
When was darkness you brought me to the light
When there was no hope you brought me strength
When I needed to confess my secrets you never judged me
and have asked nothing of me in return.

For that I dedicate my life, my soul to you. I love you for all
eternity and beyond infinity.

Judi Witherspoon

Rich In Love

I awoke one morning, the first thought on my mind
She must be out there, this jewel that I must find
I've seen her in my dreams, her smile so honest and sweet
I wonder if she knows me, this gem I'm destined to meet
Stones and diamonds, she wears them with grace
Yet they don't compare, with her statuesque face
Envisioning her beauty, her long silky hair
I pray that she exists, this treasure so rare
But still I fear, that she'll vanish from me soon
For I possess no gold, I only have the moon
And I question myself, does wealth bring her delight
My heart tells me differently, love is what's right
So I'll give her my heart, and the great sky above
For I own the greatest gift, I'm truly rich in love

Todd Coburn

License

Take this burning snack cake and give it to the masses
Bring a ficus tree to the edge of the woods and set it free...
Cry for the lost attempts of salvation
our society has license...to bake our minds
their leader is the Snackwell Cookie man...
Screeching in fear as his cookies are taken away

Brendan Koral

A Change

The Condition of our nation must change
We can all help, it is within our range
We need to have concern for our fellow man
Let's pull together and lend a helping hand
Let us not be concerned about the color of the skin
Show some humanity and be a real friend
The Conditions that we presently face
Are not prejudice, they are affecting every race
The diseases that are upon the land
Are serious and they fear no man
We have hungry among us and this they should not have to face
The food we all throw away is a total disgrace
To one another we must show some respect
You will find that this will have a positive effect
We must educate our Children to the best of our ability
Instill in them to be the best that they can be
We cannot teach our children right and then we do wrong
We must bond in unity in order to stay strong
The conditions around us may seem out of range
If we all pull together we can make a change.

Barbara A. Haynes

Abandoned Building (Jan. '96)

I am a building
Weakly standing alone;
People pass me by everyday
I used to be a home.

I once stood tall and strong
My body was fresh and new
The walls inside me were clean and sturdy
The symbol of strength straight through.

People abused me inside out
By destroying my walls and trashing the halls
No one did anything to stop it.
I'm stumbling, ready to fall.

My windows have poor visibility
The roof leaking more as I stand on
People have left me to stand on my own
Abandoned, standing alone.

Michael A. McCray

My Hamsters

I used to have one hamster several months ago,
then all of a sudden the family began to grow.

I was up at my grandma and grandpa's farm,
and my hamster was doing just fine,
when two days later my mom called and said now there are nine.

I thought only nine hamsters, push, easy
only nine hamsters, stupid me.

You have to give them water, and food, and love,
and if you think that's easy, you're dumb.

Not to mention the cleaning of the cage,
that stinks even more than your age.

Then later on when the babies grew up,
they grew fatter and fatter, they were so plump.

They got so big there was no room in the cage,
so we gave seven of them away to a different place.

There you have it, and that is how,
we ended up with only two now.

Kristin Hayden

End Of The Beginning

The gripes and trivia's of my youth;
So bitter and deceiving.
Just when I thought I left the worst at bay,
I find that my sweetest days were behind me.

I look for myself inside of everyone else,
I conform to the ideas if individuality.
I want to love myself for who I am,
But I deny myself the possibility.

The things that attract me so much to myself
Sicken all those who love me.
I search the streets for a person just like me,
But deep down I know I'm alone.

So I lock myself up to live in the dark
And only my dreams are in color.

Estie Wartenberg

Spirits Of My Heart

I remember a time not long ago,
Where the Christmas of my youth is found,
A time when businesses flourished,
A place we called downtown.

The spirit of Christmas just glistened,
As the snow made a blanket of white,
The sights and the sounds of the season,
Came alive in downtown at night.

The echoing sound of crunching snow,
With each storefront came a surprise,
A toy, a Santa, a lighted tree,
A wonderland for the eyes.

Shoppers scurried from store to store,
Pure magic was in the air,
As they chanted a Merry Christmas,
In a place that's no longer there.

One by one they moved away,
Not just a few but all,
Christmas has left the city,
And is now hiding in the mall.

Sharon L. Good

Secrets

Our friendship has grown throughout the years,
We've seen each other through many smiles and tears.
I can not imagine life without you,
There isn't anything in the world I wouldn't do.
I know my mind is not easily read,
But for once just listen to what I've said.
You'd see that I'm not as complicated as you thought,
For I'm the one that needs to be sought.
I want to spend time with only you,
Because my love for you will always be true.
Oh how I wish you'd hold me tight,
And tell me that everything's going to be alright.
I may not express my feeling toward you all the time,
But how can I when I know you're not mine.
Our friendship means so much to me,
Maybe that's all our relationship will ever be.
I know my moods can change as often as seasons,
Although now you may understand some of my reasons.
I hope that we will always remain close,
Because you're the one I care about the most.

Kimberly Christine Glavin

Untitled

Subtle colors blend
Producing shades of brightness
Symphonies explode
Joy floods the dew-dropped plains
Light is shining and everything is new
I am a prisoner of this ecstasy
Then, darkness is spotted hiding in the weeds
Observing the joyful occasion
It slowly creeps in, matting down the greenery
The dew-dropped plains are replaced with dying
    wastelands
The symphonies are resolved to eerie-operatic
    tones
Brightness fades to shades of black and white
Joy is gone, but happiness still remains
As I dance around in my dreams
I shout to the deaf mountains
"I am free"

Jonathan Garrison

Why Daddy Why

Ever since the day I was born you have been my daddy -
One day you changed from out of the blue.
Why daddy why?
Now we are not all together anymore-
I can't understand why.
How can it be just you, why not us?
Why daddy why?
All you care about is your drinks and getting high -
Why daddy why?
Can you go back to the daddy I once knew -
Why daddy why do you do what you do?

Katie Palmer

My Guiding Light

When I was small, yet but a kid,
I used to watch what my father did.
He worked hard all day, but every night,
Had time for me, to each me right.
Now that I'm grown, and on my own,
I thank the Lord for my wonderful home.
There are so many blessings he gave to me,
It's hard to live up to his legacy.
But I'll keep on trying to make him proud,
And though I seldom say I Love You out loud,
I want him to know he means more to me,
Then anyone could possibly see.
He's my inspiration, my guiding light,
and when I go to bed tonight,
I'll pray some how my son will see,
His shining light, reflected through me.

Dennis Gongwer

Tenacious Of Life

The light shines
my shoulder feels its warmth
I am not afraid
there is light in darkness, the moon, the stars
heaven
afternoon showers
sprinkling tears
grieving losses
immortality comes with popularity
I traveled alone, the road was short
the water is now cool and crystal blue
always there is fruit and I am
happy, buried beneath this fig tree

J. Carol Reiner

Thoughts

Emotions are running through my brain.
Causing me heartache, misery and pain.
It's driving me crazy, but still I am sane.
Walking through the woods and I don't know my name.
Why do I feel so ashamed?
Hatred is taunting me.
Trying to find away to set me free
Chaos won't even let me be.
If you look through your heart, maybe then you will see
why your memory is haunting me.
My feelings will never leave me alone.
Why is the only way I can touch you is through a phone
But when I hang up, you always let me down
I always seem to walk away with a frown
Why is our love such a lonesome sound?
Why are my feet still stuck on the ground?
Why are you still no where around?

Brian L. Flechner

The Soothing Wind

Humph! Humph! Humph!
My mind is filled with frustrations of life.
I run out of my house, slamming the door.

Outside I find a wonderful autumn scenery.
Leaves with many colors falling gently and
A wind that feels just right.

The wind, like magic turns into a soft whisper.
She tells me things that I can't understand.
But, it cools me down.

I open up my mind, by staying still.
I lie down and look up to the bright sky.
I watch the leaves fall gently.

Then, again I can hear her whisper.
This time I can understand what she's saying.
She tells me that I should treasure life for I will only get one.

I head back home, listening to her songs.
I take her advice and it works perfectly.
I wait for her every day.

But one day I wait to thank her, but she never comes.
I think she went to soothe others.

Jason Lim

A Rose

Sometimes, when you look in a crowd,
there is a rose with thorns all around
It is the trials of life that hurt so much.
But the rose is on top and so
is God - with all of His love.
The "Rose" - with all its beauty tells us
we are loved.
The "Rose" can't describe - the love He
has for you - it's all inside.
So stand tall - we all love you and
be proud - you are our "Rose" in a
crowd - with thorns all around.
We stand behind you through thick and thin
and with His help, we will win again.
We need you, our "Rose" in a crowd - with thorns all around.

Mary B. Davis

Anger

Some time all I think of is elimination
Feeling like I'm a victim
In a white man's brain washed nation.
All my good thoughts go through a combination
Process of evacuation and frustration.
I take anger as my explanation.
Anger is like a mental irritation
Which makes me react with no consideration
Caused by frustration and a wicked imagination.

A good demonstration of how to send your anger
On a vacation is to put your mind in relaxation
And flow with good thoughts to meditation
And you will feel a good mental sensation.

Bryan Montas

Blessed Are Two Hearts

Blessed are two Hearts
who have overcome obstacles on the path of Love
And by the union of their wills
reflect each others dignity and inspire
each other with hope.
Each the Wing of a Celestial Bird
They together fly
Beyond all wordly summits
To view the Divine gateway
And enter realms
Of beauty
And Harmony.

Vern Zuehlsdorff

The Magic Of Peace

It spoke to me as I listened quietly
The calm became one within me
My eyes were opened with wonder
Inner sounds were like music to my ears
My body came alive as I pondered

What magic have I come upon?

Beating of my heart became a mellow rhythm
With gentle ease came each breath I took
Emotions took flight soft as feathered wings
My fingers touch was like my voice spoke
So sensitive was I to many things

What is this magic I have come upon?

No age does it call to one
Only a heart is the opening key
Mystery of my acceptance
Mind of a challenged chance
At a time I chose to be lucky

Given the magic of peace I came upon.

Linda J. Bowman

If...

If everyone could get along
If we could all sing one song
If everyone could see the light
Of peace, that shines so bright
If everyone could just hold hands
Smile at your fellow man
If everyone could put down their guns
Joins together and have fun
If everyone had just enough power
There would be no more bomb shower
These may be high hopes
But it's better than sitting around with the mopes

Christy L. Baker

(The President Of The United States Of America)
John F. Kennedy

The birds stopped singing and they even stopped chirping and everybody here on earth is silent. Praying for the one man who we all knew and loved so dear, but now he's departed from us our great President John F. Kennedy, a name that will always be

remembered and worshiped by us all and never will be forgotten

From this day on. President John F. Kennedy every one here on earth is crying for you together with your children, your wish of peace on earth shall soon be granted. As for Caroline and John the are growing up fast, but how they miss you. The white house is not the same any more without The President Of The United States, John F. Kennedy, now he's gone gone from this world forever, but one thing for sure he will always be remembered by us all. But how they miss you. The President.

Terry Xanthos

Reminiscene

I await tomorrows of yesterdays never again to be relived.
I dream splendid dreams that society seems to forbid.

By dawn, through treeless forests I ride.
By dusk, under starless skies I've cried.

I've been known to ride out the waves on a waterless sea
And gaze into mirrors that seldom reflect me.

I've stared into eternal suns that refuse to set and
Sit pondering past memories that are impossible to forget.

Each New Year more promises are made that I'm unable to keep.
Every Spring fresh seeds are sown that I'll never reap.

I walk through the valleys where the winds won't blow
And wander about fertile fields where crops fail to grow.

Jean Marie Cook

The Biggest Peak

I leave the house in early morning
with butterflies alive in my stomach.
Finally I reach the mountain,
the biggest peak I've ever seen.
The mountain looms high above,
and intimidation slaps me in the face.
I begin to climb,
and feel faith's undimming light.
I'm going to climb this mountain,
whether it takes me all day and all night.
Soon I reach the top,
and feel the hero's light
shining, just on me.

Perrin Ireland

Family Holiday

We sit and gaze with wonder
  into the eyes of each other
    and are amazed at all our changes.
Some have grown taller and some have not,
  some have learned and some have taught.
Those once quiet have found new voices
  and those loudest of all are paused.
We gather once a year to put changes aside
  and enjoy a strong sense of pride
    in knowing . . . we are different yet the same
    . . . we are family, we are one.

Jennifer L. Wilson

Arrowhead

A black chipped stone in an old man's pocket.
Gone the rotted bow and shaft.
Gone those happy red rock days
No more the little boy who found it.

A simple souvenir, plucked from 'neath a cedar bough
among decaying leaves and silt.
Remains of better days for red men
conjured in the farm boys brain.

Oh come again the water days
the boys tanned toes
caressed by warm red mud,
and lightning nights on the farm.

Come but once again the cornstalk candy,
and skinny dipping with friends in the swamp,
Innocence and mischief and crisp spicy cress
gathered from ditch banks, (home to elfin frogs).

Reluctantly —
the old man gives back
what was never his to keep.

LaMar R. Johnson

Waiting For Spring

As I sit here, looking out
at the wintry scene, all about
I can't help but feel it will never end
Nature is sleeping all across the Land.
Oh when will it be, I say
Can the children go back out and play
in the days warmed by the sun
playing and laughing and having fun.
But it is just a far away dream
with many more freezing nights, it seems.
Until one day when the silence breaks
And nature bursts out, all awakes.
Until then I have to be brave
and hibernate at home, like a bear in a cave.
Oh spring please be here soon,
so that the birds can sing a happier tune.
But I thank you Lord, and I pray
every day you create, will be a great day.

Margot Craven

Christmas Is

Christmas IS the time of year. Children smiles
and bring great cheer. Opening their gifts, and
to their surprise, bring bright glee to their
little eyes. Sing and dance around the tree,
Santa has come, "Oh Mommy, come see. He
brought Danny a red truck, Willie a blue sweater,
Jane a doll, and Mommy a leather. What
did Dad get, "Oh nothing at all." You can't
forget my daddy, "Oh no, Mr. Clause." As I
kept yelling to Santa, while he went dashing
through the sky, all I kept saying was Santa,
"You forgot my dad, why Santa why?..."
Santa looked down at me from the sky,
as I stood down below, and said, "Oh no,
my child I did not forget your Dad, ho, ho, ho."
What did Santa mean, as I wonder in doubt,
What did he mean, what was that all about.
I guess I'll never know, until
next Christmas comes around, when dear
old Santa comes back to town.

Beatrice Miller

Noisy Neighbors

When looking for housing, please head my words,
Apartment-stacked housing is best for the birds
Living downstairs is worse than you think
I'm often awoken by sound in a sink
By footsteps of elephants, slamming of doors,
My rent is no cheaper (and this I deplore)
Music seeps through my ceiling of paper
How can my neighbors commit such a caper?
It's hard to complain, though often I think,
The next time I hear a plate crash in their sink,
Upstairs I'll charge, earplugs in hand,
And this from my neighbors I will demand,
If they don't stop sounding like big, clumsy bears,
The management will find new tenants up stairs.

Marc Avery-DeWelt

The Sea

The sea is like an untamed animal
    with its wild roar,
And the sea gulls never cease to soar.
Or it is as calm as the blue sky
With fluffy white clouds floating by.
The sea is deep in mystery as its depths;
The sun's reflection on the water is like
    a gold coin,
And with its grey-green color it can easily
    tranquillize anyone.
The green seaweed sways with a soft rhythm,
While shells of many sizes, shapes, and colors
    are banked along the sandy shore.
The waves lap over the sand in a salty whisper
    of tears,
Which are as brilliant as diamonds under the break
    of a rosy dawn.

Kimberly P. Farrar

As We Stand On Higher Ground

As we stand on Higher Ground,
And listen to the trumpets sound.
We'll look for Jesus in the sky,
Prepared to go, prepared to fly.
To see the Lord sitting at His throne,
Happy to finally be at home.
We'll walk thru the heavenly city at last,
Pain and sorrow are a thing of the past.
We'll meet everyone and everyone
    we'll know,
Love and joy will be a steady flow.
These things we look for a can be found,
As we stand on Higher Ground.

Donna Farmer

Sunrise And Sunset

I look out my window and see the sunrise,
The golden sun against the bright blues skies;
The smell of dew and grass fill the air,
Oh how I wish it was like this all year!
Time goes by and dinner passed,
The sun is going down at last;
As the sun sets I close my eyes,
Waiting for tomorrows sunrise.

Amy L. Boulet

Proven True With Time

Times, seconds and hours have finally
Filled a wound I thought eternal.
Crying until I stopped.
A clock held me like a mother and
Child maternal.
Friends spoke to me of these mystic
Powers of time.
Rub bottles, tall mountains I would climb.
Undaunting the pain in midst of ruin.
Never healing is more convincing than time.
Poor heart feels not the future
Only the hurt it's doing.
Once the pain is lifted then you can see.
Feelings exposed.
Was true love or just passion for thee.
Tears begin again realizing which of the two.
Always will my heart hold her, my love was true.
I wish her everything.

David M. Lopez

Volunteer Closing The Library

Another quiet day. No children came.
I missed their whispered stir, the crackling noise
Of pages turned, the swish of corduroys
In kneeling to Adventure (not so tame),
The slow revolve of Mystery's creaking frame
Was not heard today — no mystery there! Boys
And girls would rather revel in the joys
Of out-of-doors! (On that we put the blame.)

Discouragement must fold, and like this flag
That's furled within my hands to wait behind
The door for yet another day, I drag
My useless feelings home — keeping in mind
Tomorrow's volunteer may justly brag
Of those enrolled, those she served, few she fined.

Rosalie S. Jennings

The Fire Next Time

So many says, "What in a kiss?"
But, that's where my passion lies deepest
Yearning and burning
Ready to unleash my flames
As I envision setting U all ablaze

But...
My heart belongs to another
My fidelity lies centered
In my mind's eye
Unyielding in my loneliness
Yes, non-existent in your presence

Our hearts have laid claim
to one another
Thereby engraving their designs
Cognizant of the danger
should these passions
materialize

So...with regret
I resign and, patiently await

The Fire Next Time

A. Craig Matthias

I've Been Adopted

As I amble along, down the pathway of life;
Not knowing which way I should turn.
Then I met Jesus, the light of my life.
And now I await his return.
He'll come from the portals of glory above.
To reach down and take me away;
Forever he'll keep me in Heaven above.
Nevermore from his presents to stray.
Jesus gave his life to save me one day;
His pure blood was shed on the cross.
He hung in suspension, between God and man.
But that was in our Father's plan.
I've been adopted, yes, adopted.
And filled with his infinite love.
I've been adopted, yes, I'm adopted,
I'm a child of the almighty God . . .

James W. Keeling

The Next Generation

Fight the fight that women have fought
Do what is right not what you ought.
Don't run away in disgust and defiance
Act on a cause, a future alliance.

Passion is powerful so do what you must
Being viewed as a misfit can also be righteous.
It may feel lonely but do not despair
Think of those to come who will be treated fair.

Persist for the children who have suffered so much
Insist on the right of a compassionate touch
What you choose to do now may heal an old wound
Its never too late, and never to soon.

To give of yourself is an unselfish act
And cannot predict how many you will impact.
The rewards are not yours though your courage is rare
Do more than just wish and follow your prayer.

Magda E. Valco

Lost Without You

I feel lost,
Lost without you.
I think of you everyday and night
How I want to hold you really tight
And make magic happen when you kissed
Me good - night.
How I love to have you back again in my arms
Like you did when we belonged.
How I feel about you is really true
But their's only memories of us together.
Like holding each other tight when it
Was cold out at night,
And how you starred at me like I
Was an angel in the light.
So when my heart goes out,
It's going to you
And that's a good thing
When I'm thinking of you

Heather Gouveia

School Days

School days are wonderful
I'm a special kind of ways
Work hard, study and learn new thing each day
I know these are the best days
for a body too strong to grow old
But yet in this life
I spend my time for something
More precious than gold

Sherry Mootee

My Sister

Today my sister is thirty-four
But my sister isn't here anymore
We grew up together just one year apart
And she'll always be so dear to my heart
We sang, we danced, we hugged and we played
We laughed, we cried, we hoped and we prayed
She was my sister, she was my friend
And I wanted her with me right to the end
Well the end came sooner for her then for me
I just don't understand how this came to be
Because my sister had a blood transfusion
My life is filled with such pain and confusion
I thought we'd have husbands and children and maids
But in the end all she had was Aids.

Maureen McDonnell

A Decade Together

A decade together, one third of my life
It means so much to be your wife

A decade together, a lifetime of love
The two of us fit like a glove

A decade together, we've been through so much
Yet I always seem to need your touch

A decade together, through pain and fear
I always feel better when you are near

A decade together, years come and go
That you still love me is all I need to know

A decade together, you're still the one
With you I seem to have so much fun

A decade together, you are always there
It doesn't matter what you do I'll always care

A decade together, I hope you'll always stay
To be my knight in shining armour and keep the ghosts at bay

A decade together, and this is just the start
We've grown into one being, we share one heart

Jeannette Oslejsek

Taunted

In the dreary depths,
depths of my blackened heart,
there lie bloody shards of glass.

The shards, once a window,
shroud my heart, this darkness, created by blood.

Shimmering, as it gently rolls,
drop by drop, cascading to the floor,
forming a magnificent pool.

The pool ripples with each drop,
as it enters, feeding it, making it grow.

The pool of life, of death,
it will never end,
as the pool grows it transforms,
into an enchanting being.

Temptress, what I wanted to be,
what I should of been, she is beautiful.

She shimmers and flows,
like the pool,
alluring, forbidden fruit,
she promises beauty in the form of death.

Angel Aleen Smith

The Sky

What do I see, way up aloft?
    Blue as ocean, with white that is soft.
        The wind blows the clouds, moving leaves as well,
            The clouds melt away as the sunlight fell.
Still I wonder about what I can see,
    So gigantic, much bigger than me.
        I stare in awe at this space,
            My mind begins to race.
This sight is quite beautiful, there is more than meets the eye,
    There is so much more beyond this wonderful sky.
        It is true, this is hard to describe,
            An object so plain yet so very wide.
The sky nags in the back of my head,
    Telling me things that can't be said.
        The sky may be silent, but it is very loud,
            To the person who feels, not listens for sounds.
You must listen with your heart, not with your ear,
    To the nature that surrounds us, year after year.
        Hearing those sounds is an everlasting prize,
            For those who can listen are considered very wise.

Timothy Ficklin

The Scribe

I sit on the banks of a still pond
Memories of you sting
like the prick of a thorn
from the most beautiful rose
I bleed and my heart sheds tears
The only tears prevalent to a heart
So from the rose I pick the most radiant petal
The softest most beautiful petal
By it's majesty I am hesitant to disturb it
And I would not
But there is none other to tell my story
I take the petal and absorb the tear of my heart
I then lay this adorned petal on the mirrored pond
And as I leave
I turn and take a last look
    a last breath
And there inscribed on the petal
    Is my story

Dale D. Singh

Seasons

Spring is life, begins anew;
Like a golden drop of dew.
Nature wakes from icy sleep;
To bear the fruits we care to reap.

Summer is heat that's hard to bear;
Lying around without a care.
Kids are out and they do play;
Dreading that first fall school day.

Fall is leaves so dark and gray;
Not like those you find in may.
We prepare for winters blight;
With pilgrim meals and one last fright.

Winter is wind that blows and blows;
Then it freezes and snows and snows.
Sometimes we like it and sometimes we don't;
But when we want it, it can't or it won't.

Seasons change like the life we live;
Never fully knowing, what it will give.

Jon M. Witt

Untitled

You were in my life,
Now you've gone away.
I should have said the things
I always wanted to say.
Should have said the things
You always needed to hear.
If I would have said these simple things,
You might still be here.
No more of my loneliness,
No more of my sorrow,
I'd keep thinking of you
I'd look forward to tomorrow.
But now I am alone,
No one seems to care.
I wake up so lonely,
It's almost too impossible to bare.
The memories keep me going,
They're all I have sometimes.
I've got to stop this thinking
This thinking you are mine.

Dan Kalmar

Heaven And Hell

His eyes are a glowing shade of red
Below this earth lies his fiery bed
His eyes look upon us with hope and love
His kingdom lies in the heavens above

The love of his life is to see the evil within
His passion comes from the committance of sin
He is expected to answer all of our prayers
Especially those in the pit of despair

With a cynical smile he paces down low
As one more evil soul is taken below
An angel from above descends down to earth
As it takes a soul with him to make room for a birth

There is a race against time to save the lost souls
Heavens or hell no one will know
The devil laughs as he walks amongst the hot coals
God shines his love down on them below

Kelli Thomas

Lonely

We met in spring's youth.
We wed in summer's heat.
We laughed and loved through many seasons,
yet we were lonely.

Our lives were fulfilled
one bright summer's day,
we adopted our daughter.
We laughed and played through many seasons.
We were lonely no more.

Your illness came,
our lives were changed.
We knew the end was near.
We laughed and loved through another season.
We were not lonely.

Then you were gone.
Two of us left
to laugh and love through the seasons,
and we are lonely.

Bobbie Halverson

Plants Of The Future

Water those plants I say,
For they are dying.

Panting for relief,
They are dying.

Withering,
And with little life.

Give them light,
Let the sun shine down on their souls.

Let their roots spread far and wide,
Through every countryside.

For if we let these plants die,
Then who shall carry on our future.

Equip them with the tools for success,
Tell them knowledge is the key to it.

But as of now they need water and sunshine;
But; they'll be fine.

Then they will rule the world.

Our children, our future, our generations, to come,
can someday bring the world together as one.

Sarad Davenport

Untitled

Words beyond definition, too often used without meaning,
Embodied by you!
There is magic in your being.
  Beauty
A man for a woman, and a woman for a man;
The man that you are...
I need to be woman that you choose.
  Always
Eternity in a moment
Yin and Yang
Powers of difference perfectly balanced:
  Harmony
Welcome into my body
(my Heart, my Soul)- -
A perfect song of creation, being, and completion,
  Ecstasy
Such indescrible joy in loving you
Equalled only by the bliss of being loved by you
Sweet, sweet lover.
  Happiness

Stephanie Lynne Gray

Irony

The war was long — never going to end.
The troops all starved, haggard and thin,
With leaders fattened and well,
Hoped and prayed for an end to this earthly hell.

The East had but one chance at avoiding loss,
And so a carrier bird to wing forth the cause.
The secret plans of battle, placed round the foot of the bird
Would bypass all spies; no secrets to be heard!

Meanwhile by the river among threes so bare
Huddle the sickened Eastern troops, their faces one morbid
stare.
Till one man with a musket, chanced to glanced overhead
And noticed a small pigeon - -oh, sacred bread!

So he placed the sights, without pause or waver,
Shot the bird his would soon savor.
And so it fell from the sky, the last hope of the East,
Sacrificed for a lowly yeoman's feast.

Ross French

"When Even My Grave Is Remembered No More"
- Jose Rizal

When our children of the living land toil
Let their plows and spades churn up the soil
Over my grave, till my ashes are borne
To the surface to rest, the earth to adorn
And bask in Your sun in an era of light
Of which were my dreams, for which was my life

Till a breeze comes along, in heed of my pray'r
I know 'tis Your breath, as I ride the air
Disperse me throughout, Scatter me wide!
To cover my Fatherland, my dream as I died.
Once again with my brothers, though known to no man
An eternal reward from my god, my Land

Then shall I be complete, only then to be whole
That my mortal remains be unwittingly sowed
By my brother's hands, born free and living free
And then to die free in land beloved redeemed
For then shall my soul from death be released
And reincarnated into lost Paradise retrieved

Roman Gonzalo L. Ranada

The Watermelon

Hot August days and ice cold watermelon go together.
I looked at it and (I swear) it winked and grinned back
Daring me to taste of its fruit.

Round, firm and fully ripe
(Like my stomach)
It was ready to be cut and opened
Its fruit released to be enjoyed
Its fertile seed to reseed...
(Like mine would).

Dad, Hubby, and Uncle sat on the porch
Waiting to sink their teeth into
the ice cold watermelon.
I wanted it, too.

I raised the knife to plunge it into the ice cold
watermelon, to plunge it into its sweet meat
But it bounced off my round, firm and fully ripe
belly; first one way, then another.

Frustrated, I cried; whelped with self-pity
Then groaned with sharp, low pain.
We named him Michael Martin.

Eva J. Koch

Subjectivity

Houses snaggletoothed along the roadway
  Show us promises of a welcomed warmth.
It's not as if we have to search them out;
  They're serendipitously spread around.
From each kitchen flue, spider webs ascend
  Into well-seasoned-washtub-colored skies.
Shafts of light from country kitchen windows
  Lay down their strips of golden apricot
Across November's early evening snow.
  What's the power behind these pseudosunbeams
That keeps the eye from turning back away?
  There are some things in an evening kitchen
That share the golden glow of lamps of oil.
  (This surpasses being busy-bodies;
Perhaps a search to fill nostalgic hearts).
  The sun-like kitchen light across the snow
Has built-in information like as that
  In any up-to-date computer chip.
Down the country road we make our way, and
  Programmed as we are we read the print-outs.

Leonard R. Lively

Fallen From Grace

I'm so tired of trying to impress girls
the same routine and the fancy talk
now I know I found the right girl
'cause you're good and kind and make me feel good
I see into your eyes, I see myself
you're so beautiful, darling
just by looking at you, I'm taking my chances
I'm so glad I held out for someone like you
Heaven must have send you, I know
I feel good when I'm next to you
I'd be such a fool, if I let you go
there's something about you
I can't live without
I've had fast talking so many woman
that with you I don't know what to say
so maybe you are my curse
for all the woman I hurt
because when I'm with you
I just don't know what to say.

Jose Medrano

Foolish Wife

I dug those things left in the ground—
  small beets, small carrots.
"Too small to store. Leave them," —
  so says my man.
Says I, "Too bad to waste." Later as I pass
  him with my brimming pan,
He shakes his head, and
  I'm sure he muttered, "That's foolish!"

Even so, I brush and scrub each tiny thing,
And stew from them a "foolish meal."
He dines content, as husbands should,
Looks up at me, and says, "That's good."

Lucy C. Pratt

The Three Simple Words

I love you in a special way,
It's not all about your looks,
But it's what you say.

You're always so sweet,
Though I don't know why,
When I'm feeling gray
You know just what to say,
To make me see
That now is not my time to die.

So I go on to live my next day,
Not because it's how I feel,
But because of what you say.

By now you know that when I'm blue,
You just whisper those three simple words; I love you.
They are so simple yet so strong,
I haven't heard them in so long.

Amanda Brousseau

Fears In My Tears

Fears-fears-fears are in my tears when I cry in my sleep I
think of my fears. When I'm in my room I start to think of my
fears like heights and bites. When I'm lighting flairs I
think of fears like burns from the fire of fears.
When I'm out, camping I think of my fears in my tears.

Ernest Thomas Shine

I Can Find My Dreams When I Desire

Oh no, I'm lost in the meadow!
There are blossomed flowers everywhere.
Where will I go? What will I do?
I know my ways, I will follow my heart.
The dreams I wanted, the future that I am waiting for.
Spring is the season that I yearned to seek!

Fall, what a beautiful place to be!
Leaves changing colors,
Lakes glistening in the sun with passion and pride.
Look at me! I found my way through, I am home at last.
I don't have to worry about where I will go and what I will do.
I already found my dreams and I am so close to my future.
Look at the different wonders that I had gotten to,
Look at what changed my life and how I put all my worries behind.
I adore Spring and Fall,
Because they are so passionate with adventure and excitement!

Jennifer Halat

Listen Up!

Busy people, tall houses, only birds soaring free,
What a modern, sophisticated sight to see!
Concrete sidewalks, gray grass, a twisted, gnarled tree,
Cars honking, people shouting, what a place to be!
Not much creation, no conservation at all,
No one can see the beautiful colors of fall.
Buildings and construction, no room for nature,
So many people, their faces a blur.
Where is the tranquility in this huge town?
No nature unspoilt wherever you look around.
Luxury and comfort is what you find,
Building, and building without future in mind.
When will we learn to preserve what we've got,
And not treat Earth as if it were bought?

Zeenat Hasan

Reflections

Who is this woman who stands before her?
The years gone by are just a blur
Forty plus years have come and gone.
She's done mostly right, but yet some wrong
Now she sighs she's satisfied.
She's done her best, she always tried.
She shrugs and wishes things were clearer,
For the woman who stands there is in the mirror.

Daniel M. Volden

Untitled

As I climb to reach my destination
In me you may find much determination
The snow covered mountain top is where I want to get
I know I can do this, my mind is set
The joyous singing of the birds can be heard throughout the air
The weather is a bit cool, mild, and fair
The powers of nature will let me go on my way
Hopefully no horrible forces will ruin the day
I am out of breath, my body aches
But I still know hope is what it takes
It starts to get dark, the wind starts to blow
I am a bit scared the temperature is low
Now I should worry, things don't look too clear
The horrible forces of nature are coming near
The heavy rain starts pouring from the sky
All I can do is run while I cry
My journey is over, I got to get down
The faster I go, the faster to town
The forces of nature were too strong for me
The fact that my task is incomplete is what will have to be

Cortney Schlosser

Goodbye..., Goodbye

Goodbye..., goodbye;
Those words I will never forget,
For God knew, and I knew, and he knew,
That would be our last goodbye.

I said words to fill the void,
The many miles created more helplessness,
To not be able to reach out and touch,
To end only with goodbye.

I sat alone that night,
It's memory will never fade,
It will never leave me,
For that was our goodbye.

The disease was taking him,
The foreboding in his voice told me so,
His pain that went beyond the body,
It was so clear in his goodbye.

Too few days passed before he left,
We stand around to console others,
While we writhe in our grief,
But he didn't leave without saying goodbye...goodbye.

Elizabeth M. Pillari

Reaching

Spending our lives,
Always in search of;
Looking towards the heavenly.

Dare we to grasp for the clouds,
The ethereal, the spiritual,
Our souls yearning for release —

Spending our lives,
Always in search of;
Knowing our bodies are rooted to this earth.

Dare we to dream, to leave this reality;
Scratching, crawling, stalling, falling,
The truth be known for what we are —

Spending eternity,
Always in search of;
His loving mercy and grace knowing no bounds.

Dare we to realize our Father,
Knowing since before the dawn,
Down to us He reached instead —

Benjamin Scott Jr.

Remembering Momma

Born only to scorned for being a product of a weak father
and an angry mother. Father weakened by the liquid that
contaminated and controlled his mind, body and soul. Liquid
that became a dictator. Dictating his violent actions and
soothing his corrupted soul.

Mother angry and scared runs for shelter and a new
beginning. This product pays the price, being forced to
wear here father's shoes because of her mother's memories
and inability to cope.

Although she resists, deprivation, echoes from the past and
the environment force her to seek freedom in a marriage.

Lack of knowledge and freedom, motherhood, fear and pain
coerced her to seek a way out. She escapes to the shoes her
father once wore. Shoes that became the death of her flesh.

Her products have a choice. Stand strong or become victims.

Marilyn Smith-Bahari

Cycle Of Life

Night so quiet, so dead
Children crying, longing to be fed
Towering trees stand dark against the sky
A heart turns to stone, someone dies
Clouds floating past the radiant moon
A soldier is praying the war will end soon
Soft breeze blowing a sweet morning scent
Countless minds twisted and bent
White picket fence, swinging gate
People living in fear and hate
Endless fields of wheat and corn
The miracle of birth, a baby is born
Crickets chirping at a low rhythmed tone
Someone is lost left alone
The night is fading, soon will come the dawn
But the Cycle Of Life goes on, on and on

Michael Dinunzio

A Far Better Place

There comes a time in our lives when we
Lose someone dear;
For each one we lose, we shed some tears.

But, the angles waiting upon the wing,
Raise their voices and sing, sing, sing.

So, when you lose someone you love;
Look up to the heavens so high above.

Envision the smile on your loved ones face,
And you'll have no doubt, their in a far better place.

Gone to heaven, yet still in our hearts;
Remember this and your healing can start.

We cry cause we miss them; but we mustn't be sad;
For this is the best day they've ever had!

Susan M. Martinez

Disconnected Telephone Lines

Mother, hearing from you is like
   you hearing my first words.

Knowing you are there feels like the
   armed force protecting me from evil

Not having seen you for so long makes
   it seems as though the telephone lines
   were down all over the world

Now, the longing to see you makes
   the day seems like eternity and
   the nights like the breeze from the wind.

Jennifer Trent

The Call Of A Little Girl

She screamed and cried,
And then she died,
Nobody answered her scared voice,
Some people didn't have a choice,
Now when they look at her they just glance,
They say she didn't have a chance,
Now people look back and say why oh why,
Why didn't I answer her cry,
We all regret what we didn't do now,
We look at her grave and take a bow

Jennifer Snow

Seasons

Seasons are like the birth of a child
A new beginning, a gentle breeze, a loving smile

The birds that sing, the flowers that bloom
Winter has passed, summer is soon

Seasons pass quickly, before our eyes
were getting older, to fast to realize

Seasons are like life, a beginning and an end
life is so fragile, so little time to spend

Fall will be soon, leaves fading away,
the cool breeze on your face tending to stay

Pumpkins and turkey this season brings
family's and hearts together to sing

Seasons are short as winter nears,
A sign of death, or so it appears

Trees with no leaves, grass covered with snow
beautiful flowers, were does it all go?

It will be back as seasons come again,
seasons are lucky, Life just ends.

Robin Pulver

Melodic Relief

Breathing . . . closing my eyes and falling back
On a pillow of cottony melodies.
Fingers dancing, pressing lightly as the music flutters.
Fingers striking, loudly pressing out lightning and screams.
Out the tips a stream of freed grief flows,
And through flying arms excitement is transferred
To the black-and-white world of drugless highs,
And troubleless nonsense noise.
An earful of pitches and tones is only deafness.
A body full of music is believing, seeing, fleeing.
Swimming through the thickness of the song . . . an underwater
World of Color and Brightness.
Closing my eyes, I can see so much.
As my heart belongs to the water, my hands
belong to the keys.

Sarah A. Wood

Dark Places

it's cool and quiet here and you're all alone
stay very still; don't move around
you're safe
no one can touch you in your dark place

dark places deep in your soul
safe places no one else goes

someone's knocking, you let them in, you say
"stay very still; don't move around"
it's not safe
someone's touching you in your dark place

dark places deep in your soul
safe places no one else goes

banging into things unknown; now you're not alone
no one's still; you move around
no longer safe
bruising yourself in your dark place

dark places deep in your soul
safe places no one else goes

Kathryn Dianne Jackson

My Promise

I promise to give you the best of myself,
   And ask of you no more than you can give
I promise to respect you as your own person,
   And realize your interest, desires, and needs.
No less important then my own.

I promise to share my love, my time, and my attention
   to bring joy, strength, and imagination to our
relationship.

I promise to keep myself open to you,
   Allowing you to view my world,
Of innermost fears, feeling, secrets, and dreams

I promise to grow along with you,
   to face changes as we both change,
in order to keep our relationship alive.

I promise to love you in good times and bad,
   with all I've to give.
Completely and forever.
     David L. Weist

Why

Why do I feel so lonely tonight.
   Why does my heart always get broken.
    Why do I put my trust in someone
     And always get hurt.

   Why, why, why!!!

Why do I get depressed over it.
   Why do people treat me like garbage.
    Why does it always hurt when someone leaves.

   Tell me why, why, why!!!

Why do I love, care, and feel so much.
   Why do I make love on a bed of roses.
    Why does it always hurt.
Just tell me why...
     Shawn C. Greene

Song Of Lamentation For The Earth

Today I stood upon my grave,
Fear assailed me, wave on wave.
There were no clouds or sun on high,
I could not even see the sky.

The warm earth felt snug around my feet,
"I love you earth," I cried. My echo did repeat.

I stood all day, and all night long,
No moon or stars or cool wind song,
And when there should have been a dawn,
It did not come, it just was gone.

The cold earth felt snug around my feet,
"I love you earth", I cried. My echo did repeat.

Today I lie inside my grave,
No fear assails me, wave by wave,
I cannot see clouds or sun on high,
I cannot even see the sky.

I am the snug earth around all feet,
"I love you earth", I cannot cry. No echo can repeat.
     Ethel G. Bauer

Among The Warmth

Among the warmth nestled between
   Pine and moonlight.
A warm glow beacons its call
A togetherness of one becomes quiet,
   as the midnight soars.

Among the warmth, a fire stone grey turns
   To crimson red.
We huddle together like sheep with eyes
   a fixed on the dancing serenade.
The colors amber and gold capture
   a soft parade while shadows chant
   songs of long ago.

Among the warmth, life becomes clear
Where there is love
The circle embraces and inner hearts grow near.

Inside, the warmth warms the heart and soul
Outside the body and mind
The warmth is a gift of God
A presence to be shared for all mankind.
     James La Manna

Lost In The Woods

Lost in the woods, in the darkness of night,
With a candle to light my way.
My vision is limited to the length of my nose,
Yet I can almost hear you say,
"I am with you, Miley, unto the end."
"I will guide you all of the way."
I know not who He is, or from where He comes,
But I can clearly hear Him say,
"Have faith in me and you will find,
A solution to your dismay."
I follow, He leads, to the clearing of the trees,
And I lean towards Him and say,
"I believe in you and all that you are."
"Dear, God, you have shown me the way."
"I will follow you down the narrow path."
"Dear Lord,...I have been saved!"
     Jonette A. Holtz

Dance with the Dolphins

I wake early to see the sun rise
I see the dolphins jumping in the bay
As the early morning sun hits the water
It looks like gold
As I watch the dolphins play
I suddenly desire to swim with them
I row silently in the clear blue water
Not wanting to disturb them
As I slip quietly in to the water
I am greeted by a dolphin
I have come to know as zues
As I swim along side them
I feel their silky smooth skin
Under my finger tips
As I look up at the sun
I see it starting to set
As I sit on the beach watching the sunset
I see the dolphins jumping in the bay
As the late sun hits the water
It looks like gold
     Sierra R. Cagle

A Light Way Of Looking

I look at you cause I like your style and I smile
Way out wide open you drive me wild.
Thinking of old times and you I begin to miss
Come closer with open arms and a southernly kiss.
The way I feel is like an old tradition
Memories of you and me and I start reminiscing
You send me for a loop you leave me twisted
Making my hot summer nights just right and real misty
In the night there's a light shinning very bright.
And with that light I for once see something that I like.
I'm so serious hot dam you've got the look.
Now I want to study your body slowly like a very long book.
I look at you first with a glare then long with a stare
What I see you've got I want and nothing compares

Howard Randolph

Grey Flowers

Through a bouquet of grey flowers
An elusive nymph studies me.
Though the flowers are deeds of mine,
Whether thought or action.
Called opinions and other ganglies,
In truth they are of me.

Dear Nymph your perception is unfailing.
I'll not hide from you again. Knowing of me as you do,
Peering through my shell, and seeing what you will.
Though the quick denial, that the flowers are of me.
How can I misled you, when you are central to my dream.

So in view of truths you know of me,
You essence remaining still.
To touch and speak to me, through my very soul.

To even know that you exist, if only in my dreams.
Gives me joy I'd not thought to be.
And never knew was there.

So I thank you little Nymph.
for the pleasure of your being.
The knowledge of your existence smiles upon my heart.

John Joseph Anulies

Follow Your Dreams

Life isn't what's on the surface,
or the things that one can see,
It's more greater than that,
for someone passing through like me.

We all have dreams in our hearts
that we someday want to achieve.
All we need is faith
and with that one must believe.

That dreams can become a reality,
with the right foundation,
Everything perfected by "Him",
who in which made all creations.

If you build upon a "Rock",
your dream will stand,
not like the fool who built his house out on the sand.

So, follow your dreams wherever they may lead,
with God as Rock and Foundation of your life,
you are destined to succeed.

Vickie L. Barrett

Heaven's Child:
An Ode To The Children Of Bosnia

Bullets
blanket the globe
with blood stained sheets
as salty tears
trace lines of war
down her face
on their journey
toward the lifeless body
lying at her feet

The mother
of heaven's child
no longer weeps

But her soul cries out to the child
who can no longer hear...
genocide - like Satan
must never be revered...
lest the world become an orphanage
filled to capacity with heaven's children
and their never ending tears

Richard J. Martinez

Dove

Jah children trust positivity
   cause this reality of mystery
      iniquity, hypocrisy, is a liar
         and I know soon come the fire

      until then we grind down babylon
     stumbling blocks with independent
  thought energy: we shall overcome
at this precariously balanced moment

          truth is
            anathema to
            oppression

so this is the emanation of Iyah
    Qi energy manifesting through Jah
      cause who feels it knows it Lord
        health and wealth unknown before

      a mastery over the mysterious and thus
    the unity necessary to resist the chicanery
  taught us in babylon; beginning to exodus
a valley of decision into a reality of fertility

Christopher Johnson

After Work

The sacred love, that we feel at the end of the day.
That once was a working man's lust,
or do I know? I pray.
What I feel towards you, is what
drove me to work every day.
to see you, to be with you.

There is nothing wrong with this feeling,
there is nothing wrong with wanting you,
there is something with my feelings...
even though I am not an Epicurean as you are,
wanting to get to know you expands my mind.
I search for hopes and dreams that will make
this existence for that happiness, which you are.

Do I want you forever?
I don't know, but I want to spend some time naturally
together as we grow.

There is something about you,
as though our steps seem to rhyme?
That makes me want to, get to,
know you for the rest of time.

Michelle A. Depew

What Do You Do?

What can you say, when it's all been said?
How can you keep going, when there's nothing ahead?
How can you see, when you're out of the light?
But when you step in, it's much too bright.
What can you do, all alone with fear?
Why should you smile, when it's really a tear?
What's the point of a dream, when it's already come true?
But once you're at the end, what is there to do?
Do you just say goodbye, and wave it all away?
Or do you go to sleep, and pray for yesterday?

Kodi Klein

Photo Album

Soon I shall be; but, a shadow in your memory;
My face remaining ageless to time;
Captured in photos of memories;
An never ending smile endures;
Eyes glossy with that moments life;
Never to pass all life shall.

Carrying secrets of ancestry; names;
Lost in caverns of minds;
Never again to be reclaimed;
But in the silence of your days,
Dreams of your nights;
Passed on through tales from a moments memory,
I shall live as a shadow eternally!

Katherine Johnson

Untitled

It's raining again today
I should be happy, no way!
The tumbling noises from the drain pipes
Singing a song so sad, "Be glad" says my mother.
She starts counting: "It's good for the crops."
What a pity
We live in the city.
"Rain is G-d's way to
Wash the world"
"Turn on the sun" says me.
"Then it's outdoors I'll be"
I mope and give up hope
The rain's song's too long.
Blip. Quash. Drip. Mosh...
Dull. Dumb. Rain.
Will it stop
Before we float away?

Thelma Ribnik

A Reunion Journey

Over the mountains and through the snow -
Luggage and bags and boxes with bows.
In a truck, a van and a 4-runner we have been -
Men, women, and children who number ten!
An Ol' fashioned Christmas we did seek -
A family brought together one wonderful week!
A beautiful chalet for our vacation sojourn -
A blessed child was born this Christmas morn!
So many "thanks" to our wonderful hosts -
With our cups full of joy, we raise a toast!

Kathryn Anne McGuire

Don't Look At Me

Lovely Eyes, don't look languidly at me!
You are playing a dangerous game
Which can release a very hot flame,
And cause great damage in burning fury.

You know that you are terribly seductive,
That you won't stay unnoticed to me.
Day after day I think of you with ecstasy;
Your image makes my lessons less effective.

It's thrilling to be attracted to each other
By dreams and fear of some unavowed desire.
But love, when not allowed, will spread like a fire;
It will burn up whoever dares to come closer.

And I'll be blamed for the frightful indignity
Of misconduct in an erratic love affair.
A true teacher can't breathe the fragrant air
Of genuine feelings, because he is not free.

So, let's have a truce, and work faithfully
To enhance the learning for your advancement.
Our talk must be class-centered and innocent,
And from now on please, don't look languidly at me!

Theodore Tran

The Howl

Glitters in the moonlight,
as he howls up to the moon
in the dead of the night.
He looks up to the sky,
with pain on his face.
The artist who sculpted the howl
had to kill the Howl
with his own bare hands
that lone moonlit night
with the Howl howling at the moon.
He howls up to the moon
with years behind him being hunted by man.
That one 'lone moonlit night
When the artist was watching him
he knew something would happen.
He was waiting quietly
that one love moonlit night.

Sarah Sellers

Every Mother's Son

After your day's work is done
Do you ever think of some mother's son
Who may be lonely, sad or blue
Just yearning for some word from you
So, just take a few minutes that's not long
And fill some lad's heart with song
It's all so simple if you really care
To see that each youngsters get's his share
Perhaps he can't tell you, for now he's a man
And so can't cry like his sister can
Perhaps tomorrow he may go
Out to battle, and meet the foe
He doesn't care if he has to die
Because he loves you, yes that's why
So sit right down and drop him a line
For it may still reach him in time
You may not know, but he takes it hard
When he doesn't even get a card
So let's get together each and every one
And write a letter to every mother's son

John Muth

Our Dad

We love you dad, so much,
But your so busy with your life and such.

You never rest, you seldom play,
It makes us sad, but it's your way.

We look up to you dad, and respect what you do,
But we wish you could share with us, some of you.

But you work so hard, and we never see you smile,
We'd like to spend some time, and talk with you a while.

You are known by many, and respected too,
You've accomplished so much, we are proud of you.

We never wanted for anything, we had it all,
You were there to pick us up, whenever we would fall.

You're at the top of the list, above all the rest.
You are our dad, and you're the best.

We wrote this poem, just for you,
We wanted to let you know, how much we love you, too.

Linda McCann

The Prism

Within the infinite prism
endless and unbounded,
Dispersing light mentally and spiritually
Life begins in transparent form.

Where a man should be equivalent
adequate in power and degree
ability of knowledge
created are we equal.

Manifested by metabolism
adapting to environment
The mind becomes separated
as water diverts into streams

Consumption of wisdom journey's endlessly
and life ends in transparent form
dispersing light in the spiritual sense
within the infinite prism.

Jenene Worrell

The Winter Of My Life

I longed for the day when I would be free,
My last child grown and away.
For years I dreamed of how it would be,
Of how I would become settled and gray.

No longer having to need a man in my life,
Able to be on my own, comfortable and warm.
Capable of handling life and strife,
And keeping myself safe from all harm.

As I grew older, I knew it was true,
No doubt was in my mind at all,
I let everyone know it was what I wanted to do,
There would be no man for whom I would fall.

But alas, my plans did go astray.
A man in my life, how could it be!
But he came, and is here to stay;
And heavens, he is so much younger than me.

As I enter the Winter of my life,
A man in the Spring of his years,
Has taken me for his wedded wife,
And has calmed all my hidden fears.

Mary Randolph

The Dawn Of The End

We make love with our eyes,
Contact lasting only long enough to crave more.
The temptation of a future and a past,
Present themselves before us.
With the beginning, the end will not be long,
Before we are one, no longer apart.
Finally, together, stronger than the whole
The world will become only us.

We link our souls,
Fitted together,
Intertwined.
The piece of the puzzle we are both missing,
Redeemed and finally fulfilled.
The end of two,
But infinitely stronger as one.
The dawn of the end of life apart.

Phillip Absolom Harris Jr.

Life Flower

Life is just a budding flower
Yet when it rains we never enjoy the shower
Starting our life as a small budding seed
We always want to and have some unimportant need
next in line is a stem and a petal
that's when our heart turns into some kind of metal
now we become a full blossomed flower
Yet we still can't see over our own built in tower
Last but not least we wither away
Then we start praying for just one more day
think about what you have just read
Put love in your heart and smarts in your head

John R. Bobik

What Is A Friend?

A friend is a person who is always there.
Time, place, or anywhere.
A friend can be a girl or a boy.
Who come to you in greatest sorrow, or in greatest joy.
A friend can be young, or even very old.
A friend can be weak not always bold.
Friends tell the truth and have nothing to hide.
Friends care about who you are inside.
My best friend are like family to me.
Friends are very special people as you can see.

Cassandra Lopez

Another Day

God made another morning,
When I got out of bed,
I could here the birds sing,
The babies waiting to be fed!

God made another afternoon,
The sun wasn't as bright,
I could tell the evening was coming soon,
The sun was a beautiful sight!

God made another night,
Up in the sky the large north star,
I was blinded by the beautiful light,
From which the wise men traveled afar!

God made another day,
And it went real good,
So it went his way,
Like he knew it would!

Sara Marie Scott

Rainbow

Brother do you believe in Rainbows
Do you believe in dreams, in love
   and togetherness — do you believe in tomorrow?

Brother do you believe in colors
   in the rays of the rainbow
Brother do you believe?

Brother share your faith with me,
   help me to see the colors
   of the rainbow thru your eyes.

Help me believe in a better tomorrow
There is so much need for serenity,
   for peace in our homes all over the world.
A need for togetherness — so that all people
Will carry in their hearts the rays of the Rainbow.

Brother put back in our soul
   the blessing of God.
Share with us the rays of the
   Rainbow.
     Schelika VonBernuth

Connection

Man,
WoMan,
ManKind . . . Kin.
See a connection?
RacISm, DIScrimination, DogmatISm,
Is leading us in one direction . . .
In the destruction of,
Man
WoMan,
ManKind
Kin
An Armageddon, that can only have one end.
Educate, appreciate, tolerate the difference and the beauty.
For inside of you, there is a little piece of me.
We share in one another,
Multifarious is the word . . .when I call you brother . . .
Man
WoMan
ManKind
Kin . . . see the connection?
    LueWana Bankston

Mother's Day

What kind of mother are you?
I have something to ask,
I have something to tell;
I hope the good things,
relate to your trail.
What kind of mother are you?
A mother is one who, cares for her children;
In sickness and in health.
A Mother is one who
helps her children;
In the time of trouble,
even when we don't deserve it.
What kind of mother are you?
Are you a mother who,
comforts her children when crying?
Are you a mother who,
protects her children;
from all danger and harm?
Do you have that motherly love?
What kind of mother are you?
    Tangelior Thomas

Excepts From The Upturned Glass

Once, within this with'ring wilderness astray,
I found a hermit's cave and begged to stay.
But from its haunted depths a voice replied:
Not thou! I am thy dream of yesterday...

Old mosques and towers of another day
Loom cracked and crumbling o'er the narrowed way;
Then suddenly a thunderbolt descends
And clears illusion's rubble all away...

The sages knew the wisdom of our faiths
From Babylon and Ur to Samothrace.
Where speech was stilled, and heart and soul were one,
A thousand Gods but wore a single face....

The hills of ages mark the paths we trod
In futile quest of why we sweat and plod;
But now and then we reach a crest and see
The course of time that changes clod to God....

The truth, my friend, is very much like wine.
The taste of yours is different than mine.
But make and vintage cannot change the fact
That both are from the same Eternal Vine...

    Stuart James Byrne

Amity

Shh, listen...patience is near
Hush, quiet...the sound so tranquil

Wait, calm...they now have meshed
Stop, feel...they soul is refreshed

Hush, speak...release forth your tears
Shh, pray...for he lends an ear

Stop, write...let your mind begin talking
Wait, freedom...let your spirit begin walking

Smile, win...the kindness of others
Reach out, give...to all kindred brothers

Breathe, deep...the thoughts of your life
Release, exhale...your pain and your strife

Reach out, hold...for moments on through
Smile, happiness... Feel enveloping you

Release, unleash...the anger apart
Breathe, love...inwrapped in your heart
    Shannon Kabeary

One

Eyes that shimmer like emeralds
A smile that could brighten the darkest day
A voice as sweet as a bird's morning song
A heart that is kind and giving
From the moment I saw her
I knew she was the one.
Tick... Tick...
A year has passed and the world is seen in a different light.
The once ever present butterflies are gone
Security and comfort now remain.
These new feelings are rooted in love,
A love that grows stronger and stronger everyday.
It stands like a mountain
Stable and Sturdy through the test of time.
The clock still ticks,
Yet one has visions of it stopping.
Fear, anxiety, anger wonder of what the future holds
One knows not what to expect,
Though, with love in our hearts
we will remain
   One.
    Jeremiah P. O'Donovan

Oh Lady, Oh Dear, Oh Love

Oh lady, oh dear, oh love,
Cry, pray Proteus, tell me of my sweet.
To where have these ocean waves carried my dove?

I advised you, lady, to stay within our cove,
But down the door you beat,
Oh lady, oh dear, oh love.

Mast swayed from ten to two or a quarter of,
Even the captain and sailors did retreat.
To where have these ocean waves carried my dove?

I screamed, I howled, looking to God above;
The ship did thrust you off your seat,
Oh lady, oh dear, oh love.

I extended but your body I could not move,
Your body, my soul, and the sea did meet.
To where have these ocean waves carried my dove?

I trust these waves will bear me to my dove.
Where is Triton, I urge we meet!
Oh lady, oh dear, oh love,
To where have these ocean waves carried my dove?

Kimberly McElhatten

Blue Stars And Red Balloons

Feelings saunter, dancing on the fingertips of flames,
An emotional jaunt throughout the dark and twisted clouds.
The closeness desired only pushes them further away,
Leaving conflicting temptations, a dance all alone.

The last tango under the pale blue star
Ignites and incites a whirlwind of passion,
Bubbling over into a pink champagne fountain
Tickling the pearly insides of our lost souls.

Laughing, the interpretation of the dreams of fools
Reveals a lighter side to everyone's downfall:
An upside that fills the red balloon with spirit,
Only to burst over the drunken night.

Then her confetti smile brightens the room like a lantern
Sprinkled from the roof top of the universe,
Teeming and gleaming, sparkling an inner glow
And covering the ground in a warm blanket of love.

Blaine Hummel

Logic Of A Carousel

Times as we know is like a piece of gold,
And only for a moment we want to behold.

In the distance we hear the ticking of a
Clock, yet when will the door be retired and
Locked.

We've been given the choice to execute our
dreams, but if we're not careful we'll clip
Our wings.

Tediously we move like a second hand, yet in
The dark we probe for a more stable land.

And in the struggle for a day, unnerved we
Falter, kneel, and pray.

As we travel down the winding road, we're
Finding out time is an eternity we want to
Behold.

Lisa Thomas

Viet Nam

He had this body, and I thought it was beautiful.
He was my boyfriend, and he was true to me.
I knew this through his honesty,
for this is what he said:
"I want only to be with you, for no one else will do.
In my mind, and through all my heart,
I cared for you from the start. See in my eyes the
devotion for you. You must believe me, for these
feelings are true".
So I gave him a chance; he gave me romance.

Day by day, months gone by,
through the years, he stayed at my side.
One cool night, under the stars we sat on the
grass, by the sea that was calm.

Then one day, he went away.

Now for many years I have wept many tears,
for he was shot in Viet Nam.

Kelly Jean Herron

Another Day

God made another morning,
When I got out of bed,
I could here the birds sing,
The babies waiting to be fed!

God made another afternoon,
The sun wasn't as bright,
I could tell the evening was coming soon,
The sun was a beautiful sight!

God made another night,
Up in the sky the large north star,
I was blinded by the beautiful light,
From which the wise men traveled afar!

God made another day,
And it went real good,
So it went his way,
Like he knew it would!

Sara Marie Scott

The Winter Of My Life

I longed for the day when I would be free,
My last child grown and away.
For years I dreamed of how it would be,
Of how I would become settled and gray.

No longer having to need a man in my life,
Able to be on my own, comfortable and warm.
Capable of handling life and strife,
And keeping myself safe from all harm.

As I grew older, I knew it was true,
No doubt was in my mind at all,
I let everyone know it was what I wanted to do,
There would be no man for whom I would fall.

But alas, my plans did go astray.
A man in my life, how could it be!
But he came, and is here to stay;
And heavens, he is so much younger than me.

As I enter the Winter of my life,
A man in the Spring of his years,
Has taken me for his wedded wife,
And has calmed all my hidden fears.

Mary Randolph

Seductive Death

Seductive eyes bring her in,
knowing she hasn't the idea of death.
She hopes to find love to begin,
But she doesn't understand she has all but the best.

Among the hot night's steamy mist,
She sees him standing, waiting there.
She stands scared with a clenched fist,
In the wind is blowing her beautiful hair.

Softly she walks over to him,
She doesn't even see what is really there.
He rubs her face, so sleek and trim,
Then she screams in pain as her skin begins to tear.

A soul who thought that she had found,
Lonely and hurt, she sought out love.
If she only knew her ties had been bound,
But now she is free - free as a dove.

Paul Black

Cosmetic Brain Surgery

Should I put concealer on my mind,
then foundation?
Should I put powder on my mind after that?
Should I put some eye shadow on my mind,
then eye liner?
Should I put mascara on my mind after that?
Did I forget to put blush on my mind?
Did I forget to put eye brow pencil on my mind?
Should I put lip loss, lip liner, and lipstick
on my mind?
What about color and kind?

I'm not really sure at this
moment in time.
Maybe I should make-up my mind.

Ryan Reyes

I Wonder

Life to me can be good or bad
But lately I've felt sad.
I wonder if my marriage will survive
But I thank God to be glad I'm alive
I have my family but alone I am still
I wonder what it is I need to fulfill.
You get out of life what you put in.
That's probably why I've felt like I been.
What I have done was lost sight of myself.
I put all my needs up on a shelf.
I have to depend on myself as a friend.
I wonder how my life would be then.
It's me that will help my self-esteem
Rise.
It's me that will change from grey
to blue skies.

Monica R. Gramby

Courage

I look for courage in me and you
and all I see defeat.
Then I look inside of me and
see hate that has no need.
But you share the love that's
Inside of you and that's all the courage I need.
To have a life of you and me and the
courage conquers the defeat.

Teresa Conaci

Our Promise

To you, a promise, a simple word
this day I make to you.
To be support, your Pillar of Strength,
for life, in all you do.

To Me, I promise, I'll always hold
our vows in high regard
To cherish you, and stay your friend
through easy times and hard.

To Us, we promise to always stay
as one in harmony.
From dusk 'til dawn, our whole lives long,
we'll keep "us" company.

To Everyone, who shares this day,
A promise is what we give.
To love and honor one another
As long as we both shall live.

Robert J. Blair

Grandpa

I see an old man,
Laughing and joking.
Each wrinkle tells his past,
The lessons he has learned.

This man, my grandpa,
Tells the tales that has made him great.
His eyes twinkled when he sung me a song.
When I hear his voice, I hear love.

This man, my grandpa,
Has shared his life with me,
Which made each moment a memory forever.
His wise words touch my soul, makes me see,
That the good begins in the mind,
And love begins in the heart.

This Great man, my grandpa, my hero,
Has made the impact in my life,
And has filled my heart
With peace and love.

Cynthia Grace Golightly

The One I Want

The one I want doesn't know I'm alive,
but I often dream of being by his side.

I know he probably has a girl,
and I wish I could replace her.

I haven't told him how I feel,
and don't know if I ever will.

My friends know how much I care,
but they will never tell — they wouldn't dare!

He has the most gorgeous green eyes,
and he's not quite like the other guys.

He knows how to draw me near
just by being a little sincere.

Yet he can always get to me,
and make me feel like a bird — free.

I can't believe life can be so cruel
as to not let me have the one I want — you!

Marsha Dean

Winter

Snow and ice,
Is very nice.
Children of all ages play,
All through the day.
Building a snowman,
Who's name is Fran.
Trying to shovel
A large, white bubble.
Having lots of fun,
Making homemade cinnamon buns.
All people young and old,
Go out in the cold.
But there is nothing like a nice hot drink,
To give someone's face a smile and make their eyes wink.
Snow and ice
Oh, it's so very, very nice!

Daniel Groth

The Locker

I don't understand.
"What don't you understand?"
You're probably wandering.
Come close; I'll tell you.
I get slammed each day.
Then locked up.
Sometimes even kicked.
"Why?" you ask. Isn't that what you would have said?!
Huh, I knew it.
Don't you get it?
These "kids" abuse me! Yes, your darling little angel.
I get jerked open, stuffed full, slammed shut,
and then I hear that dreadful dial!
Now, what I am about to say may
not be suitable for immature audiences.
This is to all you dreaded teenagers. I read your notes,
tell all your secrets, steal your homework, and Ha!!!
that sweet ol' innocent dog gets the blame!
And I just sit back and laugh!
    For I... I Am The Ultimate Locker.

Annette M. Bellerud

Tears

I go to my room and slam the door
My tears fall, unnoticed on the floor.
Where is the balance of my life
When someone has in my back a knife?
The hurt spills out to unopened ears
This confirms my deepest fears.
No one cares, I'm all alone
No one listens when I moan.
I plaster a smile on my face
And hope no one will see the trace
Of anguish that rips through my heart
I begin again and make another start.
As days drag on, my sorrow appears
But who will wipe away the tears?
All of those friends that said, "I'm here,"
Are now the ones who mock and jeer.
They don't have problems, their lives are great
But part of my load they'll never take.
So now I sit in my room surrounded by fears
Knowing no one noticed my hidden tears.

Christy Haven

Wonder

A slice of bread I do behold,
it's soft, and fresh, and square.
It's yellow, like a piece of gold,
it's small, but it's all there . . .

And every particle of it,
and every nook and cranny,
reminds me of the baking wit
of my beloved granny.

She mixed the flour with the milk,
and made the magic dough;
The dough came out as smooth as silk,
I don't know how she did it, though . . .

O, bread, thou will not stay here long,
but you've deserved this little song.

Gregory Razran

Goodbye For Now...

Thank you, my darling daughter, for being there for me.

When the days and nights were long and hard you
were there to comfort me.

I never told you thank you. But, please understand why.
Even though I was there, my mind had already said good-bye.

Thank you, my darling daughter, for being there on that night.
When the Lord came to me and said, "it's time to say goodbye".

I knew that it was your loving hands holding my tired head.
And that your loving husband was standing by my bed.

Cry no more, my daughter. For I look at you and smile.
Heaven is such a peaceful place. I think I'll stay a while.

I'll be waiting patiently, not only just to see. But to
touch your beautiful smile and know the Lord brought
you to me.

Lori Camp

The New Coat

One day late fall, a girl like a doll,
Decided her old coat didn't fit her.
The first snow was nearing, and she thought it endearing,
To be warm when the weather turned bitter.

She'd save up her money, and though it was funny,
A new coat was all that she longed for.
When she put on her old one, clouds replaced noon sun,
And an icy blast met her at the door.

The girl headed down to the nice part of town,
Seeing what all the stores had.
Finally seeing what she was needing,
The girl was no longer sad.

She walked outside glad, to go home and show Dad,
As a snowflake landed on her head.
On the corner of the street was a man who looked sweet,
And she decided to stop instead.

His eyes looked tired and he'd built a small fire,
Looking sad and lonely, she thought.
Thinking only a second, to him she beckoned,
Taking out the new coat she had bought.

Amanda Rybin

I'm A Rainbow

I'm a rainbow up in the sky,
Over the clouds and very high.
Blue is for hearts I broke in the past,
Red is for love that will always last.
Green is for our lives with each other we live,
Yellow is for the gifts to each other we give.
Orange is for me, I love you,
All my colors shine for you.
Purple is for you who I love to hold,
I'm a rainbow and you are my pot of gold.

Brian Raines

Colorado

Rocky mountains God lavished up and down,
dressed in white and lofty wedding gown,
betroth to the world in love and peace
invited to come and share the wedding feast.
By the millions they came from all the earth
lusting for her secrets and hidden treasures.
Downhill virile sensual motions gave birth
to rhythmic caressing curbs loaded with pleasures.
Back again to the top just for one more run;
'tis addictive when you are swallowed by fun,
and why not? She is seductive. She is enthrall;
like the traditional marriage of old,
loving rhythmic motions mounting the blood,
firing romantic eruption of passion for all.

Luis Armando Divas

Wathem

The day is beautiful, the time has come;
Walk with me.

Our love is strong, the time has come;
Walk with me.

Come - wear the stars on your head,
and wrap around you the pure white clouds;
And come walk with me.

Come hold my hand, and stand by my side;
Stay with me until I die.

Even after death, put on your golden robe,
so you can walk with me.

James Leach

"What Happened to Us?"

What happened to us, and the love we felt?
The caring words said that made us melt.
It up and went, that love we preached
It's hanging above us out of reach.
But it's still in sight as I can see
Maybe there's still a chance for you and me.
We can fix things you told me when it was time to go.
But how can we fix what we don't know?
Our feelings have changed, and so have we.
We need to take time and live life free.
If it was meant to be, it could come back again,
And then we would know, there must be no end.
We found those feelings could be for no other,
Now we know they are meant for each other.
Neither of us knows what in the future lies.
All we can hope is that it contains no good-byes
In the race through life there are no guarantees,
But I know in the present, there's only you and me.

Robyn Podkul

The Treasure Of Love

The ultimate wonder of our mysterious world
Is the unknown passion and glory in the loving of each other
This is a glory of a treasure which far surpasses the value
of diamonds or pearls
A unique feeling which binds two people together, such as a
sister and brother

This love is what unions us with someone who is especially dear
A parent, a child, a friend or even a lover
It provides us with an eternal commitment from others who
are sincere
We give in return a commitment of love to our
significant others

This wondrous joy of love when it is shared, is indeed our treasure
So hold on to it with every fiber of your being and
experience the never ending pleasure

Vernell Leeks

Opened...

In the quiet stillness, sitting, I wait
Longing for the beauty surrounding to manifest
Nights glorious shield from the powerful burning of day
Time is here and gone
All within a stream of gentle cleansing moonlight
Alone under the shadowed clouds as the sky parts again
Moon, barely visible, brings conscious dreams to light
Tarnished logic and hidden love send these dreams away
Born anew as a lingering dim soul
No longer waiting, arising now to the call of the sought after
The call not verbal, perhaps not made at all
Returning now to the quiet stillness, the manifest beauty sleeps
Every breath drawn in taken from the spirit of love lost
Sadness and bliss stream forth into the night
Madness illuminates the night and darkness has no meaning
Darkness gone, daylight forgotten, the gentle cleansing ceases
Angelic screaming conceals the demonic homilies of the wind
Feeling... Numbness... Infinity..
A strange journey never taken as the intense flame of day ignites

Ryan Cinalli

My Heart's Prayer

Here Lord Jesus take me as I am,
I know I'm not deserving to hold thy precious hand,
So take me as dainty and simple as can be,
And make me O Lord full of purity.

O God of creation, my Saviour, my friend.
The one who is with me till life's journey end,
Touch me, heal me, and save me O God,
Hear my humble cry near and abroad.

Sovereign father, just God, Kings of Kings,
Listen to what my poor heart sings,
I know I have sinned,
I'm not worthy of thee,
Praise to God you love even me.

So as I cry in shame and despair,
I begged thee, O Father, my prayers to hear,
Search my heart and see my needs,
Take me, O God, where ever your path leads,
Teach me to be more of what you want me to be,
Pure and simple, faithful, Lord to thee.

Carol Baptiste

The One I Adore

Her curly blond hair shines like the sun.
Her smile is contagious to those near her.
Her charm makes me long for our hearts to be one.
A kiss from her lips would make my heart stir.

Her touch is as soft as a bed of roses.
Her eyes are as clear as a sky of blue.
To be near her is to want to hold her close.
My life, my hope, my eternal dream is you.

To hear her voice is to relax my soul.
Her laugh often fills my life with joy.
Without her my life is like an empty hole.
Her company is something that all enjoy.

Just an acquaintance she could be much more.
If only I knew what life had in store.

Luke Riffle

My Sweetie Pie

It was a warm rainy day,
When young love came into play.
I met my husband forty three years ago
I wish our time together would move more slow.
He looks at me with love in his eyes and
Says, "Honey, you're still my `Sweetie Pie.'"
It was a busy time together with the events of life,
Not long ago it seems, when he asked me to be his wife.
With our children of eight and out on their own,
We have more time to just be alone.
Now we enjoy our golden years together and
Are warm with our love, no matter the weather.
My husband never misses to tell me he loves me,
And adds with his special sigh,
Honey you're still my "Sweetie Pie."
I know our time together is getting short,
And wonder how a separation will stand.
Me at 17, my husband at 19, when he first took my hand.
Life is great and I can tell you why,
Until the day I die, I'll be my husband's "Sweetie Pie."

Elizabeth Dolges

Aching Dreams

Chant the sweet language of my love,
  like wind blowing mist from the sea.

Whisper, like delicate rain pounding the bareness
  of my lusciously smooth shadow.

Wants shake the sweat from tiny petals
  and flood the moans I lie within.

Beneath the elaborate forest of aching dreams
  the moment screams through my blood.

Frantic beauty sleeps under me as the symphony
  of his lust plays upon my weak visions.

Stare into love's power with a lake of cries
  behind the bitterness of life and death.

Rebecca D. Montgomery

Morning Sun

As the morning sun glimmers off the
rolling plains of dew. The sky looks like
the doorway to the heavens.
With streaking rods of gold light which seem as if
they're giving love and warmth to our mother earth.
Soon after the morning dew arises from the
ground. The trees seem like they are trying to
reach up and hug the soft white clouds above. It looks
as the vast shades of blue and green come to life once again.

Bryan Gibbons

My Friend, Anne Townsend

Some thoughts of my friend I'd like to express
A neighbor to me who's one of the best
She always seemed pleased to have me drop in
And we'd enjoy a good visit now and then.

I always felt free to knock on her door
And she often would phone and we'd talk some more
If I lacked an egg while making a cake
She's gladly give it so I could bake.

When I worked at school and her boys were there too
Sometimes there were favors she's ask me to do
I'll never forget how she gave me a gift
For those favors to her — to me 'twas a lift.

Anne made me rich with her friendship so dear
Many friends I have, but she was so near
When returning from work no light do I see
Her house is so dark, a reminder to me.

My friend left this world for heaven above
I can't wish her back even tho' she was loved
Yes, I'll miss those visits and her not here
But the memories I'll cherish year after year!

Esther Snyder

Farewell

I cross the room, I look at you.
Then I pray God what must we do?
My heart breaks, I try not to cry
Then I'm selfish, please God don't
let him die.

Such proud man, 'neat loving and tall,
You are outstanding among them all.
So proud of your journey through life
Including two sons and a wife.

Now my dear, life took its toll on you
And only God can pull you through.
As I plant a kiss on your brow,
God I ask please take him now.

You would not want to live this way,
Slowly passing each dreaded day
Putting your family through such terrible woe
You wouldn't want this I know.

Bonnie Kemper

metamorphosis

want became a (silkworm) so
and crawled forever,
soft and slow
and danced with all upon a leaf
(looking down) eyes open (in disbelief)
for seasons quick did play their part
and (walked away)
with friend at heart
and soon a new thing (even odd)
hung sure and solid
a (golden wad)
no princess eyes or fairy kisses
came close around this thing
but far within a (something) moved
sensing change not quite the same
this want this silkworm this something odd
was not what it was,
nor same, nor small
with wings outstretched and wind about
want flew away as will

Darren J. Davey

221

Wind

I take words
  and form you
  eyes, hair, flesh
  and bones
from the space of dreams
  where you touch lightly
  the places I have sculpted
  a world of
    sand and stone.

I take the earth
  and form thoughts,
  words you will speak,
the motions of your movement like shadows
  across the desert floor
  and as we walk home
    under clouds that
    ease the light
    of this world,

I know something of myself
  reflected in your eyes.

Elam Raymond

To Say Bye

Staring at the sky in an indefinite stare,
My best friends up there in his own solitaire.
I miss him so much, and his special ways,
I miss his smile, his laughter, as I recall
those days.
When they told me my best friend was gone,
I thought of what you would say "Keep
the faith, carry on."
When I look at the clouds, I think of you,
What you're doing, I wish I knew.
There's so many things I wish I could do,
But most of all said "bye" to you.
Here's the last words I have to say,
"In my heart you'll always stay."

Teesha Verrinder

Who Are You

Who are you my regal sister?

Are you the product of mighty Dahomey Kings
or was it the proud Zulu's royal blood line that
gave you the majestic grace you wear so well?

Was it the womb of your ancestor that once
cradled mankind's first born? Were you taught to
move with the Nile's undulating rhythm
by generations of sun-kissed madonnas
or is it that your very genes are stamped
with the serpentine movement of that timeless
stream of life giving flow?

Who are you ebony goddess of angelic beauty?

You are the syncopated heart beat of mother Africa
as she rests in the color drenched setting sun
calling to her sons, "come home from distant shores?"

It is you that commands the central place of
both my daydreams and night visions.

What is it in you that fills that deep well in me
that has long been boarded up and allowed to....
give refuge to silken webs of disuse and little else.

Jon D. Jennings

The Tears I Cry

Never in my life did I feel such a pain
The tears kept falling, falling like the rain
You said that you wanted to talk
But when the time came, all you did was walk
Away from me there at the fair
Just leaving me sitting there
Sitting there on the bench ready to cry
I just wished and wanted to die.
My dreams were shattered, my hopes were crushed
You left there in such a rush.
Talking to you meant a great deal to me
Even though I knew it would not be.
I see now that you did not care
That miserable day at the fair
And with every tear that I cried
I realized more that you lied.
I wish that day would never have been
That terrible, horrible, sad day when
I cried a hundred-thousand tears
That will fall everyday for the rest of my years!

Kayce Swenson

War

Why do we have war, please answer this question.
How can we stop it, I have a suggestion.
Just stop all the violence and all the hate,
If we do not we will all meet our fate.
Our brothers and fathers are drafted to war,
We'll never see them again as they shut the door.
But now there are gangs out on the street,
And yet, more hate we have to beat.
So how exactly can we stop this war,
It will take you and me and a whole lot more.

Rebecca Hill

Listen To The Children

"Children should be seen and not heard!"
This saying how old and absurd!

They will take today into tomorrow,
mending our broken world of sorrow.

Children watch with fresh new eyes,
Seeing truth we have covered with lies.

Children are not born with anger, prejudice, dishonesty,
insecurity, or conceit.
Possibly in their generation these feelings they will defeat.

Listen to the children,
do not fear...
Their new words heard in our world are Very Dear!

Jerri L. Hauenstein

Out Of The Thorns, God Gave Me A Rose

I was born into a life full of mistrust and hate,
Even those with good intentions were always too late.
Each path that I took, each road I went down,
I found patches of thorns and people that would frown

All the way to adulthood there was no peace to be found,
After Vietnam I wondered, why was I around.
Why was I still here, why did I even survive,
Did God have some reason for keeping me alive.

Now here I am just sky of my fiftieth year,
As I look back on my life, God has made it clear.
I have survived for wife, it's as plain as my nose,
For, out of the thorns, God gave me a beautiful rose.

Richard W. Dunlap

I Wonder Why?

A little girl runs to her mother,
Clutching a picture that she is so proud of...
She waits for her mother to look down and see her shining face,
Her mother turns and ignores her again...
Why?

Bullets fly through the air over a wounded man...
That no one sees,
They all retreat silently through the brush,
He is all alone, left to die...
Why?

A man gets on a train bustling with lots of people,
He doesn't like trains, he says they are too dangerous.
They start going and he realizes that it isn't that bad,
The next moment the train crashes.....he dies.
Why?

Sometimes I just wonder so many things,
Why do people do this or that,
Or why is this, this way...
Sometimes I just
Wonder.

Jill McBride

Our Love (To Maria)

All will ask, some shall seek,
but few will find of what I speak.
A love to last the test of time,
A love as sweet or strong as mine.

For you, my love, the sun does rise,
The wind blows softly, the willow cries.
For you, my love, make the planets turn,
the summer rains fall, my heart churn.

You are all, and all is you,
The moon, the stars, the morning dew.
Each day begins and ends the same,
With thoughts of you . . . or your whispered name.

Our hearts held captive, but of free will,
Upon our love lay the final seal.
And join two beings, two souls as one,
A knot drawn tightly, and never undone.

Chris Boatwright

Oh Gentle Smile

Oh gentle smile, never lose the rays of happiness.
Pierce the gray dawn and cast upon it, Heaven's gleam.
Melt away the sorrow that blankens the faces,
And kindle the coldness of hearts with flames of delight.
Oh gentle smile, how far and endless you reach,
Touching all who catches it by reach.
No matter how great the pain is, the smile endures.
No enemy of disease can banish it,
The wrath of fear can not hover it,
Nothing could ever destroy it.
Time has passed and it is dawn, again.
Oh, how it glistens, now.
Oh gentle smile, my dear,
No longer here, yet always near.
Guide my heart in this way,
So that I may be as light and gay.
May my smile be as gentle, as yours was.
Oh gentle smile, Heaven has you now.
Look down upon me,
And always, will I see your gentle smile, reflecting from the sun.

Kimberly-Ann Kateri Ragonese

Life's Journey

Life is a journey we all must take
from the moment of birth there's so much at stake
each day of our trip, be it great or unkind
we have problem's and worries often hard to define
will it rain today, or will the sun shine
will I have a small hill, or a mountain to climb
will I stumble and fall, will I laugh will I cry
"yet" why do I worry, why do I sigh
with God's understanding and mercy divine.
And his love so tender, and so very sublime
My final big mountain, I surely will climb.

June Stear

Mother

This is a story about my dad's wife.
The story of the woman who gave me life.
She worked a lot way back then,
but being a mother she was a ten.
She could never be paid what she is worth,
there's not enough money on the earth.
She's worked hard all her life,
a wonderful mother and wife.
Not only a mother had I had,
but as time would pass she'd take over for dad.
This is a story twenty four years old,
a story my mother could have told.
But modest she is most,
so about her I must boast.
I want her to know I love her dear
and thank her for the past twenty four years.
Just one thing left I'd like to say,
thanks to the man above
for giving me a mother with so much love.

Y. Renee Doub

Forgiveness

I forgive you. Often accompanied, by an
embrace, and often a tear. Words spoken
from the heart, or solely for others
to hear.

Meaningful, I forgive you, if spoken from
the heart. For someone to know, the
friendship remains, and with life, a
refreshing new start.

A heart given forgiveness, can bring
such joy and meaning to each and
everyday. Complete forgiveness, medicine
for the heart, the soul, and to heal
the hurt, no longer here to stay.

Gary W. Huffer

King

To be the king,
with clothes of gold.
To wear a smile,
instead of dirt.
To call and be answered,
To hope and be heard
clearly and quick,
To have many men
die in your service,
and proudly,
while you stand back.
To be loved
is not always to be King.

Walter Quinn

Who Are You

Who are you my regal sister?

Are you the product of mighty Dahomey Kings
or was it the proud Zulu's royal blood line that
gave you the majestic grace you wear so well?

Was it the womb of your ancestor that once
cradled mankind's first born? Were you taught to
move with the Nile's undulating rhythm
by generations of sun-kissed madonnas
or is it that your very genes are stamped
with the serpentine movement of that timeless
stream of life giving flow?

Who are you ebony goddess of angelic beauty?

You are the syncopated heart beat of mother Africa
as she rests in the color drenched setting sun
calling to her sons, "come home from distant shores?"

It is you that commands the central place of
both my daydreams and night visions.

What is it in you that fills that deep well in me
that has long been boarded up and allowed to....
give refuge to silken webs of disuse and little else.

Jon D. Jennings

I Think I Lost My Way

At the twilights last gleaming...
Allegiance, liberty and justice?
No, hatred and hardship are the undying evidence,
Of pearls turned to sand, of dignity to dust.
And I want to get to heaven, but I think I lost my way.

It's an enigma of chastisement for a little ones rights,
When contemplated disregard perpetuates their hunger,
Or when pompous authority share their might,
By bestowing a penny in the name of compassion.
And I want to get to heaven, but I think I lost my way.

Anarchists, armies of liberation and of wars,
Wreak rage in their crafty ways,
To godless, unfree souls of darkness,
Like they, impiety reigns.
And I want to get to heaven, but I think I lost my way.

Nomads are we all, seeking the truths,
And somehow the stones will unturn,
The freedom will reign and justice prevail,
When we all agree to just love.
And I want to get to heaven, but I think I lost my way.

Kathryn Swanson Garner

Demonstrator, 1963

We're hoping to be arrested
And hoping to go to jail
We'll sing and shout and pray
For freedom and for justice
And for human dignity
The fighting may be long
And some of us will die
But liberty is costly
And Rome they say to me
Was not built in one day.

Hurry up, Lucille, Hurry up
We're going to Miss Our chance to go to jail.

Elizabeth Thomas

Ozymandias II

Blackness ruled when I was awoken
in the restless hours before dawn
By Ozymandias, dark and brooding
"They want to roll back the stone.."

"What stone?" I said from my darkened bed
But he seemed not to care nor hear
"The stone that kept Him among the dead",
Was his reply to my ignorance and fear.

"All that we have learned, all that we have loved,
we owe to the victory o'er death.
But if the stone slides back to its mold-embossed groove,
You will have drawn your last mortal breath."

"I?" cried me, "And who is they?" I asked
Though a separate person in me already knew
"Yes," Ramses nodded "they are but one in the same—
those desperate centurions are you."

"Lessons of love, the growth of spirit, seeking
the birth of your soul's next stages—"
"Accept these reflections," this was me speaking
"For what is learned steals the death stone's dark wages."

Jason M. Kelley

Best Season

I've yet to know my favorite season,
But love them all for many a reason.
When a child, in spring, I'd go fly my kite,
Play marbles, go fishing and hear "greenies" at night.
In summer there were picnics and ice cream galore,
Fourth of July fireworks, baseball, hopscotch and more.
Autumn meant Halloween pranks and would I be a witch or a ghost?
Thanksgiving at Grandma's and who would be eating the most?
Winter brought my birthday, sled rides and trimming the tree,
And wondering what presents Santa would be leaving for me.

When a woman, in spring, this season seemed best,
With its beautiful bulbs, flowering trees, a robin's nest.
May ushered in lilies of the valley and anniversary surprises,
Then summer beaches exuded beauty in all different sizes.
In autumn one would see the most magnificent views,
With leaves in all patterns and flamboyant hues.
Then winter was here when the leaves were all done,
And there were Christmas carols, mistletoe and all of that fun.
Now that career days are past and retirement is here,
The season that's best is in every day of the year.

Gladys Yeager Pavlock

Grace Bedazzled

With her heart hewn in half
    and a soul stripped silent
Her years ripple onward with a force uncontrolled

Listen-
    Could this be the sound of a
    Youthful hope having grown in power?
No-
    'Tis liquid frustration echoing
    through the caverns of necessity

Crystallized anger unknown dripping throughout

This is all she'll ever know
"Could-have-beens"...."Should-have-beens"...
    Recognized with a sweet smile of regret

But life is never so gloried as in renewal
Choices made where rewards are deep
    and satisfy the soul

Rippling onward - This sound of
    Youthful hope growing with power

K Curry

Be Yourself

When the sky is too cloudy, your hair is too frizzy
to style and shine your beauty,
do not be afraid to try to hold the tree.

Try to create a new face, challenge your race,
make a new line, a new trace, something brand new to enlace...

Because...Because, life is a battle,
an immense, beautiful struggle
that we all should cuddle
and be strong "together" to handle..!

..Every one of us has a spirit to pamper,
a good reason to be stronger,
   and go further, to meet the stranger...

Because....Because, what we do call destiny,
   it's not our beauty,
instead, it's life simplicity
that some of us refuse to admit as a reality...

Never live for an environment.
Live with a self encouragement...
And always take a moment, to appreciate a compliment...!

   Be yourself...!
   Yveline Fung Cap

Natural Treasures

The wild timber wolves run
And sing to the moon
This land is their own
Don't let their time end too soon

Our forefathers who roamed
this land wild and free
respected this land
much more than we.

Are we too far above,
are we too blind to see
Man and nature must work together
To live in harmony.

From the majestic mountains
the sparkling streams flow out to sea
the golden fields and great woodlands
God gave to you and me.

From the snow leopards and soaring eagles
to the rainforests lush with trees
we must preserve our natural treasures
or our world will cease to be.

   Joyce Davis

Gods Way Of Touching

Deep in the soul of every man
is a need and desire so desperate to be filled

Maybe only possible by the creator
Yet man wants to be touched...to feel and to kiss

So he searches lifelong to many painful regrets
for that one person to reach in
and fill but a corner of the emptiness within

No...not a love...not a romance
not a passion that burns
until the wings of morning snuff her out

But a treasure so great
built on days of joy and sadness
of tears and sharing laughter and caring

It must be God's way of touching
a kiss from above
He has given me a friend to love

   Diane Balog Helferich

When This Has Passed

I looked for then when this has passed
Look in my eyes you'll see my history
From my eyes you can see what's been
While they show me what's still yet to be
Took a wrong turn so long ago
My habits of then have destroyed my now
Living now in the certain wreckage
Of my future
Just around the bend

Flames that dance in front of me
Ignite my ship that will carry me
I've been to the moon and I've seen both sides
Now I spiral towards earth to crash with destiny
Caught between my life and space
I feel the stars still calling me
In my quest to return
I've imprisoned my life on earth in misery
Like a dream trapped in a bottle
Rub my life with love
And set me free

   Joseph A. Safrany

Spring

It's the most thrilling time of the year
When winter is gone, and spring is here;
When spring-birds sing their refrain,
And things are coming to life a-gain.

The world that's been so bleak and bare,
Is now being decked in beauty fair;
Bare trees will no longer be seen,
They're dressing now in robes of green.

The tiny flowers along the lane
Are peeping out to welcome spring,
We can-not see just how things start,
But surely it is the work of art.

The soft warm clouds float along with ease,
Looking like sail boats up-on the blue seas,
Warm rains will take the place of snow,
To make the grain and flowers grow.

The golden sun shines warm and bright;
God has fixed it all just right
Without the winter, spring would not be,
Such a thrilling time for you and me.

   Minnie Scyphers

Death's Last Dance

My lips kissed your cheeks, deeply sunken in,
And your forehead of frozen ice.
Kneeling, hunched over you in your coffin,
No words of comfort could suffice.

A rosary of red roses covered
Your body, so wasted away.
For the last time, over you, I hovered,
Etching you in my memory.

The heaving sobs drowning in my numb ears,
The lump in my throat choking me,
My eyes clouded over, sight disappeared
As I left you, in misery.

You were cheated, and stolen from your friends.
We weren't given a fair chance.
AIDS is the only winner in the end,
It whirled you into death's last dance.

   Nicole Scotton

In A Friends Memory

There are so many times you stood by my side
You were there to stand tall and full of pride
But, then you were taken the way many have been before
Now, you are gone, you're not here anymore

Many times we shared a special trust
And, the truth is your death was unjust
And, now there is something that needs to be done
Our fight for justice has only just begun

Many people grieved when you were taken away
Now in your memory we all must pray
That in our lives you played a special part
Now you and your memories will always stay in our heart

With your memories we hold a special bond
One that takes us above and beyond
Remember we had a friendship that always stayed true
Remember my friend, I love you.

Brandi Jolliff

Custer's Last Stand

The Indians sat upon the surrounding hills.
Custer's face turned deathly ill.

He knew that death was close at hand.
The war drums were beating to beat the band.

They came rushing down the hill.
All of Custer's men stood still.

Their faces turned a pale white.
They were coming from the left and coming from the right.

They let out an awful cry-
the horses, they seemed to fly.

Down the hill they came,
and then,...it began to rain.

There was no hope for Custer and his men,
even though help was just around the bend.

The only survivor from Custer's side,
a horse that Custer can no longer ride.

As people learned of this terrible battle,
the Indians were back on the reservation raising cattle.

The sky overhead is no longer blue.
This is a sad tale, that is true.

Dustin Drumheller

Wall Of Glory

The raindrops upon the wall of names
reflect the tears of those left behind.

The names upon it become the bridge to those lost,
it serves as their bodies in physical presence.
So we might touch them and the memories of love,
of laughter, of smiles and of pain.
Of words not said and of words that were.

Remember them all, all who died for what ever the cause.
Are they justified only in memory?
Did they believe in what they fought for?
Indeed they did.

They are the heart of our country, the shield behind
which we live in freedom.

Remember them with love, honor, respect and glory.
For they are the red, the white and the blue.

Shelayne M. Kidd

My Other Mother

I have another mother,
Who's as dear as she can be.
She's never baked me cookies,
Or held me on her knee.
She's never praised me for a mark,
Or held me close when it was dark.
She's never taught me right from wrong,
Or sang to a good night song.
But, she has loved me many years,
And helped me through so many tears.
She's listened to my tales of woe,
And always said, "I love you so."
She's been there for me since I've grown,
The only mother I ever known.
I'd never trade her for another,
To me she is my wonderful "Mother."

Betsey Kohlhoff

Musings Of An Artist

And it is gone.
Relinquished; faded into a garble
of pencil and paper crumpled on the floor.

I watched the music dancing with the sky,
across my starry eyes—
through my open fingers.

The magic dispersed
leaving an awkward
imitation
on the floor,

And I only wished
to catch a hint
a whisper
an aftertaste
of notes that rang
behind my pen.

Why can I create only
dry empty eggshells,
brittle, devoid of residue
of substance?

Rachel Swift

Words Will Never Hurt Me!?

"Sticks and stones can break me bones,
But words will never hurt me"
So please be careful what you throw,
Or something just might break me.

Yes, sticks and stones can break my bones,
But words can break my heart,
So choose them with the greatest care
Before you let them part.

For nought you do, or think or say
Can e'er recall them once they're gone,
When you've winged them on their way
They linger on and on and on.

So keep in mind dear, loving friend,
Long after bones are knit together,
My heart may still be on the mend,
The hurt could stay with me forever!

Mary A. De Graw

Tomorrow

Excited, scared
New City - New State - New Faces
Fitting in, feeling inadequate
Yet proud

Workshops, field trips, classes
Filling each day
Camping, caving, canoeing
Adding adventure

Reaching, adapting for tomorrow
Diane Psaute

Untitled

Here I am,
Ready for view;
You don't know me,
I don't know you.
I ponder why you smile,
You wonder why I frown,
You appear so happy,
I seem to be so down.
As you stand across from me,
I see how you are presented.
But what you seem and what you are
Makes you awfully resented.
Why do they loathe you?
Do they really know who you are?
No, I don't think so,
They only view you from afar.
You hide behind your smile
And still receive no affection.
I ask, "Why do they treat you this way?"
Staring at my own reflection.
Julie Whitley

Untitled

A silent canyon
Awoken by an echo
Is able to speak
Vincent LaCalamita

The Crusades
(The Battle For The Field)

The sun rise's on a silent field
Armor gleams bright on the sod
The battle starts with sword and shield
A fight, they say, for God

The battle rages to and fro
It's hard to tell who's winning
The dead, they look like fallen snow
Yes, Satan is a grinning

The sun sets on a silent field
Armor gleams red, by moonlight
A broken sword, a shattered shield
Their eyes, they have no sight

The field is sown and washed in red
The reaper comes with scythe
Black cowl will harvest up the dead
Still think he's just a myth

Hell's gate creaks open very wide
The demons laugh and grin
The dead march in a crimson tide
The Devil; gets the win!
Daniel H. Sharp

Life

Why does life have to be so
   lonely and cold?
It's not happily ever after as
   once told.
Friends and families it may be
But right now it feels like only me.
The sun is shining, the birds
   are singing -
Still only heartache is what
   life seems to be bringing.
The kids are all grown and
   live away
Yet in my heart and on my
   mind they will always stay.
Nancy Stanton

Thanksgiving

Let us be thankful on this day
God has given us so much.

Let us slow down, not rush
Enjoy the time we have to share.
On this Thanksgiving Day.

Its a time to really care
and give a heartfelt thanks.

Let us all Pray
not only for a wonderful day,
but for His guidance
on this Thanksgiving Day
Linda Eckert

Peachland

   As I wonder through
my life, I smell
something sweet inside,
the fresh scent of peaches,
limb by limb, together
in bunches, they flounder
the fields in peachy colors,
and outgrow the blossoms
on leaves nearby. They have
a casual scent, nothing like
others, juicier inside and
sweeter to the mind. Peaches
are God's treat, nothing
better to eat. They seep over
the ground, and into the
woods, finding a place to put
their roots. Peach trees everywhere
trying to survive so
animals can hide.
Sena Johnson

America The Salad Bowl

America is a salad bowl,
With a variety of different vegetables
That all come from different farms.
Each gives off its own flavor,
Which adds to the salad's uniqueness.
Alone, the vegetables can be bland,
But if they're tossed together,
And share a common dressing,
A flavorful and wonderful salad is made.
Donald F. Yap

To My Grandchild

   Sweet little grandchild of mine
God took you before your time.
   I'll never know your gentle touch
This grand baby I loved so much.
   There must be a reason
   one we cannot see.
I know you are in heaven waiting for me.
   Some day when I pass this world
full of pain
   We'll be so happy forever again.
So little baby be patient;
Just wait and see
   We'll be together, forever;
   in eternity.
We love you little baby.
JoAnn Kaminski

Christmas Morn

Hello Teddy Bear
This is Pooh
Let's have a party
It's Jesus' birthday to-day

We'll call Lauren and Sarah
and Steven and Danny
And Micheal and baby sister Pam
Let's invite Julia and Christopher too

We'll sing some carols
and read the story true
How Jesus was born
and come to live with me and you

He is the Prince of peace
God's gift to us all
Just follow in His footsteps
and listen for His call
Meta S. Davis

Amy

A morning does not go by,
   with me not wishing you at my side
Morning, noon and night,
   without your presence, I've no light
Yearning for your love,
   I go on only by my breath
Searching for your hand,
   without it, I've found death
Many nights that I've spent with you,
   are pointless if you don't care
Every minute I'm away,
   I dream when you were there
Never shall you leave me,
   and never shall I leave
To every person there is love,
   to every love there is a seed
Every seed I have searched over,
   and I have found the best
Kissing your lips endlessly,
   sweeter than the rest
Christopher Allen Ogren

Change

The seasons of life
Like autumn leaves
Change
Lynn Thompson

Welcome Baby

Welcome baby
Welcome
It's so nice to have you here
Your innocence and sweetness
Bring a bit of heaven near
Welcome baby
Welcome
May life be good to you.
May your days be bright and
sunny
May your skies above
be blue
May you grow to love
And learn to love everyone
around you.
And always may I love you
and may you love me too.

Amy Neely

Our Gift From God

The path that never let you stay
The bride you never gave away
Now new doors will open
For I was always hoping
At last the babe is on its way
We call you grandpop
They call me grandmom
God's gift to us
We both will cherish
For God's love will never perish.

Italia Giancola

The Greatest Artist In The World

With a single thought in mind.
He visioned a perfect plan.
Without a blueprint he designed.
A beautiful world for mankind.

Just look up at the sky.
It is a dazzling color of blue.
There is no way one can deny.
The work of a great artist, but who?

He used no erasers, or, ink.
And he penciled nothing in.
With perfect precision he linked.
Each color to a perfect blend.

Awesome! I thought amazed.
Excitement build as I observed.
Only God, could have made.
So much beauty with this word.

Ethel Brewer

As I Sit Alone

As I sit alone I want to cry
for the love I had has
gone and died
She left me here in this
cruel world
with no love, and with
no home

Maybe someday we will reunite
Until then I'll try to sleep
through the night
it will be hard cause
I sit alone

Scott M. Creager

Broken, Broken, Broken

Broken heart day
I waited for the never call.
I jumped at the rings
All day not for me.
Broken heart day
I called myself stupid.
Stupid heart broken
for believing one
who cannot tell truth
without at least one lie
in the middle.
Sad heart day
woman waiting again
quiet, no broken left.

Janaki Severy

The Tornado Is Here

Down it came very fast,
every one was in at last.
Down in the basement we would stay,
until it was away.
Once we came out,
a tiny spout came down and started to
destroy.
We prayed very hard,
finely it was but sight,
and that was when I saw the light.

Bethany Twarozynski

You Are Needed

You don't feel important in the
    grand scheme of things
you crawl instead of flying
    high on soaring wings

Let the birds soar according
    to their very need
but you are important
    right here indeed.

Your smile may be a beam
    that's heaven sent
to someone you never guessed
    was in need of encouragement

The ripple effect you have created
    multiplies and goes on unabated
it boomerangs from one to another
    creating love or hate to a brother

Can you now see how very
    important you are
because everyone of your
    actions reaches so far!

Hedy Harrison

Cool Summer Breeze

She lifts me up and carries
me away. It feels so good,
yet can't be explained.
    As we ascend above the leaves
of the trees, I think of
irreplaceable thoughts of which
cannot be perceived.
    She enters my soul and
takes me away on a voyage
drifting deep into space.
    As we start to descend I
feel her faith, a presence so
strong, never to be replaced.

Raymond W. Marshall Jr.

You Are This

You are the breeze gently blowing across
a field of spring daisies
The melody of a songbird at dawn
welcoming a new day
The flame of a fire warming the
desert at night
The dampness of dew resting
lazily amid morning grass
A hint of fog creeping silently
along the peaks of mountains
The sound of distant thunder
echoing heavenly splendor
The flash of fearsome lightning
glowing for all to see
The unmeasurable joy of laughter
a smile could never create
The honesty in a child's eyes
looking humbly to wiser elders
And the sincerity of a single tear
drop flowing down a grieving cheek.

Terry A. Powell

Date 1-08-96 2:00 Am To 2:25 Am

What would I do with Annie Lennox,
in my room; this very moment?
You know, I wouldn't lie to you;
about my feelings, and the
truth is plain to see. How
does John Lennon feel at this moment?

Insecure fried bacon, is sometimes
what it is I feel, dear Annie
She said: you know; it's a one
way ride; and as I listen to
her plea, at this moment;
how is it I feel.

Now that I have her strapped to
my chair; I know I don't have
to cut her hair. Monumental
feelings; make us both disappear -
To a love so long ago, yes I know
My dear Annie at this moment

Chris Bailey

Life

Life is a game with one
roll of the dice your life is
changed. Now every thing is different.
Your life is changed. You don't know
what to do. Then Boom! Your life
has changed again you go insane
like everyone else in the world.

Vanessa M. Lujano

A Retirement Plan

Streets of gold
and many treasures,
diamonds and rubies,
whatever your pleasure.

A pension plan
that's already been paid,
a mansion, a bed,
that's already been made.

So before you go,
make reservations,
because you can only get in
on eternal salvation.

Faith Bowman

Summer

Summer is the time of
year for Baseball Hotdogs
and Rootbeer. The crowds
can't wait to fill the stands
and jump around and clap their hands.
The ball game is a fun
night out, it's played in sun
and rain and drought. The players
run out one by one, then our
National Anthem is clearly sung.
Peanuts popcorn cracker Jack yell
the vendors, have a snack.
Voices of cheer are heard out
loud, as the game is played
with a rooting crowd. The ball
game is and will always be
a game enjoyed by all of thee.

Joyce E. Saporito

Little Sister

Right on little sister,
cause you know just what you are.
You're a lovely piece of heaven,
You're a fiery shooting star.

You bring gladness to your babies,
with the milk of life's sweet breast.
You bring comfort to your man-friend
when he lays his head to rest.

You're a cleaner and a cooker,
and a mender and a friend.
You've been handling heavy circumstances
since this world began.

And I love you little sister,
whether near or whether far.
You're a woman, little sister.
Oh, but most of all — you are!

Prather Blackmon

Untitled

Everytime you start to cry
An angel falls from the sky
I should have been there just for you
But I wasn't now you're so blue

Although I've been in your shoes before
I can't stand to see you hurt anymore
I will find him take him down
I'll make sure he's put in the ground

Sandra Perry

Unfeeling Felt

If I created my heart
I would have made it of steel
It would never have to hurt
Because it would never have to feel.
If I had made my eyes
Beauty they would not see
It wouldn't hurt to look at you
Because I would only look at me.
If I designed my soul
Love would not be there
I guess I could think of you
Without falling into despair.

Amanda M. Spears

Fly Away

Fly away little Angel
Fly away little Angel
We will see you in another day.
The calmness that you exude,
No matter the chaos,
Spoke loudly in a manner soothing.
Your quietness and
Mystique
of a smile
Has left an imprint
That will last
Forever.
As if to say:
Peace
Be still
Fly away little Angel
Fly away little Angel
We will see you in another day
Rest in Peace
My Dear One

Evelena Reese

Erik

You gave joy and brought love
We didn't know
Until your light went out
How much joy and love you gave

Oh child of confusion
How much you must have anguished
For we didn't know
Until your light went out

Now we understand, and now we know
Our hearts are heavy
We miss your special glow

You will be missed
You will always be loved
We are sorry
For we didn't know

Claire M. Jernigan

Christmas Eve

On window panes,
The icy frost,
Leaves feathered patterns.
Crissed and crossed.

In our house, the Christmas tree,
Is decorated festively.
With tiny drops of colored light
That cozy up this winter night.

Christmas songs familiar and slow,
Play softly on the radio.
Pops and hisses from the fire,
Whistle with the bells and choir.

My brother now is fast asleep,
On his back and dreaming deep.
And when the fire makes him hot.
He turns to warm whatever's not.

Propped against him on the rug,
I give my friend a gentle hug.
Tomorrow's what I'm waiting for,
But I can wait a little more.

Shivani Ghoshal

Flannel Night

Flannel night moves down over
the peachy cheeks; fresh and young
are they, because that is what they are.

Move over my friend, your side of
the bed must be warmer, because
you are there...and I am here
waiting to cover our comforter
with picnicy things
Apples, peaches, baskets of paper
flowers
And if it rains, will we get wet?
And will it smear the chocolate
icing on your face?
And when I awake from such
sweet dreams of you
will you be there to comfort me?

Lisa Benjamin

Watersheds

Water is running
Rain is falling
Unto the watershed

Watershed oh watershed
Please capture the water for me

Falling rain falling rain running
Unto the watershed

Watershed oh watershed
Please capture the water for me

Water is running
Rain is falling
Unto the watershed

Watershed oh watershed
Please capture the water for me

Heather Bell

Lost In Traffic

When I'm driving to and fro,
The lane I'm in seems always slow
But I don't let that faze me
As I change lanes with a grin
I'm right proud of what I done
Now I can move - well son - a- gun
The one that's moving fastest,
Is the one that I was in

I travel East and West a lot,
But North or South, it matters not
I go from town to town,
And rest my body in between.
It's all the same from coast to coast
I think what blows my mind the most,
Why traffic lights are always red
Much longer than they're green!

Wendell M. Phillips

Romance

Heartbeats in the moonlight
on a warm summer night
Palm trees gently swaying in the breeze

Shadows dancing 'til dawn
A rose on a summer morn

Maria Santos

229

Beauty

He sits along the wall
  watching her go by,
he smells the sense of her perfume
  and twinkles in her eye.

With a red velvet dress
  and silky white nose,
and black and white shoes
  that does not cover the toes.

Her long blonde hair
  moves from side to side
she's smart and intelligent
  and very very kind

The beauty of her self
sweeps him off his feet
and when he looks at her
one day they'd like to meet.

Nicole Homeier

My Friend

I wish for you:
A never ending thirst for knowledge,
A lifetime of happy tomorrows.
The discovery of a true friend.
The adulation of your children.
The joy of a trouble free life.
A true love for someone.
The revelation of that love returned.
The memories of a legendary past.
The hopes for a love-filled present.
The dreams for a beautiful future.
These few but precious gifts,
I endow for you.
For I wish you to experience
What I already possess.

Carol P. Kane

A Room

That day was so hot
  Your room
My picture stuck on mirror
  Your room.
A fan blowing hot air
  That room.
Dark cloud full of death
  That room
Papers blow in thick air
  The room
It was him we could feel
  Dead room.
Small boxes of his life
  Now.
A room.

Alice Powell

Sea Shore

The sun sets low, the fire glows,
the seashells are a glistening pink.
The gulls fly over head, as you
wash your sandy hands, the ocean is
your sink. The smell of salt
water is fresh on your face,
and your eyes get heavy as you
stare into space. I wish I could
spend more time at this place.

Kendal Gregg

The Stalker

Death is stalking everyone,
Eventually he will have won;
Clasping life with steel - cold hands,
He banishes dreams and foils plans.

He stalks in silence one by one
Until man's earthly life is done;
He never tires nor does he sleep,
His mission quest he's sure to keep.

Like a hound following scent of prey,
Death trails man by night and day;
He is the monster who will succeed
Without regard to how one pleads.

Melba L. Paul

Bit Of Sweet Sorrow

He calls, I miss him,
He sings, I wish I could kiss him
He talks, I listen.
He totally glistens
My ears rings of happiness
My heart rings of sadness

My eyes are waiting
While my heart is aching

He does know that I exist
but loves another that close to me

How shall I bear the pain
Maybe some sweet day
he'll be listening
And then I'll be glistening

Christina Battistella

Break

The darkness reaches
into my soul
touching me
in places I have never known.
Gripping my heart tightly,
the paradise lost
the images shown.
pleading promises
unkept, unwanted,
except for the pleasure that lied ahead.
The pain,
that came after.
So full of it,
I couldn't quite see through,
your untold secrets
they killed me
inside.
I should know.

Rachael C. Hilyard

To My Boy

I love you
When you kissed me
I layed on my back
you gazed in my eyes
I felt your hand brush
  with mine
we looked at the sky
  and the stars came
  out to play

Amanda Spurlock

Untitled

Dark seas of thought part before me
Revealing the deep dark secrets
Of the inner soul
Hidden deep down in the inner regions
Of an enigmatic mind
Who plots and turns
With little regard for pain
Scarring flesh
From self-denial and torture
No release from the hidden darkness
Where he lurks and plays
At horrid sinister games
Called love and hate
Manipulating the feelings
As if numbers on a page
Without heart or soul
Just cold hard facts
Of life and beyond

Stephanie Wang

Finding The Son

His mind is glowing
Like the sun.
Forever flaring never done.

The world is not kind
To those like he.
He walks alone,
Oblivious to what they see.

He cares of course
But not of them.
His aim is higher
Careless of where he's been.

Do I know him?
Nay not I
An enigma flickering in minds eye.

The road he travels only he knows.
Darkness goes with him wherever he goes.
Someday he will find the sun,
Only then will my task be done.

Barbara L. Hockett

Untitled

If I found the truth
every day of my life
there would be no mystery.

And it would not come
Surprising Reassuring
as it does so seldom.

It would echo in the towers
and eaves of abandoned buildings.

It would ring each hour
at the top of the church.

And then it would stretch
white and grey across the sky,
and fill the deepest ocean.

Even then love,
even if the truth were all these things,
in all these places;
You would doubt me still.

Judith Mascia

Untitled

To my little one
That I'll never know
Our lives could have
been filled with
so much love
but now all I
feel is sorrow.
I'll never see your smiling face
or feel your loving embrace.
I ask myself, why God
didn't take me in your place,
Give you a chance to grow,
Play and race. Why did
he have to take you away?
And never let me see
Your beautiful loving face.

Maureen E. Gardner

Alltimers

The bases are loaded,
she thought she heard,
picturing bases stacked like freight.
In the country
unaccustomed to television
until television
had no other worlds to conquer,
each generation of her women,
her mother now, grandmother before,
dissolved, erased before her eyes.
Is there a name for this?
Alltimers Disease, she was sure he said.

The bases now cleared
leaving an empty field
of weeds and shadows
in the summer's evening.
Even the Babe,
she was sure the television said,
suffered her family's fate.

Michael Adelman

Look Of Pain

Dedicated to Adam J. Purichia
Those eyelids almost down;
that smile turns to a frown.
The day turns to night;
He has a huge fight.
That face looks very old;
I touch him, he is cold.
I get scared, I shout, shout, shout;
The candle just burned out.

Tears come to my eyes;
Nobody ever wants to say goodbye.
My vision is a blur;
My speech is such a slur.
My palms start to perspire;
Him I really admire.
The flowers start to bloom;
Every king deserves his tomb.

James A. Amick

Like A Star

As I look into the sky
I often sit and wonder why
Things are the way they are
life is precious like a star
But like a star life will fade
and will we live another day.

Nick Tomaskie

Love Lost

He prefer me call him master
A name absent of base
the forced sins remain nameless
For they devoid of taste
The pushing down of your love
for the still holding hand
Oh the hurt you bring
still your greatest fan

Since the death of Your love
You haven't been quite the same
Into the bright heavens
from whence her beauty came

Yes you prefer me call you master
forgotten of the love we once had
Yes you prefer me call you master
But I rather call you dad.

Robert Bannon

My Christ

On days of steel I held the cross
To ponder that which Christ had lost
And saw his vision coming fro
With angels in the afterglow.
I thought upon his life well spent
And souls toward heaven once he sent
And nights of prayer without relief
For humans need to share their grief.
I wondered why his days were few
And how he spent them as a Jew;
I couldn't help but bring to bear
The value of his loving care.
And so I tried to comprehend
The meaning of his early end
And shed some light upon his cause,
The force of which had made me pause
To think again of loving man
And those that try as best they can
To give help to the hurting few
Like any duly chosen Jew.

David Stark

Seeing Is Believing?

What I see...
...is industry
Paving the way...
...for society
What I see...
...is the economy
taking precedence over ecology.
What I see...
...is a lack of civility
in a nation born...in barbarity
What I see...
...is a salary
determining our humanity.
What I see...
...is morality
becoming a luxury
rather than...a necessity
could my eyes
be deceiving me?
or is it just...reality?

Frank J. Nadal II

Earth

Summer ends silently like
   secrets of soundless
Words of mystery
   and faith...

Where wild winds wail
   restlessly through
   the hills up to
   the untamed peaks...

Where once I was born
Oh falling raindrops
   on a crystal moon
   lite night...

Wolves howling at
   the cold night
   air...

Vanishing through
   the wilderness
as fast as it can...

LoriAnn Sanchez

Missing You

Time heals all wounds.
I've heard it said before.
My wounds seem no less,
Yet no more.
The longing remains,
and his voice I hear.
The missing is the same,
when I feel him near.
Sometimes I see him,
in others his age.
Time, will never be able,
to turn that page.
Things that would have been,
now will never be.
The future I dreamed of,
I will never see.
Time heals all wounds.
I think that untrue.
No matter the time
I'll always miss you.

Gearldine Gregory

Mothers

Mothers you are the dearest,
Things on earth to us.
Portrait of a rose.
Face with, character that only
Love and years can mold.
Your smile hold real sincerity,
That shine pure as gold,
The tenderness within your eyes,
Show us love, caring of the soul,
The wonderful way you walk,
Each steps a work of art,
Some, old in years
But very young at heart.
Filled with faith and hope,
Give strength when things are low,
Out of the things God made on earth,
He, never made a purer soul.

Myrtle Joiner

Mary

She
was from me -
 but not of me
Our ways were one
 yet far apart.
For love
 she walked
  across
 my life
and
left her footprints
 on my heart.
Ethel Christian

A Glimpse Of It All

Sometimes
Just sometimes
There's a grand moment
The moment that strikes you
Strikes you so deep into your soul
Almost like an explosion
The one moment that changes
Almost all perspective of "reality"

Can you hear the color
And smell the sounds?
This grand moment...
Is it love?
Or shall it be hate?
But it's an emotion
Unexplainable to any other soul -
Other than your very own
Charlotte Cattell

Thief

Guilt burdens the back
that bears it, making
time internally long,
shackling its prisoner,
shunting the passage of time
away from life....
stealing its song.
Rita Oleksiak

The Gift

I walk along as I often do
with my eyes glued to the ground
to make sure each foot is planted
in the perfect place along my path.

Suddenly,
A ribbon of sound wraps around my ears
and tugs my head up . . . up . . . up
until my eyes touch the sky.

Directly above me
two red-tailed hawks
waltz in rhythm
to the pulse of life.

Their dance expands my heart
cracks open my consciousness
dissolves boundaries.
My spirit soars, wingtips brush my soul.
Doris Beresford

Drifting

The world is an ocean,
In which we are adrift.
We're always in motion,
And life is a gift.

Sometimes we have rafts,
To help us pass through the days.
Other times there are chilling drafts,
And we're tossed among the waves.

Who knows how our days will end,
And in which the way we go.
It all depends on the messages we send,
And on how well through the waves we flow.
Starsha Truesdale

A Day Outside

The day was cold;
There were clouds in the sky.
Yet we were bold
Because we had to go outside, to get by.

The wind was blowing;
The clouds hid the sun.
Yet while we were playing,
Our faces got well done.

When we got back home:
We all could tell
That the sun had come
And burned our faces very well

Some faces were just a little red,
Some were more,
Some were tan (they said),
And some swollen and very sore.

The lesson that we need to know,
Is to wear sunscreen outside,
So your face won't glow,
When you get back inside.
Shauna Thomas

The Flower

You are like a little flower.
A flower that shines in the morning sun.
You are like a little flower, that needs
 more than just the sun.
You are like a little flower, that needs
 the morning dew.
You are like a little flower, that needs
 water from the dew.
You are like a little flower, that needs
 the rain too.
You are like a little flower.
Just like my son so true.
You are like a little flower, that
 fills a mother's heart.
Like my son can only do.
Phyllis Kwiecien

Love

If I could choose from Life's shelf
the things I'd like to do,
The only one that I would choose
is just to be with you.

No promise would I beg of thee,
no task need you fulfill.
Only that you be with me
and never my love still.
doris miller

The Paths Of Hollow Woe

Upon the paths of hollow woe
we walk our lives demise
Stopping for but just a moment
to watch another rise

The paths run coarse from years of wear
the trav'lers own dismay
But still we plow them on and on
trying to forge our way

Knowing full the impending cost
our journey does not halt
Flying high a banner of death
with it we find no fault

But on these paths lie little gaps
where one can come or go
To where they go, from where they come
you or I may never know

So still we carry always straight
marching to our end
Less one can walk these paths to save
and thus his life to rend
Dan Kelm

Carl

My dear Carl has gone away
In God's hands he will stay

I brush away my tear
No one here to lend an ear.

I miss him so very much
Longing for his friendly touch

I creep around the house
Being as quiet as a mouse.

Thinking he is still sleeping
When I remember I start weeping

I will join him one day
Together we will romp and play
Beverly Tietz

Mommy's Trophy

A fair young child
Of only six years
An angelic beauty queen
But her heart filled with tears

Mommy was proud
She was living her life
Daddy was busy
At work all night

Her youth torn away
She did what mommy would say
Daddy was distant and cold
But he had riches and gold

The angel was missing
The family searched the grounds
In the dark basement
The angel's body was found

Sad her death was
But did she ever live?
Mommy and daddy
Said they created the best womanly kid.
April Henderson

A Vision

Slumber in the night,
Wake half way through the day.
I had a vision in my head
Of the reason why I was made.

It showed me tears and laughter
Of constant jubilee.
It showed me hate and anger
With moments of envy.

It showed me love and beauty
As she stepped into my space.
It showed me bored and silent
While lingering in my ways.

It showed me fame and fortune
Of goals yet unto meet.
It showed me poor and lonely
As my life came to be.

I had a vision in my head
Of the reason why I was made.
I pray it was all a dream
For me to end that way.

Timothy J. Bentz

Live This Day

Live this day
For Yesterday
Is but a Memory
Tomorrow but a Vision
But if this day
Is well lived
Then Yesterday
Becomes a fond Memory
And Tomorrow
Becomes a Vision of Hope

Teresa K. Weathers

Bruised Hands

Slap on the hand
Thin line between wrong and right
Invisible to an innocent child
Who cannot see it
Losing battle
Always disappointing
Have I let you down again?
Unfortunate errors
Never forgotten
Hold them over my head
Make me regret and repent again
Never allow me to forget
Bruises form on tender skin
Hit me while I'm down
That's how you like to play, isn't it?
Bruises on my pale, fragile hands
Don't remember how they got there
You did your best to make me forget
But I know you
And I can still remember the truth.

Julie Overstreet

Will I

If I live, will I not die
If I laugh, will I not cry
If I'm hurt, will I not heal

Aaron Joseph Sannipoli

I Love You

There I sat staring at you,
You were standing on two
Very unstable legs,
They looked like wobbly pegs.
    And I thought, "I love you."

The next thing I heard
Were your very first words.
At any time of the day
I could expect you to say,
    "I love you."

As you've gone on with your life,
That day you married your wife,
I kept thinking how
If I'd known then what I know now.
    Oh, how I love you!

You're a most precious one,
My very first grandson.
I couldn't believe
or begin to conceive
    how large the words are, "I love you."

Crystal Meier

Guardian Angel

My guardian angel,
That's who you are.
Always helping to guide me,
Whether near or far.
Wrapping your arms around me,
In the times I may be cold.
Giving me daily strength,
As my life begins to unfold.
Helping guide my family,
Undoubtedly with protection.
In times calming my baby,
With your undying affection.
Giving me a glimpse,
Of what's now a dim light.
To help lead the way,
I know a fire you would ignite.
Although I miss you dearly,
I feel safer with you up above,
For who better to be my guardian angel,
Than my grandpa so full of love.

Jannell Palms

My Shining Star

Mom my child said to me.
I'm being judge by what they see!
They don't want to sit at lunch by me.
I'm not asked to say parties,
I guess I'm not cool enough
suave, stylish, or have the right stuff.
To be in this group that they
call friends, the click, the groupies,
this little trend.
"Oh" how shallow they all are.
Not to notice that you're a star.
Because inside you really shine
your friendship and love is genuine.
They are the unfortunate ones.
Not to know you for what you are.
Not to know my "shining star".

Gail Turner

Untitled

Lonely, set astray from my usual
    path to destiny,
I mistakenly chose the route to
    destruction.
Love was once so indestructible in
    my own little world;
    but now so humble.
Left with nothing but the torment
    of being alone;
I cry, but as always no one hears
    me.
    Everyone is deaf
The solemn night leaves me to
    call your name.
    I receive no response;
    just the echo of my own voice.
I realize that I will love him
    forever, despite the pain.
    I dwell in memories
    and rest in silence...

Sara Jennifer Wilson

The Captor

Crafted in ingenious ways,
The highly geometric maze
Wafted gently in the breeze.

A beauty was this silent snare
Its mesh as soft as angel's hair,
Yet strong enough to cause despair.

For some who trespassed it in flight
In early morn or late at night,
Not knowing of their fateful plight.

They'd twist and turn to get away
Only to tire from the fray
And slowly die on their last day.

Right or wrong, we cannot say
It's simply part of Nature's way.
The little spider paused to pray.

Irving E. Morrill

Broken Man

From fragments in time
In thoughts that we would
Turn from within
If we thought that we could

As we search from within
From what it must seem
Should we make our life right
or follow our dreams

The dreams that we follow
Are deep from within
On roads that we walk
From a path with no end

To wander about
When all that seems lost
Do we feel with our heart
Or die from the cost

So reach for your dreams
If it's all that you've got
Try to feel with your heart
From a life that would not.

Frank Shortridge

Before Noon

Born of my lover's tongue,
I glide on sandy shoulders
flocked with tiny brown swans
to harvest opiates, budding poppies
sedate my lips in plume.

The sun's fingers
push through ivy framed window panes,
lightly touch the hazel pools
on the golden landscape of her face,
she breathes them in.

Sighs, rhythmic as ocean waves
from deeper than her throat,
flood my ear
with a salty mist,
cover two pieces of a puzzled world,
each curve fit to fit
as if cut from the same light.

John Davis

The Bond Of Love

My eyes open for the first time
The wailing cries never cease
I am held in her arms so gently
A bond never to be broken

She feeds me when I hunger
Catches me when I fall
Picks up the broken pieces
Rocks me to sleep with a song

She protects me from the boogey man
Lends a shoulder when I cry
She's my friend when I'm lonely
A glimpse of light when I see darkness

A supporter of all my decisions
A guide when I wander
She shows me my potential
And hugs me when I fail

Someday we will go separate ways
The bond remaining strong
Held together by wonderful memories
This is a love between Mother and child

Justin Calabro

The Sermon

The swirling clouds of awesome storms,
God's mighty works he shapes and forms.
A fearsome sight for the faint of heart,
Thunder crashes as clouds do part.
Lightnings fingers race cross the sky,
Droplets sift down as angels cry.
No mightier sermon have I partook,
My depth of soul has he shook.
Spirits uplifted I worship in wonder,
My God calls to me in the thunder.

Jean Norris Stennett

Shadows

Hear the melody of my heart,
Hear the whispers from far apart,
Stop and take a look at yourself,
Stop hiding in the shadows.

Simone Egan

I, The Least Of All

Nights in the desert —
Lonely and cold.
The knife cut of wind
Blows 'Cross my bones.'
Searing my soul
Into many grains of sand.
Over rocks, around cacti,
Blasting my lonely thoughts
Away into a billion stars,
To gaze upon my naked face.
Burning the deserts soul
Into my weathered being —
    Hot breath of survival
    To the smallest creature
I, the least of all . . .

Bill Bowman

Little Reflection

There you are,
little reflection.
Can't you be still,
just one moment,
to let me glance at you?

Inside all those clothes
that half engulf you,
behind philodendron hair
that matches sinfully chocolate eyes,
I see a little bit of me.

And when you flash
your amusingly kiddish smile,
shining at everything above,
I see a little bit of you.

There you go again,
run off in your mismatched clothes,
with aspirations of a gold digger,
I laugh at a little bit of us.

Hilary Terrell

Endless Battle Rattled Minds

Endless battle rattled minds.
Dear God give me a whole lot of time,
time to think, think of you.
Satin for sure makes me blue.
I hope and pray from day to day,
Dear God, my Lord, I want to say.
I'm waiting for the day I'll be okay.
Darkness awaits the bad in me.
Light, early mourn serenity.
The love in my heart is like solid gold.
Please dear Lord I feel so old.
Endless battle rattled minds
I pray let me do something else
    with my time.

Deborah R. Costa

The Ultimate Betrayal

People wander around lifeless
    so unaware of real purpose
To be blindly led
    by a society preoccupied
    with selfishness and corruption
Is something they will
    come to regret with sorrow

Rhett Ray Wilson

If You Knew Me

If you knew
The terrible secrets
That went on
That summer night,
If you saw,
How terror joined the hands
Of innocence,
If you knew,
The terrible secrets
That the river's soul swallowed
Then you would know me.

Una Ramey

What Is Death

What is death,
Who really knows?
Some say it's a new start
Some say it's the end.
Some say it's peace
Some say it's pain.
Who really knows?
Who knows is God!
God knows if it's a new start.
God knows if it's the end.
God knows if it's peace.
God knows if it's pain.
All we can do is wonder,
And wait for God to let us in.

Marsha Ray

In Line

Handsome young man waiting
Patiently in line.
Sixty jars of Gerber.
Two boxes of Pampers.
Enjoying the break.
Looking down content and weary.

Tall, thin woman pacing
Back and forth in line.
Two bottles of wine.
Ten microwave dinners.
Disdainfully sniffing the air.
Harried and wanting to be elsewhere.

Round, middle aged woman
Leaning on her cart.
Overflowing with food.
A family's weekly menu.
Glancing at the cheap rags.
Distracted and resigned.

Leigh Senter

The Storm

The unmerciful wind howls,
sending a chill down my spine.
Lightning flashes,
making the dark sky light up,
like the eyes of a cat.
Thunder rumbles,
shaking the ground,
like the footsteps of a giant.
I crouch next to a boulder,
watching for any sign,
that the storm shall die down.
A leaf brushes against my face,
making my trembling legs crouch lower.

David Wilkinson

Love Is All That Counts

Love is all that counts
When you're learning how to walk;
A kiss from Mom on your boo-boo,
Gentle rocking, and sweet talk.

Love is all that counts
When you have a broken bone;
A frightening cast and painful tears,
Are soothed by Dad's soft tone.

Love is all that counts
When you meet a boy you like;
Marriage is forever,
With our own little tyke.

Cynthia Wolfley

Out In The Orchard

Throw me a line,
To hang me up,
For the crimes I have committed
Out of just damn luck.
I want to be burned
I want to be tortured,
For the crimes I have committed
Out in the orchard.
The apples I took,
The wine I drank,
I must be burned,
I must be tortured,
For what I did
Out in the orchard.
I do admit it was fun.
But now I have to pay,
For what I have done.

Nicole Squassoni

Little Mountain

In the distance of the view
The sense of the summer set
On a clear mountain lake
The tranquil mountain
Will not rest
For it is alive
Alive with every creature
Of every living thing
Past and present
So that one day it may be reborn
In a child that comes to play on top
And see
What I have seen.

Robert Pilaszewski

You Loved

You love at day
you love at night
you loved in Alaska by
the northern light.
You loved in America
you loved in Japan you
loved upon the oceans
sands.
You loved in the beginning
you loved to the end
you loved life wherever
you have been.

George R. Flick

Casually Manic

To be sorrow washing
over my gaze
would mean something.

I am sure of you sorrow
lone feeling comfort.

This questing
becomes ink
One day adds up
Much of what was spoken
Attracted
This point of perspective
Often
Shadow of the eye will blue.

Jhon

Fate

Against the Clouds
I see the Sun
gone is the Dark
the Light had won
a warm, gentle Breeze
tousles my hair
I breath in
the sweet morning Air
it won't be long
'till the Morning
is gone
soon the Day
will have begun
but until then
I will wait
for now I'll Wonder
what is my Fate?

Tara Michelle O'Sullivan

Untitled

Don't close your eyes to the world,
You will miss the simple beauty...

A flower drops a seed, grows a
flower drops a seed. Not able to see
flowers bloom, caught up in our
own worlds of black and white...

Violets, yellows and teal bring
comfort to the mind, knowing
we are but a seed...

Eric T. Hoffmann

The Bookstore

The cold rain
Runs in rivulets
Down my upturned face.
The sun is gone,
Like a bear in hibernation.
The frozen rain fights my tears
As I stand in the doorway
Of the rare bookstore,
But I don't care.
The window, full of fragile tomes,
Reflects my water-logged vigil.
I am waiting,
Waiting patiently
For my loved one to arrive.
God gave him to me,
And, for him,
I will wait an eternity.

Stacy McManness

Untitled

At dawn I see the light
entering my eyes,
we can see the future
In this light,
Forever, is the change
that takes place
In a Dark corner of my mind
I hide from the light
To know the past,
The fire in the Darkness,
cools my soul
I light a candle,
for the hope of some light,
but it brings me further
Into the darkness.

Eric Sanderson

Misjudgement

My heart explodes
And bursts into flames,
Destroying my insides.
The raging red
Seeps out of my body,
Escaping my mouth as words.
The angelic sun forgives my anger
As the puddle at my feet
Reflects my stone eyes,
Drained of innocence,
And without inspiration.

Chris Mason

Alone

Alone, I reach out.
I reach out with my heart,
my arms draw back empty.
I reach out with my soul,
my arms draw back empty.
I reach out with body,
my arms draw back full.
A compromise at best...
the heart remains cold,
the soul remains empty,
and the body...
waits for ecstasy.

Shannon Evans Bickford

The Aging Painter (Degas)

The bather twists her back
as the naked is clothed
by the pull of a towel.

Alone and shimmering
in contrasting veils
of pink and green

Her solid mass,
(once a dancer's)
spun from the Sun
stands still and
cools as water lifts.

The painter's vision congealed
like the moments fireworks,
in dark sky, begin to fade.

Jonathan Nash Glynn

My Little Lullaby

Filled with fear and anger
towards herself why she had
to be for she was only a child
herself. When the day had come
to take it away she suddenly became
so afraid, while sitting in a room
filled with other's you would think
to yourself we were all mothers.
You want to cry but want no one to
see so you hold it in until you
can't breath. When they call your
name they feel no shame all because
they feel you're to blame. When you
finally awake you feel you made a
mistake but then you know it's all
to late as the tears fall from
her eyes she knew she would always
cry for she could never forget her
  little lullaby.

Dawn Patterson

Little Ghetto Girl

Little black girl sitting on a curb
up there high in the sky soars a
bird, but then there are voices
heard over to her left some are
loud and some unclear, noises to
the right, little people play and
big people fight, what is this
place her mind wonders then, like
that bird in the sky, this child,
would one day fly, little black
girl sitting on the curb, silent
when she cry's will she ever be
heard, a car is speeding by, get
her off that curb, where is this
place, she's thinking now, she'll
fly beside that bird in the sky
one day she will, one day she'll try.

Reba Collins

Magical Land

I'd like to go to a place,
where butterflies fly,
and there is always,
a rainbow in the sky,
where there is a,
beautiful princess,
and castles grand,
sometimes I like to travel,
to this magical land,
where unicorns prance,
and fairy's dance,
where dreams come true,
just me and you.

Ariana Griswold

Grandma

A mother twice over
A blossom in the clover

Unconditional love forever to cherish
With empathy and caring never to perish

Always accepting and eagerly supportive
Blind to mistakes which bear no motive

Unselfishly giving without asking for
Best hugger around, grandma, I adore.

Laura M. Chamineak Gibbs

Untitled

Once I had a paper
cut
That bled and bled
all day,
And even though I never
picked the scab,
It wouldn't go away..

Lindsey Cuneo

Someday

People come and people go
Yet in our hearts, their faces show
Times of goodness and of tears
Caring laughters and golden years
Your soul will stay in my heart
And I know we'll never part
Though you've gone so far away
I know I'll see you again . . .
Someday!

April Dawn Behymer

The Sound of the Ocean

Oh please, would you please
take me down to the sea
where seagulls fly
and the wind is free.

If only for a moment,
not even a day,
we could walk with the sand
on our toes right away!

No, we don't have to have eyes
to see beauty per se,
for we can carry it's memory
in a most unusual way...

Yes, we can hold the ocean
in the palm of our hand
if we stop for a moment
to realize how grand...

The sound of the waves
that we can always hold dear
through the brilliant instrument
of the seashell to our ear.

Kara T. Michel

Who Is This Man

Who is this man before me?
This man with the gray in his hair;
With pain in his eyes,
And a heart full of sighs,
Who is this man sitting here?

Who is this man before me?
This man with his shoulders bowed low;
The heartaches and fears
Of his sixty four years
Have made his footsteps go slow.

Who is this man before me?
He's different from all other men,
Always loyal and true
To me and to you;
My husband, your dad and our friend.

Louise Lilly Simmons

Untitled

Petals fall slowly to the ground
As she decides her fate with a rose.
He loves me.
He loves me not.
Tears roll down her face
As the naked stem rests in her hand.
He loves her not.
Blood runs over her finger.
As the thorn pricks her flesh
It pricks her soul.

Katie Wirt

Snow Power

The softest sound I know is
snow. Soft cool snow power.
Power to cripple a whole city.
Then again soft and cool
against children's faces to
bring roses to their cheeks.
Power to let us know how
insignificant we really are
and to paint the whole city
with soft and cool snow scenes
think about the snow and you
will really know who has the power!
Soft and cool.

Matilda I. Gowen

Sheltered Space

There are some loving moments
  that time can not erase
Vast, timeless memories
  that guard love's place
Each paving life's long path
  with a sweet, familiar taste

Sadly — some of love's true moments
  will tumble in disgrace
Those released remain untouched
  and slip away to waste
While others cherished are reborn
  to an elevated pace

There in love's brief moments
  that time can not erase
Destined hearts again will share
  time's infinite space
Where memories find shelter
  held close in love's embrace

Denise Lynn Baldwin

Hypocrisy

Preach, pastor, preach!
Do you believe what you teach?
You whine, you wail, but do you reach?

Jason M. Simpson

Enemies

Enemies to the end
Because you spent
All my cash on hash
And pot
I do not want to be your friend
We are now enemies to the end
Now you're buying cocaine
Now you're crying
'Cause you know it's insane

Larry Zukerman

Juliet's Lament

A miracle sent
By Fate's decree
Was it a dream
When you came to me?
Unforeseen, your soul touched mine
Thrusting me into the abyss.
Dizzying, tumbling
Basking in hopeless bliss
A magical existence
Where once there was none
Feel the warmth! See the colors!
Alive! Abloom in the sun!
Illuminating my darkness,
You are my star
But so high, up in the sky
You remain so very far.
For our distance remains immutable
Even for the Heavens above,
And I despair of imminent poisons,
Of pain, born from love

Christine Yee

Dance Of The Hunters Fire

Dance...Move...Sing...
Hear the beat
Feel the rhythm
Shout with joy
Cry...Scream...Moan...
Mourn the death
Of our brothers
Deer, Elk, Buffalo
Laugh...Shout...Yell...
Sing the tremolo
Dance with pride
Stomp the grass
Listen...Feel...Live...
Release your soul
Grasp the spirit
Of the hunter
Dance...Move...Sing...

Steven Ayers

Who Would've Thought?

Who would've thought
it would be this way?
That we'd fall in love,
I fell anyway.

And who would've thought
It would turn out like this?
That what we had
Now can only be missed.

Is this the way
All relationship go?
Do all melt away
Like last winter's snow?

Or somewhere out there,
In the world my friend,
Are some so lucky
To last 'til the end?

But even though, my dear friend,
We could not last that long
Things won't be sad forever,
They'll be better farther along.

Sarah J. Hitchen

He'll Never Know

He'll never know the silent pain that I
    carry here in my heart.
He'll never know how much he's loved
    even though we are so far apart.
He'll never know how many years I've
    lived with this broken heart.
He'll never know the pain I feel when
    it's time for us to part.
He'll never know how it breaks my heart
    pretending to be just he's friend.
He'll never know this love I feel
    will never have an end.
He'll never know the pain of an
    unrequited love.
He'll never know the prayers I've prayed
    to the good Lord up above.
He'll never know I've loved him,
    even though my life should end.
He'll never know the love I've felt was
    much more than that of a friend.

Glynda Leger

Angel And I

Angel and I
Oh how we fly
When we're together
Angel and I

We're two of a kind
Angel and I
Two separate people
Angel and I

Her brown hair
And beautiful brown eyes
Are no match
For my blonde hair and blue eyes

Her smile so becoming
And charm so cold
Meek and reluctant
I am, I'm told

Yet we do love
Angel and I
Sister we are
Angel and I

Mary McHenry

Family

She turns to those she wants to love
They turn away.

Why do they all live together
Yet stay so far apart?

Doors slam, in anger,
Childishly expressed.
Hearts weep, in love,
Kept fearfully repressed.

She reaches for a better world,
Too young to know the truth
Family bonds are tied with blood
They cannot be cut loose.

She screams to those she used to love,
Again they turn away.

Kate Cole

To The Coming Of Death

Let it be quick as a humming bird
    darts at a feeder;
Let it be soft as a puffy white cloud
    rests on a mountain;
Let it be gentle as the first breeze
    of morning at sunrise;
Let it be still as the hushed witching
    hour of midnight.
Thus, then, may the way of one
    world be forsaken
As Brother Death and Sister Life
Join hands at the entrance to
    the new.

Bertha W. Wightman

Your Love

When the sun glances
through the window
it's as bright
as the smile on her face,
I feel your warmth
watching over me,
When something's wrong
you hold me tight
through horrible moments,
The times that are good
and times that are bad
I go with you,
With every year that
passes you always
watch over me and every
moment is special to both of us.

Cassie Kornblau

The Summer Sparrow

    Coo, Coo, Coo, the summer
sparrow cries. The sunlight casting
summer shadows in his summer
eyes. Dusk comes soon and then
comes night but the sparrow he does
fly. Then a single ray of heaven's
light comes bursting through the
sky. Dawn comes and then comes
morning but the sparrow he does
sleep. High up upon a branch in a
little summer heap. But soon comes
fall and then the trees soon begin to
shed. And I woke up one morning to
find that he had fled. I miss him
dearly he's the most beautiful thing
I've found. I know he's gone to
brighter lands with summer all year round.

Sydney Roy

Death Of A Sister

Oh no, you must be wrong!!!
She's not gone!

Don't say it again until I can hear
I'll tell you again with tears and fear

Not my best friend, my sister, my hero

My sorrow, my pain, my horror
To try to live without her

I love you right down to the bone
Making your spirit never gone...

Elizabeth Scott

Nacton Shores

Through the woods I marched
very brave at heart
through the broken gate
a graveyard awaits
old and very cold
stories have been told.

Hedgerows overgrown
I fell over a stone
part of someone's grave
I felt very afraid
tall creepy trees
made me weak at the knees

Finally I was there
I took a breath of air
the sun was going down
I was so glad I found
the beautiful shores of nacton

Tina Joy D'arcy

Darkness

I sit here in the darkness
Waiting for you to come
Though I know you never will
I wait there still
Looking for some hint
A glimmer of hope
Suddenly I spy a note
You've left never to come back
I sit down blindly
With tears in my eyes
I should have been wise
To never let you in my life
Though you said you'd be my wife
If only I had known
Now my hearts cold as stone
I still sit here in the darkness
Only now I'm all alone

Jackie Meier

Eye Of A Child

A child's eye, crystalline,
reflects the world as it should be,
fairies, treasure, dragons and elves,
each a childhood fantasy.

Time traps me with ticks and tocks,
I scramble through the monster's maze—
but I cannot find the golden string,
so I wander in a daze.

My eyes have grown opaque and weary—
and it seems I've lost the way,
the dragons, elves and fairies too,
have fallen also in decay.

But on crystal quiet evenings,
the pipes of Pan project the thought
to join in the fairy dance and forget
the lessons I have been taught.

So I check my sleeping children,
snuggled tight in dreamland's hold.
My eyes reflect their imagination
and there I find the fairy-gold.

Caisa E. Pope

Of Birthdays And Goblins

As the birthday goblin
Gleefully slaps his thigh
At every added wrinkle
To shrinking souls
Gleaming hard bodies
Glistening
Golden sweat
Expressionless
Unlined
Masks
Dorian Gray
Patron Saint
Behold the glory of
Youth
Another soul collapses
Black hole
Of dried up prunes...

Laurence Moscato

Memory Of Mother

Dear Lord, bring me comfort,
Ease this pain in my heart;
Sometimes I feel the pain
Will never depart.

I miss my dear mother,
The love she outpoured;
Though time moves on further
That love will endure.

I know she's in Heaven
In God's tender care;
And someday forever
I'll be with her there.

Kay Rinehart

The Cat

See the furry cat
stroll across the street.
The obstreperous roar of the
feline yet so faint compared to
the sound of its relation the
magnificent lion. As you caress
the tabby you notice its stole
is as velvety as a bow.
You peer into her emerald eyes.
You wonder what the kitten is pondering.
The sensation of its purr is like
the engine of a classic vehicle
roaring into existence after a
prolonged rest. Witness the
frolicsome puss scamper around
the dwelling in such a sheer
fashion. When you encounter a kit
you begin to value human existence.

William A. Zadell

Tear

A tear fell from a tree
When I looked up 'twas only he.
With a far away look in his eyes
There was sorrow where only dreams lie.
Far beyond the dreams of some,
Dreams of things yet to come.

Pearl M. King

Anxiety

Is something wrong with me
I've got a pain in my stomach
And I feel so empty
When I am happy
I still frown
People tell me to cheer up
But I am still down
My mind is never at ease
And I am so hard to please
I've got this secret I can't tell
If I do my life is sure to go to hell
I can't live with this pain
it's driving me insane
I've tried to smoke it away
I've tried to drink it away
But it comes back
Stronger each day
I wish it would
Go away

Robert Miata

Moon

Oh! Bright moon in the sky
how it is that you can fly?
What it is that you can see?
Can you see my sweetest dream

Are you the one that keeps me safe
from the nightmares till the day
do you chat with the stars
or do you chat with venus and mars.

Are you happy living there?
Do you ever wish you where somewhere?
another place where you can see
some other things you've never seen.

Asenet Martinez

Trinity

Classical!
Charming, so delightful!
Colorful!
Leaves float like butterflies.
The colors of the river streaming!
The sun light glittering!
So many hues.
So deep are the blues,
Yet clear glass dripping off my body
puts ripples on the shore.

Robert J. Frolli

A Faithful Story

I wish to tell the world
A story of a little girl
She came to me one day
With confusion blocking her way
    Her life was such a mess
So she wanted it to end
But little did she know
With faith she could win
    I kneeled her down
I wiped her tears
And took away all her fears
    Little girl don't you cry
Give yourself another try
You are worthy of my love
Call to me and the father above
    Little girl just call my name
And I will comfort you again.

Gidget Roney

Untitled

Could you help me please?
I seem to be lost

I can't find my way around
I have nothing to hold onto

I am too weak to find my way out
Worn down from the many times

I need someone to help me up,
Could you carry me awhile?

While you carry me through this mess,
I seem to fall in love

But if you were to drop me now,
I'd slide back to the pit

And cry a frightening amount of tears
for I'd never get out again.

Katie Lyons

Love And Joy

The dawns of heaven
shines down on us everyday.
The love and warmth from
those rays is the happiness
of our hearts sharing
with the world.
Together they are unstoppable
over all the evil and wrong
doing in our lives. So I
try to share some of that
love with God and everyone
whom I meet

Jermey McLain

The View

As I look outward
  from within
I envision the world
  in its entire complexity
Subconsciously seeking
  to explore the known
  as well as the unknown
Hoping to identify
  and interpret
  the reality of what exists.
Discovering in my attempts
  the possible probability
  of anything
Be it real or abstract
  which can both
  influence and affect
  what mere light
  cannot reflect.

Jeannette Pope Hailsham

Manipulate

Through words
and
easy lies
you crush
me
into a
repulsive void

Bessie K. Conner

Ruins

As the darkness settles over the land,
A disturbed silence sets the world
Full of a controlled chaos.
Cities overturn.
Governments crumble.
The land is left in ruins,
  Burning ruins.
And somewhere at the beginning
  Before the darkness
  Before the destruction,
I stand
  Holding a match.

Stephanie Gordon

The Light

To the shadows I may go away
from the light, away from the
places I know too well, toward
the spacious sky close to my heart
I will keep the light that I have
left behind me. If I could only see
the light that I left so far behind
me, even if I could see the light
that glows so dim I would never
return to the past, I must look on
toward the future and I must keep
my course through life, until I
can't see the light that I have left
so far behind.

Jonathan Silberman

Untitled

I feel pain
I see red
It starts to rain
I wish I was back in bed
The horrible truth comes to me
I will never see my family again
My life flashes in my mind
All those good times I had
Everything now a memory
Everything now a thing from the past
I know that death is near
Death has come here

Indira Medina

The Garden

I am my thoughts and my feelings,
My fears, my hopes, and my dreams,
For without those, I would be
But a mere shell of what you see,
If I would be at all.
What would I be without all of these?
I hope I never find out.

When we were born, we were seeds
Planted in a mere garden.
Without thoughts, feelings, fears,
Hopes, and dreams, we would remain
Seeds forever. With those, we
Will grow, and the mere garden
Will become a lush forest.

Humans have not yet reached the forest.
With any luck, they will soon,
But they must first learn how to grow.

Katie Egolf

Untitled

These glasses are special
there's only just two,
to toast your devotion
and love so true.

When life's little troubles
make patience grow thin,
drink from THESE glasses,
not ones made of tin.

These glasses ARE special—
they are a matched pair,
to remind Chris and Ginger
how deeply they care.

Cindy I. Milner

My Love Is Gone

My love is gone, he went away
Only maybe will he be back someday
I had to go far from him
Now our flame of love is dim
My life was once but now it's not
Because my love I've no longer got
My heart was torn, ripped to shreds
My life is gone, better off dead
Nothing left to look forward to
No ambitions, nothing to do
He says he loves, but is he real?
Did someone else his love steal?
I will not know but hope I must
And his love I have to trust
My love is gone, he went away
And if I'm lucky, maybe he'll be back
Someday.

Kristin M. Lukowski

Butterfly Wings

I hold you in my arms.
You, who are just beginning.
Lost in dreams, you will not remember.
I think of our future together.
Places we'll go, and things we'll see.
You are beautiful and fragile,
Like butterfly wings.

Nathan William Gay

Lonely Mistake

Often we remind each other of the things
we do wrong,
Instead of encouraging each other
with words to make us strong.

Our self-esteem begins to decrease
and our ability to move on goes down,
You'll always be able to find me
there whenever you look around

We are overcome with negativity when
we feel we've reached the end,
only to be brought up by sensitivity
knowing in me, you have a friend

In God's will and way our minds will
be brought back together,
And they shall interlock and be
bonded forever.

Whenever we keep to ourselves, to
ourselves we must make,
And to tell each other of what's
wrong in each "Lonely Mistake."

Maria Honeycutt

December

Motionless gray clouds hovering
Over a white bleakness
That seems to pour out
On to me,
And the rest of the world.
The twisted trees are thin,
With arms of death
That wrap out to embrace us
Until they are given back their life
By the God of springtime;
Which will show its face
Sometime as I sit, waiting,
Waiting,
As a curtain of white death
Showers over me
While the outside world is asleep,
And snug in their homes,
Shielded
From the beautiful bitterness of
December

Nick Senn

Free

Death... is inevitable
It is our fate to meet one day
We will sit at the table of life
and discuss my mortal ways
I will be judged upon my actions,
some of them out of my control,
And it will be decided at that moment
the final passage of my soul

"God"... Will speak
and my soul will shriek with pain
The judgment will be passed
as I'd begin to feel the flame
And in the distance,
Fate will beckon me to follow his lead
I will proceed to receive my punishment
for only asking to be, free.

Jason-De'Sean Gregory

Dream On

The New Year comes, the old year ends,
And with it go the might-have-beens,
The dreams we dreamed,
The thoughts we thought;
Some had substance, form and grace
And found in us a resting place.

A place to grow in faith, divine,
Unhindered by the tides of time.
Encouraging us another day
To seek and trust His perfect way,
And see fulfilled the hearts desire,
Cleansed and purified by fire.

Susan R. Zipprich

I Like

I like to run around upon
the green and grassy ground
to hunt for night crawlers
late at night
to catch a fish if they bite
but the thing I like to do
the most is run around and
pretend we're ghost Boo;

Donna M. Cross

Mommy

A woman
a child
they care
but so mild

She slaps
she cries
not hate
but she tries

The pain
has become
like herself...
so numb

Memories
held nearest
of her sweet
mommy dearest

Julia A.

Paradox

My arms, they are strong
from all the burdens they have carried
Yet they are gentle.
My hands, they have traveled
the roughness of human hearts
Yet they know no treason.
My breath has ventured into
the infinity of deception
Yet it sings of peace.
My heart, a weary soldier
ballets into new life yonder your stare
My eyes so teary from the pain
are thirsty for the dew of a new dawn
The richness of my journey
bows before you
Your sight deceives you away
to barren ground.

Maria O. Vera-Gil

Time

He governs daylight,
And dominates dark.
Uprises the sun
And the moon who pursues.

Time rouses us up at dawn,
And puts to slumber at dusk.
He directs the seasons,
And brings forth the years.

No man knows the future.
No one ever will.
Who knows what betides us?
The Father of all, time!

Sarah Christopherson

Untitled

Whether poor or rich
More
More again
Which
Much more
No more
But always more
Will there ever be enough
Forever more.

Jennifer J. Sulak

Counting Days

Someday I may
get used to waiting.
Days between our moments
fall like autumn's last stubborn
brittle brown leaves swirling down.
Each in destined turn
a bright reminder of summer fire.

I do
my counting inside,
unwrapping island time-packages
again and again,
picking through carelessly
tossed ribbons of memory
left behind in me.
Each bit I once let
fall to the floor
in haste to touch you
is still here —
reassembled, and
torn apart endlessly.

Charles A. Bailey

Sweet Love

Sweet love of mine
How I love the so
Your lips
Your smile
I have engraved in thy heart
Your hands so rough
But yet so smooth
As are your arms
That make my heart beat in happiness
As days go by I've cherished every smile
And yearn to see your sparkling eyes
Sweet love
My heart beats in your hands
But freezes to say some words
That your ears years to hear
What better day to say it
If not on this day
I love you so....
Is what joins our hearts
Sweet love of mine.

Irene Hardesty

Shadows

Shadows are everywhere,
Dusk is about to fall.
I think of you and smile,
I hope that soon you'll call.

You are now far away,
But you seem so very near.
You are always with me,
Though you are not always here.

Our love binds us together,
No matter where we go.
Time and distance,
Make no great difference,
For I will always love you so.

Nola M. Boehm

So I'm Crazy -
I Can Blame It On Fumes!

Sliding through the sludge
In my great big honey truck,
Into the muck I go, axles in
All the way, dollar signs
In tow truck drivers eyes I see,
Man! Did they get bright!
'Cause he knows I just paid
For his college kid schooling tonight!
Oh septic tanks, septic tanks
Boy what a stink - I'm out
Here mucking - it's enough to drive you
to drink!

David R. Spencer

Christmas

Christmas comes.
Christmas goes.
Christmas is hear.
When it snows.
Go to the store.
To get the turkey.
Stove toping pumpkin pie.
And beef jerkey
Most kids want toys.
Like cars, G.I. Joes and trains
Watches, jersey's and air plains,
now it's Christmas Eve
Everyone in bed
Mouse sees, the mouse trap.
Snap he's dead.
Now it's christmas morning
Everyone around the tree
Now the Christmas Dinner
   Turkey

Preston Littleton

Out Of Reach

The first thing you see,
Is deemed the best.
So, on a pedestal it goes,
Much higher than the rest.

While remaining way up high,
Something suddenly goes wrong.
It spares no one hurt,
Neither weak nor strong.

You simply can't comprehend;
Its mood you can't breech.
Now only to accept
That it's just out of reach.

Kenny Griffith Jr.

Snow

Snow is cold and crystal clear,
Snow is near and almost here
The wind is starting to swirl away,
It's telling me today's the day.
I look right out my windowsill
to see that everything is still.
I want to rush right out the door
I want to see the snow once more!
It never snowed last year at all,
Not winter, spring, not even fall
I see a hill not far away,
Where we can sled and play.
I run downstairs in a hurry,
to come and see the little flurry.
Oh how I love the snow!

Rachel Joy Marcussen

Clouds

Each time I see a cloud above
I wonder whence it came
And how it got to be that way,
No two are just the same.

The friendly ones, the angry ones,
The lacy layered veils,
The fluffy ones, the tiny ones,
The ones like horses tails.

The thunder bumpers, bright on top
And scowling dark below,
Chameleons all, from time to time
Their many faces show.

We call them fog when they come down
To see us on the ground,
Their mist then dims our very sight.
They come without a sound.

The wonders of these clouds
Is there for all to see.
It's hard to think of anything
More beautiful or free.

Robert C. Newcomb

The Weed, The Violet, And The Sun

Violet said to Weed one day,
"Why grow you to block my way?
Never have I kept from you
The wind, the rain, the bees, or dew."

Weed replied, "The Sun is mine
To drink the light all the time.
If you can't grow, more for Weed;
So die, small Violet, and let me feed."

Violet said "The Sun's not ours,
Not weeds or Violets or any flowers.
The Sun is free to rise and fall
In circular patterns around this ball.
God alone controls its course,
And He is Sun's power source.
Sun provides for all, you see;
He's life for flowers, you, and me.
So if you try to snuff me out,
He'll kill you, without a doubt."

Barrett Foster Brookshire

What We Need

A sea of humanity
is not what I need.
I need a place
where my soul can breathe.
A place where not one
but all shall lead.

A place of no envy

A place of no greed.

For in this place
there shall plant a seed
and from its reapings
the hungry shall feed.

This is a place
that all people should seek,

a place of peace.

This is what we need.

Y. L. Henry

Time Again

It may seem that everything disappears,
Slowly as I said before,
But I was wrong -
It is only manipulated.
Love turns to hate
And hate to envy
Then envy, in turn to lust,
But lust is love of the heart
And the hate of the brain.
So you tell me,
Where the hell are you
At the beginning?
At the end?
Or where did you even start?
For life is a vicious circle,
Not necessarily un-ending
Because its been stretched and torn,
Yet held together by a steel thread
And the manipulation will continue.

Angela Mueller

Too Late

its over, its done
too late to go back.
Oh no, what to do
can't pick up the slack.

to late to change
what has become
of a dream, a hope,
shot down for fun.

might as well give up,
no use at all,
too late to stop
we're out for the long haul.

it's all too much,
can't deal with the pain,
too late for help,
tears fall like rain.

Amna Sheikh

I Write

I write in verse
About daily life
The sorrows, the joys
The everyday strife
Some call it poetry
What I do with words
They say it's unique
Some say it's for the birds
What name should I give
To what I put down
When some read it and smile
And others read it and frown
It's therapy for me
It helps me to cope
It makes me laugh
And gives me hope
So I'll continue to use
What some call a gift
For as long as it gives
My days a lift

J. Teal

My Little Mitsy

You fly through the air
  with the greatest of ease,
Like a little bird -
  instead of a doggie.
Coat of velvet brown
  with a beautiful sheen,
Always playful,
  and as happy as can be.
Digging out toys one by one,
  until the floor is covered by all.
Lover to all, and as cute as can be.
She's such a joy to have, you see.
Cuddles my head as I sleep at night,
  with love and warmth,
  you just can't fight.
So if you want a lot of Love
  A little Chihuahua!
  Has got it all.

Anita T. Denham

Coming And Going

People come and people go.
For what reason I don't know.

They may be gone for a short time
They may be gone forever.

You may see them soon
Maybe never.

They may have gone to a place
That is out of reach.

They may have gone to a place
That is nearby.

My advice is if you see them
Say Hi!

Meaghan Coughlin

Untitled

Together brings a madness,
You and me and sadness,
Never ever faulty clever
Leading to our badness.

Always is a longing,
Going about and wronging,
On my knees, I beg and plead
Make this no prolonging.

I look at us so sadly,
But I'll retake you gladly.
Need me, lead me, love and feed me,
I'll always love you madly.

Jamie Steinke Lindbo

Forever Sleeping

I lay here so silent
Caught by defeat
My train of thought
Banished or lost in
My sleep.
My emotions run wild
My heart starts to race
My tears flow rapidly
Each breath not replaced.
I'm going so quickly
My eyes growing weak
The world grows silent
As I'm lost in my sleep.

Julie Gentzke

One Way

Something walking
Something crawling
They are coming
To heed the calling
Evil things
From not this earth
Are reaching through
To grasp their birth
The horrid sounds
On holy grounds
Send you chills
As it kills
Run and hide
Suicide
There's nothing left
To talk about
There's one way in
And no way out!

Veronica Putnam

Divine Omniscience

Prescience, a knowing...
of the future, fear growing.
Insanity? Genius...
grasp of the present, tenuous.
My prescient self
is but half my reality,
Psychotic? Exotic?
Or basic duality?

Brize Jackson

The Dance

Music is blaring,
hearts are singing,
couples dance close by.

One couple stands out,
the glow of love all around them.

Their faces,
side by side.

Their matching smiles,
ear to ear.

Their arms wrapped around,
as they move and sway.

Their feelings of love,
dance and move,
with the beat of their hearts.

Stacy L. Martin

If Only I Knew

Open my soul
deeper than my wounds of love
are my wounds of hate
feel my pride

Stronger than the will of he
but she will choose my fate
hold my night

The harvest moon appears above
I feel this is my date
touch my life

My gaze into the eyes of she
told me my date I'll wait

Jabari Eshu Ashanti

Blue Sky

  Blue sky, blue sky
High above the mountain climb

  Blue sky, blue sky
Over top the ships at sea

  Blue sky, blue sky
shining through the window seals

  Blue sky, blue sky
making its way through darkest fog

  Blue sky, blue sky
warming the air for everyone

  Blue sky, blue sky
Taking nap in the night

Chasity Sabins

My Dream

Underneath a willow tree
I slowly drift away
To a place away from here
To a quite, misty bay
I sit upon a wooden dock
And look out toward the sea.
To watch the whales and dolphins
Dance so playfully
The water is so peaceful
There is no hate or war
Drugs and guns are obsolete
And serenity engulfs the sea
This is my Utopia
My idealistic place
Love surrounds me everywhere
In disregard of my sex or race

Desiree Pandrea

Sorry

The things I did the other night,
I know it hurt you deep inside,
and I'm sorry for what I did,
I know I shouldn't of said
What I said.
I hope you forgive me for that
night I broke your heart and
made you cry,
I hurt myself as well as you.
And I hope to God I don't loose you.

Melania Daniell Hurst

A Family Garden

A family garden is a
Place where new growth
Intertwines with old
Growth creating an
Everlasting place where
Dreams are planted, roots
Grow deep and strong, and
Beauty and love prevail:
Providing upcoming
Generations with a start
To create a landscape of
Their own using their
Start as a centerpiece to
Build upon.

Linda Minogue

That's Never Picked Up

It's not as easy as you say
living in times like this
Midnight strolls
with hands tied behind your back
like sleepwalking
through the warfields to come
lucky to live long enough to see
true termination
Demoralized
Desensitized
All feelings are shot
execution style
for the 5 o'clock news
Scarier than 13 steps in the summer
Bullets will kiss my skin
like you used to
with tear-stained lips
and puffy eyes
not like you at all
to cry for me.

Brian Collette

Storm

Fall down from the clouds
fill the air with a shroud.
Crack a bolt
from the heavens
lay it down
upon these heathens.
Steady stream
erupted in flood
beautiful cadence
disgruntled and harmed.
Soaks in the stems
which grow when it passes
brings nourishment to the masses.
Delays plans for the world
enjoyed by the lonely girl.
Upon are abodes we watch from afar
all the roads covered in water.
It will pass soon enough
then we'll relax, in all the wet
I'm all alone don't leave me yet.

Chris Jones

Moonlight

High moon shines above
Casting an eerie blue glow
On all that's below,
Creating silence in the dead of night.
I stand midst the night,
In the summer moonlight,
Warmed by westward wind.
I stare in amazement
At this light that's so bright,
While I'm alone in the dead of night.
A black lake beside
Is shining with white,
Waving specks of light.
A silhouette of geese
Float by with ease,
That are quiet in the dead of night.
A tree on a mound makes a rustling sound
In the warm unleashed summer wind.
Now breaking the silence
Of the dead of night.

Amy M. Sanchez-Hamilton

A Child And You

My child's laughter warms my heart,
It makes me think of you,
So joyously does she respond,
Just like you often do.

Her eyes lit up as laughter came.
In such a way that I,
Couldn't help but kiss her lovingly,
With thoughts of you inside.

Shirley Lind

Illuminations

Upon a lighted interest
Of the million candles burned,
A glowing interest of the morn'
Shines drollfully amidst a knighted dawn

And princes scorned by shadow's might
Gallivant the meadow's luned sight
Upon the image's encompassed night
Akin to monster's scorn

And lying deep beneath the seeping haze
Of mountains breathing sleepish daze
To Night's eternal peekishness are born
Dreams unto the midnight torn

Through the gashes of the fabric's host
And knighted souls in dreams do toast
Of dreamy thoughts and palisades
Where peace of mind and spacious malaise
Own up to echoed harmonies
Of the timelessness unpaid

E. Lee Mahoney

Cat In My Hat

There's a cat living in my hat.
He's very, very fat.
One day that cat flattened my hat.
I said, cat you'll have to
find another hat to live
in, and that's that.
The cat said, you'll just
have to get a bigger hat
and that's that.

Deborah DeJesus

Grandma's Attic

In Grandma's attic
at the top of the stairs
so many memories
are stored away up there
Boxes of photos
and old teddy bears
lots of blue ribbons
she won at the fairs

The wicker basket
she always took to the lake
delicious fried chicken
and her famous chocolate cake
Some beautiful combs
wore in her hair
when going to dances
she always wore them there
I close the door
knowing someday I'll see
all of these treasures
passed on to me

Norma Bagby

Beloved Brother

Precious boy that links us
three together.
Laughing face to fill the
endless days of childhood.

Let's play, let's have fun,
let's grow old together.

Never ever leave before me
But if you do - wait for
me and baby sister.
The circle never ends.

Marion L. DesRoches

Life

As the last light
of dawn stretches over the
hillside, pain cries out over
the land. Life itself drains
away like the setting sun.
Towering mountains cease
their existence on this molten ball.

So close to extinction
courses so deeply engraved
in one's mind become
blurred, and the treacherous
trails of life move on.

Cassandra Hillis

As

As the clouds gather,
so do my fears.
As the rain falls,
so do my tears.

As the lightning strikes,
so does my pain.
As the thunder sounds,
so does my name.

As the sun comes,
so does a smile.
As the rain dries,
so do my tears.

As the clouds go away,
you appear.
As the day warms up,
you are near.

J. R. Crespin

Ah, But If I Could Die

Ah, but if I could die,
for then I could truly fly.

To be but another wayward
spirit, floating in the featureless
darkness, like a feather upon
the midnight wind.

To be free of this earth bound
form, in a place which follows
no norm.

But guides itself and in its
ultimate wisdom, we may find
peace and freedom from the
burden which encumbers us all.

Jason Humphreys

It Hurts

When you lose your love
Where do you turn?
When your body aches
and your heart yearns.
You can not run.
You can not hide.
The pain returns,
it burns inside.
Your voice cracks,
the tears flow.
When will this end?
I do not know.

Valerie Michaelis

Upon The Sea

Upon the sea, a perilous tale
Upon the sea, our heroes sail

Upon the sea, do perils lie
Upon the sea, our heroes fly

Upon the sea, a ships a ground
Upon the sea, our heroes pound

Upon the sea, a terrible sight
Upon the sea, our heroes take flight

Upon the sea, though we may die
Upon the sea, our heroes try

Upon the sea, we risk our lives
Upon the sea, the Coast Guard thrives

Michael E. Bronson

A Winter's Morn

I woke up this morning
and much to my delight,
I saw the world around me
Was dressed in snowy white.
The trees were laced with silver
Icicles on display
A cardinal perched upon a limb
Welcomed the new day.
A host of tiny snowflakes
Were dancing all around
And softly kissed my window pane
and floated to the ground.
O, the beauty of a winter's morn
The world all wrapped in white.
Brings a peace upon one's soul
That lingers through the night

Julia E. O'Brien

Lord, Let Me Be An Angel

Let me be an angel,
Let me be of help,
Let me have a purpose,
For others - not myself...

Let me watch with love
And guide someone with care....
Let me have a reason
Just for being here....

Let me be a messenger
To someone who's in need
Let me show your greatness
Through kind and loving deeds!

Teresa L. Dawson

The Flute

I play my song,
My flute of cedar red
Carved from the heart of a tree
My breath carries my song,
To the Hawk, my brother.
He soars with it on the wind,
The golden breeze of Dawn,
Across the valley,
Still in night's purple shadow
Up the mountain,
A blush in morn's rose-gold light,
To the Great One.
My song,
A prayer for you.

Frank Sweeney

Daddy

I know you can not hear me
and I know you can not read this,
but I have these last words
that I never got to say.
No one could ever replace you, Daddy,
no one could take your spot
you are the one I looked up to
the one I most admired.
This all happened so fast
I didn't want to believe it,
now I don't know how I'll last
Please don't forget about me, Daddy,
I know I could never forget about you
I have lost you forever
but with the memories I have
we will always be together.
I love you and always will.

Love,
"Your little girl"

Reneé Heiob

Envision

The future lies beyond the horizon;
There are those that are able to
Envision the future — that which
Is enduring — by way of eternity.
Love has no beginning and
Never ends,
Much like a wedding band.
Though not circular,
The beauty in the horizon lies in
Infinity.
Attempt always to grasp the horizon
For its strength and look beyond:
There is where your love for
Each other will always dwell.

Kristen Ward

Teardrops

There are teardrops in her heart
But they can't make her cry
There are teardrops in her heart
But they can't come outside
The teardrops in her heart
   Just Want To Die
Because they have to stay inside
Teardrops can't take the pain away
So why let them out anyway...

Trena Gaye Locke Strickland

Believe

Walk silent, walk alone
the answers lie within.
Speak softly, speak truth
there's someone who'll listen.
Love freely, not bound
by thoughts not your own.
Look before you, not behind you.
Look within you, then around you.
Save yourself, then the world.

William R. Skarka

The Sea Is Peace

I will walk to the sea
Where the white sand scratches
   like a silver mice.
In a world of water ever free
Salt air, wheeling gulls — paradise.

The sea is peace
An emerald garden
   dripping crystal rain
Where the wind-whipped waves
   never cease,
But billow, peak, and foam again.

Arby Hewitt-Mulryne

Brionna

Brionna is full of sunshine;
And lots of energy.
She always likes to make me laugh;
You'd think she's two or three.

A grandma's job is lots of fun;
She gets to play and sing
Those nursery rhymes she learned so well
When just a tiny thing.

Brionna is a special gift
Sent from Heaven above;
She's always full of mischief
And unconditional love.

I hope that she will always know
That Grandma loves her "Bri";
And that I'll always try to live
So she'll be proud of me.

I hope that she will always say
My grandma is my friend;
And that our days of sunshine
Will never, never end!

Jackie Thomas

Dream

The girl sits by the window
and watches her past come by.
She sees the things she has
thrown away, things that have
caused her world to spin in
circles and things that have
made her heart fall apart.
She said "What could I have changed?"

Jamie Bowers

Why???

As I am walking
I can see you
smiling, running, playing
  To . . .
It makes me wonder
Deep down inside
What is it that you must hide?
Crying, screaming, pushing
  To . . .
Life could be so precious for me and you!

Keaunis L. Grant

Untitled

A root, a seed, the rainbow in the sky;
everybody has it:
tucked away somewhere special.
Some have lots, while others have few;
It is the basic cause to go on.

It brings to everyone a new beginning,
a new place to start,
A cause for life, that never ceases,
even though some ignore it.

But when comes the moment of truth:
and hardships are too hard to face,
we all turn in one direction:
Towards the sunshine,
And wait for it to emerge:

Hope

Runjhun Misra

Elegy

The grey-green dragon came
  And you climbed
    Upon his back
Tickled his ear
  And he carried you away
So far we could
  Not bring you back.

Play little one, play
  Until we meet again
When the grey-green dragon comes
  To help us find the way.

Evelyn Warech

The End

Time is near,
the snow has fallen,
the light is bright,
my life it's calling.

The fear so deep,
I try to hide;
I feel his touch,
far deep inside.

The sun turns red,
the stars are lost,
the leaders have lead,
we've paid the cost.

The fragile cry of the hound,
nature is lost;
to the trumpet sound.

Dale James

Questions Unanswered

Who do I turn to?
Where do I run?
What do I do?
Why is it done?

Why didn't I listen?
What did I think?
Where did it glisten?
Who's advice didn't sink?

Who told me so?
What did I say?
Where did I go?
Why not obey?

Who's to blame?
What's to think?
Where did he shame?
Why doesn't he wink?

Why does he take?
Where does he plunder?
What a fake,
I'll always wonder.

Antonette Merritt

Untitled

Locked in a room
With a mind full of doubt
Looking around
I begin to scream and shout
The world is crashing
That is easy to see
Hate and destruction
Is all that surrounds me
Search through the darkness
Where is the light
Is hope only a dream
Succumb by a bloody fight
I walk to the door
Hungry for a new chance
Visions fill my mind
So horrible they make me wince
In everyone's face
Reflections of fear
The door shoots open
Revealing a mirror.

Jeff Chapman

Heaven Sent

Words screamed in anger
Sear into my heart
Branded into memory
My confidence torn apart

Yell against the wind
Cry unto the heavens
Lord send me an angel
Adorned in your affections

Soothe me 'til I sleep
Hold me through the night
Wake me with your gentle touch
Make everything all right

Remember all the good
Banish the bad
Take me under your wing
To the heaven I never had

Angie Wullenweber

Sleepless Night

Cowardice consumes the mental
  heart
long life lingers in the moon's
  thick air
while two remain one

Forgotten but most passionate
  devices
remember songs which sweet
  hopes sings
songs that are but half done

Memories spawned at the heir to
  love
forging schemes to overthrow the
  Mind King
clashing counts of thought and touch

Courage drips upon my cluttered
  brow
this chance to die with soul
  at peace
and now to live as such.

Tim Allen

Tones Of The Earth

Green, bright or dark
Yellow, sun or spark
Near or far
Where you are
You see the tones of the earth

Auburn leaves, brown bark of trees
Red orange sky, what a sight
Beautiful to the eye

Other colors remain unsaid
Some may look bright or
Others you might dread
Near or far, where you are
You see the tones of the earth

Reena Lynne Tabita

Projection

I'm so broken.
I can't stand the sight of me.
So I look outside.
But all I see
  is a world populated by mirrors.

I can fix you.
I don't have to turn away.
I look deep inside.
But then you say
  what the hell are you looking at.

You're so broken.
I can't stand the sight of you.
So I look deeper.
But all I do
  is make myself sick with hatred.

I can't fix me.
I don't have the guts.
To look that long
I'd see the cuts
  and a childhood inundated by tears.

Kay Russell

Whitsuntide Dusk

Standing erect,
the naked tree
flails a tangle of epileptic arms

Millions, millions
vacillating in the wind,
violent black nerve-ends

Trilling out their hurts
to the bald orange tumuli
of milky light;

While replicating stoics,
a nimbus precipitates
its divinatory cunning,

Preparing to
Drown out both man and trees
with its God like thunder.

Mae Seon

Untitled

The wind gushes through
my wide open hands.
The rain falls gently
Into open streams.
The storm rages over
wide, open lands.
Through the clouds
there is a soft, gentle
gleam.
The gloominess turns to
glowing gold bands.
The sky rips apart like
a tearing seam.
The suns shining down in
long, glowing strands,
sifting, sifting softly
through my wide open
hands.

Amie Dechene

Endless Beauty

All around us
  endless beauty
it surrounds us every where
  from the snow covered ground
to the smell of fresh spring air
  and the wooded forest, you can walk
  through, without even a care
Endless beauty
  is here for us to gaze
In wonder, and amaze
  from the colorful rainbow
To the foggy winter haze
  Endless beauty
  Lets sit in a meadow, and look as far
  as you can
  see
Enjoying, what was meant to be
  just the
endless beauty

Mary Foucault

Voices

In the hollow of my mind
Contradiction shall you find.
One voice shouts, "Fight for the cause!"
Another cautions, "Take a pause."
Voices battering my ears
Till the end of all my years.

In the darkness of my head
The logic I once had is dead.
No one hears my silent call
I am lost inside the fall.
Forever crying out for peace
But the voices will not heed my pleas.

Matthew Shaw

Reflections

I look into the fountain
Hating what I see.
I can't help but think of you
And why you love to hate me.
Nobody really wants you
And why can't you just see
That the only one who really cares
Is the only nobody me.

Nikole Patson

Our Love

Enchanted!
  as with the touch of spring
As we feel this love that only God
  can give,
Shall we ever sound the depth
  or exhaust the beauty of this thing:
Oh God forbid!
  -that we should kill this love
'as long as we shall live.

I pray that as we live
  Our love shall soar
Beyond the summit of the
  everlasting sky;
Or to the deepest depths
  'that only God with us could know-
And every trial and test we'd meet
  between this height and depth
Would only help to strengthen us
  And bring us to our best!

John W. Huber

The Ocean

The ocean can be a mystic place,
Of things to do and see.
It all depends, on one's mind,
And the will to set it free.
Walking along in the sand,
The waves caress my feet.
My body fills, with such a warmth,
And my heart increased its beat.
I gazed out on the ocean,
Watching the fog roll in.
And in that special moment,
I forgot where I had been.
I've never felt so peaceful,
And I've never felt so free,
As when the music from the ocean,
Does its mystical magic on me.

Jeanette McCraney

Coquette

My neighbor's tree
across the way
Is dressed in
chartreuse lace.

But playing shy,
she pulls a veil
of rain
across her face.

Hester Overstreet

Death

There comes a time in all our lives,
When we must face the end.
Some, it's swift, some wait in pain,
Their souls for God to tend.

We don't understand the timing,
Death always comes too soon.
It steals into our very heart,
Not one can be immune.

It takes the young before their prime,
Their breath is snatched away.
It takes the old and sick and lame,
And gives them rest that day.

For some it is a blessing,
For most an unwanted cross.
When a life is stricken from us,
Man suffers a terrible loss.

It is said a life is taken,
when one life is conceived.
No one can ever be replaced,
This makes the heart to grieve.

Colleen Kellick

Teacher

She stands above the class
like the sun stands above the earth.
Her words light the classroom
like the sun's spectrum lights the sky.
She has the power of a queen,
but she does not use it.
She speaks in lecture formation
with a cold hearted glare,
having no concern for the student
who could be looking at her ways
for guidance
on how to be grown.

Shelly Rae Szymanski

Sons Adored

I miss you
My sweet young men
For I am nothing here without you.

Your crayon drawings
Your laissez-faire
Your winning ways about, too.

I do adore you
My sons, my child
Immortal may thoust be.

Forever mine
Forever yours
Forever eternity.

Ana Sanchez-Preston

Questions

Am I going crazy,
All my life a little hazy.
Am I going insane,
How can I avoid the endless pain?
My world is falling apart,
How can I heal this bleeding heart?
My nights are full of sorrow,
Will I leave this world tomorrow?
My days are full of sunshine.
But how can I ease my troubled mind?
Will I find love,
Or will if fall from above?
Questions fill my mind,
But answers I can not find.
Can I find the path,
To lead me from my troubled past?
With all the questions that I ask,
How long will I last.

Michael Matthews

I'll Always Love You

I've loved you Jesus,
For all of my days.
Each morning I rise,
I give you the praise.

Now I need your help Lord,
To see me thru.
Whatever your answer,
I'll always love you.

Friends have forsaken,
My family is gone.
Some days I feel,
I cannot carry on.

But I reach for my Bible,
Read your promises anew.
Whatever your answer,
I'll always love you.

Diana M. Dunn

Other Dimensions

Another passage, a destiny unknown,
Revealing seeds that have been sown.
A crying soul, a fleeting heart,
One binding life from which to part.
A deeper action, a changing way,
Facing reality in a wanton day.
An aching spirit, confused with strife,
Adding another dimension to the knife.
Uncertain costs, undertaking the loss,
Hence comes redemption from one cross...

Cheryl Lynn Voet

Indifference

The grey moors beckon me.
I take one last sip of the cold coffee
    And depart,
Leaving my cubicle behind,
    Susceptible to anything.
I trek across the rugged terrain,
Hands in my pocket,
    Head down.
The irregular ground beneath me hardens.
    Where am I?
Back in my chair, reading the paper.
I have gone everywhere yet nowhere.

Meg Frazier

The Savior

The rain trickles down my window.
Each one more despondent
    than the one before
Till I drown in a flood of sorrow.

I am swept away in the torrent
    of the sky's tears
wondering if they might be my own.

I plummet through my watery despair
    being pulled down by grief
and emotional turbulence.
Dolefully I surrender.

I sit in the depth of the water
attempting to gaze through
the murky unconsciousness.
Yet my desire is repressed.

Finally I see your radiance
slicing like a knife
through my dismal waters
and I am spared.

Jordan A. Collins

International Lover

Allow me to taste you
like a German Chocolate Cake,
Sampling your dreams
like Columbian Coffee
I'll take ya to Jamaica,
slurping Swiss Mocha shakes

Allow me to have you
in my arms in old Venice
Drinking your thoughts,
refreshing as British tea
Desiring to grab you
because we "match" like tennis

Allow me to hold you
whispering words in Spanish
Tasting your mind,
Tantalizing like French toast
I guess I should've told you:
Catch me before I vanish.

Quentin Huff

Vows

When two hearts like ours combine
And the love becomes entwined
It's a feeling so divine
That will last throughout all time

And because we love each other
We will always be together
It's the only way to be
I for you and you for me

May we never have a notion
That might threaten our devotion
And our love burn like a fire
Every person will admire

With these vows together marry
Distant pasts forever bury
Only future plans to be
I for you and you for me

Marilyn J. Peebles

Abandoned Fields

The ground holds truth in sorrow;
rutted roads to forgotten fields.
The path is marked by fallen trees,
hope of Spring in ruins.
And yet, the shadows haunt the hill
and whisper April rounds.
The field, unchanged from childhood,
lies nestled in the dawn.
Free-form flowers drift in dew
once viewed as diamond luck.
Now, neglect defines the frame
creating dampened weeds.
Rain etched rocks,
too large to move,
teach patience to the wind.
A spider hunts on rusted wire,
courage dancing in the breeze.

Fate is held in memory
as once abandoned fields.

Judy Aslesen-Rekela

October

October gave a party.
The leaves by hundreds came.
The chestnut, oak and maple.
The leaves by every name.

The sunshine spread the carpet.
And everything was grand.
Miss weather led the dancing,
Professor Wind the band.

They all danced to their partners.
As they gayly fluttered by
The night was like a rainbow.
Now falling from the sky.

And in the shady hollow.
At hiding seek they played.
The party closed at sundown,
But everybody stayed.

Mary B. Adams

Destiny Drops

Our world
is a cloud.
Our forefather,
the storm.
An assorted shower of billions
tumbling down from above,
epitomes of randomness.
Some land in sewers,
others in oceans.
A stream; a city.
We come to know
our H2O associates,
yet could never fathom
the fraction that we are
of the entire precipitation picture.
But if you think we're lucky now,
wait 'til it snows.
A few close friends
are worth more
than a million relations.

Dan Hargreaves

Heartfelt Love

A touch, a kiss, a momentary rush
  of life,
A life in a moment of love
Alive in the love of the moment.
I would stay if I could,
Still the moment,
A moment so still it transcends
  a life
A life so full
Its moments overflow,
I cannot stay the swell,
I cannot hold the touch,
  the kiss,
I must let go
To hold the moment in my heart.

Robert G. Schult

Friends are Friends

Friends are friends
Make amends
Don't be mean to me.
Friends are friends
Make amends
They'll come around,
You see.
Friends bring joy,
And happiness
Around the world to me.
Although they fight
They try their might
To be like friends should be.
Although it's hard to get along
We all need friends,
You see.
To bring us up
When we are down
And be like friends should be.

Jessica Rose Weiner

What Are Mothers For?

Mothers listen to all our sorrows
and woes.
And kiss every hurt from our head
to our toes.
A person who washes, cleans and
cooks our meals,
And tell us where to put our orange
peels.
She waits with a lot of love
for us
When we arrive home on
the school bus.
Then will read a book, when
it is time for bed,
So you can sleep as soon
as you lower your head.
Dear God, please bless them,
one and all.
Young or old, short or tall

Erma Crumrine

The Beggar

This day a man dies
But it affects not a soul
For he had nowhere to stay
And nowhere to go
Everyone shunned his presence
And not a man would speak
To this person and his face
At which no one would peek
So he roamed alone
In a world full of hate
Until he passed through
That very last state
But no one will notice
That he is not there
Because he was a beggar
And for him no one cared

Leah Rhoades

There's A Mouse In My House

There's a mouse in my house
I think I am going to scream.

There's a mouse in my house
It laid in the Ice cream.

There's a mouse in my house
It's in the fridge door.

There's a mouse in my house
Now it's on the floor.

There's a mouse in my house
It's heading for the cheese.

There's a mouse in my house
Someone stop it—oh please—,

There's a mouse in my house
I don't know what to do,

There's a mouse in the house
And it might come after you!

Squeak!

Billy Garver

A Song For Bobbie

Weep not for me now I am born,
weep for thyself alone.
I'm here, I'm me, I'll ever be
as now in basic form.

No wish, no dream,
no prayer will change
what God hath wrought this day.
I'm here, I'm me, I'll ever be,
yet I know not dismay.

So teach me not of spite nor hate,
I have no need of fear.
But love... Ah love,
tis love will draw us near.

Weep not for me now I am born.
accept me as I am.
I'm here, I'm me, I'll ever be
your child... And love of man.

Marvin L. Borgman

Baby Boy

*Dedicated to my Grandpa Chris
and brother Brian*
Baby Boy, Baby Boy,
  dressed in baby blue.
Hope that you will love me
  as much as I love you.
Your little face, your little eyes
  looking up at me.
I hope we will be
  the best family.
I welcome you, I welcome you
  with joy in my heart.
To see your smiling face
  makes me want to never part.

Raven Mencias

Child Of Light

Child of light, chained in darkness,
  bound with fear.
Through veils of lies, and watery eyes,
  falls silently thy tear.

'Tis but a day, thy path on earth
  a step in time.
Before thy birth, and past the grave,
  thy glory ever shines.

Wipe thine eye; be not weary; fear
  shall flee.
And ever shining, as a star, in truth
  thou shalt be free!

L. Farrell Wilkins

Albuquerque

You cracked me open
like the sun over the Sandias
in October. Pure light
melting colors into dust.

Dissolving through my blood
— feasting on my slowly
scorching heart — there were
no valleys in which to hide.

No valleys, no rivers, no ocean —
to smother the fire your
kiss kindled, and left to burn.
I blaze

into the desert.

Tara N. Mahady

Untitled

It shines,
Faintly through the clouds.
Its brightness,
Dimmed by the clouds.
It peeks through the trees
As we come around a bend in the road.
What's a better navigating tool,
Than the moon?
Always there.
Always shining.
There's a face I see.
The man in the moon, my dad says.
I see the man in charge of my dreams.
Why aren't they coming true?
I ask him at night.
He doesn't say a word.

Kendra A. Gruman

Which Sun?

Each morning
we wait for the sun
which marks us the day,
and gives us the light
so that we can see
the road to travel on,
where our life shall lead.

Often we rush,
and do not see the other sun.
Which gives us the rays of warmth,
of the life-giving smiles.

The other sun?
Yes!
The faces,
and flowers of all kind.
They are the beauty on the earth.
These all make worth our living.
Just return their rays of smiles
as you are passing by.

Zoltan Vasvary

Nature's Beauty

There's beauty around us everywhere
In things both large or small
From a little tuft of seeded grass
To a rippling waterfall.

Wild flowers in an open field
Make homes for all the bees.
From these they gather honey
Before the winter freeze.

A pink rose grows proudly
Among wild blackberry vines
With larkspur, lily and goldenrod
And fern so lacy and fine.

The cultivated beauties
That bedeck our own yards
Are everlasting pictures
Painted by the hand of God.

Idella M. Higdon

The Luckiest Penny
Is The One The Remains

Warm wetness courses through
The rusty taste of blood,
Salt of sweat, sour of fear.
Fingers mark with pain.

The mask of calm control remains
Mind and body separate.
Skin, blood, bruise, cut
Ultimate pain is not of the body.

The mind rebels, unclean
No longer of one mind
Terror of past always present
Safety yearned for

Cries of pain and fear
Gone the whole, taken forever.
Evil remains, fear remains
Pain of body releases its grip

Mind, unwhole, remains.

Katie Chaney

In Memory Of Josephine

I held a jewel in my fingers and went to sleep.
The day was warm and winds were prosy.
I said, "'Twill keep."
I woke and chilled my honest fingers.
The gem was gone and an amethyst remembrance is all I own.
Tie the strings to my life, My Lord.
Then I am ready to go!
Just a look at the horses — Rapid! That will do!
Put me on the firmest side, so I shall never fall.
For we must ride to the judgement, and it's partly downhill.
But, never I mind the bridges, and never I mind the sea.
I held fast in everlasting race by my own choice and thee.
Goodbye to the life I used to live, and the world I used to know.
Kiss the hills for me just once.
For now I am ready to go!
If I can stop one heart from breaking, I shall not live in vain.
If I can ease one life the aching or cool one pain or help one fainting
Robin unto his nest again, I shall not live in vain.

Laura Paiz

Our Walk

And so our walk is almost over, you point the way I should go,
    This time you say you can't come along.
I can't understand how your path has ended,
    When you never guided anyone else wrong.

We've stumbled on huge stones and pushed them aside,
    And many times felt the freedom to run.
Through all the darkness we've dealt with deep in the woods,
    We've always managed to find the sun.

You taught me to see simple things in an extravagant way,
    And together we've explored some unknowns.
I've followed in your footsteps,
    while you sheltered me from bad weather
    And you've watched me on our path as I've grown.

But now you tell me I must continue alone,
    your strength to walk is gone.
Our path has narrowed now, through weeping willows,
    I slowly continue on.

The flowers don't seem bright now, the sun doesn't give warmth,
    I no longer have shelter from the rain.
All the beauty you once taught me to see, now resembles pain.

Tomorrow will come, I'll still be walking, and again the sun will set.
I'll see in it your smile, hear your voice in the wind,
    And our walk I will never forget.

Carrie Horton

Hope Everlasting

The Legacy of Life was given to mankind in
Hope that he would someday mature and achieve the right to
Eternal life, to walk amongst the immortal who
Believe that (Good is better than evil) hope is better than despair

Love is stronger than hate, and believing will get you there
Ordained by the Spirit of Truth and Love.
Our hope has been blessed from above.
Destiny set if we would just believe
Life eternal the reward to receive
Interceded, because of the darkness of sin would
Never have earned the right to enter in, where (all) life begins and
Ends Never more.

Charles E. Peterson Sr.

Free Spirit

The wolf howls and the fire burns bright. My spirit
appears to me. It is wild and untamed. It shows me the way,
and I follow. It leads me to a sled with three dogs, the spirit
puts me on the sled and I shout let's go. We take off as fast as
can be. The snow shoots back as the dogs run through the forest.
Left, then right, around we go. I feel free, that I can do anything.
The mountains are all around me, covered with snow. The trees are
moved by the wind. There's no one around me so they can't see.
My spirit is proud and I am free. I am swept away by the view,
and by the speed. I am free. I am surrounded by my friends the
wolf, the bear, the dogs, and the otter. I am free, I am free. My
spirit has shown me the way. The spirit has told of my destiny,
and I will follow. This is where I am free. There's no one to
judge or laugh, it's just my friend nature and I.

Jamie Capitan

Abundant Life

When does life become abundant?
    Though its perception differs like the individual,
        it appears to be searched for in common ways.
    But wealth cannot possibly purchase it.
    Position surely cannot possess it.
    And pleasure is not the sum of it.
No, it would have to be attainable by even the poor and lowly.
    Anyone willing to move along the path of experiencing.

Living is experiencing.
    To only know depression is mere existence.
To pursue pleasure is existence with improvements.
    If abundance means much, then would not
    abundant life have to embrace all the emotions
    and experiences known to man.
To know the valleys and the mountains, and the many trails between.
    To encompass the excitement of the new, the pain of loss,
        and the hope of eternity.

When life experiences a full spectrum of emotions,
    it should be called abundant.

D. Keith Jones

Old Chicago

With right foot on Freedom, left foot on Freedom,
a careworn woman steps off the train. Pink faces, pin stripes,
stockings. Chicago. 1936.

Freedom, opportunity on Maple Street.
A glorious sea of Ebony saunters along the street.
Three piece suits, rawhide suspenders, crisp hats,
    brass pocket watches.
With a dime in her shoe and nothing else, she defied the south.
Freedom.

With her forlorn and blistered hands, she touches the window of
The Palm Tavern: Dancing, jazz, and martinis await.

The Man ain't keepin' us down. No more.
Freedom, Chicago, the Promised Land.

As oppression turns her hair gray, prejudice numbs her heart.
With hope and firm conviction, she meekly waits for her Freedom.

Coffee colored faces, silver badges, black batons. Chicago. 1946.
Airport homes. Riots. A shot is fired to Protect and Serve?
A veteran of pain, the aged black woman lay dying,
screaming out gospels and homeland songs of praise;
Freedom splits her head, turning her gray into crimson.

Marlon Sims

Life Goes On

Like a rock beneath a waterfall. I sit and wonder
    what life would be like elsewhere.
Destined to always remain among the pounding force the water brings,
constantly being beaten down.
The foundation of the earth, dirt and sand, washing away beneath me.
Digging me deeper and deeper into despair.
I ask is this what life has to offer? How may I escape?
Where the denizen of the deep and creatures
    from below the restlessness, will not even visit.
The water brings such turmoil. I can not rest.
Helpless to nature as years move on,
    with a body of rock my soul so strong.
Why can't I be like a tree so tall and bright
    with limbs out stretched for other's delight?
Growing toward heaven giving reverence to God. Laying seeds,
    yielding oxygen, so that the life and legacy of others, will go on.
To live a good life then to wither and die.
No, I'm a rock, isolated, living in darkness, longing for tranquility
With only my thoughts of faith guiding me
    through the displeasure's of life.

Steven P. Johnson

Fearful Thoughts

A great mass approaches, its triangular fin protruding out of the
    white crests.
I tread water, praying for this not to be one of the few times the
    beast might attack.
But there is always a chance.
It is a constant threat, holding a sense of danger.
It swims towards me and the greasy flesh crawls along my leg.
I close my eyes, waiting for a blur of white teeth to destroy me.
This doesn't happen. It is toying with me.
I fight to keep myself above the waves as my panic-stricken body
    begins to tremble.
If it is going to happen, I think, let it happen now so I don't have
    to fear it happening anymore.
But I really don't want this at all.
And the heartless creature drags the terror on...

The fanged widow awaits its prey in anticipated suspense.
Once received, this nightmarish creature binds up its victim so it may
    not be free.
It is helpless.
The predator then sucks the life away,
leaving only the shell of its former self;
devouring an arm, a leg, a foot,...the eye.
No individuality of its own.
It is now just a part of its consumer, an insignificant fraction of
    something larger.
The assassin does not mourn, it returns to its murdering web and
    prepares for the next kill...

A side of love.

Kelly Ceckowski

I Am A Woman

I am a woman and this is what it means:
I am mother earth, a goddess and a divinely ordained queen.
I am your mother, sister, daughter, teacher, student and wife.
I will lend you my serenity for all of my life.
I am the soft hand that caresses you at night.
And I am the voice that says everything will be all right.
So come lay your head next to my heart and your troubles at my feet.
I'll lend you my strength and soothe
    the pain till all your fears and tears retreat.
I am a woman and this is what it means, to be me.

Karla Riddle

God Sent The Word

God sent the prophets and his son Jesus, to let us all know
Follow his commandments, and be righteous,
    then to heaven you will go
Praise me I am your God, the one and only
Accept me, and I'll never leave you lonely
Follow me, for I will show you the true way
Allow me and I will work miracles in your life today
Seek me and I'll bring you out of the darkness to see the light
Love me for that is what is truly right
pray to me, give me all your problems large or small
Put faith in me for I can take of them all
Sing to me, allow your song to be heard
Believe in me for you have read the word
My son and I, your savior, your God your closest friends
My son and I shall see to it you are saved in the end.

Kenneth L. Stepp

Untitled

Had a dream that he came to town, wanted to see me, but he was afraid.
He wanted to apologize for the mistakes he made.
So many years of dismay. He couldn't do it, too afraid.
She was tough, and filled with disgust and dismay.

On that day his son came to his aid.
Delivering words, flowers and money for his dismay and perhaps
    forgiveness one day.
She was outraged at his shameful face, the son delivering and acting
    as his aid, and she turned him away.

The next day after years of no talk , his mother calls,
    oh no, bad news is on its way.
Had to say I'm sorry for his ways.
His father and I have been disgraced.
Just wanted to say hello to our friend today, and that I am sick,
don't know if there will be many more days.

Cried all night, thinking that she was ill
    and there weren't many more days.
Illness has stuck and perhaps will take her away.

Got myself together the next day. Had to buy groceries and play
310 in the lottery for the day.
310 for his birthday and where they once stayed.
310 came out in the lottery that day.

Dorothy Ann Barr

Pass It On!

When sorrow turns joy into pain
I'll find away to pass it on
Making others aware of the chance to make a positive change.

When sadness turns smiles upside down
I'll find away to pass it on
Letting others know where comforting friends can be found.

When trouble turns hope into an uncried tear
I'll find away to pass it on
Giving others the courage to face today with a healthy fear.

When death turns life into stormy weather
I'll find away to pass it on
Teaching others that strength is beneath the winds of one another.

When tribulations turns peace into a broken heart
I'll find away to pass it on
Showing others that it takes endurance on their part.

When hate turns love into an agitated sea
I'll find away to pass it on
Guiding others in the way of humility as the best way to be.

Gwendolyn R. Allen

Give Me A Woods To Walk In
And I'll Leave A Lot Of Happy Tracks

A hillside of trees where the bed of a deer is still warm to the touch,
a young rabbit sitting under a branch thinking it's hidden from view

And the thrill to see a partridge setting on a nest of eggs
Then one day seeing the nest with baby's just bursting from the shell

In the spring I can't wait to find a patch of May flowers in all
their beauty while the warm touches of sunshine has nudged
them from sleep with snow yet in the fields. I enjoy these
wonders of the earth.

Just to sit and have a friendly squirrel talk to me
a chipmunk tell me how happy he is I came quietly
a chick-a dee visit from a branch just above my head
Is a treat no one should be without

A walk in the woods in Autumn - the tangy smell - the
beautiful color of leaves, and one lucky enough to pass by
some Indian Peace pipe. A rarity of mother nature you will find
    no where else.
Yes give me a woods to walk in, and I'll leave a lot of happy Tracks.

Clarice Boyer

Bushels Of Time

If I had bushels of time on my hands through space
    I would like to fly
To catch a glimpse of the universe to God's home in the sky
It must be a majestic place to see with a throne of gold and glitter
Oh! What I would give to see his face my heart begins to flitter

I remember Him when I was young, Oh! Why do we forget
We get so wrapped up in worldly things we try to take
    on the fight and yet
Our minds, are so full of day to day things we become blind
    and deaf to the weeping
But, He reminds us every day we are in His arms for safe keeping

If I has bushels of time I would dry those tears of sadness
I would stop all of the hunger and all of the pain
I would set down with people with nothing to gain
And tell them my story and tell them my shame

If I had bushels of time over the land I would fly
To see all of creation in all of the nations, see the beauty in His eyes
What must be have in mind for me, how can I be in His plans
I am just one single person, I am merely a mortal man

But, God gave us bushes of time you see for life goes on and on
It is up to us to listen within and to sing His praises in song
Because life surely does go on

Ruth O'Neill

Arrows

Your words, like arrows, are stuck in my heart,
Try as I might, I can't make them depart.
Your words, like arrows, are stuck in my soul,
I get some out, but they leave a hole.
Your words, like arrows, are stuck in my eyes,
I still perceive light, though my focus is blurred with lies.
Your words, like arrows, zing by left and right,
I dodge them, duck them, run in fright.
Your words, like arrows, are my enemy,
Until the barrage ends, I can never be free.
Your words, like arrows, have penetrated my shield,
Our talks fuel the fire, no peace do they yield.

Dawn Lee Kilventon

A Child's Cry

Mom and Dad, I think more than the world of you.
I thought you would be for me, and help see me through.
I thought you would hug me and kiss me and make things all right.
But, instead, you're full of anger and wanting to fight.
If you don't love me, then who will?
Who will teach me Jesus loves me still?
Who will pray for me when everything's gone wrong?
Who will teach me a comforting song?
If you fail me, who can I turn to?
What must I do to be accepted by you?
Where can I turn for loving memories when the years have left me old?
When I am sad and lonely, what good memories could I hold?
If you don't teach me of Jesus, then in this world I have no hope,
You leave me no saviour to help me cope.
Please, please show that you care,
I need more than food, things and clothes.
I need your loving kindness just to help me grow.

F. Aleen Gooch Sullivan

I Wish

I wish you were here with me so I can tell you how I feel
So I can hold you in my arms and keep you safe and warm.

I wish I could wipe away the pain
Dry up the tears and make sure you never cry again.

I wish I could make you smile the way that you should
The way that you do when you light up the room.

I wish I could hear your voice to whisper in my ear
All the dreams that you have that I can help come true.

I wish you would take my hand and walk with me to the peaceful place
Where your heart yearns to be.

I wish you would give me the chance to give you all the things
That I know you need, that you know you deserve.

I wish that you could look at me in that way
That you looked at those who broke your heart.

I wish you'd let me love you in the way that I know I can
The way I've always dreamed, the way that you wish for.

But above all else, I wish I don't have to wish anymore.

Christopher M. Clark

Cultural Fantasies

Politicians are all honest and bright, and
    the worlds religions, each, the only one that is right.
Wars, by a nation, are justified for better living conditions
    and human relations.
Men sent to combat in war, are revered by those who weren't,
    for evermore.
Man is the most intelligent animal on earth, evidenced by their
    battles, prejudice, and love of material worth.
Recorded history is always based on proven facts,
    never altered to benefit singular, corporate, religious or political acts.
All mankind's knowledge can be acquired at institutions of formal
    learning, absent any experience by doing, creating and yearning.
The human race, regardless of color, is not genetically sister and
    brother.
Abuses, chemical or other, will be abolished from humanity
    by law, religion, politicians, and values of family.
Armageddon coming, is not probable, since mankind's intellect is
    not that gullible.
These negatives implied, can not be abated,
    by true compassion, love, and people widely educated.

Robert W. Gaskins

On Down

Come on down, come on get down, ride this rhythm without a sound,
feel the frost light the spark, see the light within the dark,
let go of sense, take hold of time, moments of me, body like rhyme.

Slide on down, stare me down, in my silence voice you've found,
ride the rise, collide and crash, thunder thrust, lightening dash,
inside my black, into my red, spin the madness in my head.

Break it down, break on through, hold my fears, make them true,
dare my spirit, dare me to whatever, why not, lead me to you,
born from fire of years gone by burns desire telling me why.

So let's go down, let it go, sun melt down this path of snow,
jewel within lives fire bright, cherish precious, peaceful light,
search the depth, eyes that drown, just come on baby, come on down.

Kerry Beth Doonan

Life's Miracle

From deep within my consciousness surprising bits of flotsam rose.
Buried deep, unknown to me, they challenged waking and in repose.

I found there was no true escape, no matter how I tried
By being busy, working hard; they would not be denied.
I understood the hounds of Heaven. No way I could be free.
As in the Earth-sea legacy I fled gloom on land and sea.

I knew the fractured sense of self that held me in its sway
Blinding me to who I am, held love and peace at bay.

They were within and must be cleared, they were not right or wrong.
I found they rose in memory, with a challenge deep and strong.

Rising from the forgotten past, they held me in illusion.
Hiding the truth until at last I sought freedom from confusion.

To Glorious Spirit, Creator of life, with great love, joy and peace,
I came each day in quiet time, this dark threat to release.

A moment came - a Flash of Light - with truth, so powerfully,
I turned and faced that old dark threat; surprised, it fled from me.

Thus the healing power and light were filling inner space
Until the shadow grew more small, to vanish in God's grace.

When in crisis, pain or fear, with courage I move through.
A higher great transcending power brings the miracle anew.

Sara Marriott

By Moonlight

The soft illuminating moonlight casts a warm glow
    up and down your gentle form
I lay awake and watch you and your skin
    glows with heavenly perfection
    as you are bathed in a sea of soft white
And all the while your name hovers throughout my fathomless mind
You lay silent as slumber has absorbed you
    and I feel our hearts beating completely as one
As I lay awake I cannot help but think how blessed I am
    to be by your beautiful side
Memories of the times we have shares dance vividly in my head
    and combine with my dreams and desires of our future together
Your enamoring beauty is unmatched and as I grow more and more
    content and secure I begin to drift into an afterglow slumber
And the last thing I see as my eyes close slowly
    is the soft illuminating moonlight that casts a warm glow
    up and down your gentle form
Then on the verge of sleep
    I realize that we are both bathed in this heavenly light
I smile as I think that we are meant to be
    friends and lovers in all the same right...by moonlight

John Wetherbee

A Dream Come True

The initial superficial feelings were confirmed as time flew by.
Life became richer and fuller as the "We" became priority, not me,
　　not you, not I.

We navigated various seas at first and fought all battles together.
And if the future brought rough tides again,
　　as one we'll conquer wrong forever.

Our love has been tested by people and circumstances,
But we have been there for one another willing to take our chances.

People are not always fortunate as you and I have been.
We've become soul mate and lover and of course a best friend.

Our dream came true like that of a fairy tale,
With faith and trust, with God and love as one we cannot fail.

We fell in love, we've grown so much and still have room to grow.
And I will gladly take that route with you, this you must always know.

I give myself to thee today because
　　I love you more than words can say.
Your love, your warmth, your gentle touch
　　provides the sunshine for my everyday.

I prayed to God for you my love to be part of my life,
He answered my prayer, the dream came true
　　as we are husband and wife.

　　　Lynne Schwab Schaefer

Bard's Song

They came to us one shrouded night, before the dawn had come
They spoke to us in ancient rhymes, and we felt our minds grow numb
We tried to fight their voices, as they circled in the wind
And we witnessed their mystic descent, as they rode the dreams of men
Now they invade the depths of my subconscious
Please help me to conceive what is happening to me
On the cliffs I knelt and prayed, for aid from the Gods
Soon my pleas were answered, in forms of fiery pods
They shoot across the heavens, in search of where I lay
A dagger thrust in my breast, all was black to me
One thing is sure my son, tomorrow will never come
And the secrets of the night's events are concealed in your kingdom
You have good reason to fear my friend, for you are not alone
There are others in your mind you see, and are slowly turning cold
Now I float on the edge of time, with memories of my past
I now begin to understand powers that were beyond my grasp
I think they're going to send me back, for what I do not know
Maybe to avenge myself, or repay some debt I owe
I do believe you are the one, you start to think anew
And when you walk the earth again, wonder if I am you

　　　Aaron Timothy Smith

My Firebird

Here alone I sit in the bus by and by
observing the headlights of the passing automobiles
as dusk furtively captures evening into his ominous clutches

When suddenly I looked out upon the desert-like plains over
the culture-stained trees who stood there in rigor mortis and I saw it.

Just like an angel, with outstretched wings she hovered over the
Western horizon in such libertarian brilliance, and I sat there and
watched her out of the charter's windows like a parent looking at
a newborn child.

I saw a firebird in the blue ocean sky and I quickly claimed her as mine.
Unfortunately, my apathetic colleagues could not appreciate
the beauty of the orange burned bird above us.

And as quickly as the beautiful bird came, she departed.
She disappeared into a virtual non-existence.
But I know she's still around somewhere.

So goodbye, my firebird, good bye.

　　　Hollis Webb

Remembrance Of The Holocaust

Born and raised in the era of hatred called the Holocaust.
My dreams of life gone away with the wind, and my childhood
stolen by the Nazis. Leaving fresh scars in my memory, never
again to be erased.

As if it were all a dream; they invaded my territory, and forced me
into their camps with nothing left. Separating me from the ones I loved.
My family departed into a much better world: Death!
Leaving me in the world of survival and struggle for freedom.

In the camps; it was a horrible sight. Men dressed in uniforms
carrying rifles were everywhere. A cloud of smoke filled the sky,
dogs were barking, and far off I was able to hear the screaming
of people that were being murdered; just like my family.

I was trapped with no way out. The men in uniforms were ready
with their rifles for any attempted escapes. Buildings and fences
were covered with barbed wire.

Supervised by Nazi guards; I was assigned a specific job.
We were forced to dance, witness deaths of escape attempts by
prisoners, and please the Nazis. The ones who refused were
tortured and killed.

Crying for freedom, we escaped triumphantly. We defeated the Nazis!
Hundreds and thousands of innocent people were tortured,
and didn't survive the Holocaust.

I became a survivor of the Holocaust, but the scars remain...

　　　Nelly G. Zamora

The Skies Of Tennessee

Her colors are as rich as the deep blue sea
Her brightness shines through mountains of great distance,
　　like spring giving birth to summer
She sways me; as thunder ripples across the sky - I sweat
As the moon and sun flirt, I do dream
As clouds dance around the blue, I ache for touch
Her colors are tranquilizing, almost intimidating
she has a touch of fantasy
Warm with leisure is she, yet serious with thought,
　　her innocence is tantalizing,
I have never seen anything until I laid eyes upon the skies of Tennessee

As she cries, I to cling to reason; her anger devours mercy,
　　her gentleness entails mass
A vision of sheer beauty, divinely creative was she; heavenly scented,
Her aroma is as fresh as the afternoon rain; so clean, so free
As fair as pillars of wisdom she shines, while shining her love on all,
　　she weeps for night
While embracing passion she longs for moon;
　　driven by wind she awakens hypnotizing the horizon
As new as a new born baby, as old as the ancient sea - she will be,
　　beauty is she
She never leaves you emotionless; as moody as she may be,
　　her deity engulfs her
The skies of Tennessee are as sweet
　　as a baby suckling a　mother's breast milk
How mystical; how beautiful thou art
Passionately she release, raining upon the meadow
I have never seen anything until laid eyes upon the skies of Tennessee

　　　Veronica M. Smith

Friendship

Friendship, is expensive, I've had some repossessed,
If you have one you're lucky, three or more, then you are blessed.
The upkeep's rather costly, yet considering the price,
Its worth is more than gold itself, I know, take my advice.
So, when next you're browsing friendship, there's something
　　you should know,
They're precious, they're expensive, and they'll need some
　　time to grow.

　　　Lyla F. Bailey

Tough Love

I'm struggling to pursue love
I'm trying so hard to be loved, as I am. Why does it hurt?
It hurts right through the core of my inner deepest emotions.

I feel like I shot an arrow of pain through my chest cavity.
I'm loving you the purest I can.
I'm feeling the receiving of my efforts.
I'm loving you effortously.

Touch me,
Feel me,
Hear me,
See me,
Don't stop loving me.

J. S. Okin

Let's Be Friends Yesterday

Let's be friends yesterday, makes no sense, some would say,
but it makes sense to those who choose to stay, back in time,
that's yesterday.

I knew a girl once, I loved her so, how selfish of me, I didn't
want her to go, to the club and cheat, with men she would meet,
she gave me thought on who she would keep...

It went up in a flame, not one is to blame, but she should carry
most of the shame, to hate me now for what we once had, is a
waste of time and that is what's sad.

The time soon came and our ties broke apart,
I tried to be friends, from the heart, she wouldn't have it,
the communication was dead, this girl I once knew,
was the girl I had wed.

Over the years I grew wiser and seen better days, as for her, she
grew wider and sings a different phrase, "I'm so alone, will you
be my friend?" "Are you kidding! What happen to the club and
the other men?"

Now I've been blessed from the man up above, I prayed for and
received another chance at love. May God bless this girl I thought
I once knew, so she can someday find another love too!

Lawrence Barton

Mr. Mischief

He stands three feet tall from his locks to his toes,
And just two short years past since he first showed.

He can do so much this cupid clone,
No matter what he does I'm as steady as stone.

Change this diapers, part of life, so much a bore,
Except when he tries to change his own, and surprises hit the floor.

And now comes soothing powder, how cute his tiny bottom.
He's just so quick the lid he opens, all over before you stop 'em.

Then came the potty training, use just a bit of tissue,
Now the wrapped roll's in the toilet bowl, really, not an issue.

Ahh, teaching him to color now, use a picture of a car.
But he's not drivin' you crazy, stuffing crayons in the VCR.

He looks like the youngest DJ as he handles that cassette,
The ball of ribbon now at his feet, a birds nest you can bet.

Big box of toys, all his own, overflowing at its top,
Emptied completely upon the floor, he plays with the first he got.

Looks so sweet talking on the phone, but the moment that you slumber,
Presses the buttons, and now the charge,
    a whopping long distance number.

Change Cody's name to Mr. Mischief,
    and seek help from powers above?
No not really though, cause with just one glance, all I feel is love.

Gordon B. Hanson

The 15 Elements

Let your friendship find its way to me when I have no one to turn to.
Let your hand touch mine
    when I'm down on the ground and need help to get up.
Let your understanding be great at situations that need it most.
Let your patience endure 'cause at the end of the rainbow
    is a pot of gold.
Let your words of communication reach me always
    so as not to set yourself to limitations.
Let your goals be reached because
    then you would have what you wanted.
Let your lonely day be half a day
    so that I can take over the other half.
Let your thoughts meet mine together often during the day.
Let despair occur if it must because hope often comes by in disguise.
Let your sadness not drown you over
so that you can always see the surface.
Let your tears fall silently and freely because ironically
    it sometimes lets you view where your life has been
    and where it is going.
Let yourself believe first, then anything can follow after.
Let a commitment be carried through truthfully and lovingly
    and never for it to be locked steel chain of body and soul.
Finally let your love flow through convincingly by words
    and actions because only then do others know of its existence.

Lana H. Hoang

A Summers-End Day

They came, bearing gifts, at the close of a
Long, lazy summers-end day.
The last bit of the season's light was dimming with the sun
As it tucked itself slowly, sleepily away
At the very edge of the western horizon.

I reluctantly turned my attention from nature's spellbinding power
And was greeted by smudged, smiling faces and little, dimpled fists
Clutching mixed bouquets of wilted weeds and wildflowers.
I accepted their priceless gifts, accompanied by sticky baby kisses
Seeing the beauty of the sunset reflected in their enormous eyes.

Following the formalities of their presentation ceremony,
I returned my attention to the sun and sea good-night kiss..
Now somewhat less brilliant and awe-inspiring
As the fiery glow of evening was all but extinguished
And I was having some difficulty focusing through the mist.

D. J. Calzada

Untitled

And if this was the verge or the merge of cracking up
I'd certainly think that more should be involved
Than Phillip Glass records
And a rose throat.

And if at this point
I have developed a formula
It would include punching that crying clown
Square in the mouth.

All the more reason to misunderstand:
(Respectfully and universally), the upper hand.
Held by those weighing in at 2,000 years and millions strong,
Is it a surprise that I've never had so much history hate me
    before?

If fading is tolerable when forgetting costs too much,
All the art of the pacific couldn't drag me out of this one.
But fading is too easy - effortlessly easy.
Forgetting, on the other hand, is ironic, and just enough to
    be tragically pleasing.

Worrying with intent is generally not my style,
But I guess this means that I'm man enough to face the end
    with a smile.

David J. Patrikios

Last Breath

Breathin' I feel this whezzin' wondering will it take control.
Breathin' heavier and deeper as time goes by waitin' on the next
treatment feelin' tingly and high. All messed up that's probably
why I cause more damage than I do good. Intense pain, I strain
lookin' at the light I feel hot and sweaty and my body's all tight.
Impatiently I wait while I breath heavier and deeper maintaining
control, waitin' till the next hour hopin' this one will hold. I feel
the sorrow that's in everyone's eyes as I despise being in this
situation. Wonderin' should I take another hit, but now this
may be my last trip.

Nearly in tears my late night dreams bring fears. Fidgety, jittery,
lie down, stand up, go here, go there, I don't know where I wanna be.
Maybe in his arms and maybe this in his call tellin' me to maintain
myself cause I might be the prime example of someone takin'
their last breath!

It's feelin' heavily and tight this may be that last time I see such
a light and I wonder as I hold this pipe will this be my last night,
last day, last hour, last minute, last second? The questions I ask
seem to have no answer. And I still remain in a state of confusion?
"Are you alright?" Yes, I almost took my last breath.

Devona D. Parrish

Foolish Heart

Countless nights I cry away the hours,
    wondering if I'll ever love again
For you I will always cherish, though our love has come to an end
When I needed you most, I turned to find
That you had fallen astray and left me behind
An empty heart, lost in the cold
A story of dreams, broken and untold
How can my life ever be the same?
To never feel your touch or hear you whisper my name?
Foolishly, my heart cannot let go
My spirit is bound, though deep inside I know
That all we had could never be
Alone in love, with only a memory
Of faded dreams and broken promises
Will my heart ever feel a love like this?
For even though you've gone and abandoned me
Should you need me to, here I may still be
To take you in my arms, and hold you near
Foolishly delivering you from your suffering and fear.

Jose A. Mendez

Missing

I wish you were here by my side for I miss you so!
You were so pleasant and now you're gone
    a million or more miles away.
I wish you were here for why I miss you
    is impossible to say with words.
You just can't do it, but I'll try any way.
The way your voice rang through the house.
I never will forget the way you made me laugh with your silly jokes
you will never be beat by anyone in this entire world!
The way you taught me so much art
    and stuff I can't even imagine how you do it?
You both did so much for me that only love can explain
    the feeling of missing!
If only you could know how much I miss you.
It is just impossible to explain I just can't go deep enough to do it!

Elizabeth Yahn

Cry Of Hearts

O' hero mine, of chiseled dark beauty, take not my weary heart for
it lays splintered and aching. When loneliness grows, you may
stroke the gossamer tendril I once lovingly bestowed you.
This token, you may carry close to your heart in remembrance . . .
Of times when lies of love beckoned your lips to deceive
me and dreams of our mating flesh haunted your lonely nights . . .

O', vixen mine, dancer of heated dreams, I forgot myself
when in your arms and whispered cruel magic of empty pledges.
Fool that I am, I forgot how I burned for your sweetness.
Forgive me this late hour, I'd willingly crawl the walls of hell
to reclaim you. O' hear me this time, vixen, I bestow you my
tortured soul, you are more beloved to me than life . . .

Anita D. Moore

Winter

A dry leaf travels across the frozen earth,
Past skeleton trees,
As others join it in the biting wind,
Making their endless journeys across the flat tundra

Swept away in an updraft,
The lone leaf scrapes across an icy pond,
Where children skate and build snowmen with their tiny,
mittened hands,
Their red, rosy cheeks showing the cold.

The sun suddenly peeps out from under its blanket of clouds,
And the wind picks up.
Scrambling away from its penetrating warmth,
The leaf floats past a cozy cottage.

Curly, white smoke swirls from its red brick chimney,
And suddenly, the ring of an ax cuts through the quiet,
As a man, bundled tightly in many jackets,
Chops frosty wood, then tucks it neatly in a pile.

Finally, the long, drab months of winter sweep by,
To open up to the joy and beauty of spring,
With tiny buds emerging from the once-dead trees,
And birds, sound like tiny flutes, proclaiming the new life of the season.

Stacey Ruff

One Of Heaven's Highest Ranks

Every Sunday at the Church at half-past nine,
Down by the nursery, you see Mothers in line.

With a baby on her hip and a smile upon her face,
A break is finally coming from the morning's hectic pace.

Each Mother has instructions and things she has to say
About how to care for her baby in his own special way.

So the ladies listen humbly as if they never knew
How to powder a little baby or to tie a tiny shoe.

Once again Mom's smiling for she's walking out the door
Feeling proud that she left her little one for the workers to adore.

Now Susie is getting fussy and needs a diaper change
And Timmy, he'd just love to walk if that could be arranged.

Mary wants a bottle and Lorie has thrown hers down;
I wonder how the workers spread their love around.

Oh, the babies' cries are getting louder as tears they begin to shed
For their idea of home sweet home is not a pretty bed.

Now the Service is over and Mommy comes to get
That little tiny darling that she had left.

With one last word, she whispers,
"Did you get time to sit?"

Ruby Sewell

Cosmic Sun Spots

It's like the stain on the sun shedding a new vibrant color.
Never ending trails of electric beauty, passing, but always
moving. Purple shadow's dance along the old abandoned
highways, talking about romantic love songs. The friends
all sing along remembering the galactic past. Why can't we
embrace nature instead of blind it's beauty with shapes of
plastic. Buildings built for greed with thought of only their
need. Fractured unity is the visual for the lack of forgotten
compassion. We are a part of Everything on this globe, for the
oceans which stir so violently, as for the rivers which run wild.
Somewhere a natural imbalance occurs twisting the course of nature.
Preserve beauty, respect the land and enjoy the thunder storms,
spark the mind with pure electric thought.
Crimson colored mind melting memory always strikes
with fire smile.

James E. Castro

No Second Chance

Time and time again,
Through our relationship,
I wonder what's going wrong.
To make us go through, such pains and heartache.

Should I love you,
Should I leave you?
There are so many choices,
So many reasons why.

I don't understand why you want to take me through these choices.
I can't decided what to do when it comes to me and you
because my love is true.

Where do we go from here?
I can't help but wonder,
Do we belong together?
I don't want to loose your love,
I just can't be with out you.

Got to have you in my life
Can't you see we can make if we try?
I don't know what else to do.
There are a million reasons... So many choices.

Justin Zamora

Angel Child

Lost in whirlwind, no signs of hope do tell
A lost, beloved sibling, in the beautiful realm.
Yes, I know you'll be happy, no more pain, hurting, no more hell.
Your spirit remains alive in me,
It strengthens me and brightens my soul
In you was the courage no one could ever foretell.
The trials of a weak body battling poison in its system, caused a
    child's most fundamental times to be lost in a prism.
Traumatized, and hurt by loss has put turmoil in your slow beating,
    but pumping heart.
With the crest of winter brings sickness instead of health.
Cold haunting memories come hauntingly back from hell.
No matter when the angel comes my life I would give in place of yours.
The brother of a lifetime, my soul mate more precious than gold.
The times we had, your Jim Carrey impressions,
    will remain forever locked in my mind.
Your sweet child chocolate brown eyes smile upon me and make me cry.
My life I give to you, the wings under my feet, muscles in my hand,
    healthy beats of my heart.
It's all for you.

Sarah Walker

The Revolving Door

Here comes another period of learning; another open door
here comes another series of good-byes, oh, another closed door

It's funny how life works, we always look ahead to the future,
bigger doors, wider doors, excited about what is in store

So we sit and wait, bright eyed and bushy tailed
for that fantastic person, or occurrence which we'll undoubtedly adore

But when we get there,
Oh, how laughable it seems, the door simply swung open, closed,
    and made a revolution

Have things really changed? Aren't most situations the same
Isn't simply a different time, season, and players in the game

It forces us to sit, have a hearty chuckle or two
    laugh and comment to ourselves or even a fellow or two
    "damn this feels familiar,
I guess things really haven't changed it feels like it was just
    yesterday that I was standing in this place"

Life is full of revolving doors
The key I suppose, is knowing if you are coming or going
    out of the door.

Shantelle Goodall

A Picture Framed in Time

Into the skies our emotions rise lay down upon lines remem-
bered for all times. The stories told from both young and old
embedded deeply in our minds. To read them is to travel to far
away lands.
Friendship and romance in the palms of our hands. Imagination
often lost as a child in new places. The smell, the warmth, the
smiling faces. Like a picture framed in time, emotions lay down
lines upon lines.

Jonathan Lynn Petersen

A Good Poem Should Be

A good poem should be as vibrant as a child
A good poem should be as tempting as a bowl full of ice cream
A good poem should be as enjoyable as a good book
A good poem should be as long as a meter stick or as long as a ruler
A good poem should be as colorful as a rainbow
A good poem should be as eye popping as an outrageous thing....

Robert C. Hines

The Lady Once Fair

She was fair, she was frail, she was pale, like the falling snow.
And her road, so neatly paved, was to the liking of her Virgoan way.

One day there came a storm, and tears to remember.
Untouched pebbles, pure no more, rolled to the beating wind.
The fair lady dreamed for a calm and peaceful moment,
    void of strangers eager to cross her path again.

But behold one stranger! He was tall, like the trees
And bended sweetly as the beloved willow.
And with a kind hand he created a warmth
Dusting the pebbles off along the afflicted lady's path.
Now blushed by the heat, and fair no more,
She was colored of love's roses.

But time seemed too short, and tears swayed him not,
As the stranger set out on his own.
For his journey sought more wondrous wonders,
More than his lady, once fair.

This lady did cry to the thought of her sad story
And shared her sorrow to the wind.
The wind blew and others would listen to it's roar.
But one man listened longest and took her to be his own.

Linda Marie Masters

Higher Ground

Well you say I dwell most in the past, the place of broken hearts;
Old dreams that would not last.

Owing to you is this solemn vow, that I will leave you
Someday, somehow.

Just sit back and listen to the rain, remember the sun,
It must come out again.

I had to say goodbye to you, to save us both
Seemed like the thing to do.

Alone at night - Do you miss my touch?
Yes I know, cause I miss you so much.

Well I know you hear my voice ringing in your ears.
I tried so hard to change you.
You listen now?
After all these years?

Upon your deafend ears I've grown,
The angels moved me to a place unknown.

Happiness rings here all year round.
Happiness, the higher ground.

Nancylynn Pera

My Calvary

At Calvary's Cross where Jesus bleed
It was a man beside him, a thief who said
"Come down from the cross" if you be the son of God
For why humiliate yourself before this mob
Jesus lifted his eyes toward the sky and in his spirit he gave a sigh
For he knew it was needful for man that he die
This he thought to himself, yet and gave he no reply

He allowed himself to be beaten and bruised
Laughed at for sinners pleasure and for their muse
He suffered embarrassment, humiliation and pain
That the soul of mankind may be redeemed he was blamed

Yes my Savior he could have come down from his cross
But then my poor pathetic soul would surely be lost
I'm so glad he decided to die and for my sins paid the cost

He said take up your cross daily if you will follow me
That others like you once bound may be free
Now you too can come down from your cross
But the soul you're responsible for just may be lost

Barbara A. Reed

Children

On the sobs of one child, I can awake my sorrow.
With his tears I dried my tears.
And in his arms I protect myself. I made his lap my support.
I looked deep inside his eyes, and I could see all his tenderness.

He has a wide smile on his face, with all his simplicity
And with his own celestial glare. I felt his heart beating.
In a rhythm I never heard before. I breathe love.
I wish to go back in time. I wish to sing a lullaby to myself.

I try to see everything like a child, but I am an adult.
Big enough to understand everything.
But sometimes I cannot understand one child.
I get lost inside his mischief and I lose my temper.

For a minute I become a witch but I remember his smile
And I cool down again, telling him a "Once upon" story.
I feel great, I'm a child again.

Sometimes I think the child I have inside me
Wasn't born at the right moment.
Now I can feel it with my children and I can understand better.
This fascinating world full of dreams of a child.

Rejane Lasheras

Memory

I remember bright hot sky of California, waiting to get out of school.
I remember traveling miles to see my light of love.
I remember she gave me warmth and power.
I remember seeing her shiny brown eyes look into mine.
I remember expressions on her face, delighting to see me.
I remember a light brown face of beautiful black queen.
I remember great extent of love I shared with her.
I remember dark night of Christmas Eve when she went to heaven.
I remember flying miles, a deep dream of darkness, thinking of nothing.
I remember seeing her still, a deep sleep.
Memory, this special woman. My grandmother.
I no longer see her, I feel her.

Joi N. Torrence

The Silence Of Many

The silence of many has killed them all
We love you children, we all miss you so...
Spare us the cheap grace if they're already dead
Don't pay condolence, awaken your conscience...

An endless savagery inflicted on body and mind.
Plagued by a mortal silence of timid neighbors scared of all...
Desperate and abandoned to their faith
    with whispered lullabies of death.
Part of a predictable scenario children drowning in pain...

The names of the victims
will soon be forgotten
They will not be mourned for long
and I wonder if we have the right to mourn at all...

The silence of many prisons that incarcerate
the helpless children who survive the worst...
What has love done to them
to make them grow up to be such dangerous adults.

The life of a child, the conscience of a man,
the essential human worth lost
and at the end a shameful death,
May God forgive us all.

Afshan Ali Mahmood

The Teacher's Reverie

He sat with his back to the light from the window,
Forming a silhouette as black as the night.
His students toiled over a lengthy assignment,
Fearing his wrath if their answers weren't right.

The silence was tomblike, the air was oppressive,
A fly buzzed, lethargic in the late autumn day.
He sighed and corrected a thick pile of essays,
He wished he were elsewhere, a place far away.

He dreamed of a maiden with golden hair flowing,
He imaged himself on a charger pure white,
Slaying her dragons and bearing her onward,
Into a sunset of crimson delight.

He fancied himself on a tropical island,
A castaway lolling in the hot summer sun.
Cotton ball clouds scudding o'er cobalt heavens,
At peace with himself, there was nowhere to run,

Then a sharp, clanging schoolbell burst through his fond dreaming,
Gray walls, dusty chalkboard loomed back into sight.
His students dashed madly, for the schoolday was over.
He sighed as his heavens gave way to drab night.

Peter Lundgren

An Empty Vessel

I can't believe the way I feel, as if I'd known you forever.
An empty vessel filled with thoughts of you and I together.

We sat beneath an old oak tree on a windy Autumn day,
Trading secrets from our youth amidst our childish play.

We wandered down an old dirt road engulfed in nature's wonder,
Thinking not of time or cares, just being with each other.

We made a snowman two feet tall with a tiny little face,
Then silently warmed each other's hands beside the fireplace.

Hand in hand through the park as if we were just one,
We dared the day to finish yet, although the setting sun.

We traveled to a distant beach to gather seashells from the sand.
We watched the sun slowly rise as we held each other's hand.

As I wake and face each day, the truth and I, we wrestle.
All these thoughts and more I see inside this empty vessel.

Jon Coble

I Am A Christian

I am a Christian, who loves Jesus with all my heart.
I wonder when Jesus is coming again.
I hear Jesus speaking to me in secret everyday.
I see the cross, as a reminder that he set me free.
I want to live for Christ 100% in every way.
I am a Christian, who loves Jesus with all my heart.

I pretend he is walking beside me everyday.
I feel his presence that surrounds me in times of temptation.
I touch the earth and sky as a reminder that God made it.
I worry that so many people are lost and without Christ.
I cry to think if Christ wasn't my savior, where would I be today.
I am a Christian, who loves Jesus with all my heart.

I understand that nothing is impossible when Christ is in control.
I say God is real because he has changed me.
I dream of the second coming and how the world's going to end.
I try to live for Christ so the lost would see him living in me.
I hope that every man and woman can say they're going to be with
    Jesus when he comes again.
I am a Christian, who loves Jesus with all my heart

Christine M. Dahl

Wings Of Dawn

When darkness like a veil descends upon a sinful heart,
Where evil lurks and what is good cannot be told apart,
And shadows fall across the eyes which may have held some light
For the foolish heart that stumbles blindly in the depth of night.

Where he who makes his bed among the depths
    where conscience sleeps
Surrenders his soul to the deceit where deep calls unto deep;
And hides the sinful desires of his heart beneath the impending doom,
Where friends and foes alike fall silent in the encircling gloom.

Yet just as he feels lost amidst the blackest and darkest of night,
There shines within his very soul a tiny glimmer of light —
A thought, a hope, a word remembered - spoken years before,
"Seek and ye shall find the way, just knock upon the door."

The knock ushered in a perfect light - so pure and deep and strong
That even the darkest depth of night could not seize down upon;
For in the presence of a Holy God, no sin or shadow abides,
So rise ye on the wings of dawn, wherein His hand will guide.

Sandra K. Adams

Reflections

On this day, that was sure to come,
Putting down a few words and thoughts meant for everyone.

Words soaring and whirling in my head,
What could I say that would be read.

Sand in life's hourglass, seeping through its portal, is sad,
Hoping, with class, I will remember only the best times we've had.

As a day, like this, we all must face,
I hope to endure mine with a smile and grace.

The sand in my glass continues to flow,
So I will pause, change directions, and be on the go.

If asked, what have you done and where have you been,
I can proudly say... "enjoying a family and many friends".....

    Reflections... until
    Betty Lou Drawyer Luzier

What I Have Become

Look at me.
I am your creation.
This is what you made.
Do you like what you see?
You are the one that made me like this.
I was able to do anything for you.
I could have cared for you.
You could have shared your pain and joy with me.
But now you have lost control.
You cast me aside.
Left me to my own demise.
I have sat there watching you live your life without me.
You are driving me crazy, every time I see you walking
    with someone else.
I have given up so much for you.
Now, all pain I felt had made me into a monster.
You have no power over me.
You can not stop me.
Because I'm free.
And you will never have me again.

    Charles Curtis

God's Gift

You're God's gift that was sent to me.
Now with you here, I feel so free.
God sent you from the heaven's above.
When I look into your eyes, I see love and peace.
The things you would find in a dove.
God sent you with a piece of his heart.
There He prays that nothing will tear us apart.
God sent you with all of his hopes and love.
He has reasons with him high above.
God sent you with the rivers and the oceans.
He made you with plenty of hopes and devotions.
When God placed you here with me, He knew He had to set you free.
The day you were lost and couldn't see, that God had placed
    you here with me.
He placed you down with a tear,
For he had plenty hopes and little fear.
God's gift is who you are. You are now beside me and not so far.
You are so special for which God made you with love, hopes,
    peace, and His dreams.
You're God's gift that was sent to me from God above.
God made you for me out of pure love. You're God's gift!

    Tina M. Collester

Life Or Death

There are two choices in life, you can live or you can die
For there is no life in death and no death in our lives
You can choose to be free and live life for all it's worth
Or you can live your life for others and be bound to this earth
There is no chance in our lives for we decide our own fate
The low road of damnation or the road where love awaits
You must not bind yourself to the things dear to man
If you must go by yourself then by yourself you must stand
There is only so much you can allow yourself to do
For there is a limit any man can put himself through
Life is not a game yet it must be played from time to time
And you must stare your fate in the eyes when death is on the line
The difference between fulfillment and that which knows no joy
Is the life which lived prosperously and the life which was destroyed.
You can live for who you are and live for what you love
Or you can die without a cause and be separated from above
The choices are there but the decision is ours to make
Life is the only answer and God is the only way
Heaven is a place of eternity yet Satan still has his breath
For as eternity goes with life so shall it be with death

Kevin Odom

I Am

I am a happy-go-lucky boy who loves basketball and karate.
I wonder what sport I will get a scholarship in.
I hear sounds of balls bouncing.
I see people all around cheering me on.
I want to play for the Pro's one day.
I am a happy-go-lucky boy who loves basketball and karate.

I pretend to be Jon Claude VanDame.
I feel I will be as great as he in Karate sometime soon in the future.
I touch my trophy and feel my black belt around my waist,
    this make me proud.
I worry one day that I will hurt someone.
I cry when I do not achieve the goals that I set for myself.
I am a happy-go-lucky boy who loves basketball and karate.

I understand that being as good as I am with my sport is a gift.
I say for everyone to find something that they enjoy and do the best
    they could possibly do.
I dream of fame to come to me in my older years.
I try to be the best that I could possibly be.
I hope all my dreams will come true.
I am a happy go lucky boy who loves basketball and karate.

James Douglas Lampke

Food

There're all kinds of food in the world,
that you can eat.
And all kinds of juicy meat.
There're different tastes, Like sweet and sour.
And icky ones like baking powder.
There's some people that they call health nuts.
Who only eat health food and such.
There're some people who only eat junk food.
I bet they often get sick.
But they take their lollipops along,
so they'll have something to lick.
If you ever ate so much, you would get bigger than big.
Then you would get real fat.
Then they would have to call in the fire department,
and I bet they couldn't even deal with that.
But that could never happen.
You could never eat that much.
Unless you had three course meals for dinner, breakfast, and lunch.
There're so many foods out there to try and taste.
But if you let them sit out too long, they'll turn to waste.

Matthew Corso

Destiny

At night, sometimes I will look out my window and look at all of the yesterdays. I will wonder what ever happened to the promises each of us broke. I remember the day that both of us agreed to go our separate ways. For itself, the truth spoke. It said the fire that was once well lit in our hearts, tears somehow got in, and washed away the sparks. I will admit that we did try. We wanted to say hello, and not goodbye. For there is nothing good in leaving someone for eternity, to just leave them there as if you never really cared. As we pass by each other day after day, I wonder, if we had the chance, what would we say? You taught me to live in the present and not in the past. We said that we are always going to last, it turns out that we were both wrong. Now the nights are beginning to get long. Every once in a while we exchange a glance. It's as if we are both wondering what happened to that perfect chance? Deep down inside we know all of it was worth while. Heaven shined down on us with a smile. It's like you said one time, about destiny, if it was meant to be, it shall happen. The future we shall finally see. If we all just open our minds to that once in a life time chance, everything else will come naturally, and then we can live our life fully.....

Cassie Bennett

Untitled

The first snow lies heavy on the earth.
The grasses and seeds are covered, taking away the feast of the birds.
The annual migration along the river is in full flight.
With a back-drop of blue sky and sun-drenched pink clouds
    there are many species on the wing.
Ducks and geese go by in their uniform 'V' formation with their
    present leader at their point.
Others are scattered across the early morning sky
    not sure which flock to join.
Beaks straining toward the rising sun
    they wing their way ever Southward,
Each one with a winter home on their far horizon.
Whether near or far I wish you a safe journey
    and look forward to your return in the spring.

Judith Fritz

Untitled

You were never supposed to leave me alone,
Not ever, but especially not now.

You were never just "mommy",
You were my best friend, the sibling I never had,
Overall, you were my entire universe.

The one I couldn't lie to , the one I told everything,
The one who would run out at three in the morning in the rain to
get me Burger King. At fifty you belong beside me.
I need you so much more than God does,
And yet he is the one who gets to hug you and hold your hand.

You have brought me crashing to my end of innocence,
Not by want, but by necessity.

And here I stand against the rest of my life, without you and alone.
I see your face, and I hear your voice,
    yet I need to feel you beside me.

But just because your heart stopped doesn't mean you can't love me.
I just hope that you can feel my love radiating back up to you,
    as you sit above me looking down.

You were always my whole life, as you still are.
You will always be "mommy", no matter where you are.

Carrie Elizabeth Simpson

Who Knows?

In the beginning, God created the heavens and the earth.
Then, he created the sun, moon, and stars.
Next, God created the beasts of the field, and the fowls of the air.
Last of all, God created mankind.

In the end, man polluted the heavens and the earth.
Then, he crashed spacecraft into the sun, moon, and stars.
Next, man killed the beasts of the field and fouls of the air.
Last of all, man called himself God.

Why did he who knows all things
create all things
including the things
which destroy all things?

God only knows!
Truman E. Thomas

Dearest Jim

Thanks be to Jehovah that you have decided to spend forever with me
For there is no other man with whom an eternity I would rather be

Our love for each other grows more every day
By Jehovah's loving-kindness he has shown us the way

You strive to be more like Christ in giving of yourself to others
By helping them materially and teaching them to be Bible lovers

All knowing ones see that you spirituality has increased
You apply Bible principles and of this I am well-pleased

Although our marriage has had a few bumps
By forgiving each other we've managed the humps

So let us, honey, by love and fine works for each other
As husband and wife continue to draw closer together

By loving Jehovah whole-souled as a team
And worshiping united, faithful, it will seem

That tomorrow's paradise is closer than ever before
As Jehovah's bright future is made sure all the more

I love you, Jim, as I know you love me
Together, if Jehovah wills, forever we'll be
Love, Reenie

My Beloved

My beloved, my beloved, you are sleeping sweetly now,
With the pain of the world lifted from your brow.

You're resting in the warmth of Jesus' arms,
While I, left behind, struggle somehow to go on.

The pain within my heart, so hard to describe,
Always there..., but with time seems to subside.

At time passes my soul cries out to be at peace,
As I feel your presence fading from my reach.

To continue on life's path is what you would have me do,
Wishing me happiness again...though it be without you.

My beloved, you touched my soul
and your love has made me who I am today,
and, though our life together was all too brief....
I would have it no other way.
Alberta A. Prioleau

A Child Not Wanted

It happened in the winter, during a cold bitter storm.
The very innocent birth of a child not warned.

Born with hope, just looking for love, peace, a chance to be free.
Not expecting the hell that was given to you and me.

The sadness, fear, torture and pain, all this is worth living?
Not put here by choice, but why? No reason was given.

No more torture or sorrow, no time even for crying.
Just simple peace, that's why the best part of life, is dying.
Susan A. Siegel

Julien

For Arianna
Days In...Days out...
You know
It really doesn't matter
how or where I live my life now...
Neither am I taken by my own failures
nor captured and held captive
in some far off dark and unknown region
far beyond my mind's central and familiar perception of
thought...
It's not that I do not care...
nor am I saying I stopped believing
in The Super Natural Secret of Existence
or
The Magic in the Beauties of the road...
I just want to live...
Astounded by nothing nor anybody...
I just want to live...
Julian Figueroa

An Autumn Walk

The gold of the harvest moon
lights the evening almost day-like.
The shiny bricks beneath my feet tell of a prior afternoon shower.
Leaves of rust and burgundy are plastered flush
and make no sound when stepped upon.

The wind moves softly with gentle fingers, warmly on my cheeks.
Porch lights glow of orange, from houses tucked in for night's peace.
I speed up and listen to the sharp clicking of my heels.
Interrupted only by an occasional car sound in the far distance.

Deep breaths cleanse me of the day's tenseness
and tomorrow's promises of stress.
I stop quickly and ascend steps that lead me to my own address.

Hesitating, I smile briefly, rejuvenated!
Thank you God!
For autumn evenings,
and walks that yet await me.
Dorothea Green

I Love You

In time, you begin to realize that a true and
Lasting friendship comes from the Heart.
Once accepted, this small truth emerges like a
Velvet-winged butterfly to guide the Heart on its Fool's Quest.
Every day, thoughts of you beckon, and my own Heart longs to
Yield to their Siren call and lose itself in the almost
Overwhelming Beauty that is you; and a once wounded Spirit,
Uplifted by the song in your eyes, soars on the wings of your
Smile.
Gary L. Privitt

The Storm

A warm summer's night the red-orange sky above
   the sand under my feet the sun, its going to bed
   beneath the clear-blue water.
This is the way I like it.
I'm not sure where the sky ends and where the earth begins.
Maybe, that's because I'm in heaven soon it's nightfall
   the stars scattered in the sky...are shining brightly.
If I stare at them long enough they seem to answer my questions.
Again, I must be in heaven.
Its time for the sun to rise again but it doesn't, the clouds set in.
No, not the pretty ones. The gray ones
Those clouds that make you feel like some things wrong.
And the feeling grows stronger it's windy very windy cold.
Here comes the rain.
It feels more like hell today
Lastly, comes the lightening bolt thunder crashes!
The lightening strikes before me. Hits a tree, it's down.
That tree will never have life again.
Maybe it's supposed to make me realize how lucky I am to be here,
   to be alive.
So next time I won't complain about the storm because it is the
   storm that helps us to see the calm.

    Rebecca Marie Gaudreau

God's Promise To Me

I am a child of promise
Jesus is the author and finisher of my faith
The problems that come upon the people of the world
I do not have to take

I rebuke them in the mighty name of Jesus
I bind them in the name of the Lord
I am the ship bound for Zion
And Satan you cannot get aboard

I have found favor with Jesus, He is my Savior and my Lord
Anything that rises up against me shall most assuredly be destroyed
A thousand shall fall at thy side, but it shall not come nigh unto thee
Because I am a child of promise and this is God's promise to me.
Hallelujah, Hallelujah,
Hallelujah Amen

    Emerson D. Broadnax

Happy Birthday To Me

The years are fleeting by at an exceedingly speedy rate,
It's amazing to me that, here I am, already seventy-eight!
I recall as I retired a few years ago, endeavoring to decelerate
   the fast and furious pace,
I implored a friend to search and find an eighteen-year-old girl
   somewhere in my eyes and my face!
Now, as I warily venture backwards through the peaks and valleys
   of all my years,
Dredged up memories reveal joys, successes and failures,
   deep sadness and tears.
In my acquired wisdom, I now know it's not likely
   that time will slow down,
And it's my pleasure to keep busy,
   perhaps earning a small star for my crown.
May I look forward to this somewhat limited future with a lot of humility;
Making a promise to accept the inevitable infirmity or adversity,
   whatever it may be.
This is rewarding time that has evolved, I thank God I've been blest,
May I give back a full measure in gratitude of my bequest.
May I appreciate my allotment of years on this planet so divine;
Be happy now and this time next year, when I'll be seventy-nine.

    Mary Beth Pritchard

A World Without Color

Think what life would be, if we all roamed the earth
wearing our skin folded over.
Showing not our melanin content but only
the veins and blood cells which we all possessed.
Would life still be the same. Would man still be judged by color,
Hmmm . . . this time by the color of our veins.
No! Our veins are all the same no matter what creed or race.

Could this be the solution for unity?
Could this surgical breakthrough have us see
peace, love . . . a world without color.
A world were people of all raced, of all creeds, of all nationalities,
would stand together, hand in hand, in one accord.

Quietly . . . I sit still pondering with my thoughts.
Is this the cure for racism?
Softly I sing the song of peace, "let there be peace on earth
and let it begin with me."
If folding your skin is the cure for racism,
well I think we, . . . no I will be the first to get surgery.
Peace.

    Sean I. Roach

Gone Laughter

As the air swallows my body I laugh gleefully
His laughter meets mine and I feel that everyone is happy
When he leaves I know my life will leave with him
Suddenly I turn around just to see still air
I stand there, and after a second fall to the ground
The warm summer air wisps my body up and away to the beach
The warm water brushes along my ankles and the bottom of my dress
My head falls back.
I feel as though my soul is being pulled out of my body
As I look forward I see just the splashing waves of the ocean
The shore won't laugh with me,
   though nothing laughs with me anymore
Everything is gone from my body, my soul, my smiles,
   and my laughter.

    Tiffany Turner

Her

I saw her again tonight. Her eyes are haunting.
Her tears are flowing. She looked back at me;
   daring me to act unknowing.

Her face is young; with dimples.
Her eyes have depth; they are old.
Her brow slightly furrowed . . . from suffering
   sorrows untold.

Her emotions show in her face.
Her eyes would betray . . . any lies.
There is misery . . . etched deep into her being;
   she sighs.

This woman frightens me.
She's too fragile to have to be strong.
She only wants acceptance, to be real . . .
She cares deeply for love; yet to no one belongs.

I've met this woman. I know her well.
I see her . . . wherever I happen to go.
I just glance into a mirror . . .
She looks back at me, you know.

    Sonja Lee Sletto

Cry No More

My eyes a dry lake, for I cry no more
Tears of pain gone with an endless roar.
Feelings forgot and memories destroyed
My soul long gone to an endless void.
Nowhere to run and nowhere to hide
That's what I longed for, that's why I cried.
Now I must go to that unknown abyss
With no one to love and no one to miss.
Take this dear life for how will I gain
My life's filled with hate, sorrow and pain.
Dignity, disgraced and respect denied
That what I longed for, that's why I cried.
But I cry no more cause I am a man
For I did not choose this, it was he who had planned.
To kill all the Jews and create his own race
But if I'd ever saw him, I'd spit in his face. Now I await my
untimely death I say not a word, for I'm out of breath. A young
Jewish boy with nowhere to turn I step in the room and now I must turn.
Hope for the future, that's why I cried that's what I longed for,
    so now I must die.

Jack Scaturro

Nocturne

The fiery orb slowly sinks
And the horizon swallows its light
She peeks her head from the clouds
And smiles her glow o'er the night

She looks down over her kingdom
Bathed with a soft, radiant glow
The forests reach back toward her
Their arms covered with winter snow

The lonely cry of the wind
Whistles and moans through the trees
The sound reaches her ear
With its sweet mournful melody

The stars open their eyes
And creep from the shadows of the lake
Their reflections ripple and fade
And the second night sky is awake

She sits atop her throne, where she rules a nocturnal peace
But the darkness is slowly waning,
    and her silent reign must soon cease...

She smiles one last time at her people
    as she looks to the horizon's new light
She disappears as the sky is brightened
    by the sun as it takes to its flight.

Rebecca Mindock

A Prison With No Key

The world is but a small spool of thread, spinning uncontrollably.
It tells the past, present, and future, but it does not tell why.
It does not say how to help stop the murder, rape,
destruction, and hate in this world.
But it does say we are the ones who chose this evil over good.
We are the ones who created this prison among ourselves.
We are the ones who allowed our lives to fall apart piece by piece.
Why must we live in this unforgiving world?

To bring hell to our children and misery
    to the only love this world has seen.

Cameron Ney

Where Do We Go?

This question I ask, for I have need to know. I've
been in a situation where my mind needs to know more. I looked
in the corners and knocked at the door. It's not to please others
but to satisfy myself, not to be poor all my life because I need
common wealth.
    Not riches nor fame, for I don't need the world pointing
at me with blame. The wealth that I seek is for my inner soul,
having this thought in mind, I strive for my goal.
    The Lord spoke to my heart as He took me by the hand.
With my faith and His grace, He showed me His promised land.
I found His vow to be true, in His Word was the instructions,
a kind of 'how to'.
    Here, I long to be in this place, where there are no
divisions or race. There, a man can be in His rest, not any better
than, just one of God's best.
    I see His land, it's far away. I will live my life
to be there another day. His promise I hold true, it is not
by the things that I do. For, I would fall short of reaching
this destination. Jesus died and arose to life, this is salvation.
By faith we are saved, God's gift, He freely gave.

Margaret L. Case

Simply Because Of You

The reason for being creative
The reason for a smile
The soul reason I give when I go that extra mile
The pain that I would go through
The many chances that I would take
The rules and regulations that I would so gladly break
The never ending bridge I would cross to hold your precious hand
The castle I would build from a single grain of sand
There is no such thing as risk or nothing that I would not do
Nothing that could cross my path to stop me from getting to you
These words should draw a picture that is crystal clear in every way
One that cannot be fogged even on our worst day
A burning fire that screams to rage like no one has ever known
So we can slip through the black smoke into a magical world of our own
Our snuggling nights are endless and each star offers a wish
And to have half of this come true I would be in total bliss

Michael A. Guadagno

My Muse

Oh my Darling you're so thoroughly divine
My thoughts will be of you all throughout my time
When I gaze upon your lovely face
It projects me to that special place
Where I feel the powerful urge to create
So in your honor I will sing, sculpt, and paint
Because an arrow was shot into my heart
That's the reason your likeness is in my art
When in Rome you are my Venus
Cupid brought you from Olympus
To the Greeks you are Aphrodite
To me you're the goddess from the sea
Your beauty I rank as fine
Your loving exalts my mind
I feel magic from a Unicorn's spiraling horn's spell
I hear music from Angels and Mermaids blowing through shells
Your inspiration I can use
You're wonderful, you are my muse
I am welcoming you with a reach from the beach
    and some daisies from the fields
Follow me down the path past the tree
    of apples to my castle on the hills

Jon dig Mann

The Sweet Taste Of Desire

The moon shines bright on a silver ocean of desire.
You wait for me on the shore.

Your gaze hungers for my touch.
The night becomes still as silver waves encompass
    our shadows as we fulfill the passion locked deep in our hearts.

You kiss me and look deep into my eyes.
It is apparent you love me.

And then I wake up . . .

My thoughts are of you as the rain begins to fall.

Katie Persons

My Life With My Sister

My sister is so very mean
Of course she is only a teen
I love my sister Danielle a whole lot
Even though I can't count how many times we've fought
She says that she would never be seen with me
Just with her ugly boyfriend Lee
I could never understand why she is always so furious
I've just been really, really curious
She acts like a brat when she's on the phone with Lee
She acts like he beholds the key
When I go in her room, you'd think I entered the world of doom
She tries to make me feel sorry for her when she gets hurt by Lee
I tell her that I'll feel sorry for her, but she's got to pay a fee
She thinks that I never get in trouble
She is so totally wrong, I get double
I still know that my sister is as good as gold
I also know that my poem is all told.

Jennifer Moss

The Strength Of Aleesha Quintana

It's amazing to me to see the strength of one child
One so strong on the inside, but outside seemingly so mild

In the game of her life, a monster took the pitchers' mound
And pitched Aleesha a curveball, when leukemia was found

As her parents were told their baby was faced with such a disease
In shock their hearts screamed "why couldn't it be me"

With a set to her jaw, and a tilt of her chin
She was faced with so many tests, saying only "let's begin"

So she hits that curveball with every thing that she's got
Wincing through the tears with every treatment shot

She's rounding first, with her blood counts favorably low
A warrior of a player, seems nothing can make her slow

Aleesha's doing so well trying to jump and steal bases
But sometimes a fever would set her back a few paces

Still she plugs on taking third base as her own
She knows with all her hard work, soon she'll hake home

Aleesha, when you are a hundred years old, still fit and well
What a story of unmatched courage you will have as your own to tell

Amy V. Bassett

My Love For You

   I don't know how to explain how your love drives me insane, it
caught me by surprise your gorgeous brown eyes. The things
that I say come from deep within my heart, I know its for real when
I say we will never part My sweetest times are when you're
near when you're around I have no fear. When you're around
you close out the fright you bring me joy through the darkest night.
I hope you know our love is very true if everything fails I hope
I still have you.

Ashleigh Toole

The Mirror

I looked in the mirror, and what did I see,
    the face of compassion was gazing at me.
I looked once again, and then did I see a face that
    was patterned with rare honesty.
I smiled at the mirror and chuckled out loud, and saw my reflection,
    accepting and proud.
I bowed to the mirror as I turned away,
    to cherish the woman I saw there today

Rebecca Nichols

Crack Is In The Air

There's no place like home right or wrong. All cold in the rain.
You can't come home right or wrong. Living homeless in a
world where there are homes. We are living in a world of greed.
Held the children in a violent word. Crack the future lives of
babies still in the womb are ruined by it. It's a nightmare. You
feel the chill of the cold steel. On your back...because neighbor
hoods are becoming war zones for the control of it. Those
indiscriminately slaughter...are carried away in body bags in
the aftermath of it hospital emergency room staff's crack.
Because of it...the sound of crack is in the air for all the
young children pretend looking for quick thrills the rich the
poor successful the old and the employed. Who cannot say no
to it become easy prey to it! So say no and mean it.

Cassandra Orr Romero

Untitled

Familiar is he to me
    fame and fortune he does know
A wonderful thing it must be
    appreciation for having fun
Vexing is it to me
    vaguely, I understand why
Radiance projected as he
    raises his arm to make the pass down field
Everyone holds their breath the ball is caught
    everyone cheers triumphantly as the play is skillfully completed
    by all

Favre he's our shining star
    and he'll take our Green Bay Packers far

Cara S. Shaeffer

Love Strikes

"There, right there. Don't you see it?" asked the blind man.
I lurch out of the corner of my well to hear what he is seeing.
The black cloth coiled tightly to the blond silk.
My toes feel every movement.
My toes digging further and further into the sand of my memories.
Walking with the water caressing my every leg hair to the follicle.
"Right there. Right there!!" he shouts in a cold dark voice.
Closed eyes, opened ears. Fearful heart. Mind expands.
Touch...hold...caress...engulf...
The ocean stares at me with the impulse.
The water, too rough. Dive right in.
Now, swirling in the pool, I become lost.
Voices cry out. Voices ringing in the storm.
"Right there!!!"
Now, more intense than ever.
Now blind, now deaf. Heart pumps with raging blood.
Squeeze the valve, cut off flow.
"Right...here."

Phillip G. Crystle

Untitled

You came into my life with a whisper,
slowly and without my knowing you took my heart.
I was reluctant - you were persistent,
so I let my guard down and allowed you to swallow me whole.
You filled my soul with such joy. It was the little things -
the sweet caresses, the gentle kisses, and the lightest touches.
My emotions soared, sweeping me higher and higher,
and my feelings increased.
Never had I ever felt such pleasure from just a person's smile.
I thought nothing would ever bring me down from my high —
Then the clouds came. There were no silver linings,
there was no break in the heavens above.
There was a storm brewing
I felt myself falling - falling rapidly towards the ground below.
I was no longer able to fly, life as I knew it ceased to exist,
and my world on this earth crumbled.
But one thought haunted my mind,
creating within me my own private little hell...
Why did I allow my heart
to overpower what my mind already knew?

Rozalynn S. Frazier

Prevailing Dreams

Do the dreams prevail over all humanity?
Is there no escape? Can't be left behind.
Stop running and lay your body down to rest.
Let your soul unwind.
I'm coming back to starve on the apples of the tree.
So young are the thoughts that you just can't learn to stop.
Can a grain of sand be held in your hand
    without being blown away by the wind.
A drop of blood, black to the eye,
    rolls down my cheek as I start to cry.
Life's just one big argument that never seems to end.
No one wants to hate, but they just have to pretend.
Do dreams prevail over all humanity?
Over all eternity? Will there ever be an escape?
Please don't leave me behind.
Life won't let the soul unwind.
To the past I can't let free.
I can't let go so please don't leave.
Way too wretched, too deep the hole.
When death creeps near, next to my heart, please bury my soul.

Jeremy M. Ray

When I Lay Down My Comb And Brush

When I lay down my comb and brush, and bid farewell to toil and rush
When Saint Peter says "Come my child it's time for you to rest awhile".

In my last will and testament, I shall leave
My worldly possessions, do accept them please;
Tis only love and all my blessings
For you dear ones in the beauty profession

I wish now give my instructors license
to someone whom I wish to surprise
Now I'll feel even with this old girl
I am now prepared for a better would

Now you've heard my tale of woe the time as come and I must go,
With the angels who are waiting there, wile I hobble up golden stair.

If you don't believe what I have said
You might as well just go ahead
But the time will come and you will pray
That you'd listened to what old Himes had to say

Farewell to you whom I've left behind
May fortune be yours, with peace of mind
I shall not mind to adjust "His Chair"
But I hope to heavens that angels have no hair.

Gladye Haimes

Blind Faith

Faith is the stuff that things hoped for are made of
From childhood, we are taught to believe in things we can not see,
Like hope, warmth and love.
We get what we wish for, sometimes,
And difficult situations seem magically to work out fine.

But we grow up and find that there is such a thing as,
Blind Faith.
This happened in Days of Old.
In situations when believers in miracles and God's Wonders,
Felt alone and were treated cold.
They seemed to believe as one standing against the masses.
This is how we must be no matter what passes, in our lives.

For Blind Faith, believing beyond sight,
Surpasses doctor's doubts, in sickness,
Or the extent of a lawyer's might.
Can pull you over all things,
When you seem alone in your care.
Blind faith connects the bridge to God,
That we travel across in prayer.

Barbara Cutter

Transition

Transition, they say, is in the meantime,
But how long does the meantime last?
It seems my meantime has been extended
To much longer than the recent past.

Transition, they say, is partly derived
From a word that means "move across",
But somewhere in all the movement
I do believe that I've been lost!

Transition, they say, can be through space or time
Or it can span from age to age.
If that's the case, then why am I not
With the rest of the world: In sync and on the same page?

Transition, they say is a feeling, an emotion
That permeates your mind, your body and soul;
They did not say if, you can survive this invasion
And still feel that you have remained whole.

Transition, I say, is all the above, and necessary, I must admit.
To be stagnant and static is to surely die;
For confidence and strength grow right in the midst of it.
It is transition, my friend, that compels you to try.

Jo Ann Tolliver

Jerry With The Laughing Eyes

Life is not the same without him, but I have to go on anyway,
and when I look toward heaven, I believe what I am seeing will be.
I see rainbows up above, moonbeams filled with love,
The sky so full of doves, and Jerry with the laughing eyes.
I see sunshine and stars, moonlight and Mars,
Diamonds in the sky, and Jerry with the laughing eyes.
I see fields so full of wheat, snow all white and sleek,
Flowers all in bloom, and Jerry with the laughing eyes.
I see night time turn to day, a path to the milky way,
Angels that guide the light, and Jerry with the laughing eyes.
I see love and amazing grace, and only the human race,
Trees and a waterfall, and Jerry with the laughing eyes.
I see mended hearts so pure, and happiness for sure,
Fireworks the Fourth of July, and Jerry with the laughing eyes.
I see football and baseball too, Babe Ruth up at bat,
a homerun hit for you, and Jerry with the laughing eyes.
I see Christmas trees so tall, stockings hanging from the wall,
Thanksgiving and birthdays too, and Jerry with the laughing eyes.
I see God with outstretched arms, wonder and not harm,
Santa Claus and Easter Bunny too, and Jerry with the laughing eyes.

Ardella R. Campbell

A Special People

A Special People, a special kind.
With White Man's evil, we changed their lives.
We did not try to understand them, we kept them far apart.
We killed and torchered their elderly, women, and children,
We hurt the warrior's heart.
I do admire them, we owe them a tremendous debt.
They gave us legends, myth, and romance.
We tried to take everything so there was nothing left.
It did not matter for the young and the old,
We pillaged and raped the land and their lives we stole.

What happened to the special people was inevitable,
But the way it happened was cruel and sinful.
I ask many people what can I do?
They say why should I care, they are drunkards and heathens,
They should not mean much to you.
I am a human being with love in my heart of this special kind, for
these Special People called the Indians, that still have their pride.
I have an Indian heart and that part I will not lose,
If I do not try, for when I die,
I will be ashamed of my white blood too!

April Thompson Pennington

Our Boys

I walked into the living room and took one look around,
Then heaved a very weary sigh for this is what I found.
A cap gun on the window sill, a toy truck on the chair,
Marbles scattered on the floor and clutter everywhere.
I said, "Those boys!" and Daddy smiled and said "Be calm, my dear,
Why anyone can plainly see that two small boys live here!"

When Dad went out to mow the yard, I overheard him say,
"Why must they scatter things about when they go out to play?
I have to stop and pick stuff up before I can go on!
The things those little guys can find to strew across the lawn!"
I smugly called to him out there and said, "Have patience, dear,
Why anyone can clearly see that two small boys live here!"

Myrtle M. Jacques

The Frozen Northland

In a sea of desolate white. No sound nor life can be heard
Destined to be in eternal dusk.
It is Winter. And Winter is frozen and dead.
Trees stand towering overhead. Like a stone, cold, colossus.
Yet the cold is a person, but a person darker than any imaginable.
He whirls around your neck and ears to freeze and destroy any heat.
His greatest enemy is fire for he has already conquered the sun.
But, fire is a futile enemy. But an enemy nonetheless.
Fire is heat. Worst of all though, fire is life.
Because man must create fire and man must live.
Man must live.

Art Vilassakdanont

My Favorite Time Of Day

I think I like the morning best, when all is calm and still...
The Earth's just waking from her rest, a shroud of fog still on the hill.
It's clear to me the Lord has blessed each fragrant daffodil.
Each day-break fills me with such zest! It's surely my best thrill!

My favorite time is afternoon - the middle of the day
When all the world seems so attuned ... A busy Matinee!
I know I'd be a poor buffoon if I didn't stop to say...
"Thank you, God, for broad daylight, my favorite time of day!"

I've always loved the evening most, when daylight has withdrawn..
The crickets, tuning up now, boast ... They'll serenade
'till dawn!
The stars peep out, and I'm engrossed ... Night's gentle as fawn.
I'll thank you, Lord, our Gracious Host, once more before the dawn!

Valentine

Misfortune's Wall

There's many who will judge me by the way that I appear
I'm homeless, lost and hungry, wondering how I landed here
A series of misfortune took away stability
I sleep in borrowed doorways, frozen in humility

Looking out from my dread locks and sunken blue eyes
In the mirror I see a gaunt, sad face I no longer recognize
To tourists driving by I am stoplight entertainment
Like a side-show criminal just awaiting my arraignment

But please don't judge too harshly, we are all humanity
I'm any man woman or child, I'm every one you meet
There's no protection from misfortune, life has no guarantees
Take a moment to count your blessings, you could easily be me

I hate asking for a hand out or to grovel for your pity
Just need a shelter from the cold in this dark and lonely city
Life is but perception, our reaction to events
Complaints are high in modern times from behind your picket fence

Fire and storm disaster can come and take it all
So try to feel compassion as we scale misfortune's wall
We're struggling to regain our lives, trying hard to break the chain
Please don't treat the homeless like we're strays out in the rain.

Julie K. Hughes

Reunion

I fell in love again with the children that we were
And all the Nuns down through the years
That led us on the paths to God.
I heard our echoes from the old walls of the church
And saw again the stained glass stories of the past,
Stories of Popes and Saints and sinners
Who walked and lived again.

The priests we knew were there clad in their ancient vestments
Shimmering in the light of beeswax candles standing tall.
Blue clouds of incense filled the air with fragrance from the East
As Easter songs and Christmas carols sang
From the old pipe organ absent now.

We've been here in this Church so many times before;
  Children then - old men and women now.
Our hearts are glad, our spirits soar!
  Striving to meet again some future date,
One final time, on Heaven's happy shore!

Fr. Joseph Orrin Bauer

Kids

Hey what's happened to our life?
The guns in the hands of children go off with a manly bang too much,
and the frightened elders hide behind their mothers skirts and whine
like the children don't anymore.
The stare in their eyes is not the innocent gaze of our past
and the halloween candy is no longer safe, it cuts and poisons
everyone away.
So instead the painted child burns Chicago to the ground
and goes home to the cinders to comfort his mother
grieving her burning existence.
Why the fright in your expression?
We raised them in the drug streets and alleys.
Proudly displaying them when the holidays roll by,
forgetting a few on the path.
We forgot they were children.
And they forgot to wipe their stolen sneakers off
before coming in
  from the reign...

Greg Carlson

The First Snowfall

The swirling snow falls gently on the ground, it is the first snowfall
of the season and as it lands on a piece of flesh, the body reacts
by a bushel of goose bumps
S — l — o — w — l — y
you recover and remorse by sticking out your tongue to
taste the first bright, crisp, awakening snowfall that has falling
for what seems for hours. The freezing of the
bright, luminous, over confident snow makes you bring your tongue
in, promising yourself you will never forget the coldness and that
you will never do it again, but next year's snowfall you do the same
thing . . . How quickly we forget the most harsh of things.

Crystal Brown

The Child Within

A mourning child cries out for her innocence.
Violated, she is scared by crimes committed against her.
Her spirit is wounded deep within.
Tears are spilled by her innocence torn.
Kneeling in sorrow, her spirit groans in travail.
In prayer she lays down her life at the foot of the cross.

As memories begin to surface, the blood covers the vast sins committed
   against her.
Through eyes of compassion our savior sees her brokenness.
He lays down His life to restore her to wholeness.
Are you crying out for the child within?
Are you groaning in travail for the healing of your soul?

Heavenly Father, pour down your mollified ointment,
   heal the wounds of my spirit.
Piece together the brokenness of my heart, purify the soil of my past.
Purge the dross of my soul, rebuild the waste cities of old.
Cause the desert of my life to bloom that I might blossom as a rose.

Are you groaning in travail for the healing of your soul?
Are you crying out for the child within?
Father, heal the child within.
Heal the child within.

Carolyn G. Martell

Grandparents

What a beautiful creature!
She is so tiny featured.
Her eyes are blue, her hair is dark,
Her skin is fair, her cry is like a lark.

Emily Ann is three months old.
She is to us like precious gold.
Being our first grandchild,
She makes our hearts beat wild!

We can't wait for the day,
To here little Emily Ann say,
"Grandpa and Grandma are here!"
A big hug we will have for our little dear.

We spend as much time as we can,
With little Emily Ann.
She grows sweeter as each day passes,
Filling our hearts with gladness!

There will be a time when we will have more grandchildren to enjoy.
Whether it be a little girl or a little boy,
We know they will bring us as much joy and laughter,
As Emily Ann has now and will ever-after.

Carol F. Smith

Beauty True

A diamond's clear sparkle, a skies' deep electric blue;
An ocean depth, all things beauty true;
A walk on the beach, sunrise-sunset-all things better then the rest;
Happiness is to be free, independent, one can bet -
   nothing but the best;
Look for your fantasies, wishes, dreams, true charm;
Don't be scared, shy, nervous definitely not alarm;
Expand your horizons, look across the sea;
Only then could you, fully come to be;
Evil, adversity, trickery, deceit hold you back;
Greatness, fame, love exotic is the right track;
Gain control of life or things become very lame;
Don't be alone looking to only blame;
Find your comfort, lust, true heart, everlast;
Don't forget all but, say goodbye to the past.

Justin Kotcher

An Empty Shell

They say love conquers all, but I feel it has only conquered me
as one, as a whole, as a person.
I told him once he makes my heart swell like an ocean wave.
This wave has curled and broken only to rush toward shore to leave
behind nothing but empty shells. (It's how I feel.)
But, pick up that shell and put to one's ear and hear the life and
memories of what once was, (beautiful).
Will this empty shell be picked up, brushed off,
   brought home, to be loved and admired.
Or will I be swept back to the ocean only to lay
   at the bottom of the sea.

Tricia Ducey

The Dark Of Day

The child digs in the sand,
Awaiting treasures she's sure to find.
She flinches, sending grains into her hair.
Flesh torn, a rusty fishhook, droplets of blood in the palm of her hand.

She wipes her hand on her dirty blue jeans,
Turning her attention to less hopeful activities.
Forming castles with a dixie cup,
A band-aid drawbridge is all that is left it seems.

An apple crashes down, splitting in two.
A worry free worm wiggles away, robber of fond childhood memories.

Bradley W. Van Riper

I Touched Your Soul

I looked into your eyes and I felt your soul.
I touched your skin and it felt deathly cold.
I could smell your sorrow, as you forced out a breath of air.
I feel that your heart has lost its golden flair.
I see your pain, stretched across your body so tight,
I know you're afraid to sleep, because of your demons at night.
I taste your tears and it makes my knees go weak,
I know your life needs the nourishment, that only love can meet.
I ask you what's wrong, and you tell me a lie.
I can tell your soul wants to leave, so your body can die . . .
So I take your essence and wrap it in a golden light.
I'll give you my heart fire, so yours will shine bright.
I'll give you an immeasurable love, that can't be met.
I'll give you my life, so yours won't be spent.
I'll give you the key that unlocks heavens door,
I'll open my heart for you to explore.
For your eyes will never shed another unhappy tear.
For my love will envelope your being, that my soul holds so dear . . .

Christopher J. Shelton

Untitled

Beams of sunlight in my mind-keep on breaking through
Bringing back those memories, of how I felt for you.
You have been my guiding light, the strength, that guides me home.
If you and I go separate ways; I'll know I am alone.

You don't realize what it means to have a friend like you.
A friend can make you laugh and cry and forget you're feeling blue.
You are like an image; that bounces back at me;
And when I look into a pond, your face is all I see.

The stars in heaven light the sky with a luminance so bright.
They hover in the universe; to keep us safe at night.
That is what you do for me;you keep me safe from harm.
I hope you know I love you, when you hold me in your arms.

Tell me you are still my friend; my lover and my mate.
Say all our wounds will one day mend; and that it's not too late.
Tell me that you haven't gone; and stand here by my side.
Tell me that you need me too and your love will never die.

I hope that you will think of me, and it makes you warm inside.
Thinking of the memories; that are so hard to hide.
I hope you'll always call me friend, if you need me, I'll be there.
I will hold you if you're weak; for I will always care.

    Tammara I. Cappellano

Footprints In The Sand

I walked upon the beach of life and took a little while to stand
And look back on the way I'd traveled,
I saw my footprints in the sand.
O, I could not help but wonder, looking back on the way I'd trod,
If all those steps I'd taken, had led me one step nearer God.

If someone else should choose to follow all those feeble steps of mine
Could they feel I'd let them closer to the love of Christ Divine.
Waves of trial swirled round my feet and make it difficult to stand,
In a moment, they had washed away, my footprints in the sand.

Lord, let me live a good example as I witness here for you,
May you alone be glorified, in everything I say and do.
May each step lead me nearer heaven, as I travel through this land,
Let there be more for folks to follow,
    then shifting footprints in the sand.

    Glenna Zelanak

Garden

Are you deadly exhausted? And angry? A grouch?
A strong headache? Your heart totally pains in your chest?
Don't be lazy! Come on! Leave your stupid soft couch!
Visit a garden! It helps! It's the best as a rest!

   Do not tell me, how gorgeous is the blossom of flowers:
   Any time, anyone is as nice as a bride!
   How great is birds' song — listen to it for hours!
   You feel joyfulness, tenderness, pleasure inside!

Pain's forgotten, mind clears, headache disappears,
You are eager again! So you can never lose!
A garden is the best treatment for heart, eyes and ears.
Use these "drugs"! So who doesn't — has no excuse!

   Birds fly out . . . Short day . . . Autumn brings endless showers . . .
   Hundred colors at fall . . . All leaves whisper to us . . .
   Winter makes a thick blanket from snow and covers
   Leafless trees, iced bushes and frozen grass . . .

Do not worry! Just trust in your luck and ambition:
Spring will come anyway! Winter will shortly stop!
Even if you have lost in the last competition —
Just remember the proverb: "Don't ever give up!"

    Michael F. Kharaz

Freedom

I heard freedom's cry of agony,
I saw freedom being torn apart by the claws of injustice,
I saw freedom being strangled by the evil hand of tyranny,
I saw freedom struggling to breathe the air of truth,
while drowning in the ocean of ignorance.
I saw freedom being abused by those who despised it,
I saw freedom being exploited by those who misunderstood it,
I saw freedom being suppressed by false traditions,
I saw freedom being oppressed by unjust laws,
I saw freedom slowly dying.
Freedom cried bitter tears each time a word was censored,
Freedom bled each time a rebel was imprisoned,
Freedom's heart was broken each time a young woman was
forced into the prison of an arranged marriage.
Freedom was once flying, but now its wings lie broken.
I once sat mourning the death of freedom,
yet now I know that freedom still lives,
it lies within the hearts, minds, and souls of those who believe in
   all what is true.

    Mayssa Abu Ali

Cry No Tears For Me

When the war came he went on his own, not drafted.
When the shelling started he died that you might be free.
His mother and wife did not understand, but he did.
He said cry no tears for me.
He died so a man's color was no longer an issue.
He died so others might not have to.
He died so you might go to church or school where you please.
He said cry no tears for me.
The man in the corner with the long hair chose not to go
   and that was OK.
The pregnant young girl ran away from home,
   that she might keep her child.
A man kills because he feels there is no other choice he can make,
   and it's OK.
He said cry no tears for me.
Save your tears for yourselves who cannot see through
   color to the good inside.
Save your tears for yourselves who cannot learn enough
   tolerance to let the world be free.
Shed your tears for yourselves,
   whom he died for that you might be free,
   for you are not worthy.
He said cry no tears for me.

    Ernie Ellis

Close Enough To Reach Out

Like a bird in the sky uninhibited by ties
Free and adrift like the waters in the sea
Close enough to reach out...knowing when to let go
Bridging life with heart and soul
Whether a mist or a glow
Let's not complicate things with possessions or rings
Free of disguise...way of life
I can make no promises as the future is untold till tomorrow unfolds
I'd like to be able to look back
And know I made no compromise
Let's get close enough to reach out
But know when to let go
Only then have we embraced love and allowed it to flow

    Norma Jeanne Adams

267

The Night-Time Lullaby

Pain is a memory no one remembers
A distance so far, you can feel its breath upon your heart.
A man's dream, so close to reality,
Is now as foggy as a death received by a loved one.
Promises she broke like a jig-saw puzzle,
Now fall upon the ash covered ground.

Tears fall from a stone figure that had once been a young maiden,
But a mother's spell had cast the beauty away.
When the sun rises a mysterious shadow begins to grow;
And when night bows upon the world,
the figure introduces its misery.

Silence is a gift souls cannot taste.
Pain is a pleasurable feeling hate can only produce.
Tonight I will sing the world to sleep in hopes of dreams to cherish.

Josie Callahan

The Unknown

Clouds so puffy, soft winds, skies azure. I drift away to
another place where all is free, where time does not count.
For truly though my eye's does not see, to close my eyes and
see
what I've never seen before. Where all is beautiful, reaching
into the unknown. In the twinkling of an eye, I was changed,
there was no pain, for my heart did not fear. Where the Angels
ride upon the unicorn's. Watching as they pass, leaving white
clouds of silk behind. I smell the sweetness of the roses, finding
myself in the most sparkling rose garden, not a thorn one.
Humming birds to and frow within their bud's. I go unto
another cloud, lying my head down, drifting off, how peaceful,
just drifting, and drifting. Awakening, starring up to the clouds,
how wonderful, back to my world, where pain is real, and tears
that flow. Yet just to know I can drift away to the clouds and get
away. I stare to the stars, within the nights darkness, stars of
brightness, yet there is no darkness. My heart flutter's my eyes
are open, yet I am there sitting upon a star. Hearing sounds
of the unknown and I am not afraid. All is waiting, all
is beautiful, and when my time. I'll be where I belong.

Marsha Higginbothom

An Artist's Letter To It's Soul

An artist,
a creator that has power to transform anything it handles.

The artist's hands influence the soul by creating its emotions.
Flat, sharp edges represent anger and distress; while lumpy,
    uneven surfaces show fear and uncertainty.

The artist's hands continue to work the clay, molding it and
shaping it, adding water to make it smoother and easier to construct.
Occasionally, an abundance of water manipulates the soul like
fabrications and lies, by turning it into something it isn't; then
confusion sets in. When the clump is exposed to too much air, it
dries up and the soul becomes depressed.

The artist never stops, it dedicates an even and continuous flow
of construction to the soul. Sometimes it rounds and polishes
the edges so much that it forms a sphere, a sphere that is
complete and whole with happiness and love.

In reality you are the artist, you are the one that has control of
my soul. If this is true, then why don't you maintain my shape
as a sphere? Why do you make me unhappy at times and
confused at others? Why do you make me angry and uncertain?

The truth is, you are also influenced, influenced by other artists,
artists with feelings and thoughts of their own. You can't
control these influences that change my dreams. So in the end, I
will learn to accept your decisions of emotions as I step back
and admire a lifetime of feeling combined to form a statue of my soul.

Natalie Raab

I Looked Into Her Eyes

As I looked into her eyes, I saw a tear crawl down her face.
I asked her "What's the problem?", she said "He got away."
I said, "Please tell me what happened, because I just don't understand."
She said, "I thought I had survived it, but the pain won't disappear.
Well, if you look inside your heart, the answer are with you.
The tears you feel must fall at last, to heal your shattered dreams.
Did you find yourself in trouble, more alone than you can bare?
(She was on her way to catch a plane and fly up in the air.)
And then I ran up to catch her, to tell her it's OK.
She said, "No one has my answers.", and turned and walked away.
After many years of struggling, she learned to accept the past.
She moved on to the future, she was happy at last!
The man she thought would marry her, he said, "She is the best!"

Monique K. Brewer

One Brief Moment

Darkness falls before my eyes
    all the while my tears have crystallized
Thinking back so long ago,
    the hurt seems gone but the pain still shows.
My shattered dreams from another time, every thing I ever left behind,
    swept away by the winds of change, every time that life turns strange.
In just one brief moment,
all you believe can get so turned around.
Just one brief moment, your whole world comes crashing down!
Once upon a time in your life you were sure you had it all,
    you built the ladder to success yourself,
    there is no way you could ever fall.
Securely safe, certain that you've found a piece of paradise,
nothing ever could go wrong, there's no reason to think twice.
Then suddenly it's hard to see, when the darkness shadows your eyes.
A trick of light in a twist of fate, as some thing inside of you dies!
In just one brief moment, all you love so strangely disappears.
Just one brief moment, you're living nightmares
    of all your doubts and fears!!!

Edward A. Liptak

Autumn

When we see the smiling faces,
hear the children at school running foot races.
The colors of leaves falling to the ground with the slightest of ease

The crisp wind that feels so good,
the autumn moon that sometimes
makes you wish you could be in
the arms of someone so dear
with the sky above you so crisp and clear

Come back bright moon, stars, and heaven
let me see the face,
feel the kiss, and be missed also

Brenda Baker

Time

I know you feel alone now, the world an unfamiliar place
You're suffering with grief now, sadness covers your face.
A part of your life has left you now, although you weren't prepared
You have to look back to the happy times, together you once shared.
For now you will feel your pain and be resentful towards every day,
But someday you may find the answer as to why it happened this way.
Time will release the anger and confusion you're trying to hide,
And help you deal with the emotions that are tearing you up inside.
It's then you will cherish the memories
    you were given the chance to make.
And those will bring back the smile this tragedy attempted to take.
Everything in life has a reason for why they occur as they do,
It's just harder to uncover the reason, when its someone close to you.
So take the time to heal your pain and deal with every part,
For one thing that can never be taken,
    is the love deep within your heart.

Diane Grant

Remember

The angel closes your eyes, but you fight back; you hold your breath
because you know that if you release the last breath, that God will
hold it in his hands forever

Your body will return to the soil, where the tree roots will be arms
that are reaching out for your soul; but where? Where is your soul resting?
You gasp for air, but your lungs can find none; you reach for
something to brace yourself, but your finger tips fail you; you
struggle to see, but now you are blind

There will be no more air to breath; you will need nothing to hold
onto; there is nothing else to see;

You have left your familiar world behind, memories are all you have;
all misunderstanding that you have faced in your life, is now more
clear than the crystal waters of the ocean

You understand your life but you misunderstand the concept of
confusion; now you walk with the Almighty Being and he speaks;
remember when you helped the woman that was sick; remember when you helped
the depressed man; remember when you helped the little girl who scraped her arm;
remember all the little deeds you did that were miracles for other people.

They were all one soul; thank-you for helping me all those times
"Well done, thou good and faithful servant - enter thou into the
joy of thy Lord" (Matthew 25:21)

Cheryl McKinney

Autumn On The Hill

I sit on my hill as fall surrounds my being and fills my soul.
I hear the wind rustling leaves on the mighty oak causing them to
fall like rain, covering the ground with an orange carpet.

Robins, cardinals and blue jays sing a song of thanksgiving
while they take their fill of seed that has been spread for them.
Blackbirds perch on the fence surveying the scene.

Two squirrels scurry through the yard, scratching under leaves
for acorns. I move, then freeze as one rises to stare at me, holding
his prize to his chest. Then he is gone, taking his possession with him.

The rain begins. The drearier the sky, the more vibrant the colors
that God has loaned Nature for the annual "kaleidoscope of grandeur".
I see yellows, reds, oranges, and browns intermingled with the green
of the pines. The blue ridge of hills in the background blend with
the sky while a cloud of mist hovers just below the trees to provide
a landscape too glorious to be duplicated on canvas.

As I sit, I realize there are chores that must to be done. Yet
still I linger to behold the majesty of God and to thank Him for
another autumn day on my hill.

Rachel K. Norwood

Colibry's Breadth (A Hummingbird's Breadth)

Come to me oh, Colibry
My petals will open when the sun rises, to feel you closer as the sun entices
I'll give you all I am and change your life
Have thy juices oh, Colibry! To feed you is all I need
My life is yours for as long as I live, take it soon it is adrift
Let's enjoy our reciprocal needs.
Come at sunset and say good night, let's be together is our right
and change life as nature demands.
I'll shall be yours and calm your senses, come to me without pretences
Feel the joy of common greed.
Being in you will fulfill the universe
Enjoy our ecstasy in this short life and our togetherness with no array
As long as I live I'll give you pleasure, our lives will be a treasure
and when I'm gone and you try another
as life goes by, remember me with sweetness pride
and give your life as I with thy!

Mirna Jaimes

Flying High

Floating up in the sky, floating high.
I wonder why?
The eagles fly above me
    and the finches fly below me.
I wonder why?
Sitting on an old oak tree I wonder why
    the mountains are so high.
The sun is down and moon is up.
The stars are high glimmering with light,
    High, high in the sky.
The sky is dark I must say good night.

Kathleen Perley

Dahlia

Dahlia the sunlight shined in your hair
as you popped into sight
on the grassy hill
as I grew near
my heart fell to the ground

You bloomed with love,
and fear for what you do not know

Dahlia you need look no further
for what you have searched for,
for so long

The time has come to loose your fear,
need not worry, when loneliness comes near,
don't shed a tear

Dahlia you are beautiful and elegant,
use your strength to forget your fear

Dahlia don't be lonely, your waiting is done,
follow your heart, forget your mind
we'll be together till the end of time

Jeffrey P. Landry

April Shower

Millions of flowers cover the ground,
The dirt is soft and warm,
after an April shower.
A rainbow cuts across the sky,
while the sun dries and warms the earth,
after on April shower.
A gentle breeze blows through the grass,
the trees are sprouting buds and the leaves are
    turning green,
after an April shower.

Kaylan Greenwald

Competition

As he approaches the field of combat
his mind races - no wonders
of the physical and mental abuse he has endured
to reach this day
Not dreams but vivid memories of heat,
frustration, pain and disappointment

But now the miraculous coordination of spirit,
pride and body rise from within
and victory becomes paramount
There is no pain, no frustration
only the quest for victory

His bleeding body cries out for more
and the victory trophy is but a symbol
of the burning spirit
of the man.

Bucky Sawhill

Color Blind

And why do you judge me in the way that you do?
Do you know me at all, have you walked in my shoes?

Hey, then don't waste our time fighting over colors,
Take this anger, this hate, and start fighting for others.

Fight for the homeless and for the environment, for education and AIDS funding,
Fight against illegal drugs and drunk driving, against criminals and crime,
Fight to stop child abuse and animal abuse, to stop our children from killing children,
And fight to stop racism and reverse racism, or fight for nothing at all.

We can all change the world. Hell, our future is in our own hands,
But we have to start with ourselves to make others understand.

And tell the others, for they're dying to hear what you have to say-
That God's people of all skin colors are forever here to stay,

No one cannot avoid it, so don't bother to make a fuss,
For in our lifetime color will not be what labels us.

No matter what color you may be, one thing remains so true,
It's not at all what you look like, but what in this world you will do.

So embrace your hued world! Get down with what's right!
And search hard for others to join your new fight,

To stop all the nonsense and spread yesterday's news:
Extra, Extra! In a racist world all colors will lose.

Lisa M. Girolami

Tomorrow

Forgotten youth waiting in pain; elderly folks alone in the rain.
Hordes of people obstructing my view; anguish and horror are what's
    seeping through.

Alone on his porch a saddened man waits for his children to pass
    through the wrought iron gates.
A wish I'm afraid will never come true, his children and others has
    forsaken him too.

Gunshots ring out from across the town as an innocent child falls dead to the ground.
Lying like stone, cold to the touch, deprived of his youth he has not out on much.

Parents wait in hopeless sorrow for their only son to return home tomorrow
From a war that was never intended to last, all they have now are thoughts of the past.

A world in which we must truly despise all that is good in order to rise
To the top of the pile of struggling wrecks whose only religion is the size of their checks.

Try to see it once my way; you can not ignore what's here to stay
Life as you know it may come to a halt if all that matters is the size of the vault.

Katie Kardes

Fair Weather Ends

I've never seen a fair weather friend, I don't know if I ever believed
That people could actually stoop so low, is not something easily conceived

You must have been so very amused, watching the abuse that I took
But now that you find we've made it through, I hear you're the ones who shook

Yes I have dirt, more than enough, to bring your whole house down
and in the end be the one to smile, when all you gave me was a frown

Shall I expose the people I know, for what they do and who they are
maybe decide not to hold it inside, to purposely take it too far

"Nothing I do will come back on me" isn't that the way you all thought
slimy conniving way to exist, believing you'd never get caught

Don't rest or relax and don't rely on the good nature I promised to show
Take a minute to think about how fast painful anger can grow

I let you off, thought I'd never return what destruction you sent my way
But like you I've become a fair weather friend. What more is there I need to say?

Tonia Kinney

Paradise

The music rings in my ears
Annihilating all my fears
On the ground I dance with glee
Contentment fills the whole of me
I gracefully sing the sweet melody of life
I do not know any strife
My mind fills with joyful thoughts
I know I'm in heaven, as I have been taught
I saw the light and followed it here
My arrival brings a happy tear
I am in a place that has no pain
A place where God powerful reigns
A place where there is no wrong
A place where anyone can belong
Paradise

Lindsey P. Smith

Onset Of Night

Today . . . today she died
    and deep within I felt pain
    as tears began and I cried.

Beauty should have been her name
    for she was, and though others shall come
    they can never be the same.

I long for her trying not to let go
    alas what can one do when the end is here
    naught, and thus be it ever so.

Yes, beautiful she was and shall ever be
    after she fades from the thoughts of all
    still shall she haunt my memory.

What be her name — that cause this plight
    names, she has many but simply —
    it is day now gone to night.

Dennis Salmans

The Broken Rule

In wonderments wild land
I go a searching, hoping I will find
The answers to the question of my mind
"The earth on which you live" God said
"Was made for all mankind
you are to keep it beautiful.
The sun will be your light by day
At nights you will have the moon
Stars will gleam on the Milky Way
And gentle will be the dew.
The fruits of the trees and the herbs of the field
Your sustenance will yield
The animals will you obey
Also the birds that fly
The flowers will bloom and beautify
and add fragrance where you may
For you in my image I create
To rule all here — Just keep one rule
And live forever in Harmony."

Ivy Soonfah

The Voices That Call

From the past I hear the cry, familiar voices of days gone by.
They speak of evil more than good, I wonder if anyone really understood
What can this be that rises today? Is it sleep again that calls us away?
We have allowed this sleep to fall, and we cannot hear the voices that call.

They call for truth and justice for all; for freedom too, oh, hear them call.
The evil one has lulled us to sleep; he stole the Rock from under our feet.
Remember Hitler, atrocities done, they seem so familiar as if one by one;
They rise up to haunt us, the very same, evil among us that puts us to shame.

Our forefathers knew the day would come, when tyranny would make here, its home.
Raise taxes high, invent inflation; bring poverty, to our degradation.
Problems begin when we choose not to see; freedom must reign for you and me.
We will all suffer, oh, can't you see, if we fail to learn from past history.

Those Executive orders they call laws, take freedom away from the eagle's claws,
There's enough now for retribution, we'll do away with the great Constitution.
Unless we seek our Lord's face, there'll be no good left in this place
Two generations it will take, to remove all freedom from the United Sates.

Stand now for freedom, hear the loud call; heed God's Word or we will fall.
This world's peace cannot be won, until the Prince of Peace will come.
Until He comes we all must fight, to keep and bear our God given rights
Lies of Satan have destined us all, if we fail to see what's coming to call!

Wanda F. Garrett

Just You

I was sitting on the chair watching the chimes sway as the
wind came through the door of my living room, and all I could hear
from them was a peaceful and musical song. It seemed like they
were trying to say something to me. They chimed quietly; almost
like a whisper, then they'd go into a slow sonata, and I was putting
words together in my mind.
The words came smoothly, but I cannot call your name,
because I wasn't thinking of that, I was thinking of you. Just you.
Music in chimes, the soft wind, and the smile I felt on my face,
when I think of you. Just you.
My age should tell me everything, my history should tell me
a lot, my friendships should be plentiful, my loves strong, though
few; but it all comes together in such sweet harmony when I think of
you. Just you.
I don't need a full day to accomplish a loving thought of you.
I don't need twenty-four hours to believe in you.
I don't feel pain or hurt of sorrow when I can count on you.
My whole life doesn't revolve on only you.
Yet, my happiest is when I think of you.
Just you.

Lynda J. Fernandez

The Clock Of Time

Tick tock, tick tock, what goes on in the mind of a clock?
As the hour hand goes round to the sound of tick tock, tick tock,
and the gears twirl around to the sound of tick tock, tick tock.

Hour after hour the hands go around, day after day when questioned
who cares to say tick tock, tick tock.

There can be heard the sound as the earth revolves round tick tock, tick tock.
Again and again the earth will resound the small faint sound of tick tock, tick tock.

The years are timed and slowly marked down to the old clock
sound of tick tock, tick tock, and the grandfather clock sighs - tick tock, tick tock.

Our hopes and fears are chased through the years by the tick tock
sound and the years and gears grind forever slowly to a tick tock,
tick tock, tick tick tick tick —— tock.

Malcolm Nash

Farewell

Goodnight I went to say,
But in a silent sleep you already lay.
I drew close and whispered sleep well.
With tears my eyes began to swell.
Silence fell upon us, not one word;
As the honoring shots were heard.
The horn was singing a sweet lullaby.
Slowly, the clouds began to part in the sky.
The light of heaven enveloped you
    and took you above;
Leaving me on earth your love.
Yet as you returned to your heavenly home,
I realized I would never be alone.
Though, for a short while we may be apart;
Your spirit will live forever in my heart.

Sandra Hogan Lane

Life Anew

Spring will soon arrive,
with all the scenic beauty.
But in my mind, I will see
only those you left behind.

You forced me into, starting life anew,
you promised to never leave me,
but I guess the promise,
you could not hold true.

Those of us, you left behind
will never be the same.
The tragic way you ended it,
left us wondering, if it was just a game.

I always knew that things for you,
were never truly real,
memories of your past,
kept haunting our even keel.

You forced me into starting life anew,
only now do I realize,
that it was not just for you.

Judith Kanizar

Soaring Like An Eagle

Like the young eagle in the nest,
We long to fly and be part of the rest

But before spreading our wings,
It soon becomes clear we need to learn some things.

Experiencing lifes' ups and downs,
Thus gaining knowledge to land safely on the ground.

The eagles' mother so tried and true,
Teaches the young bird lifes' lessons not so few.

From his brother always by his side,
He learns that together there is strength to glide.

Watching the eagle so majestic and high,
We can see that he never gives up trying to fly,

Each day as we open a new door,
We are like the young eagle trying to soar!

Crystal S. Marble

Buried

Buried by my confusion and rage
Shocked by the way things became
I shouted and screamed trying to be heard
finally discovering that it couldn't be changed
So now I've moved on awoken by truth
To focus on me and undig my grave.

Samantha Jarc

A Spiritual Diet

I woke up early one morning I was feeling so burdened down
So many trials that I've faced, I felt a little unfound

As I went into my bedroom to take a closer look into the mirror
When I saw my spiritual innerman, I understood the picture clearer

My soul was damaged and crying out for a successful spiritual diet
Between the good and the bad, I was going thru a spiritual warfare riot

My soul was labeled with many burdens hanging all around me
Most of which were pledging for strength, but the others just wanted to be free

So without a second thought, I prayed to my Savior, and He told me it's already done
He said, "Have faith for I took your case and your battle is already won!"

This battle I paid with my life; to be free from sin, I paid an eternal price!

As I tried not to listen, because I didn't understand just what the Lord had to say
His voice got stronger, very appointed and then my spirit man begin to relay

A spiritual diet, Oh Lord, I cried how can that possibly be, then
He begin to lead me, where I was tempted and immediately my blind eyes could see

Finally, the Lord replied, "take it only if you want to be used for
    if you fail this diet plan your soul will surely be abused

He ordered my steps and I followed His plan, He gave me His Word;
It was all in His Hand the spiritual diet was just what I needed for
my new preparation, I successfully completed it and now I am burden
free with God and no other separation

  Tina W. Hudson

The Subtle Vision

As I humble myself by a babbling brook, it's the truth I hope to find.
And a mist arose from the forest floor, and a secret was revealed to
my mind. The fact of the benevolent mystery of life is, we all have
the key in our hand. But the justice of truth must be innocently
shown, in the presence of nature, God, and of man. When we take of
this day our daily bread, and give nothing back to thee. And we strip
the land of all its trees, and we feed our waste to the sea. What
foulness and filth and an abundance of grief, as we drink our cup full
of lies. And our hearts are filled so full of the dark, that we don't
hear the animals' cries. So much greed has clouded the thoughts we
think, as one by one they all grow extinct. O let's wake up people,
before it's too late, and let life live, it's not ours to take. Or
someday soon we'll all be alone, and just like the little animals, we
too shall be gone.

  Robert L. Andrews

Holding Hands

A warm August evening, the stars were shining and the sky was black.
I walked with my new husband and my grandpa to the railroad tracks.

Stories and laughter filled the empty night as our journey began.
I walked between them, holding onto each one of their hands.

I rubbed my thumb over grandpa's hand, callused, rough, and aged.
He's been married to grandma for more years than I've been married days.

His hand, rough from farming, was used to wipe away World War II tears.
Yet his hand felt soft and comforting, able to soothe away many fears.

As I felt my husband's hand, it was smooth without scars or sores.
I pray we will never have to live and suffer through a world war.

Amazed at all the trials and triumphs my grandparents have endured together,
What makes their love so strong when many couples often leave each other?

I looked up into my grandpa's eyes under the corner streetlight.
When he smiled, they became full of life, shining very bright.

Then I looked up into my husband's deep eyes, timid yet surprised.
And I saw the same brightness which was shining in grandpa's eyes.

Holding hands on that warm August night taught me more than words could say.
I realize that marriage is a loving commitment you respect and honor each day.

  Jalene L. Miller Hornbuckle

Old Oak Tree

Way up on the grassy hill
between the willow and peach
the old oak tree stands firm and proud
with lessons of heart to teach

Rings to mark each year fought
through the snow and sleet
gashes in the old tough bark
made from a blades sharp heat

Leaves for every time he swung
on the sturdy limbs
initials carved and branches bent
spared by gusts of wind

Many times he ran to the oak
and cried a river of tears
he sobbed and clutched the wounded bark
until it subsided his fear

Every now and then he visits the place
although no one can see
he climbs to his friend that outlived him
his wonderful, sturdy oak tree

  Amanda Wiegmann

God Created Earth

God created earth, he thought it into space.
He made the land, green grass, and
trees, and beaches every place.
He made the sun, moon, and stars
oh, what a heavenly sight.
He made the oceans deep and wide,
mountains to touch the skies.
God created all living creatures some
great, some oh, so small.
Then man, God made of himself,
to take care of it all.

  Barbara J. Bateman

Fall 4 Me

I can look into your eyes and see
exactly how you feel about me

I know I can believe in this sight
because when I hold you it feels so right

I hear your soul calling my name
your heart and mine beating just the same

I'll promise you forever, if you believe
So baby, why can't you fall 4 me

You said it is hard to trust endearment,
but baby, do you know the true meaning of it

Can't you understand the love that I feel
it's not a fad, baby, this is real

You know what we share is pure
it could not be better, I am sure

This kind of feeling that we are showing
some people die without ever knowing

Open your mind and forget the past
Let's find a way to make this love last

Hold me tight and say you love me
I really need you to fall 4 me

  Kevin H. Price

The Starving Children (For All The World To See)

As the clock of time ticks death at every stroke, for all the world to
see, Despair, Sorrow, and Hunger through death filled eyes, stares at
you and me.

Pleading eyes, spirit's dying - for all the world to see,
We watch from false safety in our home's - a Collapsing Economy.

We've grown wise in our Wisdom's, living far above our means
We've forgotten to feed God's starving child, some rice or a cup of beans.

Mass Graves, Mass Starvation, How can we let this be?
Have we become this cruel and cold for all the world to see?

We've crossed thresh-old's or tomorrows, we've mixed our own minds up,
Yet, crooked Politics and failed Religions - don't fill an empty cup,

We've somewhere lost our tenderness, our loving hopes for all Mankind
- Our Dreams of Democracy for tomorrow's Children die,
While we slip back in Time,

We are the Strongest Nation, We are the USA - Awaken O Mighty Eagle,
Do not falter yet! Though your wing's be torn and tattered,
The Starving we can't forget - for if Heaven ever intended,
A job for you and me,
It's feeding the Starving Children for God above to see . . .

Robert L. Bowers

Tears From Heaven

I had a dream but I didn't see, I looked towards heaven but he missed me.
I cried to the Lord please help me, raised my eyes and saw tears from heaven.

I had a dream but I didn't see, Lord what do you want with me, I raised
my hands Lord please help me. I looked up from prayer, and saw tears
from heaven.

I had a dream but I didn't see, through tears of my own, I cried Lord,
Lord please help me. I felt lost with pain but could not see,
I prayed with head bowed, saw tears from heaven.

I had a dream but I didn't see, a heavenly being came to me. I raised
my hands to heaven, Lord please help me. I looked up saw tears from
heaven, the Lord said what do you want with me.

I had a dream looked into a child's eyes with a body broken, and weak.
I saw tears, and pain for me, confused what did I see. A child who
could not move, touched me with love, and smiles to say I have God's
promise, and I'll be free. Now I prayed, Oh Lord I do see, and I
looked towards heaven, now I believe. The Lord's tears were for me.

Mary Applonie

My Soul Mate: Sweet Flower

Flower of the night come with all your might
To over shadow all of my dreadful fright
Bloom when the moon calls you to take flight! Letting your sweet
scents cuddle my nose so tight. Oh sweet flower of the night!
Who lives in a place so desolate of delight. Where grains of soft sand
turn with a heavenly blight to shield your soft petals from my gazing sight
Vibrant flower you will wither away before day break. Leaving my
heart to quiver and shake. Oh so much is at stake! That my dying
heart just can't take. Flower you are the last of your kind. Just as
I am the last of mine now you wither way before I. Dying flower
loneliness has crept upon me. Oh to soon I will be without you
You will leave the desolate desert behind. For all of eternal time
Oh sweet dying flower your time is up. For the sun rises before my
eyes like a yellow crystal cup. Your beautiful petals
have been spread about by the wind. There is no water to keep you wet.
Or bury the dryness in my mouth now you are gone to my despair
nothing is here with me now but my thoughts and wretched misery
goodbye dear sweet lifeless plant I'll see you soon.

Marisa Richardson

Appreciation

Sea oats
swinging gently in the morning breeze
a whispering of praise and of thanksgiving
echoed
in the splashing of roaring waves,
foaming and driven, breaking and broken
playing in the southern wind....
retelling a story:
Faithfulness, anguish, betrayals, hope...
watched by a lighted sky...

...a flight of elegant birds,
searching...

O self,
in one breath embraced and kissed,
embracing all...
a moment of eternity
already changed
yet rooted and in awe....

A grain of sand
in the mysterious shore of life...

Mimmi Zamboni

Life's Tests

Life throws us tests,
One after another,
Sometimes so great,
That they seem to smother.

But I'll, hold my head up high,
And try not to cry,
Feeling weak, but trying to be strong.
Can't be all that wrong.

Faith, hope, and love.
Comes from God up above,
Without these life would be nothing,
But because of these, life is really something.

I'm thankful for the days, nights, and years,
Even though some may cause me to shed tears,
Now all I need is someone who cares.

Rita M. Berg

I Would Love To Make You Mine

I would love to make you mine,
To take care of you till the end of time.
When we're together, it's summer in my heart,
And I pray we never part.

When things go right or wrong,
You'll be there, and so strong.
I wipe away the water from my face
And you'll hold me tight in your embrace.

As time goes by and we grow gray
Our burning candle will never fade away.
When we have reached our peak in life
I'll always treasure of being your wife.

Which one of us is first seized with a sleep
Just remember our great love and don't weep.
Yet in heaven we will see each other
And will be forever, with one another.

Cathy F. Zago

Why

A soft breeze blows across the silent night, it caresses my mind and brings
to surface the same unanswered question of a thousand other nights, why?
   Why do we wound ourselves and bring pain to the heart and mind
that no other can inflict with such expertise? Why do we surge ahead,
knowing full well that what we do can only bring us unhappiness and grief
and black despair?
I found the ultimate soul, the match mate for my heart and mind.
A human who was for me both sophisticated and yet, a simple soul,
unique from others I had known.
We shared a perfect rapport, a satisfying, harmonious blending of
personalities. Together, in discussion or in silence, with an
unawareness of the passage of time.
   And yet, my heart cried out "beware", there's something missing
in this soul for you. There's something you can never share.
   A difference in values and purpose that creates a summit,
intangible, yet unremovable and unsurmountable.
   Still, knowing this, and having been forewarned, we plunge ourselves
into deep unfathomable misery for the ecstasy of being close for
however brief a time.
   Like the moth is drawn to a light, I was drawn to this love that
brought me anguish. And now, in the aftermath of my folly, I ask
myself again, "Why"? And the quiet breeze gives no reply.

Joanne Heinmiller

I Remember Mother

I remember mother-I remember when I was a little boy full of wonder,
curiosity, and trying to find my way; and ever since I was old enough,
I remember your devotion to Jesus Christ and how you instilled in me
the goodness of his graces.

I remember how you guided, suggested, cajoled, and put your foot down
when I strayed. I remember how you taught lessons of right and wrong.
Now they call it family values, but you have always valued family.

I remember how you shepherded like a lioness 14 little feet of noisy
chaos making pitter-patty around the house. You watched over and
protected your brood, but this was no feat for you, mother.

I remember when something bothered me or I felt upset, you'd just
explain it away; so I could face the day. And mother, I remember the
sacrifices; miraculously the ends would always meet and I can still
hear you say, "the Lord will make a way."

I remember how you loved me, now I share my love with others. I remember
your laughs and I remember your sweet, quick smile mother; but most of all,
I remember your sense of humor. I know, because I got that from you.

I will remember October 11, 1996 as the day the leaves all fell to the
ground, and I remember this as the day Christ and nature reclaimed one
of its own. But, my memory of you will remain like the pine tree,
evergreen-Yes, I'll always remember you mother fondly and with love.

Mark O'Luck

Love

Tender, passionate affection — it encompasses our entire world with
its benevolent power, enticing us with vain promises, drawing us
into its inescapable trap, clenching and squeezing our virtue, until
all hope is lost.

It begins to devour our souls, twisting our minds to do its every whim.
We put up no struggle.

We grasp onto it with both hands, taking it for granted, never
believing we may lose it. But, when it slowly begins to seep
through our fingers, we panic and attempt to clench it tighter,
forcing our hold to fail.

We beg and plead for it to return, our cries fall on stubborn, deaf ears.
It toys with us, pretending to show concern, but it's not there for
you anymore. You find a fraction of yourself missing.

Love is nurturing, Love is caring and forgiving.
Love is spiteful, Love is regretful and painful,
Love is everlasting — for better or worse.

Adam Pankratz

Untitled

Death comes on winged, silent feet,
Stealing part of my self with
my loved ones.
Sorrow sits quietly awhile;
Grief grabs hold, not letting go.

A shining, distant light
Beckons me thither
Christ awaits with arms opened wide
Offering comfort to my pain harrowed soul.

Gather to the light, dear one;
Bask in Christ given love
Receive comfort from His teachings
And be whole once again.

LaMerle Deca

Will You Let Me Try To Love You

Will you let me try to love you,
because you know how much I want too.

I can show things that you can only
dream about,
Even though every time I ask you, you
take a different route,

When I sit alone and think of you, people
tell me I am going crazy,
then I realize that without you in my life
it would be real hazy.

This special girl does not understand how
powerful my love can be,
I just hope God can open her eyes and
let her see,

When ever I call her I may not have much
to say.
I just hope she know's I think about her
night and day.

I can do what ever you want me to do,
If you will try to let me love you.

David Alfrey

Until There's A Cure

Until the world will change its ways
No more judging, no more hate
To save the world we love so much
Into eternity with one did not survive
Loved ones dying every day
To the place we'll never know until we go
Heaven or hell, they aren't the same
Eternity lasts a long long time
Remembering lasts forever
Eventually we'll all be gone
Safe from all the pain we left
Another generation to start again
Can they survive the inevitable
Until the world will change its ways
Remember the ones we've lost so far
Eternity lasts a long long time
Until there's a cure.

Stacy Connor

274

The Wait

The waiter passes by again. His eyes drift to your chair.
Mine do the same...my heart beats fast, and I wish I didn't care.

Ten more minutes I tell myself. My pride allows no more.
But I have to see your face again..please walk through that door.

You were my road not taken...my chapter not yet read.
And now I wait to look in your eyes, to speak words left unsaid.

You said you'd always love me, that first loves never fade.
What if my dreams had been different then? What if I had stayed?

The waiter passes by again and I order a glass of wine.
I smile at the invasion of sweet memories...you never were on time.

You were my destiny and I was yours. Ours was a love of fate.
But when I came back, my fate changed. For me, you didn't wait.

Her dress was white. She held your hand. Your eyes never left her
face. They say she cried a little that day, behind her veil of lace.

Her tears were not the only ones that fell on that spring day.
My eyes sting at the sight of it all..too much, too little, too late.

You saw me too, and I tried to smile, to hide my broken heart.
I thought I saw a flash of regret, as you made your fresh new start.

The waiter smiled. I put on my coat, thinking of what might've been.
And if I hadn't lowered my teary eyes, I might have seen you walk in...

   Marilyn Y. Vidrine

Writer's Block

I'm sorry I can't write in the journalistic style; it's just not my way.
But why should you block my creativity, just because of what I say.

I'm not trying to be a revolutionary, I don't even want to be profound.
I just want someone to read me, without the company of a frown.

Surrounded by a load of boredom, I create my own idea.
But because my tenses aren't correct, I might as well just sit here.

I write, and write, and write, producing countless stories for you.
You just tear them from heart, saying they will never do.

So, maybe my word choice was poor, you don't want to offend;
Those words are the best I know to describe the way things have been.

The disposition of an editor is to put a story at its best.
It does not involve spitting on the passion that burns within my chest

Just change a misplaced comma or two and let me be on my way;
You have no right in invade my mind, because you like not what I say.

I'll do the menial work you ask of me, I'll write the stories your way,
But, I hope, and I pray, you learn the art of writing someday.

   Scott T. Borland

Hypocrisy

Woe to they who drink their wine, they who laugh, they who indulge
in their lavish lifestyle indifferent to the reality of the outside world.
A world that did not care for them then and so now they in turn do not care for it.
A world that carries no real meaning to them any more; a world forgotten,
   a world betrayed.
And now in the safety of their riches they dare to talk of the sorrows of their world?!
Surely nothing but talks of hollow.
For now they have become what they had despised most of all, doing
nothing to correct the injustice that was done on to them but just
talking that of a talk that has no true meaning or intention, lest
they feel the dagger of guilt bleed them dry.
It is they the hypocrites that care for no one; care for nothing,
save that of the saturation of their pockets; of their bellies.
Dare they do this to a world; dare they do this to a people?
A people yearning for someone to do something to pull them out of a
never ending abyss of injustice.
Nay, instead their cries have fallen on the deaf ears of hypocrites
who have turned their backs to their people, to their land.
A land theirs never more.

   Omar Shariif

Romance

Flight from Loss

Amidst my desire for true love
came the brightness of romance
like a flame from a distance in the night
a brief, lovely, flickering flame taking me into flight.

This lovely, lonely bird opened her cage
fearing not the flame burning in the dark
for she knew the beauty awaiting
as a rare and unique painting.

The coolness upon her wings eased her pain
providing the freedom yet shelter of the moonlit sky
the mere touch of the breeze of intimate tears
removed the untold hidden fears.

As she descended gliding back to shore
the flame was still burning so brightly
and yet, she knew her refuge was her home
where she was destined to dream alone.

   Blythe Hedin

Twisted Dawn

A twisted dawn born from my lips,
each brand new vow at my fingertips.
On golden night wrapped through my hair,
one shadowed man awaits me there.

Of shallow depths this waters edge,
has lead me past each narrow ledge
and allowed my arms on moons to feed,
while suns of yours begged for my lead.

Have darkest secrets scorned my past
and buried deep my bones at last.
A spindle from the web I weave,
one reason more for you to leave.

Broken now, small shards of life
are rusted vines against your knife.
A kill beneath a mothers call,
a reason, a warning clear to us all.

While damned ones dance below your feet,
pray angels forgive their blind deceit
and wait no longer to call you home.
Born from this dawn, we're not alone.

   Josephine Green

A Child's Cry

I stand before you
But you don't see me
I begin to speak
But you don't listen
I start to cry
You tell me to be silent
I look for guidance
But you won't lead me
I need you protection
But you just tell me there's nothing to fear
I show you my talents
But you don't encourage me
I tell you the truth
But you don't believe me
I tell you I love you
Don't you know that I need you!

   Deborah Esannason

Blessed Thanksgiving

I was sitting in a restaurant in the early A.M. having my first hot cup.
People around me everywhere smiling, laughing, and generally cutting up.
When in the corner of the room something caught my eye.
It was one of the worlds, many senior citizens, and it looked as though she'd cry.
For while everyone else was having such a good time, she was sitting alone.
Today is thanksgiving I guess all of her folks are now gone?
It made me feel lucky that I was with a friend.
But I also felt compassion as I glanced towards her again.
As she ordered the traditional dinner, I thought of Thanksgiving that had passed.
How as a child I thought things would forever last.
I could tell by her brittle hands, she too had prepared some feast.
Probably with family and friends. As the waitress delivered her
plate I heard her softly pray, Thank you Lord for this meal, Amen.
I realized at this moment she was not so all alone.
For she had a special friend that would also follow her home.
As I decided to leave I turned to her and smiled. I bid her a good day and fair well.
She softly said God Bless You My Child.

Regina Turney

A True Friend

A true friend is someone who cares, and also someone who shares, all
your sorrows, griefs, and pain; so that you may gain, the everlasting
love, and the eternal flame. Joy unspeakable, that never ceases, so
you may enter into life, though maybe maned; your body does not go
into Hell's fire eternal flames. That your soul can inspire to Heaven
on Earth, taken out of the murky mire. A true friend is someone who
sticks closer than a brother; In whom you can always depend to be
there for you in times of trouble. Who always speaks to your heart an
encouraging word of cheer; If your countenance has fallen, or your
spirits in fear. Who greets you with a Holy kiss of pure love; That
lifts your soul to cloud nine like a dove. A true friend is someone
you never want to lose, someone you want to keep close to you, and
whom you always choose, To be with you forever and always, and till
times upon times indefinite, throughout all eternity. A true friend
is someone who is like a precious jewel, that is worth their weight in
gold. Who does things for you that no one else would; moving Heaven
and Earth and courageous deeds untold. A true friend never hurts or
harms you, but always keeps giving love that never fails, kindness,
tender affection, compassion, mercy, forgiveness, and understanding,
everything that a person, could ever wish for in a lifetime.

Maxine Ortiz

Pathetic Fallacy

Only six days had passed...
Six days, and the grass drank deeply the dew as honey.
A cloudless sky had given birth to the sun every day;
And every night, the darkness, to unwavering moonlight.
Mother's inhabitants still roamed Her lush Earth;
Mockingbird and deer alike fed their young and with steady eyes observed...
No traces of Frost were visible to the eyes that fluttered awake from
their solemn slumbers to embrace Spring.
The warmth granted beautiful life to all flowers- all save a solitary
bouquet lying atop a patch of sun-bathed earth.
The petals had lost their color-drained away down the stems...to the roots,
Mingling in an eternal stream of crimson amidst which lay a streak of dull silver.
Her slender fingers caressed the stone, lips delicately kissing the soil with somber agony.
Those eyes glittered with unspilled tears,
Those eyes, whose dying embers of life had long since extinguished.
She would remain for eternity in the bosom of Frost, binding our souls forevermore.
And I...I mourned in sympathy, watching Her wretched mort lie upon the ebonies
Where She took Her life over my grave, with a melancholy dagger shrouded in sorrow.
    She would remain...but t'was a beautiful day...

Pathis

I Am Your Rose

In a garden mixed with flowers of beauty
My growth come from a special seed.
Don't dig me up, please get me grow
A grand surprise I have for thee.

Pluck me quickly from my bush
Place me in your heart, my home.
Hold me with your masculine hands
Tenderly, then I shall never roam.

My body is smooth like velvet,
And my cheeks are scarlet red.
Capture the fragrance of my blossom,
As you lie there on your bed.

My petals too soon are withering.
Oh, why must they turn so brown?
The time has come for me to leave.
Don't cry and begin to frown.

Please crush me not, and toss me away,
Just lay me gently on the ground.
The winter weather will nourish me,
Come next year I may be found. I am your rose.

Elizabeth L. Hutton

Easter Lily

Yonder o'er the cliffs of Moher
    u-boats land with leadened treasures

    English landlords had reaped their tithe
    as defended by just parliament

        As if a host should owe more than
        blood to its parasite

    The vision of Home Rule,
    egos, feuds, and vengeance

  Sired a beautiful Epona
still-born

Natalie A. Kane

Just Sitting Here Doing Nothing

Sometimes just sitting here doing nothing
My heart cries out.
When will I find peace.
When will my soul rest,
I try everything I possibly can,
But I guess that doesn't matter,
Sometimes just sitting here doing nothing,
I talk to God.
Knowing that when he steps in,
  my life will seem simpler.
Sometimes just sitting here doing nothing,
My heart sings,
Sometimes sad
Sometimes glad,
Sometimes I'm alive,
Sometimes I'm dead inside,
Sometimes just sitting here doing nothing,
I just praise his name,
Because of you there's hope,
When I'm just sitting here doing nothing.

Victoria Johnson

The Battle Cry Of The Son

The Battle Cry of the son is played on the drum of the land.
Horses are mounted, blood is spilled, death comes swift,
Like crabs crawling through the sand.
Ships blow their horns, bullets fired, apologies offered.
When all is finished, there is nothing to be heard,
Except the quietness of the rain.
The narrow path leads to the open gate
Is it fate? That brought friend and foe to walk hand in hand,
beating the battle cry of the son played on the drum of the
land? Or was it one step, leading to the final peak?
Blue grass, green sky, ever expanding, never contracting,
When the leaves have fallen, there is nothing to be heard,
except the quietness of the rain.
A man plays the flute, while a friend and foe bow in respect.
A prince of peace has shown the way!
Many follow, few finish, more blood is shed.
The friend and foe continue their never ending search,
but what they are looking for has yet to be decided.
The battle cry of the son is covered, for there is nothing to
be heard, except the quietness of the rain.

Danny Gulbin

Pecos Diamonds

Pecos Diamonds sparkling in the white desert sands
Like the love expressed as they held hands
One man, one woman, one day of the most perfect kind
A pristine moment in time, now so far behind.

Pecos Diamonds sparkling in the white desert sands
Like the mysteries of life intertwined in love's strands
One memory, one souvenir, of a love felt so pure and rare
The final resolution of his betrayal made with care.

Charlcie Ann Middleton Goodman

Dinosaurs

A real bone for a budding paleontologist
Is deciding the temperature of Tyrannosaurus.
Some claim the level was almost mammalian,
While others are sure it was reptilian.

Which side is right is hard to detect,
It seems to depend upon what one would suspect
About bone growth, shape, and belly proportions,
As well as the use of some mental contortions.

And then there's the school that strongly implies
That Oviraptor was related to something that flies.
But one thought that really deserves a lot of attention,
Is dinosaur feathers - now that's worthy of mention!

Perhaps some new dinosaur site
Will prove that these fellows could have been bright.
With so little about them on which we now agree,
Perhaps we can settle their intellectual pedigree.

With these many high theories of dinosaurs in mind,
Try eating for dinner a bird of some kind!
There's no way one can enjoy eating turkey for a meal,
T. Rex's possible relative can have little appeal.

Sheldon S. White

Heaven

I'm soaring up to the sky like an eagle on its flight.
The clouds brush past me like silk on my skin.
I'm up, up, up . . . Then I'm finally touching the firefly light.

But wait. It isn't time.

I swoop down to the ground like an eagle for its prey
Now I land safe and sound on the ground.
I am now safe at last, safe at last

Meenadchi Chelvakumar

Goodnight Little One

Goodnight little one sleep safe and sleep well
Dream, dreams of tomorrow - or - of me things to tell

I watch you lying there - so chubby and innocent
That dimple in your cheek - appears heaven sent

That gurgling sound you make, that laugh, and that Coo
Means God put a lot of love and work - into the making of you

When I hold you high and firm - that strange look on your face
It is the look of assurance - it says "I know that I'm safe"

The goodness that radiates - from a being so demure
Can come only from the heart - of someone totally pure

I'm both joyful and fearful - when you fall as you walk
I marvel at the new words - while you learn how to talk

The mess that "You Will Make" - during the time that you feed
Shows that while you are with me - there is nothing you'll need

Now you have played hard all day - and I know we had fun
But, you need your rest child - for all day you had none
So don't fight it grandchild - from sleep do not run
I will be here in the morning — So

Goodnight Little One

Robert Charles Thompson Sr.

Dear Precious Lamb

Dear precious lamb at Jesus feet,
No more this world of sin defeat.
You've paid the price, your battles won,;
Oh precious lamb, you lamb of God.

Dear precious lamb the river crossed;
No more the pain to bear or fight.
A crown of gold upon your brow;
Eternal life of heaven show'r.

Dear lamb of God, so pure and free;
this life of toil your soul released.
A smile of joy, of praise and peace;
You share with love at
Jesus Feet!

Callie A. Suber

Cacophony

He turned on a soft rock station
  the moment everyone left
   me alone with him
    in the wake of their warnings
     of rumored bruises, unexplained scars
and the music's pulse sang soft
  with words of unseeing faith
   accompanying my doubt's benefit
    and the trusting melody
     of my stubborn and willful affection
and as ceaseless as the music
  he paced around the room
   stealing only one caesura next to my sitting body
   claiming my hand to pull me voiceless to him
but not by the rhythm
  of the distant faceless singers
   but only by his own,
    he a blind deaf musician
     separated from the song
in a world where he alone
  gives out the tempo and time
   to musicianless instruments
    and faceless bodies and me,
     new strings on his old battered guitar.

Deanna Welch

Tonight

Tonight as I stumbled in the dark
across my room to turn on the light,
I remembered to avoid your guitar.
I could almost see its dark form on the floor.
As I reached the switch
I reconnected my mind and realized
Your guitar wasn't on the floor.
I remember carrying it down the stairs
this morning and placing it in the back of your car.
I wish it still was on the floor
that way when I turned on the light
I could turn around and see your face.
I can still feel the sweat, thick on my skin,
after waking up from our nap.
Your body is a furnace.
Now my feet are cold.
I always feel my best around you.
Slowly as the hours slip by after parting
I slip off my pedestal
and back into the dark shadows that surround it.

Katherine Fernald

The Truth About The Road Less Travelled

Walking proudly along the dirt path,
Understanding nothing of what I seek;
Pleasure abides on my behalf
To know my journey is unique.

I stumble often as I go,
Yet I pick up and move forward
Often with scars and wounds to show,
As if I were flaunting some reward.

But truthfully, this road is aimless.
And different as I may be,
My trek often leaves me nameless
Wondering lonely as the sea.

I share my journey with no one,
On this, the "road less travelled".
For, left void of those that I can count on
The difference is that I've unraveled.

Chad E. Bush

Do You Remember?

Do you remember when you were a kid?
The whole world yours, whatever you did.

The thrill of new clothes each year to start school,
and just getting to swim in a real swimming pool.

To ride down the road on your first new bike,
or walk through the woods on a very long hike.

To win the race at the school track meet.
Remember how fast were those young feet?

The birthday cakes with candles bright.
The Christmas tree on that special night.

Getting to go to your first big dance,
with the date of your choice, just by chance.

Your first gold watch and your class ring.
Your first big love and your first big fling.

Then graduation came at last.
Ah, those were the days, the days of the past.

Do you remember?

Ella M. Barlup

Until We Meet Again

You brought us laughter, you gave us love.
You encouraged faith, in the Lord above.

Your importance in family was always shown.
The love we had was always known.

You brought us smiles, instead of tears,
You gave us hope, throughout these years.

You never condemned, or questioned why,
You were always there, right by your side.

Your perseverance, never dimmed.
You fought, you loved, your struggled to win.

With time no longer on your side,
Gracefully, you waited, for the pain to subside.

Always so humble, and willing to give,
Full of inspiration, and dreams yet to live.

Each breath, we watched you, slip more and more away,
From our hands, to His, on Valentine's day.

The importance of family, will only endure,
Your spirit, your laughter, will live forever more.

Never goodbye, we'll soon meet again.
Our mother, our grandmother, our mentor, our friend.

Kelly Bishop

To A Friend

When sun's swallowed up by an angry sea
And dark crept up from its banks,
'mid trials of the day that linger with me
I pause, for a while, to give thanks.

What would this day've had to offer;
What light to be found at its end;
If, in darkness, I woke to discover
That I'd bothered to make not a friend.

I'll not fancy you'll always be there,
Instead, play each day as though
It's the last of a life we'll e'er share,
And that friendship will help me grow.

Fondest of memories, the last funny story,
Quietly sharing a walk or a view;
To all these things you add love and glory,
By being my friend; being you.

Bobbye Lopez

Follow

The wind is whispering through my body
"Come hither" it cries
"Pledge fealty and I can make way for the sun"
My body rides the wind's shuddering, enjoying its cold guffaws
I let out my own chuckle and find my soul escapes with it
Do I even want to see the sun?
My lost soul, the wind's cold might, and its disorientation
An the damned disorientation
The south wind calls now, to be replaced by the entire compass
"Come hither" echoes more voices than I decipher
"Come hither" for the joy, for us, for yourself, for golden rays!
"Shut up" I am sick of the howling
yet my soul is floating on its freezing fury
I must follow a wind.
To foci of the Earth they may go, I must follow one
All promise the sun, all offer gentle guffaws, all happily freeze
and steal my soul, and I...
I call for the lightning bolt to break apart the wind and sweep
me to Valhalla

Russell Weisfield

The Chosen One

God planted a tiny seed in a womb,
Knowing he'd pick it before it could bloom
As parents he chose two people he knew
Would nurture and shelter it as it grew
This precious gift that came from above
Was perfect and special, surrounded with love
Loving care shined upon it making it pure
And God embraced it before it matured
He smiled with pride and said, "You are the one
Who has lived and loved like Jesus, my son
Of storms and droughts you'll worry no more
I'm giving you wings, and you will soar
Gentle and pure before petals open
You are the angel that I have chosen"
God knew the parents would be shattered with pain
And he whispered to them, "It wasn't in vain
Know that this angel who gave you so much
Had a mission to do and people to touch
The memories and love you treasure
Are more than most will ever measure..."

Sophie Longoria

Come To Town

The circus has come to town.
Clowns cheering, jabbering, laughing.
Why the somber, sad eyed crowd across the way?
Candles lit, hand in hand, softly praying.

The children have come to town.
Slaughterhouse tote boards roll and record.
Unwanted, discarded, forgotten before even born.
Childhoods head severed with a rusty sword.

The blind have come to town.
Justice chimes on a twisted unseen clock.
Unshed tears, cutting, marking cemetery signpost.
Drug dreamed vampires dining behind every rock.

The face of death has come to town
Grave-diggers hurrying, unfolding corpse crates.
Tagged, bagged, boxed, the children put away.
Deaf and dumb, the circus clowns await.

Patricia M. Hart

To A Mother

My mother was my rock
  To support my dreams come true
I returned home and never had to knock
  She was always there with the family crew.
Back when I threw a tean-age bash
  She never scolded me then
I would make it my big win
  To make her proud that I removed the trash in a flash.
She was there when I wrecked my bike
  Healing the wounds on such a small tike
My mother was never partial to me
  I had five brothers and five sisters you see.
We had picnics every Sunday
  Out at the branch, the cave or the old Sawdust mill
Just know that we have our lessons for Monday
  Because no explaining could replace that pill.
We worked together on every chore
  There was none, no not one who could call our life a bore.
And now she rests in that magnificent place above,
  Waiting for her family she thought so highly of.

Mary Vaughn

In The Black

The way I feel is like no other
What is it like when you cannot love your brother?
The starless nights go on for days,
Like a king walking through the forest haze
When you know you were defeated,
But never really lost.
Can you trade in your life at any cost?
The bleeding moon, crimson red,
How long will it take you to realize you are already dead?
The blackness of the night leads you away,
Your friends will be gone tomorrow, but what about today??
The rustle of the leaves and the cry of a cat.
How can one stand up against that?
No one knows how I feel
I must find someone to break this limpid seal

Benjamin J. Hoover

This Friend Of Mine

This friend of mine is very dear
His kindness and his innocence
Are why I hold his friendship very near

He has always been there when I need someone to talk to
Numerous times he has given me good advice
I have shared some of my secrets with him
And he has shared some of his too

He has been there to wipe away my tears
He has heard my dreams and fears
And whenever I need him most he always appears

Through the months my love for him has grown
Even though I know nothing will ever happen between him and me
Because he has a special someone, unlike me

So my love for him stays locked in heart
For he shall never know my true feelings for him
Because our friendship may be torn apart.

Stephanie ReAnn Ball

A Reminder

Time, oh friend a child is as
sweet a wine as can be coveted by
the hearts of fall, but now is merely
the fresh young leaves on your laurels
wreath, Ours is a changing nation
throughout our lives as well as yours.
Always remember your humility, and be
humble in the face of God, for you are just
another ripple in the pool of life, and you too must
come to grips with the inevitable shore, may peace be your
guidance.

Myron Hite II

Goodbye My Friend

They say there is a time to laugh,
and there is a time to cry.
But there is no time to say goodbye.
Friends will come and friends will go.
But none compare to the ones I've known.
As fall brings golden brown leaves,
And spring brings back the pretty green trees,
I will always remember our days together.
For they say, memories last forever.

Karen Engelhardt

Crystal Solace

An angel I'd made in the frosted snow,
Laying there catching snowflakes on my tongue,
Thinking as I hear the wind, in my heart I know,
Few things in life make one feel so young.

So many different patterns form on my mittens — glow!
Glancing at each one tenderly, so unique,
Silhouetted against the sky — patterns they show,
Fascinated by the stillness, something I seek.

Opening myself to this glorious display,
Watching each drift down on trees without leaves,
The sun slips behind clouds so far away,
Mesmerized, contentment lingers in me.

I'd shared secrets, releasing tears — suppressed,
It wasn't the sights or sounds — but the touch,
Of the gentle, crystal snow — none like the rest,
The time so special, so calm — it meant so much!

V. Susan Brooks

The Proposal

During an evening date at a quaint place to dine,
I decided to put the rest of my life on the line.
In my presence was a lovely lady who was so fine,
With a gorgeous face and bound for a shrine.
Her exquisite body was so tastefully divine.
To not notice her one had to be quite blind.
As we softly talked, her lips glistened with wine,
And I couldn't believe that I'd made such a find.
She was a woman of beauty - so sweet and so kind.
Right then and there I made up my troubled mind,
I'd spend my life with her if she'd only not decline.
I struggled with the words that would best define.
Those chills that she could always send up my spine.
I told her that each day of our life would be a sign,
That we truly wanted each other - at least 'til 2099.
My heart skipped a beat, and my eyes did shine,
What a life we would have 'cuz she said she'd be mine!

Shepherd

Unborn

Darkness surrounds me, utter blackness is my world
Yet I feel no fear
Comfort is my solitude, sustenance I derive from you
I hear your laughter, know your pain, cringe from your anger
But will always desire your love...you are my eyes, my ears
Through you I see and hear the world,
I am nothing without you
Swaddled by your loins, protected from the rage, the evils
A disenchanted mankind
In chambers of war creating weapons of destruction
Seeking peace...Ignoring justice
Hunger walks the streets wrapped in torn tattered bundled rags,
discarded bags...vacuous eyes
Mirrors to a tormented soul stare unblinking...hopeless...
Steel grates, a wisp of steam
Provide comfort and warmth
Crimson hope flows unchecked into the sewers of decadence
Youth forever lost...
I twist and turn, a primal cry unheard...
Stretch forth time and space
Prolong my existence.....in this, my fetal cage,

Alvin B. Layne

What Is A Man?

Master of the African nation.
Opposed to human violation.
Making a stand with God's guiding hand,
He is righteous and understands that:
The God up above is the creator of the plan.
With this knowledge, he chooses to be a man.
Giving honor and glory as he tells his story
with his humble actions, he shines his light so bright.
Peacemaker, not a heart breaker.
Uplifted through his plight, the enemy is cast out of sight.
With God the father, Jesus the son, the holy
ghost three in one. A man strives to become united
with the three. Perfecting each gift from the Lord so
you can see. Proving himself worthy of his chosen
citation: Master of the African Nation

Althea B. Leslie

Untitled

To the man I love too much:
I have you as a friend, I want you as a lover,
I want you as a soul mate, I have you as a brother,
I have you as a person, I want you as a man.
I want you as a confidant, I have you as a fan.
I tried to make you realize, I tried to make you see,
I tried to seduce you, I tried using jealousy,
These tactics you misread or blatantly ignored,
They might have ruined our friendship, and that I cannot afford.
I'm the one who's jealous, I'm the one seduced,
I'm the one who loves you, through all the pain you've induced,
I can't stand to lose you, so I'll let go in the end,
If you won't be my lover, at least you'll be my friend.

Valorie Sheperak

The Poet's Poem

A poem is a unique creation
by choice,
that paints a picture from words
by the voice.
Each poem is the reflection of a
writers inner-being,
and to read one is to know how and what
her or she are feeling and seeing.
By prose and rhythm and rhyme each poet
does convey,
a very special message to their readers and listeners
what else can one say?
Poems are carefully composed and written for
our world to share,
because it's from the heart in the well of each poets soul
that they do care!

Darrell E. Mills

The Poetry Of Life

As the ocean waves crash to the shore,
My heart begins to soar.

The Counselor of Light shines through the night.
My Deliverer is indeed in sight.

There the Cornerstone of the blue,
Remains faithful and true.

Now the night deepens into light,
What was wrong is made eternally right.

And now the ocean, the sky, the night, and I are one,
As we reach to the Son.

Keta Adams

Untitled

Sometimes there comes along a person
  who's been to hell
and somehow mustered the wherewithal
  to come back.
A person who has sloshed in the muck and mire
  of this world and managed to come through
  it all washed off.
A person who at times had no one
  but yet still had something
  for everyone in need.
A person who could rise above their circumstances,
  who never lost sight of a better life,
A person who even though surrounded by negatives
Always knew there was a positive,
  And a person just for them.
A person who never gave up
  and is a great person for it.
  That person is Penny.

   James Balliet

Untitled

Slowly as night falls the beautiful maiden
Emerges from her hiding place.

Gracing all that see her
With a mysterious glow.

Her radiance becomes the light
That fills the darkness of this night.

As she anxiously awaits the arrival of her mate.

Finally he arrives and takes her by the hand,
caressing her softly as they dance.

Engulfing her light they become as one.
Blocking out the world behind them.

As the music dies they realize their fate.

Still dancing they slowly slip away,
Sadly biding each other good bye.

Again her radiance is seen.
All though her love's meeting was brief,
She shines inside for the world to see.
Already she is thinking of the day
When they again will meet and become as one.

An eclipse of the moon and the sun

   Christina M. Kreiling

Life

To be given that bittersweet knowledge
Of what it is to live
For one short lifetime
To know the folly of oneself
And speculate the existence of others
Empathy attained by certain knowledge
Would be sublime
To know the ecstasy of the superstars fame
The anonymity of the commoner
The worriless days of wealth
The life of poverty
To feel power as a ruler
The terror of the persecuted
To think akin to brilliant minds
And know confusion as an idiot
To ponder as philosophers
To be content unknowing
All this and so much more

   Lisa Blaydes

Lost

How your voice echoes through my head,
As a spring breeze brushes by.
Wondering what will become,
As you slowly turn to me.
Whispering.

I know not what lies in store,
But I long for you to be near me.
I long for your gentle touch.

Thy heart is that of the Knight's of yore;
Noble and Strong;
Courageous and Loving.

Love me till the end of time.
Till the wind blows no more.
Till all is gone.

I never found a love as true,
That you gave to me.
The love I desperately crave.
The love of Lost.

   Carrie Peck

Visitation

Now a breath there is not a need
But a deed as yet to do
As kin of tender years come to view
To gaze and wonder, this is not the you I knew
Why now so still you lay
I strain your voice to hear
A smile or frown is not I see
In the best you're dressed and lie among the flowering blooms.
Friends are many whose tones of speech are sadden too.

This my dear ones, you shall come to know the way
that all must follow thru.
From this day on I forever away at rest
you with memories are blessed.

   George Tincknell

The Book

I sat down and took a look
at my life, as though a book,
Many things were right; some
were very wrong.

A lovely song, an unkind word
some terrible gossip that I heard.
Deeds good and bad, scattered
here and there, and through it
all, someone's whispered prayer.

There were memories so dear
of many loved ones far and near.
When one passed, a flowing tear.
Trials came, great and small, only
God kept me through it all.

Days are rushing, there's so much to do
for thee oh Lord, before life is through.
Give me strength, my faith is small,
to whisper a prayer through it all.

Now, oh Lord, I'll close my book,
but someday soon, again I'll look.

   Ruby J. Isler

Shaun

You're just a thought in our mind
But you'll be here in time
We wait for months and now it's time
You come to us but life's not kind
But we thought everything would be alright
When you were born you looked just wright
We loved your face we loved your sight
They took you away and that's not wright
for someone so small to have to fight
You went for days you did your best
but now we have to let you rest
We took you to a pretty hill
lay you down and lay you still
But you're with us for all time because
we have you back here in our mind
        David L. Surface

A Family Dream

The sky was dark blue overhead.
The snow laid white and deep like a quilt upon natures bed.

The house built upon this land
gave protection to all who lived within.

The giant trees with their large limbs
protected the house from the northern winds.

The pine trees that stood straight and tall
gave a feeling of peace to one and all.

The livestock nestled in the barns were fed
and away from winters harm.

The lights of this house reflected from windows
that were painted by Jack Frost.

The snow laid deep upon the roof,
tarnished with blackness from the chimney soot.

The fireplace set in ancient stone
blazed with a fierceness all its own.

The love of this land is shared by nine,
at this time of day around the evening and meal you'll find

Bowed heads and blessings being said
the day is climaxed by the sharing of the bread.
        Fern Zimmerman

Lone Soldier

No one sees the grueling tasks
The blood, the sweat, the tears
A soldier toils, the fears are masked
Days grow long, nights hide the tears
Lonely for Kin, thoughts of home
Guide the soldier, no need to roam
The road is rough, patience grows thin
The soldier is a beacon, a star that shines bright
Always there as a future light
        Merlene Cox

Life

    Some people say life sucks!
Some say that life is great for them!
    Some live it to its highest!
That's what I say too, although I don't do it!
    What would you say? What would you do?
Are you sure? Do you know? Can you do it?
    Why? How? Where? When? What?
Go for it? Do it? Why not? Okay? Sure? Come On?
Do it?
        Misty Aisnworth

Love

Love is a flower that begins its life
as a seed struggling to force its way
through cold, damp, earth
to the light above.
Constantly battling to survive.
Love grows, as the flower grows, day by day;
blossoming to its
height of beauty at maturity.
Love sometimes fades
and seems to die;
but, like the flower,
it drops its seeds to the earth
and continues its endless cycle
of life, death, and rebirth.
So does love's cycle continue,
enduring pain and dark days,
basking in the sunshine
of good days - surviving.
Love remembers.
Love never dies.
Love is eternal.
        Rose Jadniah

Templars

At the beginning of crusades fought,
guarding the highroads of an absolute faith.

Honor, glory, power, a gift from the city of seven hills.

The flower of the lion heart's army,
the one's who stood firm at Acre.

A barter of your freedom for our life's blood.

Cast down by a people, betrayed by a pope,
blamed by the jealous "king".

From a time now gone, to one not yet arrived,
we prosper for a returning day.

Remembering we say: We were, we are, we will be!
Templars.
        J. Scott Stallings

The Harvest Of Youth

What's in that hand?
This tight fist of rebellion
you guard with your anger,
the outcast's medallion.

The mother who never sang songs at your bed.
The father with eyes of loathing and dread.
The key to the place where you entered alone
and cried to the darkness "It's a house, not a home!"
The teacher who scolded each time you cried.
The day that you learned it hurt less when you lied.

Give it to me,
all your pain at its best.
Move this rebellion
away from your breast.

For I am your mother, your father, your friend.
My love will not fail you, nor will it end.
I'll fight all your battles, you'll know not defeat
and you'll laugh at the enemies I lay at your feet.

I know you by name, each precious one,
Says the Lord God Almighty to our hurting young.
        Martha Cosner

Frosty Fantasy

He's nimble and quick light as a snowflake
When he paints skies and treetops upon ice cold panes.
His cool icy coat is just part of the outfit
He needs to put on when on cold country lanes.

Jack's appearance is quick, his departure is fast,
And the sketch done in ice on the pane is complete
With a twist of the wrist and a stroke of the hand
Two lovers appear on a lone country seat.

The stars twinkle above and the earth white below
Makes a picture so pretty it's hard to relate
With the girl in her ermine and he in his wrap
Resting sweetly for oh, such a horrible fate!

For Jack Frost does not think of the end that's to come
Of the couple alone on the back country lane.
As they bill and coo with no more to do
Oh, how perfectly sweet till it came! Yes — the Rain!

Dolores Jean Haritos

An Echo Of Life

The falling leaves are lost souls
Floating, drifting on a breeze.
When the wind stops or slows,
They plummet with graceless ease.

The vibrant strong hues
Are memories live and bold.
But even those we can lose
If they shrivel and fade in the cold.

The bare branches reaching are those sad souls yearning.
The harsh hollow air leaching strength that keeps love burning.

The newest green and brilliant sun
Are promises of vitality and youth.
When the air warms and life has won,
The fresh leaves will tell the truth.

The bleakest days and worst pain
Can melt like mountains of snow.
The ones we lose will always remain,
In our minds, in our hearts, in a warm glow.

Paula LaFond

Climbing

Let me learn from the squirrel
He runs back and forth like a circus performer
the risk of disaster seems to phase him not
are there fears within him?

I love watching him work hard for his winter's feed
I feel this is his pleasure too
abstract conditioning, I suppose

There is total dedication and dexterity in his movements
snatching, reaching, risking, clutching and achieving
never watching for the fall.

What I saw in a nutshell
A little creature made more of his precious time than I
Hanging on to my fears
I must learn to climb more trees.

Patricia Carr

The Spit

Warm cheerful rays shine down upon me,
Slipping into the dark crevices of my rocky form,
Arousing feelings of unsurpassable strength.
Bright beams dry and bleach my long out stretched arm,
Which like child to mother clings dearly to land.
Eon after eon ceaseless lapping waters pound my shores,
Pitting its strength against mine.
When the beacon of day fades foreboding creeps in
And silver streams of night reign supreme.
A glissading eventide weakens my grip,
While salt watered winds sweep away
Grain by grain the life of me.
Relentless waters triumph over my tenacity,
Yet, from my ephemeral rocks rejoicing echos
For the privilege of having been.

Joan E. Bashford

Sister

*Dedicated to my sister Chynna Dawn Younger;
With All My Love.*
The smile of a child brightens your day.
The pinkness of her cheeks light up her face.
The power of her eyes bring you within her.
The joy of happiness brings a twinkle to her eyes.
The structure of her hand wipes away your tears.
The quiet path she follows is your own.
The laughter in her face makes you smile, just for the fun of it.
The sadness in her face makes you break down and cry.
The secrets within her are yours, too.
The dreams she dreams are left unknown.
But you learn more about her within every footstep.

Shanna Hamilton

Untitled

You draw people in like cheese on a trap;
You make people long to have you
And, then, when they are within reach,
you clamp down and ruin their lives.

You are like a pesticide:
Given in small doses you do no harm
But too much and you are deadly.

Worse than a scorpion's sting
But not as bad as a witches death,
You are illusive to some but attainable to all.

You are success.

Valarie Dill

My Peaceful Place

Off on the horizon the sun rises,
Like the miracle of new life.
The bright light permeates the blue skies,
From heaven a new day in life.

Early morning brings the soft rippling waves,
Where I can walk for miles upon miles on end.
In the distance the echo of the ocean blaring from the caves,
Where the fisherman's nets makes all my soul amends.

Looking out onto the horizon,
Each morning a precious new treasure from the See is brought.
With the luminosity of the sun,
Like a gift from God I thought.

A place where I can walk in the sand,
With my Savior the Son of Man.

Dan D'Amico

A Child's Eye View

As I lay upon the carpeted floor
Faithfully doing my exercises
My little girl comes through the door
And the situation she apprises
She positions herself right behind
Where I'm bending in an unflattering position
She seems to study very hard
My bent-over and awkward condition
Then this girl of mine, who is almost three
And, I must say, is hardly ever snotty
Places her hand upon my knee
And asks me . . . her mom, "How can you fit on the potty?"

D. M. Collins

Untitled

It's snowing outside, white softness silently falling.
My window, curtains parted, frames a picture.

Autumn leaves lie, like thousands of tiny cups,
filled to the brim with white tea.
The branches of my cherry tree have been magically crowned —
only a breath will change them — back to brown paupers.

But don't — not just yet.

Are lawns suppose to be green?
Mine isn't — not anymore.

Snow — it's oh, so quietly
changing my world out there.

Should I go out and let it change me?
Touch my face, cling to my eyelashes,
crown me with millions of sparkling, glistening flakes?

No, that will wait 'til later.
This one is to watch
to look out upon — untouched,
To dream a little by — inside me.

Jennifer Treece

Waters Edge

Sitting by the water's edge, on a starry night,
I'm compelled by past events, and how they've led my life.
First of how when I was young, sunshine lit my way.
Innocent and so naive, for my life I prayed.
Then of how my teenage years, took over suddenly.
Taken away from all I knew, dropped off in the city.
No one there to show me how, I should lead my life.
Drugs that promised nothing real, took away my strife.
Many years of running round, hardened streets of rage,
left me confused, and very sad, at such a tender age.
But there I sit on sandy shores, after many years.
A smile has crept upon my face, while my eyes shed tears.
I've left the city far behind, the drugs are memories.
The streets I crawled are just a dream, for hidden eyes to see.
The only thing that I want now, is love that can't be found,
So I sit by the water's edge, and watch the world go round.

John C. Klatt

Victim Of Myself

I am an empty shell, devoid of compassion
scraped inside and out, manipulating preconceived actions
Twisting fate and bending it to my will
yet never understanding why I feel unfulfilled

Kimberly Ann Bartlett

Sunshine's Tender Lies

All your tender lies, went straight to my heart
I fell for every line, each fictitious part

You should be an actress, a legendary star
your performance wins an Oscar, by far

You spoke of a love like you'd never known before
my heart ran rampant as my head began to soar

Your sensuous lips and eyes of emerald green
Stole my heart instantly, fulfilling my every dream

You remain eternally in my heart there's no doubt
You will always be a fire I just can't put out

You convinced me we'd be together for all time
Yet you disappeared like wind through a chime

You left, taking my heart and our unborn son
Knowing that for me, you'll always be the only one

I still wake each morning and reach for you at dawn
Feel the emptiness beside me and remember you're gone

My heart and soul tremble, although it's not from fear,
It's the tender lies, you whispered softly in my ear

William C. Johnson

Doorways

A day at a time.
Where tomorrow will lead?
I do not know.
I walk through the door like I know it.
Ahh, but we take things for granted sometimes.
The door is so very different everyday.
Even the way I walk towards the door is different.
The way I look at it.
The way it appears to me.
The way it greets me.
The way I move through it.
The way it moves around and with me.
Nothing can ever be what it was.
It can only be what it will become.
I can only have what I have now.
Nothing more, nothing less and that is myself.
I am my own door.

Kellie J. Wright

The Path

As we walk all day
Not knowing where to stay
We have our own path
That will always be there
It's the only thing that can last and must last
This path will grow and grow
It will never ever grow old
It will not change no matter how we feel
You are the one that makes everything go wrong
You are the one that stops my path
You are the one that blocks it
You are the one that tears it up
If you would not interfere
Then all my dreams would be here
After all that's all that counts
I would not want to be gone so fast
Everything would forever last and last
Isn't this what you wanted it to be
This is all that could have been oh well, what can I say?
You are the one that took everything away

Michelle Sinclair

Like A Dream

If one's life were like a dream
I wish all love would not fade away.
If one's life were like a dream
I wish all hatred would not grow from love.
If one's life were like a dream
I wish all life would not suffer through pain.
If my life were like a dream
I wish someone would stay with me.
If my life were a dream
then my life would not start where it ends.

Lisa Fang

Children!...God Love 'Em

For a very short time, they are little,
seems all they do is drink and piddle.
They learn to walk and talk, and it seems
the house is alive with laughter and screams.
Slamming doors, running feet,
little children: aren't they neat?!
Skinned up elbows, banged up knees
from roller skating 'n climbing trees.
Get out the band-aids, lavish with hugs
now they're content as bugs in rugs.
Teenagers now and rafters rattle,
woofers, tweeters, music (??) prattle!
peace and quiet, where'd you go?
Swing with 'em parents, let them know
you're young at heart and able to deal
until you find them at the wheel...
then it's gas and oil and such,
when will it end?! This is too much!
Then they're grown and on their own
Guess who made the house a home? Children!!!...God love 'em.

Geraldine Wright

Our Brave Soldier

He was a loving and caring man,
We show our respects as best as we can.
A good husband, father, and grandpa,
This is the wonderful man that we saw.

He went through a lot but Christ was with him,
He struggled and things grew dim.
We didn't give up, we said he's strong,
But in our hearts we knew it would not be long.

But God has decided it is his turn,
We have to be strong, we have to learn.
He's in a better place,
Far beyond earth, far beyond space.
A wonderful place called heaven.

Brittani Barrick

Out My Back Window

On days like this
when the snow is deep
and falling all the day,
I long to hold in my hands
something familiar and remembered.
Lost from the sights and sounds around me
found in the longness and loneliness
of too quiet of a day.

Evelyn J. Ewing

Todd

He played basketball with all the team.
His mom, oh how she did scream.
He was number one,
He shot like a pro.
A job well done.

He often won trophies
And an all-American player
His eyes would gleam when only he knew
No one had one better.
Full of life, laughter, and love
When I look at this picture and that smile
It seems all worthwhile.

Memories are great
And we cherish each one
Sometimes it is hard not to cry.
Known to many as only Ice
And signing his ball
Kool as ice, but twice as nice

Barbara Gibson

Untitled

A fiery red followed by the evocative orange
The wind gently settles the last days warmth
The water eases against our ankles as our lips touch
My heart explodes and expels with each breath

Walking hand in hand, no words need be spoken
An enchantment of bliss, the dance of two prosper
A woman that I can call a friend and lover
An angel to me, a whisper to her

I will never forget our first touch
A silver tear falling, you and I in a soft embrace
My fingertips tracing the outline of your beauty
The feeling we will never separate this state of grace

There is nothing more beautiful than an echoing
Of the water on a white sand beach
Next to the wooden church with a choir
On a starlit night with you in my reach

Michael R. Matthews

My First Crush

I will always remember you were my first true crush.
Whenever I'd see you, I would become all a mush.

We met one beautiful day on the first day of class.
You always had jokes that made me laugh.

You made me feel something new deep down inside.
I felt a sense of love which gave me pride.

Then the school year ended and I would fear,
that I'd never see you again and break out in tears.

After the summer when I went back to school,
I saw you walk by me and felt like a fool.

You didn't even turn to wave or say hi.
How could I've been so stupid to believe such a lie.

A shadow stepped in my path making me too blind to see:
A guy like you could never like me.

My friends tried to comfort me and make me forget.
But all I kept remembering was the first day we met.

Now I can say I would have done anything for you.
What I really felt inside no one ever knew.

Months have gone by and I've finally put you in my past.
But I know now in my heart no other crush can be like my last.

Yanidmar Gonzalez

So Very Far Away

You're so very far away...
  And I need you...Every Day...

Even tho...we're far apart...
  I'll keep your memory....in my heart...

I work and work...in every way...
  Trying to fill the void....in every day...

Fleeting thoughts...of You...
  Make me wonder..."What to Do"...

The thoughts of you....make me smile...
  And help me go...the extra mile....

I have a choice to stick...or go...
  And yet in my heart....I already know....

I'll sit and wait...and hope and pray...
  And never give up...on that day....

When "You and I"...will be together...
  Every day...and forever....

JoAnn Lachney

The Penguin

The Darkman prowls the grounds alone
he sees a woman in red, Simone
there he goes in hot pursuit
oops, "sorry Newt,"
"Hi, Roger, how's your family?"
"In Phoenix, on a shopping spree,"
"Did you pass your driving test?"
"I don't remember," what a pest
distractions must take a back seat
such priorities and odds to beat
I must have her, yes I will
the sun and the stars must stand still
through the crowd and around a table
like a cherished romantic fable
the Darkman says "Hi!", with a dashing smile
she screams and knocks him to the tile
"ow," he grumbles, rubbing his cheek
"was that her fist or her penguin beak?"

Roger Scott

Mirrored Images

Looking out,
a world perceived in mirrored images.
Like Nature herself, she is the seasons.

Bright hopes and dreams her spring.
Wondrous colors of flowers; rainbow's end after showers.
Thoughts soar on the currents — free as the eagle's flight.
Soft, loving breezes gently touch,
Tender butterfly wings flutter.

Passion rising, as the hot sun on a summer's day.
Shimmering heat waves — creating mirages.
Crystal and murky waters — reflections.

A chill wind blows — it will pass by
A squall seethes and boils!
Thunder erupts in the angry sky!
Doubts and fears form
Varying shades of gray clouds threatening storm.

Torrential rain of tears stinging
Heart filling, overflowing . . .

But the soul's seed; planted long ago
Bright hopes and dreams spring forth — anew!

Barbara J. Brocknau

Death

Hiding within the shadows,
Lurking 'round the corner,
He awaits;
Cautiously planning his next move.
Knowing that something is going to occur,
Painful cries - who will it be?
Voices repeated over and over in his mind.
Noiseless is his movement, his breathing.
He leaves his darkness, only to examine the passersby.
Quickly, he extends his long, black arm,
Catching an unfortunate soul.
He is neither man nor animal.
He is death and his victim is dead.

Glen Beck

Be Nice

Be nice to each other, it's not really
hard to do brother.
Try it, you will gain, just by trying there
is no pain,
smile make an effort, be nice, try twice.
We are all on the same team.
"Let's get up and go team, all the way to the
finish line."
Be nice, and show the team spirit all the time,
after all, it won't even cost a dime.

Betty Jo Shepard

Wonderment

I walk the day in early light,
I look but see her not in sight.

My heart is tired, my mind is weary,
My thoughts are racing, my hopes dreary.

She's consumed my soul, my very being,
My consciousness everything I'm seeing.

I wonder will it ever be true, or will it
Be you who comes to my resuce.

She's forever here a part of me for eternity,
Every move I make every thought I take.

She's my need, my will my expectation,
She's beauty, witty full of revelation.

But she's in the fog to dense to see,
I try and try but I wonder, will it
EVER be me.

Roger Best

The Archer

A man he was tall, thin, and limber,
Who had made his home inside the timber.
His face, it bears nights tired and long,
From countless nights without his song.
He wears baggy and comfortable clothes of thin,
Made from the deer's beautiful buckskin.
A quiver full of arrows be,
Their shaft made from the mighty oak tree.
The feathers of these mighty shafts,
Show love and care in his daily crafts.
The man of power he must be strong,
To pull the mighty hickory recurve long.
He is a man of grace, timing, and speed,
Always willing to help others in times of need.
He awaits his fate in this modern land,
With all his worldly possessions close at hand.

Kevin M. Davis

Sight Through A Man's Eyes

A man walks into a forest,
luscious, fertile, and green.
He looks up into the heavens,
And tells himself his life is content.
Days that have passed by since his wife died,
And he has cancer.
Content!?
Is he really?
Another man walks into a forest,
luscious, fertile, and green.
He gazes down on the ground,
And tells himself his life is lost.
This man is prosperous and wealthy.
He has a loving family and is in great health.
Lost!?
Is his life really?
What is the difference between these two mortals?
The man so content is looking to God and not at himself.
And the man who is lost is looking his shadow not into himself.
What man are you?

Dariush Askaripour

Where Will They Play

I was in the old neighborhood today, my mind raced swiftly to
    another time and place.
A place where laughter, joy and innocence lived.
I see no familiar face, what has happened to this place.
The playground where laughter, joy and innocence played.
Is now covered with glass, rocks, and decay, so much decay.
I wonder where will the children play.
Innocence played hop scotch here and joy ran to second base.
    But!
That was another time and distant place.
I see no familiar face, glass, rocks, and decay
    have taken this place
Where oh where will the children play?
Sliding board and monkey bars did you leave
    because of decay?
Who, oh who will help our children play?
    There is so much decay.

Yvonne E. Jackson

The Tree Of Life!

I planted a seed in the ground.
It grew into a seedling.
I fed it, I watered it, to make it strong.
The winds came and blew it in all directions,
But my firm hand held it straight.
The sun tried to burn it,
The cold tried to freeze it,
But I continued to protect it.

As it became a sapling,
I slowly withdrew my attentions.
I stood back and watched,
As the sun tried to burn it,
And the cold tried to freeze it.
But the sapling had grown sturdy roots,
And nothing that life had to offer,
Could take away my sweet daughter's smile.

She has grown into a strong young lady,
Who has complete command over her own life.
And as she walks with God through life's experiences,
She will always succeed.

Bonnie White

Musings After A Long Illness

True Oregon babe,
You have come a long way now.
Do not give up yet.

Life is not easy
Why can't I remember things
That used to be clear?

Time for every thing,
But nothing gets done just right.
Why am I so lost?

Family is my strength,
Love makes the world go around,
Loved ones see me through.

World full of beauty,
Sun, flowers, wind, trees, grass, people.
Life is fading fast.

Vernice Goodman

Long Face

"Wipe that long look off your face,"
he barked. "Little girls should look happy
and be grateful to those who gave them life."

She would inspect my face when I
came home from camp and point out
every flaw, every mole, every mark that
in her loveless eyes made me undesirable.

These days I look into the mirror
and cannot halt the freaky wish to
scratch furrows through my face, to satisfy
their withered souls' desire for my ugliness.
I am driven to peel off skin,
to pare away the surface layer,
to find the other, prettier face
that must be underneath.

God's commandment is
to honor Mother and Father,
but I wonder if he'd let me
make exceptions
for parents such as these?

Heidi M. Shelton

We Will Make It Together

It's a world of trying and struggle and pain
Laughter and love to eventually gain
What we need to exist here day to day
All times we work hard — that is our way.

For some they are crying
In a world seen as dying
Quit the struggle they say
But that's not our way.

Stop trying so hard — what's in it for you?
The big men will take care of me and you too.
Cheat and steal and lie if you may,
But not for us, that's not our way.

You talk so big but you're broke today
The big men, they just gave my pay.
Doesn't matter to me, I feel good inside
Tomorrow's payday and I don't have to hide.

Lay down and keep crying
For me, I'm always trying
I work honest today
For that is our way.

Beverly Fitts

Forbidden Lake

Sinking deeper and deeper into my plated glass,
The cool serenity of deadly beauty.
Frozen cruelness disguised as the perfection of life itself
But, oh, the deadly sadness
Who would have thought.
Not I, of course; until now
Only as I lay here still.
At the bottom of the sea.
Caught in my own thoughts and fears.
And the secrets of the mind.

Only fish surround me now
As I lay here dying, only asking a greater
   power the final question of death.

   Gina D'Angelo

Second Chance

Once in my life there was so much despair.
My troubles were many, more than I could bear.
For I never thought there'd ever be
a second chance such as the Lord has given me.

One night in darkness, I knelt in prayer.
I reached out my hand to find He'd always been there
To take my hand and never let go.
And in his eternal love, a second chance I always would know.

I know when I knock, His hand will open the door.
And my life will be so much better than ever before.
To know the peace He has given me.
With him in my life, of my battles I'm now free.

How so very different my old life does seem.
So very long ago, as if it were a dream.
When others had forsaken me I went to Him in sin.
He took it all to let me have a second chance to live again.

   Roger D. Tucker

House Of Mirrors

I ran away to find myself. Didn't like what I had been.
But the truth I was running from, just led me back again.
So now I've come full circle, the pictures crystal clear.
The images that I portrayed were cast off a house of mirrors.

Living in a house of mirrors, filled with lies and schemes.
A never ending struggle, just on the edge of humanity.
You've heard of people in glass houses. Things are seldom
  as they seem.
Living in a house of mirrors, trying to wake up from the dream.

So I took off to find my fate, and leave the dream behind.
But I just didn't get too far, for running circles in my mind.
And the thing that I was hiding from, was waiting there for me.
When I finally faced my fear I won my sanity.

Don't think you can't rise above whatever you've come from.
Living in a house of mirrors, the roads been hard and long.
But when I gave in and prayed for the faith, I know I would need
It was then I started to get answers, and I woke up from the dream.

   Debra A. Pifer

Look Around

If you look at the sun, and touch the Earth
you'll feel the nature run through your body.

If you care, why do you kill the beautiful animals
of the Earth.

Just look, just look, watch and see what they do.
If you stop killing, there will start to be more animals
to grace, watch and learn about.

   Dustin C. Newton

The Tradition's Enemy

Christmas! Shoppers greeted the sun
reflecting their spirits as curious
sprites, gathering a hopeful glance
at tradition. Viva! Viva! The tradition
hunters sang, in unison as told to them
before their time as a lesson from a hawk
teaching praise. Traditions carry many faults
of yesteryear, as oxygen is useless without
God's creations, or as the closed mind
of a war-like person sleeping with
A minister's skills; until his youth taught
his life that the gifted feelings deserve
more for demanding nothing.

   Jefferson Craig Dowdy

Untitled

The venerable oak stands ancient and straight
Preparing for the day he will fall in decay
To fertilize the ground for his saplings.
A man, who has not the roots of the oak,
Cannot stand so stolid and still. He must
Instead live in eternal spring and bloom
Vibrant and bright before he withers,
And like the day-flower, live full and
Beautiful before the coming of the night.

   Andy Ashby

If I Should Die

If I should die,
I want everyone who cares not to cry.
If anyone cares don't lay me to rest,
Just have a party make it the best,
Besides my family who would care?
Don't be scared don't be alarmed,
I'm just seeing what would happen if I was harmed,
I'm not dying just yet,
With everything that's happened what the heck,
I know this doesn't make sense,
But it's time I came to defence,
If I should die,
You don't want to see me dead,
No one would know, so don't be down,
All I am is a friend in the ground.

   James A. Towe

Death's Deception

She's won the battle and took you from me,
I have no choice, I must set you free.
She calmed your body and numbed your mind,
And knowing your troubles treated you kind.
Slowly she won you into her power and will,
Now her grip tightens, she plans her kill.
For her you will fight, cheat and lie,
Knowing the final price is to die.
As her prisoner you can't tell her "no"
And I can't fight her, I must let you go.
If your mind was clear then you would see
It's not lady alcohol that loves you, it's me.

   Virginia Zimmerman

Create Reality

Catch life with your tongue
Wash your hair with shooting stars
Reach out and embrace a cloud
Bounce on balloons
Dance with pigeons
Sing a song to dagger
Carry dreams in a secret pocket
Eat sunshine on a gloomy day
Breathe laughter at a funeral
Conduct a choir with a shoelace
Befriend an ant if you're the size of a thimble
Propel your tail and fly off into space.

Heather Clift

Whispers

I hear their whispers,
the messages they infer:
Light, yet projecting,
soft but rejecting.
Unsure of what I am doing to cause this mental anguish.
I fear them . . . I want them to vanish.
They stare at me with burning eyes, penetrating my soul.
Searing my conscience, I am no longer whole.
Pieces of my heart have been torn from my chest,
leaving me empty and unable to rest.
I cannot escape the agony inside,
tearing at my last vestige of pride.
Bowing my head in weariness,
trying to rid myself of dreariness.
Pleading for a higher power to extinguish the fire within.
The war between my heart and my soul will now begin.

Jessica Prince

Grief Turned To Joy

This is not a time to grieve, but a time to rejoice
Because of the fact that the pain is gone
The struggles and heartaches of daily life
Have been mercifully put to a stop!
Now the long awaited reunion with those whom
Have been missed so very much, can finally begin.
Although this world will never be the same
Without her heavenly light, we can take
Great comfort in knowing she is well taken care of.

Brandon Gamber

A Caring Loving Mother

A caring loving mother no one can replace. The memories shall remain deep in our hearts. The directions passed to the love ones remain in our hearts. Mother gave birth to us to cry and smile in times of trouble, knowing our mother is near to correct us to be a loving person. While in the womb, mother carried us through rain and snow so we may see life. At times of sickness, we searched for our mother for comfort and joy. Now we are adults with our own family to carry on in a loving caring way.

Melvin H. Caraballo

Ebb and Flow

Today I touched the world
  I saw skies shinning and trees bending
    forward into motionless silence
  Shimmering seas scurried off silver sands
 back then forth and back then forth
Today the World touched me.

Heather Marie Ancich

He Is Near

He may not always come when you first call,
but he is near.

There are times when he seems so far away,
but he is near.

At times you may feel that you are all alone,
but he is near.

Never give up, keep your faith and
give him all your cares and troubles.
He'll work them out, because
he is near.

He loves you very much and wants you
to trust in him with all you heart,
for he is near.

He is closer to you than you realize.
Reach out and take his hand,
for he is near.

Quileena Bryant

God's Gift

As the water flows off the mountain top,
the world is blessed from God above.
He brings in life to the lands,
and the skies so high above.

I take a drink from the stream that comes from God,
too be refreshed from a tasted of Gods true blessing.
As I walk the forest that God has given me,
I have seen nature has taken its toll.

I reach down to a wounded animal,
only to hope God has blessed me to help it.
Hoping not to hurt it; as I picked it up
Think in my mind, I can help it as God has me

I slowly attend to its hurting pain.
As God is touching me to love once again.
I feel the pain inside her only to let go.
Hoping that I have helped her enough to live on another day.

Ryan Brinkman

Geraniums

For my mother
the garden was a playhouse.
She was barefoot there,
among the oversized bougainvillaea,
fern, mint, and violet geraniums.
Her wrinkled hands knew each,
Joy was making them comfortable in the soil.
Her dolls, in their beds.

Beverly Freiberg

What's Right

Its not what's wrong, but what is right
That makes my heart inside me fight

Against the blight of wicked men
That will pay any price just to win

There's Joseph Stalin the butcher of Budapest
Adolph Hitler and all the rest

They slaughter the world for one lost dream
Don't they understand what they say or mean

Heartless men with blinded eyes
When they move the whole world cries

Give us a leader when at his best
Thinks not of himself but of the rest

Robert Fry

289

Father

It began as party for two
that ended up with a new guest.
One of them left and the other stayed
through the struggle and for the support of the new guest.
Now the new arrival has become a grown adult; now the one
who left wants to be called father, when he doesn't even know
the meaning of the word father.

By given life, does not make you a father; standing by that
child do wrong or right makes you a father.
by giving your last name to that child does not make you a
father; coming back years later to reclaim your position as a
father does not make you a father.

To be a father, you have to grow up and be responsible first,
for yourself and then for that child.
To be a father you have to teach respect and give respect in
order to get respect.
Now tell me should I call you father?
I ask for I cannot remember your face and your absentee has
been my true memory of you.

Miriam Bernardez

The Dentist

The dark, dark room gave an odor
That was somewhere between old age and mouthwash
The child sat waiting
In the room that was all too red
Too much like blood
He had heard the stories
Of what was done with the drill
His feet dangled from the end of the chair
Piles of magazines lay scattered on either side of him
His heart beat wildly as
The intercom came on, some other poor victim
He calmed himself, but his time was ever closer
From behind the translucent glass
He heard a muffled cry - the door opened with a bang
As a man came in smiling showing his perfect white teeth
Directly behind him was an elderly woman
But she didn't smile
He looked wildly at the speaker
His heart began to pound again
As the intercom clicked on...

Mark Billingsley

Blue Doors Of The Church

Fresh keys open the stale fruit
Tonight is the end, maybe
Tonight is the beginning, I think

Free green moss and bracken
Maybe this place is dark
Blocking out the fire
Spilled by capitalistic Nazi planes

Here knocking on the blue doors
Of the last building - the church
The life inside the decaying moss
Gives no thought to the stingy war, so far away

As the thick plants breath cool mist flies out
Never mind the boiling, November air
Of beer-brewed, distant war

Here nothing comes, nothing goes in the thick night
The rumbling can finally be heard
1000 lb bombs, tanks and planes so far away

Rest lightly! Eat the fruit
Tonight is the end, maybe
Tonight is the beginning, I think

Anthony Ilacqua

Like A Mother

I spoke from my heart,
you gave me your hand.
Like a mother
and said, "that you understand".
I cried so much because I was scared.
And, just like a mother,
you said, "not to worry and that you cared."
We've shared so many feelings
and we have grown so close.
We have a special bond
like a mother,
who I look up to the most.
You're an angel sent from God,
one of whom I will always be fond.
Like a mother,
Who I will always treasure.
So from this day on
you'll be in my heart forever.
I love you
like a mother.

Jennifer Pedersen

Love Of A Mother

The tears that fall, the hearts that break,
The mothers heart that never shakes,
She goes before the Lord in prayer,
Knowing God will hear her anywhere.
A fervent prayer before the Lord,
God honors and opens up heavens door.
He bottles her tears, one by one,
To let the mother know it is finished, it is done!
With mercy, grace and love so pure,
The heart of the mother will always endure.
The ways of God, love so true,
He has granted mother for me and you!

Gloria Cain Morgan

An Embraced Psalm

I awaken to your presence
    as the birds sing outside my window.

I am reminded of your nature
    as the wind howls and the giant trees sway.

I have been touched by your beauty
    as the red cardinal sits proudly on the blanket of snow.

I have learned the gift of life
    as I have struggled to stay in life.

I have shared your suffering
    as someone I have loved has said he doesn't love me.

I have known your aloneness
    as I have been left untouched for so long now.

I have grown in faith
    as you have allowed me to be a giver.

I have experienced your grace
    in my need to be a taker.

I am coming to know you
    and I am the lucky one.

I must invite others . . .
    come, waste some time with me.

Jan Donley

When Love Whispers

Sometimes when you least expect it
Love whispers in your ear
So soft and gentle you barely hear it

But soon your heart is filled with the warmth
of a sundrenched afternoon in September

The clouds appear lazier
The sky seems bluer
And at night the stars twinkle brighter
as they dance in the sky

When you awake in the morning you feel a
radiance and giddiness that lasts all day

All because love whispered in you ear

Scott Parks

Innocent As A Flower

Innocent as a flower,
    We faced the blackness of mass cognition;
Helpless before omnipotent power,
    Our souls were impaled with erudition;

Two distinct personalities inextricably juxtaposed,
    A quiescent clash of favor;
An abyssal, faceless encumbrance arose,
    Between two powers which would not waver;

We retreat into our very essence,
    Our shadow, our countenance, our being;
Our volatile emotions erupt with effervescence,
    Our conscience not agreeing,

A parasitic preponderant shower,
    Gains supremacy with nonchalant jocularity;
We anticipate the inevitable, innocent as a flower:
    A most ironic parody.

Jason Flatley

The Golden Race

Champions all - assembled in this place.
Thrilled to partake in the arduous race.
Most will lose
as drops of melted dreams stain sorrow's face.

With high held hands the victorious few celebrate
under a banner of victory.
Each beaming countenance is joyous to behold
as the best rise up to thundering acclaim
acknowledging the anthems strain
and cry tears of gold.

And some glorious day,
with high-held hands under your banner of love
as I step up before the supreme giver of awards
may I be found worthy, Lord
to cry tears of gold.

As golden tears drop before the feet of my refiner
His hand will reach out to wipe them away
so they will not cloud my vision
as I gaze upon the face
of the most magnificent victor ever known.

Betty (Newsom) Calender

Renee

Today's experience is tomorrow's voice
With daily opportunities, there is no choice
With tomorrow's voice, the future is set
With today's experience the opportunities are met
As we achieve our toughest goals
As we pull our heaviest tolls
We realize the fulfillments that life brings
The life that offers us different things
Things that satisfy our every desire
A sun to give us fire
A moon to give us light
The stars that fill the skies every night
Tomorrow's voice was today's adventure
The daily opportunity that gave us pleasure
The future that's set in its perfect place
The opportunity will be met at one's pace
The toughest goals yet to be done
Pulling the heaviest toll has yet to be won
The fulfillments that life will bring me
Are different things in life, you see

Yvonne Colon

More Angry Than Afraid

I thought of going down but where
The smell of change is in the air
Would it help or hide the truth
I hate the thought of being used
I see a plan to take away my youth
A sacrifice prepared by you
I think there must be a better way
The status quo has got to change
It is past the time to point and blame
Or sit and hope it will all go away
It is nice to think that we can dream
Here in the land of opportunity
We must stand up when something is wrong
Who is strong enough to take it on
It scares me but I have to say
That I am more angry than afraid
Just think of all the progress we have made
Just to see it all go down the drain
It scares me but I have got to say
That I am more angry than afraid.

Brian Zachary

The Stronger Side Of Love

A man stands by his loved one so fair.
Crying, crying for her life to be spared.
His pride he has forgotten.
His strength will keep him near.
For love is more contagious when your loved one is not there.
And if his one true love shall prevail.
His pride he will put aside.
For love is too powerful to ever be denied.

Maureen Withee

Dogs

On my street there are all kinds of dogs
big ones
small ones

At night time you hear dogs barking to one another
like people who love one another
but can't get to each other.

Because there is a silver lake
it is so deep
so all they can do is bark.

Nicole A. Baldwin

My Wish

Almost gave up my wish of having a friend for life.
Being an only child was lonely.
Will my desire ever succeed?
After twelve years my wish is granted.
Never thought I could hold you, my new born baby sister.
My heart is pounding.
Your body is light as feather.
Your skin is red like the sun in the evening.
Your hands are tiny.
You have a marvelous baby scent.
The new baby is so pure and innocent.
You bring the joy and happiness to my life.

Wongrat Ratanaprayul

The Day

As I look in the doorway,
    it is dark, and yet there is so much to be seen.
The visions of being there, linger on.
The gay, happy times we shared together.
The meeting of new friends, new acquaintances.
The bonding of great relationships we will never forget.
Yet, the day comes, where it all is gone.
All that is left, are memories of times past,
    as if it was all a dream.
The space you once took, belongs to someone else.
Your memories transform into theirs.
The moments you wish never to forget, will happen again,
    but never in quite the same way.
There will be new acquaintances, but it will still
    be different.
These new friends will never be like the ones
    you once knew.

Teresa Raniszeski

The Miracle Of Spring

The long cold of winter is gone.
    Spring is here. "Hallelujah!
Some say there is no God.
    How can that be?
Do they not the miracles, you and I see.
    The soft rains that cleanse the earth.
The flowers that burst forth.
    The animals that leave their dens.
And bask in the warm sun.
    The birds return and build their nest.
For the new ones too come.
    They know winter is done.
The robins sing their sweet song,
    The fragrant breezes, through the leaves.
This is what spring means to me.
    My prayerful wish.
"He" allows me. One more miracle to see.

E. J. Hill

Peace

Prayer is the doorway to God's eternal throne;
Enter through it often and you'll not be alone.
Accept the answers to your prayers as part of His great will.
Certainly He cares for you and your needs He will fill.
Even in your darkest hour: Prayer's answer - "Peace, be still."

Vaudeen Seely

Fond Memories

I asked a child just the other day,
    About a trip he'd taken down Orlando way.
A big smile brightened his gleaming face
    As he started to tell of this magical place.
"There was this castle, Mickey and streets of gold,
    Rides, and games for young and old".
In minute detail he went on quite a while,
    Painting his picture, every inch, every mile.
He concluded his story omitting not a thread
    Of an incredible journey - "Awesome!" he said.
"it's not the tale I heard from your own Dad,
    That trip to Disney had some parts that were bad".
"What about the flat tire? The line and long wait?
    Thunderstorms, high prices, and the bus interstate?"
With a puzzled look "I don't seem to recall
    Not on my special trip, no, not at all."
"Nothing went wrong. It was perfect, you see,
    Exactly, I'm sure, like heaven's gonna be!"

What a lesson I learned as he hurried away,
    One of God's greatest gifts is a "Fond Memory" of yesterday.

Garry Snider

Rodin

Are you a Rodin beauty from solid marble hewn?
Marble, luminous to eye and cool to touch,
you pluck my soul like a violin string to trembling,
till painfully, one single tone vibrating, I dare no longer gaze.

Or, if transfixed I linger, stirred to find a harmony
as ballast for that single line, which pulsing inwardly
renders me alone and isolate, as singer unaccompanied,
I think to penetrate that beauty's marble moment,
to draw a glow, a warmth, a vital chord,
an inner voice to meet my word in space, halfway between us,
to make duet our apotheosis, then I risk my life.

No echo to my strained intent replies, and fearsome feelings
warn me to avert my eyes. You are cast from simple, solid stuff,
monastic and homogeneous, of oneness pure and self-contained,
and will endure unchanged, unmoved, untouched.

My spirit fails, my soul fights mind's intelligence
which, grasping full that soaring flawless elegance,
transmutes within my head in unrelenting peroration
that single tone to toneless reason, echoing from side to side,
in fading iteration: "There is no inside, no inside."

Edwin Fishbaine

Waves Of Whispers

As I sit and listen to the waves of the sea,
memories of you touching me.
    Your skin so tender and arms so strong,
held me tight and made me long.
    I long for the day and of the night,
when you whispered to me that it felt so right.
    If it felt so right then why did you stray?
I just can't understand why you went away.
    As your tender lips caress my ear,
with the gentle sound of those words so clear,
    I want to believe and trust again but,
it is hard after you've been betrayed by your best friend.
    Those words that are whispered as we sit by the sea,
are that you love me and there's no one else for thee.
    As I listen to there whispers, I cannot see.
I'm just hoping these waves don't come crashing down on me.

Kelly Barahona

Silence

It fills the room with its awkward sound
With every breath I hear its deafening pound
Louder, louder I think I'll scream
It just seems to penetrate my very being!
Slowly, slowly it slinks away
Once again it seems a tranquil place to stay
Oh thank you Lord for my defence
To conquer the sound of silence

Kamina Singh

Winged Time

All things must end at a given time.
We have no time to think and wonder.
A thing that's here is gone the morrow,
No time there is to grieve and sorrow,
For every fair from it retreats.

And when the wind in glee sweeps by,
No time the rose to guard, prepare.
There can be no eternal joy,
For dark clouds always linger by.
Where a smile is tears stalk nigh.

For time is truly a winged creature;
Which carelessly moves on with disregard,
And with it moves beauty, youth and happiness.
Ephemeral is solitude and tranquil peace.
For after the calm comes the mighty storm.

But if things can only fleeting be;
Then aching hearts and anguished souls;
Painful pangs and stinging tears,
Soon all must cease without a doubt,
And agony is but a misty dream.

Langze Palmo Phunkhang

Lament, For Donna

Donna is gone, gone from me,
It's tough to accept all the misery,
Emotions Donna had urged,
Tides that powerfully surged
All of these has to be purged,
Now that Donna was gone.
There's no haven for me in this wide expanse
I can see no retreat and I have no chance
To forget, to forget.
Donna is gone, gone astray,
Well you can bet hell's to pay.
There's no way to forget,
Yet who wants to forget
All I can do is go on,
Donna's gone, Donna's gone

Abe Russo

Ice Doves

Like crystal ballerinas frozen in flight
Of molded ice from previous night
My eyes beheld a glorious sight

Orphans of rain, ice and storm
Each is like a glassy dove
All are distinct and pure in form
Stoical mystery lies therein of
Cold creatures aura so ironically warm

Unknown is the time in which they will stand
As elemental children so silent; so grand
These works of nature's winter wonderland.

Calvin L. Marshall

One Halloween Night

The wind whistled in the trees.
The branches bare with the ground full of leaves.
The orange array of faces glowing on the sill.
The black mansion that lay on the empty hill.
The shutters torn, the ghosts who mourn.
The man who sworn they lie.
For no one dares to go by.
The place in all tatters.
Dust from wall to wall.
It must be that spooky call.
In which the children never bother to pass,
Tonight the mothers are in such fret,
For the people they have never met.
Of course all they really want are sweets.
But do you know who they will meet?
The frowning face of the man giving them a great big fright,
Running home and never forgetting that dark,
halloween night.

Rebecca Leeson

Delusions

All these years, I've had stars in my eyes.
I never once thought that love was a lie.
I believed in hope; I believed in dreams.
I believed in love, and magic beans.

I was like a child: gullible and innocent;
And I trusted things that made no sense.
I believed in fairies and magic dust;
I believed in love, ignorant of lust.

When things went wrong, the bad went away;
And I always thought one could find a way.
I believed that faith would always change things;
I believed in the love that binds wedding rings.

I've never had proof of any of these myths,
But I've had plenty of proof to oppose.
And no matter how much I want to deny it,
That means I've been tricked, I suppose.

Maybe I've been foolish to believe in so much,
But someone's always been there with a loving touch.
Still, maybe it's time I finally grew up,
And stopped believing in the things that mean so much.

Sara Lewis

Untitled

That first night when we lay I was taken away
Your perfect words spoken, how I wanted to stay
Your hair was like sand on a glistening beach
I picked up some shells, I started to reach
'Twas then that I saw with a brush of my hand
Your eyes were like water from a tropical land
Since I know natures law and it must be obeyed
I played on the beach then I swam in the shade.

But morning has come and now we must rise
To head for our home under realities skies
The morning gold sun how it strips away lies
It tells us the truth and opens our eyes
That water so blue with a tropical hue
I see filled with chlorine to burn through and through
The hair so like sand now mixed to concrete
Surrounding those pools like curbs on a street.

Steven Cernek

293

So Glad You Got Your Wings

Angels came down to pick you up
because you could not fly.
Still don't know why you had to go
or why you had to die.

I think of you everyday
sometimes I shed a tear,
I know you're in a better place
no hardships - no fear.

I know you already came to me
where you knew me best.
I heard what no one else could hear
and now your safe at rest.

Hakuna Matata with the angels you now sing
I'll see you in the promise land
So glad you got your wings
                Barbara Anita Lane

Life

Who are you?
Do you realize what you've given me?
This innocence I thought was lost forever
has returned.
And my faith
that had burned so brightly
extinguished
resparked and struggled to burn
now shines so bright it blinds me.
And I believe
that such a love and purity exists
hovering in front of me.
For me to touch and taste
waiting
for me to swallow and be full.
                Lisa M. Dittman

My Paw Paw

I will never forget the sorrow I felt
As quietly beside my bed I knelt
In agony I cried as my heart slowly bled
I felt as if I would be better off dead

Where have I seen this before
It was outside the bathroom door
He lies there without any feeling
At first I thought he was healing

I suddenly realized it was not to be
My precious Paw Paw was about to leave me
They all held hands to pray
While the kids were wishing he would stay

My dad walked up and held my hand
We both walked slowly to the van
We drove quickly to my aunts
It got cold so I put on long pants

Then we got the call that my Paw Paw had passed away
I was sad we all wished he could have stayed
My Mom and I were all broke up
Later she came to pick me up
                Eric Clayton Wade

Love And Broken Hearts

I loved you
You loved me
But we are through,
You and me.

We thought we loved each other
But now we hate each other
So forget all the things we dreamed of
Because we don't have a true love.

I wish we were together
For always and forever
But we are better off not together
Because that green feather
Just blew away in the windy air
That's how I know you aren't near.

I try to sit here and think of you
But my heart just turns blue
So forgive me for blowing dust in your eyes.
I promise you I will never tell lies.
                Tenika McGriff

The Gift

The first time I held you
I gazed at your precious face.
I knew then and there, the reason I'm here
And I felt that I knew my place.

It's not been quite two years
Since you joined our family ways.
With your dazzling eyes, and your tooth-filled smile
You bring joy to our busy days.

Sometimes I sit and watch
You play with your cars and toys.
Sometimes I catch you, staring out the window
Wanting outside with the big boys.

After playing is over
And bath-time fun is through,
In my arms you'll be, I'll sing you to sleep,
And rock 'til your movements are few.

As you lie in your crib
All curled up with your blankie,
So peaceful and new, I thank God for you
And that He gave His gift to me.
                Tracey L. French

Untitled

Love me . . .
    and when it's dark and dim outside,
    stay and hold me.
    Look deeply into my eyes,
    tell me that I'm part of your soul,
    and lay your head close to my heart.

Love me . . .
    and I'll be there to watch the morning sun
    cascade through the curtains
    and onto your shoulders.
    Then, if we must part,
    assure me you'll hold me all day in your heart.

Love me . . .
    and when fate's cold hand bid you go,
    we'll have shared a legacy of love
    that through time and space
    will fill each other's soul,
    until we touch again . . .
                Tricia Murajda

Life Lights

Flickering light from the fireplace
Sooths my tiring thoughts of a daily routine
And warming the chill from my mind.
Shadows are cast by the dancing light
Racing around and dancing slightly
While reminding me that life is a radiant gift,
Borrowed from God with a purpose
And its warmth blankets my soul.
I long to ease back into those carefree memories
When all was new and gleaming brightly
Just to rekindle my dreams.
But for this moment I will reflect,
Count my blessings, and know
That life has enabled me a light
To share as warmth to others.
So flicker on dear light of hope eternal,
Blaze more dreams to guide me,
Fire up my spirit from within
And bring me peace to find my way.

Norma Griffin

The Production

We're the producers when the stage is set,
in a unique production we're not soon to forget.

If we could have known that the seeds that were planted,
would effect other's lives that were taken for granted.

The production would have taken a quite different turn,
and compassion for others would have kindled and burned.

But that's just the problem. "There is no reversal",
it's just one time around without a rehearsal.

We were not destined to write our own script,
'cause it's found in God's word as your guide when you drift.

The final production is all up to you,
let God be the director and he will make you anew.

We can't un-do the things of the past,
but there's room for improvement and love that will last.

Let God be the director in your grand production,
and he will turn it to good where Satan meant your destruction.

You can be sure your productions a hit,
when it's at the master director's feet that you sit.

Valerie Plyler

English

I wish I were not so good at English.
I read 35 books a day.
46 on Sunday
I have even read the worlds most complicated books
in 10 minutes.
I turned down a $40,000,000 with scholastic; so I
could teach at Middletown High.
I edited Charles Dickens books and found over 10,000
mistakes in them.
I wrote a book better than Treasure Island.
I put all the great authors to shame with English.
I have written dictionaries with over 100 added words to
the English language.
If any of this poem were true I'd be in the
Guiness Book of World Records many times, and I'd be honored
by the president, or I'd become president.

William Gaker

Your Choice

These locked doors I leave behind have left lasting
memories in my mind.
When your freedoms are left at the door you life becomes
nothing like it was before.
It shows you the things you have to lose and some
you will, but who got to choose?
It puts your relationships to the ultimate test, strengthens
the true ones but destroys the rest.
People say you're not the man you were before but they
have never lived behind these doors.
Behind these doors everything changes, always among
friends but surrounded by strangers.
You'll soon find out who your true friends are, for
they will come visit no matter how far.
It makes a man look deep into his soul and gives him
the option of returning whole.
The day you go home is a day to rejoice but always
remember, it was always — your choice!

Darryl Curtis

Symbols For Myself

I am the flower.
I am shy, like flowers are shy to grow tall as a tree.
I like to smile, like flowers are the happy plants.
I like to wear fashion clothes, like flowers have pretty colors.

I am the color white.
I am the color white, represents peaceful and careful.
I am the color white, can choose as a good friend.
I am the color white, who is quiet and introvert.

I am the boar.
I am the bear. Boar is my Zodiac animal.
Boar is a kind and honest animal.
Boar is someone finish her work on time.

I am the Box.
I am the box, I keep many things in my mind.
I keep my secrets, thoughts, and feelings in the box.
I am the box, that keep those things in.

I am the flower, the color white, the boar, the box,
And I am myself.

Beverly Her

Unspoken Words

The one I love has gone away,
there are so many words that I cannot say.
There are still nights,
I lay awake in my bed, and wonder for hours,
what I could have said.
I told you I loved you
day after day, I don't see why
that couldn't make you stay.
if only once more I could say "I love you,"
I'd know in my heart, my dream had come true.
I know I will get that chance once again,
when the Lord comes back,
and takes me with him.
I can't wait for the day
to stand at heaven's gates,
and know when they open
I'll see your smiling face.
When this time comes,
I'll know that it's true,
that I got my second chance, to say "I love you."

Elizabeth Jamie Trimble

Do You Ever Think of the Lilies in the Field?

Do you ever think of the lilies in the field
  or think of the new mown hay?

Do you think of the misty morning dew,
  before it melts away?

Do you think of the cry of a newborn babe
  or look at the sky when the sun starts to fade?

Do you hear the rippling of the brook
  as the fish gently swim away?

Do you think of the falling of the leaves
  as the season starts to change?

The beautiful white blanket of Winter,
  the vibrant color of Spring.

So, when troubles come our way
  and we need the clearing of the mind.

Just look to God and His creations
  and a certain peace you're sure to find.

Rita Lou Sizer

A Prayer For Our Children

Oh precious Lord
Take the children's hand
lead them, guide them, help them to understand

For a world like this, show them where they fit in
Oh precious Lord take their hands
with heads held down often faces with frowns
we pray for our children Lord please turn them around

For at the time of trouble, at the time of need
when guns are firing and dying hearts bleed
A prayer for the children is all they need
to stop guns from firing where dying hearts bleed

Children are searching for their place
in a world that's so cold
Oh precious Lord touch their souls

Where tears are shed and sorrows bred
a road of lost children is what's ahead
Oh precious Lord
this is a prayer for the children
take their hand, lead them, guide them, help them to understand

Cynthia Evans-Mabry

Eire (Ireland)

It is a treasure held in this mind of mine,
The scenic beauty engraved,
My native land it will always be,
The body has long since fled
But the mind will always belong,
Who could help but linger,
In its fresh cool water lakes,
Nor run through its fields
In their forty shades of green,
Climb its hills
Inhale its fresh breezy air,
It is where my mind can be found,
In its wondering ways,
Deep in that breathtaking valley of green.
I cannot escape it, nor do I want to,
Here I once belonged
And will one day belong again,
For home is were the heart is,
And though my home is here now,
The heart will always beat Eire.

Margaret Ronan

To Gold

Frost bit when he did say
that, "Nothing gold can stay."

A meadow does now fill my eye
hear those words, release a sigh

Fiery sky, a wondrous sight
darkness approaches bringing night

Eden sank down totally in grief
hearing the whippoorwill sing, feel relief

The world is changing at a marveling pace
my only fear is for the human race

Love for what's simple is hardly new
a day is coming that complexity will rue

A sermon is not what I'm about
for no one is capable of filling that mount

Still though, every hue my eye does hold
wishes earnestly to return to gold.

H. Lauritz Christensen III

Letter To The World

If only I looked forward to getting up.

Beautiful girl makes my heart dance.
Do I know true love.

I look at him, a rebel in his own mind,
thunderbolts of remembrance shoot my head.
He walks away, my heart in dust.

I too walk away, but a different yellow brick road.
I wonder who or how I will make it in everybody
else's eyes.

Quotable friends sit next to me. I wonder what they want.
Their way of living is my way of dying.

Why can't I melt things with my eyes,
predict the future or tell you exactly how many
gumballs are in that machine. Something to amaze you.

He said look into my crystal ball.
I looked into it and saw the true feelings, scary but true.

I sit in my garage and her beautiful voice sings
to me like a bird song in the mid-winter morning.
A way to find the sun through the foggiest grey.

Anthony Beardsley

Untitled

Depression is a storm. Black clouds move across
grey skies. It's cold, almost freezing. Darkness
swallows all thought, leaving a feeling of despair.
It begins to thunder, and then rain. A rain of
tears so strong that it devours the soul. The
wind begins to blow, ripping apart love and
memories. The rain continues to wage a war on
the heart, an unending, unforgiving war. The wind
tears at the heart, but the heart fights to keep
what belongs to it. The love, the life, the laughter.

When the heart is about to surrender, the
storm stops, and lonely sorrow sweeps in.
The skies remain grey, but the storm has
moved into the distance. All is quiet and calm,
but there is nothing. Only the heart remains,
standing unprotected, alone. Yet it finds the
strength to open its arms and spread what it
has protected. The love, the life, the laughter.
But the depression remains in the distance,
promising another storm. Another day.

Jenny Rebecca Pokorny

When Angels Cry

Silence greets the early riser
Sunlight pours from the sky
All seems calm, but for a moment

The day grows upon us
Our traveling companion is reality
In its face can be seen
Bitterness, hatred, pain, anger, and despair

Finally, the earth swallows the sun
The moon becomes the lamp of darkness
I urge you to look hard at the midnight blue
Listen with your soul

·You will hear the mournful sound
Each star is a teardrop fallen
When angels cry

Daniel A. Roessler

Thoughts Traveling In A Bus

I bet none of you know
This is not what I usually wear,
I says: "Might as well look like the top."

I bet none of you know
This bus fare was a spontaneous affair,
I snitched the old woman by the stop.

I bet none of you know
My girlfriend's death wasn't something mild,
I never thought she would overdose.

I bet none of you know
Randolf is the father on my child,
Not something that I would have chose.

I'm late, I'm late, I'm late, I'm late.

I bet none of you know
My husband will shortly die,
He's been tested positive with AIDS.

I bet none of you know
I just spilt ketchup on my tie,
Man, I hope this stain really fades.

Geraldine Schreiber

Touch Me

Touch me...in secret places no one has reached before,
   in silent places where only words interfere
   in sad places where only whispering makes sense...

Touch me...in the morning, when night clings at its midday
   and confusion crowds upon me
   at twilight, as I begin to know who I am
   in the evening, when I see you, and I hear best of all...

Touch me...like a child, who will never have enough love
   for I am a girl who wants to be lost in your arms
   a woman, who has known enough pain to love
   a mother, who is sometimes strong enough to give...

Touch me...in crowds, when a single look says everything
   in solitude, when it's too dark to even look
   in absence, when I reach for you through time and miles...

Touch me...when I ask, when I'm afraid to ask...
Touch me...with your lips, your hands, your words
   with your very presence in the room...
Touch me...gently, for I am fragile
   firmly, for I am strong
   often, for I am alone.

Rebecca Liesenfeld

Each Must Have His Own

Forged from the love of liberty,
to the land of the free and the brave
All race, all class, all ethnicity
could find a equal place
This land was built for you and me
to the depths of our forefathers' graves
Our children who are yet to come,
should they carry on the pain?

"Live and let live," my mother used to say,
"This world is not your home."

One must not have all
but each must have his own.

Hughroy Hendrickson Andrews

Eyes Full Of Tears

Eyes full of tears
Heart dragging in the dust
(my) Inside has dried out like a well
The rain hasn't stopped but the
Sun shines in the dark.
Grey, black, red, and orange
Sky has been covered with the
Discrepancy of evil,
A clown can't smile, a baby doesn't know how to laugh.
A life full of Emptiness, Eyes full of tears
Sliding, running, flying
(my) Outside has turned into bricks
The rain has stopped, the birds are singing songs of
"Cries in the Wind". And my heart doesn't
Know the pleasure of love because
Its full of emptiness.
Eyes full of tears
Heart dragging in the dust
(my) Inside has dried out like a well
And the rain has finally stopped.

Juanita Turner

Half Past Happenings

At half past three they climbed down
the tree to see what they could see . . .
The grey squirrels played at the end of the day,
They claimed their snack before it turned black,
And then they scampered away.
At half past five a pair of possums
posed with their noses to the ground,
Their naked tails curved,
as they meandered and swerved,
And finally drifted away.
At half past six two black crows
cuddled and huddled on a branch,
While parachuting jays cascaded down
As though in a primitive dance.

Nancy W. Levine

Untitled

A storm that brings no rain,
Just pain to a mother that has seen her child slain.
The look on her face, the tears in her eyes,
As she looks towards the heavenly sky.
No answer as she asks God why.
All that's left are the memories of a loved one.
Memories so deep that it hurts just for her to speak.
But as she recalls her memories, she does not accept defeat.
For at the crossroads they shall meet.
As for now all she can do is pray because the will
   that drove has lost its way.
It's just another sad day with one more life taken away.

Travis Bailey

Little Things

Quite simple really
I don't ask much...

A little dusting on occasion,
maybe wash his clothes some time...

I do not ask much of him...
save for common courtesies...

...closing what he opens, fixing what he breaks,
simple little tasks are all...

I do not ask much of him today...
while he dreams away the sun...

but today the roses died...
and he is still sleeping...
Michael Wisniach

As A Tree

Make me a tree.
Give me brown knots for eyes
and the shadow of a mouth in bark.
I'll take long roots for legs
that reach into the earth, sucking water.
No more walking or driving over the earth,
I grasp the earth as a tree.
I spend all day in the sun
and stay out in the rain, getting all wet,
my leaves singing.
I sway and sigh with my dance partner, the wind.
The birds sit and talk with me all day.
I live for hundreds of years,
watching people come and go,
gaining girth and height
till it seems I can touch the sun.
In death I fall and sleep on the earth,
provide a matrix for all living things.
David Burrows

The Portrait

I still think about the man in the portrait.
As I grew into a young man
did I cause my mother pain
Especially when she saw my wife with child
and held her first grandson.
He was so selfish to leave her
at the most crucial time in a women's life,
motherhood. And fatherhood,
what could have been so terrible
to die even before your son is born.
Why'd you do it, father
I needed you, I needed to hear your voice
just once, your voice. I remember hating her
and wishing you were there to stick up for me,
as fathers and sons do, of course.
She was so angry, I did not understand.
One late night, quite tanked on gin and tonics,
I learned the truth from her. How you had been found
with blood spilling from your head.
A bullet, but no explanation. I needed you.
Jessica Bursma

Never Say Never

Never again shall I live for anyone else but me
Never again shall I reach for things I cannot see
Never again shall I scream when I have nothing to say
And when I know where I'm going,
Never again will they stand in my way
Never again will I show sunshine when actually it's rain
And never again will I ever say never again.
Mikki Byron

From My Heart To Yours

To all the women who share the pain
So deep inside where no one knows
It hides and lingers onto your very soul
While life just passes as it takes its toll
We meet someone whom we love so much
And then in time becomes no more
I fell and stumbled till I couldn't get up
For the whisper of the words so harsh and hurtful
Surrounded my heart till I could not feel
We trust in love and wait in return
To just be hurt again and again
Of all the pain I've ever felt
The one most of all is the love that was beaten
I look within at a bruised up heart that once was so alive
But this of all was I back then
But now I'm here to live again
I am alive and full of love that someday I will give again
So don't stand still like I had done
I know it's easier said then done
For I am here to show you all
That being strong, was I along!!!!!!
Mari McNally

Journey

While my body lies there,
my soul flies high above the grasp of touch
into a realm of loneliness
surrounded by passionate sorrow.
As I wander farther
I acknowledge all that I have left behind
and cry for all my pains of yesterday
and for the love I've given away.
I try to collect it back, but
it slips through my fingers like running water
and the drops I save are not enough
to know from where they came.
I then gently lay down in a dry meadow
letting the scorching sun burn my face
and my life, for it all seems so fake.
Then I look next to me and see
you lying beside me.
All my sadness melts away
and I can love again.
Laura Marie Jelsone

waxing

stretching the skin between my bones
cleaning the spaces inside my heart
dabbing at tears not yet fallen
i find a way to flatten out meanings

it hurts me when i crumble my gods
and they hurt me when i beg for forgiveness
knowing all the while that
i've lost their teachings, that
dullness is sweeter than trying to feel
and feeling is only a reflection of dullness.
thoughts that tried
so hard to try
rip like dusty linen sheets
that blanket my truths
leaving them stark and raw;
the breaking of thoughts
seems to tear at them too.

is this what it is to grow
out of myself?
Priya Narasimhan

Neledi's Tale

Your little sister is sick... What would you do?
Neledi went to Johannesburgh, about which she had no clue.
It probably was a pretty foolish thing to do.
And worse, Neledi's brother Tiro went, too.
But she had to bring her mother from the "City of Gold"
To help poor Dineo, who had more than a cold.
The children secretly stayed in an orange field that night;
The orange field of a white farmer who gave them a fright.
Next day they rode in a truck that was very fast.
The children could give their feet a rest at last.
Then, in the city, the two got on a bus.
However, the driver kicked them off with a fuss.
The person who then helped them was a young woman named Grace.
She took the two to their Mma's working place.
The next day Mma took them to their very own house
To rush Dineo to the hospital; she was being quiet as a mouse.
They waited for days: One, two three
And when Dineo came back well again, everyone shouted with glee.
Now Neledi is safe, though separated from her Mma
Who lives and works in Johannesburg, South Africa.

Prashant Tatineni

A Work Of Art

Greater than the stars in the heavens above,
   Is the gift of a daughter and her special love.
Brighter than sunshine is the smile on her face,
   She's a true work of art, with her own style and grace.
Softer than a summer breeze is her gentle way of caring,
   Always unselfish and constantly sharing.
Like raindrops from heaven that moisten the earth,
   She showered us with joy from the time of her birth.
More radiant than a candle glowing in the night,
   Her God given beauty is one awesome sight.
Her heart is purer than a new fallen snow,
   And she sews seeds of love wherever she goes.
Like flowers blossoming in springtime her wisdom unfolds,
   She's treasured by her family, both the young and the old.
Like soaring wings on an angel or a dove,
   She spreads happiness, peace, hope, and love.
Loved by the Father, embraced by the Son,
   Filled with the Spirit, three in one.
She fulfills her destiny one day at a time.
   Like poetry in motion, line after line.
She's patient, intelligent, a gift we all treasure,
   We thank God for her and will love her forever.

Rody Hamen

Peace Of Mind

Every minute of each day, I hope I will find
One single minute of "peace of mind".
Worrying, wondering, dreaming each day,
Of how my life has gotten this way.
There's a saying that goes;
"Life is only what you make of it".
Is this what I have made of mine?
Never to find time for "peace of mind".
My worries, my cries, my many tears,
My laughter though few, through all these years.
Many thoughts are of tough times,
Some happy, some sad,
But the problem is.
Never a time for "peace of mind".
Where could I find this peace of mind?
With life, love and happiness,
Through smiles, laughter and a tender kiss.
Maybe one day; and it will take time,
To finally find that "peace of mind".

Elsa Howard

My Life's Dream

To be liked by everyone
To be and to have fun
Fun to be with and around
Always up, never down
Sometimes acting like a clown
Just to relieve some ones frown
To put smile on every ones face
In my life no empty space
This is one of my life's dreams
Life isn't always what it seams
People say I'm always mad
Inside I fell really glad.
I don't know how to show it
Always end up blowing it
I'll end this poem by saying I'm all right
So this way I can get some sleep tonight
Realizing this isn't at all true
I lay awake feeling blue.

John C. Shevlin

Internal Scar

Things screw me over everyday,
It just seems to fade away,
No one cares, this can't be real
No one hears the pain I feel.

I do things I can't explain,
Dreaming different, but Dreaming the same,
Darkness is here and stealing me,
I can't fight, I can't get free.

He's getting inside my head,
Killing my soul, I'm almost dead.
I'm not sane, not by far,
Can't you see my Internal Scar.

My life is over, be on your way,
People still laughing, laughing still today.
I am drained, there's no more in me,
Please God, just set me free!

Blake LeBlanc

Your Everlasting Rose

I try to clasp your image as I dream
Yet it slips away, dissipating like the morning fog
And I am unearthed, dispatched from my roots
Away from what helped me grow, flourish, continue.

Now, as a garden blooms about you, far away
I am here, withering in a foreign soil without you
I try to catch your fragrance in the night's breath
But all I feel is the cold, aseptic, cutting breeze.

Yet I must keep straining toward your fervor
For that is all I can do not to give up the fight
As the sun sets, the stars look down upon me from heaven
And pray this frail, sequestered thing can make it to daylight.

John T. Beck

Sunsets

Let the sun set in the west
sunset, the time I like best.
We like to see it, with its colors pink, orange and blue
making a quiet time for me and you.
The sunset doesn't get hot from the sun,
The quiet, cold colors tell the day is done.
The sun sets at sunset,
The birds fly at sunset
and I'm happy at sunset.

Kendra Koehn

The Shadow

Come, come and see my world;
Stand in the doorway like an earl;
See the toddler waging a war to stand —
Extend your arm and give him a hand!

See the boy striding to school.
He knows to obey the rules,
Because living without a cause
Is a bedrock with flaws.

See the light with its beaming rays
Invigorating mankind all his days.
The sea of mankind sways to a crazed exhilaration,
So, I implore someone for an explanation.

Who is responsible for this jubilation?
Who, then, can explain my uninvited isolation?
For a response I wait; yet there is no sound.
So, back to the doorway I am bound.

But the doorway has disappeared, removed by time . . .
Lingering thoughts of the toddler, however, will forever chime.

So - come, come to see my mystifying world:
My world, like me, is a passing shadow, a shadow, a shadow . . .

  B. J. Mathews

Sunlight

Every day and every night, everybody sees the same sunlight.
Everybody thinks of the sun as a different symbol,
some see it as a sign of hope, others feel it is a rude awakening
but no matter how we think of it, it's all the same.
The way I think of the sun is all the good things put into one!
So every day and every night you see the sun rise and
see the sun set I would suggest to think of all the good things
in the world.

  Chelsey Eaton

Rose

Rose, Rose, beautiful Rose
You brought me so much joy since the day I found you
With your wonderful grace you stood tall and beautiful
As you withered with age you still shone brightly
I love you, beautiful Rose
I miss you now that you are gone
But now you have no pain
Now you have no sorrow
You can stand tall and beautiful once again.

  Janet Cowart

Somewhere To Never

Wings of eagles transpose the sky,
A wisp of feeling in a sigh.
A promise felt in looks, as if to fly.
A print of magic, the caress of an eye

The weakest moment is so near,
Of happiness, love and soft lace.
Shouting to the silence of want and fear.
A look is to know the sadness in the face.

Look to the sky, the image is every near.
Dreams are the eyes of inner repose.
Sadness is the feel of natures tear.
The web of life spins the silent rose.

How lonely to stand and want and not be near.
Those eyes are like the distant sun.
Earth moves and catches loves first tears.
Somewhere to never they fall and never run.

  Losone L. Parmeter

Destiny

Half a day gone, half a day left
everything is wrong, let's make the best

A pessimist an optimist no matter what you see
it won't change, it won't change, what will or will not be

So make your move fast or slow
you still can't prove where you'll go

Play your life the way you feel
Starving at night or enjoying a meal

Because your mind is half empty, your mind is half full
with plenty of questions all of them for you

So flip a coin and hope for the best
or play the odds and take a bet

No matter what you do
it won't change, it won't change what's in store for you

  Richard Rode

I Won't Be Alone

One of these days,
I'll be on my own.
Even son, I won't be alone

The spirit of my mother
Will tuck me in at night.
The soul of my father
Will turn out the light.

The goodness of my brothers
Help me cross the street.
The kindness of my sisters
Help me when I weep.

It is said that when you die,
You just rot in the ground,
In the dirt you lie.

But, you rise to the Heavens
To watch the Earth,
The denying death,
And the miracle of birth.

There will be someone with me all of the time.
God's watchful supervision will always shine.

  Janae Biggs

My Reflections On Life

"Love of money" is the root of evil.
It is worshipped as a living G-d.
It does not lead to the peace of mankind,
Nor lasting happiness, nor quest for G-d.

Money is needed for food and shelter,
Then tricks us to think that we are secure.
It does give comfort and fleeting pleasures,
And buys us friends, (their loyalty not assured!)

What really counts are the many "Good Deeds",
We do for others, relatives and friends,
For the strangers we meet in passing,
Saying a kind word, ourselves to lend.

All our "Kind" deeds will be rewarded,
If we leave a legacy of goodness behind.
To be remembered, can be so special,
If we leave "Sweet" memories, on people's minds.

Keep on going, do not stop trying,
Do not procrastinate and waste the day!
We are on a voyage, pack in the "Good Deeds",
Do not hesitate. Today is your day!

  Miriam Lourenso

What Is Blue...

Blue is the glorious sky
On warm summer days,
And the bluebirds that sleep
In there piles of hay.
Blue is the cookie monster
With his outrageous hunger,
And the bee that fell in blue paint
Who saw a girl and stung her,
Shaded blue flannel skirts,
That everyone would admire,
Blue is the color of your little brother's eyes
Who is a big fat liar!
Blue is one of your favorite colors.
From time to time,
It is also the sad moment
When you can't make a rhyme.

Jimmy Mitchell

Remember

Did you ever wonder why things
happen like they do
You just sit back and think of the
things that someone meant to you
and how much you miss them
no matter how far they are away
you'll see them again one day
and why they had to leave you
with so much left to do
but then always remember
what they thought of you
Was this to teach you a lesson that you
already knew?
Or was this something alone you had to do
So you can't waste your time
dwelling on the past
remember them for what you had and that
will always last.

Michael John Barucky

For Those Who Love Me
Hear These Words Of Comfort Upon My Death

To those I love and those who love me
When I am gone release me, let me go
I have so many things to see and do
You must not tie yourself to me with tears,
Be happy that we've had so many beautiful years.

I gave you my love and you can only guess
How much you gave to me in happiness.
I thank you for the love you each have shown
But now it's time I traveled on alone.

So grieve awhile for me if you must grieve
Then let your grief be comforted by trust.
It's only for awhile that we must part
So bless the memories within your heart
I won't be far away, for life goes on.

So if you need me, call and I will come
Though you can't see or touch me, I'll be near.
And if you listen with your heart,
You'll hear all my love around you soft and clear.

And then, when you must come this way alone,
I'll great you with a smile and say, "Welcome home"

James R. Morris

What Is There To Say?

There is nothing more to say
   Just watching the time pass away
I look into the glass and find
   The path to the future for behind
So I say to myself this day
   It's time to search for a better way
And when I say within my heart
   This love I have will never ever part.
My heart will never become
   a stumbling block for some
a few or even many
   but will always yield to plenty
and though I may seem to be down
   the weight will never slip the crown
and when my heart becomes full of mourn
   I will flow with the wind that is bourne
and I am reminded more this day
   that there is nothing more to say.

Thomas J. Bronson III

Reality

Flying on the wings of selfish pride
I swallow this jagged little pill
and bury my face in the mud
because I have failed at life, love, and happiness
but now I'm alone, except for you
still pushing me and testing me
and then you told me you loved me

But I don't believe, with faith like a child
life is not that easy
I still don't believe and like Icarus
I collide with my reality
crucified for belief. I don't know
why, it seems ridiculous to believe
but as my world crumbles
I come to realize, and look upon the
empty cross where you were
crucified.

Derek Nall

Evilness

A teen aged girl lives in the streets
Abandoned from her home
She watches in envy as everyone eats
She's trapped in an unending dome

She remembers from long ago
The evilness from the past
Her bruises and bumps still do show
Lives on and on it still does last

She sees as people fall down dead
And as the sirens blare
Blood explodes from their head
She watches as people forget to share

The girl sees the homeless cry
She sighs as the teens lie
Everyday she sees them die
She wants freedom like birds when they fly

There is ending to this poem
We can make things better
This is our country not France or Rome
Because we're stuck together forever

Catherine McCrary

For Dad

What's a daughter to give her Dad?
I've thought so hard, it makes me sad.
At Seventy-One, what's left to get?
You have everything. You're all set!

All my life, you've given me so much.
You taught me to catch, clean fish and such...
But what's to give someone for all of this?
All I am think of is a big fat Kiss!

I know I could give you things-
tools, clothes, money or golden rings.
I wish that I could give you twenty years
of fun, joy and wipe away your fears.

We go through life and never say
the things we should say everyday.
I've never said it, but I try to show it.
I love you Dad - I hope you know it!

Peggy Jane Jones

The Struggle

The struggle is real
    Only a few can deal
        with the cards that fall
            not everyone can have a ball.
Realities unfold
    The truth is told
        The statements are bold
But be careful, because your soul can be sold
    To a bidder with a higher price
        You find yourself rolling the dice of life
And then what will you have to hold on to
    You'll no longer be among the few
The means justify the ends
    look at all those friends.
        "Pop pop" You've dropped.
because you took the short way home,
    and now you no longer belong.

Rita Holsey

They Say That They Love You

They say that they love you
They say it again and again
They say that they'll be with you
Until the bitter end

But when you tell him what you've been hiding
He says "it's not mine" and then starts denying
You say to yourself, "he's the only one I've been with
So why is he lying

Then he walks out and leaves you
Without even a word
They say that they love you
They say it again and again
They say that they'll be with you
Until the bitter end

My mom always told me about being protected
Now I'm pregnant and being rejected

A year has come and a year has gone
Although I'm older, I'm still alone
So ladies don't be fooled by love

They say that they love you they say it again and again.

Tiffany Maddox

Matthew

I felt the cold kiss of winter upon my cheek
Yet my heart was as warm as a Summer's day
For the dawn had brought news of an expected arrival
And I rushed to see what I had eagerly awaited

When I entered the room I looked at your sleeping face
It was a face of glorious innocence that only a child could have
And right there I knew I would love you with every breath I took
You are the heart of my heart, soul of my soul, my very being

Then I put my hand in yours and you grasped it ever so gently
And I sensed you knew that something wonderful had just occurred
That at our very first meeting we had forged an unbreakable bond
One that would last for all our days and beyond tomorrow.

Shirley Gulotta-Simon

Forgive And Forget

Forgive him for putting his hands on you!
To forgive would mean I would have to Forget:
    I was a child
    He was only tickling me
    I trusted him
    The pain
    I told them
    They let him do it
    He wanted to father my child
    His rough face so close to mine
    The tears I cried
    The fear I have
    It haunts me day to day
    My anger
    He's my uncle and step-father.
To Forgive might be possible, if they could make me Forget.

Rebecca Oppermann

Sacred Cow

Notion, potion, motion, devotion
What is this time,
When poems don't rhyme?
Life, strife, blade of the knife!
A time so cut apart
From the song of our heart...
We don't feel warm when it's sunny
We only feel warm when it's money
The sun, and a gun, and a bun, stun gun...
Blind lies ride the waves
Heard by deaf ears persuaded to crave
...What a sweet treat to eat meat...
And have a hunger for murder...
God, mud, blood...and a burger.
Sacred creation, Holy as thou
Holy creation, Sacred Cow

Robert Linden

Angels

Angels will guide you if only you ask
They'll come to save you when you need them most
She'll whisper sweet songs and help with a task
They walk down the aisle and cheer at the toast
Angels will stay by your side when you're ill
They'll comfort your heart when upset inside
She'll sing in harmony from your windowsill
They chase away evil that lurks and hides
Angels will lead you with welcoming arms
They'll take you to God when the time is right
She'll hum soft tunes that will frighten what harms
They fly to your side in day and in night
I know where my angel will always be
I know my angel watches over me

Renee Donovan

Benedict Arnold

Benedict Arnold in charge of West Point,
Must of been way out of joint,
Because he had the plans in his hands,
He was a real greedy man,
Then he sold the plans to the hands of the British,
But General Washington wasn't very skittish,
So he stopped the king's men,
And Arnold was never seen again,
But his name is still around,
Although he left American ground,
Before he died in England,
He got up and pledged by our land

Tim Rutledge

Forgive

If I smile at you will you be my friend?
If I knock on your door will you let me in?

Can the past be forgotten? And a new start begun?
Can we say things are different, and what's done is done?

Life is too short for holding on,
To past mistakes and imagined wrongs!

Blood is thicker than water I have always heard,
And our hearts can be heavy with unspoken words.

So let's look to the future and our time left on earth
Let's live to the fullest and prove what we're worth,

By laying aside old griefs and thoughts
And coming together before all is lost.

Then someday in heaven when this life is o'er
We'll all be together as a family once more.

V. M. Barcus

Stand, Your Fate Awaits You

Stand tall
Your ghost is walking now,
    ahead of you
Fate has you in its grasp
    do not close your eyes
        or like a child turn from what

Awaits now in the final hours
    these loose moments, seconds
        spent splitting hairs and wondering

You, cold eyes and lonely
    with fatigue as deep as
    the mud you have sunk
        your worn bare feet into
            what a joke
            you seem

Chris Davidson

Targets

A cold, sad morning
it was when you walked with fear
your heart dark and tired
your soul worn out and weathered
we were targets
they took our money
they bought our time
your smile faded
your teeth yellowed with age
Now you say you
never cared a wink for the game
but who knows anything except that
you'll never play again

Dan Osgood

Benedict Arnold

Benedict Arnold in charge of West Point,
Must of been way out of joint,
Because he had the plans in his hands,
He was a real greedy man,
Then he sold the plans to the hands of the British,
But General Washington wasn't very skittish,
So he stopped the king's men,
And Arnold was never seen again,
But his name is still around,
Although he left American ground,
Before he died in England,
He got up and pledged by our land

Tim Rutledge

Forgive

If I smile at you will you be my friend?
If I knock on your door will you let me in?

Can the past be forgotten? And a new start begun?
Can we say things are different, and what's done is done?

Life is too short for holding on,
To past mistakes and imagined wrongs!

Blood is thicker than water I have always heard,
And our hearts can be heavy with unspoken words.

So let's look to the future and our time left on earth
Let's live to the fullest and prove what we're worth,

By laying aside old griefs and thoughts
And coming together before all is lost.

Then someday in heaven when this life is o'er
We'll all be together as a family once more.

V. M. Barcus

Where Is The Love?

Where is the love that shines so bright?
Where is the love that turns darkness to light?
Where is the love so much like a song?
Where is the love that made right out of wrong?
Where is the love that made people smile?
Where is the love that makes life seem worthwhile?
Where is the love that turns war into peace?
Where is the love that makes enemies cease?
Where is the love that helps us to understand?
Where is the love where we walk hand in hand?
Where is the love that makes life worth living?
Where is the love where we offer thanksgiving?
Where is the love we were granted from birth
Where is the love to make peace here on earth?

Pamela R. Redick

Sisters

Sisters through marriage, friends as well,
Future memories to make and to dwell.
Days of talking, laughter, and tears,
Sharing, caring, sisters for years.
We'll discover one another as friendship grows strong,
Strength renewed through our family bond.
A new friend among many and a love newfound,
Wishes for my brother and sister that love will abound.
Wherever your home you both shall make,
Sisterhood, family memories are cherished keepsakes.
A seed has been planted, a garden of love for life,
I will gain a sister, my brother a wife.

Vicki Lynette Brown

Angels, Come Quickly...

Angels, come quickly and gather around,
My little boy is saying his bedtime prayers now.
Collect all around him with one at each side
And watch him for me, while I go rest my eyes.

Let's put his favorite teddy up here by his head
And straighten these covers while he snuggles in bed.
You must pay close attention when he is sleeping about,
That a bear or a tiger doesn't fall out!

Now, one of you make sure the night light stays lit,
And if he should get thirsty, here his water glass sits.
To make sure he stays warm against the evening chill,
We must draw down the shade at the window sill.

He may need a "comfort" throughout the long night,
And should a bad dream upset him, you must make it all right.
If it happens to rain, make it silent and light
And save the loud thunderstorms til after the night.

So, come guardian angels, my little boy yawns
Your attention is required until the new morning dawns.
Then I will take over with a new day to start,
And you may return to heaven after doing your part.

Linda Schweitzer

New Beginning

I have emerged from my cocoon,
A beautiful butterfly,
Free to fly with the wind.

I am scared at first.
I've never had wings before.
I try my wings out slowly.
Do I let the wind take me in its currents?
Or do I choose my own direction?

I flap my wings,
And do a dance.
A silent dance of peace and anticipation,
Anticipation for what awaits me.

I look at my brightly colored wings
And somehow I know
I am ready for this journey.
I am strong.
I can finally be me.

Marisa Villar Sampson

We Are The Village

We are making history, today at Miles,
That's the reason you are here.
If it takes a Village to raise a child
Parents and Elders, are needed, that's clear.

We need your help and confidence
And together we will work each day.
We will be the Village, and raise the child,
In a most successful way.

In your work at home, and our work at school,
We must try our very best.
We must help the children see the light;
We will help them meet each test.

We must teach them well as children
We must help them learn to grow;
After they become the Village,
They will teach, because they know.

Dominic Bornino

My Stars

At night as I gaze upon the stars,
I wonder at how far away they are.
Dazzling us with their brilliant light,
They light up the sky when day turns to night.

In the mountains on a clear and starry night,
The stars bestow upon us a special delight.
One will zip across the sky,
And leave us to wonder where it goes and why.

In my dreams, I am high up above,
Riding the wings of a heavenly dove.
Spreading it's wings in glorious flight,
Sprinkling starlight through the ebony night.

As a new day comes, I realize,
The stars are disappearing from the skies.
But I know within his heart of mine,
Tonight at sundown the stars will shine.

My stars, my stars, how bright they glow.
Giving a wondrous display to the world below.
And though I know they really aren't mine,
For me in my life they always will shine.

For to me, they are, my stars!

Marijke Eline Ellert

Woman In Love

When I first met you, I looked in your eyes;
The feeling I got, I never wanted to say good bye.
We dated and had a good time;
When we were together I felt so fine.

Loving you the years went fast;
I looked back and two years had past.
You asked me to be your wife;
That was a beginning of a whole new life.

You gave me a child and a home;
Then no more your love could roam.
It was hard adjusting the first five years;
The pain and suffering brought a lot of fears.

I didn't know if our marriage would last;
I kept living to much in the past.
You changed and treated me right;
Then I had no more fears and frights.

You know it took a lot to bare;
But it all went away when you showed you cared.
Thank you for changing and making me glad;
Now there is no room to be sad.

I love you and want you to know;
Many years has past, I still love you so.

Debbie Mays

My Second Tear Was The Sweetest

My child was born and I shed a tear
For an innocent baby born into sin and fear.
Not much to offer a child for tomorrow,
For a world that's full of pain and sorrow.
With any luck the child will go through life;
And not have much care and strife.

Then I shed a tear
When my child is born again out of sin and fear.
For our dear savior died to set us free.
So their eyes were opened and they can see,
Through His blood and water so pure,
He gives them life that is sure.
So my friends, I tell you this:
The second tear is the sweetest bliss.

Dwight M. Ashbaugh

Ooky The Eskimouse And His Adventures

Fairy tale king gave the order. "Nero, take this egg.
Fly over mountains high, over little hills
where no animals can ever fly by."

Nero did as he was told, but the egg was so heavy.
Puffing, panting, much sweating, he reached the
goal. Nero's claws became very cold. The egg
slipped from his hold.

Pumps! The egg fell on the ground! Cracked open
with a big sound! All the pine-trees were in awe
at what they saw!

The shock made room to wonder! What is in this
egg so small? It's a cute furry animal. Wooden
skies are on his feet, handy ski-poles, gloves,
pants also checkered white keeps him cozy and
bright!

Finally, the furry animal tells the pine trees.
"My name is Ooky The Eskimouse! I'm sent by the
fairy tale king to bring happiness to this animal
snow-wing!"

Kenneth Timur and Tanit de Buday

Judged By My Cover

Life is our open book
To read it, is to live it
To live it, is to understand it
You cannot tell what your book is about
From the tittle page
You cannot live without knowing what you title is
My title is "The Expressioner"
For that is who I am, what I am
I am but a single thought whispered among many
I am a page with unreadable words
It is unnecessary to read or understand me
Just know that I am what I am
I am as One will see and then vanish
One who will shine as brightly as a star
And then void my visibility through the
Blackest of all holes
I will hide and defend my soul from
Those that dare burn through me with
Eyes of trickery and deceit
I Will Not Be Judged By My Cover

Quan Southall

My Problems Aren't So Bad

My Problems Aren't So Bad
when other people are starving, or when they have been shot
My Problems Aren't So Bad

My Problems Aren't So Bad
when there's child abuse,
and physical abuse
My Problems Aren't So Bad

My Problems Aren't So Bad
when there's children standing on corners dealing drugs
My Problems Aren't' So Bad

My Problems Aren't So Bad
when there's homeless people living on the streets
My Problems Aren't So Bad

My Problems Aren't So Bad
when someone loses a loved one to AIDS
My Problems Aren't So Bad

My Problems Aren't So Bad
when a drunken driver runs down your only child
My Problems Aren't So Bad

Deanna Thompson

Child's Play

To Douglas
We drive a thousand miles a day, every day
On winding red dirt roads
Carved neatly with a garden hoe
In places where Bermuda grass isn't
Under blossoming honey locust trees
Growing in Grandpa's yard.
Small cardboard box houses spring up, create towns.
Twine laced matchstick fences mark boundaries never breached.
Virginia Creeper leaves become pretend palms shading
Backyard swimming pools.

Today, you are the truck driver; I am the movie star.

Innocent, small, grubby faced misfits
Imagine life beyond rusty clouds
Swirling in forever wind,
Dream the unreachable, create perfection,
Pick and choose the best best,
Escape reality of three times patched,
Earth stained,
Double kneed Tuf-Nuts.

Karen Snitker

Pain

I'm so sick and tired of things that go on
All I ever hear is voices of evil
I tell myself, you don't hear it
But yet it is so crystal clear

As it continues, its size increases
"Why should this go on?" I say
But it is not me
It is what I hear and what's being
thrown at me

I then think yes, it could be me also
But the feeling in which I get is something
of disgrace
Maybe wishing I wasn't of life

Of course this isn't always the answer
In my words, I wish not to cast pain,
But in them, I shall show of my hurt
And the only to then understand, is who
cast of such hatred

Wendy Anthony

Son

I am sitting here reflecting on you, my son
the pride and joy of my life.
Of the countless moments of laughter
that you've brought me.
Your smile brings one to my face...at any time.
Your laughter is infectious and free
it reaches down into my funny bone and causes it to wiggle.
Your questions and comments awe and inspire me.
You are a priceless treasure, that no jewel could rival.
You have honored me, by respecting me.
I would have chosen you as a friend
I like, as well as love you.
When I look at you now
I see the husband and father you will be.
You have given my life a completeness
that no one or anything could,
And when I leave this world
I know I'm leaving it a better place
for having left it you!
I am so proud to be your mother.

Karen A. Anderson

The Skeptic's Prayer

I wrote a prayer, one day . . .
  Conceived in gratitude, and love
To the Magnificent Creator — of life, and living beings,
  And all the endless mysteries above.

So much misunderstood, misworshiped, misbelieved —
  Maligned and vilified without contrition,
And worst of all, perhaps, ignored, denied,
  By any sense of deep and True cognition.

To this mysterious, all pervading power,
  So far removed from petty human strife,
I said "I thank you, God, for I am small, diminutive,
  Yet I appreciate my tiny speck of life."

And even more, the gift of love . . .
  (Whatever God may be!)
For I am but a tiny atom part —
  A brain-cell in a brain I cannot see . . .

These things I thought, and wrote . . . then asked myself,
  When I was done, while feeling light as air,
And will the World and life be different now . . .?
  Or only I, the better for my prayer . . .
  Sullivan Cook

Who Am I

I am a woman who through God's will
Has suffered heartaches and troubles
I've been through the mill
But, I've learned how to live
I've learned that when I have a little
I can still give
I give of my time by caring for others
I share my experiences with other single mothers.
Who am I
I am a woman who God has blessed
With a good attitude in the middle of a mess
I can call on the Lord without any fear
Always knowing that He is near
Who am I
I'm just a loving, caring mother
Who raised my children alone
Willing to help the poor and the needy
With more than a bone
Someday I'll receive real forgiveness, wealth and real love
I see my victory, coming from heaven above.
  Mary Slaughter Little

Behind My Eyes

I look at the world
  from behind my eyes
I must not let you see
  the pain I feel inside.
I must stay alert
  there's a big world out there
Full of dragons, demons, and beasts
  waiting to consume me.
I must not let them in
  yet—
This keeps me locked inside
  full of pain behind my eyes
No one to care for me
  when I have difficulty doing it myself
Unable to speak
  I cannot let them know
  that I am dying inside.
  Penny E. Harris

A Life Fulfilled

If I should die today,
Not live another minute;
My life would be complete,
Because of the time that you were in it.

If I should die tomorrow,
Live for just a little while;
My thoughts would always be of you,
Your lips, your touch, your smile.

If I should die ten years from now,
And that time was spent with you;
I'd be the richest man in the world,
Because you've given me a heart brand new.

If I should live to be one hundred,
And you're still there by my side;
Such joy, such happiness, such pleasure,
Like a life-time roller coaster ride.

If I should live for all eternity,
And have all joy and blessings too;
Nothing in that eon of time,
Would compare with loving you!
  Douglas A. Alberts

The Sad Man

The night time is the hard time
I sit alone in my room
Not knowing what to do
I search my mind looking for away
To convince my love to come home and stay
We had a love that was beyond compare
But now its gone and life seems so unfair
What shall I do how long will it last
I wait in agony with memories of the past
The tears they come and cloud my eyes
I lost my love and only God knows why
I'll try and be patient and understand
Good times are coming don't be sad
I want her back and that's for sure
But the day will come and I will know
The memories I have I'll have to let go.
  Thomas L. Blanchard

Lucky Seven

She looked like an angel standing there,
As I fought to hold back my tears.
Our love was right but our timing was wrong,
I hadn't seen her in seven years.

So I asked her to have a drink after work,
She met me around five-thirty.
It felt so right being there with her,
That we both got a little flirty.

We sat and talked and then we danced
And then I finally bought her a flower.
She said I have to go, I feel like Cinderella,
We had been there for seven hours.

I told her I had spoken to my spirits
Because I was having trouble with my Love life.
I believe they listened and sent her to me,
Maybe this time to be my wife.

I talked to her the very next day,
She said, I feel like I'm in heaven.
I was reading up on my horoscope,
It said my lucky number is Seven.
  David Ferrell

Eternity

My eyes were drawn to the clouds in the sky
The beauty of the sun shining through brought tears to my eyes

I just could not help feeling that someone was on their way
Going to meet the Lord in heaven today

I never saw the sky with so much detail
It looked like a much traveled trail

Many must travel that long journey home
To the heavenly place where you're never alone

Some are anxious and cannot wait
To get to that heavenly gate

Others may feel apprehensive as they draw near
Waiting to sense your presence near

Help them Lord to win the fight
And let them know it will be all right

Thank you for the promises to each of us who believe
Life eternal to receive.

Deborah Fisher

Love's Whisper

As I silently listen to the whisper of love,
My heart soars higher than a spirited dove,
A Godly treasure so sweet and so dear,
So I ask you...Can you hear?

It is larger than mankind, wider than any sea,
Standing proud, with open arms, as does a tree,
With winds of power and peaceful eyes of bliss,
Even a gentle caress of a warm kiss.

Untouched and pure with the glow of the sun,
All of life's laughter, all of life's fun,
A bond between mother and child, and a father's dream,
A path for lovers, and a child's gleam.

It's a fresh breath of air, or a kind word,
The wisdom of song, full of beauty that's heard,
Fields of flowers, and a lot of dancing bees,
A reborn day full of warmth and glee.

Let's always embrace love with our very being,
And share it with all God's creatures, as birds sing
It's then that special doors open, thru soul and heart,
That love whispers to us, like a work of art.

Concetta F. Miklai

The Field

I've seen you in my dreams again.
I've felt the cold wind whistling in my ears,
The peace of heart my soul has missed,
And the softness of your voice calming my fears.

The field wants me to touch you once again.
It wants me beside you as our thoughts meet
In the cold wind that becomes love,
Our love that melts the snow of my dream.

It is not you crying, just your heart bleeding
As I see you running to our dark lake
Where we both swim on our bed,
A bed of thoughts which can not fake
Your feelings, my feelings, for they are real
Even for the field in my dreams,
And for my heart in your tears.

Ruben M. Saenz

My Halloween

You may think I'm wacky with Halloween
Seeming so dear to me,
But on that special night, just once a year,
You can be what you want to be.

The bill collector's not after a witch,
The kids won't talk back to a clown,
And your husband can finally have his french maid
(If he specifies upstairs or down).

The crisp night air and rustling leaves
Just add to the magic for me,
And there's no harm pretending there's a ghoul at the window,
Not the branches of a tree.

Sure it's a little crazy
To hope a witch just might fly by,
And believe jack-o-lanterns protect us
From evil spirits lurking nearby.

But when candy-eating goblins turn back into kids
And my ghost once again is a sheet,
Reality may have to move back in,
But I still think Halloween's neat!

Heather Lapine

My Dream House

If I were a young man, I know what I'd do
 I'd build a great house, all red, white and blue.
I'd plant roses in the yard, vines on the wall,
 There'd be a picket fence, and that isn't all.
I'd have a small rill, yea, even a brook
 I'd plan it all out — go right by the book.
There'd be gardens galore, all pretty and pink,
 To describe it all, I'd run out of ink.
I'd have a flag by the door to welcome our guests,
 And high on the rafters, would be fancy birds' nests.

Now that I'm old, I know what I'll do,
 I'll build a small house, all red, white and blue.
I'll fix it up cozy for my wife, and me—
 We'll have friends dropping in for 4:00 tea!
We'll be happy, I know, in our little castle
 Without all the frills and a lot less hassle.
Home is where the heart is; I know that's true,
 So wherever you're happy, that dreams for you!!

Le Snider

A Mother's Memory

 The first cry with joyous tears,
our pain quickly forgotten.
 God has prepared us for this coming.
 He knows within the seconds
that follow no other love
can bear witness so strong,
as a mother's love for her son,
 He has appointed us guardians over this life.
 To shape and mold in his image,
to put the essence of love,
for that's the most important
ingredients and most precious gifts
a mother can give.
 All too quickly the years pass,
like a wink of an eye.
 Little by little loosening out ties.
 Seasons come and seasons go,
but like a tree our love will grow.
 The finished product we will see,
bears witness to thee.

Connie Herman

Basketball Has Two Sides

Ten men on a basketball court,
There for one reason
To win their territory.
We had won two games before,
Now it's time for the third.
Whose funeral is it going to be. Their's or ours.

The game has begun
Our enemies are gaining ground.
Therefore there's no turning back.
My soldiers are aging as the war goes on,
And wonder when is it going to stop.

The ball is in bounded, our time is up.
It's passed to the man which I am guarding.
He looks down at the three point line,
One second later he looks at my eyes and sees fear.
He leaps and releases the ball in one motion.
I closed my eyes knowing there will be no rebound.
As I walked out of the court, with my team by me.
And said, "the war has not come to an end".

Eden R. Labriel

The Event

The day has finally come
Nervously you put your shoes on
Shots keep ringing in your quivering ears
It's time, you say.

You arrive, your there
You wait and wait
They call the event
It's time, you say.

Standing there at the start like a wasp
Shaking, shivering, scared
Ready, set, go, pop!
Your off and then . . .

Nathalie Conte

Nocturnal Creature

I am a nocturnal creature
I like living alone
The night is my prairie
In the darkness I roam

I slip into the darkness
Never needing the light
I see through the darkness
I have keen insight

I know where you are hiding
The night is my friend
I see into the darkness
I can see the end

With the morning light
You'll expect me to hide
You don't know the metamorphosis
That took place in the night

Now there's a new turn a mysterious loop
I can transcend into light
Never missing the hoop

I can have both worlds, the night and the day
And each has its virtues, I'll not cast them astray

Sarah Parlett

Torremolinos

I long to find those rolling hills, of luscious cypress trees.
The perfect air would fill me up, and bring back thoughts of you.
We could share again, the sight of our best friend, the crescent moon.
It hung so low, that it could see, the
dotted houses of white washed walls, and arched rooms.
Remember drinking sangria in the village streets?
You had to hold me up, I could hardly feel my feet.
With all that love, we had no need to communicate.
Our only wish, was the beautiful sight of
the starlit beach, the crescent moon, and
the lighthouse, just to the right.

Gail E. Cohen

Codee

I found a picture of you and Chris from my trip out west.
It brought a smile to my face.
Now is a different day.

Dee Dee's news has shattered the everyday rituals that fill
My ordinary life.
Reminded me of the specialness of a life and how it can impact
Another's.
We were just two everyday souls getting by.

Living for weekends,
And reminding ourselves that we shouldn't wish our lives away.
Thinking ourselves a long way from drawing a conclusion
To this life's span of time.
But time is unrelenting, it creeps at first, and then gradually
builds momentum.

I could wish we had stayed in touch.
But I would rather be grateful for having shared
Our banter across the phone lines
And enjoy the memories of our few face to face encounters.

Time is easy to wish away hoping for a bitter time,
A more meaningful time, but all we have is this time, precious
And fleeting. How we squander it.
But perhaps that is part of the process of becoming,
Wiser about its value.

The lesson of your leaving will not be lost on me.
Nor will you.
The banter quietly echoes on.

Joan Gargiulo

A Valuable Lesson

Like so many young people today,
you do not take life seriously.
You feel that you were put here to take.
But you are wrong!
You were put here to give
of yourself to others.
You must learn how not to think
only of yourself.
You must learn how to help
others without expecting anything
in return.
You must learn how to love others
for what they are and not for
what they have or for what they can give you.
If you do not learn anything else
in life, I hope you learn that
a person is happiest when he knows
that he has done something good for others.

Gail Steele Collins

Time

Time is such a special gift that money cannot buy.
It really can't be borrowed, though we so often try.

We always try to manage it and save it as we go,
But how much of it we truly have no one will ever know.

We strive to spend it wisely, but often in our haste,
Most of us don't realize how much of it we waste.

We all take it for granted, so often we lose track,
And miss those precious moments we never can get back.

Live each and every moment as if it were your last,
Don't worry about the future, or dwell upon the past.

Take every opportunity to show someone you care,
For tomorrow holds no guarantee that they will still be there.

Never leave until tomorrow what you should do today,
And be thankful for the time you have before it slips away.

Jeanie L. Pitrizzi

The Splendor Of Life

There is the pristine sight of snowcaps on
   The mountains so high
And the meadows so rich with clover
   That it staggers the eye

There is the glistening of the dewdrops
   Welcoming in the early morning
And the endless fields of flowers
   They are adorning

There is the sunlight kissing the splashing waves
   Of the ocean
And there is the serenity of the sea
   Calm without motion

There is the rich smell of the earth after hot summer showers
   And the music of bees gathering nectar from the flowers

There is the singing of the birds ushering in the rising sun
   And the quiet silver of the moon when the day is done

There is the star-studded night sky further than the eye can see
And in the midst of all this magnificent beauty
   There is the gift of life called me.

Ulla Cummings

Can You Believe It's Actually Been A Year?

Many years and a long time ago,
I could never imagine, I didn't know.
That the day would come after such a defeat,
To where you and I would ever meet.
I'd often sit and wonder "why?",
And when I couldn't answer, I'd start to cry.
I grew up feeling so alone,
I didn't know I was a clone.
I was nothing like the people I was around,
Not the way I act, look, or sound.
The time we've spent I've learned so much,
About my ways, my feelings, and such.
This past year I've learned a lot,
I've learned more than you ever thought.
I know where I'm going, I'm no longer lost,
I will be a success no matter what the cost.
I just wanted to thank you for making that call,
Because without it this would not have been possible at all.

JoAnna Tawney

A Child's Prayer

Alone, on my own
As I walk through the streets,
My head hanging low in despair.

Alone, on my own
With my small frame shaking
From the cold, cruel world that engrosses it.

Alone, on my own
Only my thin hands to blind me
From the violence and hatred my eyes always see.

Alone, on my own
No longer can I be,
All my strength finally faded from my soul.

Alone, on my own
Asking you to love me;
Opening the gate to my heart.

Alone, on my own
I'd no longer be
If you'd give just one chance.

One chance.

Hill Hector

Painful Love

Did you ever love a person,
   but know they didn't care.
Did you ever feel like crying,
   though from it you'd get nowhere.
Did you ever look into their eyes,
   and say a little prayer.
Did you ever look into their heart,
   and wish that you were there.
Did you ever feel like crying,
   with the lights dimmed way down low,
   and whisper, "God I love you,
   and don't want you to go."
Don't ever fall in love my friend,
   the price you'll pay is high,
   and if I could choose between life or death,
   I think I'd rather die.
Don't ever fall in love my friend,
   you'll hurt before it's through,
   you see my friend I ought to know,
   I fell in love with you.

B. J. Sharbutt

A Birthday Gift

A Good Friend of mine will be celebrating a
birthday on December 25, I was wondering
what I could give him for a gift:

I thought how about a map of the whole world,
but he is the whole world so that's out:

Then I thought how about a cross, but he is
already hanging on one so that's out:

Then I thought how about a boat and a fishing
pole, but he is already a fisher of people so that's out:

Then I thought I would just wish him a happy
birthday, and to thank him for all the laughter
and sorrow that we have shared together.

Patrick M. Gale

Antennae Tuned

If you can still yourself a moment,
Open wide in soul,
Be ready for response;
Engage perceptions
So they're clarified and magnified,
You'll net the butterfly of people's beauty,
Capture loveliness through love,
Achieve a headiness you'll want to keep.

But, in possession, know it's fragile this experience;
Try not to hold it captive for too long.
So, as you would with purple emperor or zebra swallowtail,
Do treat it gently, cup it, do not pin,
Enclose it, take care not to bruise
Since you, by accident, in hunger,
Just might snuff its source,
Its glory-flutters down to solids, peace,
Harmonious, exquisite-formed design.

Release it, then recapture it again.
Re-studies' freshness bring to it.
On any day on such wings — you can soar!

Mary M. Grozier

Everyone's The Same

Now I lay myself to sleep and now my minds
at rest.
I pray that my judgement is based on what I
am inside.
Who I am is what really represents my life.

I pray to God without race, so being black
won't help.
The God I serve has no pastor, so I only can
represent myself.
Only the people who taught me will come deep
within.

So I can be judged by that and the color of
my skin.
In death there are no races, there are no
blacks or whites.
So why would there be a difference in the way
I live my life.
So why others see the racism won't fade.
I pray to God everyone the same.

Delicia Lacy

November Twentieth

As the lightest footprints through snows of winter,
Silently you creep through my mind.
The sweetest memories leave pain behind,
The smoothest wood has a sharp splinter.

The cold wind blows in a bitter air,
I hear your voice in a breeze.
My throat fills with the biting freeze
Of things I wish I could share.

The brown leaves crunch their barren cries
As emptiness fills my head.
My visions are coated with pure, deep red;
Bloody tears fill my eyes.

A cold and bleak November day,
And yet the sun is shining.
My eyes are dry, my heart is crying —
I hear time pass away.

Angela M. Kayl

Wendy Lynn

I have a little grand-kin,
Her name is Wendy Lynn,
And when she comes to my house,
I can't wait to let her in.
So I open the door and there she stands,
Clutching her blanket in her hands.
Silently she watches my face,
Waiting my greeting and my embrace.
So I give her a hug and her little face smiles,
She takes away heartaches she takes away trials.
We play with the toys, the puzzles and books,
Then she runs to each room to have a good look.
As time goes by she may get cranky,
That's when I'm glad that mama brought blanky.
Soon mama will come and call for her baby,
I'll be grandma no longer,
I'll just be the lady
Who waits for Wendy to come again,
To give me the pleasure of being grandma again.

Bernita Becker

Your Like A Rose In Bloom

You're like a rose in bloom.
A sunny-field-day.
Every-day my darling
That's why I-love you,
That's why I-love you,
Your sweet love is something-beautiful
You're like a rose in bloom
A sunny field-day
Every day my darling
That's why I love you,
That's why I love you
Your sweet love is something
In your heart.
Filled with sincerity
And-darling you show it a million-ways,
That's why I love you
That's why I love you.
Your love is something beautiful.
You like a rose in bloom a sunny field day
Everyday my darling that's why I love you that why I love you.

Sybil H. Hedges

Life

Life is that period between
Birth and death, within that time.
One seeks his wealth.
Who knows in what field his goal will be made,
Or the manner of work for which he'll be paid?
For many there have been burdens and tears,
But happiness will follow through the years.

In some phases of life we
Try to succeed, hoping to accomplish many good deeds
Working hard ere we go, even if success might be very slow.
One keeps striving until his goal is set;
Then he is happy for doing his best.

Whenever there is an unhappy day,
Keeping faith will drive the clouds away.
Life holds much we are told,
work on and on seeking that goal.

Life can be joy, life can be sorrow,
In life there is much for tomorrow.
Take some good pleasures and with them take heed,
Never turn back, always take the lead.

Nancy L. McElroy

So, Who Are You Calling Normal?

It happened on the bus one day,
When a man, his fare did pay.
"Oh no!" He loudly shouted and much attention gained
"I dropped my souvenir coin that I recently obtained".
Laughter came from this man's plight, but not from me,
He was a pitiful sight.
A laughing lady asked of his bag's contents -
And I said to myself now this is nonsense
"It's my dinosaur I bought along
with the shark coin I just now lost".
The more he talked the more they mused,
Now which one is normal?
I'm not confused.

Elaine Heaphy

The Journey

A cold, damp air settles in and puts
a hush on early evening.
Blossoms close, capturing the last
hint of sunlight.
Nuthatches call out a last song,
until morning,
as their young are nestling in.
The fires' hot coals soon turn to ash.
Nature encourages rest and a gaining of strength
for the next day.
And as with life, each dawn brings
a new awakening,
a fresh beginning.

Catherine A. Kramer

My Mom Says

My mom says I act like a monkey,
but I have no idea why.
For if I was a monkey,
I'd climb trees five miles high.

My mom says I'm acting like a wild Indian,
but I have no idea why.
For if I was an Indian,
I'd have arrows sharper than knives.

My mom says I'm bouncing off the walls.
I know this isn't true.
For if I could bounce off walls,
I'd be black and blue.

I wonder why
my mom says all these things.
Because if they're true,
I wouldn't be talking to you.

Zachary Halter

O Young Black Girl

O young Black Girl don't you know
your land for thee is for you to stand and be free;
just believe in thee.
I'm proud and I'm saying it loud.
Just believe in me this land
is for you and me just stay in unity.
As Martin Luther King was trying to tell thee
freedom is for you and me and not just some of thee.
It's time out for all the slave I'm not a servant;
I'm not a maid all I am is a person who need a lot of loving
because God doesn't have a respect of person
all he do is just keep on loving.
He give us that special covering
so that He can help us govern and show everybody
what His word say about loving, and again I say God
doesn't have a respect of person.

Yolanda Denise Owens

The Keepsake Of Paradise

There is a fire on the water of the sea of my heart;
One that has been there ever since you lit the spark.
It flickers and glows and lights up the dark.
It burns strongly when we're together
    And wildly when we're apart.

I live in the wake of your smile;
And the air of your words makes breathing worthwhile.
You are my cold rain falling on the hot desert sand;
My strength of stability in the heart of this man.

I never could imagine finding a soul
To keep and to share, to have and to hold;
To calm me down when I'm out of control.
To say those words that I've never been told.

But I'm still chasing rainbows,
Lost in the sand.
I wish you were here now,
Because I could really use a hand.

Steve Whitmire

Him

As I sat alone
All I could do was think about him
I thought about how I felt, the
feelings I had for him
Whether he feels the same way,
I don't know, I have no clue
All I know is my mind can never go for
a second without his name running
through it
As I sat there, my body yearned passionately
for him to be near me
I wanted him badly, more and more
I missed him so much
I wished he could hold me tight
And never let go
All I know right now is that my heart
belongs to... him

Marissa Griffin

Loving You

Your smile lightens up my day,
Your hugs make the world go away,
Your kiss leaves me breathless
Your being here make my problems seem less,
Loving you is so simple.

Even on the days when nothing seems to go right,
And on the nights when the moon and stars don't light.
Even when we're to busy to spend five minutes together,
And even the times that we're away from each other,
Loving you is so simple.

When we bicker and fight,
And we both look affright,
When everyone is against us,
And everything comes before us,
Loving you makes so much sense.

I'd give up my dreams and fantasies,
I'd give up my goals and family,
I'd give up everything I own for you,
I'd even give up my life for you,
Because loving you and having you love me is all I need.

Stephanie Nipper

Make Me Remember

Make me remember, the things I've done
Make me remember, before all is said and done
Is it true to believe, can you really say

The days go by but I still don't know
Make me remember what I must do
Tell me how it must be done
What journey must I make - on what road will I take
Which way must I go
What will I behold

From generation to generation
and generations to come
The words you will say must all be said and done
The words you speak must not die
The future of this family depends on you
The story of this family must be said on this day

Latisha Brown

Winter

Winter, and the day breaks to my face
Winter, and I see the dark
Claim terror to this place
"Winter," she said, "Doesn't have to last this long."
Winter is the only thing that keeps me holding on

Winter, and I feel like getting old
Winter, and the life I knew
Turns to shame and soon runs cold
"Winter," I think, "Blows flurries in my eyes."
To shield me from the pain of the laughter and the lies

Winter, and I know that I've been sold
Winter, and the storms come
And I drop the hand and fold
"Winter," I know now, "keeps me falling in and out."
Winter — it means swimming in the deep end of my doubt

Shareef Elfiki

Untitled

To live alone is a life of unhappiness
To live with someone you love is a life of joy
To be without you is not to be,
for there are times to see a sunset
but alone it's just another day gone by
To sleep alone is the worst thing of all,
for why should we wake if we are
   still to be
     alone . . .

Bryan Denton

Then And Now

I look back at my life these past one hundred years.
I've seen my children born into slavery
  and my grandchildren born free.

I've watched my people pick cotton.
Then came the cotton machine.

I've gone from slave shacks to dream homes.

I remember the feel of the whip on my back,
because Master caught me learning to read.
Then, to see my grandchildren get a college degree.

Lydia M. Qualls

Basketball: The Dance

When I was a child, my mother thought
That I was strong enough and sure enough
To someday be a dancer....
But when I was five or was it six,
I couldn't dare to dance, didn't want to dance
Unless I was dancing on the court.

And then when my father passed me the ball,
And that ball was shaped as the whole world to me,
The thing that mattered the most was to do my best.
The ball flies down into my arms,
I score a basket,
And at that point I finally realize,
"I am what I want to be!"

To be who I want, to go where I can
To be wild, to be loud,
To be defensive and to be aggressive,
Strong enough, sure enough,
I am free; athletically free!
Just like a dancer.

Lindsay Margaret Dicker

Breathless

I can't breathe! I can't breathe!
I need air to breathe!
My respirator isn't working!
What is wrong? What is wrong?

Nurses coming and going in an intense rush.
Nurses are crowding all around.
What are they doing?
What is wrong? What is wrong?

I am frightened. I am scared.
I need air to breathe, now!
The light grows weak, weak, weak.
Life fades out.

The light shines again.
Doctors and nurses look at me.
The scalpel burns my throat as a new incision is made.
Life fades out.

Time passes; the light shines once again.
Breaths come and go easily.
The respirator is doing its job.
Thank you God.

Evan Edwards

Untitled

What's it like there Stevie?
Is it pretty as they say?
Is it everything we've hoped for
or nothing but a grave?
Are there bubbling brooks, willow trees,
soft green grass and a cool summer breeze?
Do you know that we love you and still care
even though you're a million miles away from here?
Can you see us, Stevie?
Do you know what we say?
Do you know what will happen to us
each and every day?
Do you know that trials and tribulations we must face
and how to overcome this silly human race?
Do you know now Stevie, the meaning of life and death?
Is there something better after or only nothingness?
Is it what we learned in Sunday School and should we
follow the Golden Rule or is that all meaningless?

Carla Bates

The Lady Downstairs

The lady downstairs is quite weird,
She even has an azure beard.
The lady downstairs has an eccentric green car,
Covered with flamboyant pink stars.
She consumes strange meals,
For dinner each night she eats fried seals.
The lady downstairs has a grotesque house,
With eerie cobwebs and a revolting mouse.
The lady downstairs has an alligator for a pet,
She takes it every decade to the vet.
The lady downstairs has fraudulent teeth,
She has dusky hair that reaches her feet.
The lady downstairs is certainly queer,
Shhh! Be quiet, or she'll hear!!!

Nivi Pinnamaneni

Remembrance

Twenty one years ago...
Departing from my motherland
On the road of exodus I went
The heaving Pacific Ocean below
Couldn't overwhelm my sorrow

Distraught men, women, children
Crowded in the overloading ship
Tormented by the waves striking the hull
Swallowed bitterness all along the trip

Oh! Hell and Heaven were so nigh
Only a moving line separated sea and sky
Screaming waves of human beings' lamentations
Deity of compassion only might understand

In the midst of distress and sufferings
A mother was just delivered of a child crying.

Hoa Bien

The Evil Weaver

"Not again!" the weaver cried
Afraid that this time, he might be fried
Hopefully not
The weaver thought

For stealing money, he could be whipped
Or his teeth, they could be chipped
A breath of fresh air just might help
If he were ducked near the kelp

And then he saw his worst nightmare
"Oh no!" he cried, "This isn't fair!
Perhaps I should complain to the mayor
No! That wouldn't even give him a scare!"

"To the stocks with you!" Cried the man
The weaver could run through the sand
But then he saw that his hands were tied
"Not again!" the weaver cried

John Myers

Undying Love

To the one I love,
Love came so easy when I looked into your eyes,
the thought of spending my days in your arms
brings me so much joy. I've been told that
nothing can last longer then forever. As I stand
here looking at you smiling at me I know our
love will always be true, no matter what the
in coming seas bring us or the harsh rain pours
down on us our love will be there to part the
clouds and let the light shine down on our
undying love.

Dawn Walsh

Clouds In The Sky

Clouds high in the sky
You can see them at night
They look just like they're glowing
In the air it isn't right

Nature did not put them there
Factories belch them into the sky
They look as if they belong there
At night they float so high

As man we should not make these clouds
Nature's original beauty we soon shall not see
The night skies should be clear
For these clouds should not be

Lamont Powell

Waving Back!

My flight is long, but I shall be strong,
As I see through the windows,
The clouds look like fresh snows.
I wonder where my mother could be.
As it is she, I long to see.
Mother whom I so recently have lost,
what a price it has cost.
I look out the aircraft's windows,
Trying hard to keep from pressing my nose.
Against the glass as I look,
To see if my mother doesn't frolic.
Through the clouds all lined with silver,
On her way to heaven she is delivered.
To be by my loving grandmother and brother Jack.
Look! Isn't that her waving back???

Wanda LeLea

The Beach

Oh what a wonderful place to be
Fun for you and fun for me
Running along the burning sand
Or sitting and talking hand in hand
And with the glowing sun up above
We can't help but feel the presence of love
Footprints walking side by side
Being washed away by the ocean's tide
Listen carefully and you will hear the sound
Of coconuts falling to the ground
The seagulls are up so very high
Soaring; or just passing by
When we hear the crashing waves
We'll know it's the ocean and how it behaves
And now I ask you could there be
a finer place for you and me?

Linda Moneypenny

Love

Love is like a rose that is always growing.
It was there when you were born,
and there when you die.
It's in the air, it's everywhere.
You hear it, you feel it,
You know that it's there.

So, why don't you express it to someone you care about?

Don't keep it in. Just let it out.
In a letter, in a note, out loud.
Show the person you love how much you care.
Send them a flower, a gift,
Or just be there.

Michelle L. Soriano

Saint Michaels

The scenic route is beautiful, this cold and sunny day.
I left the winter snow behind, to meet him by the bay,
To bridge a gap of forty years, an imprespicuous task,
But since fate crossed our paths once more, the dye it
    seems, was cast.

I wait for him out on the deck, the warm sun on my back.
The winter breeze is ever still, the water cold and black.
Now, I hear him call to me, soon he's by my side,
Together by the fire we watch, the bay's outgoing tide.

A candle glows, two glasses touch, a drink to warm the heart.
We try to think of why it was, back then that we did part.
Moments filled with tenderness, music we hardly hear,
Just the beauty of ourselves, the joy of being near.

How can two hearts as old as ours, be as young as this
Or find the magic that we have, in each others' kiss.
I touch him and his energy, flows through my every vein,
He touches me and life is born, in my soul again.

We count the stars and try to name each galaxy we see
Walking back from dinner thru this dark infinity.
A chilling wind blows in on us while we are fast asleep
Disturbing not our oneness that, flows thru the either deep.

Nancy Hannan

My Butt

I asked her what to write about
She said, "My butt" I laughed

I thought about it and wrote it down.
She said, "You're silly" I agreed

I squeezed my eyes and wrote these words.
She said "Go to sleep" I wished

I clapped my hands and wrote vigorously.
She said, "Having problems?" I sighed

I told her about the poem and pretended to write.
She said, "Sounds exactly like me" I nodded

I didn't tell her I was going to write this part:
To Jo-Ann (-ie, sometimes), the great from Hawaii soul friend
and silly Roomie that will always be in my heart

Christina Y. Pai

Thank You Mother

Did I ever thank you mother for creating my soul?
Did I ever thank you Mother for helping me grow?
Thank you Mother for picking me up, when I had fallen down.
Thank you Mother for listening to my problems
    when no one was around.
Thank you Mother for healing my wounds, when I was in pain.
Thank you Mother for listening to my ideas
    even when they seemed insane.
Thank you Mother for when I thought the world had blinded me
    you opened my eyes and showed me that I could see.
Thank you Mother for when I didn't want to hear the truth
    you took my hands from over my ears and said "I Love You".
Thank you Mother for when I said I can't, you said I could.
Thank you Mother for when I said I won't, you said I would.
Thank you Mother for helping me learn not to follow.
Thank you Mother for showing me a better tomorrow.
Thank you Mother for telling me you loved me everyday.
Thank you Mother for when you were mad, you said it anyway.
Thank you Mother for because of you I can succeed
    and realize all I have to do is to just be me.

Vareece Jackson

These Crying Eyes

These eyes have been weeping and done less sleeping
Never have they won and cryin' ain't no fun!!!
Now I have been in a race with tears runnin' down my
Face only to accomplish last place...

No sorrow or pain do I have to gain when my life has
Been a crying shame,
Now I truly understand the weeping willow as I see
My tears on a stain - proof pillow oh! Willow

But blessed it be for this company to have found me
For my poeticism would let me see through these
Crying eyes a payday and a heyday the same way

And finally I could really see what life would be
Without crying eyes befalling me
So dry your eyes and cast your vote and help this
Brother get out of this drowning boat!!

Seriously,
    Anonymously,
    Tearlessly,
    "W.E.E.P.Y"

Venoil Joseph

An Evening Prayer

It's nature's time for prayer
    Her silent praises of resplendent skies
And earth's blest hymns profoundly high
    To God, their breathing's bear.

With them, my soul must bend,
    In sacred reverence before Thy throne,
Trusting in thy Son alone,
    His sceptre's power to extend.

My God, if I have turned away
    From grief or suffering I ought relieve,
Careless a cup of water ere to give,
    Forgive me Lord, I pray.

Oh teach me how to feel
    My wayward wanderings with deeper smart,
So more of grace and pity to impart
    All my offenses, swiftly heal.

Oh Father, my soul would be
    Pure as evening's unsullied dew.
That as the stars night course be always true,
    So must I ever be to Thee.

Vincent T. Goble

At Midnight

I'll be thinking of you at midnight on New Year's Eve
With my heart still pumping out a reason to believe
We're flying high over the big city
you're so smart and so achingly pretty
although visibility is zero
you are my sight and my unsung hero
Through your eyes I can see for a million miles
Through the years you've given me a million smiles
above dark and dirty streets slicked with rain
a dove glides safely away from the pain
In me such beautiful feelings you have aroused
awakened desires I had long ago housed
a hint of moonlight touches your soft skin
I wouldn't let you down if you let me in
I realize for your hand others they vie
But they don't understand for you I'd die
I live in fear that there'll come a day
When you're gonna let us slip away
as I wait for your blessed sign I live to receive
I'll be thinking of you at midnight on New Year's Eve

Shawn Butler

Untitled

I want to take you away to a magical place
A place where we can be all alone
No friends, no parents, no phone
We would never be apart
And love would fill our hearts
I know him not the smartest guy,
   the funniest, on the best
But I'll love and care for you more than
   all the rest.

Mike Schwabenbauer

Why?

Part of me says he's still there.
Part of me knows he's not.
Why did I take it so hard?
Why didn't I realize we were so close?
Why did I go into shock?
Why didn't I cry right away.
Part of me wishing I hadn't heard.
Part of me glad I did.
Why don't I like hearing about it?
Why don't I like talking about it?
Why don't I like even thinking about it?
Why did I have to know?
Part of me wanting to cry about it to everyone.
Part of me only wanting to write my feelings on paper.
Why that place?
Why setting a day aside for death?
Why that path?
Why did he have to end?
   He's gone. He's gone.

Jamie Vorves

Mother's Day

Once a year loved ones come together
To celebrate a certain event like no other

If not for her to whom would we turn
When days become hard and love seems unlearned

She brightens the days and nights just by saying "hi"
She's always there ready to listen, to understand
and always there when we cry

Things become rough like the holes in a road
But with a call or one of her hugs
she takes the whole load

Ready to mend a heart, broken and torn
With all her love she has to give
Never to be worn

She's that very special person, with that one certain place
Always a smile on her beautiful face

Giving the support one always craves
Never to scared to share her ways

She's my best friend, she's my mother

Belinda Hodgdon

Mothers Are Special

Mothers are special.
Let me counts the ways.
Mother's always listen.
Mother's give you praise.
Mother's knows when you're sad
and always tries to make you feel glad.
If one does wrong mother knows.
She will forgive and friendship grows.
When one is sick and can't go out Mother will always be there.
When we have problems mother will be someone to cry to.

Gloria Pinter

You Treated Me Like An Angel

You treated me like an angel
That God let walk on this earth
I want you to know how I miss you
I know you're a man of God's worth

I listen to hear you knock on my door
And watch you as you walk by
Then I remember you're in heaven
When Jesus took you I didn't know why

I know you're watching over me
I can feel your presence around
I see you picking four leaf clovers
And I see you picking them from the ground

I wish you knew how I miss you
But somehow I know that you do
I know you remember our good times
And all the happy times we laughed through

I had so many good times with you
I didn't look for the bad
That someday you would leave me
And that I'd feel so sad

Ruth Shelton

Iron Treles Bridge

Stone cold soldier, wrapped and standing at attention,
Bridge of sighs, fortress of pride,
ride with no unnatural suspension on high
Iron Treles Bridge, high spirited, breeze way,
Gunship avenger, afore and aft earths shaky earthwork
Chieftain with an imaginative fore front
Ancient gateway for the traverse
Avengers on the road
Iron Treles Bridge, stationary flagship, ladyship
Lady finger gatepost
Eagle easy gun-whalen drawbridge
Silhouette crossing, eagle gated detour
Iron Treles Bridge

Vickie Chisolm

Turn It Over To The Lord!

Help me to turn it over to You Lord.
Let me feel peace again within.
Help me to turn it over to You Lord,
Free my soul from turmoil again.

I have seen Your miracles performed,
You have answered my prayers in the past.
So, help me to let go,
And turn this over to You Lord.

The beauty of Your world,
The peace and solitude it brings.
To walk and gaze at the creations,
Only You, Lord could bring.

Trees don't fight to be the tallest,
Birds don't tell other creatures to stay away.
Butterflies don't pry into the bumblebees affairs,
Here I am, Lord - Hear my prayers.

Take these painful issues,
Let me lift them up to Thee.
Free my shoulders from this weight,
Let me turn it over, and - Be Free!

Carol A. Oesterbo

What Silent Thoughts

I know not what silent thoughts feed your mind.
I don't know if what you say is truth or lies.
You say you love me more than anyone in your entire life.
You say you want me to become your forever loving wife.
But thoughts of pain that's come to past haunt my mind.
Is it me or just my heart that makes me blind?
You say to just leave the past and begin anew.
But for me that is somewhat difficult to do.
The fear of another heartbreak fills my head.
And I cry before I go to sleep in bed.
For I know not what the thoughts in your mind shall do.
Are the words you say to me when we're alone true?
Or am I a fool whose heart gets in the way of truth?
Or is my name inscribed in your heart as yours is in mine?
Oh, if only I could know what silent thoughts feed your mind!

Leandra Lee Kerr

The Why Poem

I do not understand
Why my friends tend to fight
Why boys like to fly kites
Why the sun is sometimes bright.
But most of all I do not understand
Why I need to go to bed at 8:00 every night
because I don't like my bedtime I agree with 9:00.
What I do understand is
Why I'm here on this earth
it's because God put me here to
or so that I could serve Him and
someday be living in His home.

Shelley M. Bolton

The Old Man

I knew an old man who was all gray and blue
I asked myself if there was anything I could do
I could see in his eyes he just didn't care
I wonder who left him totally bare
I decided to give it may best shot
I walked up and shook his hand and told him it was hot
I figured the small talk would provide a good start
I could tell by his expression he wanted no part
I explained I didn't come to take anything he had
I just thought he needed some cheering he looked very sad
I was just about to leave and be on my way
When he stopped me and begged that I stay
We sat together on that hot afternoon
I began to understand why that old man looked doomed
After we talked and had some cookies and tea
I could tell after all he really liked me
I then told him I had to go and be on my way
He looked up and smiled and said have a nice day
The following day I went to see the old man but he was not there
He was dead — Damn life just isn't fair.

Angela M. Ferguson

When I Say I Love You...

When I say I love you...
...it means I want to share everything that our heart's and
soul's desire, our goals, dreams and fantasy . . .

When I say I love you . . .
it means I want to deepen our understanding and together
become something greater than we ever could have by
ourselves . . .

When I say I love you . . .
it means that we will be in love from now until eternity.
I want to be with you forever.

Valerie Renfro

Earth

As the wind blows through the trees,
A soft call is heard.
Soothing and fine it chills your soul,
Making you want to cry out.
The love it sends and hate it takes,
Calms the earth of a terrible place.
The grass is short and trees are tall.
Making it the calmest of it all.
Cold winter months and hot summer days,
Changes your life like a passing maze.
The air is swift and takes your place,
As you stare in a peaceful grace.
Small and tall as dark as night.
You say to yourself,
I'm glad I'm here because,
It hold's my soul and leads the way.
This is a wonderful place to be,
Because it's the only place you can walk,
FREE.

Lacey Ryan

Free

Last night I dreamt I was a bird and the whole world I could see.
I was soaring above it all. I was truly free.

Free from my problems, free from my pain.
Nothing to bind me, no walls, locks, or chains.

I did not feel anger, nor sorrow's abuse.
These words did not exist to me. I needed no excuse.

I heard no whispered secrets, only the whistle in the wind.
I heard no lies or objections. I saw no reason to descend.

So I soared higher and higher and felt restless no more.
I was filled with love and peace. No worries to endure.

Then I awoke sadly to my world of lies.
I wished to dream again, and quickly closed my eyes.

I then realized in my thoughts, that I could never truly be.
Content with my life, as was the bird.
Never satisfied or free.

Amanda Wasnik

Hoping For Them

It is said a country divided cannot stand alone.
But what of a family living in two homes.
Nothing is more difficult than the loss of a child.
But what of a loved one who becomes gang wild.

It is said the meek shall inherit the earth.
But what if the affliction is acquired at birth.
Nothing is more difficult than being physically impaired.
But what if a person becomes just plain scared.

It is said the world is on a course for disaster.
But what of a country selling a nuclear reactor.
Nothing is more difficult than facing fear itself.
But what of an epidemic which risks world health.

It is said judging the color of people has no place.
But what if those judging think they're a superior race.
Nothing is more difficult than being judged by one's looks.
But what if no one has learned from all the great books.

It is said that we live in troubled times.
But what of a world not using all its great minds.
Nothing is more difficult than achieving world peace.
But what of tiny minds - teaching prejudice must cease.

Richard A. Barbian

There It Goes

There it goes, it went flying by.
I caught a glimpse of it out the corner of my eye.
He's beaten and ridiculed it right out of me;
it's over there in the corner, so far out of reach.
I know I need it, I need it to get strong;
so I can pack my things and move along.

There it goes again, it's going the other way.
I didn't have enough strength to grab it today.
I want it back bad, I can feel it inside.
Between the walls of this house, I can no longer hide.

I didn't know this was in the plan, when I left everything
to marry this man.
But, that heart that loved no longer has a gleam
cause over there - out of reach,
    is My Self-Esteem!

Ula D. Brown

Song Of Remembrance

Render unto me the sender of a song
To make my heart swell, is been perilously long
since I've had any such happening in my quiet abode
and a contentious youth is not carried to old
but sustained are the memories not of days
but of years of traditions, of feelings and ways
I long for a sweet moment to feel what I felt
as a child a young women, innocence as I knelt
before God and the world but now I am weary
the pureness of spirit it sang everyday
now even some respite just for a day
let me feel in my hands the world like I did
the freedom to stand up for anything or something
amid chaos or happiness it really didn't matter
a song or a sonnet
unto me please will you render
and open the heart so the mind will remember

Kimberly L. Neisch

A Gift Of Etiquette

I thought that you would like to know
The gift of etiquette that we should show
That nine letter word the synonym of manners
A treasure that will earn you so many banners
Day by day the gift you will get
Minute by minute you shall never forget
With jewels of knowledge it will present
Many good values you shouldn't resent
And when that day comes you will need your gift
From the memories treasures
It will all come backs swift

Marleena Scott

Silly Things

Children do some silly things!
They eat worms and rotten beans,
Pickle juice and Apple peelings,
They eat cobwebs from the ceilings!
They climb on top of monkey bars,
They jump off of roofs trying to get to mars!
The swing on vines across a lake,
They stick their finger hooking bait!
They try to read upside-down,
They always act just like a clown!
When barefoot they try to walk across glass,
They are always full of sass!
Children do some silly things!

Lizzi Eargle

No One Knows

I cry,
But no one knows.
    They see me smile.

I ask for help,
But no one knows
    They hear me say, "I'm okay."

I get mad, full of fury,
But no one knows.
    They hear me laugh.

I fall apart; I become a mess,
But no one knows.
    They think I'm their "perfect little Jess."

My emotions are unseen;
My plea is unheard;
My tear invisibly flows.
Only because
    No one knows.

Jessica Morgan

What Is Love?

Can you catch it in the air as it flies by?
Or do you hide it in your heart of despair and cry?

What is love?
Do you give it to all and then be still?
Would you give your child to be beaten and killed?
Would you suffer pain and die for all?
Even if some do not stand tall?

What is love? What is love?
Jesus Is Love!

Who is Jesus? You say. I'll tell you who He is.
The one that said, "I'll go. No let it pass, but
no I accept. My love will last."

If you're depressed, oppressed or distressed,
Jesus loves you and no questions are asked.
Whether you love him or not. He loves you still.
He suffered, bleed and allowed himself to be killed.

Elaine Parish

Bell Aire

So much spoken but not so much said,
Hearts been broken, through tears I have bled.
So much lost with nothing to gain,
Empty in confusion, I struggle with the pain.
My spirit is fading as my troubles become clear,
No one beside me to help me through my fears.
Everyone is with and I am without,
Everyone is sure and I am in doubt.
Why do I feel weak while every one seems strong?
Why do they seem right when all I feel is wrong?
In seclusion I suffer, with no one I will tell,
Nothing seems important once you've been through hell.
To hell and back, I have returned,
Still breathing but badly burned.
Burned not on the surface, but burned deep within,
Trying to live happy after all of my sins.
Too sad to cry, too angry to scream,
True serenity and joy come only when I dream.
But through all the despair, I can still find some peace,
Through faith, love and kindness my spirit will increase.

George Scott Lamphere

317

Spiral Of Being

The sun's path, along the cloud speckled sky is shortening, giving up all hope. The trees, release their power to live and grow, for the cold winter long is coming. And you will fall, for all power has vanished, but the fierce cold, and strong wind. Your limp body shall float and the chill of the wind will carry you afar, until nothing is meaningful to you anymore. Every thing is just a spiral of life starting in the center and winding outward. And now your time has come; you have been loosened off the edge of the world, where mists and skies meet together as one. And here, at the edge of the colorful world, where everything is grey and dark and a mystery, you will slowly melt into unbeing and you will collapse and disappear into the world of nothingness. But have hope, oh venerable one, for a creature will be created to thrive upon you, so that your energy and spirit will begin at the center of the spiral, once again.

Claire M. Stoscheck

The Marathon Called Life

A pat on the back,
  A punch in the face,
Is there a reason,
  Why I'm running this race?

One warm, happy smile,
  Three cold, cruel glares,
I often-times wonder,
  If the world even cares.

Why does the sun tease me with a grin,
  Just before the clouds begin to frown?
It frustrates me so,
  And I often break down.

But I must keep charging,
  And master this feat.
For the end will come fast,
  With the surrender of only one beat.

Erin M. Wilson

The Greatest Feeling

Watching the sunset every night;
Hearing the waves that are not within sight.
The greatest feeling it could ever be;
If the one I love is always with me.
Feeling the cool breeze on a summer evening;
In that moment nothing is deceiving.
I feel as if I'm on cloud nine;
As if everything in the world is mine.
The stars look just like silver sparks;
Nothing is so extravagantly seen in the dark;
And the black contrast of the sky,
Makes the night seem like a lie.
But I know in my heart the memory will always be there,
If the one I love will always care.

Dawn Viglione

The Rose

I once asked the Lord why did every beautiful rose have thorns that can cause us pain, and I heard his voice speak in a whisper to my heart as I stood silent beneath the rain; he said it is a symbol a tribute of grace, I then held it close to my heart, my eyes were then opened as he spoke of the rose, and explained to me each part; He said the seed represents the tiny baby, that in Mary's womb was placed, and the petals represent the softness of his heart, and the love upon his face; the thorns represent the crown he wore, on the day he was beaten and bruised, and the stem represents the stripes on his back and the pain from the whip then used. The fragrance represents the oil brought to the tomb where my son laid, and the beauty represents the day he arose with every sin of mankind paid; Every rose that blooms is a symbol of grace to the heavenly work that was done, through Jesus Christ the Rose of Sharon, my risen and holy son.

Elizabeth Holowasko

Jar Of Clay

Each mind is a formless piece of clay waiting to be shaped.
Willing to listen to words of wisdom and hungry for truth.
Trusting the potter to press it firmly, yet ever so gently
Cutting out the rough edges and smoothing out the rest.
Every moment is precious to the future of this clay.
Movements unnoticed still affect its end result.
After shaping and perfecting this matter, it is
Time to let go. For what comes next is the
Choice of each child. He will be thrown
Into the fire and put to the test. Standing
Firm on his foundation will be his only
Hope. To make it through will be a
Challenge, yet when he does he will
Always remember the hands that
Formed him into a jar of clay.

Tricia White

Hidden

To escape his troubles,
he resorts to paradise.
A rock holds him on its lap;
a tree races the sun to block the mysteries out;
and a lake which draws him a friend.
Armed with a branch, some string,
and a piece of metal
he out stretches his relationship with nature.
Although his whole purpose is to get away
he finds a warm companion in being
one with the water.
The peaceful setting allows time
for the eyes to close.
The ringing sound of the bell awakens you,
you smile with admiration
followed by tears, from being happy
this has been your first catch in all
your twenty-one years
and no one is there to share your joy but,
suddenly when letting it go, the tears become of anguish.

SalV

Behind The Glass

Darkness, total and complete, engulfing, cold darkness,
An eery wind brought forth from shimmering light,
Into which he emerges, floating up from the abyss,
Staring blankly into the demonic face, pale and putrid,
Behind the thin film of glass sits in solitude,
Hunched, a beaten hag beneath the assailants lash,
Lost, lifeless, a weary face, pinched and placid,
With void expression and hollowed eyes, it turns on him,
Uncoiling and slithering forth with the smell of living death,
A deep aching emanating from within, gasping for breath,
For life, for death, but yet has neither the strength nor will,
Raising a decaying hand towards him, straining,
Desperate, it flattens the withered palm against the glass,
Poised and pleading with animalistic longing,
He stiffened, the cool, smooth glass against his skin,
And there it stays the starving beast, palm to palm,
Face to face, two identical pair of eyes,
Frozen together in the looking glass.

Lizabeth Jackson

Voices

The crowd's echo,
Are words without essence that drain the soul.
Only the endless blue sky speaks essence,
Essence, but no words.

Wanda Cruz

Morning Love

I wake up every morning to the sky's dullish grey
Preparing to take upon another day
As the sun comes from within the ground
You arise from the slumber you were bound
A day without you by my side
Would be a day the sun doesn't shine
A world I would truly miss
Without your loving good morning kiss
Oh how I wish I could stay
But we have to start our day
We say our goodbyes
As I pull out of the drive
I think because of you in a way
It's going to be another glorious day

Steven M. Rutkowski

Worthless

All my life, one way or the other, I had been told
Or made to feel, worthless
This curse seemed to go with me wherever I went
No matter what I did, it just was not good enough
After hearing it for so long, I believed it to be true
So why even try, said I. They are right
and I am wrong. I am worthless
I just might as well give up and face it
I am worthless
Then is when the good Lord above stepped in
He gave me the truth. What He said sure woke me up
I do not make anything that is worthless and I made you
I gave my only son for you
What a price I paid for you
So, don't you ever believe it again
That you are worthless
No amount of money can buy my Son
Yet I gave him for you
To us you are worth a lot
Together we paid a high price for you

Yvonne Michael

Lonesome Heart

Somewhere out there there's a lonesome heart.
It's in despair, it's torn apart.
That lonesome heart belongs to me, its in grave pain.
Can't you see? It's as torn apart as torn apart can be.
It hurts so bad I can't stand the pain.
The tears come out and it looks like rain. Can't you see?
Probably not. So it may as well be that this is one
heart that must forever stay lonesome and forever torn apart.
This lonesome, lonesome, lonesome Heart.

Amber Crowder

Love's Fool

My noisy heart sleeps, while now it sleeps alone.
Yet close to my ear, the pounding tune is grown.
Beneath the softness skin, under my soothing breast.
In her chambered room, she quivers without a rest.
Thinking only him, tongue pressed to tongue.
Eyes seen through eyes, souls becoming one.
Kisses to the boy, he whispers to my ear.
If my heart should love, then death should I fear.
A payment to my own, a thousand kisses I plead.
And to whatever you wish, should give all that you need.
My lonely heart is found, now she is fulfilled.
But with my kissing him, kissing him has killed.

Lana Diliberto

To The Mountain Daisy

To one that is so fause and fair,
and to the drooping locks of angelic hair.

Outcropped on a mountain top, overlooking as if divine,
there she sits between the Edelweiss and the vine.

O' the power has thee, and helpless am I,
and there she sits between the Edelweiss and the vine.

On a cliff, there she sits toying with the mind,
and helpless are we
as we sit between the Edelweiss and the vine.

O' the beauty has the daisy,
a beauty so divine,
that she makes the rose jealous in the summer time.

Outcropped on a mountain top, and helpless am I,

the daisy sits between the Edelweiss and the vine.

Kieran Murphy

The People Who Dared To Believe

This is an ode to the people who did change the world,
Who carried on in spite of the cries that they heard
Of disaster and failure, no matter how loud,
Who were frightened themselves, but triumphed anyhow.

This is ode to the people who never gave up,
Who kept to their path no matter how rough,
Who worked hard and long and were often afraid
So that those coming after could walk what they'd paved.

This is an ode to the people who suffered and died,
Who stood up and spoke out rather than live with a lie.
They kept on despite knowing the price that they'd pay;
Risked their lives to tell everyone how it could be someday.

This is an ode to the people who dared to believe
That love conquers all and that they could beat the machine,
That in a world scared and cold, they could light a small spark,
That would burn everlasting and light up the dark.

Rebecca Moreland

Untitled

Why do people put you through so much pain?
Why do the ones you love and hold closely to
your heart, always are the ones you end up hating.
All the pain and misery those one's put us through.
The depression that bonds all of the lonely and wounded.
We have all backed down slightly.
But even though slightly, it was just enough to push
us off the cliff from which we were dangling.
We are now falling into a never-ending hole.
All of the time wondering. Worrying. Searching our
minds until our heads hurt. At this point,
the darkness, the blackness, is our closest friend.
Something for which we can confide our deepest
and most burdensome feelings. Some people never
confide in that darkness, therefore, they never exit
that black hole of theirs. But some do. The strong
find the way. The weak never know.

Samantha Krassow

Untitled

My beautiful daughter's a sight to see
her pretty blue eyes, she get's that from me.
Her smarts are from mom, that's plain to see
We love her so much, and that's from me.

Dave Intartaglio

"Wounded Birds"

Why do I want to help wounded birds
when I, myself, can't fly?
Why do I see a rainbow
when there's just an empty sky.
Why do I live in a dream world
made up in my mind?
Afraid to face the truth because of
what I might find?

But, perhaps, without my knowing,
there is a bird who flies and
perhaps a hidden rainbow way up in the sky.
And, perhaps, I live in a dream world,
my heart safer there, because the truth is . . .
I always really care.

Judy Savoy

My Heart Is So Confused?

You just walked out of my life
Turned away, didn't even say, good-bye
Left me here to face the pain alone
What did I do wrong, why did you turn away?

I'm sitting here in your favorite chair
Listening to, "Our song"
Trying to recall what I said or done
Tears begin to fall

I meet you on the street
You don't even say, "Hello"
As you walk on by, a tear falls
I wonder, do you remember at all?

When you left, I didn't understand
I believed our love could never go wrong
It's been quite a few years
But, still my heart is so confused!

Shannon Moser

If

If I were a bird, to your window
I'd fly and every night I'd sing to you a
different lullaby.
If I were a vineyard, no grapes would
be as sweet as mine as when you pressed
them to you lips you'd taste the sweetest wine.
If I were a flower, in your garden I'd
grow I'd be a beautiful flower, a big
bright yellow rose.
If I were an apple tree my apples would
be sweet so anytime you wanted you
could pick yourself a treat. I am only
human and as for from perfect as
can be but I can love for you and
care far you and the rest is yet to see.

Judy Brewer

Dancing Leaves

Leaves blowing one cold night,
There a crunch and a plop and I here the wind,
The wind sounds like a whistle,
I can almost feel the roughness of the leaves,
It's almost a spooky feeling,
I jump in the leaves and fly with them,
I can feel the wind blowing in my hair,
They fly round and round and round some more,
And that is how the leaves dance.

Amanda Schwind

Elaine E No Tegami (A Letter To Elaine)

Although our lips have never touched
I do feel your words when we talk
They help me to know the joy and pain that you live.

When you tell me your dreams
I hope you know I dream them too
And I pray they come true for you.

We were never intimate
And this is not my goal
But you are more special to me than my lovers of the past.

I smile when I see the calmness of your face
Because I know it is just a mask
To hide the softness and warmth of your heart.

You give much more than you take
And I admire you for this
You truly are a special person in deed.

In college I only knew your name
I could never imagine knowing much more
Now I know you as my dear friend...Elaine.

Shawn Jackson

Within My Dreams

The wind blows gently through my hair.
It sweetly kissed my cheek.
I walk along the sandy path, beside a crystal creek.

The sun is warm upon the leaves;
It dances through with grace.
It leaves a shadow on the ground
That looks like ruffled lace.

I love to sit beside the creek and dip my toes within
The water bubbles o'er the rocks
And tickles on my skin.

the flowers grow in patches there;
They are a sight to see.
the colors are magnificent, surrounding every tree.

A robin lives there in the glen:
It chirps a happy song.
The music is so sweet to me; I listen all day long.

This special place I like to go
is filled with happy things.
I simply close my eyes and nod.
It's deep within my dreams...

Lorri Vancott

Par-For-The-Course

For Sandra - From Mother
Boating and fishing, beer with the boys,
   All his pleasures, not one of her joys.
With cooking, cleaning and children to care,
   Her daily chores left no time to spare,
      The children are grown,
      All needs are sown,
      Time now to be seen,
      Onto the green,
      No stops to go,
   Golf like a pro.
With patience and candor,
   the years she meandered,
Her time now for play, to their remorse,
   a lack of fairness, Par-for-the-Course!

Jeanne Barbato

Macabre Listlessness

Throughout the lives of mortal men she lolls,
Engrossed in that which heaven seldom cedes;
Requesting those with grief inflicted souls,
Consumed by exponential heart string needs.
She taunts and flouts in unrepressive might,
Resembling children mocking olden ways;
A likeness gained from unrelenting slight,
Antagonistic love she dares portray.
Although her force of will I cannot win,
My healing heart anew will now be filled;
For retribution I obtain from sin,
So shall her reign of careless slay be stilled.
·Afflicted by the channeled rays of hate,
My need for her no longer worships fate.

Robert W. Pretlow

Forgotten

In this land, we find ourselves
Long lost forgotten.
Our lives conquered by our allowance.
Each day, diminished in our "civility."

I go among the sentinels in the high country.
They are there, waiting to be called upon
   to protect and help.
From them comes my foundation,
   my sturdiness, my life.
From them I know myself.

The land waits for us to remember our connection.
We remember the bliss of silence,
How peaceful and at rest life can be.
We glimpse the long lost forgotten.

Martin Daniel Wittenberg

Wild Weeds

Tall an green, too young to scheme
So many bright lights, send them climbing to evil heights.

Seeking, searching, hoping to find a way back to
singleness of mind. Their counsels are in the mist
of them - oooh, but they can only turn and twist.

Where is the truth, where is the truth they cry...
we are held in bondage, locked in a world cold and dry.

The voices, the voices, traveling in the wind, extending
the invitation to our children to sin. Wild weeds,
wild weeds, take not heed to the voices sowing the
evil seeds.

Listen little children to the voice with all power,
who can deliver you, this very same hour . . . Ps. 29; Act 2:38;

Oh His name, His name, it is still the
same . . . Jesus.

Dalphine Cade

The Butterfly

Follow the butterfly to see where she will go, where and when
she will land, only she knows. Her bright pretty colors may
enlighten your eyes, however she is cautious and eager to rise.
She may flaunt about you and tease you for play; when you hold
out your hand, she will then fly away. Sometimes she will land
but only to see, what it is like to be stable, not quite so
free. Seldom, sometimes will she land on your arm, daring the
risk that you mean her no harm. If you were to catch her and
hold her too tight, you would hurt her wings and capture her
flight. Be gentle to the butterfly and admire her art, so that
the joy of this creature can flutter your heart.

Kelly Kovel

To My Best Friend

She is alone again,
he went away and she is sad

Each week they meet, and then she feels
as though some part of her wakes up.

But when he leaves, she dies her little death
again, again, again.

Sometimes she screams, deep in her soul,
"Enough with pain, enough with hurt!"

Her senses sharpen, and pain is real but then he comes . . .

Smiles and touches
And with each move, each look, each touch
She feels reborn, like little child.

Her essence brightens; she is charmed,
by loving look that worms her up.

And even though the words
that make the difference to her were never said,

She's filled with love
that makes it worth to be, to see, to live.

And when you take one look
at her, you see it is all she needs!

Karina Magakyan

Curmudgeon Though I Be, You Wait For Me

I think today of what will happen when,
Retired, later, nothing pressed to do,
Quite gaily, I'll annoy my wife daily
And sleep till noon as youth was again new.

I'll be a mailman later in my life!
One who whistles and walks by the flowers
Going through the trip with bag on my hip,
Flirting on females with all of my powers.

I'll look at the mail and see who gets what
At the women who get Playgirls I'll stare
Never ordering magazines again,
Knowing when Jenny Mae gets her welfare.

I'd get those black shoes two pairs at a time,
And wear my hat brim rigid straight across.
I'll chase the dogs that still show scary teeth
A growl of mace will show them who is Boss.

I'll take the invite to drink lemonade,
And lounge on all the porches I can find.
Napping in the sun as soon as I'm done,
Or day dreaming there, Uncle Sam won't mind.

Scott C. Henkel

Here's To 20 Yrs. Together Forever

I've given to you 20 years of my life.
I'm glad you chose me for your wife.
Through good times and in sad, and never bad.
We stayed together loving each other.
You are the sunshine in my days.
The smile in my heart.
How I dream will never part.
You love me in so many ways.
I hope to do the same for you.
Without you I would be blue.
So happy Anniversary to You.
May we be happy for always, and forever true.
May our Love shine together, to brighten our days.
And bless us in so many ways.
I will love you always.
Together Forever.

Debbie Peterson

321

A Second Chance

Growing old is a fact of Life,
It's something we must all do,
But when there's nothing to gain,
Living is no longer true.

Life is full of addictions,
Life is full of lies,
So how do we see the truth,
With no room to compromise?

Where there's sadness, there's pain,
Where there's pain, there's despair,
But where there's darkness, there's light,
A light that reaches out to care.

Life can be such a burden,
A burden I wish not to endure,
So I choose to think positive,
And give myself a life once more.

Life is too short,
Too short for a passing glance,
Yet it's so easy to ignore,
But worth a second chance.

Michael V. Rippo

Just For Charlie Mildred

I wanted to write a poem just for you.
I sat and thought.
The words wouldn't come.
I pondered. I strained.

Enjoying the sounds of daylight and
Emotions of nightfall.
I envisioned a smiling sun and crescent moon
Neither of which would aid me in my search.

There has to be a poem
Just for you!

On the day after forever
When you'd gone far, far away from me,
I found the words in tears and smiles.

I decided to keep the tears.
The smiles are words just for you.

Carolyn Foster

An Angel Born . . .

An angel born on a summer's night
Blessed this man with the gift of sight
I opened my eyes and saw the light
An angel born on a summer's night

An angel born to relieve my pain
Wipe the tears I cried in vain
I'll never again feel the strain
An angel born to relieve my pain

An angel born to help guide me through
To help me accomplish all I could not do
Showed the difference between false and true
An angel born to help guide me through

An angel born to become my wife
Filled an empty space in my life
I now no longer live in strife
An angel born to become my wife

An angel born to have my child
One day on my face will put a smile
For this I'd wait the longest while
An angel born to have my child.

Gerardo Gomez

Before You Came Along

Before you came along
My heart was filled with sorrow;
The days went by
slow, sitting alone,
waiting for tomorrow.

Before you came along,
nothing really mattered all of the time,
my heart was torn and shattered.

Before you came along,
I never believed in
love - but when I saw
you, it was heaven up above.

Before you came along,
every day was blue;
and now that you're here
each one is like a dream come true.

Before you came along
I always felt so cold; but now my life is
different, you made me warm and bold.

Maria Barone

Ocean Survival

In hope of surviving, I jump off the speedboat,
knowing the huge shark is after me.
I furiously pound my arms in the cold, black water,
I try to move faster, but it seems like I'm going nowhere.

Suddenly, I feel an intense jab of pain,
the shark has dug its teeth into my left leg.
As much as it hurts, I continue to the shore.
I start to slow down in pain from my bloody leg.
I feel myself sinking, drowning in the ocean,
I pull my head up to the cool, midnight air.
My arm freezes and my legs stop moving.
My black hair starts to drift off in the cold water,
My mind flashes my parents awaiting my arrival at the shore.
I can't let them down, I think, I'm almost there.
Out of breath, I chug along, my injured leg behind me,
Nothing will tear my parents and me apart,
As I swim closer to the destined island, I see faces in the sand,
My mother and father glow in the dark night.
When I come upon the shore, I'm greeted with hugs,
And I tell them what an adventure I've had.

Ashley S. Mitchell

The Bond

As time drifts in this forever wind
I sometimes hear whispers of you coming back again
When I saw forever it was in your eyes
Just like the heavens our friendship will never die

So strong and so pure this bond between friends
That all we know all we felt will never end
The sun never felt so warm as your smile did
And there was nothing we held or didn't give

More beautiful than all the worlds gold
More rare than rubies wrapped in silver bows
So perfect and new as every morning sunrise
Bonded by trust and caring with loving ties

It's a friendship never to be broke
As your burdens become my yoke
When I saw friendship it was in your eyes
Just as the heavens our friendship will never die

And there is nothing we hold or won't give
When with you there is so much to live
For because we know all we felt will never end
With this strong and pure bond between friends

Trevor A. Jacobs

How Are You?

So how are you now?
Are you okay? I wonder how you feel,
in time I shall see you, but for the time
I don't see your face,
think of the feelings you put me
through, close your eyes and carry
your ocean to the hole of mine,
and see clearly the black petals that
have been thrown on the memories of
you, feel my drops of tears that only
you shed on me, your impact of
words, put me on the diverse brink of melancholy,
but as always, the moon takes me back,
as to where the stars
shine down on me, and as you feel the
me that was, think....
How was I?

Ashley McKenzie

Seasons Of The Heart

Winter is upon me, the snow is in the air.
My soul is feeling icy, like no one really cares.

I long for Spring to come, I know it always does.
The daffodils and tulips lie waiting, like God's patient love.

In Summer, I will run and play in the days so long and warm.
Each day's precious moments erase memories of the cold.

The Autumn arrives - fiery beauty — the hint of a chill.
I'll plant the bulbs of spring to prepare my heart for love.

Kathleen B. Polo

The American Woman

She's an angel in truth, a demon in fiction
A woman is the greatest of all contradictions.
She'll take you for better, she'll take you for worse
She'll split your head open, then be your nurse.
And when you're better and can get out of bed
She'll pick up a teapot and throw it at your head.

She's faithful, deceitful, keen sighted and blind
She's crafty, simple, she's cruel and kind.
She'll lift a man up, she'll knock a man down
She'll make you her hero, her ruler, her clown.

You fancy her like this, but find she is that
For she plays like a kitten and fights like a cat.
In the morning she will — in the evening she want
And when you start to, she says, "Darling, don't!"

Timothy Gassaway

Untitled

I sat there staring into the sky
wondering if he was going to live.
I never thought I would have to say good-bye.
All I had was love to give.

He walked into my life two years ago
a sweet and gentle man.
I knew that I would not say no
because I was his biggest fan.

Our love grew thru the years.
He never left my side.
He even made it very clear,
that he would always be my guide.

I got a call later that day,
and that is all I have to say.

Rose Andrzejewski

Together Forever

Though you are literally gone,
you'll be with me 'til the end of time.

There are so many happy memories,
you used to read me stories,
you taught me to draw,
you were always ready to listen,
willing to help in any way.

Even though you have left me,
everything you have taught me will stay forever.
You have taken a piece of me with you,
And I'll never be complete again.

I look at pictures of us together,
and tears fall to the page,
but then I stop and realize,
that even though your body isn't here,
your soul and wonderful memories still are.
And we'll be together forever,
until the end of time;
until we meet again,
at the gates of heaven.

Amanda L'Allier

She's Still Waiting

She remembers how it used to be
Hoping and waiting for the day he'll see
All she ever needed the love he gave
Nothing more does she need today

She's still waiting for him to see
All she ever wanted was for them to be

She's still waiting for him to hear
All she ever needed was for him to care

She's still waiting

She's still waiting for him to conceive
All she ever wanted was for them to believe

She's still waiting for him to remember
All she ever needed was for him to be with her

She remembers how it used to be
Hoping and waiting for the day he'll see
All she ever needed was the love he gave
Nothing more does she need today

She's still waiting

Tina M. Busey

You

You said you cared
  You lied
You said you'll always be there
  You never tried
You made promises
  You never kept
You made excuses
  You always wept
You look to me
  You think I understand
You see, I am a child
  You are a man
You need to stop
  You need to think
    You need to put down that alcoholic drink

Jeffery A. Thomas

New Millennium

Homeless people out there starving in the streets
Picking through your garbage
Trying to find something to eat
The condition of this world makes me want to holler
We're killing our own brothers
Trying to hoard a dollar
Fighting overseas there has to be a better way
The children are our future
Will they have a place to stay?
Destroying what God has created
How much longer can you take it?
I've got another question
Are we going to make it?
There's got to be a way
To set examples for the children of today
Give them something to believe in
Renewed pride in a world filled with disarray
More positive adult role models to show them the way
Starving, fighting, destroying, contaminating, when will it end?
God save the world this new millennium

Harriet L. Hines

"Heaven's Most Beautiful Angel"

The snow was falling softly on the day they laid
her down,
On her head now lay a tombstone, no longer a
feminine crown.
The snow was the cause of her destruction, that
forced her untimely rest.
Forever she leaves behind her friends, especially
her sister, who was in fact her best.
Imagine all the heartaches her family will go
through, as they watch the children make their
angels in the freshly fallen snow.
And come to quickly realize, their daughter, their
sister, their friend, has left to become one of them,
to only be seen in heaven though.

Marybeth Clark

Untitled

Questions rotating like tiny soldiers
Marching to the beat of the blues,
Empty spaces filled with masked existence
People only leaving tiny impressions
over a hidden meaning of time.
Scars brought to life,
like the rekindling of a bonfire,
Leaping with determination
into the unknown depths of space.
Hoping to escape
to dwindle and finally extinguish itself
from our memories
and once again
fall into peaceful undisturbed sleep.

Debbie Haskins

A Dark And Gloomy Night

The night is dark and gloomy.
Not a star in sight.
The owls hooting are the only delight.
Mother reads a frightened little child a bed
time story.
While father listens very closely.
Rain will soon be falling.
The day that comes will be bright.

Kelly Greene

If I Could

If I could...
   I would be a child again
   And build castles in the sand
   And play in the snow
   And seeing Grandma, through the white fields I'd go.

If I could...
   I would rise with the morning sun
   And before the day was done
   Make mud pies and swing to the top of the tree
   With my favorite doll gliding with me.

If I could...
   I would run to meet the ice cream man
   And empty the pennies from my can
   And a banana popsicle I would buy
   To share with my friend standing by.

If I could...
   I would give a magical toy
   To every girl and to every boy
   Always would be the magic of childhood
   If I could do this, I surely would.

Doris J. Lacey

Are We Aware, Do We Care

Plates moving below,
Rifts on top, magically grow
The ground shakes, an earthquake makes,
Bedlam for all in its wake.

Storms from Hawaii come on land,
Continuously, as if on demand.
A veritable lake, even a sea.
Beyond understanding, for you and for me.
Roads, houses, lettuce, and grape.
Disappear, as if pulling a drape.

Blizzards roaring across the plain,
Causing innumerable aches, and pain.
They just keep coming, or so they tell,
Wind blowing straight out of Hell.
Snow to the rafters, roads are blocked.
Makes a person want to get crocked.

We are sadly amiss in our Devotion,
The living God is weary, of the notion.
People can exist, any way they say,
What is the Zip Code of Sodom, U.S.A.?

Emmett W. Johnson

Birth of Something New

In spring I sit waiting for the birth of something new.
Till one day I notice green buds growing on the ends of you.
Soon the sun will sit high in the sky and its
rays will make you grow to potential size.
In summer, on a hot hazy humid day I thank
God for the gift of your shade.
Enjoying the beauty all summer days through,
I feel warm wind on my face and hear soft
music the wind makes with you.
In fall days become shorter bringing morning frosted dew,
soon I'll be seeing beautiful red, orange, and yellow color
bursting through. Now all have fallen from your limbs under
skies of grey and gloom. When all on
one winter day blankets of white fluffy snow
will cover the beauty you and I once knew.
So for a time, knowing I will miss the
beauty in you, I'll sit waiting for
spring and the cycle to renew.

Brenda L. Glidden

Battered And Broken

Silent tears of a battered child,
All her fears, but no one hears.
Can't they see her bruised as can be,
no one there to set here free.
To afraid to say a word,
Where were they, when they all overheard!
Battered and broken, there was no more
hoping, she was barely coping.
Silent tears of a battered child,
With all her fears, and still no one hears!!
No one there to dry her tears,
And chase away all her fears.
Silent tears of a battered child,
Being left in all her pain.
For no one hears, they just close
their ears, and ever so silent become her tears.

Kim Taylor

The Hill

When you awake, what do you find?
A Hill ahead that is hard to climb?
And many obstacles are in the way
With the aches and pains you feel each day.

The Hill may be high but with each step we take
We are forging ahead for the Lord's sake.

Some are burdened more than others,
So feel compassion for our less fortunate Brothers.

Remember He's there when you're in need,
Your prayerful wishes He'll try to heed.

Make each day one of joy and pleasure,
And He'll give back to you in equal measure.

Eleanor Bajt

God's Gift

In my heart there lives a love
Given to me from the one above,
Sacred and true it will always be,
For to the door of life He holds the key.

"Go", He told us one and all
"Go and live until I sound the call.
Roam this earth wild and free,
Mould your life as I do a tree,"

"Make it strong and all worthwhile
And face your troubles with a smile."
Now, I hear His call from high above
And I turn my face to the one I love.

Connie Dalton

I Choose . . .

I choose to see life with all that's good
   To keep it as precious as it really is
To keep that glass "half full" and my "rose colored
   Glasses" securely on my nose
I choose to take joy in the "simple stuff"
   That so many take for granted
To watch a dolphin swim or a setting sun
   To hear children laugh — see flowers that grow
To treat people the way I want to be treated
   To live each day as if it were the last
   With no regrets when that day finally comes
And to know at the end of my life
   I may have made a difference
   Because of the person
   I chose to be

Geri Murphy

What Is It?

Is it a mouse in a wall, or a bouncing ball
Is it a train in the distance, with such persistence.

What is it?
Is it a baby crying, or just a bird flying
Is it a bear, that I see over there.

What is it?
As it opens the door, I want to know more
As it steps into the light and I'm filled with such fright.
I realize it's just my mom, and dad coming
to tuck me in and say GOOD NIGHT!

Ashleigh Kitts

I Want A Horse

I've dreamed of owning a beautiful horse,
With a tail that touches the ground, of course!
With a mane that flies,
As it touches the sky,
When she wins the race — whizzing by.
And only me will she look at and nuzzle,
With her dark, gentle eyes and soft little muzzle.
And to me, what I really, really hate
Not having a horse is a terrible fate.

Natalie MacNeil

Through Our Eyes Only

Possibly known by the many as few,
I see myself through
The light of the stars,
And have to ask why
In the lots cast for life,
We were the chosen to know we are here.
For if all out there
Inanimate be,
Where lies beauty
With no soul to see?
Save for some higher dimensionality,
Through our eyes only.
If so, mark us lonely,
For as twilight sets in,
Finite vision grows dim.
While the stars endlessly sprinkle the night
With twinkle of sight,
Yet destined, they see
Heavenly brilliancy
Through our eyes only.

Ronald E. Sherrod

The Intruder

I try my best to keep it out and still it enters in.
I laugh and say it isn't there and yet it always wins.

It enters sometimes suddenly without a warnings note.
Engulfs me like a shroud and tightens round my throat.

It fills me with an emptiness and leaves me weak with fear.
I don't my mask of pretense in hope to stop my tears.

I play the part quite well and few can really see
the agony I feel or hear my desperate plea.

It comes in different forms in any given place.
It fills me with a dread and sets my heart to race.

This intruder that I fear is known to all mankind.
We all have been its host, a prisoner of our mind.

What is this thing that takes me down into a deep abyss?
The intruder has a name and its name is loneliness.

Patricia J. Norvold

Virgin Love

Love forever lost in between the stars
it's written somewhere in time
but the moon blinds the eyes
to beyond the sign of Jupiter

Lies our unrested souls
longing for freedom but nobody knows
we weep no sorrow
For the lose of gravity has no hold
on these two hearts
they're too strong like our souls

Hoping to share in the sprinkles of light
falling in love like two falling stars
burning out of sight.

Ecstasy of bliss, forever being kissed
Forever in our arms, forever doing this

'Til the sun covers the moon
another sunrise with you

Two hearts revealed not concealed in time
we wait patiently our raw hearts pealed

Pure serenity at God's will
Our virgin love be stilled

Leonetta Milton

In A Catch 22

Down the highway speeding on through the night,
I search the horizon seeking you; was it right?
I feel your presence even though I'm alone,
The flower of love gone as though the seed never sown.

What went wrong that you should leave with no trace,
If only you'd look, you'd see the tears on my face.
Faster I go chasing the wind through the night,
I must see if I can find you before morning's first light.

You took my soul and let me a shell,
I must find it or see neither heaven nor hell.
Just a little bit faster and I will be there,
My spirit saved, but does anyone care?

I inch down the pedal it's touching the floor,
It's not fast enough I need a bit more.
You're just out of reach and forever will be,
But am I so blind I can't possibly see?

The faster I go the farther you get
And I haven't been able to catch up to you yet.
My heart and my soul were stolen by you,
And I will always be caught in this Catch 22.

Otto Martin Ludecke II

She Appeared

She appeared as an image, a silhouette you might say.
Always at night or late in the day.
It would start with a glow of bright golden light.
An amazing experience, a beautiful sight.
I kept this to myself for a very long time.
For society labels beliefs as if they were crimes.
Her images were so perfect, her advice so sound.
Her appearance and purpose had been justified and found.
She was sent to assist in every which way.
To guide my decisions all through my day.
When she felt I was ready, she would then depart.
At which she promised to remain within my heart.
Her departure was sad and I expected it would be.
But I knew she got her wings and would live eternally.

Ted Schreiber

Lover And He

Yesterday, yesterday He laid in bed
Yesterday, which was Sunday He was ask to go out instead

The choice to stay in bed was far too easy
His lover, now upset says, "just nice will you please me"

Many words were spoken that He wish he did not hear
"It's better this way," he thought but, of course everything was
now becoming clear

Not having much in common is beginning to take its toll
Not having very good sex well, that's contributing to the whole

Lover is very astir not able to keep still
He on the other hand is static he can keep still at will

He is content, anti-social and meek
Lover is the opposite not to mention elite

Lover's career is demanding, work of the plenty
Lover's constant business trips doesn't help matters any

Lover's financial means may not be hurting
Now paying for two is now becoming a burden

There is no doubt that love and he loves each other
Sometimes love is not enough, with that I guess
    who would want to bother

It might end up that lover and He will love from afar
Because they do what they do, because they are what they are

Erick D. Griffith

She

She is mine to have and to hold
She has chosen between love and gold!
All the joys life can give
Shall be hers, while I live,
For she is mine to have and to hold!

She gave me happiness - deep down within,
Serenity with each sunrise
She added success in each facet of my life
With love that never ends.

She gave me eyes, she gave me ears;
And humble cares and delicate fears,
A heart, the fountain of sweet tears;
And love, and thought and joy!

Nagla El Gindy

Amid A Secret

Look no further for amid you is a
    secret, maybe even a lost dream.
A once in a lifetime memory that will keep always and forever.
A beautiful sky stretching before you, A world of experience.
The most exquisite sunset, draped in glorious gold and
    dressed in the finest jewels and gemstones.
Flowers, an emollient lullaby blowing through the cool breeze.
What was once a world of security, is now a place of doubt.
Searching deep within one's soul, you may find peace at
    home and comfort in that peace.
There are sad stories to tell about a broken heart,
Or happy stories to tell about a higher rank.
To hope is to dream, and to dream is to continue a secret,
A lifetime commitment, a promise to never be told,
For to look beyond a secret means to destroy that
    trust that you once had.
A dream can be no more unique, unless found in a
    world united, that once stood divided.
For this reason, among you stands a secret...
A secret to never be told.

Kelly Makovec

The Man

I stand alone on the quiet shore,
  and watch the rolling of the sea.
The waves are dark and tipped with white;
  they're lonely, just like me.

For you are no longer with me,
  to comfort or to guide;
Where once I heard your laughing voice,
  there's just an ache inside.

You closed your eyes in sleep,
  from which there is no waking,
And left me with a loving heart,
  that I feel slowly breaking.

My life is just a gray day,
  that never seems to end.
But my sorrow I hold inside;
  to the world I just pretend.

Yes, my life is full of tears,
  and I know that I am sad.
For I know I'll never see him,
  the man that I called "Dad."

    Janet I. Shrive

Hope

  She sat rubbing the top of her knuckles,
mind blank,
pain shot through her like a thousand needles,
pricking,
pricking,
stiff,
sore,
knuckles bloody,
fingers bloody,
face tight,
mouth almost forced to shut,
body hard as stone,
was she a gargoyle,
was she a stone carved goddess?
No, just a prisoner of a very vicious disease,
Then her last breath, heavy,
suddenly, painlessly she was free,
Free . . .

    Lauren Schultz

The Fight

I know a special person
Who meant the world to me
She was a best friend, a confidante
Her smiles could light up a room.

She was ill, sick, dying of cancer
She suffered deep inside, but,
was still strong, courageous, and a hero
She fought the battle of her life
with great persistence.

You think you are ready for death
You talk to yourself, you ask
"How will I cope?" "How will I deal with this?"
It was as if life
Just came to a sudden stop for a moment
But when you think about it
After all of the suffering and pain she was in
She is now in a place of glorious wonders
I will never forget the impact my grandmothers
Life and death has had on my life
I only hope to be half as wonderful as she was.

    Jennifer Michelle Harrison

Anita

I've looked into the eyes of despair
Of love lost and her golden blond hair

I've heard that sweet song she sang
On every note my broken heart hangs

As the wind sneaks through the heath
I smell that sweet memory and weep

Her soul would caress and hold me
With distress she would crop and scold me

I close my eyes and think of her
On abated notions I twist and stir

I'm tired of dreams and wishes
that don't come true.

    Heath Van Fleet

My Seashell

As I gaze into the cone shaped shell
It attracted my eyes with its peachy color
Then it is like a rocket in the vast space
And then it is like an icicle in Greenland
And then it becomes a tornado from Texas
And now it is a regular seashell
And now it means nothing to me
And now I'm bored of the shell

    Omar M. Masri

One Of My Favorite Past-Times

Eight Bushy eyebrows.
Wiry standing hair.
Ears all at attention.
Like antennas in the air.
Large hands with long fingers stretching.
Reaching and grabbing for all
Hey! Don't take that one!
Oops! See, you made me fall.

Four little jogging suits.
Each one brightly colored.
Socks twisted off their heels.
Name-brand shoes, oh! Brother!
Jumping, tumbling, running, laughing.
All that happy energy.
One of my favorite past-times,
My Godson, my Grandsons, and me!

    Sharon Kay Henderson

Waterfalls

Waterfalls of life
Trickle and sometimes rush
Down the big pathways we live in
Picking up things that might waver aside.
Beautiful and so deep
Never ending
And if you open your eyes and can't see
Try opening your heart and you will find
Waterfalls of life.

    Michelle Burmeister

Nowhere

Welcome to the land nowhere,
Where they crucify the sincere.
It's the useless drag of another day,
and there are hidden thoughts in every way.

Fall into a deep hole of despair,
where thoughts and feelings you never share.
Then gauge into your reckless life,
and face toward you the useless knife.

All they can see is a frightened child,
one in which is a little to wild.
It's all the emptiness of your youth,
but no one else will believe the truth.

Just lost inside life itself,
took an oath upon hates shelf.
Eclipse of terror into the mind,
all lonely mistakes you will find.

Close your eyes now for the sleep,
but it's your fault if you fall to deep.

Timra Blake

Pocket Change?

My life, this time allotted me,
Is like a pocket of change
And loosely folded bills.
I have no way of knowing how much was
Placed in my earthly change purse.

Much has been spent in foolish endeavor.
That which has brought far more satisfaction
Was given unselfishly to others.
As Scrooge, hoarding it to myself,
Kicking and screaming for my time,
I loose it. At best,
It becomes only tinkling coins.

There's no room to be spendthrift,
Neither is it wisdom
To indulge only myself.
Me thinks it wise to
Give what I cannot keep,
Therein gaining that which can't be lost.

Leslie Williams

Jesus I Need You

Jesus, I need You, please don't let me astray.
Send Your Holy Spirit, fill me today.
Send Your Holy Spirit, send Him I pray.
Without Your Holy Spirit, I'll only go astray.
Jesus, I need You, You're my first love, You're my last.
You've blotted out bad memories, You've forgiven me of the past.
Jesus, I need You, I'll love You to the end.
You're my "Lover" and my "Counselor"
my "Healer" and my Friend.
Jesus, I need You, be with me night and day.
I need You to protect me, and to show me the way.
I need You, dear Jesus, Your kindness and Your love,
Your goodness and Your mercy, and the power of your blood!
Jesus, I need You, be with me to the end.
Without You, I won't make it,
I'll hit a dead end.
I need You, dear Jesus, I need You, oh so bad.
We need You, dear Jesus, won't You take our hand?

Sally L. Scherer

Country Roads...

A quilt...barns, cows, garden rows,
    pigs, chickens, geese...

A yearning to go home
    to the land flowing with milk and honey,

To places in my heart
    from days long past.

Days of sunshine, porches,
    and number two tubs.

Days of Granny's cookin' and
    charming chickens and finding ladders to lofts.

Days of wonder at each angle in a barn,
    each bend in the root of a tree on the bank of a creek.

Days of playing house in wondrous plum thickets
    with cousins and pretend friends.

Country roads...
    a yearning to go back to places from the past.

Places which are no more...
    save only in my heart.

Lavonda Vincent Mann

If I Were A Bird

If I were a bird, I could see,
    A thousand miles down a tree.
I'd look all around, all over the
    ground,
And wonder what all this stuff would be.

If I were a bird, instead of me,
    I'd fly all day from tree to tree.
I'd spread my wings high in the sky,
And for miles and miles, I would fly, fly, fly.
Until I was on a branch near the sea.

Oh, if I were a bird, I would
    try to sing,
A sweet and warm and gentle thing.
I'd park myself on a fence,
With two lovers on a bench.
And all of a sudden, their lips would ring,
When they would hear the song I have to sing.

Bessie E. Wyche

Sweet Song

The sign declared boldly, **TREASURE - DO NOT TOUCH.**
It was so intricate, so delicate, so beautiful that such

Desire arose, prompting closer inspection
of this curious artifact so close to perfection.

The crowd moved on, awed by its mystery,
But I lingered behind to take part in its history.

So detailed! So smooth! So that neither were hurt
I cradled it gently in the front tails of my shirt.

And the music began, angel chorus to my ear,
reaching my heart as I held it near.

Its light flickered on my soul to expand
and I felt the lamp's warmth in the palm of my hand.

In the midst of the light appeared a small door
opened, I knew inside was much more.

The art still displays with the same bold sign,
But I touch her gently and the treasure is mine.

Thomas J. Anderson

Life Must Be

And you told me it was love at first sight,
But like a rose fresh cut,
Its life was short though sweet;

For if your love to me was true,
You would still be here with me.

Your love for me has gone away,
Vanished now as twilight in the dawn,
But never will you see me cry,
For I must carry on.

Though my heart is set on you,
Your heart cares not for me;
And to my heart I must be true,
For life must be as life must be.

But no one else can touch my heart,
Not quite the way you do;
For should I search eternity,
I'll find not one like you.

Tammy Jenkins

Walk With Me

Walk with me through a field of corn
One hot, humid, mid-summer morn
The stalks over our heads, unfold
As we pass through a sea of green and gold.

Stroll with me through the fallen leaves
That autumn demands and nature concedes
They crackle, swoosh and rustle so
It's their last hurrah you know.

Spend time with me on a cold winter eve
As the sun makes way, a full moon to receive
A stage made of freshly fallen snow
Exposing countless gems that sparkle and glow.

Give yourself to me when spring comes along
And the stately robin sings its song.
The flower of love will born anew
In the spring as all growing things do!

Larry T. Carroccino

For Lucan And Clementine

An old man dressed in white,
Who hardly felt that winter's bite.
And sister too as young as dawn,
Their friendship everlasting long.

Never booked there was always time,
The apple never bitten to give a dime.
Many stories there are to hear,
If one should have an open ear.

And the rock has now been broken,
And now heard proverbs clearly spoken.
Angel of death once in the past,
Now guardian angel to everlast.

He was an elder yet just a teen,
With wisdom that could just be seen.
Her faith was bold and without flaw,
But not from what the gardener saw.

He knew it was time and left in peace.
She too went soon so her sorrow would cease.
And now together joy they still bring,
So listen at night and still hear them sing.

Alberto C. Gomez

The Jungle

The pounding of the drums,
The flashing of reds and greens.
As I pull aside the leaves,
It's not what it seems.

Natives dancing around a fire,
A humming deep within their chests.
I'm drawn into their haze,
With their brightly colored feather vests.

I am their slave.
The humming goes on.
It's in my head do what they say.
I'm like their little pawn.

I am to be their sacrifice.
They have me lie in a sand circle of white.
They pray to their God's,
It's to be this night.

Debbie Minckler

For Branwen

Touching an angel in a forest of oak
Watched o'er by the blazing lone pine
Coddled by the feelings of fire and of glass
And of soft sweet breath on my arm

Made conscious of passions so long retired
Encouraged by fear and with love
Forced by a need to reach out and discover
To give and to take and become

Awakened by a realization of truth
Who I am not, not who I am
And of what I can become, not what I was
A vacuum that nature abhors

I turn wholly to you for deliverance
Hoping to find peace in your arms
Hoping to ignite the same passion in you
That burns within me as we kiss

Pol Heiney

Coles On The Water

The clouds; the armies of the righteous
March on; no destination
The sky; a river of life
(Armies) Marching on; along its bank

The windowpane of the world
A crack in the clouds
Opens wide the gasping void
To the infinite blackness

The earth; the worthless masses
Work on; no understanding
The trees; a natural pyre
(Masses) Working on; despite the flames

The one sitting near the water
A desperate yearning
To leave his human form
To lead the armies of clouds

Kempton Van Hoff

The Bad And The Dead

A tree grows in the ground.
Evil men come and knock it down.
They kill anything that gets in their way.
Only the dead leaves of the trees stay.
And whoever challenges them always loses.

Jared M. Johnson

Differences

I have a friend. We are different.
She is from Russia, I am from America.
She has green eyes, I have blue eyes.
She has blond hair, I have brown hair.
But we are still friends.
   I have another friend. We are different.
She is black. I am white.
She has brown eyes, I have blue eyes.
She has short black hair, I have long brown hair.
But we are still friends.
   Don't you think it would be boring if all your
friends were only just like you.
Everyone is different. There is no one just like you.
Even twins are different.
Everyone has gifts and faults.
If you want to be their friends you have to learn this.
Everyone
is
Different!!!

Mallory Patrice Horejs

Mother Nature

If you were to look up into the blue skies,
What would appear, but a beautiful sunrise.
The sun and its glow, puts on a great
big show.
To my frightful eyes comes an unexpected
surprise.
As the sun goes away, soon coming is
the sky of gray.
Falling from the sky is rain sounding
like the roaring of a train.
Hoping the sun would appear, comes
a great glare.
Out from the sky comes a glow from
an enormous rainbow.
In the skies I see a swarm of
butterflies.
As the day begins to end I must say
that April showers bring May flowers.

Timothy Abrantes

Breathe

You were like me in my seat,
fidgety and uncomfortable.
Did you want to stretch
so you could see the world?

The one thing that kept you alive
took the gift of life away.

I'll never know you.
You'll never have the chance
to grow, to learn, to smile.

I cried when I saw you.
I expected you to open your eyes.

I sense your presence.
I feel a surge of tranquility.
It passes through and I feel warm inside.
I know it is you, watching.

Switch with me.
I have breathed.

Rebecca Beausoleil

Infinity

It's such a small thing,
and yet, you find
that in one breath, or one heartbeat
you can gather all the love of a lifetime.

You can give no more,
love no greater,
know nothing more beautiful,
than this moment.

Some would trade a moment
for a lifetime
I would trade a lifetime
for this moment.

Phyllis Remington

The Shores Of New England

   I stand and gaze out upon the ocean with
wistful eyes. I breathe in deeply the scent of the
salt air. All around me the seagulls squawk and
the waves crash against the nearby rocks. The icy
water of the tide swirls around my bare feet and a
cool, gentle breeze ruffles my hair. The warm amber
glow of the setting sun causes the sapphire billows to
shimmer like diamonds. All of this picturesque beauty
and wonder are what make up the shores of New
England.

Rose Arszulowicz

Dreams

Dreams take time.
Like everything else they require patience.
Dreams are goals in which you must strive for,
never giving up, and always hanging in.
Dreams are promising.
They are filled with wishes and hope.
Dreams can come true, but you must believe.
In order to be a dreamer you need confidence.
Never let failing keep you down,
Instead stand tall, be stubborn and brave.
Dreams can be achieved,
but you must be strong and rise above all fears.
Fate nor luck can control your dreams,
only you can make them real.

Kristin Kugler

Broad Shoulders

Time passes too quickly and I sometimes forget
to show you how special you are;
as you carry the weight of so many hearts' burdens
sometimes more than broad shoulders can bear.

You are charming and handsome, considerate and fair
with a wisdom that heals wounds of the heart;
your smile undaunted by life's little troubles
eyes dancing like stars in the night.

The friendships you've made are many,
gathered through time, year-by-year;
so precious the gift of love you offer
to those you hold most dear.

Tina Kay

I Am A Woman Of Color

My roots come from many lands.
I suffered from oppression under the dominant man.
My visions are clear
My hopes are here
Even when the way seems drear.
My thoughts are my thoughts and not another.
I have concern for my brother.
Laughter sometimes comes hard amidst tears,
But a still small voice calms all my fears.
Red and yellow, black and white,
There is hope even in the night.
My fight did not just began,
It happen when I was born a woman and not a man.
A woman I am proud to be,
Even when others do not see.
My destiny is unhindered by any force,
Because I chose not to boast.
A Woman Of Color I Be,
Alive And Happy And Free.

Dorothy Marie Greene

Untitled

Your old convertible rattled and creaked
As we drove down the winding
Country back road.
You said something funny, and I
Laughed
And I folded my arms under my chest and
Seduced you,
And you asked if I was cold.
The stars were bright, clear and the
Hills were backlit by an invisible moon.
I didn't know where we were.
When we parted, I knew you wanted
Something.
A kiss? An embrace?
You compromised with a slug on my shoulder,
Old buddy, old pal . . .
So, where are we? Most satisfying
I don't know, but I know that
I'm the only girl in America you've
ever kissed.

Randee K. Brar

Emotions Of Hate

Oh how I thought of it so well, whilst long I waited
Stuck in the hell which I've created
Hope and love seem so jaded
Respect and pride have long faded
The anger in me will not subside
The fear builds up inside
My emotions have no laws to abide
This is my wild ride
My senses are sharp I know this is not a dream
The voices in my head turn to a scream
I hear every whisper, I feel all the pain
If I don't scream soon I'll go insane
I realize my secret fate
As I go through emotions of hate
Now I must say goodbye
For in the end we all die

Angeline Moore

Pure Revival

Gently the river flows
Quietly the wind blows
Alone with music we drift
Empty days are the past
Moments like these will always last
Nature is hearing this song
She's shining down whispering words
Dancing and chirping are the singing birds
Fresh skies above are inspirational
No longer with precious time we'll dismay
These gifts unwrapped will be used starting today
A time of revelation
If only we can share
These emotions come from something in the air
The essence of life is in our eyes
The final note had strum
A new day has now begun

John J. Rutter

What I Am

I'm little more than what I am,
but not exactly what you see.
For I am more than just a man
I'm a raging sea.

A raging sea inside of me,
a clash of hot and cold,
A ship at sail to heaven from hell
the ship is my poor soul.

God bless my soul and keep it whole -
Don't let me fall apart.
Keep me strong and away from wrong,
and keep love in my heart.

My pounding heart is where I start
to feel for ones like me
For they're little more than what they are,
but not exactly what you see.

Patrick Chisolm

Flowing Forever

While fishing on my boat,
The water of the bayou rolls.
In this water, my grandfather once fished.
A tug on my line;
My fish has been caught.
I look at my fish;
There I see my father holding this same fish.
But my children are unaware of their history,
So this fish shall live on.
And this bayou will forever flow.

Adele Perrin

Where Did He Go

Where did it go, this man's soul?
Dead is the gleam in his eye.
Where did he go, this man I know?
Good-bye, Good-bye, Good-bye,

Will it come back, the lift to his chin,
or the heart for his work
through the day? Will he try to
survive by staying alive and
wait in passing away.

Where did it go, this man's soul?
Dead is the step in it's stride.
Where did he go, this man I know?
Good-bye, Good-bye, Good-bye,

Barbara Touchton

Good-Bye

Good-bye my old dear friend.
  I've loved you and hated you,
  though I miss you now still.

Just one cup of you was never my fill.
  I could not hold you for very long
  before needing more. You helped
  me close the door on things I did not
  want to see or feel. Although our
  friendship was long, it was never
  real. I would not see what I truly
  sought, yet it was always there.

I looked for it in you — to never be
  found. It finally showed up when I
  hit the ground. It was inside me, and
  my Lord saw to me and never let go,
  and loved me as I am and never gave
  up on me. He saw past you.

I've left you behind. I will never forget
  you or stop respecting you for what you are.

Good-bye.
  William Dahn Jr.

Garden Creature Features

Insects are the smallest creatures of all,
some are big and ugly,
some are cute and small.
Crickets, grasshoppers, and butterflies,
Oh my! So many creatures are flying by.
A snail as you know,
isn't fast, but moves so slow.
Polkadots, stripes, and colors that vary,
can make garden creatures look oh, so scary!
Rays of sunlight pass through painted wings,
of butterflies that dance,
and crickets that sing.
Busy bumblebees gather pollen from each flower,
as they wait anxiously,
for the next spring shower.
Each morning dew droplet,
offers a water supply,
to tiny little insects as they pass by.
How fun it is to watch Mother Natures creatures,
star in the latest, "Garden Creature Feature."

  Cassie E. Dillon

The Hudson River

The deep purple of the Catskill Mountains rise
to meet pinkish orange of sunset skies.

Apple blossoms bloom and Bluejays sing
as the Hudson embraces the welcome Spring.

Who can deny the glorious sights
of the diamond-like stars of warm summer nights.
Life is beautiful along the Hudson.

The orange, red, and amber leaves
adorn like garments, the Autumn trees.

The snow is falling all around
while its soft white blanket covers the ground.
Life is beautiful along the Hudson.

With the snowy cold that the winter brings,
we remember, soon again it will be Spring.

All of nature's beauty this valley delivers.
Life is beautiful along the Hudson River.

  James K. Bowers

To Lilac

I worship a purple woman
in her summer moon gown,
with frantic symphony of delirious language
through a gorgeous moment together.

From behind white mist
I stare at the forest vision of goddess power.
Let her tongues not want time to recall
the next thousand delicate springs.

My dream goes...whispering;
still seeing elaborate wind shadows
in a languid lick of light,
beneath cool diamond rain.
  Victor E. Wakefield

The Past

People think I'm made of glass,
They don't realize it's because of my past,
Can't you see,
That these thoughts and feelings really aren't me.

My trust was shattered,
And with that my feelings scattered,
I had to put up a wall of protection,
Just to keep me safe from rejection.

I can't seem to explain,
My feelings or my pain,
What once I cherished,
Has all but perished.

Uncapable am I,
Of those feelings I see in your eyes.
  Marisa Martinelli

Where Will I Be When I Am 73

The year will be 2015 and where will I be?
My creaks, cracks, and aches will let me know my age
Although my spirit will be free
Will I be hooked up to a beeper and a page
Or will I still be able to smell the roses
And climb a tree
Will my grandchildren be many or none
Will they love their grandmother
The world will be a different place
Yet still the same in many ways
I hope I am here to share the days
With family and friends by the sea
Oh, where will I be when I am 73?
  Christina M. Duron

Untitled

When the winter winds leave the valley
and there are new fresh winds on the way.
You start to hear children's laughter
as they play in the warm winds.
Now birds start to sing the warm songs
of summed and babies are born.
Now the world turns to a beautiful place.
Before each child goes to bed the
song of summer is playing
the warm winds are now blowing and the children's
laughter will never die.
  Emily Messer

They Always Said

They always said you'll never know,
Until you have a child of your own.

At twenty-two right out of college,
How was I to have parental knowledge,
A teacher in my own classroom of twenty-four,
Twenty-four children for me to understand, mold and sculpt,
The vast curriculum I am to impart to children who I do not know,
Then after ten months I must let them go.

Meeting with parents of my students I learned the most,
The parents enlightened me with information of which would help,
The children worked hard to learn, make friends and please,
While left undone were so many child related needs.

Ten years did pass and that means ten times twenty-five
  children a year.
Upon looking back it is all so startling clear,
The words I never could understand,
  the times when parents bared their hearts,
  the times when all my efforts failed, the times
  my struggles were in vain, no matter what it was always the same,
Until I left teaching to have a child of my own...

How true the words, All you parents understand,
  you know the moment your child is born,
  how special a job you have to do,
  the words they said were unjustifiably true,

Now I understand, now I know, I have a child of my own.

   Patricia P. Nolan

Confide In Me

Confide in me when troubles come your way;
Confide in me, let me help to make your day.

Regardless when, our what the case may be,
Won't you please? My love, please confide in me;

When things go right, and your days seem bright and gay,
Share your joy with my heart, for there shall you always stay;

Just how much I love you, sweetheart, anyone can plainly see,
Though, I love you even more when you confide in me;

All your dark days are just as dark to me;
For you're my very life, and always shall you be.

   William J. Hopkins

Hidden

Pondering.
Questioning.
It's an addiction; like the drugs.
It doesn't stop.
It emerges everywhere, in everything, every situation.
Need for answers, truth, meaning.

It brings ephemeral satisfaction which diminishes into
darkness,
sadness,
confusion.
It's a disease which liquidates any happiness.
No smiles.
Depression has evolved.

There's no escape, no more chances . . .
Once deep within.
To not know, not ask, is good.
Somehow this is wisdom?
What is wisdom?
Perhaps wisdom isn't wise.

   Patricia Bickley

What If...

What if the trees weren't green?
Would they look as divine or serene?
What if the land was wet and the water dry?
Would I listen to the land for a gurgling lullaby?
What if the rooster didn't crow?
How would I know when to get up and go?
What if the animals could converse?
Would they speak a splendid verse?
What if the moon didn't come out at night?
Who would meet the dawn and twilight?
What if the birds could swim and the fish sing?
Would the salmon sing as sweet a thing?
What if yesterday came instead of tomorrow?
Could we right the wrongs we owe?
Maybe so!

   Bethany R. Canver

Woman

Woman is a diverse, feminine creature...
Oh my yes!

She has many qualities
One would ne'er guess.

From the sureness of her walk,
And the set of her "jibs"...

'Tis fair hard to realize,
She was once Adam's rib!

She cries when happy,
And smiles under stress...

By gosh! She can be a most confusing female...
I must confess.

But she's the most wonderful companion
A man e'er had...

For she can draw at his heartstrings...
Make him feel wanted, and glad!

Chase away clouds of Doom
From the start...

With our little words:
"I love you, sweetheart!"

   Lorin John Hamilton

True To Myself

The night so dark, I could not see.
The day so bright, It blinded me.

My heart so wild, It yearns to be free.
While my mind so true, Knows that cannot be.

I need to be noticed, Yet still love to remain unseen.
Good and evil, I tread in between.

I may be crazy, Or totally sane.
Whatever I am, Or have become, I'm the only one to blame.

   Alan M. Pelt

My Clumsy Grandmother

I have a grandmother who can fall off of the bed,
Go around the corner and bump her head.
Walk through the house and bump into the door,
Step on a loose rug and fall on the floor.
When in the kitchen she's a total disaster,
In dropping dishes and glasses she's truly a master.

   Jeana Lyn Pryor

Sad Sam's Story

Seven salty sailors sailed southern shores
Singing several sad sailing songs
Ship swaying surf spraying sea splashing
Sad Sam shouted-start swimming ship sinking
Six salty sailors said stay sad Sam
Sing some sad sailing songs
Sad Sam started swimming south
Six salty sailors sank save sad Sam
Sad Sam's still swimming south singing sailing songs
Singing some softly singing some sweetly

Francis William Doyle

Sister Mystic

Saturn whirls   shady Olympus   scintillating stars
storyteller is born   scarcely morn
Sable skies   sabbath eyes   see and sigh
season's turning   stirring into warmth
Salamandrine fires   sanguine and subtle   serenely arriving
sprinkle star dust   stammered tidings
Patricia's hues   so close a connection   so full within
so dearly cherished   so longingly sought
Splendors unfold   sound, light, movement   seeing, listening
feeling, forming   subtly reshaping seductive
Saints, scholars, explorers   poets, mystics   evangelists
semi-precious eyes   speaking volumes
Silent touches   sobs, sniffles, smiles   soft whispering
scribbled lines   seamlessly linked
Shadows and shrines   souls unshelled   scenery divine
simple abundance   swaddled in song
Short-numbered hours   spellbound seconds   spent lights
speed the parting guest   smilingness
Silent bedstead   smooth caress   silver-feathered sleep
shadow, flame, breath   stamps Himself afresh

Susan Marie Printup

The One That Got Away

She walked in beauty with every graceful stride
for she was natural beauty personified.
She walked with an aura of dignified style,
her fortes were her magical charms,
her charisma and her dazzling smile.
To make her a beautiful dream in totality
Nature endowed her with a knock-out personality.
Although seldom indeed is such rare beauty seen,
into and out of every man's life such a lady has been.
With memories of her, every male will say,
"How could I ever have let her get away?"

Nasario R. Rodriguez

The Clouds Of My Life!

There is a city in the sky of mass proportions
at first it is as red as the flames of hate and hell
then it turns gold, like the most beautiful palace ever seen
but it goes through yet another change . . .
It turns white as if all the angels of heaven were there.
and all the evil was forever wiped out
it floats so majestically through the vast sky
it's as though it was running water,
flowing off into eternity and beyond . . .
Then, finally, it turns black, the darkest of death
with a slight outline of blue hope . . .
Again the next day will come
my life will be reborn
the clouds will turn all colors
and I will live forever in some shape
or form!

Ryan Fritts

Yesterday's Moments

What can you find from a family tree
Take a closer look and you will see

For there is a key that will open a door at last
To explore and discover the events of the past

The sun rises and sets as the days pass by
Remember yesterday's moments so they won't die

We may find our ancestors of long ago
They maybe friend or they maybe foe

And you may not be able to choose your genes
But you are the navigator of your dreams

So always try to do what's right
Strive for that with all your might

For when I am placed on my family tree
I want my descends to be proud of me

Starlene Ross

My Red Headed Boy

On the beach he would sit with no shoes on.
Watching the waves all the day long.

I wonder what he was thinking or what he could see.
This little red headed boy who belongs to me.

The twinkle in his eyes as excitement grew.
What he was wishing no one really knew.

In a moment he would be up and gone.
He could play and run all day long.

Then at night he would lay sound asleep.
Like a red headed angel without a peep.

His shoes by his bed and his dog in the floor.
I knew tomorrow he'd be out the door.

Another day to jump and run.
This red headed boy just having fun.

I look around his room and pick up his toys.
And I thank the Lord for red headed boys.

Teresa Christolear

The Lighthouse

The waters are coming down.
Your ship is still afloat, but on my face
there is no smile because you are still
not around.

I am still looking toward the horizon hoping your ship to see.
Hoping that forever you are not lost to me.

The storms have been rough and as strong as I have seen,
but I still love you with all my being.

Are you in trouble on the waters still?
Where is your ship, my Love?
Is there still a chance to guide your vessel
as your captain;
To be the man who spins your wheel.

Let me help mend your sails and be the man on whom you can lean.
As the wind speaks, listen... Hear...
... Believe.... My love is strong and clean
for only you.

Irene K. Cox

Those Good Ol' Boys From Rabbit Creek

Years ago some good ol' boys lived down on Rabbit Creek.
They were some of the best for friends you'd wanta pick.
Since then some have moved away,
And then again some have chose to stay.
Some died young and some died old,
Either way we sure hated to see them go.
So there will always be good story's told
About the good they would always show.
Therefore we honor these good men
With a few of those stories as often as we can.
About how they joined forces,
Saddled and mounted their horses,
To roundup and work the livestock.
They were always there to help, as sure as a rock.
Other times they would meet at the fence line
And talk for awhile sharing good times.
There are many more stories to be told.
About when they were brave and strong and bold.
So we will share their stories over bread and cup
And remember they ride in the final roundup.

Michael Randall

Sailors Of The Sea

Our sails are in the wind, we are back out to sea again.
For we are sailors of the sea and that's
Where we got to be.
We weather a storm day or night
Our ship gets tossed around like a kite
Bow up down ruff sea our ship gets
Tossed around, tho the sea is tuff but
   so are we, cause we are sailors of the sea
And that's the way its got to be
At a days end the sea is calm again
Just a breeze as we head for the Florida keys.
We sailors feel free when we are out at sea.
Just us and the sea that's the way its got
To be cabs we are sailors of the sea yes sir-ree.

Phillip D. Keele

Love Dot Com

I peer into the gapping hole of my solitude,
unwillingly open, allowing others to intrude.
Carefully searching the false, and the rude.

Endlessly seeking that which cannot be found,
through years, weeks, and seconds. Is this profound?
My endeavour for fulfillment, will not be bound.

I have gazed upon their words so discreetly.
Many say nothing, only one spoke so sweetly.
I pray it is from her heart, and soul completely.

Although I feel we may never be acquainted.
Her purity I hope, shall never tainted.
If we could, or would. Imagine the picture painted.

It matters not, her beauty to behold.
Of me she knows, for this I have told.
"The treasure within, is worth more than gold."

One can only wonder, or maybe assume,
had we sown a seed, what would it bloom?
A fragrant flower, or a weed destine for doom?

James William Ludwig

Survival Of The Fittest

Young and trusting, I walked through the jungle
where you stalked me -
scaring me with your growls and maiming me with your claws
Frightened and wounded I limped on

Defenseless and bleeding, I fell from exhaustion
legs numb so I couldn't run, arms broken so I couldn't fight back
I heard you returning for me

I crawled in a cave to die
but instead just lay there mute, shivering
afraid to go back out, afraid to stay in the dark alone

I played dead for what seemed an eternity
growing, thinking, learning - practicing a growl
I grew stronger

I remembered how cunning you were
seeking out my weaknesses and preying on them
Jackal. You fed on me.

Wise to the jungle, I stepped out of hiding
hunted turned hunter, but you were gone -
God help you if we should meet again
because it's spring, and I'm hungry.

Laurie A. Mielcarek

A Modern Tragedy

Day is done; Gone the sun
So much to do; so little has been done
The man on the street stands alone

They see the bright lights; the colorful signs
But the true hues of the city are seldom seen
The red of blood
The brown of dirt
The black and blue of destiny lurks
The gray of despair
All colors are plentiful but green; the only one that is rare

City of angels; no halos are worn
Again they pass the man who stands alone
He stands in the darkness biding his time
Waiting for a better place for his soul to reside
He helps a lady across the street
Then returns to his wishing place

The days go by; the nights get long
The temperature drops; the colors fade
The people go by one by one
They pass the place the man used to stand alone

Laura L. Gudbrandsen

Time For Me

She awakes early everyday
tired of work and life's problems.
Her time is precious
but she still finds time for me,
Late at night, in bad weather, or on short notice
she takes me where I have to go.
I have really never thanked her
but her warm smile shows me she knows.
Her lessons will remain with me forever.
She taught me the value of a dollar
and that hard work rises above all.
She is my grandmother
and I will always love her.

Charles Flippin

Untitled

Start with the oil, which is olive by plan
Add garlic and onion, plus herbs to the pan

Saute the mixture, 'til barely translucent
Resulting aromas, as though "heaven-sent"

Toss in tomatoes 'n mushrooms, 'n flavored "stock"
Simmer concoction, all to be timed by the clock

Don't ever overcook, 24 hours is sufficient
Listed on the chart, is there a co-efficient?

The choice of pasta, must be "Thy" favorite
Certainly cooked "Al Dente," to everyone's delight

On the plate, heaped astonishingly high
Pour over with sauce, don't splash in your eye

Cover entirely, with aromatic grated cheese
Exercising taste buds, down to one's knees

Include a sour loaf, with that earthy crust
Covered with garlic butter, a demanding must

What is the desire, to enhance thy "Spaghet"?
A fine vintage wine, like "Jug-Red" "you-bet"!

C. L. Wilson

Son

I kissed Alan good-night and bid him farewell
for Alan was leaving me that night
I lost my baby and was too devastated to see
the light that was within my sight.

On January 7, 1973
was borne unto the world my son
the light and hope Larry brought with him
we knew he was second to none.

Blessed were we as each year he grew
Inca mystique blazed in his eyes
thirsty for knowledge each year he grew ever so wise.

In 1977 he started his journey
towards his life time goal
as I closed my eyes the years flew by
it was '88 and high school now embraced him.

I will always love you and hold you dear to my heart
now it is time to kiss you good night
this is not a good bye
soon you will return a healer of body and souls
as you conquer your bachelor's degree.

Matilda Cabrera

My Nurturing Venus

With whispering eyes, I feel her,
A taste of beauty sighs from my heart.

A gift given, dear love received,
what gestures to warm my soul.

Her breath carried sweet breezes across
my being with symphonies in my mind.

As cascades flow down,
silky rivers cradle the altar where
windows to this angel's heart I may view.

As far as eternity, as brief as a breath,
I live and die a thousand years with one touch.

I will flourish.

Glenn L. Cooper

Raised In The Country

Mama was home all day long,
doing her chores and singing good songs.
The golden rule was taught in those days
and having no worries, how we did play.

Hop scotch, leap frog, rolling in the hay,
rock school, paper dolls, time passing away.
The old swing in the big oak tree
was sure in use instead of a T.V.

No electricity but an out house for use,
cold weather or hot no bills were due.
Cows were milked, gardens were hoed,
Oh! I stepped on that glass and cut my toe.

Swinging a chicken 'round and 'round
turn him loose, watch him fall to the ground.
You know what? That chick was drunk,
he couldn't walk straight after what I'd done.

School days were fun way back then,
jumping rope, hat ball and teacher joining in.
We drank water from a dipper 'till it was dry,
and down the dusty road homeward we said, "goodbye."

Mildred S. Boze

Beast

I lay singing lullabies
trying to comfort the beast from
within. O, stop calling me, I'll
not answer. The damage you've
caused are so vivid in my
imagination. Cries from within come
beneath and spread. The flames they burn,
the wounds so deep I can't see the end.
He rips my flesh and feeds
on my soul. My mind won't
conceive my thoughts for
I don't remember yesterday.
O, that someone believed
me. I'm deep within a darkened
child, no light, no hope,
no existence.

Krystal Bryant

God's Portrait

What is more beautiful than a bird on the wing;
A field full of daisies, or a bass on a string?
What is more beautiful than a mountain of stone;
A forest of Fall colors, a deer standing alone?

What is more beautiful than a full harvest moon;
A star-studded sky or a rugged sand dune?

What is more beautiful that the ocean's churning waves;
A spectacular sunset against the sky's crimson haze?

One thing surpasses all these in quiet beauty;
A life scarred by sin, transformed for God's duty!

A life once meaningless without fulfillment or purpose;
Changed into Christ's likeness, no longer hopeless.

A more beautiful portrait can hardly be found;
That reflects God's peace where love and joy do abound

Lanis E. Kineman

Love

Of loves there are many.
Some are filled with joy
Others, quiet and at peace.
There are the wild and free
Like birds in flight.
Romantic love,
The most glorious of all,
Brings enchantment to life
As though God has blown a kiss.
This love, exquisitely fine,
Like a gossamer web
Sparkling with dewdrops of love;
Now, fragile to the touch.
If nourished ever, ever so gently
Turning delicate strands of web to steel,
Ensuring life's most treasured love.

Van Klink

Words, Words, Words

What are words without a focus?
Are they more than what is physically seen?
Some call it vision and some hocus-pocus
But there is magic in the words of a writer that is keen.

What are feelings minus words?
Words are expressions of what is deep down inside.
Without words what would be heard,
Who would we know, and how could we confide?

Words can make a blind man see,
Words can cause an adversary to agree,
The most powerful potion known to man
Are words, just words, written down by a hand
Or passed down through a voice,
Mortally concocted through an 'Every mans' choice
Of how to express what he wants one to see,
With the right words anything can be!

Richard Cassford

Hawaii

The sun shines a fraction of the time,
As I sit with a Chuba-Chum that's flavored lime.

As the waves crash and break out at sea,
I observe a lizard the size of a pea.

In the wind palms whistle, flipper and flap,
One day a coconut fell on my dad's lap.

Outside it is hot! But inside with my fan,
On me I notice a nice golden tan.

As I leave the islands a tear rolls down my cheek,
I know I shall return but for longer than a week.

Danny Driscoll

I Dare To Live A Full Life

As I've lived for almost five decades now;
I reach inward and outward for higher planes that
I've neither seen nor been before.
Knowing surely there are countless blessings and
joys still to be attained somehow.

But, then I remember that to experience those
new joys, may ultimately lead me to new losses,
more sorrows and heart rending pains.
Oh! But again, I'm willing to take that chance,
because sorrows and loss can only come to those
whom have known great joys and been receivers of many gains.

So! I look forward with great anticipation,
as my life continues to blossom daily in new directions.

Joyce Beal

The Teenage World A Dangerous Place

Growing up as a teenager is hard
these days, like watchin' your back
and tryin' to be saved from all this
killin' and hurtin' everyday overshoes,
clothes, and petty lil' thangs.

Don't use hate, try to use love, cuz God
is watchin; you from above. Don't
play with guns and other people's lives
and especially kids, don't use knives.

Know right from wrong and you will be strong
when ya in a confrontation,
don't use harm.

Now all the things I've said today
ain't no joke, so instead of using
the choke hold on one another.
use the talk hold to get even
closer. Peace and Love!

Tiffany McDonald

The Great Escape

A hoopoe picked a worm for lunch one day,
He sat in a garden sweet and gay;
Shaken, the insect suppressed his scream;
The hoopoe went into a waking dream.

In the insect's mind rang a bell,
He began to mumble, then to yell.
Enraged, the hoopoe flew around,
'Cause the creature made a cacophonic sound.

"Sorry", said the worm to the hoopoe,
"My yell is all but rhapsody,
My speech has no charm nor melody.
Highness! Your voice is tidy and you sing so well,
What I present is merely pell-mell."

Puffed, the hoopoe burst into a song:
Hoo-po-po, hoo-po-po
Hoo-po-po, hoo-po-po
Which had melody and no note was wrong.

The wise worm fell off the hooopoe's bill,
And ran for his life to the nearest hill.

Manzurul Amin

Love Forever

When I saw her from a distance
I realized that she could be my next mistress.
Seeing her hair glow in the sun
she might be more then just the next one.
We went on our first date
it was well worth the wait.
Something told me it was right
her beauty was a noticeable sight
Her long legs made her my height
she really would be worth the fight.
We enjoy spending time together
no matter what the weather.
It was time to pick the one
I was praying that I would be her new Hun.
We got into the car and went for a ride
all along the country side.
Then we were back home
snug up tight without a phone.
Now we are together
and our love will be forever.

Michael Stephen

My Love, My Heart (The Wedding Poem)

Never will I deny God my first Love.
For he has given me one other soul to love
besides my own.

Our eyes which have seen the years of unsatisfied
charity, will be no longer.
The music your heart echoes makes my heart
resound with lyrics.
And the timing of our thoughts are like the
sea knowing the shores.

To find the mirror image with its own reflection
Never seemed to be a reality.
But with a smile that sparkles as a single star
and passion that rises from our bones
we have found grace, beauty softness and strength

I give to you this day, forever,
My love and my heart for your own.

Sistine Gardner

A Child With No Name

I do not live, exist is all
so a child with no name I shall be called.

Who is he, I have asked?
I am told he lives disguised in a mask.

Where is he, why isn't he here with me, I have questioned?
But only to be turned away feeling empty and puzzled.

When will he come to see me, I deserve to know?
I wish I could tell him how much I love and miss him so.

How is he doing, I really would like to see?
Does he have a wife, a girlfriend, or children like me?

What was his purpose in leaving me here?
I promise I would have been good, a wonderful dear.

It's quite disappointing and from time to time I am saddened,
to think I may never in my lifetime see this ghostly man.

I am one of many children that have to proclaim
Yes, I too am a child with no name.

Sheryl Anderson

The House That Once Was Home

Today I saw a dream come true.
And I saw it all alone.
I drove one hundred miles in the country
To a house that once was home.

I pulled into the driveway.
I thought I was alone.
But all at once I had sweet memories
Of all the love we had known.

I had the strangest feeling.
Filled with so many joys
I could almost hear the footsteps
Of our little girls and boys.

I slowly opened up the door
So sure I would see a face.
But in that long dark hallway.
There was only empty space.

I stood there in the door and cried
I was so all alone.
But I closed my eyes and thanked the Lord.
For this house that once was home.

Grace Tucker Butler

Grand Canyon Or Bust

I am a woman who works at the "Y"
And plan to gander at the Arizona sky

Although I am slightly older than most
I know I have to get busy and not just coast

Troy was encouraging by what he said to me
"It will be a breeze, if you do your
Sit-ups and keep bending your knees!!"

So I worked out everyday in spite of my years;
And endured all the pain—
The blood, sweat and tears

I am sure the Grand Canyon is one of the God's best creations
But I hope I didn't get myself into a difficult situation

My feet may get sore-but my sight will be clear
Pondering nature; holding things dear
A rock on the ground, or a leaf in my hand
I am sure to be amazed at such a beautiful land

But I hope a few days into the trip
These words aren't falling from my lips
"I am tired of drinking and eating from tin,
I want to go to the Holiday Inn"

Nancy Kowalski

Life Hurts

Life hurts when your father is one to leave
Life hurts when his love is hard to retrieve

Life hurts when you've been up to no good
Life hurts when alone you've stood

Life hurts when you try to get out
Life hurts, but you can't sit and pout

Life hurts when you've given one your heart
Life hurts when you are now split apart

Life hurts when you sit and wonder why
Life hurts when all you can do is cry

Life hurts when you feel you're alone
Life hurts when love is not shown

Life hurts when you're stuck in between
Life hurts when your cries are not seen

Life hurts when your mother says you'll always be with her
Life hurts, she lied and chose her lover

Life hurts when your mother is also gone away
Life hurts, there's nothing left to say

Marcie Erin Marvel

To Baby - Rebekah Rose

Oh precious baby, tiny and sweet
From your little nose, to your tiny feet.
We welcome you here with lots of love
and our "Thanks to God" from up above.

Your Mommy and Daddy, have waited so long
To love you and nurture you, and help you grow strong
They will watch you and teach you to know right from wrong
And with God's help, keep you from harm

The Joy you will bring to all of us here
Will enlighten our hearts and make us smile ear to ear.
Oh precious baby, our baby so sweet,
With your little hands and dimpled cheeks we all love you.
Godbless,
Grandma

Charmaine Mathias

Untitled

One day after arriving at my house
I turned on the T.V....
The announcer said:
"Act now, it's only $19.95
....$3.00 for shipping and handling"
So I ran to my phone, dialing as fast as I could,
then spoke, saying, "send me that wonder,
  that marvel of life,
   ...please give me your
   Invention of 'Armageddon in a bag.'"

John S. Szymanski Jr.

The Silent Witness

If I could speak, what a tale I may could tell
of brave Indians
who ate at my bounty
or soldiers of blue or gray
who used me as a hitching post
when stopped for rest,
My bark has served me well
Through the heat and harsh winter's cold
I have bent and swayed under the savage winds
But always straightened tall and bold
No one knows my true age, just that I am old
Through the seasons I stand stately
As if to give watch and comfort
To those who gaze upward through my leaves
I have been witness to births, deaths
  laughter and tears,
of many families throughout the years

Wanda W. Fox

Quietude

A gentle breeze whispers its path through
  fallen leaves then disappears
Daylight, once endowed with radiance,fades
Twilight and dusk ensue.
Stars adorn the sky
Moonlight, destined to diminish their glow,
  slowly prevails.
I sit and listen.
Mockingbirds mimic with perfection, a
  promise of quiet serenity
Staccato barks of distant coyotes soon intrude
  joined, restlessly, by a lonesome dog.
A confused cock crows twice
An owl hoots its displeasure.
Then magical silence as falling stars singe
  their trail across the sky.
Only then the faint laughter of children floats
  gently on the breeze.
I am content.

Vernon G. Higginbotham

Moonlight

Peaceful darkness lights the night,
  broken by the sunless light.
Moonlight rays cast haunting figures,
  though still the night in darkness lingers.

Through closed eyes the watcher listens,
  to the drips of ice that glistens
in the moonlight, tranquil peace,
  as if the night will never cease.

Of course the night will take its tolls,
  and cast its rest upon all souls
Sleep will come to all this night,
  despite the moon's purest light.

Thomas Davenport

You Say

You say time heals all wombs.

But after many years of heartache and pain
everything is still the same.

You say that things would change.
But why do I still feel empty.
You say that time will tell just wait and see.
But nothing has become of me.
You say you would always be by me and help
me through.

But hay you said you'll say a lot of things
That doesn't mean that they will come true.

Lakeya Sewer

Special Friend

Whenever I need that special friend
To talk things over at day's end,
I know that you are always there
To give advice and show you care.

Thank you for being there all these years
Through my anger, happiness and tears.
Extending your arms and giving to me
The love and strength that was meant to be.

I know that our friendship will grow in every way
As we travel that winding road each day.
I love you, friend, and thank God for His plan
Of bringing us together throughout life's span.

Linda Cooper

Time Will Not Impair

Some people always tell us
That everything always dies
But some things are eternal
Such as your beautiful eyes

Your brilliant smile will never fade
As we travel day to day
The beauty in your gorgeous face
Will never go away

From your stunning beauty
To your silken hair
There are many lovely things about you
That time will not impair

But aside from your exquisite looks
And your enchanting charm
There is a better thing in this world
That time will never harm

For as each day passes
And people pass on too
The most important thing that will never change
Is my undying love for you

Josh LeHuray

Untitled

Money comes and money goes
Each month I pray my account won't close
The gas, electric, phone or rent
Before I know it, it's all spent
None left for food or washing clothes
Stuff for my hair or pantyhose
It's just not fair, I work so hard
Still have to borrow, my pride is scarred
Another payment this month is missed
Tenth IOU goes on my list
Each month's a gamble, so I place my bets
In hopes that I'll pay all my debts

Milagros Suriano

My Imagination

My imagination is a great place to be,
because all I have to do is be me.
In my imagination there are many places I can go,
If I want I can go to a broadway show
In my imagination I can go anywhere
If I can't I can float in the air.
In my imagination sometimes it will rain,
but that won't cause me pain.
I don't won't to be a pest,
but my imagination has to rest.

Lillian DuBois

Love Is...

Love is caring, as well as sharing.
Love is when two people join together in marriage.

Love can make you feel blue, as well as feeling brand new.
Love is the feeling shared between me and you.

Love is a part of life, and life is worth living.
Love is why many people spend their life-time giving.

Love has brought happiness to many, and has helped
Many to obtain success.

Love is a word that should always be heard.

Love is just being a friend when in need.

Knowing that there's someone who cares and is ready
and willing to share.

Share many secrets, now all a part of the past, knowing
that our love is one that will last.

This is what love is!

Mary Randolph

Missing You

I fell in love the first time we touched.
I'd never have guessed that I'd fall this much.
Now it seems every moment without you stretches too long.
So I dream that we're dancing to a slow country song.
Being in your arms feels oh so sweet,
As we move across the dance floor to the two-step beat.
I whisper in your ear to tell you just how much I care,
Then I open my eyes to find that you're really not there.
I wonder and wonder what I'm going to do,
If I have to live another day being without you.
As the minutes pass on it makes me miss you all the more.
So I close my eyes to drift off to dream like before.

Corie Lund

In Awe And Wonder

I know I have always admired the beauty and majesty
    that is a tree,
But never so much before since now I am growing old.

The deep blue sparkle of our oceans and streams,
But more so now that I am growing old.

The white clouds wafting through the soft blue sky,
But it's a poignant beauty now that I am growing old.

Do stop and appreciate, in awe and wonder, this
    beautiful planet God allows us to share,
    tend and nurture it with loving care.

Then you too may enjoy its many splendors unfold
    and feel your own poignant thrill as you grow old.

Tama McCann

Mountain Peace

I behold the magnificence of Thy handiwork,
Overwhelmed with the kinship to my being:
    The joyful turbulence of the river,
    The peaceful murmur of gentle breezes,
    The stolid serenity of the mountain-
        daily changing with the time, the season,
        a solace, a haven, ever present.

Though I frolic in the summer of earth's goodness,
Or shiver in the winter of misunderstandings,
In the valley of Thy strength and Thy wisdom,
    Faith is reborn .....Life is good!

Lois Batson Rodgers

My Precious Love

As time goes on my love will lift
for you inside I present this gift
My love is forever and will never end
and so is this gift I'm about to send
So when it looks at you I hope you will see
what's really there is really me
Like any other there are two sides of me
one you observe and one you can't see
So look at them both as you read each line
and feel the essence that I have in mind
For I am no master with the gift of love
but know what I seek and search for above
I call on you now and sing you our song
to see if its right and if we belong
For I do not look in a manner of lust
but simply a woman I know I can trust
As I pass by and see you each day
I wait for the moment that you might say
With all your compassion you look for one too
So offer your love as I do to you

John L. Johnson

Two Night Candles On A Texas-Sized Table

Bridges and absences
Anoint persuasions
Things you wouldn't say are
type—
cast into flesh of alabaster
black

Look for the light and
cessation of precipitation
Look through the windows and the lowering plants

Ever have your eyes dilated
on a sunny day?

Where are the two pink tissues
to be used to out the candles?

Eleanor Dennis

A Cat On My Window

A cat on my window can be really rude
A cat on my window eats all it can find
A cat on my window knows no limit
A cat on my window out in the rain
A cat on my window all wet and muddy
A cat on my window is now on my floor.

A cat on my window can wake a whole city
A cat on my window does not want to rest
A cat on my window looks up at me
A cat on my window walks over to my door
A cat on my window now sits on my floor.

Elizabeth A. Embree

A Nightmare In Dreamland

It seemed so real and true,
But my fantasy was a dream and the nightmare was you.
I didn't miss your soft touch and your loving care,
But in my dreams it came back and the magic seemed to be there.
I loved you with a love that was pure
and you gave me heartache without a cure.
I gave you my candy heart and sweet soul
and you gave me cold satisfaction and coal.
I watched you, but in a haze.
Now I realize that you were just a faze.
I used to wish that you were still by my side
but now every time I look at you I want to hide.
You had taken over my life and mind.
When I think of you, grief is all I find
If you asked to go back to the way things used to be
I would think about the way you treated me.
Then I would once again feel that pain, that heartache
And at that moment in a cold sweat - I would awake.

Rajvi Patel

Life's Regret

Through all of my life I'll have one regret,
many nights alone I have wept,
a tiny child I had hoped to conceive,
for this chance my heart will always grieve.

To someone else a tiny life was given,
and they chose to do the unforgiven,
they took away your right to live,
of themselves they would not give.

You know there could have been another way,
if they had just chose to let you stay;
you could have been raised by someone like me,
I'd have given you love, you'd have been my seed.

There's no one now to carry on our flame,
my heart is sullen and filled with pain;
there's nothing in life that would give more pleasure,
than God's gift of life, it's the greatest treasure.

There are things in life we can't explain,
there are things in life we'd wish to change,
things will be the way they're meant to be,
this is just life's cold, hard reality.

Sandra Marino

A Dream Of Ingredients

Add a little self confidence and a lot of self esteem.
These are the main ingredients to starting your dreams.

Put in some goals, with a few limitations, the skies
the limit, with no hesitation.

Turn down the heat, stir in some reassurance now you
have something tasteful, it's called endurance.

Mix it well over the years too come, by being successful,
and then some.

By having all this you surely have pride, there is nothing
wrong with taking it all in stride.

This is all it takes to make a dream of ingredients
garnish it with prayers, patience and obedience.

Yvette L. Holland

Expression Of Love

Love is a beautiful thing created of many splendid things
As beautiful as a snow white turtle dove
Love was created from the heavens above
Love is an emotion that can be felt or spoken
Love can make the world go round
Sometimes love may never be seen or found
Love can make World War III stop
Feeling of love can be solid as a rock
Love is a bundle of joy
A baby girl or baby boy
Love is treasured in the heart
Or priceless till death do you part
Love is worth more than money
And sweeter than honey
Love is a kiss on the cheek
And God's gift for all mankind to seek

Lloyd Starks

A Myth

When we first opened our eyes
to behold the light of the garden
overcome by its splendor
witless in our bliss
it was enough for us
to bask in the sunlight
reveling in the youth
of our unblemished humanity

Then at dusk when the light began to fail
we cried out fearfully
for what seemed to be
the last rays of the sun
the most courageous among us
so moved by our terror
stole fire from the heavens
to comfort us with its light

And in this one act
the triumph and failing of our destiny was contained
we had never learned
to face the night

James Joelson

This Girl

I look at this girl who used to be fun
I look at this girl who used to weigh a ton
I look at this girl who was smart and bright
If anyone even knew her plight

I look at this girl and all I see
is a trapped soul trying to run free

I look at this girl and what used to
seem simple
is now just all a dream

I look at this girl who was full of life
but all that is gone now
and she can't get it back

I look at this girl who used to be
Strong and brave
but all she want's to do now
is run to her grave

I look at this girl and I'm
starting to finally see
could this girl be me?

Brianne Parish

Going Home

Standing against the reddish desert sky
His brown duster rustles in the breeze
Boots worn with time, laced over with rawhide
Blue denim shows thin, at places where they breached
A black and green checkered shirt that was once his Sundays best
At the waist a tired leather belt,
But a polished buckle does him proud
Hands large and strong, tremble with the years
A gold ring on one finger, a reminder to his heart
A crisp and dusty brim covers his once brown-blond hair
Lines like craters dress his rugged face
Now hard and sunbaked he takes a weary gaze
Blue eyes so deep and clear, you could look into his soul
Once strong shoulders now sagging down and low
Slowly turning to the setting sun, he bows his mighty head
Back to mother earth, who gave him so much life
With night fall he'll find peace, the final resting place
In her arms in heaven
With weathered lips
  He smiles
    Richard O. Wimmer

Unconditional Love

It's when you love someone from inside out, and
you know nothing about them or what their life's about.

But for one brief moment a long time ago, they
took the time to hold you when you needed someone
to hold. An left you with a feeling you can let go.

They took the time to kiss you, when you needed to
be kissed. The warmth an passion in that kiss is what
you long for is what you miss.

They were just a stranger that passed in the night,
but took the time to hold you tight.

They told you you were special no matter what anyone
said, and for one brief moment you believed him an
the loneliness was dead.

But now he's gone, but somewhere deep inside, it's
the unconditional love you just can't hide.

Just to think of him is all you need to do, to
kill any doubt you have inside of you.

So he left you with this precious feeling an memories
you just can't hide. That unconditional love down inside.
    Lisa Shuburte

Yearn For You

You are so wonderful
I just wanted you to know....
You set me on fire and melt me like snow...
You always lift my spirits...
Brighten my darkest day....
If only I could hold you in my arms....
And you would never go away...
I want to make you happy...
Fulfill your every dream...
So look into my eyes the way
  Only you can do...
The fire in my veins yearns for
a view.
    Jackie Pohehaus

Pictures

When you see a waterfall
you imagine it's a fairytale.
The stepping stones become your royal footmen,
and the water becomes your royal carpet.
The trees become your castle.
But when you wake up your in your own bed.
You say I was just Dreaming!
    Nicole Zangara

Christmas At Our House

Bells and bows draping the staircase
Stockings hanging above the fireplace
There's lots of presents under our tree
The weather is cold and they're sipping hot tea

Friends and family gathered 'round several tables
Listening to Grandpa telling us his old fables
A room full of laughter just before Grandma Pray
Giving thanks to God as we celebrate Christ's Birthday

While eating cake and singing songs
Christmas wishes are sent on the phone
Pictures are taken as we open our gifts
The love that's shared give our hearts such great lifts

Later that night after all has gone
I get on my knees to Pray while alone
Again thanking God for such a great day
You see "Christmas At Our House" is always that way
    Sheneka Bothwell

Grandma

The definition of "grandma" is unconditional love
They are one of God's angels loaned from above
They are unfailing kindness and everything pure
Their caring is always constant and sure
They're on your side even before they hear the debate
All in all grandmas are absolutely great
They love you for whoever and whatever you are
In their adoring eyes you're always a star
They always have a warm hug and kiss to spare
They are constant by your side showing you they care
They support you in every aspect of life
They ache with you through life's toils and strife
They are life's greatest treasure so hold them dear
They always listen with a compassionate ear
"Grandma" is a name better than all the rest
So here's to you grandma, the person I love best
    Jessica Tobolski

Ever Again?

The smoke rises behind me but I do not see it,
My eyes look only to the forest.
Its peace, its tranquility, I drink it in
The beauty of dappled moss soothes my soul
While chiming brooks erase the factory from my head

Will I ever again sit against the oak
Or eat nuts with the squirrels
Will I ever again hear the birds sing
Or watch the butterflies swirl
Will my life be with out this beauty
Will it be forever gone to me!

The adult world calls to me, but I do not heed it.
It pulls yet I don't come.
Paint is no substitute for life, nor brick for stone.
When the loon's call pulls me no longer
then I'll only be dust and bones!
    Kristina Sullivan

342

Take Time

Take Time to look at me
not my frown or grin
the style of my hair
or the color of my skin.

Take Time to talk to me
don't assume I'm dumb
just because I answer
with my hands my fingers and my thumbs.

Take Time to listen
when I need to talk,
don't just look away
because I can not walk.

Take Time to hold my hand
and be a friend to me,
don't think I'm nothing
because I cannot see.

Take Time to notice
that I'm human just as you,
and because I have a handicap
doesn't mean my life is through!!!!!!!!!!!!!!!

Diana L. Bennett

Discovery

Dawn broke today. The warm streams of sunlight, hidden
beneath the clouds which blinded me,
filled my being with new joy, new life, new desire.
My step became lighter as the soggy sands
disappeared from beneath my feet.
The gentle mist from an ocean of delight
hushed my doubts and fears and refreshed my heart.

In today's dawn, I touched the sun
and gathered a handful of warmth
to take along with me through life's journey.
For today I rediscovered your Love for me,
and its warmth resurrected my life once more.
Its eternity enkindled joy such as even distance cannot impede.
Its sincerity breathed peace into my soul.
Your love has once again set me free
to laugh at life and at myself:
Free to love the truth, and above all,
to treasure you with every breath of my being.

Nothing can ever stand between our need for one another.

And this is life...for this is Love.

Loretta Saladino Hastings

A Fleeting Moment

I had a wonderful feeling today,
like I could make a difference in the world...
but it faded into nothingness.

The words were there,
and I thought I'd remember,
but they quickly slipped away.

For a fleeting moment
I knew how to make a difference,
but then it was gone.

I felt a spirit inside me
struggling to break free...
but then it was locked away by the world.

I hope I find that feeling again,
sometime soon.
I hope next time,
that feeling will stay.

David Beatty

Paradise

Sparkling, silvery, shiny
stars;
Glimmering in the dark, violet, moonlit sky.
On a soft, still
night;
The waves crashing on the shore,
whispering with the wind.
Cool, calm.
Trees shaking, shivering.
All is alive, at peace with the spectacular blue sea.
A paradise.
A feeling of
Freedom.

Leisha Williams

Parade

My mother's hands, once comforting, lie wrinkled
pale and paper thin upon the coverlet
as if they have no life to call their own.
The thousand tears those hands would wipe away
are gathered hot behind my eyes.
My lover's step, once quick,
comes slowly now, unsure and stiff.
I search his face to find a sparkle
of the thousand stars that led my life.
Old images return
a tiny room, my mother bending down
to wake her child or smooth a dress;
a busy train, my lover's words
"Come, let me show you Paris."
I have no time to weep but take instead
my mother's hand to help her hold the glass,
and kiss my lover's quiet lips to feel him here.
Dear God, I'm not prepared
to be the head of the parade.

Natalie Babcock

Awesome

Hush be quiet and listen close
While your child sleeps you can hear his heart beat
When you do so you soon will see
There's nothing in the world that could ever compete
No such match for this miraculous feat

Tina Marie Sanal

The Forgotten Victim

The empty shelves spoke to the Soul,
Sending the heart reeling in despair
Loneliness seep like poison through the veins
Eyes alight with unshed tears.

A toy lies unforgotten on the floor
A lonely testament to past joys,
Hands tremble and clutch to the heart
A frayed shoe with laces all gone.

Eyes desperately seek a picture in a frame,
Forcing a smile to trembling lips,
Fingers gently caress a papered cheek
Seeking comfort from the inanimate.

Minutes become hours dragged into days
But anticipation mounts with the passage of time
Until a knock on the door sends the senses flying
Arms open wide in a welcoming embrace.

A whirlwind of activities is packed into days,
Fearful of wasting a drop of precious time
And just as life appears to be fine
The empty shelves speak to the Soul...

Annabell Mitchell-Henry

Clouds

Clouds are like mountains and mountains
of marshmallows from high above.
They're white, white, whiter than a turtle dove.

Clouds are white with some blue from the sky,
angels with wings go floating by.
Clouds are huge and great,
there is not one thing about the clouds that I hate.

Planes go by all day and all night,
but the clouds don't mind because they are so polite.

From the ground the clouds look like
different shapes and sizes.
Every cloud has a picture to show
They never tell you no! Go away! Go!

There is just one thing,
that is the clouds main favorite thing,
is to make it rain.

Clouds are amazing and fascinating,
they have so many jobs and they are so polite,
so look at them at night and you will see them show off
that they are all white and bright.

Molly Schulman

Untitled

He helped me dream.
Fire devoured my soul with each sweet kiss given;
Angels welcomed each warm embrace.
He enveloped me in powerful devotion;
In delicious laughter;
In love.
Then raindrops washed away laughter.
Tears remain.
His lies...
Stinging...
Became everything.
Aching loneliness.
A whisper of terrible pain.
Fear.
My trembling soul,
Defenseless,
Given but a tender dream,
Betrayed,
Cowards.

Heidi C. Rummler

Embered Skies

Luminous skies, embered clouds
Thunderous roar, to the flame that flows
Through time etched, carved
On her naked soul
Journeys a blink, a tear, a pause now it's gone
Out of darkness, its furnace aglow
Ever so gently, patient, touching the shore
All its rage, fury, spectacular blaze
The grace of birth, ones hearts adores
Waves greet her, rhythms fierce, melodic
Constantly soothing, nurturing the fountain erupting
From the oceans floor, rooted firm
Strong, engulfing, yet respectful
As it emerges in the early dawn
Smoke, sizzles off the surging seaside
Sun does reflect, echoes her mother's cry
Beauty from depths, none can define
Yet the heartache, love it implores
Still calling calling — deaf
She still calls

Augustine Montiho III

Then

Ten, where were we then...
Transfixed, caught in the spell of one another's gaze,
unable to escape each other's consciousness.

Ten, where were we then...

Lovers, untamed and passionate,
emitting pure, unadulterated love.

Ten, where were we then...

Dreamers, soaring the heights of possibilities,
eluding storms, defying logic.

Ten, where were we then...

Vines, flourishing, singular yet intertwined,
strength for the other, beautiful as one.

Ten, where were we then...

Fertile, our love tilled,
awaiting new growth, offshoots of our passion.

Ten, where were we then...

Exuberant, thankful to be us,
delighting in love's daily gift displayed.

Ten, we were there then.

Then... again.

Donna L. Camera

Octet: Dylan Thomas

What servant god has carved the naked howl,
Curved root through leaf to sculpt a verbing ram?
What tongue and fork with break have made this jowl
The breather of the drunken anagram?
In flooding dram, what nerved the seed and pinned
The verb into the wounds, made waking scars?
He's not mute to mock the living wind
That shock has cast a curtain round the stars.

Ann Robbins

Fear Of Death

I sit, I think, I look.
Two walls covered in glass
Small windows on the others.
Tubes, buzzers, alarms, machines.
A foreign place without heart
Breath like wind through the trees
echoes through the room.
Chill of death waits outside.
Keep it out, block the doors, cover the windows.
Seems to be a clean place
soap and cleaning utensils everywhere.
Foods rotten, sour, can't eat.
Odors of sickness, sadness, medicine.
People weeping, talking in horror.
Bacteria, virus,
Could this be is this a hospital,
is the baby going to make it.
Love, and happy thoughts, prayers to keep her alive.
Stay strong, keep going.
We all love you.

Tamra Solien

Lost Love

Engulfed within blue waters they heal their wounds,
By sailing a ship infected with faulty tombs.

Blind with lust they giggle and fiddle,
Under the unforeseen shadow of sweet caress,
Flying on an imaginary carpet of a mad princess.

They fear the narrow walls of fate . . .
Yet love slowly licks the cast,
As they find new ways to mate.

Compressed between thoughts, they slip to shore;
Dry and safe, sure to hate no more.

Now at land they must part,
Doomed to walking winding roads with a swollen heart.

Dry streams of sightless scream!
Grinding words with no meaning!
They are sucked by clouds of crying cream.

Lost in everything,
Strolling through the chaotic thread of sad lament
Which is to part in multiple directions with no end,
They day dream,
Asking to the mute wind: when shall we again meet?

Denise Karin Johnsson

Letter To My Love

Dear I loved you from the start,
I just wish we needn't part.
I had fun in those days,
But you thought of it as play.
I had hoped and prayed that you would stay,
But my wish was too much to relate.
So now you want to make it all the past,
The pain is great and will last.
Till one day God will seek me out to end the pain.
My tears they will fall like rain.
I know you never knew,
That one day you would say.
"I loved you, too."
"It just wasn't meant no other way."
I told you that I would go back to her one day.
But your pain will ease at last.
When it all is in the past.
You will find another love!
"And I pray that one day you will understand,
The way I felt about you."

Valerie Moore

Country Sunrise

When I wake up in the morning, the
house is still and quiet
I steal out of bed and tiptoe down
the stairs.
The kitchen is dim with the rising
sunlight
I silently walk out the door, to greet the
sunshine
I feel refreshed as my feet land softly
on the wet, dewy grass
I stroll across the misty lawn to
settle on my tree swing
I turn my face towards the ascending
sun, and watch it rise, spreading its warm
rays over the fields of golden corn as it lights
up a new day
I smile as the rays of the sun warm my face and remind me
that another country morning has begun
I turn back towards the house to join my Mother in the kitchen

Jennifer Marquis

The Lawnmower

Whence graced the golden dandelions divine,
and where beloved buttercup doth bloom,
amid white daisies dear and wild woodbine,
the callous blade with careless cut consumes.

Whilst whizzing, rushing wheels all rent uncaring,
with rasping sounds repeat the grinding round,
the naked lawn now like a garment's wearing,
a cloak of purest green, so bare, profound!

None pity petal-less stalks that spit, come clean,
or see their spirits' shadows shake the grass,
a shrieking heap upon the sick'ning scene,
in silent sorrow sweetest life doth pass.

The rites of spring bestrew a holocaust!
Is thereby beauty gained, or beauty lost?

Debra L. Smith

Destiny

Destiny is defined as one's fate
Paths we lead based on choices we make

Whether it's wrong or whether it's right
We walk into darkness or into the light

Remember the saying in God we trust
Living life to the fullest is always a must

Believe in yourself and the things that you do
The best things in life are waiting for you

My future is bright as far as I can see
Choices I make determine my destiny

James Norwood

Dirge

And then there was silence.
The bell tolled for thee.
Lying in the arms of death.
Untouched by the light.
Standing at the scene in confusion.
Finding comfort in the ones left behind.
Praying to the so-called man who is responsible.
Asking why.
Tears rolling down their own tracks.
Misshappening our future.
Destruction now lies ahead,
And the whistle begins its final blow
Before the incident is faced.

Lisa Ventre

How Long Will I Love Thee

Until the night is day and right is wrong
And the birds no longer sing their morning song
Until the thunder and rain can no longer touch the ground
And the end of the rainbow is easily found
Until the highest mountain moves as dust in the air
And hearts are no longer meant to share
Until the waters of the earth are turned to sand
And the stars above can be reached by hand
Until the sun no longer sets in the west
And the earth and sky are laid to rest
Until the end of eternity is all that we see
That's how long I will love thee

Chuck Clark

Why

From the moment we as babe's, learn to talk,
Our most frequent used word is, "Why?"
"Mommy Why do we learn to crawl then walk?"
"And Why do some people continue to Baulk?"
And some say, "Well it is all their own fault,
For if they could somehow learn to halt,
They might take time to think, about how they ought,
To stop an ask "Why not instead exalt,
Our Heavenly Father, Whom us He sought."
Then on that cruel cross He bought,
The price that all our Sin's had wrought.
And Not Even Once Did He stop or baulk,
To take the blame for which we ought.
So when your own precious child ask, "Mommy Why?"
You must smile and say, "My loving one, "Why?"
"Why, because it is my duty to my Heavenly Father,
For you to be told, showed and taught,
The Love and Forgiveness Our heavenly Father taught,
To all who believe he died on that Old Rugged Cross,
Because He loved us so much, Our sin's, He freely Bought.
Amen
Corrie Carson

Goodbye

There is a new land of milk and honey,
Where the sun shines everyday.
That is where you've gone,
Where the cares of this world fall away.

Follow the rainbows,
climb to the top of highest bough.
Leave your smiles in the stardust
and on the shadow of a cloud.

You started before us
on a new and glorious path.
You are a traveler now,
your soul a carpetbag.

Your warm hands will be there to greet us
along with someone else,
She too has gone from this world,
but not from my heart or my self.

You've both gone to a land of milk and honey,
and will be the brightest stars in our night's sky.
You were so excited though,
you forgot to say goodbye.
Melissa A. Faber

Tears For April

Trying to write with tear filled eyes.
With the thoughts of pity, remorse, regret
With the memories of a little girl holding my hand
  as a little boy holds a smile.
The hands of time have taken us down opposite paths.
Hers with the pride of a husband and three children
Mine with just many of life's tests.
Some of the tests not given to myself are given
  to her and are unknown to me.
She is dying and I weep.
The loss is unmeasurable and holds to no boundaries
No value to my pocket - but everything to my heart.
The time will come for her to rest beside Kenny.
Seeing this happen is unseen in my minds eyes.
But looking in my eyes - the tears tell me otherwise.
Paul Metcalf Jr.

Nothing More...

A sultry look, laughing eyes,
The smell of your perfume in the air.

A dream...nothing more.

The feel of your body against me;
A soft touch, a softer whisper.

A dream...nothing more.

A harsh alarm shatters the scene,
Bringing me back into reality.

A dream...nothing more.

But the images persist, the emotion remains.
All through the day...a feeling.

A dream...nothing more.

I smile, then feel sad.
A grin, then I get angry.
Because it is...

A dream...nothing more.

Then a decision, a feeling of resolution.
Another smile, and I feel at peace.

This won't stay a dream forever.
Scott W. Kniss

Faces

I sit across from them each day,
Those smiling, quizzical probing faces.
Glowing with anticipation of things to come.
Asking, sensing experimenting,
One after another they challenge,
No barriers, no fears nor hesitations.
Chalky white, mellow yellow, burnt sienna, ebony
Or cerise means nothing in their world.
Honesty in its purest state is what they seek,
To challenge whatever the future brings.
Not to one, but to all of them,
Those smiling, quizzical probing faces.
Silence sometimes follows their questions,
Not one of quietness or despair but one of
Contemplative desire, hope in its truthfulness.
Desires, not out of reach but based on reality
A search to make acceptance universal.
A light to guide their expectations,
Never to stop those smiling, quizzical probing faces.
Robert C. Warkomski

You're Never Alone

No judgement do I pass
Eternal love was made to last

All your troubles you may confide
God sent me to walk by your side

We shall never be apart
For I connect with you deep in your heart

I keep records for God above
With all of us he shares his love

I promise to help all I can
But faith is truly in your hands

I'll hold your hand through laughter and tears
Be your lifelong friend for all your years

...I'm your Guardian Angel
Kerri J. Incitti Walkinshaw

Afterlife

On this night, by the vague light of the glowing moon
I hear whispers of secrets yet untold.
I only see your face by the shadow in the room
But I feel your heart, shining like gold
To me it is all to good to be true
And I know you feel the same
But still I have my greatest dream, you
And you hear me calling out your name
In the night, where the shadow of your heart lies
I hear the voices in my head
And just as the last one falls out and dies
I realize that both of us are dead
That's how we are together now
In this huge world unknown
And now I know, beyond the shadow of a doubt
That never again will I be alone

Nicci Sprinkle

Time To Remember

He walked and talked at one year old
He was potty trained when he was two
His favorite toys used to be mold
But then he got too old
His favorite hobby was playing games
He would never participate in calling names
When he was punished he used to scream and shout
But he grew up and joined the Boy Scouts
His first day of school was very horrendous
His first Little League game was very tremendous
At his graduation you were very proud
But now he's drafted
His commanding officer is loud
He earned almost every medal there is to own
He died trying to save one of his own

Josh Ormonde

The Smell Of Your Body

I love the smell of your body, as we lay together at night.
The scent is always pleasing and on you it smells just right.
It's not strong or overpowering and is pleasant as can be.
I really don't mind saying that "you smell good to me".
After we finish making love, the animal smell is just great.
As we lay side by side, I think "I'm glad you're my mate".
The smells are all so different in everything that you do.
And it's one of the ways I can tell, that you are just being you.

Robyn L. Cornelius

Untitled

Death is the brother of sleep
And love is the sister of Life
Where is my mother, my soul?
For in her arms I have peace from strife

Wings of angels enfold my soul
Touching my heart are the lips of God
Pain and joy are my relatives all
They walk before and beside me where I've trod

Leaves of pain descend upon me
As the chill in the winter rain
Tomorrow the warmth of the summer sun
Enters my being, helping me to sustain

Little sparrow, cuddly bear and soaring falcon
Who fills my day with dreams of the 'morrow
You have given me the most precious kin yet,
Hope — the father who kissed my tears of sorrow.

Alana Negri

Sometime Soon

Lily white smiles
   travel with me for miles,
   as do blissful dreams
   and sunshine beams.
A wind composed song
   breezes me along,
   a grassy, forgiving path
   which knows no wrath.
It is an angelic trail,
   quite old and frail,
On my left, the deep blue ocean
   and its whispers of gentle motion,
On my right, gardens so plush and green-
   only angels eyes could have seen.
I freely continue on
   into a translucent orange dawn,
   where my tears and blackest fears were forgotten,
   and my seven deadly sins forgiven.
Time has stopped here, I do see
For my maker's crystal eyes have looked upon me.

Mary Thorne

Our Fight For Freedom

You captured us
and we came with a fight,
Is what you did really right?

You took our people to fenced in places,
We didn't have that funny faces.

Our sign has six sides,
Your sign has four,
But who really cares whose sign has more.

You killed us in many ways,
Guns, labor, hunger or gas;
We shouldn't have died first, but last!

Some of us did survive
But for the others, their poor souls died.

And now you are back,
We all know what you're doing is not right.
So like we did before, we came with a fight
and we will leave with a fight!

Michelle Gina Kletzky

Far But Near

Sitting here, alone
With you on my mind
Wanting you near me
Longing for your gentle touch
Remembering your sweet breath
Whispering "I love you"
The day my thoughts become reality
Seem too far away
So far that it almost blurs in my mind.

Sitting here, alone,
Scared
Caressing your picture in my hands
Hoping you will always be there
Waiting to hear your calming voice once again
Knowing that you're always with me in my heart.
Even though I'm sitting here alone.

Tammy L. Beacom

Untitled

Take me back to the times where
we would live with never care
the curious air and fleeting feet
the wills abound for the sky to meet
in every purpose, in every stare
our virtues true and thoughts sincere

How the years have changed from them
to only glimpse now and again
I can't believe it's been so long
Since I've heard the wind or tasted a song

With tired eyes we yearn for such
we work so hard and pretend too much,
for if we'd captured moments there
we'd always smile and never fear.

Christopher W. Maitland II

Entering The Light

Beyond the horizon, just below the canyon
There emerges a trio of wild horses
One of them a vibrant stallion
Dark and sleek as midnight
Daringly entering the light

I begun to paint a picture of extra-ordinary beauty
My soul is calm with serenity
What exquisite beauty to behold eternally
The splendor of freedom so serene
Captures my soul majestically
The silhouette awaken the moonlit night
There emerges a trio of wild horses
Daringly entering the light
Upon my canvas a splash of golden sunshine
Bathe each horse in a special ray
A moment in time is captured
Forever and a day

Latoya Jonee Phipps

Faith

His tender touch can be felt
Whispering words can be heard
Faith to keep as a token
The promises he has spoken
All souls shall rise above
Shining graciously in his everlasting love
Forever
And
Intimately
Trusting
His word...

Eileen M. Hanus

I Have The Right To Be Me

In someone else's steps, some people stay,
They mimic every move, can't turn their own way,
I am like no other, not my father nor my mother,
I have the right to be me.

Some try to make me like them, to control my mind,
Toward individuality, totally blind,
I don't mind a push or pinch, 'cause I won't budge an inch,
I have the right to be me.

Nothing will stop me from doing what I please,
I like to weather the storm, sail the high seas,
No matter what they might say, no one can take away,
My wonderful right to be me.

Parth Venkat

From The Porch At Dusk

Through wooden slats and rocking
we looked out.
I saw the orange road
return to the sky
its color and
I felt my smile.
I felt my smile
like the way you smile.
That was nice and
the sky is full with frosted clouds.
I can hear their cutting edges
clip by the moon's crust.
You are looking at that long naked
row of trees; a silhouetted
gnarl, of twisted lines.
I know that horizon by heart. It looks
like the hair nets the lunch ladies wore
in grammar school.
The school bus seats always got your hands smelling
like pennies. Tarnished.

Beth Krumholz

Back To College

The oil underground is nearly all pumped out,
It's hard to make money with cows and cotton during a drought.
A feller must search for some type of new livelihood,
Other than watching the sand blow, and cows chew their cud.

So you load the furniture, the dogs and the horses,
And enroll once again in some educational courses.
Seeking more wisdom and knowledge,
You move, to attend John Tarleton's College.

It has been ten years, but school hasn't changed much,
They still teach English, Math, Science and such.
But wait, they have new fangled machines that compute,
And Economics and Accounting - tough as a boot.

It's plain to see, it will take some time,
And some days it takes a toll on your mind.
But hard work and perseverance will pay,
With a proud feeling of accomplishment on graduation day.

Van Spikes

I Ask You

Hold me like you used to
Kiss me like before
"Can anything come of this" I ask
You reply "This and nothing more"

My heart begins to tumble
I can feel it breaking in two
"Can't you feel it" I ask
"No it's only you."

Why don't you want me
Don't you need me with you
"Don't you love me" I ask
You started to laugh "You think I love you"

"Yes, oh yes I do"
And with hesitance I ask
"You do don't you"

You reply in a whisper
I can barely hear you speak
You say "I ask you"
"Why do you love me like you do"

Remy Kole

The Storm

On the horizon, ominous clouds begin to form,
And droplets of rain fall from the angry storm,
Sprinkles splatter in the cool, dry sand,
Water deluges the unsuspecting land.

Wild waves are dashed against the shores jagged rocks,
Gulls take to the dark sky in massive flocks,
Upon a grassy hill is a tiny white house,
Nestled quietly like a napping mouse.

Against its small windows the icy rain splatters,
Creating a loud but joyous clatter,
And laying alone in a bed cozy and warm,
Sleeps an old man oblivious to the passing storm.

Aaron Mortensen

The Chessmaster

The game is on, two armies fight;
one is black, the other, white.
The pawns make up their armies' front rows;
ready to stop the approaching foes.

Both armies have two knights so brave;
they send one another straight to the grave;
the rooks or castles in the corners of the board;
there to protect the king, their Lord.

The bishops of the game, the saints of them all;
will protect their liege, if they must fall.
The queen herself; the most powerful role;
her mission, to kill every living soul.

The king of the army; the "Alexander the Great";
if you don't watch out he could end up mate.
The battle rages on until one side wins;
then the pieces reset and play again.

Jeff Hein

Rose

My tears fall,
Upon the rose you left for my broken heart.
Slipping perfectly into its own petal,
Like dewdrops in the early morning sun.
Your touch, was so perfect.
Your voice, was so sweet.
Bringing light into the darkest of places.

Though I am alone now,
I search my soul
And parts of you are there,
Chiseled forever in stone.
This stone is with me now,
And forever.
Where my mind and body go.

Diana Courtney Scott

True Friends Last Forever

True friends last forever.
Of course that's what we are.
We've been through thick and thin together.
We are always there for each other.
We're like birds flying south.
We get lost along the way.
But I know we will always be together.
In my heart that is what I pray.
We will eventually go our separate ways,
But in the end, we will hold on to each other.
And be able to say the right things to comfort one another.
True friends are what we are.
We are the best kind.
We will be together forever.

Tiffanie Kellner

We Are One - You And I

That day
I saw the hunger in your eyes
That I had not allowed myself to see
And felt the tears spill hot against my cheeks
And knew that somehow you were part of me

That day
I felt the pain within my arms
As though I too were holding tight
The tiny life you held and wept with you
And raged with anger - as we lost the fight

That day
I heard your silent cry for help
And felt the desperate hopelessness you knew
That we were worlds apart - it mattered not
For deep inside, I was part of you

That day
Lives in my heart and in my soul
The feelings and the memories have not died
I can't explain - nor understand - yet this I Know
We are somehow One - You and I

Elizabeth J. Bajew

Someone I Knew

When knowing someone all our lives
Our ignorance could not understand
That things we tend not to learn
Is most of the time given from the hand

I'm very sad in this life
'cause I came to love someone through time
For that someone was very special
Yes, was also special to a daughter of mine

That someone special will be missed
By those who loved her very much
We must realize she's now in peace
And that her smile brought a certain touch

Her gentleness will be remembered
Her thoughts will be carried on
For now she's in a place called "Heaven"
At peace and happiness where she belongs

Gilbert Minguela

Innocence Lost

To be young with the innocence of children.
To run free not worrying about the future.
To be new to life and its hardships.
Innocence lost to never be regained.
To play under the willow wisps,
   for an eternity of youth.
To feel the sun on my young innocent face.
Alas the lost years, ode the lost freedom.
But all should cry when the innocence is lost.
Oh save us Diana from our gone years,
   protect us from the hardships of the world.
Weep with me now world as a new generation
   of children die and give birth to adults.
Children of the world never lose your innocence,
   for once the world takes your's away,
   may the God's have no mercy on our souls.

Eric Brown

349

Death Is A Part Of Life

Behold the lilies of the field
Have you seen their beauty fade?
Seest how these flowers yield
To the ground in death they're laid?

Have you seen the bright spring robin
Flying through your trees?
For worms the bird does go a bobbin'
But from life he too will flee.

And what of the world's boys
Killed in the crazy wars?
They'll no more experience this life's joys
Into the blue sky their spirit soars.

There's so much death around us
We've seen it everywhere,
Yet humans beings make such a fuss
Death is for them - a horrible scare!

But death is just a part of life,
There is more to come soon after.
When this is gone so is the strife
All that's left is joy and laughter.

Joe A. Henry

The Pain Of Birth

Oh, Lord Jesus, it hurts so much
To feel the pain of loss and grief.
When all around this house his touch
For our emotions does compete.

A trophy here, a model there
A picture of him with uncombed hair.
A flower pot he made at camp
And soccer shoes worn when he was champ.

He never got to drive a car
So therefore didn't travel far;
And yet wherever he hung his hat
He made a friend or two, like that.

The loss is ours, for him no pain
To ever again feel the strain
Of one more breath upon this earth,
For Dustin's received the ultimate "New Birth."

David E. Benshoff

Never Forgotten

You gave this world a lot of life
You never stopped smiling
You caught the eye of everyone
Your spirit was admiring

In life you seemed so happy
As if you would never want to be anywhere else
Oh, but then you flew away like a warm summer breeze
Up to heaven everyone would say
But did you really want to be on your way

I know you didn't mean to cause all those tears
I know you didn't like all those ten-year-old fears
I did not understand then, but am old enough now
I know you hadn't left on purpose, it was just your time

I have never forgotten all those fears
But now there are no more tears
And I'll be loving and remembering you
For all of my living years.

Kate O'Neill

To A Friend

If you were me, and I were you,
  I do not know what I could do
To prove my friendship more sincere
  Than you have done throughout each year.
You cheered me up when I was blue;
  It's you I brought my troubles to.
A truer friend could not be found
  If all the world I went around.
Your friendship can't be bought or sold.
  It's worth much more to me than gold.
I think you're great! I think you're swell!
  I love you more than I can tell.
Words fail me when I try to set
  A value on your friendship, yet,
Its value you could easily see
  If I were you, and you were me.

James O. Hillhouse

Only God Knows

We're living in this world of Hell
Which way will I fall
Which way will my depression dwell
Will I fall victim to the demons
And do myself in
Or will I be a victim
Of a come up by someone else's Mac-10
Will I live to see 21
Or will I die a violent death from a gun
Will I live to see my newborn
Or will I die in another war like Desert Storm
Who will judge me when I die
Will all my people miss me, will they cry
Let them take me to my grave
In this world we're all still slaves
Living in this world under God's command
Who can judge me but that one man
So as we live and die
Stay close
And always remember God and live right

Cory Mathews

The Wounded Tree

My asylum's window o'erlooks a burial ground
where a single tree stands tall.
Limbless, almost to its top,
it still shades the graves
from Autumn's sun.
From a deep gash in its trunk,
it bled its life-sap.
Yet from its branches,
lifted up in prayer,
it lets fly a thousand winged seeds
hoping that one,
shielded from snow by a protecting leaf,
might grow into a perfect little tree.

Lee Roberts Durgin

Houses Of Stone

We gather in houses of stone
And talk of times that shall never return
Of stars that once brightly shone
With flames that no longer burn
Yet we are of true mind and heart
And though our numbers may be few
We hold the fire for flames to start
Lighting long dead stars anew

Joe Hartford

Impressions

The cousins have only to close their eyes,
And instantly, they're caught up in the past,
A past as soft as a Monet painting —
Impressions of their beautiful mothers.

They hear the poignant sounds of the music
Played on the little harmonica
Held to the lips of the youngest sister,
Her face a mirror of innocent pleasure.

The older two move to the waltz-time rhythm,
Their nineteen-twenties dresses
Swaying gently about their slender legs,
Damp, unbobbed hair in tendrils on their necks.

The daughters so briefly revisit their childhood,
Each with a vision of Mama, as she was —
In a time of spontaneity and youth,
Shrouded in a mist of enchantment.

The mothers fade away with the haunting melody —
Gossamer shadows of tender retrospect.
The cousins sigh, and with knowing glances,
Share their precious memories.

Thelma D. McKinney

A Trip In My Mind

A trip in my mind can be so siblym
as to;
radiate warmth from a sun unseen and to smell
salt air from a downwind breeze.

A trip in my mind can be so siblym
as to;
See gentle swells, that hint of stronger weather
flows from deep below the sparkling expanse of
green-blue water, dancing, it would seem, toward
the horizon's boarder.

A trip in my mind can be so siblym
as to;
picture the cove in the island's lee where fun
can be had and spirits fly free.

A trip in my mind can be so siblym
as to;
conger up joy when reality says I must stay behind
for I'll be on board, as long as I have a
trip in my mind.

Lois M. Hubbard

A Heart Breaks Too

A Heart is a special part of life,
It is the key to life.

It is the one that holds our precious future.
It is our emotions everyday.
It beats a little rhythm to keep us going.
It is the invincible one,
So we think.

When we love someone,
We become blinded by it.
It shows them that we will always care,
And keep them safe.
It mourns for them,
In their time of need.
It shines for them,
When they are happy.
And it cries for us,
When the ones we love,

Breaks the Heart.

Jaime Marie Walker

A Grandmother's Love

A grandmother's love is unconditional:
No matter how far you fall,
She will be there to pick you up
So don't give up.

She bails you out of trouble
But if you choose to ignore,
Your punishment will double.

She listens and lends a shoulder to cry on,
Just her love will keep you going strong.

No matter what happens in the future
Whether she lives or passes on
Her love will always be with you
Through all the years long.

Amber Mabry

Changing Life

When I was young I spilt my milk
I got spanked and then threw up.
Middle age I became
I saw a deer in my head lights
Times changed.
I didn't want to buy that new sofa
A chair would be fine.
My kids spill their milk
I laugh
I jump
I shout.
Watching them is better than TV.
A pencil in hand is like laptops over there.
A new life.
A sound beginning.
I can't go back.
I can only swim up stream.
Cooking pot roast can be fun.
A new day
I have changed.

Yoon Joo Mager

Unconditional Love

As I sit here thinking of you I think of those eyes
so blue- your touch so soft- your words so kind.
These things of yours are no longer mine. The endless
days together, the lonely nights never spent on the
phone. I loved you before and I always will. Wouldn't
it be perfect if you loved me still???

Jaime Sekusky

Modern Man

Man so high looks back upon the sphere and sky
across a continent with time enough for a quick bite and a movie.
Add the bill, subtract, divide before you can blink an eye.
Wall to wall
Hot and cold
Gas, electric or microwave.
Water hard, crushed or soft in plentiful supply.
Garage door moves up and down: Flip a switch.
Too hot? Switch cool!
Too cool? Switch hot!
Press a button. The whole world's in your Net.

Yet,
dirt, cool sand still clings.
Mud slips and splatters.
Food goes in, crumbs on shirt and tie.
Look back in times far, far in the past;
And...
We are just the same.

Kristyn E. Kazmark

Life Dreams

With sun in my face and thoughts of life faith
I take a breath of fresh air, and wait
Getting through one day
Hoping for another.

It isn't hard to see what this broken heart has done
to me
I stood tall and refused to fall
When it felt there was nothing left at all.

I close my eyes and count to three
To say "oh please this isn't me"
Life goes on, not always fair
Sure would be nice if someone was there.

Long walks, silent cries
With memories of those loving times
Not enough blue skies
Hoping for one more try.

It isn't hard to see what this broken heart
has done to me.
I stood tall and got through it all
Refused to fall and opened life's doors.

Debbie Henderson

Out The Window

As my heart does it beat,
the time does go by,
cars pass on the street
I let out a soft sigh.

She asks of a number, that I do not know,
she asks of this number, as I look at the snow,
the snow does not talk, and ask things of me.
the snow does not need to because it can see

See what is meant, by the things that are done,
the snow does not need, words to have fun,
they do their job without any fear,
they fall from the sky which was once clear.

They have faith in the whole, that lives in the sky,
he is the soul of people when they die,
he lets the snow fall as the children all play,
they giggle and laugh, as the snow falls all day.

My heart does it beat,
as the time does go by,
cars pass on the street,
I let out a soft sigh,

Sabrina Layton McCabe

Blinded By The Truth

We refuse to open our eyes,
The fear we face is far too great to erase,
This fear is the truth.
We close our eyes tight,
Afraid of what we might see,
For the real truth is calling out to you and me.
Curiosity burns inside,
Longing to be set free,
Stubbornness stands in the way of true reality.
Our minds are blocked, our eyes bolted shut,
Fear steps in the way,
Curiosity takes over me.
I must open my mind and my heart,
And push aside stubbornness,
But to my surprise there was everything I already knew.

Denique J. Morris

Far From Soe

Thin could not describe the man it seemed too soft
for there was only skin strung taut on a frame
draped in cloth oily with threads near transparent.

His walk mimicked a glide
pavement hot — with perhaps
no sensation through his leathery soles
hardened with time and purposes unknown.

To return to Soe was all he asked
and even that was hard
2000 rupiah
for his remaining pride
denied even a photo
least it carried his remains abroad.

His fear of a riding memory
going higher toward Soe
where he felt he should be
could not defy his knowledge
that the tug of the red soil
was growing stronger everyday

Thomas C. Cope

Tribute

I saw so many empty barns along the way.
Where horses once stood and ate their hay.
They plowed the fields and mowed the hay.
And played at the end of the day.
Oh to see the horses in the fields to graze.
And to think back to what they have done.
You'd be amazed.
And the cowboy that set in the saddle,
The horses help herd the cattle.
They were warriors in our wars.
And the duties they done was by the scores.
To them we should be so grateful,
They're friends that are so faithful.
They're like old soldiers, they never die.
They just fade away.
Where would we be if it weren't for them.
Just let them run free and live.
For we owe it to them.

Dolores K. Guffey

Goodbye

Well here I am on this dark and gloomy day
Still wondering why life has to be this way
Day in and day out
We wonder what it's all about
Only to find that in the end
God chooses his own unique trend
But helps our hearts heal and mend.
He decides when it's time for us to go
And how he does this we'll never know
For now my stomach is the bottomless pit
Where my lonely heart could desperately fit
Because I am tired of the time
When not saying goodbye is an awful crime.

Kelly Boyd

The Place

The far mountains holds the place. The place that I alone know.
The place where I laugh and live. All alone am I...
This place were I stand looking upon the animals that scurry.
I know that I shall never leave in a hurry,
This place I have found, I have lost for now.
But it will return I know.

Betsy Logan

352

Truly Blessed

I often think of that lonely road, the misery,
the pain that seldom showed.
My dreams, my wishes all were crushed,
all because I wanted a rush.
Not thinking that one day I could die,
the months, the years went racing by.
Before I knew it, the time had gone.
I had no wish to carry on.
When in defeat, I sought His face, a way of
escape, to leave this place,
In the midst of darkness,
there was light, a passion, a burning, a will
to fight.
I gave my life to him above,
I was filled with hope and God's great love.
Now I know that in God there is rest.

I am very thankful and truly blessed.

Kayla Spears Walker

Does He Know You

The Lord gave me shelter, the Lord gave me wings.
I have not the need for material things.
He gave me his love, salvation too!
I gave him my heart, and said, how do you do?
Now he walks along with me, every day,
And by his side, always, I'll stay.
You may think that this is just another story.
I tell you the truth, I give him the glory!
He gives me strength, in my time of need.
Yes he is in me, yes in me indeed!
I am a man, not of fortune or fame.
I'm just a man, I am what I claim!
But the Lord knows my heart, he know that it's true.
So tell me my friend, does God know you?
To the kingdom of heaven, can you enter in?
You can not go there, if you practice sin!
These words the Lord gave, that you might see.
He gave up his life, for both you, and for me.

Carl Tapp

He Beckons

In creation God speaks, His sweet voice we hear,
Saying "Come my dear children, come and draw near".
We find him in forests, in ditches, on hills.
He beckons, he bids us, he comforts, he fills.

From a soft summer field of white Queen Anne's Lace,
Comes his whisper "Grow with me in beauty and grace".
And as green leaves of August turn crimson and fall,
His voice murmurs "Change comes, but trust me for all."

He waits in each tree-covered hollow or glen,
Bidding "Come rest with me, your companion and friend".
From the ocean's expanse in great wisdom he speaks
To the longing we feel saying "Tis I you seek".

Great blessings burst forth from rich fertile fields,
From seed and black earth his bounty he yields.
And amidst the tall trees and birds bright with song,
We hear "Fear not, be like them, to me you belong".

God's presence we sense when in splendor and light,
He grants sunsets and full moons and wild geese in flight.
How amazing his love, how he longs for our all,
May we humbly and joyfully follow his call.

Lou Gallagher

Heaven's Gate

I had a conversation just the other day
with my father about heaven's gate
will I pass through to the other side
after knowing how very hard I tried
to do your will in all things
will I hear the angels sing
you've given me so much right from the start
touching me deeply in the heart
I look forward to every day
knowing you will guide me along the way
I feel good having done my very best
when the time comes for me to rest
my father assured me that all this is true
I will go with him feeling brand new

Serena Mattox-Freeman

Winters Past

How the winter can be so long and cold,
I fear it will never end;
my love for you only grows stronger as we get old.
I am living each day to my fullest content,
Life is short;
Our love grows stronger everyday that's sent.
Leaves are turning green again,
Changes in the weather outside;
Summers warmth is where our love will begin.
The years come and go all to fast,
Fading in and out;
We find our love now only in the past.

Staci Morgan

Daybreak, Nightfall

Daytime is nice, warm, and pretty
Birds fly by, animals are active
Humans walk, talk, and have fun
Soon night falls and darkness appears

Nighttime is nice,
All dark and motionless,
It's creepy and sleepy when nothing goes on.
It's lifeless and yet,
There are motions now and then.
In that weird, creepy darkness called night.

Whether you like day or night better,
That doesn't matter to anyone but yourself.

Jen Randall

Look Up And Know

Look up, look up and know;
When the dark clouds loom and the sun shines darkly.
Look up, look up and know;
When there's no one besides you.
Look up, look up and know;
When silence is all around you.
Look up, look up and know;
When the sun ray crest you.
Look up, look up and know;
When the sun's directly over head,
that you're in a circle of hope.

Barbara B. Miles Jackson

Night Dreams

While looking towards a far off town
With the full moon shining down
And the stars that brightly glow
While the breeze does gently flow,
I saw the night speed on its way
And I heard someone say
'Tis time for bed and not for dreams
Too soon will the sun be giving its beams.

But as I lingered on
The voice and echo both had gone,
And far below, lights disappeared
The depth of night enfolding me:
Then down I came from my magic spell,
To wonder if I'd always see
The night, with all its mystery!

Edna L. Demler

Don't Cry When I Am Gone

Don't cry when I am gone.
I want to live on and on.
Don't put my pictures away.
In your world, I want to stay.
Death comes to us all,
And when I travel that hall,
Don't grieve because my body is no longer here.
My spirit will always be near.
Don't forget my words and my face,
And I'll be with you no matter the place.
Remember the mistakes I have made,
So you want make some of the same.
Keep my memory in your heart.
Keep it and never part.
Don't let it fade through the years.
Don't fail to keep me near.
I want to be remembered when I am gone.
I want to live on and on.

Kimberly Schriver

Just Open Your Eyes And See

Just open your eyes and see
What's inside of you and me.
Sometimes sad, sometimes happy,
Sometimes we all see things differently.

Just open your eyes and see,
How the world was meant to be.
A place full of people, happy and friendly,
No fighting or hurting or being ugly.

Just open your eyes and see
All the ways we are free.
Free to talk, free to pray,
Free to be you and me,
Free to see what we can be.

Just open your eyes and see.
Not all things are what they seem to be.
We are all just more than he or she,
On that I think we all agree.

Ross Freeman

Perfume Love

Perfume is like a bed full
of Roses, Tulips and Lilies smell so
good you'll want too become a silky
flowers too. You'll grow strong and
healthy to become the most gorgeous flower
in the garden.

Jennifer Richardson

His Love

Life upon the sand was all I ever knew,
Building castles as my shelter: Seeking not
a strength around me when the tempest blew
Footprints of others I soon forgot,
And my weakness made it hard to bear
Kindness, slowly washed away in the tide
Of lonely time. Seasons changed, but the care
for brother, sister I found not: I cried
Out in murmur, wanting to be heard
Yet clinging to my aged walls of sand
He listened, He knew, without voice, a word:
Love complete and free I now understand;

As I give up my will, my problems each day,
He leads on, blows my castles away.

David A. Wood

Sonnet

Empowered by truth the multitudes sing
As one clear voice they penetrate the night
Soaring, ascending to heavenly heights
Pure harmonies linger and sweet dreams bring.

As servants they labor praising the King
As soldiers they battle claiming the fight
Shining, combining as torches they light
The flames spark change; weary souls they do sting

Passion transmuted to beauty a'flight
Renders man's soul convicted with sorrow
Oh, radiant voice, your melodies raise
The song of humanity's wrong turned right!
Glory to Him who ordains our 'morrows,
Gives purpose our psalms, and reason our praise.

J. Wilcove

Nature's Earth

You have one life, try new things.
It does not matter, try it all.
There are a lot of different people, different weather,
Different times, it never stops.
Only one childhood, enjoy it.
Cherish thoughts and happy moments.
It never stops, never.
Cherish love, smiles.
A different, never stopping world.
Enjoy it, enjoy it all.
Times are different, always changing, always changing.
All yours, ours, everyone's, everyone's world.
Don't stop now, never stop, never.
Love for you and me and everyone.

Sarah Cohen

Untitled

And darkness reins upon the land,
the evil ones are close at hand
the cows and lambs are full of fear.
Birds are quiet because of things they hear.
And all is silent, for they have come near.
The ones that don't die, who live for the ages.
Who's presence brings terror to the brave.
Who's voice turns the strong into weaklings.
Who's actions brings fear to all.
Men, women, children, all are prey for these ones
The ones whose names are not important.
Just the name of their evil empire
The ones that we call vampires

Adam Chapman

Ode To Women

Is there any sound sweeter than a woman's moan or sigh?
What can be compared to it,
except the cry of a new born or the rustling of the wind.

And what is more tender than a woman's tear?
Only the dew upon the morning grass,
or the rain falling upon the parched earth.

And of a woman's beauty, what can be likened to it?
The stars on a clear night,
or the deer running free in the wild.

Is there any art greater than woman?
I think not!

For when God took the rib from man and made woman,
he took the rib closest to his heart,
closest to his dreams and highest aspirations.

When God created woman he rested,
for his work was done.

    Bob L.

The Scar

A scar, a blemish, a memory,
  the remains of a smudge of life.
Like an inkblot on a paper, it distorts
  and remains forever.
The scar cannot be erased,
  for its impression lasts forever.
That little mark may go away, may fade away
  may hide or stay,
But once that mark has found its place,
  the previous path has been displaced,
From that point on, life makes a change
  who's roots are in that scar.
The scar may not last forever, but
  its effects will never ever depart.
Like the inkblot on a paper, the paper no longer new.
The newness of that paper, now distorted to the eye,
For the inkblot changed the paper's course,
  it can never be brought back.
Since it's gone, the scar has made its mark, never to depart.

    Susan R. Mast

Best Friends

When you think the world's
  against you
When you think you've had
  enough
When you feel the road to
Happiness is getting far too
  rough
There is someone you can turn to
They'll be there till the end
They'll be with you through
  thick and thin
That is your best friend
When you're cramming for a finals
And you're feeling really stressed
Give your best friend a call
He'll help you pass the test
When your other friends all leave you
And bring you lots of tears
Your best friend will always stay with you
He'll stay throughout the years

    Nate Hall

What Does Love Mean?

Does love burn your flesh so deep?
  Is it dreams when you're asleep?
Does it heal you when you're hurt?
  Does it warm you like a shirt?

Is it made to break your heart?
  To take your life tear it apart?
Is it the loss on a winning streak?
  Is it the bad day of a perfect week?

Is it the success on your very last try?
  Is it the sparkle in your eye?
Is it all the good things we get out of life?
  Or the pain we get from a sharpened knife?

Maybe it is both
And maybe it's not
And the lessons of love
Will never be taught

So whether we lose
  Or whether we win
Depend on the person's
  Heart we are in

    Stefanie Warren

Just Reminiscing

In town, years past, neighbors often met
To discuss future events, and yet
Today these events have caught up with us
Very few now left these events to discuss.

We used to know each one by name
Our thoughts and days were much the same.
Today we no longer are remembered by name
And our days and ways are not the same.

Our lanes are now traffic-laden streets
Paper works done on computer sheets.
What happened to all those pastures so lush,
Will they all be lost in this every day rush?

Maybe not lost, but times change they say
As all towns keep painfully growing each day
So just remember the past, give future the way
For it's their turn now, and their own day.

'Tho' man has tried in his tiring ways
To combat these uneventful growing pains,
We now must look to future's ways
And leave behind us those old-time days.

    Lillian Hawley

Thirteen Years

It took me thirteen years
to digest what you did to me
while I dreamt in innocence.

I thought I was safe, curled up, warmed by a quilt,
on the soft velvet couch in your living room.

But relentless you were, night after night.
The floor creaking with your immoral footsteps
alerting me to another night of hell.

I laid there, opening my eyes only enough
to see your manipulative body hovering above.

How many more times tonight, I would think to myself,
will I have to endure your deviant games?

Thirteen years later we sit across the table at thanksgiving.
And you still have the power to make me feel helplessly exposed.

There in a room I haven't seen in years
yet keep visiting night after night in my mind.

    Christa Buberel

Play Me That Song Again

Play me that song again telling
Me the tale of how we got over,
Bent backs, aching tired feet
Heavy hearts and tired souls.
Hymns of freedom song down long hot dusty rows.

Play me that song again child
Tell me that tale of how we got over.
Drowned babies, sold husbands, widows, brothers
And sons whose blood runs warm through pure veins.

Play me that song again child of the star that
showed the way for the Wise Men three.
The child that gave his life for me
Upon some lonely distant cross
I open my wings to fly.

Play me that song again child
Of the promised land and the home beyond the sky.
Take my burdens upon the backs of beast
Wipe the sweat from my aged and worn face as I
Pray to hear those timeless songs of old once again.

Shirley A. Honeycutt

The Fourth Of July, 1863

It is July 4
The day after the deadly battle
The noise of the previous days still ringing in our ears
The booming of cannons and screams heard over and over
The smell of the rotting flesh
Mixing with the waste of the unknowing
Cherry eating Confederates
Assault our noses
As we work to drag the bodies off of the field
Bodies bloated
Decaying
Dead and wounded
Remain strewn across the battlefield
The corpses pile high in places
Draped over fences
Rocks
And any other obstruction preventing the bodies from lying on
the ground
Helping the wounded burying the dead
Experiencing the hellish torture brought upon by war

Jason Powers

Opposition

Nothing in life is free,
Nothing but death is captive,
Good may prevail over evil,
But evil will always be around,
The cravings of one's heart is futile,
While generosity lingers like a cat,
Stubbornness might get you by once,
But cooperation will get you through a life-time.

A sinful act might be forsaken,
While a just act is merited,
There are a zillion and one choices to choose from,
As there are two faces to a coin,
One face represents opportunity,
While the other suggests failure,
In the end, however, the reality is that opposites do attract.

Kamala Grey

Vaulting The Prow

Black - the night is black
A painter in wild, thickly laid strokes
Laugh - the people laugh
They hide their cries; try to change their wild lives
Smile - so many have lost soft smiles
Exchange soft skin for a knife
While I run away to find a seashell in the grass
Blue - rich blue and light blue coalesce to form the sky
Hey now why the wide eyes
A cloudy day can paint such a scene as well as I

Follow me or do I follow you
We each have our own path, so everyone knows exactly what to do

If days are windows, look out your front yard
Where you can see me chanting in the rain
Look in the back yard if you want to see me playing
Try not to slip on your path but make sure you take liberties
If you want and need a change of scenery
And if you want to get there, you can eventually

Jimmy Wilburn

The Umbrella

Traveling through an imperfect world,
  hoping to escape its horror and pain.
The storm of life caught up with me
  tripping my exhausted feet.
The hail - the rain
  They batter my weakened body.
The wind - the wrath
  They tear at my dying soul.
I fall to my bed of infinite rest,
  wishing the end would come.

I notice a translucent warmth of perfection
  Like an umbrella shielding me from the storm's rage
My child, - a voice spoke - don't despair
  Just believe and my hands will always protect you.

I never met up with that storm again.
  For when I believed, the Lord's hands protected me.
In fact, he always did - I just never had the strength to believe
  To believe I should always carry an umbrella with me.
Now I do - now I do
  wherever I go.

Duane Maxwell Vincent

God's Creation

I caught a glimpse of the moon last night,
As it made its way across the sky.
Just what did God say as he charted its path?
You must follow this course exactly each day.

There are people who have never conceived,
That there was One Great enough to plan the world.
They still say it was wrought by a mighty blast,
That placed it all just where it was hurled.

Just ask one of the astronauts who walked on the moon,
If he feared to alight on its soil?
That it might move away from where he stood.
How foolish! He knew God made it all.

In the eons of time since God made the world,
No need for change has ever been made.
It all rotates in the course it was laid,
God still has control of it all!

Carrie U. Meacomes

Terrible Beauty

I can remember peace
that took me captive
when those eyes
seduced my coldest thoughts.
Having security
as a hushing baby in mother's arms
wanting to acquire agape devotion.

I can remember verbal foresight
which inspired novels,
the detainment of crowds
without asserting intonation,
her lamentation, longing for love and dependability,
My counterfeit passion, as a
result of her perfection.

I can remember her love,
falling into deafness, longing for consent,
disgracefully discharged;
the desire to be implicit
which evolved frustration,
this,...I do not want to remember

Troy Heitsman

The Fatalist

A fatalist I know I am,
A mere one score and five,
As easily led as a new born lamb,
For my spirit is not alive.

As I float along on the sea of life,
In the eddies of fate I am crushed,
I no longer feel the wound of the knife,
Nor the strength with which it was thrust.

And I sit and I think of Omar Khayyam,
And wished that I'd lived in those days,
When sorrows were drowned in a keg of good wine,
And one staggered around in a daze.

For nothing's worth fighting for not any more,
One's life, one's home or one's friends,
As over my sorrows I sit and I pore,
There's nothing for me but life's end.

Alma W. Coats

Who Am I...

Who am I
I'm a person
Still searching
Still growing up
Still making mistakes
Still asking questions
Still confused
Still wondering
Still daydreaming
Everyday I ask the some question, who are you
And to myself, I answer, I don't know
Why is it that I don't know, is it that I'm scared to find out
Or is it that I see myself one way
And the world sees me another
If I don't know myself, then how am I suppose to act
As myself or, as the world sees me
Who am I
I'm still asking who am I
It's just a question
A question many people ask themselves.

April Francis

Forgiveness

I have wounded you my friend,
Forgetting that you share the God within me.

I have claimed for myself what was ours,
destroying a part of my own soul.

I have misused the earth and her children,
denying the fruit of my womb.

I have been careless when you were hungry, lonely and sick,
thinking I could be whole while you were broken

I have refused to honor the divinity of your being,
ceasing to exist myself.

Forgive me.
I cannot know life without you.

Paula Diane Feiler

My Child

My child has soft pale pink skin,
his hands, feet and body grows within,
when he is born he'll have to go,
not because he is not loved and not because
God will take him above.
It's because I'll say so.
I will love him until the day I die,
even though I will not be there to hold him
when he cries.
I have no job and I have no home,
If I keep him I'll raise him all alone.
he is a part of me now and always will be,
and I hope that someday he'll forgive me.
But for now he has a new mom and dad,
that will care for him, love him and hold him
hand-n-hand.
And when he get's older and takes him a wife,
then and there I hope to be part of his life.

Patsie Smith

I Shall Know My Love By The Seasons

If Spring, he will come to me with
sentimental reasons.
As birds fly high, as nature prepares
to bloom
I pray that you will come soon
Come summer, I thought my wait
would not be this long.
Tis fall the leaves trickle slowly
Across my face, I still wait patiently
for your embrace.
It's winter now my love where are you?
I've waited, I've prayed, what more can I do?
Winter, spring, summer or fall
might not my love come at all

Juanita Gibbs

Mountain Top Encounters With Life

The gently flowing mountain stream mirrors life as being
    placid and serene.
Of its own will, the spring torrents rush and spill
    its roiling contents down the sloping scene.
Not unlike life's unprotected upheavals, nature's pathways
    can combine to change control of the ends it seeks.
Oftentimes its own devious response to circumstances bring on
    the beginning or the end of visions.
Some of them, many humans had hoped and planned for
    others not.

John B. Slocum

357

He'll Always Be Misunderstood

Deep in an alley behind yesterday's papers,
A man lives his life.
He sleeps in the moonlight, with worries of tomorrow.
Hoping to get his food,
this time, without a fight.
He cries himself to sleep.
In the winter,
He can only shake to keep warm.
No one thinks about his struggle,
No one keeps him out of harm.
He's on his own,
This time without a guide.
He only possesses petty, worthless objects he can find.
He's lost everything he's known.
Pride, dignity, and truth.
It all means nothing,
Now,
For he'll always be
Misunderstood.

Alicia Schaeffer

Sadly Looking Back

Fathers are our saviors,
In our greatest times of need.
Just like our Lord Jesus,
They help pick up our pieces.

They love us with their greatest might,
And give us all they can.
Wrongly we condemn their mistakes,
They are only mortal men.

Often we speak words in haste,
With our youthful thoughts in mind.
Suddenly we age and mature,
And regret the things we find.

Every human makes mistakes,
And what we see in our hindsight can make us sad.
Fathers are learning the same as kids.
Now looking back we realize the love we feel for Dad.

Brandon S. Thacker

Guenevere's Lament

When Arthur came, his gaze warmed me.
He was in awe of the woman who would be his bride.
So long ago —
Long before Lancelot set eyes
    on the woman whose soul had died.

His gaze burned me.
It lit a fire whose blazing flames consumed all.
And somewhere deep inside me,
I knew Camelot must fall.

Forgive me Arthur.
You let me walk, and I ran
so fast, there seemed to be no place on earth I couldn't go.
And now that I know what lies beyond these walls,
they can't chain me in again.
My spirit soars to places they'll never know.

Forgive me Arthur.
You let me speak, and I screamed.
My heart echoed like thunder through all the land,
when I dared to dream.

Tricia Simpson

The Ballad Of The Sloth

I saw a sullen, Slimy sloth
secluded in a tree,
till suddenly, he fell right off
and came down rapidly.

He landed with a hearty thud
I thought he had been hurt
till I got close and saw the sloth,
he said his name was Bert.

"Oh no!" said the sloth
my nose fell off
and went where I can't see
and the next thing I knew, the sorry sloth
was crying by a tree

"Don't cry!", I shout
I'll find your snout
wherever it may be

And the sloth looked up
then dried his eyes
and smiled pleasingly

Marc Jeffrey Flynn

Rotten Cheese!

It smells, it dwells in the house
until along comes a little mouse.
The mouse says "Wow!" The people say "ew,"
and then the mouse starts to chew.
The stink goes up, the mouse goes down,
and then the people start to frown.
The mouse does down, in the hole,
and then he said, I feel like a mole,
so he came out again and again,
and that is the end
of the rotten cheese and the mouse called Ben.

Sheena Polam

What Is Guidance

Guidance is a gentle handling in a
    difficult situation
Guidance is a gentle caring without
    reservation
Guidance is the soft pedal when the world
    is spinning
Guidance is an arm around you when
    you aren't winning
Guidance is necessary for you to know
That what you fear is not necessarily so.
Guidance reaches out for you to see
That there is someone there for you and me
It can come quietly in the form of love
But I'm truly convinced that it comes
    from above

Mary W. Kline

Nature...Nature...Nature!

Nature is...
Green-filled trees with an autumn breeze...
Birds chirping...
Flowers blooming, and...
Oceans looming...
Throughout the beauty of nature
and life.

Ashley Ferguson

Answers In A Day Well

Upon the shoulders of the driven
  the invite of opinion
To a whom it may concern
Born from an empty well
It directs
To a whom that inspects
From an ignorant spell

And from the points through chosen pawns
In an acid that eats what's not their own
But insists in this the only base
and returns its weight to its owners face

From beginning to end
Through a drivens own defend

And from here must be asked
  were they ever really there

In a mind who questions now descend
Now sets loose
A pivoting role
To later be played again

    Brandon Ivie

Song Of Mourning

Come weep and wail, ye winter winds,
And howl in mourning round his bed;
But touch ye not his pale, cold brow,
Nor breathe upon his noble head.

Lament, ye clouds, and grieve for him;
Let softly fall your rain of tears.
Stop, sun and moon, your heedless flight,
And mourn with me his vanished years.

Ye mountains, hills, bow down your heads,
And groan aloud your grief and woe.
And all ye rivers, lakes, and streams,
Cry out your sorrow, keening low.

For he is dead, is dead, is dead!
And I must live, I know not why.
The blackness cloaks me like a shroud,
And all are fled but Death and I.

    Linda Waugh

McKensie Rose Age Of Two

Little hands fooled in prayer
with thanks to God she'd like to share.
It's night - night-time for Mckensie Rose
and this is how her little prayer goes.
Must be on her knees at the side of her bed
then she folds her hands and bows her head.
She says, Thank you God for my Mom and Dad
and my baby dolls that make me so glad.
Thanks for our home and my doll house too.
How sweet is this angel, age of two.
She touches or points as she goes down her list
with a little soft voice that God can't resist.
She wraps it all up with a little "Amen"
then it's under the covers, in bed again.
Another day is over another day ends
she'll be up as soon as a new one begins.
When I say my prayers she's on my list too,
"Thank you God for Mckensie Rose" age of two.

    Michael P. Callahan

Two Flames United

Our flame burns fiercely to the world,
Yet in its core it withers and wains.
It seems to emanate strength but embodies doubt.

One flame flickers unsurely in the world,
Yet in its core it has a strength still unknown.
It seems naive and weak but possesses a secret courage.

As the two flames meet, they burn higher and higher,
Forming a pure fire of strength within and without.
They are now one and burn with new found power and courage.

One large flame burns like a torch for the world to see,
Proudly announcing its passion and power.
One amazing flame that will last for all eternity and never be
extinguished.

    April Dunkum

The Three

At 0600 the doors do slam,
As I wake, I remember where I am.
Liberty and justice for one and all,
even when you stumble and fall.

All seems lost and without hope.
Can I find the strength to cope?
All I need is to hear their voice.
I know that this is not their choice
or they'd be on the phone each day
asking me when we could play.

Does anyone know or even care,
the pain, the three of us, do share?

I once risked life for liberty,
now it's been taken from us, three.
Our love can never be put to death.
We will fight this battle with our last breath,
and my sons again are at my side.
They are my life, my joy, my pride.

Someday soon we will surely meet,
because the three know not defeat.

    J. Pablo Arias

Weaving Colors

God has a special way of weaving all things
Into a collage of colors that he brings
He weaves them into the day all bring and new
He weaves in each color like me and you
There was not a special color that he had in mind
He just wove a rainbow which he called mankind
Colors which spread across this entire earth
Bringing a new beginning, a new birth
He never gave it a thought of what his colors stood for
He only knew that they were his to adore
So to make each one special he gave them some land
To nurture and flourish as he has planned
Because one day he wanted them all to be
Different, but the same for all the world to see
That everything he made was equal and good
So in your hearts remember this if you would
God made mankind many colors from above
For each one was a color that he loved
And when his tapestry is all but done
We all shall glitter and shine beneath heavens sun

    Diana Irish

65 Roses

65 Roses is what Mommy calls it,
What a pretty name,
So why does it make me feel this pain?

My breaths are short, my lungs are full.
Too weak to walk, no breath to talk.

Mommy said everything will be O.K.,
If I pray to God,
Maybe I'll see my tenth birthday.

Maybe I was meant to go,
I can see Mommy crying,
I wish she wasn't hurting so.

Leaving my family has made me sad.
Like a cloud, I'll be watching over them,
It really isn't that bad.

As they will always love me,
I will love them,
This is a twist of fate, can't you see?

Now I can breathe, jump, run and fly,
I wish it could be like this on earth,
Was I really meant to die?

Meghan Hukowicz

Grandpa's Farm

Grandpa was born right on his farm,
In the old house that was moved away.
A rock marks the spot where the house stood,
On the farm where he still lives today.

Grandpa followed in his father's footsteps,
And made farming, and family his life.
Faithfully working beside him all the way,
Has been his devoted, and loving wife.

Grandpa worships in the country church,
Built by pioneers on the prairie grass.
It still stands as a refuge to country folk,
And any other searching souls who pass.

Grandpa worked long days on his farm,
Raising crops, cattle, chickens, and pigs.
But he says the most rewarding task,
Was helping grandma raise their five kids.

Grandpa talks about his eighty years on the farm,
Calling farming honest and honorable work.
And he expresses joy and satisfaction,
As he sums up his days on earth.

Alice Sathre

To My Love

"Oh, ___ I love you so
How do I tell you, I don't know

I want to be with you, days on through
I share with you, my company, too

To be with you the rest of my life
I want to be your wife

So please consider my thought
For you are the one I sought

To be with me through the years
Even though there will be sorrow and tears

These will be memories to treasure
Our whole lives forever and ever

Say never, never to forever true
But "I do" for the years on through.

Dana Louise Benson Verdin

Untitled

Teach me.
I offered up my innocence
naivete to be written upon
the risk in love.
I met once a boy who gently touched my chin
as my enamored eyes peered deeply into his.
I saw once
the tender blanket of human emotion
evoke no less that all my soul's affection.
At that I emptied myself,
basking my naked heart upon the glass platter
that I so shyly presented him.
He beckoned me with honest embraces
through fields of gold,
the summer gone, fields of white.
I inhaled none but the sweetness of lips
dressed red and dampened with wine.
"Teach me," I pleaded, "life."
He accepted, instructed, fled.
Broken, I emerged — taught.

Debby Maddock

The West/Women Who...

Thinking about women who talks to chickens
way out on the prairie
in the lone star state. Or anywhere.
Some time...
middle of the nineteenth, early twentieth century...
or anytime
that a woman got so
dried up
with loneliness and need
that she would take companionship in her hens
and they would possibly, probably
listen
as the dust blew around her yard
and the darkness settled in
not quite, but nearly,
killing her with silence.
So grateful she was just for their soft clucking...
scratching out existence
on the wide Texas plain.

Melanie Rae Voland

Tears With Fear

It's all but a tear can't
let no one here, a silent fall that's
what I wish of all...
So much inside I no everyone
needs to cry, don't want anyone
to see, just go away and let me
be....
Thou all that I doubt why
can these feelings finally come out, hoping
for a tear can that be what I fear....
For there's so much in you can
call it a sin, then why can I express
with all that is left...
No way to stop when my tears
don't even drop, hidden deep in my
heart that's were it first starts,
but not from my eyes, Lord can
you tell me why....

Lisa Rollod

Sandcastles

We strive for perfection,
And when we don't get this confection,
We lose direction,
And make a connection,
With a sandcastle place where little children hide,
And dreams we had are set aside,
To let the moment be our guide,
And in our hurry and in our rush,
In our fret to keep it all hush-hush,
We build our sandcastles too close to the waters edge,
We live unrealized lives at the tip of a ledge,
And our last breaths are taken in protecting,
The clump of sand we've been erecting,
The leaders we've been electing,
But not the dreams we've been neglecting
So we'll let it ride,
And hide inside,
But drown come high tide,
Protecting our sandcastles,
With sandcastle pride.

Shane Pangburn

Everything

Everything you want, anything you need
I'll do for you, I'll do the deed
I love you so much, I really care
I couldn't hurt you, I wouldn't dare

You light up my life, can't you see
You're all that I have, you and me
I want to marry you, be my wife
Live with me, the rest of your life

I'll give you a hug, I'll hold your hand
If you're in trouble, I'll take a stand
I'll do what you want, I'll help you out
I'll be there through fights, even shouts

I've loved you always, from the start
I'll love you forever, with all my heart
If you ever want something, I'll be there
I'll do whatever it takes, to show I care

Everything you want, anything you need
I'll do for you, I'll do the deed
I love you so much, I really care
I couldn't hurt you, I wouldn't dare.

Daniel Carriger

Cry Of Thirst

The hot sun burns the ground and melts
everything as I look around
the trees burn bright and cry of thirst as
the cactus' insides begin to burst
the pavement burns the soles of my feet, my
face drips from the intense heat
the flowers are dried and the grass is dying
and so am I as here I'm lying, lying alone with
you close to me how did I let this come to be
my soul is crying for what it lost
my mind forgot just what it may cost
my heart is gone, I don't know where
yet nothing inside me seems to care
my mind is somewhere far away
my soul is longing for another day
I did as I pleased thinking only of me
and now I stand alone like that burning tree,
crying of thirst dying of pain
all of which I brought thinking of what
I may gain.

Jennifer Hughes

A Very Special Night

The air is cool, the wind is calm,
The stars and moon shine bright.
Could it have been like this back then
On that very special night?

He came in quiet and left in glory
To the amazement of many men.
One born from love yet killed by hate,
He died for all our sin.

Now He's exalted by the God of Gods,
He sits at God's right hand.
His job is done, His work complete,
He awaits God's final command.

Who will go and who will not?
Knowing God's Word is a must.
For salvation's not based on what you do,
It's based on Who you trust!

Jesus is the name I love to hear,
And I long to hold His hand.
To see those shiny streets of gold,
As we walk through the promised land.

Dwayne Thompson

My Son

How good it feel's, the love of a son.
His call to visit, laugh or cry...
Sharing his day, his week, him month...
His caring, his concern, his genuine love....
Respect filters through and touches the heart...
Just like the hug... The grin..
That mischievous look...
His spark for fun....
Such joy and pleasure he brings to life...
My son.

Susann French

My Lord Understands

My Lord understands each trial I bear;
He knows of the burdens that I so much fear;
He feels the deep sorrow that makes the tears flow;
My Lord understands for He lived here below.

He knows how it feels to cry and be sad;
He knows what it means to be misunderstood;
Above other men He was tempted and tried;
My Lord understands 'tws for me that He died.

"Come all ye that labour and you'll find rest;
My yoke upon you assures you are blest;
My promise to help you stands sure every day."
O wonderful Lord, I shall trust and obey.

Kathleen Newman

Him

All the strings of nothingness are sewed into my heart.
He tears and rips and drains me until it falls apart.
I burrow my head in darkness and try not to
dream of dreams, but he always find a way to
play his little schemes.
He melts his thoughts of evil into my twisted mind.
I feel his desires twining all throughout my spine.
I long for a comfort and not for his disease.
He makes me crawl and beg for it on my broken knees.
I bow my head in tears while laying at his feet.
He blows away my fears until again we meet.

Sarah Davis

The Cowboy

Cowboy hats, knives, guns, leathers, and an iron horse—
You came riding into my fantasies, dreams, and my heart.
Now I lay in your bed, feeling so safe, secure,
And so loved in your arms.
You touch me in ways no other could ever have.
I see your eyes looking at me, from under that cowboy hat,
I feel the strength of your arms and hand,
When you wield your knife and whips.
I know the feeling of satisfaction and pleasure
When you make love to me.
I lose control of my senses and my head,
When you touch me.
And when we ride out on your iron horse
The feelings of freedom and oneness overwhelm me.
You call me "Lady" despite my past.
You call me "B***h" in your bed.
But your eyes call me "Lover" in your heart.
I know only that this woman-child
Dreams and desires to please the Cowboy.
And when you ride away—I pray you'll take me with you.

Darilynn M. McClure

Release

I have left the note where it will be found,
not that any will care once I am gone.
I hold the blade in my trembling hand
(is it from the cold, fear, or excitement?)
I have second thoughts, but nothing to loose
and all to gain (an end of pain?)
I proceed. All I feel is a gental tug as the frail skin
puts up a futile resistance to the razor. It yields.
My ice numbed flesh is slowly warmed
by my life blood trickling down my arms,
and pooling in my palms (it kind of tickles).
I feel light headed, and I softly smile,
for I know the release from pain is close at hand.
I close my eyes and silently wait . . . for the sweet . . .
kiss of death . . . to be placed . . . upon . . . my . . .
lips . . .

W. A. Fleming

Original Family Name

Written in the spirit to those who have
The problem with black, because they
Are not and those because they are

No! No! My lost brothers and sisters, I
Repeat my lost brothers and sisters there
Is no one in my family named that.

However there must have been someone
In yours. For I have heard many many many
Of your family members call many many many
Of my family members by what I truly
Believe to be your original family name

N***er! N***er!

Jamel Myers

Untitled

There was a woman proficient at stitching.
Without needle and thread she'd be b***hing.
To soothe her guilt,
She would quilt.
Now, ain't that bewitching.

Court H. Bentley

Take My Dreams

Take my dreams
    into your hand
and crush them to bits
    Let them sift through your
fingers like sand

I said, "It would be always you!"
I don't care about memories
    or none of that s***!
I know that it's over
    I know this is it!

But you took it all
    and threw it all away
You know I still love you
I see our future's end
And if it's any consolation
I just called to let you know
I'm gonna take my dreams and go

Calvin C. Gonzales

My Angel

She comes to me, my angel,
With pleasure as her goal.
Her eyes so captivating,
They penetrate my soul.

Her breath upon my neck,
My will I cannot keep.
Lost inside her desire,
Passion extremely deep.

She takes my self-control,
Excitement so intense.
Washing me with hunger,
Worth every consequence.

I've never felt such pleasure,
Until she came to me.
Now spread your wings, my angel,
Evoke your spirit free.

Lysa Marie Sharp

Behind Bars

It was a set up.
Police-Police-Police
Blue and red lights flashing...

Three bare walls,
Bars on the front of the animal cage.
Cold cement floors,
And a wooden bench to rest your head.

Orange jumpsuits,
Brown sandals, and handcuffs, too.
They've reminders...

Lost souls,
    Lost faith,
        Lost hopes and dreams that never return.

Yelled at, cussed out
Treated like a piece of S-*-*-t
It's no wonder the people come out
    Worse than when they went in.

They've got no
    more
        self-respect.

Christine Rouse

Untitled

You ranted and raved when you first brought me home
I was clean and pure and white as the snow, bedazzling to the eye.

I gave you a sense of comfort and security inside your home,
  I never complain!
Rarely do I get the care I deserve, the only time you adorn me
  now is when strangers come to pay they're respects or if I
  become offensive.
I'm always calm and cool when you are slumped over my shoulders,
and really, must you worship me so!!

Now!! I'm tired of your s**t!

If I hold my breath you will surely wade through
  my vengeance with a mighty stench!!

The ravings of a mad toilet
  Suzanne Riccelli

Light Of Dawn

He said, "Don't do it. Your mom will kill you."
In the end, his words had come true.
She put the gun to your head,
Then you lay on the floor, bleeding to death.
She did the same to your sister, and set fire to your home.
The fire consumed your mind, body, and soul.
Although you've been dead for years, I still feel pain.
After that, no one's life was the same.
It's not fair, it wasn't your time to go.
You could have been someone everyone would know.
They never got your mother she killed herself.
You don't know the pain everyone felt.
Everyone misses you more than you know.
She was the only one who wanted you to go.
I remember all the good times we had.
Do you realize everyone is still sad?
The police came and took pictures and names.
She must have thought it was all just a game,
But she soon realized how serious it was,
Then she took her own life in the light of dawn.

  Mandy Gettel

The Beat

We met dark-haired as before, when somber clouds shut season's back
door. Then cold winter's wind blows in the mascara-smeared eyes of
gritty snows. Our sweat-soaked palms held close as we secret-sharers
shyly pose. She of strong jaw, sharp eye (in haste) and thighs
larger, rounder than my waist, with high heels, long-legged she stood
a female colossus in coat and hood. Then, unclothed, bare from foot
to have, her vast curves - belly and breast enslave. In uncertain
with horizontal passions unflung, I surrendered to her white mounds
covering my pale cornse without bounds fever and frenzy filled my
heart; trapped within, I played my part. My fate: To hold her close
heat for heat, our eager forces pulsing to the beat.

  Ralph Haworth

Cubby Holes

Empty faces
Used to fill empty spaces
Digesting my sorrow
Choking on contradiction
Promising tomorrow
Is my worst addiction
Broken, I stand before you
Aware of my condition
I don't want to hear it from you

A circle of bulls**t
Flowing in motion
Repetitive ignorance
Reveals the notion

  Matthew Rogers

Prelude To A Suicide

If death has meaning
and my life have none
then I lived so-called life
for my only son

Do not love me
I have no need for it
and if you warned me
I would not heed it

Cross my arms
I'll be on my way
using my charms
on judgement day

You may not see
the things that I know
but I will be free
of this world of a****es

To my son I leave only this
I am sorry I couldn't give
One last good-nights kiss

  William Augustine

Black Queen

You are the daughter of Cleopatra
The sister of Nefertiti and the cousin
  of Tiye
Just like them you are a queen your
  kingdom is the city
Such a pity that you are every man's dream
As you walk all heads will turn
Do I smell the scent of roses when you
  sway your hips
There is so much to be learned
One can only fantasize of kissing your lips
Are they as sweet as your skin brown Suga
The Lord must be praised for the
  creation of this beautiful black Sista
I notice there is tattoo on your chest
You have a delightful round butt that
  I would love to caress
Oh please my Black Queen you have men
  on their knees
You are the woman of my dreams

  Grover Brown

Get To The Light

It's dark — dark,
I'm lost in the ark — the ark,
Who knows, who knows,
What will happen next — next?
Will I die? Die.
Stick a knife through my eye, my eye.
I will die, die.
  It's loud, loud,
I'm floating on a cloud.
Who knows — knows,
What will I do next — next?
I will fall — fall,
Fall from my cloud;
To the ground,
Now I snapped my neck,
My neck.
  It's light — light,
Run towards the light,
Don't fight — don't fight.
Get to the light, the light.

  Courtney Kowalewski

Ode To "An Angel Here On Earth"

As I sit recollecting the smooth curves of your beautiful face
Not believing that I am on the ground, but somewhere in space;

And I watch the clock as each second and minute slowly passed,
Not flinching, because I know you soon would be in my arms, at last;
Going crazy with anticipation, as I await your alluring presence,
Exclusively you occupy my mind, as I recall your wonderful essence;
Love is in the only emotion my whole being wants to experience.

How do I begin to describe the ways you make me feel extra special,
Even at times when the cares of the world appear almost sensational?
Realizing that with the passage of time, my love grows ever stronger,
Eve never had such a hold on Adam, although their time was longer.

One hour or one day at a time is how I resolve that I must now live.
Next to my heart, a special spot as a token of love, I unreservedly give.

Enter into a pact of love and be my special earth angel of light,
And always will I be joyful whether or not you are in my sight;
Ready am I, here for you, come love me, and please don't fight,
True love is hard to find, so when it finds you, it you should not slight;
Here I am, come to me, take me and let me show you that I am right.

Hugh O. Stewart

The Flower

I saw a flower in the rain, its petal bent and torn.

I gathered it my palm so it would not feel forlorn

As I held the fragile shape, it came alive;
to my surprise it turned to look me in the eyes.

It smiled and winked and from my palm I did hear

"Oh person so kind, I am glad you are near,
my life would be lonely if you where not here.
Many storms I have seen with rainbows aglow.
And from my soul, I want you to know.
Petals cannot unfold without sun to grow the edges of my being.
Leaves cannot sway in the breeze of the day
When your heart you cannot give away.
You held my strength in the palm of your hand
I feel that you can understand.

I am the rainbow, the color of love, the color of light from above.
If God did choose me to gather a bouquet,
I will give it to you, I will not be far away."

Gently I lay the petals beside me, gathering
the essence of love within the rainbow above.

Joanne Young

Saying Goodbye

Ambitions strongly fill my mind
Of dreams that remain untold.
Urgingly,
They touch and inspire me
Asking me to speak out.
I reach within the depths of my soul
Trying to find the courage I have always doubted myself of having.
I slowly but surely
Take cautious steps,
My pulse beating rhythmically in my ears.
Suddenly, I tightly clench my fists
And just as suddenly,
I relax.
I approach the still figure lying there
With tears resting on the brims of my eyelids.
My emotions flare
But I strongly fight to hold them back.
They close the coffin and I walk away,
Never stopping to look back.

Angela Pringle

Goodbye Vietnam

As the end of my tour grew near, time was filled with anxiety.

Days seemed eternal and dampened with fear,
as I slept my mind subdued the atrocity.

Alas! The day appeared, I quickly packed and bid farewell.

To all those guys who never feared,
for too their day was coming - The End Of Hell.

I can see their faces cold and gaunt, memories in a hazy cloud.

Still in my dreams they haunt, I hear their voices - not aloud.

For the men I left behind to die, in deep distress and loneliness.

Today I find I still do cry, for my comrade dear is emptiness.

Ten thousand miles create the distance,
thirty years to a time - to a place.

While the miles do widen that great expanse,
nothing can ever erase those Hero's embrace.

No hero's medal to adorn this chest, just an empty void within.

Just an empty void I hold within my breast,
for those dear, dear men - those lonely men.

Oh Shout for joy my fellow vets, don't ponder how or why.

No time to morn or have regrets, Vietnam — Goodbye.

Larry L. Conwell

A Sad Life

A sweet, fresh baby new to
the world soon goes from thoughtless
to carefree to a school child with
troubling teachers and too much homework.
Then more with soul breaking schoolmates and back stabbing friends.
With only some peers to trust and only some family by her side.
Going through life in fear, crying herself to sleep
and desperately trying to solve
each treacherous problem step by step, day by day.
No time to think for herself or accumulate a future.
With rapid thoughts trembling through her
mind she tries to grasp the truth of reality,
but instead of fretting with her confused life she ends
all worries and harshly leaves the world she so gently entered.
As she lays in her final rest bed
bloodshed rings her like a wreath of new born roses.

Melissa Spanos

If I Had One Wish....

If I had one wish right now, I know what it would be.
I wish that all the pain I feel would somehow be set free.
Free from the confinement of my soul, that is about to die...
Please set all my sorrow free, so my heavy heart can fly.
If I had one wish right now, it would be to trust again.
After all the times I've been hurt and betrayed,
I want my heart to mend.
If I had one wish right now, I'd wish that you could see,...
this worried, sad, pathetic girl, is not who I want to be.
I have built a shield around my heart, so it shall be hurt no more,
because I know without this shield of mine,
it would have broken long before.
If I had one wish right now, it would be to take this shield away,
so you could see the real true me,
and my heart could be free someday.

Nicole Edinger

Black Friday

The happy crowds, the marching bands
He smiled and waved, and clasped their hands,
"You are so loved today?", she said - The land words he would hear
In the twinkling of an eye there was panic, rage and fear.
"Oh no" she cried, and held him cradled on her breast,
His life's blood ebbing, the stains imprinted on her dress.
"Oh no" we cry, we're sure it can't be true
No one would dare to harm this man our country loved and knew
But all the powers that be have failed,
Our tears flow free, our grief's unveiled.
She kissed his lips, and placed within his hand
Symbolic of their life and love - Her wedding band.
We are a nation stripped of pride
Helpless, outraged, sick inside
For us the sun has dimmed and waned,
A once proud nation ever shamed.
We pray forgiveness, and while he sleeps
A sad stunned Nation weeps!

Sylvia R. Soraparu

The March Of The Locusts

Oblivious to space and pressured by time, the large army of locusts
advances seeking for the lame guiding the blind.

Forthcoming is the message that engenders paradisaic delight.
Not one implement of war was raised, not even a fight.

The hungry must be fed, the thirsty quenched.
The fight cannot be relinquished, the darkness must be wrenched.

Onward! Onward they advance. There is no turning back.
The light gets ever brighter even though the opposing forces
   would turn it black.

There are still some that cling to life as if they were newborn
   infants sucking nutriments from an infinite source.

It is of no avail for their search is futile, their journey empty,
   their fruitage coarse.

They feed on nourishment that is tantamount to lies.
What is so perplexing is that even when they have been enlightened,
   they still perceive their half truths as vindicating cries.

The locusts tread ever forward. Their progress cannot be impeded.
Their message is from an infinite fountain that cannot be depleted.

Listen! Do you hear their march, march, march.
Ever treading never parched!

Hector L. Quiles

Feathered Friends

Have you ever sat and watched the birds as they gather their stock?
To prepare themselves for the Winter cold and make their nest with
   humble a bold.
To protect their young diligently until they are able to take flight
   with their gallant wings.
Then as the cycle unfolds their work is done and gone untold.
But oh then, to be like our feathered friends...
To be able to take flight as the storm comes in.

Juliana Lee-Perez

To My Darling Children

To my darling children, I will always pray for you,
I will ask the Lord to bless you, in all you say or do.
I pray that you all will walk worthy, according to God's word,
And the goals that you each set for your lives, never be disturbed.
Remember this always that God is merciful, full of truth and grace,
So, if you falter or stumble along the way,
   get up and continue to run the race.

Ola Eason

Silhouette Of A Soul

Days roll by like the dice of a compulsive gambler trying to break
the addiction to the game of chance. The chance for love. The
game of love. Which seems to be all rained out by the tears of
the multitude of fools, who once believed in fairy tales and
forevers. Now waking to a tequila sunrise, facing a stranger in
the mirror, who's eyes burn through the cynicism to bare the
heart, soul, essence, and aura of the waiting, wanting, hoping,
nonviolent warrior poet. Who's armed only with words, roses,
and the desire to experience truly returned love.

Matt Crile

I Had A Daughter

I had a daughter

Her morning melodies were lovely, lilting, with the songs she would
sing, her laughter filled our house and our hearts,
her childish cares and concerns put our problems in perspective,

She was cute as a child with winsome ways that stole your heart,
and pretty as a young girl,
innocent and sweet standing in the sun
with copper highlights in her hair, as the gentle breeze blows,
I can see her still.

She loved the woods and the fields,
walking alone with her dog there was something mystical and peaceful,
it made you realize her time with you was a gift,
and she really belonged to God.

I have a daughter

She is busy with her life, it is full of friends
and work and her own family.
She goes happily on with her daily routine,
not realizing my presence with her,
not knowing, sadly,
we won't always be together.

Marilyn L. Kaholi

Nick

You're gonna tug on my fingers, kid.
You're gonna tug on my hair
Cause I've seen how everyone's waited for you
And I see that you're finally here
And I've seen four babies before you,
   and I know what it is babies do.
They tug on your fingers and pull on your nose
And make playgrounds out of you
they stare at your big boy hands and
They crawl on your big boy feet
and as far as things to chew on go,
Big boy fingers are pretty neat
So I'll let you bite on my fingers kid,
   and I'll let you tug at my hair
And I'll make funny faces and smile down at you
And wave you around in the air.
But soon you will be much too heavy,
To be waved around in the air
Soon you'll start walking,
Your coos turned to talking and
sometimes you're alone out there
But by then I'll be at where I'm gonna be
While you're looking ahead future too bright to see
If it scares you, all right
it's a real scary sight
To see one's whole future before him
just tug on my fingers
Put your hand in my hand and together, we'll get to walking.

Bernard J. Dolan

365

Go With The Poet

Equipped with thoughts, feelings, paper and pen he is ready to take the adventure again.

Whether he seeks new horizons or the past to escape and hide he invites you along for the emotional ride.

He may bring you to the point of tremendous fear or explore the pureness of a child's tear.

You may walk with him down memory lane but please take an umbrella as he might stop to smell the roses despite the rain.

You may be caught up in wonder you may laugh or cry but don't be surprised when he wipes a tear from your eye.

Or you may sail with him far above all hopelessness and despair and soon realize you're riding on God's loving care.

He may take you to a lovely garden, but you may sense something out of place, as he pulls back the flowers to reveal a scar that has been hidden from every face.

The scar appears so jagged and deep you will both want to see it for only a quick peek. But go with him and explore the scar of sorrow and pain, when you have gone through it and learn from its wisdom something in your life will never be the same.

No matter where you want to go or where you have been, get ready for a new adventure as the poet is picking up his pen.

Timothy A. Johnston

The Road Is So Bright

No matter where you are right now, day or night,
Whether you're sitting or standing, take a look outside

Look for as long and far as you can...and don't look back

Everything you want is out there,
Only now it just takes a little more energy to find

If your dream is to become a ballerina
than you must learn to dance

If your dream is to become a pilot
than you must learn to fly

If your dream is to become a flower
than you must learn to grow

And if your dream is to become a boxer
than you must truly learn to fight

The road to that dream is different this time, it's long and rough,
Yet it's simply an obstacle, the kind you have faced before,
 and will face again

Your keen sense of humor and smile will help you through each day,
And each day will take more courage
 and determination than the one before

One thing's for sure
The light at the end of that road is so bright... It is blinding!

Nina L. Fadelli

Burnt Sienna

Burnt Sienna is like sugar sweet brown chocolate
 dirt mounds which cause floods in Bangladesh

Burnt Sienna is like the smog that fills the air
 at 4:00 a.m. rush hour in D.C.

Burnt Sienna is like an African drought,
which looks like baked clay

Burnt Sienna is like a person's mind drifting away into the dream land
 in a pig pen in Kansas

Burnt Sienna is like a Native American's skin
 which stands for a warrior of knowledge

Burnt Sienna, Burnt Sienna is like no other
It's only what you make of it

Josef W. Blankenburg

New Years Eve Reunion

So he's the one you're going to marry
not Joe, Marty, John, nor Harry I under rated him
Thought he was just a whim
That in a while he'd go too
And like the others he'd be through

Nice looking fellow you made a handsome
couple when you danced by
I didn't mean to stare
But couldn't help it when I caught your eye

I recalled our nights of splendor
Broad way shows Coney Island
Easter Sunday in New York
"The Music Man", Seashore trips
Niagara falls Canada
Gallaghers, Lindys, Army - Notre Dame
World series games

I felt the eyes of friends upon me
And knew they felt a little sorry for my sake

But I quickly yessed, someone laughed a hollow laugh
 and had another drink
But hoped the music was so loud that no one heard my heart break.

Harry J. Agnew

When Children Ask

A child whose skin was dark as coal, kissed one whose skin was white,
Fortunately for both of them, they had not learned to fight.
A crippled boy led up the street, a man who could not see,
Their friendship grew experiencing, life's cruel adversities.

A large girl who had almond eyes, leaned on a thin man's arm,
The difference in their races sure was no cause for alarm.
A tattered teen who saw a fire, saved kids from pending harm,
The mansion burned down just as fast, as if it were a barn.

A Moslem knelt in prayer with Jews, a pastor with a priest,
Religion helped them all to see they fought a common beast.
A homeless man helped those on drugs, enriched their lives with hope,
Addictions caused awareness of, the need for them to cope.

A man with aids consoled a boy, who he had never met,
They shared the errors they had made, and treatment they could get.
A mother gave an organ to, the victim of a wreck,
So that she'd know, God willing, death wouldn't conquer yet.

So many of us speak of how, we want the world to be,
But it won't change unless, you know, it starts with you and me.
When children ask if people are, as different as they seem,
Point out to them we're all the same, and they will live our dreams.

Mary E. Washington

What Have You Done?

What have you done for the Lord today?
Have you stopped to kneel and pray?
Have you met someone along the way,
In need of a smile and a kind word to say?
Have you visited the sick, the elderly, or have you helped the poor?
Have you witnessed to the one who lives next door?
Have you helped feed the hungry, the thirsty the weak?
Can you put someone in need, on your schedule this week?
Have you went to the prisons, to let them know God cares?
Have you shared with a stranger that God is always there?
Have you given a child a helping hand,
 or just scolded him and condemned?
The least on this earth, men despise.
But the least on this earth, are precious in God's eyes.
When we do service for the least of them;
Aren't we doing service also for Him?

Lynnette Hilliard

I'm Me, Not You

Why do I have to be like you, when I can't even do what you do.
Walk, talk, sing, and smile, you need to think on that for awhile.
I don't have to be like you, God told me what I have to do.
I have a purpose, and you have a purpose,
we all have something to do on this surface.
    Shoot, you aren't my idol, so I can get my own title.
    I can be and do whatever,
but from the way you're talking, you seem to be under the weather.
    You need to get a life, because I plan to have kids and be a wife.
    You can be a mocker, but I'm going to grow up to be a doctor.
    You may work a part time register,
but I can be a full time hair dresser
    You may think you're funny, but you got another thing coming.
    I don't want to be like you, when I can do my own thing too.
    Hm! You make me laugh, from the things that you say last.
    Girlfriend, you need some prayer, so please don't even dare.
    Stop telling me what to do, and start trying to make a difference in you.
    You know you're my friend, so don't let this relationship end.
    Look! You can be you, but I can do what I want to do.
        Amber M. Likely

Life's A Bear

Life's a bear it's not fair, but that's the way it is.
Keep on looking, keep on cooking, there's a place for you somewhere.
Be careful, beware of the lions lair, they lay there lurking,
Waiting for you to appear so they can tear you down.
There they lurk and stare in their lions lair, the smell of blood
in their hair. Waiting, waiting, for the poor soul who may
be different than them.

Take a care of what you wear, watch the way you wear your hair.
Be careful of the way you walk, remember when you make a dare
To be different from them, you'll cause the clicks to talk and stare.
If they stare and creep toward you, they'll tear your face apart.

So, beware, beware of the lions lair and remember life's a bear
It's not fair, but somewhere out there, there's a special place
For you, where there's a hunting season...for lion's hair!!
        Nancy Staten Gregory

Lately Grey

I often dream in antifreeze green.
My sense of smell is keenly tangerine.
My memory is taking in Polaroid snapshots.
My hearing is in deafening, panoramic and pristine clarity.
I'll soon leave behind this biosphere
Of the world that revolves around "the green."
Damn my lost religion, morality of blasphemy.
My emotions are released into the wild plains of riveting Naivete.
My touch sensitive, and my feelings free,
Become confused and tangled tumbleweed.
I taste hazelnut Irish cream.
I see in rainbows, Roy G. Biv and Me.
No more dreams, I feel depressingly blue. Is this life worth living?
My misleading voice, unkindly guide inside my mind,
Unbleached cotton should I die...
And dye it red?
My last few days have been
Lately grey.
        Minh Bui

Virtue-Al Windows

If the eyes are the windows to the soul,
    why do you keep the shades down so low?

I've placed mirrors in my windows.

Rare and few are those who want to know you with good intentions;
    they would rather see reflections of themselves...
        or harm you in ways too evil to mention.
        Lourdes Plumey

Just Because

In the mind lives a beast of self-destruction ready to explode.

At times the soul grows weak, the heart turns black,
    unable to burden the load.

Sometimes we find refuge in a wonderful bliss of confusion,
    a torrid blur.

The alleviation is enticing.
But, the cruel pureness of pain is all that endures.

The beauty of human contact in the midst of this pain
    is so selfish and primal.

It's one broken being looking for solace that makes the pain so final.

The soul tends to follow the mind, instead of the heart,
    creating foolish fantasies of love.

Yet, we continue to subject ourselves to all this just because.
        David J. Lovern

An Angel

There lies an angel in thy heart.
Thou is a part of thee now,
and I pray to God, that thou will be evermore.
Thy face is full of the beauty of an angel,
thy eyes, like stars, lighting the darkness in my life.
The light of God appears clearly in thy sensitive skin.
Thy hair like silk, blown in a gentle breeze.
When she cries...so dost the Heavens.
Thy life would be hell, if not for her here.
My heart is embraced with pure love and joy, when thou art present,
and bleedith it does, in darkness when thou art banished.
Though thou probably doesn't know...
I would dost anything for her.
So come thick knife, and strike thy heart!
For thine love forth her shall end never!
If thy were made of thee purest poison,
I would press the poisoned chalice against thy lips,
and drink of thee, so thou wouldst be part of me always.
Show me a man that loves a fair lady so much as I.
For there is no such man!
        Ben Colwin

Family

From the very beginning each and every day
you're told of great men and women that you will never know.

You yearn to know what you think you've missed out on
What they could have taught what you could have learned.

You imagine angels and stars beautiful soft clouds for them,
to rest their heads on while they watch over everything you do.

You believe because it's what you've been taught and told,
it's what everyone thinks and believes they are a loss
    to you in your life.

Even when you grow up and find that what you've been told
isn't entirely true, that these were not great loses to you.

You will always wonder what if I had been there,
What if I had known, what if anyone had known.

Would it have changed anything, could it have been different,
Would the pain go away, would I stop crying.
        Melissa Mazurkiewicz

Life's Perplexities

No, I do not have alzheimer's
My colander encased brain
Is just slow in its synapse transmissions.
And life is so terribly confusing
With difficult technology and new terminology
Such as windows and viruses and internet.
My head is a file for numbers
As telephone, credit cards, securities and more.
One lived at a simple address once but, now it's www.com and such;
On a planet, in a solar system of a galaxy.
Happy days are not here again,
'Twas much easier in the thirties
When we coped with trapezoids
And, "Parlez-vous francais?" And paniculata grandiflora
Even though, we had Copernicus, Galileo, Keppler, and Einstein.
The new millennium is so very frightening.
I must learn to sandpaper my irritations!

Theresa D. Trezza

Mother's Day

Each year around the middle of May;
Our very special ladies are recognized on that day.
They aren't all rocket scientists,
computer programmers, or such;
But to some of us, our lives in special ways they do touch.
Daughters, sisters, wives, or friends they may be;
To each of us a special place in our hearts they hold you see.
Through the miracle of birth and their tenderness of love;
They use a special guidance from our dear Lord above.
They have nurtured, molded, and guided us to be what we are.
We all need to reach out and praise them from near and far.
For many sacrifices have been made for us one and all;
Hugging, kissing, caressing, or picking us up when we all fall.
Their unselfishness and love, day in and day out;
That is exactly what being a Mother is all about.
Take her out, buy her flowers, and treat her special in many ways;
But don't forget, to us she is our Mother the other 364 days!

Steven H. Lee

Elusions

As the mountains feel the imprisonment, of the grounds mighty chain.
And the wind for a storm feels, the heartache and the pain.
And as the droplets of water, are ordered sadly from the sky.
And the sun sheds a tear for he, caused a plant to die.
We curse these many things, as the age and times roll by.
Thinking only of our broken hearts, and tear filled eyes.
We should stop for a minute and think, of all these things.
Of how we would feel without nature,
and the joys that she brings.
For if the mountains didn't stand still
and the storms didn't blow
and the droplets of water didn't fall or the sun didn't show
Then the times wouldn't roll on, and we would not be here.
To share the laugh of laughter, or the sadness of a tear.
It's not a bowl of roses, or a cave of broken hearts.
We must take and give in both, a little perfume and some parts.
Either way it is life, in which we must live.
For the good and the bad, we must take and then give.

Sharon Mitchell

Dear Momma

Dear Momma,
How can you love a friend that's so bad;
Everyday she makes you happy, then you're sad.
Right arm, left arm, left arm, right; Oh no!
It's gotten so bad now, you need her every night.
Near-at-hand is the end of your life!
Momma, read the first letter of each sentence and you will see;
The horrible, ugly friend that you put before me.

Latisha Richardson

Mother, A Gift Of Love

A mother's love transcending any words to measure.
An unconditional love that's been a family's treasure.
A love steadfastly guiding us through laughter, pain and tears,
An endless love that kept on giving year by passing year.

How often did we take her caring love for granted?
This heartfelt love she gave to us so graciously;
Unselfish love encircling us each day and ever growing deeper,
Please God, grant each mother's child with eyes to really see.

To see that as we grew within her wisdom,
And progressed from childhood to maturity.
This priceless mother too was growing older,
Can it be that someday with us she'll no longer be?

The twilight of her years; the smile still sweet upon her face;
Age crowning her with beauty, gentleness, and grace,
Her spirit shining forth with strength and dignity.
As Lord she contemplates a new life spent with thee.

Can it be the happy, nurturing, years have swiftly passed away?
A family closely gathers her to honor;
    their voices in remembrance softly say,
"Mom, this wondrous gift of love you've given us has come full circle;
They celebrate her life of love - filled blessing; with love,
    a family says goodbye today.

Joan R. Taylor

Watching From Above

Sitting here at a desk thinking of the days when you were here.
Looking at pictures of you, wondering how you are, if you're happy in
The heavens above.
You are our angel who watches down from the clouds above us.
If only you could know how much I hurt,
I know you can see, but can you actually feel my pain.
You're an angel of Grace, always smiling whether you're happy or sad.
You are my bright light that helps me go on with life.
I believe you are helping me stay alive.
If it wasn't for you I'd be almost dead.
I still have dreams about your car accident,
I can see everything you went through.
Sometimes I feel like I'm the one who's dead.
But we know that's not true.
The day of your viewing, I couldn't stand
To believe that was you lying there. I can remember saying
"Daddy why is she so cold?" Having to see all those bruises and
The expression on your face. It was full of pain, misery and
Confusion. It looked like you were asking God why.
Why did this happen to me? That's what your expression told me.

Andrea Kay Tidd

Chains

The cry of a woman comes from a distance
I run towards the sound
Stop at the gate and peer in
I see nothing

A movement, a scuffle of feet is all I hear
A deep strong manly voice yells "who's there?"
I keep quiet and duck from view
The man strikes a match and lights a lantern
He looks about, but sees nothing

So he continues as he was
I spot a kinky haired, big nose, big lip male
Cracking his whip at the back of a white female
Then I am awakened from this dream
I realize I am still the oppressed

Solely because of my kinky hair, big nose, big lips
Bondage at birth, bondage at death
Bondage in mind, and Bondage in chains
A dream is only a dream but I pray to see the day of equality for all

Fatima Abbas

Love

Once upon a picosecond, God,
Seated on His ubiquitous throne, decided
To bestow happiness to a random undeserving soul. He chose me.
God was in a jocular mood;
With His infinite tongue in His infinite cheek, He said:
Let there be love in him!
For I have ordained love to be the prime directive
   in this part of my Universes.
And for one thousand picoseconds,
   longer than one thousand years to you and me,
Infinite God looked (or whatever He does with His infinite eyes)
   into the Earth.
And He found you . . . and He gave me to you . . .
   and He gave you to me.
God was a jocular mood,
   with His infinite tongue in His infinite cheek, He said:
Let them be happy and suffer in their joy,
For I Myself could not attain a painless love,
   some thousands years ago,
While visiting this place in human form.
And then, the picoseconds gone, God thought,
Among His other infinite and simultaneous thoughts:
My work complete, Creation in My hands,
   I must return to other tasks undone.
Let these two souls stand on their feet.
I gave them all there is to want. The rest is theirs . . .

Daniel Grau

A Year And A Half Ago...

A year and a half ago my NaNa was here,
A year and a half ago I felt a lot of fear.

A year and a half ago I was very sad,
A year and a half ago I was also very mad.

A year and a half ago I felt a lot of pain,
A year and a half ago all I could think about was her and her cane.

A year and a half ago I remember her coming
   and ringing our doorbell chimes,
A year and half ago I remember all the good times.

But she's still in my heart even though she's gone,
And I still miss her deeply,
But I will always remember her as I move on.

Jaclyn R. Reilly

Life Get's Better With Time

No matter how difficult your task may seem,
You must follow your golden dream.
Though you may be afraid of the road that lies ahead,
The answers come not, by staying depressed in bed.
For there are many opportunity's that await's for your arrival,
In order to make in this world, you must be a survivor.
Things in life may not always go according to the way you may plan,
Focus only on the future, and then you will be able to stand.
For God himself has given us all a very special gift called life,
We must cherish it morning, noon, and night.
There is nothing that one can not do, if one truly and
honestly believe's.

Life is not perfect, nor will it ever be.

Leslie Lawrence

Still In Love

I'm still in love with you. I can't deny it,
   on the inside I'm slowly dying, you got me crying.
All the pain and heartache doesn't seem to go away,
I think of you night and day. As we move on, we change,
And nothing will ever be the same. I know in my heart you will
   always be, cause you were the one to always look after me.

Andrea Roberts

I Cry

Sorrow is among us, hate is closing in, blackness is
spreading, happiness is but a shadow of our past. I use to cry
salty tears now my tears are bloody with sin and hatred.

I'm lost in a sea of sorrow and despair. I'm drowning.
It looks as though there is no light at the end of this tunnel.
I can't survive anymore, there is no change. I can never go back
to the way it was before.

I cry tears of sorrow, of defeat. I have lost the joy of life.
it no longer flows through me. My heart can break no more.
My life is mourning a death that will not come, my death.

My generation is occupied by lost souls, wandering the earth.
They have committed the ultimate sins. No one will take them in
because their cursed. This curse is from the sins they have
committed and this will kill generations to come.

As we die both you and I. With my head in my hands,
I sit and cry. Now I have told my sad story, so many tears I have
shed because of it. Now go, please go and don't end up
as I have.

Amberlynn Porter

The Rape Of The Black Man

Oh! What fools we were to believe we are too illiterate and
couldn't be taught or to think intelligently. Tricked into darkness
with our eyes wide open. Taking advantage of used and
abused, made to work from sun up until sun down to service
others in every way possible with our bodies and our minds and
not being able to refuse raped in every way imaginable, men
Strong Black Men.
We stand in the light of time and nothing changes we are still
being raped with no defense, with the justice system turning it
head. Why have we giving up, lost our faith sunk so low,
because no one hear our cry, no one see the blood spilling into
our streets,
no one feels our wounds. So we throw up our legs and open our
arms and embrace the rapist trying to easy the pain. The result
of these rapes end also in pain and hurt a lot more than the
victim it hurt his love ones and all those like him. Because there
seem to be no better tomorrow and the disease keeps spreading.
Oh! What a crime this is. Oh! What a lost. "Black Men
Strong Black Men "Raped"

Jeanette Curry

Black Roses

We stand face to face, yet we are in totally different worlds,
Not knowing what river to cross to venture towards the other side.
Time is stilled, seasons are silenced,
Our lips utter no words.

You seek comprehension of the crevices of my mind,
Crumbling fortresses of lingering hurts and insecurities.
You dispel the myths of lacking gentlemanhood,
Your intentions are pure and sincere.

I stand before you, completely mesmerized,
Disbelieving your heartfelt plea of true sensitivity.
If it be a dream, let me slumber in peace,
I've never known a man to care so much.

Our hands touch nervously, yet our hearts journey no more.
The path of our souls cross, ascending higher than heaven.
Our reflections mirror the core of eternal illumination,
No distractions, just an awaited embrace,
Amidst the petals of black roses.

Angela D. Adams-Hemphill

Old Chinese Rose Jar

Cherished old Chinese rose jar, what is your magic?
Your lifted cover releases a potpourri of memories
Far surpassing any lingering trace of spicy petals.
Loving memories, warm as the gentle hands
    that gathered each blossom.
Memories so beloved, unshed tears blur eyes,
Insistent memories lump behind tight throat,
Heartache of love once known, now gone beyond.
Do you know who cherishes rose petals now?
Are you glad dried blossoms can recreate your aura once more?
Rustling petals go back to sleep.
Tenderly, lid presses down on petals and emotions,
Put away, to be released another day.
How many ways our resurrection comes.
In memories, love and a cloisonne bowl.
Who needs a grave?
Man cannot be contained!

Barbara Jane Vanderwarker

A Simple Glance

His mind I cannot read, though his face I can.
His body sends the languages of a cruel, cold hearted man.

He was not always this way to me. He used to show me love.
Now he won't even speak to me and I doubt I'm spoken of.

It hurt to see him pass me with rarely even a glance.
Each time I see him pass, " Is this my chance?"
The chance he'll give me to show him love once again
or maybe even the chance for me to be just a friend.

I would hate to see it pass me like I let it go before,
but from then till now, I've been just glance and I'm
afraid to him I'll never be more.

I thought we would last forever, but it seems
forever doesn't last. I'd give anything if he
would look at me the way he did in the past.

Now the past is gone like the snow in spring and I
let go of my chance, so it seems from now until forever,
I will remain a simple glance.

Christy McRae

Switch The Rails

In this life of speed and chaos,
We rally round to meet its churn,
Forever marking time with rancor!
Forever losing time in Fear!

When 'ere we grasp a moment's lone,
We journey quickly to our special place,
Of calm, peace, harmony, joy and Love.
So tranquil, and so devoid of all we fear and hate.

Stop! Why wail along this glorious gift of life,
When all we wish is but a moment's span?
Why not switch the trail we travel
Making Love our life and fear a foggy and forgotten failing?

Oh how quickly justifications rattle forth
Against life's joys and for its tragedies!
Old fear triumphant in its strangle hold.

If we would but recognize
The shallowness, the weakness of fear's dominion,
Versus the pure strength of Love's expansive endowment,
Then would we enthusiastically embrace and live our gift of life in
full, with innate calm, peace, harmony, joy and love!

Addie Claudia DuLaux

I Always Love Someone, But I Didn't Know

I always love someone, but I didn't know they didn't care.
I always tried to cry, but I knew I'll never get nowhere.
    Sometimes I'll watch them walk away. Not wanting them to go.
I whisper I love you. But never let them know.
    I cried all night in misery. I went insane,
there's nothing in this world that can cause such a pain.
    If I could choose between love and death, I think I'll rather die.
Love is fun but it hurts so much. The price you pay is high.
    So I say don't fall in love. You'll get hurt before it's through,
You see, my friend I ought to know I fell in love with you.

Tanika Dickens

The Belly Of Life

It began 9 months ago
The mystery seed was planted
A life will soon emerge from
The belly of my sister

It began 9 months ago
Its body starting to form
We can now see its feet, its hands and its head
It's starting to bud from within
The belly of my sister

It began 9 months ago
I swear that she willed the conception
Soon a child will be born, for all of us to spoil with love and
    affection
This baby inside
The belly of my sister

It began 9 months ago
The excitement builds with each day and unfortunately the difficult
    pains seem to build as well inside
The belly of my sister

It began 9 months ago
This special treasure will soon appear for all of the family to
    splendor and to think this wonderful gift began to grow
    into a little person inside
The belly of my sister

Diana Healy

Home Sick

Take me home I want to sleep in my own bed tonight,
She closed her eyes and turned off the light.
But he still sat on the bed, waiting for his gift, a kiss,
    a kiss that would cost him his life.

They all said stay away she's much to young!
Find some one your own age son.
But, he would only smile and wave oh,
    this girl will send you to your grave,
    they warned him and hurt him but the idea never sunk in.

He just kept loving her. Nothing really matters he said.
If I die my love for her will be dead.
She can't bear the thought of me leaving her alone every little
    detail will haunter even my cologne.
But its too late to reason we will leave in the blink of an eye.
We will run away with out saying good bye.
Just a note to say that you can't get us to say our love has fell.

No, I would rather be sentenced to life in blistering hot hell,
    nothing can stop this love inside.
Not even if you tried. Our love is deep the hill is to sleep.
So, if her parents read this. We say by the time you finish
    reading this we will be far and long we will be gone.
And say love sees past age and life. It sees what's inside.

Sarah Alderman

Realm Of Love

Romance the walk under the stars
  on a half moon lit night.
With a peaceful femme, of laughter
  and much to our incredible delight
We seem to be enjoying the west sand between our toes
  Of glimmering ocean shores.
I myself am in total awe of her womanly essence
  Because holding her hand is a gift, and reassures our presence.
Wow!....She orchestrates whispers of soothing sweet tones
  Giving me so much inspiration I just knew that she'd be the one.
I tell her she's a creature of great enduring beauty
  She says to me I could have just her forever! I mean that truly!
With which to my surprise! Of Why?
  Things aren't what they seemed.
Suddenly it hit me!?!
  It was just another crazy dream.

  Brad Leach

Possibilities

Thinking of brings it on - the feeling that maybe the past isn't gone,
Or someone just might live on Earth forever.
I turn my head and face the day, but the sky's already turned to grey,
And my heart is wrenched away as by a lever.

I drift back into my pensive stupor.
The chores and bills wait. Must I be their suitor?
The dreams of a lifetime and the ghosts of the past,
The fallen hopes, how love doesn't last...

I sift through it all and pick up the shards.
I'd shuffle the deck, but no new cards
Could turn away the hands of time and fate,
Or open up another clenched in fear or hate.

Suddenly, I look inside, puzzling at the great divide.
I see an open door or two - a narrow, cobbled avenue.
Though my body is at rest, my mind's endurance is put to the test.
The heat brings welcome, cooling sweat, as I fall into a safety net.

Dichotomies and diplomacies, abilities and possibilities,
Streaming through my mind, my heart no longer blind,
I go on day by day, standing in the fray,
Knowing strife is just one word for life.

  James J. Gvozdas

A Silhouette Of A Promise...

Dreams make the spirit grow and fulfill it.
Ride on, charge at any broken path at will.
Even if you cannot take it to the highest point
Aim high and you, with God, fulfill's it.
Mistakes are common upon the earth's children.
So never be frightened of failures, they will always be.

Come fourth, rise above your ancient masks,
Overcome each obstacle and path.
Madness may endure you, but come fourth and pray,
Endure the powers of your mind.

Trying, trying, trying...ritual that may haunt you too!
Until you make it to the heavenly land of your precious promise.
Even when your blunders overcome you, do not fret yourself to death.

Soon you will find the right path, also.
Fair is the goal when it is achieved, and one, who has
  achieved it and taken it to the highest.

Mine, theirs, even yours...
Arising from their broken worlds comes light.
Fearless beauty overcomes the miraculous spirit.
You will find it, you will see it; you and your silhouetted promises.

  Laura M. Cook

A Black Women Distinction

I was born into this world.
To grow into a strong black women.
To have pride in myself, to survive for myself.
In this life time I will face many disagreements.
But I will not let that harm me, hurt me,
  or reverse me of the person I am.
I have a destiny that no man can take away from me.
A destination to become a form of life,
to teach our black children that we are not the enemy of this earth.
A destination to be the back bone of others
  who are not stronger then me.
A destination to glide through life without being
  treated like a mondar on same type of life
  that God put on this earth to be treated like an animal.
A destination to reveal that I am a image of freedom
  a fisty spirit that can show a positive way to life.
As a growing black women. I will educate, an bring together a
  unity of followers, who are strong who are not a shame of their colon.
Destination to educate sisters to be proud of there race.
Show that black is beautiful.

  Sylvia Patrice Lewis

Behind The Pane

Inside this darkened room
is fire with such ardor that it puts the sun to shame
can you see it's flickering
through the cobweb laced pane?

In this forgotten locked away place...this empty and lonely space
candles of fiery intensity brightly burn,
and shimmer, and flutter and...yearn

But there's no one out there to see
abundance of nothing...inside these walls... for me
gazing out this casement window in the light of day,
in the moonlight, when the sky's gray,

Waiting, hoping...for someone to come tapping
at my window sill to unlock the latch
let me find someone who still feels the fervor for life I do

Someone with a heart that's kind, and pure, and true
stranger passing by...is it you... who'll unlock the lock
shatter these pains and help me to walk through?

  Morrie W. Greene

Can I, Or Should I Dare Say A Letter Of Love

How are you? For some time
I have admired you from afar
yet I am wondering if I should be writing you now.

But like the chemist if I am to find the formula to this dilemma
Why procrastinate. Or tell my heart be still when you are near.
If the research must begin why not now, with us.

Beauty is in the eyes of the beholder
Unlike the tide that roll away never to return, I must take my chances

If there must be a tomorrow for me
Less love while there is life with in us.

Somehow the beauty of it all is in you and I

Simply beautiful, forgive me if I seem straight forward
How else are you to know

By quiet flickering fire I sat dreaming of you.
You are crowding my mind, more than I should admit.

Would it be a total catastrophe to say, come my love.
Take my hand walk through love garden with me.

But wait the lane is long.
The rose are sweet why not gather a few along the way.

Come my love awaits you.

  Illia L. Daniels

There Is A Time For Rest

While driving, I saw it — an unfamiliar site on a familiar road.
A man driving a tractor pulling a rake.
My mind began to wander — I pulled off the road.
I watched and before my eyes the site became a familiar one.
The man on the tractor was you, dad the field - the farm I grew up on.

Then all the memories came rushing back — memories of many
haying seasons, some better than others.
The smell of home cooking permeating from the kitchen.
The sight of all of you sitting down to eat the food so lovingly
prepared by your wife and daughters.
It seemed just as quick as you came in, you were all gone.
Back to the fields - no time for rest.
Mom, Grandma, Liz-Ann and I would eat our dinner, cleanup
and begin preparations for supper - no time for rest.

At the end of the day, the hired hands had all left and the cows
  had been milked....
But the sky began to darken - so again no time for rest.
We would all hurry to the field and bring in the remaining hay.
Before the first sprinkle all the bales had been put under cover.
We would all sit on, the front porch watching the rain, drinking
rootbear floats and then finally we would rest.

I realized as I watched the rain that I was no longer on the farm.
I began driving again and then the scene became clear.
There is a time in life for work — when we are young and able.
And then there is a time for rest....

Jennifer N. Bird - Father's Day '96

Mother

One little girl who wants to grow up and be just like.

One who waits nine months to become and did twice.

One who grew up and now is.

One knowing that the worries and heartaches will come and go,
  but the love and memories will last a lifetime.

One who teaches us right from wrong. ABC's and 123's.
Watching our every little step until the time
  for the yellow school bus to drive us away.

One who prepares us for that step up from grade school to high school,
  wishing that we could stay little forever.

One who cherishes every moment possible before graduation,
  knowing what comes next.

One who sits and dreams of a better life for each of us,
  just like the one her mother gave to her.

One who loves and takes care of us,
  sometimes better than she takes care of her own self.

One who watches her only two daughters walk down the aisle,
  and hoping that she has taught them enough to make it on their own.

One who keeps in touch with us as the years go by, helping and giving,
  sometimes neglecting things for herself to benefit us.

As we look back through the years, we realize how lucky we were,
  and still are.

This is what we call a mother.

Kimberly A. Ross

The Light

The light is bright and in my eyes I know it is coming time for me to die.
As I walk I prepare for Heaven or Hell which ever will be there.
A angel of mercy stands upon a cloud
  beckoning me to sit upon her shroud.
My clothing is then shed now I know that I am dead but I am not fearful.
For the light is comforting the light is eternal life.

Daniel Steenbergen

Colors Of You

I may not know what love is or about,
But what I do know is it's not when people scream or shout,

It's not the colors black and blue,
And then to cover up for the colors you tell me "I love you,"

It's not making water puddles every night,
And then saying "I'm sorry" and trying to hold me tight,

My inside feels so much pain the outside shows the pain,
The colors everywhere just now scaring up,

Leaving would be impossible because I'm trapped in a cage,
And you know I can't come out,

You told me you loved me and that love hurts,
But I have to draw the line somewhere I just don't know where to start,

I do know that I love you in my heart,
Trying to believe that isn't true is the hard part,

I have to get away from these colors that's what I need to do,
But it's impossible when I've come to know I do love you.

Jessica Lyn West

Tumble Weed

Until I can master emotions that lay deep inside of me.

Like a tumble weed. Driving by a ghostly wind,
that continuously blows with no respect to where or when.

Only then can I be free, no man can
measure the height or depths of me.

Emotional maturity is what I strive to reach,
because without it I'm not really unique.

Life is full of hurt and pain but our response is what keep us sane.
Emotions is like a powerful game.
If left uncheck can have such a staggering effect.

Because I know not where trouble may arise.
I'm not afraid. Being truly in touch with my insides.

This is why I strive to be like the tumbling weed,
rolling oh, so care free. The wind doesn't bother me.

Jean Shepard Williams

A Look

It starts with a look, long or short, in between there's: warmth,
  touching, despair, and frustration; we need, we want, there's
  tenderness; there are feelings and giving and taking and sharing.

We show compassion, generosity, and patience;
  we're proud and mad, right or wrong, happy or sad.
Communication, thoughtfulness, and kindness;
  there are moments, seconds, years, and lifetime.

We kiss, hug, touch, talk, sing, and make love.

We walk and taste, hope and breath, shout and listen.
There's evil and goodness, jealousy and conceit, yet joy and faith;
  we hold, we trust, we accept and defy.

Caring, demanding, breathing in and out; being super, tremendous,
  and wonderful.
Gifts, greatness, healing, all in time.
Experiences, teaching, always perfect.

Exceptional, nonstop, forever and always!
Dreams and goals, all in your eyes; man and woman,
  gold and black, touch again; midnight, midday, it doesn't matter.

This started with a look - it turned to love; this is the path it followed,
  it was the day I met you; today is that same day,
It will never end.

Stephen J. Morgan

Love Is . . . Lost

Love is a shapeless entity by which man can be brought
   to the edge of heaven, or suspended over the depths of hell.
Love can be seen a far, when it is witnessed in the lives of others.
Or seen up close, when it is felt in ones own life.
Love has brought people up, and torn them down,
   given them wisdom and drove them to insanity.
Love is overwhelming, yet so small that people search all their lives,
   and never find it.
Love can warm the heart,
   but to stand in its shadow can freeze the soul.
Love is unpredictable
People who search for it find it only in those
   who have never looked for it
Love is peace and chaos.
Love is addictive, to have known love, is to want it forever . . .
Whatever Love may be, it no longer presides in my soul.
I am the shadow of love. I lost it and know not where to find it
I can see it in others, but cannot feel it in myself
I have dwelt in heaven, now I preside in hell.
I have cursed all that love is, yet I still long to feel its touch
I have prayed for my own destruction, yet I am still allowed to live.

   Daniel G. DeSautell

Mirror Image

Victorian nobles face, soft and unblemished, it is the only white
thing which you possess you with the disorderly crows feather
hair, snake burrow eyes, stoplight red mouth and small rounded
body of mushroom when you line your eyes with war mourning
paint all you can see is a little girl, in long braids and eyes of
saucers staring back
People, parents, boyfriends have proclaimed you beautiful for
years but you can't put stock in it, it won't clothe, feed or warm
you and when men look you over, fresh calf in the market place,
that's exactly how you feel, led to slaughter by enthusiastic
hands so you have marred this flesh with inlaid needle point
sketches in an attempt to call it your own
and you have pierced long elfin ears and sculpted nose
time and time again to mark private property
Yet you are as hypocritical as a political candidate
as you pose nude for drawing classes
claiming that it's not your soul or only in the name of art
which is, when it is boiled down, your one true platform
for the words can never hold a mirror to your face

   Miriam Wiederhorn

Untitled

Endless days billowing into equivalent nights.
Always going.
Never stopping.
The scrutiny goes on.
Forever so it seems.
Can't the pain stop?
When does the suffering end: If ever.
Tiresome moments race into dreadful misbecomings.
A race to the finish.
Not knowing what the end holds into store.
Frivolous thoughts cloud the minds of those who oppose just that.
But why disagree? To fall into the hands of others is not
Completely
Wrong. No struggle is too great, no insecurity deemed.
What to do? Where to go? How to know: Some never will.
Others ponder over the thought to insanity.
Then there are those who have had the answer all along
But do not wish to succeed.
And never will.

   Nicole M. Hipple

The Segregated Paints

Sally sat quietly at the table before her.
A table covered with a rainbow of paints and blank paper.
Mama taught her how to mix colors to make other colors.
Sally remembered that yellow and red made orange.
So Orange, orange was the color of the bright shining sun that
Sally painted at the top of her white paper.
Green, green was the grass below the hot, orange sun painted by Sally.
Weren't no mixin' when it came to green, she thought.
Blue and red combined made the deep, deep purple of the lilacs
sprouting from the green, green of the grass Sally had painted.
Sally looked at her paints and wondered
   what color did black and white make?
No such color is what mama had told her.
As she began stirring the white liquid into the dark,
   black paint her mama walked in,
Sally turned questioningly to her mama and asked,
"I thought you said that black and white don't mix?
That's not true mama. Look here, I made a shade of gray."

   Natalie E. Carbo

Lights

The moon crawls across the naked sky, dressed with only
   random clouds strolling along as if they had a destination.
A child stands on the street corner with the moon and a street light
   peering down upon him, forming two distinct shadows.
The lights are different.
The child's eyes gaze into the moon and a deep space unfolds —
   soft, gentle, thoughtful.
He turns toward the street light, but quickly looks away.
Colored flashes sprint before his closed eyes.
He looks up once more and his eyes have adjusted to the street light —
   its brightness and intensity.
As he looks closer, the non-focused eyes see a small dark spot
   resting on the bottom of the oval-shaped light covering.
And the child realizes that it is a pile of rotten insect corpses.

   Thomas Grimm

Another

It looks like love
That's what it seems
She fills your days
And invades your dreams

But it's not your heart she wants, and still your love for her grows

Your love for her
So pure and whole
It's in your heart
It's in your soul

But it's not your heart she wants, and not one part of you knows

You know it's so strong
This feeling you feel
That no matter what happens
You'll love her still

But it's not your heart she wants, and you could love no other

But you're never happy
You just get sadder
Because now you know
your feelings don't matter

Because it's not your heart she wants, she wants the heart of another.

   Nathan C. Sexton

Togetherness

What is togetherness?
To you it may be one thing, to me it may be another
Togetherness is something rarely found in this world today

To me, togetherness is standing by your mate, friend or relative
   Yet not putting pressure and stress upon them
To me togetherness is someone to hold you up when you are down
   Someone to encourage you, not discourage you
If you have someone on your side,
   you should not take them for granted
   For just as easy as you came together, you can fall apart
Togetherness with your spouse should be a special feeling
A feeling beyond feelings that you can't put into words
A feeling above the rest in which your quest should involve
   Communication, laughter, and love
   Love that passes all tests of time
   A love to bind, from now to the end of time

Look, find, and hold tight to that something special called
   Togetherness

   Elissa Edwards

The Loss Of Innocence

The life of a child is a gift from above,
They're brought into this world with innocence and nothing but love.
Sometimes they're taken to a strangers home,
But the parents still love them as one of their own.

The family loves the child with all of their heart,
And a promise is made that it will never depart.
A child brings happiness for so many years,
with good times and bad, and quite a few years.

Sometimes people drive when they've had too much to drink,
Their mind is so intoxicated, it has no time to think.
You might have been lucky, driving drunk in the past,
But if you drive away this time, it might be your last.

So many children have been killed, by people who are drunk,
It hurts the parents so much, it feels as though their hearts have sunk.
Hopefully drunk drivers will someday realize this
When you drive drunk, the child you kill will be missed.

A drunk driver can take a child's life in a blink of an eye,
So if you are going to drink, please don't drive.

   Alex T. Hartsell

The Harbor Side Warrior

In myth and legends found a certain strength forewarned;
From dreaded seas so fearce saved by only Zeus's son.

To surge her oceans deep her ominous soul they quench;
A sacrificial mate she seeks for the spirited heart they send.

On the bow of his warship sails his bearded face unfurls;
No captains' mate dare guess, to protect, Hercules' eternal quest.

Weathered on this wooden hull the warship veteran vessel sails;
Crisscrossed the seven seas, she knows now his presence well.

Sixty-seven years last they met, his eyes always to be transfixed;
Stony Brook to guard his harbor safe his back forever against its bay.

Lest he glance the waters blue, in his heart a depthless yearn;
Nor feel his hull break waters thru, or taste spray of her salty
   breath.

   Debi Joy Burghard

My Happiness

I found my happiness in God
He loved me in spite of, and I thought it was odd

He cares for me like no other can
He understands me and has the patience of no other man

If you trust and believe he'll set you free
He's like no other you'll find, just try him you'll see

He'll make your gray skies sunny and clear
Your heart's desire's and prayers he'll always hear

You'll never be in darkness; because he is an everlasting light
He captures hearts and frees souls like a thief in the night

Accept him
Never ever reject him

He will supply each and every one of your needs
If you love him and have faith with just the size of a mustard seed.

   Cheryl Verna Rose

When I...

When I arrived you were there to welcome me.
When I opened my eyes you were there for me to see.
When I fell you were there to catch me.
When I started walking you were there to guide me.
When I spoke my first word you were there to listen.
When I started preschool you were there to hold my hand.
When I was afraid you were there to hold me.
When I needed a hug you were there to give me three.
When I couldn't sleep you were there to tuck me in.
When I was told that I couldn't read at grade level you were there
   to fight my battle.
When I brought you "A" papers you were there to say great job.
When I brought home bad report cards you were there to tell
   and ask me why it was this way.
When I turned 13 you were there to tell me what to look out for.
When I had troubles you were there to see me through them.
When I felt down you were there to say just the right thing.
When I cried you were there to dry my tears.
When I was happy you were there to be joyful with me.
When I needed a friend you were there to be that friend.
When I was small you were there and even now you're here.

   Tanya Carr

Idol Of Night

Come midnight's wary calm I make escape,
Enter a dark place, between the beams of time and space
Through listless hours spent upon this Earth; blazing rose
That bloomed then withered in my palm,
And scattered lofty dreams upon my toes.
O vision! Dead leaves,
Sweet wish born to nothingness
As the wind reaps willow seeds!
How strange my barren sight
Should summon this comely ghost
Which haunts my dreams each wicked night;
Whose porcelain face framed all the mystery of the Mona Lisa's grin
In every picturesque expression.
And glow did the divine blueprint of her form.
The hopes of every dreamer's dreams swirled in her storm.
And dormant mind and dry pen stir
To sample life's first quiver.
Sweet idler of night,
Sometimes she plays a loveless rhapsody
That keeps my weary mind from sleep.

   Christina F. Romero

Years Change

It is strange how everything changes from day to day,
I ask myself why does it end this way?

I watch my children as they grow,
By watching them I learn so much more.

I realize life is way too short,
So benefit from it for it is your own.

I see the population growing so fast,
When I was young it wasn't this bad.

I listen on tv about all the headstrong gangs fighting each other,
Whatever happened to love thy brother?

I hear about molesting, rape, and murder,
I wished I knew of a way to not let it go any further.

I sit in my home feeling safe as so many others do,
But if you really think about it we are targets to.

It is hard to understand the wars we have overseas,
By seeing that, still at home we have no peace.

I know at one time there was respect and trust,
Now everyone thinks they need to cheat one another,
they think it is a must.

I am getting older and I probably will never understand,
But hopefully one day we can all wake up, reach out, and
give one another a hand.

Evelyn L. Sanchez

Resplendent Shrine

I never thought that I could feel the way you've made me feel
I never thought that I could deal, I never thought it would be real.
I always thought the entire world was a monsoon of pain
   and so I shut my eyelids closed and ventured blindly right
   through the pouring rain that would lead me into your reign.
I never thought that I could see, I've lived my life obliviously
   guessing which door I shall open next to reveal my destiny.
I was a naked soul riding midnight blowing winds,
   a poor pathetic ghost floating, prancing, roaming free . . .
   and no matter what I did, all my actions became sins.
I never thought that I could love, but you've become my shrine-
   my precious saint of gold, so resplendent and divine
   you are the one who's turned my bitter blood
   into the sweetest brand of wine.
I always thought I'd die alone a wrinkled mass of aging past,
   an empty fool on shattered glass, upon a bed of burning grass.
I never thought there would be you,
   abundant flesh of flourished wounds, invective grief
   mutating slow into the sky's fluorescent blue...

Alexx

Hello

Hello
said the bug to the flower
   You look dull
said the ocean to the sky
   And why is that?
Said the body to the soul
   for you cannot judge me with your eyes
   although you are the life, we are the existence to always being,
   with us, there wouldn't be any of you,
   you being the scents of laughter and beauty.
   But without you
said the color to the page
   there wouldn't be any strength, or wisdom through all ages.
And said the heart to the rose
   Remember my dear, without the two of us,
   there would be no world,
   for what is a world if there is no love?

Alfie Mullins

Each Has A Reason

Each has a special brand of job on which their sights are set.
A way of life, a certain goal, for which they work and sweat.

What some regard as happiness, others may overlook
For there are many different scenes, in life's great picture book.

Each has their own conception, of what constitutes real pleasure.
Some cast aside the very thing, that other people treasure.

Some find joy in variety, some thrive on wedded bliss.
I think the greatest thing of all, is true love's tender kiss.

Indeed, there are so many things that fashion happiness,
It would be quite impossible to list each sweet caress.

So life goes on its merry way, each has a reason why,
some never find true happiness, but everyone must try.

Romuel E. Crishon

The Fires Of Life

First, there is Joy.
Then, there is sorrow, pain, grief.
Each, challenging me to survive.

Clutched from the bowels of tranquility, I fear for life.
The painful voyage seem endless.
Terrified am I, of the all consuming darkness.

By sheer will, I struggle for that first breath.
The outside air, cold and frigid, numbs my senses.
Freezing am I, in this purified wind.

Suddenly, darkness gives way to the blinding lights,
   burning in my eyes.
Strange noises I cannot understand invade my senses.
Fear I, the loud voices.

Confused am I, in this alien world.
Fight, this challenge must I,
As the journey through the fires of life inspires me to birth.

Jose M. Viera

Embers

As the flame begin to dim, but the embers won't let it die.
The wind is wildly blowing, not a star up in the sky.
Time passes, time goes on,
time to live, time to love
a bottle of wine and music for the soul
If you're lucky, someone to closely hold.
The night is here all dark and sleepy
People are getting sentimental and weepy.
Take your lover by the hand, share the warm feeling while you can.

Now the embers are almost gone, soon it will be beginning of dawn,
A new day is on the way, make it the best in every way.
Keep your love close but also let it be free
You just be you and let me be me.
If our paths someday cross and we again meet,
Back to the fireside we will retreat.
As the fire slowly burns, the embers appear.
Renewed friendship and happiness are here.
We'll re-kindle our flame and allow love to bloom
Will it bring ecstasy or gloom?
Time passes, time goes on with one thing certain, the flame
into embers will burn.

Barbara Kusserow

The Blue, The Grey, The Red: A Civil War Lament

Summer hues of brown and emerald shift gaily: full, warm, lush;
Drops of diamonds dance on flower faces;
A Day: Bright, Soft and Calm.

Mighty waves of Midnight Blue surge forward: tall, sure, intense;
Sparks of sunlight flash on golden guns;
A Leader: Hard, Brash and Bold.

Steady walls of stone-set Grey hold fast: firm, calm, quiet,
Darts of shadow play on silver swords;
A Leader: Proud, Brave and Sad.

Ugly spurts of dark red blood stain soldiers:
    twisted, torn, trembling;
Shreds of flesh hang on broken bones;
A Body: Battered, Bruised and Dead.

Shivering silence of sadness-settles down, grieving tired, alone;
Shrouds of death press on hollow hearts;
A Country: Faded Blue, Stained Grey and—Red.

Carol L. Allen

Whether or Not

Whether it be freezing cold or whether it be hot
We're bound to have weather, whether or not.

You may have fair warning of an oncoming storm
So keep the home fires burning so you will keep quite warm.

When you don't like the weather, just what are you to do?
There is no way to change it, so here's a plan for you.

Learn to enjoy the weather, whether it be foul or fair
You will find enjoyment, for weather is everywhere.

Take a brisk stroll in the rain or a leisurely walk in the sun
Go for a swim in the water or skate on the pond for fun.

Play around in a snowdrift or enjoy a bright summer day
Cherish the flowers of springtime, get out with the weather and play.

Thank old Mother Nature for the blessings she has wrought
For we must tolerate weather, whether or not!

Ernest L. Moody

Taken From

From the start... A new beginning,
A chance to get to know you in a very special way.

From the future.... A promise,
The promise of all the things that come with each new day.

From my hands... A warm and reassuring touch,
To comfort, warm, and keep you safe, on any given night.

From my lips... A kiss,
To ease away your fears and assure you that everything will be all
    right.

From my eyes... Visions of you,
To show that you are always in my thoughts.

From my soul... Priceless treasure,
All the things in life that cannot be sold or bought.

And taken from my heart... All the things that words cannot say,
To let you know I'll love you always, and not just for today.

Norris J. Darby

The River

Eventually all things merge into one. And a river runs through it. The river banks shape and direct the water through time. As children our parents guide and protect us as we shape ourselves into one and they run through it. The river banks are our parents, and the river is our childhood. As we grow new branches open up with happiness and opportunities. The water there is so pure and clear you can see your reflection, both parents are one, yet they're not on either side of you. The river banks have eroded away, as human beings fade and die away. The memories are put under the rocks so the water can flow freely and openly. As time goes by we as individuals will someday be the banks of life to a child so the river runs through it.

Leanne Bonalumi

Roots

I look for the roots
which can explain
my way
of living

Back to my childhood
back to my baby
those growing
years

In this mirror I see no colors,
I see only thoughts
In tears that back up
My conscious life

Who I am, I'm the result of those commandments?
Were they fair, I know they couldn't be "cause life didn't turn
out
to be fair to me"

Was I fair to people,
Or to the thoughts they taught me to think?

Am I fair
to myself, is it fair, were they fair?

Am I fair to my roots
Or to myself?

Patty R. Calvillo

Shattered Love

A little girl so sweet and shy
Where deep inside a sadness lie.
A little girl who tried her best to appear as normal as the rest.
Her unhappy home life she did hide.
Ashamed, embarrassed, she had her pride.
A secret she must always keep.
Don't get too close she must not speak.

A flowery meadow, a deep blue sky,
White billowy clouds go floating by.
A special place where she can dream and wishes for a life serene.
A promise to herself she'll keep to one day leave this life so bleak.
Never to return again. A shattered love beyond her mend.

The darkness pierced by rays of light.
Streaming inner peace with warm delight.
The pain, the sorrow, the fear now pass.
Her heart's uplifted. She's free at last.

A little girl so sweet and shy no longer does she live a lie.

Francine McAree

My World

Nothing ever comes here
No one ever comes here
No way out, no way in
Anger stands in my way
Don't love, it only brings pain
Don't get attached
They'll leave if they know they can hurt you
They always do
Close your feelings off
Be numb, don't feel
Don't let people reach out
They'll leave if it gets too intense
My friends say they'll stay but they won't
Sometimes I think it would easy to be six feet under
But I don't try anymore
I used to think I could open and close my coffin
  as many times as I wanted
But I don't try anymore
I'm stuck right where I am
No way, in no way out
This is my world

Tatyana Olicker

Mankind's Paradox

Since the beginning of earliest recorded time
Man has added to the world's beauty and wonder
With statues, church towers and cities filled with homes.
Man built long, slender roads to join cities together.

Harvesting the stone from mountain and wood from the forest,
He created bridges, palaces with towering walls.
With skills and patience, he turned barren fields
Into fields of potatoes with corn and wheat growing tall.

In his search to reach the Lord Eternal above
He built beautifully designed and inspirationally spired churches.
In his search to eliminate physical pain and replace it with love,
He developed medicines, treatments and preventive living.

Yet rising behind these beautiful vistas of his achievements,
Like hideous gargoyles of some dark Netherworld,
Stand mankind's incongruent monuments to stupidity and depravity -
  Wars
Wars that recruit the youths of all nations in the world.

Wars that take the youths in their prime and destroy them.
Wars that sacrifice these youths on the altar of hate.
Wars that slaughter these youths in manner most gory.
Wars that sugarcoat their horror with a word called "Glory."

Arthur W. Dubois

To My Father

I went to visit my dad today - I hadn't for quite some time.
I just wanted to tell him about some things that were on my mind.
I told him he wouldn't believe it - how I wished that he could see
All the good things in my life that The Lord had granted me.

"I'm really quite successful - not like power or wealth.
I have a lot of friends who care plus a fine family and my health.
Your friends say I'm a lot like you - and mom says she agrees.
It makes me very proud to know there's so much of you in me."

I told him about Linda, how she came into my life.
How I felt she was so special that I asked her to be my wife.
I told him of my children and how they would make him smile
If only he could be with them for just a little while.

"I Love You Dad", I said - "maybe sometimes it didn't show."
I just felt it was important to be sure that he did know.
All these things I said to him as my eyes welled up with tears,
That fell upon the grave where he lay for 18 years.

Anthony J. Smerk

Untitled

In the embryo of my soul-lays dormant-a love.
Waiting the ecstasy of birth.
Its golden light-dimmed. Flickering in despair.
A tiny voice weeps. And echoing through my heart
I can hear the faint sound of its far distant cries.
Spiritually united...eternally bound...we are one.
Enveloped in this entity of uncertainty.
We long with all our being to embrace the comforts of true love.
To enter that realm within us that allows no doubt
and knows with full promise-we can captivate this passion.
So how-how do we succumb to these mortal chains,
and embrace Heavens gifts?
I yearn so to touch once again where we have been.
Faded through and worn heavily by time-it has slip through our
fingers.
And I know without shadow to caress and restore
this one held rapture I must learn to love you unconditionally.
But first I must learn to love myself.

Tami Bannester

Kevin

I have one Son and a Daughter too
But I also have a son that I never knew

He was born on March 3rd and his name is Kevin
I think of him often up there in Heaven

The day he was born was the same as his brother
You couldn't tell them apart one from the other

It was the happiest day of my life, but still I was sad
I just wish that one time he could call me Dad

I miss him a lot and I wish he were here
Still I know in my heart he is always near

Kevin, I Love You so much and I'll always remember
The way that I held you so warm and tender

You were asleep in my arms when I held you that day
I will never forget it is all I can say

Maybe in the future I'll understand why he had to go
If you ask me today I'd say I truly don't know

God, please take care of my boy and I'll take care of his brother
for he is Loved faithfully by me and his Mother

I hope you can see me when you look down from Heaven
I'll always be your Dad and you my Son Kevin

Mark V. Douglas

Love Is A Precious Thing

Love is a very precious thing,
It's more than just a wedding ring.
It's in your heart and in your soul,
It helps you meet that special goal.
Love is like a paradise,
It happens only once not twice.
The rest may have been puppy love,
But, when it's real; it's like heaven above.
Love is more than a steady date,
It's more than never having to wait.
It's caring and sharing and living for him,
It's standing beside him when things get dim.
It's standing behind him in whatever he does,
And being thankful for what he is and not resentful for what he was.
It's giving him all you have to give,
And learning to love him more as you live.
It's standing by to catch him,
And being there when he falls.
It's loving him dearly and treating him good,
And supporting him like no one else could.

Kasandra Umphlett

A Tribute To My Niece

A little bit of sunshine,
Left our lives one day.
It was when a niece of mine
Kara Hammerstone, passed away.

No more on this earth,
will our Kara roam, You see! God took her up above
Into her permanent home.

And knowing Kara, to God she would say,
for Mommy and my Brothers, Lord
"I love them, so we'll pray." I'll pray that they'll be happy
And please, don't be sad, tell them, I'm with my Nanny,
And also with my Dad.

And I'm not sick, any more, there's nothing here but love,
With Nanny and with my Dad and God in Heaven above.

The deep sick feeling in their hearts and with eyes, full of tears
Tell them, I'll be with them all, in the coming years.

Then we'll all be happy, for we will be with each other
All the ones, I love so much, Mom, Dad and all my Brothers.

When you look up, to see a star shining bright
Just think! It could be me. And you know! You might be right.
  William L. Silvers

Last True Island Paradise

Warm sunshine
Tall palm trees line
Shimmering pink sandy beaches
Fragrant tropic breezes, powder blue clear sky
Aqua shaded vivid sea, no other place on earth I'd rather be
Than here where, rainbow colored orchard's cover every little hill.
Towering majestic golden mountains stand so still.
Musical water falls fill winding tranquil stream's
Gently their dance flow's through valleys a most beautiful
green, the prettiest mortal eyes have ever seen.

How I love this land this last true Island Paradise

Some nights brilliant bright fluffy white cotton candy clouds
circle sparkling stars
Positive energy beams radiate an amber like, glow.
Heaven's mighty Angels watch over these miracles
Such peace, all of life's problems are released

How I love this land, this Last True Island Paradise.
  Roderick Moore

What's It All About?

Why did my daddy have to die, before I was one year old?
He loved my mom and his four little girls so much, I've been told.
Why do accidents happen and cause such pain and terror?
Sometimes it's mechanical failure and sometimes human error.
At times lives are shattered when Nature rages.
It's nothing new, it's happened through the ages.
We ask questions about these things and more.
From day to day we don't know what's in store.
Each must try to find his answers and his peace.
Sometimes it's hard, but we mustn't cease.
When the point is reached: "I'll never understand";
May all realize it's in Another Hand.
Believers can accept and know, there is a Father who loves us so.
Maybe someday questions will be answered; maybe we'll know
Love is what's important, as through eternity we go.
  Pat Berry Taylor

Farewell

Gentle breezes stirred the evening air,
  while the setting sun cast its golden glow.

It was a place with fond memories.
We had happy times here on this beach,
  many hours spent in the sunshine

This is the place where you wanted to rest,
  for all the days and all the years to come.

And so we gathered, hand in hand
  and arm in arm at the edge of the warm surf.

The time had come for last good-byes and setting spirits free.

After a day of sadness, there came, in that moment when your ashes
  joined the sand and the sea, a feeling of tremendous joy.

It came from wishes fulfilled and from the peace and love of family.

Then, as if to greet you, the dolphins did they dance upon the waves.
  Linda Hanie

"The Indian In The Cupboard"

My story is a fiction book, the author is Lynn Reid,
So why don't you take a look, and listen as I read.

One day was Omri's birthday, he got an Indian doll
He put it in the cupboard, so the Indian wouldn't fall

When he woke up in the morning, he heard a noise inside
It sounded like a snoring, he peaked and said "He's alive".

He said "I think it's magic, oh how can this be",
Then he thought once again and said "I know it's the key!"

Omri tried to talk to him, but the Indian was full of fright
He said "If you come near I'll kill you" he said "You know I might

Later the Indian befriended him, his name was Little Bear
The boy said "I am Omri", but the Indian didn't care.

Omri gave him many things, including a cowboy friend
At first they were enemies, but became friends in the end.

Little Bear was so confused, he wanted one thing in his life
The thing he wanted most of all was for him to have a wife.

Omri put in an Indian girl, they waited till she was alive
Then Little Bear saw her come out, she gave him a big surprise

Then Omri put them back inside, and sadly began to cry
Then he closed the cupboard door, and quietly said "Good-bye".
  Angela Zeoli

Angel

  It's a place where butterflies fly,
animals run freely through trees.
Flowers bloom beautifully.
  In the pond sit two turtle doves in the center of heaven and earth.
Beautiful fall night, the sky so dark with the dull moon light.
A shooting star pass through the night.
  A silhouette of a woman dressed in white appears to him on the
path of life and death. She whispers to him in a friendly tone.
He's afraid and confused, doesn't talk back.
She takes his hand to guide him into the light,
just as this happens the machine that's giving him life cuts off.
His family cries and his body is left behind.
  Arriving in heaven, its so pretty, smell like sweet roses.
Everything looked so pure. He follows the woman until they come
to a big metal door. The door opens slowly bright light in his eyes,
blind he asks where am I. A heavy but friendly voice spoke to him...
welcome to hell.
  Michelle S. Sutton

A Monarch Moon

Tonight the waves are crashing
Beating, thundering against the shore.

Tonight the full-moon is shimmering its reflection on the
dark dancing ocean,
Electricity lighting up the deep blackness of an evening sea
Illuminating life from its depths.

Feathering silk clouds roll pass, trying to cover the blue moon, yet
the radiance of the moon's glow manages to push through the
grey white cotton shapes emerging in a ballet type motion
moving rapidly as if to say "hide me if you can" and
the illuminating reflection on the sea below proves the
moon's victory.

Yolanda Mancino

Her

Can love break this wall?
Or is it just too tall?
Seem's I've been thru it before
she'll continue to move the door

But I know it's not her fault
hidden feelings in a secret vault
cares and thoughts she can not mention
what's it take to relieve this tension?

All my heart, all my affection nothing compared to perfection
Please release her of this sin please let her let me in

Her happiness more important to me that my own life could ever be
If my absence is her only cure then take me now, away from her

I've seen the future, I know how it will be
I will know her, as she will know me
and all the meaning we'll understand
as the cool sea breeze crosses the sun warmed sand

To her security, to know that she's my one and only
in that truth, she shall never be lonely
beyond it all, thru all her days
I'll be there, forever always

Tyler Martin

Come Goodly Turn-Of-Phrase

Come goodly turn-of-phrase which came to rest,
With coffin glaz'd in euphemistic earth;
Like death from friendly fire, 'tis hardly best,
One's just as dead: Can poet gain rebirth?
As (Hen's son's) "Bonny's the sod o' the Goodman's taft", o' needs
Which means, placate th' Devil, as a debtor
"Winged her flight from this (our) World, in...", reads
Beth Abby, "Expectation of a better."

Touch of double pun, borne magic land,
The smile in Devil's groan, I rest my case;
There's none so dead but that, true poet's hand,
Divinity crawls out cocoon's debase.

   Your beauty my desire, your poetry
   My ink, bewings your immortality.

J. M. Whitehead

Best Friends

We planted the seed of friendship many moons ago.
With a continuous amount of kindness, support, and love.
The roots have grown deep, allowing us to grow strong and tall.
Yet never knowing the full growth here on earth.
Only when our spirits meet will we know true friendship and the words
"Best Friend."

Denise M. Maxwell

Smores

A wisp of smoke stung my eyes and darkened the fire's furtive tongue.
She watched me talk too much as her marshmallow sparked;
   dripping into the ashes.
Hissing like a cat.

I chose a gnarled branch, whittled it into a white point,
   to poke inside my own wad of goo.
How hot were the coals?
Show me!

My boots began to melt, my shirt smelled like a country ham.
She looked at her watch, and kicked apart the ring of stones
   that I had placed to contained the heart's wanderlust.
She smiled.

I took an old pail and filled it is a nearby pond.
The black water swirled as it mixed
   with her fallen sweat and my broken elm.
Steam smeared the air.

Walking out, I noticed an old Smokey the Bear sign.
He had a stern look on his face, and
   a burning match in his paw.
I smiled. (while ripping it down)

G. A. Prewitt

Echoing Words

Echoing words of my father, once told me
   wait for your time, learn thy adapt to that time, patiently
Adjust to that time it's life's secret key.

Now, I try to pass down, the learned lessons, I'm still trying to
   teach thy, the hard times we've had, the cries I've made.
Nothing seems to move thy, nothing makes you happy.

Oh, why can't you see,
Why don't you understand, it's not all about you.
There's a path or a place that we both must meet.
Oh, why are you so blind to see.

As two individuals, let's try and defeat, what we can foresee,
   let's beat destiny.
Why do I then feel it's, defeating thy.
Let's not let our small desires beat us to part, for lets
   not forget, our other small part.
He's only a small child needing understanding and yearning for love.

We've both felt the same drowning states, the same traps,
   the same pressures, don't you see.
I'll tell you, what my father told me, it's only temporary. Should
   it last any longer, let's pray a rosary, for out heavenly father,
   to hear and foresee.

Neith D. Sostre

Untitled

Since the day that I was born you've been right by my side,
You've shared with me my happiness,
   and you've held me when I've cried.
Your the one who has helped me to stand up very tall,
And when I fail your the one who catches me when I fall.
I wasn't even sure for awhile if you still were there,
When I was hurting so very bad, I didn't think that you still cared.
The one day I cried until I couldn't hang on no more,
I couldn't see my life going back to how it was before.
Then right before I gave up and threw my arms up in despair,
I turned around and saw you and knew that you still cared.
I felt you put your arms around me and take my pain away,
You helped me to be strong enough to face another day.
I wish I would of turned around and saw you standing there, before,
I'm sorry that I doubted your love, I'll never do that anymore.
So now whenever I feel bad I know just what to do,
Just say a prayer to God above and know he will help me through.

Kathy Primeau-Bailey

The Dreaming Song

They're all together now the brothers of the past.
Hand in hand they meet him, Dream Weaver, who was last.
He couldn't wait another day, the music called him on,
For while he lay there sleeping, he heard the dreaming song.

Can't you just imagine, the pow wow in the sky.
The brothers all are dancing with sisters standing by.
The rhythm of the drums, like rain drops pounding down.
The excitement in their hearts, like lightning crashing round.

It's all quiet now, as they smile from above,
They stand and watch the tears, of those they all, so love.
They know that they will guide the way, when all our time is gone,
When we too, lay and sleep, to hear, the dreaming song.

Judith K. Abacherli

Comfort Me

Tears of pain trickle down upon my saddened face.
My paths of prolonged fear, I shall no longer trace.

My heart burns with fire, raging against the wind.
Mischievous thoughts linger to be sinned

My sadness comes upon a shredded tear
Loneliness haunts the mind of words I wish to hear

Embrace yourself upon the heart of mind
Raise my lifeless body above fire and ice, and say that I'll be fine.

Shawna Smith

Children

They laugh,
They cry,
They are the reason most of us go on living from day to day.

They are the wind that ruffles their fathers feathers,
and the gleam in their mothers' eyes.

They are there when you need them, there beside you with
unconditional love that is there for you when you need it most.

Some wear little ruffles and bows in their hair.
While others are at home in overalls and baseball caps.

They love to cuddle up at night to read a story by the bedside light.

They understand a lot of things, that you wouldn't believe,
if we only give them the chance to listen.

They are the future of our world. So don't let anyone waste
their bright inquisitive minds. If we waste their minds now,
the world will be left with the ones unwilling to work.

So be kind and gentle but strong when need be.
But please remember, they are only children.

Children are the light of our lives.

Shelby Evans

Untitled

One thing about days like today,
They are sometimes the antithesis of yesterdays,
In turn, spark the genesis of tomorrow.

The cloak of the days of rain bind the shapes on the street to one,
While, days of endless sunshine accentuate their differences,
To share the bond of oneness in universal energy under the sheets
of precipitation, to be lone in identity basking in the suns
golden rays, these are choices each of us often make.

Jon T. Middleton

Leaves

The breeze that cools the evening,
   blows some leaves down from the tree.
Are these leaves really dying, or is the tree setting them free?

As I reach out to touch one, guiding its way down,
I'm searching for an answer, if one is to be found.

If I were not standing here watching them this day,
would they dance so beautifully, or kiss the ground this way?

Why didn't I seem to notice them as they clung up in that tree,.
And now that they are falling, why do they matter so to me?

The leaves fallen yesterday, cool my feet and sooth my mind,
they make me think of days gone by, memories harsh and kind

To lives I've touched and those I've loved, this tree is teaching me,
to appreciate the leaves, each one, while they're still in the tree.

Dorothy C. Steir

January Is Beautiful

The paper says a contest is being held,
For poets across the land.
Subjects of every kind will meld
Into a book to hold in our hand.

So here I sit with pen and ink,
Trying to get my mind to think.
This is January, it is cold winter time
I should be able to write a rhyme.

The snow is new and glistening white,
This is a good subject of which to write.
I like the snow, it is clean and soft and bright,
Everyone should see it. It is a most beautiful sight!

It falls so quietly on houses, land and trees.
It covers up everything, and blows in the breeze.
Children like to sled ride and play in it,
They have their fun, and they get cold; but they don't care one bit.

So January is winter time, so many beautiful sights,
Children playing, old women crocheting to music that delights,
The old men eat their fill, find there favorite chair, to pet the cat
This is snowy winter time and life is just like that.

Edith D. Brown

The Bedmaker

Oh for the uninterrupted beds of petless people!
Lakes iced over on a windless day, frozen in creaseless welcome;
   sheets, blankets, pillows — all lie serene beneath the pristine spread.
Eye-delighting, uninterrupted bed!

Not so my own. Mine is a chaos of cratered pillows,
storm-tossed sheets, with spread avalanched to one side,
and blankets seething upward under the mobile mass
you not surprisingly mistook for magma.

"Magma?" you asked. "A volcanic bed?"
In denial, I shook my head.
Seconds pass; a glacial quiet has settled where once upheaval reigned.
Deftly, I part blankets to reveal a uniquely charming terminal moraine:
   Furry it is, with forepaws folded under chest.
   Eyes locked in sleep, it exudes innocence, fragility.

All four pounds mine, I boast.
My kitten, fellow-bedmaker, totally dedicated to this art;
   he pursues it with the unexpectedness of genius,
   never assisting twice in the same way.
Do you wonder my interrupted bed is here to stay?

Anne S. Williams

Autumn Dreams

The time has come again for changes that must be made,
The sweet sounds of the song bird is silenced,
The trees are bare and the multi-color leaves drift proudly and
    gracefully on top of the crisp swift wind that beats upon the earth,
Lakes roar with monstrous waves that slap the faces of the shores,
Playgrounds are filled with only memories of gleeful children,
And the sun that smiled for all the day is now hidden by light
    fluffy clouds at play,
Night is called by an earlier hour,
The blossom is gone,
There's not one flower.
Mr. Moon glows with great luminous powers,
Along with diamond like stars that you can count for hours,
The changes are here,
The dream is dear,
And the time, the time is fall.

Rhonda Hills

Blame Goes To Who?

I must have missed the calm, but I think I started the storm,
We're supposed to be a family, caring, always smiling, and warm.
I'm very little, if any at all, of the solution,
    but I'm the number one problem.
Fights and arguments, from all my actions stem.
If you think this is true maybe I should leave,
For you don't listen to me, even if I tell the truth you don't believe
If you can't trust me and the things I do,
You should recall who raised me and you'll remember it was you.

George Nowak

Ten Months After

Six years ago I began a journey on what I thought was a lifelong love.
I was building what turned into a fairy tale relationship based on
    friendship and trust.
Ten months ago, I was forced to make a change in my life.
Ten months ago, my love was no longer mine
    and the master plan of happiness had crumbled.
My emotions overran with anger, blame, and betrayal.
I tried my best to turn that emotional switch off by speaking
    of the tragedy and convincing myself that I was the victim.
I socialized heavily to keep my mind off of the hurt.
I bed women that would have me trying to bury the miss.
I became monogamous to fill the void.
I have tried and failed to keep that switch off.
I dearly miss my love and want to hold her like it used to be,
But it could never be the same as trust was violated.
I am being torn by a wonderful past and a road that fate
    has destined to be my journey.
Over time, I thought I would be free from this emotional turmoil,
But ten months after, I am still a captive of a dream
    that wasn't meant to be mine.

Marc A. Sbaraglia

Flight Of The Eagle

Take flight and soar, do not look down
Look out, look up, fly high, fly proud
You are adored by many, cherished by God, loved by me

Let me be the air by which you soar through the sky
Elevating above mountains and bursting through clouds
Let me be the branch upon which you rest
Restoring your strength for a new flight
Let me be the nest where you can return and feel safe

Venture to the sky and discover the endless boundaries of the world
With me as your wind, search the oceans, the valleys,
    the mountains and plains
Letting nothing inhibit your flight

Brett Pullins

A Man And His Dogs

The agony in my heart pulls me and I'm forced to look away.
I've seen him before, a man made of torn clothes, worn shoes,
    and blisters on his feet.
With his dogs, his company, his friends,
he walks the lonely walks ahead.
He may be perfectly happy with the life he's living now,
But I'm saddened to see him walking down Main Street,
    shuffling so alone.
I'd like to write a song, a story, a miracle and make him smile out of joy,
To help him see the other sides of the world that he might never have
The chance to see otherwise.
I want to help him, but I'm locked in a position of the watcher.
But at night, I will cry for him,
And I'll pray that God will watch
    over his long walks through the city
With his three dogs.
And I'll remember to somehow feel blessed.

Angela DiIulio

The Land Of Wishes, Hopes, And Dreams

Tell me where you have been
And I'll tell you where I'd like for us to go.

There is a magical land, a beautiful place, a place where wishes do
    come true.
If you have aspirations and fantasies, Come with me to a magical land,
The land of Wishes, Hopes, and Dreams.

Open your window on a clear night and catch a glimpse of the
brightest star,
Now close your eyes and repeat after me:

    "Star that shimmers, Moon that glows,"
    "I believe, Oh I truly believe,"
    "In The Land of Wishes, Hopes, and Dreams."

Now clap your hands and stomp your feet,
    open your eyes and enjoy the view.
This is a world of peace and solitude.

A place of color, with green grassy fields,
A place full of flowery flowers of red, blue, and gold.
As you can see, there is a bounty of trees,
Whose boughs seem to reach for the sky,
It is truly a magical land.

This is a mystical land, so ask away for you shall receive,
Whatever you want is within your reach,
In The Land of Wishes, Hopes and Dreams.

Connie Rubalcaba

Recognition

A tear starts as rain in sky's pattern, too heavy for the soul to bear,
    but with Freedom as the reaction of relief.
Winds are life's willows . . . Light and Shadow.
Ideals, expectation of oneself, without Presence of the other.
As a solo performs.
Ideals, expectation of the other as individual as lives birth.
Something due?
As a womb delivers . . . or is it you forgot to fulfill yourself?
Satisfaction . . . to grant or give what is Needed for them or of yourself.
Abundant supply of Love and to Give. What is due?
Only when recognition of the other and if life's windows
    have you recognized the other holding no grudge for the morrow.
Grief and Sorrow, ingrained with thinking.
No understanding when one expects as Themselves.
Perfume, just a memory. Acceptance and respect come day by day.
Our beginning . . . and today is now! This hour to embrace.
Not the same, for one is uniqueness, but with combination,
    many two find a common cause.
Expectation, recognition, try to do what you think others
    should be doing for yourself.

Ada Jennings

Do You Love Me?

Kicking small gray pebbles deep into the sand
A gold locket twisted frontward and back in my hand
The metal cold against my warm skin
I stood there watching him
His brown hair
Tucked under a forest green baseball cap
Worn backward
Layers of blackened ripped masking tape wrapped around
The broken plastic band
He wore a green jacket
Unzipped, blowing in the breeze
His cheeks reddened like a child's after a day playing in the snow
Was he nervous or just cold, I could not tell
His flannel old and frayed
Colors faded and loose threads hanging from the seams
Looked like he spent many days with it on his back
He wore it the day I met him
I remember the gray and blue plaid
And the pocket with the brown button

Lauren E. Leone

To Grasp A Straw

Sing out o rain!
Augment the disappointments in my brain,
Crash loudly mighty thunder and lightning flash,
To rent and tear my heart asunder with distress,
Beat down with intrepid fury;
Permeate the very dungeons of my soul and sear it with despondency!
Fight, struggle, work, conspire, climb up, fall back, try again,
Fulsome hope return dissemble, bubble burst anew,
But don't desist, consort with fate in secret risibility.
Offer cryptic formulas, enhance my road with mellifluous penchants.
Let me reach the fantasy, embrace it, seek to pry it loose,
   then let it evanesce,
Cast me out once more upon the merciless sea of emperical futility.
What power can I seek to evince this fleeing sophistry,
This Lorelei escaping with impunity?
But I remain impervious to despair, defeat.
Impale my hope, inculcate my heart with specious thoughts,
   behold a travesty.
Asperse me with dejection, condemn me for defection,
Condole me not, but inundate my dreams unkindly fate
   with your vindictive law,
Yet I shall fight to rise again to grasp a straw!

Harry Maraldo

The Real Me

I try to hide the way I feel
I try to say my feelings aren't real
I try to be everyone's friend,
I try and try until the bitter end,
Until all is said and done,
And the good guy usually hasn't won.
People laugh and walk away
Nobody really listens to what I have to say
People ask me what I think and I tell them what they want to hear
No one knows the me away from school when no one else is near
I like to sing and dance and act from this I show the true me
But at school most of the time, I'm someone I don't want to be
They think they know me but they don't have a clue
To who I am inside and away from all of you
If I can't do it how can she?
If they can do of why can't I, why am I so afraid to show the real me?

Bernadette Martinez

Soul Deep

It haunts me, and reaches into my very soul.
Touching a part of me that I am not even in touch with myself.

An ageless, mournful sound.
Echoing through the deepness and vastness of time.

How many years has it traveled to reach my ears?
Touch my heart? Bare my soul?
Waking in me the the possibilities of forever?

Striking a chord deep within this shell I call a body.
It beakons me onward, outward . . .

Urging me to strive for a better way. Quieting me, giving me peace.
Making me want to dance and sing.
Wishing to pass this feeling on to all who happen to cross my path.

Is this what it was meant to do?
If so, than why doesn't every ear hear it? Every heart feel it?

With smooth heart-felt tones. Long, low, full of calm.
Sending its message to all mankind. A song, hopefully without end.

Such huge, gentle creatures. With their simple, basic song.
Vibrating through the cool waters.

Like a beacon in the dark for those who have become lost.
Who are searching for the way home.
Listen, let the whale song guide you . . .

Karen Wantland

Waiting

Intently I gaze upon a room full of happenchance colors,
blended, striped feline coats longing for touch, admiration.

Green-eyed ladies and golden-eyed gents silently pleading
through crowded glass window; childlike, melancholy, beguiling.

Lost, forgotten, unwanted; I cannot comprehend!
For such grace, stealth and beauty possess no other like it.

Sheltered from the storm, yes, but waiting...waiting oh so long!
For hearth, for homestead; cabin, cottage, castle all the same.

Free at last to warm the master's lap and heart,
and if so pleased, to purr a symphony of love, unconditional.

Laurie Roberts

Touched By An Angel's Hand

Crystal flakes
a gift from heaven
fall from the evening skies.
Whiteness silently fills the hushed air
and creatures magic in front of my eyes.

Gently, delicately and so very slow
like feathers dancing on the twilight
the air filled with millions of tiny white flakes,
in continual flow falls snow on snow;
muffling the sounds so no one wakes,
while wrapping nature in a mantle of the purest white.

Tranquil flakes, settling softly, continue to fall most of the night
painting a picture with a magic brush
created at midnight, when there was no rush.

Overcome with joy, on my breath a prayer
I take the time to reflect anew
and see my whole life in His care
sharing it with you.

In this winter weather, touched by an angel's hand
we stand, together.

Hildegard Wendt-Caringi

Glowing Sins

So many things have happened, so many things changed.
I have to stop to think for a minute, to figure
    out what's happening today.
It all started so very long ago that I don't know how it started.
All I know now is that things can never be the way
    they once were.
I sit thinking about that for hours. And feel a great
    sadness on my shoulders.
Not too long ago, I saw a light. I asked the light to come to me.
Sadly all the light did was tell me that it was already within me.
I told the light it wasn't with me because of the sadness.
The light then told me that the great sadness that I felt
    was really the light itself.
I told the light that I did not understand this.
It then explained to me that the "power" of the
    sadness was really the light holding me back
    from the sins that I was doing.
I then saw the light disappear
    and my sadness was replaced with a glowing light.

   Carli Gibson

The Saga Of Warrior Coleman

I'll tell you a story about a warrior that's fact a warrior
    named Coleman to be real exact.
A warrior, a wizard, a fisherman true; a hero and hunter of
    ginseng root too!
One day while hunting, a root he did see; he soon discovered this
    root had a bee.
The warrior so brave and so bold swore, "Gosh dang! There lives
    not a bee who'll keep me from seng."
But down went the warrior from eight mighty blows; down under the
    tree where the seng root still grows.
So hail to the warrior that's fallen from grace, you see now quite
    plainly the welts on his face.
For the gold growing wild he sought that day, is no longer
    there; it's been taken by "A."
This treasure he hunted but still couldn't claim, has brought
    this new hunter fortune and fame.
So buy Warrior a drink, his pockets are barren; his treasure's been
    claimed by the hunter named Aaron.

   Matt Coleman

Existence

The diversity of our small community lying in birth here before
my very eyes, seems to exemplify the perfection of the world we
constantly search for but consistently eludes us. Because we
look so hard we negate the obvious opting for the hard edge as
opposed to the subtle gentleness of what is inherently evident.

Before my eyes I feel in my heart The diverse commonality occurring
Amidst these four and one quarter walls, which houses African
American, Native American, American American, in no particular
order Mind You. There Is No Priority Here, There Are No cast,
no classes, no racial ties that bind us to an otherwise artificial
society created for the benefit of few and the demise of many.

In this room and one quarter wells, we hold the essence of
cultural mischief. My writing, his reading, her magazines, our
love, their lives, all compiled...combined...integrated, separately
into a fusion of cooperative coexistence. We slip into dialogue
paying attention to each other as much as we payed attention to
our separate issues, Just as quickly we combine with the
rhythms of each other our own moving, swaying, flowing in and
out, up and down, sideways.

It is amazing the transference of energy vying for attention,
surface, room to stretch and breath. Harmoniously behind?
Confined? Within these four and one quarter walls.

   Wendy Stewart

The Birds Meeting

Have you ever noticed when motoring down the highway
How the birds seem to congregate in such an interesting way?

There will sometimes be about 35 or 40 just sitting on
    the telephone line
Seeming to discuss the world's problems,
    and considering yours and mine.

How fun it would be to be sitting with them
    and hear what they had to say
And if they thought we looked funny to them in some silly kind of way.

We hear how smart the animals are — I've heard it all my life
Wouldn't it be fun to learn what they know — to hear it twice or thrice!

What an interesting discussion they could surely have
Seeing how we act sometimes when our behavior is very bad.

Maybe it's better after all that we really can't know
For we would be driving down the highway embarrassed so.

   Judy C. Wiese

Burning Bridges

I have crossed many bridges over the years.
I realized to late I fear.

That so many times I was told.
Don't burn your bridges you may need to cross them when
you're old.

I see now to burn a bridge, it means an end.
You forever loose a lover, partner, family or friend.

You can't go back again you see.
Forever things are changed for me.

I go over and over the past in my mind.
Sometimes wishing I wasn't so blind.

Some of the many bridges I crossed, I were best burned,
    and meant to be.
The ones that still hurt, I guess, I was to learn from my destiny.

I sit back and see you burning your bridges behind you.
I want to help, to say something, yet knowing
    there is nothing I can do.

Only with time. As I found will you see.
How burning your bridges alters your history,

Sometime told me once, don't burn your bridges
    you may want to cross them again.
Don't ever forget that to burn your bridges means, forever an end.

   Vickey Bailey

Tiger

During the day he slumps over and hibernates
    in the solitude of his dreams
When he wakes, his pain and in liquid form cascades
    down the innocence of his skin
He wanders from day to day fenced in by his own misbelief
When you look into his eyes, you can see the swirls of frustration
    cyclone endlessly around his ominous pupils
He'll run as fast as he can, his anger racing into energy
Like a football in mid-flight, he suddenly explodes into the familarness
Of the ground, as he picks up his weary body he recollects the days
    when his happiness was as plentiful as his own tears
He brushes the shadows of seclusion from his eyelids
    and looks into the discomfort of his reflection
All he sees is darkness, which is his only companion

   Lauren Czachor

383

Always And Forever

You broke my heart the day you said good-bye; I am still wondering why?
When I think of the fun we had I could just cry.

The days, the nights, the weekends away, are they gone forever?
Will I ever forget them? Never!

I keep hoping and praying you'll come back to me.
Should I give up and let you be?

You keep saying you have to be free, but why can't you still see me?
You say that you miss me but won't even kiss me.
I thought we were meant to be.

Can't you give in just for a night? All I want is to hold you so tight.

Am I asking for too much? Don't you miss my special touch?
I try and try to not think of last summer, but without you life's a bummer!

As I come to the end I guess I should realize I'll never be more than your friend!

Friend or no friend and this is no lie, I will always love you 'til the day die!

Just remember "my friend", I'll always be here for you 'til the end.

If ever you're lonely and the sky's not blue, look up at the stars
   and you'll see my arms reaching out for you.

   Joan Borgese

Young Black Women

It's time to take a stand, to claim the prize of success that is now at hand.

Being young and black is a challenged alone,
   but being a women well, you know the song

You've watched and seen others do well,
   and now you're dreaming of your time to excel

You know being an achiever is a difficult task,
   but black women should know because they've always been last

You've wanted to stand and to be counted,
   but instead you were harassed and embarrassed

There's a lot to do in this country today,
   that's why young black women must press their way.
Looking to move beyond those stumbling blocks of ghost gone,
   hoping to prove society wrong

Young black women must now realize
   that the true bridge of success starts inside

Self-esteem is a big key, that will open many doors of opportunity

Bringing up new generations of offspring will help to put this country
and economy on the upswing

Giving them leadership from our perspective
   will give life meaning and a positive objective
Let us now take a stand to help build this great land
   with a black women's plan withe focus of her success at hand.

   Regina Hudson

A Tribute To Dr. King

   The name Martin Luther King, Jr. became a symbol of courage and
hope for oppressed people everywhere. He had a dream, a wonderful
dream, his name was Martin Luther King. And a preacher that was he;
he marched for mankind, died for freedom singing we shall overcome,
yes we shall overcome. He fought for equality for blacks and whites,
and jews and gentiles. He always believed that the United States
would not be a truly democratic nation until all people of all races
were given the same rights under the law.
   Martin Luther King strive to improve ourselves spiritually,
morally, mentally, socially, politically and economically for the
benefit of ourselves, our families and our nation. Dr. King, said,
"Man must involve for all human conflict a method which reject revenge,
aggression, and retaliation. The foundation of such a method is love."

   Travis A. Harper

Each And Every

Whether you go North or South,
   Or whether you go East or West.
Each and every way you go,
   You get there trying all your best.
Whether you use crayon or paint,
   Whether you use paper or wood,
Each and every way you do it,
   It always comes out good.
Whether you like thin or thick,
   Whether you like big or small,
Each and every thing you like,
   It doesn't matter to me at all.
Whether you like playing or reading,
   Whether you like eating or sleeping,
Each and every preference,
   Is the choice that you are keeping.
It's all right to stay the same,
   It's all right to change your mind,
Each and every choice you make,
   Some answers you will find.

   Lisa Riva

A Saving Love

Hiding and lying to no one but myself
I walked through life without a care
Keeping my emotions on the highest shelf
I was in a river of despair

People see things that they want to
I see things from afar
When I look and see in you
I see things as they really are

You came in and saved my life
From a very certain end
You did more than anyone
You are my very best friend

You're a loving, caring woman
A woman with whom I'm in love
You won't ever try to hide from me
For what's been given to us from above

I can't cease my writing as thus
Because I would always be blue
All I want for eternity is us
For all I think about is you!

   David B. Potter

Thought It Was You

So honestly can be so true
Patience is often virtue
My dear to me
Love is found
Like one's wonder
Digging underground
Finding the world at last
Full of treasures and pleasures
But too some this is worldly terror
Often to many unknown
Joys they took
To search and grow
One will search, look to find
A constant pleasure
Something they can small "mine all mine"
A shape to fit their own measure
Oh! This task holds so many defeats
Only hoping to find a perfect pleasure
Just for me.

   Nexus Sams

My Personal Prayer

Oh Lord I pray for peace upon me and for TRUST in You be more
than A RAY . . . for things that really now seem impossible; through
YOU; ALL THINGS ARE POSSIBLE. In YOUR time; and AT YOUR PACE,
in the meantime, sometimes, my heart does: JUST RACE . . .
Not trying to be an insult to You, TRUST and ASSURANCE; I must
LEARN I'll get through . . . all the obstacles and trials that
before me I have, ARE NOT reasons for which to be sad.
TRUST and OBEY, for there's NO OTHER WAY; but to be HAPPY in
You JESUS, I want to DO AND SAY.
I can only PRAY; for You to guide and DIRECT ME ON THINGS TO SAY
AND DO, and to TRUST and ADORE only YOU. I pray that You may
TOUCH my life in a way; and produce PEACE in my LIFE and in my
HEART, by You be directed, on what to SAY. To RELEASE me of
BURDENS that are HARD to release . . . of SECRETS THAT WERE KEPT,
that were FOR SOME USE . . . to NOT BE SILENT: to make not ANOTHER
excuse; but to PREVENT: to HELP, for life to BE HAPPY: EVEN
AFTER ABUSE. TEACH me PLEASE: TRUST and to be wise, and to see
through so many a disguise. PLEASE, for FAITH: that has already
been STRESSED; and to be like You in and THROUGH You; to be wise.

Miss Robin Rose Carlson

Glowing Memories

Do I see them, once again, through this tall misty doorway, I walk
past, dark vague colors fade to clarity, eyes focus to clear, shapes
of shadows take forms of once living lives. I've been following a
secret, a vision created inside my dream, at once alone in silence,
this sky that is my mind, turns from a hazy fantasy, to the touch of
a solid reality, this doorway becomes rivers of splashing silver,
mountains of the purest of gold, I'll swim this fresh water ocean
before me, never too deep, all to reach a destination, once for me I
could never believe in, lest ever hold. Dripping with crystallized liquid
reminders, as it forms warm puddles beneath and around my naked feet,
I look through the distant years gone by, never could I listen to those voices
becoming silent cries, to ones who assured me of nothing more than an unkind fate.

For all around me, like friendly trees spouting from a field of gifted
seeds, they've come to gather and embrace, a feeling of warmth inside,
I see them all now, their pictures generating the goodness within me,
 I'll remember those moments forever, for neither death nor darkness,
can swallow my sight, this bright light of days gone by, never lost,
never to be forgotten, but always right beside, with these glowing memories.

Andy Kumpon

Pain, Anger And Unforgiveness

I'm in a state of nothingness. Nothing comes in, nothing goes out.
I'm just an observer, looking out from behind stained glass walls; a
toy puppet waiting to be maneuvered; a robot waiting for its next
command. My walls are ever standing. The prison within my soul
keeps me from even daring to venture from beyond its overprotective
boundaries. It's too late for anyone to shatter my overpowering
walls of defeat.

My soul is full: of pain, anger, and unforgiveness. Although I try,
I still can't seem to hide from the feelings I possess inside. They
consume my whole being, my whole soul, my whole universe. Never
letting me rest, never letting me go.

The pain is too deep; the anger too violent; and forgiveness too far
gone. The core of my soul was wounded long ago. What could I now
possibly do or say to make this nothingness ever go away.

If you gaze into my soul this is what you shall behold; happiness —
a fading memory; hope — crushed beyond repair; and love — was simply
never there. My dreams have long since been shattered. My tears
better left repressed. And in the end there is only my nothingness
left, that won't ever be at rest with the pain, the anger, and yes,
the unforgiveness.

Elizabeth Aundrea Thomas

Unexpected Fate

As I sit here and wait
I see the darkness of the sky,
I wonder what is my fate
Am I here to die?

The sky then turns red
And I see it coming through,
With nothing she is led
Is she coming for me too?

Then she halts in front of me
And sees me it there still,
She glares and lets me be
Then my body with fire she does fill.

She seats me in the chair of death
And across the land I see her,
I pray and take my last breath
As she announces, I am Lucifer.

As I sit here and wait
I see the darkness of the sky,
I now do know what is my fate
I am here to die.

Benjamin Hurley

Death

A knife in a heart,
a bullet in a brain,
water in lungs,
and a rose by a grave,

A tear on a cheek,
a child left alone,
a feeling of worthlessness,
and another matching stone.

Gina Sullivan

Night Dreams

I look above me
and see the silver moon
underneath the twinkle of the stars.

I realize your love for me
is but a distant glow.

But wait...
I see a shooting star.

I can only wish your love for me
will someday grow
and shine bright like the midnight sky's
North star.

Janice Quintero

Untitled

I cut my wicked line
beneath the late moonlight
I weave my deadly basket
I bleed myself a song
I cut my wicked line
across this late moonlight
I wind my ticking clock
My tick, my tick, my tock.
I grind my pearly whites
Across this moonlit night
I burn my sinful crosses
I purge my higher self
I blend with these surroundings
And spend some time alone
with only my panting breath
I cut my wicked line.

Jacob David Odgers

Gloria, Gloria

Sadly, the night comes again and with it, the whispering of the wind.
"Gloria, Gloria," the darkness cries, then slowly, painfully, tears
fill her eyes. Late at night, she cannot hide from all the pain she
retains inside. A pillow pulled tightly over her head doesn't hinder
the memories of the dead.

Big sister, come to hold her brother's hand; more pain and sorrow
than the heart can stand. "Gloria, Gloria," little brother cries, he takes
his last breath and then he dies. Life's most vicious lesson she has
to bear and guiltily wonders why she was there. Too much for
A sister's eyes to see, she carries the images endlessly.

She never speaks of the torment that she saw, thus shoulders the
burden for us all. The bed shakes with her sobs of pain and then
she drifts asleep when her body's drained. The sunlight pushes her
anguish away, relief enough to endure the day. She rises slowly,
clears her head, and tries not to think of he who's dead.

Big sister, not so big after all when faced with the death that she saw.
And time can never take away the words of her brother on his last day.
Late at night, I too hear the winds call and slowly, painfully, my tears fall.
I weep for my brother who had to die and then, "Gloria, Gloria," I hear myself cry.

Donna F. McDonald

Satan's Sting

Satan's sting has reached the "hill". Great men's lives with pain are filled.
Citizens born in times long past unite to pray for help en masse.

Let no man feel he perfect be lest he destroy our imagery.
May no action the world to rule, destroy our faith—add fire to fuel.

Temptations raise their ugly heads, decisions based on good—soon dead
Ambitious ones—no faults are known. Soon bitter seeds of doubts are sown.

The complications of our lives, our status in a world of hives.
Have patience with our fellow man. Humility—an inbred stand!

Our Nation great did not become because of lack of decorum.
The standards set in years gone by—endangered—one by one to die.

God, please hear our desperate pleas. Alas, not all of us agree.
There's good in everyone, tis known. Bring harmony to seeds we've sown.

Unite our Nation, make us feel purpose. High principles are real.
Lift our people from their miseries. Help us join hands across the seas.

The world is far beyond our scope. But never shall we give up hope.
That men can concentrate on faith, and Nations drop to knees and prayeth.

Jane Colley Gayle

My Creed

I believe in God. His formation is like that of an oak tree. His
many colors are vibrant like those of the leaves during Autumn. His
voice is soft and wistful that welcomes each individual. He is like
a lake, strong and encouraging, but not forceful and demanding like
that of an ocean. God is a close and everlasting friend who will
always be by your side through thick and thin.

I believe in Jesus, Son of God, who speaks the words of His Father.
Like His, He is also a close and everlasting friend who is bonded with
you throughout your life. He extends His hands and sends out His
heart to all of us. He is the blind, He is the deaf, he is the
children. He is everybody. His love is for all eternity. It will
never die, just like His presence in our lives never disappears.

I believe in the Holy Spirit, the Spirit and presence of God. He
showers us with the gifts of life, love and forgiveness, which in our
hearts will never be taken away. He gives us the courage to understand
the messages in the Holy Bible and the strength to live up to them.

I believe God has called upon me to live up to my highest potential
and to help those in need along the way, such as the poor, the
homeless, and the sick. I believe He has called upon me to help protected
the environment and take care of it, just as He protects and takes care of us.

I will continue to believe in God and His call of nature for me.

Stephanie R. Kayea

Reality

You pray that it's pure,
the disease with a cure.
Believing there's love,
granted from above.
You've assumed wrong,
there's no love in this song.
You trust those who betray,
finally seen is snow in May.
Realization has stuck,
looks like you're outta luck.
lay down in your dreams,
"all's good" it seems.
Engulf all these lies,
while reality cries.
Then give up the truth,
diminish the root.
Numb this pain,
be a coward again,
for when you awaken it'll be the same.

Talha Idrees

While I'm Away

While I'm away, hear my heart say,
"I wish I could be with you today,"
While I'm away, I hear your heart say,
"I truly am there - in a way."
Yes in this hour,
You give me the power
To do what is needed to stay.
The day will come when my work is done,
And we can share our love
while we're both away.

Anthony Scire

Blame It On The Stars

One night the stars were bright
Your hand reached out for mine
You kissed and held me tight
Blame it in the stars.

We talked of yester years
Of days gone by with bitter tears
Happiness and things held dear
Blame it on the stars.

God knows what's in our hearts
Why must we be apart
I've loved you from the start
Blame it on the stars

What will tomorrow bring
Happiness and everything
Sorrow or broken hearts
Let's just ask the stars
    Why not ask the stars?

Dolores DeBord

Break the Chains

Once I was alone and afraid
praying for the day when,
I'd have a voice for my fears
to break the chains, that
hold the tears.
To be the one who's soul is free
and to know what is meant for me to be.
If only I could find my way,
I'd have no more reasons,
to be afraid.
My voice would cry in happiness
My soul would finally beat rest.

Sharon McGrath

Forever With Me

Dedicated to Daryl Turner, R.I.P.

Our minds clouded with madness pain and sorrow, nobody knew that
there would be no tomorrow. We ask ourselves over and over why?
Why today? Why'd the Lord have to take my partner away? I try to cry,
but my tears are deep within their holder, I'm here for the family if
you need an extra shoulder. Now all I have is memories to carry me
through these trying times. It seems like all my good family and
friends are dying. People always asking, are you Okay?
Damn, another tragedy today. They say it'll be alright,
but to them he's just a victim of society,
they don't know what sadness really follows me.
Every day a life is taken and someone dies,
listen close you can hear the world's cries.
The shadows of darkness shower us in gloom, keeping the happiness
out sealing us in a tomb. Friendship is forever and we'll forever be together,
cause the friendship we had death can't even sever.
As I look at your family many cries pass their eyes, but don't worry,
we'll meet up on the other side. From C.A.S.K.E.T. to the G.R.A.V.E.,
without a doubt you'll forever be with me. We all have regrets.
Maybe one or even a ton, but when you think about it
there is nothing no one could've done.
This loss is very deep and puts a great streets on our hearts,
but we have to let it go or this stress will tear us apart.
I know it's going to be hard to get over his tragic end,
but I know we will, our wounds will mend.
It seems like so many of our youth meet their end so young,
being locked in a cell or killed by a gun.
To God I thank you for the times we had with
each other and for the family I'm sorry one to another.
Six feet under if you can hear me this is true. I'll never forget,
I will always remember you.
And as they say, ashes to ashes and dust to dust again,
you will forever be with me together as friends . . .

Ian Searcy

Your Love

Your love is like a pot of gold, hard to get and hard to hold
Your love is like heaven's star in the sky, so sweet, pretty, and twinkling up high

Your love is like a wild animal, yet to be tamed, but I hope it will always stay the same
Your love has got me confused, for I don't know what to do

I can't find what I'm looking for, that's because you took that part of me with you.
Your love is great, your love is grand, your love is rare, your love is walking hand to hand.

Your love is like an angel from above, it warms you, comforts you, like a glove.
Your love is like the sun gleaming, like watching the mountain waters streaming.

Your love is like a deep sapphire pool, anyone who disagrees is a fool.
Your love is like a grabbing sea, I wish it would grab a hold of me.

Your love is what I love, it must of come from the heavens above.
Your love is what was meant for me, meant to stay, meant to be.

When I look in the mirror guess what I see, I see your love calling for me.
I follow your love like a shadow, when it is deep or when it is shallow.

All your love is easily seen by me, all your passion and purity.
Your love has nothing to lack, it has filled your body from front to back.

Your love is like a forest floor, so many corners unexplored.
Your love is like a rainbow bright, so enchanted you could take off in flight.

Your love is one of life's little things, it must be a gift that God brings.
And you lay forever to rest, I'll remember your love as #1 as the best.

Joshua Ryan Catron

My Separation, War, And Reconciliation

"Death" is a thing with fierce eyes
There's a certain Hint of stench,
I like to hear them moan and cry,
hardened criminal's of the past
I never knew Jimi
To tell the truth I don't want to
overdoses for all man kind
I see the funeral, in my soul,
When Kurt died a bee did sting me
because I could not allow death
my life was lived, but not complete
The coffin in the dirt
Much madness is rock industry
as undetected as is grief
My soul doth recall one J. Garcia
Gratefully dead he now must be
The space of death remains still here
That was my wisdom, know it all.

T. Murphey

Trust

Come with me
Up into my head
See what you will
But please take nothing
It goes against all my training
To unlock these doors
And allow your entry
So please be gentle
Don't break anything
It has taken me lifetimes
To repair all the damage
So look don't touch and
You shall see my soul
I hear it is beautiful

Pindi Sparks

One More Doubt

The book of life,
That I often read,
I try so hard,
My mind just doesn't conceive.

Though I love my Lord,
And all He's about,
Sometimes I explore,
So that often brings doubt.

Some say that's the same,
As committing a sin,
But I truly believe,
That's what makes a man.

So God I ask you,
For your guidance and help,
Please give me enough strength,
To understand myself.

William Lunn

The Cookie Jar

Thump thump
Thump! Here comes
the children.
Top off! Here
is a cookie
from the cookie jar.
Go outside now. Bye!

Emily Ruth Doll

Searching For A Light Beyond The Darkness

Here I am wandering down an unknown path searching for even the
slightest bit of light, but the only visible trace
I could find was provided by the moon.
I continue to look everywhere the human eye can see as
I wander down this dark and dreary path,
but still there is no light to be seen anywhere around or near me.
I wander through a thick dense fog that seems to close in around me
so my vision is obscured, and with this I can see not even the little bit
of light provided by the moon.
Now I wander in total blackness staggering about now looking for a light
to guide me, but all I do is stumble and fall not knowing where to search.
I manage to break free from the total blackness created by the fog
and continue my journey, and now I am striving
to succeed even harder than before.
I now feel weak and feeble thinking that the journey I have started is
too impossible to continue, but somewhere I find the strength to go on
and continue my search for a light.
Then I looked up and saw the dim lit moon start to fade away into the
now brightly lighted sky, and then I realized that the dreadful path
I was wandering on had finally come to an end.

Diana Boccio

Love Doll

You are my love doll now and forever. I have been injected with
passions I've never dreamt existed. Just as I was about to give in to
reality as it seems, you arrive and like a strong and penetrating wind
you fill my soul with love and make me believe in fairy tales again.
Now I see forever and I realize our love can never die. It is a deep
and universal, infinite and eternal love. It can never be changed.
Now I'm consumed with ecstasy, just as it was then it is now and for
always, I never knew I could love and be loved so deeply. I never
felt such a permeating touch. To be together and separate at the same
time. If only true feelings had words of expression.
So don't wonder of me, because I now have the ability to soar beyond
the barriers. I am finally free of the torments of desire, my cup has
been filled and I can drink throughout eternity in remembrance of your
sweet and sexual soul.
Soul meeting soul, only words of the spirit can describe it, a feeling
unrelated to anything physical. I came to you a seed needing to be
nurtured and left a perfect blossom.
Continue spreading your rays of love to the world and now I can do the
same. In the next moment the universe will sing the song of lovers
and they too will know why they believe. I thank you my soul
inflaming love doll with all that I am.

Kafi Mosby

Something Is Wrong

The trees are upside down, snoring complacently in their status quo gowns.
What are the colors of the underground? Prismatic Illuminations or muted tones?
What is the depth? Six feet or four? No one knows. No one knows.

   Something is wrong. Something is wrong.

Leaves and branches are buried in concrete and mortar,
   the birds of enlightenment have no place to nest.
They are frighten of collectivism's duress.

   Something is wrong. Something is wrong.

When are the wooden giants going to learn...they're upside down?
Upside down? A fire of protest has been lit
   but the rains of laughter have damped it! Damped it!

   Something is wrong. Something is wrong.

The flowers bow their petals in mourning...for they are the pallbearers.
The ice age of apathy is creeping into the soil of life.
Where's the sunlight, the sunlight? The forest is sleeping, sleeping.
No one hears the little flowers weeping, weeping.

   Something is wrong. Something is wrong.

Ruth F. Smith

Have You Seen My Valentine?

Have you seen my valentine?
I know he's out there somewhere.
I need to find my Valentine
To tell him I still care.

His tender smile and loving face
The way I felt in his embrace.
His arms of steel and heart of gold
The plans we made for growing old.

The broken heart, the shattered dreams
The reality of life, it seems,
Can never once again be mine
Until I find my Valentine.

Have you seen my Valentine?
I know he's out there somewhere.
I miss his kiss - I miss his touch
I miss the man I loved so much.

Say you've seen my Valentine.
Please tell me if you do.
I need to find my Valentine
And I was hoping it was you!

Peggy E. Criqui

Lily Love

I have waited only to
think it would be the day
of my death. Love that
has been isolated has
gave me reason to never
shed a tear. Your absence
taught me all but love
and happiness. I was only
believed on lies. I burn
with this yearning not
wanting this great thrush
of imaginative emotions.
I take away thoughts and
thrive on what will come of
it. I await on reactions I
know I'll never receive. My
mind comes to a halt, only
to find myself in your arms.

Justine Johnston

Fear

Height's too high,
Water's too deep;
Wall's closing in,
No room to speak.

Death's all around,
No air to breathe;
Ground's falling beneath,
No place to weep.

Too many people,
Not enough time;
Chaos within,
Strangers behind.

Trust has no meaning,
Darkness, no light;
Change is coming closer,
No friend in sight.

Words kill,
Violence reigns;
Nature's self-destructing,
Fate has no change.

Christine Alt

A Life To Hide (A Tribute To Marilyn Monroe)

Beyond the image, under the skin, naked disaster lies within
Taught to speak lies, keep truth hidden deep, raped of innocence,
   nightmares forced to keep
Misunderstood and mistaken by the crowd, ashamed to believe, could
   never be proud

Under the soft skin and smiling face-an insecure, unbearable disgrace
Faced with fears, unsurprised more would come, fought the war alone seeking freedom
In a world alone, still hears lots of noise. The outside is fine, yet the inside destroys.

Faces are hidden and unknown to all, there's nothing to look back on nor to recall.
Deep is the word, almost buried inside, emotions are there, but the control has died.
Courage was fake, another face to wear, little time to think and even less to care.

Diagnosed with depression, with reality to blame, was never a waste
   but always felt shame
Trust was impossible and too hard to find, disillusion entered, became totally blind.
Drugs were a lie which confused her heart - then brutally robbed and pulled mind apart.

We know your name, can't forget your face, too bad you rushed yourself to keep up the pace.
Felt so empty, yet engraved inside, this is what she lived and was forced to hide.
Goddess of secrets, lived more lives than one, interference over, it was finally done.

Ashli Avonne Mees

He, Whom We Loved

The pain that I see in everyone's eyes is nowhere near the pain he had known
While helplessly dying, his heart gently cried for the wife he'd be leaving alone.
Just why he was taken no one can quite say, but dear friends, he loved not in vain
Although hard to accept, take comfort in knowing that now he lives without pain.
So the tears that we cry need not be of sorrow, but of joy for the life he has now
As I'm sure he is watching over us all and he'll help us get through this, somehow.
We must now find our strength and try to move on, he's in a much better place than we.
And do not feel bitter towards the Lord, for his pain is gone, so thank Thee.
Just remember the next time you feel the wind or see the sparkle of new-fallen snow
To open your heart, because he's a part of it now, with the love that we've all come to know.
And if ever you think you won't see him again, know you will, just a different way.
In our hearts we will hold him while knowing in fact that we too, shall join him someday.

Maria Renee Giallorat

Silent Music

The swing in my step seems to quicken, as I sit here alone with my thoughts.
And the pleasure my silent music brings can not be sold or bought.
The smirk on my face seems to widen with each bar of every deafening
riff. Yet when my silent music ends, the grin on my face grows stiff.
The pleasure will fade from within and reality will soon return.
And though I long for contentment the anger inside will still burn.
My loneliness will still haunt me. My hidden talents remain lost.
And the price I would pay to be happy is an unbelievable cost.
I feel alone, for there is no one who really can relate.
And so far no one has come along, I guess I'll have to wait.
And time ticks by, and I'm still here, playing silent music in my ear.
And do not feel sorry for me, cause this music is quite nice. And
Though I must be alone to here this music, I'll make the sacrifice.
For the songs I hear have no words, yet say all that need to be said.
And to go one day without silent music, well my friend I'd rather be dead.
So here's to silent music and all of those miserable things. And
someday you'll here your silent music that no one ever really sings.

Priscilla Lopez

Only One Person To Talk To

My friends all hate me,
My mom really doesn't
care about me, only about,
her boyfriend. There's only
one person to talk to,
I get ignored everyday,
I feel like crying on
someone's shoulder, no one
cares about me. There's
only one person to talk to,
I hate myself, my only
friends are looked up in
there boyfriends and when
they need someone to talk
to, I'm there, but there's only
one person to talk to, she's smart,
funny, kind, sweet, caring, and
helpful that special person is may
7th grade teacher, Mrs. Conkling,
she's the best.

Amanda Hook

Untitled

The minutes pass
I wait
for days endless in time
to go by
so that I
may go to the day
when I find you
I wait
I always do
for something
for you

Kristina Hope Amonson

Seasons Change

As the seasons falter
and fall to the ground,
the songbird's sound
is no longer around.
Just the sound of the wind
as it engulfs and surrounds,
the wide open nothingness
when I look around.
It is a dream.
I can not believe,
the beauty that I see.
The wind has brought
pleasure and bestowed it on me.

David A. Miller

Let's Live A Dream

Dream the dream
Ride the tide
Hold your hands up to the sky
Touch your lips near to mine
And there you'll find
A love real and pure.

Let's live our lives
And pass the times
Let's join our hands
In swimming sands
In the stillness of the night
As the stars do shine bright.

Andy M. Smith

The Edge

I hate a lot. I just hate. And I hate hating. What's happening to me? Oh God!
I feel like I'm at the edge of an endless pit and I keep on getting sucked in. I'm
fighting and fighting and using up all my strength trying not to get pulled in. But, my
stamina is wearing thin and I know that any minute now
I'm just going to fall into this deep black endless nothing.
And I'm going to just forget how to be, and I'm going to forget everything. I'm
going to be nothing in this huge empty space.
And I don't know if I can handle it. I know that when I finally do get pried away
from my tiny, narrow, rock hard ledge I'm going to lose everything that's important
to me, and all the protection it gave me.
I'm going to lose sanity. I'm so afraid. But I can't concentrate on that.
I'm too preoccupied thinking of all the people
I would like to see or hear from before I totally lose it.
But then I could see them,
I'm sure my ledge would widen and I'd have more strength.
I'm so sure! I can almost hear their voices!
I can almost hear the laugh! And now!
There!
I can! I can! I can!
Or can I?
No!
Don't let me lose sight! I was getting strong!
Don't tell me it was the wind howling in my ear!
Don't! Don't! Don't!
Oh, God! What did I do? I've been good all my life!
Or I've tried to be as good as I know how.
Don't do this. Please don't. Please...
I just let go.

Kamentha Pillay

Ode To My Generation

There is an Array of emotional torment and self-induced pessimism and
Cynicism A premature surrender of those exiting before triumph
I also find a tremendous amount of creative intelligence and aspiration
A ferocious hunger for meaning and knowledge and for some, wisdom
A time for perspective and challenge and a mourning for the lost
Comfort of the hand that tucks them in at night
A wildly delicious and painful collective humor given birth out of many open wounds,
monotonous work and meaningless hours spent on TV.
Looking for comfort in Other's Mistakes
Searching for hope in Other's Fortunes
Happy, but too afraid to enjoy it for long because the child-like
Present moment wonder has faded into an ability to look beyond the
Glory of it all to see only the doubt and disappointment
Hence, the exit before triumph

A misfortune of the intellect I believe, that at times, prevents one from
Truly being committed to one's own heart, intuition and true self out of
Fear, instead of love and faith

Kristan Olivas

To My Darling Daughter

Oh I remember when you were born, your dad wanted a son and I was so
torn. I wanted that little girl with all my heart, I knew that when
they said I was Pregnant right from the start. I knew that you would
look pretty in pink and with your eyes of Blue, and when I saw you
the first time I knew! That God had rewarded me with this little girl
with twinkling eyes of blue. You grew so fast our little bundle of
joy, we would go to the store and all I would here is I want this Toy.
Of course I would buy it and spoil you rotten, but it didn't matter
because look what I had gotten. Then as you grew older and went to
high school it was mom I have nothing to wear what am I to do. but
time has sure gone by fast, it seems like yesterday that you were born
and now it is in the past. Soon you will be gone from me and that is
so near, that you will become Mrs. Fournier. So daughter my dear what
I am trying to say is that I will miss you when you go away. But
Fathers and Mothers are only here for a while, to guide you while you
walk that extra mile. To find that right man that enters you life,
and now you both become husband and wife.

I love you mom

Linda Remaly

Swift As A Bird

Swift, Swift
a bird has flown
into its nest
safe at home
I won't cry
I won't shed a tear
I just wish I could fly
up above
and think...
Of nothing but nothing itself
by myself
all alone
I am Me!
And me alone
I am a person
gazing up at the sky
Not a bird.

Jessica Weiss

Night

Night is but the
absence of light
night, night is dark
night is betrayed
bad, evil but night
is for saying not for
crying!

Trevor Clark

The Establishment

Wronged
Perpetrators are bold
Laughing
Standing up high
No rungs ascending their tower

Saved
Persecuted must be cleaver
Smiling
Standing down below
We shall go fetch a ladder

Brian K. Gresham

Throughout The Day

Early in the morning
When the grass is wet with dew,
The only thing I can think about
Happens to be you.

And in the middle of the afternoon
When the sun is out and blazing,
I tell everyone
I think you're amazing.

In the evening
As the sun begins to set,
I still haven't quit thinking about you
Not even yet.

And in the middle of the night
When the moon is out to shine,
All I can do
I wish you were mine.

David M. Roderick

100,000 Poems Of Life

100,000 poems in the sea of life,
Some of them with lots of love, some with lots of strife
You don't need to go after them
with a spoon, a fork, or a knife.
Ideas coming to you from here, there and everywhere
You can gather riding in a boat sitting in a chair,
or flying in an airplane in the air.
Thoughts are like sun beams and moon beams everywhere.
You can keep them to yourself
Or with other's share
When you travel and roam
You can always end up with a poem.
From shore to shore or sea to shining sea
You can gather ideas about the flowers or about the bee.
Sitting around the coffee table or
having afternoon tea, baking cookies
or at a quilting bee.
Some of the things, you hear
Some of the things you see.

Earle Baillie

The Name And Arrows Of Edw. Oxenford

Since this is now, which will become to-morrow,
And that to-day, what was just yester-year.
What bank is this? Who cannot lend nor borrow
'Tis Endless Time, although long gone is here.

All-healing Time bind-up his wounded name,
Refute up-lock'd lie in history,
Expose the one who did usurp his fame,
Explain the why, resolve the mystery.

Old Sluttish Time, did you besmear the page
"In praife of Ladies dead, and louely Knights"?
Did you behold and note the Queen's fierce rage
So he denied the works that are his right?

O, Hope! It is that in black ink some way
That Time will come and give us truth one day.

Lafayette Lee Foland

Hope

Hope is a child looking through a toy store window,
hoping for that perfect toy at Christmas,
the sun trying to shine through on a cloudy, rainy day,
for the children have a desire to go outside and play.

Hope is the girl in the hospital,
praying for a cure for her disease,
the lone bird with an injured wing,
desperately, silently, waiting for help.

Hope is the seed,
hoping to grow healthy and tall,
the doll that's being ignored,
while the girl does her schoolwork.

Hope is the waterfall of life,
hoping to fall and keep searching for that big, body of water,
searching, turning, and swaying,
always living and hoping...

Kathleen McCormick

God's Gift

I don't know what you are yet
But that doesn't matter to me
Cause I know your very precious
And the world will soon see

I'm counting down the weeks
Till you're in my arms
to see your little features
And all your loving charms

I can't wait to see you look at me
And give me that special sweet smile
I know that I'm the luckiest
Mother to be alive.

Carolyn Brown Spalding

Untitled

They tell me you are gone.
As if I didn't know.
As if I didn't need to be reminded.
Why is reality so real?
Why is death so final?
Why not like TV, the movies, books?
I could change the channel
or turn the page
and you could be there waiting,
as I wait.

B. G. Twiname

In Memory Of Jim Snipes - My Beloved Uncle

Until I was born,
  He waited for me;
  I loved him dearly,
  He liked to be with me.

I enjoyed going to visit,
  How I loved him so;
  He used to tell me,
  That I made his roses grow.

Then he left me,
  I wanted the answer,
  So I was told,
  That he died of cancer.

Catherine Taricco

The End?

Ride the dreaded final moment,
Wrangling it down and breathless
To float freely
In an endless, tender black
Of the unknowable.
And thus released,
All wonder of your being not denied...
But loved.

Liz Thompson

Tall Talk

The tree-tall giraffe
up to its neck in
brown and yellow
patchwork quilts, turns
tail and shuffles away
on wooden stilts.

Jade Turner

Single Visions

I stand here, dry on the desert sand for it is a peaceful place of
mind, most often when the sun has done it's daily shift and the moon
covers the midnight rise, here I lay, bare on the ground under the
stars, counting the many planets and visions in the sky, laying here
warm on my blanket, I feel an abrupt, yet crisp blow rush violently
across my back, which is open to the sky, my toes rub against each
other, feeling the moisture within, breathlessly I lay, picturing the
faces of my children...my daughters, who shall carry on my name,
their nonchalant attitudes, but earnest and benevolent personalities
as fast as the image glimpsed through my imagination, it fogged into
the mist of a small cactus in the distance, beyond the mountains a
swift breeze leads me to cover myself, for I look around this vacant
land, I touch my face, to come to the conclusion that I am the only
human on this dry sand where my feet come to rest, I am the only human
on this island, one salty tear slowly roles down my left cheek, for it
is not the tear of being uncourageous enough to complete my island
journey...but it is the tear of knowing that I have been faced with
the challenge of completing it alone!

Adreena L. Ogle

Mothers Cry

A Mother's cry is a caring cry.
A Mother takes everything to heart.
A Mother's cry expresses a lot of love.
A Mother's cry is a special cry that shows her kids
what they mean to her.
A Mother's cry is a dearing and soft cry.
A Mother's cry shows her kids that she cares what happens to them.
A Mother cries when something bad happens to her kids
because she hates to see them suffer.
They care so much and so deeply about their kids that they
begin to cry.
I'm not saying that it is wrong for them to cry.
I think it's nice to have a mother who cares about you
so deeply that she begin to cry, when something bad happens to you.
I know that cares very deeply about us because if she didn't
she wouldn't bother to express her feelings so deeply
that she begins to cry.
I don't know what I would do without a mother who cares about me
so deeply that she begins to cry.
Without her I would rather die than to suffer
in a world without care!
I love her so deeply but I don't express my feelings as easy
or as deeply as she does!
I find it hard to express my feelings out in the open.
What I'm trying to say is
"I Love her more than this God forsaking world!"

Joseph Jones

Love

Love unrequited
Love still united
Sharing space adamantly
With grace I depart cautiously
Strange thoughts pervade my consciousness
Wanting another while laying with a chosen lover
In confusion I desire the touch of an unloved heart
By infusion out two souls are now, once lifetimes apart
In love I fell, out of love and back in love
And now I love another and yet another
From the past who is no longer
My heart cries painfully
Nearing dreadfully
Love still united
Love unrequited

Mary Green Dialinakis

Let It Be Said

Let it be said
that he wrote some lines
that redefined
the way some look
at a pond

What was once a puddle
is now a subtle
reflector of the sun's
flashing song

He wrote one verse that broke the curse
of the way some look at being old

Now they run just for the fun
and don't even try for the gold

Before his poems
They say a bird flying

Belying

The red tailed hawk
Cruising in the drafts of the cliffs
Wings tips up

In the soft raw air of the sea

Tom Pattinson

Time

The world is a timeless place where
minutes go by eternally. People live
in a time pattern. As the clocks ticks,
life is going on. We often forget that
every time the clock ticks something
new is coming, we live in a world of
past and a time of future. We are
surrounded by time, and the words
of our grandparents stay in our minds.
The stories they tell are of the past
yet remind us of our future.
Time is Everywhere. Time.

Amy Haack

Oreo Reality

It started long ago.
When people had no heart.
Families were broken.
Lives were torn apart.
They were sent all over the world.
They were chained and sold in spite.
Our eyes were dark and clouded.
When it was clear as black and white.
Laws were set and stated.
We thought an end had come at last.
But little did we know,
you cannot change the past.
Lives had still been ruined.
People tried to change.
It never really disappeared.
The hurt was too wide a range.
Our only example, a cookie.
Black surrounding white.
A combination of pure goodness.
A time when races shall unite.

Allyson Pritchard

Within

Within your heart, is the only place,
  To find the Good in everyone,
And the world will become a face that
  Will belong to
    only One.
  Colette A. Christie

A Mother's Questions

When we finally meet,
Will you recognize my face?
Will you know me in your heart?
Will you run to my embrace?

When we finally meet,
Will I know who you are?
Will it be as if you never went?
Like we've never been apart?

Have you ever looked down upon me,
through heaven's shining light,
And prayed just one little prayer,
That I can live without you in my life?

I often look toward the stars,
And wonder if you see,
The weeping, lonely mother,
The one you see in me.

I cannot wait to meet, us two,
On that very special day,
When two worlds join as one,
And I look into my child's face.
  Amie D. Stephenson

▬▬ ▬ ▬ ▬

Trap, trap, trapped
miss, miss, miss you.
Wish you could, maybe I would,
would have,
Would have not had I known,
You . . . lost lost
I'm lost, pain rain once again
Yell . . . please
I said
you yelled at me for them.
I'm not, never, won't
be them. Even when I tried.
Wish you a good bye.
Bye when someone you love gives
you that
sigh,
Sigh away my life when
you look at my bad blind eyes
eyes that never really see . . . you.
  Jared Elliot Cardon

Rootbeer Foam

Scratch scratch on the side of my head
11 o'clock comes it'll be bed
Scratch scratch on the back of my skull
My scalp is dry and my hair is dull
Itch itch hours nonstop
Drink and chug and gulp my pop
This describes an evening at home
Ahhhh, burp, rootbeer foam
  Colette Sacksteder

Thoughts

Empty thoughts creeping in my mind,
thoughts of nothing thoughts of lie.
Couldn't think of any thing, no I can't
not a bit nor a sigh

Thoughts of love all over me
yearning burning inside of me
Thinking of you both day and night
wanting you every night

Thoughts of fear coming to me
running, hurrying thru my veins
Can't you see it thru my eyes!
I feel so cold, as cold as ice.

Thoughts of joy, oh! I feel so good
I just think I'm in the mood.
Lifting my feelings oh so high
lowering my pressure down inside.
  Alfredo Sy

Time Past

I was raised on the East Coast,
We vacationed at the shore,
It was a place called Reisterstown,
And that's near Baltimore.

I had lots of fun there,
It was a great place to grow,
And as a kid I would be happy,
If in December it would snow.

I started working at,
The age of fifteen,
Soon bought my first car,
and thought I was keen.

The days they pass quickly,
And I grew up fast,
At least that's the way it seems,
When I think of the past.

The years come and go,
And now in Texas I'm found,
But, I'll never forget my childhood,
In Reisterstown.
  Gary E. Mercier

Life

Life is young, carefree, and gay
Live it to the fullest,
always remember to pray.

Life is treating your neighbors kindly,
and never going astray.
Being mindful of the Lord,
because he'll
show you the way.

Life is opportunity,
dreams to pursue.
Follow your spirit,
and let it guide you.

Life is always striving,
and forging ahead
Climbing up the ladder
and being prepared.

Life is wonderful,
treat it with respect.
Because when it's over,
you'll want the good memories left.
  Olivia Vega

Brief And To The Point

Money
  avoids me
Doesn't even know my name.
Isn't that a shame!
  Gladys Perrina

What Christmas Is To Me

Christmas in my mind
Is meant to be fun
Not everybody rushing
Just trying to get done.
It shouldn't be about gifts
But about love.
Not fruitcakes or cookies
Or even turtle doves.
This time of year
When kids eyes seem to glow
Because all they love to do
Is play in snow.
It's the time of year when we celebrate
The very special birth
Of Christ our Lord
Who came to save Earth.
So if you read this
You know it's not a hunch
If you say I love Christmas
Very very much.
  Tyler Sidwell

Blessings

How often I begin my prayer,
"Lord, Thank You for the many blessings
You give me everyday."

When my daughter says "beep"
as she touches the tip of my nose.

When I forget, for awhile anyway,
that my son is different
and needs medication twice a day,
You let me think of him as just
a little boy.

So, "Lord, Thank You for the many blessings

You give me everyday,
and help me Lord
to recognize them for what they are,
gifts from You."
  Melody Gettel

Scared

I'm scared to look forward
But I don't want to go back
Back to my past
Scared to move away, alone
But I can't stay here
All my life
Scared for what might come my way
Scared for what never does come
Where do I turn
Left, right, or straight
I can never go back
I can never go back to my past
But too scared to go forward
  Kelly Margaret Boyd

Christmas Alone

There's a chill in the air
The North winds are beginning to blow
Christmas time is drawing near
I'm hoping it will snow

What's the true meaning of Christmas?
For many it's not clear
Celebrating the birth of Christ
Or reveling and spreading cheer

So when you're sitting around the tree
Enjoying this holiday season
Just remember why you are there
A show of faith is the reason

Loneliness can invade the soul
but I have learned not to fear it
Although we're thousands of miles apart
I'm there with you in spirit

So don't worry about me this Christmas
I've been away for a long time it seems
I want you to know that I miss you
I'll see you in my dreams.

James R. Alberts

Seasons Call

There it is once again
when the seasons call,
was that sound that's heard
the killing of snipe, grouse
or quail?
Shots ring out and echo
over hills and dale.
That one who's song
will not be heard, is
the Bobwhite Quail,
Oh how I dislike the
noises that ring out before
sunset and sundown.
These eager hunters make
Awesome sounds,
Whenever the fall seasons, comes
around.

Vida Durham

My Friend, Babe

Oh, how I love my friend, Babe!
The most faithful friend I ever had!
He loves my humble home.
He lives with me in the most littlest
    castle you will find....
He is always happy and cherry....
He always obeys every rule I say...
And when I say No to his
    whining desire...
He looks me in the eye, speaking
    his desire:
"Master, forgive me I am only a dog"
Then licks and kiss my lips.
Oh, how I love my most
    faithful friend, my pet.
His name is Babe.

Ella Orth

The One That Cries In Silence

Pain is the sorrow
That burns inside me,
That huddles me and
    encloses me
Within its black,
    satin veil.
I wish I could escape
But it holds me back,
Reminding me of my
    suffering,
Throwing away my
    joys.
I have everything I
    could ever want,
Except the thing that
    matters most,
The thing that makes my blood run cold,
It's my soul that makes me pretend
    to be,
No one knows the real me,
The one that cries in silence.

Heather Ashley Nirenberg

Socks

I was walking one fine day,
When I discovered something very naive.

There were socks everywhere!

There were socks on feet,
And socks on floors,
There were sock-filled hallways,
And socks spilling out of drawers!

There were socks of every style,
Mile by mile,
And socks of every shade,
Purple and jade.

And they lay everywhere just like a...
Dream! Oh my!
This story is not real,
But then why do I see socks of teal?

Carmen T. Bertasi

Memories

As I sit here and think,
memories of old times rush back

I thought about old games,
Homecoming, prom, wishing I was queen

I sit and start thinking
about old boyfriends

Mark Thompas, 4 - months
DeWayne Campbell, 4 - ever

I start thinking about collage
How I wish I went

I start to drift back and I'm
glad things turned out the way
it did.

Tiffany Kinsinger

My Heart

My heart is full
of smiles and sunshine
My heart is full of laughter
Tears of joy
My heart is full of fears and worries
Playful and unique
Blue eyes I'll forever keep
Sometimes sad, sometimes stubborn
Most of all I'll always love him.
My heart, my son!!

Regina Sexton

Then And Now

I remember long ago
When I was just a child,
I had so many chores to do
No time for running wild.
I always helped my Mom and Dad
Around the old homestead,
And never thought of talking back
No matter what they said.
But now it seems that children
Have a mind their very own,
And as they grow into their teens
they wreck our lives and home.
We see them for a little while
When they run in or out,
And if we need a helping hand
They seldom are about.
The only thing that we can do
Is pray for them each day,
That God will always guide them
Along their future way.

Mary Nardone

Untitled

Summer is over
the cold is settling in
I feel the warmth dying,
the chill coming in.

Winter's approaching
I feel its cool air
And along with it all
I sense the cold despair.

I find myself recalling
Memories of seasons past
Regretting the reality
That these moments wouldn't last.

Summer is fading
And so is the memory
What once was you and me
Seems gone in my reverie.

Carla Camins-Macapinlac

Summer Wind

The wind so warm and soft,
touches my face as I walk,
The ghostly wind I cannot see,
But I know it's really there,
because I can feel it blowing
through my hair.

Laura Pyle

Goodbye

As I sit down by my window
I see the birds fly by
I feel a tear in my eye
As I remember the happy days we had
We said this wouldn't happen
The day would never come
I remember sitting in the field
Just you and me
One we were to be
I never thought
This awful day would come
The day we said goodbye
I remember I started to cry
As we kissed
goodbye -

Adam Parise

The Logical Way?

Aye, I say
without a nay,

We could make,
and have a stake,

In a car that lasts more
years than a half score.

But to build by decision
to expire by precision,

Would meet with objection
and only derision.

For it wouldn't be nifty,
to be going fifty,

Have the car disappear
and land on your rear!

There was a day
for the One-Hoss Shay,

But it went the way
of the hoss' neigh.

Thomas A. Huls

Loneliness

Loneliness is something
    that few understand
It creeps through your very being
    taking over both mind and hands

It can turn a great king
    into a poor wretched soul
It can reduce a talented young lady
    to little more than a whore

It has the power to maim
    and the power to kill
It leaves you with a void
    that nothing can fill

It will tear you to pieces
    leaving nothing alone
It has the power to break you
    to make you a drone

Loneliness is something
    that few understand
Loneliness is deadly —
    she's the destroyer of man

Lyssabeth Mattoon

Dreams

Dreams are your goals,
They cannot be forgot.
In your heart and soul,
They have a special spot.

These very special dreams,
You wish to complete sometime soon.
They are just stuck with you,
Like and unwanted tune.

Some dreams,
You feel are just right.
You set your mind and move forward,
Sometimes you put up a fight.

And these dreams give your spirit,
They let your mind flow.
But my best advice to you,
Is to just start slow.

Just keep dreaming,
Eventually it will pay.
Everything can be accomplished,
Somehow, someday.

Rachel Riddleberger

The Looking Glass

Not long ago I lost my life
My husband passed away.
The loss is monumental
A struggle every day.

One's unexpected kindness
Sometimes catches me off guard.
My eyes well up - my heart beat pounds
Just breathing in is hard.

Memories are all I have
The help to ease my pain.
For even though he's left this world,
Something beautiful remains.

His face, now framed where he'll reside
Behind the "looking glass"
Smiles beyond that great divide
To say "this, too, shall pass."

His pain is all behind him
His life is now his past.
I'll smile as I acknowledge
That he is "home" at last...

Virginia Endresen

Aliens

Aliens
are there?
Where are they?

I am one
An Alien,
is writing this

Don't
believe
me?

Well then
look behind
you

Watch out...

I strike best at night

Missy Chatfield

Fading Shadows

Walk in my shadow, Alice Mae.
Give me the strength to face each day.
Seek not love, learn to stand.
Walk in my shadow, do not cry,
Wipe the tear, from my eye.
The music of life, I can not hear.
Wipe away another tear.
The years are long, the people weak.
Walk in my shadow, I shall not speak.
The kiss of death, hold my hand.
With God's love, you can stand.
Tomorrow is yours.
Walk in my shadow, Alice Mae.
Take my hand, seize the day.
Seek not, but give your love to me.
I am meant to be. Walk in my shadow.
Time plays life's rhythmic tune.
Gifts from God, forever to bloom.
Walk in no man's shadow, son's of mine.
Tomorrow is yours.

Alice M. Lindquist

Uncle Ken

My love ones are dying
To which I regret
I wasn't ready
At least not yet
I'm empty inside, but I look just fine
Hiding the sadness that is of mine
What can you say
What can you do
When a loved one disappears from you
There's a gap in my heart
Where they used to be
Now there's bundles of anger filling me
Death is sorrowful, death is sad
When you think of the love you once had
As I sit here and cry this night
Hoping your here my last goodbye
My loved ones are gone
To which I regret
I wasn't ready
At least not yet

Madeline Gehrlein

Ask Me How I Feel

Where do I go from here
My thoughts disappoint me
The addiction has me strapped
Peace is no longer felt
I'm never alone, yet very lonely
Grasping on to my dreams
All I seem to have left

Life is more than this
My destiny I can choose
An Angel has come
On my journey I have begun
I am alone
And I will be okay
There will be brighter days

Rebecca Dauenbough

Sight

The unpretentious thing it is
Of loving now and for the while,
The torment that it brings to us
When once we find our love has eyes.

Emily Radford

God's Heaven Above

I wonder what it's like in God's
Heaven above, it must be like the
sunshine that shines with love
It must be like the small children who
are happy with glee, where there are
no worries but a harmonious sanctuary
It must have daylight all year round,
where there is no darkness or nights around
It is a spiritual place that God created
himself, for the people who would
appreciate goodness and health
I wonder what it's like in God's
Heaven above, it must be so pleasant
and full of love

Sabrina-Yvette Powell

A Moment In Time

Life is but a moment in time,
Clutching to windswept dreams,
Toe-tapping through silly charades,
And breathlessly searching for love.

Each passing day is a new dance,
Some of us needing a second glance,
As we peer through clouded glass,
At the many shades of love.

With just a simple touch,
Others find common thread,
For an everlasting romance,
In this moment of time we call love.

Dianna Hendrickson

Snowy Wonder

Storm clouds roll in
   winds howl through the night,
But morning dawns calm
   and a wondrous sight.

As I gaze through
   my frosty window pane,
Sun glistens on tree tops
   down in the lane.

All around me there lay
   a breathless scene,
A blanket of snow
   so soft and clean.

With fluffy white pillows
   piled so high,
Under morn's beautiful
   bright blue sky.

I look up and thank Him
   for our great nation,
And for His morning's
   snowy creation.

Elda Jean Olson

"Portrait of Grace"

In deep recesses of the heart,
   Where desire and passion impart,
The struggle to cling steadfast
   To virtuous and noble paths.

With determination and resolve,
   Though conflict persevered;
Eternal joy prevailed —
   'Twas loss of heaven I feared.

Valerie Bordelon Pyle

Sweetie Pie

I have a cat name Sweetie-pie
With a name like sweetie-pie,
You would think that she's nice,
lovable and quiet cat in fact,
She is anything but quiet.

She play with bounce ball, carries
bones around the house just like a
dog and chews up my dad's Sunday
shoes. We leave her in
the house at night.

She wakes my mother up at 3:30 AM
to be let outside, sweetie-pie is
black and white.

Sarah Griffin

I Am

I am hidden and unknown
I wonder if anyone will ever find me
I hear God's call
I see the chains
I want someone to find me
I am hidden and unknown

I pretend to know what's going on
I feel their tug
I touch heaven
I worry for the loss of my sanity
I cry when I am alone
I am hidden and unknown

I understand that God is in control
I say "here am I"
I dream the American dream
I try to walk my talk
I hope I am not the only one
I am hidden and unknown

Michael J. Maleto II

Fusako's Magic Touch

It thrills me thru and thru
your magic touch

I can't live without it
I need it so much

Sensations that have never
been felt before

Engulf my body
and my hearts door

Such feelings that well
from deep inside

Like released phantoms
on a mystical ride

Where did it come from
this erie glow

Such powerful emotions
you'll never know

Frederick Aldred Miller

Untitled

Tree tree it's beautiful to me.
Love love a turtle dove.
Flower flower you have the power.
Rose rose set me a pose.
Leaf leaf you give me relief.
Weather weather a cool little feather.

Ashley Wilhelm

Lovely Valentine

Valentines, a day for love,
like heavenly words from above,
I love you on a card I write,
Our love and friendship is so bright,
Candies and hearts I give to you,
I want to say I love you too,
Sharing the times of years have passed,
I hope this day will always last,
Will you be my valentine?
Please, I hope you will some time,
A balloon, candies, or just a kiss,
This valentines I'm going to miss,
But don't worry it's coming again,
A valentines day like it's always been!

Shana Reid

The Mountains

There is poetry in vistas
That majestic mountains hold,
As the sun-set paints the tree-tops
With its emerald - tinted gold.

There is restfulness in mountains
With their gurgling, tumbling streams
And their soft, cool whispering breezes,
Quiet rest and peaceful dreams.

But the blessing of the mountains
That you feel you have to share,
Is the silent, prayerful reverence
For the Power that placed them there.

Caswell Ellis

Peace And Plenty

Peace and plenty
Was it ever there
At anytime, anywhere?
It never was and never will be
Except it man's goodness and care
For
If men do share
Their surplus fare
There sure is
Peace and plenty!

Raju Muchimilli

Year in haiku

Leaves on the concrete
crunch and fizzle, grinding to
a soft, silent dust

Mucus running down
my nose can't feel my lips, but
I can taste the salt

Moist, musty topsoil
seasoned with earthworms. Special!
Today on mud pies

Icy sweat trickles
down slick glass through my fingers
tracing curlicues

Alison Park

Honor The Women's Garden

Through the windows of the garden
Images and reflections, fleeting...
Of women whose spirits are
This creation.
Their presence, quiet and powerful,
Garden spirits, the essence being one.
Whispers and murmurs of the women,
Giving, tending...loving,
Come to play on the gentle pine breezes.
A dance of life...a circle,
Creation and re-creation.
Caretakers of this place, we are...
Partners and friends sharing the spirits
Of the women.

Robert A. Greene

Fatherhood

Sovereigns of the cure,
Lords of global peace
Looked upon with all the answers
Victors of the beast

Protect from fright of darkness,
Provide with needs of life
Guide the future of the world,
Through good, through bad,
through strife

Mold the minds of hope,
Advise with wisdom and reason,
Show the path of which to take,
Direct the way for goodness sake

Thrust upon broad shoulders
the fate of things to come,
Do not despair,
Life's all good
Stand up, Speak out for Fatherhood

Lavall V. Woodhouse

Smile

It was an Eve in December
My friend and I went to eat
At a cafe in Hartland, Michigan
We had to stand in line
What did I see watching me?
A little four year old girl
I gave her a big smile
She smiled back
Then stepped over to her sister
And said, "She smiled at me!"
It made my day.
What must I say
A real smile will pay.

Glozella Bowman Meyer

Where

Ware do you go
in the thickness
of travel
once you will know
the former flights
farness
From familiar to Zaire
no room for comfort
in your carry
    on to wear
you begin

Brenda S. Hart

The Untended Garden

He planted his seed
waited for them to sprout
and as they grew
he quietly slipped out.

The warmth of the sun drew the plants
and they flourished.
Scattered rains brought drink,
and minerals that nourished.

Although untended
Mother earth never let go.
She gave them solid footings
Letting them branch and grow.
Despite scars and blemishes
these plants bore fruit,
which they nestled in their leaves
and secured with their root.

Then He happened by,
and took pride in the life
which he had little to do with
'sept abandoning to strife

Joy Galletta

The Bride

An impassioned woman,
So ardent in her pursuit
for this extraordinary man.
She seeks him out with such fervency.

Her love for him increases
as she awaits
the imminent intermingling
of two hearts, two souls.

Her mind is filled with the essence of
his character and truth,
Her heart saturated with
his tenderness and passion.

Deep within, she feels
the marriage of their spirits.
And she anticipates
the consummation of their unity.

Julie Landreneau

Holding A Dream

They reach and stretch and
Grow with time.

They will come and they will go.
For without them the day can be an
Eternity.

They take time and effort.
They come easy and go
Hard.

Like the wind some are gentle,
Others are harsh.

To control them requires
Determination and
Strength.

To own them is heaven on earth,
To be owned by one is torture.

Everyone has them but yet only a
Few have held their
Dreams.

David L. Larson

This Is Just To Say

I have painted your
picture
backwards and
put

It on the wall
opposite
my big
mirror

So that I could
see
you as
you

Are; not as I
want
you to
be.

Margaret Alliet

The First

The first child is so precious
Your hopes, your dreams, your fears,
The first child is your future
Through all the pain and tears.

You want so much to give them
Everything that you had not
The things no one can give them
Whether borrowed, loaned or bought.

You love your little first one
With a love that is unknown,
To watch her learn and see and live
To love her beyond grown.

To see a little baby girl
So fragile in your arms,
To see the smiles and the tears
Her special kind of charms.

To you, her mom, she'll always be
The first bundle from above,
To you, her mom, she'll always be
The meaning of your love.

Debra J. Bingham

Untitled

Can I imagine still
A life
Without your presence
Beside me

While a stream tumbles down its bed
I sit in silence
Waiting for your return

From one waning moon to full
A love grows new
Everlasting

Could it be
This love so tender
Shall light the path
To follow together

A rose garden
With endless rows of thorns and blooms
Flourishes with summer's warmth

But the springtime
With all its beginnings
Is the key to its success

Joyce N. Andersen

My Birthday

Another year has come and gone
And still I linger, carry on
My purpose lost, it passed me by
And went its separate way

One more year etched in the wall
The scratches there that mark my fall
Their meaning clear within my eye
And still I wonder, why

Another year will soon begin
With all its pain, watch it grin
My final moments I spend alone
As time weighs down my bones

Just a year like all the rest
None are Great and none the best
There is no past, no future bright
Surprise, I made it through the night

Existing now within my fear
The memories are O so clear
From them I hope to find good cheer
So I can make it one more year.

Forrest Seals

Untitled

Our lives are but a drop of sand,
    among this world, upon the land
We waste away below the waves,
    when water fills our lonely graves...

Ksenia Potapova

Kittens

Kittens, kittens, kittens
your eyes shine in the dark,
kittens, kittens, kittens
you're frightened by a spark.
Kittens, kittens, kittens
Get off the table!
Kittens, kittens, kittens,
if you are able!
Kittens, kittens, kittens,
Like all cats, you are lazy,
kittens, kittens, kittens,
and sometimes you go crazy!

Sean Begg

True Love

If my love were to be
expressed in words, to show
my love is true,
    it would be written,
heart; to be able to love you
    and feel the joy,
mind; to know that I Love
you and why,
body; the essence of which
allows me to be attracted to
you, and
soul; for the love will be until
the end of time and we shall
always be one.

Norman Lee Grayson

Untold Love

One can look at the other
But neither can say a word
As if by unveiling a cover
Would set them free as a bird.
Their eyes are their only connection
But that is all they need
For by this conversation
Both know where it will lead.
They can stare from across the room
Even smile at one another
But when they speak none too soon
One can only look at the other.
For in this affair
No words consume the air.

Christopher Ragland

Mom

No matter how low I get,
I always look straight up.
I cling to my life's rope and say,
"Just how full is my cup?"

To some, my life's a nightmare
That I never will control.
To me, it is a learning tool
With which my soul can grow.

I've been to hell and back again.
It was a nasty trip.
But even that couldn't hold me back
Or loosen up my grip.

My rope keeps getting shorter, though
And my patience, too.
But if my rope should leave me,
There's a net below called you.

Emily Kuntz

My God Is My Anchor

My God is my anchor.
He's my strong arm.
My God is my anchor.
He'll keep me from harm.

My God is my anchor.
He'll save me from sin.
My God is my anchor.
With Him I will win.

My God is my anchor.
He has saved my soul.
My God is my anchor.
With Him I will grow.

My God is my anchor.
When my flesh will die.
My God is my anchor.
In his arms I'll lie.

    Amen

Ricky W. Primm

Trumpets

    Trumpets are very fun to play.
Trumpets don't give a powerful ray.
If you stay with it,
You won't have a fit,
And soon you will learn how to play!!!

Michael Gagliardi

My Miracle

Painful days,
Tormented nights,
Haunted by questions
and unsolved answers.

What is wealth?
What is joy?
What is a smile
or what is happiness?

Conceiving is a miracle!
A dream come through!
For you're my wealth,
My joy,
My reason to smile,
My happiness and my dream
for the future.

Saveeta Seenauth

Daddy

Father, don't you love me
I'd really like to know,
If you really love me
Why don't you let it show?
You don't call that often
I haven't seen you in two years
Then you never understand
the reason for my tears.
I've grown up so much
you were never there to see
now that I am 15
You don't even know me.
All this time that you've been gone
I've learn to understand
That me being a part of your life
Was never in your plans.
I've slowly forgotten about you
You may question how
But you see, that's ok
I have a new daddy now.

Brandy Leigh Burns

Sisters

Old but young
Poor but proud
Beautiful but never married
Black or white
Never a slave
Sisters for life
But never the same!

Lauren McGhee

Nocturne

Under the dome of night,
Naked, I sleep.
Suddenly, out of the void
A glow from which emerges
you - floating down on me.
Rising to enfold your softness
breathe in your nectar
Lie back in mutual embrace,
While away in our pleasures.
Suddenly, even as you came,
you are gone.
Ah - to be dreamless!
Wherefore
Whence nirvana?
Does Succubus Incubus delight?
In dream, day and night?

John V. Pollack

Our Moon

Our moon looks just like Swiss cheese,
Can't see it if it rains,
I know it has four phases,
It waxes and it wanes.

It spins along an orbit,
Gosh, is this the one that tips?
Depending on just where things are,
Sometimes it will eclipse.

The maria and craters,
They weigh more than a ton,
Some planets have a lot of moons,
Our earth has only one.

Whenever it is visible,
I just look up and stare,
To think that in our lifetime,
Men have taken steps up there!

It has a Sea of Crises,
Its gravity is low,
It really isn't far away,
Some day I just might go.

Rosemary Laporte

Untitled

The ripples begin to mesmerize me
Capturing my desires and holding them
Prisoners of confusion
The drizzling rain stains my eyes
Only to leave me drifting on
My wooden ships of loneliness
Creaking by
And evading the paths laid out for me
Alone at sea
But as I obey the archaic sign
I notice the shore which
I have chosen, the warning,
And attach myself
Never to sail free

Charlie McCarter

Who Has Seen The Heat?

Who has seen the heat?
Neither I nor you;
But when the leaves hang fading
The heat is passing by

Who has seen the heat?
Neither you nor I;
But when the trees bow down their heads;
the humidity has risen high

Who has seen the heat?

Minnie Castro

Search

How many tear drops? wasted
On lonely dreams.
Too many yesterdays, not enough today.
We love the light, we indulge at night.
Eagle tree water birth, gone like the
Snow in summer.

Damien Lance Gayle

The Final Day

You live a life, so short and sweet,
No place to go, no one to meet.
You take that life, so plain and boring,
And live it over, dusk 'til morning.
But nothing you do, and nothing you say,
Will keep away that Final Day.
That Final Day, when all shall end,
And Death becomes an age old friend.

Life is like a simple game;
You live, you die, it's all the same.
But once you take that Final breath,
That life of yours belongs to Death.

Kyle Griffith

Written In The Sand

On a beach with miles of
    area to be covered,
We don't possess anything much,
    except each other,
And "I love you" written in the sand.

You showed me the open land
    and we breathed the great ocean air.
All of this would have meant nothing
    if you had not been there,
With "I love you" written in the sand.

The ocean tide comes and recedes
    as you hold my hand.
There are shells on the beach and
    the sand is ruffled from feet,
With "I love you" written in the sand.

Colleen Sharpe-Tibbles

Love

Love is not something
that would fill up a
box; just as candy
does. That is not the
right place to keep it.
Keep it in your heart.
Share it with others;
just like sharing a
little pack of Sweethearts
with your family.

Anne Otto

Sarah

She was as gentle as a wisp of air,
loving, tender, and full of care.
In her eyes everyone could see,
humor, kindness and her love for me.

Comfort was there whenever needed,
compassion flowed forth unheeded.
Goodness poured from her heart,
she was both witty and so smart.

God claimed her; oh, much to soon,
she is up there, near the moon.
Her star shines brightly in the sky,
but we still ask God, Why? Oh Why?

Sarah was not know for her fame,
but life won't ever be the same.
There can never be another,
for you see, Sarah was my mother.

Sarah L. Halligan

The Time My Heart Was Broken

The time my heart was broken
Was the saddest time of all
The time my heart was broken
He answered the Lord's call.
The tragic night he left us here
Was the worst time ever yet
The tragic night he let us here
We never will forget.
He charmed us with his presence
That I never will let go
He charmed us with his presence
That will always, always flow.
Soon I'll see him, you just wait
Cause my life is in God's loving fate
Soon I'll see him, you just wait
He'll be at that pearly gate.
The time my heart was broken
Was the saddest time of all
The time my heart was broken
Kurt was placed in victim's hall.

Kelly Rice

Insecurity

The soul is an exponent of itself
Revealing truth to so few
Calculating steps of meaning
Undressing one's essence anew

Find my meter; find my rhyme
The land of Heaven has no time
Cancel the order; I've changed my mind
L.A.'s city lights help me unwind

Poet or bard is next in line
One in the same unequally framed
Viktor Frankl crossed my sign
Logotherapy's death; what a shame

Visions of grandeur dance in my head
All alone, is love really dead?
Pilgrimage takes me back home
To contemplate my soul alone.

Christopher Todd Mason

Blind

The sun comes up
Yet another dawn
Unfortunately things said yesterday
Are never gone
They hang in the mist
Like early morning fog
And some bother you
Much like city smog
Regret is something
That follows in the footsteps of living
Sometimes you have to stop taking
And do a little giving
But you must be careful
And not give too much
Or you'll find yourself crippled
Without a crutch
It's times like these
When you walk the line
But keep both eyes open
Because you'll fall if you're blind.

Robert Swartz

The Dance Of Denial

Shadows visit from the past
And call him into lonely rooms.
They taunt him in his solitude
And leave him in the empty night.
He fights the darkness, breaks the cast.
He cries "I will not live in tombs"!
He clings to all that he can be
But all that he can do is fight.
Like Jason lashing to the mast
He finds the strength to face his fears,
And like a fighter, he goes down
And stumbling, awaits the bell.
But like a dancer he will rise
And knowing he may fall again
He keeps the measure of his stride
And in his heart, he never fell.

Jefferson Wainwright

Mom

I would like to hug you tight
because you help make all days bright
you love and trust me always
through the good and bad days
you have always gave and shared
even when its not always fair.
You have been here when I am sad,
mad and most often glad.
Through all of my happy years
and all of my happy or sad tears
you were always here for me
that's why I love you.

Rachael Langstaff

Inner Conflict

The castle of my heart has a moat
bottomless and broad
Yet only a rod down falls between.

I search for a way to reach
the inner gifts within,
That beseech themselves to me.

My intellect struggles with my heart,
here a battle rages on,
As a dart is ready to glide
through the air
Piercing the side of the inner cares
withheld deep inside.

But no I will not allow the dart
to soar so close
Prepare to destroy all the
love, joy, sadness, and zeal,
That awaits it meal
of ample supply.

My heart will live on
till the passing of time.

Coral Mills

Dancing Feet

I fly through the wind,
I bounce on the floor,
then I come to send,
not even one bore.
The crowd starts a wave,
I smile so sweet,
this memory I save
of dancing feet.

Heather Jones

Last Call

Across the room his vision skims,
Broken heart just reads old hymns.
Betrayed again and triple charms,
One last look for living arms.
A work of art or masked aggression,
Eyes say all 'cept for confession.
Pain and past are fused together,
Even smiles say she's no better.
Attempt to hide it or ignore,
That o.k., it's at her door.
Growing strong with every thump,
Torment in love's lifeline pump.
Approaching dark and 'neath a tree,
Shadows of yore hold you and me.
One voice in charge, its name is fear,
Taunts "love is lost, get out of here!"
Hope lives to try, but she revealed,
No need no cry and hate to heal.

Tyrone Charles Millhouse II

My Pleasure

His voice on the phone
A rendezvous late at night

Our eyes meet
We kiss.

Our hands touch each other,
caressing so tender.

As he softly kisses
and slowly undresses me,

I quiver with expectation
of the ecstasy to come.

The hugging, the kissing,
the touching, the loving;

My world seems so wonderful
when I'm in his arms.

If only our meetings
could happen more often,

But for now I will settle for
"It's been my pleasure"

Penny Ingles

Memories

   God has taken our mother
But has left our father.
   I remember the mother we had
that makes me feel sad.
   I remember her pain
But never again.
   I remember her eyes
They remind me of mine.
   I see her smile
But only for a little while.
   She's here in my heart
Right from the start.
   I miss her dearly
But I have her in my memory
   She left her family here
Now she's waiting for us there.
   She went to heaven with out a fuss
Now she's waiting for the rest of us.

Cathy Landon

Life Is But A Dream

Life is but a dream
Walking through the stars
Trying to find happiness
And finding out our flaws
Life is but a dream
A journey through our lives
Through the good and the bad
The week and the strong
We will find it to our homes tonight
Life is but a dream
Merrily, merrily, merrily, merrily
Life is but a dream
Merrily through our lives
We drift to other places in the night
To the ocean near Jamaica
And the cold winds in Canada
Asia in that faraway place
And Greenland up above
Life is but a dream
A gateway to the means of imagination

Melissa Keenan

My Garden

As I look upon my garden
Under neath the leaves, I see
Thousands of little fairies,
Looking back at me!
Immediately they scamper,
From one place to another,
Their little dresses fluttering,
Changing places with each other.
And as the sun grew brighter,
They seemed to disappear
I wonder where they went too?
Will they be back next year?

Florence I. Stark

All Alone

I've been left alone
with words I don't understand
lying on the paper,
which makes my eyes dirty.
Insomnia is the disease
that kills my own dreams
in my bed, which seems
so cold to me.

I've been left alone
with thoughts I can't keep in.
I want to shout them in the dark,
shout them into the black night,
that keeps my secret,
that swallows me,
'cause I've been left alone.
   All alone.

Daniel Sandor

Soul

Soul
   Invisible
      Sought after
         Yearned for
            By passed
            Ignored
               Forgotten
                  Dreamed of
                     Desperately

Ruth Shaw

Untitled

Sunshine falling,
showering everyone,
it's always calling,
the birds to sing.

It feels as though,
your heart's on wings,
will it last
or soon be the past?

You frolic and play,
you wash your worries away,
how can you
forget your grief?

Time has passed,
but that doesn't mean,
that you can act,
as if you hadn't seen.

Her face white,
as the coroner's sheet,
her body lifeless and cold,
like a stone.

Brittany Gotschall

My Answer

You are my shepherd
guiding and leading
thorns my be thick
but you're always there
caring and helping
every step of the way.
Your light always shown
my darkest path
Your care always healed my
deepest wound
Your touch made me feel very
secured
Everything you did meant something
special
you are my
Shepherd, my Messiah
and
Answer

Josleann Negron

The Wave Of The Senses

O sun
you caress
glistening ocean
where birdies fly.

O my wild ocean
you kiss so smooth
the velvet sand.

And the wind
blows from far
the tender dunes
into a sandcastle.

Be silent
smell and listen
dream your dreams
and open your eyes.

Bernice Annette Lampton

New Tomorrows

I start a brand new job today
What's in the future, I can't see
I've made good friends along the way
Along the paths of yesterday.

It's hard to leave and go away
But something new is calling me
Around the bend - and if I stay
I'll never know what's down that way.

I leave safe pastures, through the gate
To unknown trails, for what will be.
I'm older now, is it too late
For me to go? - I've shut the gate!

Still, I'm afraid, dear God, I pray
I've made the break, it's up to me.
I stand alone, with only faith
And tread down paths all new today.
What lies before me?——

Patricia Foster

Through The Eyes
Of A Farm Worker

Though I till the soul
I see no reward.

I have shed blood, sweat
and tears.

My hands show the signs
of aging with each year.

And every breath that
I take, I feel it is my last.
My lungs are filled with
poison.

The only rest I will receive
will be my death.

Though I till the soil
I see no reward.

Esther Santibanez

Rain

Burly, barreling, bellowing clouds,
Slowly sailing, slipping by.
Weighty, watery, weathery billows,
Covering, coloring, climbing high.

Daintily, deftly, delicately raining,
Flying, flowing, falling down.
Teeny, tiny, tender flowers,
Nurtured, nourished, never drown.

Lowly, listless, little seedlings,
Hapless, helpless, home is dust.
Gasping, grabbing, gulping droplets,
Mining moisture midst the crust.

Steven J. Olson

The Man In Black

In my bed I sit and weep
I know better then to sleep
I know that I can't hide from him
Even if the lights are dim
The man in black has no shame
It is my soul he wants to claim
So if he wants my soul this night
I don't think I'll put up a fight.

John Boone

So-Sad

I wish I could be a happy poem
the kind that sings when said
but the days have bled my color
and fewer poems are remembered when read

There are no balloons on birthdays
only blues and leftover joy
days of weak and weary parents
fumbling pictures of dead girls and boys

"Potentials this..., potential that.."
and what their babes might have been
had they lived
to kiss away their tears again

I wish I could be a happy poem
the kind that sings when said
but the days have bled my color
and fewer poems are remembered when read

Quinita Edmonia Good

The Life That A Leaf Had

There was once a leaf bud
When new was the mud
In Summer the leaf was new
And it grew and it grew and it grew
And then newly bound
It fell to the ground
It fell from the tree
But no one was there to hear or to see
It fell to the grass
It thought it had finished its task
But the leaf proved wrong
For the very next day a boy came along
He picked up the leaf
And forgot he was troubled
All of his joy and happiness was doubled
The boy and the leaf found a connection
The boy kept the leaf for his collection

Rebecca Callahan

Not As Others

Broken glass lines the inside walls.
Behind the hazel eyes,
the truth lies.
Love and hate,
divided we fall.
Now we must sever all ties.

Kiss the past goodbye.
loneliness once again,
close friend.
The future will not allow another try.
With time my soul shall mend.

Tears of sorrow drop.
Anger and hate,
with just a touch of rage.
Bang,
the gun goes pop.
Twenty-five to life,
in a stinking cage.

Virginia Alanna Reece

I Try To Remember...

I try to remember
What it was like for me
I try to remember
How hard it could be

Everything happens
So quickly so fast
One day I'm little
Then that's all in the past

The toys are still there
I'll never give them away
But to play, I don't dare
There's no time not today

Mom and Dad they don't listen
They don't always see
The changes, the feelings
That's happening in me.

I've tried to remember
What I had to go through
So we can be closer
My daughter, "I Love You"

Bob McNamee

Settle For Me...

As you lay down in bed
are you dreaming of your life
the days that lie ahead
is love what's on your mind
finding someone just right
in a world with so many wrongs
for a woman with so little time.
Once you were my search ended
sadly grown apart in time
but, when my life needed you
you're there right by my side
I know you need your time
for an open heart to bind
if it's love you can't find
put aside my imperfections
for a friendly heart
that looks at you so kind
settle for me

Carlos Vega

"Winds"

The Crime of surpressed passion,
Held in the palm of my hand;

Threaded beads of desire,
Spreading grains of sand;

Howling winds are screaming,
Tingling through my limbs;

Confused feelings livid,
Stifled cries and whims;

Secluded sands are moving,
Scattered across the land;

Caress the palm before you,
Gently hold it in your hand,

Threaded beads will mold,
Secluded sands will stand;

Howling cries will quiet,
As we hold each others hand.

Ruthie Durrin

Running Away Train

Go to Mexico on a train
Turn around, come back again
Jump the cars, wind rushes by
Now I feel that I can fly.
All those eyes stare up at me
For a minute I look to see,
Just to hear, "Is she insane?"
I thought this much when I began.
What would they say if I ran and ran
Between the cars of a train
Headed to Mexico and back again.

Christine H. Doty

A Mother's Vanity

You are the sun
that warms my spirit;
You are the air
I breath.

You are my rainbows
in the universe;
I signify
your foundation.

My blood,
In your veins...
I cherish you
with love.

When heartache
strikes you,
I feel your sorrow...
When you sparkle,
I feel your glitter...

You are my daughters,
A Mother's vanity,
Through you, I live again.

Linda Richardson

I Can't Sing

I use to sing
but, look at me now
notes just mean nothing
I've even forgotten how

I can't carry a tune
I'm a basket, cause of leaks
when I try to carry a tune
My voice box only squeaks

I've forgotten about the treble clef
The musical scale has faded
I'm all mixed up, too, with
Notes that are dear or shaded

Line France

Untitled

Seeking go hides
Was never so fun,
Though losers were keepers
of weeping
Finders of
Truths that never
lacked beauty they
somehow earned.

Jimmy Martin

Ode To Dreams

Come, sweet dreams,
Embrace me with
Your gentle touch,
And we shall dance
The night away.
Sweep me upward
To the unknown.
Fill my yet unfelt desires,
Which lie dormant
In some unsuspected
Chamber of my soul.
Come, sweet dreams —
And we shall dance
The night away.

Dale S. Rogers

The World We Live In

The world we live in is
full of hate, crime, poverty,
and destruction

The world we live in
needs love, understanding
patience, and brotherhood

The world we live in is
not perfect, but there is hope
for the world we live in

The world we live in is
your home and my home
So let's make our world a
wonderful place to live in.

Mickey R. Backus

Side By Side

Evan and Tillie,
Side by side,
They've run their ranch
With grace and ease.

Branding stock,
Riding the mountain,
Raising kids,
They've done it all
Side by side,
With grace and ease.

Side by side,
Evan and Tillie.
Have done it all.

Watched colts grow,
Calves grow.
Their children
And grandchildren grow.

They've done it all side by side
As they will always do.

Alishia Kingsbury

Nature's Violinist

Sweet music wafting up
through the tall grass originating
from the cricket, nature's violinist.

Paishann Curtis

Time Heals

Nothing heavy
within
this battered soul
can be lifted
without
time
An
abundant commodity
that I
cannot afford
to lose

Baron Koral

Just Wanted You To Know

I stand amidst his shadow,
The one I'd hope to be.
I looked to him throughout my youth,
A source of strength to me.

Not only childhood hero,
I still look up to him.
So much of him is part of me,
Is seen in who I am.

To him my life I patterned,
And stepped the steps he trod.
Looked up to see if he noticed,
Await approving nod.

Perfection never claiming.
I wonder if he knows,
What he truly means to me,
And how he helped me grow.

I hope when all is said and done,
Someone in me will see,
The same as I saw in him,
And continue the legacy.

Carey Ford

My Broken Heart

In the summer when it's hot and
in the winter when it's cold, like my
heart when it's broken; you know it
can't be resewn, like a pen when
it drops, you know you're never
far from my heart, like the sun when
it rises and like a leaf when it
falls. Like the way you said we
would be forever and I believed
you because I knew no better.
I felt like a fool when you dumped
me that day. I felt even worst when
you didn't call me, and I often asked
myself, what did I do to deserve a
girl as beautiful as you.
With your smile so sweet and your
hugs so gentle. Girl I know I am
getting too sentimental, but the love
we had you can't ever forget.

Muhammad I. A. Brown

A Poem From Me To You

This poem is like a kiss,
It is short, sweet, and simple
And it says
"I love you"

Eric Cothern

Cool Summer Things

Cool summer things
Great summer fun,
Bathing suits
Warm pools
Hot summer sun.

Real cold water
Straight from the hose,
Swimming and diving
water up your nose.

Dripping fruity popsicles
Cold twist rainbow ice cream,
Beautiful summer wildlife
What a wonderful summer dream.

Holly L. Baranowski

The Dream

Darkness surrounds me as,
    the night begins to fall.
Voices seem to whisper as,
    death to me he calls.
He does not judge me,
    nor the ones before.
He leads me from the light,
    and through an open door.
My life flashes by me and I
    recall my lost loves.
With tears running down my face
    I pray to the one above.
Yet death, he laughs at me and
    says my child it's to late.
This is my worst fear, but I
    must accept my fate.
As he takes me to the fire nothing
    is as it seems.
Then I'm woken by the sunlight
    and realize it was a mere dream

Armecia D. Stroud

The Nightmare

The sun is falling away
Calling an end to my day
Night will seep into my world
Again my terror to be unfurled
How I long for light to stay

I must not drift into sleep
The terror lies within it deep
Waiting only to be released
Hoping never to be ceased
Awake, awake I must keep

Each moment I painfully hunger
To embrace peaceful slumber
Not to know my terrible dread
Only to encounter sleep instead
And my heart pounds as thunder

I think of lighter things
Yet the heaviness still clings
No escape can I find
Sleep imprisons my mind
And again its terror brings

Janet Morrison

Untitled

Grass grows greener on the other side...
of my mind.
Split personality, oh what fun
Who will I be...
Tomorrow?
Today...
Give me a crowbar
to spent the evil twins
And to form a move perfect union
Our forefathers would want it that way

Barry Koral

The Wedding Feast Of The Lamb

This whole thing is oh so
    Oh my goodness
these angels dancing on everything
and the Spirit leading the festivities,
the procession,

And the ministers
(and ministresses)
like King Dave's wife appalled
and the Spirit wild,
and with a long white beard

Pauses stares, waits,
bursts into laughter
over legalistic matters,
throws a ripe peach at them, saying,
You've met the Master
(oh joy and oh cheer)
come sit and dine rules are no rules here

Andrew S. Plymale

Lullaby

Wind in the willow,
Tiny head sleeping,
Fast on its pillow,
Blanket of blue.

Soft are the moonbeams,
That fall upon him,
So softly he dreams,
Tiny and new.

It could befall him,
In his deep slumber,
That angels call him,
Like angels do.

But I have told him,
How much God loves him,
His arms will hold him,
All the night through.

Robert C. Nash

Pershe Ode To My Black Cat

Beautiful Black Persian
    that you are,
    nothing is too good for you.

But in dire circumstances,
    must you spit up on
    my oriental rug?

I would not cringe, oh!
    if you would not use
    the fringe so.

Ardis O. Hunt

Ages

It seems I've spent a life or two
Stumblin', tumblin', muddlin' through.
How distant and how hard it seemed
To know of what the stars had gleamed,
And as these days eat up the year
I find I'll never 'scape the fear
That fills my pores and takes my air,
And steals from my every hair.
'Cause nothing seems to stop this crime
That murders cold and robs our prime,
And takes of us just what it deems
Of warm young hope and fresher dreams.

Dennis Dillingham

That Cat

I have a very stupid cat,
He always wears a cool hat.
His hat is very tall,
When he walks down the hall.
his hat's always on
his mat.
He is a very cool cat,
He likes to play with his bat.
His bat is on his mat,
When he lays there looking fat.
He has cool looks on his mat,
When he lays there with his hat.
When he plays with his bat
He looks cool with his hat
That is the end of that cat

Jeff Miller

The Bible

The bible is true
The bible is nice
The bible is full
Of good advice

When you are troubled
The bible will help
So read the bible
And see for yourself.

Joshua Meier

Tonight Is The Night

Tonight is the night,
Stars are so bright.
Presents are on their way
Pheasants are cooked today.

I sit alone,
And wait for the phone.
That or eat alone
for it's Christmas day!

Pretty angels fly.
Beautiful, swift, and silent.
In the clouds above

Jessica LaPensee

My Heart's Plea

If in time you do decline,
Then on bended knee I would proceed;
To beg and plead by love's decree.
That you are mine and I am yours.
Listen closely to the beat.
One and one is two, then one.
Oh, how sweet and complete.

Michael Ostrander

Suriel

He came,
silently creeping,
silently stealing,
taking to deliver
souls to rest
in silence.
Giving peace,
leaving tears,
snatching promise.
He came
for the old,
for the new,
for the strong
and the weak.
with surprise,
answered prayer,
sweet release.
He came.
Suriel.

Juanita DeShields

Glory

Written in honor of
Laura May Jones & Lula M. Joyce
I have asked as a little girl.
And still I find no answer.
How can I bring glory to God?
Even through my strife and anger.
This world is like a foggy glimpse,
of what there is to come.
I have love in my heart.
You will find hope there too.
But still I ask.
How can I give glory to You?
Now, my day has come
for me to see His loving face.
And He tells me,
You brought me glory, going not astray.
But staying on my narrow path.
And making love, your way!

AmberLee Kay Ingersoll

Stewart

Misty droplets unfurl
Giving hair a ringlet curl

Silver streaking in a line
Magic myriads thru the pine

Fingers trace the endless sky
Empty now the gourds on high

Streaming down in great relief
Gently washing every leaf

Angels rinsing off their wings
Worms soaking earth bound rings

Tiny droplets gently seep
Into the mystic ocean deep

Lightning splits the sky in two
Half for me half for you

Pearls of rain upon the rose
Gather there in sweet repose

Drenched caterpillars scurry by
We hurry home you and I

Splash thru puddles soak our feet
Playing in the rain is neat.

Mary Ann Kerr

My Day

I got up from bed.
I got on my feet.
I bunked my head.
It was time to eat.

I looked at the clock,
It was so good,
I put on my sock.
I put on my hood.

I made a big fuss.
I tripped over some stairs,
I got on the Bus.
I went to some fairs.

I got back home
I stared my brother in the face,
I had to write this poem.
I need some space.

Jason Shovan

For Avery

Clouds,
Aura contained.
A racy sky,
Surreal blue
Dark light day,
Appearing as those
Written
About in novels
Felt,
More than seen

In this eclectic
Brightness
Your leaving
Has just become
Vivid,
And the road
Is whispering to me
The way it use to,
Your hand,
Right outside my wind shield.

Cecil Gray

Timeless Moment

With the ocean
on an August
full moon night,
I stand barefoot
where the dry sand
meets the wet.
Out past the surf,
an oval of undulating silver flakes
is matted on grey black.

A quicksilver ghost
cavorts at the foot
of a rising wave
and disappears
before the breaking,
before the cannonade
advances down the beach,
and the ocean's tongue
slithers up the beach
to kiss my feet with ice.

Fleming James

Memorial

A ray of light,
A spark,
That's how you came,
That's how you were
In our lives
Bright
Cheerful
A symbol of Hope
and joy.

You came for a time
For a special purpose
To open our eyes
To love
To truth
To God
You served your time
You fulfilled your purpose
Shine on!

Ina Morrison

Winter

Life is suspended for now;
The poles have reached yet farther

Life is suspended for now;
Beseech the unclothed arbor

With rounded belly, I
Lie down in lax and labor

With girded, layered skin
I reach for warmth of brethren

The hearth burns bright eternal;
With faith in constant lyre:

A song of bird reminds me
That spring will soon be here.

Merri C. Hunter

I Am

I am a star with several
    different rays of light.
Sometimes I am Nurse
    and shine for my patients.
Sometimes I am church
    and shine for my Lord.
Sometimes I am Volunteer
    and shine for my community.
Sometimes I am Mother
    and shine for my girls.
Sometimes I am wife
    and shine for my man.
But, most of all, I am woman
    and I shine laughter, love,
    joy, sorrow, mischief and fun.
I am life, I shine light.

Roxanne Shelenberger

What Life Is All About...

Life goes on...
despite trials and tribulations,
for being positive
is what really keeps you fit.

Life only comes but once
so make the most of it at once,
for tomorrow might never come
or God will be the one to come.

Leonardo Saligumba Torralba

To Be?

So little time it takes to live
To breathe, to cry, to laugh
A screen of flesh, growing big
Too soon - too great - too fast!
A darkened spot! What will it be?
If anything at all
A seed that grows from choice of youth
May soon be made to fall!
Time is short, torn hearts will feel
No matter what is done
True pain so real, a soul can steal
Love from everyone!
Yet, life and death both wait for us
So should we not be scared?
Not if death means life to us -
Life that can be shared!

Maryann Kershaw

Unknown

The warmth of her body immense,
    her love deep from her soul.
She is the one that I love,
    my love she never will know.

The love in my heart burns wild,
    her's a forbidden zone.
The fire in which she ignited,
    the flame in which she controls.

Her love is all but forbidden,
    to my heart, she holds the key.
My love expressed in a whisper,
    an expression she never will see.

Ricky Huddleston

The Miracle Of X'mas

    Once again its
that time of the year,
    when a baby arrived
on a midnight clear
    The magic came from
very far,
    following a particularly
brilliant star.
    When they saw that
it shone down on a certain
place,
    They rushed to a stable
to see a sweet babies face.
    Giving him gifts, they
heard angels sing,
    that today on earth
is the newborn king!
    Now we gather with
tender love, while
Jesus smiles down from up above.

Robert McGovern

Volcano

I have never seen a volcano
After it erupts
But I have imagined
The smoothness of the rocks
The sight of great bare trees
Tickles me in the breeze
As I see my mighty mountain
Turn to hardened rock

Mikaela Crane

Freedom

The wind will always set my spirit free,
but when the wind dies,
where will I be?
I could be anywhere,
but no one will know it's me.
Even if it's sunny and clear to see,
nobody will know it's me.
People will be thinking
"Where could she be?"
But only I would know,
I was free.

Minka Hoogeveen

Stormy Day

It's a stormy day,
but I want to play.
There's nothing to do,
I'm feeling blue.
I want my friend,
but she's away for the weekend.
The power went out,
I think I'm going to shout!
Ring-a-ling,
The phone rings.
Sam's car broke down,
She's staying in town.
She can come and play!
Like I said, what a great day!

Gracie Lynn Shatzer

Lines Of The End

Lines of the end
open the story.
A glance upward
to catch your friend.

A forgotten fork
for an empty seat.
Trade an hour
while souls do meet.

The furnace is lit
a theme is set.
to rumors tonight
with Olympic kiss met.

Two winds blowing
create a storm.
Neither cloud knowing
Spring is born.

Jason Bryant

Only You

Only you....
    Were always there
Only you...
    Would always care
Only you...
    Knew when I was blue
Only you...
    Were there when I didn't know why
Only you...
    Were there to help me try
Only you...
    Could ever see
    Everything inside of me.

Nicole B. Jackson

405

Rainbow

Colored,
Negro,
Afro American,
Black,
African American,
Which one are you?
Are you like the rainbow,
A spectrum of colors so true?
You have a choice you see,
To be or not to be.

Larzetta Jenkins Smith

What Love Means To Me

When I hold you in my arms I
fell like a cloud floating in sky.
Away from the lonely night
and days making my heart open wide
for your love.
Love for you is bigger then to think
bigger then the world.
The world is made of love so am I
made of love just for you my dear
I am so sweet, and play full.
I understand why you love me so
because I know what love is
all about.
I was born to love and be loved
born what in my heart to love all.
Like I love myself.
That way I love you so much.
Love never end, we do.

Lupe P. Berry

At Peace

I cry for what, I no longer know;
the pain so great; I can't wait to go;
Chameleon I am, this today,
that tomorrow no is the wiser,
I scream, I yell, I cut, I bleed,
I swallow, I shout but no one hears,
no one sees.
Under the ground, deep beneath, is where
I want to be,
At peace.

Debbie Welever

Untitled

The moon is shining bright, my lovely
Others see it, too
We both sleep beneath it, my lovely
And watched as the darkness grew.

It shines on different faces, my lovely
It knows how wrong we are
No matter what we be, my lovely
It pries our doors ajar.

The moon sees us as we are, my lovely
Wherever we may be
That which hangs above us all, my lovely
Sees the human in you and me.

Even if we're different, my lovely
We sleep beneath the moon
And it is the very same, my lovely;
I hope to meet you soon.

Bounphone Chanthavong

Where Has My Friend Gone?

In nineteen hundred and fifty eight,
I met and married my life's mate.
He became a friend I thought for life.
But God thought, oh no not quite.

My friend of fifty eight you see,
We had some sons, the number is three.
We lived together for twenty five years,
At his demise, there were many tears.

Thirteen years he's been gone away,
Sometimes it feels like yesterday.
He used to say that he was the "Boss,"
I'd let him be, if not for the loss!

Maxine Ashner Polk

Mind Over Matter

Don't come to me
With your grumblings,
Your whining and fretting.
Out! Satanic thought! Out!
You're not welcome here!
Stay and be my footstool
For I shall trample you underfoot
And prove that you're not worthy
Of my mind's attention!

Don't waste my time
With your dark clouds
Trying to overshadow
My purpose and destiny.
Your murmurings are lies
And your evil thoughts
Are dust for the wind.
For there is no lack or want in me
I am all I need to be.

Alison L. James

In Memory Of You

It has come the time to say goodbye to
someone very dear.
The memories we will cherish,
Our hearts we will keep near.
For the love brought to all our lives,
Has made it all so clear.
Precious is the life we have,
With no promise of another year.
So keep in touch with those you love,
Lend an open ear.
For it has taught us how to live,
without a given fear.
With this we thank you, oh so dear
our eyes are filled with tears.
Goodbye Goodbye
and may the Lord keep you near.

Yolonda Jordan

Tourist

I
saw a fish
fly.

A fish,
with wings for the
sky.

Yes,
I saw him.

In Barbados,
in mid-July.

Noel Michael James Ashton

Mr. Dad

I call you "Mister".
Why? Because to me,
You've been nothing, but,
a great, big, "Mis-ter-y"!

You never were around
When I needed you to play,
You have never heard me
when I knelt down to pray.

Now that I'm getting older,
you want to come around;
You want to be called, "Dad"
Now, just how does that sound?

You say, you're my dad,
Am I to give you glory?
You, who never held me
or told me a bedtime story.

You never even was around
when I was lonesome and sad.
Now, you have the nerve,
To want me to call you, "Dad", Mr!

Mary Kay Pringle

Mother's Dance

Pow! Punch! Whack! Smack!
I did not want to dance with you.

Yell! Scream! Roar! Shout!
Please don't make me dance with you.

I was little, you were big,
My legs could not carry me away.
I was little, the world was big,
No one believed me anyway.

Then I ran, with the others,
To the only place there was to hide
With more violence came more others
Inside my head we would reside.

Now I am big and I am gone
Because I cannot live with you.
You are weak, your poison's gone
I have started my life anew.

So, pow, punch, whack, smack
As I undo the dance with you.

And yell, scream, roar, shout
Mother, I'll never dance with you.

Angela M. Kroll

In This World

In a sea,
painted colors
swirl to find
intertwined.

In a stream,
lost reflections
dance to see
dreams.

In a drop
shadowed lights
blink to discover
one another.

In this world,
fragment persons
huddle to obtain
sameness.

Sara Masenheimer

Sweet Winds

Sweet whispering winds
That blew the lone leaf from a tree
now bare,

Take me down a path
That is so clear and let me breathe
The air.

Sweet whispering winds
That spoke when I chose not
To listen,

Echo strong a breeze
The now returns strength of
Conviction.

Sweet whispering winds
Take my soul back to ideals
I knew

Before I struggled
'gainst the force of whispering winds
That blew.

Susan C. Schulz

Credit Card Blues

Tempting words, so enticing
Like a cake that's all icing!
"Have fun now can pay later"
So much to feed this alligator!
As when later comes too soon
And more dollars are on the moon
So consolidate, get a loan
That will throw the dog a bone
As a rabbit running frantic
Last hope gone, in a panic
All the shelters blizzard buried
Snow and ice and cold winds married
Searching, seeking, endless quest
Always, always there's the test
Tear them up, do it fast!
Final, blessed, peace at last!

Ileane Smith Murray

Flying, Part I

Earth, fell away.
It's a new way, world.
Longing to stay,
in a blue sky, world.

You, flew away,
given wings my butterfly.
Still so much to say,
to this angel, butterfly.

Take me now, away,
upon wings, yes, flight.
Let me feel everyday,
the surreal journey of flight.

You watch from far away,
steel wings climb, mine.
We are closer for today,
descending fleeting, time.

Earth, fell away.
It's a new way, world.
Longing to stay,
in a blue sky, world.

Lisa Lachler

There Is A Silence

Each year we are touched
By the ultimate voyage
Of those we are so fond

Each year we come
That much closer
To God
And, the great beyond

Each year, a scar is left
In mind
Body and spirit

But living with scars
They wouldn't want
We must go on life
And live it

John C. Williams

Morale Booster

She's a ray of sunshine
On a dreary winter's day
Her smile has a "wattage"
That lights a weary way

She pauses to encourage
Each fearful doubting one
And leaves the warmest feeling
Not knowing what she's done

God has blessed this lady
With a very special grace
Inner beauty shines anew
With each smile on her face

Her deeds are done in secret
With a charming humble air
And all while she is sitting
In a specially fitted chair!

Margaret Lodge

Grow Old With Me

I'd give you my eye's;
    if you would only see me.

I'd give you my lips,
    if you would only
    say you love me.

I'd give you my arms,
    if you would only
    hold me.

I'd give you my hand's,
    if you would only
    touch me.

I'd give you my heart,
    if you would only beat
    for me.

I'd give you my leg's
    if you would only
    walk with me.

And I'd give you my soul,
    if you would only grow
    old with me.

Faye Marshall

The One Pearl

The one pearl, formally dressed,
Strung on a strand of others,
Decorates the elegant neckline of
A beautiful woman.

The pearl sits there while the woman
Speaks of all her love stories.
The necklace breaks, sending the
Pearls in all directions forming
An artwork of chaos.

The one pearl, formally dressed,
Round, perfect, rolls over an old
Worn wooden floor, landing in a
Deep crack, never to be seen again.

The one pearl, formally dressed,
Keeps the love stories forever.

Delome Greenwald

The Fox Hunt

A fox darts across the woods
A horse and hunter jump fence
The fox, as a hunter's trophy?
Is the future
unless the fox can vanish and vanquish
his adversary.
The tail bolts.
The gun points.
A hit? A miss?
To take a life or receive frustration?
The fox will live to frustrate again.

Dan Daly

A Dream...

Quietly
the ripples of water
wait while I think.
So quiet, so peaceful,
so scared of the yards ahead.
So quiet, so peaceful,
before I enter
the dead, motionless water.
I hear a tone; I go;
I leave that platform
above the water.
I feel, I think: Will I win?
After what seems like a year,
but is merely 29 seconds,
I touch the wall.
I look both ways,
yet don't see anyone.
I've won! I've done it!
I've achieved success
in the dead, motionless water.

Mary Beth Metrey

Petite Terror

Such a tiny little creature,
    so delicate by design,
Can cause so much commotion,
    created by us, the human kind.
Your prehistoric ancestors, who
    once roamed the earth,
How majestic they were from the time
    of birth.
From dinosaur to petite delicate lizard,
The sight of you can make me move
    like a blizzard!

Debra T. Urquhart

Love?

Just sitting on my window pain
  thinking about the day
When inner peace and happiness
  will finally come my way
I fought a fight to no avail
  an answer not achieved
I found the love in others
  that I couldn't find in me
Babies born know not of love
  but seem to show a sign
Grown ups posses the knowledge
  but not the peace of mind.
The dawn brings on another day
  our destinies unfold
The dust shows only emptiness
  of the love I've never known
If I die before I know what
  love is really like
May justice serve its mighty blow
  this moment as I write

> *Michael Bell*

Rite Of Passage

See me
through unlying eyes
with truth
with clarity
See me
as I am now
no longer a girl
but a woman...
  a woman
    scarred
  a woman
    strengthened
In loving you
I've lost
that which bound you...
  my softness
  my naivete,
  my youth

> *K. Lynn Purdy*

A Dream

  Baby, you can bring me down,
like no man has ever done. You're
a woman that knows what she
wants out of life, a woman
who strives for happiness and
meets life's goals head on.
  Baby, you have a smile and
a heart of solid gold, you make
me feel alive - something I've
never felt in years.
  If you and I were together,
together as one, I would love
you as no one could. I would
cherish the life we would have
together - but most of all,
enjoy the love, you have in your
heart for all.
  But then again, if this could
only be true - a dream, a dream
from a lonely man.

> *Anthony Taitano*

Untitled

Lord shine your light down on thee.
There's so much animosity in the air,
Lord touch their souls so they can care.
The hostility is there,
You see it everywhere.
Oh Lord lead us in the right direction,
Before the time comes for resurrection.
It's not too late to change our ways,
And ask the Lord for happier days.
As we kneel down here and pray,
Oh Lord it's not hard to say.
Bless me and my neighbor,
And let the Lord be our savior.

> *Betty King*

Goodbye

I can't believe you're saying goodbye
I'm sorry if I start to cry
I'm sorry that you have to leave
It's just too hard to believe
We never really knew each other
But to me it felt like forever

I can't believe you're going away
I really don't know what to say
I've only had a few friends like you
I'm sorry if I look so blue
I hate for you to see me this way
But this is what happens when
goodbye, is what we say

Please be careful when you go
Cuz I honestly love you so
Now it's time to say goodbye
Please remember me or try

> *Erik J. Smith*

It Awaits

Silence echoes
Doubting thoughts
Fear crowds my mind.

...It's here

Oppressed feelings
Hopeless cries
I'm alone

...It stays

Screaming pain
Chained emotions
A touch of love comes..

...It attacks

Death is considered
Overwhelming fear
A deadly rebuke

...It left

Unconditional love and forgiveness
comfort and hope, found
Angels protect and surround

...He died for me.

> *Nissa Engstrum*

My Brother, Mark

When I was growing up
There was a person like no other
The person I am referring to
Is none other than my brother

As the years went by and we got older
My brother moved away
We cried a lot on each others shoulder
I wish he could have stayed

We were many miles apart
But he was always there for me
That was the kind of man
He was meant to be

My brother is in heaven now
It has been almost a year
They say that time will heal the pain
For those who are left here

I know that death is a part of life
And some die sooner than others
Someday we will be together again
I love and miss my brother

> *Deborah St. Andre*

Everywhere Forever

You are everywhere.
Like skin, like breath,
like thought, you are in me.
"Whisper in my heart,
tell me you are there, "Carole says.
Daydreams become night
dreams and I am only
as big as my thoughts.
And the moving pictures
are of you and me
studying each others faces
and looking deep into forever,
and forever was never a never.
Your image is tall and you
are a smile and a poem
being spoken forever.

> *Cynthia Africano*

Martin Luther King
(A Drum Major For Peace)

"Whiteness is a true color
blackness is a fake"
For everyone should know
prejudice is a big mistake
For we are all created equal
black, white, or blue
for it does not matter,
which color is true
Dr. King had a dream
that we are all created equal
White men, black men,
Jews, and other people
I ask myself questions all the time
then think about what King did
he always believed in fairness
even when he was a kid
King's dream lives on
and that shall never cease
for Martin Luther King Jr.
was a drum major for peace.

> *Craig Sams*

Gravediggers

The grey, a brawny-made farmer,
who tilled the swampy lands;
The blue, a city bred teacher
with soft, uncalloused hands;

Sat drenched, in the chilling rain,
beneath the lone pine tree;
amid the blood and pain,
sharing the same destiny.

They compared no philosophies,
but spoke of common things
and they clung despairingly
for comfort touch brings.

They prayed for their daily bread
and swift release from pain.
As the vultures circled overhead
waiting to make their claim.

Joined in death, by duty bound,
deaf to tongues that rave;
now oblivious to killing sound
of philosophies that dig graves

Helen R. Hawthorne

The Print

Caulk, focus, snap
  one million words, one second,
    you are the historian.
Reel, drip, dry
  one million meanings, one shot,
    you are the magician.

The image conceived grows
  beneath gentle fingers
    caressing,
    you are the artist.
Live! Breath! Become!
  Each print exists as
  an inviolable component
  of you.

Sarah L. Ramey

Eternity

The waves on the shore
The warm summer sky
The sand that's adored
By the wondering eye

The softness of the notes
The stroke of the keys
This which provokes
The sounds of the seas

Wondering who we are
Guessing where we'll go
Wishing upon a star
Remembering what we know

The silence of the moon
with clouds that form near
As the wind plays a tune
Am I really here

Love that wouldn't die
and bells that would ring
Who am I?
And what will tomorrow bring

Michael Pascullo

Lioness

Cool paws
pass upon crackling grass.
Eyes
sway from side to side.
Ridged deep,
like rivers long dried,
jaws grasp life,
young cub.
Shadows flicker
among brown blades,
but she waits,
rises,
squints into the sun's
fiery blaze . . .
walks into the wind.

David C. Lankford

Grown Up

  Once a child, sweet and nice
now a grown up mean and dead,
all grown up forgotten memories
of fun and games of hiding go seek.

Now the only thing hiding is
your heart under a pile of
responsibility, money and costs,
you scream help but no one
answers, you kill and no one sees.

Everyone's silent and everyone knows
of evil and anger started on
an apple tree. No one is
perfect everyone ought to see
what's wrong with me.

Tabitha Connelly

Christmas Day

It's lots of fun on Christmas Day,
You open presents and then you play.

The Christmas Tree is all lit up,
Under it, you may find a pup.

If you're good, you get lots of toys,
So try your best - girls and boys.

Stockings are hung with toys and candy,
Mom's cooking, is really dandy.

On the table there's lots of food,
It puts you in the Christmas mood.

Outside, in the snow you play,
So have a happy holiday.

Jonathan Figueroa

Steadfast

Life is like a carousel
spinning round and round;
emotions soaring up
and also plunging down.

We often run in circles,
going to and fro;
seeking our solution
when we already know.

Our father holds the answer,
we only need to ask;
He's willing and he's able,
so hold your faith steadfast.

Kathleen Elliott Blackburn

Don't Let Go

Don't let go
I need you so
More than you'll ever know

I need you here
Erasing my fears
Lending your ear
Easing my problems
Erasing my tears

I need your friendship
I need you giving a darn
About who or what I really am

Please don't hurt me
Please don't let go
Stay here with me
I'll always need you so . . .

Daniel Jara

Who Am I

My body
Temple of the living God
Bought by Him
Belongs to Him
Paid for
By His precious blood
Priceless.

My body
Controlled by Him
Redeemed by Him
Lives through Him
My body
Washed by His precious blood
Priceless.

My body
Serving Him
The Lord on High
Master, Savior
Honoring Him
My Body — Priceless

Hazel Fraser

Screaming Inside
To The Winds Outside

While looking round about him
He wondered for what he was waiting,
Standing alone where he was
Crying to his heart unlistening.

Screaming inside to the winds outside
He tore himself apart,
Knowing that it soon would come
Yet he could not hide.

Looking to the sky above
He wondered for what he was waiting,
At that he thought he saw a dove
And things like this could not survive.

Screaming inside to the winds outside
He tore himself apart,
Truth too beautiful to be alive
Things like himself should not survive.

Timothy P. Frey

Longing

Shh! Listen!
. . . Can you hear it?
Hear what?!

I hear it every time you
Gently stroke my face,
every time I long for your warm embrace.

Your endless patience, your gentle ways
From my path please do not stray.

I always need to have you near,
Your absence is my biggest fear.

Whenever though we are apart,
I can always hear your beating heart.

Daniella A. Pompella

The Light Of The Sun

The light
of
the sun
is very
bright
gleaming
shining down
on everyone
glowing beautifully
until
night falls
and darkens up
the towns
below

Angela Franzino

Christmas

At Christmas, I find presents under
the tree and stockings by the chimney.
At Christmas, I hear bells tingling
far and near, carolers at my door and
Twas the Night Before Christmas
which I've heard before.
At Christmas, cinnamon meets my
nose and pine from the tree
and peppermint from the candy jar.
At Christmas, I taste hot cocoa in
my mouth. Cookies fresh from the
oven and goose for dinner.
At Christmas, I feel joyful, and
happy, and excited all
at once because it's Christmas again!

Christopher Ponder

Winter

Winter is a time of fun,
No flowers or a bright, hot sun.

You can catch a cold or fever,
But you can't catch a frog or beaver.

In December, deck the halls,
Or go outside and make snowballs.

All the birds will be flying south,
As I drink hot cocoa with my mouth.

Build a snowman, or go sleigh riding,
On the ice, you'll be gliding.

Later at night, there will be a moon,
Winter will change to summer real soon.

Matthew Di Gioia

A New Day Has Just Begun

I hear the ticking of the clock
I see the rays of the sun
Rising up to tell me
A new day has just begun.
Running water every where
Brushing teeth and combing hair
Getting ready for the day
There ain't no other way.
What a life we have to live!
Ain't it great to be alive!
On such a lovely morning,
Oh! That sun lets me survive!
Do a good deed and pass it on
To your neighbor standing by
And see if it makes them smile,
And almost makes you cry.
There's a feeling going 'round...
Don't know what it could be
Maybe a kind of love
That's made for you and me

Mary Ann Herman

Financial Bind

My wallet's empty hope is gone
Wonder why I carry on
Tried so hard but now I see
This is what is left for me

I am being cuffed by dollar bills
Quarters fall from my finger nails
I'd like to leave it all behind
Can't you see I am in a financial bind

Somehow I knew it all along
Every thing would turn out wrong
My monthly rent is over due
And my bank account is empty too

Restraining bolts are in my neck
I am being gagged by a rubber check
Bills to pay mouths to feed
A little cash is all I need

This situation can't go on
Must find a way to carry on
It's not easy I know this fact
Must break the chains that hold me back

Titus Paris

Untitled

Nobody understands
Who I've become
Especially me
Questioning what's wrong
Blind to my pain
They don't know
I am lost
I am nothing
Everything is tainted
My thoughts torrid, twisted
Out of my control
My soul drowning
Terrified of reality
Surrounded by darkness
Nobody sees me
I am gone

Ursula Olszowski

Toys

I like toys of every kind.
Some are good for your mind.
I like to play with basketballs,
And also shop in the malls.
Dolls and skates are really fun
To play with in the rain or sun.
Every girl and boy likes toys,
Especially ones that make lots of noise.

Amy Beth Fernandes

The Monster Dream

One dark and gloomy night,
A monster gave me a fright!

He was big, ugly, and hairy.
Boy was he scary!

I tried to hide under my bed.
"What's the matter?" my mother said.

"I'm afraid of that gruesome thing."
He might take me away 'till spring.

All of a sudden, I woke up,
It was a dream - oh what luck!!

Amanda Smith

Sometimes

Sometimes when I'm thinking
About the color of my skin
It becomes rather frightening
To believe it's just melanin

Sometimes when I'm looking
Trying to find myself within
I really get to wondering
If it's really just melanin

Sometimes while I'm walking
I see others at me a looking
Do they see the good within,
Or just good old melanin

Sometimes I think to take a stand
Show the world I've got a plan
And very soon is the hour
They'll see more than my color

I then, like the Phoenix will rise
Put an end to all the lies
Ain't just melanin, no demons within
I'm more than the color of my skin

Sherwin Corbin

Restless

Sitting in a tree as a
hideous but cool breeze
Flows through my body like my
thoughts, though I am not lost.
I am here wherever here may be.
For in my search for a
place to hide from life's
uncertain insanity I have
found this place of refuge,
blessed with comfort
and tranquility.

John R. Bramos

Glue

Sticky, slimy,
                wet,
                       white,
                              glue.

What is there to do with glue?

Big glue,
    small glue,
    any size will always do.

Colors, colors, colors
        galore.
Different colors in the drawer.

Everyone uses it.
Everyone choose it.

Glue, glue, glue.
            E. E. Dooley

Untitled

From what we give
It is not life we live.
Within the heart
(merely blood)
Within the soul...
(the deepest love)
Where we walk upon rose petals
And the breeze carries lilacs.
Familiar images
(Images within imagination)
I never smelled lilacs
nor walked upon petals
My feet are on pavement
And for this I create...
    my lament.
        Brian Shaw

My Existence

Worker, worker
Run run run
Do this
And hurry

Mother, mother
Run run run
Do this
Don't do that
And hurry

Wife, wife
Run run run
Do this
Don't do that
And hurry

Where am I?
Who am I?
Who knows?

        Annette Barnhill

Always With Me

He is there
Always with me,
The passion never dies.
He is there
Always with me,
Love and friendship never end.
He is there
Always with me,
Sorrows and problems cease to exist.
Endless love never fades.
He is there
Always with me,
By my side,
Our love can overcome boundaries and
Survive many dangerous obstacles,
That lie ahead each day.
For the future holds our time
Together, but still, he will always be
There, always with me!

        Christine Vick

The Garment

Life is simple and delicate
A precious garment we wear
Each strand fit to a certain character
Imperfect in its make,
Yet harmonious in its fit
Swaying elegance
Stained by our secret sins
And unwashed deeds
Concealed with adornments
Of shallow success

Some hold tightly to the garment
Selfishly stretching its worth
Some wear it loosely,
Dangling it before death's jaws
Some complain of its length
Loving the sun and cursing the moon
Claiming that life is too short
In its passing days
All missing its true essence
Harmonious imperfection

        Desmond Jennings

The Ski Hill

The air is crisp
the season is here
it's time to get out
your old ski gear

Now find the old iron
and get out the hot wax
so when you go down the ski hill
you won't get stuck in your tracks

Now in Michigan
the weather is a pain
sometimes it snows
and sometimes it rains

But thanks to the ski resorts
on a fine job that they do
the hills are all ready
I hope you are too.

It's time to get ready
to the ski hills we go
to have a lot of fun
and play in the snow.

        Joey & Cindy Brower

I Am

I am a woman
Fulfilled and grateful you see

For I am a wife
With love that is shared equally

I am a mother
To teach, to love, to watch him grow

For I am a daughter
Taught to respect, admire and to let go

I am a sister
Youngest of three

For I am a child inside
Still with maybe a dream to achieve

I am a woman
Fulfilled and grateful you see
        Diann Turner Mulrenin

Luke's Just Not A Farmer Owen...

When I was in 2nd grade,
and we would hit
the playground,
I was always Luke or Han
or Darth. Well, it was usually
a good guy, but
on the playground,
I was always Luke or Han
or Darth, and all these
other kids played
stormtroopers or
R2D2 or C3P0.
Now, when I look back,
I realize that I can't
understand why
these people were
such silly characters
in the playground
Star Wars game.

        Sean Perry

Time Passes

The sun fades away
    Darkness steals in
So ends another day
    New journeys to begin.

New ideas to ponder
    New schemes to perfect
New miracles to wonder
    Old memories to resurrect.

Life is what we make it
    To an extent, so is time
To be genuine or fake it
    A nightmare or dream sublime.

The hours pass by and are gone
    Never to return again
Were we kind to everyone
    Did we make one new friend?

The sun fades away
    While the world amasses
The wealth of our day
    As time passes.

        Love Joyce LeFlore Schuster

Reflections

When I look into the pond,
I see a reflection of me.
It looks like an illusion,
But it's all a part of me.

I wave my arms in the air
And feel the cool breeze.
Making my way through,
I pick a few lovely flowers, too.
Throwing them up in the air,
Beautifully they fall down on the pond.

I look at the pond
And I think I look goofy,
It looks as if I have a twin.

Then I sit back and relax.
Just having a little fun.

Linda Cheu

When I Saw You Last

No words of goodbye,
but I didn't cry.

My heart that was with you,
has now left me too.

I thought you'd be there,
but now you're "up-there".

You said you wouldn't go far,
but then you got in that car.

You never saw that tree,
or the hurt you caused to me.

I watched in disbelief,
as my soul filled with grief.

I saw them take you away,
I've not seen you since that day.

Now one year has past,
since I saw you last.

Almost everything is okay,
because I look at this way:

When the time comes for me,
you again I will see.

Sarah E. Pollard

The Recluse

The house is without the slightest sound
Except her heartbeat's repetitious pound
That echoes and fills the room around

She maintains the house tidy and prim
The lights are kept low and dim
Her glass of wine up to the brim

The rocker she sits in begins to squeak
It forces the floor below to creak
A river of tears flow down her cheek

The massive drapes shut out the sun
Sounds of people having fun
A roaring jet plane on the run

On the hour the clock will chime
her weary eyes gaze at the time
She senses she's nearly lost her mind

No solace rests within her soul
as each lonely day unfolds
Another recluse growing old

Janet M. Reeves-Valdez

Mixed Feelings

I'm glad I don't live
Where it's sun and rain,
The sun
And rain
Again, again!

I'm glad that I live
Where there's ice and snow,
And fall
And spring
And summer glow.

I'm glad that I live
Where seasons change;
I like
my world
To rearrange!

Shelly Martz

Charlottesville

The islands in the mountains,
It is a different world.

If you need a job,
    go to Gastonia.

If you need some kindness,
    go to Kings Mountain.
If you need a bargain,
    come to Bessemer City.

If you need some recreation,
    visit Dallas.

If you need some fresh air,
    try Cherryville.

If you need a date,
    try Lincolnton or Shelby.

If you need the big city life,
    go to Charlotte, at night.

Everything you need is here,
    in Charlottesville,
The islands of the mountains.

Irene Davis

Untitled

You shut us out,
when we were there.
You couldn't see,
that we all cared.
Today is hard,
to say goodbye.
For all I can do,
is to weep and cry.
As this day,
comes to a near.
I wipe away,
one last tear.
But before I go,
I must stare.
Up in the heavens,
I know you'll be there.

Nancy Quinlan-Westerman

Unfulfilled Love

What have I done,
to be hated by you.
I thought you were the one,
Now what do I do?

I showed you,
How much I care.
And all you do,
Is just sit there.

I thought you could care,
And know how I feel.
Its not fair,
My heart was yours to steal.

I see you every day,
walking with your friends, in school.
I don't know what to say,
I feel like a fool.

I guess I should give in,
And let you walk away.
I guess I'll let you win,
And never talk to you after today.

Nicole Pronto

Answering Machine

Hello this is the McRumple's
We can not come right now
We might have heard the phone
But just sat there and groaned

We might have went off to the store
Or maybe we went to the shore
We could have went on a plane trip
Or maybe went off and did some flips

We might have went off to Brazil
Or we might just be cleaning the grill
We might have flew to Slovakia
Or maybe even Bosnia

We might be playing some basketball
Or maybe just running down the hall
We might have went to go sledding
Or maybe we were just laying our bedding

So you know we can't come right now
So please don't have a cow
You know what to do at the beep
Because we probably just fell asleep

Dale B. Snitgen

Grandpa

You have gone through
    much as a little boy;
From war to death, you saw
    it all.

The time when my Mom was
    born you were delighted;
Torn feelings when India had
    its Independence and
    when Gandhi was assassinated.

Now your life is at peace,
    but you still remember it all;
All the blood, wars, and tragedy;
All the love, and happiness,
    it is all in your heart;
All is in your heart and even me.

I love you, Grandpa;
That pleases me!

Anita Desai

Boundless

I came upon a feather one day
and a thought came to me; what
travels and wonders, have thy seen?

Foreign places, vast open spaces
seas of glimmer, and earth that trimmers;
Travelling on "God's great breath", you've
probably witnessed more of what is left for us
to see; those who choose to walk with thee.

Are your travels great in number"
Your stories filled with joy and wonder?
Smiles and laughter touch every heart;
If you were there, why did you part?

· For down here on the ground
we've turned wicked and wild, no
regard for life of mother or child; so
you see, you are lucky that it is me,
who has come upon thee!

And a voice softly spoke; "I have
seen the "Peace" you are to see in the
Eternal"; I turned, and the angel went away.

Chester Brown

A Sudden Bloom

Struggling to survive, seemingly on its own this time,
this precious plant had been given up on by the gardener.
It seemed to have no hope, its beauty had been but dim,
forgotten by the cares of life, it was placed in a corner.

The only friend the lifeless plant seemed to have,
was the ray of sunshine that gleamed through the pane.
No doubt it gave just enough for the plant to live,
was there any hope or had everything been done in vain?

Today, the gardener noticed for the first time ever,
a beautiful white bloom, as pure as the very first snow.
The Master Gardener's timing had been so very clever,
for only confidence and courage did the plant now show.

The gardener never imagined such a burst of life,
to come from this plant so suddenly and unexpectedly.
But it gave the gardener a renewed hope for life,
for this the Master Gardener was getting all the glory.

Never again would the gardener give in to life's gust,
without asking the Master Gardener to come and befriend.
For it's in Him we must always and continually trust,
because it is Him that will always be there to the end.

Stephanie Hardesty

Katherine Jean Riddle

Dedicated to the Riddle Family
In loving memory of their daughter and sister
My very best friend Katherine Jean Riddle
April 25, 1971 - November 26, 1995
Kathy Riddle will always be my best friend
Though now gone our friendship will not end
Through all my laughter and my tears
She will always be a part of me
As an angel she does now fly
Ever watching from the skies
My joy and sorrows I know she shares
For in my heart I know she is there
For knowing her I feel quite blessed
As a friend she was the best
We were friends but more like sisters
So it shall be forever more
Now at this time our paths do part
Forever more she will live in my heart

Dorothy-Marie Wilson

Friendship Means Forever

We always try something new,
We're friends through and through.
No matter what color you are,
We'll be friends near or far.
Our friendship is a treasure,
It's beyond all measure.
Open your eyes and see,
That there's a friend in me.
We're great friends I know,
Because to me it shows.
We always laugh and smile,
Which are as long as the River Nile.
We always show we care,
We always try to share.
We always help each other out,
And that's without a doubt.
We'll be friends til' the end,
No matter how rough its been.
We'll always be together,
Cause friendship means forever, til' the end!!

Teryn Rivera

You Mean So Much To Me

At the beginning I thought you were just my boyfriend;
But now I know you're mine till the end.

You might not understand what I'm telling you;
I'll simplify it: This Love Is True!

All the fun times we spend together;
I know we will be together 4-ever.

Baby, "You Mean So Much To Me"!

When ever I'm sad, and feel down and blue;
You always make me smile by doing the special things you do.

There are so many memories between you and me;
And you are the only one that holds that key.

Every second, every minute, every hour of the day;
You're stuck in my head and I want it to stay that way!

Baby, "You Mean So Much To Me"!

Stacey Tsepelis

The Voice Of An East Indian Girl

In whispering voice I said my name.
O! Wind do not blow my name for no passion,
But laughter there is for this name.
What fragile age when I was just a damsel
And the bell chimed to send us to our nook.
I ran the grass to my little nook for solitude
Did I seek. But admonition about them that
Laugh my name all there was for me.
I renounced the country as their own
So vain a place for me, and in a pensive mood
I painted delusive pictures of my ancestors land.
And waited for him all dressed in gold.
For him, who would put his seal upon my finger
And bound me to his joy, fear and anger.
But then, I yielded to my yearning and quit the
Waiting and joined those that mocked my name.
And together we accepted diversity and put our
Hand within the link and molded the land.
Blow wind, blow, blow my name for there is harmony

Cynthia Haynes

Untitled

"Did you see her?..." he said to himself. Her beauty passed through him as she went slowly past. Captured, he stared, not knowing that her face and smile were forever embedded into the very soul of his heart. His feelings for her so strong and so quick that it was as if he was hit from behind, whiplashed by love.

"Did you see her?!" No one seemed to answer. As quick as his question she was gone. He could find her, or so he thought, but he was still in shock from her rude enter and exit routine. For he himself did not know if he had indeed seen her. Though, he could still faintly smell her perfume;
intoxicating...
inviting....

Gone.

John Evenson

The Sounds Of Home

The small whimper of a baby
The loud T.V. in the family room
The sound of laughter in the play room
The smell of pie in the kitchen
The sound of voices in the living room
The sound of music in the bed room
These are all the familiar things I hear in my house
But the sound of quiet is a stranger to me
The sound of nothing I have never heard
If I heard nothing it would not be home.

Maggie Ratterman

Playing Hooky

Looking out at a grey flannel sky,
My mind began to play.
I skipped barefoot through misty clouds,
It brightened up my day.
I caught a ride on a fast moving wind,
Such fun I do declare!
I laughed as that wind did the loop-de-loop;
We made the strangest pair.
I must stroll back through the clouds to my home,
We will surely meet again.
There's a pussycat soft patter at my window now;
I think it's begun to rain.

Jean Whitmore

Surfer's Paradise

On a beach with sand as white as
snow;
In an ocean with water as blue as the
endless summer sky;
Rides the setting of the Surfer's Paradise.

On a board so finely shaped like a heaven
sent God;
In a massive wave carved by the overwhelming
forces of nature;
Rides the power of the Surfer's Paradise.

On a high indescribable by mere
words;
In a fantasy unbelievable to one's
eyes;
Rides the Surfer in his Paradise.

Nichol Makowski

Day Stone

Five o'clock
and the red sun
meditates its death
its descent into the infinite dark.

Five o'clock
and the plastic junk hairbrushes
and the torn pantyhose
and the couch stuffing
prepare for another night
in the gutter with yesterday's paper.

Five o'clock
and time to drink to our regrets
over the circles we danced today
time to drink to our wonder
at how our day could have possibly ended.

Midnight beast
stumbling blind in the indigo
lost again in dreams
of blood on the stone
I once used to spark fire.

Chris Martin

I Am

I am a creative girl who likes dancing.
I wonder how long I will continue dancing.
I hear music playing in the background as I dance gracefully.
I see the crowd cheering after I perform on stage.
I want to achieve my goals in life.
I am a creative girl who likes dancing.
I pretend to be on stage when I'm just dancing in my room.
I feel pain after I've been dancing on my toes.
I worry about how life will be in the future.
I cry for help when I am unable to accomplish my goals.
I am a creative girl who likes dancing.
I understand how much practice dancing involves.
I say you must work hard in order to be successful.
I dream that I will be a great dancer one day.
I try my hardest to be successful in whatever I attempt.
I hope to reach my goals in life.
I am a creative girl who likes dancing.

Melissa Catto

I Wish, I Hope, I Wonder

I wish gangs weren't bad,
I hope designer clothes aren't just a fad,
I wonder if it could happen

I wish I could help the world instead of it helping me,
I hope I'll live to see tomorrow,
I wonder if it could happen

I wish children wouldn't fight,
I hope they'll behave for just one night,
I wonder if it could happen

I wish my wishes would be filled,
I hope my hopes are fulfilled,
I wonder if it could happen

I wish I could grow up and be successful,
I hope I do,
I wonder if it could happen

Christopher J. Ungureit Jr.

Memories Of You

My heart calls out your name
Your blood pumps through my veins
I still feel the power of your touch
Time will not erase these sweet memories.
Rushing to your warmth at the end of the day
Knowing once I'm with you everything is O.K.
I still feel the power of your tenderness
Time can't erase these sweet memories.
When sadness and tears consume my soul
Sinking into your arms becomes my goal
I still feel the power of your understanding
Time shall never erase these sweet memories.
Talking to me softly in that sexy voice
Starting my engine I have no choice
I still feel the power of your seductiveness
Time doesn't ever erase these sweet memories.
Hearing the words, "It's over, goodbye"
Shocking my senses not knowing why
I still feel the power of your unfaithfulness
Time to move on, time to grow, time to let go.

Allison Kay Flamish

Listen

Shh! Listen!
Hear not the weeping!
As a child whimpers in fright.

Shh! Listen!
Hear not despair!
As a child cries into the night.

Shh! Listen!
Can't you hear!
As darkness closes, pushin' days light.

Shh! Listen!
I hear!
As the child runs, bringin' teddy tonight.

Shh! Listen!
It's alright...
As a kiss chas'n fears and
song rock'n heartbeats til nigh.

Shh... listen...
Ahh... sweet gentle lamb.
As a child returns to sleep
without the light.

Nancy Mangine-DeSaw

God Bless Our Love

Our love is a product of God's undying love
Sent down from Him to each other
From Heaven up above
I asked God for someone
With qualities just like you
I had faith in my prayer
I believe it has come true
Because those who are believers
Are definite receivers of blessings from above
That's why I thank God for you, Love
So, I can't help but pray to Him each and every day
I can't help but ask Him to increase
In us and to have His way
I pray that we'll always be able to put God first
And that in our hearts for His knowledge
We will always thirst
As I keep praying to Our Precious God up above
I'll ask continually in my prayer
God Please Bless Our Love

Jannice Thompson

My Prince

The tears on my pillow can speak a thousand words.
It seems like only yesterday, I was a little girl.
Life's not everything, I read in those fairy tale books.
I'm 31 and yet wondering, Oh! Where is my charming prince?
I wish he would come and take me a way.
And make my life ever so sweet.
But can he swim? For my tears are a pool.
They have become a room full thick. Hush up woman!
Fret not yourself, and realize, life is what you make of it.
I wish he would come and take me away.
And make my life ever so sweet.
But can he swim? For my tears are pool.
They have become a room full thick.

Valerie Ann Sutton

Angel

To the angel unfettered
who drifted through my nights
with cyanide dipped wings
sprinkling fairy dust
of the white powder that is ecstasy
(in all its forms)
spawned hatred for the twinkle in your eyes.

Mornings came without sleep
and your voice left a tingle on my tongue
but the grains of bitter memories
have drifted out with the tide
sandcastles are built now out of weathered love alone.

Dethroned, Now, with your wings torn from your back
You were my own creation
Sculpted, on an imaginary pedestal
the throne you never asked to sit upon
But there is beauty in your eyes
shaped with the grains of reality
And love that remains solid in my mind -
love, for my angel unfettered.

Jennifer Martin

Friend

As I sit and I ponder
I allow my mind to wander

Through the fields with grass and leaves
Through the forest filled with trees

And I come to a great lake
And let there be no mistake

That in that spot, yes, there, I found
As I gazed upon the ground

A peace that I had never known
A peace that I could have only grown

With the help and nurturing care
That I have when you are there

So to this lake I go and sit
If only for a little bit

When you're not near, but far
And I gaze upon the stars

And they shine into this lake
And I know there is no mistake

That it is you I call my friend
And you who will be there until the end

Catrina Ballast

Tooth For An Eye

Insolent dissenters mocking the walls of stone
Silent stagnation challenging the weak equity
we allow to flounder
Wire tangled barbs contain their pompous
contempt
Slowly, we abet the perpetrators
Their hollow laughter rings through the
cemeteries, echoing off souls of innocence
shattered, casting a brooding shadow across
their trophy ruins
The obscene reversal of just intention hangs
heavy in our shame
We bow to our captives in impotent forgiveness

Peter J. Lemieux

Precocious Love

I prayed for you, and you hath come, but ill
The time, for here precocious love takes form.
So time and fate have left us here to mourn,
As we embrace the fleeting love we feel.
I love you though my youthful heart strays still
From love so pure as in my heart was born.
My youthful acts know not how to adorn,
The passion that is lying in me still.
So please withdraw, oh falling sands of time,
And give us refuge in true love sublime.
And here my aged endearment will arrive,
For all my candid passions could then thrive.
Alas, there is no truth in dreams this kind
So, I am consoled in this, our mere time.

April Longley

Beyond This Wall In My Life

Beyond this wall there is life.
A life that beholds love, truth and happiness.
In my life love is what I give,
    happiness is what I receive,
    faith is how I live,
    hope is what I perceive.
When I got to my new life, I
    knew I paid the ultimate price.
I left a life of family and friends,
    rules to break and even to bend.
Then I realized the grass is
    never greener on the other side,
    especially beyond this wall
    in my life.

Tiffany J. Malcousu

Fear

When that sound enters your ear,
It tells you that someday you can fear
As the sound swells the fear inside you follows
Making you forget there is a tomorrow
To frighten you is the world in which it lives
Terror and hate is that which it gives
To understand and accept is the only way
To live with this thing that fills your day
But when you are ignorant to the reason
This thing called fear is always the season.

When you understand you will be free
Someday you'll wonder how it came to be
That a thing so obsolete rocked your boat,
Separate you from the world, like a castle in a moat.

Fear will always be there 'til the end of time
Like the things in life that don't seem to rhyme...

Alan Reddy

Natural Things

Radiant sun beams are shining across
    the far horizon
So beautifully splendid there's no way
    of disguising
Grass vividly green rippling in the wind
Religious songs in the minds of men
Crystal clear water flowing onward
    to the sea
All of nature's beauty fascinates me
The things of nature are sometimes
    Hard to understand
The creation of "the Master's" great hand
All made of beauty so rich and rare
To Heaven's land none can compare
There's a fountain of life freely flowing
In God's domain so wide
Meet him yonder on Heaven's side

Raymond Smith

Untitled

A full moon shines above me
speaking with her beautiful halo
Reminding me to always be thankful
I ascend the ancient stone stops
To find a room full of love
My heart soul mind and body tingle with joy
I no longer yearn to know why we
are here
Now I long to share what I learned
To spread the good news
To give my love

Lynne Biebel

My Road

I was a child and sat at the table by the windowside.
I saw blue skies and clouds pass by.
I saw trees and all greens, my cat and dog running around.
I saw a road and dreamed about going away.
I went one day to find the end which I
Could not see, laughing, dancing, and singing all the way.
It was my dream of journey all days.

I look through the windows again.
My children are playing there, looking at
flowers, butterfly's, and birds. Dreaming of
the same blue skies and clouds.
My journey went on and the road neared its end.

Now I'm window side again, sitting wheel chaired alone.
Through which I see a beautiful world.
With God's help, I journeyed a wonderful,
wonderful and exciting world.

Aili S. Cattorini

Refusal Of Goodbye

Not a day without night, a morn without eve.
The presence of a Father will never leave.
His laugh, His smile, the smell of his being,
Bored deep in the heart but never freeing.
Oh Daddy I miss you and your silly acting ways.
But I know beyond the horizon immortality lays.
As the weeping wept, time stood still.
Years gone by, tis God's will.
One day we shall meet in that heavenly sky.
For Daddy I refuse, I refuse to say goodbye.

Mindy L. Thomas

Psalm

No sweeter sorrow than this exists.
My sadness overcomes me. How am I to
control such thoughts? How can I be put
to blame? With no control over my
sorrow, I feel the same. Weather I
run or weather I hide... The deep dark
sadness is sure to find. Oh please dear
Lord, whom I adore, find me in this
dreadful place...and take from me all my
disgrace. This pain that hurts me so,
And of all my pain you surely know.
Lift me up! And with you I'll go. This
pain that robs my joy, for all that
satan has tried to destroy. My Lord,
I know you're always near, leaving
nothing left to fear. I know my
prayers you surely hear. Lift me
up oh Lord, and take me far from
here. This dreadful place, where I
can never show my face, your love I'll never cease to chase.

Alison Benson

A Grandmother's Prayer

Dear Lord, hear our prayers, please:
That there may be again, World peace!

Let evil Nations go unknown
Let them fight their own wars alone
Hear the prayers of the young and old
Bring our loved ones back into the fold.

Heal the pain of their broken hearts
Soothe with balm their scars and smarts
Dry the tears of every babe and lad
Brighten the hearts of parents who are sad.

Cleanse this your world of every wrong
Keep us always well and strong
Have mercy on us all, I pray
and with your blessed hand lead us day by day.

Susie B. Cobos

My Eternal Love

I wake up in the morning
thinking about you.
It's like a dream when we get that feeling.
I look in crystal water
and see your face
In the bottom.
I smile because I love you.
The same as I love myself
In the evening
when the sun
Goes down, your eyes are
the one think that I see
and they give light to my dark room.
Our love is more tall
than a mountain that rises
High in the sky, and like a giant
that is hard to move.
The only think I want
is to wake up, next to you all my life.

Jose Garrido

Unconditionally

As I looked at your sandy brown hair and ocean blue eyes
I knew you were the man of my dreams the stars in my skies

When you spoke your voice was as if it came from heaven above
My body froze in time and my heart was beating love

When your hand compassionately caressed my tender face
Was a moment in time I wish would not erase

When your lips softly touched my cheek
I felt if I never learned how to speak

Your wisdom was as sharp as each of your features
Unmistakably one of God's finest creatures

Anything is possible with you by my side
Any goal is achievable with you as my guide

I have not a care in this world with you in my life
Unconditional love is what made us man and wife

I Love You Don

Suzanne Dickinson

Darkness

There was silence in the forest
Until, alas! I heard the trees rustle
and the branches away.
I ran steady and still,
Darkness dawned upon my quest.

The wind raced through like the waves of the ocean
Sounds of fear echoed around me,
The leaves swirled in the foggy mist
And the full moon was hidden in the dark clouds.
Darkness dawned upon my quest.

My pulse raced and my body shivered.
Something was ahead beyond my reach
I anticipated an illusion, but to my surprise it wasn't.
The biggest deer I ever saw looked at me with dreary eyes.
Then suddenly raced away in the blink of an eye.
To me it was pure manipulation.
Darkness dawned upon my quest.

Gavin Ramoutar

The Last Christmas

I'll never forget that Christmas day
The last that my Father would see,
For in a short time and merciless way
Cancer had taken over entirely.

As our family all gathered for the noon meal
I began to focus on how valuable life can be,
I was so concerned how he must feel
And asked myself what is it was me?

As we bowed our heads and began to say grace
I held his hand to show my love,
I saw the tears streaming down his face,
As we prayed to our Heavenly Father above.

I sat there on that Christmas day
With so many questions of why this must be,
And knowing not to question God this way
I prayed that my Father would be set free.

The next day God came and took my Father away
Delivered him into a better place,
Into Heaven where I'll be someday
Again to see my Father face to face.

Devona Humphries

Life, In General

I woke up, with new eyes
An walked with my mind
To a corner, in life
Through the grasses, roses an blue skies
When I could go no further,
I had to stop to realize
Why have I come?
How long will I stay?
It was easy to get here, to easy I say . . .
Then I looked around,
All was afraid, for my world was now changed
The grasses were now blades,
And roses all thorns,
My skies closing in, twisted and torn
When then before me, stood my savior, my Lord
Come now my son, do not be a afraid
I will always love you, even though you do stray
An then I walked out, without hindrance or harm,
Using my mind, for the first time
Into my Lords arms.

Gary Thomas Hoag

The Doors

Several doors,
They stand around me.
Door number one,
Children play ball, laugh.
Having a great time.

The second door.
A dark building with boarded up windows.
Along it, a street, without a trace of light.
A moon in the sky makes the broken glass on the pavement
sparkle.

Third door is green trees.
Dandelions fill the field.
To the left, a waterfall,
Spraying the trees as it crashes against the rocks underneath.

The fourth door,
Fire surrounds me.
I feel heat, evil laughter.
I can't stand it.

I run to the last door.
Ghostly, thick clouds
About to cry the night away.

Michael Krivyan

In The Name Of Sisterhood

My two sisters, in the name of sisterhood!
Mother's passed away seven years ago.
Who's going to explain this feeling I have,
Of wanting another child,
That came over me two years ago.
If it returns, what will I do with it?
In the name of sisterhood!
Did mother ever feel like this?
How did our foremothers overcome it?
Seven years before mother's death, Grandmother died.
We don't know about Great-Grandmother's death.
Maybe it was seven years before Grandmother's death.
In the name of sisterhood!
Great-Grandmother! Grandmother! Mother! Aunt!
Our sisterhood hasn't been kept alive like the women we know.
We can ask any woman or doctor — everyone has a remedy.
We should've had one from our ancestors to foretell our daughters.

Eartha Porter

Untitled

So you're spiraling down a black hole
waiting to hit bottom
and when it can't get darker
you realize the black hole is inside you
withered, dried and rusting
like the acid of fresh fruit in the pit of your stomach
because another knocker walked away
while you wait for the man with the ax
alone in your small white box
where it is safe
alone
and you sit in the box
with no doors and no windows
and wonder why nobody can see inside
and nothing gets outside
oh yea, no windows, no doors
and you listen to the polite knocks
on the outside from the inside and wait
yelling, screaming
but the cat's got your tongue

Julie Button

In Memory

Melancholy moves into the space
where you were, but aren't anymore.

No longer in love, unable to find our way
Hope gone, joy broken.

Loss is a knife
severing the specialness
that once was our life.

Together no more
fumbling in emptiness
that was full before.

Unable to explain
Impossible to understand
Unbearable to feel

We move apart

Not knowing the why of it.
Only that what was
isn't anymore.

Both of us knowing what is lost,
both unable to bear the cost

Of finding the we in us again.

Grace Meyer

The Dream!

Like Martin Luther King . . . I too have a dream! . . .
I am but a human sent down from above,
Sent to reason, and wonder and think and to love!
Yes I am only a human, I'm proud of this fact,
I'm proud to be young, to be gifted and black!
I'm proud to have made it this far and this high,
I'm proud of the moments that slowly drift by!
I'm proud to have lived til this very day.
I'm proud that I'm proud and I'm proud to say!
My wish is to be happy, to always walk tall.
To always be able to stand up from my fall!
My dream is to stay proud until my judgment
Day for someday I will be on the top, and I
Will lead the way! So as I am ending this poem
And as I say this out loud . . . Stay young, black
And gifted, but also stay proud!!

Sharon Shelya Wells

The Power Of Love

God is love. His power is great....
With Love: Man - He did create
He intended for man; to have peace,
joy, and a happy life. He gave him
freedom of choice... And, from his
own body: God, made him a wife.

Although "man"...Satan deceived and,
caused, him, "God, to, dis-obey. Is the
reason why, humanity; is corrupted today.
Inspite, of the confusion, hate, and iniquity.
Life shall continue perpetually..as the
scriptures; says...for, God's love for man
never ceased. That's why, He sent His only begotten
son; into the world....to redeem man's eternal
life, lost. His name was "Jesus"; Who died on
the cross, rose from the grave, and ascended to
heaven above. All because of; "The power of love".

Alma D. Dargan

Untitled

Beauty - a silhouette precious as gold
Exuberant smiles are God's kisses from the sun above
My heart beats with joy and song
Arms reach to comfort from loneliness, despair and the cold.
Warm bosoms caress my soul with serenity and love
Compassionate hands touch and nurture foundations
    built with devotion
Voices whisper and speak in silent tongues at night
Lips gingerly respond of both young and old
Laughter echoes in the sky on its journey in time
Sacred spirits dance carefree in motion
Smooth satin silk bodies like cotton pillows
Innocent, secretive, passionate entities unite
Moving, floating, drifting, fast, slow
I forever yours and you forever mine

Bernice R. Kendall

Dear Brother, Richard (1963-1995)

I thought of you today, with love.
But that was nothing new.

I thought of you yesterday,
And the days before that, too.

A thousand prayers won't bring you back,
I know, because I've tried.

Neither will the million tears,
I know, because I've cried.

So may the winds of love softly blow
And whisper so you can hear.

I will always love and miss you
And wish you were here.

Barbara Efteland

'Tis That Season Again

Here it is, that season again.
We fill out our tax returns and send them in.
We figure and remember and plan
To deduct everything we can.
Finally, we have it all written down,
Take our labors to the post office in town.
Then comes that time in May
When we learn, much to our dismay,
Our refund check has been stopped,
And we can't "shop 'til we drop."

Daisy C. Neuber

My River

My life is a river
Flowing freely through time

My river has had some strong currents
Some falls
Some dams
Some calm waters
Some obstacles that forced it to find another route on this land

My river has crossed paths with others
The rivers have shared their supplies
My river has tried to leave its mark by nourishing all around

My life is a river
Flowing freely through time
giving thanks to my source, which is how my river survived

God is the source of my river
When my river runs out
I hope I leave enough branches to sprout

Aijalon Gomes

No Greater Pleasure

No greater pleasure could there be!
Then to hold your babies tenderly

My little girl, oh so sweet!
With little hands and tiny feet!

My little boy, with eyes so bright!
They light the stars that shine at night!

You fill my life with joy and love!
I'm so, so thankful to the Lord above!

No greater treasure could there be!
My boy of 6, and girl of 3!

When I put you both to sleep in bed
So many thoughts run through my head.

Some day soon you'll both be grown
And want to move out on your own!

A scary thought, oh this is true!
But I guess its, part of raising you!

You both well go and have children of your own!
And then you'll see!

No greater pleasure could there
be.... Then to hold your babies tenderly

Cheryl Smigielski

Untitled

our wind owes us as before us the land
and land the sea before the wind except after i
and i wasn't the land but perhaps the c
our land windows us this land with two c's
one sea or was it another way which way
a sea a mer as the french would sayica
blessed land bless this day our breadly day
and dare to see through our windows
owing wind sees the sea and has seen
la mer on its way around this space
pacing in a way and away again une mer
they sayica pacing through space
never daring to window us owing to
this land and a dog named Jingo

John Watson

Lunatic Brook

This is a story that was told to me by a small time crook,
About what you'll find in a city dubbed Lunatic Brook.

Candy-Coated beetle drops and come-true dreams,
Lots of giant committees and little midget teams.
No kindly kings, no presidents, no one is allowed to lead,
Everyone is treated as equals, regardless of color or creed.

You find things like this wherever you look,
In the marvelous town known as Lunatic Brook.

Cat-dogs and bird-mice and other bizarre pets,
Products of the radiation in the water where it's kept.
Crazy green monkeys swing in the trees,
Lions walk in natural cages with roots around their knees.

Things like this you'll find in every cranny and nook,
In the peaceful city that we call Lunatic Brook.

Cures for all diseases and functioning mind probes.
Psychokineses, ESP, and living snow globes.
Businesses run by computers, and robots for protection.
Found throughout the town, in each and every section.

These things, as crazy in sound as in look,
Are every-day sights in Lunatic Brook.

D. J. Annicchiarico

Friendship Eternal

From the earliest days in the lives of those near,
  To the persons who always could smile,
  And with bad news as well could rile.
But in all those moments, a soul which was dear.

And through all this time which has weathered great storms,
  As well as blue skies.
  Many hello's and good-bye's.
The diversity of life was showing all its forms.

And when the multitude of paths turned the road upside down,
  So many of us took the way,
  Of frolic and fun with nothing to say.
Only to reflect on our travels, and try not to frown.

Whether we stray or we stay is truly not profound.
  We all did what was done.
  Which created sadness as it did fun.
For in the Universe itself, forever we will abound.

So the season will come to a close and refrain,
  When this leaf shall fall,
  And grief shall overcome all.
But oh - the love shall forever remain!

Glenn Fischer

Seashells

  Somewhere on a distant seashore,
we shall run barefoot across the soft sands.
  Someday we shall slip silently through the
caressing waters of the night-still sea.
  Sometimes I can hear the distant surf pounding,
and as I breathe, the swift breeze,
alive with the sting of salt, tickles my nose.
  Somewhere on a deserted isle,
the sun casts its sunbeams down upon the waters,
playing a sparkling game of catch with refracting light,
and somehow, the splendor of the sea is displayed
on our sun-bronzed faces.
  Someday when the sun shines down,
and as gentle breezes play tag around us,
we shall search the shoreline together
for seashells.

Christa Eastvold

Just The Beginning

To dream a dream with life and hope
To live a life with disappointments and cope
To cry the tears of pain and sorrow
To know the truth of the realistic tomorrow

Each brief stab of pain and doubt
Each painful realization of what life is about
Each want for success and each want for pride
Each fear that we will try to hide

To be confused of which path to take
To know what is for others and to know what is for your sake
To know what is right and to know what is wrong
To remember that life doesn't last very long

Time will keep going it won't stop for you to cry
So dream while you can and aim your goals high
Keep your chin up always and work with more than life has given
Do not dwell on the past and always see your life worth livin'

This is just the beginning
So don't even dare to quit now
Make your dreams succeed
Anyway you know how!

Cheryl Brennan

To You (Again)

At what point did I slip up,
did I fall?
I used to be whole,
I used to be a loner.

But now, when my eyes fold,
I feel weight.
It's not lust or anger,
not pride or pain, it's you.

It's your cool touch on my chest,
it's your legs nesting beside me,
and your cheek on my heart.

It's my hands slipping through your hair,
stroking your neck,
pulling you closer.

And it's not there any more,
accept in the moment,
when the silence blows in, and my eyes slip,
And now, now you've got me leaning.

Edward M. Forman

He Or She

What is more valuable than a pearl
Than in mommy's arms a little girl

It must have seemed so long before she arrived
But think of the women who have been deprived

You two now are as proud as can be
And no longer matters if it's a he or she

Annabell Schmuttenmaer

Stumbling

Winding road curved straight
and infinite line as if there is any other kind
nothing greets her as she touches the ground
then again nothing knew she had left
colors have smell and smells are colorful
she loves her everlasting delicate whisper
more than her absent family
she leaves and walks down the circular road
she couldn't love this blindfold more, it's her salvation

Leigh E. Offutt

No Changeling

At two, a blue-eyed pit-a-pat,
  He went away.
One day...the sun, the next...a somber shadow.
  Just like that

There came another;
  Black-eyed, imperious,
    Yet not, or so it, seemed to us,
      Not, in truth, another. Not really Davy's brother.

Instead, our first-born,
  Who, wheeling in his headlong flight,
    Looked down into our hearts, grief-torn,
      And so returned...contrite.

Two now, our black-eyed pit-a-pat,
  Unlike, imperious, yet not, it seems to us,
    A second child, not that....
      Steadfast, we claim it's Davy...
        Our Davy, first and last.

Valma Clark

Untitled

The storm rolled in
Just as its cousins had done before.
I could hear the wind begin its assault on the trees
And as the rain began to fall I asked if I could endure anymore.

Storms were a plague
Yet I had somehow survived.
I dreaded most not the storm but its wake,
The repair that was needed once the wind cleared the sky.

Herein lies the struggle and pain,
The picking up after the storm goes its way.
I have struggled before and surely will do it again,
But I will always dream of a day this vicious circle will end.

Bethany Jean Schaefer

What Sort Of Life Do You Have?

When you grow so rich, you get many friends,
When you become famous, you make many friends.

When sickness comes, you lose those friends,
And when poverty comes, you lose those friends.

You are passing away; they are going away,
You are suffering much; they are sneaking much.

Everything you are will pass away,
Only what you do for God will remain.

What sort of life do you have if your friends
can only be counted on in good times?

Declan C. Onuoha

A Scary Detail

Dark drizzle fall from the sky,
Infinite tears always I cry?
Life holds such strange things
Forever in my mind the bell rings
A sound alone that causes such hate,
Dying or living, the great debate.
The choice is within us all,
Forward we leap or down we fall.
Scary as this may sound,
It's a factor of its own, to this we're bound
I don't wish to choose,
for my answer may lose
All sense of morality,
Also to discover, this is reality.

Cassandra L. Elms

My Comfort

If I ever have a worry, a care, concern, or fret,
I can always turn to Jesus, he is my safest bet.
He answers all my questions, quiets all my fears,
He heals all my heartaches, and dries up all my tears.
No matter where I am, no matter what the day,
I can always turn to Jesus, there's only one thing he will say,
"I died for you, my child, and no matter what you do,
I hope that you will always know how very much I love you".
I know this in my heart and I think it every day.
Do you think and feel the same?
Will you after today?

Nichole Nading

My Love For You

I like to hold you close, I like it when you're near
I like it when we whisper in each others ear
When you put your lips on mine, it's a feeling I can't explain
It sends the message "Gee I love her" straight up to my brain
Every night I sit and pray
that I'll be with you till my dying day
Whenever I think of you and me
My thoughts of life are clear as can be
My feelings for you are like the stars up above
Beautiful and bright and filled with love
The more I'm with you the better I feel
About finding a girl for whom my love is real
Everytime I see your beautiful face
I know I'm in a wonderful place
I use to think God had it in for me
But you were in His plan, now I see
I often wondered if there was a girl like you
To make me want to live my whole life through
Now that I've found you I can see
My life is worth living for you and me.

Jacob Zigler

Untitled

Red is a color of a frightful fire,
Orange is a color of burning desire.
Yellow is the color of glowing so bright,
Green is the color which all seems so right.
Blue is the color which enriches our minds,
Purple seems deep no thoughts will it bind.
A sea of colors which we hold so dear,
losing them all is out biggest fear.

Rosemary Fanelle Smith

Demo Of A Plastic Guilded Dream

Drained to the core
Who would have known I had wanted more?
Symbiotic matrices wait for me in the hall.
Engage in rheumatic battles and explode at your own will.
Rockets landing warm us of the new age.
Palpitating genes drip from my soul.
Who would have known?
Filled to the brim - I am a coffee machine
Waiting for the mustard - save me from my roots.
Stand beside my newfound hide
Awaiting the arrival of the sunken one.
Who would have known?
Aged to perfection
A flotation device awaits you now.
How could you pass up an opportunity
To see the bees and stand on shells made of glass?
The sky will be plaid
All the trees will be glad
And acupuncture won't work.
Who would have known?

Amy Floretta

What Do You Do?

What do you do when your heart's about to break?
When you're hurting more than you could ever take.
When your feelings overwhelm you,
When you realize they are true.

When the one you love has hurt you so deep,
When you lie there at night and never go to sleep.
What do you do when your life feels incomplete,
When you made a mistake you wish you could delete.

When you said something you wish you could take back.
When the meaning of your life you now lack.
What do you do when you're so much in pain,
When things in your life are driving you insane.

What do you do when the one you love is gone?
How will you go ever carry on?
When you feel so empty within your heart,
When you can't take it anymore — being apart.

Melissa Davis

Alone

I sit here all alone, can't help wondering,
when you'll be home. I hear the door,
could it be you? Only the wind, where are you?
I fall asleep, not knowing you'll never be
home again.

Ann M. Showers

Jean ValJean

Racing from misdeeds of the past,
leaping from village to village,
rapidly departing from each establishment,
continually running into old aquaintences,
winning after each encounter,
barely escaping death,
perpetually altering his identity,
feeling like everyone is against him,
Jean Valjean turns toward his only happiness
his beloved Cossette.

Jeffrey D. Keller

A Mothers Love For Her Child

I think of my child
  And my heart soars
And thanks God
  for what he has given to me,

To see how much she has grown
  And then watch and wonder what she will be.

She wakes in the morning
  with a smile on her face,
Ready to explore a new day.
  She laughs and giggles with
Her toys all in place,
  Wanting me to sit by her and play.

The day when your child looks to you
  And says "Mommy",
Is the day that you will know
  That this true gift from God
Will always be a part of you,
  And will forever touch your soul.

Gina Buckenberger

Indian Past

As I walk through the canyons and the
wind blows through my hair, I hear the
spirits calling me from I do not know where
they said come stay awhile and learn about
your past, of how the Braves and Chiefs died
in the tall buffalo grass. Of how they lived,
how they died with tears upon their faces, and
how it was our people were left in such a
disgrace. So if you ever feel that the world is
holding you down, think of us then and
think about us now.

Daniel S. Thrasher

Only In My Dreams

I'll never see you nestled in your crib... Only in my dreams.
I'll never see you with ribbons in your hair, or dressed in
frilly pink dresses... Only in my dreams.

I'll never smell your soft scent after a bath... Only in my dreams.

I'll never see your cute little expressions, or smiles...
Only in my dreams.

I'll never cuddle with you, or hold your soft tiny hand...
Only in my dreams.

I'll never get to see your first steps, or hear your first words...
Only in my dreams.

I'll never see your first day of school, your graduation,
or your wedding day... Only in my dreams.

I'll never see you again until we meet in heaven...
Only in my dreams.

Lisa Tucker

What Is Life?

Only a breath in Humanity...
Only a moment
Our moment in the spotlight
Some live for their religion.
Hoping their God will bless them,
After life ends.
Some seek only pleasure,
Oddly enough their lives usually end in pain.
Some are seekers,
Questioners of known facts.
Some only look at where they are,
When they're there.
Almost as if they're always asleep.
Some people think,
They've got it all figured out
Wish they'd clue me in.

Jean Marie-Anne Richman

...Nevermore

N ever hearing the sound of a crying child again..
E veryone achieves their goals..
V anity is forgotten..
E ase to the sorrows of the poor..
R est to those who can't sleep..
M oods of sadness be lifted..
O verworked be compensated..
R isk of disease is lowered..
E den be no farther away than home..

Ryan R. Morris

To Phyllis Evelyn

On your second birthday, you were in our arms,
And we sang your birthday song,
On your third birthday, you were in Heaven,
Did angels sing your birthday song?

The tenth of April is a dreary day
As each year it rolls along,
But, in Heaven, you are happy,
Did angels sing your birthday song?

Daddy joined you in 1993
And I feel so all alone,
But rejoice that you are together,
Did angels sing your birthday song?

Lois Bartynski

Us

A measured time we have to use
A Journey which past generations trod
Time often spent was time often abused
Where is the link — the generation to generation sod?
It should have grown and flourished thick

A family diary of lessons learned
Of singular lives as time proceeded forth
Such prose would allow one to discern
A clearer vision of happiness and self worth
We would have savored a simple truth

I and Me must relinquish to Us
For in Us there is a sharing warmth
While I and Me will stand alone
If only we as youth had known

An honest family journal kept
could educate the masses so
For richer we receive, having given
So simple — I and Me must go

Monday through Sunday have been traveled before
But too often by I and Me, instead of Us.

Lawrence C. Stratton

The Innocence Of Jessica

It is the celebration of her sixth year here on earth;
She is like a fragile flower, with a super under girth.
They are going on a holiday, to the great atlantic shore -

I say to her, "My dear, I have walked out there before",
With a smile - she replied. "Cool Grandma" —— and then,
I'll look for your footprints and I will walk in them!

Ah, the innocence of the child.
I marvel at the sight.
I review the things that life might bring.
I strive to make them right.
My spirit of protectiveness, wells up within me... when
That Angelic smile appears - on Jessica again.

Phyllis Eakins

Delicate Days

Bobbles and barbies and baths full of bubbles
Kittens and kerchiefs and boys are just trouble
Pink parasols and white dainty gloves
Afternoons gazing at clouds above
Beautiful ribbons and baskets of bows
Sweeping green grass tickling your toes
The beauty of life a child does know,
Admiring one flake in a field full of snow

Angela Collins

Sunset

Looking out the upstairs window met my eyes a spectacular sight
In the west the colors red and orange shone so bright
Dare my eyes to look straight up not as good a sight would be
The dismal gray, a cloudy sky is all my eyes would see
But oh those colors called my eyes away from cloudy gray
I looked, for what I saw was unlike any other day
Danced before me fire embers leaping in the sky
Swirling, twirling towards the heavens reaching up so high
The brightest orange, deepest red, and pink put on a show
Spectacular and more amazing than I will ever know
Held my fascination did the sight so far away
What a way to say goodbye to an ordinary day
A grand finale gave the embers, then the show was done
But my brain is still alive with the setting of the sun

Heather Lori Pizzi

Is It End Or New Beginning?

Is the fig tree prophesying
    That the end of time and dying
Is much closer that we think?

The third millennium may usher in
    The quantum that signifies
The long awaited brink.

In setting straight the dairy
    Of events before the fiery
End of time in Earth's ill-fated state

We may suffer through our capture
    Or we may hope now for the rapture
Prophesied in holy Scripture as our fate

But first we must erase the marks
    That separate us through the quarks
Of doubts and fear that cut our lives asunder

And then must pray our souls won't stray
    From plans of change, but stay
On course to meet the thunder

Of our failures, then to use them
    For a brand new working stem
That restores our lives to Eden's wonder.

James C. Crumbaugh

Vision In The Wind

Under the heavens the wind whispers.
Secrets it wants known;
Look and see thru the window
This place we call home.

The mountains echo thru out the land.
Let love in the window;
Like flame of a glowing candle.
Don't be afraid cause in the shadows
appear a vision.
A light shines on everything;
It's time to open the window
And hear the angels sing.

So, what's the use of cryin' makin' trouble last.
While thinking only of the past.
Open the window let love in
And see a vision in the wind.

Alice Sutton

Wishing Upon A Star

Wishing upon a star gives you the power to
keep the faith and hope in your heart.
Wishing upon a star helps keep the happy
Gleam in your bright eyes.
Wishing upon a star gives you the power to
Resist the pain and sadness that comes with life.
Maybe if everyone knew the power of the
stars, there would be peace and love all around, in every town.
All you could do is gain, never lose.
If only people knew the power of the
stars, life would be better wide and far.

Valerie Hoyt

Congratulations

A miracle sent from heaven, a baby girl
   to love, to teach her, to watch her grow,
   to dress her in lacy and frilly clothes.
A prayer was answered, took a long time,
   God knew what he was doing all this time.
He saw two hearts broken, He felt that it was time,
   to mend those hearts,
So he sent this tiny infant baby to mend those
   broken hearts this time.
He tested your faith, saw it was good,
   so he gave you both Ashley,
   to complete your family now.
Congratulations

Beverly Zdrojewski

Angels

Lord my God and shepherd of all.
You know my life as I stand.
From the beginning to the end.
It's all in your plan.
To see my dreams and know my fears,
You know my end day and year.

You feel my love that is near.
My two angel's that keep me here.

One is my heart that pumps the blood,
The other is the blood which feeds the soul.
My soul is yours that always to be true,
You give the hope that sets me free.
From this world and the beast.

I know you love me for I see,
You sent two angels to be with me.

Stewart K. Barrow

You

All of my thoughts are of you
The very sound of your name,
Is sweeter than any substance that man can obtain
Even sweater than the morning dew.

Your voice is like that of an angel
With every word you speak
Even the strongest become strangely weak
While leaving their minds in tangles

Your beauty surpasses all
Not even the perfect rose could compare
Toward the beauty which you bare
All competition will fall.

You dwell among my mind and thoughts
and no matter what I do
all I think and talk about, is you.

Chris Vert

Memories

How many times I've dreamed of, days of
long ago
Of children that I played with in sunshine
and in snow
Of all the funny games we played, and how
fast we could run,
Of all the lovely trees we had to shade us from the sun.

My dreams have gone on farther to the days
I was a teen,
Of going on to high school to meet faculty
and Dean
Of going to the Senior prom with a young
man of my choice,
And listening to the songs he sang with his sweet tenor voice.

Now that I am old and gray, my memory
seems to dwell,
On all those wondrous days of youth, that
I found really swell
And as I sit and day dream of the days that use to be,
I often wonder if there's anyone, who ever thinks of me!

Edna L. Ries

Forgive, Me Mom

Yesterday I lived, today I died
It didn't show on the outside.
But on the inside, I cried.
I came to my senses to give mother thanks
and to beg forgiveness for all my silly pranks.
I hope you will forget, the foolish son
I've been.
It's too late now, I wish I'd never sinned.

Each night before I go to sleep for you
I always pray.
I hope to see you tomorrow and we will
start a new day.
From sun up to sun down you run through
my mind.
For without you mother I'd be totally blind.

Mother there's only one so special, that's you my maker.
When she falls from life Jesus, you be
sure and take her.
One of these days, in another place we will grow.
If my mother is around Lord, you be sure and let me know.

Andrew Wallin

Every day, every hour, every minute . . .

Every day, every hour, every minute, someone in the world is
dieing. An old disease, in which no cure and death by
shooting there's more and more. Harsh words with no real
meanings and depriving children of their childhoods.
Gang-bangers and over-doses.

The government says there is too much sex, drugs, and violence
on tv. Though I beg to differ, I believe there is too much
sex, drugs, and violence in our minds, hearts, and souls.

This world is a strange place with rape, hate and racism. We
have all lost the sense tranquility we once fought to
express, violence has over thrown the peaceful nation we at
one time were proud to be a part of. There's no where to run,
no where to hide and no where to escape the troubles of everyday life.

Afraid to walk down the street with your head held high. So
many old problem with new twists. Our world will never get
better it will simply change because it is our world and our
world is a crazy place.

Melissa Savino

The Cloud

The Cloud shrouds a mystery.
It reflects every bit of my fantasy.
Its shifting moods echo
Deep inside of me.

The Cloud orchestrates nature's symphony.
It brings rain and snow.
It fills me up with a soft glow.
It colors my life with a rainbow.

It watches too — even the hue
Of my distant memory turning blue.
It renders a subtle clue
That part of me I never knew.

Dennister Martinez

Our Changing Love

Our tender moments of our loving care,
so many times we did share.

As I remember the good times we had,
I cannot help to feel a little sad.

It's because of what we both should know,
we won't have each other as we grow old.

But for the love as we might part,
It will always be kept here in my heart.

As a caring person I am to say,
God bless you always each and every day!

Dave Obermier

Loves Broken Heart

Why is this happening again in my life
I thought we were meant to be, to be husband and wife
You're a special part of me, one I don't want to let go
I see you next door and through my window
It hurts my heart to have to let you go
But to prove how I love you, I must do what I must do
If it's to say good-bye and that I love you
I'll do what I have to, whatever's best for you

I'll try to go on without you in my life
My heart hurts as I cry through the night
I wish you were here holding me tight
And with a gentle kiss, you kiss me good night
It's so hard to get up and face a new day
But I seem to do it, in my own little way
I pray that you'll come back, into my life one day
But if not, good-bye I must say

Alicia Vivian Velasquez

Disavow Me

Touch was called in the morning
Touch of mind and soul
I awoke to the sound of no one
I awoke to an empty glow
How could I be but a corpse of undead
My love is broken, alone and unwed
The reaper stays near but far from me
I think it's my time but he doesn't want thee
I can't seem to shake this uncontrolled terror
of myself, my look, my unghostly failure
my perverse moods of alternate enthusiasm
and melancholy swing has got me in a bind
I plead each day for some simple piece of mind
To keep on my feet and keep me untwind

Lou Carter

The Fisherman's Dilemma

This fisherman is out in his brand new boat.
Oh! What a day to be alive.
The boat is packed and already afloat.
For a great catch of fish, he's all a-jive.

The sun is shining on the sea blue carpeting.
The live box is all cleaned and ready for fish.
The poles are all baited and waiting
To grant this fisherman's fondest wish.

All the instruments are programmed and set,
But there's still a ways to go.
He's not at the fishing hole yet,
But his eyes are alert and all aglow.

Then all of a sudden, there's a spluttering hiss.
The great boat shuddered its last.
You'll never guess what went amiss.
You got it! We're out of gas!

Thankfully, our fishing pals are among our ranks.
They towed us to shore, and saved the day.
To town we went to refill our tanks,
Then back to fish in our favorite bay.

Lorraine Genett

Through Glass Eyes

Every night before the dream shade fell,
Bethany placed me on her ledge
Whispering to me I was her favorite.

Fearful of looming shadows in sleep,
Bethany left a ladder near the bed's edge
Down which my doll brothers could climb to protect her.

Bedposts snagged my lose bindings,
Tea parties bruised Carlee's Spanish dress,
And dog plucked out Tongo's beady eyes.

We were simple toys,
Tattered and torn through hours of restless play:
Constant happiness, our purpose, our duty.

We couldn't respond
With our mended bodies: no soul, no mind
No defense from her world.

We couldn't have warned her,
Nor match the swiftness of snatching hands:
Her stolen innocence shown brightly through glass eyes.

Matthew Louzau

Untitled

So moves the lack of color in her sky,
A spectrum gray, devoid of crystal blue,
An atmospheric hue to span the miles
And reconcile obsessive points of view—
Thoughts so inane in sickly trains ingrained,
That grooves do deepen all the livelong day.
No matter how I rail against dire strain,
Proclaim monopoly over the fray,
My failure steams ahead at total speed
To lacerate this convoluted reign.
Within black notions fueling abject needs,
Lick sooty flames engorged with frozen rain:
Her ice, her storm, destroying from behind,
My life, my calm, negated in her lines.

Fawn Howard

425

Where Are We Going?

We hurry to get there and quickly we leave
It seems there is no time to breathe.
We can't take time to just sit still
to pray and reflect upon God's will.
But, where are we going?

We hasten along as years pass by
no time to laugh; no time to cry.
There's things to do that just can't wait
Because tomorrow would be too late
But, where are we going?

Why can't we slow down to love and care
And visit with mankind everywhere.
Loving our family and others too
Instead of inventing things to do.
Because, then we might know where we are going!

C. Denise Phillips

Good Deeds

This world has faces we will never see;
Strangers pass by that I will never know
Memories would I like to leave from me...
Will they remember me, watching them go?

And in the shadow of their departure
I'll become fully aware of their needs;
Helping hands I'll give to somehow capture
Their thoughts and memories of my good deeds.

Often I reach with what I've to offer,
To one who refuses acts of kindness,
Or to the ones that their hearts so suffer
Seeing with just eyes, their hearts have blindness,

Money isn't everything, nor knowledge gains:
When I die, I'll be known for helping their pains.

Angie Leigh McElreath

Miss Margaret's Hands

The hands that held my newborn babe
were hands brown skinned and wrinkled,
each fold telling a story.

The hands that held my newborn babe
were hands gnarled from years
of working for others.

The hands that held my newborn babe
were colored with the wisdom
attained only through living life.

The hands that held my newborn babe
were full of love . . . warm, gentle and accepting.

My babe will never know the woman,
but her hands have left an imprint on her soul.

P. J. Messick

Untitled

Listen beyond the listening.
Listen beyond the leaves,
Beyond the humming bird's wing's.
Listen to the earth sigh at your awakening.
Listen to life's song, hear beyond the crunching pebbles.
Listen through the wonder of the waterfall.
Listen, listen, the earth is crying.

John A. Schwab

Freaky Little Noises

Freaky little noises in the middle of the night,
Squeaky little voices when you're home all alone,
Freaky little noises can chill your toes with fright
In the middle of the night
With their tapping and their rustling
And occasional moan.

Freaky little noises when you're lying in your bed,
Sneaky little noises when no else is home,
Freaky little noises can fill your soul with dread
Make you cover up your head,
With their slamming and their slurping
And occasional groan.

Freaky little noises when you try to go to sleep,
Creaky little noises, like an Edgar Allen poem,
Freaky little noises, a burp and then a beep,
You're afraid to fall asleep.
Till your parents or your roommate
Finally wander home.

Marion Michaels

Like The Wind

When I breathe,
I feel clear and free.
It's all you,
You make me new.
Your touch makes me want to sigh,
Like fresh snow, just fallen from the sky.
You are the one that gives me air.
You are the one that is always there.
If you whisper softly in my ear
I will cling to everything that I hear.
You put oxygen in my chest.

I will, for this, give you my best.
You are like the gust that blows my hair free.
You Are life to me.
The breeze that I feel from you, is all too clear and true.

Brandy Lynne Russell

This Travel Life

Took the time made a holiday
I'll settle back and wait for a new day
However I try can't see beyond this way I'm livin'
I've shared the back seat with the world

I told the time I take her reaction
All the way - like everyday seems alright
Along the way I fed the sky this life I've found

I've read the line I take my own way
Gather 'round for one time only
For one time only...

Tommy Mullins

Untitled

Now I lay me down to sleep
I pray to God her sole to keep.
To keep her safe and away from the bad
to be her father, take the place of her dad.
I ask him to hold her, as I would,
and or take my life so I could.
Give her cover from the rain, and
ease her every pain
take away her sorrows, and
lend me strength for tomorrow.
When she shivers at night
pull up her covers
and when she cries lend
the arms of her mother

Bobby Grabowski

426

Free Indeed

The prisoner sits, plenty of time.
Days flow past, they're all the same.
Why, you ask, did I do this crime?
Now you're a number, no more a name.

The same old talk, who's new today?
Some are fixtures, others disappear,
Some pointed out, they're here to stay,
Rules always changing, nothing is clear.

Then one day, you hear about Jesus.
He was here too, long time ago.
You thought you were alone, but he see's us.
There is something he wants you to know.

He stands at the door, just ask him in.
In pain and suffering he did bleed.
Confess to him and you can begin.
Then you'll be free, free indeed.

William Grimes

The Prince Of October

Light shadows, dark slices of moon light.
Leaves, falling upward from the ground.
Dirt, falling down like heavy raindrops.
Polished wood and cushioned linings.
Lips, sewn together with silver thread and
golden needles.
Moaning, crying winds.
Silent, flustered figures.
Dark figures.
Colorless figures.
Dry and watery paleness.
The people of October march to the midnight
funeral of a prince.

Ryan C. Ducharme

Awaken Little Ones

Awaken little ones,
for you have been sleeping too long.
You have forgotten who you are,
and thus have forgotten Me.
Awaken little ones,
it is time for you to remember;
Who you are,
Where you came from, and
Where you are going.
Awaken little ones,
open your eyes,
embrace My love,
feel My presence,
for a new day is dawning
and I will guide your spirits
to another tomorrow.
Awaken to your dreams and the reality of;
Who you are,
Where you came from, and
Where you are going.

Jennifer Lynn Kautz

Niña

The breeze blows across the grainfields.
The waves break the shorelines,
And the birds tweet happily.
But no one notices the dark, lonely death
Of a little girl named Nina.
The darkness was on her side always,
For she was friendless,
Which is a thing no person is.
She was missed only by herself and loneliness.

Keegan Lerch

Your Child

May your child be born with a heart full of love,
His skin as pure and soft as a dove.

With eyes only to see the good,
In the rich and the poor as everyone should.

From his mouth only the truth be told,
His touch will turn the worthless to gold.

His ears to hear a Robin sing,
A mind to remember everything.

Strong legs to carry him straight and tall,
His laughter will bring sunshine to all.

Little arms to hug when the day is through,
A soft voice to say mommy I love you.

Penney Russell

The City

As she rode there in the back,
her face pressed to the glass.
Eyes in awe of what she saw,
buildings blocked out the sun, so tall.
A strange place, with no green at all.
With people so many, no place to play,
could the children really want to stay?
Everyone in such a rush it seemed,
in search of their elusive dream.

As she rode there in the back,
her face pressed to the glass.
At every turn it seemed the same,
no sun, no green, no place to play,
she knowing she would not want to stay.
Let's hurry to get away, her thought,
before within this maze she too was caught.
Looking for what her future would bring,
In search of her own elusive dream.

Ruth Ottenschot

Lasting Friendship

My friend came often during the cold, long winter nights.
How good to see him, to talk by the fire's glowing, warm light!
The days and nights of that cold winter deepened,
And with each visit, our friendship grew and strengthened.

We spoke of the past, of our very long ago,
How the ties that bound us could never let us go.
Words rising and falling, like the crackling bright hearth fire,
Far into the nights we talked and laughed, not growing tired.

He held out his hand and heart to help me pass through
A time so sad in my life, that winter that turned dark blue.
Who dare price friendship that is strong, true, and deep?
In his arms I was held, comforted, allowed to sob and weep.

As winter will it give way to the green of another spring,
The world turned fresh, my life began, birds were singing.
Ah, Life! So good with my close friend and mate.
But, oh, who knows what is in the great hand of Fate?

Now you are gone! My heart aches on this windy spring day,
I pen words that are hard, hard, to say...
"Goodbye dearest friend, buddy of mine, mate so kind,
I'll look for you when I reach the Tomorrow Side!"

Judith W. Umberger

427

Pain

I came to the hospital, they said go to room, 10,
so I went to see and I saw. I saw machines hooked
up and tubes in my best friend, I couldn't take it,
I stepped in the hall. Every time I try and be
strong I tumble to my knees. If I can't take it
I'll have to go. I hope she forgives me, please!
God, give me the strength to always be strong and
always be there by her side, I know I said I'd
be there forever, I know, I know, I lied. So I'll
try and be there, for her I will, I really will try.
But when I see her laying so limp it just makes me
want to die. People tell me just be strong and her
strength will gain. But now I know for the very
first time I've experienced live, true Pain.

Stephanie Saw

And Nothing Less

Old pleasant memories haunt me with happiness,
And nothing less.
I hold my heart waiting for you,
Do you know what to do?
Joy opens every day,
But still here I lay.
I am waiting for you to show,
Is my voice too low?
When will you come to me?
Can you not see?
I want to hold memories with your arms.
Do I not bring you through charms?
Deep emotions put you to the test,
And nothing less.

Brooke Winder

What Forever Meant

I can't blame you for the way you feel,
Even I never dreamed the feelings would fade.
I guess the feeling just wasn't strong enough.
Hate never entered my mind that night,
When you called to say we were through.
I don't think either of us truly knew
What we said as we mentioned forever.
We both promised it to each other,
Never knowing we couldn't make it last.
Forever is supposed to mean eternity,
A never ending cycle we couldn't comprehend.
We promised each other forever;
Never knowing what forever meant.

Norman Clark

Our Times

As I look towards the future and
   reflect on the past:
All I see is the times we had

From our first fight to our last insight
   on life:
All I see is the times we had

From my first cry to your last smile:
All I see is the times we had

As we journey through our future;
I hope that all the times we had
Will be all the times we will have.

Kesha R. Roberson

My Nanny

My Nanny was a strong tree protecting her children
and grandchildren from unpleasant things. Strong she
was, yet not strong enough to fight the illness that
ravaged her careworn body and reduced that strong
tree-liked body into a withered mass that could barely
Stand without the help of others.

As her body withered away, her strong will to live
withered also. Crying to God to take her home and end
her misery, her excruciating pain and anguish over
not being able to do for herself, her willpower gone,
she just lies in bed awaiting her Father to take her home.

My Nanny, pillar of strength in my childhood, and now
a withered mass who depends on others as they once
depended on her.

My Nanny.

Tara George

My Children

My first child was a darling baby girl
and my first thoughts were
I want to give her the world.

My second child was the most cutest little boy
All I wanted was
To fill his life with joy.

My third child was a wonderful baby girl
when I held her in my arms
I knew she was more precious than a pearl.

My fourth child was charming little boy
when I looked him over
I knew that this was one priceless toy.

I didn't have many toys to play with,
never had real pearls to wear,
and joy in this world is hard to win,

But my life has been filled with
Love, Happiness, and Fulfillment
Because of my most cherished children.

Shelia Anthony

Justice

Perfect justice would be a sonorous canon.
As if from a dream of Amos,
A liturgy in plainsong.

Envision the prophet's plumb line
Taut and true into the firmament.
Chord of psalm and response, a funiculous;

Holy Truth clear in mortal rule's intent.
Against Pol Parrot's squawking chant,
Counterpoise could not relent.

For Truth's not in Pol's shrill descant
Of fable promise and incantation,
His funicular cant and recant;

Perfect Justice comes through supplication:
"Kyrie eleison; Christie eleison".

Robert N. Eastman

The Swans Ballerina

Perched on the lakeside,
Waiting for the ballet to begin.
Swans as performers.
They move slowly into the lake as if it were a stage,
Gliding around as to a grand orchestra.
Never out of step.
Slowly they glide and then turn;
Stopping as if to bow.
Once again they circle.
No ballerina could have more poise or beauty.
The play ends.
We the spectators,
Sitting in the choice seat, upon the limb of a big oak tree.
Tomorrow the show will be repeated.
Will you have the choice seat?
Upon the limb of the oak or beneath the marble grave.

Jeanette Kirk

When Two Equals One

One never knows, where or when
You might stumble across, a precious gem.

The most beautiful girl, I'd ever seen
I thought to myself, could this be a dream?

We were destined right there, to be together
Through life's happy times, and stormy weather.

I can well remember, our wedding day
And the vows we made, were so easy to say.

It was made in heaven, it had to be
We were meant for each other, just you and me.

When tragedy struck, and we were in shock
We held each other close, in a vise like lock.

We loved and cherished, through all the years
Through happiness and laughter, and many tears.

The years ticked off, the minutes and hours
Just like the wilting, of a beautiful flower.

And now we can see, the end is near
But with our love, there is nothing to fear.

For God will save a place, you see
For you and I dear, for eternity.

Charles Guarniere

The Procession Marched On

Although she was in a sea of deep black,
She walked alone that day.
Her head hung low and her eyes were full.
Her pinched cheeks were damp with tears.
As the tears ran down her face,
Memories of him ran rapid through her mind.
Her heart was heavy in moaning,
And the procession marched on.

The rain beat against the pavement.
The wheels of the carriage turned,
As the horses pulled the lost love.
The horseshoe pounded on the wet cement,
And echoed through her ears,
She heard the crying and moaning of the ones around her.
Their talk was of her strength,
And the procession marched on.

Amanda Leigh Lackey

Evolved Mind Creation I Am Belief
(As I American Free)

I am, I believe, I sing
Of a different reality
Not this world of illusions, shadows, dreams
But one where truth illuminates, freedom's destiny
Not one where humanity is enchained, to their limits tyranny
One where the mind is as free as one can believe
Because the essence of humanity
Is in what we believe and we conceive
And the paradoxical truth, dualistic reality
Is that in all its eternal possible improbability
If we conceive and we believe, then it can come to be
Our will, will have created, that which we've conceived
We will exist as creators like The Creator, as in its image we've been conceived
Because throughout One Mind Creation is the power of belief.

I AmErican Free

Reflections Of The Past, Visions Of Tomorrow

Enveloped by the darkness, her captured soul cries out.
Illusions fall around her, shadows of a doubt.
Encapsuled by the fear, searching, but no way out.
Visions of dreams smother her spirit.
Cries from the pit, Shh, can you hear it?
Whispers of demons penetrate the darkness.
Her spirit is filled with all of their sadness.
When will it end, how long will it last?
Reflections of the past.
The sound of light trickles through her soul.
It pierces her spirit and won't let go.
Caressing the darkness and cleansing her fear,
Whispers of angels are drawing near.
Releasing her sorrows, visions of tomorrow.

Tangue Girard

Sometimes

Sometimes when Alone His Heart begins to rome
Alone along the hallway of lost souls.
Wondering what and how he does wrong,
His appearance is Glim and Love is Endless
Yet no one sees his true being he is.
one of a kind, yet all the same as the next,
with enough love for the world but,
not enough heart for himself, confidence,
courage, words he does not know, for what
reason no one knows. For all he needs is
a little love in return before all his glory falls.
All he wants is someone!
He tries without victory and fails and fails again
He cries alone to God at night but that's the way it's been.
He wishes oh so much for love, someone to kiss, and hold and hug.
"Why" but that is the word he chooses to say.
He can't explain it, that's just the way.
Maybe in the future until there's a change,
For now it's just simple it just stays the same.

Philip J. Winthrop Jr.

Being Hidden

Here I am in this dark and lonely world.
That's what you would say when you're being hidden.
I try to escape but there's no way out.
That's what you would do when you're being hidden.
I try to look for the sun but there's no sign of light.
That's what you see when you're being hidden.
I try to scream but there's nothing coming out.
You would do the same thing if you were being hidden.
Where am I?

Carlos Planas

Untitled

The Chaos begins as the darkness shows
Its ugly face, into our lives this day.
The Monster lurks behind the shadows of
Our souls. His accomplices of Lust and
Idle Curiosity plaque our fears,
While all is silent and calm throughout
The distant vastness of dreams and wonders.
The Evil fears not of light, but of Hope.
If Hope is all we have, we need no more.
Not bravery nor strength, but the thought that
There is a tomorrow. If we survive
The night, with all we hold dear to our hearts,
The Monster won't be able to steal us
From everything familiar to our eyes.
We must know that the world will overcome
The terrors held by the eyes of Evil.
If we believe in Hope, the winds will take
The death and despair to a place where it
Can disappear without causing more harm.
The Monster must fade if we are to shine.

Millissa Dawn Thomas

Charade

I can not share this which is vivid in my mind, buried
   in my heart, silent on my lips.
I thrill, knowing that I alone possess so great a secret.
I sicken, fearing others will discover.
I weep, longing to tell; to whisper — then to shout until
   the air is swollen with the sound.

Oh, God — I must have strength to lift my head when he is near.

To smile and nod so all who see will never know.
I must clothe my naked yearning in folds of foolery;
Veil my hungry eyes with nets of nothingness.

These things I do — to satisfy the whims of all whom passion
   passes by.
But now, I laugh and weep in one;
For while they, watch unknowingly...
I love.

Barbara Oglesby

Like A Leaf In The Rain

Alone among many, grounded in flight
   I feel it building again.
The slightest of drops, no more feather - light
   Stuck down like a leaf in the rain.

The skies have all greyed, from summer to fall
   The winds have all shifted the vane.
No more echo or distance, no weight in my call
   Washed away like a leaf in the rain.

But Oh, how I used to shudder and fly!
Distant horizons adrift in the sky;
The merest attachment, strong and bold
Let me reach for the heavens, while safe in the fold.

But now I have fallen an end to my season
   No more to know laughter or pain.
With a smile and a kiss, I've no need for the reason
   And I fade like a leaf in the rain.

D. Scott Wilson

A Blessing

A walk through sand, a peaceful sound of the sea;
I search for the hand, that has been security to me.
The warmth of the day strikes a pleasant touch,
like the words that say that one cares so much.
The color of the rose is beautiful to the eye,
as eagerly shown by a loving, gentle smile.
Your beauty is held, both outward and in,
expressed by your love to all your children.
How can I thank you? Can words be all?
For all the wonders you do when I stand or fall?
You have the gentle hand, the beauty of the flower...
The words that stand in my heart every hour.
A child is granted a mother, the Lord's gift from above.
I would never choose another. I am blessed with great love.

Wendy Maniaci

Will We Forget The Elephant

It is said that an Elephant never forgets
But will we forget the Elephant

Gliding along like great wrinkled clouds
They're remarkably intelligent

It is said that an Elephant cries salt tears
But will we ever cry for the Elephant

Piano keys, statues, and brooches
How elegant
All made from Ivory
The tusks of an Elephant

Gold is a metal
From the Earth it is tilled
"White Gold" is vital
For which Elephants are killed

Love, fear, rage, pride, happiness, and despair

All emotions we share with the Elephant
How can we not care

It is said that an Elephant never forgets
Will we forget the Elephant

C. J. Barnard

Spirits Of Christmas Past

Night falls as I peer out my window to the yard out in back,
The birds, stopped their feeding of seed now scurry to shelter,
away to their rack. The trees stand erect are awaiting the dark,
The snow on the ground lies silent and stark.

It's so quiet and still on this cold Christmas Eve,
As I watch the night enter, and the day take its leave,
It's a time when a man seems to stand all alone
With his thoughts, and his feelings and soul, all too prone

Of others somewhere, who were once of this place,
Who have vanished from view, but my mind sees their face.
I think of them now, as I bow to their being,
And smile of the memory of each, that I'm seeing.

I reach out my spirit to embrace one and all,
And I whisper to each, yes, to each, I recall,
"Go on now sweet spirit, unto you I must say,
Have folly and singing, and love on this day.

For oh, that you all may have passed from our view,
Please know that this evening I'm thinking of you".

Paul L. Fornicola

Mirror Image

Look deep in my eyes, I'll tell you what you'll see,
a reflected image in the pupil, a mirror image of me,

Moving to the left, a little to the right
looking at my reflection that can't be quite right

So much sorrow mixed with joy,
feeling such hurt hopefully love will destroy

Do you feel pain the way I do?
I really hope so because there's enough for two,
It's not fair you look as I do,
trapped in this mirror which is a prison for you

If I just take a deep breath and blow it at you,
maybe you'll come to life and make me into two,
for I have had enough to bear,
looking and talking to others who seem never to have a care,
wishing and hoping to trade places
with this mirror image but leave no traces

But I know this is never to be,
so I'm just stuck here with this mirror image,
that's just me

Deanna Carter

Love

Love should be shared by two
Just another way to make it true;
It shouldn't be in vain,
'Cus when it's all over there will be pain.
Brokenhearted is the after-shock of true love
It should only be with the man you love
Love isn't true if it's only said and not felt
Relationships are built by trust
Love is only real when it is from deep within the mind,
body, and soul.
If love is true, nothing can split up the two.
The Pair,
The Duet,
The True Lovers,
The Couple.

Autumn Cleveland

More Than Ever Before

I see your image
and I'm filled with fear
I remember your smile and it brings a tear

You were a big part of me
and meant so much
and often seeking to remember your touch

I loved you then
and love you now
I wanted to tell you but didn't know how

Now you're gone
and I'm still here
missing you more and wanting you near

Still in my thoughts
Still in my dreams
holding them closely for all they mean

Missing you now
and wanting you more
loving the memories
More Than Ever Before

Jean C. Kunisch

A Dreamer

Please look past the mask I wear,
Look straight into my eyes.
Somewhere beneath all of this cover,
A different person lies.

Outside I am photographer,
There are many things I see.
Inside I am a writer,
Not perfect, but as good as I can be.

Outside I am adult,
Sure of my life's direction and way.
Inside I am still a young child,
Not sure of even the end of the day.

Outside I am a learner,
Attempting to conquer life's many themes.
Inside I am a thinker,
A wonderer of many dreams.

Both outside and in I am unique,
I am different, special, defined.
No one else is quite the same,
For my life is only mine.

Elizabeth Carr

The Valley Of Unnamed Fears

There is no sound in the valley
in the valley of unnamed fears,
A comedian doing his act in the void
no laughter rings back, only tears.

A cry for help in the valley
is answered with silence appalling,
The boy who cried "wolf" in his desperate hour
not even an echo for calling.

The nights are cold in the valley
day after chilly day without the sun,
A dying host whose guests have fled
no recall of joyous memories, none.

A hand lifted me up on the mountain
far above the valley below,
Eyes blinded by the dazzling sun,
a trembling ache when strong winds blow.

I've so long yearned for those echoes of life
there remains only one last quest,
To be free from the valley forever
and set a struggling soul to rest.

Arlene M. Bell

Band Of Gold

Dark expressive eyes hide behind
    his impish school boy smile.
His smile conceals the hurt
    that engulfs his lonely heart.
The eyes tell the story of hurt
    and loneliness in his life.
When he talks of his search for love
    his pain exudes into the room.
Though he still wears the band of gold
    his broken heart cries in remorse.
He clings to the hope that he and
    the one he loves will come together again.
He still loves her, in his words I can
    hear his hesitation and wonder.
Would she, is she going to hurt me
    and break my heart again.
He mumbles to himself, can I go through
    this again or should I just walk away?

Lois Kimbrell

431

White Coats

Do not feed the animal
This sign hangs around my neck
Viewed by me only through glass
It cracks upon reflection
One moment, one word
Eyes still see, only now a new vision
A voice still speaks, only now words of cynics escape
One moment, one word
They gave it a name
Faceless white coats of generations past
I give it a new name
Every pain
My wardrobe now is wires and tubes
Don't you find me attractive?
Wisps of hair tossed from my head
My body spits out the invisible beast
It's growing
Reigns over my body
Do not feed the animal
Unless it is poison designed to cure.

Nicole Denmark

As Time Goes By

As time goes by.
You can see it in a cloudy sky.
As each cloud passes with the gentle breeze.
You lay back and watch with ease.
The warm of the sun upon your face.
Your thoughts saying what a wonderful place.
Looking around and you see that there's
no where you'd rather be. Just watch the sky.
As time goes by.

Ruthann Giron

Breaking The Tape

Clop! Clop! Clop!
The sound of a runner on the hard blacktop.
Wind in your face,
Hoping you win the race.
The clock is ticking,
Sweat is dripping.
Runner panting,
People chanting.
Sprinting down the stretch,
Like Ken Griffey trying to make a catch.
Feeling like a heavy sack,
Ahead of the big pack.
Running as smoothly as a silk cape.
Breaking the tape.

Nicholas Bunnell

Wish Upon A Star

Bonding flames does make one complete.
The swaying and caressing of sensitive pretty feet.
Secrets swell in my bosom are true.
I'll never tell, how about you?
Confidants we are, inspire others to know.
A secret admire I am, makes me good to go.
With all that I've said, a sensual imagination
Could never be better fed.
Infatuations blind-love being the mystery true.
When fulfilled receives its due.
Guess who? I've been watching you!

Ronald Johnson

I Can't Read The Cards

He was dealt first a generation ago.
I don't know what he's holding.

When they are read, the understanding may not be visible.
Will there ever be a meeting of the minds?

Why can't he read my hand?
He has held this hand before.

As he teaches me to see the future,
Maybe I can help him remember the past.

Once I held his cards, sometimes I played them right,
sometimes I bluffed, sometimes I fell hard.

Why can't he learn from my mistakes?
If he would only listen and hear.
I'm only trying to help him.

Wow! He is a man. He wants to find his own way.

Is this me talking or is it my father?
I wonder, am I talking to my son or to myself?

Eventually, when the time is right - emotions, understanding,
and feelings will come together and a winning hand for all
generations of players will be on the table.

George Tilbe

What Happened, I Can Not Accept

My Angel, my Friend, my beloved Mom,
What crime have two of us done?
Who took you from me, tell me, tell
Who turned my life into a hell?

I can not believe that the answer
Comes just from one word, that is cancer.
How could possibly those six letters
Take from me you, who mostly matters?

My soul, my body, my brain
Were struggling for you, in vain.
No smiles, no laughs as before.
Hopeless darkness inside, nothing more.

Magic stars, sinless sky, sinful land,
What happened, I can not accept.
Why the devil has won, evil force,
Is he stronger than the sun, the life's source?

Irina Lioubenko

The Man

Mysterious mystery unfolding in the night,
A spark to flame lights his pipe.
The murderer is loose and evil runs round.
Evidence collects and he lowers himself to the ground.
A shiny bloody knife has done the deed;
He works unceasingly and seldom rests or feeds.
The suspect is nervous, terror in the night;
The sleuth is patient, confident by gas-light.
A misty shroud covers the tower-clock,
But the boom of the hour does not stop.
Tension mounts and an uproar pounds the heart,
The net whispers shut on the unfortunate lout.
The desperate criminal shrieks in guilty retrospect;
The gaunt man smirks; the superior intellect.
On the mantle hangs a strange slipper where tobacco sleeps,
As the doctor, in his notebook, the fantastic tale he keeps.
Victory is sudden, unmerciful and sweet,
Triumph belongs to the man of Baker Street.

Georgina M. Garcia

The Bum In The Corner

The bum in the corner sitting down drinking his liquor,
He hears screaming and crying
He stands up and looks around.
He hears screaming and crying
He is so frighted that he runs and runs
  till there's no place to go.
He hears screaming and crying
He hears his name more than five times.
He hears screaming and crying
But he replies with cursing and bad language.
He hears screaming and crying
.The man is obviously insane
Since he hears screaming and crying.
He will hear screaming and crying till the
  darkest day of his life!

Giselle Rivera

Miss You

I miss you,
Like children miss the summer,
Desiring to revel in the warm light,
Longing to play without the worries of life,
Waiting to be joyful at the freedom,
Yet, all the while,
Trapped in school,
Missing the summer,
As I miss you.

Andrew Donofrio

Peace Of Mind

What is this thing called depression?
This mental anguish and oppression!
It eats at your mind like a cancer soar.
Leaving your broken heart in tiny pieces on the floor.
It overcomes you in the emptiness of your days
and creeps up in the stillness of the night.
Your mind screams at you for release and your heart beats
against your ribs like a bird in a cage, seeking flight.
You can't explain it or restrain it.
Your tears fall like a spring rain,
Offering little comfort for your pain.
Your loved ones try in vain to give you some release.
But you know there is only one who can give you peace.
So on bended knees and bowed head,
Let Jesus take this burden of lead.
For even the most educated will find,
Only our Lord can offer true "peace of mind."

Regina L. Wethington

Wintery Song

The air's turning cool, the wind's growing strong;
  The greenery around us can't last for long.
The world's settling down for a winter's rest,
  Putting our strength and endurance to the test.
Families together in from the cold,
  Hands are held and secrets are told.
Dreaming of summer through the long wintery night,
  Birds of a feather held down from their flight.
Yule tide season and New Year's cheer,
  So quickly it seems to be once again here!
So quickly it's gone, only memories remain....
  Yet no two winter's exactly the same.
The land seems to die, barren and dark.
  Soon spring will renew each living spark.
The cycle continues as life goes on,
  Keeping the rhythm of a wintery song.

Catherine Copeland

Wonder Of Nature

You can feel it, and see it, the
trees and plants come alive in the spring,
  blossom for the summer,
change color in the fall, and they rest
  in the winter.
The birds coming for spring, the butterflies,
  chipmunks, squirrels and rabbits
and the rest, busy collecting food all summer,
  so they can rest in winter.
The birds fly south, a few stay behind to
  cheer us up on a lonely winter day.
Listen, watch and experience the mystery,
  and wonder of nature.

Freida Dvinge

La Cancion de la Paloma (The Song of the Dove)

So present, piercing, yet wanted
Misunderstood, fallen unwanted?
Why pursue that which enlightens, exhilarates, uplifts?
When such pursuit deceives, encroaches, met with sand rifts?
The fancy, the flight, the demands of our souls for such joy
Only then are we betrayed, give us this day our daily annoy?
It hath no meaning, no armor for strength, indeed overrated?
Those who indulge in this ominous lie, oh! The scars serrated
They who come to taste of its inviting poison, depth unknown
Receive its soothing perceptions, destroying its soft tone
Ah! The trust that we have longing for here now arises
Trust, wanting, the longing for someone no surprises
Finally the peace, the bliss, the joy, the song of the dove
This thing, this feeling, makes us sad, but oh! The joy of love!

Raoul G. Sanchez Sr.

My Friends

Branches of the same tree,
growing from a trunk rooted in the soil of adolescence.
Shared dreams and tears;
hopes and fears.
From the trunk we grow outward,
apart and together,
stretching,
bending,
upward.
Direction determined by choices we've made.
We become individual branches,
yet, we are similar.
Because we are branches of the same tree.

Timothee Jean Kearns

A Camping Tip

They warn you in capital letters
in the User's Manual:
'Never Touch Or Rub The Inside Skin Of A Moist Tent.'

If you do,
you'll bruise the invisible skin,
and tear drops
of rain and dew
will weep through.

But I could have told you that without a manual.
It's something I learned
the few times my own inner skin wept,
when love,
seeking shelter,
set-up camp

And carelessly touched the inside of my heart.

Marshall F. Thompson

Amy

I lay under a black shroud awaiting the sun to
cut through the thickest of early morning
fogs. Throughout the denseness, I sense
more than actually feel, a warm breeze babbling
insistently to my ears. The wind carries a jumble
of sound that leads me out of the fog and into
the blinding rays of a southern sunrise. As I begin
to bask in the warm glow, my mind begins to
assemble the winds constant chatter into a single,
unfamiliar word that reverberates back and forth in my
head. With a slow exhalation of breath, the word makes
its way to my vocal cords and passes into the bright
morning, naming the great light above that has broken
the fog that covered my, until recently, tortured soul.
The only sound escaping me is "Amy"

Joesf Heffner

Packages

Consider us all as packages of every kind and shape.
It's a wonder we make it through - a lifetime to relate.
Some packages rattle and shake, have little within.
Others, solid and firm, feel heavy and grim.
Some, so securely wrapped in self-satisfaction,
On the inside there is no attraction.
Some take special handling, "Handle with care"
Inside an explosive that may go off anywhere.
Those too heavy to lift, lost in self-pity,
Often lie in a corner getting dusty and gritty.
Occasionally packages fall apart, though the number is few
Compared to the millions that daily get through.
Especially the packages, fragile but firm,
Holding treasures of happiness for which we all yearn.
Check that your wrapping and ties are sound
So you will not end up among the lost, not found.
Try to package your life the best way you can,
Wrapped in kindness, love, and "Goodwill to Man".

Ida M. Heller

This Is To My — Forever

This is to my love,
   the angel God sent from above
     the lady that watches over me forever

This is to my fantasy,
   the dream I cannot wait to see
     the lady that keeps me pure forever

This is to my hope,
   the faith that helps me cope
     the lady who believes in me forever

This is to my tears,
   the woman that waits through the years
     the lady I will cry with forever

This is to my spouse,
   the keeper of my house
     the lady who shall keep it forever

This is to my wife,
   the love of my life
     the lady I will love forever

Randall Haws

My Blanket

I have a blanky that sits on my bed
Many believe that this pastime should be dead
I've been told to grow up and throw
it away, but me and my blanky
used to play everyday

I used to sit and rub my face,
with the part that's soft and silky
It was there, right with me, as I
ate my cookies and milky.

It's like an old friend if lost you
would cry, that's why I stuck by it
by and by

When I go to college, blanky will
definitely come too, it's kinda
of a good luck charm
that gets me through and through and through.

So when I go to bed at night
and hold my blankly tight
I know that it will be
with me awaiting mornings light!

Meghan Sullivan

Forever Grateful

Nine months you carried and waited for me.
'Twas before Christmas, I was born to thee.
But am I as patient as you are to me?
I may or may not, maybe.
But this I assure thee,
I'm forever grateful for having me.

I grew up and thought now I'm free
I am my own self and what I wanted to be.
Yet you stayed and was a guide to me.
But did I give back what you gave me?
I may or may not, maybe.
But this I assure thee,
I'm forever grateful for standing by me.

Now I'm far away, to a land across the sea.
I have my own family, we fit like a tee.
Still I feel your warmth around me.
But did I make you feel what you made me?
I may or may not, maybe.
But this I assure thee,
I'm forever grateful for loving me.

Peter Angelo C. Lim

My Beautiful Memory

The roses climbing and clinging to the wall
Roses stand so beautiful and tall

Red ones pink, blue, yellow so bright
Making such a beautiful lonely sight

Fragrant spreading through the air
Roses red as the ribbons in your hair

Roses pink as your lips so sweet so fair
Roses blue as your eyes that shine so bright.
Roses yellow as the gold in your hair

Roses climbing, clinging to the wall
So beautiful and tall

Lorena Runnelis

Dreams

Dreams are of truth and of lies,
never told to those it could hurt,
but always expressed in every ones cries.
Dreams are what people live by,
always hiding the truth,
and always telling the lies.
Dreams tell us the future,
telling us the truth,
yet telling us a lie.
They tell us who are friends,
but yet are enemies,
and of whom we shall love,
yet are only friends.
Dreams are sent from our hearts,
and from our fears,
and always from our darkest thoughts.

Jaime M. Foor

When The Pen Hits The Paper

When the pen hits the paper I have nothing to hide
When the pen hits the paper I tell what I feel inside
When the pen hits the paper you will truly understand
The thoughts and the feelings of this caring young man

When the pen hits the paper I am not among my peers
When the pen hits the paper I release all of my fears
When the pen hits the paper you will feel my pain
The love that I am yearning is driving me insane

When the pen hits the paper is when I open up my heart
'Cause the paper understands what's tearing me apart
The pen writes the words that I want to say
And the paper always listens, each and every single day

When the events of life are too much and the clouds
  begin to come.
My pen hits the paper till my heart can overcome.

Kristoffer James Elliot Tillery

Wind

I reminisce you, but only on the days my heart
throbs and I respire, do I spot the space.

You are who I think of, when I reminisce love.

It's quaint, the other's I allowed into my heart,
I mislay their redolence, the twinkle we're apart.

It appears as though, before time arose, that's when I
adjoined you, and your redolence is never ending.

It endures to exude throughout the fixes of my mind.
Through the span of day, through the duration of time.

Your occurrence is forever on my mind.

The flicker of your eyes, created my hair to gasp in the wind,
The curvature of your smile, compelled my day to begin.

The torridness of your feel, has branded my soul.
With fervid amorousness, never to be glacial.

I reminisce the hairs on your chest.
As you post yourself upon my breasts to rest.

My soul wept for me, the day the wind blew.
My soul acknowledged, it was bellowing to capture you.

Time screamed for further, the wind stilled its plea.
You became entangled, and loss, never again to embrace me.

Now my days arise reminiscing you, somewhere entangled
in time, never to be freed, somewhere forever.
      "Captured by a breeze"

Ann Marie Simmons

Tower

Love is a tower
It takes a good foundation to build it
But without a good foundation
It may never get off the ground
Love is a tower
It takes time to build it
But can be destroyed
In a matter of seconds
Love is a tower
It takes strong steel for it to last
But even the strongest steel
Will not make it through a great blast
Love is a tower
It takes people who trust each other to build it
But may be weak if someone tries to take a shortcut
Or forgets some bolts and nuts
Love takes people like you and me
For love to last

John J. Triggs

The Power Of Love

Who'd have thought love could revive
A spirit that was not alive.
God hand picked an angel with power to free
And sent that powerful love to me.
The faith and hope I thought was dead,
Rose like a ghost and lives instead.
So I can believe in me again,
Thanks to my special, miracle friend.
Who'd ever think that love could save,
A wounded heart that never forgave,
Life for the losing hand it dealt
Or love for pain that it had felt.
Healing at the slaughterer's hand?
My hearts physician is a man?
Love has cured what love had failed.
Now love has won where it had failed
The respect I gained for love was this:
There was no touch, there was no kiss.
God, how I wish that it could be
That such a man was meant for me.

Joan M. Hagans

More Than Friends

We were friends and that's all there was
But now my feelings are starting to change.
We use to laugh and talk about things
But now a touch of your hand
Is like a needle to my skin.

I want to tell you about the way I feel
But I am held back with my own fear and guilt
"What should I do?" is a question I ask myself,
So whatever I do, I should do it soon.

Should I tell you and lose a friendship?
Or should I keep it to myself and let you slip through
  my fingers?
How would I feel when I see you in the arms of
  another girl?

How I wish that you can feel the same way
that I do about you.

But if time is at war with us
Then I'll cry in my heart
And let you know that a friend like you
Is worth waiting for.

Claire Macauley

Awakened

Mirrors around the sun, shine a heavenly light down upon us.
We grow from the radiant wonder that's inside us.
Feel the love it sends with each sunrise and sunset.
To grasp that moment in the sun - to find it's always been there.
To be awakened from a dream to find another world, still without a love.
Talk to the wind and let it bring your thoughts to someone who cares.
The sun will always shine with a heavenly glow to remind you
    that all is not lost.
Mirrors around the sun, find my love.

Joseph L. Attard Jr.

Poppy

Because we have known you, we have known Angels.
You taught us how to love and comfort and care for each other,
    our family and friends;
To sing joyfully and dance passionately and play without guilt;
To learn all that we can and apply it to life;
To believe in ourselves and take pride in what we do;
To grow as individuals with character and integrity;
To draw and play music and create things with our hands for our
    pleasure and others;
To respect God's creatures and all things in nature;
To work hard and realize that family always comes first;
But you never taught us what life would be like without you.
Together we learned that memories must be cherished;
That your voice and song, laughter and smile were unique;
That you live each day through each of us;
That ringing church bells bring tears to our eyes;
That we are proud to have been a part of your life;
That we will again be reunited, in God's time and in His home;
Because, Poppy, an angel taught us.

Shirlee Morton

I Will Arise

I want to be in the sun, to feel its warmth; its embrace.
I want to fly with the wind, have it kiss my face.
I want to walk freely in the fields, sing with the birds
    as they come.
I want to be their song.

But I can not.
Fear chains my heart.
Memories engulf my mind.
I knew a world of a different kind.
Where there was no freedom and no choice.
Where I had no voice.
Falsehoods and lies encircle truth as
I face the dark clouds of my youth.
Yet, I will obtain that which I long for; that and more.
The storm I'll not break me - I am a survivor.

Come dark clouds, rain, and storm.
Come that I might withstand the bitter winds, the
    flood of emotions, the howling cries.
So that the flower within me can arise
    to embrace the sun, to kiss the wind, to begin live again.

Pat Ozaki

An Autobiography

I'm
Independent, resplendent,
Provident, despondent, liberated,
Educated, emancipated, frustrated, administrator,
Arbitrator, coordinator, procrastinator, baptized, modernized,
Popularized, fantasize, solicitous, ambitious, superstitious,
Specious, sociable, sensible, invincible,
Unpredictable, emotionally, devotedly,
Contentedly, lonely,
Woman

Vanessa Lathon-White

Two Years Back

Two years ago when we
were young
we laughed, and danced, and
loved each other all through the night

Two years ago when we begun
we never fought,
or yelled
and we never threw things at
the wall
we got married and gave it our all
and now two more years have
passed us by we had
a son, Nathan Douglas is his
name — yeah — that was the
best thing we ever done
now another two years has
come and gone and everything has fell apart
and all I care to remember now is
the two years back when we were young
and two years later — when we had our son.

Carla J. Craft

My Two Worlds

I live in two different worlds
at two different times.
One is everybody's
and one is mine.

One is a world of screams and shouts
and animals and houses all about.

It's a world of hustle and bustle
and the sound of cars going by.

But as for my other world
it's hard to describe.
To get into this world it's not really hard
all I have to do is step in my backyard.
It's a world of flowers, trees, birds and bees.

But in this world of fantasy,
there are things I have not seen yet,
I still have to discover it.

This world means a lot to me,
if I could live in it forever
I would be so happy.

Whitney Taylor

My Husband, My Hero

The man that I'll cherish forever
died nearly five and a half years ago,
and on that day, my whole world changed
it's a loss only a widow could know.

By age thirty five, he endured so much
living with a disease since age seven,
together we shared sixteen years
our son had just turned eleven.

Wayne was strong, sincere and full of faith
with a sense of humor that wouldn't quit,
he accepted the life he was given
even when he couldn't make sense of it.

He appreciated the littlest things
and found blessings in every day,
with a truly Unconditional Love
limitations didn't stand in his way.

He was an inspiration to all he knew
to his family and those he'd befriend,
I Miss You...My Husband, My Hero
with a love that will Never end!

Denise Schermerhorn

Feelings Within

Thrown into a world, no part in creation
lost feelings of want, hopeless sensation
a life just to view, slowly then fades
helpless when watching, a pre-written fate

Wrongness inside me, answer not there
feelings of changes, beginning to tear
painfully intense, an urging to cease
reaching acceptance, someone help me

Laughs they beat hard, sweat from cold singe
taking out my "demons", with hateful revenge
laughing now lost, spirits long down
jokes at my expense, life without sound.

Ryan S. Michel

The Silence Of Love

The stars at night, twinkle your name,
beauty and love are two cherished things.
The flowers grow, during the spring,
they blossom, they bloom, not in between.
The mountains are high and covered with snow,
the love I have, will always grow.
The sea is deep, long and wide,
the night I kissed you I nearly cried.
Sheltered in your love is where I will be,
I hope, I pray so endlessly.
Something I hide deep inside,
just for you, the silent cry!

Nicholas Martin

Untitled

I should go inside right now
  It's getting late and dark
    But the sky is charming
I dare not leave.

While the spell of twilight is being weaved
The dusk gives the heaven a small reprieve
  Between day and night
I dare not leave
'Til twilight becomes eve.

  The clouds of the day become mountains at night
  Purple and blue, capped with white
    Or flaming torches of gold and orange
    Or perhaps a unicorns silver horn
  Or the pink wings of a pegasus flying high -
I dare not leave
  'Til they're covered by night.

  So I stare at the sky with a dreaming eye
    I am captivated once again
I dare not leave
  So I sit and stare at the sky

Rebecca Jo New

Ellis Island

The rush of sapphire waves
Lightly crashes against the wall
The ebony wall, the wall that reminds us
That here we are honoring America's immigrants
People who came to pursue their dreams
Dreams of opportunity, of freedom, and of
  prosperity
The lime green Statue of Liberty stands tall
Reminding us that this is the land of liberty and
  freedom.
This is a place worth remembering -
Ellis Island.

Nicole Mancini

Pain

The day dawns bright, the rain is through
a cloudless day, so fresh and new

Many rejoice in this sun so bright
playing and singing in the sparkling light

But some dread the beauty this bright star brings
We hide from its light that blinds and stings

Shadows and clouds are the stuff of our days
we are robbed of the joy of the sun's warming rays

it crushes our spirit, suppresses our soul
we lose hope in the dream of being healthy and whole

Some are told "nothing's wrong", "it's all in your head"
"I just can't help you", is all that is said

If only they tasted our life that is hell
this misery that flows from a bottomless well

Their tune, it would change - their apathy flee
their eyes, they would open - and then they would see

We want to join those who laugh and are free
and drink from a well where there's no agony

But, we are survivors, and we'll make it through
as we pray everyday, our dreams will come true

Tréci M. Collender

Oh, Suppressed One

When will the chains be broken
  When will victory appear
When will the realism cease
  When will the daydreams draw near?

Will there ever be self gratification
  Will Glory ever return
Will there ever be justification
  Will there ever be reminiscing times yearned?

Where is the restitution
  Where is the peace in your soul
Where is the reconstruction of self
  Where is the time allotted to grow old?

How much injustice will reap
  How much sowing will undergo
How much lingering on to monotony
  How much lonesomeness to unfold?

Question not the thoughts of your soul
  Oh, suppress one look to soar....
The joy of the morning is coming
  So continue to strive forevermore!

Wendell J. Powell I

Song of Praise

Winter is coming and Christmas is near.
Jesus, my Savior's birthday is near.
He shares His birthday with good girls and boys.
I love my Savior and share His joys.

Welcome! Welcome! One and all!
Enter into His banquet hall!
As you sit at the table He'll feed all your needs.
Dear Jesus, your words we will heed.

A crown and a mansion are waiting for me.
I'll walk streets of gold in good company.
I'll hear Jesus' stories and sit at His knee.
Oh Jesus! I'm glad you love me!

Sandra L. Wray

Before And After

You would believe if you could hope,
You would wish, but you dreamed of cope,
You didn't lie, 'cause the truth would hurt,
You want to die, so you let out a cry,
You couldn't live, to give it no use,
You wouldn't wish, others in your shoes,
You want to see, what you saw before,
You want to hear, what you heard long ago,
your dreams are so bright,
but the suns never light,
towards the winters so cold,
towards the fire so low,
that even ashes won't glow,
You wouldn't say right, 'cause right sounds so wrong,
You wouldn't come near, 'cause of the high wall,
You wouldn't fit in, 'cause your hands aren't so high,
Your mind isn't stretched, to reach the high sky.

Natasha Dzhanashvili

Shadows

Looking through the window of tomorrow
From the pain of joy and sorrow.

Pain, laughter, and love
Embraced together from the Father of Love.

Standing on the outside looking in
Things look so shadow, but it's where God begins.

Things of the past come to present,
Things of now come together

Yesterday, and tomorrow are gone,
But with God on your side,
You are never alone.

Things gets bad, so often they do
We sometimes stumble and fall.
Giving up on everything and refusing to give God a call.

The grief, pain, hurt, and downfall are now replaced
with hope, joy, and love.

Yes God saved me and He come from above.
He is the key to happiness, and eternal life.
All you have to do is invite Him into your life.

Tommie Hellen Odom

Hand in Hand

They walk down the path hand in hand
    Not knowing what to expect
Not knowing any lies, not knowing any regret
    The smooth pebbles of the path
Gently massage their feet, subtly calming them
    For all that's brought to meet
The goddess of love, the God of fortune
    Live together as one
Giving light to one another
    Like heavens star the sun
Her rosy lips form a smile
    While his eyes dance with pride
As they walk hand in hand,
    Side by side
They don't know where they are going
    Their feet lead the way
They follow one another
    As night follows the day....

Nicole Garcia

Think About It

Not having the ability to read or write;
not having the undoubted pleasure of sight.

Not being able to feel be it pleasing or pain;
not being able to hear the rain.

Not having the freedom to say "that's not what I want to do."
or not having the right to say "that's not true."

Not having the ability to think of how to build a plane;
this could not be possible if you did not have a brain.

To say you dislike or hate what man did not create;
shows the Creator's gifts, you do not appreciate.

What you don't use, you lose;
and what you don't value, you abuse.

Life is not something to be taken for granted;
each life is like a flower that God planted.

Jeff D. Walker

Pages of Memories

Into the depths of darkness, I have often looked.
Not willingly, but always took.
Pages of memories, and a child not old.
Pages of memories, and her mother to hold.
Are with the Angels, walking their streets of gold.
Their innocence, their charm, their smile
Made their moment here all worth while.
Here I am and I wonder why
I can't understand, and it makes me cry.
Under the sunshine, so warm and bright.
Walking the beaches on a moonlit night.
There must be a reason, though yet untold.
That I too, am not walking those streets of gold.

Charles Payne

Requiem

From night an orchid dawn arose
And blushed the early morning light
Etching peace to the new beginning
Yet a sad reminder of time in flight.
A lonely daffodil caught in a golden beam.
Stood regal in the changing haze
As in tribute to the one that toiled
To add its beauty to spring-filled days.
Life is a journey to time's acclaim
But the treasure of each is need to know
How God's gift of creative hands
Lends such joy by the seeds they sow.
That lone daffodil with its golden charm
Stands loyal against the orchid sky
As in honor to one remembered
And a requiem for time gone by.

Genevieve Sparks

What You Want

I:
Can't feed.
Birds dropping
Tired leaves
Melting from,
Worn eves,
Pressed,
Into
My thigh
Gaining: Flying
Shot
For getting/ for being/ for hoping/ for looking/ too high

Jennifer Barcus

To Debbie

On a February morning
Almost 15 years ago
God smiled and remembered springtime
Amidst the winter snow

And he took a bit of springtime:
The song of birds returning
The laughter of melting snow
The smile of a dew-kist morning
The kiss of the winds that blow
The love of falling raindrops
And the color of the sky
The smile of the sun in treetops
And a bit of the eternal "why"
And he put them all together
And made a little girl
A girl with hair of sunlight
And eyes of the skies own blue
With a heart as sweet as music, a mother's dream come true.

My sister is the springtime and, if I be winter snow,
It makes but little difference for she loves me, that I know.

Robert C. Fath

In The Garden

I went to the garden of people today;
It was silent.
Though it was solemn, I was spoken to in voices.
They told me their joy;
I felt their sadness.
They told of gentleness;
I felt their fury.
They told of their happiness;
I felt their loneliness.
But when they spoke of wisdom,
I felt like a child;
A deaf blind child standing in the light,
My heart was moved.

John H. Petrig II

Class Of 2000

Those who are going somewhere in life,
Those with imaginations,
Those with dreams,
Those who daydream,
Those who hope,
Those who worry,
Those who care,
Those who life has a purpose,
Those who love,
And so on.
You are the ones who will lead us into the
Future.

Bethany Baer

Rebecca

Shivers run through my every pore
Still when you cross my mind
After so long you've left me alone with only emotions
In this cage I've been sentenced to you
Like no other know
My heart has been jaded
From the recidivism you promised not abandon me to die
And still haunt me with crumbs of sanctuary
Forget you I cannot but pretend I may
Not for my love of you to let you at peace
Even though my back you will not scratch
Put my heart under the knife no more can I
For rolls are bound to switch and see how sharp my pain
can be will I

Joe Thorn

The Old Guitarist

Here I sit, alone on the cold floor.
I am too weak to stand and walk, so here I sit.
I am old; lonely and my bones are so worn.
I can't see anything, everything is colorless, lifeless,
except you.
I still have you, yes you, my only true friend...
In fact, my only friend.
In a dark room all I need is the shattered light,
which enters through the boarded windows.
This is just enough light so that I may see you,
but nothing else.
I must persuade you with a warm embrace
and persistent, although gentle caress.
But how I love the sweet melodies that
echo through your cavern.
As a result of my over-whelming compassion,
each note you release represents a single tear
dripping into my river of sorrow.

Jennifer Smith

In Loving Memory Ashlee Marie Currin
May 8, 1985 - January 8, 1996

A harsh grave, an early end,
A brief but beautiful life, my friend.
I miss you - Why did you have to go?
Although God had his reasons, I know.
When they told me my best friend had died,
I felt so cold; I hardly cried.
Where the truck slid, there's still a stain.
As, in agony, you had lain.
The people don't notice, drive on.
I want to yell "Please, cry
with me, she's gone".
I'm going to cry again.
Goodbye, my friend.
I will miss you.

Elizabeth Newcomb

Give

You people, lying to each other,
Too caught up inside yourselves
    to feel another's pain.
Prisoners are people who love each other,
But fear the future that
    truth would bring.

Freedom is spawn of submission,
By sacrificing yourself into
    another one's arms.
Life isn't felt until it is given,
Until you give the pulse of your own
    beating heart.

Tear down your walls between each other,
    give when you've nothing at all.
Pay the price, whatever is needed,
    for the needs of love
    are always small.

Thomas Ford Bullock

Rain

The rain beats hard against my back.
It is a just punishment, though not a harsh one.
And in it, I find the most bittersweet of all messages:
Gaea cares not whether I be flesh or stone,
Only that, in time, I will erode away.
Such is the ordeal of my trespass,
My vain attempts to hasten her manner.

Jonathan Hart

My Daughter

You came from within
not knowing your impact on my life.
    Yet you gently and consistently
fulfilled all my needs.
    As I hold you tightly in my arms,
our warm breathing once again unites.
    My heart continues to beat for you,
as we rock alone in endless peace.
    Our dark eyes do meet occasionally,
and we see into a deep mirror.
    Who I once was and who you will become:
We stare silently into ourselves.
    My daughter, I will teach you all I know,
as we share our lives together.
    Your soft eyes close in quite contentment.
Instinctively, I rock, and rock, and . . .

Kimberly Lisowski

1040EZ

Do you have at least one qualifying child?
Yes.
Stop.
Were you at least age 25 but under age 65 at the end of 1996?
No.
Stop.
You cannot take the credit.
Was your home in the United States for more than half of 1996?
Yes.
Go to question 5.
Can your parents claim you as a dependent?
No.
Stop.
You cannot take the credit.
Subtract line 2 from line 1.
Add lines 3 and 4.
Earned income credit.

Tom Forman

Christmas Vacation

Only once every year do we all get together,
but then again, it's in stinky weather. We
all do have fun sharing Christmas cheer, but
gosh golly it's only once a year! When we
all leave life fills up with tears, but hey it's
only one time a year! We all gather 'round
the Christmas tree, and pass presents around,
and hey, there's even one for me! Then we have
a feast, and we pass around home made roast
beasts, and hey, you should see all of the meats
we have at our feast! Mom, dad, and Mariellen
too, they get presents too! Well that's all for
now, it's time for tears,
    But hey, it's only once a year!!

Kati McCracken

Charlie

While in 'Nam looking for Charlie
I felt a searing pain . . .
Charlie had found me

I could not hide or run
So I lay on the ground
And realized my waiting had begun

I waited for the air-raids to fly through the sky
Dropping their bombs
I lay there waiting, waiting to die

Justin Angert

This Old Jagged Rock

This old jagged rock that I sit on, it holds no beauty.
But, if you look deep inside, you will see many things,
The grains of sand a loving couple once walked on,
The diamond dust from a ring that once was lost,
Dirt from a grave where people once mourned,
Gold from a mine shaft that took many lives.
Silver from a bracelet that was thrown into the river
Over a first love lost,
Coal from a camp fire where many lives were taken
Because of the color of their skin.

So, the next time you look at a rock,
Look deep inside at the many treasures within.

Melissa A. Lee

One Morning

One morning I woke up at seven o'clock
When I found out I was missing a sock

It's seven fifteen
And I haven't been seen

Because I still can't find my sock
That's been missing since seven o'clock

It's seven twenty-five oh great!
I guess I'm really running late

I'm having a really really big fuss
Cause I think I just missed the bus

Now it's eight o'clock
And I just found my sock

I found it in my shoe
My brother, Lucas, just threw

I'm going back to bed
Because it's Spring break my mother just said

Samantha Schnider

Today And Tomorrow

Along this path I walk the earth
beneath my feet. For I don't walk alone,
But there's no strangers I will meet.

My days on earth have come, and gone,
But I'm in a much better place,
I now sit beside God, and Jesus
around the throne, and we will
meet again when you to come home.

Steven G. Phillips

A Family of Love

The hands move slowly or hardly at all
for I watch and wonder and think of it all

When we're finally together each moment will glow
with laughter and sunshine and love — overflow.

But often my heart feels weak and alone
for a family apart does not make a home.

The letters, the calls, the packages, too
are all quite wonderful but can't replace you.

I try my best to be patient and strong
but time is not moving, it just drags on.

But soon the precious day will come
when we're together again, a Family of Love.

Sheri Quintana

Lonely Nights

My cell is lonely and cold,
in the nights darkest hour I've no one to hold.

You cannot see my sorrow as
it escapes my lonely eyes

These nights are forever alone,
is it only an illusion to see my love of true?

These feeling I've locked forever in my mind
for eternity to seek who holds the key,

Confusion is nothing new, for
one day this person I'll find.

I vow with all of life's will, I'll not
look back if at last they'll open this door,

This torment I'd leave behind, never
to return once more.

When will freedom reign I ask?
The word "never" only to be told

Here comes yet another lonely night, with no one to hold!

Barry F. Gibson

Fantasy

What do you look like? What would I see?
Are you very different or do you look like me?
Do you smile easy? Do you laugh real loud?
Would you care, if you knew I was around?
Will you give big hugs, if I skin my knee or
would you shrug and turn away from me?
If I needed, would you let me cry on your
shoulder? At three in the morning, would
you say, "come on over"?
All these things I need to know, all these
things I want to know, I'm just not sure
if you'll ever show.
Do you not know of me as I don't of you?
Or won't you accept me because that's what some men do?
If I knew where to find you — I'd be there tonight
because once we find each other — it's sure to be alright.

Deanna Shoults Maples

Love Lesson

I have become what you hate.
I can look you in the eyes and lie to you.
I can walk away and leave you in pain.
I can avoid intimacy and retreat should you get too close.
I can push you away with my words.
I tried to show you a different kind of love than you understood.
You would not accept it.
I've spent years learning how to love you your way,
the only way you understand.
Now I love you the same way you have taught me to.
You looked into my eyes and lied to me.
You walked away and left me in pain.
You avoided intimacy and retreated when I got too close.
You pushed me away with your words.
I have learned my lesson well.
Now I am what you despise most, I am what you hate.
I am you...see yourself in me.

Elisa A. May

She

She hears
Every night 'til dawn meets day
And understands my thoughts to say

She hears me.

She knows
Remembers both my faults and fears
Combined with many troublesome tears

She knows me.

She inspires
Untangles my head while clearing my soul
A guiding light to help mend the hole

She inspires me.

She touches
Her soft spoken words; her soft silky feel
Broken pieces will take eternity to heal

She touches me.

Every night 'til dawn meets day
She'll always hear my thoughts which say......

Jaime Heather Rembo

The Red, Red Rose

The red, red rose has no fingers, legs or toes.
It boasts not of its beauty,
But sways as the evening breezes
Pass and sing in unity.

As the bluebird sings her love song,
The red, red rose listens peacefully to the days long
And smiles, always gladly,
Never thinks a thought badly
Or of the troubles to come.
It is always bright and brilliant
As the sun.

Days come and go, and yet,
The red, red rose tells its tales
Of days past,
And looks forward to the promise
Of tomorrow's last.

Rebecca Maidl

To Believe Or Not To Believe

Is life a burning hell that is eternal?
An which surrounds us day by day.
Or is it a heaven that blinds us with a love that we
  take for granted?
I guess we'll never know, because we are only human.
Do we make a mistake in believing all that is meant
  to be believed?
Or do we make life easier by believing in the
  unbelievable world?
Is there a human that is wise and can answer all that
  is meant to be believed?
Or only thinks thee can answer all.
Are the crazy people of the world the only living
things to truly understand all of this?
Is the reason why we push them away when they
  have an idea because we don't understand what they
  are telling us?
Who knows? No one knows.
Not even the man in the moon.
Oh, one more thing, is there really a man in the moon?

Carrie Binkley

Future Vision

The World will be a better place
If only we would learn
To apply ourselves to be productive
And not sit around and yearn
About the things we wish to accomplish
If we only had the time
Like giving of ourselves of others
Without costing us a dime
To love our neighbor - forget about greed
Help each person who is truly in need
Greet everyone with the warmth of a smile
Accept others as they are, go the extra mile
The warmth that surrounds you will seem heaven sent
When at last we abide in Peace and Contentment.

Bertha Aebischer

Sonnet II

Your spirit, I'd often feel it brush by
dancing, knowing we'd met before. Sad, shy
you, I. Catch it? Never! It'd flit, I'd eye
then be off to garner ill fare. Good-bye.
Companion, you return in my love lines.
Travel weary of refreshed we dine
on theology fare, mesh past, future scenes.
Yet, Graham vigor heavens gaze denies.
Love had grown vulgar. We, leg and crutch, beg
joy return, walk without knowing mirth we'd
killed! Then cold heaven's eye, thought blind to ink,
twined our glance and of sadness gave us leave.
　Ere you and I walked a common path, still
　we never met 'til eager eyes drank full.

Roger A. Waid Sr.

America's Future

We've joined together and all held hands,
For the starving children, we've done what we can.
Banning together to help out the poor,
Now open your eyes, to your own back door.
Let's all join hands and hold on tight,
For all the world, let's make things right.
Money won't help, no matter how much we make
Our children's lives are what's at stake.
Wrapped up in overselves, we have no time
For hugging and holding and saying you're mine
Can you remember, when did you say
I love you my darling, how was your day.
Screaming and yelling is what we do best
Pushing our babies right out of the nest
Suicide and drugs are where they've turned
When our love is all that they yearn.
Bringing them into this world, their lives we should share
Hug them and hold them, tell them you care
All of our babies, a gift from above
Open your eyes, all they need is your love.

Rose Early

Our Son

Our son's name is Marc
Whose life has been a lark.
To have fun and play he is quite the plotter
His life is spent much like the otter.
His dream is to be on stage as a star
Like Hoffman, Roth and Clapton
Because he also plays the guitar.
Helping him grow up has been an adventure
To which our lives have been indentured.
Soon and very soon a man he will be
And life he will face with youthful glee!

Marti S. Moodie

She Makes Me Feel

She makes me feel like the days are brighter.
I see light where darkness prevails.
Love and intellect are bonds that hold comfort near.
I greet each day with happiness to see what it will tell.

Days without her seem a world away now.
The past left far behind.
Years of low self esteem seem non-existent.
Faith told me "one day true love you shall find."

Since the day we walked into each other's lives,
I have and do consider time a true friend.
No longer do I wish for the end to come near.
I told despair "My heart, no longer shall you rend."

It's strange how one can know something,
But due to relativity can know it that much more.
She makes me feel like the most beautiful shell,
On life's vast and wonderful sea shore.

Brandon L. Donnell

One Question Never Answered

No matter how intelligent you are
there is one thing you will never know.
Why do loved ones have to die and why
do we have to let them go?

Why do some people know the answers to almost
everything but not something important such as this?
Why do people have to die and the rest
of their lives they have to miss?

I still can't figure out why this is
the way it will always have to be.
Why the close ones I loved
were taken away from me?

This is a question whose answer may never be known.
It's a question I'll ask myself even
when I'm grown.

So why do people have to die?
It's not for me to know.
I can only trust and believe in God,
and see them all when I, too, shall go.

Kim Ketchel

The Grapefields

　As Ireland's morning sun beams through the
morning mist upon these gullible grapefields, it
paints such a picture across the endless sea. I
only come here to engage with your intimacy and
memories of what used to be.

　Only impetuous memories of much worth evolve
here and are entwined within these vines. As
children, we'd wander through these rows without
hindrance, watching the essence of these future wines.

　As I come upon these dying vines, I reach
for your hand, but it's all illusion and you're
a phantom in the air. I see the nature that had
once bloomed as a laughing child too fair.

　I seemed to have filled this very ravine
with tears I have wept with interminable flow.
With each tear that has fallen upon this
soil, a new vine shall grow.

Shasta Riley

Tears Of Joy

The dreams of a child, so real and so true,
what you are dreaming, I wish I only knew.

Never a whimper never a peep
as you lie there so fast asleep.

As I stand here watching you, what I'd
give to know what's in store for you.

To be a doctor, or a clown,
or be in space,
to watch the world go 'round.

For all that life will bring I cannot say,
but you are young so enjoy your time and play.

Oh, my child, how I weep as you sleep,
these tears of joy because you are
"My little boy."

Tiffany Knight

Vision

The fine scales shimmer silver light,
like armor of ancient warrior knights.
They shine and blind his watering eyes,
struck by reflections of piercing moonlights
that fly like comets in twilight skies.
His shaking hands hold its dripping weight,
diamonds drop liquid, and fall like rain,
the gills, a trembling flicker of flame.
Its long tail is sweeping, carved in rings,
jade fins spread like gilded wings,
the fish,
opens wide its mouth, its scarlet throat,
arches armored back...and sings!
When that voice of wind, and distant waters
speaks, his heart
within him, falters.
Then the man set free his glorious find,
he watched as it vanished into water like wine,
perhaps to follow there in time.

Lisa D. Hilliker

Untitled

The train has departed
I've just arrived-
Why is the time always wrong when I'm concerned?
I wander through the thicket
to an unknown town
Only to find the backside of my mirror at home.
You see, we're all connected
by this or that
and I guess the railroad tracks
don't run through my town anymore.
It's weird-
looking at the world through your own eyes
Via the back door.
Is it possible that you follow my thoughts?-
Is it equatable to ask
if you know where I'm headed with this?
I'm not sure-
I just know everytime I turn around
I hear a train whistle nearby.

Bridgette Parsons

Its Hard To Say Good-Bye

It's hard to say good-bye
   when at home so long,
It's hard not to cry
   when they leave the home,
It's hard to smile
   when all stressed out,
It's hard to drive away
   when your mind is all spread about,
It's hard to look back
   when you remember the times you had,
It's hard to stay straight
   when saying your last words,
Such as Good-bye, I Love You, And Good Luck.

Catherine L. Fitzgerald

Facade Of The Ice Cream Man

All that is good. All that is suburban.
   All the facade of the ice cream man

Tree-lined streets and back street forests
   So many places. So little time

All that needs to breathe. All I don't have.
   All the facade of the ice cream man

The sound of traffic just faintly up ahead
   So much that doesn't make sense. So what?

All your sweet lies. All that cuts me deep.
   All the facade of the ice cream man

Erik Thibodeaux

Protect The Animals

Men are afraid of the wolf and the lion.
Men are afraid of the tiger and the bear.
Men are afraid of the stampeding wildebeest,
And the ferocious birds that swoop through the air.

So they go out with guns and with bullets.
So they go out with weapons galore.
So they go out to kill all these animals,
Until these animals are no more.

Come, let's save the wolf and the lion.
Come, let's save the tiger and the bear.
Come, let's save the stampeding wildebeest,
And the ferocious birds that swoop through the air.

Come, let's stop the men who shoot the animals galore.
Come, let's stop the men who shoot, before they shoot some more.

Jennifer Kaeser

Memorandum

So much for your promises, so much for your lies,
Too bad for your words cause you can't hear my cries.
I don't want to see your face,
I don't want to hear your voice,
But they haunt my life, so I have no choice.
Worst of all is your ghastly stare,
You think I don't notice, you think I don't care.
I am not stupid, I know your games,
You are a sick minded boy and I am your train.
The control is in your hand, you love the power,
As you drive me around your track hour by hour.
I wait for the day when I can be set free,
No longer imprisoned, for then I'll have the key.
One of these days I will get off your track,
Leave you for good and never come back.

Sarah C. Hamilton

An Abstract Picture Of Reality

Once there was a strong, beautiful
piece of golden fabric. The fabric
shined bright and became the envy
of all the eyes that fell upon it.

After some time, the golden fabric
became soiled and began to appear
tarnished from neglect. The fabric
was cleansed, and once again shined
bright but, not as beautiful as before.

Then the fabric was once again neglected,
and it began to fray around the edges.
It was mended but the size could not
be saved, and so remained smaller.

A long period of neglect passed and
the fabric became a single strand of
golden thread. This tiny thread tried
to uphold its past reputation of being
a beautiful piece of golden fabric
but, it had not the strength to stand alone.
Hence, in its last hour, it snapped.

Jody A. Eckrich

Storm Ahead

Sitting on the veranda overlooking the grassy dunes;
whitecaps splash playfully along the sandy beach.
Dark clouds from heaven above hide the glorious sunshine,
strong harbor winds blow fierce and menacingly.
Never before has this peaceful harbor been so
full of sinful nature or the sea so evil.
Looking out into the foggy horizon — there,
one lone and tattered vessel sails innocently
while monstrous waves beat ferociously upon its sides.
Being thrown to and fro the weather — beaten ship takes on
great amounts of water.
The storm ahead will swallow the sailing vessel and all aboard.
Overcome with love and compassion — the clouds part,
a ray of hope shines down on their broken ship.
Out of the blue the ocean calms,
two of the most beautiful rainbows appear
stretching as far as the eye can see.
The thankful sailors' lives are saved and all is protected, for
eternity.

Alaina Allen

Races

There are different kind of races
some are black, some are white
some are rich, some are poor.
It's like a river that flows and always shows.

Trying to leave without a fight
race is a gift that shows character
and grace, which shines bright, and bold
throughout the human race.

The blackness of the night
white cloud of the day
The rainy afternoon that turns a clear sky gray.

There are many colors like the one that
lines our faces whenever we feel disgrace.
Whether we are black or white
as long as we never give up the fight.

If there were no colors,
everything would be gray,
no fussing, no fighting not a lamp would be burning

No screams no shouts no one
would know what the earth is all about.

Cherilyn Gordon

Chrysanthemum

A chrysanthemum is a flower
Which has the smell of a soap in a shower.
It blooms in the summer and in the fall
And sometimes grows in a field as big as a mall.

Chrysanthemum for short is called mum
Indeed, it's the favorite flower of my mom,
You can find it in parks and city hall
It's an inspiration for employees and all.

It can be red, it can be blue
So if you smell it you won't catch the flu!

Jason J. Cristobal

Love Your Neighbor

We are in this world but not for very long.
So be good to your brother and don't do him wrong.

Feed your neighbor if he don't have food to eat.
You may even humble yourself and wash his dirty feet.

Whatever you do, do it in the name of love.
For our God is watching from heaven above.

Do unto others what you would have them do unto you.
This is what the Bible tells us to do.

Don't even think yourself better than a friend.
If he is cold take him in.

If he has no coat and you have two.
Then give him one is what you should do.

Help him with his burdens when they are hard for him to bear.
Then we will all be happy when we get up there.

Bernice Brown

Sweet Name Of Jesus

I bless your name, that wonderful name.
That sweet name of Jesus!
I love that name, I get peace when I say that name.
Oh! That sweet name of Jesus
I worship that name, I bow down to that name.
Love! That sweet name of Jesus.
I sing to that name, I rejoice to that name.
Lord! That sweet name of Jesus.
I praise that name, that one and only name.
Hallelujah! That sweet name of Jesus.
I get excited when I hear that name.
I jump for joy for that name.
Praise! That sweet name of Jesus.
That name saved me! That name delivered me!
Glory! That sweet name of Jesus.
That name is wonderful, that name is awesome.
Yes! That sweet name of Jesus.
That name, that name, that is above every name.
In case you didn't know!
It's that sweet name of Jesus!

Sharon Whittaker

Joshua

I begin every day the same

Loving you.
On every breath I hear a song
Verbalizing the depths of my affection,
Ending only with your sweetest kiss.

Yesterdays and todays are smiling memories
On which I will depend
Until my dreams of tomorrows with you come true.

Jessica Erin Sykes

Not African-American

My mother was born colored Down South,
Words of pride in her race never left her mouth.
I was born Negro, raised in a northern ghetto,
Embarrassed by my blackness, shame my credo
My daughter born a child of the 70's,
She was referred to as black - her complexion I envied.
Oh, my son, struggling the life of a young man,
Wonders why he is an Africa-American.
Nigra, N***er, colored, black,
All are words that feel like attack.
Attack because though I and my ancestors are native here,
Kept under attack because our difference in color must
always be clear.
I work, raised children in a home I own, doing all I can,
I am not an African-American but an American

Katherine A. Smith

The Moment Has Arrived

The rose withers in the night,
while the stars shine so bright.
The love I have has no fear,
through the tough times I shed many tears.
The flames of passion that we once endured,
now are nothing but a memory that I still mourn.
The clouds turn black, the thunder roars
as for this heartbreaking routine,
I can't take anymore.
The moment has arrived!
The beginning of the battle cry,
nevermore will I sigh.
The sun comes up, the flowers bloom.
This fight will never end,
until I heal this wound.
The battle has been won,
but the war will never end, until we become a unit,
together again.

Peter J. Castro

O Mortal Rose

I held in hand one day a full gowned rose,
It's rich and rare perfume enhanced the air.
Throbbing with life and in purity clothed,
could death decay, belong to such so fair?
Each clinging cloak, a cup of yearning hope;
"The quest of life is life, its cease it's fear."
O truth tho faith be strong, soon sounds its note of death;
Shrinking, its dusk of fate rides near.
I crushed the rose, and one by one its wings of breath
I dropped below, and thus it died.
This cruel, thought I! But whether lingering or fleet, its end,
could it always abide?
O mortal rose, God's will, withhold thy sigh,
All things are born, equipped to live, then die!

Daniel B. Weaver Jr.

The Gift

A special child, from above,
comes to us to see, if we are
ready for pure love.
With wings of silk, and a head piece
of gold, you know you are never to young
to feel bold.
You know God loves you just
the same, and he knows us all by name!
Treat every one with respect, even
if a different race, for we were all made
in the same place!
So treat every one the same,
even if a different religion, race, or name.

Stephanie Gregor

For You

I'm so confused and I'm not sure why.
Every time I see you, I always want to cry.
I love you more than I wanted to,
and now I'm not sure what to do.
You have never had a problem turning away,
when you didn't want to hear what I had to say.
I don't understand how you could feel that way,
you are the reason, why I make it through the day.
Please don't turn away that fast,
don't let me become just another person from your past.

I've tried all I could think of
to prove to you His love,
but still today you try to ignore
the pain He went through before.
He died for you, that's not a lie,
I've tried to explain His reasons for why.
It's hard to believe you didn't know,
and now you want to let life go.
Don't make today your last.
Don't end your life that fast.

Carrie Resor

Lunacy

His eyes do not pant with the power of the sun and
There is no brightness in his countenance.
His darkness looms even as I leave
A fiery soul has blistered and blackened his eyes
They never burn my face.

He lets me walk without a word
Runs his fingers down my spine and
Through his rain damp hair
Gray sketches and reckless care
Couldn't keep him in this place.

Moonbeam madness breeds an unreflected love
The desire for all dreams
to be a sunset
We float on a flooded street
Reeling towards the dark
And what he is not.

Alison Carley

Threads Of Life

The Wheel of Time spins round and round
Weaving us into its web
Ever constant, ever changing
No two paths exactly alike.

Struggle like salmon against its current
Or succumb to the flow
Others learn to steer their course
Those are the privileged few.

We weave ourselves into the pattern
Each step tenuously connected
A thread so delicate it cannot be seen
So strong it binds us like iron.

The Wheel weaves as it wills
We cannot escape our destiny
Destined for greatness, others mediocrity
Each soul an integral thread in the fabric.

Fear not your path...your destiny awaits
Hold out your arms and embrace it
Become one with The Wheel, enter its flow
So as not to be drowned in its wake.

Jerrilynn Schenck

Truth To Color

At birth color is ones complexion of the skin
Yet has no bearing on the person within
Ones color does not matter, so long as they are there
To feed, bath, protect, caressing the importance of care
The gentle voice that consoles your woes
Color you cannot see - their shadow is where your eyes go
So when you can focus, color you still is unable to see
It's the love in the smile that allows you to be
As you grow in the environment you are exposed
Racism you learn the cons and the pros
Still not gasping what color is about
Someone else's hatred you begin to shout
From their experience is where it comes from
Honestly from your lack of experience this has come
To develop an incident to say this happened to me
As a form of acceptance of the crowd you would want to be

Betty McMickens

Love Of The Game

We are the offense line.
We can not get scared.
For if they passed us
No one will be spared.

While we are in the huddle
We all start to holler.
For when we go to the line
We all get in the mud and waler.

For when we fire off,
And hit them really hard.
We know they can not stop us,
So we gain ten more yards.

For I know I can do better,
Each time I play and play.
My love for the game grows stronger
Each day after day.

I know but that I'm getting tired,
But I never give up.
There's this little voice inside me shouting
Don't settle for runner-up!

Justin Vanover

The Accountant's Son

One plus one "Daddy, can we go have some fun?"
Just one more minute son.
Just one more minute until I am done.
The patience of the accountant's son.

Two plus two "Daddy, what shall we do?"
Two choices for you son.
Two choices from which you can choose.
The decisions of the accountant's son.

Three plus three "Daddy, what will the future bring for me?"
Three dreams for you son.
Three dreams that you should seek.
The anticipation of the accountant's son.

Four plus four "Daddy, what is outside the door?"
Four mountains to climb son.
Four mountains that you must explore.
The ascent of the accountant's son.

Five plus five "Daddy, to where should I strive?"
Five more yards son.
Five more yards further than you can survive.
The goals of the accountant's son.

James Hood

La Bella Luna

And I awoke
  just before dawn
to spy the red hot sun rise
  - like an orb over the mountains in the east.

And then I turned west - and wept,
  as a huge full round milky moon
dipped between the palms
  dangling above the bridge
pouring shafts of white light
  across the rippling water
- casting a lacy silhouette upon the incandescent river
  - Japanese and magical
shimmering watercolors of orange, pink and blue dots
  Amazed!
And then one rose and the other melted simultaneously
  - the sun and the moon,
  in tune with each other
And I wanted to shout,
  "wake up, everyone; you're missing it!"
  - another day's miracle

Karina

Undone

You are the pain that I've come to know
A fading memory I can't let go
I've grown older but I'm still a fool
How easily we lost what was true

A raindrop for every tear you cried
while I lay asleep at your side
I should have listened while you were there
Just didn't realize how much you cared

I wish I could change the past
To somehow make you last
But your perfect reflection in the mirror
Has left in my mind lingering fears

We made it to the mountain
looked up and didn't try
We were going different directions
Thought I'd find you as time went by

I blame myself everyday
Because we were torn apart
But I've hidden myself from the pain
To heal my broken heart

T. J. Chopelas

Untitled

A hero is he who holds high
that which is weighed good and great.
He lives a life of love and light,
dedicates his days, wills his weeks
to caring, sharing, loving and living.
A father to my mother, a follower of God:
Never to need but wanting to give.
Calling to reveal a joke he receives,
a smile shows on many small faces.
He makes magic with his painting pen,
drawing and dreaming up picture stories.
Soldiers march out of his magnificent mind
onto war-game tables they walk together.
My grandfather is he, a great man to all,
and worthy is he, a hero indeed.

Cortney Baisey

As If It Was Yesterday

As if it was yesterday,
I could clearly remember
that beautiful kiss I had
in the month of December.

No, not at all was it meant to be,
it just happened out of nowhere.
I really know that it meant a lot to me,
and after all, we both seemed to care.

As we moved from side to side
in the music we both danced,
my heart felt in some cry
thinking it might be my last chance.

Memories like that are incredible.
Memories that really fill a persons heart.
For me, that night was unforgettable,
such beauty will never break apart.

A dawn will rise tomorrow
upon another day,
and I will remember that moment not as sorrow,
but as if it was yesterday.

Orlando Ricardo Jr.

Bear Planet

A helicopter hovered, made completely of glass,
Broken in two panes by silver, metal cylinders,
each one spewing a cloud of green gas.
The gas gave the crew of the helicopter a surprise.
Its affect was them being hypnotized.
Only the pilot was left unaffected,
but soon from his hands the controls had been wrested.
The helicopter was sent crashing to the ground
and the crew escaped harm.
"Fire a few more cans!" yelled the Orange Bear
waving his arm.
His orders were carried out on his whim.
Another cloud of gas formed around the crash site,
orange like him
The last thing I remember from my dream Bear Planet,
was the Orange Bear arguing with the Green Bear.
Who did the helicopter and crew belong to?
Both took credit for bringing it down
and neither was willing to share.

Michael Hall

Death Came Calling

Death came calling at the beginning of this year.
He took a Dear Old One, follow by many tears.
He's come back again I fear.
I can hear Him whispering softly in my ear,

"Be ready for the grieving that follows in my wake!
You cannot escape it asleep or awake."

Death came calling, there's a chill in the air!.
I can feel Him close, as He quietly waits there.
Standing by the bedside, patient and enduring.
Waiting for the Old One to do His ancient bidding.

This Dear Old One is Mother of My soul.
God please help me, I must let Her go.
The Light is calling, Heaven's doorstep waits.
Death is ever patient to take Her on Her way.
The time is close, I can feel the chill.

I pray for the strength that only God can give!

Linda Joyce Aceves

Deers

Deers have antlers. People have hands.
Deers can't speak. People can't keep quiet.
Deers have their own season. People don't.
Deers eat grass. People smoke it.
Deers can sense danger. People are dangerous.
Deers can run very fast. People can't run much of anything.
Deers roam the land without any cares or problems.
People roam the land with too many problems and no cares.
Deers raise their young and protect them from the world
People have children and can't protect them enough.
Deers have their own crossing signs on the freeway.
Peoples show signs of crossing too many lines.
Deer have an extreme sense of hearing.
People have a hard time listening.
Deers are shot and killed for their meat and horns.
People are shot and killed for no real reason at all.
It seems a lot of times that things appear in reverse.
Where people are the animals and the deers have it all together;
Perhaps that is why the deers are shot at because the people are
jealous of them.

Rodger E. Dupree Jr.

When I Call

Lord, when I call, you are there
And I thank you for being there for me.

I thank you just for having an open ear
And understanding me.

For helping me through my times of suffering,
trouble and trials you are there
when I call.

At times when I question my life
and am ready to give up,
I can't, because I know you have a purpose for my life.

I can call and you answer in a soft sweet voice saying,
"My child, I am with you always".

Tanya Norton

I Stand Alone

I stand alone, uncertain, unknown,
unthought of, unheard, and
oblivious.
Just thinking of things,
not happy nor sad,
thinking of what will become of us.

Then I decide to straighten up and fly.
I spread my wings up toward the sky.
I think of where I want to go, not wanting to stand here
sad and alone

Then with one little jump I soar through the clouds,
flying over hillsides,
valleys, and mounds.
I flash back and think of my nest in my tree,
at the same time thinking what will become of me.

Then finally the end,
along way from my goal.
I stand here alone with no place to go.
Yet I stand feeling nothing not the slightest pain,
tomorrow is tomorrow I will try again.

Tristan Clarke

Untitled

At times there are days when I feel low,
And it seems my depression continues to grow.
Life acts as a mountain; an insurmountable peak
The forecast for my life's weather is bleak.
It looks like my boat will go over the falls,
And I look at my house - the crumbling walls.
The walls fall down, the roof caves in,
I can't catch a break, I just can't win.
I think my whole world has fallen apart,
As I pick up the pieces of my shattered heart.

But I won't give up hope, there will be new light,
The gray skies will dissipate, the sun will shine bright.
I'll conquer the peak, turn my boat around,
And rebuild my house from the rubble on the ground.
As for the pain of my broken heart;
It slips to the past and thus comes a new start.
I realize this is life's tricky way:
Deviating emotions day after day.
So whenever I'm down, if the day has been low;
I have hope for better times, the bad ones will go.

Patrick J. Ellard Jr.

Tree

The bark of a tree is peaceful and cool,
You know how you feel when you touch one,
I have a tree, his name is Tree.

I love my Tree, I see him every day,
If you fall in love with one,
It will play with you.

Don't cut down the tree,
Oh please, oh please,
I fell in love with it.
He watches me play on Saturday.

My soccer ball hit Tree one day,
So I gave Tree a hug.
I really miss my Tree right now.
My dog watches him each and every day.

Sarah VanSchoick

Flight 800 Explosion

God only knows what happened on the "jumbo jet"
Their journey was so short the flight never met
A tragedy of promises all met with fate
Radiating from all levels of societies so great
Flight 800 explosion very devastating news
Bodies so hard to find and still yet no clues
Oh God we feel the pain families and friends endures
Our loved ones departed but now they are yours
We do not have answers only know where to start
Beginning with prayers and love from our heart
Strengthen their faith God with all hope
Make their families soon be able to cope
Let our prayers all around be made known
That even in our darkest hours we never walk alone

Marge Owens

Morning Sun

As the sparrow sings so sweetly in the morn,
And our Heavenly Father sends us a greeting
by the rays of the early sun,
As the morning sun reaches down and kisses the dew,
My thoughts will all be on you,
Entwining our love into one.

H. Lee Britton

Say A Little Prayer

Don't ask God for an easy life
...ask him to keep you strong.
Don't ask God to clear a path you choose
...ask him for the path to take.
Don't ask God for the things you want
...be thankful for the things you have.
Don't ask God for instant success
...ask him to help lead the way.
Whenever asking help from above
help yourself - he'll give you his love
Reach for your dreams
...and maybe a little more.
Look beyond the obstacles
...focus on the goal.
See inside your greatest ambitions
...and don't be afraid to fail
Wake each morning with a positive attitude
...and say a little prayer.

Tammy Foster

Firenze

Mid-day summer bakes the lusty rose
which folds upon its own velvet lilting.
No more movement, no more fevered dance
for innocence or pain or romance.
And no one weeps, and no one prays,
and no one tries to look away,
but the heavy air heaves a wretched sigh.

Yet midsummer eve redeems the rose
which breathes the newborn air uplifting.
Night drops the dew, heals parched lips to kiss,
to part, to whisper a breathless wish
before a hazy shaft of morning shine
steals between the lock and key,
beckoning the heat and soul to rise.

Kelly D. Belmonte

Tears

Tears
flow and ebb like the tide in the great sea
uncontrolled by human hearts or words.
Tears
of pain, pain unlike any I have known before -
all consuming pain that drowns me
Tears
of sorrow once so strange to me
now swallow me whole like Jona by the whale.
Will I ever see daylight again?
Tears
once reserved for happiness and joy
now hold only grief and bitterness.
Tears
wasted in my mourning -
a mourning as vast and deep as the great sea.
Tears
once shed, now lost
become my sea of lost hope.
Can I ever see daylight again?

Jennifer L. Briggs

Spring

The flowers are blooming, pink, white, and red.
The butterflies are fluttering in the soft flowery bed.
When the birds sing, soft sounds float in your head.
Spring, spring, spring what a wonderful thing.
Lilacs, violets, roses all bring the beautiful memories of the first spring.
Crystal clear water floating in the meadow,
oh how joyous spring can be when you're in the meadow with me.

Nadia Khan

We Remember

The sons of liberty are now at rest
They gave their lives for freedom best
They gave their lives to Him above
For liberty's cause and their country's love
Awake ye people - raise anthems on high
To honor those who for us did die
Their names shall live in the halls of fame
But their forms - we shall never see again

Lee Corn

Renewal

How special to celebrate this time of year;
to express appreciation for all wonderful things.
Look, see the buds on the trees and the infant blands of grass.
Listen, hear the birds singing.
Wait, take a deep breath; smell the scent of fresh new air.
Touch something and feel the greatness of being here.
Stand still; let out a shout.
Once this is done, there will be no doubt
that it's 'spring fever' - and oh, what joy to spread it about.

Barbara A. Bartley

Sweetheart's Soliloquy

Oh, stars of the sky, shine your light on me,
While I wait for my love under our pecan tree.
He gives me reason anew to smile, He who makes
The conservative heart wild.
The animals of the wood all know the reason,
For they have witnessed the love
That has passed here between us.
With my blue cotton sweater wrapped around,
He scoops me up, loathe to ever put me down.
As I contemplate his fox-colored hair,
I silently thank him
For this smile that he has repaired.
Though we don't speak each other's language,
It's of no concern,
Some things remain constant
No matter what we have learned.
With him, I feel no need to make amends,
With no audience to notice us, but winter and wind.

Elizabeth Barton

Love Me Now

If you are ever going to love me,
love me now while I can know.
The sweet and tender feeling
which from true affections flow.
Love me now while I am living
don't wait until I'm gone.
Sweet words in ice cold stone.
If you have tender thoughts of me
please let me know.
If you wait until I'm sleeping
never to awaken, there will be
death between us,
and I won't hear you then.
So if you love me even a little bit
let me know while I am living so I can treasure it!

Melanie Renee Knudson

Look To Jesus For Light

When the storms of life hit,
In Jesus' lap we can sit.
When our lives to Him commit,
Then our path will be well lit.

When the storm clouds assail,
Take hold of Jesus, He will not fail.
We can trust Him to provide on the trail,
He is faithful to protect us from Satan's hail.

Do not follow the mist in flight,
Stand firm and tall with a giants height.
Not by power or by might,
With His word shining bright,
To open the heart that's been closed tight.
Follow Jesus, it is right.

When the ocean waves surge and swell,
Come to the waters of the living well.
He, your soul will save from hell.
Share His light, go and tell.

Jim Cates

Mementos

When autumn gathered her rustling skirts
And fled the chilling grasp of winter,
She spilled an armful of treasured leaves
In my back yard.

They shimmered there
In every nuance of red and gold
Till ravin winter claimed the radiant hoard.
With icy strokes and frosty sighs,
He turned those bright mementos brown
And strewed their brittle splinters
With a yawn.

L. Gwen Ruthven

While You Still Can

Who'll shed a tear
When the time comes
Husbands, wives, and God's little children
A final goodbye
Cause we don't know when

Time goes forever
Our memories will too
But, what of the memories
Of loved ones barely two
Who never get a chance
To say "I love you"

Who'll shed a tear
When the time comes
Brothers, sisters, uncles and aunts
A final goodbye if we had one more chance

Just say "I love you" while you still can
Parents, friends and relatives it's never the same
But, if you never say it then, who's to blame

Who'll shed a tear when the time comes "I will" said I
With a tear in my eye another loved one said "Goodbye"

Timothy P. Ross

449

On Perfection

"Were you abused?"
  Yeah, but...I consented.
"Ah...promiscuous."
  Well...

"Substance abuse?"
  Sometimes.
"Denial!"
  Not Really.

"Relationships?"
  One or two, but they didn't last.
"Repeated your past, didn't you?"
  The past repeated itself.

"Stress?"
  I manage.
"It shows."
  It's the nineties.

"Tough life."
  I survived.
"We'll help you."
  But I'm fine...I'm just not perfectly fine.

    Cynthia Frey

What Is Happiness?

What is happiness in the world we live?
  Is it triumph and beauty to receive and to give?
Is it a smiling grin from a familiar face?
  Or is it just an open heart, regardless the race?
Could it be that happiness is just a figure of speech?
  Or is it an achievement for an individual to reach?
Maybe the tranquility of quietness alone,
  Or the acquaintance of a friend long once known.
But wouldn't it be happiness for the world to live in peace?
  Wouldn't there then be happiness if this chaos would cease?
Yes, happiness could be any of these we find,
  But, to exult in peace would be happiness, for all mankind.

    Teri Lynn Pigott

To Fellow Countrymen (1993)

Many a man is born with different talents,
And many are opportuned to exercise these talents.
But many lay waste their useful talents,
In a country where opportunities prevail.

Let's struggle genuinely for hidden talents to use.
Make endeavor for more heroes to produce,
With numerous idle elements to reduce,
In a country where opportunities prevail,

Think about numerous disgruntled elements,
Who shy away from duties of their government;
Idling, gossiping and wearing false helmets,
With less contribution to country's economy.

Our country is blessed with boundless wealth.
And talented persons should train to tap these wealth,
That would better our economy and our health,
In a country where opportunities prevail.

Let's resolve to build a virile nation,
Devoid of hate and discrimination.
And strive to produce enviable relation,
That generations may hopefully live to enjoy.

    Sylvia Akosa

This Is For You

This is for you
my withering flower.

Once you were a beautiful yellow flower
with a pure heart.

I cared for you, watered you
and you made me happy.

Your perfume filled my head
with hazy, purple smoke and
we became flowing lines of innocent.

I share my love with you and
the petals dropped, twiddling to the ground.
The color rushed out, yellow brown black.
An innocent heart, now is corrupt.
My flower of yellow was taken away,
the remains of my soul with it.

I won't try to see your yellow petals once more.
It is hard to see past the rain
and hard to trust your weak petals
that have fallen in a pile on your yellow-stained hands.

    Barbara Vickers

A Man With Aids Saved My Life

I learned about AIDS at school today,
Without my help it may never go away.
Standing before us was a man who'd achieved it all
Now he's suffering through life's greatest fall.

This man's travels are many but not for fun
He is just spreading the word until his life is done.
A cure is the prayer and the hope of many
But a cure for AIDS; there may never be any.

It is sad that we do not realize
That AIDS could indeed be our demise.
We bury our friends and they turn to dust
We still do not think that it can happen to us.

We continue to let our natural desires
Consume us with their deathly fires.
We must abstain if we are to succeed
We must break the bonds of AIDS to be freed.

Today a man came and spoke with his wife,
I believe that his speech saved my life.

    James Ashley Wilson

People these days

People these days seem to be in a race.
You pass them by and barely notice their face.
As fast as they can, they are in such a hurry.
If you get in their way you will know by the fury.
Keeping up with their work and friends.
Seems as though it will never end.
After many busy years
They stop and shed some tears.
And wonder where time has gone,
For the children have grown up and moved on.
How much of their lives did they miss?
When was their first step, first game or first kiss?
Please do not wait,
Until it's too late!
Go spend a day with your child and have some fun.
Whether it is in the rain, snow, or sun.
Because memories are truly a pleasure
That you will love and always treasure.
Having a child is a wonderful precious gift
That not all of us are lucky enough to get!

    Sherri Orman

Afraid

A child's nightmare locked in a darkened closet.
The child anticipates from his bed in fear as he watches the
Door slowly creep open.
Like the imagination of hearts and the dense sensation of
Darkness, to be afraid is to be blind.
Blind like the rotting corps under the crazy old man's
Basement.
The old man's fear blinded him, put him into a suffocating rage.
Letting evil overtake him and the darkness began to create in
Him,
The image of his mother staring down at him as a new born.
With a twinkle in her eyes from the tears she cried.
She took one last look and left him lying there in the ditch.
Tears burning in the babies eyes.
Fear growing in the child's heart.
Blindness clouding a young man's mind.
Rage and evil possessing an old man's body.
While the child watches the closet door waiting for the fear
To take him away to blindness.

Miranda Anderson

The Heart

They tell me when a bit perplexed to search within my heart.
The brain is just too logical to sense the feeling part.
But the heart is just a muscle like my deltoids or my lat.
Why don't they say to use my quads when figuring this or that.
And the heart is not as pretty as the ones on valentine's day.
And in light of this it's surely not on a gift I'd give away.
Yet every time I ponder, people send me to my heart instead.
They never say to search your brain or feel within your head.
But my brain can clearly tell me that one plus one is two.
And surely it is there that I can figure false from true.
Perhaps that's why so many hearts have broken from the strain,
Of taking on so many tasks belonging to the Brain.

Paula Graves

But For The Grace Of God

Businesses flee the country in droves rationalizing
Leaving thousands out to fend in the cold.
Years of employee loyalty mean naught to corporate down sizing.
That's just the cost of doing business, we're told.

Since getting laid off, he can't make ends meet
And bills, whew! Has he got a plenty.
It's been a steady decline since he was on top of the heap.
Without bad luck, he would not even have any.

He's considered too old for the current job market
But they say he's too young to retire.
He's a walking ghost with resume and cannot forget,
He's become valueless and unfit to hire.

Quite thoroughly he weighs each available option.
Inescapable conclusions remain.
How bitter the taste of life's unfair concoction
That it may drive this poor man insane.

Over the weekend, I made certain inquiry
And from the shocking news was taken aback.
It seems that he sketched a broken heart in his diary
Then died of a heart attack.

Muriel L. Johnson

Untitled

I can kick up a dust with a quick gust.
Create a breeze as I rustle the leaves.
I can stir romance with a soft whisper, or . . .
become calm and still after raging all night.
All of the seasons I transcend.
I am the almighty wind.

Annie L. Simpson

Forgotten Warning

The world is depressed and unforgiving,
An abandoned child refusing its mother's love.
Harsh to those that who would dare to dream and care.
Struggle for the light and for warmth,
The world's creatures try to survive.
A delicate web has been wrought for the survival of all.
Man in his arrogance has tried to change the picture,
And has broken the fragile threads that binds us together.
But there is light in the darkness,
There are those who try and repair what has gone wrong,
Yet many lives cannot be started again,
And much damage cannot be undone.
The children are the future,
But what world do the parents leave for them?
A shadow haunts us all.
Will we listen to warnings in time,
Or will the world, as many frightened and confused children do,
Take the decision out of our hands
And take the life that is its own?

Elizabeth Hibbard

The Evergreen

It's winter here. I stand alone
Among the barks whose leaves have blown
Far off their limbs with season's winds.
For I remain the evergreen
And once a year my wish is seen;
To catch the lights from in the sky
On sleeves of my branches as they pass by.
It's at this time I come to know
I really do not stand alone.
For on my coat still dark and cold
Gather from a distance lights new and old.
It's from their warmth in winter's time
That lets me know this season's mine.
For I remain the evergreen
And once a year my wish is seen.

Donna Bonavita

Seasons

Spring is so meek,
    blossoming, blooming, creating anew;
    at first seeming weak,
    but then tapping summer's shoulder to say, "Here's your cue."

Summer is so proud,
    opening our eyes in the morn;
    its voices burst out loud,
    like a child in a storm.

Autumn is so humble,
    with its array of peaceful, golden hues;
    watching the wind stumble
    in its dance with the leaves to amuse.

Winter is so majestic,
    present in all its glory;
    creeping up quietly, slowly,
    transforming the world into a fairyland story.

We thank our Father for the magic He displays,
    in a forest of spring blossoms, in a meadow of goldenrod.
    In the secrets of nature His glory He portrays—
    Holy Father, Prince of Peace, our Creator, God.

Jennifer Ruth

The Abused Wife

She wondered if anything would
be different tonight as she came in the door.
Would she see anger on his
face and feel harsh blows once more.
She couldn't please him no matter how she tried.
What could she do or say to keep him pacified.
Her self esteem had been destroyed.

She wanted to run and hide.
Her family would not believe her when she tried to tell her side
To them he was so pleasant he appeared the caring kind
He had convinced them she was in a fragile state of mind
She smelled the whiskey on his breath
and could see his bloodshot eyes.
She heard him accuse her of being out with all the guys.
She tried to explain but his patience was too thin.
He grabbed her by the hair and slapped her again and again.
She struggled and fought him and this inflamed him more.
He grabbed her by the arm and threw her to the floor.
He drew the gun from his pocket and waved it above her head.
I'm ending your worthless life he said.
The gun went off and now she's dead, if only someone had listened.

Jessie M. Erwin

One More Tear

Into the long hours of the night
I lost count of all the tears I cried.
They are so painful; they hurt;
They come from deep within my heart.
My gut wrenches with each deep breath.
When will I ever sleep? When will I rest?
Friends tell me I'm on the front lines.
Front lines of a battle, and I can't run and hide.
There is no time to retreat.
To do so would mean a sure defeat.
I've grown weak, my strength is almost gone.
Pressing forward, I pray it won't be long.
When this battle comes to a close
Will I say, faith and integrity I chose?
Help me to endure; give me the strength I need.
God, be my guide, show me Your way, I plead.
Will you, Lord, carry me out from here
As I cry one more tear?

Terry Lamb

A Little Gift From Heaven

Once upon a time the Lord above sent me a gift.
He said that it would bring me strength and give my heart a lift.
He sent it at a time when I was not so sure of me.
I kept on asking what it was, but God said, "Wait and see."

Then all at once it happened and I got my big surprise.
And when I saw the package I could not believe my eyes.
I wanted to unwrap it, but then wondered, "Do I dare?"
For a closer look revealed a sign which read, "Handle With Care."

But God said, "Just be patient and unwrap it nice and slow,
For there are precious gifts inside to give your heart a glow.
The gifts that you will find within are more than what they seem,
And you will come to treasure them more than you'd ever dream."

So with these words I got the nerve to do what must be done,
And found the inside shining out like little rays of sun.
And day by day, and piece by piece, I'd discover something new.
Then all at once it dawned on me — God's gift to me was you!

So when God sends us little gifts from heaven up above,
Accept them ever gracefully and nurture them with love.
For once God sent a gift to me so rare and ever true,
And when I count my blessings — I begin by counting you!

Julie Ann Hammond

Sleep

I heard the roar of the robust wind
And sensed the faint sigh of the clouds.
The misty madness of night rolled in
To wrap the warm world in its shrouds.

I touched my head to a pillow of down,
My mind humming with thoughts of the past.
Will there ever be a day again?
Will tomorrow come at last?

I slowly gave way to the arms of sleep
And traversed the great span of dreams.
The things that had been were no more,
Carefree thoughts like bubbling streams.

I heard the rustle of a fleeting bird
And smelled the fresh fullness of dew.
The specter of night releasing her grip
As blackness was turning to blue.

Jack E. Everling

The Old Men Of Asbury Hall

Every afternoon the men of Asbury gather.
For many, indeed for most, the gait is slow and halting.
Canes and walkers aid the journey,
Hips and knees have been set upon by time
The smooth skin of youth is no more.
Lined faces speak of long eventful lives.

Conversation is quiet, raised eyebrows and laughter punctuate
the long afternoon.
To the very young they speak a foreign tongue -
WPA, ration stamps, and rumble seats.
A wistful look, a smile as happy memories are recalled.

They came to work on time
No calling in sick.
They paid their taxes
They defined "Salt of the Earth!"

It's as if they know they've done well.
Look at these men, these old men of Asbury!
Dignity is in their speech - it is in their bearing.

The way they've lived their lives
These men are role models for all.
These men are my heroes.

Tom Norris

Bridge

There's a bridge in the middle of a forest,
    And it's holding my name,
I sit on one side of it, waiting for my claim;
The side I sat on was my childhood,
    With all my childhood fun, and I always wondered,
    On the other side, would it all be done?
Until one day the time had come,
    for me to make my way across,
As I took my first step,
    I looked back and thought my childhood was lost;
Ahead I saw my future,
    And the confused girl was me,
I was sad and different,
    But that's not the way I wanted to be;
Once more I looked back,
    And astonished I saw my childhood,
As I tried to turn around, I realized I suddenly could;
I walked back over the bridge, and regained the memories,
But turned to see my future,
    And saw the confused girl was laughing and happy on her knees.

Stephanie Kowalski

Tree Of Life

I am awakened by soft gentle showers
Kissed by the warm sunlight.
I suckle the spring rains and absorb the
warm rays to nourish my distant branches.
I have awakened from a sleepy winter.
A new birth of buds adorn my branches.
Soon my limbs will be covered with full blown leaves.
I am green splendor against a blue sky.
My branches will be home for nest and shade
for the soft swaying grasses below.
I am nursing a new birth of seeds.
The first fall of frost will embrace my leaves.
Vibrant colors of red, yellow, orange and brown,
will enhance my beauty.
Soon my leaves will drop to the waiting grasses below.
A new season of saplings, I have reaped.
I'm in the twilight of seasons past.
Standing stately, I braze the bitter chill.
On the edge of winter's eve,
I am embraced by a winter's coat,
With snow covered boughs I sleep.

Shirley Pomer

The Light Of The World

If I employ my life to light just a corner,
    That someone else may see,
If he engages his life to do the same what
    a bright world this would be.

Life was meant to be shining bright and shine
    each day as you go,
Children's trends would follow yours and the
    right way they would know.

Reflecting light is a chain reaction, reflecting
    from life to life,
It keeps everyone from stumbling and saves a
    world of strife.

If everyone would light his candle and pass it
    on from there.
The one to whom you pass it, his darkness would
    certainly disappear.

The Lord is my light; the Psalmist wrote, and
    may this light be unfurled.
His light brightens every life, Jesus the light
    of the world.

Roy M. Alamon

For All Those Apologies Undeserved

For all those nights I lie awake.
Going to Hell, What do I make?
Repent, be good, make peace with the ghost,
But who is the one that dares to boast.

For all those tears of worry I cried.
I'm sorry I stole, I'm sorry I lied.
Confess, devote, be one with the scene,
But what if it all is a siren's scream?

For all those apologies undeserved.
You forced a confession, now what is it worth?
Let go, be sane, bony fingers retract.
Aren't you ashamed of the way that you act?

For all the accused who are damned and away.
The red cloth protect thee from the coming day.
Ones judged, deemed wrong, the clergy ignites,
And all who are left are the ones that will fight.

Melissa Schultz

Rain

Rain.
My heart feels like soft droplets falling never
    endlessly into a black hole.
Rain is supposed to make things grow, and it does!
All my hate, all my anger have found a watery escape.
It flows, never stopping, into my mind,
    sending me into a trance, forcing my hate and anger
    out on those whom my mind says I hate.
No where to run!
No where to hide!
You can't escape your mind, your thoughts, your hate,
Yourself, you cannot escape yourself.
Rain.
I can feel it!
It's coming!
It beats on my chest like a drum,
Pounding...
Pounding...
Until my heart explodes, and out comes the hate...
the anger...
the rain...
out comes the rain...

Amanda Moose

What Is Love?

Love is someone special
    that never questions why;
Love is a rainbow that stretches
    across Gods blue sky;
Love is its pot of gold
    that's hidden deep within;
And love is for all the world
    never to hate again.

Love is a rose that blossoms
    in the spring;
Love is a snow white dove
    and a diamond ring;
Love is a newborn child
    and a happy couple;
And love is giving help
    to someone in trouble.

Love is caring for others and love is forgiving;
Love is for the whole world and love is believing;
Love is for the crippled and the ones who can't see;
Love is for the unwanted; love is for you and me.

Cheyrl Clark

Untitled

With age comes wisdom
In love there's a song
Music brings reality to life that's newly born
Feelings flow toward content
Caring forms a friend
I believe the best gift comes from within one's self
Always give a little bit of you to someone else
Life's given to each individual to lead as they wish
Never settle for anything less then your best
Inspiration comes through careful thought
And peace of mind
Simple pleasures should be shared
There's a special gift each of us bares
That gives us a quality beyond compare

Peggy Kolstee

Locked Away

It doesn't come easy for me to say.
I'm feeling disappointed in you, in all but to many ways.
Hiding your feelings deep down inside, making it so hard
for you to tell me why.

Looking at you heaven and hell.
I can see all your pain, but it's not enough to tell.

Running around hiding inside,
closed up so tight, you can't fight
nothing but hate, anger locked away,
all of your fears are here to stay

Carrie Green

Mindless Understanding

As days drift slowly by down the lazy
river of life,
   Millenniums pass soundlessly into the
oblivion of time.
   Shadows dance perilously on the brink of
consumption.
   Into the insane rush of history.

Time is history,
   but history is lost.
Mangled, distorted bits of life's untold truths
flitter in, out, dying and living again.
   Failing resurrection in faithless destiny
now and forever.

Valerie Ann MacNeill

Memories

Try to catch a memory going by
   See the spirit fly
The old man shows his smile
   There's a bride walking down the aisle
A feeling of pleasure or pain
   This way, we all stay sane
These thoughts of histories past
   Our lives we live go by so fast
    So fast

Sometimes its hard to remember
   Even the fire's last burning ember
All the things we've learned, there is too much
   And what about all the soul's we've touched
So many names and faces I no longer know
   I am only sure I miss them so
Now as I go to sea, the sail climbs the mast
   I can feel my heart finding peace at last
    At last

Greg Smith

Seaward Bound

The rays of morning shine across the hills,
a freshness comes from off the open sea,
the salt spray breaks upon the rolling deck,
a spanking wind is blowing fast and free.

The captain stands upon the quarter deck,
his stance attuned to every sight and sound,
the white sails fill and billow in the wind,
and white gulls swoop and circle all around.

Now all the rushing channel lies behind,
beyond them rolls the wide and boundless sea,
from this day forth the ocean is their home;
above them flies the black flag, blowing free.

Diantha James

Untitled

Remember the fields?
The pastures of yesterday?
The rambling, the running?
The timelessness of summer days?
Where did they go, those wondrous moments.

The fields are still green,
The pastures still there,
The creeks still run their course.
Have we just grown old, aged?
Do those memories change with age's vision?

I want to run through those fields,
Recapture the carefree spirit of then.
But we cannot return to days of old.

It is gone. The past is gone,
Never to return. It is gone.
Gone beyond me, gone beyond you.
Yet the memories linger.

Oh! It is all still there
Waiting for others younger than we.
Yes! To become their memories.

Ruby Jones King

Strength

As I sit and think of you,
My heart is filled with longing.

I miss your touch, your embrace;
   The tender moments that have become all too scare.

I am weak in your absence;
   The complexity of day to day life overwhelms me.

I have come to depend on your guidance;
   The encouragement that I receive from you gives me
    Courage, and strength.

I look forward to a day in the future:

The day that I can again feel your touch, your loving embrace;
   And share the tender moments that I have come to enjoy.

The day that I can again seek your guidance;
   And the encouragement that helps me through my weaker
   moments.

    The day that I can again be strong!

Lisa Gerstenberger

Genesis 2000

From an invisible and spaceless space I came,
Into a visible presence - contained and framed.
Solid and senses, a spiritual extension.

Now I know that I know, yet search to remember
That I have a time and a season - a rhyme and a reason,
To practice the presence
Of God
In these five and more senses.

When I was seven, about then I was told,
Your father's in heaven —
Now practice the presence,
Of God in your senses,
And slowly began to spiritually unfold.

When I knew what I had always known
That my soul was complete and whole,
Then it was done and off into spaceless space I spun,
To come face to face with infinite love - Our Father -
And as below, it was from above,
Thy will be done
And God and I were always one.

Jean Drews

Dear God

On cold, crisp nights you make me warm. You have given
me a love that no one could ever give me. When I'm sad you
make me happy. You know my every thought, wish, and dream.
You know my future and my past. When I'm lonely you bring
me to the light of joy. When I'm happy you make my smile
run deeper. Even when I go against you, you are there. You
lead me back to the path of rejoicing. You are wherever I
am. You listen to me always, never tiring of my meager
voice. I look up at the clouds of silk and you are there.
I look at the ground of clay and you are there. I look at
the trees, and flowers, and all I can see is you're wonderful
and generous being. People say you are not real, that you
are just a hoax. But I know you're real, as solid as a line.
I give you my life to do as you please because I know you
know what's best for me . . .

Melissa A. Swiecicki

Spring

Spring is here you can always tell,
by the way the flowers in your garden smell.
Birds in the trees singing their songs,
they seem so happy, they can do no wrong.
Many colorful kites all across the sky,
Watching as the breeze carries them high.
It's a wonderful time to enjoy natures sights,
warm beautiful days, and soft cool nights.
The sun slowly goes as night starts to fall,
it's nice to know Spring can be enjoyed by us all.
Looking at the full moon so shiny and round,
listening to the crickets as they make their own sound.
Nature is beautiful, done the Lords way,
how I wish Spring could be everyday.

Francine Ganious

Together Forever

We all have friends that live off each other,
trust, hate, and hurt one another,
we cry, scream, feel each others pain.
Some move away, some just don't get along
We all thought that we were a family,
we took care for one another.
Until one day one moved away,
then one went away.
Ever since that two months,
nothing's been the same.
But in our hearts we will always know,
that through sun, dark, rain or snow,
together as friends that will always show.

Wendy Weigert

Night Sea

The sun sets into the ocean

Like a shade drawn down to hide a lit room
The dark sky is pulled down around us
Until finally the last flicker of light goes out

Clouds make the sky unusually dark

Like the crack of lightening through a still sky
Frothing waves beat against the sand with a thunderous sound
Returning to the sea only to repeat its destiny

With passing of time the clouds have parted

The moon and stars reflect upon the now calm sea
Waves have turned to ripples
Thunderous sounds are now but a whisper

Gail Lynn Farnsworth

Angela

Trying to remember
what it was, or why,
that pushed me over the edge.
Which was more like a slope
(because an edge would be too easy)
sliding down and all of a sudden
the water is up to my pierced naval
distorting my feet into two swollen,
wavy masses, cold water
jerking my body awake
from the sedative of hallway sounds,
pushed down my throat like your words.
Looking up for a face to say; "it's ok"
But all I see are glossy pictures
cut from some 3 dollars and 50 cent' magazine,
Save a lifetime of embarrassment,
if you order now, hanging in quiet drama on the wall.
Like my hair did before the wind won the battle over
the sticky chemicals, before I dyed it,
because God forbid, I by myself.

Tara Trevoy-Vieira

Falling

Leaves of gold, striving for red
Racing the wind, defying their end
Crisp, frosty mornings, horses puffing steam
Wisps of fragrant smoke
Wise, old leaves scurry into the stream

The sunlight reminds of summers golden days
A breeze pushes clouds across
Whispering, it was just a phase

Creatures moving quickly
They seem to know what is to be
Darkness coming sooner
Squirrels run through the trees

With a heavy thump
Apples echo each other
As they fall to the ground
A chill turns children's faces red
Though many smiles are found
Leaf piles are toys of the season
A scattering of powder gently falls
Hinting of winters fun.

Joseph F. Zielke

Solid Silence, You Soothe My Soul

The jumbled, jangled remnants of the day can find voice and
    escape into your space.
Fated to bang around in my head no more, the words can
    slowly leak out or stay to dance in dreams.

Dreams are funny things, finishing undone events, or
    starting those not yet begun.
Combining segments of past and future in puzzle pieces of your life.
We are not meant to see the finished puzzle.

The empty silence of night lets the dreams fly to their
    non-existant limits.
Silence is endless and dreams are too.

Rhonda L. Stephens

The Love That Was So True

They met and loved in an instant,
They grew together as one,
Through good times and bad,
Their hearts were full of love,
Like no others have had.

There were things they did not do,
Things they did too much,
But neither of them could deny,
The love that was so true,
And forever in their lives.

Not everything is perfect,
And this love was not left out,
Things did get bad,
Way out of hand,
And left one mad, one sad.

Over time the love,
Began to show its way through,
The two were brought together,
To start again,
The love that was so true.

Lori Schwartz

Living In A World Of Darkness

Living in a world of darkness,
So dark that I can't see.
Dying in a world of shadows,
won't someone just kill me?

Surrounded by a world of deafness,
Can no one hear my screams?
Dying in a world of blindness,
Will I ever be seen?

Trying in a world of hopelessness,
Falling into a pool of despair.
Dying in a world of cruelness,
Why isn't anyone there?

Dying in a world of darkness,
So dark that I can't see.
Dying in a world of shadows,
Someone just killed me!

Tiffany J. Wysong

Broken Dreams

I found myself in a strange and wondrous dream,
In a dark, elfin forest of giant trees and moonbeams,
Of knights and dragons, beauties and beasts,
Where unicorns play, and kings feast.

I dream of castles that rise from the mists,
Tragic loves and the last bittersweet kiss,
Of waterfalls and sparkling pools in fern-filled glens,
Of hearts that are broken and do not mend.

I dream and yearn for a love that is forever,
Of whispers of love and two souls together,
That even death cannot overcome;
This love I know has been found by some.

I awaken and reach to find it all a dream,
Back in the reality of my world I could scream,
What is lost is not to be found,
Of love's whispers, there is not a sound.

I try to recapture that fantasy so sweet,
But dreams and reality will never meet,
And I find my way is empty and lost,

Cheryl Allison

LIFE

I look at myself and I see no smile, I guess it hasn't been there for a while.

My feeling inside are of sorrow and pain, just of incredible emotional strain.

I once was a person filled with happiness and care,
but through years of heartbreak, it's no longer there.

I've tried so hard to be real strong but these years of being a
walking mat, I just can't go on.

Can't they see what they've done to me?
They've ripped and shredded my sanity.

I just want to run so far away and never look back on mistakes of today.

I can't be this rock they expect me to be
because with years of erosion, there's nothing left of me.

It's sad to say I'm at the end of my rope,
I look back over the years and say, "Man, how did I cope?"

What did I do to deserve all this?
I never thought my life could become such a mess.

I try to pull myself out of this hole that I'm in
but they keep pushing me down and kicking me again and again.

One of these days I'll come back and be strong.
I'll be the person they expected all along.

Then I'll kick sand in their faces and walk out the door.
I'll have my life back, and that's what I live for.

Sarah Bays

My Little Girl

Looking back at my life and all its changes,
There were many, some good, some bad.

But, it's easy to say, my proudest moment,
Was when I became a Dad.

The birth of my daughter, my little girl,
So special in every way,

Her eyes so bright, as blue as the sky,
And her smile as full as the day.

So full of love and the spirit of life,
She blooms like a red rose in spring;

A voice that fills the air with joy,
Like the sound of birds when they sing.

Thank you God, you've given me a miracle,
In her I see my purpose for each day;

Through you I pledge to her all my love,
And together our faith will show her the way.

C. Richard Donlavey

I Am The Same

I may not see like you,
or hear like you,
or walk like you,
but I am the same.

I may use my fingers to read because I cannot see.
I may use my hands to talk because I cannot hear.
I may use a wheelchair because I cannot walk
but I am the same!

Do not be afraid of me you see...
I do hurt like you,
and cry like you,
but most of all,
what I really want is for you to come talk to me...
play with me and be my friend.
You see,
we are the same!

Lori Groth

456

My Dream Dog

My dream dog
The golden retriever
With the soft golden fur
That rests so gently on her.

Her long floppy ears
Hang so delicately from her head,
Her tail sways gently
As she sits in her bed.

She stares out of the window,
Lost and confused
She does humorous tricks
As peoples pass, rather amused.

I beg my parents,
To buy my dream dog
They say no, no, no,
But my mind does not fog.

More days pass by
The dog still is lonely
She needs an owner badly
I'm going to be her owner one day, me only.

Meghan Doherty

My Garden Of Friendship

My friend, you're such a flower rare,
Growing in the Garden, which I have groomed
For you bring such joy, to the things you touch
By your loyalty, I assume!
So, I'll take good care of my flowers, be they such —
For I know, twill always be one there —
Who grows dearer and means to me, oh, so much!
And, as I walk among my flower rare,
I will find but such a very few,
That I'd never, never trade
The old one for the new,
So, as the old years pass away
And along comes the new;
There will always be room in my garden
For a dear friend, such as you!

Doris Walker

The Voice That Whisper

Reach for me, only if you will, the scars
you have to bare, there is a price you
have to pay, the load would not be heavy
and your eyes would not be teary.
Reach for me, there is hope for the weary.

Time just moves things along, you may say,
time is a measuring stick.

Time give nothing back, ahead time goes,
never looking back, time has no pity about
events as she moves at the same gait, something
always trying to keep up, with time, time outlast
them all, reach for me, it I, not time you should pick.

Time has nothing to share, time just runs,
never tiring, never reaching its end.

It is not in time, people tries to be like me,
"In their own time" reach for me, I am the friend.

Reach for me, I have outstretched hands, matter
of fact, I am standing at your door knocking.

Reach for me, you will struggle, you have tried it all,
in me is where it's at, not in time, you see time is just ticking.

Donnell Linthecome

A Gargoyle

She sits perched above for few to see
Her heart and skin made by you and me
Ever so vigilantly she stares
always expecting the unaware
through day and night
she dreams and prays
of one more chance
to let her sweet heart take flight

The city she see's
through her large vacant eyes
watching closely to one final beat
as images of her countless rapes
streak through her mind
as her body and soul
plummet to the street

Finally she is in peace
and as the coroner makes one final sweep says
Poor Poor Margo now you are dead
little did you know that this was really self defeat

Juan H. Zamudio

Something's Missing...

Feel empty deep inside here...
Feel sad...lonely...needy...full of strife.
    Something's missing from my life.

Heart is heavy...weighted down.
Smile has lost its way to my face.
    Something's missing from my life.

Clouds hanging over...following me around.
It's always raining in my space.
    Something's missing from my life.

Joy ran away. Love escaped.
Heartache took their place.
    Something's missing from my life.

I've tried and tried to ignore the facts.
But there's nothing I can do.
    Something's missing from my life...

        And I know now...It's you.

Oseye Mchawi

Running Away

I am running, it is all I seem to know.
Your always there, yet still I run away.
I run away to try to hide,
but you always find me!

Why do I continue to run?
There is no place to hide,
    that you will not find me.

What am I scared of?
You are so loving, and understanding.
You will always be there.

I know I need you, yet I run.
You have picked me up out of the rain.

Please Father, humble me, remind me, how you rescued me.
You rescued me from the bottom.
Help me to be thankful and humble.

I'm running, but not from you - To You!
And there you are,
With open arms ready to rescue me again.

Whenever I start to run from you
Humble me, remind me, how you rescued me.

Rebekah Melton

Time

In youth we wondered if time could pass fast enough?
If the years ahead would hold our dreams?
The future seemed far and hard to grasp.
Pondering anxiously, trying to peer into time.
Running and pushing to catch the future.
Turning around the find it has caught up with you.
Suddenly realizing it's passing too fast.
The hopes of youth become adult reality.
Some as we expect, but most an alarming disillusion.
The anticipation for the future decreases with the lack of
  lives vital visions.
Time races by with out direction.
The only way to impede times velocity,
  is to discover new expectations.

Carolyn Stewart Simpson

The Sun, The Moon And The Angel

Gasping at the top of my lungs as if the moon were my
diary and the angel was my witness, I give my soul to the sun,
the moon and the angel. As for my pity, I spit on the Devil
along with my humiliation and my cries. I refuse to live my life
with rules to live by and philosophies of how I will turn out.
The sun, the moon and the angel are my sky. My eyes are blind
but I can see. I am paralyzed not by movement but by fear of
how to live and how to die.

I am not a doll which you envy. I am the sun, the moon
and the angel. A piece of wing, a smile to make me cry, and a
rock to hold me down in the heart of the world. I am the
beginning of a new creation.

Stutts

Because Of Our People

It has been our fault, you know it was
We never gave them a reason, why, or because
We took their land, freedom, and their nation
And we put them away on a reservation
Yes, we changed their way of life and being
that's what I wish, everyone was seeing
We never gave them a right, to do what they pleased
Instead of love and friendship, we killed and seized
We blame them for wrong our people did
We auctioned them off for the highest bid
We abused them and beat them until they were red
And this is something our history books haven't said
We did the wrong, instead of the right
We never gave them a chance to fight
We built our houses, roads, and towns
And in their lives, these things weren't found
They can make the rain come down from a dance
They know enough to be given a second chance
So now you know about our nations past
For the years have gone by, all so fast...

Lynnette J. Choate

My Big League Boy

As my son plays ball as best as he can
I know it won't be long before he's a man

He'll hang up his glove and his baseball bat
And go out into the world to "see where it's at"

There will be no more trips to the Little League Park
Or coming home from practice way after dark

No more gleaming "That's my son"
The little boy who just hit a home run

No more running bases as fast as he can
That Little League player will soon be "my man"

Alexa McCartney

What Life Means To Me

What life means to me
There is a part of my
life where the spirit is
  allowed to be free
and indeed it's something
to be seen I am always
the same as for many it
seems like they are
striving for this inner spirit
I have in me I am
problem free and my
life is tranquil like
a calm sea for most
it's hard to perceive
I can indeed say I have
freedom like ray's of sunshine
beaming down on me
and like fresh cut flowers colorful and arranged in
a vase for they may not last long as for my spirit every
day it keep's me strong.

Alberta Williams

Untitled

So young, so pure
going way before his time.
Never knowing, never seeing
what life would bring by.
He was brave, he was strong
never shedding a tear.
But all the tragedy, all the pain
aged him before his years.
Why go so soon
stay and fight.
Let someone special show you the light.
You had your friends, the people who care.
But more than that, I was there.
I tried my best, and I let you down.
Yet all my efforts you got around.
All my pain and all my tears
You've seen from up above.
But while you were here,
you never saw my love.

Brook E. Hull

Anybody There

Is anybody out there? I'm asking in pain
My life is dreadful and I'm going insane
The name calling and grief it hurts;
The unhappiness and sorrow is worse.

People don't know the way I feel
They don't understand that my pain is real;
My prayers aren't answered, they just drift away
I'm always begging for happiness to stay

I'm really very lonely and I need a friend
So that my battle with happiness will win
I cry myself to sleep at nights
Just dreading the heartache at the next day's light

Is anybody out there? I need your love
Not your pushes or even a shove.
I'm begging you to answer me please,
So that all my pain can rest at ease.

Allison Bowling

Our Love Can

Our love can cause tears of joy to flow down smiling cheeks
into a steamy pool of passionate desires.
Our love can sink into the deep abyss of a silent argument
only to rise on the waves of apologetic expressions.
Our love can soar high above the bombardment of daily stress,
past the ozone layer of unforeseen failures,
and rest on the pillowy clouds of our comfortable companionship.

Our love can be static clinging together, electrically flowing,
charged with excitement, and forever letting the sparks fly.
Our love can accelerate down the love lane of sorrow, past the
salvage yard to broken hearts, and pull safely into the parking
lot of commitment, trust and compromise.

Our love can be counted on when you add up years of devotion,
when you multiply moments of ecstasy, when you subtract anger and
anxiety, when you divide time and energy.

When it's all summed up,
Our love can never end.

Paul L. Johnson

Computer Cowboy

Howdy, I'm Steve, a computer cowboy,
   an real compact an sturdy.
Yeah, I'm all booted up
   an wearin' ma big old stepson hat.
I'm a good old boy and a real straight shooter
   out on the internet.

Herdin' about 10,000 long horn mega bytes
   an 100 K's a ram.
Switch on early, don't never surge,
   until I've had ma coffee.

Ride an ink jet printer,
   a real fine dos.
An pardner, can he ever rom.
   Wipe em down with a floppy disk.
Then feed em a big red apple.

Wanna watch where ya walk'n, son.
   Ya jist stepped in a micro chip
An that's jist plain mo-dum.

John Allan Dodds

From A Mother's Eyes

Life is created; a child is conceived.
Oh, the miracle of birth and life!
It has always been and is still believed
The greatest joy of a husband and wife.

The excitement of watching our child as it grows.
Yet, it wasn't hard to have guessed
That only the Giver of Life truly knows
How much we have both been blessed.

Our baby's first smile as I tickle its face.
It responds with a "gaa" and a "coo".
A memory that time on earth can't erase.
"Oh, Hon, it looks a lot like you!"

Unexpected, our child takes that first shaky step.
Oh, to suspend those moments in time!
Running and jumping - such energy and pep
Developing strong like a flowing rhyme.

As its mother, it comes as no surprise
And it's just my opinion, you see,
That envisioning from a mother's eyes,
It'll grow up to be as cute as me!

Dan Myers

First Love

Relationships are like roses,
they are beautiful before they die.

When they are in bloom they will make you smile,
when they are gone they will make you cry.

Red in the rose symbolizes passion and love,
which only you can earn.

Or perhaps a roaring fire,
which can also make you burn.

People choose to ignore the thorns,
from the rose that's far from plain.

Not realizing that even beautiful things,
can cause you grief and pain.

Diane Croteau

The Lonely Tree

Where's my family, said the tree all alone!
Bulldozers and men took them.
Now, they're all gone.

They chopped down the forest
that provide the shade.
Products, they said, needed to be made.

They forgot about the oxygen we make,
and the soil erosion we prevent.
Bent on making money - that's not heaven sent.

The land will turn to dust.
Then they'll remember us.
They have to! They must!

Navada Heflin

A Place To Go

While you're away, I have a place to go
a place where only, you and I know
I'll go there when I'm feeling blue
I'll go there as I'm missing you

This place is filled with memories spent
of places where, you and I went
this place is held within my heart
where memories of you, will never part

Until you return, I've a place to go
a place of memories, you and I know
I visit there, as I'm missing you
I visit there as I'm feeling blue

As I travel to this memory place
joy comes to my heart, a smile crosses my face
for these memories are, so filled with you
I'll love you darling, all eternity through!

Joseph E. Brown

Relief

My life feels like a jar
with the lid closed tightly on my emotions;
making sure that none of them escape.

At any point, trying to open this lid
and let a particular emotion out,
causes a mass exodus of feelings
which usually results in a tearduct leak.

But now I have found relief,
a way to open the lid one emotion at a time.
all I need to do is to ask my Lord and Savior for help:
He stays with me through it all — emotion after emotion!

Angela C. Fix

A Call To Character

Deception, lies, they bring not peace
Desertion, shame, one can't release

A family whole of one accord
Fragmented family, and then ignored

Voices, choices, we all hear
Justification, selfish motives fear

That which is wrong and told its right
Don't help the tears in the depth of night

Philosophies dictated by fraudulent morality
Leaves a home a statistical fatality

A noble nation falling to desolation
Foundations of home with new interpretation

Ancestral folly of generations past
Now are worse than the first to last

Oh who will rebuild among the ruin?
Hearts once true and genuine?

Jhodi Riggins

Miracles

Miracles happen every single day
The Lord touches our lives in a special way
With Angels at His command night and day
He brings his Chosen ones back to His narrow way

A way that only is narrow through this world's view
With people so blind who cannot see
The greatest Blessings await them from His high view
Just believe in Miracles one cannot see

Only believe with all your heart
With your eyes fixed on the Star in the sky
The mountain will fall into the sea
The Miracles will happen right before your eye

Not by Might nor by Power
But by my Spirit says the Lord Almighty
For when you are weak, he'll make you strong from Heaven
No mountain, however high, can stand says Zachariah 4:7

The people of this world say seeing is believing
But God in Heaven says believing is seeing

Monique Yannotti

Eyes Of The Unseen Wolf

There's a sound in the distance
    dropped
    like a rock
      yet soft as a shadow
    darkly running
    down cliffs

A moment...a stillness...a shift
    then it's gone.

...No sparrow's scion ever hears
    the Indian, who misses the twig
    the steel trap, unsprung by its prey
    or
    the cry of the one not stung by the wasp.

Lorraine Barrie

Do Not Worry

In the early morn, when at first you awake,
If I am not there
Do not fret, for I am safe.
If throughout the lonely day, I never show
Please do not search me out,
For I am not alone.

Renee Odom

As I Cry Out To The World

As I cry out to the world no one hears my call
No one pays attention when I stumble and when I fall

I want someone to love me, I want something to care
I want to know they will always be there

I am so lonely I don't know what to do
I only wish I had a wonderful life like you

If you share some of your joy, I'll share my sorrow
I promise I won't keep it long, I'll give it back tomorrow

As I cry out to the world I want someone to hear
To pull me close and to let me now they'll always be near

Jessica Jefferson

Sonnet

Fruitful branches open wide,
Reaching to the solitary, helpless leaves.
A new place for me to hide,
So different from all the other trees.
Why did you love? Why did you care?
A withered leaf, a broken heart,
Repairing the pieces, this tree is rare,
Until the wind blew, and tore us apart.
Why I fly the way I do,
I left you lonely as I once was.
I had no choice, the wind just blew,
I never meant to fly, no leaf ever does,
Life: quicker than the wink of an eye.
The story of love: hello and good-bye.

Caroline E. McDaniels

To A Child

Dream a dream, oh silent one, the peace child you may be,
   occurred from in thy mother's womb the future's held in thee
As a child you will observe the colors of the rod,
   bold and lustrous profound by the eyes of God
Time abiding, let it not, or linger in the mist,
   reach out beyond your boundaries leave no border to resist
Ponder all creations with strength unsubdued,
   pour your soul into the earth and shower every hue
Follow every rainbow to the lucky pot of gold,
   for in the midst of emptiness through eyes of His behold
Look over every crevice and stitching of each cloud,
   and under Heaven's glory lope against a daisy shroud

Sara McMinn

From The Tree

I know you are watching me from behind your veil
Your head bent down toward earth,
Beckoning to me and the sword that I carry,
Longing to be pierced and filled with my life.

Stalking you with a magnet heart
According to instructions from before time that were
Burned into body memory with the heat of the first explosion
That brought the dance of opposites.

You in your rain forest
Dripping with juices of forbidden fruits
So sweet to the taste
Impossible to refuse.

I spy you from the tree at the edge of my desert
Across the gulf of an endless river
And I long to fall on you hard
To drink the blood nectar of your flowering.

We are bound to solve this unsolvable puzzle
Let us build a bridge across the river.

Matthew Fox

Visions

I am searching for microscopic visions.
Butterfly wings, to dance in my minds eye.
A dream perhaps of fuzzy cattails,
dividing the skyline.
Which in all its greatness,
has no beginning,
nor an end.
Lily pads that float in their own dimension.
Enduring only the space to survive.
Tiny yellow budding flowers,
To meaningful to pick.
Dare I tempt my fate,
The exception in my mind,
To pick the yellow sun.

Laura Kraklau

The Writing On The Wall

A masterpiece each and every day
Divers colors all array
Shining so bright and perfectly clear
sights to behold awesomely dear.
It's the writing on the wall.

As time has passed no sights has changed
a thought to gather unsealed unarranged
Some unaware of the benefit of it all
Cannot see the writing on the wall.

In troubled times when things aren't fair
lift up your head to glance and stare
at the wonderful works where blessings fall
Look up! Take courage,
see the writing on the wall.

The door has been opened, your wishes sent
Now wait on the answer and all that is meant
for soon you will see and understand it all
It's in the Master's hand, who does the writing on the wall.

Gloria Young

Love Is Never Really Black Or White

Life's experiences happen in many shades of gray,
For Love, is never really Black or White.

The Choices I let you make and the Paths you let me take.
Sometimes we stray, but silently for the other we pray.

At times you are the rock that will not break,
White, I am the willow that will not weep.

The promises that you may want to make and keep,
I've chosen to let sleep.
And the choices that one may often times regret,
You choose gracefully to forget.

For we understand Our love, Our life we give,
That the other may live.

Together Our Paths will always flow.
And Our thoughts, the other will always know.

The mountains, they are not so steep
When the Colour of our eyes meet.

You and I apologize to each other not.
For our past to touch, we know would be unfair.

And as Friends, the burdens and joys we will always share.
After all, Love is never really Black or White.

Kyrna A. Ball

Terrell's First Day Of High School

Today's the first day and everything's gone wrong.
But I have to admit, I really look the Bomb.
I need my program card, I gotta get to class,
If they don't give it to me fast,
I'm gonna kick some a.

I'm tired and sick, I'm sick and tired
they keep messing with me
I'm gonna get them fired.
When I saw all those people in front of the place,
I couldn't believe that I didn't know anybody's face.

I went in the store and bought a lollipop
when I came back out, the fear just stopped.
I walked to the front, marched up the stairs,
when I got to the top, I knew all the people there.

All the people I knew were from the "5", (JHS 145),
they were all swarming, like bees to a hive.

Now it's time for me to end this rhyme,
I can't be late, It's Lunch time.

Terrell Vickers

Prophet's Song

To hear the faint and distant cries
of headless men to be,
'tis to rectify the weeping eyes
of prophets that could see.

The home called earth has stood for time,
but longer 'twill no more.
So yes indeed, take this in head,
go barricade thou door.

When eyes doth see impending doom,
dark days ahead await.
'Cause evil known in hell to loom
shall bust the cosmic gate.

Now I have come to warn with song,
thee young and eager ears.
To pass abroad the torch so long,
forever through the years.

Necrosis with its devils bring
the end to all that's seen.
So remember time, thy pleading psalm,
forever mote it be.

Christopher W. Valentine

Life's Blueprint

I fall asleep at night saying my prayers
Hoping against hope and asking
That tomorrow I can just climb the stairs.

I awake in the morning wondering about the new day.
Wondering what is in store for me.
Wondering if I chose the right way.

I guess I feel that whatever has happened to me
Is just another step in God's master plan
And what He wants me to be.

And if I can only make the best of wherever I go.
And if I can only see the good in whoever I know.

I feel that perhaps I will have taken my space,
And made the world a much better place.

Just like a blueprint of a house not yet a home,
Until God is finished with me,
I will continue to roam.

Radona

461

Sitting At The Window

Sometimes at the window I do sit,
Pondering over the when's, why's, and where's,
In hopes to answer life's bouts of fit.
Miles I dare say I can see,
Some as real as you and me.
Most, however, are as far and distant
As yonder images in my head.
People gone, people yet to come,
Flutter through my window
Like haunting spirits that make me dumb.
Answers for this world, to me do elude,
So persist I will to sit at the window
And ponder I shall to conclude;
Life is not of what you make it,
Life makes us all as we take it.

Stacy A. Olson

The Power Of Our Love Together

The tears that fall are for the one that I love. Wanting
to be near you, needing to feel your love with-in me. Seeing
the love in your eyes hoping it will never end. Hearing
those soft whisper's of, "I Love You", beneath each other's
breath; hoping each other can hear.

Listening to the notes of our love that we have created
together; knowing deep inside it will last forever.

The soft words, the gentleness of your touch, and your
love for me and mine for you.

The happiness that overwhelms each other's soul keeps
us strong when we're apart, and loving each other when we're together.

Knowing we will be together when we are
apart allows our love to overpower anything
that comes with-in each other's soul.

Together we walk in the power of our love, forever!

Carisa Thesing

D-i-v-o-r-c-e

Divorce Lyrics are written about in popular songs
Divorce We hear in headlines from news stand and t.v.
Divorce Lawyers encourage. Courtrooms agree
Divorce The wife seeks to be free. To allow growth with in
Divorce Husbands hate to force, alimony to pay
Divorce Oft-talked about at ones place of work
Divorce Children complain, feelings of hurt, hard to cure
Divorce A word that means a breaking of a home
Divorce Effects hot just one, but a family as a whole
Divorce The course of pain, tears, emotion stirred
Divorce So common, yet hard to face, to understand
Divorce Sets apart a very special vow
Divorce Importantly talked about in a Sacred book
  Many unaware of this, that is why we see
Divorce Lyrics are written about in popular songs
Divorce We hear in headlines from news stand and t.v.
Divorce If analyzed from God's Sacred Book "The Bible"
Divorce It wouldn't be so popular, it would be
  More of a rarity!

Dorothy Strode

Departing

I wish you didn't have to go,
I know I'm going to miss you so.
You'll be gone before I know it,
I'll feel bad, but I'll try not to show it.

I really love you with all my heart,
and I really hate to see you part.
But this is something that has to be done,
If only it could be more fun.

Michele A. Veliky

The Sun...

Today the sun will set, but not on
the world. On a life, a life that touched the
hearts and souls of someone, somewhere.

Today the sun will set with a hope for
a better tomorrow, with a hope for peace. The
sun will set one last time on someone special,
who had a gift.

The gift to touch the hearts of everyone
he knew. The distinguishing way to tell
a person he knew what you were going
through or how you felt.

Today the sun has set for one last time,
leaving only a memory, but it will set
with a glimmer of glory and faith, with peace
hope and love.

Today the sun has set for the last time,
one someone special who loved everyone
and everything. Tomorrow the sun
will set with love and compassion.

Michelle Schobert

Hearts

Hearts are soft hearts are tender
But that's a whole different gender
Hearts can love and hearts can give love
But nobody loves the heart that I love
Hearts can be given and hearts can be taken
But that gives life to the human race
Hearts beat fast and hearts beat slow
And that is very clear
People only have one heart
It's a jolly heart gives you life and love
Some people say hearts are fatal
Some people say hearts are famous
Hearts can do glorious things if
You use them right
Hearts are good hearts are great
That's what keeps the human race

Holly Hughes

Disrespect

Stiff, rough, always there . . .
The shell of the void which covers them,
Which keeps me out, which keeps me out,
Has driven me away.
And in my place a sobbing child
Desolate over the sorrows of everyday human interaction,
Pitiful because of the wrongs she has not done,
Miserable as she cannot be what they require.
More than tears, and more than a frown, and more than the world
    which casts her down
And more than the others that "just say no" . . .
Just more — that's all that she can be.
And they tell her that there's nothing she can do.
They tell her that "some people are just like that!"
She wants to say
    "You're as bad as them,"
But she just walks away.
Goes home to bed, and then to sleep . . .
Wipes away her heart so
she won't fall to pieces.

Jessi Harper

Who...Me?

Meaning is just a word expressed through thought and action
Feeling disappointed, ashamed, or loved is more than one's
satisfaction.
The hurting pain of your rejection
a tear peeks from my eyes, knowing you're my creation
but, is it me who casts the feeling
of bitterness to show you're my last and only meaning?

My creation, why have you darken so?
Is thee eyes blurry or I just don't know.
Am I too old to realize and understand
true love I have for no woman nor man

Yet, meaning is a word expressed through thought and action
but this feeling is Me with pure bitterness and no satisfaction.
So...Who am I?

Sierra Cotton

Loved Ones

Loved ones is a precious group,
They are sometime narrowed to a very few.

Different things happen to them,
When their lives seem lost and dim.

Loved ones you cannot forget,
They live and dream of things not yet.

They gather sometime to pay tribute
to the ones gone on before,
Rejoicing and reminiscing with each
other once more.

Misfortune comes sometime without any warning,
But rest assure, God is right there
just before the dawning.

Happiness flows when loved one meet,
That is how it is going to be,
When we sit at Jesus feet.

Willie B. Fleetin

Sleepless

I'm trying to get you into bed
but dear heart I'm already there
then let me climb in behind you
yes that would only be fair
to warm and embrace you gently
to aid in your sleep throughout the night
as I would only consider leaving
at the first hint of morning's light

To dispel all said rumors
of what's lost won't be found again
free your mind of all conscious efforts
and throw said rumors into the winds

In a moment or two you should be sleeping
dreaming of lands so far away
embracing new bodies and kissing new faces
and giving your heart a chance to be swayed
experiencing all these new sensations
long past the streets where you play
to be awaken by a nudge and a soothing voice
wake up, time to begin a new day

Paulette Bryant

Who Is She?

She's someone who is always there,
Someone who listens and someone who cares
She's watched me grow, from day one,
And she's helped me with my own son

She's there for me whenever I call,
Whether I am happy, sad or have taken a fall
She's talked and laughed with me through my tears,
What would I have done without her all these years?

Through these years, we've grown quite close,
And shared lots of love and fun
Can you tell who she is now or
Need I go on?

Who is this person, you might ask?
She's someone who's like no other.
Not only has she become my friend for life,
But you see, she is my mother!

Sharon K. Tuohy

Erase The Hate

Hatred still grows more and more,
And won't stop until we seem to even the score.
Crying, bleeding, and aching with fear,
The songs of love we do not hear.
Still bleeding from the bullets of war,
And we don't even know what we're fighting for.
"Hey, that's life," the old men say.
They're lucky . . . they've grown old and grey.
"Why?" a little boy thinks . . . "Why me?"
"All I want to do is see
Why we hurt each other like this.
Why can't we fire and then just miss?
I wish that we would look around,
At what we've done and what we've found.
I think that we could change our fate,
If only we'd "Erase The Hate."

Samiera Kookasemkit

Fisherman's Twenty-Third Psalm

The Lord is a Fisherman,
So I'll not want for good fishing.
He maketh me to lie about my fishing,
He leadeth me to fish in still waters,
He cleaneth my fish.
He leadeth me in paths that lead to the best fishing holes.
Yea, though I hike in the Rocky Mountains,
I will still catch fish.
Thou art with me when I fish in the Gulf of Mexico,
Thy rod and thy reel and Thy Flies
Are my best fishing tackle.
Thou preparest a table before me laden with catfish and hush puppies,
Thou annointest my head with fish oil,
My cup runneth over with joy at every good catch.
Surely good fishing will follow me all the days of my life
And I will enjoy the great outdoors forever.

Paul Eugene Ehly

Books

Books are like magical places far, far away.
They are like brain surgeons opening your imagination.
Books are like the bait on a fishing pole and you grab it,
then you're hooked, and you can't get away.
Book are wonderful tools that are always there.

Janelle Wadas

Summer Days And Nights

The sun was hot and bright today,
So we swim in a cool, clean pool.

Afterwards we were very hungry,
So we went inside and ate lunch.

We layed on a hill and saw pictures in the
clouds.
We decided to draw the pictures that we saw.

That night the sunset was so beautiful,
We stayed out and watched it as we felt the cool
Gentle breeze of the night.

Lisa Schultz

The Mind, The Truth

A journey of a thousand miles is formed
with a decision - a decision that will
take you almost any where; for if you
don't stand for something on the game
of life then you'll fall for anything
that is not there.
    The mind maybe magical; for dreams often do come
true for you will achieve the very things you believe
as these things and more will surely come to you.
    The old things we must let go because in every
thing there is a reason; in that appointed time
"Only God knows" for in everything there is a
due season.
    Remember that prosperity begins with a state
of mind so with it try not to faulter
for there is no reason why we should
settle for anything less than the Best!
that life has to offer. My mind/my truth

Cherecia Phuller

Farmer Joe

Once upon a time, there was a boy named Joe
For it seemed he always kept his parents on the go
His dad taught him what make things grow
His mom bought two tools a shovel and a hoe
He made himself a garden with the tools
You know planting things a row-by-row and now
He is known as Farmer Joe

Paul Billie

Birth of an Angel

The sunshine is gone from her small, glowing face;
her bright, warm smile - covered in black lace
The backpack she used to carry and swing,
was replaced by two gorgeous angel wings.
Her body is gone, he spirit still here,
she seems far away but is actually quite near.
In all of our hearts, we see her warm smile;
the one on earth for such a short while.
It seems unbelievable; this wonderful life gone,
her heavenly soul rose with the dawn.
Nothing we do can make this pain end,
no flowers, no blessings, or gifts that we send.
All we can do is weep, cry and mourn.
A child has passed; an angel is born.

Stefanie Smolen

Acorn

Patch work fur, eyes a blur of different
shades of green, softly you walk through
the snow like an angel without wings.

The burning flame inside your heart,
your simple love that plays a part of
my life forevermore, never leaving never torn.

For in day night shall break, and my
heart you shall take, your dainty paw
ten times in mine and never claw
skin so fine.

I've held you close and never lost,
summers blaze or winters frost, springtime's
green or season's change, for my life you've
rearranged.

Now my friend when you go, your paw-prints
are still in the snow. I remember all these
things and at last my angel's found her wings.

Amanda L. Norden

Angels Watching Through Heaven's Eyes

*A*s night unveils a shadow of darkness thru the sky
And heavens slowly begins to open it eyes,
I wonder if angels are watching from the other side.
Can they witness the pain and listen to the cries
For love and happiness we need in our lives,
An angel watching through heaven's eyes.

*D*o they know how dif0ficult the moments have been,
trying to control the anger and frustration within
And through this crisis we may turn to a friend.
Who's trustworthy, caring, though older and wise
And angel watching through heaven's eyes.

*T*hrough visions and dreams which could come true,
I have prayed with assurance this angel is you.
I've kept these thoughts in my heart for a while.
Your kiss, touch, and specially warm smile
And with your guidance I will continue to strive,
You've been my angel watching trough heaven's eyes.

William L. Poindexter Jr.

Precious Memories

My mother, Mary, so young and frail
Raised with brothers, the macho male
Walking to school from the old sod house
Long way to go in a middy blouse.

Education was her first desire
She was a teacher now for hire
My dad swept her off her feet
Teaching, for mother, took a back seat.

A wedding date was soon to be set
The time arrived and then they met
This was the day the two become one
My dad and mama were so much fun.

Mama is now quiet and growing so old
Frail as a child her stories untold
All of her needs are a loving arm
Someone to hold her and keep her from harm.

Time goes so fast along with the past
She gave so much love that would always last
I was so blessed having her so long
Loving and caring for my special mom.

Lieutitia Volene Heft

State Of Mind, Or Is It Not

A vast expanse of nothingness, far as eye can see
void, nothing neither high nor low
seen by none, yet is there one,
spirits, souls of every race
not as minds perceived this place,
it is not.
That it is not a comprehendible state of mind
no dreams, cares, or knowledge of time,
it is nothing.
Names of objects, all to see emptiness,
dark a million miles everywhere.
Beyond these boundaries where no soul has wandered,
we can not know or think or want.
The freedom of life, experienced once so long ago is
forever lost.
The time we had, to choose our existence,
gone for eternity.
Somewhere in this state of hell, I shall meet and end
no soul, neither here or not
I shall never know, have not as tried, but found it yet.

Chad R. Fisher

The Party

Night life is live and that's no jive.
Heart beats, toe taps and hand claps!
It's a party on the dance floor!
Before they get their groove on the crowd
Inhales a little more.

People lookin' around; up and down, tryin'
To see who's the most grand of them at all
When a male couple and a female couple comes crashing the ball.

For they look the best, their blue/pink are clean and pressed.
The crowd hearts are racing
As they notice couples warm embracing!
Their moves make you jump! They do little grind'n' bump.

Over the music there was a loud shout
The crowd kicks the female and male couples out!
Later the eve. The man who started the fight
Was about to be struck by light.
Saved by one of the girls he kicked out, Club Music World.

What I'm saying and I'm not playing
The choices we make has an out take
Big, little, small, or tall God created us all!

LaFayette Bernard-Acevedo

Forbidden Memory

In a dream,
the pictures and sequences of memory
seen by the mind's eye,
come in more detailed
than a slide viewed by the strongest microscope.

The edges of objects long forgotten
cut through the mists of time.
Their shadows are reflected
and bounced between the two worlds
of now and then.

Shifting silhouettes
outline the blurred shape of a loved one,
taken,
forever from your grasp
by your own selfishness and pride.

Lindsey Grant

Little Innocent One

To be formed, to be fashioned by the Master's perfect hand
Tiny toes, sweet smiles, and quite cute coos —
To those who wish to erase God's beautiful design,
we must take a stand!

God steps forth and casts His vote unmistakably so.
By creating this life, His plan is a life
To be born and to grow!

Chosen parents make a choice and babies birth is denied.
In his own defense, "Let me live!"
He wished to have cried.

Angels receive the innocent one before his birth.
God's freshest gift never experienced his life as God had planned
For here on earth.

Many tragedies happened when his life was taken away —
No future memories of first steps, of tender good-night kisses,
Or of shuffling "footed jammies" on a cold winter day.

In the Heavenly Father's Arms, love and joy will always be.
The sadness comes in not knowing the life he could have lived
Or the memory of his God-given family.

Cheris Gaston

To The Young Sisters And Young Brothers

Hey, are you my young sisters and brothers of today
Can't you do a little better Grand-ma used to say
Listen, my young sisters and my young brothers

Be the "Do something generation"
Or become the negative other
Remember Mama's advice is always good
Apply it quite often, make sure it is understood!

Don't do a crime
In some jail you'll spend your precious young time
If you really want to be cool
Make sure you graduate from high school

If you have big plans
And want to go somewhere
Make sure you include
The Lord, God, Almighty in there!

Brenda Scott

Living A Deception

The beauty of your body is an appearance that deceives
where enjoyment, is the game
satisfaction that comes and goes
sometimes leaving an eternal creation
that doesn't have any blame for a night of pleasure
living in a world of regret that after a failure
without the boasting of an experience
doesn't know how to appreciate a true love
carrying to the end a pagan life
where the deceit and the suffering is always present.

The anxiety of having you is a an uncontrollable pleasure
because the figure of your body
attracts attention, being your world
an illusion of fantasy because in your skin runs
the sweat of adventures, past times
that have left, marks in your life
ones that reflect roads without directions
and other that are visible of illusions full of inaccuracies
that make you a love that is not worthwhile.

John Leon

So Beautiful

So beautiful it is, oh yes! You can see
the beauty. So wonderful. So nice, so
beautiful! So pretty and attractive! Oh
yes! So gorgeous. So glittery. So attractive
So gorgeous. So beautiful. But you can't
see the beauty, I can, in the dream world,
in peace. Where your dreams come true.

Lana Moore

Fast Enough For You

When you thought that you were going fast,
I was slowing down.
When you thought that you were catching up,
I slowly slid around,
Right on by without a sound.
You were so busy trying to pass me up,
Should have you stopped and looked around,
Because the best thing's in life aren't going fast,
But merrily slowing down!

Mark Lynn Sims

Unworthiness

What source is deteriorating our love,
Destroying you and me,
This invisible force that has taken control,
We use to be devoted to each other,
Now I live in one world,
And you seem to live in another,
Two lonely people staring at the stars,
Standing beneath the heaven,
Lost in an innocent space, we blew everything,
To unworthiness,

You no longer have any faith in me,
And surely I can't rely on you,
Afraid to trust, all we do is fuss,
We have to be direct,
Even though we can't detect,
How or why this has happened to us,
In retrospect we might wonder,
When our hearts began to wander,
And in due time we might both confess,
To unworthiness.

Robert Michael Davis

Waiting, For Her Love

Breathing, again.
The grass will grow,
The breezes will blow,
But how will I ever know?

She is me in so many ways,
But this game runs me like a maze.
Sooner or later it's going to rain;
And light will shine on future days.

Right now it hurts for it's a strain.
It feels as if I should go,
To a place where waters flow,
I would take her with me, but she might say no.

It's like I am on a farm to graze.
But since I've been in my deep daze,
All I feel is powerful pain.
While my head spins in constant craze.

Benjamin Shamsi

Relationship

Like a blossoming rose bud on a warm Spring morning
A feeling like no other the human soul can feel
Making you feel wanted by someone
giving you happiness or grief.

Like a sunset
Dipping into the ocean on a Summers eve
A beautiful sight to behold
A wonderful time to begin a relationship.

A moon lit night
Laying in the grass, looking at the stars
Sweet whispers of love to each other
giving you happiness.

A quiet rainy Autumn day
A telephone call disturbs the silence
Those five heartbreaking words
"I can't see you anymore"

A dying red rose on a frigid winter night
Ripping apart at the heart
Making you feel lonely
giving you heartache

Jake Bigham

Are You Here

I am now scared because I don't know
If my angel is near

I sometimes wonder if I did something
wrong, should I live in fear.

I don't know how I will survive living
on my own

I just can't bare the thought of being
all alone.

Did I say the wrong words, did I act
the wrong way

Was there something I was suppose to do
Or something I was suppose to say.

Maybe there is a trip of discovering I
must take

Or am I just dreaming and soon I will wake.

I am now hoping my angel doesn't stay far away.

Because I know the day I will be judged, it
is the thirty-first of May.

Camilla Roberson

Tears Of Joy

With tears of joy, I cry.
For you are my children, my light.
Sent from Heaven above to bring,
love and laughter into my life.

My heart sings for you,
and for the One,
who gave you to me,
I will cherish you for all eternity.

I will teach you right from wrong.
I will strive to protect you from all harm.
My precious little ones,
You keep my light strong.

When I hold you in my arms so tight,
and I feel your warmth and love,
then I surely know that you,
were sent from Heaven above.

Dianne Wallace

Down The Seashore

Down the seashore, life is never a bore.
You always see the ocean, looking out your back door.
The beach is always fun, it is never a chore.
The pretty girls are plenty, who could ask for more.

Down the seashore, the water is blue.
The ocean is pretty, what a wonderful view.
You can have a cook out, enjoy a lobster too.
They have a nice life guard, his name is Lou.

Down the seashore, the board walk's great.
It's the ideal place to take your date.
The rides are a blast, you can always stay up late.
Down the seashore, nothings second rate.

Down the seashore is where I want to be.
The boating and fishing are always free.
You can enjoy a swim, there's never a fee.
Down the seashore is the place for me.

Ron Marcella

The Woman In The Wheelchair

"The Woman In The Wheelchair;"
has one of the warmest smiles, her clothing
is filthy, and she has no legs.
I give a dollar or two to keep her from
having to beg, she has her pride too.

"The Woman In The Wheelchair;"
smokes the butts from cigarettes real
smokers throw on the ground, never complaining.
Never hearing anyone call her by name,
"only the woman in the wheelchair,"
as they stare.

"The Woman In The Wheelchair;"
when she looks into my eyes I hear her
spirit, saying; "I'm just glad to be alive!"
Where does she go when the corporate
doors close? Only God knows;
The Woman In The Wheelchair.

Calvin J. Kelley

Sisters

We grew in the same womb.
Hearing the thumping-rhythm of the same heart.

We all four called her Mom.
We are forever linked.
A bond stronger than gravity.

Our shared memories...of laughter
The fear of his punishment.
And, those long lonely nights
we laid awake in the darkness.

This is the cement that has bonded us
through the storms.

We are grown now
Supposedly on our own with our own families.

Yet, sometimes I know it is one of you before I answer the phone

I smile as I finish your sentences and you mine.
I am not surprised for we are still connected

We are like the awesome colors of a rainbow.
Each color can stand alone.
Yet, when connected is always complementing each other.
Making the other colors more beautiful and mystical.

Like the Rainbow...Neither time, age nor distance can weaken us.

Dianna Johnson

Back Then And Up Now

Back then, our people plowed behind mules,
Back then, our people knew who ruled,
Back then, our people wore frowns,
And we all walked with our heads hanging down.

Back then, our people had pride.
And for that good people, innocent people,
Died.

But up now, my people up now,
No more mules,
No more of their rules,

Up now, my people wear crowns with our heads
Towards the sky, saying
Look, black people, look white people
Look everybody, look what we found.

Up, up now, my people,
We see our pride, we can walk our pride.
We can talk our pride,
We now can clearly speak our pride,

We now after all these years can "Feel" our
"Pride".....

D. E. Machild

A Wolfe's Christmas Poem

They lived in a house they built together
And hoped it would shut out the bad bad weather
Then came the babies, one thru six,
Oh how they loved but just couldn't quit.
Each one was loved the best they knew how
No matter how big, no matter how small

Christmas's came and christmas went
And to think of all the money that they all spent
One christmas came and they all got together
Each one buying presents for one or the other.
None of them would know how Christmas would be
If there were no presents under that Christmas Tree
Why can't they remember how Christmas should be
"No one gave presents" all they gave was thee.

So let us now give what we can
Even if its only just a helping hand.
And let us not forget next Christmas Eve
That a part of giving is giving of thee.

Heidi Burns

Home

Home is a place of love and happiness.
Home is a place of disbelief and grief.

Home is a place for two to become one and control the peace and
    the mutiny.

Home is also a place where sometimes one must stand and control
    the field of life alone.

Home is where the positive side of life is instilled in you and
    you're taught to watch out for the negative side.

Home can also become the negative side and you start to believe
    that the outside is the positive side.

Home is where the future lies and the children are our future.

If we don't start joining together and helping one another, in
    the future there won't be any children,
        just a wooden structure that we once related to as Home.

Cassandra Chenevert

A Dark Night

As the white pearl of darkness rises,
The cold eerie shadows of the night
Come alive in all shapes and sizes
Swallowing all colors of light.

As the black skies crawl over the land,
The dark, blankets creatures big and small.
Is the Darkside in command,
Blinding natures beauty from us all?

Will the darkness be our only light?
Will we feel the warmth once more,
Or will we live in the cold shadows of the night
From shore to shore?

We wait for a new day.
The days can not be bought.
For night is here to stay,
Or is it only a thought?

Anthony Donato Root

Untitled

In the fall I see rocks, leaves, nuts, rocks, leaves, nuts,
rocks, leaves, nuts, I can see in the winter snow,
trees, ice, snow, trees, ice, snow, trees, ice,
I love fall, I love winter I love fall because of the leaves,
I love winter because of the snow, that's why I love
fall and winter, and in the fall I see rocks, leaves,
nuts, in the winter I can see snow, trees, and ice.

Craig McCarthy

V.C. DeMarco

Often things happen we cannot explain,
along with them follows sorrow and pain.

We think to ourselves, "If I had one more
day, what could I do or what would I say."

As time passes on the pain will subside, your
memories grow fonder and deep in your eyes.

When you need them most friends and family
will be near, don't be afraid of your dreams or fears.

Life is something to be cherished and more,
never walk away and close the door.

Jill Solorzano

A Drifting Little Boat

Tonight autumn is coming
On horizon fog's falling
A little boat on the stream
Like you who comes in my dream
In the trees cold wind's blowing
Through leaves and branches swinging
Pine trees 're crying far away
How I love you I can't say
In the wind the little boat is moving
On cold Thuong River with two streams
Tell me, little boat: Where are you going?
Tell me, river: How deep you are?
Seeing fog falling makes me sad and cry
I can't see you, my love, in my dream tonight
You don't come to me, my love, tell me why
Under the dim moon light, little boat I can see
I beg you, boat, to bring her to me.
*Thuong River is a river in N. Vietnam
Part of the poem is a translation from a Vietnamese
classic song "Con Thuyne Kong Ben" written by
Phong The Dang*

Thien Bao Nghiem

The Story Behind Christmas Delivery

It was an eventful day last October
We were hunting and all were quite sober.

Through steep canyons Bill's horse led the way
We'll never forget that fateful day!

Then, through the air a shocked Bill did fly
Thrown into Limbo between earth and blue sky.
The impact was fast and very severe
With cuts and bruises and so much fear.

But Bill, our old cowboy, he's very tough
And of adventure he can't get enough.
A talented artist we know out west
He captured the moment and it's the best.

We hope you enjoy this gift of "good cheer"
Delivered with wishes for a great new year!

Ursel Hulse

Nature's Trail

Boughs of cedar carry nourishment to
nature's animals

Branches of oak, elm and maple seem to molt
Shedding feathers
Of persimmon, tangerine, and honey-colored leaves.

Limbs shelter lady hornet until the first flight
Of downy white flakes. Then her guardians
Abandon her to her winter sleep.

Layers and layers of leaves rush
To an oily death beneath thick pond scum.

Nature's camouflage protects
Turtle, chipmunk, and snake.
Glossy leaves send mankind to an itchy frenzy.

Still...we are the lucky ones.

Every artist uses nature's palette
Stroking topaz mornings and indigo nights.

Every musician borrows from her tunes
Playing bubbling brooks and trickling streams.

We have only to look and listen...
Don't you love her melodies?

Astella Streety

Winter Is Coming

Every year Fall comes before Winter
  As everyone knows
But then comes Winter with . . .
Christmas and Christ.
Christmas is filled with . . .
Happiness and Cheer
Trees and houses light up . . .
  So . . . Dear
Messages sent to bring love and joy
Then Santa comes with a toy
for every good girl and boy.
But the real reason we have
  Christmas is . . .
Because Jesus our Savior was . . .
Born on Christmas Day.
Jesus was born in a manger on a . . .
cold winter's night.
But when He was born his mother sang and smiled
This Is Christ The Holy Child!

Stefanie Roche

Untitled

Performance rises and falls with the temperament of the audience
Strange faces underneath masks that appear human
Can anyone understand the words of the actors themselves
All I hear are leaves moved by the wind
Leaves that otherwise are lifeless

John David Weekly

For My Love

It started with a kiss
   Something I could never miss

You were everything in mind
   And never unkind

I have cared and shared things
   With you that I never have dared

I see your face and feel your heartache
   I see the trace of the tears you have cried

The silent sound of the hurt left unspoken
   You were strong enough to hide.

We have waited for this day
   Without a word to say.

It does not matter how far apart we are
   As long as we are in each others hearts

The caring and sharing will never be missed
   Because I will always remember our
    First Kiss.

Cindy Coomer

Untitled

White birds dipping, blue birds fly,
The whisper of a willow tree passes me by,
Small children frolicking, laughing in the leaves.
Their innocent gibber, flying on the breeze,
A deer goes jumping, a squirrel euns by,
My body feels so light: I'm sure that I could fly,
My eyes close softly and I start to drift away,
I'm walking on a beach now, in a sandy bay.
I sit here now like never before.
The wind is in my ears, the waves are on the shore.
I am standing in a spotlight now, or it is just the sun?
Small children are running, all are having fun,
White birds are dipping, blue birds fly,
The whisper of a willow tree passes me by.

Stacey Bertsch

The Unicorn

Oh, mythical beast of legends untold
What mysteries does your form enfold?
Have you danced along the Milky Way
And watched Irish leprechauns at play?
Have you entered the sphere of a maiden's dreams
And cooled your hooves in Utopia's streams?
Elusive and shy you hide away
In the twilight colours of yesterday
And never to a human eye
Show the grace of your flight as you go by.
But, as Morpheus grants dreams sweet and mild
To the innocent mind of a sleeping child,
You wait in the shadows of days yet unseen,
Never revealing where you have been.
In that magical place where the soul roams free,
By the shores of the gold Eternal Sea,
Will we earth children awaken one morn
And see the enchanted Unicorn?

Pamela Bestianich

Baby Jake

A seed was planted, a child conceived
A whole new reason to pray and believe

God gave us a miracle, this newborn life
And shined upon us His Heavenly light

The seed grew so quickly, healthy, and strong
We knew in our hearts that it wouldn't be long

That we'd soon be holding this newborn life
Created in God's image, myself, and my wife

The angels came down from Heaven above
To take back the baby we so dearly loved

Our hearts filled with sorrow, tears, and pain
A child we loose, but an angel we gain

Now our baby's in Heaven, he's in the Lord's hands
Our worries are over now, for God has special plans

He has shined upon us His Heavenly light
And spoken to me these words of delight:

"I've come to tell both you and your wife
Baby Jake is waiting for you in eternal life."

Greg Gittere

Untitled

I think of you often and miss you so much,
The days feel like years when we don't touch.
The sweet moist kisses that I can still taste,
Every moment together is never a waste.

Please run away with me and I'll love you forever,
As long as you're mine we'll always be together.
Your warm kind smile keeps me going day to day,
And fills my head with love every time you're away.

You are the angel sent to me from heaven above,
Even if I died today, it is you that I'll forever love.
There is always a place in my heart only for you,
And though I don't know what to say, I know what to do.

Let me take you away from all of this crazy world,
My heart and my soul will be given to you totally unfurled.
Loving you would be so easy because of who you are,
You are the sweet rose of life, a lone shining star.

Phil Sibbald

Coming Out Of The Dark

Coming out of the dark,
Where I have roamed for many years...
Into the light of life,
Where I can release all my fears.

Coming out of the dark,
From that path I've had to follow...
Learning by suffering,
From things I've found hard to swallow.

Coming out of the dark,
To that puzzling junction in life...
But unlike the others,
I know which path will hold no strife.

Coming out of the dark,
Following a soft voice calling...
I walk toward this voice,
Now no longer scared of falling.

Rebecca A. Davis

The Song From Somewhere

A song playing somewhere, brings only a trace
of a memory dim, of a warm smiling face.
The sound of the rain, brings a memory too,
of pure golden days when I was brand new.
Those times are all gone now, those days in the sun,
when we blamed our failures on just being young.
We never thought those days might end
and that moment by moment we begin to descend.
The sound of the music brings only a trace,
of a memory dim in some long ago place.
And the faint sounding tune rolling 'round in my head,
brings back the laughter so long ago dead.
Now is now and the past is the past,
it was all too perfect for it ever to last.
And so the memories are where they belong,
I can only remember that I once sang the song...

Bonnie Barton-Novak

Ecstasy

A chain smoker.
She was.
When things were depressing.
Sitting..making love to a cigarette.
Wondering.
What went wrong?
Sitting.
Thinking.
What happens if?
Where did it go?
Problems fading as smoke hurls.
Up to heights unknown.
Depression.
Exhaustion.
Fading thinking.
Loving things unreal
in a world of realities.

Deanna Joppa

Ever Since I've Been Driving A Bus

Ever since I've been driving a bus,
I no longer have any reason to fuss.
The things I've once took for granted
"Poof" - have all disappeared,
Ever since I've been driving a bus.

I hit the highway at the crack of dawn.
I see the sun set.
I see the sky turning ever so blue,
As majestic mountains come into view.

I see pillars of clouds suspended in air,
As birds spread their wings and glide through the air.
I, too, am free, God's gift to me,
Ever since I've been driving a bus.

Many of my students may not see what I see,
Or hear, or talk, or walk like you or I do;
But oh the look on their faces as they board my bus,
Simply tells me that God watches over all of us.

I no longer dwell on having it all. The pay is less,
But oh now I'm blessed,
Ever since I've been driving a bus.

Clara J. Murrels

Minutes Of Freedom
(For Shanyigana Shanyigana)

The storms of a nightmarish languor come visiting oftentimes
Amidst the thanksgiving of a violent harvest. Could it be true?
Dire extrication of nocturnal tortures!
Then I will make the return flight into glory land.
Because the winds have subsided. And,...
Hear the voice of the ambushed drum beat,
Joyously mimicking Miriam Makeba and the Dark City Sisters.

On the shores of the Atlantic ocean, the Cameroon Mountain towers,
Harbor for the U.N boat on which I live and pine for sea weeds,
My dreams as those of the licensed fisher-man that I am,
The expectation of a return wave.

When the sun rises from the horizon,
A reposition will also come.
Then can I take my probation to the Walvis bay and the Kalahari desert,
Embodiments of a scuffle with hertzog's waves.

Enjoined. Are they?
The A.N.C and S.W.A.P.O.
Fist fisted in the risen sun, verb phrases as masthead for
anniversaries revisited, progeny and parents can flock together.

George Atanga Bamu

Untitled

He left. Put everything down before collapsing.
A day to remember—Friday the 13th—a bad luck day?
Shockingly unexpected. Looking back, had a last supper
In an Italian restaurant with him and our granddaughters,
Had a rare potato pancake breakfast prepared by him
    before I went to work.
Had an almost imperceptibly longer hug "good-bye".
My heart had lifted, misconstruing a revival of our love and affection.
Only a letter on the dining room table—a coward's way out.
Months of tears, of hope, of hopelessness, of helplessness.
Months of receiving cards, notes,
    and letters saying "I love you..., but..."

There's no turning back. Long term trust
    and commitment inexorably destroyed.
Looking ahead—Friday the 13th — maybe a good luck day.

Maria Z. Sedmont

Untitled

If you saw me on the street could you tell what kind of person I am?
By the way I walk? By the way I stand?
From my type of shoe? Or my pale peachy skin.
Could you tell what kind of mood I'm in?
Would you wonder if I was honest and kind?
What wandered through my mind.
If I said hello would you think I was odd?
Reply with words or simply a nod.
Would you ponder on where I was going? Or where I've been?
Will I return there again?
If I'm good? If I'm bad. Do I posses something you wish you had?
How about where I work? Where I live? What I take? What I give?
Would you care where I'm from or at least my name? If I'm normal.
If I'm insane. Do I look simple minded or hard to please?
I'm actually neither one of these.
Before you go judging you'd better think twice. Count your own
    virtue along with your vice.

Amy Boring

God And I

I looked across the desert sand, and wondered how this could be.
Of all life's fears, and all my doubts were face to face with me.
But, then I realized I was not alone, as the sign came from the sky.
To face each new tomorrow, there was God and I.

Barbara E. Penrod

As Long As You Stand By Him

Every Sunday you go into His house.
And for that same reason, I go there my self.
And you don't even care, that I'm sitting there.
I love you more to see you carry out your affair.

You live with me, but you live for Him.
And it bothers me not, 'cause I know it's no sin.

I'll Stand by you, as long as you stand by Him,
And I respect you so much for living with two men.
Your heart's open to Him although it's full of my love,
And when I'm looking out for you, He's always watching from above.
You serve Him in everything that you do,
And that never stops me from wanting to too.
And because you stand by Him, I'll stand by you.

You fold your hands, but your arms are open to me,
And when you close your eyes at night, I know you can still see.

He's given me more than I can ever give you,
And as you get closer to Him, it draws me closer to you.

He's the only thing that comes between you and me,
And He's the main thing that keeps our love in one piece.

Tel Saucerman

The Face Of Me

Your arms do not embrace me, your heart won't let me in.
Your hands will not caress and save me from the depths of your sin.
You have soiled all my waters, and have darkened all my skies.
My fields are still and fallow, dusty from your greed and lies.
My sons live in hatred and my daughters are in tears.
My children ever hungry; and my babies full of fears.
Speak to me of honesty and trying, hold hands in thought of me.
Count well all of your sorrows, learn from all you see.
Take heed of your tomorrows, you thoughtless men of antiquity.
See me, hold and love me, I am the face of humanity.

Carolyn Tratensek

High Above

Beyond the sky, behind the clouds, farther then the moon,
    and higher then the stars,
There is a place where I can rest and have Peace, Love
    and Togetherness.

From the beginning of time, there has been hate without reason,
    marriage without love.
Beauty on the outside and ugliness within.

We speak the truth, but is it a lie?
Have our wants taken over our needs?
Does the mirror on the wall reflect person that we really are?

Behind the mask that we wear; we try to cover up our mistakes,
    but higher we must rise
    above the rest, because we want to be the best.

Take me from this world of foolishness and the masquerade;
The truth no longer holds power the lies have taken reign.

Where is the beauty that was once placed on the earth?
I close my eyes to imagine and it hurts.

Do we still love thy neighbor?
Do we love thyself?
Can we love one another and have peace on earth?

Beyond the sky, behind the clouds, farther then the moon
    and higher then the stars there is a place where I can rest and have
    Peace, Love and Togetherness.

Nicole L. Montez

It

Is IT an embryo, or an unwanted baby?
One month old, or a six-month old, or one year or two years,
    or an abused child of any age?
Is IT a surviving teen tortured by a home with no love?
Is IT an alcoholic parent, the product of an unhappy
    one parent or two parent home?
Is IT the next "news flash"?
    "Young father charged with the death of his one month young baby."
    "Mother takes child to shopping center
        and he never goes home again."
Is IT a gift from God drown in a bathtub, beaten by an electric chord,
    or burned a by cigarette and dead from an infection?

What is our infection that leads to death?
    Lack of interest . . .
    Unconscious observer . . .
    Unloving to the unlovable . . .
IT is not just an IT; We are talking about a child of God of any age,
    be IT embryo, child, teen, young father, young mother . . .

Linda Dunning

Peace

She seemed small — only four — tucked with that field of
    beautiful ox-eye daisies

That vivid memory — so serene — it was like the protection
    of a picture — not reality

The field was tamed — the ox-eye daisies disappeared —
    she grew older — less protected

She married and moved away — my family and I moved —
    she was in my thoughts — though not protected

At the site of our new home I saw the field of ox-eye daisies —
    memories of that long ago year refused to be crowded

Destruction of the serenity now finished by the machines —
    there by the curve of the road stood one ox-eye —
    so beautiful — so tall —
I rested more easy with the curve of life —

James Powell

Dreaming At Night

While you lay, and think at night, about the things that are a fright.
All the things that come out,
The things that make you scream and shout.

Sometimes night can let your heart sing,
    something like a nonliving thing,
    it brings up mystery, magic, and power,
But all that is gone within an hour.

Within an hour, different things come alive,
    things that can jump and things that can dive,
    things that come from inside your mind
Things that can hide, and things that can find.

Although you cannot run and hide.
From all the things that come from inside.
The things that come only at night,
Things that can run out of your sight.

Things that can bring you love and joy, but yet not always a small,
imaginative toy, these are the things that know your fears,
These things come from imagination and peers.

Things that can walk, and things that can talk.
Things that can run, and things that have fun.

So as you lay and think at night, about the things that are a fright.
Just remember this one thing, imagination is the best thing.

Jennifer Schonschack

Oh, No!

When I came to school after Christmas break,
I don't know why, but I realized there must have been some mistake.
The mistake was that my teacher wasn't there.
Grrrrrrrrrr! I was ready to pull out my hair.
I just sat down and looked at what to do next,
But when I looked at the board I couldn't read the text.
I heard the other kids saying, "I don't know what to do!"
Then they came up to me and said, "Do you?"
Then all of the sudden my bed began to shake.
Next, I heard my sister telling me to awake.
As soon as I sat down on my bed,
I realized it was all in my head.
Then I said to myself, "no way!"
Oh, no, it is that school day.
When I really got to school,
It seemed to be pretty cool.
I really seem to like math.
To tell you the truth I like it better than taking a bath.
I really like my school.
I also know that you'll think it's pretty cool.

Andrea Eicher

Conquest Of 20 Lions

"Who the hell are you!" Knock, knock, knocking on my mind's door
"You demand, what!" Arouse the dragon, asleep on my mind's floor
In yonder den he lies, blood red eyes, within green envy skin
His jealous fangs drip my soul's blood, "Please, won't you come in?"

"What's that!" You ask I fight him, with soul chained to 20 lines
"To hell with you! It's suicide!" But my soul can't stop from trying
Dragon's breath reeks literary vomit, regurgitated from past feasts
Of poets devoured before me, who have tried to kill this beast

Yet they still come in packs and droves, like Mongols in a horde
Armed only with weapons, thought to be, mightier than the sword
Weapon at the ready, my soul tiptoes into demon's lair
Disturbing not the skeletons past, (multitudes have died here)

Silent deceitful blackness, Dante's Inferno lies await
My soul feels the demon's eyes, and turns to face his fate
Feverishly I lash and slash, choking back mortal tears
Deceit cuts deep, soul's blood runs sweet, releasing all my fears

Staggering from demon's lair it screams, "I hope you're satisfied!
For I have ventured into the hell, of past poets who have died!"
Now my soul's blood lies before you, splattered across this page
For you to scrutinize and criticize my imaginary rage

Steve VanAllen

Two Lost Souls

The water rushes past me
I see it crash against hindering rocks and burst into white flames
As it rushes along I stand
    not daring to take a step
Something holds me back - not fear, but fascination with this water-
Always rushing
    with no place to go

I steal my gaze back and force myself to continue
A weary journey down the endless riverbank
And as I am alone
    the salty stream offers its companionship
It is graciously welcomed by a fellow wandering soul
I leave my footprints as a mark on this place
And though I do not look back on them
I know that they fully represent my role in all this
Parallel to the river, the two of us
    never touching but following the same endless path
Wandering, questioning
    with no place to go

Claire Cook

The Mirror

Tonight you and I said some words that I know our hearts
didn't mean.
So I walked out with a slamming of the door, hiding eyes full of tears.
As I walked the city streets I thought about what we had said
    and done through the years.
The people we had met and the places we had seen, together,
    then I imagined doing it all again, alone.

That thought made me turn and walk home to you.
I could see the relief on your handsome face when I walked
    through the door holding a flower I had picked just for you.
That look told my heart that what I had been feeling was mutual
So we both gave in to the words on the tip of our tongues,
    and I softly whispered I love you too.

The night as I held you tight I thought about the flower
I brought you and about how your smile reflected the beauty
    of it's soft red petals.

And how the silky leaves reminded me of the bright beckons
    of love shining through your eyes.
Through the darkness I reached up and touched your face and
    was reminded of me softness of the rose.
And silently I thanked the Lord for all things pure and true,
    but most of all I thanked him for the love of my life, you.

Lisa D. Shaulis

The Desire To Love

I have grown, learnt, and admired
but never doubted my confidence
I have seen beauty and shrugged
but never loved it.

As time lapses and nature ages
loves matures and lust rots away
I feel my emotions pressing and my conscience fighting my instincts
but my heart's beat calms them both.

From this I have come to realize
that I have fallen victim
to a cause no man ever understood
but what should I do?

I pondered for hours but to no avail
I asked myself again and again
Am I wrong to feel the way I do?
I am not the first and won't be the last.

Deep down in me I see a new self
an old self attached to a new self
reaching new heights and experiences
but the fear of change keeps me aback for fear of disappointment.

Benjamin Roberts

The Sweet Sounds Of Spring

The sweet sounds of spring awaken me in the morning light.
And put me to bed in the dark of night.
The sweet sounds of spring give me a strange feeling of
    happiness I love that feeling.
The sweet sounds of spring brings happiness to my life.
And heals me when I am wounded.
The sweet sounds of spring are soothing and happy.
They are joyful and sad. All the feelings you want are there.
I listen to the birds chirp and sing, I learn the birds song.
I see happy families playing in the playground and the parks.
I love watching baseball games at the baseball stadium
    on the cool spring night.

Michael Quay

To My Daughter

I was there when you first saw light
I loved you then as I wanted to hold you oh so tight

I was there when you first learned to walk
I loved you then as I watched you learning to talk

I was there when you fell and injured yourself
I loved you then as I did my very best to help

I was there when you first learned to ride a bike
I loved you then and felt great when I saw what your smile was like

I was there when you first started school
I loved you then as I saw you growing and glowing and playing it cool

I was there as you became a teenager
I loved you then though at times I thought you were a little too eager

Though I am here as you go through this pain you are bearing
I love you now and I will be there when your pain is ready for sharing
I love you with every fibre of My being

Dad

Thomas I. Andrews

Life... It's Going To Take A Miracle

It's going to take a miracle, for life to be right, it's
going to take a miracle, for life to be nice, life is like diamonds
and pearls, a new born baby in to the world, treasure the
moments that we have. To ignore the smell of fresh flowers, the
birds, the bees, fresh cut grass, and tall trees. Just see for
yourself, and just believe, God made things for you and for me.
Nuclear bombs, does us harm, man is not the master, war is not
the answer, creating disaster. Here's another chapter, starving
people, homeless people, wickedness, that no laughter. Listen
to this, I would like to say to all the people of the world here
today, the things goes on in our lives this may killing one
another like a game we play. The worlds out of control, and
gone astray. Remember the song, "Lift every Voice and Sing",
dedicated to a hero Dr. Martin Luther King, ring a bell or
sound familiar. We are our own number one killer. "It's going to
take a miracle", robbing, disease, getting one drugs, fighting for
your life, now that's bugged. Just as he started, we must be
departed, it's hard to understand, with greatest demands, and
God on our side, we know where we stand. The world is his, and
will be missed. The world he created, the world he taketh. Let's
all get it together so we can make it. Love one another, help
each other, and destroy hatred. Enjoy life and think twice, its
going to take a miracle, its going to take a miracle, for you and
for me...

Dawn L. Walkes

The Country Cow

All day long I stand in a field.
Damn kids, it's only a dirt road but, can't they yield?
In the summer, I reap what the rancher sows.
One day, I'm not going to look up, whenever a horn blows.
City folks, they all slow down and scream moo!
Country folks, their music filled with trues, blues, and yous.
I can't complain though, I think I've got it pretty good.
I'm not crazy about winter, in fact, I'd go South if I could.
I hear Texas is pleasant this time of year,
Lush meadows, warm ponds, and no wind chill to fear!
150 of my friends moved there a while back,
Yep, the South must be nice, 'cause ain't none of 'em ever come back!
For now I'm living, doing the best that I can.
Each year I'm a little more wind burn, and a little more tan.
I think I'll stop talking now, I've said my spiel,
Chew on my cud a while, and just stand in this field.

Matthew Edwards

Immaculate

Idyllic City of Charms, fragmented souls drifting blindly through
Cimmerian canals, wayward pieces of a pictureless puzzle.
Ephemeral spirits circling underneath the Bridge of Sighs,

Guided solely by a connection divinely resplendent;
Perfect concordance eclipsing limits imposed the evil Time to Part,
Two halves reunited by a power transcendent.

Minds secretly intertwined on Venetian rooftops,
The World frozen on its axis, a toy globe stopped by a child's
sticky hands, until Daylight unmasks the celestial magician.
The Sunlight unkind, leaving in its wake frozen moments of beauty,
Mere snapshots in the Mind, until only fond memories exist.

With the onslaught of Daybreak, the Mind works to molest,
Incessantly rationalizing the enchantment, groping for the tangible,
Unjustly putting the ethereal to the physical test.

Extend your hand open into the sewer water,
    and let the spirits seep into your pores.
Floating remnants of Hope hidden in aqueduct mazes,
The barriers imposed by the Warriors of Time and Mind
    can be slaughtered.

Maria DiBenedetto

Winter Night

I sit at the window and stare at the stars for the lights are off
    on this winter night
The one I have fallen in love with no longer exists
This time she has changed and I will be with her no more
She no longer remembers me as I was before

I sit in an empty house with the radio on,
    only wishing I could return to the day
It was when she liked me but I know it was not that way
For she liked the person I pretended to be, but it really wasn't me
I fouled up and was not aware, this person did not care

Never would I say yes for someone else to change my life
Our feelings were not the same and that is alright
I will show no regret to only be friends once more
And go back to what I had before

Why was I mad at my friends, for they betrayed me
    and told her what I said
It is no longer that I think of the disappointment at the end
I remember the good times with her
I can still call her my friend and hope she can do the same for me

Many a night I return to the window only to look as I did before
    and wonder what is out there
I can't say what it is, for I have never felt it and do not know its power
It took what was inside me for one moment and ripped it apart
Once more our eyes will never meet and forever goes my heart.

Michael A. Ziser

Time

I welcome the sweet release to fall down upon my cheeks.
I close my eyes to feel the dampness caressing my face as it strolls
to a new destination.
    A part of me falls with each drop, as I let go.
Each one belongs to a heart deeply buried in feelings.
    Warmth and comfort abide in this unknown chamber.
I, and only I, know the warmth as I spin around in this pool of
    emotions.

    Time is my only companion on this long journey upon which I travel.
She keeps ahead of me, getting farther and farther away.
    I am left alone in this dark haze as I stumble along, searching,
This road is traveled by few as I await company.
    I slowly walk onward, time is slipping away.

Chad Trauger

The Dream Maker

A vivid figure dominates the dream throne;
   timelessly pondering every possibility to be shown.
Understanding and witnessing the wonders one can do alone;
   that man's only restrictions are those they create on their own.

The mission is to profess our history, trying to guide
   eager wanderers to their destinations far and wide.
Appearing momentarily, speaking words to abide by,
   it is continuously watching through the mind's eye.

Bouncing between each wander's soul unseen;
   this force becomes a boiling fire,
   combusting energy one could not believe.
Inhuman, however, living cancerously within all that be,
   it ambitiously awaits for answers to the endless possibilities.

Traveling nomatically, it accepts all cultural bands,
   feeding off ambition, aspiration, and the need for expansion.
This spirit, within every cell throughout the lands,
   forever directs our souls through the times of the sand.

   Michael A. Riley

A Child Lost

I cry a mother's silent tears, I feel my aching heart.
I feel a part of me slip away as your soul from this earth departs.

No other pain is quite so strong, no other hurt so deep, to
watch a child you love so much lie in such a deep, deep sleep.

Not to hold you in my arms again, never to fill this empty space.
Not to hear your voice, not hear you cry, not to look upon your face.

Only a mother could ever know this hurt,
   only a mother could feel such pain.
Only a mother knows the days ahead will never be the same.

But the memories you've left here in my heart
   will help me make it through.
Not an hour will pass, or a day go by that I won't think of you.

As I lay upon my bed at night I pray God keep you near.
For you've received my heart, my love, my life.

You've received my child so dear.

   Gayle Colbert

My Dream

   A child dreams of sleds and dolls, their favorite
super heroes to hug. An adult dreams of less snow,
more pay and the next meal. What about me I'm not old
enough to vote so I can't be an adult. I'm too old for
the playground at McDonalds so I can't be a child.
What about my dreams, do they not matter? I write to
the president and he ignores my ideas. If someone old
enough to vote wrote him he would probably respond
hoping to gain another vote on election day, so I will
tell you my dreams please don't ignore me. That's the
adults job. I want everyone to love each other, to stop
fighting over peaceful problems, for example killing
someone because they called you a bad name is sad,
sure they won't call you anything else, but I bet allot
of people will call you worse after. We tell young
children to share, but what do we do, fight until we
get what we want. So, I guess I really wish for peace
among each other, that's the first step to world peace.
Maybe someday the president will listen, but for now I hope you do.
Love is wonderful, but we first have to stop the hate to feel it.

   H. Leiterman

A'Gape

   As he gazed deeply into her beautiful eyes, he saw a
beautiful creature in disguise. She had eyes that told stories of
her backward past, and she looked as if she had found love at
last. He gently reached out his hand for her to hold, for he felt
his heart tell him to be bold. As his hand reached to meet her
hand, she remembered her mother saying "Trust no man".
Confusion was truly on his mind, his gesture was suppose to be
nothing but kind. What could he do to earn her trust, he would
have to be honest and not lust. She could see that his heart was
beating every beat for her, but other men made her insecure.
The men of the past had taken all her trust away, maybe he
could earn it back day by day. He went to her house and gave her
a red rose, and tears of happiness ran past her nose. She had
never had someone who truly cared, and at this moment both
creatures stared. They felt the chemistry and rapport growing
between one another, she went to introduce him to her mother.
At this time he proved that he was a worthy man, and the both
Of them embraced each others hand. You could hear the Angels
In Heaven sing their joyful songs out loud, for it was a true love
Found, and one that would last all eternity.

   Anthony James Manha

He Hears Us When We Call

There comes a time in all our lives, when a loved one has to die,
   And through our tears, He hears us say, oh Lord, oh dear Lord why?
Even though we think we know what's best for you and me;
   The Lord above has reasons for all that's done, you see.

And though we may not understand the reason for it all,
   The Lord has everything in control, His love won't let us fall.
Our loved ones see the beauty, and they never see the rain,
   They walk only in sunshine never feeling any pain.

They walk along the golden streets, seeing flowers everywhere,
   In Heaven, they have peace of mind and they are free from all
their cares.
They will live with joy and singing, there is just no other way,
   And the Lord will take good care of them till we meet them
there someday.

So when we think of loved ones, and a teardrop starts to fall,
   Reach out to God, for He's our strength and He hears us when
we call!

   Marti Neidigh

Life Is A Simple Thing

I'm beginning to think life is too complex.
I'm beginning to think that man has done himself
   a great injustice by complicating his surroundings.
I'm beginning to think every invention is a step backwards
From the happy and simple time of long past.
When people could be happy and not know why.
When people were content with being content.
When all that was needed to be happy was love, food,
   and a place to sleep
But here we are, drowning in a sea of unimportant details
Trying so hard to keep up with the constant changes
   that we can't breathe
In a time where it requires a philosopher to comprehend life
In a time of Yoga, hypnotic trances, and relaxation techniques.
Even relaxation is complex in our world.
I'm beginning to wonder why man is the only animal
   compelled to make its life more and more complex.
I'm beginning to think this poem is too complex.
I'm beginning to think life is a simple thing.

   Michael P. Gallogly

A Ten-Thousand Mile Adventure

Checkers of oil and sparkplugs and too-loose chains
We were cactus riders and patchers of tires and tubes
Readers of road signs and crumpled roadmaps
We were befrienders of kittycats and candy-gnawing rats.
Sleepers, we were like trolls under bridges, tents and tarps
Under ice and stars and rain
We whizzed behind countless trees and bushes
And under old motel roofs we watched reruns of the Munsters.

Beneath some sun and clouds
We rode and ate and played
Grinning with red-black faces
All the way to Mexico and Florida, then back.

Pleasantly we filled our pockets full of pennies
And our gastanks full of memories
As we retold our trip to friendly old geezers as windy as the weather
Gosh, but I wish you all could know
   the spirit of bummery in which we rode.

   Larry E. Laws

A Daughters Lost Love

Mother, how I wish I could turn back the time,
To live precious moments together.
We lost some years together to enjoy life's pleasures.
Because, you were away, sacrificing your life to help another.
While you could have spent those precious years with your daughter.
Though we had our ups and downs, but love
   was deep in our hearts to mend our sorrows, to love one another.
I've always forgiven you, because you're my one and only mother.
But, when you got sick, my life felt so bleak.
I enjoyed taking care of you, but inside I was dying too.
God was there to comfort you.
For if he wasn't, it would be a dreadful thing to go through.
For, when the end was near, you were in my arms, holding you near.
Peacefully you left this world, for my heart cried a million tears.

   Geraldine L. Freitas

Forever Wanting

Stranded in a large open field
I realize in my state of loneliness that my fate is forever sealed
With the light of the moon I can scarcely see
Which way should I go it is all up to me
With a pout on my face I look up to the sky
I stared at the brightest star and wondered why
Happiness layed at the edge of this hell
I began to run but often I fell
I continued on for what seemed like days
The ground stayed hard and flat below me not the slightest raise
I grew very weak the stretch to happiness was to long
I fell to cold ground and my moans sang a heart-breaking song
I tried desperately to crawl but my body fell down
My face in the dirt and my fists hitting it with an awful pound
Tears slid down my rosy cheeks with the thought that I would never
   reach my goal
Will I ever have enough strength to reclaim my lost soul

   Stacey Howard

Untitled

The long drought left the land barren; then you came
with a refreshing rain that produced life and vegetation.
Years of suffering made the children hard and untrusting;
At the sight of you they opened their hearts
and befriended each other without hesitation.
The everlasting war brought forth the unyielding presence of death;
Bitter foes came together and embraced after you took your first breath.
My prolonged isolation left me a sad and broken man;
Then I was rejuvenated by just a kiss and a touch of your hand.

   Bill Cuff

Garlic Cloves Spill Chemicals

A form or some similarity to loneliness
   will occur, it will take some place, within some day.
I've exceeded the capacity, strung-out and drooled out
   excessive amounts through my mouth.
Thrown to be aloof in some corner to stroke myself in some sorrow,
   in some way.
Douse the dimming translucent orange of the flame.
My green eyes engrossed with fluids of pain.
A trial of meetings, I slept alone with my feelings sustained.
A form or some similarity to loneliness
   will occur, it will take some place within some day.
The bulk of my tomorrow will be spent battling this in some mentality,
   in some way.

   Michael Craig Berg

A Day With Grandfather

I see him sleeping all covered up and snug,
I really want to reach for him, just for a hug.
He lies there helpless with his eyes shut in pain,
Wandering what to do with no strength to regain.
He reaches his hand out and tries to say hello.
I sit down beside him, but I'd rather go.
It hurts me deeply to see him this way,
I try and keep him company with no words to say.
I ask God to help him over, over and over again.
I ask God if he slips through life's fingers, to free him from sin.
I sit in question waiting for him to sleep,
Then leave the room with God at his feet.

   Chad Cross

It Takes A Village

The sacred journey traveled by the human
   crosses a bridge above annihilation...

Exploring future destinations, our global climb may reach the real

In search of symptoms to our ills, we walk a path known for cures
Turning the wheels of destruction back for the seeing
   opens the view to kind medicine and healing

Hope as the Herb of remedy is greatly needed in each community
   of this age
Our children will prosper with power of observation
Guided by people of moral character and courage that show the way
Smiles given freely brighten emotional decay
   easing the struggles we face each day

To share the wealth of knowledge breaths new life
   and strengthens vision
These kernels of corn bring health to the system
   Illuminating and nourishing our mission

It takes a village to create this magic of gentle power
As each individual finds life and standing in their own
   personal tower. Mistakuye-Oyasin (we are all related).

   Lois Elsensohn

More Than Words Can Say

There are just no words to tell you, what you mean to me,
And just to be around you, shows me how sweet Heaven could be.
   And the glow I feel, when I'm with you, the blind could even see,
There are just no words to tell you, what you mean to me.

Like the flowers need the summer sunshine,
And like the precious roses need, the sweet kiss of the dew.
   Like the evening sky needs the stars to brighten up the way,
That's how much I need you, more than words can say.

Like the glow of a rainbow, when the storm in finally through,
And like the meadows need the kiss of summer rain.
   Like a golden sunrise greets a newborn day,
That's how much I need you, more than words can say.

   Nancy J. Stoner

Snow Star

I heard a snowflake fall yesterday,
it was a soft, sweet sound.
I saw music begin to play,
but where from couldn't be found.

A taste of cold hung in the air,
and threatened of menacing snow.
The weather was bad and the wind was fair,
until then came a strong cool blow.

I bowed my head and pushed on tough,
but then fell to my trembling knees.
I still crept on my heart was rough, till I saw my soul to please.

There lies ahead a beautiful sight, my eyes filled full with tears
my heart was glad and took full flight,
it did 'way with my most wicked fears.

There lay in the snow a sparkling star
that had fallen from the sparkling sky.
I wonder how hot it had fallen so far, to wave not a single goodbye.

That is why I sit here today, in my wooden rocking chair.
The star has kept me alive to say, that it held me in loving care.

So if you ever see a golden, snow star that
has fallen from the lonely sky.
Pick it up and take it far, and keep it till end of time

Elaine Lanphier

The Final Frontier

Once I met a psycho, he hid it all so well
Outside he was an angel...inside his tortured hell.
He had a thirst for anti-freeze one hot summer day
but all it did was make him sick, didn't take the pain way.

Inside his head were voices that told him many lies
And with a knife he let it spill...bleeding slowly, again he tries.
A friend came by to say hello, a sight he had to face
And once again the boy was saved to continue in this race.

And then one day he bought a gun, his father's favorite toy
Just another game to play, one more struggle for the little boy.
That night he felt the pain so deep...the voices scream in his mind.
He couldn't take it anymore, a bullet was not so kind.

I woke that morning all alone, deep cries brought me from sleep
Frightened, I enter the other room...this pain will hurt me deep.
I see my lover slowly dying, blood leaking from his head
Now I can't stop myself from crying, now I wish I were dead.

Gloria Knoll

The Firefly Of Nozual

Abnormality is a constant misconception
and an unseen cause of intimidation
the subjects do not always wish
to frighten others in their appearance
but rather they wish to express their increasing concern
regarding individuality
often the subject feels overwhelmed
by the sea of massive trendiness
and their reaction is often a result of this common feeling
many interpret this behavior as an act of rebellion
but the truth remains that these "rebellious youth"
only wish to expand their horizons and follow in no one's footsteps
this new direction in life
is destined to be adopted by others
who have strayed from the norm
but who lack the esteem to venture out on heir own

Ian Andrew Mance

Angel To Spare

Lord do you have an angel to spare
There is someone I know who needs special care
Even though she has been through so much
Her compassion's still shown with a loving touch
Sometimes I fear you have given more than she can bear
But I know you are near so I implore
Lord do you have an angel to spare

For I've never seen such undying faith in you
No matter how much pain that she is in you won't hear her complain
So at times she is fearful of what may lay ahead
and once in awhile tearful
But has the wisdom to know what you want her to do
And even more so the courage to follow through

You don't have to be told she has a heart of gold
With a loyalty she'd defend you to the end that some would call bold
And an honesty of as many years as she is old
Lord do you have an angel to spare
For my mother an angel in need of some special care

Judy Boyer

For Our Dearest Daughter Alexis

Alexis, I shall not think of the bad days just of the good.
If I could make you live for an eternity you know I would.

Of course all power is in God's hand.
Before you arrived God knew his plan.

I'm glad your mother and I were blessed with you.
This experience has made us as one instead of two.

This I am about to say for certain is no lie.
Our love for you will never die.

Out dear Alexis, this precious time we had together,
will remain in our hearts and minds forever.

I have heard people say, a child as special as you can only be
sent to someone who is capable of a great love.

Well, if this is true, your mother and I are the ones who are
blessed for having you.

So, with these few lines I'll say, it is better to have loved you
for a short while, than to never have loved you at all.

Love Always, Your Dad
Eddie E. Blue

God Is Our Love And Strength

God gave me love to be a blessing to others,
And without his love, in this life I could move no further.
Through his love I find strength to carry on,
Each day is a blessing, and nothing can go wrong.
God gave me a heart to feel and listen when his presence is there,
And if I take heed, I can find that his presence is everywhere.
I can find it in the grass and the trees, and in the sun so bright,
And when I find his presence, he becomes my guiding light.
He is my hope and he is my future where ever my future stands,
He is one to be praised and he is my helping hand.
For my Lord so sweet I can be a vessel of honor,
God can use me in his works,
Where I find God, nothing but goodness and grace does lurk.
Working for the Lord leads to so many blessings,
And it is so nice to know that in him there can be a time of resting.
We have a chance to serve our Lord, and this is what I wish to do,
The rewards are grand and I know that God loves both me and you.

Terrie Humphries

A Team

It isn't just a forward, a captain or a goalie that will make you win.

It isn't the glory from the fans that will make you good.
It isn't the constructive criticism that will help you out,
And that state title isn't won by tradition anymore.
For there is only one thing that will take you to the top.
It is a team.

A team who holds the hands of the despaired and praises the achieved.

It is a group that when the tough gets going, they go.
For without a team you are just a forward, just a captain or just a goalie.
And after we have won the championship,
Remember how you got that medal around your neck.
Because you surely can't pass to yourself
There was someone else
It was your team.

And after the dust has settled, look at that trophy

There is a picture that goes along with it.
It is not a picture of the girl who scored the winning goal
But a picture of twenty-two other girls.
It is a picture of a team.
That team could only have been as good as their weakest player.

Kelly Jean Pinke

An Irish Lass

'Tis the wearing of the green this very day that makes you Irish
 so they say
But you my dear are in every way Irish each and every day
So take these coins and put them away and soon you can go
 your own way
They will grow and you will see, you can be what you want to be
You can go to college or buy a car or go on a trip oh so very far
But remember my dear to put them away so you don't have nary a
 rainy day
You are an Irish lass for sure getting big and bold
And oh so mature, for someone who is almost four
We sometimes forget to understand some of the things you demand
When you are older you will see life is not always as it should be
Be a good girl, smile, be proud for an Irish lass should never frown
We will walk with you and take your hand and say be of good faith
 and cheer
For your an Irish lass today, tomorrow and each and every year,
 for sure

Judy Ann Costello

The Young Girl Speaks Of People

I've known people:
I've known people as old as the world, or so their minds work in
such a way.

I have learned from these people.

I have looked past their worst experiences, and tried to forget mine.

 I laughed with them, and cry with them.
 A laugh can turn golden in the sunset,
 while a frown can turn the smallest cloud
 into a ragging thunderstorm.

 I've known people:
My soul has learned from these people.

Elizabeth Castillo

There Is Hope

When the whole world seems to be against you,
 When you just don't know what to do,
 When no one seems to understand all that you're going through . . .
 There is hope.

A dark cloud covers up above,
 But in the midst of the dark you can see a beautiful white dove,
 It is then you will realize, with God, there is always love . . .
 There is hope.

Hope for today,
 Hope for tomorrow,
 Hope to dry all your tears and calm your sorrows.
Hope that will last an eternity,
 Hope that will be there for you and me,
 Hope that our Heavenly Father has granted for us . . . can't you see?
 There is always hope.

Brenda Chambers-Ruth

The Truth

As it is, the shining piece of glass.
Shimmering and glowing from the sunlight.
Everyone admires it, but no one knows the truth
hidden between the lines.
They marvel at its beauty, but do not know its story.
That is all they know.
All they remember and all they care about.
Stop looking at the outside.
Look deeper, look inside.
It has more to share than just lines and shapes.
It has a story to share.
A story that will mesmerize and shock you.
It will draw you in and make you feel the pain and glory.
Go deep inside and see the happiness that is fleeting
 and the pain pouring in.
Watch as it becomes nothing but a story.
Not a statue. Not a masterpiece.
The glimmer has come out of it.
There is no more beauty.
Just truth.

April Fernandes

Penny Wish

I wish I had a penny, for every wish that's made
from the beginning of this era, right through this very day...

I'd rush it to the bank, into a fat account
and when somebody needed it, I'd gladly draw it out.

I'd spend it oh so carefully, and not waste one red cent
to see no one went hungry, or got behind on rent.

Then anything not needed, to be spent on today
I'd wisely invest in stocks or bonds, and keep it put away

The next time some one had a need, it'd be right there just waiting
to be retrieved with great great speed, there'd be no hesitating.

Dear one each day we have, more precious than riches told
much more precious than rubies, or of the purest gold...

A penny's worth of time, often left unspent
in the moment that it's gone, we don't know where it went.

Never to be used, to benefit a friend
to look a loved one in the eye, and say how have you been?

A hand outstretched to meet a need, to feed a hungry child
or comfort lonely strangers, giving warmth for just awhile...

We truly are so rich, but blinded to the fact
that every day as time goes by, we wonder where it's at.

Beverly Jo Meyer

Of Mice And Men

There was a time I thought I knew the ways of mice and men
But as I grew I found I knew that there had never been
A time, a place a certainty of universal blend,
And so I know that as we grow, will come changes to the end.

The race of men will fight and run their game of 'let's pretend,'
  they'll turn and squirm and sometimes ruin
    their chances in the end.

They'll turn on friend, they'll turn on foe, yet faster still they'll go,
To curb a fate that long was set like stanchions in a row.

Blindfolds in place, hands flung out in reaching,
Stumbling ever on the way for the answers they are seeking,
Blinded thus, they cannot know where the answers lie, well hidden.

'Tis in their hearts, as from the start,
  the yearn to do God's bidding.

  Frances Y. Rollin

Love

His sweet voice
His sexy lips
His wonderful smile
His sweet smell
His strong arms wrap around me
Then he's gone
I'm never in his arms again
I'm losing him.
My man is slipping away slowly
I try to get him back, next thing I know he's gone
What will I do without him
I can't imagine living without him
It's like the saying a rose without water would die and without you
  so would I.
I try to hold back my tears
I just want to lay dawn and die
It's not worth living without him
I love him, I miss him
But where is he, who knows
It hurts to see the man I love walk out
Why does love have to be this way?

  Chantal L. Esperance

A Winter's Night

The wind is shaking all the trees
To snatch away their dancing leaves
and fling them gayly through the air
To spin, and swirl, and linger there
Before they flutter round and round, floating softly to the ground.
The moon is playing games tonite behind the clouds as they take flight
Scudding in flurries before his face, as across the sky they skip and race,
Seeming to search for a better place.
There's a shuddering ripple across the pond which some of the leaves
Have settled on, as a lonely owl sits high on a bough
  where the leaves are newly gone,
    he makes a dismal hooting sound as though he's only recently found
His green habitat, suddenly stripped and bare like that.
'Tis an eerie quiet night, with a shivery chill like a winters blight
the streets are empty, the sidewalks bare,
not a person stirring anywhere,
the only sound a mournful whine of the wind
as it glides through a stately pine,
then suddenly rushes far away
to seek the dawning of a new day.

  Betty J. Petersen

Pain

I feel like I'm tied down and strapped up
does anybody give a damn?
All that I feel is pain because my life is such a strain.
Yet, then why is it so easy to maintain
carry on and don't complain,
as I hear voices in my brain, knowing I'm not insane.
I just can't take this pain who else is there to blame?
I often feel like my soul is on fire,
or I'm stranded with a flat tire, or I'm stranded with a flat tire.
Growing up there was no one to admire everyone I knew
were liars, now that I have grown up I just blame it on back luck.
Could it be I'm the only one that lives this way,
experiencing pain in major ways?
It's like the temperature
it changes everyday, but never goes away
there is so much pain!

  Adrian Deane

Ingredients for Life

Once in your life, two seven two seven five,
you're sure to fake like you made it; no doubt deny
The fact that you lived half your life a lie.

The Laws of Love, the Laws of Life,
Ain't all about safeguarding your rights; albeit years of strife
Stammer by, still shackled in situations skin-tight; note this:
  might ain't right.

You say you want freedom from the wed-locked cage, exit stage
Left fractures in the relationship, cracked jaws from the knuckles
  slipped, anguish, rage;
Bearing the right choices will bear newborn freedom,
  or risk a life of slave to sin, not sage.

Muddled in a slough like Muddy Waters, falter, got the blues?
Might it be you who must alter, deluge of amorous booze?
Blood, sweat and tears must weep to become a fortified Gibraltar,
  unassailable like Zeus.

Although many alike had gripped tighter than the untamed night,
  a noose,
Rebel in what you believe as once did John Hus;
Albeit death jostled destiny, Hus was set free,
  for he had uncovered the Truth.

Chafing friction in your own mission for recognition,
  the prodigious potential;
Right mentality bound by respect, passion and pride
  side by side essential;
Believe...believe and you shall see far behind, beyond the mind,
  past the eyes of Einstein immortal, Monumental.

  Jo Hoon Seuk

I Remember

I remember when I was small, how Mom and Dad thought me to crawl.
I remember the joy they got, when I would toddle from spot to spot.

I remember my Daddy when he took me on his knee,
How he would smile and say-you are my little baby!
I remember when I was ten, how mother would always win,
When I would go out to play, and come back covered with clay.
I remember when I was twelve, how Mother would always yell,
About the things I did, and didn't do to well.
I remember when daddy left to that great big building in town,
Never to return again, because of what they found.
I remember when I came home, and no one was ever there,
The cold lonely hours I spent were more than I could bear.
Then I met a wonderful person, who into my life he came,
He is a man of strength and might, and Jesus is his name.

  Maria Richardson

Dream Dancer

Our time together was short lived, filled with laughter and whimsey.
The days were joyful and the nights dreamy.
That night we danced together lives in my heart.
The wine glasses clinking, music to my ears.
My heart soared at your very touch.
I ached so long to touch your face.
Slow motion memories of our embraces.
The night was warm and dewy,
caressing my skin as you caressed my heart.
So many times you've danced in my dreams.
I rush to sleep to see you there.
Once you were in my life, but now you are miles away.
The distance so great, my heart aches.
I long for the days so long ago,
When I danced in your arms in a world of hope.
The hope is gone, but the dream lives on.

Frances Mueller

Acceptance

When I was still a little girl, - I listened to my mom,
I did whatever I was told, - no sign of things to come.
She chose what I would wear each day, - and fed me from my plate,
and all she ever did for me, - I would appreciate.
I don't know when this turned around, - that slowly I would be,
much more concerned with friends of mine, - than all my family.
For me, it was the third grade, - I became aware of friends,
and all the little fights we'd have, - and how we'd make amends.
Yet when I reached eleven, - it soon became quite clear,
that kids could be so hurtful, - and never even care.
I wanted to be popular, - with girls, who in my school,
were thought of as the prettiest, - the ones who were so cool.
I wanted them to like me, - and did everything I could,
to be accepted by my peers, - so hopeful that they would.
I tried to copy how they dressed, - so they would notice me,
but they would cruelly laugh, and say, "You're such a wannabe"!
So maybe you can understand, - dilemmas that we face,
when kids like this, reach out to us, - not put us in our place.
Decisions that we often make - are influenced by peers,
because we want acceptance, - being left out's what we fear.
The pressure that we feel from friends, - is sometime's very strong,
that's what it's all about for us, - to feel like we belong!

Sandra Rand

God Sends Us Special Friendships

Did you ever find a friendship that you found hard to describe?...
It had no definition, strings or any tie!

But you felt that bond anyway, and knew that it was there...
The kind that is unselfish and you know you'll always care.

You want to share 'just everything' because she'll understand...
You can be 'just who you are' that's what makes it all so grand!

And if you find it, always know, it wasn't made by you...
But by the gentle, loving hand of Jesus, that is who!

He leads us down life's pathways and if we'll just trust His way...
And look at all He's given, we'll see blessings everyday.

Special bonds are made in Heaven 'cause He knows we cannot go...
Along this path called lifetime, without help to ease our woe.

And if for a special blessing, God gives a special friend...
And helps you both to see it, and share your life within...

Thank Him for His favors He has given just for you...
And take care of this special gift 'cause He would want you to.

If we can thank our Father and give Him credit as we should...
Our life will be much better and our friendship always good!

Debra Wade Sacran

If I Lived In Atlantis

If I lived in Atlantis I would become a gladiator in the arena.
If I lived in Atlantis I would be the king.
If I lived in Atlantis everyone can breathe underwater.
If I lived in Atlantis our guards are sperm whales.
If I lived in Atlantis all people are equal
If I lived in Atlantis I can communicate with fish and ocean mammals.
If I lived in Atlantis cephalopods will only eat plankton.
If I lived in Atlantis limited resources will become unlimited resources.
If I lived in Atlantis coral reefs will be protected.

John Paul O'Neil B. Atienza

I Thought Daddy's Were Forever

I thought Daddy's were forever not just every now and then,
Daddy's are so special and fathers are just men,

Mommy, couldn't live without us and my father just moved on,
I guess that my father didn't have a mother's bond,

I still remember the day when Daddy broke her heart,
Mommy said, "I'm sorry we have to split apart",

Mommy knew about it from the hairs left on his shirt,
I guess Daddy didn't care if Mommy got hurt,

My father is just now and then but still I'm glad he's mine.
But I'll never forget my mommy's job cause I got her love full time,

If Daddy's were forever then the love would never stop,
but the hardest part about it was to watch Mommy's teardrops.

Michael Killion

She Smiles At Nite

I hear the sound of crickets outside our window
   and I snuggled closer to protection from the world.
I can't sleep for fear of some thing or someone stealing
   you away so I'll stand guard all nite.
As I lean down to look at you I hear you breathing
   and it seems with every breath you call my name.
There's a smile on your face which tells me you are happy and as I
   gently kiss your head I silently promises to love you forever.
Now I feel the presence of your arm around my waist and it feels
like you softly squeeze me to let my know the smile is really there.

The time has passed by now but with each nite the
   smile on your face remains the same.
But now the smile is for a better reason.
Now you're thinking of the life you carry inside and you
   dream of how it will be.
Will she have your loving eyes and sun filled hair
   or my sly grin and laughing gestures.
She's ours so it doesn't matter.
There is one thing I hope she gets, I hope she gets your smile then
she can make someone happy when he is with her
and she smiles at nite.

David R. Elliott

The Sea Shore

The shore was beautiful, with the sunset casting a metallic glow,
It looked like a scene from a movie or television show.
The water was so lovely, I wanted to dive right in,
Little did I know that's what I would do the next day with my kin.
The sunset was gorgeous as it cast its radiant colors,
It was bright and luminous, like it there would be no others.
The sand was sparkling,
But the sky was darkening.
I knew the day was over, as I saw the sun sink low,
However tomorrow I knew as always the shore would show.

Jeff Jolly

479

Untitled

In a room full of emptiness you fill the space
You lie motionless in the midst of countless candles flickering
   in the dense darkness
As if your face were the 'man on the moon',
   it smiled to the dancing stars all around you
Shadows are cast upon your body like crevices
Deep ravines descend where once windows
   to your soul were filled with light
I could feel your breath that lightly play with the rhythmic motion
   of your chest
As my feet anchor earth, my arms lift off into space to feel
   the warmth of your soul
As my effortless grasping kill my strength, I was forced to admit
   the distance between us was unreachable for my mortals hands
The burning question remain . . .
Should I close my fist and warm thy fingers?
   or release anchor and risk being lost in space?
One Small Step For Man, One Giant Leap For Mankind

    Stacy Lynn Strack

Ode To A Redwing Blackbird

Oh, beautiful Redwing blackbird, what memory recalls,
   Of a gentle breeze, one bright summer day; oh, I remember it well.
Out of the blue, the flash of wings, the rush of your coming,
   For at your appearance, my heart still sings.
And suddenly you were there,
   Black as the night.

Oh, lovely Redwing Blackbird, quickly, across the green meadow,
   I saw you there; so beautiful, and yet you came,
As a messenger over the hill, singing your lovely song,
   Above the rill.
And suddenly as a shadow,
   You were gone.

Oh, Beautiful Redwing Blackbird,
   Someday, oh what a day that will be!
The sun will shine and the flash of wings so free,
   Will cross the meadowland again.
Oh, ship of memory, oh death will carry o'er the Bar
   For once again shall gaze across the celestial meadowland afar.

And for a certainty, we shall see,
   God and eternity!

    Robert Williams

Perception

"Life has its ups and downs." Once said by some great mind.
But what has failed to say is, "It happens all the time."
It is the wise man who sees life for what it is.
It is the fool who only sees the riches
But what are those who only see themselves.
Well they have a name, too?
To understand this theory, you must first open your mind.
To get a better understanding, let these words come entwined.
You can not be respected, if hypocrisy, rules your life.
You can not be loyal, if you can do nothing but lie.
To reign, authority, is a fantasy within itself.
But to achieve your wildest dream, is a dream with being conceived.
For one will never know, unless one experiences.
And without experience, one will never know.
The object to reality, is to master it blind.
If you know what is expected, there is nothing left to find.
To wither from perception, is to wither from the mind.
But to wither from the heart, only happens in due time.
Do not expects a fantasy, for that is nothing to believe.
But the answer to your miracle, is to get down on your knees.

    Ca'Nisha Faye Taylor

Time To Care

Violence and slander's around, that's for sure,
Presidents, preachers, leaders are soon caught with a lure;
It's all happened in the past, but let's not dwell there,
Take it to heart, there's time to care.

Children wander aimlessly, who could have been nestled in love,
We watch them search for blame for their thoughtless shove;
While, in the meantime, they gather shocking things to wear,
Take it to heart, there's time to care.

Come on, it's not so hard to talk, when each was born crying out,
Don't let us lie there, saying we're too tired to shout;
If we hurry, we can truly share,
Take it to heart, there's time to care.

Shall we reach out to others with arms and soul,
After all, we could probably reach the same goal;
We all have enough room to bear,
Take it to heart, there's time to care.

    Mary Fran Fewell

Imagination

A thoughtful smile lingers as the days go by,
A love increases as the Sun sets in the evening sky.
Hard to imagine a Love like this,
For years on end, I have known no such bliss.
Hard to imagine what might happen with just a kiss,
Still, I think such thoughts and I have to wonder.

Heart-warming laughter from behind a sweetly, seductive smile
Gently piercing eyes, sparkling like sunshine all the while.
Hard to imagine a Love like this,
A Beauty beyond what beauty is!
Hard to imagine the Love that I so dearly miss,
Yet, such thoughts are always in my mind and I have to wonder . . .

For now, I can only dream about that Kiss,
But I look forward to that day when this dream, I no longer need ponder.

    Eric Hohn

Rodeo

He's a rodeo man,
He sits on the bull and ties the rope around his hand.

He looks up at his wife and child,
As the bull starts to get wild.

The gate opens and they're on their way,
His wife asks God to please give him another day.

As the bull begins to kick and turn,
She's about to cry, and the knots in her stomach start to churn.

It's been seven seconds, only one more to go,
All of a sudden, through his chest comes a horn, with a great blow.

With his arm still in the air,
He falls to the ground, only dirt to bare.

He had only one second left in order to win,
But he didn't make it, and he'll never be able to ride again.

Tears falling from both of their eyes, like rain,
His wife runs down to comfort his pain.

From the beginning she knew in her heart that there was
   something wrong,
That in this arena her husband did not belong!!

    Jessica Gail Kirksey

Time Extinction

It was the time of regression
In which the silent noises deafened
Those who did not hear...the tough time.

The slow haste of the minutes was
running fast towards a nonexistent space...time out of time.

Weak voices cracking the silence,
unfolding of shadows hiding the day while a dull scream erupted
from the world immersed in pain.

Fantastic moans in the wind entangled laments of agony.

Is my thought immortal that foresees
some day's catastrophe? Or is it time's
time which inopportunely got out of its axis falling ill?

And the marks of time in the invisible
were slipping, bound for nowhere,
as if they were losing their balance in an eternal fall.

It has happened! It is here!
It was true! Life's inertia...zero time. And there is confusion.

Second by second time dissipated and it was soaked in an obscure
light when in a mad rush echoes pursued one after the other
and a huge silence exploded!

Cesar A. Quiroz

Void

I guess things are just never the way they seem
I guess I'll never be as happy as I think
And I guess I'll never be loved quite the way I love
Yet all of these things are not so bad in and of themselves
But what resurfaces time and time again is the same question
Is it me?, but already I know it must be, and I am condemned
Who else but me?, her?
If I ever dreamed of her as such, I would have never tried
But I did, and of course, I am still alone
Perhaps I fall too quickly for those who seem to touch me in ways
   that no one else does
I suppose it is a heartsend, with one flaw
I always seem to be on the sending end
   and never have anything returned
After all these years, I wonder if I have anything more to give
And I wonder if I should even try to be happy
For it seems each time I begin to, I am pushed back two steps
And after being pushed so many ties I really cannot remember what
   happy is really like
And it pains me to say these words, to write this down
To write of how I'll this whole life can be
But for now, pray just for now I cannot foresee my heart being
   brought out
Out of a closed, locked, empty heart for even a tinge of enjoyment
Just locked away, and no one has the key...or even cares to...

Jon Monahan

Music

Music is my antidote for anger.
I use it the way I'd use aspirin for a headache.
It soothes my soul and makes things better.
When I need an escape from reality, I turn to music.
It helps me in my time of need, and it's always there.
In some ways it can be similar to a friend.
Music is my salvation.
Music is the link that connects all cultures because we all
   understand it.
It's a world-wide communication.
Therefore, music is important, and without it there would be nothing.

Melissa Campos

Sometimes

I fear
I'll take the smile from your lips and the laughter from your eyes
Sometimes
I fear
I'll take the song from your heart and the joy from your soul
Sometimes
I fear
I'll lose the magic of your love and the warmth of your embrace
Sometimes
I fear
I'll lose the strength you shared thru the years
Sometimes
I fear
I'll lose my wife and best friend
Sometimes
I fear

Harold J. Rowbotham

The Disrobing Of Summer

Majestically they stand, clothed in crimson and crowned in gold.
In the late autumn sun they glow in a last desperate attempt at
glory and splendor. They hope not to be forgotten. Regally
they tower above us making a last impression before disrobing
for the long winter rest.

Lightly and calmly they drop their coats, soundlessly laying
them on the ground in a blanket of color. With their covering on
the ground they beckon us to enjoy their garments: the sight of
the rich hues of the season, the sound of the crunch under our
feet as we pass, the feel of their brittle crispness as we role and
play, and the pungent smell of mildew as they turn to feed for
the earth.

Yet, in all their attempts to cheer us with their colorful splendor,
they are still a grim reminder of what is yet to come. Cold, bone
chilling winds and frozen skies will be their only companions as
they stand naked before the world, silently designing their
spring wardrobe.

Katherine J. Nally

Common Choices

Time is fading, yet moves slow; heart is racing, forced to go.
Feelings passing, tucked away; rain is falling, what to say?
This is the language I must speak
Lonely is the journey; I'm too weak.

Memory's burning, stripped and bare; fate left standing, how to care?
Season's scowling, gone unknown; names are calling, slip the stone.
A cause for celebration to the night;
All covered up: The sun is out sight.

Power's crossing, slight of hand; heart is sealing, change in plans.
Count the hurtings, hidden smiles; courage, soul on trial.
Can there be a reason why we cry?
Will this door be opened - come the sighs.

I can be everything I want. I can see all the things I want.
We live. We move. Clocks run; only hearts can beat.

Time is fading, lights are low, breath is pounding, can't go slow.
Feelings holdings, deeply prayed; courage asking, come and stay.

So if we live this life we choose
With other pathways taken: Much to lose.

What then is this lesson, common learned?
As passion holds our season - feel it burn.

Paul E. Martin

Alone?

Upon the vast shadows of the dark, he lays there.

Terrified, neglected, lonely, miserable,
  for what the world has brought upon him.

He crawls up to his family's window. They don't even miss him.

I watched him every day knowing that he needs a friend, but as
I looked at him, his face was gnarled with deformity. I turned
away in fear. His melancholy eyes looked up at me.

All of a sudden, I wasn't scared any more. I hugged him.
A smile spread across his face.
He had finally been loved for once in his life.

In an instant, his deformity faded, and a handsome,
  charming boy appeared before me.
He came up close, and whispered in my ear: "Thank you."

Always remember: Don't let anything stand in the way of love.

    Angelica Colon

Expression

Its the start of a new year and everyone looks to start a new page.
Clearing the slate is a necessity when moving ahead.
It bewilders how silence can come so naturally to you.
Could you for one moment have thought I'd forgotten my abuse?

And I, questioning my life fully, from every facet...
Its evolution within secrets where helpless lessons are taught...
My innocence fragmented from my foundations on.
Twelve years in though, just thoughts and spiteful comprehension.

Confused emotions still broil when reminiscing my incest.
I bravely brought myself to the conclude that I'd forgive,
for that simple reason that made it simple to you.
Reasons that yet wait to be spoken for by you.

I can wait no longer!

          Santiago D. Caraballo

Fragile Breath Of Life
(The NICU Journey Of A Mother And Child)

After giving birth to my son at six months along,
The Neonatal team rushed towards him with respiratory care.
His body so tiny, weak, and frail, his spirit alert and strong,
I asked daily, "When will my baby take in air?"

As weeks passed and months appeared,
Under bright lights, vital signs and piercing alarms,
My aching arms to hold him has neared.
Already bonded with love, he introduced me to his behavioral charms.

Witnessing his struggles, pains, and knowing his survival rate,
God help me, I dared hope to hear him breathe on his own.
Without life support, I knew there would be a homecoming date,
That one day soon, I would be caring for him alone.

I set up his nursery and layette with anticipated pleasure,
Took every instructional care to become his full-time mother.
The day has arrived to bring home our sweet treasure.
It was through our journey we learned about each other.

I love you so much, my precious child.
On Christmas Eve you will be coming home to me.
The miracle of life and his breaths still mild,
I thank God and the NICU staff for helping Nicholas join our Family!

    Monika Livell

Flashlight Tag

As children we ran across the wet field
  covered by the endless night sky.
Each star above our heads was a dream of our adulthood
  yet to come.
Although our minds immune to the harsh realities
  of responsibility, love, and the standard of society we captured
  our victories through finding each other.
Sometimes everything in life is hiding,
  you just need to look hard enough.
Though unlike when we were kids
  all we had to find was each other.
Eyes bright and reflecting the same splendor that there is to find.
Your friend in hiding, when I was a child,
  anyone who played on my playground was my best friend
  and we were always told we can be whatever we want.
It's just that when we got older our lights became dim
  and most of us lost our way.
But the rules to our old flashlight tag game stayed the same,
  only there's more of us in hiding than will ever be found.
Tag, you're it.

    Dustin Patterson

To Carol, After Our Conversation....

For me now, the feel of sister love is like rain in the aspen, (and
all the while, our frail words fluttering) - I could not mistake the
tears in your voice... "Long ago..." (- I long to point to some
memory, some moment beyond now when we both knew who we
were were and what we would become - inevitably, containing
the smell of horses and loose, black soil - and that emptiness
belying nature..) I wish we had practised when we were young
standing open to the rain white barked, bare leafed, shuttering in
the breeze...so that even now, when one spoke, the other moved,
seasoned to the dance...and our hearts would flow into each
other - uninterrupted...and we would be impossibly free - but I
am not prepared for this moment, and I stand without memory,
feeling the rain, feeling the soil, still afraid to even open my eyes -

    Luann Sessions

Off To War

Five soldiers march off to war, Their names are Billy, Fred, and Phil.
Next come Joe and Johnny, All march off with good will.

First one to fade,
Under the pat of the spade,
Was Billy from the small pox.

One was sheared,
When a cannon was heard,
Fred comes back in a box.

Four months of cold,
Two arms to fold,
Was Phil from the harsh chill.

Next to go,
Was poor old Joe,
And left another hole to fill.

None to save,
Johnny comes back with one arm and leg,
But he survives the war.

Without tears but sad,
Poor Johnny's mad,
None dare touch his door.

    Nathan David Little

Let Freedom Ring

As I stand like a ghostly figure that no one can see,
I stand with pictures in my mind of men and boys leaving their homes
to go to war, leaving their wives and children in tears,
not knowing when they will see them again.

As I stand like a ghostly figure no one can see,
I stand with pictures in my mind. Not knowing where I am,
I see men and boys, all of a sudden, falling to the ground screaming.
Like the good Samaritan, other men try to help their friend and
although they know their friend won't make it
    they will not give up trying.
I hear the screams, I see the blood.
I now know where I am.

As I stand like a ghostly figure no one can see,
I stand with pictures in my mind of people dancing in the street
and people crying with sorrow.
For the people crying out with sorrow have just found out
they've lost their loved ones and the people in the street rejoice
for we have won the war.

Let freedom ring!

Rachel Martin

A Step Bound From Hell

In a pit one day, amidst all of my sins;
A voice said to me, "Please let me in."
As I opened the door of my heart; with sweet patience, He took a part.
But - in that instant I could tell; I had taken a step bound from Hell

He cleansed me - through and through,
    then He gave me something to do.
"Be Filled!" He said, with my saving Grace.
It surely will keep you day by day.
And in my spirit my feet it fell another step bound from Hell.

He said, "Watch and pray both day and night;
And all your battles I will fight.
Be kind and gentle, meek and humble,
Stay on your knees and you will not stumble.
And in my mind like a sounding bell,
I knew within, another step bound from Hell.

So study His word and do His work;
To be a good soldier you must be alert.
No greater Love, than His life He gave,
That through His blood we might be saved.
So step by step up to higher ground,
Not just from hell, but Heaven Bound.

Gail R. Lively

Sheba

Larry has a great big intelligent collie dog
    And Sheba is her name
Although she and the queen of Sheba live far apart
    their needs are all the same.
Whenever Larry drove his car, Sheba sat front too.
    Although in back, if others came, she'd be friends with all she knew
Now, Larry has a friend named Paul who adores that Doggie too.
And fed her many market bones mostly by the bunch;
First, a milk bone at 10 o'clock - at 11 she got her butcher bone
And a ham bone at 12 - ended her Thursday noon day lunch.
Now I like Sheba too but I like to shake her paws
    But she wouldn't do it till Paul gave me a clue.
"Show her a piece of candy - that's all you have to do."
That did it, but she - with two front paws did
    not know left paw from right.
Till Larry told me, "Don't say left paw say the other"
That worked just fine. She is so cute, oh brother!

Elizabeth Bechtel

Rain

I can feel the rain coming down on me,
and as it burns my tongue, ooh it tastes so sweet.
Almost as sweet as blood, but with a twinge of fire,
that is the pleasure I seek, that pain I desire.

When I mound the salt upon my wound,
the pain is so overwhelming that my soul's thirst is quenched.
The feeling of release, take the pressure off,
let it all gush out, out of my beautiful gash!

Slice thru the skin, wait for the blood,
here it comes! Watch it drip!
There it goes! Down my finger, on my nail, down to the tip!
As it drops, it pools, on the cold, linoleum, kitchen floor.

It falls like rain, out of my sore,
then I tire of the pleasure, and slumber once more.
When I awake, I look outside. The rain is falling like someone died.
I, of course, am only newly coming alive!

In the rain I will dance, and for happiness I will strive,
for the rain pools with my blood, and my blood flows like rain.
I feel whole again after I realize,
I am not insane!

Emily Sue Inkelaar

Rocks: Shades Of Gray

Hot crimson molten streams bubbling from the earth,
Cold black embers pressed in graves beneath mountain turf.
Brilliant gleaming beaches, glistening from foaming surf,
Porous grains cemented by lustrous transparent crystals.
Dazzling coral reefs hidden in icy blue waters,
Silver cities stretch against iron clad foundations.
Brown tortoise shell stone embedded in lush green pastures,
Sparkling chips in golden sun lying upon newly turned sod,
The etching of time revealed in splendor upon marble faces.
These are the core of our globe.

The silent gray rock forever sleeps beneath our feet,
Yet rises in majestic canyon for tempered eye to see.
All the shades of gray I search for are every color of the spectrum,
And man is paralleled indeed to rock of cliff and crag and sea.
Composed of very much the same but as different as each name.
And while the rock in shades of gray upholds man for all his days,
Man is Rock to one another not to be judged by his brother,
But to be held in high esteem so he may shine and sparkle and gleam.

Shirlette Joy Tinsley

Live Each Day

Our lives today are filled with things we cannot understand,
The sickness and the sorrow of man throughout each land.
We hear each day that those we love have died on far off shores,
Yet we cannot explain, the reason for these wars.
Some say the world is growing worse with little left to love,
Yet could not those who say such things fail to seek
Guidance from above?
Let us live each day, as a new born child
Grasping all that is in sight,
Let us hold on to the things we love
Throughout each day and night.
Let us live not for ourselves alone,
But for our fellow man.
Let us try to understand this world, all the suffering in each land
And if we can do just this each day and build upon the good,
Surely then, with guidance from above..
Each day will bring what it should.

Joan Temple Graff

Morning On Ocean City's South Beach

I want to recreate the power of the sea,
Changing its shape, filling all void with its fantastic disguises.

I feel the rush of the salt air clinging to my hair,
Making it sticky soft.

I smell the wetness of the sea, until it abides in me,
Whipping me off my feet, spinning my arms and legs into the air.

My hands plunge down, slicing through each wave.
Seaweed in my hair, jellyfish at my finger tips:

The power overwhelms me.

Courtney Miller

Nightide

Silver light, illuminates ebon waves,
  splaying foam finger, o'er wet sand.
Surging frantically, retreating slowly.
Endlessly, the sea washes me, as I crouch beside the tide.

Night (blown) sea, sky and landscape.
Dark winds' inky seafoam whips through my hair,
  shattering my nightsoul against the reef.

About my body, ebon waves swirl and flow,
  bringing million year old visitors to join left behind eons ago.

Nightide rolls in beckons whispering, darkly onward home with me.
Dare I wait?

Nightide waits along the shore.
Quiet and at peace, I walk into the sea.
Each step, the swirling higher 'round my head.
I clasp my brother, nightide's hand and head home.
Home to the cold black sea.

Linda C. Choubaili

The Rising Tides

As I look out upon the majestic yet massive ocean I see many things
I see the beauty, the life, the endless horizon
I see God's perfect creation that so perfectly yet solemnly
  defines my sorrow
The depth and weight of this mass is my burden of pain
  for the loss in my life
The sparkling light reflecting from above
  is a warmth always felt from one I loved
The life that this creation holds is the diversity that time holds,
Good and bad, joy and sorrow, laughter and pain,
  that were all, always shared with one
The full moon rises and takes with it the water, my soul
The rolling waves that move in and out against the shore
  depict my times of great sadness
They are sometimes so graceful and yet at times
  too powerful to approach
Eventually, the calming of the sea returns
  and my sorrow transforms to laughter
The sun shines once again and the birds live freely
  above the soft waves
At last for a brief moment my soul is free once again
And so is the way of nature and the way the Lord God
  commanded the cycle of life to be
The ocean shall not cease until his command
And the sadness I feel shall not end
Until he takes my last breath so precious
So, in all of its rising tides, the ocean lives in me and abides

Maria Deann Manson

January

The holidays have come and gone and decorations put away.
Looking outside at the snow, my thoughts begin to stray,
I dream of sunshine palm trees and lying in the sand.
Where warm breezes caress my face while I work on my tan.
I dream of putting on a snorkel, mask and fins
To look below the water surface and watch pretty fish swim.
Perchance to take a quiet sunset sail out on a lagoon,
To watch the water turn to sparkling gold from the light of the moon.
Suddenly I'm brought back to reality by my barking dog,
Announcing the arrival of the mailman coming
  through the winter fog.
His bag is packed with all kinds of mail,
And tons of fliers announcing all those after Christmas sales.
Christmas sales?...I'm all shopped out
  and don't want to see another store!
Because, you see, the mailman also brought Christmas bills galore.
So I use the junk mail to help me start a cozy fire,
And to my comfy recliner I will retire.
I close my eyes and my mind drifts to very pleasant things.
Like...perhaps when I awake it will already be spring!!

Maryann Dwyer

A Christian Mother

Whispy brown hair mixed with gray frames a small loving face.
Kindness looks from within soft, deep blue eyes.
Hands now worn from years of daily toil,
Once held the tiny fingers of her little ones.

A free and easy smile spreads across her face.
It becomes a laugh that loses control,
A laugh, this minute, with no hidden worries
And an appreciation for life.

Her small frame is a contrast to her huge heart
That, every day, gives a family love in deed - not word alone.
Her love knows no bounds;
It expects nothing in return.

In the humid summer heat, wearing a simple cotton dress,
She spends some of her most treasured time in her garden.
Few can appreciate the earth's yield quite the same...
The soft pink blossom of a crab apple tree or a dahlia as bright as
  the morning sun.

As her garden thrives - grounded by solid roots and light from above,
So does her daily walk in faith.
A Christian mother's life is like the huge oak tree
With branches of influence reaching out to those around her.

Veta Wilson King

Cry Freedom

Crime, drugs, and unemployment
Lack of any societal sentiment, black on black crimes
Racism reminding us of long ago times
Crack babies cry and some even die
Affluent society sits on its collective hands and wonders why
Government indifference to civil rights
Yet, they have the nerve to campaign for third world human rights
What about the blood of our own black males
  flowing in our own gutters
"It's their own fault," a diamond clad socialite mutters education,
  treatment, and then eradication
Educate the mind to the evils
Treat those already afflicted, then and only then can there ever be
Hope to eradicate the need
For this instant gratification, single parent homes
Absentee fathers who choose to roam
Rather than stay and be responsible for being the positive role model
Therefore, young brothers walk a path straight to hell
For no one hears the cry for freedom, from this life, that they yell!!

Isaac Clay Jr.

The Gamble

I know it's hard, I feel your worries and it ain't easy darlin'
Never easy when it comes down to taking a chance
Where u may lose it all, including the only thing
That makes it possible for u to give and receive
What this insane world really needs - so much, so much love

But take this chance I offer u darlin' - gamble your heart
And I'll be your luck, as long as u and I can play the cards right
I'll make sure the gamble u take will be nothing close
To another heartache, another great mistake
But what u and I truly desire - so much, so much love

Just as long as u can take that winning chance with your heart
For my heart, for it all - this is the gamble we must all make
The chance u must be willing to take to having it all - u and me

Me and u, chillin' in our throne like queens and kings of hearts,
Side by side, hand in hand with an ace up our sleeves
And the cards laid out on the high roller's table,
Feeling the cold rush of a gambler's addiction
But with a single comforting thought on both of our minds
"This time, I'm goin' home not empty handed
But with a pocketful of love, sweet love, oh yeah..."

Mark C. Taberna

Treatment

Yellow, chalky pills make lolling circles in white paper cups,
    like Weebles wobbling (but they don't fall down) on a tray
    precariously balanced.
Up the hall, down the hall, I look for Ted; three stocking hats,
    four-day beard, one trench coat, and a face with a map of
    Schizophrenia's long, scenic vacation etched in grooves and lines.

Ted's out back, smoking his relief, pulling the nicotine and tar in hard,
    get it there, get it there, it burns but it's oh so nice, it
    makes you forget the crawling, the eyes, the wires.
He knows I do not understand but he humors me,
    even manages a smile.
It's time for Communion.

The bread is the bitter powder, all neat and sweet
    in its little machine-manufactured disc, and the wine is water
    (tastes like pennies) in a sterile, disposable paper goblet.
In an unspoken pact, we perform the rite
    that helps keep the voices at bay.
Later, he may vomit and his mouth will feel like burning sand,
    but to keep the voices quiet we will try, we will try,
    every day, he and I.

Heidi J. Bloem

Life As A Single Mother

God has given me three gifts...that are my life...
They're my joys, heartaches, best friends, and everything to me..
Because without my kids...life would be so boring...you see.
Sam, John Paul, and Steven B., are my little ones which in this
Life I have to teach, 'til God decides to set them free.

I have raised my three children on my own since day one...
It has been hard, wonderful, and a life of hope,
To be single and play both parents raising three children on my own.

My eldest, Samantha, is eighteen now...
She's very pregnant and slowing down,
John Paul, who is my eldest son,
Has always kept me on my toes...
My youngest one is Steven B.,
He lectures me on life each week.

If you have children...be good to them...
Nurture the time you have with them...
Take full advantage of your time with them...
Because someday they leave and sometimes never return.
Teach them good values, patience, and love...
And someday, my friend...you'll see results.

Carmen Falcon

Operation Desert Storm

It all started on a bleak and sandy field
    what we all came to know as, Operation Desert Shield.
They were dug into their bunkers, deep within the sand,
    hidden from our soldiers, but we were determined to free this land.

So we moved on inland, with guns and tanks of steel
    those Iraqian soldiers knew that this one was for real.
Saddam Hussein's the man, that we all hate and scorn,
    so that's when the war became, Operation Desert Storm.

We blazed on through that front line, like it wasn't even there
    we were met with little resistance, and we had 'em runnin' scared.
From there we moved on to Kuwait, and the Elite Republican Guard,
our commanders and our generals knew, we'd have to hit 'em hard.

With excellence and strategy, as only America knows
    with our coalition forces, dealt the heavy blows.
Husseins' Republican Guard, that was supposed to be so tough,
    were surrendering by the thousands, they had had enough.

We fought a war that was feared by all, and will be written in the books,
    freedom was won so proudly, and one hundred hours is all it took.
The artillery has ceased on the deserts early dawn,
    what we all have been waiting for now is called,
Operation Desert Calm.

Roxie DeLong

The Mere Likeness Of Reflection

Enduring an endless array of fears
learning to understand through a million tears
Cruelty is a gift from mankind its edge of reason is somewhat blind
Somewhere man has planted his flower only to neglect it
    in his search for power
Long ago my rose was planted
Traveling through time I must have taken it for granted
Perhaps I left it on a shelf thinking it would take care of itself
Not realizing it too needs care to survive
    and nourishment to keep it alive
Still my flower is a beautiful as ever seeming
    as if it were forgotten never
Honesty will confess that it was not my touch that has
    maintained its essence as such
Its roots were there all along allowing it to grow, keeping it strong
This way you, the strength of two
This was love shining like the radiance of the purest dove
Engraved here in my heart valued as priceless art
What have I to give here in this life I live
Only the mere likeness of reflection
Only this which never displayed rejection I offer this rose to you
    an eternal symbol of love both constant and true

Corinne Gagliardi

Sleep Tight

You're sent to your room with no dinner before bed,
Lack of nutrition makes one crazy, you said
Your nightlight, a beacon, dims through a tear
You plunge into darkness to conquer your fear
Alone and afraid of what might really be there.
Possibly demons- possibly nightmares, things conjured in your head
You advance toward the unknown realms of your mind,
Hoping you'll not come out dead
You come armed with courage that dwells in your soul
The shaking and sweating you just can't control.
You finally realize what was once in your head
Is really a monster hiding under your bed.
Sleep Tight

Cary McDonald

And The Angels Weep

Angels weep to empty cribs for the loosened soul of innocence.
Sharpened lies slice the darkness, like obsidian raven's claws.
Babies have children, dead before they're born,
because we're all dying somewhere on the inside.
The times have seen too much to speak,
the swollen tongue of truth.
Little boys die, in little games of war,
as their fathers kill fathers, in their inherited passion.

An angel cries out, a silent scream,
as she watches her world burn to dust.
Poisons of the brain run rampant, amuck, as they inhabit the sane,
and leave the crazy to rot, in a putrid world of corporate filth.
Where what's right is wrong and what's wrong is law,
and children die at the hand of their parents.
Where walks in the park are interrupted,
by gunshots overhead.

An amazing world, we live in now,
where we can't live in harmony, for we don't know how.
The children have seen too much to cry,
so let them be, and then let them die.

Andrea Walker

Imagination's Legacy

Peace toned petals flow
Then float from amber skies
They drift through perfumed clouds of lacy fragrant mist
Guilded by a torchlit night
As one mind frolics in pleasantries of spirit known only to oneself
Envelop soul with positive illusion
If one must need imagine at all
Let go the troubling toil of day
To enter hidden chambers of the mind
Those templed shrines molded in obedience
To the Gods of love and peace and harmony
Listen for the heart strings plucked harmoniously
By falling bits of stargazer dust
Sent from higher worlds as comfort for all the ills of Life
Listen for the beauty of creation as it unfolds
For those with time to hear...to reach...
To remain afloat amid the current's pull
Where all who play can win
If only for one spin

Marie Dixon

Pepper

You were always much more than met the eye.
My wonderful freckle face guy.
Looking beyond the face,
Claiming goodness - if only a trace.

Judgements weighed on a delicate scale
Never tipped for personal need.
Monday's courage and Wednesday's giving
All week loving minus greed.

Watching your arguments unfold,
We could hardly wait to push the pace.
Back and forth, yes and no, Do you remember long ago?
I still recall those joyous debates, along with your freckle face.

We shared our loneliness, we shared our pain,
Cried, prayed, and hoped again
That love would pulls us through the rain.

You left us in such a haste,
Only now do memories slow their pace
So we can paint that freckle face.

Esther Acker

What Love Is

Love, it is something that you should never take advantage of.
It's something that one should cherish for as long as you live.
Love is what every girl waits for,
    it is what every guy isn't ready for.
Love is what you need for a relationship, as well as trust and respect.
Love will raise you up to great heights,
    or bring you down to the depths of despair.
Some people can't afford to lose love but some people can.
Love can be cold and harsh, a nightmare that won't stop.
Love is a dream that happens to everyone,
    and it is a promise that isn't broken.
Love is like a swinging door that swings both ways.
A memory that can't be changed.
Love is like a tear of blood from the heart,
    that only time can heal the pain.
Love is a friendship, a whisper that only you can hear.
In these crazy times we are living, love can turn into regret.
Love is like a game, when you get hurt the game is over.
When you're in love, you can see it in your eyes.
Love lasts with every beat of your heart and everyday without an end.
Love should last till the end of time
    and that should be a promise to keep.
If a guy is in love, he will make you his world and love only you.
Love can be a teacher and you learn from it
    or it can be an enemy and you can avoid it.
All in all love is the greatest gift from God!

Kristina Barlett

My God

O' my God, rid me of this love,
for she takes control of my life, when I lift her up above.

She comes in many colors and she comes in many shapes,
but she does not care for me, or my body which she rapes.

She comes to me at night when I am full of hate.
She is always there for me with open arms,
    but she will not keep me straight.

She is there for me the whole night through, over and over again,
but she will not stop coming, though my blood is running thin.

She controls my every move and she controls my every way,
even though she is always there, I must learn to push her away.

When I try to push her away, it seems that she will never move,
but living without her is to myself, what I must prove.

I must say to myself "I can do this, I can make it through this day,"
    and this is why I am here, and this is why I pray.

To live without her is why I pray, for Your every willing grace,
    and this is why I ask of you, will you please take her place . . .

J. W. Cornwell

The Moon

As the light turns to darkness, the horizon gets dim;
Over the hills and mountains in the sky,
    just past nine o'clock there is the moon!
The moon sits and has a glow you can see from miles around.
It's surrounded by stars — stars that protect it from
Harm or danger, but it always stands out!
Even when the clouds get dark and gray, and the nights are cold;
You can see it peeking through the corridors of the gray flames.
The moon is used as a guide.
It's brighter than any street light, and its features are sharp!
Sometimes it can be different shapes — quarter, half, but it
    still can guide you through the roughest storms.
So as you watch the sunrise from the valley, and the moon disappears,
Just knowing you will see it again
Makes the day go by just that much greater.
The Moon, there are still questions
Unanswered about its existence.

Melvin F. Shearin

Looking Back

Back when I was very young, I could never understand,
Why you'd get so very ugly, at the many things we'd planned.
I always knew, as sure as not, when we traveled for the day.
You'd end up with a headache, somewhere along the way.

I wished so many, many times, again, again and again
That somehow I'd get lucky; a younger mother I would win.
I was too young to see it then, the trouble eight of us could be.
But, I am sure of one thing now, I'm glad it wasn't me,
If you could live your life again, I'd hope you'd choose to do the same.
If you had chose another path, I might have had lot less to gain.
One thing I feel you gave to me, was the ability to work and read.
And with those simple talents, I'm sure that I'll succeed.

I only hope you'll get that feeling, before it comes your time to rest
That you can feel, deep down inside, that I have done my very best.
I really want to Thank You, for all you've done for me.
And hope that time will make you proud,
   that I'm an apple of your tree.
Amelia F. Manter

The Lie

Some song springs forth from hallowed ground, where few
   will ever tread, corrupts, contorts, and twists around,
   then finally leaves for dead, pure intentions, nurtured long,
   and harbored in the soul.
Sparked, then dimmed, then mirrored the wrong seen but never told.

Creeping forth, the lie begins the dance which had no end.
Shackled down, the virgin sins, and takes the lie as friend.
The babe holds fast to ample breast, like dew holds to a flower,
Then rues the day she came to nest, when all the milk turns sour.

The eternal sea of emptiness engulfs the bitter child.
Devouring with scornful bliss, and mocking all the while,
   lessons learned when things were new,
   and the horizon still showed light.
Those held dear with dreams too few desert her in the night.

The ruined sapling kneels to pray, in the blackest mass.
Winter's demons come to stay. The pod is dead at last.
Pitched upon the hallowed soil, and in a pool of red.
Some song springs forth, and then recoils as silence takes the dead.
Daniel C. Bohen

A Year Ago Today

A year ago today I lost you in the fire
While on the phone with 911 it burnt right through the wire
The smoke was thick, the fire was mean, you could not find your way
At last you found a doorknob and you began to pray
Dear God I'm only eighteen and what about my mother
I hope that all the ones I love will take care of one another
You knew that they were on their way and hoped it would be soon
To make time go by faster you thought of our favorite tune
You remembered all the happy times we had since we were six
And wondered what I'd do about my problems
   you wouldn't be here to fix
I know I would have saved you because I have no fear
Or I would have died, in that closet, with you, my dear
As I sit here and think about you a year ago today
I yearn to tell you something, I have a baby on the way
It's due three days before your birthday,
God must have a special plan
He took you away and put more life in me, figure, if you can
For all those years you nurtured me and helped me make it through
Now I'll have someone to care for with a name the same as you
Sharon Raedelle Wolford

The Illusionist

You ask me for a token, a gift, a soft insinuation;
I give you the halo of my hands, the rose of my lips,
The candour of my languid gaze.
You want me to recite poems to you at dusk
And to sing sonatas of desperate love at dawn
With double flat and sharp tones in si and do; quavers and allegros;
Like the nightingales of your dreams,
Or the wind that strains through the bushes of the poplar grove,
Perhaps the notes dispersed for the rivulet that
Disembogues in the ocean of my affection.
I immersed in my spasmodic-metaphorical-utopian thoughts,
Naked before you: "My infinite space, volcano of
tenuous-warmth-fervent (light)",

Manna is drought, nectar of my life;
Covered with silk veils, scarlet masks
And velvety capes in the present of a mundane world;
Concealing the erotic-ethereal-eternal corporal fragments,
That belong to the rider of my galactic steed.
The tamer of the golden unicorn that flies in the magical-ephemeral-
   (intangible cosmos)
Where my delirious and longings float.
Clarena Moreno

The Day

The Sun is beginning to rise, it's a new day, not a me day, but a we day.
Let us be wise so it won't cause our demise, that will be the day,
   all that is Pure and Innocent will be here to stay, nor will it fade away.

The breaking of Dawn is near, so where do we go from here -
   with no fear.
Only a tear of joy, it could be a girl or a boy. They are who we hold dear.

Will it be a chance to advance into time,
   with the devine Dance of Romance
The day of a love affair.
It's not a toy that will break, nor put away.
The day is calm on the water's shorelines, on a warm summer day,
   children are ou to play.
In hopes for the day, that has come to a full circle.
Without worry of a delayed reaction no strays or distractions.
Just a refreshing breeze to put us all at ease.
The day - not me - but we will all be free
To see the day of connection, perfection and resurection.
The day the light shined brighter than stars of a moonlit night.
The day that ended the fright of fight, that wasn't right.
Now we stand with the day of correction.
Mary L. Robinson

Names

Names, names, I wish I could remember a name!
While I'm trying to recall, one and all think I'm lame in the brain.
I talked to a lady down at the pool, I'm sure she has a name.
You know, the one with the white curly hair, she's an attractive dame.
Is it Marian, or Barbara or June or May?
I think her last name begins with a J.
I wanted to call that bald headed guy, the one that walks a little lame.
It sure would help to find his number, if only I could remember his name.
I went to introduce my friend the other day,
   one I have known for years,
I could not come up with his name, I was almost embarrassed to tears.
My mind is a blank when it comes to a name
   but I have some friends that are the same.
The way I am failing, it sure is a shame,
I can remember a poem as long as your arm but I can't remember a name!
And when I die and go to heaven, where there will be no more pain,
And I finally get to meet my Jesus, I hope I can remember His Name!
Don Higgins

Untitled

I look into the mirror and see a blank face staring back at me.
I see a young woman with too many problems and worries for her age.
Her hair is starting to grey and her skin is a strange whitish color.
Why she is looking like this is a mystery.
Life has been rough on her and now it's starting to show.
As I look at this desperate face I wonder what I can do the help.
Just as I whisper this, the woman disappears and in her place is God.
Then, I realize that God is in me and always with me,
And at any moment ready to take my problems away from me.
So I let him.
The woman reappears in the mirror with no wrinkles and no grey.
Just a bright, shinning, smiling face that warms me down to my soul
And I realize that everything's going to be okay.
As I turn to leave, I see someone behind me,
A loving, caring, generous being.
He bends over and engulfs me in His arms.
I look up at Him and, in that moment of
    silence, said everything that I was feeling.
Now words were spoken,
    but we both knew how much we loved each other.
Before He vanished away again,
He placed His hands on my cheeks and
    gave me a gentle, loving kiss on my head.

   Leslie A. Harvill

Waking Up To Vietnam

Waking up. In the first light. Good. Morning. Morning dawns.
The clock yawns. The street trembles. In sun rising traffic's din.
Steel beams of glowworms in motion. Flood the cracked concrete.
Veins fill up with a streetbeat. Aorta chokes in the overflow.
Smog bites! Memory stroke! Surveillance camera watches.
Intersections of quicksilver. Fire tide runs through the rifts.
Infrared detector interrogates. The rolling coaster of feelings.
For eventual hospitalization. Resuscitation of hope fails.
Wobbling pedestrian stumbles on the fast walkway. Defeated.
Dazed and confused! Morning!! Good morning!!! Vietnam!!!!!

   Juliusz Zajaczkowski

Wilderness

Wilderness can be defined as God's way of expressing
    his feelings

Sometimes there are rocks, jagged as a knife,
    or rocks smooth as silk
Maybe there is water, a huge powerful waterfall,
    or an innocent little stream
Then there are the animals, fierce mountain lions,
    or little birds who are always high on life

Wilderness can be defined as God's way of expressing
    his feelings

Many times I see trees, some towering and mighty,
    then those that are sick and weak
The sky is sometimes clear and blue, but when bad weather
    comes, it becomes dark and filled with rain

Wilderness can be defined as God's way of expressing
    his feelings

Out of all the things in the wild, my favorite are the
    mountains
They rise up above everything, watching over everything beneath them

Wilderness is God's way of expressing his feelings

   Tate Brown

The Contemplated Truth

The earth is ever changing and evolving.

As it evolves, it gives up its possessions to those who are worthy.

Those who are worthy, are determined to be those who are wise.

Those who are wise, are determined to be those
    who have become responsible.

But, who are truly wise and responsible and,
    who are truly worthy of life's creates possession-wealth?

Is wisdom acquired or learned?

If it is learned, why to we constantly repeat our mistakes?

If it is acquired, why can't we progress forward?

If there are those that truly possess wealth,
    then why do they always find themselves coming up short?

And, if we are always coming up short,
    how can we be considered truly responsible?

I feel, that true wisdom comes when one sees that,
    one's greatest gifts are not truly great,

Until they are truly shared with those in want.

By sharing with those in want, we make them truly rich thus,
    we become truly wise and greatly responsible.

For we have learned the true meaning of true wealth
    for a gift to have meaning it must be given.

It must be shared-wisely and responsibly.

This man, then, will be found to be truly worthy
    of any of life's many gifts to come.

   Bianca Tate

Snow

It is white in color, its season called winter.
Used in comparison — as white as snow
Makes people who like it excited at the first sight of it and those
who hate it panic because it makes them feel cold.
Makes the roads very slippery and slow down traffic whenever it falls.
Causes school closing when the temperature is below freezing point.
People have frost bite when they expose their hands
    and legs as well as ears.
Skiing and skating are good entertainment during the snow season.
Sculptors cut out designs from ice.
People entertain their eyes in the different sculptures.
This season of snow is called winter.

   Celestina Ndukwe

She Waits For Me

The night is filled with memories, and I am searching for a ghost.
Awaiting still some sign from her that she exists beyond the grave.

The bond between us was first borne, when we two shared a single life.
And I thought death could not destroy the silver cord that bound us so.

Yet when Death called, he left his card,
    a still white body—cold and hard.
No breath of life, no spirit oozed from matter that had ceased to be.

For Death had stamped upon her face the certain look of nothingness.
And horror rose within my heart, for the visage promised nada.

Yet something in my inner self said there is more to life than death.
And somewhere in eternity she watches, smiles, and waits for me.

So here I wait, in vain perhaps, for proof of an eternal life
From she who was the world to me—
    who may be naught but dust and air.

   Kathryn Linda Wickett

Thy Kingdom Come

For Nathan Joseph Embry
The absence of your presence seems to grow stronger each day
I stare blankly out the window letting my mind drift away
You left my life so suddenly, and the pain of our goodbye
   leaves me empty and alone
Each night I whisper to your ears, please come back
   and patch the quilt we've sown
My memory of you is peaceful as I recall the love I felt from you
Two years and yet I can't stop hurting and feeling blue
The rain has come and the smell eases my mind as cheerful
   thoughts of you clutter my brain
I look in the mirror each morning wondering what's wrong
   and am I going insane
This disaster in my life has taught me a greet deal of things
It's hard for me to trust people but my trust is simple
   and only for you darling
These days go by slowly as I remember something new all the time
My king is gone, my heart is empty,
   my soul as sour and as bitter as a lime
I wait patiently until the day we shall be together once again in harmony
Until then my love, I'll be here thinking of you and being lonely.

Michele Renee Lester

At The Changes In View

How changed is our Homeland from the place we once knew
Now I look through tall grasses at the changes in view.
Where our children grew up in the splendor of nature
   and our cattle roamed free
Now all things are so different from the long ago that use to be.

How green were the valleys we planted,
How purple the hills at twilight we beheld
How golden glowed our meadows with a blue sky tracing through
Now I look through tall grasses at the changes in view.

Looking through the window of this empty cold house,
   where once we called home
To up on the hillside where our cattle did roam.
I see there a tree gnarled and twisted from the weather of past time
And my fingers trace the initials and hearts you place there long ago
   so lovingly entwined.

In sadness and sorrow we placed you in the tall grasses and soil
In the heart of the land you had served so well
Now I bend low to look through tall grasses
At the changes in view.

Geneva Bell Truesdale

Color-Blind

When we met I begged to search your Soul;
you pushed me aside and replied "not today."

When we met I pleaded to feel your Spirit;
you ignored the request and responded "no time my friend."

When we met I longed to journey deep within the depths of
your Mind; you weren't up to the challenge and simply walked away.

When we met I hoped to encounter your Energy;
your Do Not Disturb sign was hanging from your
door so I decided to return another day.

When we met...
I clutched your hand and held it in mine
and cornered you with a glance like the
passion of an undefeated champion; "Kind Friend",
I replied ever so softly, "it is a pleasure
finally meeting you; Let me introduce myself
I'm color-Blind".

Our colorless silhouettes pounced the pavement as
we bid each other adieu and went on our separate
journeys. Mission Accomplished: Fulfillment...

D'Andrea L. Jackson

Nightsong

Perfect green treetops swayed effortlessly by the kiss of a star goddess,
Who bestows on us for one sweet moment
A faint scent of the beautiful perfume blown on her breath.
Pale gold moonlight spills out of the porcelain bowl too small to
   contain it,
And covers everything with its soft caress,
Creating shadows amidst the fingers of the mist.
Suddenly, the scene is drenched in darkness
Like the shades pulled down by a suspicious man who tries to keep
   out the staring eyes.
A single dog's lonely howl pierces the black like the cry of the lost,
Until the moon peeks out from behind the cloudy tendrils,
Showing its face once again.
And slowly the stars twinkle on to join it,
As their happy inhabitants click on the lights, chasing away the
   darkness so many of us fear.
Come.
Embrace the night and its beauty.
Cherish its soft touch and savor each moment.
For soon, day breaks and morning comes, and night exists no longer.
It's majesty and mystery fading with the last star.

Danielle Kohler

A New Life

What would happen if you could recapture
All the untried ideas and goals of a lifetime?
Coax them and coddle them and prize them out of the dark shadows.
Remold them like lumps of clay,
Mix the still damp and pliable with the crumbling dross.
What would you get?

A new life?
An alternative to the familiar, the comfortable?
A more exciting, fulfilling, unfolding wonder?
Or a journey through a land of unease
And "I told you so's?"

Or maybe after all, you leave this virgin mass
On some side road, never to be tried
But left instead with the regrets and reliefs of travels *not taken.*

Do you try it?
Try it and find you are the person you've longed for,
Or not, and realize you always have been.

Shirley Hambrick

The Whitest Breath

Running passions and twisted turmoil flooded through me
I wondered what to do, what to think, what to see
The winter's offspring seemed to know my flesh away
But though I dashed, whipped and scorned, it did not end that day

I wondered what, in my mind, I could not understand
And dreaded fear of Nature's hand and what man had done
   with vicious hands
And yet, I lingered upon the breeze flying high and sweeping low
Swiftly flying upon a wind losing battles with vivid snow

A blanket clean of whitest pleasures tear apart the sky
Making muffled sounds of an unbearable and frightened creature's cry
And upon a field of golden grain I lay beneath the ground
Wondering to what oath my wretched soul was to be bound

I learned an important lesson in both life and on that evil day
That life could be fearful, scared and timid,
   something that winter's threats gave away
I learned as I lay beneath a stone inside the frozen field
To treasure life, to understand love, and to be never forced to yield

Sharon Cabana

Paper Tiger

Clutching a bathing suit in her small hands
  a child stares at the moving water.
It looks so cold, unknown.
Suit on she again approaches the water.
Bare feet timidly toy at its edge.
A shiver ends itself in a shudder as she wades to her knees.
Goose bumps spring instantly to cover her body with a new texture.
Anticipation begins to yield to smile,
  knowing that the decision is at hand.
Fear finds her stomach as water creeps past her thighs.
Teeth chatter, eyes merely tight slits; a gathering of will.
Under the water then quickly back up; a new intense joy!
Back in again and up, deep breath more relaxed.
There's exploring and freedom and fun!

From the shore a question, "How's the water?"
From the child "It's warm."
From the heart "It's a paper tiger."
From the soul "I have grown."

  Nancy Bostian-Dolge

I'm Coming Home

How long must I remain captive to this life,
  shackled by the confines of humanity?
They look at me with awe and surface compassion, yet they are
  unconcerned; thankful that they are more complete than I.

In public...the stars, the whispers, the scuffling of feet to create
An unobstructed path for me to travel.
Forced to endure the constant barrage of insincerity.

Secret to all are my feelings. So few over stop to share.
I am bound to a lifestyle I had no part in making.
Forced to live in life's shadows...
Unable to participate; condemned merely to observe.

All alone in a world so full of people.
Alone, yet together, in search of something more...

I reflect on the past: The pleasure, the pain.
The experiences of life; some lost, some treasured.
I am thankful I believe in the promise of the ages.
Someday I will be restored to my full stature.
Soon to be unconfined by the limits known to this world.
Destined to be whole...Again.

No longer will I be alone; no longer will I be the source
  of the unwanted attention.
No more the focus of the lengthy glances,
  the topic of the silent whispers,
    the unwilling subject of endless conversations.

As my testimony comes nearer its end, a heartfelt "welcome"
I will proudly issue to this limited existence.
 I have much to look forward to as I boldly await the time I can say,
"Lord I'm Coming Home!"

  Robert P. Posey

A New Beginning

Life is taken, the pain has ended.
Grieving children, family and friends fear not,
For the soul is lifted to a higher plain.
When the end comes it shines a new beginning.
What was brought at birth is returned to God.
What's left on earth is the love, the family, and the goodness
That you have created by living.
Fear not; our sorrow will end, our tears will stop,
But our love for you will remain for all our lives.
So go on and start your new beginning, of this place you are released.
You're not forgotten, so go in peace.

  Michael Keith Sanders

Thoughts and Actions

Because each of us is an eternal being of infinite light,
energy is given to every thought we think and everything we say,
and this power penetrates the eternities every second of every day.
And no thought can ever be recalled from its flight
or changed from its consequences of right
for right and wrong for wrong, moving on its way
gaining momentum to forever remain, to forever stay
in its designated cycle, where it attains its height
to inevitably play out in all our tomorrows.
It is our own power that brings to life our passionate affirmations,
our own self that leaves us drowning in our collected sorrows,
each of which we individually created with our internal repetitions
and expressions of depressions or passions or dreams or desires -
ultimately ordaining ourselves to outer darkness
  or degrees of eternal heavenly fires.

  Irene Jones

My Soul's Dispersion

Let me hear you listen to me, and then I'll feel your voice,
Can I look into your hurt
Then smell the fear that you disperse

Understand my soul's confusion, take a space in my heart,
Feel the illusions my mouth projects
Consume the pain my aura must disperse

The weakness that must be contained,
  and the strength that's now unleashed,
May know the man that tastes no fear
When his thoughts must be dispersed

Knowing not what should happen next, if my heart should understand,
The power in which my soul confides
As emotions are dispersed

Thoughts are cluttered by what you say, as I try to feel your pain,
But I can not taste the smell of hurt
When your love you must disperse

Confusion is the key to that, which has no mortal being,
Fear not the sight that you can't hear,
Just grasp into darkness until seclusion fills your sense of touch...

  James Thompson

My Mother

A beautiful black woman, so divine in every aspect of her life
Blessed is the man who has this "Pearl" as his wife.

A woman whose very image reflects that of God above,
Carefully taking every moment to show forth her love.

For each day has shown her many things,
Experience having posed as a brief struggle

Yet she journeyed on in the wisdom of God
Having both roles as a parent to juggle.

A virtuous woman, my mother have you not heard?
Leading and guiding me as ordained in the 22nd proverb.

She set aside self, and lacked things seemingly good,
In order that I'd have an opportunity to trod the path of manhood.

What courage? What love? What care?
Willing to accept the responsibility that was there.

Contributing her honest opinion, while lending a listening ear,
Is the most important way she's proven to be a friend that's dear.

For God knew exactly what I needed when he placed me in her hand
He knew there'd be times like these in need a strong black man.

Now, as a father I can fully appreciate all that she's done for me,
For she set the perfect example of how a real mother ought to be.

  Aundre Stanton

The Storyteller

Winter has been vastly approaching.
The preparation of fall's final days was now complete.
The Canadian geese were flying overhead singing a warning to us.
This singing gave the northern winds the go ahead.
They came that evening, thickening the sky with clouds and turning
    every animal to its den.
This dreary, cold nothingness was just the welcoming of our old friend
    Jack Frost.
He didn't waste any time letting everyone know he was in town
    when he covered the place with bits and pieces of ice.
Like Santa, Jack would bring his own bag of tricks.
That night he put on some music; music he could dance to.
We heard a piece that he would play just for us to hear.
It always started with the howl of the wind going through the trees,
    then the crackling of the ice on the branches
    bending by the force of the wind.
After the introduction there were no sounds at all.
During this time it gets very cold, so cold you could see his finger
    drawing on all the windows.
He was really a very good artist.
He would even drawn himself a stage to dance upon.
After everything was complete, it would start to snow.
I believe Jack was shy.
He didn't want anyone to see him dance,
    so he made it snow so no one could see him.
I also believe he was proud of his work because after he finished,
    he would put the clouds in his bag
    and wake up the sun extra early to
    let it see his wonderful creation.
But he was never seen; only his works were left to be melted
    and forgotten by those who shine.

   Mike Pilkinton

Who Am I

In the past I judged myself as a nobody.
It was never brought to my attention I was a somebody.
I stood distance away in a far away land.
I found myself going in circles,
    so I stopped in the middle of nowhere and asked myself

   "Who am I?"

I continued to walk and look ahead.
There were so many paths not taken.
I really didn't know which way to turn or where to go,
    so I did an "about face" and followed my footprints;
    which led me in the same direction I had just left.
My journey seemed meaningless and my where about's were worthless.
At this point in time, my life really had no meaning at all.
It seemed as if my surroundings were caving in on me.
Furious with desperation I asked myself

   "Who am I"?

Out of nowhere a voice spoke to me and said..."Come My Child".
It is I who walked over mountains and looked over plains.
It is I who treaded the still waters and watched the skies so blue.
It is I my life to see my father live and watch my mother die.
I'm slowly understanding why some things happen in life
    and for what reasons (though they remain unknown)
    but through it all I answered with a great reply

   "Who am I"?

   Chifonna Dionna Mitchell

Tormented Hearts

For all I long to hear is loving words and fairy tales whispered in my ears
Never be ashamed to call my name and tell me I'm the one you treasure,
You look at me and all you see is a girl, who lives inside
    of a golden world and you believe that's all there is to see,
For you will never know the true me
I wade in insecurity, and dream of whom I will never be.
I harbor my fears, and smile through my thousand tears.
I could not breathe. I could not speak.
You unclouded my eyes for me to see, you are the only one for me
Wandering through misery, you set me free
I once was a prisoner unsteady
    and cold locked inside of a dark dark world
And the skies cleared up, and washed away my uncertainty
    while your sweet love rained upon me.
The dawns ribbon of light burst through the dark,
    and finally I saw your golden heart
Shadows of your pictures watch over me,
    and I fantasize that you will one day be mine
You change like the tide, and only I can see
    the burden which you have for me
Many of your friends may come and go,
    but you will never know how much I love you so.
As the clocks keep ticking, and each day in time passes
The wind will change, and soon blow backwards
    and when we must part,
    you and I will finally see each others heart
For later on in years you will then see how much you truly mean to me.

   Ida Churchill

Bloomin'

Throughout the year, all years and time; within each season,
within the minds; of lovers, elders, spirits and travelers;
Minstrels, violins, essence and dabblers; admire and sit,
in wonder and learning, at the strength and the wit, the stay and
the strivings; hey bloomin' pollen on!...
Leaves dirt-rooted, dig the fervent colors of nostrils lathered.
As sunlight dances, prances and prowls; o'er the stemmed leaf
    of vine branched flowers.
Held, in the lapels; labeling the lace of lovelies.
Gold flakes red ribbon'd crimson violeted hues, of blue - the glowing
    vibrance, flower blooming.
The organic shadowed life, a fragrance overwhelming. And True.
Deities of antiquity tomorrow, will flow life finding health,
    only in their borrow, from the beauty of bloom, itself true sublime;
    honest to the rainbow of a chaos, Divine.
Tomorrow, it will fly, and the following day, it will die.

   William A. Bannenberg

Till Death Do Us Part

The sandhill cranes have arrived, at long last.
Spread across the sky in flight a welcome sight to see.
Dropping one by one among the many sanddunes.
To this their winter haven in the west.
The very young and old alike eagerly await their coming.
A big event for all to witness natures way of life.
Unconcerned, red heads bobbing they make their vows.
Dancing with total joy of being with one another again.
Lives forever intertwined, together.
To death do us part, is their commitment.

   Margaret E. Kelly

Que Passa?

The times—Good, Horrendous—they're reported Best & the Worst,
With flood, fire, drought, the Devil Itself has upon us all burst.
Big Evil—flicking peep shows, doped mania, doing all the dancing,
The elbow, fist, the finger and ego-jeer, go diabolically prancing.

Times are the best, proclaim bulging builders of golden piles,
Dazzlingly they reap: slashing all with their yellow-devil smiles.
Times are the worst so prate the poor drugged host of no sayers,
As they entomb and smash the darker light of the Nation's prayers.

GOD CAME TO AMERICANUS WARNING:
YOUR GOLDEN PILES AND GOLDEN LIES, HAVE RIPPED FROM YOU—
THE SIMPLE GOLDEN TRUTH, WHICH NEVER DIES.

Evil zips down roads, in hostile cars, jeeringly, madly arrayed,
Like Dung bug pile heapers, counting: when and where to be paid.
Ye measure not in coffee spoons, but in cursing THE LOVING SCHOLAR,
With howling profit, more-more, more and more, of Devil-Dollar.

Your politics, your view of the games, of fiend, friend and foe,
Sad valuing earth, spirit, kin and kith: simply measured in dough.
In the room, women come and go, bragging up the fondest yellow,
With alloyed attention to really almost any kind of devil fellow.

GOD CAME TO AMERICANUS WARNING:
DRIVE OUT THE YELLOW DEVIL STORY, RENEW ANEW,
LONGLIFE, LOVE, NEIGHBOR: THESE THE OLDEST GLORY.

Charles F. Smith

My Gift

I opened my present and inside was God and he gave me myself.
And I asked him, "What should I do with this gift?"
And he said, "you can use it in my kingdom where there's an abundance
of joy and of sorrow, and love enough to meet your every need."
And I said, "but I'm a tiny speck; why would you need me in your kingdom?"
And he said, "if a tiny speck were in your eye, your whole body would
    know, would it not?"
And I said, "okay, but please tell me more about the sorrow,
I don't think I could handle much more of that."
And he said, "you could give it a try; besides, outside of my kingdom
    the sorrow is much worse."
I said, "I believe that is true, but I'm still not sure."
"You know, I could really botch things up for you;
I wouldn't want to get in the way."
"Yes", he said, "I suppose that's a possibility,
    but ultimately you will serve my purpose."
"Then what more could I want my God?," I said.
And he said not a word, but a tear came from his eye.
I took it as joy, 'cause I felt it too. And I just wanted to give some to you.

Gayle Berthold

Baby

In the beginning I made promises hoping somehow you could hear me.
I never meant to lead you in the wrong direction, or to make you
believe that somehow I was right. Where ever you are I hope you know
that I'd die to undue what I did to you. Somewhere floating above
the earth, I hope you knew how much I loved you. Every tear that
fell for you still falls for you today. I know that you were loving,
but I just wish I'd given you the chance to prove it. Society may
condemn me but maybe that is truth. I hope you understand that I
thought it was best for you. Sometimes I feel that it was I that was
saved by sparing you the pain. Please love me only for loving you
and not to heal the pain of losing someone near to me. I never gave
you the chance to be all that you could be, instead I stood in your
way. Please look down on me and see that I suffer, could you love me
today? A precious life and a perfect soul taken away from one so
worthy and deserving. I loved you enough to say that even though
I never knew you, I gladly take your place. To give you the chance
to be as special as you were bound to be.

Rachel A. Wilson

Enlightened

Life liberty
pursuit of happiness
Mother Earth
The universe
created by God
The Spiritual Being
Who we all know
But have never seen
Love death
The air so fresh
The moon the stars
The beasts below
The sunflowers majestic in a row
Black holes planets too
We all know
Were made by you.

Greg Candelaria

Lonely Looking Sky

I want to jump
into the miles of intense blue
    it crawls to all corners
calling me in.
    Can I dance with you?
I want to share your loneliness
    it's so beautiful
Can I fill my heart blue
and sleep on your pillow at dusk?
Your pure, flat silence
    is music.
filled with your alone-ness
    I am happy.

Philippa

Depression

Inside me there's a prison
I've built each wall with care
Inside the darkness of my cell
Are many secrets hidden there.
The pain that rips
When nights are long
The soul that cries
Wishing to be strong
A heart that breaks
But hasn't died
The river of tears
Refusing to be cried.
The many voices
Reaching into my cell:
Screams of injustice;
And dark threats of hell.
Only one light, in dreams do I see -
A voice softly whispering....
Telling me - that I alone hold the key -
Getting out of here is up to me...

Jessica S. Clark

A Child

The moon shines bright above
A child runs through the trees
chasing shadows, being chased
The darkness surrounds him
    it closes in

The moon is gone
there are no more shadows
    the child rests peacefully

Heather D. Cole

Reflections

The woman sits in her wheelchair...thinking...
she is filled with many thoughts and fears of what is to be,
In her mind, she travels to many far-off places where she has been;
  she relives many special times that she has lived.
In her mind, she wonders, "Why me, God? Why me?"
Oh, she's loved and does love...but now longs for her "better" days.
After all, what hope is there now? What is there to look forward to?

Things do happen; none of us are guaranteed anything.
It's natural to have thoughts and fears of what is to be.
As she tries to make sense of all this, she begins to realize, "Why not me?"
It's time now to find ways to go on—to reach out and Live
Hope and strength are available through Jesus Christ, who gave His
  life to give us hope, purpose, and a new life.

Friend, cherish your dreams your loves, your experiences, your past,
But find joy in those big and little "surprises" God brings you daily
  through friends, family, nature through Life itself!
Those things we often "expect" in life, take for granted, can be gone in a minute!
Life is strange, often unfair; yet with Christ hope, purpose, and life.

So, friend, think in your wheelchair, but go beyond your cherished past
Give and reach out to Him; find hope and love through Life in Him.

  Patricia E. Lokker

Tree Of Love

A moment passes—
The supple leaves of Springtime green, so soft and gentle on my eyes,
Now burn their passage with Autumn's fire, ashes soon, as hope in
Winter dies.
Take me back to Springtime where I once beheld your face,
And time for that brief moment stopped, or seemed at least to slow its pace;
Onto my soul your essence sear, in mind your image burn,
And cling again as tree to leaf, whose parting fate they've yet to learn.

Let us together that moment find, where in held hands 'tis coaxed to stay;
We can halt t'ward Autumn the ruthless march and dwell forever in a day.
As green in Spring, our bonded love if strong and pure might rise,
And in Forever softly pass, where leaves are green and Springtime never dies.

A moment passes —
Millenniums of season's endless march have come and gone;
Yet as we lived and died as one, the tree of love lives on.

  Robert Nicholls

Rage And Betrayal

I thought of us as friends, I guess it wasn't meant to be...
Always there to talk to, you now claim jealousy towards me?

A true friend is a confidant, somehow you just won't trust...
You stand behind me smiling, our "friendship" turns to rust.

Boys followed gradually, we hardly ever fought...
You've become a distant stranger, saying friends can just be bought.

My mind drifts slowly through your past, where did you stumble and fall...
Our frowns and tears so frequent, once we raced smiling down the hall.

I try to understand how hard your life must be all the nuisances that
  cause you so much strain...
Your personality lit up the room, what's giving you this pain?

My eyes fill with tears that you will never see, cold reality slaps your face...
Dreams that are forever lost, you will never fill a certain space.

The warmth of your smile, do you ever use your head...
Passing notes and looks during every class, you live and yet you're dead.

You're fighting with my sister, now you say that I must choose....
Friends becoming enemies, in your envy you will loose.

I thought you'd be a friend that I'd cherish, rage and betrayal are there..
I hope that you're happy, with one sigh ours is a friendship I don't share.

  Amanda Needs

Memories

Autumn winds are blowing
The trees will soon be bare
Let us enjoy this beauty
For this beauty is so rare

Like a sound from a bird
In the still of November
Is a magical sound
And nice to remember

Memories that are beautiful
Will never change I'm sure
Its like owning a prize possession
Because to me this is pure

So I'll keep all this beauty
In my mind I arranged
Stay on the road of memories
Which can never be changed

I'll create beautiful pictures
To hang on my wall
I'll love and enjoy them
From the spring through the fall

  Sal Caccavale

She

She stands,
  alone.
In a world filled with hate, hunger,
greed and passion.

She stands,
  Tall and proud,
proud of what she is,
and what she represents.

She stands,
  and thinks.
Those who pass by
  tease her,
  scorn her.
But still she thinks,
  and dares to dream.

She stands,
  forever.
There before the beginning,
and still there after the end.

  Lindsey Harlow

My Friend

No spoken words passed
The last time we met.
My feelings were masked
Though I'll never forget.
Arriving that night
I could not believe my eyes.
I stood there in fright,
What do you say when a friend dies?
They made him up well
No visible scars.
From that night of hell
That brought him to stars.
Not a day can go by
Without thinking of you
I can only ask, "Why,
Why did He take you?"
I do miss him so
But my heart will mend.
When its my turn to go
We'll meet in the end.

  Paula Chagnon

Sue Sea

Take me to the sea where the air is clear for my eyes to see.
The calm shimmering sea awakens my spiritual being,
An essence of peace within my heart.

I close my eyes visualizing the sea, I can feel the tides enrapturing me.
The touch of Neptune's hand guides my physically into a world of serenity.
I fall deep into a trance, frightened if I opened my eyes to a world of mankind.

I am transformed into a mermaid,
A creature of breath taking galore which my imagination has over soared.
My soft brunette tress flows effervescently in the control of the current's sea,
I am surrounded by tropical fishes to deliver all of my wishes
As they swim towards my direction.

The name Sue Sea is echoes throughout the ocean,
A name that was familiar to the under creatures as they swim towards my direction.
I do not know, how it came to be,
How the fish and the mammals inherited a queen named Sue Sea.
I realize now why there are tranquility,
While the people dressed in suites are in misery.

There is a numbness sensation as the people throw my ashes,
While my underwater creatures,
Gather my Soul to live eternity as Sue Sea amongst the ocean.

SueLee Hope Smith

A Rose From Rosemary's Garden

A burning orange haze replenishes the fragmented dawn
Morning dew drops cascading off long slender blades of prominent grass
Absorbed into rich soil, cultivating the endless splendor
Young blooming orchids smug in an angelic fog of heaven's cool crest of lament
Whispers through the winter's wind soothe, calm and anointed
Flying carpets along with majestic butterflies cover-coat the dense
  aroma of alluring omniscience
In the midst of the prosperous garden a delicate sincere rose basks
  erect in the eternal limelight
So pure and benign the angels sulk in envy
A heartwarming smile and pair of glistening eyes nourish the surrounding wild life
The atmosphere, so serene and tranquil, remains glazed with harmonic overtones
Jovial sprites abound from tiny indentures, scattering the sky with
  vivid purples, blues, and reds
Nature's masquerade massage adoring souls, lingering in the meadow
An animated life and goodwill towards humanity, constructed these Babylonian Gardens
The massive gates always beckon and entice our longing with its luster
As we walk naked back into the world, sweet rays of cordiality ease our aggression
Although the glorious moon has arisen from its daytime slumber
The rose, an archetype in its way, dances amongst the fiery shadows
Never to give way to the dying embers, striving through against the
  midnight candlelight.

Jeff Comeau

The Greatest Love Affair

My pen, the lover of my life, make love that only the two of us can
understand. As I hold Mr. Pen, he trusts me and believes that I would
never steer him wrong. As I push, he never inserts a stop or caution
sign and as he glides across Mrs. Paper to gently soothe her waiting
emptiness, she never goes away feeling unsatisfied.

But, the bet part of this relationship is my Sister Imagination.
Sister Imagination loves Mr. Pen and adores Mrs. Paper. As Mr. Pen
allows Imagination to leave the confinement of her thoughts, she
eagerly explores those mysteries far beyond the stratosphere of comprehension.

When Sister Imagination takes flight, Mr. Pen dashes pass
unforgiveness and whispers mercy, He dances pass confusion and replaces
it with peace, He cruises pass insecurity and showers it with
strength, He circles about pleasure and graciously lands in love —
a love which surpasses all human understanding.

As Mr. Pen gently penetrates Mrs. Papers existence, he bleeds
joyfully in her presence. Only then does Mrs. Paper sigh with relief,
knowing that once again, she has experienced a small taste of Heaven
here on Earth!

Kecia A. Hill

My Sorrow

We, Immigrants, are also
part of your community,
my community, our community.

Don't treat us harshly
We have feelings and dreams
the same as you.

We don't want to impose
our culture or our language
We want to share with you
if you let us.

We all live
in the same country
and We all want
the best for all of us.

We strive to be the best
the same as you.

We look and sound different
Yet We have human feelings
the same as you.

Estela Delgado

Snow

Many winters we've had snow
Before it comes we rush to and fro.
Some people like it,
Some people don't.
Some go out in it
Some say 'I won't.'

It snows and it snows,
Children's faces glow
They go outside and they play.
For what seems like all day.

They make snow angels,
Have snowball fights,
They wish they could play
All day and all night.

Work places close, school lets out,
Rushing, rushing all about.
When snow comes, it usually stays
And it won't go away
For a number of days.

Rhonda Barton-Joe

Things I Love

I love the ocean's roar-
the sea rushing to shore.

I love babies of all kinds
Trying to understand their minds.

I love things made of lace
stitched with love and grace.

I love people of all ages
watching and waiting for all phases.

I love a moonlight night
Oh, what a lovely sight!

I love the stars above.
These are some of the things I love.

Vadie Lockhart

My Dad

I miss my Pops.
I'll give him a call.

Robert Duron

At My Pool

At my pool there's lot's of fun,
but my lifeguard tells me not to run.
At my pool there's a slide.
That's the only ride.

Best of all is the view,
But the most is the pool.
Annette Kowalczyk

Meetings

Thank you for your kindness,
   your humor and your smile.
And thank you for your courage,
   that represents your style.
It isn't easy meeting,
   talking on the phone.
And is there any reason,
   for feeling so alone?
Angels come from far above,
   they just find things to do.
But can I take, and is it fair,
   the time I ask of you?
But if it's not to wonder,
   and now it's time to try.
There isn't any moisture,
   in the hollow tears I cry.
Daniel Williams

Abide In Gratitude

It is expected of the pressures of life
to trample down our attitude

But it takes a special kind of person
to abide in gratitude

We often overlook simple gifts
that we should be grateful for,

And focus on what we do not have
to increase our final score

There's no end to what we stress about
We let our inner peace elude

For every moment holds a miracle,
if we abide in gratitude
Linda O'Neil

The Path Within My Mind

When evening comes and all alone
I close the door behind
And open the door to yesterday
To a path within my mind

'Tis not a lonely road
For every turn I find
Flowers and breezes and berries
On the path within my mind.

And for the hour I dwell again
In a place so long ago
Where friends and food and laughter
Made these memories grow

I walk with you once again
And feel your breath on mine
And curse the morning's closing gate
On the path within my mind
Mary L. Brennan

Three Years In A Day

Leave me to hide
Down so long
Did she save me
When I died

In this lie
Nailed to the floor
Can't explain
What I'm waiting for

In my eyes
I haven't forgotten
The bleeding tries
leaving me wasted

Sickness in my chest
Spinning me through
Part of your mess
feeling so dirty

Tried to be your world
And you needed more
set me free
Cause you feel not a thing
Damian Carter

Steak

I don't like the steak,
It's juicy and red.
It's bleeding on my plate,
I don't think it's dead!

There's grizzle on the side,
A bone in the middle.
I don't want to eat it,
Not even a little!

Please send it away,
It's making me sick.
Send it to China,
Or a place of your pick!
Karen Panunzio

Epilogue

From across the room
He watched me in silent appraisal,
Wide eyes fixed in that wordless realm
Wondering who I might be.
Erect he sat, and serene
Midst his loving fold
Holding the object of his curiosity
And radiating a precocious strength
For one just four months old.
How to describe that insistent stare,
A bonding moment so profound,
A moment when with eternity we share
That cosmic force to which we're bound.
His mother brought him to me,
And after a moment
Sitting in my lap
Head tilted, staring up
His cherubic face softened -
And I said, "Hello Grandson".
A. Zitlaw

Children Of Innocents

Children! Who do you turn too.
You look towards your youth
for guidance
For adults are not to be trusted
Beverly Houston

Corporate Take-Over

The Company gets bigger,
Everyone should be happier,
After long days, long hours,
Fourteen years, altogether.

Co-workers want to go,
Where? They do not know,
But, the C.E.O.s,
To cash their dough.

For C.E.O.s, all is past,
For workers, will it last?
Changes made too fast,
Can shatter everyone's forecast.

C.E.O.s, your liquidity
Is in your work force quality!
Do not dismiss human dignity
Like your inventory.
Benny Fits

Simple Things

Simple things in life are free
an unbridled horse, a crashing sea
the desert sands, a hummingbird
a silly grin with one kind word

Simple things in life are good
a roaring fire, a stack of wood
a rustling breeze, a child's smile
fallen leaves heaped in a pile

Simple things in life are true
a thunderstorm, the morning dew
an apple pie, a loving note
a fish on a line in a small rowboat

Simple things in life are fair
a mountain stream, a baby bear
a shapely cloud, a babbling brook
a hearty laugh with a knowing look

Simple things in life are lost
a power's surge on computer's DOS
a snail's pace, a look around
simple things in life abound
Patricia L. Vanourney

Melody

There's a melody in the shadows,
so beautiful and so clear.
Beyond the mountains and the meadows
a song fills within the air.

The sound overcomes you
with its rhythm and rhyme.
This melody will bring you through
the hour glasses of time.

It caress's your soul
with a delicate sensation.
Making your body take a toll
of awe and relaxation.

Close your eyes to wonder,
will this melody be forever here?
In your heart and soul, dig way under,
it's there, always ever so near.
Sheena Grierson

Untitled

Accordion frenzy fills the air.
Harmonized with clarinet and sax.
A colorful, vigorous rhythm.
Tantalizing costumes capture the eye.
Hypnotized by pretty girls.
Three quick steps and a hop.
Inebriated with joy.
Around and around they twirl.
Seeming never to tire.
Possessed with excitement.
Til the wee hours of the morn.
Hot sweat bodies.
Reluctantly retreat from the floor.
These exhausted polka dancers.

John R. Forsell

No Apology

I am what I am.
I am what I am since day one!
   It is deep.
   It is determination.
   It is joy.
   It is love.
   It is strong.
It's beyond me, beyond my control,
Can't help it! It is in my nature.
It leaves me no choice, but to be
   What I am,
   Me!

Rosemarie N. Lucas

The Tree

The tree
the tree grows
the tree grows pears
the tree gets mighty
just like it should
but then the gas
comes through the air
it comes to tear
up that mighty pear
the tree hangs on
with all its might
but it can not
bare to fight
that mighty gas
that is in the air,
so it dies.
That is what pollution does
to innocent people,
nature or grub.

P. Caren

Life's Fault

It's the fault of life that I can't
see thee anymore.
Though I feel you.
It's a lie's fault that I cannot
touch you.
I don't know what to do.
Are you upset with me?
Are you looking down on me ?
Hoping ... Praying...
Even missing me.
All these things I have
to wonder, my friend
For these are everyday
Thoughts for me, that will
never end.

Rita Marlene

Life

The morning light shines so bright
Through all of God's Glory and might.

Our work we do day by day,
Knowing God will show us the way.

With his love and gentle care,
We know we can go to him in prayer.

All our problems seem so blue,
But with his guidance he is so true.

Then as the evening sun goes down
And night falls all around,

We will sleep ever so safe,
Knowing he's there when we awake.

Beverly Creel North

Lonely

Lonely as can be, no one to care for me,
So sweet and kind, with a lot of time.

Marvin Jones

Peep Hole To The Soul

Eyes caressing, feather light,
Searching for that window.
Pray for the gift of second sight.
A peep hole to the soul.
So easy to assume what's right,
To focus on a goal.

Walls that hold them out,
Am I on the inside?
Do we know what we're about,
Do our souls ever collide?
Walls translucent, yet stout,
Let them see that we hide.

E. J. Conn

My Twin

   Our hearts and souls were
connected at birth, when the time
came for us to be placed on this earth.
   From family to family as the
two of us were passed, we hoped
to have a love that would last.
   Life was tough for us, this
I know, leaving us with pain
that we were never able to show.
You were taken so soon at
the young age of thirty five, much to
young for you to die.
   Now that God has got you
firmly in his grasp, the pain that
you suffered is indeed in the past.
   In peace as you rest my dearest
twin, always know my love is deep within.

Melissa Armstrong

The Lords Bidding

When I've completed all to do,
The Lord will take me, to be with you.
The Lord will whisper in my ear,
Not only me, the world will hear.
For in heaven I shall ascend,
To be with Jesus, at the end.
   God Bless

Raymond Ruland

Drowning

Fear
Anguish
My fists are swinging wildly
Discord
Detest
My mind is filled with hate
Stress
Anxiety
The anger now is killing me
Hope
Curiosity
What will be my fate?

Rob Paterson

Isfahan

Stars streaking clover skies
Wet flakes winter white
Sulphur gauze sweeps
Across cobalt east
River a mirror
Of black
Brushed with leaves

Roses on Isfahan's old
Bridge
Silk and doves
Turquoise mosque
Wild moss.

Bees swarm around
White orchid moon
Where my grandfather's
Pistachio trees
Bloom.

White Cloud

Dedicated To Billie Holiday

Captured so gently
in the glow:
the bird with
fluttering wings
is silent
and magical.

The shattered halo

of the angel
of mercy
responded
frantically;

And yet, she
never arrived
soon enough
or did she?

Tommi Massey

My Favorite Place

My favorite place is in my room,
Where never I think of gloom.
There, I can be, a dragon rider,
Or a ninja, master fighter.
I could even play the sax,
Or sit back and relax.
Then if all goes awry,
Sit back and carelessly sigh,

   In, my room.

Amile G. C. Wilson

Alluring Warmth Of The Soul

The summer's morning grass
Is sparkling wet with dew,
The sun peers o'er the horizon
The tender earth still cool.

The sun's rays gain strength
And the world warms end to end,
A warmth that touches both of us
As you become my friend.

The rays grow warmer rapidly
Each flower looks to the sun,
Our friendship grows ever stronger
Now we're no longer two, but one.

The sun dries the delicate dew
And opens every flower;
You opened your heart and dried my tears
With love, the strongest power.

Angela Eckerly

My Heart-Shaped World

Tolerance is a chisel,
To carve this world of stone,
Forgiveness is a mallet,
Let's not use it all alone.

The tools of compassion, common sense,
And compromise we must use,
Be positive, use all of these,
We have no choice but to choose.

It's not black or white at all,
Only colors in between,
With these tools day by day,
The shape one day will be seen.

Use these tools day by day,
A great deal or a little,
We'll have some fun along the way,
But this shape it is no riddle.

It may take days or maybe years,
To shape this world of old,
And when we do, then look around,
You'll see our heart has turned to gold.

Donald Ray Liescheidt

Birds

Birds are often debonair,
as they glide softly through the air.
With exception to the vulture,
proper eating manner is bird culture.

Birds are pretty,
birds are nice,
some have the colors of paradise.
Birds are big,
birds are small,
some birds are the biggest of them all.
Birds are ugly,
birds are cute,
some birds are as melodic as the flute.

You can see birds in the street,
you can see birds in the park,
you can even see birds in the dark!

Laila Muhammad

The Last Good Bye

I live in a sea of loneliness
in this house with you
Silence blankets the room
I am alone tonight
even though you are sitting here
you are remote
Television is your companion
it comes to life
and takes your thoughts
further from me
you have turned me away
I embrace loneliness
I can not relate to you
I must find meaning
for myself
you have abandoned
the woman in me
you deny my existence
It is "Good Bye" at last

Anne Elizabeth Barber

Cape May In March

I stayed here to find me
against the sun wall
of the sea,
with a sea gull in my hand
and the wave's sounds
full of sand.
Endless corridor of sound
to make the world shape
round
pulls the moon in me to change
with a tidal
rearrange
as pebbles, shells and shapes that lie
like constellations in the sky,
riveted upon the sand,
with ridges round on every side
til gently moved
by some spring tide.

Jean MacKay

Corridors Of Darkness

My Soul — haunted
by a thousand
shattered pieces
of obscure memories;
Existence that lay
in somber shreds
merging with darkness,
in secluded patterns
like fragments of coral,
growing where nobody sees.

My Heart — vulnerable
from tests of fate
always revealing
the dark surfaces;
making futile attempt
to navigate passages
like dim corridors,
in quiet desperation
to reach the untouchable
place in my soul.

Jeani Ekkens

Visitation

A statue, I sit
a silent shadow frozen
in layers of
suffocating ice.
Barely breathing, I feel
his eyes
dance over me
and mark me with fire;
they smolder and burn.
Sparks scatter
across my senses to melt my mind,
and ice cracks
as I awaken to feel the flame
from his fingertips;
he touches my smile.

Laura Cole

From The Mouth Of A Broken Babe

It was not you who grew up
Afraid to go home, afraid to sleep,
Afraid of making microscopic mistakes.
It was not your voice trying out
(silently within your mind)
Into the night for freedom from fear,
With wide-waken eyes.
No. No,
You never had to sit
And explain how "falling"
Broke your arm,
Or how the "door" blackened
Your eagle eye.
No, you did not...did you?
Then how can you
Judge me? You outsiders.
You lawyers, doctors, teachers.
How can you be my judge?
It was not you who grew up...

Melinda Rigby

The Wanderer

I'm ashamed and sorry
I had broken up the team.
I even turned my back on you
To follow up a dream.

I tried to open many locks,
But it took me time to see,
That when I left you far behind
I had also left the key.

In my deepest sorrows
I tried to walk dry land,
But when it was the mud I found
You still took my hand.

I thought me independent,
A sheep that walks alone,
But when I became lost and scared
It was you who guided me home.

I'm sorry I ever wandered,
I'm sorry I ever strayed,
But with you to love and guide me, Lord,
I don't have to be afraid.

Roberta J. Howard

Bunco

The bell has rung at
table one
who reached the score of
twenty one

We roll our dice with strategy
for three sixes are
what you want to see

You grab and yell
for all to hear
Bunco
as it was just
rolled right here

Patricia Rivera

Window Of Life

Standing there, painting what I see,
through the window of life,
through you to me.
I see you waiting,
waiting for what?
Waiting for a trolly,
I wonder what?
Waiting to hitch a ride,
or just to wander?
I watch, I wonder.
I watch you,
waiting, walking,
as I watch you,
I paint,
I paint my window,
My window of life,
through you to me.
I watch and I wonder, then I say,
My window, my life,
from me, to you.

Trinity Sloan Lache

Still Needing Her Love

I'm filled with too much anger
eating away at my being
I hate her
for her leaving

I still cry
what did I do
my eyes are dry
sick of dying over you

I love you mom
but I can't forgive you
I can't accept who you have become
until you admit what you have done

Dawn Bondi

Life

Life is like a game.
No matter how you roll the dice,
it's never the same.
Play by the rules,
and keep your business discreet.
Whether you're playing at home,
work, or even in the streets.
Keep your faith in God;
don't forget to pray.
And you'll live long enough
to play another day.

LeConya C. Jones

Reality

Everyone can be happy
Just don't face reality

You can't think about
Bad, evil and the crime

To live in this world
Just don't face reality

Be happy for what you have
not for what you don't

You can smile
Just don't face reality

It sucks no matter how you look at it
Abuse, violence, hate

You can have everything
Just don't face reality

The world is cruel
we all must change

We all have masks on and
Just don't face reality

You can be dead
and then face reality

Katie Nellen

Violent Violet

The sky, a canvas
streaming with
violent violet
the rain disturbs
its silent, silence
my purple prose
a wilting rose
its beauty fading, left unseen
unknown
no one cares
about its thorns
there's no one there
to grieve or morn
my store bought dress on sale
is soiled and torn
alone I am
a violent dying rose,

Elizabeth Erskine

Transience

What once was ruby
is now dim
will blacken and die
after it glows again

He who had crawled
can now walk
will crawl again
and stumble and fall

The leaves had turned
and now fall
will reappear
at April's call

The dust had breathed
and now lives
will quicken one day
at the hour God gives.

Christopher Melton

Losing Our Unborn Babes

Oh, my unborn baby,
So small and so tiny;
Never a chance in this world,
Just in my womb did she curl.

We dream, we hope, and we pray,
For what the future will be day to day.
And then the tragic moment comes
When no heartbeat can be found.

There is no grief to compare,
The terrible feeling of despair,
When you lose your little one,
In the womb or full grown.

But continuing on is a must,
And in our God we must trust,
That there will be a better day,
And another babe will come our way.

Sheila D. Hoker

Common Goal

As onward to the common goal
I pray it won't be long,
I fight the fight and stride the race
until I reach my home.
So may I bear some burden,
for those along the way,
whose faith begins to waiver,
whose life begins to fray.
I'll remind them of the Savior
whose breath so long has past,
and of the pow'r and the glory
which is His to last.
And should I start to stumble
and for Heaven no more care,
may one come to my rescue
and point me to the Heir.

Jennifer Arnold

Untitled

Every time I get the confidence
to turn my back on the world
I get a knife stuck in it.

By what?

By whatever's behind me.

My past
My failures
My mistakes

Jeremy Joslin

My Love

How much do I love you
The words can not explain, but
everyday you're gone from me my
heart can feel the pain I
need you every morning to help me
through the day, but now I must help
my self since you're so far away.

    I wish you were by my side
so I could hold you so tight and every
time I kiss your lips I'd know our
love is right, but now I must leave you
and I must let you go still keep in
mind my darling.
    I'll always love you so!

Theresa Natale

Thinking Of The One I Love

I go to the river
Late at night
Sitting and thinking
In the bright moon light

Thinking of the one
I love so much
Waiting to feel his
Loving touch

He tells me he doesn't
Love me anymore
So I went to my room
And closed the door

As I lay on my bed,
All's I could do was cry
But deep down inside
I wanted to die

I've always heard, there's
More men in the sea
Maybe someday there'll be
A special one for me

Pamela Christene Beard

Why I Hate Bees

Why I hate bees
Because they're worse than fleas
They make me sneeze
They give me a chill
This is not a thrill
Then they start to tease me
This does not please me
They sting me on the knees
I'm still not pleased
That's why I hate bees!!!

Onika Williams

God

By myself, but I am not alone.
He stands and watches over me,
Since I have grown.

He is my caretaker, my guardian angel.
He loves me always, yet I am a stranger.

Knowing all my secrets and my sins,
He lives up above,
with the great winds.

I go to him,
when I am afraid.
Looking to the sky, in a great gaze.

Who is he,
And why? I can't answer this,
so I cry.

He comforts me,
with all his love,
and tells me to look,
up above

By myself,
But I am not alone.

Jennie Wisner

Untitled

Is everything always your fault?
I know you think it is,
I must admit I do too,
But it is not always you,
Sometimes it is me,
Sometimes it is others,
I just want you to know,
That I love you with all of my heart,
And I always will.

Lauren O'Connor

Hate

Let it out in a rage
Feel as if I'm in a cage
Locked up tight let none escape
Dark and deep, I hate hate
Kept up in my soul forever
Until my mind begins to tether
As it grows it hurts more
Til all strikes in down pour
What kinds of satin spell is this
One of a sad fearful kiss
Breath of death creeping down my neck
Myself is whom I must protect
From this sin I brought upon myself
I also brought a psychotic wealth
A blanket of hell rapped around me tight
Save me from this fearful fright
What ever it takes to set me free
Help me now, I do plead
Until this day, in my future - never
Hate is what I see forever

Sara Haddad

Untitled

One morning I woke
In the wake of an
Unforgotten storm.
She wrapped her arm's
Around me like a hangman's
Noose dangling in the sun.
For days I struggled
But freedom took no form.
Hatred grew and faith was my son.
I escaped and I ran but
The storms never left my side.
I never surrendered
And the icy hand
Of fate compromised.
I found an uncommon
Strength to survive.
There is reverence and
Hope in the warmth of dreams.
No matter what dilemma you face
- there is always spirit to Believe.

Trey Outlaw

Friends

Friends are forever.
Friends stick together.
In good times and in bad.
Friends should respect, love,
and appreciate.
We laugh and cry with
each other.
They are like brothers
and sisters we have never had.
They come and go but
"Best friends stay forever."

Jennifer Wong

Nobody

Invasive
Sensations of warmth
creep along my limbs.
To center
my spine
my heart.

Foreign pulses
radiate through me.
Pulses
louder than mine.

Grasping panic
Energy forcibly gushes
into my mouth
filling my lungs
Permeating existence.

Until
there is no pulse
no breath
no body
nobody.

Cailyn Gray

Follow Your Heart

In times of worry
    when skies are grey
The world seems darker
    with each passing day
Follow your heart
    it has something to say
Your heart is wonderful
    always at play
It knows only goodness
    never will it stray
Full of love and truth
    help is on the way
Follow your heart.

C. E. Huggins

A New Face

A new face
A new name
But the feeling remains the same

Getting alright vibes
From down inside
Letting the feeling grow
Making it show

I just wanted to tell you how
My thoughts of you are right now
So please don't go astray
And turn me away

You're like a guiding light
That I want anytime
Day or night
You're so fine
Can't get you out of my mind

Tammy Learned

Thunder Poem

Sometimes thunder makes me glad,
Sometimes thunder makes me sad.
Sometimes thunder makes me proud,
Sometimes thunder is too loud.
Sometimes thunder goes around,
Sometimes thunder hits the ground.
Sometimes thunder is scary,
Sometimes thunder is merry.

James C. Bakken

In Your Eyes

In your eyes I see a world
it is so beautiful
it is a place where we can go
a place to be free
a place with just you and me
I long to be in this world
this world in your eyes
free from life
free from care
no longer a body
just a spirit
floating endless
in a sea of heaven
together forever

Robert M. Pagel

Midnight Star

The flowered fields of love,
Once cherished but now dead,
The sardonic psalms of youth,
The patron'd rhymes have fled.
The terrific smiles of chided lips,
Once open but now creased,
Are but shades upon a sheet
For the heart of him has ceased

The withered bouquet upon his breast
Gleamed brighter than his eye,
And upon him fell a chill'n tear
From the mourning sky.
No more his past will haunt his soul
Nor his present be marred
For he made that Faustian pact
And became a midnight star

Mike King

We Are Talented People

We are talented people plucked
up from our home land shackled
thrown into belly of ships the
strongest survived the weakest
thrown overboard food for
things in the sea, set foot in
America sold as slaves could
not be families because of the
powers of being, the powers of
being have always been afraid
because we are talented people
whether it's work, sing, dance,
or play we are talented people
we don't have to work at it as
hard as they were are talented
people we are talented people
talented people

Yvonne Pugh

Mother

Mother has pretty brown hair,
and nice brown eyes
she's as beautiful as the stars,
and as important as the sun
I love her because she's my
mother oh! she is the one.

Benita Henderson

Untitled

Waiting, am I like
Flowers
Whose petals bowed
With moment of
Gift
The dew
Endowed,
Spread open my heart
To
Life's staircase,
Then down
Down
The darken space
What spark of
Light be
I?
One step more
Before
I
Die.

Karol Wehrley

The Tree

A sad little tree I was the day
They came and cut me all away.
I knew not what my fate would be
I would just have to wait and see.
My Creator had greater dreams for me.
The shelter for His Son, I would be.
I was made into the shed
in which he made his little bed.
Sweetly singing the angels came
to honor great His Holy Name.
Oh how proud I am to say,
I gave honor in a greater way
Than all the trees that grow so high
and never even reach the sky.

Mary Satink Hughmanic

Dad

He gets up each morning to race the sun
like a bee whose work is never done.
He is not but another drone
he does not grouch
he does not groan.

For it is obvious to see
he appreciates the work
God has given him.
It may give him pains
yet you will never see him complain.

Once work is done
he still yet races the sun
for his family will have to wait
to see his shining face.

For each day when he comes home
we should seat him upon a throne
for he is why I am here
instead of on the streets with fear.

That is all, I have to say,
I'll write again, another day.

Robert Huneycutt

Falcons

A falcon can be caged
But cannot be paged
A falcon has claws
That looks like saws
A falcon hunts with a mate
He does not hate
When a falcon is angry
It can be very scary
When a falcon is sleeping
You are peeping
When a falcon is hurt badly
You watch it die sadly
There's nothing that lies
Of a dead bird walking
That's not really talking

Brandi Nicole Ferguson

Angels

Miracles from the sky.
Gee I wonder why.
They help us out when were in need.
They're spectacular people yes in deed.
They tell me right from wrong.
And help me to be strong.
I'm glad they're on my side.
And that is why I strive.
To be the best that I can be.
For people just like you and me.

Amanda Annette Beard

Waiting

Sitting here
   in the thick dark

Remembering

Remembering
   the pain

And yet

I have only to lift my eyes
   to the stars

Cool
Waiting
Waiting

Barbara Preston

Momma

Momma you made me
the person I am today
Even when the skies
were grey you said
it would be okay.
Although we didn't
have much you made
sure we made it with
what we had.
When everybody came
down on me they judged
and criticized me, you
spoke up and stood up
for me. For that I really
admire and thank you.
Even though there's no
way I can repay you
Momma thanks for
being true and
Momma remember I will always love you.

Marlon Gillespie

Songbird Song

Pretty bird
singing so lively
with humor
looking for adventure
seeking love
everyday she dreams
and hopes her dreams
for she is smart and kind
gentle as a calming wave
soothing sore feelings
loves those close
friend and a sister
she has hope for another
she mustn't give in
it would darken
the shades of life
keep on singing
dear little songbird
your dreams will come true

Kristal Sparks

About Gordon

He challenges himself
And inspires those around him
To improve upon their best
And follow where he leads them

He's creative, an achiever
Both a thinker and a dreamer
His smile's warm
    His touch is gentle
His laugh's infectious
    His love is tender

He's quick, and he's curious
He sets his standards very high
He's disciplined, he's in command
And he's strong enough to cry

Sharon Lawson

Untitled

The birds came together
They didn't worry about the weather
They wondered about their friend
And wondered when will it all end.
This beautiful duck
Who swam in the pond.
Early every morning
From dusk till dawn

Could not be found.
They searched and searched to no avail
Then all of a sudden one saw a
A brown and purple tail.
Here was their friend
Coming from behind the bushes

Their friend Gail.

Florence D. Schmalke

Just Da 2 Of Us

She's my hubba bubba bubble yum
    Sugar bugar honey bun
We rub a dub in a tub of love
Cuddle together like a hand and glove
Heavenly love above da clouds
Heart to heart so happy and proud
Wedding bells and marriage vows
If our love was money
    We could afford a child
    It's Just Da 2 Of Us

Ernest Tyler

You Are One...

You are one and I am two,
You are proud and I am true.
You hold my hand when I am scared,
I open my heart to yours when bared.
You let me fly and I look below,
You're always there, I have a shadow.
You hold it in and I let it out,
You let me go when I scream and shout.
You are one and I am two,
You are proud and I am true.
You comfort me when I cry at night,
I'll never let you give up our fight.
And when you soar, I feel so free,
You are what makes me, me.
You are one and I am two,
I am nothing without you.

Jody Nichols

True Understanding

Understanding is a deceiving term,
Cloud like, ever changing, subjective.
When I understand do I condone?
When I understand do I allow?
True understanding rips away fear,
Opens the heart, smashes bigotry.
Few understand — they've not been
understood. The scar tissue builds up.
So don't understand unless prepared to
love unconditionally.

Sandra Janson Perkins

Snowflake

In a population of
billions
She is unique
Intricate, beautiful
She is free
Drifting by the
dependent clusters
She is pure
In solitary glee
She trickles to her
destiny
Ready, willing
She is the single magic
droplet
That springs fervent
new life
from the glacial earth

Jeannie Ralston

Searching For Melanie

    It's been a long time
since we've gone our own ways
    Myself, and my friend
from my childhood days
I think of her and wonder
    "What did she grow up to be?"
And do you think she ever wondered
    the same about me?
I'm reaching out and hope to find
    my dear childhood friend
And pray I didn't miss the chance
    to be her friend again.

Rori Ettleman

Goodbye Sweetheart

Goodbye my darling we're parting
I know this will break your heart
Sweet Jesus just told me this morning
That tomorrow we must part

My mother is dead and in heaven
My father has gone there I know
Sister has gone to meet mother
And now it's my time to go

Goodbye my darling I love you
Love you with all of my heart
I'll wait for you up in heaven
The days won't be far apart

Goodbye my darling I'll miss you
I'll miss you with all of my heart
I'll wait for you up in heaven
Never no more to part
Goodbye Sweetheart

Clair Forney

The Man With A Master Plan

There was a man
Who had a dream
A dream that would be heard
Word for Word
By every boy and girl
Throughout the foreign land
Black and white shall one day unite
To let everyone be free
In the eyes of every girl and boy
From sea to shining sea
This man was great
Yes sir indeed
Dr. Martin Luther King Jr.
Through those perils days and nights
So that each and everyone of us
Here today
Would be able to pray
To praise this great man
Who united a country . . .

Lloyd Gyamfi

Peace

    Under the sky,
In the world,
    There is prejudice
everywhere, not a single
    place is peaceful.

    But on the
islands, full of
creatures and no
human beings, you
can always find peace there.

Sophia Wilson

Stars

I see the stars.
Their shining bright.
They are so pretty,
Under the moon light.
They shine tonight.
They shine tomorrow.
Hopefully they will stay,
forever in my sight,
under the moonlight.

Hannah Phillips

So Sad

So sad are the moments when I
remember. There was a time when I
thought our love would last, as we
both would move ahead of the past.

So sad are the moments when kissing
you my heart would skip a beat, when
I could have put the riches of my
love for you at your feet.
But now all I have are memories
to keep.

So sad are the moments when love
has to end, when we break instead of
bend, when my heart weeps and no
longer skips a beat.

So sad are the moments, when the
thoughts of loving you where so crystal
clear and losing love was always that
hidden fear.

Kymberli Roberson

To Be Alone, I'll Never Be

To be alone, I'll never be
While the Spirit of God abides in me
To sit at night with dark around
I can't be lost when I am found

To feel the cold and dampness near
And see all others full of cheer
Sometimes makes me feel alone
Til a voice within me makes Him known

The wind He sent to feel its breeze
The trees are bent to touch their leaves
The stars He made to shine for me
To be alone, I'll never be

Yet sometimes anger fills my heart
Until I say to it "Depart"
For while the Lord hath love for me
To be alone, I'll never be

Yea God has made man over all
And if I fail or should I fall
There's comfort in His word for me
To be alone, I'll never be

Charles R. Enos

The Anointed One

I see strange faces staring at me.
Like if I am anointed in my disease.
I am not poison, I do not bite.
To people I am the quiet parasite.
I am not afraid of what is inside me.
One day in my life I want to feel free,
Free from all agonizing pain.
On the last night I will close my eyes,
questioning the path.
God chose for me.

Justin Burns

Floppy's Hop

We opened Floppy's cage today
I wanted to pet her, she wanted to play.
She hopped in the kitchen
She hopped in the hall and bedroom,
Just like a big furry ball.
She hopped in her pen.
That's ok - she wanted to hop today.

Troy Bowers

Reflection

The reflection on the water
blends the horizon with the sky.
As sunset turns to dusk,
a gentle breeze blows through the eve.
Peacefulness settles over the lake
and moves my soul.
It slows my pace, and quiets my spirit,
so that I may see majesty.

Cynthia J. Ellis

White And Black

As a white angel flew by
I saw a tear drop from her eye
I wondered why
she had to cry.

I look up in her world above
to see pretty sights, clouds and doves
and I wondered why
she had to cry.

Then I realized, a big black cloud
with crashing thunder, it was so loud,
I looked in the sky
and started to cry.

This thing in the sky wasn't a cloud
but it was pollution, crying out loud
Now I know why
she started to cry.

Katherine Hilline

I Will See You In Paradise

An entirely blind man sees reflection
   in closed eyes.
Ignorance is bless to those
   who are wise.
You pray, you pray
   not wishing to die.
Paris or Entebbe awaits you
   on the other side.
You sigh, you cry;
   for another sunset, another sunrise.
I'll whisper gently
   as you close your eyes
I will see you there;
I will see you in paradise.

Donald Chapman

My Heart

You said you weren't lying,
I can't believe I actually thought
you were for real!

Did you ever wonder how all
this would make me feel?

You're not even trying!
You think you're out of my league.

You can't just make a promise,
then break it like a twig!

You expect me to just forgive
and forget, it's just a little lie.

Maybe that's what you think,
but that's my heart you're playing with.

Heather Lewis

Throne

Sitting on a throne of lies
I wear this crown of bloody thorns.
And inside me hides,
A man that sits and mourns
What have I become?
A shattered man, with feelings numb.

Inside I sit and cry.
I pray to God that I will die.
Now I live with this pain,
not even knowing,
when it came.
Now I sit all alone.
And think of the people
I had once known.

Sitting on this bed of tears.
My whole life is now a nightmare.
I hold the scars of life's betrayal,
All this torture, without bail.
You don't just stab, but twist.
Don't know how I got into this.

Nate Hamilton

Special Guy

You walk towards the sunlight,
Your hair is flowing in your face.
You try to find a special guy,
In a special place. Don't try so
hard to look for him, he's found
to find you first. But if you attitude
is straight, and you never
tell a lie, chances are, if you find
someone, he'll be your special guy.

Samantha Hathaway

The Call

Don't feel sad for now I'm free
I have gone home, God called for me
I could not stay another day
It was my time, I heard him say.

There was yet much to do
These things, I must leave for you
Perhaps a child, an elderly man
Needs you now to lend a hand.

A touch, a hug, a kiss we've shared
A sign to me you really cared
A child's arms around my knees
"I love you Nana" was sure to please.

Perhaps my leaving will bring you grief
My time on earth seems all too brief
But when God called, I took his hand
It was time to see the Promised Land.

Lift up your heart, look to the light
Share his love and seek his might
Seek his mercy and peace to thee
Sooner than you think, you'll see me.

Phyllis Robertson Fry

Untitled

Love you, I do,
I knew it would be you...
Needing love and care,
is what we will share...
    Please don't ever go away...
I would die on that day...
Go to the heavens above...
    If I could no longer
have your love...

Lea Anne Walker

My Great Admire

Admire him when he,
walks on by.
Admire his beautiful,
smile.
Admire his eyes as he
looks into your deep soul.
Admire him when he holds,
you close to him in winter's cold.
Admire him close by the sea as,
he sings you a love song to you.
At night he'll hold you close,
and say "I love you" by,
the warm fire.
And you'll say "I love you"
back the smile,
So when you see this person
Admire him,
He is sweet as can be.

Laura Dinh

I'm Sorry

I tell myself
I'm not going to cry.
I say I don't have anymore
tears left to cry.

But when the pain starts,
Tears don't hesitate to fall.

I tell myself to hang on
and I won't fall!
But what if I can't
hang on any longer, and I fall!
Like a thousand bricks?

It doesn't matter.
If I do fall,
I won't have to deal with
my pain and sorrow!

I'm sorry, but I can't
hang on any longer.
My rope is too short.

Eileen Dezalia

Fall Colors

More leaves turn color every day.
The air is crisp and cool,
And as we take our morning walk
The colors seem to sing, to talk.
Ochres and russets murmur soft;
The golds and reds shout out aloft,
"See me, see me, look and see.
We'll soon be gone, but then we'll be
Back in the Spring". So the cycle goes:
Bud - to leaf - to jewel.

Ann Van Veen

My Dreams

I have so many dreams that no one can
take away

My dreams are my hope and they help me
day by day

They make me strong and never let
me down

You may call them weird and may call me
a clown

But they are my dreams and they are
fair

I see you laugh at them but
I don't care

Sara Vasquez

The Hour

One glass dry red wine
one hour lost in time
lost in soft memories of you
you alone
intoxicate my night
and caress my dreams beyond
for you were the dry red wine
I, the hour lost in time.

Briggin Lyford

Life

It's knocking at the door,
Each rapping grows a little louder.
Time is rapid, yet stands still.
We're afraid to answer,
But want to know the truth.
Go ahead and open up, let it in.
Never live if you don't risk it,
Can't help but wonder,
Which way will the cards fall?

Emily E. Fleming

Can You See Him

Can you see Him in a sunrise
When the golden glow appears,
In the dawning of each new day
When we are free from fears?

Can you hear Him when the wind comes
So silently at dawn,
As you feel His hand upon you
And you know things won't go wrong?

Do you feel a sense of peace
When you look up to the sky
And you know that He is near you
And will hear your every sigh?

There is peace, and joy, and comfort
And a total lack of fear,
And none are ever left alone,
For He is always near.

Verna R. Stroehl

My Empty Vase

My love is empty,
Empty as a vase,
How I long for someone
To fill my vase,
I see him in my dreams
But when I awake,
My vase lies empty.

Alicia Sara Ann Fennemore

My God

My God is certainly powerful,
The creator of all things.
When I think and dwell upon him,
Oh what a joyful feeling it brings.

I want to be with him always,
And have him dwell in my heart.
I pray I never fail him,
I always want to do my part.

To be in his presence,
Is the greatest thing I know.
And I pray I'll be ready,
For in the rapture I may go.

Cleanse me, mold me, guide me Lord,
Is the prayer I pray each day.
Lead me and forgive my sins,
In my life have your way.

For you are all knowing,
And some things I don't understand.
But I know I don't have to worry,
For we walk hand in hand.

Karen A. Young

The Wake

The body is bloated with fluids
The face is powdered and calm
The mourners shuffle by stiffly
The priest is reciting a Psalm

...And couples cling close
to each other while loners
seem very alone...

The corpse is quickly forgotten
The talk turns to children and things
The crowd feels an uneasy closeness
The specter of death always brings

Milo Bowen

Whispers

With the wind only a whisper,
the whispers only a shriek.
When do they come to end,
at what forbidden peak?

Shall the two come together?
Can they never learn to shout?
As within the world of a storm,
only one secret that life's about.

Only happiness to keep calm
the storms of a loving sea.
For the hatred to lie within
the whispers of love shall be.

To calm the heart of the wind,
as she settles down to sleep,
always to hold with her
the whispers she shall keep.

Stacy Barnes

503

Lost Soldier

I walk among the living dead,
I ponder and I creep.

Among the living, I just watch,
But it's their lives that I seek.

I fight the darkness of days gone by,
because I know the years.

They've followed me in my thoughts,
And vanished in my tears.

I've seen the soldiers come and die,
And change in their command.

But it isn't life that they have lost,
It's freedom they demand.

And now this day, whatever year,
Still watching time fly by.

I look to God for all the answers,
And the meaning of mankind.

Christina Hornby

Look Beneath the Surface

Look beneath the surface
Even take a second glance
Baby who knows just what you'll find
It might just be romance

Outward beauty's just skin deep
It's the inner strength that lasts
Open up your eyes and see
a love that's true to last

One who truly loves you
may be hidden deep within
Look beneath the surface
Look beyond the skin

You're searching for that perfect girl
The one you'll never find
The body beauty fades away
there's never stopping time

Once the beauty is all but gone
what's left but what's inside
Look beneath the surface
Who knows what you may find.

Sharon Erkkila Pietila

Our Last Year

Our time has come,
our last song has been sung.
We have been here for years,
now we will all shed tears.
Now that we are going to a new school,
will we still be as cool?
Will we act the same,
or remember each others name?
Since it is our last year.
We all have the same fear,
will we be accepted,
or just rejected.
When we just started to be close friends
it starts to come to an end.
So I hope when we pass in the hall
I still hear that familiar call...
"Hey! What's up?"

Susan Corter

Their Misinterpretation

Don't tell me that you understand,
Don't tell me that you know,
Don't tell me that I will survive,
That I will surely grow.

Don't come at me with answers
That can only come from me,
Don't tell me how my grief will pass
That I will soon be free.

Don't stand in pious judgement
Of the bonds I must unite,
Don't tell me how to suffer,
And don't tell me how to cry.

My life is filled with selfishness,
My pain is all I see,
But I need you, I need your love,
Unconditionally.

Accept me in my ups and downs,
I need someone to share,
Just hold my hand and I let me cry,
And say, "My friend, I care".

Michelle Felix

The Spinster

Alone she sits.
Alone she ponders.
All alone
waiting for something
that'll never come.
Alone she hopes.
Alone she prays
waiting to feel something
that'll never reappear.
Alone she grows old.
Alone she ages.
All alone...
Alone she dies

Danielle Palser

My Mocking Bird

What does he want or maybe she?
Is there a purpose or need?
Perhaps he seeks warmth and is chilly
Or hungry and wants some seed.

Did he miss his flight?
Is it that he's just lonely?
Is he coming toward the light?
Does he think it's his territory only?

He pecks on the windows
And flutters all around,
He puts on quite a show
Then flies at a movement or sound.

Sitting on the back of the chair
He watches his reflection in the window,
Then squawks and flits through the air.
He mocks the other birds, you know.

I hear his mimicking trill,
When other birds are near,
His presence gives such a thrill,
When his persistent pecking again I hear.

Jane Cole

To Be A Friend

You came into my life
When I needed a friend;
Prior to that there seemed no end.
To the weight of the burdens
You graciously lifted
And lessened the pain
As the problems were shifted.

You're reaching out slowly
Was really a must
In rebuilding my soul
And rekindling my trust.

There were hours spent listening
As the deep hurts came spilling
Where another might find
The details too chilling.

But you my dear friend
Proved worthy the name
Just know when you need me
I'll do the same.

Daniel Andriesse

They Call This
Freedom Of Speech!

They pull "old glory" from its staff
To trample under foot
They cover it with gasoline
And turn it into soot
They say that this is freedom
A constitutional guarantee
Written many years ago
Just for you and me
Will someone kindly tell me
So that I may also teach
How this very overt act
Can ever be freedom of speech.
To take the very symbol
Of red and white and blue
The final "Cover" of hero's
Who died for freedom too
Is what they are trying to tell us
To me it seems quite plain
That those who died for freedom
Have surely died in vain!

Joseph P. Tozzi

Hidden Memories

To touch the rays of another day
  and linger upon its beam
To hear the rain and its pain
  filled with voices unseen
To clearly see the fallen tree
  give in to silent birth
To smell the air that always cares
  to bring along its mirth
To taste the green the skies have seen
  that caress a mark on me
The forest's heart I've taken apart
  and learned hidden memories.

Carmalyn Harwood

Emotional Heart

You just don't understand me,
I can't figure out why.

Everytime I look at you,
inside I start to cry.

Tears run down my face,
when no one else can see.

These's nothing, but confusion,
building inside of me.

You say you care.
You say you are concerned.

Put aside your pride;
Show me the affection I have earned.

I can't play this game much longer.
I refuse to be played a fool.

Sooner or later
my emotions will shatter;

All this will prove,
is a love which never mattered.

Michele Gabrielle Lanzone

Lotto Fever

Life sure would be easy
For many a year
So thought those millions
Wishfully hoping

For many a year
Some emptied their savings
wishfully hoping
To win all that money

Some emptied their savings
So thought those millions
To win all that money
Life sure would be easy

Jerome J. Van Den Berg

Untitled

What an awful life we lead,
controlled by this thing called greed.
A Deliverer is what we need,
To save us from ourselves.

"Give up all and follow me".
Says this man from Galilee.
Is this the way to be free?
I can't really tell.

Oh, how happy now am I,
Since to myself I've learned to die.
That man, Jesus, told no lie,
He is my Deliverer!

Even now still I am learning,
For to myself I keep on turning.
To solve the problems that are burning,
Deep within my soul.

O Jesus, teach me to follow Thee,
And keep my eye away from me!

Jesse A. Carrier

Till We Meet Again
At The Pearly Gate

As mom and dad lay in the ground
  we hear a voice of familiar sound.
You ask us to forgive when you
  weren't there but in our hearts
  we knew you cared.
You now remember the things you
  had that made you happy and
  now your sad, a pool, bike and
  a ping pong too for those we
  loved and you know who!
I know you feel bad and you're going
  to cry we like to join you
  but our tears are dry.
Remember you were thought to love
  and not to hate.
Till we meet again at the pearly gate.

Alfred Ingrassia

My Dear Friend

Walk with me...
To a place away.
Forget dreams lost;
From yesterdays.

Hidden tears fall;
Gently like rain;
Slowly light a fire;
dry the pain.

New roses blossoming;
All around.
Catch the fresh petal;
Before it falls to the ground.

Open your eyes;
To the new dawn.
Let go of the past;
It never made you strong.

Don't put down the book;
Just end the chapter.
Once you turn the page;
Behold new love and laughter.

Jennifer Lynn Claycomb

Suicide

Sick of your life out on the ledge
ready to jump over the edge.

Freeing yourself ending it all
it could be over with a simple fall

One last scream but not a tear
you've left behind all your fear

Everything you loved now is gone
you have no reason to go on

Your chances diminish now you say
maybe this wasn't the only way

Too late now down you go
a final smash is all you know

All the problems in your head
have just been solved but now you're dead

Stephanie Sue Gallagher

Your The Best Mother
There Ever Was, Because...

Your the best mother there ever was,
because...
You are beautiful and elegant
and very intelligent
You dress really nice
You are made of sugar and spice
Your the best mother there ever was

Fatima Alibana

Untitled

You try making a bed
with a two-hundred pound man
in it.
Try frying an egg
in a dirty skillet.
Try running a mile
flying to Spain
Catching a snowflake
with lead weights on your ankles
If you know a way . . .
Tell me.

V. Mott

Upon A Winters Night

I feel the warm and gentle breeze
brush past my upturned face.
It's cold although, those being only
cherished memories of last years
summer's place.
The birds that sang and the
gentle breeze did seem so long ago.
I ache for summers sweet
release to feel the hot and
radiant sun beat upon my upturned face.
In this wintry clutch a longing
and a wonderment of what will
take its place fills my mind
and a smile now forms
upon my upturned face.

Patricia Ingles

Swiftly, Time Slips

Time swiftly passes through
Infinite portals of space,
Marked in the minds of
Each man by a memory.

When time idles,
All things idle.
If life stops,
Time goes on;
So act now.

Fun times in life
Offer to everyone
Recollections from the past.

Nobility is given to the humble;
Optimism, to the meek.

Memories are
All we have to
Nurture life itself.

Vernon A. Warner

Confusion

Random thoughts enter my mind
thoughts that mean nothing
where do they come from
what is this feeling I get
when phrases enter my head
it confuses me
makes me feel like I'm someone else
in a different body looking out
getting that person's thoughts
when I look in the mirror
it's me
yet it's not
it makes me feel strange when he comes
the man I was before

Matthew D. Bonk

Burnt Trees

Hate erupts with anger
flowing like
new spewed lava through
young forest growth
burning and searing
all it touches.
The longer it flows,
the more it destroys.

Pray
let the cooling waters
of understanding
peace staunch
its power and advance.

Then a new day
of gentle rains
will restore the land.

Woodrow Foster Jr.

Coexistence

Rise to reason,
neighbor, stranger;
come to truth,
neighbor, stranger.

In man's culture,
much to differ;
in man's peace,
much to offer.

Rise to purpose,
sister, brother;
come to trust,
sister, brother.

In man's practice,
much to care;
in man's future,
much to share.

Sol Wolfert

Time For Peace

It's time to forget the past
    and learn to live the
future. Time to forgive and
forget those who gave us pain
and sorrow. Time to learn to love
and be a family on this special
day. It's time to bring the New
Year in with a good positive
and good feelings from our hearts
time for joy and happiness, and
love.

Penney Murphy

The Children

He found the cure for cancer
And She, muscular dystrophy, too
This one found the final answer
Uniting Arab and Jew
All problems of human endeavour
Finally solved, at last
Famine, aging, poverty
Are now the woes of the past

But He will never find the cure
And She will not join in the quest
And the final answer will long be sought
For they have been laid to rest

These heroes were never created
To see the sky of blue
For they were never fated
To join both me and you
They were never allowed to laugh
And join the others at play
These ever loving children

Abortion, has taken away

Marvin H. Whyman

Rosebuds

I am a flower of life
and I am destined to survive,
but I need another life form
to rise and bloom into this world.

You are the vim from the sun
once you shine your light on me,
please don't hide me in the shade
you, the sunshine, makes me grow.

You are the calm and peaceful rains
saturate me with your showers,
once you have quenched my thirsty roots
do not tease me with a drizzle.

If you dare to create me
you must always remember,
you're part of my existence
never leave me to starve and die.

If you help to glorify me
I will forever be grateful,
by giving all of me to you
my rosebuds will burst with beauty!

Juliana L. Meyer

Untitled

The fallen angels, dark and cold,
sing ancient hymns of tarnished gold,
of innocence both lost and found
in pleasures palm, where flesh abounds.
To gorge upon red, ripened lips
and fill one's cup with passion's fire,
to taste of sweet forbidden fruit
with coursing veins of pure desire.
Fear not the sting of bitter pain
from love's eternal ebb an flow.
Embrace the burning in the soul
and taunt the flames that burn below.
Drink deep the essence of this life
for we know not how long it pours.
So breathe each breath as if the first
and die to live for seconds more.
If fallen angels dark and cold
sing ancient hymns of tarnished gold,
yet ate life's feast and drank its wine,
I'll take my gold of little shine.

James Corcoran

The Spirit Of The Stone

Oh wondrous and mighty spirit
Who speaks to me with the wind
Allow me the privilege
Of knowing and seeing
The spirit of the stones of which
    I seek.
Allow my hands the power
To release that Spirit
To its fullness.
Guide me along the paths of
    righteousness
In my thoughts and deeds
Where-by the act of gathering the
    stones
Helps raise me above my weaknesses
Into thy Light.
Teach me the true meaning
Of the oneness of all things.
    I shall then hold
The most precious Gem.

Howard Doughty

Why Do I Weep?

A miniature in white
    Against a clear blue sky —

A symmetry in marble
    Set with precious gems —

Strong enough to survive death,
Fragile enough to breathe life,
A temple erected to love alone —

    This I truly comprehend and
    This is why I weep.

I should rejoice;

    I have lived in your love;
    I have seen the TAJ.

Mary Elizabeth Smith

A Tribute To My Mother

I was a young girl
When my mother went away
My mother now an angel
Heaven she will stay
She was always kind and gentle
I pray to her every day
She was strong and silent
Clever in a shy way
Always helped people
In a loving manner she gave
Respect, hard work, and lots of love
To also believe in God above
And to think of others as he does
God guided here to keep me strong
Always away from earthly harm
My mission here on earth is clear
I should try to be my mother dear

Sheila Bird

Untitled

And he said to me
    "Goodnight Sweetheart..."
And it was Night...
    Forever.

Linda Sippel Martin

Guilt Of A Gunfighter

He stood tall in the wind
Above the body of the twelfth man
Six shooter in his hand
Guilt above his head
Born to kill
Born to murder
Drooped his gun in the dirt
Mounted on his saddle
Rode away singing
A song about his last killing day

Edward Lake

My Everything

For someone so sweet and tender
So elegant and rare
You touched my heart
the first time I caught your stare
I caressed your soul
For one lonely night
You broke my heart by
leaving my sight
minutes hours and days went by
I missed you so much
I couldn't help but cry
Day and night you run
through my head
Many lonely nights I
lay alone in bed
without you I might as
Well be dead
You complete my mind
and make me whole
oh how I wish to caress your soul

Joe Wessel

Safe Place

Tucked away in a corner
Bundled up real tight
Hidden in a safe place
Well out of sight

Told them I wanted you
Wanted you real bad
They put me in a safe place
said I was mad

Friends come to see me
Saying everything's fine
But I can see it in their faces
I can read their minds

Hidden in a safe place
Far away from you
Strapped down to a bed
there's nothing I can do

Cards are on the table
and I'm not looking to good
wasting away in a safe place
Nothing more I can do.

James V. Hudson Jr.

The Ocean

So blue and never ending
Miles and miles of sandy beaches
The wind rustling through the palm trees
Sea shells scattered along the sea shore
So full of life and spacious
The water sparkling in the sun light
Quiet and cool in the evening
Beautiful sun set on the horizon

Mick Sturtevant

Rainfalls

Rain falls,
Dew drops,
Fog hangs in the air —
When I walk with wet hair, —
When I go to meet my maker, and
quite possibly a town baker, I
will sit and stare, through my hair and
at the air waiting —
Waiting for those whom I adore
to converse with me once more.

Nicholas Curry

Remember When

Remember when we were together,
all the things we did?
Remember all the fun,
we had in the sun?
Remember the days,
We would always say,
"I love you or I missed you?"
Remember when I would be sad,
How you acted so big and bad?
So all I'm asking is,
Do you remember when?

Stephanie Grosjean

My Melinda Jo

She came so slow
and left so fast
I didn't really know
my Melinda Jo

All the things I know
to you I could tell
if you hadn't had to go
my Melinda Jo

Yes, before the first snow
one of God's smallest angels
came amid a crescendo
my Melinda Jo

Why is my heart so low
you came though not to stay
yet knowing God has given a halo
To my Melinda Jo

Al Hockaday, Sr.

I Live Each Day

The world is all around me
Each morning is all new
I open up my eyes,
And wonder what I'll do.
The answer is so easy,
My routine and my meals
But what will help my friends most,
That will show them how I feel?
I can give them a happy smile
and say, "I'm so glad to see you!"
I can lift a load for them, or,
Can somehow help them, too.
But most of all I love them
And want them to know I do,
For aren't we all brothers, God's children?
His Love will see us through!

Margaret Clark

Body Language

To touch the skin so lightly,
to tease, to tantalize.
Leave nothing to the imagination,
to dream, to fantasize.
To kiss the lips-not hard, not soft -
to keep him wanting more.
To give the mouth all of the things
that it's asking for.
To hold you lover lovingly
in a warm embrace,
To feel the chills all down your spine
as you stand in place.
To stare into your lover's eyes,
for these two do not lie
You see in them the things you know
the heart just can't deny.
To love your lover all night long,
your bodies become one.
Then to rise the next day
with the beams of the sun.

Tanisha Fossett

The Road Home

I'm coming home
   I'm coming home.
It's been a long journey,
   A weary road.
Searching all the tomorrows,
   To find my way.
The quest wasn't so far,
   as it took to be.
My road to someplace,
   led back to me.
My wanderings in thought,
   my pilgrimage.
Now I am home,
   I, completely me.

C. Michael Barry

His Will Is The Way

The wicked way is easy
   The righteous way is tough.
So why should we walk the narrow path?
   Isn't eternity reason enough?

To follow the worldly is a breeze,
   But I'd rather walk His way
For the more I follow His footsteps
   It gets easier day by day.

Satan says to follow The Lord
   Is not the smart thing to do
But I've lived my life Satan's way
   So I know what he says isn't true.

So remember as temptation besets you
   Keep your mind firmly on Him
The Lord has more than strength enough
   To save us from all sin.

And if you feel downtrodden
   And your faith is starting to sway
Just lift your heart to Jesus
   And let His will be your way.

Robert L. Klingenberg Jr.

On My Own

Confusion.
Racing through a maze.

He's nowhere to be seen.
Slipping away.

Insecurity.
Living without him.

Wanting to be free.
Yet needing him there.

To care for me.
His hand in mine.

Sharing feelings, emotions.
The warmth of two hearts.

The reality of separation.
A nightmare come true.

Becky Hadrath

Immortal Angel

I lay here on my bed listening
To her royal voice
With the soul and body of
An immortal angel
Rising to the heavens above
Making all things happen along the way
She lives a fantasy life
And I can just lie here
Dreaming that one day
I will meet this immortal angel
Of my dreams
Then, silence struck my room
A bright tunnel of light
Came down from the heavens above
Then, she emerged from the bright light
Stepping forward she took my hand
And said "come, it's time"
And she dragged me into
The bright tunnel of light
And we left the earth for eternity.

Douglas Seymour

Grandma Angie

Grandma Angie I love you so,
Why you left,
Lord I don't know;

I didn't get to say goodbye,
although I knew you were going to die;

I will always miss your angel eyes,
your body, soul and mind,
may not be with us in our lifetime;
But grandma your soul is so very kind;

Grandma Angie I love you so;
Why you left Lord I don't know.

Casey Jo Hillesheim

Do They Care

As the water runs through its trail
I sit and wonder have I fall;
As I sit alone and no one is there
I sit and wonder does anyone care;
As I sleep at night in fear
I wonder is death near;
As the well runs dry I dive in
I sit and wonder where have I been;
As I awaken another day
I ask God to show me the right way;

Charles L. Corley II

Echo

The eagle's scream
Echoes...again
Echoes...and
In the silence dies.
The sands shift
Losing time.
Time lost for The Spirit.
The Spirit cries out like
The eagle.
Echoes...again
Echoes...and
Falls on deaf ears.

Angela Senyard

Goosebumps
Dipple-dapple my skin.
Toes remind me that it's
Growing too cold for bare feet.
Sunshine
Baptizes my room, all
White and clean, tip-toeing
Across my floor like a
Traveling evangelist.
A warm, puppy kiss
Paints my cheek, while
I grow tipsy
Drinking in
The sharp aroma hanging,
Ghost-like
On the fall air,
Hinting
At winter's blooming.

Melissa Barnes

Travel Brightens Learning - Listen!

Travel enlightens
Travel brightens
The monuments, the statues,
The points of interest, and the museums
A yearning for America's past
Learning about something that will last
Questing for knowledge
In a raw and natural college
Stand back and listen
To the gold leaf dome that glistens
A wealth of information
Drives to transformation
Words touch the eyes
They trace the ties
To just see and to be
In the spaces
All embraces
Of all there is to show
The mind will grow.

Steven R. Croft

If I Decide

If I decide to leave tomorrow.
Remember all I hide inside.
If I no longer sit in sorrow.
Know what I had inside has died.
If I decline my pain and power,
know my dreams subside.
If I erase my trace of tears,
you'll know my heart no longer cries.
If I find comfort in the sun,
you'll know this battle I have won.
If when you speak I no longer hear,
then you shall know I'm no longer near.

Yni S. Miranda

Memories Unfold

Oh Lord up high, only you know
the pain I bare.
Only in you my hope that
you can repair.

It seems the more I try
to do what is right
it seems the devil goes onto flight!

Her face and her laughter is such a joy
why should we be punished,
when they are at fault.
Is there any way you can bring
the devil and the pain to a hault?

The memories are a treasure to behold
and in the back of my mind,
they constantly unfold.

Carla Shawn Quisenberry

Empty...

You tell me I am beautiful
    But you will not look at me

You say I am intelligent
    But you ridicule my thoughts

You tell me I am funny
    But you do not laugh with me

You say you know me
    But you do not

I am empty with you

Kelly A. Magruder

Happy Holidays To All

'Twas the night before Christmas,
And all through this plant
All of our wishes
We hope Santa can grant.
Yes, you could say
We've been good big girls and boys
And it would be nice to work
In a place you truly enjoy.
Now, Santa may not be able
To grant each and every request,
But we all surely know
Santa will do his very best.
As the New Year approaches
Let's all hope for the better,
But remember - we really all
Must work at it together.
For All of you
I hope the best in every way,
And may you All
Have a safe and happy holiday!

Susan Cade

My Love

Like an angel that was sent to me
from way high up above
You came to me with open arms
and filled my heart with your love
With childlike hopes and dreams of us
I wish on each star I see
That you should never leave my side
and together forever we will be
You are my heart, my soul, my self
You're in everything I do
For the past, today and eternity
I will always, always love you.

Christy Stevich

Hidden In My Heart

If only my heart could speak
What would it say
If only it could talk to you
I know it would find a way

Letting you know the thoughts
That race through my mind
Leaving me jealous
Thinking things unkind

I envy the woman
That lives in your heart
If I were in her shoes
We would never be apart

Hidden in my heart
Are all the things you need
Just give me the chance
I know I would succeed

First to win your love
That's the easiest place to start
Never would I give in
Until I've won your heart

Karen Guilbeault

A Fragile Heart

Suspends a tear
in my heart
hanging in effigy
to my lost child.
A tear,
aloof, unreachable,
wanting to drop
to the place of hopelessness.
A silver, polished,
gleaming bead,
shivering in the emptiness
of a guarded chamber.
I won't allow it to fall.
My life
would quake.
My psyche
would shatter.
And so I pray....
it will evaporate
in God's mercy.

Charlotte A. Desiderio

For I Was Not Born

Born not was I
To live out of cry
To hurt in this way
As I do day to day

Born not was I
To away and be shy
To be cast and be shunned
From help I do run

Born not was I
To hide behind lies
To conceal as I do
My feelings thought through.

Born not was I
But now, I ask why?
Hurt as I may
Why I live through this day.

Adam Saunders

I Go Back To 1979

I go back to 1979
When life was so happy,
So free and sublime.
I was so happy and free.

Free from my problems,
Free from disease,
Free from religion,
Confusion and worries.

Free to play and sing and live,
Free to be a child, very young—
To not give up being a kid,
To have the heart to be forever young.

I go back to 1979,
Back to my favorite
Moment in time—
Just to be a kid.

Lissa R. Hayes

My Black People

My black people
we are killing one another.
We have to come together as one.
To increase the peace and
to decrease the violence.
My black people
there's more to life than guns.
There's more to life than death.
My black people
We have to put down these guns.
To join our hands together
among one another.
My black people
we as strong black
African-American's have to
stand together as one.

L'Tanya D. Hatchett

You Went Away!

You went away
The distance wasn't far
From the door to the car,

You were not gone long
No more than a song

You did not say goodbye
And I did not ask why

You were just gone for a while
And in your usual style,

You left with a smile
And a wee trace of guile

Some day I will learn
You will always return,

But my heart skips a beat
Until once more we meet

Though you went away
Our love is here to stay!

Louis N. Rozakis

Closed In

As I walk
I feel closed in
As I walk towards my bedroom
The feeling never ends
As I sit in the floor
Or lie on my bed
I sometimes dream
Of the life I once had
As I sit in my room
I wonder what could be
What could possibly become of me
I think of the friends
That I once had
The memories we shared
The good, the bad
Yet I feel so closed in
And I wonder why
It's a mystery
Why do people die?

Kellie Pollard

Missing Tara

A mother's love
So sweet so pure,
I miss you my darling
I find there's no cure

The love that we shared
Over 14 yrs. ago
Is gone now my baby
But I still love you so.

You were so special,
So sweet, so kind
I love you my baby
I miss you all of the time

God has you now
In his arms so strong
I'll see you again my love
It won't be so long.

Linda L. Black

The Waters Of Life

Just when my heart seems so empty
Just when my world seems at end
His words come from deep within me
It is on His word I depend

His love keeps me from straying
The power of His arms lift me up
My life comes from His sayings
I just cannot get enough

The waters of life taste refreshing
They cool and delight the heart
But it is a matter of requesting
This is where it has to start

Come taste the waters from Jehovah
From them you will be satisfied
He gives you things dreams are made of
For God cannot tell a lie!

Cheryl Burton

509

Heaven's Glow

As I cradle you
And look in your
Sparkling eyes so blue.

It is though, I
Can see Heaven's hue.

If only you could
tell me something new
Of God's plan for you.

Before the vale comes
to cover your tiny soul.
Leaving only the vaguest
Inclining of your pre-existence.

Fluttering of angel wings
I can almost hear.

So blessed and protected
Are you by all
Of God's chosen ones.

It's as though
All around you
Have a small piece
Of Heaven's precious glow.

Cara Dayhoff

The Dark

The late night is like a black cat,
Moving slyly without a sound.
Wait, I hear something!
What was that?
I don't dare look around.

I feel its claws in my back.
It slowly creeps up my spine.
I can't open my eyes,
For it's courage I lack;
Even though this bedroom is mine.

I pull the covers over my head.
I am trying not to shake.
I heard a noise,
From under the bed.
What an awful sound it makes.

It jumps out and eats my arm.
And I scream and scream and scream.
Mom wakes me up,
With great alarm.
For it was all a dream.

Jessica Dorato

The Birth Of A Smile

One more year nears
One more tear clears
As she grows and smiles
As she plays so proud

Why cry near the ground
That berried your smile
When on top she plays
Oh! She plays so proud.

As one flower blooms
And dies near your grave
Oh! She plays so proud
When she hears your name

One more year nears
As we celebrate
The year of her birth
The year of your death

Dolores C. Conte-Merino

Untitled

I move across the land with ease,
using up what's in my way.
When I come up to a pond,
at the edge I'll always stay.
The grass lands I like.
The forests I love.
And I dance with the wind
when it gives me a shove.
Many men have tried to tame me.
But I'm still in control.
And I show proof of this
when threw dry lands I role.
I am many years old.
But I'll never retire.
My forces are strong,
because I'm a Fire.

Edward L. Lockhart

Thank You

Thank you for things I've seen
Thank you for trees so green.

Thank you for stars above
Thank you for your endless love.

Thank you for my children's life
Thank you for my loving wife.

Thank you for the time to play
Thank you for another day.

Thank you for the things I've done
for the life of joy and the life of fun.

Thank you for my mom and dad
Thank you for all I've had.

Though life is not always fair
I must be thankful beyond compare.

For all I've seen and all I've done
is overseen by the Father's Son.

So be thankful everyday
take the time when you pray.

Thank Him for all He gives
and remember too that Jesus lives.

Robert Losee

A Special Star

I cannot imagine where you are.
As I stand gazing up at a star.
It twinkled bright and caught my eye.
So now I wonder and question why,
Our lives have crossed now at this time.
You in there and me with mine.
This star now twinkles so very bright,
As I stand gazing here tonight.
I'm lost in thought life's so unfair.
But through this poem, you see I care.
So as each day draws to an end.
Watch for the stars above, my friend.
The one that twinkles oh so bright,
Is the star I saw this night.
I thought of you and prayed out loud.
That where you are there are no clouds.
And think of me each time you are,
Gazing up at the stars.

Linda D. McKown

My Reality

Your reality,
is someone else's dream,
My reality,
is someone else's nightmare.
What you have,
you don't deserve.
And what I have,
ought to be better.
If you were to,
take my place,
You couldn't stand it.
You're not strong enough,
to fight the hatred and sorrow.
I can stand up to it.
It cannot penetrate me.
And so I am left alone,
to fight against it.
Forever in my reality,
Someone else's nightmare.

Niome Rideout

Children

The dawning sun
peacefully streaks the hallway
while, through the swirling vapors
of my coffee,
come small people, with sleepy eyes
and bare feet,
following, slowly
the smell of breakfast cooking.

Later,
as they climb aboard the school bus
and vanish over the hill...
I find my thoughts
are still with them.
Somewhere, inside, I sense theirs
with me.
They are my heart
...my life.
I love them.

Jimmy Moore

Learn To Be Lonely

To taste sweetness on my lips,
my mouth dost adore;
but to end in bitter denial,
I can take no more.

And no more tears fall
from eyes so dry,
Lost love is soon forgotten
and at night, I do not cry.

My heart no longer hurts,
for cold stone feels no pain,
but rock can still be broken,
and my heart will break again.

Ignorance in love is a blessing,
disguised as it may be,
I wish I didn't know love hurts,
So that I may again love free.

I learn to be lonely
and never show how I feel,
because only my dying soul
should know what is real.

Daniel E. Jenkins

A Writer's Goal

I want to write.
I want to write right.
All right.
If it takes all night
to get into the rite,
I want to write.
And I want to write right.
All right.

Pamela Carson

Agony And Ecstasy

Agony

Sleepless nights and
restless days
Wondering,
Wandering,
Searching for answers
Seeking solutions to what
should have been
    or ... Could have been
    or ... Would have been
if only...

Ecstasy

Knowing you are there in the
Sleepless nights,
Restless days,
Wondering,
Wandering
Searching and Seeking
with me.

Pamela J. S. Challis

A Disabled Person

I sit in a wheelchair
my legs can't walk
but I still enjoy
a friendly talk my speech
is slow and sometimes is
hard to know what I say
my eyes maybe blind
and my ears don't
hear but things aren't
so bad as they appear
I like to go places
and have fun even when
I'm told it can't be
don't so many of us have
something to share but are
ignored by those that don't
care there are many
thing I can't do but
there is no difference
between me and you.

Larry L. Giddings

He And A Bright Sunny Day

Dedicated to my late Grandpa Etzel
He was like the sun on a bright
    sunny day.
His hair shined like the sun on a bright
    sunny day.
His teeth were as white as clouds on
    a bright sunny day.
His eyes shined like the sun on a bright
    sunny day.
My Grandpa was like the sun on a bright
    sunny day.

Amanda Etzel

In Love

I swore to myself it wouldn't
happen to me.
Until you came into my life.
When you held out the key
to my heart.
I knew I was in love
When you came in my life
you made me change my mind.
Just when I thought I could
never fall in love.
I thought it was impossible
for me to fall in love.
But oh you proved me wrong.

Crystal Gail Colbath

Twenty Oh Oh

It is nineteen ninety seven
    as men record...
in the year of our Lord
    and perhaps in heaven
look at the nineties
    a century of war
and "men" in nighties
    ignore morals like a whore.

"Product of conception" swept away...
    save the grey cells
cure for aids someday
    then they will ring the bells
help the sick terminate life
    will produce a master race
hustle...bustle so much strife
    I can't keep up the pace.

Nineteen hundred ninety eight
    and nine time spins, oh!
I'm not ready! I'll be late!
    here come twenty oh! Oh!

Patsy Yob

When Our Father Calls

God wants me in heaven
For he called me today
No more be a wanderer
He has shown me the way

My Lord He has promised
Home in heaven with Him
Tho the pathway be narrow
And my vision it's so dim

Shed no tears at my parting
For I'm a victor, you see
By His grace He has saved me
Sins forgiven, spirit free

This thought for my loved ones,
Place your faith all in Him
He will carry your burdens,
Eternal life, you will win

When we all meet in heaven,
After our journey is run
How wonderful 'twill be,
To be at home with the son

Dwight W. Holman

Untitled

I'm searching for your voice
I'm sinking in its quietness
it blows me away like a wind
maybe because I am
a sad lost leaf
scorned by life
about whom nobody cares
having no hope
a twopenny a tiny nothing
without a chance in the world
lonely and empty
nobody's
I need your help
and you're not here
but I know how to love
even though I'm different from others

Agnieszka Swiszcz

Falling Ivy

Thin,
    delicate
        tendrils
Kissed by
    heart-shaped
        lips,
        Flowing,
            Curling,
                Entwining
Like reaching,
    grasping
        fingers
    Yearning
        to touch
            again

Resa Cirrincione

Family Band

My family is like a great big band.
Mom's the director,
Waving her hand.
Dad's the bass drum,
Keeping the beat.
Sister's the piccolo,
Sounding so sweet.
Where does that leave me???
I'm big, loud, and strong.
Let me think for a moment—
I must be the going!!!

Julie Ritter

Ode To The Lord

Blessed be the name of the Lord
He is—
    The Beauty of the Day
    Harmony of the Heart
    Peace of Understanding
    Gladness of Life
    Joy of Salvation
    Hope of the Future
    Wisdom of Love
    Gift of Life Eternal
    The Wonder of God's Care.
He Loves us so much.

Ruth Ayers

Friendship's A Gift To Self!

A hand extended reaches out
with friendship's, we claim.
Bringing joys innumerable
and little pain
when we act sane.
Like mirrors cracked,
Images distorted,
Results are usually not afforded.
Oh wonder of wonders
when we act sane
and friendships reign.

D. Marley Ruhf

Abortion

Have you ever thought
of what abortion means?
You kill a precious child
Its hopes and all its dreams.

It wasn't the baby's fault,
It never had a chance.
Its blood cries out to you,
You couldn't control romance.

The abortion is over,
And you've had your fun.
Looking back in the past,
You see what you have done.

You did it out of passion,
You did it out of love.
The boy will probably leave you,
That you thought so much of.

Years and years will pass,
But you'll never pay your dues.
Your mind will always wonder,
If the baby looked like you.

Crystal Johnson Stobbs

John Foster Golden

Who is this precious jewel?
A treasure from above.
Sent to bless a Golden family
with happiness and love.

His visit to earth was brief,
And why we may not know.
But this much we can be sure of
Heavenly Father has called him home.

His smile was warm and friendly.
Messy diapers - they weren't a chore.
And all that long black hair
Made you love him even more.

He was always so alert.
And as newborns often do,
He'd keep his parents up at night,
But with his smile say, "I love you."

Yes, who was this special spirit
We remember with tears of joy?
John Foster Golden
Our precious little boy.

Randall A. Kenworthy

A Seasoned Life

I rocked my sleepy babies
In the pale moonlight
As the snow fell softly
Upon a cold wintry night

I chased my laughing toddlers
Through the flowers in the spring
In time to watch the butterflies dance
On delicate magic wings

I watched my golden children
In the sun at play
Running barefoot in the green grass
On a long ago summers day

I waved good-bye to yesterday
As the autumn leaves fell fast
Leaving my nest empty
Feathered with memories of the past

Shelley Barrett

Untitled

Love is a box of chocolates
    on Valentine's Day,
Love is something you do
    or something you say.
Love is the sweet smell of flowers
    on the very first day of spring,
Love is waking with the sun
    and listening to the birds sing.
Love is walking on the beach
    with the moon shining bright,
Love is a romantic dinner
    with the single candle you light.
Love is dancing in the dark
    to our favorite song,
Love is you making love to me
    all night long.
Love can last forever
    just as my hope for you and me,
Love, My Love, is true
    and someday I hope you'll see.

Jackie Huth

He's In Eternity

Underneath the midnight sky
I look up to the stars
And my soul cries out "Why"

Underneath the weight of grief
I search the darkness for relief
And my spirit is made meek

Underneath the burden of sorrow
I seek a refuge for the morrow
And my heart begins to weep

Calm surrender of his soul
Restless warrior set to go
He's in eternity

Heaven now near, had seemed so far
Gone to just beyond the stars
Body broken no more to scar

Calm and gentle from above
Hand to hold me in His love
And bring me peace from the Dove

He's in eternity

David L. Bradburn

A Tribute To Mom On Mother's Day

Thank you for the opportunity
To know what life can bring,
To know the joys of living
To laugh, to talk, to sing.

To see the birds out on the wing
To hear the babbling brook,
To smell the flowers along the way
Of life's path that I took.

I thank you Mom for all you've done
And I thank Father for his part,
I thank our Lord for both of you
And my life right from its start.

William E. Theobald

Why

How would we live
    in this world of ours
were it not
    for the dreams ahead.
For thorns exist
    with the blooming flowers
no matter which
    path we tread.

Each one of us has
    that treasured goal
which reaches
    far into the years.
So forever we climb
    with hopeful souls
as the smiles
    erase the tears.

Andrea Tremblay

Ode To Dr. ———

Strong coffee
Talkative teacher
Do keep me awake
Me — hearing
But not listening
My mind floats out the window
Melodious birds singing madrigals
Free butterflies soaring high
Strong coffee still hot
Talkative teacher still loud
But my attention follows —
White butterflies in the air
White daisies on the ground

Hsing-ju Wei

Friends

Friendship is laughter,
Friendship is fun;
Friendship is a friend,
When you really have none:
Friendships are near,
Or they can be far;
It's a feeling of closeness,
Wherever you are;
It can show up in a letter,
Or just with a smile;
Friendship is a feeling,
that lasts a long while.
It's shared with someone caring,
And it makes you feel divine;
A friend brings happiness,
All the time!

Diane M. Bunn

A Growing Church

I think that I shall never see
A church so "perfect" as to be
No place for folk like you and me.

Rather, a church that seeks to know
More of her Lord, and wants to grow
In grace and truth to others show.

A church that heeds her Master's call
To servanthood that's shared by all
Who in His service can stand tall.

A church where youth and children walk,
Where strangers need not wait and knock,
But all find welcome in its flock.

A church that holds a world-wide view
To keep its sense of mission true,
While tending to its local few.

A poem is built by folk like me.
'Tis Christ who builds a church, yet He
Needs building blocks like me and thee.

Robert J. Bracey

Forever

When it's time for the crocus to
bloom, so it is the cogent of the
resurrection of the Lord. To
ponder and consider what He has
done for us. What it would be
like? What wonderful thoughts
of our bodies to ascend from
the grave just as He, with power
and glory from the Almighty
God who created us. To be
with him forever! The
beautiful many blooms
that come from one bulb
of the Amaryllis, so it is when
we tell one of His Salvation it
multiplies and blooms to others.
Then look up to the heavens
were He will gather us together forever.

Terri Riggs

The Quiet

In an easy chair
an old blanket lays.
Asleep underneath it
a man with a book
on his lap
deep lines crease his face
gray hair tops his head.

The rain pours down outside
A fire crackles inside
a cup of tea sits on a table
by the man
half empty.

The room is silent
except for the ticking
of a clock
and a soft snore from the man

Then it all seems to stop
as the man dies
    alone
in an easy chair.

Suzanne Miller

Silence

No noise,
No words,
It's a power to remember.

Silence can hurt the heart,
But help the mind.
No one said it would be easy.

Strong and deaf,
It has moments of boredom.

Silence can relax you,
And make you think.

Emotions stir in the silence of a room,
Yet you sit still.

Sarah F. Sudakow

Untitled

From where I stand a new day breaks
a silent voice in my heart wakes

The ground below me disappears
and with it takes my darkest fears

I hear a graceful fledgling's song
as calming winds tow me along

From here beneath me nature greets
a dance of wisdom wildly beats

A passing cloud envelopes me
angelic wonders whirling free

Above its majesty of bliss
I've felt the everlasting kiss

I've seen the trees below me sway
the river's muddy waters play

I think it's here I wish to stay.

Leticia Torres

My Shoe Box

I have this little shoebox
Full of precious memories,
That keeps us well connected
Where ever we may be.

It has no magic powers
It has no good luck charms,
But I wish it could protect me
Like when you hold me in your arms.

It's not out on display
for all the world to see,
What's in there is very special
Meant for you and me.

But, when I look around me
You are the most important part,
So I guess the biggest shoebox
Is the one that's in my heart.

Diane Samanica

Just Like You

I love you just the way you are,
Because your beauty is like a star.
The skies are blue when you are near,
They know how much I need you dear.
I want you darling, can't you see
You fill my life with ecstasy?
In my heart, I'll hold you true,
For in all this world, there's no one,
Just, like, you

Joseph Turner

Wither

The stolen gifts
Of lake delusion
Harbor beliefs
Malignantly
And with sharp angels
Tears in pair
Lotion my shoes and thoughts
Beside others I peer
Into the grove of promise
To find the rusted gaze
Of truth
I beg for the hands
that affect me.

Ross Leach

Love Always

If my heart is broken is because
of you. The tears I fall for you
is because I love you so much
But what can I do to get you out
of my heart. Everything remin's me
of you why do I feel like I was
the cause of our break out but
I hope you will always have
me in your heart but for
me I will love you always
and I'll drop every tear for
you to have you back.

"Love Always"

Mayra Cruz

Nothing Can Be Said

A witness to horror, or just existence.
But what can be said.
Broken lives cast by the wayside.
One chance to live.
One chance to be.
One fall, and you
lost it all.
Mangled and torn,
left to exist like that.
Like a scarred face,
like a scorched soul.
Hopeless and discarded.
Thrown away like a wilted flower.
Abandoned like a dying fire.
Empty now, left to burn itself out.
Empty now, soon nothing but ashes.
No one will remember.
No one will know.
No one can say anything.

Yuri Fyodorov

How Can I Forget?

The gentle kisses, the firm embrace,
I won't forget the words or the place.
The things we did, the things we said,
    how did it all ever end?
It's been harder than you know,
I will never completely let go.
The life I had, the things I knew,
I easily found it all in you.
Now you're gone, what will I do?
I will never find another you.
The love we shared, the way you cared,
by God's grace alone we were paired.
You and me, me and you,
maybe again it will come true.

Kelly Kostock

Untitled

Caring and nurturing the body
and soul through the seasons
of life. Essential physical needs
prepare purpose and meaning.
Then one lives to survive...

To feed a soul is of
a spiritual nature. It is
the fountain of life that
flows endlessly. If cannot
be seen with the naked eye.

Nature, listen, explore
Nourish the soul through the
senses to the heart and mind
creative expression, sharing
finding the passion deep inside
Then Live To Thrive

Michelle Pastore

Homes

Homes are what keep us warm,
They are where we sleep,
They keep us safe in storms,
They are where we stay when
Snow is three feet deep.

Homes have yards,
Where little kids play.
But what about the people
Who do not have homes,
Where will they stay.

Kristin Renee Corder

The Castle And The Cabin

Behind gates sits a fine old castle
Stone upon stone perched there on a hill
Attentions are held with the dazzle
The servants so precise in their drill
Rushing everywhere, such a hassle
Tick, tock, tick, tock....

At the slope's foot rests a cabin
Simplicity nestled in the trees
No one's looking, no one's botherin'
Work is slow but it gets done with ease
Wind and water whisper soft therein
Tick, tock, tick, tock...

Time drops away when you're not looking
So much to do while the stones crumble
But wind and water are still moving
Hidden with the one ever humble
Learn and live, this wisdom invoking
Tick, tock, tick, tock....

Julie Sumwalt

For Father

You were always there.
From the time I took my first breath
Until the time you took your last.
We had bad times and we had great times
But they were our times.
You were someone I belonged to
And now you've gone and left a hole
Where you always were.
It cannot be filled by anyone else.
But I can play our memories and smile
Until I see you again.

Susan Whitmore-Hennigh

Love

It's hard to understand
this thing between a
woman and a man.
It's an everyday role in life
between a husband and
his wife
It's not often you will
find it true
first it breaks your heart
then it leaves you sad and
blue
No one knows because it
won't go away
so before you go thru this
make sure it's true
because the person you fall
in love with, might fall
out of love with you.

Tomeka James

When The World Was New

In a time, long ago
When everything was new
True blue seas, light blue skies
Everything was true.

Unicorns, with silver horns,
shining in the sun.
By the lake, Dryads dance
Just to have some fun.

Over there, in the sea,
In the clear blue water
Is a horse, with golden wings
Pegasus and her daughter.

Magen Coleman

Boundaries

Driving by I see
two horses sprinting, at
that moment my heart felt
as free as they did. Yet they
were bound by fences, not
able to feel as free as they
wanted. And my heart suddenly
felt pain. Because it was bound
also, by my body.
Life's known boundaries sometimes
visible, but not always understanding.
Yet angels of God are free. Death
frees them, opens the doors of
life, as the coffin closes.
You don't just die, you learn to
live again.

Holly J. Helsten

To See The World
As A Grain Of Sand

To see the world as a grain of sand,
it's best imagined if we stand
along the shore of Milky Way,
and with Odyssean view of bay,
connecting us to boundless space;
then peering down from such a place
to find our earth and galaxy
as dust that winds might blow away:
To weep for those of this vast land
who cannot see our grain of sand.

Robert Cotner

Recipe For Friendship

A dash of laughter,
A bunch of gab.
A little bit of tenderness
Anger...well just a tad
A whole lotta love.
Spread over the years,
generously sprinkled...
with each others tears,
lovingly warmed by
remembered smiles,
served too seldom when
distanced by the miles.

Girlfriend! You made the
best cup of coffee...
I miss you

Marilynn Gonyea Smith

Death Of A Hero

Hot lead pierces his skin,
He sees his life spill on the ground,
He is sorry for his sins,
Soon the pain will be gone,
He is at rest,
Some one notifies his next of kin.

Douglas Baker

Only In Mind

I reached out to touch a rain cloud
and tried to feel the rain
but once inside the darkness
all I felt was pain

I lay motionless in layers of calm
waiting for a ray of light
when I awoke, alone, on my own
my thoughts passed on into the night

Now all that remains is the temptation
to move on to another day
but perhaps in this cloud of destiny
I will find I will have to stay

For never in my stay here
through the darkness could I find
the one simple truth I searched for
was only in my mind

Kirk E. Hobbs

The Mysterious World Created

Many people,
Many of you,
What a pity
Can it be true?
You said it would be great
I believe in you,
With all my faith
and trouble too.
You make the world what it is today
Or can it be man
that made me stray?
Whatever the time,
whatever the place,
there is never a large space
for me and you.

Kristen Tansits

514

Snowflakes

Children are like snowflakes
A gift of beauty from above
A treasure we are given
Given to respect and love

And like a fragile snowflake
They must be handled with special care
They are held for just a moment
And their gifts are ours to share

They bring us special riches
That money cannot buy
They bring us joy and laughter
And some can make us cry

They grow up so very fast
And the time oh how it flies
Today they are just children
Tomorrow adults leading separate lives.

Pilar De La Cruz

Untitled

Times are rough
As you grow older
But have no worries
It will all smooth over
Just think positive
And keep your head up high
Don't give up hope
Or your dreams can die
So follow your heart
To the end
And you will find
Your happiness again.

Richard L. Higgins III

A Promise

Your touch -
An ocean's wave of passion.
Your smile -
A star on a cloudless night.
Your eyes -
Piercing but warm, see through me.
Your heart -
As pure as a winter snow's white.

I promise to love you always;
I promise all I can give
Is yours now and forever,
As long as we both shall live.

Tina Murphy

Streams Of Pavement

Lead me far away
to calm the silent waters by
So in time I may remove
this filter from my eye
With the haunting sounds beyond
I never could trespass
Or travel this endless path
through tremors in the grass
Against every darkened stream
of quite shallow rain
Are lost and shaded secrets
of love I must regain
Designed to be a memory
Close my eyes in time to see
A falling star that fell to far
Cross my heart and there you are

Nathan Fowler

Real

Sometimes when I meditate
in the middle of
my soft glowing peace,
a large round tear
will gently fall
from the corner
of my eye.
I don't need to know
if it is born of
joy or sorrow
it does not matter
for it is a sign
that God is near
and close to my heart
and He understands
for it is His tear.
He weeps with me,
in joy and sadness.
God is love
God is Real.

Christine Gilley

Untitled

I know this year
You're sad and blue
But just remember
He loved you

Be happy today
And all through the year
For in your heart
Were all so near

Life is to be lived
From day to day
Trust in God
Come what may

Robert R. Kelly

Tashi

Startled, I wake from a sleep
That takes me back in time
A dream so wonderfully deep
I remember the furry black cat
For me to forever keep.

Food she ate I can recall
The way she slept and walked
Down the long, dark hall
But between us now exists
A barrier, an unbreakable wall.

Beth Harrington

In My Room, Peacefully

So strange am I to
fly so-low?—
Alone with everyone
not here but me,
in my room,
thinking quite quiet thoughts
about nothing in general;
not quite finding
what it isn't
that I'm missing.

Royce Welford Chen

Love Is...

Love is sometimes lost
but not always a treasured find.
Love is often confused
with what matters in another mind.

Love is sometimes weak,
it takes two to keep it strong
Love is music in the making
and not just another song

Love is like mentality,
it can be shallow, it can be deep.
Love is like falling,
look before you leap.

Love is like happiness,
something very few have got.
Love is sharing your heart
and "forget me nots."

Love is life's mystery,
finding each and every clue.
Love is the worlds biggest wonder
and I'm in it with you!

James King

I Can't Sing

I use to sing
but, look at me now
notes just mean nothing
I've even forgotten how

I can't carry a tune
in a basket, cause of leaks
when I try to carry a tune
my voice box only squeaks.

I've forgotten about the treble clef
the musical scale has faded
I'm all mixed up, too with
notes that are clear or shaded

Lincoln E. France

Someone

Someone lives and someone dies
Someone laughs and someone cries
Someone prays to God to let one live.
Someone pleads to God to bring one back.
When someone's gone from you forever,
You know deep down in your heart
you will forget them never.
Unless you let the cherished memories
slip away,
You can believe they are in a far
better place, far far away.

Dana Schmidt

Death

A knife in a heart,
a bullet in a brain,
water in lungs,
and a rose by a grave,

A tear on a cheek,
a child left alone,
a feeling of worthlessness,
and another matching stone.

Gina Sullivan

Cringing Under The Rage
Of A Wilting Soul

From under the frosty pale pink moon,
curiosity opens its eyes.
Like the birth of a bluebird,
whose feathers lift the wind.

A hazy light storm
peaks around a mountain of frowns,
chilling the breath
beneath the love.

With craters of day
burning an orange tear.
Cradling the soft voice.

Still sounds of endearment
hover by its ears,
and shivers of snow
only freeze the soul.

Helen Beeson

Untitled

My thumb are
suns rising
through prisons
of bars.
My toe
is the
tone
of a
hundred
guitars
my
heart is
a rose in
a sparkling
wine
my soul
is the
 smell of
a billions of
stars.

Christopher Chapman

The Handi Work Of God

As I walked along the pathway
 the moon was shinning bright
As I talked with my Savior
 In the garden last night

I'm so thankful that I'm living
 Where it's free to worship God
And have eyes to see the beauties
 of the handi work of God

He made the flowers in the gardens
 So their beauties we could see
He put the snow upon the mountains
 and the water in the sea

He made the hills and the valleys
 He put the leaves upon the trees
He gave us the freedom to worship
 To worship as we please

I'm so thankful that I'm living
 Where its free to worship God
And have eyes to see the beauties
 Of the handi work of God.

Freda Lee Jackson

Will You Be There

Will you be there
If I should call
Will you be there
If I should happen to fall

Will you be there
If the need arrives
Will you be there
To be by my side

Will you be there
To lend a helping heart
Will you be there
And never forever depart

Will you be there
To help a friend
Will you be there
Till the dying end

I want to thank you
For being there
And for being someone
Who really did care

Marsha F. Greene

One Journey Of Life

You stepped into a new realm
As the clock ticked on for us
The shock, disbelief surrounded all
As you started your new journey.

One breath away to a haven of faith
Left us in a tide of grief
But a richer more loving life for you
Of this we all believe.

Now within that split second change
A new life we all receive
One spent in loving memories
And a loss beyond belief.

On you go, as do we
To the out reaching arms of eternity
Glad for time shared, wanting more
As we journey to lives many shores.

Susan Rhoades

Berry Good

What's big and red
Makes life more merry?
Nothing less, than
A ripe strawberry!
Crushed on some shortcake
Smothered in whipped cream,
You have created
A dessert supreme.
Sense the fragrance
Of homemade bread,
This ruby substance
You must spread.
In a breakfast bowl
It's a go getter,
Makes every morning,
Much 'more better'.
You see its real cool
To select the right berry
Its nothing less
Than a red ripe strawberry!

Marshall N. Smith

Of Leaves And Love

As I watched the leaves
come swirling down,
smothering my still-green lawn
I thought about love
(I do that sometimes)

My mind went back to springtime
when buds are born,
and the earth is full of hope
and promises of color,
like new love
when it starts to blossom.

Like the few leaves
that cling to barren branches
until strong autumn winds
force them to let go,
we don't always know
when it's time to say

Goodbye.

Mary L. Pirozok

Christine M. Boss

I didn't know you long,
But I knew you enough
To know you loved everyone.
You said bad things about no one.
You were a mother to one
A second mother to many.
You lived life to its fullest and
The cancer rarely slowed you down.
You were full of life
Until the final hours.
You will always be cherished
For the rest of our lives.
No one who knew you
Will ever forget you because
You cared for so many
And they all cared for you.
Dave and John will really miss you
And the rest of us will, too.

Brandi Jo Echelbarger

Dragonfly

Have you seen the dragon fly
Far up in the sky?
Can you truly find
The image from the mind?
Can it really be
if eyes do not see?

Of it you have heard
or read in written word.
Sadly though, it seems
lost in a world of dreams.

So close your eyes
before it dies.
Keep it alive
and let it thrive.
This mythical beast
has not deceased
if your inner eye
sees the dragon fly.

Sharon Bode

I Send To You

I send to you,
something so true,
and it is called love.
I think of love,
whenever I see a pretty dove.
It is so true,
that most of the time,
I think of you.
You said that you would wait,
but only until God opened the gate.
I did not want it,
but yet it came.
Not even my love or memories for you,
will ever fade.
My heart is broken,
I feel like I'm choking.
Now can you see how much
I did love thee.

Janine Keghlian & Rosemarie Leek

Greyshadows/Like-Me-Deaf

Windows-dirty
no-hear-eyes
souls-inside

White-bright
open-no-how
door-lock

See-hear
open-how-know
hands-hearts

Touch-meld-free
light-white
brain-searing-bright

Wraparound
sob-sing
heartbeat-warm-like

Butterflies
in
the
sun.

Marene Mattern

His Heart

Inside his heart
there are many things left unsaid
Thoughts that haven't been released
words that haven't been said

He puts on a show
every single day
Yet once in awhile
he'll let his guard fall

He will tell me his deepest fears
and share his thoughts with me
Of everything that is near
of everything he holds dear

Memories from the past
that he's afraid to relive again
Memories of loved ones
that according to him were lucky
enough to have gotten away

Inside his heart I can see many of my fears,
many of my thoughts, and feel almost all
of his pain.

Shawnna R. Whitson

My Prince Charming

He did not ride a big white horse
or shiny armor wear;
But I knew from what I saw
I'd be his maiden fair.

He came a courtin' many times.
And handsome? That he was!
I'd thrill at just the sight of him.
It seemed my heart did pause!

We'd walk for hours by the water;
Of this he seemed quite fond.
Sometimes he'd even pick for me
A lily from the pond.

One day while we were picnicking
And having so much fun,
Quite suddenly, to my surprise;
Up he hopped and off he run!!

I followed him and found him
Just sitting on a log.
It was then that I did wonder
Had my Prince once been a Frog?

Delores Magnuson

A New Dawn

To wake up in the morning,
Without a single warning.
No clue on what lies ahead,
Ahead down that road we dread.
Lying here with so few dreams,
Unrelenting are my screams.
Looking through my window pane,
I see my sky shrouded with pain.
No more decadent wishes,
No more romantic kisses.
No longer is she by my side,
Just last night she was my bride.
No more laughs or joyous cries,
No longer does love shine in her eyes.
Her words may no longer echo in my ear,
But her essence will always be near.

Peter Bruno

Daddy Please Don't

I have always loved my daddy so
more than anyone could know.

There are still secrets that we share
of things he said no one would care.

The words inside my head today
are words I still need to say.

Daddy please I'm so scared
Daddy please don't touch me there.

Patricia Holloman

In The Darkness I Spy Trees

In the darkness I spy trees.
Through the forest, lightening glares.
Bubbling water sings my name
Through whispery breezes, yelling young.
Words escape me when I call you
And I cannot see the wind.
If the dreams I hold, appall you,
Then those dreams I now rescind.

Amy L. Kurlansky

Christmas Eve

On Christmas Eve
The stocking are hung.
The children are laughing
But soon they'll be gone.
Because Santa Claus
Is coming soon
Off on his sleigh,
Zoom, zoom, zoom.
Down the chimney
All full of soot,
Stepping out
Foot by foot.
Filling the stockings
One by one.
Then in a flash
He will be gone.

Jaclyn Watson

My Child

The masterpiece I dreamed of when
I was young
You are the one thing I have worked
on all my life
A shining star I tried to reach for
in everyday life
With in every day life you are
the fulfillment
All the things I try to write, paint
or draw you are
Now with all I am blessed, because
you are my child.

Heather Clark

Spirit

The last rays fade over the horizon
Crickets set the stage,
The ringed moon enhances the feeling
The star light brings you home.
I drive through the town
Death makes me feel eternal
I ride in the heavens
On a twilight cloud
I look to the east
And feel the day
Morning comes
And I am gone!

James F. Murphy

When Elephants Play

I saw an elephant in my yard today,
Jumping and tumbling, how he could play.
Standing only four inches tall,
He was no bigger than a softball.

Look! Watch him leap,
The wind carries him there.
You would swear he had wings
As he flies through the air.

Oh, little elephant at play,
Why did you go away?
I blink my eyes and you are gone,
A leaf in your place flies along.

What joy for a moment,
What fun in my day,
Time well spent,
When elephants play.

Janet K. Edens

Man's Decision

Yesterday as I strolled this way
Stately pines and sturdy oaks
Towered here, cooling the earth
And absorbing pollution
Being friends to mankind.

Today they have been desecrated
They lie in a huge, dying heap
Pushed there by the bull-dozer-
Man's tool of mass destruction.
  Gone forever from my world.

No longer will I see them
Bow before the summer storms
Their great limbs grazing the ground
To rise again in awesome beauty,
Their leaves dancing in defiance.

Now I wonder-will we cross
America's bridge to treeless plains?
It's not too late for songs of birds
In forests lushly green and deep.
That decision rests with man.

Ella Fay Stephens

Purple, Red and Blue

There's a painting in my house
of purple, red and blue,
looking of frost and cold snow
an old barn is there too.
Birch trees are scattered along,
and a road meanders through
the smoke rises from the horizon;
of shadows there are quite a few.

So look at this cold clear painting
Set in the gold gilt frame
Give thanks with your heart,
and all of your soul
for the warmth you yet may retain.

Charlotte Christensen

Cannon

The explosion
was a deafening bomb
whizzing like a train
through a tunnel.
Consumed with angry power,
the cannon ball
hurled through the air,
startling as lightning
in summer.
Crackling smoke
filled the air,
as the sky
burned with haze,
the stillness
becoming dark.

Chase Meyers

Winter Wind

The early wind blows,
The morning sun glows,
When the wind blows its leaves,
Hush! Listen! It is the sound of winter.

Venetia Papaioannou

To My Love

Through the years that we
have been together, I have
learned so much,
From looking into your beautiful eyes,
To feeling your sweet soft touch.
My darling you have showed me that,
true love is very dear,
and how much it really means to have,
the one that you love near.
So from this day on,
I'll make this promise to you,
I will love, honor, and cherish you,
I'll do the best that I can do.
And as always,
My heart belongs to you.

Kelly Binns

January Winter Eve

The day dies suddenly
Darkness constantly at 5:30
Dawn will be distant
Seven thirty before brightness
Fourteen hours of nightmare
Only ten choices till daylight -
More time for reflection
More time for family things
Its not all bad - TV and fireside
Hot snacks and books to read -
Early to bed - warm as toast
Up at six - sunshine and snow -
We grumble and wait for winter to go!

Byron Porter

Together Forever

Together forever
In your arms
Under the stars

I tell you until my voice is gone
I love you
And my love will always be strong

So never forget
These words I say
"I love you Babe"

Jeanne Michelle Snoddy

Moon

The moon is glistening;
while I'm listening,
with an open mind.

I whisper into the sky.

The moon wouldn't respond;
I am lonely trying to stay strong,
Finally the moon response.

Jennifer Nicole Seymore

My Loving Dad

To my loving Dad,
Who yells when I am bad,
Who truly loves me,
And is starting to let me free.
To my loving Dad,
Who loves me with all his heart,
And I know our love and bonds
Will never break apart.

Jessica Marinelli

A New Day's Dawn

On the horizon,
I sense a light.
It's almost time,
to watch the end of night.

I hear the birds,
and their morning song.
I enjoy the melodies,
that I've missed so long.

I hear the scurrying,
of tiny feet.
Owned by a young animal,
in search of something to eat.

I now notice a glare,
that is more profound.
And watch the rays dance,
across the dew on the ground.

I now hear the sounds,
of civilization returning.
And I say out loud,
"Hello" and "Good Morning"!

Tony Nickell

The Soul

The lost soul
looking
desiring answers
searching
lost, but wanting to be found
Wait, I am not a lost soul
everyone else is lost
they have forgot
the language
of spirituality
love, and
live
for what we give
will take us to were we belong
don't lose your soul
discover it

Lindsay Heath

The Dawn's Awakening

Hush . . . The dawn's awakening
  is too clamorous to bear!
Oh, let me linger softly
  A moment longer here
Let me memorize the magic
  Of midnight's moments before
For all too soon the sun will peak
  And the morning thrush will soar!
Oh, let me take this sweetness
  And press it to my soul
To unwrap and savor
  When I have grown old!
Oh! Hold the sun!
  Refuse the dawn!
Let me linger — on — on!

Jean M. Might

Spring Is Born

Today I saw the season change
As nature gave birth to spring
All new and tender, filled with hope
It was a wondrous thing.

A robin searching for a mate
A daffodil in bloom
Blades of grass peeking through
The sun was warm by noon.

So reassured was I today
That love is all around
What else could prove it more
Than the spring that God sent down?

Gaye Hughes

Sublime

Pleasures to her thought
gifts to her heart
all thee I sought
fire into the arrow
skies have fallen
heads have turned
lips have spoken
but inside they burned
grace underfoot
lace flies above
tastes have forebode
stories never told
flowers fray the silence
love overflows my heart
I take her hand...
we live upon the land...
exploring her beauty grand

Rick Miller

Heaven Is Near

Heaven is near and blessed
When I think of home.
Childhood memories so vivid
Where tender love was shone.

Each little nook and corner
Leads me to reminisce.
Could anything quite equal
This simple arbor of bliss.

Each flower in its formal place
Each face with perfect radiance.
From time to time I shed a tear
When dreams of past I chance.

Snow flurries on a winter night
The hills and streams now sheeted.
With unaided hands, by God alone
The peaceful bit of earth He created.

Carmel Leavitt

Breaking My Heart

As my hearts break inside
my tears flow down my eyes
how could you break my heart
and just walk away.
Are you that cold?
Are you that cruel?
To break my heart
and walk away.
Was it fun for you to break my heart?
How could you break my heart
the way that you did?

Maria-Eneida Flores

Life

You would take me to school
and take me to a pool,
We played all day
till we were out of breath,
it would be late
but we still found time to play.

But you had to smoke
and you started to choke,
you new what was wrong
and you finally told me,
I tried not to cry
but you started to cry
and I wish you hadn't told me.

The day had come to pass away,
you left us now,
you're in our hearts night and day
I still try not to cry,
you were my grandpa
we all loved you,
why oh why.

Anthony Velasquez

Untitled

As I sit and wonder why
what it is that I've done wrong.
The clouds go slipping across the sky
making me wish that I were gone.

My love has left, there are no others,
I turn and look - they have fled.
All my wives, friends and lovers,
have left me with a sense of dread.

No lips to kiss, no heart to pound,
nobody to press so close to mine,
I will not beg, I must be proud,
soon all eternity will be mine.

My life is short, the end is near,
there are no sobs, nor a fear,
I've loved the best, this I know,
with those fond memories, off I go.

A twinkle in the eye,
a grin on my lips,
through eternal darkness,
I now slip.

Richard A. Fredrick

They Call It Angel Oak

We call it The Hanging Tree.
As many as eleven Black bodies
Dangled here at once,
In South Carolina,
The South, near the sea.

Seventeen hundred years it's lived,
It's seen hangings and hurricanes.
Old before Columbus got here,
It stands witness to life and pain.

Men have met beneath its leaves,
and changed each other's fate.
The air's eerie feel is not its fault.

It only stands and waits.

Deborah H. Payne

From Now Until Forever

As the sun comes up
in the morning and the
glow beams upon my face,
I know that God is watching
and filling me with his grace.

It's a joy every morning
to wake and see my family
alive and well again. It fills
me with cheer and lets me
wake up with no fear.

As night falls and I go
to bed and pull the covers
upon me, I thank the Lord
once more for protecting me
from my enemies so good night
my friends and please remember
to pray for me and know that
God is always with thee.
From now until forever.

Jessica Eaddy

A World Tomorrow

As the years slip slowly by
I sit and ask myself why
Why is the world in the shape it's in
will it change will a new world begin

If it does I hope I'm here
so the new world can bring me some cheer
I hope it takes away, all the pain
And gives me a life worth living again

I hope the world we have this time
will be rid of all it's crime
And that the people can get along
To make this world right not wrong

If we all would just pull together
We can make this world even better
There would be no more pain or sorrow
If we could have this world tomorrow

Josephine Luwanna Stotler

Thanksgiving Time

It's that time of year again
When leaves change color and fall
And the air is very crisp and sweet
And the trees stand bare and tall

It's that time of year again
When sweet smells fill the air
Of roasted turkey and pumpkin pie
And cobbler, oh so fair

It's that time of year again
When children bundle up
And play in autumn leaves that fall
Of red, gold and rust

It's that time of year again
when we reflect on past
And thank God for our many blessings
And memories that last.

It's thanksgiving!

Tim Steinbuch

Cabin In The Field

I sheltered those who tilled the soil,
Gave them respite from their toil,
Heard children shouting while at play,
Kept them safe at the end of day.

I heard the newborn infant's cry,
and sadly watched the old ones die,
I knew their secret hopes and fears,
Heard their laughter, saw their tears.

But silence now pervades my halls,
And clinging vines possess my walls.
With loneliness each year is filled,
For now the voices all are still'd.

E. B. Dittmer

It's Life

Oh my life is like a river.
Always running, always tripping
Never really following a path.

It is like the vast blue sky
Never dying, never ending
Although it's always changing.

My life is like the green rolling hills
Sometimes up and sometimes down
Never just plain smooth.

Oh my life is like a good many things
And though not all of them are good
They make my lonely life complete.

Theresa Capito

Free

I am a free feather on the open tundra,
the rolling fog,
the falling caribou,
the gentle snow on the frozen plain.

I am lost and alone,
one with the wolves,
a follower of these magnificent animals.

I am a free feather on the open tundra,
the rolling fog,
the falling caribou,
the gentle snow on the frozen plain.

Kristin Slade

Mystical Oneness

Valleys edge I go to meet
amongst the forest trees I hope to sleep
calmed by the dripping sap
I nestle in a meadows patch.

To touch the hardened earth beneath
softened by some baby's breath
I long to find a sacred space
away from life's crazy pace.

Night breeze, calm caress
sky wings open to embrace
sparkling are the shooting stars
planets unite not far.

More scenes I long to birth
with you oh Mother Earth
You are the One I do desire
burn deep within, Your Mystical Fire.

Diane Eller-Boyko

The Eternal Sea

To men I'm just another sailor;
Here today, tomorrow, another port,
But just like they, I have in me
A lonely longing in my heart.

The sea can be so beautiful,
And yet, so desperately mad;
She can take a life away,
From honest man or cad.

She has no respect for man,
Nor the ships in which he sails;
They take the bitter and the sweet,
Tho she hands out wind and gales.

A seafaring man is a lonely man,
But the ships and the sea are in him,
And a landlubber's life is dull!
It will never completely win him.

So when my life on earth is done;
Don't put six feet of earth on my.
Lower me gently and calmly down
To the waiting lips of the eternal sea.

James C. Leischner

I Listen But I Cannot Hear

I listen when you say,
I should get away.
I listen to you cry,
when he blackened my eye.
I listen to you yell,
he should go to hell.
And I listen when you say,
he'll kill me one day.
I listen about how much you care,
but still you're so unaware.
He'll never let me go,
this I already know.
So I know you're my friend,
when you say leave him once again.
And I listen to your tears,
But I simply cannot hear.

Anna Lee Riley

The Perfect Age

A little plump girl
playing with her doll
caressing it, singing
in her hands swinging.
   Oh, what a perfect age!
Young lady, blond hair.
Dreaming about her man
the one that will come
and make her a madame.
   Oh, what a perfect age!
Mother giving birth to a baby
who sends a smile, bird's chirping,
Warm milk in round breasts,
near which her baby rests.
   Oh, what a perfect age!
Grandma, still young
taking deep breaths
straight gate, hair grey
Enjoying life in her own way
   Oh, what a perfect age!

G. Ehrlich

One Life One Death

One life One death
There's no in between
One life One death
There's no middle to this crazy thing
One life to live
One death to die
I'm gonna live with honor
And die with pride
I'm gonna love my life
And treat it right
Then I'll deserve a good release
From the Black Night
I crave my life
But I don't fear death
It's gonna come anyway
My life won't leave my soul astray
One life One death
There's no in between
One life One death
There's no middle to this crazy thing

Mellysa L. Meier

Uncaring

So beautiful it hardly seems fair
Earth's destruction; and no more air.
Can't breathe my body in fear
Can't see; where are you my dear.
It's yesterday glad to be alive
Now today; why must we all die.

So beautiful it hardly seems fair
Why earth; has no one to care.
America America land of the free
Chaos, war has come to be.
Can't hide it'll soon see
Just know you'll die with me.

So beautiful it hardly seems fair
No ones living; nothings left here.

Dawnielle Haines

Leave Yesterday Behind

Leave yesterday behind
Look for tomorrow...
We can't relive the memories
Or forget the sorrow.

We smiled; we frowned;
We laughed; we cried.
But, the times we had
Were filled with pride.

We made mistakes
We now regret.
Those times, however,
We can't forget.

The friends we had
Were the best, we know.
But in years to come
New friendships will grow.

Leave yesterday behind
Look for tomorrow...
For it is happiness you'll find
And only memories you'll borrow.

Lauren S. Swalberg

Things Are Better Still

When sour seems your view of us
Think back I pray to how it was
Before we tamed the wind and rain
Before our lives were easy made
The age when life was wild and free
The age that you would now to flee
When time's regress lays in your will
Remember things are better still.

Zachary Forrest North

I Have A Place

I was lying in a gutter of sin,
beyond the help of human hands,
until one day I asked my savior,
if his hand, he would extend...

Yes! He saved me,
Yes! He saved me,
Save me by his loving grace,
he washed away my sin's forever,
now at last, "I have a place"...

Randall Blevins

Why?

I ask myself several times,
Knowing there is no answer.
I tell myself not to bother,
But confusion is such an intoxicant.

If it were for me to say,
The right words wouldn't be said.
I could call out for wisdom,
But I'm satisfied being perplexed.

I'd rather he who knows doesn't tell,
The truth is a bitter pill to swallow.
I'll peacefully dwell in the unknown,
For I realize the reasons Why.

Brian K. Finch

Daybreak

Day is coming, night has gone.
As you cried yourself to sleep.
The tears dry upon your face.
When you feel the
one you need, you see they're
not there to wipe the tears
on your face.

As you look around you
realize the sounds are not
a comfort to your heart
they're just their to put
tears on your face, so the
you love can wipe the
tears from your face of
fears.

Shannon Snapp

Valentine's Candy

Oh valentine's candy
You are so sweet.
You taste like momma's
Biscuits of wheat.

Eddie Humphrey III

My Husband - My Friend

The passage of years only served
to enhance the treasures of our life
together. Our relationship as one
still has many exciting adventures.
Knowing I can look forward to my
future with you gives me a
terrific sense of security and joy.
You have such a way with your
protective soul over my peaceful heart.
I'm not afraid of the ever changing
times with you in sight. If I
searched the valleys low and mountains
high, I'd never find a person like
the one at my side.

Kelly A. Chaffins

Untitled

River running wild
    images
        impulses.
Filling the caverns
    depths
        darkness.
Reflections of
    today
        tomorrow.
A remembering of
    days gone by.

Cathy Randecker

Sunset Love

The sunset hues burn bright,
picturesque colors fill the sky.
A splash of orange,
a dash of yellow,
slight shades of purple,
as nature's masterpiece
hits its bedtime
and slowly fades
from view.
This scene does not compare
with true beauty,
your smile beams bright
from a warm glowing personality.
Soft lips,
tender as a newborn
glowing eyes showing love.
The inner beauty you have,
more beautiful than
a setting sun.

Steven Lomax

Untitled

If you look inside this gift,
A package you will find.
And with this package, goes a question
That's really been on my mind.

A question meant for only you;
A question to you from me
I want to know if you'll be my wife
From now 'till eternity.

Now if your answer is a yes.
I'll see it in your eyes.
But please say it out loud
Dear Judy.
For a nervous wreck am I!!

Michael L. Doyle

Corny Lover's Poem

The corny lover's
    are so sweet.
It is almost everywhere
    that they meet.

They stay together
    through pain and pleasure.
They don't care,
    as long as they have each other.

The corny lover's
    are so truthful.
They never lie,
    and are never deceitful.

I envy the love
    that they share.
Oh well, as long as I
    have a man who cares,
I'll be happy. I swear.

Zelda Castrow

Gray Hair And Wrinkles

We wear our Gray Hair
    and Wrinkles with pride.
They are our badge of courage
    to the world
That is at battle outside.

A trophy of endurance
    for each front-line
        explosion
            sabotage
                and loss
    we have come through.

Decorated

A Medal of Honor

for the person inside.

Terryl Lieffers

Man's Soul

As he walks,
He stands alone.
For inside his soul drives.
Within that soul,
There is a heart,
That he uses.
No question, no doubt.
How could you or I judge this man?
For he does not lie,
Neither to us nor to his soul.
If only we were so fortunate,
To walk and stand alone.

Kristin Schierwagen

An Evening Promise

Touched by twilight,
The night comes gently.
Forever guilty for the darkness
Of the present and the past.
Time stretches endlessly.
With the evening a peaceful serenity
Drifts upon the shadows.
Stars dance across the sky,
Illuminated by the moon's bright light.
But eventually the night ends,
And tomorrow begins again.

Dianne Brannon

Daily Reflections

As the sun is slowly setting
I reflect upon the day
Of things I should have said and done
And made the time to pray.

As busy as our life may be
The Lord is the only way
Take your cares to Him in prayer
Do it each and every day.

Our burdens He will gladly carry
Because Jesus died for all
To save us from eternal death
He will not let us fall.

Everything will turn out right
Of this we can be sure
If we ask Him that His will be done
We know His Love for us endures.

So take a moment every day
To say a prayer or two
Pray from your heart to God above
For all that He has given to you.

Kristine Gegner

Pizza Toppings

What I would find on my
Pizza pie are some
Squirmy worms which
Are still alive,
Moldy cheese,
Rotten peas,
And week old lima beans.
Spoiled mayonnaise home to filth,
Flea infested fish heads,
And two scoops of spoiled milk.
Curdled cottage cheese,
   Ketchup left in the
Sun for days,
Mustard which we had to peel away,
But absolutely no anchovies.

Mallory Cerny

By Myself

I am alone
a woman at home,
my sought-after solitude won.
I worked very hard
to get where I am,
escaped the confining
love of a man.
I must never go back.
I will move on and along
under my own power
and keep growing stronger,
the stronger the better.

Daphne A. Sayers

Secrets

The wind blows secrets,
Only some can hear.
The sky holds the future,
Out of reach, but so near.
The ocean holds the past,
Drifting away day by day.
For soon we'll be happy,
He'll show us all the way.

Alison Diamond Long

It's Christmas

It's time I celebrate
The birthday of a king
What kind of gift
may I give to "One"
with everything?
The gift is deep inside me,
A humble, loving heart.
Give Him this most
precious gift,
Then let the season start!

It's beginning to look like
Christmas.
It looks like Christmas -
everywhere -
With Christmas Peace
and Christmas Holiness
Then Love
   will be
   in the air!

Lea C. Debalty

A Mountain Blows

Mt. St. Helens,
Why did you blow your top?
With such fury and rage,
It seemed to never stop.

Was it because handsome Rainier
Never looked your way?
And Mt. Adams was agog
With Three Sister's fine array?

Better quit your stomping, Gal,
And stay settled down.
You have everything to lose!
You have already lost your crown!

You have spoiled your lovely trees
Where animals loved to hide.
You turned the rivers into mud;
There all the fish have died.

You have destroyed homes,
Camps, lakes, and streams.
You have demolished forever
Men's hopes and lovely dreams.

Muriel L. Richter

Rejoice

Rejoice ye heavens and the earth
Give praise to God of Virgin birth
Sing hallelujah and Amen
We praise the Father yet again

Lord give me wings that I might fly
Oh let the angels lift me high
Give mental view of heaven's height
To bear me up through earthly night

And through sometimes my spirit bows
Accepting pain as Christ allows
I hasten on to sing His praise
And feel that lowly spirit raise

Until again with bellowed voice
I sing, give thanks oh earth, rejoice
Give praise to God of virgin birth
Rejoice ye heavens and the earth.

Edith Kidd-Willis

October First

As the summer sun
becomes the fall
cherished times
become a memory

Though life moves on
with branches bare
you are still with me
forever
on an Indian summer day

Molly Elizabeth Brown

Words On Paper

I saw her walking
   In a garden fair
With flower and fragrance
   And beauty rare
Petals were falling
   On the path at her feet
As if by chance
   Her step would meet
A song of beauty
   From her lips arose
That made the sun shine
   And the flowers grow
A vision of love
   She is to me
The moon in its quarter
   Her fullness to be
Sweet gift of God
   A wondrous treasure
A maiden of life
   And love without measure

John Deal

Dead Princess

I fall asleep...so sad
Only to dream of toads and princes
The path is dark...
Still waters cold...
The princes are all dead
And toads have melted into lily pads
As I awaken...slowly
No chivalry to speak of
Only ripples on the water
And swords that have no masters

Lynn Kehoe

Morning Glory

The mist that drapes the hills
the river so calm no force to
   reckon with
the birds start to chipper
but some how the calm, the mystery
   and the beauty of such, morn
engulf my soul with glee

So I ponder amid the clutter
Look to see whats the matter
all of a sudden
two haggard strangers
   befuddle to say the least
ghastly how could I help I said
   although I can tell they were
   already dead
so help help I said
Oh morning glory how dread,
   how dread.

Helena Ward

One

I am one with the universe.
Me.
I am one.
My individuality is my best feature.
I am the one.

I am one in nature.
All creatures are my friends
All creatures belonging to the earth
I adore.

I am one in love.
Love runs through my body
like water through leaves.
While death is cold
Love keeps me warm.

I am one with the world.
I am one.

Jennifer Garson

Eloni

Trapped blue endless light
Made free within confines.
Content to be imprisoned there;
Infinite love stored in time.
Eternal blessed; eternal spring
Of love that never ceases.
The wind that stirs the soul, the heart
This wind wrapped round my heart.
Its storm sets free
The glory of two hearts made one.
All air, wind, earth, and fire
Made strong within your clasp.
This love I cannot own
It belongs with both of us.
Everywhere flowers felled
(Their drabness not equals us.)
This magic of Eloni
turns nothing quite the same
This force stronger than any else
Is the birth of first new love.

Vera A. Feistel

Renders

A rose sires
a torny thorn;
a suckling youth
and prickling render.
Growth! Growth!
An infinite twisting at the viny spine.
A prickling youth
and suckling render.

Danny Barrious

Untitled

When the sky is blue as blue as streams
I hope that you'll have special dreams.
When the sky was blue as blue as streams
I did have very special dreams.

In the special dream I had
a lady appeared and said,
"Your dreams are like wishes,
your wishes are dreams
that are filled with happy things."

Jennifer Thibodeaux

A Mother's Silent Love 1954

I wonder does God grant the right
To a mother who's gone to rest
To touch her child's small baby band
And bold her to her breast.

Does she guide her steps and thoughts
And help her play and grow?
Does her heart reach out with love
As she walks on earth below?

Can she touch her fevered brow
And hold her small hot hand?
Can she kiss her little mouth
And say "I understand."

Or does God do all the work
And let the mother rest?
I think to ease her heart
He says, "Hold her to your breast."

Grace Shelton Dukeminier

Our Dog Bo

It's kind of funny,
Our dog has a bunny!
He takes it wherever he goes.

He's a brawny boy,
But he needs his toy.
It's never far from his nose.

Floppy ear and all,
The rubber rabbit is small.
Inside his mouth it fits.

Don't hide Bo's rabbit,
It's become quite a habit.
If lost, he would lose his wits.

Although he won't share
His white tailed hare,
We love him, he's our dog "Bo"!

Beth Loughry

Neptune Rising

The ocean roars loudly
And casts its anger
Against the helpless shore,
White seagulls cry out
And careless winds
Bandy nests of dried debris
On wings of swirling sand,

Scepter bearing Neptune
Riding curly maned Teranos
Seeks a storm raped prize
For his grandiose cavern
Arcaned far, far below
Rotting ships and divers eyes,

Where laughingly he toasts
Man's human frailties
And centimeter existence.

Noree Liang Pope

Winter

When every thing is white
With cousins buildings snow forts
Snow glistening every where
The best time of the year
Sledding down icy hills
Every one is warm by the fire

Melissa Ruben

Black Child's Cry

Black child cries out in the night,
In search of hope and joy so bright.
Tears falling from tiny eyes in despair,
   but he dare not rise.

In a world of poverty and violence,
Justice he longs to see.
Little black child, dry your eyes;
Don't despair! 'Tis hope is here to
   brighten your path.

For you hold within your soul
a potential to unfold and fly...
Yes, soar like an eagle in the night!
Unlease your power and dreams.
Yes my child, you hold the key to
a life unforseen.

Barbara D. Lynch

Crossroad: U.S. 81 No

Tinker Tavern Road!
Where the Yankee peddler
   of pot and mug
Rested his horse
   and drank a jug
of stout, or ale
   while telling a tale
of the wilderness trail...
Then he'd doze a bit
   before he hit
the lonely road
   with his jangling load.

Anne Laughlin Smith

There Is Someone

There's a reason why we live
Take a moment to believe
If this world tomorrow will die
There must be reasons why

Have you ever wondered why
Something sparkle in the sky
Some will try to conquer the star
To find the reasons why

There are blessings we receive
It's a reason why we give
Yet there were times
That didn't look bright
No matter how we tried

Yes I believe there is someone
I do believe there is someone
Yes there is someone
Behind it all

Jaime B. Quilala

See Through The Skin

For those who read this
My advice to you is
Try to find a friend
That is true
Look past the cloths
And through the skin
To find the person
That lies within

Sandra Adkins

Fake Flowers

She looks like the real thing,
She tastes like the real thing,
But fake flowers . . .
Still glow.
But I can't help but feeling,
If she were the real thing,
It would be me,
she'd outgrow.
I don't have to care for her,
Don't need to be there for her,
Because fake flowers . . .
Don't grow.
But at least when I'm home at night,
In absence of life or light,
I know my fake flower . . .
Won't go.
Away.

David J. Rodgers

Memoriam

Though a year has passed
    Since you left our side,
Happy moments with you
    Will never subside.

Many times we sit
    Alone and we cry,
The Lord took you from us
    We still don't know why.

But one thing the Lord
    Cannot take away,
We feel you are near us
    Each night and each day.

Some day in the future
    We'll pass through the gate,
Then we'll all be together,
    Though we know not the date.

Madeleine M. Riska

Spiritsmoke

Sparks flee the
    Heat enraged
As the smoke dances

I am the smoke
    And cannot be harmed
The hotter you make it
    The higher I'll charm

When I'm attacked
    I've all the more style
As arrows slip through me
    I can't help but smile

The gentle flame
    Upon their heads
Will always be with me
    In His path I tread

From Him flows
    The life eternal
Separation is death
    Alone infernal

So find the flame and life discover
Unmatched and unsurpassed united forever

David M. Curri

Untitled

When the light at the end of the tunnel,
Seems to be dim.
Let me be the light that guides you,
When your days seem to be dark,
Let me be your sunlight
When you can't seem to find yourself,
Let me be your guide.
When you fall down.
Let me be the one to pick you up,
When you go to pieces,
Let me be the glue that binds you,
When you're wearing a frown,
Let me turn it upside-down.
When you shed a tear.
Let me wipe it away.
When you need someone.
Let me be there for you...

Marc S. Berke

Bittersweet

I'm haunted by the dreams I dream
The dreams that died so young
I'm haunted by the songs I sing
And the songs left unsung

I'm haunted by the memories
Of chances that I missed
I'm haunted by the pretty girls
The ones I held and kissed

I'm haunted by the pressed red rose
Between pages without sun
It reminds me of a lovely girl
I wish I knew which one

I'm haunted by life's mysteries
Can't say I solved e'en one
I'm haunted by my long gone friends
Who also never won

I'm haunted by fates final blow
To those so tired and weary
I'm haunted by her parting gift
Life's binomial theory

Daniel Skandera Jr.

Upon Superior's Shore

Upon her shores,
I calm my mind.
The struggles of life
wisping away with the wind,
crossing the blue expanse of beauty
and sunken groves.

She moves in a dance
of her own,
with rhythm of the waves
sliding upon the shore,
an everlasting partner.

The work of Mother Nature
no man can tame.
Beautiful she is,
and wild with grace of eagles

Supporting life of land and water,
taking what is hers.
Enchanting the hearts
who sit upon her shore.

Andrew James Watt

What Is Wrong With Me?

And like a lost soul she rises again...
Looking at the mountains so high,
looking at the sea so deep
What is life with a soul
if you can't feel your flesh.
Looking at the mountains so high,
looking at the sea so deep
What is wrong with me?
Am I a ghost, a lost soul
who wants to be free, or just
a person who can't feel complete.
What is wrong with me?
I feel deep in the ocean,
and I want to be free.

Wanda Rios

Something New

All I think
Has already been thought
All I say
Has already been said
All I see
Has already been seen
All I hear
Has already been heard
All I feel
Has already been felt

Looking for something new
To think
To speak
To see
To hear
To feel
All for myself
and no one else

Christopher Clements

The Excitement Of Love

My hand goes shaking
Now hidden in its pocket
Exploring the crevices
Trading the traits of oneself

Thinking and pondering
With no place to go
Around in circles
Sometimes spinning in infinity

My lip goes trembling
I ask of my boldness
Courage to face my opponent
Is there love to give away?

Jason Hale

Untitled

I look out side and see
my life pass before me.
I wonder why such things
happen to me.
Then I think of a place
I want to be.
With someone I love.
Someone like me.
Then I wake and
come to my senses,
and go to my life imagined or real.

Jeff Robert Hargrave

Love

Young and precious it starts
Simple and sweet it grows
Enjoying and learning it goes
On and on
Fulfillment to the highest it knows
It comes unexpected
But when it comes its great
No one can explain it
It is much appreciated
Because it is a joy
It comes to a girl or boy
You know what I'm talking about
You've felt it before
It's love
It's something you must explore
It's something that will endure

Adriene D. Brown

September Child

Born of the fires of winter
A heart skipped beat
In silent awe
The breath
To fill first sound uttered
From lips formed of a
moments melting two hearts to one.
Love, love's child
Forged of the depths of a
Soul's yearning,
My loves perfection.
Walk with me
My September Child,
For we are one.

Shona Woram

The Barn At Bread Loaf

We enter the heart
of this campus
through doors
that open and close

Open and close,
like two valves.
Under the ceiling
ribbed with beams,

We circulate through
chambers, take in air.
Our muse fueling us.
So when we leave,

We can pen
the blood
of our lifeline.
The pulse steady.

Nancy Manning

Where Is The Snail?

The snail left home.
He disappeared!
Left his shell alone,
And in despair.

Empty and not filled,
I found the shell.
I took it home
And treated it well.

Heidi Schellenbach

We The People

I sit and I wonder,
what "we the people" mean
does it mean all of us?
Or only ones in the mainstream
Do laws that apply to you,
apply to me?
Or are they just a mockery
When will "poker face" politicians,
stop sending us crumbs?
Shall we ever overcome?
"We the people" like Humpty,
might have a great fall
is it justice for some...
or justice for all.

Brian O. Smith

The Battle

The sword goes up,
The battle's on,
As darts fly everywhere.
Satan's lurking on the prowl
To unnerve our every care.

The lightning's flashing,
Swords are clashing,
The angels stand and fight.
Each warrior of the Lord is strong,
They protect with all their might.

The demons tremble,
The warriors bold,
As the battle begins to grow.
There is victory in Jesus
From the blood that once did flow.

They demons flee,
They are defeated,
This battle has been won
By the warrior of all warriors,
The great and holy one.

Donita Ortega

My Hungry Dogs

Dusty and Arrow,
cute as a kitten,
and are more playful
than mice in a mitten,
wait at the table,
as still as a tree.
My mother said, no!
Don't feed them the food.
Louder than a train
bellowing through.
So I'll wait till we're
done to feed them
the food.

Samantha Williams

Eagle

I sit and watch with wondering eyes
as in the sky the Eagle flies

The sky is like an endless field
a field of hopes
a field of dreams

For an Eagle finds hope in every dream!

Ashleigh Skye Hickle

Souls Meet

Summer came
and so did you
quietly, like a misty fog
sweeping over a silent city.

Your assumed sophistication
could not hide
the goodness in your heart.

Your smile, your looks,
your ways - thrilled me.
I deliciously wallowed
in your attention
which was short - spanned.
I loved you forever - yet
no one knew...
not even you...

Joan I. Brennan

Untitled

I sit alone
Waiting for day
I cry with no reason
Maybe tears of sadness or
tears of happiness.
I cry out
but with no sound
My room is dark
lit only with a flickering candle
I stare at the flame
orange glow twinkles in my wet eyes
I realize that I have stared at the
flame all night
I see the first rays of light peek
through the darkness.
The feeling of joy sweeps over me
but it is just another lonely day.

Heather DelCollo

The Oil War

Thick and black it oozes out,
a madman steals the day!
The world in disbelief does shout
as oil contaminates the bay.

The "Oil War" takes another turn
in Saddam's ruthless mind,
from wells that he has tried to burn
to terror on mankind.

The dolphins, fish and waterfowl
have played no part in this,
and yet they too are victims now
caught in his black abyss.

What untold terror lies in wait
for soldiers on the line,
when liberation of Kuwait
is fought with grunt and grind?

But fight we must with all our might
to quell this evil man
and restore the just and the right
unto this troubled land.

Jeffrey T. Wilson

Fallen

I see him sitting all alone
Treated like a piece of bone
He wonders what he did wrong
He wonders for so long.

A woman passes and says "Hi"
He just stares with one eye
He doesn't understand her well
I was the only one that could tell.

I went to see this fallen man
And tried to find out all that I can
As he came closer to me
He began to feel happy and free.

He fell down before my feet
And began to sob and weep
He fell down from the sky
He had his turn and lost his try.

Marian Otil

Kids Today

You say, 'These kids today —
There go all my hopes.'
I say, 'Look at you,
Sitting there watching soaps!'

You say, 'Don't like their clothes,
Baggy pants, dyed hair.'
I say, 'What of it,
They show love and they care.'

You say, 'It was different
When I was their age.'
I say, 'You are wrong.
I'm angry, full of rage.'

You just choose to forget
what we had to face:
Assassins and war,
The hate for a race.

You berate and rag them
And don't want them near.
I am not that way,
I think they're quite dear!

Deborah Gardner

I Have A Dream

I have a dream that I
will get my life back

'Cause right now what the
world is spinning I know it's
gone bad.

I dream that the life I'm living
will come back and be the way it was.

But now it seem that it's gone
bad I feel can shed my blood.

'Cause nobody can feel the pain
I'm going threw not my teachers
not my friends and not even you.

As I say how I feel with this
lost principle lead if only I had my
life back I wouldn't have to
put me to my final rest.

Darrick Parkins

As The Rain Falls Gently Down

As the rain falls gently down,
softly touching the ground,
like our love, quietly unspoken,
our marriage vows won't be broken,
no other man will come between
all our hopes, all our dreams.
This short time we'll spend apart,
creates more fondness in my heart,
although these days I'm missing you,
I know that when my time is through,
Our strong love will still be there,
the rest of our lives we will share.

Chancey Bridges

Promises

Life is full of promises
Some are fulfilled,
By the one's we love
Some forgotten
As time goes on
Yet life continues,
We keep on moving
Year to year
We part as friends
Where will we end?
Friend or foe
We really don't know
Are we being true to ourselves
When we declare our love is
    never ending
As time passes
Will we start to think
About all those forgotten promises
    that were never kept?

Eileen P. Leach

Stranded

I sit,
Stranded,
Deserted.

My car, gone
I feel so alone.

My Wallet, Watch, Pride-
    Removed,
    Stolen,
    Swiped.

The night embraces me.

I see a light,
So dim - yet so close.

A car! I enter.

My driver, so mysterious....

The light of the moon appears
I see my driver....

Listen, ever so carefully,
And my cries you shall hear,

For Death drove me home that
    Lonely, dark night.

Robert Jessup

Sister

Loyal but persistent
there through it all,
priceless as a porcelain doll,

My heart and soul my
number one,
my heaven on earth
through rain and sun,

Together we are too much
but apart we are even worse
being this special must be a curse,

If she was to leave there's
no doubt I will miss her,
she is one of a kind she's
my baby sister.

Regina J. Berry

Grandma's Prayer

I pray that risen from the dead
I may in glory stand.
A crown, perhaps upon my head
But a needle in my hand.

I've never learned to sing or play
So let no harp be mine.
From birth until my dying day
Plain sewing's been my line.

Therefore accustomed to the end
Of plying useful stitches
I'll be content if asked to mend
The little angels breeches.

Marguerite Siemieniewicz

Song Of The Mother

Mighty Mother, womb of darkness.
Blood moon mistress of water's tides,
Hear the Serpent calling loudly,
Filled with echo's touched with life.
A breath, a touch, a fleeting shadow,
The spiral call of an ancient dream,
Sparks the heart within the shadow,
Touched with life, the Mystic Queen.
For now I see thy coiling essence.
Now I feel thy crystal breath,
Giving forth the highest mystery,
The touch of life, the brush of death.

Gina Green

Resolution

Hide the tears behind closed doors.
Your pride is at stake.
Counter all those hurtful remarks.
Your courage is at sea.
Forgive the masters of domains.
Your freedom is the bait.
Open the shades and the windows.
Your maturity is the key.
Conquer the goods all in hand.
Your future is to take.
Resist temptation now and then.
Your security is the fee.
Protect interests of the souls.
Your death is away.
Shelter the love inside yourself.
Your lover is to keep.

Niti Vaid

Only You

If I fall in love with you
Would you love me too
   Or would tears fall like rain
And our hearts be filled with pain
   Would you tell me the truth
in all I ask
   And leave the past in the past
   Would we forget all about the
games and the lies
   Would I only see truth in your eyes
   At night when I dream I dream
of one thing
   It is only you, you and me
When I awake, awake I will be

   Only us together, I want to see,
   With all of this its plain to see
   What one day we could be.
   Tonya Williams

The Heart Turns In

The heart turns in
On itself and swallows;
Its mouth is big
And its stomach hollow.

Jump down its throat
And watch it turn blue,
Kicking and screaming.
Tear it in two.

Navy blue sleeps in red.
Navy's bride sleeps in my bed.
All numbers and lines are dead;
Time to splatter-paint instead.

Do not fear the lightning bolt
Or the thunder cloud.
The great white hunter killing things
He's only read about.
   Joseph St. Louis III

Peace Is . . .

Peace is when there are no wars
with silence all around.
Peace is when a lake is calm
and has no waves or ripples.
Peace is when I hear
my daddy's car drive up
into the driveway.
Peace is holding Jesus hand
and sharing our thoughts together.
Peace is knowing the
Prince of Peace
and how He saved me.
Peace is the eternal life
with my God
above in Heaven.

God Is My Peace
   Kristal Branscum

Sadness Through The Years

The tears keep pouring out of my eyes,
Forming a huge puddle,
The size of an ocean.
For I have cried too much.
And now I must drain the ocean,
By bringing out the sunshine,
Which brings happiness to my eyes.
   Jennifer Szlag

Empty Words

Does anybody hear me?
Can you see what I see?
I didn't think so
Because my words are empty.

Do you ever listen to the rain?
Or look outside from a windowpane?
Do you ever look into a child's eyes?
And see what they dream and fantasize?

The world rushing here and there
No one has a moment to spare
Take a risk, open your mind
Explore the earth, see what you find!
   Keia Fulgham

Donkey

She is small and brown
I like to ride
Her around town.

When she starts to bray
Usually people turn
And run far away.

Her ears as long as can be
Longer than the distance
That she can see.

Clarissa is her lovely name
But chasing boys
Is her favorite game.

She is in trouble all the time
And if she could read
She'd despise this rhyme.
   Collin Burt

My Self

I can not see
What happens to me
When I hold the things inside me,
For all I know is that I hurt
And the hurt will never leave me,
Anger that comes will never go
It always stays inside me,
From time
To time
I slip away
From all this hurt and pain,
But then again
It will never leave me.
   Joey M. Hildebrand

Silence

Darkness filled the room
Voices hushed the children
Silence
It seemed as if the silence
Was louder than the
Children's shouting
Silence
Silence so heavy it was
Thicker than the England fog
Silence
What I most fear
Silence
   Abby Geis

A Friend

Is a special person of love
Who is a friend in need
And a friend at need

Who is like a dove
Warm, loving, and kind
And doesn't mind

Who we may honor and cherish
For the rest of our lives
Until we parish
   Nancy Newman

My Love

My love for you is so great and
   strong

Your strength and your love keeps
   me going on

I watch and I wait knowing
   that you care.

Because "God" up above help us
   to share

The joy that we have between me
   and thee

God Himself made "you for me"
   Josephine Malone

Memories

I tried to clean some shelves today
And much to my dismay
Their contents held a part of me
I could not throw away

In between the knickknacks
Were cookbooks tried and true
Craft supplies and magazines
With decorating how-to's

I looked thru photo albums
I hadn't seen in years
As memories came flooding back
I blinked away some tears

Brushes, paints, and sketch pads
Reminders from the past
Tempt me still to recreate
That masterpiece at last

So I sat there contemplating
What to toss and what to keep
My head said "throw", my heart said "no"
And so I went to sleep!
   Shirley A. Galusky

Smile

Tiny little zipper muscles,
   cramped up like fetuses in gestation.

Now stretching out of hibernation
   with a popping of joints.

A tingling - not quite pain.

It felt so funny to smile that morning
   after a night of just crying.
   Matt Bandel

Will I Ever Understand

There she sits dying,
but she smiles what's the use of crying?
She shouldn't have been so careless,
She was shot by a man who is heartless.

He cares nothing about her pain,
as he listens to the rain.
Being as peaceful as ever,
looking back? Never.

He's a selfish man,
with a gun in his hand.
One shot to the chest,
and you know the rest.

Will anyone wonder why,
She had to die?
Will I ever understand,
What happened to my best friend?

Jessie Ann Horton

A Toast To Her

Allow me to propose a toast
To someone very special to me
My cook, cleaning lady, seamstress,
And gardener too;
Plus spiritual leader, mother,
And wife, to name a few.

I toast to her, who for many years
Has been so under-rated

I toast to her, who for many years
Has been so under-estimated

I toast to her, as we both have shed
A few tears

I toast to her, who has put up with me
For all these years

I toast to her, hoping and praying
She would keep me for life

I toast to her, the gal
I proudly call my wife.

Frank B. Redondo

No Pains

No pains are as bad as mine
the deep dark winds that carry
the sea don't come close
the crash of a car
the mind spinning music
the heart breaking news
the death of my brothers the
last of the clues
No pains are as bad as mine

Katie Flees

Untitled

If you are lonely
how would you
feel. Would you
be lump on
a wall. Will you
feel sad or happy
if you are a
plain person act
yourself don't
act like someone
you're not.

Mars Hawn

Treasure Your Memories

It comes so fast
  the days we grow old
Treasure your memories
  like they are gold
We live for today,
  and don't think of tomorrow
We think of the joys
  but never the sorrows
When we grow old
  we have nothing but time
Keep all of your memories
  in the back of your mind
They will always be there
  till our last resting day
When the Lord comes and takes
  our dreams and memories away

Jane E. Schubert

You

I looked for you,
But you were transparent.
I reached for you,
But you eluded me.
I smelled the air,
And that was all it was.
I listened to the wind,
It sang only of the Earth.
I tasted of the soil,
But you were not its savior.

I prayed for you,
And you answered me.
I cried for you,
And you sent me peace.
I lived for you,
And you made me whole.
I will die for you,
And you shall give me life.

David Pizzuto

After Father Died

After Father died in eighty-nine
Mom became a grieving widow
Who in all consuming sadness
Became our new fallen leader.

My sisters saw an opportunity
And sought to take advantage
Of her grief and weakened state
With a weapon known as guilt.

The accusations came right and left
And they shocked her when they said:
"You spanked us when we were small
And you often screamed."

They took her on a bumpy ride
All of them but me;
The second born, the bonded one,
I made her fight my own.

I sharply cried, "you can't say that
Our mother was a good one
For in the days when we grew up
Discipline was expected."

Joan Norgord

Wish Gardener

My garden grows.
My spirit knows
  the seeds will fly
  and I'll be gone.

The bitter leaf
Of love and grief
  will wither from
  the burning sun.

When rain first falls
To quench Thirst's call
  I'll pack my bag
  To leave this garden
  of you.

Gather the fruit
Of pain and laughter
  crying, a little
  for tears and rain
Will only come after
  I'm gone.

Nicole Lu Casale

Thoughts Of You

I filled my head with thoughts of you
To fill my heart with this love too
I changed my mind to your point of view
I traced your steps to be so true
  And you're my only love
I climbed the staircase of debris
And I ran until it was you and me
Across the valleys of humility
I cried the rivers to your sea
  And you're my only love
I imagined the treasures of no grief
I held onto this beauty with such belief
Filling my head with thoughts of you
Tracing my steps to walk with you
  And you're my only love
  You're my only love

Matthew A. Schemkes

Sometimes

Sometimes it takes the rain
To make the flowers grow
Sometimes it takes real pain
Before real joy one knows
Sometimes it takes tomorrows
To understand days gone by
Sometimes before the laughter
There comes a heavy sigh
Sometimes it takes the midnight hour
To value morning light
Sometimes it takes the longest mile
Before things come insight
Sometimes you often wonder
Why your heart can get so sore
But it's the rocky paths in life
That make you cherish smooth roads more

Leslie J. Datcher

My Loving Son

Today is your Birthday
My loving son
Today is the day
You turn twenty one

May you always
Be happy
May your dreams
All come true
Remember I love you
And so proud of you

God bless you
And keep you
My loving son

This one special day
You turn
Twenty one

Mary Louisa Aldana

Unconditional Love

Jesus loved the little children,
So why don't you love me?
I may be just a little odd,
With problems you can't see.
I can't read and I can't write,
I'm not as smart as you.
You point and laugh, it really hurts,
But I have feelings too.
I know I talk a little weird,
And sometimes very slow.
It's hard to make you understand,
You really couldn't know.
So many times, I'm very clumsy,
Then I trip and fall.
The awful taunting words you say,
I cry, you laugh, I crawl.
I cannot help the way I act,
Or control the things I do.
But I always try to remember,
God made me, like He made you.

Debra M. Adkins

Fear

As the darkness creeps into
My sparsely furnished room,
I quietly quiver beneath the covers.
The lone chest shakes
With every powerful gust
And the splintered headboard
Rattles in reply.
The constant clicking of the furnace,
The dripping of the faucet,
And the clattering of misfit windows
Seem to intensify in the dark.
Outside, the leafless branches
Bow to the wind
And carelessly scratch the roof.
When the wind finally subsides,
The stillness is overwhelming.
I cannot sleep.
Is it the darkness
That I fear?
Or fear itself?

Julie Nichols

Sovereign Sun Hero's Que

There once was a hero
  of many a knight
Who fought for the freedoms
  of liberties plights...

He went round the earth
  with his weapons of war
Known only to those
  of gentle valor...
With chivalrous flower
  scenting the air...
He made many aware
  of its beauty and power...
    Climbing its highest towers...
As he danced in the dance
  of the golden white light
Atop the waves of wondrous delight
  by the sea - by the sea
    victories great rights...

Yolanda Theresa Marroquin

How Easy It Is

How easy it is to hide the pain
and emotions deep inside
from one's words or another one's acts
that tear at one's self pride.

How easy it is to hide the hurt
only hanging your head in disgrace,
but how hard it is to hide the tears
that trickle down one's face.

David Ganser

Fishing

When you arrive at
The lake you tie your colorful
Sharp lure on your pole.

You throw out your lure
in the lake. Bam! He has it,
Quickly set the hook.

You're fighting for life
To pull, pull, and get him in
He must weigh a ton.

It is sunset now
You have caught your catch and more
You're gliding to dock.

Now one more long look
The shimmering lake glistens
You're on your way...Home!

Brandon Harris

Holidays Come And Go

Christmas is all over,
But the tree still trimmed
And gifts scattered everywhere,
Now where do I begin!

We're in a New Year now,
And of course we all hope we fare well
But let's just take it a day at a time
And with God's blessing, we hope we will.

Emelia Ames

Red

The color of roses
On a cold and misty day
The color of blood
That takes or gives life away.
The color of our country's flag
Whom many have fought for and died.
The color of your face
When someone knows you've lied.
The color of cheeks in the winter
As you walk down streets full of snow.
The color of Valentines day
When love is all you know.
See red has so much importance
That we pay no attention to.
It has love, hate, fear, and honor.
But then again so do you.

Ashley Fladmo

Ocean Songs

Softly the song of the ominous ocean
Murmurs its melancholy melody:
  Sweet and subdued,
  Obedient and obliging,
  Rippling and rustling,
  Mystical and musical.
    Then suddenly-
It whispers its wavering warning,
Gaining more vigor and vitality:
  Surging and swelling,
  Lusty and lively,
  Bulging and bursting,
  With fervor and force.
  Daring and deafening,
  Crashing and clashing,
  Vicious and vile,
    Then again-
As rapidly and it came, it subsides
To a sweet, soothing, simple song
  Once more.

Kathleen Reilly

A Shadowed Image Of Two

With the plight of the moon
In duress under mist
Less the light has been strewn
From the stars

Adrift without eyes
In a mind without heart
Unremembering ties
Go untold

No canter brought day
But a struggle in darkness
And thus we shall slay
For the life

The gasp in the breath
For the future beyond
And to reach unto death
For the light

Meredith Cochran

The Special Times

The old man lay,
Beneath striped blinds,
Began to whisper,
What was on his mind,

Got it figured,
After all the years and lines,
What really matters,
Are the special times,

Not the nickels and the dimes,
It's blood red sunsets,
And fishing lines,

Helping hands from a friend,
When you thought at the time,
It was over, this is the end,

Life is an uphill job well done,
When you work as a team,
Not just as one,
His face was craggy with the lines,
One for each of those special times.

Y. D. Lott Jr.

When My Time Comes

When I am sadly told the fact
  that I have-"cancer"
  and that-"we're sorry to say-
it's-well-terminal!"
When my time comes,
  how shall I react?

When they no doubt suggest
  that I at best could have
  an outside chance with "chemo"
  or at least extend my time down here
  six months or more before I-die,
    what shall I reply?

(I make no judgment as to others'
fear or faith or sad or glad consent)

  but as for me-
When my time comes,
  I hope I happily refuse,
  and midst the pain
  hold also to another fact:
    "to die is gain!"

Jack Yonkers

Attitude

They no kill me!
Me not die for what I did.
State no kill me; that is wrong!
The woman me killed?
That is a different song.
Me be a man, a man I say!
They dis me, and they pay!
The judge say she, that no way to be.
Me be a man, a man I say!
You be no man that way;
To rob, kill, and prey on us.
A man be of honor and trust.
Me be my man, I say!
The judge say she cry for me.
Only thirty years, they no kill me!
My man I be; no tears.
Oh God, thirty years!!

A. R. Waterhouse

Weather

When the rain's about to come,
You can smell it in the air.
Thick clouds tell you also,
That it will soon be there.

You can hear the soft patter,
At the window panes.
I love to hear the sound,
When it rains, rains, rains.

But when it starts to get bad,
With lightning and thunder,
I tell myself it's Ok,
And then I begin to wonder...

How does weather work?
I guess I'll never know.
But as soon as it lets up,
It begins to snow.

The sounds of the rain are soft enough,
To put asleep a baby.
And when I think "will it stop,"
Then I say "maybe".

Jeffery L. Chancellor

Nestor Of The Park

Espy, did I, one day a man
Afar, I waxed agape.
An august one, a noble son,
A soul to venerate.

'Twas in the park, nearby a pond
Upon a storm-tossed bench.
There nestled he, beneath a tree,
But swelled within a wrench.

Those eyes drew near, upon my face
With brow I ne'er forsake.
Then motioned he to counsel me,
And wide flung I the gate!

I romped to him, ere swift afoot
To reap the words divine.
So like a child, my eyes a wild,
Wayfaring back in time!

Regarding me, his mien evolved
Into a pale November.
Did he begin, a glance within,
Yet strain, "May...I remember?"

Bart Rippl

Betrayal

You see an image
Only a reflection
You see a friend
Only an image
You see a reflection
And it
It's you alone
And it's for there
But not your own

Robert B. Hedenberg

Think Of Me

When you're feeling lonely,
and there is no-one near,

Just close your eyes and think of me,
and then it will be clear.

When things are going wrong,
and you feel like no-one cares,

Just remember who was there,
when no-one else would dare.

If you ever need someone
to just give you a clue,

Just think of me when you're in need,
and I will help you through.

Karmella Carlson

A Little Levity About Reality

Did you
Ever notice
That when
You finally
Manage to
Poke a hole
In your
Mental shell
And you try
To peek out
To see if
The world's
Gotten any better
Since the last time,
There's always
Someone there
Waiting to
Poke you
In the eye?

Erik Isaksen

What I Feel

When I'm with you,
it seems the sun shines bright.
I look at you,
and I know what I feel is right.

I think of the oceans blue,
and the stars bright shine.
And I think of you,
and I'm glad you're mine.

Our times together,
they seem so rare.

They get better and better,
I hope you know how much I care.

My hopes of love,
will soon come true.
But I think they have,
because I love you.

Our love is pure,
and its here to stay.
Because I'll love you,
day after day.

Jonathan Brunjes

Moonlight Love

Staring into moonlit mirrors,
We wished upon the Star bright senders.
With loss of hope and sorrow mended,
I prayed for peace, then it ended.

Friendships come and fly with the wind
With longing memories to condescend
The happiness that we once did share
Under the moonlight's darkened glare.

When we decided to depart,
No longer caring for his dear heart,
I tossed aside my sweet love so bright
And danced into the night's moonlight.

We danced together then apart,
And smiling I looked into his heart
Only to find love for another.
To this day it makes me wonder.

The star bright sender heard my prayer
But his heart was gone, no more he cared
To stay by my side, always be there
Under the moonlight's darkened glare.

Emily Best

Eventide

At eventide, we sit and gaze
Upon the cobalt sea
As humans wend their homeward way
And seagulls sound their plea

Softly breaking waves roll in
Upon the quiet shore
Replete with myriad foot prints
Of those who've gone before

Darkness with its subtle brush
Subdues the brilliant hues
and then as with a final hush
Obliterates the views

Sally Raach

Being Thankful

All we can think about
is how life would be,
if there were no parents
in our society.

Life would be fun
no rules, no chores,
you could stay out late
without sneaking outdoors.

But then we realize
what would we do,
if we got hurt
and needed you.

There would be no mom
there would be no dad,
no one to go to if
we were feeling sad.

Then we become extremely thankful
when we see all the things that you do,
to make our lives much easier and better
and that is why "We love you!"

Jason Barnes

Friend For Me

Friend for me
Fight for me
Fly for me
Frighten not me
Fail not me
Forge ahead for me
Force not your world onto me
Forgive me
Fulfill my wish for me
Fill joy around me
Free me, fun for me
Feel like a rose for me
Familiarize yourself to me
Friendship give to me
Face my eyes to reflect me
Forget not to smile for me
Forever let me be me
Friend for me . . .

Mary Ann Wilson

Kentucky Wonder

Field of flowers, perfect fragrance
Tiny violets, lilies tall.
Valley blanketed with blossom.
Springtime freshness for us all.

Church-top steeples, dot the surface
As we view the countryside.
In a cabin or a mansion
We are neighbors, side by side.

Crickets chirping to the rhythm
Of the wild bird melodies.
Newborn "critters" scamper lightly
In the morning country breeze.

Warmth of sunshine peeking through
A hazy morning in the hills.
Waking up, breathing deeply
Fresh air from open window sills.

Helen E. Weber

The Storm

Thunder roars,
Lighting crashes,
Rain pounds,
A dreary night to most eyes.

But ohh to comfort
It gives to a sad heart.

The storm inside
Finally released.

Winds howl,
Cold rain beats upon the world.

With each blow.
The heart breaths a little easier.

Thunder rumbles,
Lighting fades,
Rain becomes drizzle,
All to soon the storm ends.

And with it goes
What little comfort it gave
To a breathless heart.

Jennifer Ward

The Way I Love You

Love is sensual,
Love is joy,
Love is the way I love you.

Love is sexual, love is exciting,
Love is destiny,
Love is the way I love you.

Love is good,
Love is action,
Love is a word,
Love is the way I love you.

Love hurts, yet cures,
Love is unsure, yet sure,
Love is impatient, yet patient,
Love is the way I love you.

Love, it's you and I,
Love, it's the babe,
We both will share...
Love..., that's how much I love you.

Claudine A. Crosdale

Baren At Sea

There is a ship sailing lonely at sea.
Sailing for land if there may be.
The water is cold and miles deep.
The height of the waves so very steep.
The cold wind on our face,
"Please shelter us Dear Lord,
There is no ship captain,
Just a women an child aboard".

Lisa Erickson

Clouds In My Backyard

Brilliant ramparts white as white
Cast black the sunsets ebbing light
Drawn deeper in dusks shading hues
The phantom fortress light imbues
The black of night which it belongs
Sunset past and it is gone.

Karil Wade

No Matter Of What Is Made

Despite the pressures of life,
The future entails a lot
Of what we do now.
We must go on
Regardless of the
Problems and Situations
We may encounter.

Life is what one makes it,
No matter of what it is made.
Life is very precious, and
We should live each day to the fullest.
We will never know
When it will be our last.

On humble and praying knees
Is how we should be,
Sending praises up to the sky
To the Man on high.
For God is the reason for the seasons.

Katrina Johnson

What Your Mother Would Say To Comfort You

I went ahead my dear one
To make a place for you
So we can be together someday,
Whenever your life is through.

Remember what I taught you,
To be loving, good, and kind.
Always think of your fellow man
It doesn't cost a dime.

I know that you will miss me,
And you know I will miss you too,
But my work was all completed,
So my life on earth is through.

I cannot hold you in my arms
Or kiss away your tears,
I cannot take away your pain,
It is a pain you will have to endure.

I always knew you loved me
And you knew I loved you too.
So when God comes to bring you home,
I'll be waiting there for you.

Patricia Ann Bolton

Only Trust The Best In Me

The surges went by,
You didn't know?
It need pure heart,
to let stars glow.
Like glitter, gleams,
in truth it rest's.
The prophet's inborn wisdom.
Go West, he knows,
to find the flock,
had long ago astray.
Return them as a precious stock,
use trust, your mind, confined,
to grow,
for, them as well convey.
Hence love will stay,
and lies decay!
When Prophets walk on water!
The sweetest song of all.

Joachim Fritz

My Forever Friend

My friend loveth at all times,
Be it good or bad
Happy or sad
My friend always understands.

My friend must forever
Speak the truth
Although, at times
He must remain aloof.

I could pray for
No better end
Because, I love, and understand
My forever friend.

Shirley M. Robinson

To Howard - My Dearest Love

You came into my life
When I was sad and lonely
I knew from the first Hello
That our meeting was God's way
Of bringing two lonely hearts together

You brought sunshine into my life
And shared with me
Your delightful sense of humor
I will remember you always
With fond memories

And now God's angels have
Taken you home
But, your sweet, gentle, loving spirit
Will be with me the rest of my life

And so, sweet gentle Howard
Crawl upon the lap of Jesus
And give Him a hug for me
I will see you soon, dear one.....

Peggy Weaver

An Endless Desperate Attempt

Sitting thinking
about a long time to go
till there is no thinking to do.
Looking through an empty eye glass
watching the rocks beat up the water
that can't stop flowing
Watching the endless light beat down
and burn my skin, nothing to stop it
but a baseball cap and a empty
bottle of lighter fluid.
Caring to much about the future
Ahead.
Writing to fulfill my need to
Think.

Derek Kelley

Untitled

We are born into this world
With a God-given will
A heart that is full of innocence
And a mind that is made of steel
Along our path of life
When faced with wrong or right
We can love or we can hate
Lend a hand or we can take
But we all live together
In this world of day by day
Some of us hope
And some of us pray
So in good faith
We will soon see the day
Where wrong is thrown from right
And we lead the way
In happiness and harmony
From the one up above
Believe me I know
God gives us his love.

Wayne Arthur Hecker Jr.

Don't Ever Fall In Love My Friend

A heart is not a play thing,
A heart is not a toy,
But, if you want it broken;
Give it to a boy.

Boys love to play around with things,
See how they will run,
But when it comes to kissing;
They do it just for fun.

Don't ever fall in love my friend,
Don't ever go astray,
It causes broken heart my friend;
It happens everyday.

Don't ever fall in love my friends,
The price you pay is high,
So if I had the choice of love or death;
I think I'd rather die.

So, when I say don't fall in love,
It hurts so much that's true,
You see my friend I ought to know;
I fell in love with you!

Charlotte Davis

Lizards, Lizards, Lizards

Bad lizards
mad lizards
Lazy playful, fast lizards
slow long blue lizards
Those are just a few
Tall lizards
small lizards
sleepy, old, green lizards
smart, short, baby lizards
fat lizards too!
Skinny lizards
red lizards
And don't forget excited lizards
Last of all
Best of all
I like cool lizards!

Maile Lathrop

The Daily Theme

Me against the world.
All eyes on me.
My one and only.
Myself, I and me.

I am moving up in the world.
Alone and with a mission.
With passion and pride.
Holding "mad" recognition.

To those up support me.
To those who said,
"You can do it, my dear,
Go right ahead!"

A wise man once said,
"Do nothing for free."
My knowledge you won't get,
Without acknowledging me.

I look up to myself.
But he looks up to me.
I look up to the world,
And that, you will soon see.

Rochelle M. Howard

Mother's Embrace

The words of a mother and her embrace,
the sad and troubling times can erase.
Oh, how I miss my Mother's smiling face.

I, remember though the winter snow,
when I was young and sometimes low,
that smiling face and her warm embrace,
it picked me up and changed the frown
upon my face.

The seasons they have come and gone,
I'm older now and I've lost my Mom,
but the memories of her smiling face,
helps me feel her warm embrace.

I miss you my Mother, but rest in
peace with your Mothers before you
and their Loving Embrace.

Marnie Johnson

Be All That You Can Be

When everything seems to go wrong
And nothing in life seems fair,
Take an inventory of your blessings
And chase away despair.

Remember the beautiful story
Of two footprints in the sand,
You never go through life alone
God carries you in his hand.

Get up every morning
With a smile on your face,
Go out and greet the world
With love for the human race.

Your days will have more meaning
You'll be much happier by far,
If you use the gifts God gave you
And reach out for your star.

Nothing would make God happier
Than to look down and see
All his beloved children
Being all that they can be.

Roselyn J. DePofi

Fear

Planes, are you insane?
Crash, boom, you have to assume
I'm afraid of that.
Even if I wear a hard hat,
I'd be dead.
I wouldn't be in the sky,
not up high,
but going down fast.
I'd be in the past.
I don't want my last words to be,
"Oh, dear Lord, please help me."
I couldn't be calm,
how could I?
knowing I was going to die.

Amanda Mabes

My Hero is He!

My hero
is he who comes upon
me the one who died for
my sins. I praise him day
and night, spring and winter.
But who can this hero be?
My lord Jesus of course to me!

D. Trevor Weathers

Untitled

A simple ripple can become a wave
  Big waves can produce hurricanes
Destroying small cities and towns
  With its torrainian rains

A simple ripple can end up in a wave
  So so justifying or not
waves can become abusive
  just looking for the right spot

Ripple here and a ripple there
  can wraught devastation
flooding flooding and flooding
  can lead world to hallucination

A simple ripple can end up in a wave
  such strong gales blowing and blowing
die is cast for, nature's damage
  cause waves don't resort to clowning

Nicholas Lucarrlli

Untitled

I walk...
barefoot in the snow
The sun
just about to start the day
I am going towards nothing
with only a robe to keep me warm
The cold of the snow cannot compare
to the freeze of my soul
My feet are numb
I keep walking...
waiting for it to reach my brain
so as not to think anymore
I am tired
I reach up to the sky
My face streaked with tears
I can go on further
I wake up
A shiver passes through me
I am alone

Theresa Gran

Broken Heart

Let the rain
disguise the tears.
For I have years.

As I embrace my emptiness
all I hold is loneliness, instead of you

What pain must I bare
so deep, so profound, so unfair.

Yet what lies I be still
in my broken heart
Perhaps is the foolishness
on my part.

To believe for just a moment
that you love me still

That no one can take my place
in you heart and never will.

I still find myself walking
on a road that has no end

Hoping in the midst of it all
I will find you, my friend.

Sandra Jaramillo

Carolyn

A little girl of fantasy
A quiet little face,
A child born into mystery
In a silent place.
She never knew nobody
Not a friend she ever made,
She was so very pretty
As she pretended and she played.
My dearest little Carolyn
We all know where you're from,
A tiny little angel
Who awaits for death to come.

Kimberly Weathers Rosser

The Giving Time

The giving time
Strikes its toll.
It eats away
At the heart and soul.
It touches us all
Yet touches so few.
The giving time
Seeks someone like you.

Joanna Young

Listen With Your Heart

Standing in the shadows
of a love that can not see.

Someone came along one day, he
smiled and rescued me.

He came to me with so much
love and compassion in his eyes.

That deep in my heart
I had to recognize.

The smile, the love, the caring.

The message it was clear.

It was the Lord God the Savior,
telling me he was here.

He said my child, please be
strong, don't shed another tear.

I'll stay as long as you
want me, I'll always be near.

I'll walk with you, and I'll talk to
you, if you listen with your heart.

I'll stay with you forever and
we will never part.

Barbara Mohler

The Moon

My favorite planet is the moon.
You rarely see it at noon,
You usually see it at night,
But that is not always right.
Sometimes it is cloudy out,
Then the moon is not about.
I think the moon is very cool,
I'd like to learn more about it in school.

Lauren J. Keeffe

Untitled

Waters calling in blue and green
rushing shores of blackened white,
watch the sunrise in the evening
see the rainbow fall from sight.

Stars crashing in a yellow sky
clouds angry with the dawn,
listen to the crying winds
singing clocks on magic wands.

Bluebirds red and planets blue
white bleeds itself a river,
smell the sweetness of the heavens
reflections growing into quivers.

Lost is paradise in a lover's dream
on the sand in the naked moonlight.

Nathalie O'Reilly

"Aching Heart"

It pours from deep down,
within her aching heart,
the agony of bitter sweet pain.
Of love that she has lost.
Memories of her beloved.
Pass often through the mind,
the loneliness unbearable,
as time keeps passing by.
In quiet moments she recalls.
His gentle loving ways.
A touch upon her shoulder,
reminder of his love,
not a day has she regretted,
sharing the years together.
He her husband, she his wife,
now he has gone forever.
She believes in her aching heart
that one day they will meet.
to continue the happiness,
they saluted in their youth.

Meryl Keswani

Devoted Sisters

Dedicated to Anne and Mary Calhoun
Of all burdens that exist
  these shall resist
With valor side by side

Whose hearts shall break
  the turmoil in life's wake
Keeping each other above the tide.

What dreams out of reach
  each shall meet
Never leaving the other behind.

J. L. Bailey

"Portrait of Grace"

In deep recesses of the heart,
  Where desire and passion impart,
The struggle to cling steadfast
  To virtuous and noble paths.

With determination and resolve,
  Though conflict persevered;
Eternal joy prevailed —
  'Twas loss of heaven I feared.

Valerie Bordelon Pyle

Spring's Hope Prevails

In the light of winter's day,
When the ground is white
  and the sky is gray,
When patience is gone
  and tempers rise,
Therein, depression lies,
Causing hope to slip away.

We clear away the fallen snow,
Keep watch for tiny buds to show,
For in those buds,
  Spring's hope prevails,
  and with the Spring,
  Depression fails,
Giving hope a chance to grow.

Lori J. Lamb

The Kiss I Never Had

You loved me for a little
Who could not love me long

You gave me wings of gladness
and lent my spirit song

You loved me for an hour
but only with your eyes

Your lips I could not capture
by storm or by surprise

Your mouth that I remember
with a sudden rush of pain

As one remembers starlight
or roses after rain

Out of a world of laughter
suddenly I am sad

Day and night it haunts me
the kiss I never had

Kristina Waible

As A Child

As a child
You used to roam,
Run, and play,
Living life was easy,
All careless and free.

You're growing up,
Life is tough,
There isn't much
Time for play,
You still make time
For having fun
But still it's not the same.

You're all grown up
No time for fun,
The world won't
Wait on that,
Still you have fond
Memories of living life
All careless and free,
As a child

Heather Gattis-Payne

Like

Like the petals smooth, bright
Growing, living like the stem
Like the waves cold, sweet
rushing, forcing beneath my feet
Like the wings pure, true
watching, helping each thing I do
Like the drops new, cleansing
falling, raining wash my face
Like the blades sharp, fresh
growing, dying coming back
Like the leaves colored, soft
blowing, flying turning hard
Like the clouds soft, free
drifting, changing above my head
like the stars white, many
glowing, blinking attracting eyes
Like the moon perfect, round
leading, floating in my dreams
Like a rainbow bright, eternal
Colors giving endless smiles

Rebecca E. Wochnick

AFTERMAN

I DON'T KEEP IT BUT I NEED IT
I'M YOUR GARBAGE MAN
I NEVER STOP TO THINK YOU THINK
A LOWER FORM I AM
IS THAT YOUR GARBAGE CAN?
WELL, I'M YOUR GARBAGE MAN

I KNOW ABOUT
YOUR SECRET HABITS
HOW YOU SHOP AROUND
I KNOW ABOUT
YOUR PRIVATE CHOICES
WHERE YOU GO IN TOWN
YOU'RE INTIMATE
WITH INFORMATION
YET I'M NOT YOUR KIND
I BET YOU NOW WE MEET AGAIN
SOMEWHERE DOWN THE LINE

YOU ONCE USED IT
NOW I GO THROUGH IT
AND IT GOES BACK AROUND
THE DIFFERENCE BETWEEN
ME AND YOU IS
MIXED INTO THE GROUND

Scott Brown

Lament

Oh the night the endless night
No sleep, no sleep for me
The words, the thoughts,
Come on pour out
Pour out like rain
Rain from the heavens
Gray —
Like the gray days of autumn
Cold—
Like the cold days of winter
So gray and cold
A match for my soul
The swollen rivers, no mystery to me
Swollen from my tears
As my soul flows to the sea
The emptiness that is left,
The void,
The void that can't be filled
A part of me is gone.

Janis Ortman

Friends

1.)Friends know you through a relationship of a sincere communication;
   as Friendship progresses on,
2.)Friends are there, when you need their support, advice, love, or
   Friendly laughter, and so on.
3.)Friends understand your deep hurts, your ways of expression and such,
4.)A Friend has a way of bending an ear, and keeping in touch.
5.)Friends will do anything for you, and you do likewise for them.
6.)Friends will call, write, or visit you; also be there for you now and then.
7.)Then, you can always trust, depend on a true Sincere Friends who is
   unselfish, caring, forgiving with no greed and they are loving and kind,
8.)Friends will be there when you call them, when something is on your mind.
9.)Friends form a bond, sometimes hearts are broken, but there is repair,
10.)Friends will express God's unconditional love all the time; because
   they are forgiving, they display they really do care.
11.)Friends care about others, and not themselves,
12.)Friends' compassionate love is something that you treasure:
   and just don't put it on a shelf.
13.)Friends go through deep hardships, also wonderful, great times together
14.)Especially when it's very stormy weather.
15.)Genuine Friends back you up when you ask them to,
16.)Friends are really great, when you hear those warm words, "I Love You."
17.)Friends should be honest with each other and never try to offend.
18.)Friends with a sincere, happy, delightful, positive attitude,
   humbleness, integrity: is always the one you can depend.
19.)Friends understand your ups and downs and your mood swings,
20.)Friends will bring you laughter, joy, happiness;
   just as you hear God's beautiful birds sing.

Agatha Cecelia Rollins

My Shelter

Life emerging from the ground as the sun and rain blanket the land;
the summer's cool breeze racing across warm skin;
the gleam of an infant's eyes in the security of mother's arms;
the relaxation from the symphonic sound of soothing soft music;
or the air beneath the wings of an eagle suspended above the still earth.
Each is comforting yet dependant on the other for existence.
You have been the one to shine on me and give me life;
you have been the breeze which has shielded me from the heat;
you have been the arms to keep me safe;
you are the hypnotic music to calm my spirits;
and you have been the wind which has lifted me to new heights.
Most of all you have been my comfort.
If love and appreciation were measured in dollars,
my wealth would exceed the riches of the world.
Thank you for your strength and giving me the will to continue.
And most of all...thank you for your love which has given me life.

Mike James

City Blocks

Four million and more were inside its core, thousands of blocks
each with twenty houses or more. Each block had a boundary, a line
you dare not cross. Where the streets are the ditches, the lines, the sidewalks.

There she sat on this curb, a free spirit happy and young-just
sittin'-resting and fearing no harm, entirely quiet and calm-just
sittin'. Without warning it hit her so hard and so fast, she wanted
and wished it to go right on past. But there it stood this reality,
right in her face. You all want this spot? Tough sh*t! This is my place.

She willingly defended her rights and beliefs, she plainly just kicked
ass on those hard rugged streets. She had to make it known, she was
not afraid to stand alone. It didn't come easy this right to survive,
she got tough and hard just to stay alive. Somehow a miracle, she
wasn't afraid and many enemies and/or friends out of this were made.

Wherever she went her pride went before. They all knew who she was
and believed all the lore. Not many would try her, call her out one
on one. It took five or six to get the job done. They knew even if
they beat her to death, she'd still defend her rights with her last dying breath.

She wanted no followers, not even a friend. Just leave her and her
spot alone and the fighting would end. We all learned the hard way,
how to give or get, and that spot on that curb she would and could freely sit.

Kelley Lin Minnick

Untitled

Love of my life, where are you?
The phone rings, but goes dead
To live on without you
A dying seed.

To hold you, the soft touch
Hand upon my head
As I lay on your shoulder
Soft goes my heart
Which sings - of joy.

I pray to the father
You will return,
Endearing to me with love.
The look in your eyes
When you see me there
Dimple in cheek - a smile.

I call you again
Via telephone pin
Hang up - chagrined
With sorrow.

Margaret A. Copenhaver

My Dream Man

My dream man should be romantic
and his eyes should be magnetic
I like him to be realistic
he is the man I always think.

My dream man should have a sense of humor
that will amuse me when I'm bored
the type of man I'm looking for
will make my heart beat double trible.

I like a man who is clever
who knows what to do
when I have a fever
fever in my heart that is not so severe
the only medicine is to go to the theater.

My dream man must have a personality
that will attract my heart easily
he need not be handsome or wealthy
but he must secure me so tenderly.

Yolanda Y. Odulio

Biographies
of
Poets

ABELL, CHARLOTTE B.
[b.] January 31, 1925, Philadelphia, PA; [p.] Dr. Chales H. Bender, Henrietta S. Bender; [m.] Ernest G. Abell, January 31, 1948; [ch.] Richard B. Abell, Stephen G. Abell, Constance Ann Abell; [ed.] Green Street Friends, Germantown High, Temple University and Immaculata College; [occ.] Retired - Executive Financial Vice-President of Abell Engineering Co.; [memb.] National Society Daughters of the American Revolution, St. David's Golf Club, Miles River Yacht Club and St. Luke's Lutheran Church; [hon.] Honorary award for 12 years of volunteer work for Cancer Research Institute at the Fox Chase Center. Graduating Class Salutatory speaker at Roosevelt Junior High.; [oth. writ.] I write inspiring notes to my children and grand-children hoping to guide them through life—they encouraged me to express myself in poetry.; [pers.] My studying the heavens bestows spiritual guidance for me, hence, "Star Dust." May more poets of today look to the heavens for inspiration!; [a.] Saint Michaels, MD

ADELMAN, MICHAEL
[b.] June 6, 1940, Cambridge, MA; [p.] Ben Adelman and Sally Adelman; [m.] Amy Adelman, June 15, 1962; [ch.] Robert and John; [ed.] Univ. of Michigan, Univ. of Michigan Law School; [occ.] Attorney; [memb.] American Bar Association, Mississippi and Michigan State Gan Association, Southeast Miss. Legal Services Crp., Trea., Bd of Directors, 1978; [hon.] Univ. of Mich. Hopwood Award (1963, Miss Essay), Ralph T, Abernathy Award, Jackson County (MS) SCLC—1978; [oth. writ.] "The Deputy," The New Renaissance, November 14, 1981, "The Detention Center", The New Renaissance, November 23, 1989 . . . short stories.; [a.] Hattiesburg, MS

ADKINS, DEBRA M.
[b.] July 10, 1957, Cleveland, OH; [p.] Frank Dargay (Deceased) and Belva Naskoviak; [m.] Charles W. Adkins II, May 1, 1981; [ch.] Charlie and Ryan; [ed.] West Tech High School; [occ.] Self Employed, Crafts; [memb.] Ascension School Council, Chairperson; [hon.] Outstanding Service SCC - Cleveland Public Schools; [oth. writ.] Poem published - Good News Christian Publication; [pers.] God is number one in my life. This reflects in most of my poetry. "Unconditional Love" was written for my son Charlie who is artistic; [a.] Cleveland, OH

ADKINS, SANDRA
[pen.] Sandra Adkins; August 21, 1984; South Charleston, WV; [p.] David Adkins, Susan Adkins; [ed.] South Charleston Junior High 7th grade; [occ.] Junior High Student; [oth.writ.] Several other poems but this is my first ever published; [pers.] Friends are a blessing. Hold them close and treasure them dearly; [a.] Dunbar, WV.

AFRICANO, CYNTHIA
[b.] June 9, 1950, Kankakee, IL; [p.] Reba K. Johnson/Glenn O. Johnson; [m.] Divorced; [ch.] Nick Johnson Africano; [ed.] Eastridge H.S., Illinois State University; [occ.] Artist; [memb.] American Cancer Society, Breast Cancer Support Group, Past President Mulberry School; [pers.] Do what you long to do. If you didn't have the ability you wouldn't want to do it.; [a.] Normal, IL

AGNEW, HARRY J.
[pen.] Harry J. Agnew; [b.] May 4, 1918, Penns Grove, NJ; [p.] James and Mary Collins Agnew; [m.] Kathryn E. Imese Rip, November 30; [ch.] 2, 1 Dead Daughters; [ed.] Graduate Niagara University, Niagara, NY, 1943; [occ.] Work for Bob Camiac Stable, Retired El Dupont, Retired from Garden State Race Track; [memb.] Sakima CC Penns Grove, NJ, Salem County Sports Men's Club, Penns Grove, NJ, Sona Song Writers North America,

Central Board Basketball Official; [hon.] Basketball all Western NY (Nigeria), All Tri County Forward St. James High, Penns Grove, NJ, cartained and coached established Penns Grove 1st President Little League; [oth. writ.] St. Patrick Parade in Savannah - Lovato's Home, First at the Wire - get a ticket to win or camac - poem "I Might Have Said," poem "Ain't Gonna Reign No More", song, "Nice of You."; [pers.] Satchel Page said, "Never look back someone or something high beginning on you" —you only come by here once, be sure to smell the roses.; [a.] Pennsville, NJ

AGUILAR, CONSUELO V.
[b.] May 5, 1941, Mesa, AZ; [p.] Maria J. Valenzuela; [ed.] High school; [occ.] Manufacturing Operator for (Motorola SPS Wafer Process FAB) going on 30 yrs.; [oth. writ.] "Hearts Desire" being published; [pers.] I am trying for goals in my life, the reality of life's tragedies and strengths. Hoping it will help someone along their way. I know now I may achieve something in my life. Knowing I have touched someone's heart. (I am a survivor).; [a.] Mesa, AZ

AKOSA, SYLVIA
[b.] February 2, 1932, Jos N., Nigeria; [p.] Mr. and Mrs. E. O. Asika; [m.] Dead, 1951; [ch.] Emmanuel, Loretta and James; [ed.] Higher Elementary Education, Yaba-Lagos, Nigeria; [occ.] Retired; [oth. writ.] Newspaper weekly columnist Renaissance/Daily-Star, Enugu-Nigeria, "Essays for Primary and Secondary Modern School," Nigeria.; [a.] New Orleans, LA

ALBERTS, JAMES
[b.] October 18, 1948, Dearborn, MI; [p.] Ervin Alberts, Carol Alberts; [ed.] Michigan State University; [occ.] Sales Manager, USA Today; [memb.] Sierra Club; [hon.] Academic Scholarship, Michigan State University; [pers.] My poetry is dedicated to my family: Ervin, Carol, Karen, Jenny, Matt, Joel, Nate, Donna and Jim.; [a.] Stanwood, WA

ALEXANDER, ANNETTE
[pen.] Morning Star; [b.] December 11, 1957, Germany; [p.] Mr. and Mrs. John Alexander; [m.] The Late John Alexander; [ch.] Two; [ed.] 12th grade, would like to attend college to become a social single worker.; [occ.] Mom and Care giver of Handicapped child, also 17 year old son.; [memb.] I attend Church in Akron, OH.; [hon.] My rewards are being the best Mom I can be, and helping people who are hurting.; [oth. writ.] Thank You God, Life and a Flower, I Cry Out, There Is a God, True Friend and Torn and Shatter; [pers.] God made us all, to love and to help one other and to reach out to the hurting in this world.; [a.] Akron, OH

ALFRED, JACQUELINE
[b.] August 10, 1952, Guyana, South America; [ch.] Michelle and Lennox Jr.; [occ.] Customer Service Representative; [hon.] I received awards for perfect attendance as operator of the quarter at work, and awards for volunteering with pre-school children.; [oth. writ.] I have several unpublished poems.; [pers.] My poems are based on everyday experiences. I hope they can make a difference in people's lives.; [a.] Brooklyn, NY

ALFREY, DAVID
[b.] March 6, 1976, Ironton, OH; [p.] MaryAnn and Roger; [ed.] Ironton High School; [oth. writ.] Many poems written but none have been published: One's Like, Can I Hold You, How Long Will I Be Alone, Remember Your Dreams, etc.; [pers.] I only write about how I feel about myself, life and love. I want to thank a very special person, because without her telling me to do this, then no one would have ever read my work. Thanks, Talley Harvey.; [a.] Ironton, OH

ALLEN, PEARL K.
[b.] November 15, 1922, Illinois; [p.] Deceased; [m.] Harold A. Allen, 1941; [ch.] Three; [hon.] Award of Recognition from Famous Poets Society of 1996; [pers.] Throughout my life, I have enjoyed putting into verse peaceful thoughts about my family and friends.; [a.] Stanton, CA

ALLEN, TIM C.
[b.] June 9, 1975, Aurora, CO; [p.] Charles Allen and Laura Allen; [ed.] University of Colorado (2 years), United States Naval Fire Controlman Training School (1 year); [occ.] Student; [memb.] United States Naval Reserve Officer Training Corps; [hon.] Distinguished Military Graduate, Class President 1991-1993, Rotary Student of the Month, March, 1993; [pers.] Writing should always stimulate the mind. I try to use my emotions and experiences to enlighten others.; [a.] Aurora, CO

AMIN, MANZURUL
[b.] January 14, 1926, India; [p.] Bismilla Khan (Principal, Teachers Training School, Mrs. Bismilla Begum, Head Mistress, Girls School); [m.] Rafia Amin (Writer, Painter and Sculptor), October 2, 1955; [ch.] Two daughters - Zishan Samiuddin M.D., Farozan Warsi; [ed.] M.A., LL.B.; [occ.] Visiting Professor, Mass Communication at several universities of India; [hon.] 1. Unesco Fellowship (Paris) for training in television production at BBC, London, 2. Director-General (Retired) Television India, 3. H.M. Malak Gold Medal on securing first position among all the first division students at M.A. Exam., 4. UP State Academy Awards on my two books; [oth. writ.] Author of three books—two have won State Academy Awards, published several essays poking fun at the absurdities of modern age, written and produced number of musicals for radio and television.; [pers.] I inherited love for knowledge from my parents who were teachers. They were my spark plugs. My mother used to say that two English women, Miss Thompson and Miss Pascal, helped her start a school for girls seventy-five years ago. They used to tell my mother: he who opens a school, closes a prison. I believe that armed with education, we can demolish ignorance and crime. Fact is, what we know is nothing, what we do not know is immense.; [a.] Hyderabad, AP, India

ANCICH, HEATHER M.
[b.] August 24, 1971, Tacoma, WA; [p.] Diana, Wally Brasfield and John Ancich Sr.; [ed.] American School of Madrid, Spain, George for University, Management of Organizational Leadership; [occ.] Johnson-Lieber, Inc., Marketing Manager - Food Broker; [hon.] Phi Beta Kappa; [pers.] The greatest part of life is that you get to create it.; [a.] Milwaukie, OR

ANDERSON, CARROLL C.
[b.] March 2, 1920, Cedar, MI; [p.] Chris and Mary Anderson; [m.] Edna M. Anderson, January 23, 1945; [ch.] Jeffery Anderson; [ed.] Barnum School, Birmingham, Michigan - Baldwin High, Birmingham Michigan - attended University of Detroit, Detroit, Michigan; [occ.] Retiree - Ford Motor Co.; [memb.] Edgard Desmet Alumni Assoc., Sun City West Men's Club, 3 yrs. US Navy; [oth. writ.] Fantasy, Anticipation, The Door with Glass, Champagne Honeymoon, The White House Memories of Freedom, The Unsuccessful Inventor; [pers.] Use the wisdom of today as the gateway to tomorrow.; [a.] Sun City West, AZ

ANDERSON, KAREN ANNETTE
[b.] April 5, 1954, New York, NY; [p.] Deceased; [ch.] Justin Christopher Williams; [ed.] B.S./M.S. in Education, City College, N.Y.; [occ.] Teacher; [memb.] UFT/AFT United Federation of Teachers/American Federation of Teachers; [oth. writ.]

Several poems and articles (art) published in family magazines.; [pers.] "As you walk through life, leave your footprints as many places as possible."; [a.] Bronx, NY

ANDERSON, POET
[b.] March 2, 1920, Cedar, MI; [p.] Chris and Mary Anderson; [m.] Edna M. Anderson, January 23, 1945; [ch.] Jeffery Anderson; [ed.] Barnum School, Birmingham, Michigan - Baldwin High, Birmingham Michigan - attended University of Detroit, Detroit, Michigan; [occ.] Retiree - Ford Motor Co.; [memb.] Edgard Desmet Alumni Assoc., - Sun City West Men's Club, 3 yr. US Navy; [oth. writ.] Fantasy, Anticipation, The Door With Glass, Champagne Honeymoon, The White House Memories of Freedom, The Unsuccessful Inventor; [pers.] Use the wisdom of today as the gateway to tomorrow.; [a.] Sun City West, AZ

ANDRIESSE, DANIEL
[pen.] Daniel Andriesse; [b.] June 17, 1924, Queens, NY; [p.] Fred and Charlotte Andriesse; [m.] Rose Andriesse, February 23, 1952; [ed.] 3 yrs. H.S.; [occ.] Security Officer; [memb.] Knights of Columbus, D.A.V. #18, F.O.E. Pres. 2 yrs., Dist Pres. 1 yr.; [hon.] Knight of the Month; [oth. writ.] When Tomorrow Starts Without Me, Christmas in Fla., To Walk the Path, Dear Lord ("Please"), Mother.; [pers.] I do these writings out of a clear blue sky as I work nights.; [a.] Bradenton, FL

ANDRZEJEWSKI, ROSE
[b.] September 28, 1978, Toledo, OH; [p.] Richard and Mary Ellen; [ed.] Central Catholic High School; [occ.] YMCA of Greater Toledo, Counselor; [memb.] Girl Scouts of United States, YMCA of Greater Toledo; [hon.] Lifetime Member of Girl Scouts; [pers.] With love to Scott James, who always is behind me in all I do.; [a.] Toledo, OH

ANNICCHIARICO, D. J.
[b.] April 4, 1982, Concord, NH; [p.] David and Lynn; [ed.] I am currently a freshman at Rundlett Junior High School; [occ.] Student; [pers.] I try to include a wide range of subjects in my poetry. I want to make my mark in several ways. I've always believed that it's not "to be or not to be," but how to be.; [a.] Concord, NH

ANULIES, JOHN
[b.] October 25, 1943, Riverdale, MD; [p.] Francis Water and Valeria Mary; [m.] Cheryle Ann, April 17, 1997; [ch.] Brian; [ed.] B.S. Engineering Univ. of Connecticut - 1974 US Naval Submarine service 1963-1970; [occ.] Professional Engineer; [memb.] American Society of Civil Eng., American Society of Mech. Eng., American Welding Society; [hon.] Professional Engineer in Conn, Ohio, South Carolina, Florida and Georgia; [oth. writ.] Unpublished poetry; [pers.] It's grand being human and I've had a wonderful time.; [a.] Rincon, GA

ASHBY, ANDY
[pen.] Andy; [b.] June 7, 1976; [p.] Mark and Susanne Ashby; [ed.] Junior in college (Indiana University); [occ.] Chemistry Lab. Instructor; [memb.] Royal family of Qatar, Duke (just kidding); [hon.] National Merit Scholar, Chemistry Dep't. Honor; [oth. writ.] Poems for Cecil's poetry class (unpublished); [pers.] I enjoy the fact that I still believe in many things, words give me solace from the rest of my hectic lifestyle.; [a.] Bloomington, IN

ASHE-HAGANS, JOAN MARIE
[b.] December 12, 1964; Brooklyn, NY; [p.] John N. Ashe, Flora C. Ashe; [ch.] Eric, Joavan, Joshua; [ed.] George W. Wingate H.S., Brooklyn College; [occ.] E911 Dispatcher, New York Police Department; [pers.] This poem was written for, and is dedicated to my best friend and fiance, Charles Christopher Browning. The power of his

love has allowed me to dream again. I share this reality with you all; [a.] Brooklyn, NY.

ASHTON, NOEL MICHAEL JAMES
[b.] December 9, 1966, St. Vincent, The Grenadines; [p.] Fred Ashton, Elma Ashton; [ed.] Bishop's College, Kingstown St. Vincent; [occ.] Security Officer; [pers.] I try to draw upon subject matter from the human experience overall, rather than any singular, being male, black, vincentian, etc.; [a.] Brooklyn, NY

BACCHUS, NIKKI
[b.] December 29, 1983, El Paso, TX; [p.] Rocky and Cathy Bacchus; [ed.] St Clement's Episcopal School; [memb.] National Junior Forensic League, First Baptist Church, Youth Council, Pen and Ink, School Band, School Speech and Drama Team, Border Region Library Association (BRLA), Young Writers, school journalism staff; [hon.] Headmaster's List, Honor Roll; [oth. writ.] Literary and art works published in local newspapers, poems published in church newsletter; [pers.] I believe that communication is one of the most valuable skills to be obtained. Once it is, you will find it easy to express yourself—it's fun!; [a.] Santa Teresa, NM

BACKUS, MICKEY R.
[b.] October 24, 1943, Miami, FL; [m.] Charles A. Backus, December 4, 1985; [ed.] Bachelor of Science, Master of Education, Tennessee State University; [occ.] Teacher - Matoaca Elementary School, Matoaca, Virginia; [memb.] Virginia Education Association - Chesterfield Education Association, Delta Sigma Theta Sorority; [hon.] Who's Who of American Women; [pers.] My writing depicts the world as it is, and hopefully it will encourage or inspire people to work together because there is hope for the world we live in.; [a.] Chester, VA

BAER, BETHANY
[pen.] Beth or Bethany Baer; [b.] July 4, 1981, Olean, NY; [p.] Robert and Paula Baer; [ed.] Graston VA High School freshman at this time!; [occ.] High School Freshman; [memb.] Financial Club, Odyssey of the Mind; [hon.] Various school awards, 3rd place in Odyssey of the Mind competition this year - 1997; [oth. writ.] "Death", "Home Work", "Spring", "Heaven", and many others.; [pers.] My poetry comes from deep within my mind, rather than from the heart.; [a.] Yorktown, VA

BAILEY, CHARLES A.
[b.] April 21, 1948, Pueblo, CO; [p.] Charles Rayfield and Margie Helen Bailey; [ed.] George Mason University, Fairfax, VA, Bachelor's Degree English Lit.; [occ.] Journalist; [hon.] Decorated for valor in combat by US Army, 101st Airborne Div., Vietnam, 1968; [oth. writ.] Several poems published in literary magazines such as the Washington, DC based Potomac Review, news articles published in wide array of newspapers, magazines.; [pers.] I focus my poetry on the feelings and common experiences of my generation.; [a.] Alexandria, VA

BAILEY, RIPTON
[b.] May 19, 1923, Jamaica, WI; [m.] Lema Bailey, December 14, 1957; [ch.] Althea Bailey, Raymond Bailey; [ed.] B Sc (Economics) London, Cert. in Eduction and Geography, Institute of Education University of Southampton; [occ.] Math Teacher, Mahalia Jackson Intermediate School (Retired).; [a.] Brooklyn, NY

BAKER, BRENDA
[pen.] Brenda Lawson Baker; [b.] November 22, 1945, Sullivan Co, TN; [p.] Willard and Emily Lawson; [m.] Robert Lynn Baker, January 25,

1964; [ch.] Daniel Wesley Ly Baker; [ed.] Church Hill High School, East TN State Univ.; [occ.] Holston Valley Medical Center - Discharge Analyst; [oth. writ.] Working on two books - Clay Roads and TN Romantic Plantations.; [pers.] I am a romantic person. I strive to reflect this in my writings.; [a.] Kingsport, TN

BAKER, JOAN M.
[pen.] Joan M. Baker or Joan Baker; [b.] November 27, 1932, Nanticoke, PA; [p.] Henry W. and Gussie (Warren) Myers; [m.] Roy K. Baker, January 31, 1975; [ch.] Paul E., Kathleen M., Charles D., Kenneth R., and David D.; [ed.] High school grad. - 1950, Battin H.S., Elizabeth, N.J., attended Ocean County Community College, studied and received Real Estate Licence; [occ.] Retired from Wissahickon School District, Ambler, PA; [memb.] Penna School Board Assn., Penna Assn. of Secretaries/Office Personnel, International Society of Poets; [hon.] Editor's Choice Award in 1996 and 1997 from National Library of Poetry.; [oth. writ.] Written over 50 other poems compiling them for publication. Working on a biography about my mother, the late Gussie Edna (Warren) Myers.; [pers.] I feel we often get caught up in our interests and forget that the wants of the little ones are sometimes much more important.; [a.] Glenside, PA

BALDWIN, DENISE LYNN
[pen.] Denise Lynn Bernal; [b.] October 9, 1954; Gardena, CA; [p.] Ronald D. Rodom and Marcia A. Metzger; [m.] Darryl E. Baldwin; May 9, 1996; [ch.] Nikki Anne, Samantha Marie, Melissa Ann; [a.] Trabuco Canyon, CA.

BALLIET, JAMES L.
[b.] July 19, 1930, Saint Louis, MO; [p.] Jacob and Alma Balliet; [m.] Penny, September 5, 1996; [ch.] Diane, Patricia, James Jr., Mark, Teri, William, Chad Locklear and Lex Locklear; [ed.] High School, AA Financial Planning SW Missouri State Uni., attended Southeastern Bible College, National Staff College, USAF-CAP-Squadron Officers School and Command and Staff College USAF; [occ.] Business Owner; [memb.] Mason-York Rite-Shrine, UP Meridian Shrine Club, 1st Bap. Church, Score, Retired US Army 24 yrs. CAP 20 years; [hon.] Outstanding Commander (CAP) Squadron Officer Year (CAP) Army Commendation Medal, Listed in: Who's Who Southeast, in America, International Biographies, and in the Universe; [oth. writ.] The Devil Made Me Do It, The Final Deception, The Mouse And Knobby Knees.; [pers.] Life is what you make of today.; [a.] Meridian, MS

BALLINGER, KRISTINE
[b.] September 18, 1978, Westminster, CO; [p.] Daniel and Darlene Ballinger; [ed.] Arvada Senior High School/Trapper Creek Job Corps; [occ.] Student at Trapper Creek Job Corps; [pers.] I strive to give everyone a piece of my love, to put a smile on their face and brighten their day.; [a.] Arvada, CO

BAMU, GEORGE ATANGA
[b.] April 16, 1972, Buea, Republic of Cameroon; [p.] Susan Ndongwa Bamu and Jing Bamu; [ed.] Student in Denver, Colorado (U.S.A.); [occ.] Cameroonian student studying in Denver U.S.A., Freelance Writer/Critic; [memb.] Founding President of University of Buea Young Writer's Club "The Muse," Cameroon; [oth. writ.] Several articles/essays published in local newspapers in Cameroon and a collection of unpublished poems.; [pers.] Translating my thoughts and life experiences into the living testimonies of poetry is my greatest joy in life. It is an activity I am prepared to die for at any one moment.; [a.] Denver, CO

BANGO, MARGARITA
[b.] April 29, 1966, Albania; [ed.] I had been educated in Albania and I am still in school in the U.S.A. I am a student at Anna Maria College, and my major is Foreign Languages.; [occ.] Student; [hon.] Last year my poems "To Be Thirsty For Liberty" and "I Left You Forever Albania" got published in Gdulash magazine at Anna Maria College; [pers.] I got in the U.S.A. in 1993. Since then I have worked hard to do my best for my life here, especially about my education, I love to write poetry.; [a.] Worcester, MA

BANNENBERG, WILLIAM A.
[b.] March 21, 1968; [p.] Al and Marie Bannenberg; [ed.] MA in Philosophy, The University of Wisconsin, Milwaukee; [oth. writ.] (All published) The Roots and Fruits of Solitude, The Confucian Musician Rhapsody, Jacking Uncle Walt, Analectical Variations, For Water, Philo and Sophia, Namagon's Briolette, Rainbow and the Panda.; [a.] Cedarburg, WI

BAPTISTE, CAROL
[pen.] Angel Kelly; [b.] February 27, 1978, Kingstown, SVG; [p.] Beather Baptiste; [ed.] Dorsetshire Hill Gov't. on Bishop's College Kingstown; [occ.] Nurse's Aide; [hon.] Gold Medal for drama; [oth. writ.] Never been published; [pers.] My writing allows me to express my point of view on the things in my surroundings and personal life. I have been influenced by writers such as Mark Twain and William Shakespeare.; [a.] Brooklyn, NY

BARLETT, KRISTINA
[pen.] Indian Maiden; [b.] May 19, 1982, Butler, PA; [p.] Jeff and Cyann Barlett; [ed.] High school - still attending; [occ.] 9th grader at Karns City Area Jr./Sr. High School; [hon.] Citizenship award; [oth. writ.] I have written other little poems but only for fun, this is my first poem published.; [pers.] My poem "What Love Is" was influenced by my own experiences and also watching my friends' experiences!; [a.] Petrolia, PA

BARNES, STACY
[b.] October 9, 1968, Boston; [ch.] Ashlie Barnes; [ed.] Quincy College; [occ.] Secretary, Comprehensive Development Corp; [hon.] Graduated with Honors; [pers.] I hope to touch or improve someone's life through my writings.; [a.] Hull, MA

BARON, ISRAEL
[pen.] Saul; [b.] April 17, 1919, Boston, MA; [p.] Harry Baron and Dora (Nee Breger); [m.] Phyllis (Nee Gilbert), June 20, 1942; [ch.] Donald (Deceased) and Myrna Ann; [ed.] H.S. Lexington MA. AAFTTC Chief Instructor-Teletype Maint. Self taught unto mechanics Electronics mtg equip maint dielectrics experiment/new process and applicate; [occ.] Retired; [memb.] AAF - 4 yrs - Temple Board, Randolph, WA, Chairman Golf League, AARP; [hon.] Certificate of Merit Florida Anthology, National Poetry Radio, Treasured Poems of America; [pers.] Love life. The greatest gift to the human being is arising to another day with good cheer and good health. An added blessing is a loving companion for all these many years.; [a.] Lantana, FL

BARRETT, RAIN FAWN
[pen.] Rain Fawn Barrett; [b.] August 7, 1950, Dayton, OH; [p.] Leonard Bud Burton, Phyllis Edra Ward; [m.] Gaylord A. Toombs (Companion); [ch.] James Mark Hahn; [ed.] Hawthorne High, Barthmore Beauty College Cometology License in 1968, took speech for 4 yrs in high school and loved it.; [occ.] Hair Dresser - but always wanted to be a writer; [memb.] Was a volunteer for R7 Bid Recording for Blind and Dyslexia and a

Volunteer for LAX Airport Travelers Aid; [hon.] Six poems published in a book out of Stockton, Calif. in 1980 World of Poetry, I lost my own copy, but gave so many away.; [oth. writ.] I don't write music "only words" for a song. I've written 3 country songs and one funny rap song. But no one has ever heard them. I've been writing since 1975. I design my own greeting cards. I had called a Greeting Cards Inc., a very well known one in the 70's and they turned me down to be an artist and writer for their company.; [pers.] I don't read very well and I use my dictionary to spell words right. But I feel that I'm a writer in mind, soul and body. I write about life, love, happiness and despair.; [a.] Lawndale, CA

BARRETT, VICKIE LYNN
[b.] October 14, 1966, Richmond, VA; [p.] John Barrett, Ruby Barrett; [ch.] Shakita, Chamere, Charles, LaQuita; [ed.] Franklin Military High, U.S.A. Training Academy, I.B.T. College; [oth. writ.] Poem published in Brunswick Times, and jail and prison ministry; [pers.] I strive to comfort the hearts of the souls that are lost and dejected. I pray that through reading my poems they are enlightened and taken to a higher level of spirituality.; [a.] Richmond, VA

BARRICK, BRITTANI
[pen.] Brittani Rene; [b.] May 31, 1981, Indianapolis, IN; [p.] Brad and Denise Barrick; [ed.] Brownsburg High School; [memb.] Brownsburg Christian Church, Brownsburg Tennis Team; [hon.] National Honor Society; [pers.] I express my thoughts and feelings through poetry. Therefore it comes naturally. I dedicate this poem to my grandma and in memory of my grandpa.; [a.] Brownsburg, IN

BARRIE, LORRAINE
[pen.] Lorraine Lochner, L. Johnson; [b.] July 27, 1954, Salt Lake City, UT; [ed.] University of Southern Calif. - B.S., University of California, Berkeley - Telecommunications Engineering; [occ.] Analyst/Consultant; [memb.] Maui Live Poets' Society, Writers Connection, Amateur Radio Relay League, Society of Women Engineers, Animal Protection Agencies; [hon.] Magna Cum Laude - USC, graduation with honors - UCB, Special Achievement Award - SWE; [oth. writ.] 'Lorraine's Corner' - local column, Carson City. NV ('84-'86), agency newsletter stories, proponent research for animal rights, professional engineering manuals, poetry for local readings.; [pers.] Poetry drops me into a vortex where the pain and love in my heart converge in a palpable magma. The 'writing' is the struggle of the head, then, to knit this energy into expression. Truth is 'heart' telling 'head' what to do.; [a.] Kihei, Maui, HI

BARROW, STEWART K.
[pen.] Stewart K. Barrow; [b.] May 28, 1959, Martinsville, VA; [p.] Fred and Dale Barrow; [ch.] Michele and Ashley; [ed.] Laurel Park High School; [occ.] Sara Lee Knit Products; [oth. writ.] Dreams, Many Delights, Light House, Training of the Heart, Give Me Rest, Water and Light; [pers.] I am a single parent who loves his children very much, they are without a doubt the one ray of sunshine that I have.; [a.] Eden, NC

BARTHOLOMEW, MICHAEL DAVID
[b.] September 8, 1974, Connecticut; [p.] Dorothea S. and Paul D. Bartholomew; [ed.] Mt. St. Mary's College (MD); [hon.] Alpha Mu Gamma, Tri Beta, Dean's List, Msgr. Tierney and other honor societies; [pers.] Although equally important to know others, you must first know who you are. Through self enlightenment and work you may find your ancestors, culture cultivating pride as a strength. A strong sense of self is the first step on the road to freedom and equality.; [a.] Bantam, CT

BARTLETT, KIMBERLY ANN
[pen.] Kimberly Ann Bartlett; [b.] November 30, 1969, Hampton, VA; [p.] Clarence Bartlett and Beverly Bartlett; [ed.] Warner Robins High School, Thomas Nelson Community College, and Macon College; [occ.] Service Manager; [a.] Carrollton, VA

BARTON, LAWRENCE G.
[pen.] Le'Gene; [b.] May 16, 1965, Oakland, CA; [p.] Henry L. Barton, Clara M. Barton; [ch.] Kenyatta D. Barton; [ed.] Hayward Adult School, Chabot College, Cal State Hayward; [occ.] Peer Instructor and Student at Chabot College and CSUH; [hon.] Scholarships, Inc. Award, featured in Daily Review newpaper; [oth. writ.] "My Dream That Came True", "How Soon We Forget".; [pers.] I want to say thank you to my father, the late Henry L. Barton, who inspired me to further my education and who worked very hard to mold me into the man I am today.; [a.] Oakland, CA

BARUCKY, MICHAEL J.
[b.] June 21, 1973, Scranton, PA; [p.] John M. and Carolyn Barucky; [ed.] Lakeland High School, Lackawanna County Area Vo-tech; [occ.] Mechanic; [memb.] Volunteer Fire Fighter; [a.] Carbondale, PA

BATES, CARLA
[b.] July 10, 1963, Pittsburgh; [p.] Dolores Just and Carl (Deceased); [m.] Clifford Smith, May 27, 1996; [ch.] Carrie and Courtney Katie (Step-children); [ed.] Hempfield High; [occ.] Self-employed, Leather Smith; [memb.] St. Barts Church, American Cancer Society, Lupus Foundation; [oth. writ.] Other death poems, none published; [pers.] I write of death. Not because I am obsessed with it, but because I believe it's the most fascinating and intriguing thing that happens in a person's life.; [a.] Latrobe, PA

BATES, DORTHY B.
[b.] June 19, 1919, Yuma, CO; [pers.] The poem "My Beautiful Memory" is the original work of Dorthy B. Bates, my Mom. The poem is my mom's memories of me as I was growing up. It was a gift from her to me. When I read it, I new I wanted to share it with others letting them know just how much it has touched my heart.; [a.] Clifton, CO

BAUER, ETHEL
[b.] September 25, 1915, Pomeroy, OH; [p.] David Eugene - Florence (Russell) Smith; [m.] Deceased, February 1934 and April 30, 1954; [ch.] Eugene, Roger, Thomas Willoughby Margaret (Bauen) Adams, Mary Bauer; [ed.] High school (Pomeroy HS), some college courses—Arizona State University (worked there 18 years); [occ.] Retired Secretary; [hon.] Poem published in 1996 by The National Library of Poetry; [oth. writ.] Short stories and poems, also prose.; [pers.] Poems to me are painting a picture with words.; [a.] Tempe, AZ

BAUTISTA, VIRGINIA ANNE
[pen.] Gina Bautista; [b.] February 18, 1972; West Covina, CA; [p.] Virginia and Sacramento Bautista; [ed.] William Workman High School, City of Industry, CA; Computer Learning Center, Los Angeles, CA; DeVry Institute of Technology, Pomona, CA; [occ.] Encryption Operator, TVN Satellite Entertainment, Burbank, CA; [memb.] San Diego Wild Animal Park and Zoo Association; American Diabetes Association; Dean's List at DeVry; Workman High School Space Shuttle Club President 1987-1990; Epsilon Delta Pi Honor Society; Sigma Beta Delta Honor Society; [hon.] 1st place essay contest winner for RTD Los Angeles; High School district sholar; Cum Laude and pefect attendance at Computer Learning Center; Dean's List at DeVry; [oth. writ.] Poem "The Clouds" published in Scholastic publication

"Reflections" Volume VII-1985, Poem "Ocean Wavers" published scholastic publication "Reflections" Volume VIII-1986; [pers.] I have been greatly influenced by such artists as Shakespeare, Edgar Allan Poe, Jim Morrison, and Dean Koontz. My writing reflects my life, my mind, and my ideas. It's all continuous autobiography; [a.] Temecula, CA.

BEACOM, TAMMY L.
[b.] June 7, 1978, New Haven, CT; [p.] Corrine and Robert Beacom; [ed.] Sheehan High, Bay State College; [occ.] Student; [memb.] American Red Cross; [a.] Wallingford, CT

BEARD, AMANDA A.
[b.] May 28, 1985; Jacksonville, FL; [p.] Richard and Patsy Barry; [ch.] Brothers 2, Sisters 1; [occ.] Student; [memb.] Teams; [hon.] A and AB Honor role. Contestant in Miss Team Pageant. Won County Art Contest at age 8; [pers.] I will always strive to be the success that I know I am capable of being; [a.] Jacksonville, FL.

BEASLEY, BECKY
[pen.] Becky Beasley; [b.] July 31, 1982, Palm Beach Co., FL; [p.] Linda and Tracy Beasley; [ed.] I'm currently in the 8th grade at Jupiter Middle School going into the 9th grade.; [memb.] Middle school band at school, International Order of the Rainbow for girls, cheerleading squad at school; [pers.] I would like to thank Davis Campbell for encouraging me to submit one of my poems. My hobbies are creative writing and debating.; [a.] Jupiter, FL

BEATTY, DAVID
[b.] September 23, 1973, Auburn, NE; [p.] Rex Beatty, Kathy Beatty; [ed.] Auburn High School, University of Nebraska - Lincoln; [occ.] Student - Elementary Education; [memb.] Phi Eta Sigma, Pi Lambda Theta; [hon.] 1993-94 Outstanding Student Leadership Semi-Finalist, Dean's List, The National Dean's List; [pers.] The journey to excellence never ends.; [a.] Auburn, NE

BEAUSOLEIL, REBECCA
[b.] May 3, 1977, Colorado Springs, CO; [p.] Ray and Cathie Beausoleil; [occ.] BA in English and Linguistics at University of Maryland, College Park, expected May 1999, Tolland High School Tolland, CT; [occ.] Student; [memb.] Phi Sigma Pi, National Honor Society, Alpha Beta Chapter, Children of the American Revolution; [hon.] Dean's List, Lions Club Outstanding Service and Leadership, National Honors Society, Mark Twain Chapter.; [a.] Beltsville, ND

BECHTEL, ELIZABETH B.
[b.] October 6, 1906; Harrisbury, PA; [p.] Robert Brown, Helen S. Brown; [m.] John Bechtel Jr, died in 1971 (heart); November 9, 1926; [ch.] Nancy, John Bechtel Jr; [ed.] Reading high, Hood College, MD. Nancy my daughter went to Hood for 2 years and then became a nurse at a school in Mass; [occ.] I was a Latin Teacher now Retired; [memb.] I joined Calvary Reformed Church, Reading, Several Colleges took some lunch. I had a poem in my year book; [oth.writ.] I am in the mood now to write poems in the near future, I hope you like them as much these; [pers.] I want to thank all of you for the wonderful results you gave me; [a.] Reading, PA.

BEGG, SEAN
[b.] February 18, 1985, Sacramento, CA; [p.] Keith Begg and Cheryl Begg; [ed.] 6th grade; [occ.] Student; [memb.] Christian Life Center, Royal Rangers, Builders Club; [hon.] Festival of Oral Interpretation, Twice Eldorado County Spelling Bee; [pers.] I was greatly inspired by my savior Jesus Christ. Someday I hope to write

something to contribute to the salvation of mankind.; [a.] Pollock Pines, CA

BEHRENS, SAUSLEY
[pen.] February 15, 1983; Bryan, TX; [p.] Linda Brandenberger, Monroe Behrens; [ed.] Stephen F. Austin Jr. High; [occ.] Student; [memb.] St. Anthony Youth Choir S.F.A Bronco Band; [hon.] Gold Medals (Academics) U.I.L band patches and trophies, exceptance into Hammond-Oliver. (Medical High School), All City Band, All Region Band; [oth. writ.] Several poems not published, one story published in school newspaper; [pers.] A persons literary work is reflected upon their life. The longer the story, the better the life; [a.] Bryan, TX.

BEHYMER, APRIL
[b.] February 16, 1981, Cincinatti, OH; [p.] Todd and Reba Behymer; [ed.] New Richmond High School; [memb.] Great Rivers Girl Scouts; [hon.] Archie Griffin Sportmanship Award, American legion Runner-up; [a.] New Richmond, OH

BELFORD, CURT
[pen.] Cherokiekid@aol.com; [b.] March 18, 1949; [m.] Phyllis R. Belford; [ch.] Dawn Belford; [ed.] University of Life; [occ.] Domestic Male Engineer; [memb.] America On-line, Assistant Editor for Poetic Voices newsletter; [oth. writ.] Articles on adult mental retardation for local newspaper, research articles on Guillain Barre Syndrome for National Occupational Therapy newsletter.; [pers.] Life is an illusion, time the only reality, one man's (woman's) garbage is another woman's (man's) supper. I am a simple man singing a simple song.; [a.] Yukon, OK

BELL, DONNA
[b.] March 2, 1997, Woodbury, NJ; [p.] Frank T. and Lillian Smith; [m.] William G. Bell III, September 18, 1982; [ch.] Kim Marie and Thomas William; [ed.] High school; [occ.] Housewife, Home School Mom; [memb.] Belong to International Society of Poets, was elected into The International Poetry Hall of Fame on Jan. 6, 1997.; [hon.] Two Editor's Choice Awards for Death's Last Grip in "A Delicate Balance". I have my Mother's Hands in "Best Poems of the "90's"; [oth. writ.] One in church newspaper as a teen. The other in a Shore Mall Walker's newsletter.; [pers.] I have faith in God, don't let your failures get you down. Use them as lessons instead. Do not be afraid of criticism. Try to prove that person wrong, always with God's help.; [a.] Egg Harbor Township, NJ

BELL, MICHAEL LEE ANTHONY
[b.] July 1, 1964, New York, NY; [p.] Beverly Bell; [ch.] Debra Bell, Michaela Bell; [ed.] John F. Kennedy H.S., S.U.N.Y. at Farmingdale, C.U.N.Y. at Lehman; [occ.] Bridge and Tunnel Police Officer; [memb.] United Way Fraternal Order of Police N.Y. Shields; [oth. writ.] Several poems not published.; [pers.] Striving to love myself a little more each day.; [a.] Poughkeepsie, NY

BELSKY, RICHARD
[b.] December 3, 1940, Gardner, MA; [p.] Frances and Charles Belsky; [ed.] Worcester Junior College, Associate Degree, Fitchburg State College, Major in Education - both in MA; [occ.] Retired; [hon.] National Library of Poetry - Editor's Choice Award; [oth. writ.] First Snow, City and Town.; [a.] Orange, MA

BENSHOFF, REV. DAVID E.
[b.] May 20, 1950, Meyersdale, PA; [p.] St. Clair Benshoff and Pauline Benshoff; [m.] Deanna Benshoff, June 20, 1970; [ch.] Darin David and Dustin Grey; [ed.] Masters in Pastoral Care from Ashland Theological Seminary, Ashland, Ohio; [occ.] Pastor, St. Luke Brethren Church,

Woodstock, VA; [memb.] Woodstock, VA. Lions Club, Upper Shenandoah Valley Chapter of The Compassionate Friends; [oth. writ.] Poem published in 1996 edition of "Poetry From the Valley of Virginia," Loft Press.; [pers.] My desire is to grasp the realities of life in a simple form.; [a.] Woodstock, VA

BERG, RITA
[b.] June 27, 1948, Lindsborg, KS; [pers.] I believe that poetry comes from within one's self. Expressing from the soul, on life, love, beauty, joy and sadness like a song that never ends, always to enjoy.; [a.] Salina, KS

BERKE, MARC
[b.] June 22, 1965, Columbus, OH; [p.] Allen and Lenore Berke; [m.] Robin Maria Berke, November 28, 1996; [ch.] Cassy and Stephany; [ed.] Miami Sunset Sr. High, University of Florida, Florida International University; [occ.] Management; [oth. writ.] Several poems that are yet to be published.; [pers.] I try to capture the essence of life and translate those thoughts into my writings.; [a.] Homestead, FL

BERNARDEZ, MIRIAM
[b.] December 24, 1974; Honduras; [p.] Norma Bernardez, Kennedy Brooks; [ed.] High School Graduate; [occ.] Home Health Aid; [hon.] Second place in poetry contest in school; [oth. writ.] Virgin, Soledad, Tragic,Burglar, Black Souls (slavery), Mother, Silent Poet, Unspoken Llego A Creer, Ever So Often. None has been published before; [pers.] Do the best for yourself and you'll do the same for others; [a.] Brooklyn, NY.

BERRY, BETTY S.
[b.] July 10, 1933, Wallace, NC; [p.] Thomas Boyd and Virginia Schley; [m.] Wm. Clayton Berry, August 4, 1984; [ch.] Linda Fowler and Virginia Becker; [ed.] New Hanover High School, Wilmington, N.C. with some UNC Wilmington courses; [occ.] Homemaker; [pers.] I began to write poems late in life—they just seem to pop into my head, I seem to reflect on my past. I try to refer to mostly positive aspects.; [a.] Broussard, LA

BERRY, LUPE
[pen.] Lupe Berry; [b.] February 24, 1947, Hunter St, LA; [p.] Hemry and Guadalupe Perez; [m.] Gale A. Berry, February 20, 1970; [ch.] Grace, Gale, 8 grandkids Mario, Persolla, Reben, Jessica, Sera, Anthony, and July, Samlle; [ed.] Gandmares, Soto St School, LA, CA, JH High Robert Lousis LA, CA 7-9 gd, high school, El Monte 11-12 gd, Rousemeat High El Monte 9-10 gd; [occ.] Extra talent, for Premiere Casting, homemaker; [memb.] Casting; [hon.] One for working with kids in school; [oth. writ.] Yes, but, I left it in my car and they sold it for me for a song, called "A Birthday Kiss."; [pers.] Yes. To do all of this for my family and grandkids to show them if I can do it so can they, they look at me, I love them.; [a.] El Monte, CA

BERTSCH, TIM
[b.]October 28, 1981; Calgary, Alberta, Canada; [p.] Tim Bertsch (Dad) Tracy Bertsch (Step Mother); [ed.] Currently in grade 10, maintaining a 95% grade average; [int.]Basketball, Track and Field, Enjoys opra music (Favorites: Les Miserables and Phantom of the Opera), Enjoys playing guitar; [per.] Always works hard and try to be honest with people.

BESCHONER, JUDY
[pen.] Jude Bridges; [b.] July 16, 1956, N.W. Ark.; [p.] Hubert and Mary Beschoner; [occ.] Cleaning Service; [oth. writ.] "Judy, in the Skies," "Ode to the House Maid," "Bill," "Brandy," and others; [pers.] I would like to thank my parents for

teaching me to be independent, and yet there for me when I need them. A special appreciation, also, to Dale Spain, my partner and lifetime friend.

BEST, ROGER A.
[b.] July 25, 1959, Oneida, NY; [p.] Donald Best and Barbara Best; [ed.] Crestview High, Pioneer, Vocational, Daytona Beach Community College; [occ.] Leadman, Crane Cams, Inc.; [memb.] The Nature Conservancy; [pers.] First I must thank the Lord Jesus Christ, I believe the reflection of life through words inspires others to grow and learn.; [a.] New Smyrna Beach, FL

BIGGS, JANOE L.
[p.] Jann Biggs, Tom Biggs; [ed.] Currently a freshman at Oak Ridge High School; [occ.] Student; [hon.] Eighth grade Fine Arts award, Superior Rating in oral interpretation; [oth. writ.] "The Window of Wonders" published in the Anthology of Poetry by Young Americans in the 1994 edition.; [a.] El Dorado Hills, CA

BIRD, JENNIFER NELL
[pen.] Jenelle Thomas; [b.] October 26, 1955, Gouverneur, NY; [p.] Earl B. Jones, Marjorie E. Jones; [m.] Robert P. Bird III, April 5, 1986; [ch.] Kristen Jennifer (7), Daniel Robert (3); [ed.] Gouverneur Central High, Powelson Business Institute, Montgomery College; [occ.] Secretary/Office Manager; [memb.] Salem, United Methodist Church of Cedar Grove, Lifetime Member of Weight Watchers International; [hon.] Powelson Institute Academic Scholarship, The National Secretary Award, Department of Energy Integrity and Excellence Award; [pers.] This poem was written while my Dad was ill with lung cancer. I was trying to let my Dad know that he had worked hard all his life and done for others, now it was time for him to rest and let others take care of him. He died 2 days after reading it!; [a.] Germantown, MD

BIRD, MARY EMMA IRELAND
[pen.] Mary Emma Ireland Bird; [b.] November 26, 1931, Florida; [p.] Leo (Deceased) and Ruth Ireland; [m.] Robert C. Bird, June 3, 1954; [ch.] Steven, Timothy, Sandra, Carol and 8 grandchildren; [ed.] Whigham H.S., Whigham, GA, Valencia Comm. College, Orlando, FL (AA), Univ. of Central FL, Orlando, FL (BA), School Social Worker Certification, graduated Summa Cum Laude, 1980; [occ.] Retired, worked as School Social Worker for 2 1/2 years; [hon.] Dean's List, Summa Cum Laude at Univ. of Central FL, Orlando; [oth. writ.] Poem published in child abuse prevention publication, poem published in World of Poetry, anthology - Great Poems of the Western World, Vol. II, poem in The National Library of Poetry's anthology, Into the Unknown titled "Kaleidoscope."; [pers.] Inspiration for my writing has come from family members. It is a way to convey my warm feelings for them and, in essence, to "freeze" their experiences.; [a.] Tallahassee, FL

BISHOP, HEATHER
[pen.] Heather Bishop; [b.] February 27, 1978, Saginaw, MI; [p.] Gloria and David Bishop; [ed.] I attended New Lothrop High School for 4 yrs, and am now graduated. Currently, I am attending the University of Michigan.; [occ.] I model for Avante Modeling; [memb.] St. Michael's Church, Member of Girls Track Team (4 yrs.), Member of the 1996 Interlochen Chamber Singers, Member of ML Cheerleading (4 yrs.), Member of D.A.R.E. (4 yrs); [hon.] National Choral Award (because I also sing), I've had many poems published in school newspapers.; [oth. writ.] I've written many other poems. I started writing poetry at age 12. Some of which are, "Tommy," "Unborn," "It Wasn't My Time," "These I Have Loved," etc.;

[pers.] "A bit of fragrance always clings to the hand that gives you the roses." "Impossible is a word only to be found in the dictionary of fools."; [a.] Chesaning, MI

BISHOP, KELLY
[b.] July 21, 1970; Milford, MA; [p.] Thyra McPhee; [m.] Norman Bishop; August 24, 1996; [ed.] Bachelor of Science degree in Special Education, Sign Language Certificate; [occ.] Treatment Coordinator in an orthodontist office; [memb.] Community Companion, Battered Woman and Childrens Shelter Volunteer, Special Olympics Volunteer; [hon.] Deans list; [oth. writ.] Several poems published in the Attleboro Sun Chronicle; [a.] North Atterboro, MA.

BLACK, PAUL M.
[b.] April 7, 1979, Huntsville, AL; [p.] Bill and Pat Duke; [ed.] Satsuma High School; [occ.] Student; [memb.] Historical Society; [hon.] Beta Club, Honor Student, Band Elite, Senior Class Rep., Peer Leader; [oth. writ.] A New Life Waiting, The Choice, Paul, Waiting, This Man, Who Is This Person, My Special Place; [pers.] Life is full of happiness, but you have to make it happen.; [a.] Saraland, AL

BLACKMER, ANN HUSKISSON
[pen.] Ann Huskisson Blackmer; [b.] June 9, 1946, Ashley City, AR; [p.] Winnie Huskisson, James Huskisson; [m.] Robert Blackmer; [ch.] Robert, Richard, Kenneth, Kevin; [ed.] San Rafael High, San Antonio College; [memb.] Chairman of Pineywoods Regional Girls Camps Committee, WMU Scholarship Selection Committee; [pers.] God is my inspiration for my writings, my husband is my influence. This piece written several years prior to his thoughts of marrying me!; [a.] Huntsville, TX

BLAKE, TIMRA JO
[b.] April 16, 1982, Charleston; [p.] Lisa K. Blake and Charles Blake Jr.; [ed.] Nitro Elementary, Andrew Jackson Jr. High and Nitro High School; [hon.] Little Miss West Virginia State, Volunteer at Americare in Dunbar, Finalist in Miss Teen USA, Newspaper, Yearbook Staff, and Multi-Media/News Show Staff.; [oth. writ.] Many, but none published.; [pers.] I want to thank my mother and my friends for love and support! I love you all!; [a.] Nitro, WV

BLANKENBURG, JOSEF W.
[pen.] Joe B.; [b.] November 28, 1978, Willingboro, NJ; [ed.] Northern Burlington High School, Columbus, NJ Class of 1997; [occ.] Restaurant Cook; [memb.] Church of the Assumption, New Egypt, NJ; [hon.] South Jersey Group II Division Champs - High School Football 1995, Burlington County Secondary Principals and Supervisors Association Academic Achievement Award - 1997; [oth. writ.] Other poems published in the Northern Burlington High School "Kaleidoscope" spring 1995, and Gloucester County College "Scarlet Freight" poetry anthology - spring 1995; [pers.] When I write, I hope it will touch someone. I write just for the satisfaction of writing thoughts or fantasy.; [a.] Wrightstown, NJ

BLUE, EDDIE E.
[pen.] Dad; [b.] November 28, 1968; New Haven, CT; [p.] Eddie and Ella Blue; [m.] Catina; April 2, 1992; [ch.] Alexis, Brittny, Daissa; [ed.] Eli Whitney Tech; [hon.] Crowned Mr. Black CT on September 8, 1997; [oth.writ.]Daddy's Angels; [a.] New Haven, CT.

BOLTON, PATRICIA
[b.] February 16, 1942, North Little Rock, AK; [p.] James Joseph Davidson, Mary Alice Davidson; [m.] Jack C. Bolton Sr., August 4, 1972; [ch.] Brian David Bolton; [a.] Texas City, TX

BONALUMI, LEANNE
[pen.] Leanne Bonalumi; [b.] July 16, 1975, Saint Francis Hosp., Hartford, CT; [p.] Robert and Joyce Gregoire; [ed.] Avon Middle School, Avon High School - Graduated in 1994, went on to get my certificate as a Nursing Assistant; [occ.] CNA; [memb.] I'm not currently in any. At age five I played ice hockey and at age fourteen I joined all girls hockey team that represented the state of Connecticut. The biggest membership is my family.; [hon.] I have won three awards in my live so far. One—when I was eight I won the three star award in a hockey tournament. Two—I scored a hat trick which is three goals in one game. I lead my team to a national championship. And three—the Student of the Month in seventh grade.; [oth. writ.] I basically started writing poems at age seventeen. None of them were noticed, only by my therapist named Ethan and slowly I began to form my own style of writing by learning more about myself and how to live and be happy. I was encouraged to keep writing to express my feelings more. I was greatly influenced by a man that went to great lengths to help me find my inner self and find hope.; [pers.] To say the least I'm an average young adult. I'm an incest survivor. I can really understand how life has its highs and lows. I owe a great deal to my family and friends that have supported me from day one. And a very special person who believed in me and gave me a chance to change the bad into something good. I would not be here today if I did not have the support from family and Ethan. Thank you. So basically it all comes down to courage and the higher power to live life to the fullest and the rest will fall into place.; [a.] Avon, CT

BONDI, DAWN
[b.] April 7, 1973, Iowa; [p.] Eugene McGuire and Judy Huinker; [m.] Aarun Bondi, June 1, 1996; [ch.] Madeline Kathryn; [ed.] Fairview High, Colorado Community College; [occ.] Housewife and proud Mother; [memb.] St. Francis De Sales Catholic Church; [oth. writ.] I have several other poems, that I share with people often.; [pers.] I write what I feel. My father and my dear friend Margaret inspired me for they gave me hope.; [a.] Denver, CO

BONK, MATTHEW D.
[b.] December 20, 1978; [p.] Donald J. Bonk, Christa M. Bonk; [ed.] Attending Lockport Township High School, senior. I plan to start college in the fall of 1997.; [occ.] I am a loader at U.P.S.; [memb.] I am a member of the Writer's Digest Book Club. Also I am a member of the NRA.; [oth. writ.] I have a total of 121 poems and 2 short stories. One of my poems has been published in "Visions," a magazine published by my school. I hope to have a book of my own soon.; [pers.] I believe that there is no tomorrow or yesterday, there is only today. Everything happened today. Also poetry comes from experience, everything you see, hear, feel, taste, smell, think and dream is what poetry is.; [a.] Lockport, IL

BORDEN, BARBARA
[b.] December 3, 1947, McColl, SC; [p.] Hazel McLucas - Richard McMillian; [ch.] Deborah, Annette, Tracy and Shannon; [ed.] E.E. Smith Sr High (N.C.), Katherine Gibbs (N.Y.); [occ.] Packer - V.A.W. of America - St. Augustine, FL; [pers.] I strive to reflect the true feelings and emotions of one's heart into something beautiful to read.; [a.] Hastings, FL

BORGMAN, MARVIN L.
[b.] August 1, 1939, Sheldon, IA; [p.] Elmer Borgman (D), Geraldine Borgman; [m.] K. C., September 18, 1967; [ch.] John, Laura; [ed.] BA Univ of Nebraska, Omaha 1971 Mged - Univ

of Southern California 1976; [occ.] Coordinator, plans of projects, Montgomery Assoc for Retarded Citizens; [memb.] Air Force Association; [oth. writ.] United Nations Command Historical Summary 1984, 1685 - Republic of Korea; [a.] Prattville, AL

BORLAND, SCOTT T.
[pen.] Cnewanda Knox; [b.] February 19, 1980, Warren, PA; [p.] David F. Borland, Dana Lou Borland; [ed.] Copperas Cove High School, three years; [occ.] Student; [memb.] International Thespian Society, New Power Generation, National Forensic League; [hon.] National Forensic League, Degree of Honor, Degree of Excellence; [oth. writ.] The best is yet to come, I hope; [pers.] This is my first publication (Thank you, thank you, thank you!). May you live to see the dawn.; [a.] Copperas Cove, TX

BOTHWELL, SHENEKA
[b.] October 2, 1985, Gadsden, AL; [p.] Harry and Rosemary Bothwell; [ed.] 6th grade student at Gaston School; [occ.] Student; [a.] Gadsden, AL

BOWEN, GLENN
[B.] July 8, 1956; Hanover, Jamaica; [p.] Ezekiel Bowen, Blanche Bowen; [ch.] Jason, Ronda, Talijhe, Tara; [ed.] Cornwall College, Church Teachers College, University of the West Indies-Jamaica, St. Thomas Universtiy-Miami, FL; [occ.] Graduate Assistant (on leave from job as Public Relations Consultant); [memb.] International Association of Business Communications, Public Relations Society of America, Public Relations Society of Jamaica (Past President), World Federation of United Nations Association (Former Executive Member); [hon.] Press Association of Jamaica journalism prize, Public Relations Society of Jamaica awards for best magazine and employess annual report, United Nations Association of Jamaica leadership/award, Carribean Festival of Arts bronze medal for acting, St. Thomas University/Academic Support Center "Tutor of the Year 1995-1996"; [oth. writ.] Poetry, short stories and feature articles published in newspapers, journals and magazines in Jamaica and the U.S.; [pers.] "I do my best and leave the rest to God"; [a.] North Miami, FL.

BOWERS, ROBERT L.
[pen.] Bobby Bee; [b.] August 2, 1947, Knoxville, TN; [p.] Ercile E. Lillian Bowers; [m.] Divorced; [ch.] Christina Gail and Robert David; [ed.] Greenback Public Elementary School, G.E.D., through Univ. of Maryland, Baltimore, MO, TN, Voc. - Tech., Knoxville, TN; [occ.] Commercial Vehicle Owner/Operator, Nationwide; [oth. writ.] 12 Gospel songs unrecorded, 65 songs country and blues and/or bluegrass unrecorded, 37 poems. All material previously (as is/was). "The Starving Children" unrecorded and unpublished.; [pers.] Revelat.ons of all our destinies are written—with each passing age, mankind exceeds, excells and history is rewritten by the turning of the page.; [a.] Greenback, TN

BOWLING, ALLISON LAURA
[pen.] Allison Laura Bowling; [b.] November 1, 1981; [p.] Gordon and Adrienne Bowling; [ed.] 9th Grade (Freshman) Randolph Middle School, Charlotte, NC; [occ.] Student; [memb.] Member of Oddovy of the Mind, Explorer's Clubs, Red Cross Club and a member of Morningstar Presbyterian Church; [hon.] Studying voice for 2 yrs., Art Contest Winner, Certified Baby Sitter with Red Cross; [oth. writ.] I enjoy writing poems and short stories for fun.; [pers.] I strive to help others in need. I enjoy working with children with special needs. I would like to be a Special Ed Teacher and I'm going to reach all my goals.; [a.] Matthews, NC

BRADEN, MICHELLE
[b.] June 14, 1956; [p.] Phillip and Hester Rendon; [m.] Lyman Braden, August 3, 1974; [ch.] Linda, Sue, Scott, Andrea and Phillip; [ed.] Eastwood Hills Elementary, Pittman Junior High School, Raytown High School; [occ.] Sales; [oth. writ.] "Me" published in Memories of Tomorrow; [pers.] Without knowing it, my family and friends have inspired my writings.; [a.] Kansas City, MO

BRADLEY, GAYDELL M.
[p.] Matthew and Sabra McDaniel; [m.] August 3, 1963; [ch.] Janice and Jessica Bradley; [ed.] Decatur High School, Decatur, IL; [occ.] Homemaker; [oth. writ.] Several poems presented as gifts, memorials, and read at various functions.; [pers.] My poetry is influenced by daily life experiences, childhood memories, nature and my faith in God.; [a.] Hopewell, VA

BRADY, BETH
[b.] September 4, 1985, Tulsa, OK; [p.] Patti Robertson and Jack Robertson; [ed.] I'm in the 5th grade at Kerr Elementary.; [memb.] I'm a member of the Lewis and Clark Middle School Quarterback Club.; [hon.] I make Honor Roll list sometimes BS (in Math); [pers.] I enjoy cheerleading and playing softball. I'm 11 years old and have a sister and brother.; [a.] Tulsa, OK

BRANNON, DIANNE
[pen.] Dianne Brannon; [b.] December 23, 1956; Hampton, VA; [p.] Maxine and Edward Goode; [m.] David Brannon; February 14, 1984; [ch.] Michelle, Wesley; [ed.] Kings Park High, L.I., N.Y., University of Texas at Arlington; [occ.] Sales person, actress and playwright; [memb.] Alpha Chi Omega Alumni; [oth.writ.] A one-act play, several poems; [pers.] I'm inspired to write poetry by the beauty of everyday life; [a.] Arlington, TX.

BRAUN, DINA
[b.] October 10, 1965, Long Island, NY; [m.] John Braun, September 30, 1989; [ch.] Jessica Lynn, Jonathan Tyler; [ed.] Patchogue-Medford High, Suffolk Community College; [occ.] Bank Teller; [memb.] PTA, Scouting; [pers.] I like to convey deep-seeded emotions. To learn and grow from past experiences.; [a.] Midlothian, VA

BREWER, JUDY
[pen.] Mary Blasser; [b.] July 13, 1979; Hobart, IN; [p.] Laura Childers; [ch.] Judy, Jennifer, Jessica; [ed.] Chesterton High School; [occ.] Ponderosa; [hon.] 2nd place medal for the 300 yds dash - Cross country 1st, 2nd, 3rd place ribbons for running, Trophy for 2nd place - Basketball Tournament; [oth.writ.] I have written several different poems but I have never attempted to go public with any of them; [pers.] This poem is dedicated to my loving sister Dannyelle Joseph. May our love continue to grow stronger and let nothing come between us again; [a.] Valporasio, IN.

BRICCA, ANTHONY J.
[b.] September 29, 1950, San Francisco, CA; [p.] Les and Jo Bricca; [m.] Lynn E. Barnhart, June 21, 1981; [ch.] Kelly Jo and Steven Anthony; [ed.] Redwood High, Continuing for a college degree; [occ.] Sergeant Major, United States Marine Corps Reserve; [memb.] American Legion, VFW, Native Sons of Golden West; [pers.] "To seek, to strive, and not to yield".; [a.] Austin, TX

BRODMANN, JEAN LUCAS
[pen.] Jean L. Brodmann; [b.] June 15, 1934, Kansas City, MO; [p.] Guy D. and Alma Sarah Lucas; [m.] Otto Diedrich Brodmann, November 15, 1952; [ch.] Sarah Diedra; [ed.] Attended Missouri State Teachers College in Warrensburg, MO. (Independence MO Branch), graduated 1975 from Savannah Voc. Tech Nursing School, one year

business school at Sav'd Voc. Tech; [occ.] LPN (Disabled); [memb.] Faith Lutheran Church, Arthritis Foundation; [hon.] Georgia State Student, Gold Award for Nursing Students, Who's Who Among American Vocational and Technical Students 1974-75; [oth. writ.] Ben Mayo (c) WTOC FM radio quoted my poem "Reach Out" on his broadcast with classical music in background. I've written many, many poems since the age of 8 or 9. Much of my poetry has been read at various gatherings. I've also written various short stories. Recently my twin sister and my niece put together a children's book called "Legend of the Snowflakes," one of my poems.; [pers.] My writings have always come from my heart. I have met so many people during my life and some poems are based on people I've actually known and others are poems of people I've brushed shoulders with but somehow they left impressions that I've written down. Others are of places I've seen and many are based on my faith. In fact I consider my writings truly a gift from God.; [a.] Savannah, GA

BROOKS, ANITA
[pen.] Yetta; [b.] Oklahoma; [p.] Easker Brooks, Josephine Brooks; [m.] Leo Okeke; [ed.] Degree in Business; [occ.] Singer, Writer; [oth.writ.] I have a collection of unpublished writings and songs; [a.] Tulsa, OK.

BROWN, ADRIENE D.
[b.] May 28, 1970, Bronx, NY; [p.] Charlotte Brown and Levernis Brown; [ed.] John F. Kennedy H.S., Baruch College, BBA; [occ.] Investor Service Representative (Nuveen) Chase Manhattan Bank; [memb.] American Marketing Association; [pers.] I want my parents and family and friends to know that they are much appreciated.

BROWN, CHESTER
[pen.] Ras Ches; [b.] July 20, 1954, Greenville, NC; [p.] Inez and Chester Brown; [m.] Mrs. Jewel C. Foggie Brown, May 1, 1989; [ch.] Ceresa, Kenyetta, Corrine, Ms. Eboni Ashanti and Niahamu; [ed.] Fleming St. Elementary, C.M. Eppes Jr. High, J.H. Rose High School, University of the District of Columbia; [occ.] Roofing Mechanic; [memb.] American Institute for Transportation and Technology; [hon.] High school and trade school valedictorian; [oth. writ.] Other poetry, plays for stage and screen and phylosophical writings, most are still unpublished.; [pers.] Life is like a garden of flowers, each with its own shape, size, and color, yet they co-exist with each other in perfect family harmony; maybe the human race should take the hint!; [a.] Washington, DC

BROWN, DENISE M.
[b.] October 21, 1970, Bear County, San Antonio; [p.] Terry and Rose James; [m.] Lee Curtis Brown Sr., September 8, 1989; [ch.] Vanessa, Terry, Iva and Lee; [ed.] Aladdin Beauty College; [occ.] Hair Stylist; [hon.] Was a house wife and more married once 9 1/2 years. Diploma for Finishing Cosmetology School. I've played for my kids at there school and they all made a book with a heart for me on it. With all the kids making a pitcher and saying how they would like to write so good.; [oth. writ.] Started writing in 1988 have many more. My writings are from my heart and no other writings are alike my writings are all original and feel that they will be some day for every ones enjoyment to read.; [pers.] When your young be young, find time to learn and just plan be the age you are, because we grow up so fast and wish we were young again. People go so fast these days working is all we do but finding it pays to. Baby's grow up so fast, no time to look back memories never go away, just time how it seems to pass, why are time is worth money there's so many dreams and dreams are good.; [a.] Hurst, TX

BROWN, EDITH D.
[b.] May 4, 1922, Shadyside, OH; [p.] John and Elizabeth Datkulia K.; [m.] Berlin Brown, September 25, 1944; [ch.] John, Robert, Cecil, Ralph, Marvin and Clara; [ed.] Steinersville Elementary School, Powhatan Point, Ohio High School; [occ.] None, I live on social security; [memb.] Walcrest Brethren Church; [hon.] A devoted husband, love and respect from all of our children. Hugs and kisses from all eight grandchildren and five great grand-children smiles and hand shakes from our relatives and friends.; [oth. writ.] Poems on the church bulletin.; [pers.] A good name is rather to be chosen than great riches, and loving favour rather than silver and gold.; [a.] Mansfield, OH

BROWN, GROVER
[b.] October 21, 1971, Cleveland, OH; [p.] George H. Brown, Rosa L. Brown; [ed.] Lincoln-West High, Cleve, OK, B.A. Arts and Science - English Lit. University of Toledo; [occ.] Chrysler Jeep; [memb.] Student Health Advisory Comm. Univ. Toledo, Porthany Baptist Church; [pers.] I was influenced by many other famous black authors/poets . . . Langston Huges, Maya Angelou and Nikki Giovanni.; [a.] Cleveland, OH

BROWN, MOLLY ELIZABETH
[pen.] M.E. Brown; [b.] August 10, 1967, Everett, WA; [p.] Margaret Leighton, Chuck Dean; [m.] Allen David Brown, July 10, 1993; [ed.] Everett High School, Everett Community College; [occ.] Receptionist, University of Washington Medical Center; [memb.] Irish Heritage Club; [oth. writ.] Several poems published in local newspaper.; [pers.] When I was eight, I wrote my first poem. When I was nine, I wrote my autobiography. Since then, I have always wanted to write. Now I am making my dream come true.; [a.] Seattle, WA

BROWN, SCOTT
[b.] March 12, 1948, Virginia, MN; [p.] Joann and John Sheldon Brown; [m.] Sandra (Schwartz) Brown, January 27, 1974; [ch.] Richard Davis and Michael Sheldon; [ed.] Wilcox High, University of California at Davis; [occ.] Public School Teacher; [memb.] NEA/CTA, Cal Alumni Assoc.; [hon.] Phi Beta Kappa; [oth. writ.] Assorted poems and short written pieces; [pers.] It came as quite a surprise . . . that the power pulling galaxies apart would charge for service. I try to pay with poetic observations.; [a.] Davis, CA

BRUNO, PETER
[pers.] Blessed are the meek, for they shall inherit the earth. I would like to thank Christina for her inspiration, for she is the only woman that I will love.; [a.] Miami, FL

BRYANT, QUILEENA
[pen.] Lady Quileena; [b.] April 15, 1953, Brooklyn, NY; [p.] Joseph Bryant and Dolly Bryant; [ch.] Floyd, Jamaal, Earl and Tiayona; [ed.] Abraham Lincoln High School, Medgar Evers College; [occ.] Teacher, Stanley Eugene Clark School, Brooklyn, New York; [memb.] Triumphant Full Gospel Assembly, Boy Scouts of America, Sunday School, 67th Youth Precinct Youth Council, Royal Priesthood Ministry, Drama Society, African Dance Troupe, Summer Youth Camp (counselor); [hon.] UFT - Para/Teacher Award, Good Scouter Trophy, Bible School Award, Grant Award for writing Puppet Proposal, Outstanding Educator Achievement Award; [oth. writ.] Several poems for educational plays and church programs. Some have been used for Black History Women's Month and other Holiday Programs within the Bd. of Education.; [pers.] I want my poetry to touch the souls of my people in a way that would change the negative things in their lives to positive. I want each of the readers to feel that the poem they read is a personal testament of them.; [a.] Brooklyn, NY

BUCKLEY, BELLE
[b.] Tenn.; [p.] Taylor and Aretha Buckley; [ch.] Darryl; [ed.] Douglass High - ICT College; [occ.] Secretary; [oth. writ.] Co-write children's stories, will publish my first book of poetry, "Exposed Emotions," in the near future.; [a.] Los Angeles, CA

BULL, CHRISTINA DIANE
[b.] December 13, 1976, Fort Smith, AR; [p.] Diana and Ricky Bull; [ch.] Stephen Lee Bull; [ed.] Poteau High School, Kiamichi Area Vo-Tech, Carl Albert State College (Degree in Business Administration); [occ.] Carl Albert State College Financial Aid Office (Work-study); [memb.] Phi Theta Kappa—Two Year School Honor Society, and Member of Immaculate Conception Church; [hon.] President and Vice President's Honor Roll at CASC and All-American Scholar Collegiate Award; [oth. writ.] This will be my first published poem.; [pers.] I enjoy writing because I can express my emotions and feelings that I hold deep inside. I write in order to understand my thoughts and relieve stress.; [a.] Poteau, OK

BURGHARD, DEBORAH JOY
[pen.] Debi Joy Burghard; [b.] June 23, Queens, NY; [p.] Joseph and Muriel Cervone; [m.] Raymond, June, 1989; [ch.] Joseph Charles and Brandon Michael; [ed.] A.S. Queensborough Community College Business Admin. - The Institute of Children's Literature.; [occ.] Vice President of Monetary Advancement Int'l, Investment Banking Pan American; [memb.] World Wings International - American Museum of Natural History - The North Suffolk Christian Women's Club; [oth. writ.] Staff writer, "The Beechhurster," Editor, "The Robinhood Gazette."; [pers.] I try to write from the soul, it emits from me an intrinsic feeling of accomplishment and immortality.; [a.] East Setauket, Long Island, NY

BURNS, BRANDY LEIGH
[b.] May 4, 1976, Stanford, CA; [p.] Linda M. Vaca; [ed.] Vanden High graduate, Fairfield, CA, Solano College, Fairfield, Calif.; [occ.] Student; [hon.] Numerous awards in Advanced Choir, Concert Choir, and Show Choir for Best Performance and Most Improved; [pers.] I feel that everything that happens in one's life, happens for the best, although at the time we cannot see it that way or sometimes cannot understand why.; [a.] Vacaville, CA

BURT, COLLIN
[b.] April 25, 1985, Northampton, MA; [p.] Jairus Burt Jr. and Carol Burt; [ed.] Conway Grammar School, grade 6; [occ.] Student; [pers.] I dedicate my poem "Donkey" to my pet donkey, Clarissa, and to my family.; [a.] Conway, MA

BUSH, HEATHER
[b.] November 13, 1982, Pittsburgh; [p.] Mr. William and Mrs. Deborah Bush; [ed.] Carmalt Elementary, Millions Middle School, Brashear High School (9th Grade); [occ.] Student; [memb.] Student Council, Western Pennsylvania Girl Scout Assoc.; [hon.] 7th-8th Grade National Junior Honor Society, Principal's Award; [oth. writ.] Several poems of my own kept in a notebook; [pers.] If I'm bored and I have nothing to do, I find things to write about that interest me.; [a.] Pittsburgh, PA

BUTLER, LAHOMA
[b.] October 18, 1915, Lawrence County, IN; [p.] James A. and Ora E. Hildum; [m.] William Glenn Butler, June 3, 1933; [ch.] 4 daughters; [ed.] High school, I finished the GED test in 1975. I completed 3 years of high school - eloped, but I was a student.; [occ.] Widow at home since March 19, 1993; [memb.] I am a member of the Oolitic Pentecostal Church. Have been and still am the piano player for around 40 years.; [hon.] Was on the Honor Roll in high school. My husband and I were married 59 years and 9 months when he died. We had a wonderful life together with love in our family.; [oth. writ.] I made a high score on GED test; [pers.] My husband was a dedicated man. Everyone who knew him loved him. He was a great soloist. I played piano for him and our daughters sang with him too.; [a.] Springville, IN

CABANA, SHARON
[b.] September 15, 1983, Methuen, MA; [p.] Glenn Cabana and Denise Cabana; [ed.] Currently an eighth grader at West Running Brook Middle School in Derry, NH; [occ.] Student; [memb.] Drama Club, Chorus, active in Religious Education program, Math Club, Student Council; [pers.] All my life I have dreamt of teaching and someday teach through writing - now I truly believe I can.; [a.] Derry, NH

CALDWELL, EARLINE
[b.] March 4, 1932, Miller County, Tuscumbia, MO; [p.] Earl and Mamie Thompson; [m.] Charles Caldwell, May 23, 1952; [ch.] Two sons and three daughters; [ed.] Finished high school 12 yrs, Certified Med Tec. Nurse's Aid; [occ.] Housewife; [hon.] I had a small writing in Cappers on the subject "What I Like About Being a Grandma" and received $50.00.; [oth. writ.] I have other unpublished songs and poems, some written from the Bible in hymn. I have loved poetry all my life. I like to try writing songs and poems.; [pers.] My purpose for wanting to write is to benefit others somehow. Or maybe to lift a burden someone may have.; [a.] Tuscumbia, MO

CALE, MARY
[b.] November 29, 1937, Harrisonburg, VA; [p.] Leta and Claude Berry; [m.] Thomas J. Cale, May 3, 1958; [ch.] Thomas J. Jr., Steven Paul; [ed.] George Washington High, Alexandria, VA, various secretarial courses; [occ.] Executive Secretary, Dept of Defense, U.S. Air Force, Sheppard AFB, TX; [memb.] United Methodist Women, First United Methodist Church, National Notary Association, Executive Secretaries Group; [hon.] 1996 Civilian of the Year, Field Training Group, Sheppard AFB, TX; [oth. writ.] This is a "first" publication. I write for family and friends.; [pers.] My father wrote poetry. I feel I inherited this "gift" of writing from him. I mostly write about the meaningful events in life.; [a.] Wichita Falls, TX

CALLAHAN, JOSIE
[pen.] Jo-C; [b.] August 11, 1980, Pahrump, NE; [ed.] Finishing up my junior year in Mohave High School; [occ.] Student with internship at radio station; [memb.] I am currently involved in speech and debate; [hon.] World Peace Award presented by my teacher during my sophomore year. Most Valuable Attitude at Mohave High nominated at Mohave High. Nominated by teachers and principal.; [oth. writ.] Just poems about the effects of life; nothing fancy.; [pers.] You are introduced into life as a stranger, only you can produce an identity.; [a.] Bullhead City, AZ

CALLAHAN, SUSAN E.
[b.] March 19, 1978, Fort Knox, KY; [p.] Barry and Claudia Callahan; [ed.] High school; [occ.] Business partner with father; [memb.] ATA-American Tae Kwondo Association; [hon.] Who's Who Among American High School Students; [oth. writ.] No other writings published in public, except for in the school literary book.; [pers.] Believe in yourself, trust your heart and listen to your soul.; [a.] Millington, TN

CALVILLO, PATTY
[pen.] Lilian Reuheim; [b.] June 8, 1958, Brazil; [p.] Marisa and Thore Magnus; [m.] Felipe Calvillo, July 20, 1991; [ed.] Literature Bachelor, Faric - Caratinga - Brazil; [occ.] Actress, singer, hostess,

writer and producer; [memb.] "Coolness Show" at Century Communications, Santa Monica, CA.; [hon.] Trophy for Director, Costume Designer and Writer of the adapted plays "Rapunzel" and "L'Iemanja," premiered at the Unique Theater in Los Angeles, CA.; [oth. writ.] "Laybrintus" columnist in "A Voz De Isanhomi," "Every Child is Noble," children's book, several songs for the "Cool Mess" band, "Sispell," script, "Synapsis," book, Best Brazilian Poets, in Calmaria "Shogun Poem, Arte.; [pers.] To God I offer this work.; [a.] West Los Angeles, CA

CAMP, LORI A.
[b.] September 15, 1962, Tampa, FL; [p.] Scott and Betty Hardy; [m.] Huck Camp, March 30, 1996; [ch.] Matt 14, Kelsey 9; [ed.] Opelika High School; [occ.] Sales and Marketing for Laboratory Corp. of America (Lab Corp); [hon.] "President Club Award" eight consecutive years with my company; [oth. writ.] I have written (7) other poems, but have not sent them to anyone.; [pers.] My poetry is inspired through emotions, and my husband, who inspires me every time I see him. My daughter has been an inspiration during a recent illness.; [a.] Hamilton, GA

CAMPBELL, ARDELLA RAE
[pen.] D. C.; [b.] October 5, 1933, West Virginia; [p.] William and Mary Riley; [m.] Jerry C. Campbell Sr., August 2, 1968; [ch.] Cheryl, David and Jerry; [ed.] High school graduate; [occ.] Charity Fund Raising; [oth. writ.] "Lie Low Lie Low," "The Ultimate One"; [pers.] "Jerry with the Laughing Eyes" is a dedication to my beloved son Jerry C. Campbell Jr., who went to God December 2, 1996. I give all the glory to God, for without his divine help, this would not have been possible. This is what I've prayed for.; [a.] Akron, OH

CANVER, BETHANY
[b.] January 28, 1985, Williamsville, NY; [p.] Charles Canver, Renee Canver; [ed.] Edgewood Campus Grade School; [occ.] Student; [memb.] Edgewood Campus Grade School Leadership Council; [hon.] Citizenship Award 1994 and 1995; [oth. writ.] Anthology of Poetry by Young Americans 1994 edition, Anthology of Poetry by Young Americans 1995 edition; [pers.] Writing is the way I express myself, it shows who I am. I write about what I'm feeling or about the world around me.; [a.] Verona, WI

CAP, YVELINE FUNG
[b.] April 7, 1960; Haiti, WI; [p.] Marie Erna Lelievre/ Fung Cap Fung; [m.] Separated; October 1988; [ch.] Jameson P. Gabriel and Melissa Gabriel; [ed.] Two years college degree in year 1982 at EFCTEC (Haiti); [occ.] Service Coordinator at the Prudential Ins. Co.; [memb.] N/A. but, had participated in albums: a) Peace and Love b) Time for Change... and another one soon to be released. All from Michael Ange Bazile; [hon.] A) From GOC (Group Oliver Co) as the best employee, b) From Melodias Romanticas, for service rendered through my talent, c) From Club 60, for service rendered through my talent; [oth.writ.] Several poems in French, Creole and English. Creole and French at a certain time have been published in Ilan-Ilan...A Canadian local magazine. And one time in Haiti Observateur, (Haitian newspaper). Certain of them will be soon used for music; [pers.] My dream in my writing is to leave Unity between us, and enjoy one more time the blessing of my country as a little paradise. I want to thank "God" for inspiring me. Thank my family, specially my children: Jameson and Melissa Gabriel, My mother, my sister Carmel Lafontant, my brother Essud Fung Cap. Thanks to all my dear and true friends... My co-workers at the BKQN Prudential Branch, specially (Jerry Killebrew and Lucille Scatto) whom had lead me to you... My last and special thanks to

these dearest whom had helped me climb the ups and downs to my success: Michel Ange Bazile, Wagner Bellevue, Claire Fortune Ketlie Guillaume, Lourde Moncoeur, Yvonne Marc, Mireille Beauvery and family, junie valbrun, Magalie Gabriel Claude Charles, Yvette Metellus, Rodrigue Plantin and Yvette Dupre. and the kids at Melodias Romanticas; [a.] Brooklyn, NY

CAPITAN, JAMIE
[pen.] Jamie Capitan; [b.] April 19, 1981, Owasso; [p.] Tom Capitan and Mary Kay Smith; [ed.] Sophomore in high school; [occ.] Dog Musher; [memb.] M.U.S.H. Dogsled Club, Melissa Etheridge Fan Club, and the Poet Society at Owosso High School; [oth. writ.] Several poems, but haven't entered them in anything.; [pers.] I look at the simpler things in life and learn to appreciate them.; [a.] Owosso, MI

CAPITO, THERESA
[b.] March 1, 1968, Pontiac, MI; [p.] James and Carolyn Grenke; [m.] Edward Capito, June 6, 1992; [ch.] 2 - Veronica, Nicholas; [ed.] High school graduate from St. Mary's Academy, St. Marys, Kansas; [occ.] Creative Memories Consultant/Artist; [pers.] Life's too short to spend it on adversities.; [a.] Pasadena, TX

CAPLOW, FLOYD DAVID
[pen.] Captain David Freed; [b.] January 19, 1934, Cleveland, OH; [m.] Toni Ross, July 4, 1976; [ch.] Irving, Julie, Randi, Lisa; [ed.] M.S.W.; [occ.] Retiring Social Worker; [memb.] Sanrobles Traveling Nudist Club; [hon.] Second Place: Nat'l Library of Poetry Best Poems of the 90's contest; [oth. writ.] Numerous poems yet to be published, many of which are yet to be read.; [pers.] (From 79 The Point Be Fine:) Mistakes - Could I list 'em. This takes - only to name . . . If not to blame - The whole system: Psychosexual Disequilibrium (Fancy name for "Please, I beg you, gimme some").; [a.] Vacaville, CA

CAPPELLANO, TAMMARA LEE
[b.] July 25, 1958, Vancouver, WN; [p.] Marguerite and Russell Lee; [m.] Orlando Cappellano, July 18, 1992; [ch.] Crystal, Marguerite, Michael; [ed.] H.S. in Portland, Oregon; [occ.] Dispatcher and Trainer for alarm company; [hon.] Apprehension Award for 50 crimes with intruders imprisoned, responsible for National Dispatch Tape for Training or Correct Police Dispatching; [pers.] This poem is dedicated to my lover, friend, husband and soulmate, Orlando Cappellano - for without him there would be no passion in my heart or thrill in my eyes.; [a.] Oakland, CA

CARABALLO, MELVIN HECTOR
[b.] August 22, 1958, Youngstown, OH; [p.] Israel Caraballo, Lydia Burgos; [m.] Linda Rosa Caraballo, August 31, 1981; [ch.] Amica Renee Caraballo, Natira Chandel Caraballo; [ed.] East High School, Adjutant General School, Central Texas College; [occ.] Police Booking/Property Dept., Retired U.S. Army Personel Sergeant; [hon.] 3rd Army Commendation Medal, 3rd Army Achievement Medal, 5th Army Good Conduct Medal; [pers.] Dedicated to our mother on "Mother's Day" 12 May 1996, 21 November 1953 to 7 April 1996.; [a.] Aurora, CO

CARLSON, GREGORY A.
[b.] January 17, 1966, Bristol, CT; [p.] Lanny and Carol Carlson; [occ.] Artist/Poet/Musician, Tattooist, Photographer; [oth. writ.] "The Remnants of a Crowded Picture" (Poetry from the Other Side) '97, "Officially Strange" (Spoken Word) '93, "Salacious Thorns" (Spoken Word) '95; [pers.] Without aesthetic expression we are nothing but clones, looking for life in each other's empty eyes, looking for ourselves in a passerby.; [a.] Bristol, CT

CARLSON, JON
[b.] August 2, 1980, Peoria, IL; [p.] Phil Carlson and Cayte Frye; [ed.] I am currently a junior at Dunlap High School.; [occ.] Student and musician; [oth. writ.] Other poems in a private collection.; [a.] Edelstein, IL

CARLSON, MISS ROBIN ROSE
[pen.] RRC; [b.] December 5, 1950, Galesburg, IL; [ch.] Amanda Rose Garcia/Nicholas Alan Garcia; [ed.] Grade school, Bowlake Elementary, high schools were many.; [occ.] Seeking self employment: Cleaning done by: Robin Rose Carlson; [memb.] Mt. Olive Missionary Baptist Church of Joliet Inc. Support group Thurs. for the abused, P.H.P. Depression Support Group, Silver Cross Hospital Bipolar Support Group, Silver Cross Hospital Lutheran Family Services; [hon.] Graduation from high school, $500,00 sales in Junior Achievement, J/V Cross Country Track, "My personal prayer" accepted! N.L.P.; [oth. writ.] "To My Parents Wherever They Are," "Did You Know?" for others that didn't know, "To My Aunt: I Miss I Love You, That's Sealed with a Kiss," "To my Friend," "Prejudice," "To My Uncle Bobby," "When a Child Screams," "This Poem Is from Someone You Know, in Writing, I've Grown"; [pers.] God is to be in our lives, to help us through, for direction and guidance. He knows best. What happens or has happened in a person's life is not for us to comprehend or understand, we are to be of love, to give, to show, and be a witness of our talents need to be identified, and utilized: not for self gain, but to be pleasing to God! Secrets that are damaging need to be released and utilized. Abuse is a thing that can be repeated, or stopped, love must live.; [a.] Joliet, IL

CARR, TANYA
[b.] February 12, 1981, Washington; [ed.] Evergreen High; [pers.] When I write I put the truth in my writings. All my writings are from the heart.; [a.] Ferndale, WA

CARREIRO, JOSHUA
[pen.] J. C. Lazarus; [b.] May 26, 1977, Fall River, MA; [p.] Lazaro Carreiro, Yvonne Carreiro; [ed.] BMC Durfee High School; [occ.] Currently a Dietary Aide, Sarah S. Brayton Nursing Care Center; [oth. writ.] Other unpublished pieces.; [pers.] It is my great wish to draw out the inner feelings of all who read my writing, opening their minds to new, honest thinking.; [a.] Fall River, MA

CARROLL, CHRISTEN E.
[b.] September 19, 1983, Mansfield, OH; [p.] Harry V. and Direnda J. Carroll; [ed.] 7th grade of Greenspun Junior High in Henderson, NV; [occ.] Student; [pers.] The inspiration for this poem was the sudden death of my sister's dear friend, Amber Lyn Robey. She died in a tragic car accident January 5, 1997. I wrote and then read the poem at Amber's services.; [a.] Henderson, NV

CARTER, CONCETTA
[pen.] Capri; [oth. writ.] I have written several poems and am hoping to have some published in the near future.; [pers.] I believe that poetry is an expression of one's inner being and that there is beauty all around us if we only take the time to look.; [a.] Pennsauken, NJ

CARUSO, JOANNE
[pen.] Joanne Caruso; [b.] November 17, 1941, Boston; [p.] Richard Duffley, Elinor Duffley; [m.] Anthony Caruso, October 12, 1962; [ch.] Anthony, Richard, Stephen and Lisa; [ed.] Cardinal Cushing Central High, Boston City Hospital School of Nursing, Emmanuel College; [occ.] Disabled R.N.; [memb.] Americans Diabetes Assn., Nurse Association; [hon.] Received many awards in high school; [oth. writ.] I have written stories that so

far have been rejected.; [pers.] I seek spirituality in the stress and turmoil that surrounds the world today.; [a.] Weymouth, MA

CARUTHERS, MICHAEL
[pen.] Austin Forrest; [b.] May 31, 1951, Crossville, TN; [p.] Fred T. and Anna-Margaret Caruthers; [m.] Loretta A. (Bice) Caruthers, April 27, 1974; [ch.] Jason Wayne and Jamie Le Ann; [ed.] Cumberland County High School, graduated 1969, Vocational School - 1 year; [occ.] Self-employed; [memb.] 4-H Club 1966 and 4-H Honor Club, Member of Future Farmers of America 1966; [hon.] 4-H Honor Club Award 1966, Editor's Choice Award 1997 National Library of Poetry; [oth. writ.] Faces in a Crowd, Expressions, The Wishing Well.; [pers.] I enjoy writing poetry, it is very relaxing and very entertaining. I am inspired by the early poets, whose poetry touches the soul.; [a.] Keokuk, IA

CARY, PAULA ANN
[pen.] Chicken Little; [b.] November 12, 1980, Plymouth, WI; [p.] Ruth Cary and Dale Cary; [ed.] Elkhart Lake High School; [occ.] Student; [memb.] Spring Valley 4-H Club and International Society of Poets; [hon.] High School Honor Roll, Gold Medal for solo ensemble, Conference Champs, Girls Basketball Manager, and 4-H project award for the arts; [oth. writ.] Other published poems: "Fearless" and "Forever You".; [pers.] I'm influenced by the way of my life. If you have a special talent don't let anything stop you from getting the gold.; [a.] Glenbeulah, WI

CASSELL, DANNY E.
[pen.] D. E. I'Machild; [b.] January 5, 1971, Fayettville, NC; [p.] Dorothy Cassell, Edward J. Cassell; [ed.] Seventy First Elementary School, Fulcan American H.S. (West Germany) apprenticeship (Celinary Division) Art Institute Atlanta; [occ.] Private Duty Nurse; [oth. writ.] Working on a poetry collection (Taste and See); [pers.] If you want to do anything in life, you must do more than want it. You must strive to achieve it. You must pray, be very persistent and have a purpose.; [a.] Atlanta, GA

CASSFORD, RICHARD
[b.] December 26, 1976, Long Beach, CA; [p.] Miriam Keene and Robert Keene; [ed.] Coconino High School, Hobbs High School, West Texas A&M University; [occ.] Student, Scenic Carpenter; [memb.] International Thespian Society, Alpha Psi Omega; [hon.] Best Actor - Hobbs High School 1994, Best Actor - Hobbs Community Players 1995, Branding Iron Theatre Award 1996, Irene Ryan Nomination 1996; [oth. writ.] Several poems and songs, a few short theatrical pieces, book and lyrics for "Casted Off," a musical.; [pers.] I write with talent and inspiration on loan from my Heavenly Father. I attempt, in writing, to reveal to others the truths I have discovered through my own experiences.; [a.] Canyon, TX

CASTRO, MINNIE
[pen.] Minnie Castro; [b.] January 18, 1945, Eastover, SC; [p.] Mr. and Mrs. Henry Greene; [m.] Alberto Castro, March 14, 1964; [ch.] Gilbert, Kenneth, Dwayne; [ed.] Hunter's College undergraduate Bachelor Degree Arts of Science; [occ.] Registered Nurse Private Duties; [memb.] Universal Temple Church of God, B'klyn, NY, Board of Education, Committee, Veteran, American Heart Association; [oth. writ.] Of Women she was Mildest to her kin the Kindest, and most beloved, Keenest for Praise.; [pers.] I like writing poetry that makes mankind pick it up and read it. That touches the soul. I love a good poem or poetry.; [a.] Brooklyn, NY

CATE, LINDA D.
[b.] October 15, 1941, Norwich, NY; [p.] Edward Dempsey and Naomi Dempsey; [m.] Garte Cate, June 4, 1966; [ch.] Susan Lynn and Karen Anne; [ed.] Norwich High School, Robert Packer Hospital School of Nursing; [occ.] Homemaker, Inactivern; [memb.] Robert Packer Hospital School of Nursing Alumni Association; [oth. writ.] Several poems, nothing ever published till now.; [pers.] I love God, my family and friends, people in general, and I love life.; [a.] Norwich, NY

CATRON, JOSHUA RYAN
[b.] September 13, 1982, Somerset, KY; [p.] Timothy and Debora Catron; [ed.] Monticello Independent Schools, 8th grade; [occ.] Student; [a.] Monticello, KY

CATTELL, CHARLOTTE
[pen.] Charli/Chaz; [b.] April 7, 1971, Virginia; [p.] Charo Crouse, Joshua; [m.] Christopher Warn; [ch.] Cleo Morgaine Warn; [ed.] Herndon High - Sarasota School of Natural Healing Arts; [occ.] Bartender, Monterey, California; [oth. writ.] Writing has always been a quiet love for me. This is my first outward expression.; [pers.] I love to express trust in the "mechanics" of the universe, as well as trust and love of your own true self.; [a.] Marina, CA

CERNY, MALLORY LAURA
[b.] October 6, 1985, Norfolk, VA; [p.] Kerry and Patricia Cerny; [ed.] Still enrolled in school. She was in fifth grade (96-97) when "Pizza Toppings" was written.; [occ.] Student at Hampton Oaks Elementary School; [memb.] Mallory is a Junior Girl Scout; [hon.] Mallory had a poem entitled "Tiger" published in a school district publication when in 2nd grade. She won Honorable Mention for a watercolor of Belmont Plantation in an art show. This was in fourth grade.; [a.] Stafford, VA

CHACON, DEBORAH
[pen.] "Mo Duinne"; [b.] February 26, 1970, Tacoma, WA; [ch.] Julieta May and Luisa Marilyn; [ed.] Completed my G.E.D. in 1993. The world and my children continue my education.; [occ.] Student and keeper of my children. Dreamer.; [hon.] Heroism Award given to me my Anderson Is. Fire Dept., 1995; [oth. writ.] Many written but none published as of yet. I have written many songs for friends and family.; [pers.] "Venerability is the time between learning and knowing. Never forget your dreams, for they are the rainbows of life."; [a.] Anderson Island, WA

CHAFFINS, KELLY ANN
[b.] April 17, 1965, New Milford, CT; [p.] John and Josephine Lynn; [m.] Eric Chaffins, February 4, 1994; [ch.] Tiffany Lynn Chaffins; [ed.] New Milford High (Ct), Midlands Technical College (SC), courses in Keyboarding-Photography; [memb.] I'm active in our local Riverbanks Zoo - M. Columbia Museum of Fine Arts; [hon.] Certificate of Achievement: for photography, floral, Community Service - in the school system; [pers.] Harmony sounds nice . . . .; [a.] Gaston, SC

CHAGNON, PAULA
[b.] December 4, 1978, Malden, MA; [p.] Frank Chagnon and Gail Chagnon; [ed.] Arlington Catholic High School; [hon.] Creative Writing Excellence Award; [oth. writ.] Poems and stories published in Arlington Catholic's Literary Magazine; [pers.] This poem is dedicated to the memory of Jody Bucher—March 10, 1977 - September 6, 1996.; [a.] Medford, MA

CHAMBERS-RUTH, BRENDA
[b.] December 28, 1964; camden, SC; [p.] James and Joyce Chambers; [m.] Bobby L. Ruth; June 25, 1994; [ed.] Lugoff-Elgin High School -

Honor Graduate Columbia College; [occ.] Administrative Specialist / Blue Cross / Blue Shield of South Carolina; [memb.] Ephesus United Methodist Church; [hon.] Honor Graduate, 2nd place winner Optimist Oratorical Contestry; [oth.writ.] Several poems written for birthdays, weddings, wedding anniversaries, church-related programs/activities, i.e.; Church Anniversaries, Choir Anniversaries, Mothers Day, Fathers Day. Poem published in "MADD" publication (Music, Arts, Dance, Drama); [pers.] My poetry is divinely inspired. All of my writings deal with "Life ingeneral" and how God promises to never leave nor forsake any of us; God is always there; [a.] Lugoff, SC.

CHANTHAVONG, BOUNPHONE
[pen.] B.C. Ozolinsh/Willow Red; [b.] September 24, 1982, Nakonpanom, Thai.; [p.] Khamsone and Oulayvanh Chanthavong; [ed.] Oconee County Schools K-8 (Watkinsville, GA); [hon.] Presidential Academic Fitness Award, Duke Talent Search, Honor Roll, OCMS Citizenship; [oth. writ.] Several school and national publications for short stories and poetry. One world-wide poem publication. Also working on future books and novels.; [pers.] Mine is the type of beauty that takes a lifetime to realize, that lifetime I will gladly give.; [a.] Bogart, GA

CHAPMAN, DONALD
[b.] March 22, 1955, Bennettsville, SC; [p.] Johnsie Hooker; [ch.] Guyce Hayes; [ed.] Midwood High School, Brooklyn, NY; [occ.] Operator of Patient's Elevator at Harlem Hospital - New York City; [pers.] I believe wholeheartedly that the Creator will make earth a paradise, New York City is a United Nations of people, and truly a writer's inspiration.; [a.] New York, NY

CHAPMAN, JAMES
[b.] June 23, 1946, Cincinnati, OH; [d.] November 12, 1993; [p.] James and Stella Capman; [m.] Rondi Lightmark, August 10, 1985; [ed.] BS in Architecture, University of Cincinnati 1973, [pers.] James Chapman was an architect and an educator who had a deep feeling for nature and loved children.

CHATFIELD, MELISSA
[pen.] Missy; [b.] December 20, 1983, Baltimore, MD; [p.] Donna and Jim; [ed.] Parkville Middle; [occ.] Student; [memb.] Girl Scouts, Art Club, Science Club, "The Believers Club" (secret society among my friends); [hon.] Voted most likely person to be abducted by aliens!; [oth. writ.] "My Life," "You're the Only One," "I'm Over," "Jupiter," "Mom and Dad," "Sunflowers" and "Spring Fever" (all not published); [pers.] Do you believe?; [a.] Baltimore, MD

CHELVAKUMAR, MEENA
[pen.] Meenadchi Chelvakumar; [b.] May 25, 1984; Glendale,CA; [p.] Latha and Kasi Chelvakumar; [ed.] 7th grade; [occ.] student; [hon.] straight A student, Speech contest winner, 1st place in Brains Competition in 6th grade, performed parts in Nut Craker Christmas production, received Smartest and Most likely to Succeed Award in 6th grade; [oth.writ.] write good stories, speeches and articles for school; [pers.] I would really like to win!; [a.] Buena Park, CA.

CHERNEK, LYNN
[pen.] Lynn Chernek; [b.] July 1, 1971, Erie, PA; [p.] Judith and Frank Chernek; [ed.] B.S. Gannon University, Certified Physician Assistant Erie, PA., Employed at State Correctional Facility, Mercer, PA; [occ.] Physician Assistant; [memb.] Pennsylvania Society of Physician Assistants; [hon.] Quill and Scroll 1989, National Honor Society 1989; [oth. writ.] No other published works. This poem is my first and only attempt for

recognition so far.; [pers.] I write for emotional release of the joys and sorrows of life experiences. I have been influenced by religious philosophers and early American literature.; [a.] Fairview, PA

CHISOLM, PATRICK E.
[b.] September 5, 1961, Columbia, SC; [p.] John B. and Rozeller; [m.] Rena S. Chisolm, September 9, 1990; [ch.] Karon John and Josh; [ed.] Criminal Justice (AA); [occ.] Store Manager, Hawthorne Medical; [pers.] I'm just the average cat—everyone is entitled to their own bug—the secret of life is peace, joy and love; it's up to us to spread it as much as possible.; [a.] Gaston, SC

CHMIELOWIEC, JOHN
[b.] August 30, 1982, Toms River; [p.] Deborah Philip Vomero, John Chmielowiec Jr.; [ed.] Current Sparta High School, Eighth Grade; [occ.] Student; [oth. writ.] 100 Word essay in "New Jersey Students' writing about reading"; [pers.] Nobody ever lies, they just realize their own truths. A personal thanks to my inspiration, the girl I love, Christina Tomchik; [a.] Sparta, NJ

CHMIELOWIEC, JOHN
[b.] August 30, 1982, Toms River; [p.] Deborah Philip Vomero, John Chmielowiec Jr.; [ed.] Current Sparta High School, Eighth Grade; [occ.] Student; [oth. writ.] 100 Word essay in "New Jersey Students' writing about reading"; [pers.] Nobody ever lies, they just realize their own truths. A personal thanks to my inspiration, the girl I love, Christina Tomchik; [a.] Sparta, NJ

CHOPELAS, T. J.
[pen.] T. J. Chopelas; [b.] April 20, 1976, Rooseville, CA; [p.] Tony and Kathy Chopelas; [ed.] Bella Vista High School, American River College, California State University Sacramento; [occ.] Server at the Olive Garden Restaurant, Sacramento, CA; [oth. writ.] I have written and produced a collection of 11 songs for my band fellow. I have also written hundreds of poems and songs which have never been published.; [pers.] I want to thank my family for being so supportive of me in all the decisions I've made. Thank you to the girl who gave me the inspiration and experiences to write this poem. Thanks to my best friend and my brother, Sean.; [a.] Fair Oaks, CA

CHRISTENSEN, ELEANOR L.
[b.] November 14, 1914, Chicago, IL; [p.] Fran and Anthony Gawkowski; [m.] Bennett V. Christensen (Deceased), October 24, 1934; [ch.] Eileen; [ed.] Limited formal education; [occ.] Retired; [oth. writ.] I have written hundreds, mostly like the one submitted: "The Great Exchange"; [pers.] The development of my talent was the result of the inspiration of faith in the Lord Jesus Christ.; [a.] Holiday, FL

CHRISTIAN, ETHEL ESTELLE
[pen.] Estelle; [b.] July 14, 1914, Enid, OK; [p.] Elsie and James Caywood; [m.] Jess M. Christian, August 17, 1933; [ch.] Carol, Arla, Kathleena and Phillip; [ed.] Associate in Arts, Grassmont College 1972, Grassmont, California; [occ.] Retired, Wesleyan Methodist; [memb.] Church; [hon.] Only this: I graduated from college with Honors!; [oth. writ.] Two poems published in 1974 by "Vantage": a book called, New Voices in American Poetry.; [pers.] I write for the pure joy of expression! I believe it is a gift from God. I aim for "visual rhythm" to enhance my poetry.; [a.] Lakeside, CA

CHUAN, EUGENIA
[b.] June 26, 1921, Cincinnati, OH; [p.] Dienna and Isadore Sevilla; [m.] Dr. Raymond Chuan, April 23, 1982; [ch.] Mitsei and Kendall Nishimine; [ed.] Western Hills High School (Ohio),

Golden West College (California), Orange Coast College (California), Cal State Long Beach (California); [occ.] Retired; [memb.] Walteria Business Women's Club; [hon.] Students and instructors at FRA's graduation exercises in the L.A. Home Furnishing Mart, Outstanding Work awarded, in the association's course: "The visual Techniques of Interior Design."; [pers.] Ancestors born in Spain, parents born in Turkey, married 28 yrs. to Japanese Designer, married 10 yrs. to Chinese Physicist.; [a.] Hanalei, HI

CINALLI, RYAN
[b.] May 29, 1979, Cleveland; [p.] Ronald and Rose Cinalli; [ed.] Trinity High School, Syracuse University (Summer College), People to People (Marine/Culture Studies); [occ.] Student (Senior); [memb.] Soccer Team, Ski Club, Retreat, Group Leader, and Advanced Choir; [hon.] First and Second Honors throughout high school, Perfect Attendance 4 year award etc., Science-Chemistry Award; [oth. writ.] Various unpublished poems and philosophical dissertations.; [pers.] "Reflect and amplify the universe inwardly and outwardly."; [a.] Maple Heights, OH

CIRRINCIONE, RESA
[b.] January 29, 1960, Monterey, CA; [p.] Ross and Terry Cirrincione; [m.] Stephen Schaffer, June 6, 1996; [ed.] Holy Cross Academy, B.A. Mary Washington College; [occ.] Lead Software Engineer, Research Institute of America; [memb.] International Women's Writing Guild, Oxford Historical Society; [hon.] National Honor Society, Dean's List, Mu Phi Epsilon; [oth. writ.] Poetry, short stories, fiction; [a.] Orford, NH

CLANCY, JIM DOUGLAS
[b.] March 3, 1952, Corpus Christi, TX; [p.] Trace and Harrieta Clancy; [ch.] Tracee Johnson I; [ed.] High School; [occ.] Truck Driver; [oth. writ.] Wiping Away Your Tears (for my Mom), Forever Beautiful And Young, Wishes Do Come True, Believe In Rainbow, The Boys We Loose, The Dark Promise, Forgiven Drugs - Death Of A Soul Still Living, My Calf Texan; [a.] San Jose, CA

CLAPPER, CAROLINE
[b.] January 6, 1964, Detroit, MI; [p.] Carmen and Manfred Grech; [m.] Randel H. Clapper, September 25, 1982; [ch.] Brian, Brandon, Megan; [ed.] BAS - Madonna University; [occ.] Legal Assistant; [memb.] League of Catholic Women, International Rett Syndrome Association; [hon.] Grad with honors; [oth. writ.] Nothing published at this time, presently working on "Meggie"; [pers.] Look beyond the physical.; [a.] Plymouth, MI

CLARK, CHRISTOPHER M.
[b.] November 28, 1974, Elmont, NY; [p.] Elizabeth and Robert Clark; [ed.] Bachelor's Degree in Broadcast Journalism from the University of Miami. Piper High School in Sunrise, Florida; [occ.] Advertising Executive; [hon.] Dean's List, Fraternal Order of Police Scholarship, "Guardian Angel" Award for community service work with abused children; [oth. writ.] UM Newspaper and yearbook, two features for WSVN-Channel 7 in Miami.; [pers.] This is dedicated to a very beautiful young woman. I wish I could give her the world.; [a.] Tamarac, FL

CLARK, CHUCK
[pen.] See See; [b.] December 11, 1961, Jackson, MS; [p.] Ouida Joy Clark and Curtis C. Clark; [ed.] Callaway High, Hinds Jr. College; [occ.] Engelhard Corp. (Chemical Div.); [hon.] First Mississippi "Man of the Year 1987", Mr. "United States Man of the Year 1995"; [oth. writ.] Several poems for various friends and short stories.; [pers.] My writing has to be inspired. It is the inspiration that

creates the substance. Truly a sift from God!; [a.] Brandon, MS

CLARK, JAMES R.
[b.] December 21, 1973, Scottsbluff, NE; [p.] Dr. R. D. and Jamalee Clark; [ed.] Gering High School, Nebraska Wesleyan University, Northwest Missouri State University; [occ.] English Graduate Student; [memb.] S.P.E.B.S.Q.S.A.; [hon.] Sigma Tau Delta, Semi-finalist in International Barbershop Singing Competition; [oth. writ.] Several as yet unpublished short stories.; [pers.] Music, poetry, literature, drama, the fine arts. These are the threads which connect the human spirit through the ages, and make our hectic lives of today worth living.; [a.] Gering, NE

CLARK, MARGARET
[b.] March 13, 1911, Texmo, OK; [p.] Charles W. McCoy and Winnie McCoy (Both Deceased); [m.] John S. Clark Sr. (Deceased), February 20, 1937; [ch.] Carol M. Lemke and John S. Clark (Deceased); [ed.] Graduated from high school in Oakley, KS, 1929, one year college Hays, KS - 1929-30 depression hit. Taught country school 3 years.; [occ.] Retired; [memb.] Have demitted from all of them - Eastern Star, Beauceant, Daughters of the Nile; [oth. writ.] Greeting cards for friends and family with my poems and original arrangement on my computer, also my biography.; [pers.] During my working years I was a retail clerk, a school secretary in San Diego and a Deputy Clerk in Wyoming and in El Cajon Community Court, California.; [a.] Mesa, AZ

CLARK, MARYBETH
[pen.] Kristen Blake; [b.] January 22, 1978, Huntington, NY; [p.] Thomas Clark, Carol Ann Clark; [ed.] St. Philip Neri, St. Anthony's High School, University of Scranton; [memb.] National Honor Society, Spanish Honor Society, Duns Scotus Award, Academic Scholarship to University of Scranton; [pers.] Through my writing I try to encounter my true feelings and present them in a beautiful, unique way which words can only convey.; [a.] Northport, NY

CLARKE, TRISTAN
[b.] 1983, Syracuse, NY; [p.] Cherylin Clarke, Kevin Clarke Sr.; [occ.] 8th grade student at Tenakill Middle School, Closter, N.J.; [oth. writ.] Many poems written at home; [pers.] There is a way of acting and a way of being. Those who act what they are not, are considered what they are not, and the way they are is lost within themselves and those who know them.; [a.] Closter, NJ

CLIFT, HEATHER
[b.] December 19, 1979, Toledo, OH; [p.] David Clift, Pamela Kelley; [ed.] Currently attending new School for the Arts in Scottsdale, AZ; [occ.] Full-time Student, part-time Hostess/Cashier; [pers.] I believe that individuality is the greatest power one can possess. It is the highest form of inspiration.; [a.] Mesa, AZ

COBOS, SUSIE
[b.] December 13, 1915, Laredo, TX; [p.] Both Dead; [m.] Jesus Cobos (Deceased), November 30, 1932; [ch.] Eight, 28 grandchildren, 16 great grandchildren; [ed.] Urbhan Elem., Laredo High School; [oth. writ.] Vietnam Veteran, Published "1990 American Anthology of Southern Poetry," have many unpublished both in English and Spanish.; [pers.] I am 82 years old and have been writing poetry since I can remember. It is my way of expressing my trials and tribulations.; [a.] Laredo, TX

COGHILL, JOHN A.
[b.] September 2, 1930, Kingsville, Ont.; [p.] Allan Coghill, Isobell (McDonald) Coghill; [m.] Joyce

Elaine, August 4, 1951; [ch.] Michael, Cheryl, John, David; [ed.] Graduated from Ryerson Inst,. of Technology in 1953 (Toronto Ont) Electronics; [occ.] Retired - taught Electronics at Fanshawe College for 30 yrs.; [pers.] If man uses his intellect with love, all will be well. If he uses his intellect without love, it could be disastrous.; [a.] London, Ontario, Canada

COLLINS, AARON
[b.] May 14, 1979, Huntsville, TX; [p.] Ron and Jody Collins; [ed.] I am presently a Junior in high school.; [memb.] Bible Quiz, Church, University Interscholastic League, Number Sense, Mathematics, Computer Science, Spelling, Microcomputer Applications, Calculator Applications, NHS, American Scholars; [hon.] Bible Quiz, 5th in nation; [pers.] I am a devoted Christian and believe that anything done without glorifying God is worthless. I thank Him for everything He does for me.; [a.] Bryan, TX

COLLINS, GAIL STEELE
[b.] October 6, 1950, New Orleans, LA; [p.] Elizabeth and Percy Steele; [ch.] Bryan K. Collins; [ed.] G.W. Carver Senior High University of New Orleans; [occ.] Language Arts Teacher; [memb.] Greater Asia Baptist Church, United Teachers of New Orleans, Greater Asia Baptist Church Education Committee; [hon.] Dean's List, summer scholarships to Innsbruck, Austria; [pers.] Thanks to my son, Bryan, who inspired me to write this poem.; [a.] New Orleans, LA

CONATSER, AMANDA JENNIE
[b.] December 14, 1983; Anaheim, CA; [p.] Virgil Conatser, Alice Conatser; [ed.] Walter Elementary School Attending 7th grade at Dale Junior High; [occ.] Student; [hon.] School Honor Roll 4 years in a Roll. Recognized by Michael L. Rosten Creative Writing Committee; [pers.] I am influenced by all lilving things. I like to reflect the natural beauty of the world around me in my writing; [a.] Anaheim, CA.

CONN, ELWOOD JACKSON
[pen.] Woody; [b.] July 16, 1960, Doniphan, MO; [p.] Thom and Hazel Conn; [m.] Jamie; [ch.] Kevin, Jennifer, Juston, Courtney, Brian and Ryan; [occ.] Sub-Contractor; [oth. writ.] Unpublished short stories—currently working on an epic novel—various unpublished poems; [pers.] I am an average fellow with an overactive imagination!; [a.] Grand Junction, CO

CONTRADES, STENET K.
[b.] April 27, 1979, San Jose, CA; [p.] Linda Contrades, Randy Contrades; [ed.] Southaven High School, accepted to University of North Dakota (Grand Forks); [memb.] Drama Club, Foreign Language Alliance, Foreign Language Honor Society, Art Club, Church Assistant Youth Director; [hon.] 3rd Place Poetry Portfolio in Word Quest '96, English Honors Award, Who's Who, National English Merit Award, National Science Merit Award, French Award, All American Scholar; [oth. writ.] Poetry works for school literary magazine, articles for Charger Flash school newspaper, poetry in publication of Word Quest '96; [pers.] Writing helps me express my feelings when I don't want to verbally express them.; [a.] Olive Branch, MS

COOK, CAROLYN GRESHAM
[b.] January 9, 1944, Bernice, LA; [p.] Lewis David and Estelle S. Gresham; [m.] February 21, 1964; [ch.] Andy, Stephanie and Robert Cook; [ed.] Two-year Associate Business Degree, Louisiana Tech University, Rustin, Louisiana; [occ.] Owner-Operator Cook's Seafood, El Dorado, Arkansas; [memb.] Union Grove Baptist Church, Lillie, La., International Society of Poets; [oth. writ.] Several poems published in local

newspapers, American Poetry Society, and National Anthology of High School Poems and the Poetry Guild; [pers.] I have been greatly influenced by my mother and father. I grew up in a home full of music and good books, and a lot of love.; [a.] Lillie, LA

COOK, CHRIS
[b.] August 8, 1980, Indianapolis, IN; [p.] Kathy Cook, Alan Cook; [ed.] Carmel High School; [occ.] Student; [hon.] National Honor Society; [pers.] "Try not. Do, or do not. There is no try." - Yoda; [a.] Carmel, IN

COOPER, LINDA
[b.] April 24, 1942, Winthrop, MA; [p.] Jerome and Doris Moore; [ch.] David; [ed.] Southwest Miami High, Miami-Dade Community College; [occ.] Executive Secretary; [memb.] Chairperson, Family Service Committee, Wayside Baptist Church, Director Family Services, Miami Baptist Assoc., Secretary, Support Staff Council, Miami-Dade; [hon.] Recognition as Woman of the Month at Miami-Dade Com. College; [oth. writ.] Several poems written to make original birthday cards for friends and family; [pers.] The Lord gives us strength and love by which to live, teaching us that we are never alone. I try to put that concept into the poems I create.; [a.] Miami, FL

COPE, THOMAS C.
[b.] September 6, 1953, Marshalltown, IA; [p.] Don and Suzie Cope; [ch.] Alexander and Nicholas; [ed.] BA Oregon State Univ. 1981, MA University of Denver 1989, MA Ohio University 1989; [occ.] ESL Instructor/Faculty/Oregon State Univ.; [memb.] Tesol, Ortesol, NAFSA; [hon.] 1996 Senior Fulbright Lecturer to Timor, Indonesia, 1988 FLAS Fellowship for Indonesian Language, National and International Presenter, focus teaching English to speakers of other languages (Tesol); [oth. writ.] The True Meaning Behind Internationalism, several fields (Tesol) specific writings.; [a.] Albany, OR

CORLEY II, CHARLES L.
[b.] July 15, 1981, Detroit, MI; [p.] Charles and Eva Corley; [ed.] Northern Senior High School; [memb.] D.E.C.A.; [hon.] Anti-Drug Campaign Essay Contest Winner and softball trophies for All-around Player and MVP; [oth. writ.] Other poems, rewrite of Romeo and Juliet and anti-drug story; [pers.] I am a well-rounded person and excel in most sports.; [a.] Detroit, MI

CORNELIUS, RICHARD D.
[b.] November 13, 1919, Billings, MT; [p.] Mr. and Mrs. Fred Cornelius; [m.] Ethel Cornelius, August 17, 1946; [ch.] Dr. Darrell Cornelius, Sheila Pollock, Marie Townsend, Daniel Cornelius and Lois Marshall; [ed.] B.A., Seattle Pacific College Divinity Degree, North Park College Theological Seminary, Chicago, IL; [occ.] Retired Elementary Teacher; [oth. writ.] Two selections in Time Out, a men's devotional book, printed in 1980. I wrote a book of my early life entitled, From the Farm and off to War. Had fifty copies printed for family and relatives.; [pers.] Currently I am writing a book of jokes and funny stories. I have written a number of unpublished poems.; [a.] Simi Valley, CA

CORNWELL, JAMES W.
[pen.] JWC, Wes C.; [b.] April 18, 1979, Nashville, TN; [p.] Lisa A. Cornwell-Collins and Robert W. Cornwell; [ed.] Good Pasture High School; [occ.] Student at Good Pasture High School, Madison, Tennessee; [hon.] Senior Superlative - Most Distinctive, United States Achievement, Academy National Art Award Winner, Member of School V Jazz Band, Concert Band, Honors Band and Marching Band - State Champion and Southeast Regional Champions, Nationally Televised

Choral Performance, Drama Director, Makeup Artist; [oth. writ.] Numerous unpublished songs and unpublished poems; [pers.] "Individuality is the key to live your life to its fullest, don't follow the crowd. Let your imagination run free."; [a.] Madison, TN

COSTELLO, JUDY ANN
[b.] June 23, 1953, Evergreen Park, IL; [p.] Robert F. and Virginia N. Costello; [m.] Herbert C. Doody Jr., October 20, 1990; [ed.] Fox Business College; [occ.] Purchasing Manager F&F Foods, Inc., Chicago, IL; [pers.] This poem was written for my niece, Heather Lynn Costello, for her 4th birthday. I would like to dedicate this in loving memory of Heather Lynn Costello, Born—June 7, 1988, Died—April 14, 1995. We miss her dearly.; [a.] Oak Lawn, IL

COTNER, ROBERT
[b.] November 10, 1935, Ligonier, IN; [p.] Annabelle and Blaine Cotner; [m.] Norma J. Cotner, September 1, 1956; [ch.] Jon A. Cotner, Erin A. Stuedemann; [ed.] HS - Kendallville (IN) HS, BA Taylor University, MA Ball State University, Ph.D. University of MD (ABD); [occ.] Senior Executive, The Salvation Army, Chicago; [hon.] Fulbright Lecturer in English, University of Liberia, 1971-72; [oth. writ.] Editor, Caxtonian, monthly journal of books and literature for The Caxton Club, Survivors (1997); [pers.] I believe in kindness, gentleness, intelligence, and carry these out in devotion to people in word and deed.; [a.] Aurora, IL

COTTER, DAMIEN
[b.] June 7, 1966, Offaly, Ireland; [p.] Partick and Maureen Cotter; [m.] Beth, June 15, 1996; [ch.] St. Brendans Community School, Birr Co., Offaly, Ireland; [ed.] Exterminator; [occ.] Exterminator; [pers.] Always listen to what people say and do, it could be an idea for a poem.; [a.] Melville, NY

CRAGLE, DEBRA
[pen.] Debra A. Pifer; [b.] January 28, 1965, Berwick, PA; [p.] Harwood B. Pifer and Shirley E. Pifer; [m.] Carl C. Cragle Sr., May 23, 1994; [ch.] Crystal L. Cragle and Carley C. Cragle; [ed.] Horticulture Columbia - Mountour A.V.T.S.; [occ.] Housewife; [oth. writ.] 23 Songs (poems) copyrighted; [pers.] I would like to have some of my songs recorded by a major recording artist.; [a.] Beach Haven, PA

CREAGER, SCOTT MICHAEL
[b.] October 22, 1982; Indianapolis, IN; [p.] Karen Weasner-Creager of Indianapolis, India and Michael E. Creager of Elwood, Indiana; [ed.] 8th grade at Ben Davis Jr. High School in Inidianapolis, Indana; [memb.] Charity Tabernacle Church in Indianapolis, Inidana; [oth. writ.] Hopes to do some writing for childrens books someday; [pers.] I enjoy basketball, football, writing, travelling, drawing, and sailing. I would also like to be an Architect. I enjoy sharing time with my older brothers and sister and to my families. I enjoy helping out with all the children; [a.] Indianapolis, IN

CRIST, DEAN
[oth. writ.] "God's Earth" in Tomorrow's Dream publication, "Jesus Christ Our Sin Bearer" in Best Poems of the 90's publication.; [pers.] To God be the glory.

CRISTOBAL, JASON JEREMY
[pen.] Moonwalker; [b.] August 3, 1986, Manila, Philippines; [p.] Jesus and Margarita Cristobal; [ed.] 5th grade Hesperian School, San Lorenzo, CA; [occ.] Student; [memb.] Scholastic Book Club; [hon.] Certificate of Recognition from National Parent's Day Foundation for participation in the essay contest, Certificate of Achievement

for Outstanding Participation and Perfect Attendance in Hesperian School, Honor Roll, 1st and 2nd quarter 5th grade, certificate for having read the most pages (2,340) in his class during the school-wide reading program on March 3-10, 1997; [oth. writ.] Essay entitled "Why America Needs Parents Like Mine" won during the contest sponsored by the National Parent's Day Foundation.; [pers.] Humor is always included in my poems because I want to make the readers laugh.; [a.] San Lorenzo, CA

CROFT, STEVE
[b.] February 13, 1957, Augusta, GA; [p.] Thomas Croft and Evelyn Stout; [ed.] Piper High - Sunrise, FL, Broward Community College, Davie and Pompano Beach, FL, University of Florida, Humboldt State Univ. - Arcata, CA; [occ.] Library Page - Regional Library, Savannah, GA; [pers.] Be thankful for each day, that you gave it your best. Enjoy and love life, and embrace laughter and happiness as much as you can.; [a.] Savannah, GA

CROSS, CHAD
[pen.] Chad Cross; [b.] July 5, 1975, Elkins, WV; [p.] Kenny and Linda Cross; [ed.] Under graduate of Marshall University; [occ.] Student; [oth. writ.] Other poems; [pers.] Believe in God and good things will happen.; [a.] Elkins, WV

CRYSTLE, PHILLIP G.
[pen.] Bailey Titus; [b.] December 13, 1975, Media, PA; [p.] Walter and Beverly Marschlowitz; [ed.] Brandywine High School, University of Delaware; [occ.] Waiter; [memb.] Surfrider Foundation; [oth. writ.] Self-published collection of poetry entitled, "Montage"; [pers.] You will live for a second of earth's life, yet your words will last forever, just write them . . . .; [a.] Wilmington, DE

CUFF, BILL
[b.] July 23, 1992, Milford, CT; [a.] West Haven, CT

CUMMINGS, ULLA
[pen.] Enid St. John; [b.] January 25, 1940, Orange, NJ; [p.] Carroll Williams, Virginia Williams; [m.] Divorced; [ch.] Miles Leslie, Melanie Louise; [ed.] Kean College, Union County College and Caldwell College; [a.] Vauxhall, NJ

CUNDIFF, JASON
[b.] May 13, 1976; Washington, IN; [p.] Jay Cundiff, Charlotte Cundiff; [ed.] Schools Community High School; [occ.] Line Worker-Jasper Plastics; [oth. writ.] Another poem in the book "the Coming of Dawn". Poem published in school newspaper. My poem was roted for the Senior poem; [pers.] Write poems to express my feelings emotions on life and love. "Life Alone" reflects on a break-up of someone I truly love and always will; [a.] Shoals, IN.

CURTIS, DARRYL LYN
[b.] July 25, 1965; Salt Lake City, UT; [p.] Allen Curtis, Sally Curtis; [ed.] Alta High School, C.C.I; [occ.] Construction Supervisor; [oth.writ.] Several Poems not submitted; [pers.] I write about subjects that touch my heart and those of others; [a.] West Jordan, UT.

CUTTER, BARBARA
[pen.] Barbara Britton Cutter; [b.] November 21, New York City, NY; [m.] E. Cutter, September 1980; [ch.] Two children; [ed.] Bronx High School of Science, Bronx Community College, York College; [occ.] Lab Tech; [memb.] HT (SACP) America Society Clinical Pathologists, Nat'l. Society of Histotechnologist; [hon.] Awaiting word from New York Foundation of the Arts on fellowship grant. This may help with publication of first collection of poems.; [oth. writ.] Have written book called "Growing," a collection of

poems written from childhood through adulthood reflecting changes we all go through growing up. Working on second book. Presently looking for a publisher.; [pers.] Some funny, some serious, I write poetry that reflects experiences and situations I hope we all can relate to. Through the years, teachers, family and friends have urged me to try and publish my poems.; [a.] Queens, NY

CZACHOR, LAUREN
[pen.] Lauren Czachor; [b.] February 27, 1979, Chicago, IL; [p.] Ken and Sharon Czachor; [ed.] William Fremd High School; [memb.] Illinois American Pleasure Saddlelored Horse Association (IASHA) ASHA - American Show Horse Association, AHSA - American Horse Show Association; [hon.] IASPHA State Champion; [pers.] I write poetry to emphasize my emotions. I have influenced myself.; [a.] Barrington, IL

DAHLMANN, DEBORAH ANN
[pen.] Deborah Ann Bourgeois and LaNelle Kelley; [b.] April 7, 1958, Baton Rouge, LA; [p.] Dolores E. Boone; [m.] E. J. "Jack" Dahlmann, December 27, 1995; [ch.] Michael Louis Bourgeois and Michelle Elizabeth Bourgeois; [ed.] Tara High School & Spencer College at Baton Rouge, Louisiana; [occ.] Exec. Admin. Asst.; [memb.] Landmark Church; [hon.] Dean's List 4 years; [oth. writ.] Various community papers; [pers.] Here's to Motherhood and all that I didn't appreciate during adolescence when I knew it all!; [a.] Woodstock, GA

DALTON, CONNIE
[b.] April 8, 1942, Galesburg, IL; [p.] Kenneth King, Bessie King; [m.] Wayne Dalton, September 15, 1961; [ch.] Cathy and Jeremy; [ed.] Yates City High School; [occ.] Secretary at United Methodist Church of Elmwood 17 years.; [memb.] UM Church of Elmwood, Lay Speaker of UMC of Elmwood, Finance Committee of UMC of Elmwood, UMC of Elmwood choir member; [pers.] Caring is sharing God's love.; [a.] Elmwood, IL

DAMROTH, TIM
[b.] November 4, 1982, Martha's Vineyard; [p.] David and Mary Jane; [ed.] Fessenden School; [occ.] Student; [a.] Chilmark, MA

DANIELS, ILLIA L.
[b.] October 27, 1932, Pitt County; [p.] Dellena Joyner; [ch.] James Daniels; [ed.] GED; [occ.] Home Health Care Worker; [memb.] Freemount Freewill Baptist Church, Treasurer, Choir Member; [oth. writ.] Collection of thirty poems to be published.; [pers.] It has always been my desire to have my poetry published.; [a.] Washington, NC

DAO, TRUNG
[b.] March 2, 1976, Saigon, Vietnam; [p.] Quan Dao, Anh Tran; [ed.] Loara High School, Anaheim University of California - Irvine; [occ.] Student, Manager of Teletech Paging, Anaheim; [memb.] National Honor Society, California Scholastic Federation, Who's Who among America's High School Students, G.A.T.E. Club - (Gifted and Talented Education), Key Club, Leadership Academy; [hon.] Principal's Honor Roll—Gold, President's Excellence Award, Academic Honors, Golden State Exam—Honors: Geometry and Chemistry; [oth. writ.] Poetry writing is an enjoyable pastime and hobby.; [pers.] From time to time, and rhyme to rhyme, there is an ebullient part in everyone. So it is with knowledge and a love for words would that next poet be recognized.; [a.] Anaheim, CA

DARBY, NORRIS
[b.] August 6, 1969, Orangeburg, SC; [p.] David Darby and Mattie Darby; [ed.] Edisto High School, Orangeburg, Calhoun Technical College, (Degrees) Engineering Graphics and Computer Program-

ming; [occ.] Computer Operator; [hon.] 3rd Place - Computer Application, Phi Beta Lamda State Leadership Conference, Dean's List; [pers.] I have always loved poetry as a way of communicating my feelings and I hope that someday my work can inspire others to reach for their dreams.; [a.] Orangeburg, SC

DARGAN, ALMA D.
[b.] January 17, 1934, Virginia; [p.] Deceased; [m.] Deceased, February 23, 1955; [ch.] Seven; [ed.] High school graduate; [occ.] Senior Companion, Home Health-Aide; [memb.] Calvary Baptized Church; [oth. writ.] I can write "essays" but my favorite is "poetry." I can write "poetry" best, relating to any subject or imagination, fictional or non-fictional.; [pers.] This is my way to testify, as a believer in "God and Jesus Christ," to influence others of the True Living God.; [a.] Baltimore, MD

DASILVA, NICK
[b.] June 19, 1980, Bay Shore, NY; [p.] Bruce and Tina Lamb; [ed.] Tomah High School; [occ.] High School Student/ Musician/ Poet/ Grocery Bagger . . . perhaps a Bard?; [memb.] A local garage band: Man-Goat; [hon.] Honor Roll, 2nd place in the 1996-97 American Legion Americanism Test; [oth. writ.] Several unpublished poems, some song lyrics, and many persuasive essays.; [pers.] When in doubt, revise . . . anything is possible.; [a.] Warrens, WI

DATCHER, LESLIE J.
[b.] August 29, 1976, Baltimore, MD; [p.] J. Adrian Datcher Jr., and Maxine S. Datcher; [ed.] Dunbar High School, University of Maryland at College Park; [occ.] Undergraduate student; [memb.] Golden Key National Honor Society, Alpha Lambda Delta National Honor Society, Mount Pleasant Ministries, Maryland Gospel Choir; [hon.] Phi Alpha Epsilon, Dean's List, UMCP Honors Citation, Benjamin Banneker Scholarship, Golden Key Scholarship; [pers.] I desire to glorify God and edify individuals.; [a.] Baltimore, MD

DAVENPORT, SARAD
[pen.] Buck; [b.] June 30, 1979, Charlottesville, VA; [p.] Lena Davenport, Roland Davenport; [ed.] Charlottesville High School; [occ.] Working in the Omni Restaurant; [memb.] Kappa League Leadership Club, Future Business Leaders of America; [hon.] Presidential Physical Fitness Award, Chemistry Merit Student Award, Biology Merit Student Award, History Merit Student Award; [oth. writ.] Many other writings but only "Plants of the Future" published.; [pers.] People need to dig deep within themselves and look at the harsh reality of this world. The only hope to preserve the future is for the children to obtain the knowledge to somehow save the world.; [a.] Charlottesville, VA

DAVID, JON
[occ.] Musician; [oth. writ.] "Don't Ever Dream," "Eternally Blue," "Lost Days," "Let it Grow," "Opposite Ends of the Spectrum," "Utopia," "Meals in the Nude," "All You'll Need to Know," "She Hasn't Left Me Yet," "Amenya Dreams in Flames," "Lamenting," "Here I Stand," "The August Sun," and "Eighteen."; [pers.] Writing poetry, for me, has not been recreational, it has been a passion and is as necessary as air.; [a.] Hauppauge, NY

DAVIDSON, PREETI R.
[pen.] Preeti; [b.] April 19, 1978, Madras, India; [p.] Mercy and Terence Davidson; [ed.] Freshman at Barnard College, Columbia University, New York; [occ.] Student; [hon.] (1) Creative Writing Prize at Stuyvesant High School, (2) 4th Place runner up in Poetry - Bertelsman World of Expression; [oth. writ.] Compiled a 250 page anthology of poetry and prose of my writings and other

person's works.; [pers.] Writing is my life!; [a.] New York, NY

DAVIS, CARRIE
[pen.] Carrie; [b.] August 7, 1966, Salinas, CA; [p.] Joyce and Jim Davis; [m.] Divorced; [ch.] April Marie and Kathlene Jeanne; [ed.] Lake High School, Garden Grove, CA, Mountain State Tech., Phoenix, AZ; [occ.] Licensed Sales and Single Mother; [hon.] President's Honor List, Director's Honor List; [oth. writ.] The Awakening, Our Children, My Friend, poetry contests and religious hymns; [pers.] My writing reflects my own focus as an energy life force that walks a path to destiny's waiting arms.; [a.] Mesa, AZ

DAVIS, JERRY D.
[pen.] Jerry D. Davis; [b.] September 22, 1942, Morrisvale, WV; [p.] Ermon and Ruby Davis; [m.] Dotte Davis (Deceased), July 31, 1992; [ch.] Brandy Maeker/Gabrielle Davis; [ed.] Scott High School Madison, W.VA., Austin Community College; [occ.] U.S. Air Force (Retired July 1, 1987), Manager, Housing Authority City of Smithville; [memb.] American Legion Veterans of Foreign Wars, Vietnam Veterans Association, AARP/Baptist Church; [hon.] Vietnam Callamby Cross, Vietnam Campaign Medal, Meritorious SVS Medal, Presidential Unit Citation, AF Outstanding Unit Award, RF Commendation Medal (5), AF Good Conduct Medal/AF Training Nat'l Defense Service Medal, Vietnam Service Medal/Professional Military Education, Small Arms Expert, Vietnam Service Medal, Overseas Tour Medal, AF Longevity Medal; [pers.] I want to inspire to the living that we should never forget those that have influenced our lives but are no longer among us, and remember they still live within our hearts.; [a.] Smithville, TX

DAVIS, ROBERT MICHAEL
[b.] October 1, 1949, Ahoskie, NC; [p.] Robert and Elaine Davis; [m.] Naomi Toleta Davis, October 26, 1986; [ch.] Melody Esper and Jessie Davis; [ed.] C.S. Brown High School and Columbia School of Broadcasting; [occ.] Publication Specialist; [pers.] My inspiration does not come from current events or history. I am inspired by the visionary creations of my imagination.; [a.] Norcross, GA

DAVIS, SUSIE L.
[pen.] Suzy Q.; [b.] October 8, 1948, Deerfound, LA; [p.] Louis and Daisy Square Sr.; [m.] Alvin B. Davis Sr., June 29, 1985; [ch.] Kenny, Shunda, Al, Fred and Desiree, Chaneyville; [ed.] H.S. (Zachary), Southern University, Baton Rouge, LA; [occ.] First Grade Teacher at Rosepine Elem., Rosepine, LA; [memb.] Mt. Zion Baptist Church, Lea-Nea; [pers.] I observe the world around me. Saying very little about what I see. I race home—put paper and pen in front of me. This is my "therapy" and a way to let my mind unwind.; [a.] DeRidder, LA

DAWSON, TERESA L.
[b.] October 15, 1948, Kissimmee, FL; [p.] Lois Brooks (Deceased); [ch.] Richard Ala and Tara Lyn; [ed.] St. Cloud High School, Gadsden Jr College, Gadsden, AL, Amer. Paralegal - Paralegal Certificate, several computer related classes completed; [occ.] Office Administrator; [hon.] Beta Sigma Phi, Dean's List; [oth. writ.] Many poems for special people or special occasions written solely from the heart.; [pers.] I have become an avid collector of angel items: books, figurines, etc. They strengthen my faith.; [a.] Grand Rapids, MI

DEANE, ADRIAN R.
[b.] January 5, 1974, Barbados; [p.] Barbara Deane; [ed.] English High School and Boys and Girls High School; [occ.] Security Guard; [memb.] Youth Build

Boston; [oth. writ.] Jigaboo, It's the Joint, My Project Window, Government Tactics, Who Knows Me?, Stranger, Suicide, Roots of My Soul; [pers.] My childhood in New York City inspired me. When alone a lot you pay attention to things often ignored: life, death, fear love and hate, all form the atmosphere which surrounds me.; [a.] Roxbury, MA

DEBORD, DOLORES
[b.] May 27, 1928, Saint Joseph, MO; [p.] Lawrence C. and Beulah F. Nelson; [m.] Ralph L. De Bord (Deceased, January 3, 1992), August 24, 1946; [ch.] Nancy Fay, Ralph C., Phillip G., Richard A. and Patricia Kay; [ed.] Barstow Community College, A.A. and A.S.; [occ.] Retired; [memb.] Foster Parents CA, Landmark Missionary Baptist Church, Barstow, CA; [hon.] Cum Laude, Barstow College, various appreciations; [oth. writ.] Poems and songs including "Steps of the Stairway"; none published.; [pers.] My faith in the Lord, and the faith and love of my family and friends in me.; [a.] Barstow, CA

DEGENER, MARTIN H.
[pen.] Tony; [b.] June 14, 1961, Boston; [p.] Edward and Josephine; [ed.] 3 years - UNM, Certificate in Manufacturing, Associates Degree - Electronics; [occ.] Production, Entrepreneur of small business; [memb.] Distinguished Member International Society of Poets; [hon.] Editor's Choice Award; [oth. writ.] A Walk In The Forest, Oh River Running Wild, Meow Finds A Home; [pers.] Writing is relaxing to the mind. I hope my writings will inspire others as they have inspired me.; [a.] Rio Rancho, NM

DELCOCO, MATTHEW J.
[b.] July 27, 1979, East Stroudsburg, PA; [p.] Eugene DelCoco, Rebecca DelCoco; [pers.] My writings are just my thoughts, emotions, wishes and dreams expressed in the only way I know how.; [a.] East Stroudsburg, PA

DELGADO, ESTELA
[b.] November 7, 1952, Tucuman, Argentina; [p.] Armando Delgado and Cruz Carmen Lezarte de Delgado; [m.] Divorced; [ed.] M.S. in teaching English to speakers of other languages. M.S. in TESOL from Florida International University; [occ.] High School Esol Teacher Dede County Public Schools; [memb.] Flatesol, TESOL; [hon.] For serving the AEGIS Project - Adult Esol Education (Presenter) Florida Writer! School Improvement Plan. Miami Edison Senior High School. Dede County Public School.; [oth. writ.] Unpublished poems and prayers. Working on autobiography.; [pers.] As a humanistic, multicultured educator, my mission is to guide my students with love and respect towards the fulfilment of their own individual potentials providing them with the perspective our youth need to become mature, sensitive adults.; [a.] Miami, FL

DELONG, ROXIE M.
[b.] June 12, 1940, Siloam Springs, AR; [p.] A.C. and Alice Harding; [m.] Kim DeLong, February 14, 1975; [ch.] James R. White Jr.; [ed.] Winfield High School, Winfield, KS; [occ.] Raytheon Aircraft, Wichita, KS; [oth. writ.] I presently have 3 songs with copyright in the Library of Congress, Washington, D.C., also numerous other writings that could be set to music.; [pers.] Writing is great therapy, it's a talent that enables you to express feelings from your innermost self. Although I have not had any great successes from what I do, it's the most rewarding thing I could do for myself.; [a.] Derby, KS

DENNIS, ELEANOR M.
[pers.] She is a daughter of King Jesus.; [a.] New York, NY

DeSHIELDS, JUANITA
[b.] April 12, 1951, Balto., MD; [p.] Charles & Ernestine Diggs; [m.] Febuary 11, 1973; [ch.] Gerald Andre, Eric Damien; [ed.] Northwestern Sr. High, Coppin State College; [occ.] Retired; [memb.] Burning Bush Spiritual Temple - Mother's Board, Board of Directors; [oth. writ.] Working on other poems in addition to short stories and plays; [pers.] I would like to make a difference with my writings. My heroes are Maya Angelou and Toni Morrison; [a.] Balto., MD

DEZALIA, EILEEN
[b.] September 28, 1982, Albany, NY; [p.] Brad Dezalia and Tina Eagle; [ed.] Stissing Mt. Fr. Sr. High School; [oth. writ.] A article about my father was published in a newspaper.; [pers.] Being defeated is often a temporary condition. Giving up is what makes it permanent.; [a.] Pine Plains, NY

DIBENEDETTO, MARIA
[b.] September 14, 1970, Long Island, NY; [p.] Gregory and Isabella DiBenedetto; [ed.] Walt Whitman High School, Villanova University; [occ.] Analyst, New York City, New York; [memb.] Kappa Kappa Gamma National Sorority; [hon.] Magna Cum Laude Graduate, Phi Kappa Phi Honor Society, Dean's List, English Honor Society (Villanova University); [pers.] I strive to touch another with my words.; [a.] New York, NY

DICKENS, TANIKA
[b.] December 15, 1982, New York, NY; [p.] Robin Sanogo; [ed.] St. Helena Commercial High School, 9th grade; [oth. writ.] "Of My Years Living," "This Is for My Guy," "The Truth," "What Happen," "Finally," "Mr. Wrong," "Him and Her," "Lovers" and "What Is Love"; [pers.] I really like writing poems and I would enjoy writing more poems for this contest.; [a.] Bronx, NY

DICKINSON, SUZANNE
[b.] June 11, 1971, NJ; [p.] Eileen and John Bogle; [m.] Donald Dickinson, May 11, 1996; [ed.] Saint Jude's Elem. School, NJ, Paul VI High School, Widener University; [occ.] Teacher/Bartender; [memb.] Phi Sigma, Sigma Sorority Volunteer Association of Widener University; [hon.] Honorable Volunteer at Widener University; [pers.] The world would be such a friendly place if we all wore name tags.; [a.] Sewell, NJ

DIECK, C. W.
[pen.] Will Degan; [b.] March 18, 1978, Livingston, NJ; [p.] Craig Dieck and Viola Dieck; [ed.] Lacey Twsp HS, York College of PA; [occ.] Student; [memb.] The Planetary Society; [oth. writ.] Numerous unpublished poems and a play; [pers.] I believe every human has equal capacity for good and evil. It is by our choices in life that we determine what path we follow. I've dedicated my life to the goodness of nature, but my curiosity leads me to take glimpses into the darker side of the human soul.; [a.] Canton, MI

DIEHL, CYNTHIA M.
[b.] May 7, 1965, Smithtown, NY; [p.] George and Emilie Diehl; [ed.] Hauppauge High, Suny at Stony Brook; [occ.] Human Resources Administrator; [memb.] Diakonia; [pers.] Thanks to my family and friends, without your encouragement I couldn't share this great accomplishment with you.; [a.] Smithtown, NY

DINH, NHUNG
[pen.] Laura Dinh; [b.] January 10, 1984, Austin, TX; [p.] Savannah Nguyen; [ed.] Currently a 7th grade student; [occ.] Student; [memb.] Jr. ATODA Club, "Best Friends," Sholes M.S. Choir; [pers.] I love writing poetry because it is fun and it makes me happy. I dedicate this poem to all my teachers that help me.; [a.] Milwaukee, WI

DIVAS, L. ARMANDO
[pen.] Oscar Miron, Onda Mar; [b.] February 1, 1926, Guatemala City; [p.] Martin Divas, Natividad Carleto de Divas; [m.] Twice divorced; [ch.] Dr. Ellen Webb, 4 grandchildren, Richard L. Divas, 2 grandchildren; [ed.] B.A. in Philosophy, Maryville College, Maryville, Tenn, 1952, Master of Theology, Princeton Theological Seminary, Princeton, N.J., 1962; [occ.] Retired Presbyterian Minister recycled as real estate agent; [memb.] Denver Presbytery Realty Executives International, Treasurer Denver Community Re-investment Alliance; [hon.] First prize - Alexander oratorical contest (college). Plaque for outstanding service to cuban immigrants stationed in for macoy, Wis. by the synod of takes and preries, numerous certificates of recognition by community past organizations; [oth. writ.] A collection of unpublished sermons—I'm Mexico City (1957-61), collaboration with a magazine called "Verdad" (Truth) dealt with religious, political and social issues. I have a dozen or so poems both in English and Spanish that may see the light one of these days.; [pers.] Harsh realism has replaced youthful idealism. Stretching the imagination and creativity I hope in future work to use images to amplify and expose what I see as good as well as evil.; [a.] Denver, CO

DODGE, DAVE
[b.] December 31, 1959, Jersey City; [p.] Edward and Annie Dodge; [ch.] Jackie, Michael, David, Brett; [ed.] Finished high school; [occ.] Self-Employed ABC—Always Better Cleaning—Maint.; [oth. writ.] Several poems; [pers.] I enjoy writing poems for friends who need a poem for their loved ones.; [a.] Piscataway, NJ

DOLAN, HOLLY
[b.] March 27, 1980, Stirling, NJ; [p.] Judy and Thomas Dolan; [ed.] Junior at Sabino High School; [occ.] Student; [hon.] Honor Society - freshman year, Honor Roll 3 years; [oth. writ.] Poem published by Random House, poem published by Sparrowgrass; [pers.] "The time you enjoy wasting is not wasted time." - Bertrand Russele. Life is puzzling even to the simplest people, take the time to live happily and exist honorably.; [a.] Tucson, AZ

DONLAVEY, C. RICHARD
[pen.] R. Donlavey; [b.] September 7, 1948, Richmond, VA; [p.] Phyllis and Junie (W.C) Donlavey Jr; [m.] Sandy M. Donlavey, June 28, 1996; [ch.] Ashley Donlavey, Brent and Zach Harper; [ed.] Southwood College, Old Dominion Univ., V.C.U.; [occ.] Consultant, Writer, Father, Husband; [memb.] Asbury Methodist Church; [hon.] Nascar Winston Cup 1984 World Pit Crew Champion with Jr. Donlavey #90 Winston Cup Team; [oth. writ.] Various poems and many song lyrics.; [pers.] God rewards those that give something back, so in life, be a giver.; [a.] Chesterfield, VA

DONLEY, JAN
[pen.] Jan Leigh; [b.] August 25, 1949, Columbus, IN; [p.] Barbara and Donald; [ch.] Michael age (30), Alex (18), Nick (16), Megan (13), Erin (13); [ed.] BA Univ. of Cincinnati, M. Ed. Xavier University (Cinti. OH), Ph.D Candidate, The Union Institute (Cinti. Ohio); [occ.] Education Consultant (Leadership and Curriculum), Asst. Director, Cincinnati State College; [memb.] ASCD (Assoc. for Supervision and Curriculum Development), Trinity Lutheran Church (Mt. Healthy, Ohio), Ohio Career Education Association; [hon.] Honor Citation by Ohio American Cancer Society for Program in Education entitled "Breast Cancer, What if it Happens to Me?"; [oth. writ.] Avid journal writer since 1982, newsletter editor; [pers.] The essence of life

can be experienced most abundantly in the process of transferring our innermost desires and thoughts to paper through the joys and habits of writing.; [a.] Cincinnati, OH

DONOFRIO, ANDREW
[b.] September 11, 1977, Queens, NY; [p.] Neil Donofrio, Alison Donofrio; [ed.] Walt Whitman High School, currently enrolled at St. Mary's College of Maryland; [occ.] Full-time student; [oth. writ.] Various poems and short writings; [pers.] This poem is dedicated to my beloved, Felecia. Without her, I would be nothing.; [a.] Huntington Station, NY

DOUB, YVONNE RENEE
[pen.] Yvonne Renee Doub or Y. Renee Doub; [b.] August 13, 1970, Ranson, WV; [p.] Marvin and Marlene Kelley; [m.] Shawn Phillip Doub, September 29, 1990; [ch.] Christian Anthony Doub; [ed.] North Hagerstown High School, Washington County Career Studies Center; [occ.] Hairstylist, Sagittarius Hair Designs, Hagerstown, Maryland; [hon.] Who's Who Among American High School Students; [oth. writ.] Other poems, all unpublished; [pers.] My writing would not be possible if not for those who inspire it: my family, my friends and my Savior, Jesus Christ. Thank you all.; [a.] Hagerstown, MD

DUBOIS, DENIS P.
[b.] December 27, 1941, Saratoga Springs, NY; [p.] Blanche and Wallace; [m.] Kay Stewart; [ch.] Nicole and Paul; [ed.] High school - Bkg Night School (AIB); [occ.] Semi-retired - former Intl Bkr.; [memb.] Knights of Columbus; [oth. writ.] Dawing of Mid-Life, Evolution of Life: The Beginning (many unpublished poems).; [pers.] I write about life, good and bad. I intend to publish a book of Poems by 1998.; [a.] San Francisco, CA

DULANEY, KARENANN
[b.] August 23, 1944, Detroit, MI; [p.] Rev. Willie Griggs and Louise Griggs; [m.] Eugene Dulaney, January 10, 1966; [ch.] Eugene, Michelle, Stefanie and Brian; [ed.] University of Detroit Mercy, Wayne County Community College; [occ.] Medical Secretary Olsten Medical Services, Southfield, MI; [memb.] Literacy Volunteers of America; [oth. writ.] I wrote a human interest article for the school newsletter. Also, I designed a newspaper and wrote articles during my internship; [pers.] "I would encourage others to enhance their lifestyle through knowledge because the beginning of knowledge is wisdom."; [a.] Southfield, MI

DULAUX, ADDIE
[b.] March 13, 1947, Winnipeg, Man., Canada; [p.] Mary and Menzo Claude Loucks; [ch.] Liana Jennings and Dan Sutherland; [ed.] St. Norbert Collegiate, Reiki Master - 3rd Degree Certified Metaphysical Teacher, Certified: Financial Manager, Information Systems Mngr, Administrative Mngr, Human Resource Mngr.; [occ.] Travel Manager and Corporate Executive Assistant, Human Resources; [hon.] Corporate Spirit Award; [pers.] Unconditional Love! Imagine this scene: each one of us focused on striving to live our lives filled with unconditional love for ourselves and all living cells. The result? Wow! We would be One with all and it would be unquestionably the most spectacular, the most sparkling and pure gem of our incredible universe. Imagine and this will manifest! Each one of us is so empowered!; [a.] Siesta Key, FL

DUNN, DIANA M.
[b.] January 16, 1944, Portsmouth, OH; [p.] Sam and Bonnie Johnson; [m.] Gordon E. Dunn, November 7, 1995; [ch.] Tammy Leach, Bobbi Hodge; [ed.] Graduate Jackson High School, Class of 1962; [occ.] Office Manager/Bookkeeper; [memb.] Dis-

abled American Veterans Auxiliary, Church of Christ in Christian Union Church; [oth. writ.] Several chidlren's stories, several poems published in local newspaper, poem published in 1997 Poetic Voices of America; [pers.] My writings are for my 6 grandchildren so I may leave a part of me behind that will hopefully help them in times of need.; [a.] Jackson, OH

DUPREE JR., RODGER
[b.] August 16, 1972; Queens New York; [p.] Rodger Ellis Du Pree (deceased) and La Venne Parham Du Pree; [ed.] Graduate Hillcrest H.S. Queens NY 1990: Queensboro College NY; [occ.] Customer Service Rep at Time Wanner Cable NYC; [hon.] Decca Club award for Citywide Business Orientated Competition; Awarded six month grant to study business adminstration through the Walt Disney Program, Orlando, FL; [oth.writ.] Writes own comedy; material has performed standup comedy at numerous venues and events; [pers.] "Animals are the best teachers of survival, and humans are the worst students"; [a.] Ozone Pk, NY.

DURHAM, VIDA
[b.] June 9, 1932, Weymouth, MA; [m.] Alfred Durham, June 28, 1976; [ch.] David M. Drew and Eric W. Drew, Joyce Cronin; [ed.] Whiteman High, Cape Cod School of Nursing; [occ.] Homemaker; [memb.] Paddle Wheel Steam Boatin' Society of America, National Children's Cancer Society; [oth. writ.] Poem published in school newspaper; [pers.] Like to write on a variety of subjects, especially nature's wonders.; [a.] Farmington, ME

DZHANASHVILI, NATASHA
[pen.] C.K.; [b.] November 15, 1983, Tbilisi, Georgia (Former USSR); [p.] Mzia and Alex Dzhanashvili; [ed.] Literate in three languages, Pikesville Middle School, Baltimore MD; [occ.] 8th grade student; [memb.] Greenspring Tennis Raquet Club; [hon.] Principal's Honor Rolls; [oth. writ.] "Maybe" will be published by Iliad Press in "Sensations"; [pers.] Was I the one who never knew that a limit to good is a dream come true.; [a.] Baltimore, MD

EAKINS, PHYLLIS
[b.] August 18, 1929, Lapeer, MI; [p.] William and Julia Dill; [m.] Roy L. Eakins, February 18, 1984; [ch.] James Francis, Paul David, Mary Lynn, Jo Ann, Glenn Matthew, Julia Katherine; [ed.] Shepherd High School, Michigan State Continuing Ed.; [occ.] Retired; [memb.] AFSCME Retired - Amazing Grace Fellowship; [oth. writ.] Articles for church paper; [pers.] I strive to reflect the goodness of God. The Blessing's that are ours are free gifts for the taking.; [a.] Cincinnati, OH

EARGLE, LIZZI
[b.] March 30, 1982, Newberry, SC; [p.] Mr. and Mrs. Dale Eargle; [ed.] Current Freshman at Newberry High School; [memb.] Newberry High School Concert Choir, Southeastern Stomper Clogging Association, Faith Lutheran Church Youth, Woodmen of the World; [hon.] United States Achievement Academy - 1996, All-American Scholar - 1996.; [a.] Newberry, SC

EASON, OLA
[b.] June 26, 1954; Newark, NJ; [p.] Samuel and Ethel Eason; [m.] The late Willie E. Fordham; February 15, 1986; [ch.] Lucy, Danny, Jeanette, Tharon, Danniele and Mecca; [ed.] Essex County College (Bus), Evangelical Bible Institute 8 yrs. seminary- Masters in Religious Education; [occ] Foster Mother, Professional Clown, Pastor, Fellowship Ministries Assoc.; [memb.] Memorial West Presbyterian Church -Bd of Session - NAACP Nat'l Black Presbyterian Caucus; [hon.] Poetry Award graduating class of 1972-South Side High School

Nwk. Best Cook Award some year; [oth.writ.] Theme for 1972 HS yearbook. Several poems entered and won contest. Write poems for special occasions, birthdays, anniversaries etc.; [pers.] Each one should teach one using the ability and potential that was given us by our creator; [a.] Lakewood, NJ.

EASTMAN, ROBERT N.
[b.] April 10, 1943, Mount Vernon, OH; [p.] Kathryn N. Eastman and Robert L. Eastman; [m.] Jackie F. Eastman, November 23, 1973; [ch.] Alex F. Eastman and Sarah Eastman; [ed.] B.S. Journalism, M.A. Communication and Theatre, M.A. American Literature, Ph.D. Administration of Higher Education; [occ.] Chair, Dept. of Mass Communication, Professor, Stillman College, Tuscaloosa, AL; [memb.] Kappa Delta Pi - National Honorary in Education, Alpha Epsilon Rho - National Honorary in Radio/TV; [hon.] Bronze Medal - International Radio Festival, Certificate of Merit - International Radio Festival, Certificate of Merit Gabriel Awards, Gold Medal - Freedom's Foundation, Certificate of Merit - Southern Education Communication Assn.; [oth. writ.] All unpublished poems, "June Boy," "Whim-Whom Whimsey," "Rounds," "Blackout," "Adventure."; [pers.] A poem is never finished.; [a.] Pelham, AL

EATON, CHELSEY
[b.] November 21, 1983; [p.] Greg and Joni Eaton; [oth. writ.] I have written many short story's, and a few other poems.; [pers.] I dedicate this poem, "Sunlight", to my grandma Janet Gaswint, I love you with all my heart!; [a.] Snohomish, WA

ECKERT, LINDA
[pen.] L. L. Wade; [b.] Oberlin, KS; [p.] Alfred and Minnie Wade; [ch.] Gary Dean Orr Jr., Jade Orr; [ed.] Decatur Community High-RS, Nurse Aide - Cosmetologist College NB, Jay's Trucking School - Modeling Study of Chemotherapy and Alopecia; [occ.] Care Giver; [hon.] Insurance Training, Most Spirited - Barbizon Modeling Top Honors - Cosmetology College, Learning Disability Children; [pers.] Truth and Honesty are my #1 ways in Life. Also the Love of the Lord Jesus Christ.; [a.] Phoenix, AZ

EDENS, JANET K.
[b.] June 10, 1955, Hoodriver, OR; [p.] Late Kenneth Ball, Pauline Robinson; [m.] Larry Edens, July 19, 1974; [ch.] David, Jared, Nancy, Daniel, Anna, Late Michael, and Late Joshua; [ed.] Graduated Commerce High School, Commerce, Okla, 1974; [occ.] Homemaker; [memb.] Lighthouse Baptist Church Awana Club; [hon.] Parent Volunteer at Faith Christian School, Eagle Award for parent volunteer at Emporia Elementary School; [oth. writ.] Several short stories, two plays, several poems just shared with family and friends.; [pers.] Jesus says they shall know we are Christians by our love. That's what I'm striving for. If I've put a bright spot in someone's day or made them think, I'm happy.; [a.] Newberry, SC

EDWARDS, ELISSA
[pen.] Lisa; [b.] November 14, 1968, New York, NY; [p.] Dorothy Smith; [ch.] Michael A. Edwards Jr. and Gregory M. Frierson; [ed.] Jane Addams Vocational High School, Drake Business School; [occ.] Secretary; [hon.] Valedictorian of Drake Business School graduation; [pers.] Never forget where you came from, one day you may have to go back. Also, I wish the world love and peace.; [a.] Bronx, NY

EDWARDS, STEPHANIE
[pen.] SAE; [b.] September, 1971, California; [p.] Jessie Brock and Donald Brock; [ed.] University of Phoenix; [oth. writ.] I have several writings but this will be the first time that my work has been published anywhere.; [pers.] Writing poetry is a passion, an art and a great way to express all of your secret inhabitions.; [a.] Rialto, CA

EGOLF, KATIE
[b.] June 30, 1981; Youngstown, OH; [p.] James Egolf, Georgia Egolf; [ed.] South Range School; [occ.] Student; [memb.] Drama Club, Academic Challenge, Key Club, Panda, Youth Ministries; [hon.] Various Academic and Art Awards; [pers.] "Our greatest glory consists not in never falling, but in rising every time we fall." Oliver Goldsmith; [a.] North Lima, OH.

EHLY, PAUL EUGENE
[b.] August 8, 1914, Concordia, KS; [p.] August Michael and Lucy Victoria Ehly; [m.] Esther Rebecca Bentley Ehly, May 21, 1937; [ch.] Linda Rae Whitney and Victor Ehly; [ed.] Enid High, Phillips University, BA, MA, BD, DD, University of Edinburgh, Scotland, University of Tubingen, Germany; [occ.] Retired Minister, Christian Church (Disciples of Christ); [memb.] Christian Church (Disciples of Christ), Broadway Christian Church Christian Concerns Department, IMPACT of Missouri; [hon.] Errett Newby Award in New Testament, Phillips University, Legion of Honor, Order of DeMolay; [oth. writ.] Several poems published in Lenoir Community News, evangelistic sermons published by National Evangelistic Association of Disciples of Christ, articles in Front Rank Youth Magazine, book reviews in The Disciple; [pers.] I try to express optimism and humor in my writing, as well as promote appreciation of nature and its conservation.; [a.] Columbia, MO

ELFIKI, SHAREEF
[b.] August 27, 1982, Saint Louis, MO; [p.] Dee Elfiki; [ed.] K-8 McKinley Classical Junior Academy Middle School; [occ.] Student; [memb.] Ethical Society of St. Louis; [hon.] Honor Roll, Second place in Mississippi Valley Poetry Contest; [oth. writ.] A large collection of unpublished poetry, an unfinished novel, several essays and short stories.; [pers.] If you don't live a little, you'll never live a lot. My writing is greatly influenced by Adam Duritz, the greatest poet ever.; [a.] Chesterfield, MO

ELLARD JR., PATRICK
[b.] May 30, 1980, Boston, MA; [ed.] Dedham High School, Dedham, MA, Grades 9-11; [occ.] Student; [memb.] National Honor Society, Peer Leadership, Varsity Cross-Country, Varsity Indoor Track (Team Captain), Varsity Baseball; [hon.] Boston Fire Department Scholarship Award 1994, Delegate for Oddfellows and Rebekahs United Nations Pilgrimage for Youth, Cross-Country Bay State Conference All-Star, member of 1996 Class D Distance Medley State Champion Relay Team, 1996 Dedham Rotary Club Cross-Country M.V.P.; [oth. writ.] News articles published in The Dedham Mirror, several unpublished poems and essays; [pers.] Life is a long race, if you run poorly for a few laps, don't dwell on them, just keep running. Poems dedicated to RS, TD, SL, VB, JR, JD, MW, SP, MM, CA, AF, NB, MP and EB.; [a.] Dedham, MA

ELMS, CASSANDRA
[b.] March 28, 1976, Wabasha, MN; [p.] Kenneth and Judy Hielscher; [pers.] Writing takes you on a path of discovery, it allows you to live a life of imaginative creations that can be all your own.; [a.] Red Wing, MN

ENGLE, JESSICA
[pen.] Jessica Engle; [b.] Jessica Engle; [b.] November 14, 1984; San Francisco, CA; [p.] Susan Truax, Kevin Engel, Dennis Truax; [ed.] Bancroft Elementary, Oak, Groe Middle School, G.A.T. E. program; [memb.] National Scholarship Foundation, Layfayette Orinda, Presbiterian Church Youth group Advanced Chorus; [hon.] Young Authors Award, President Educatin Award, National Scholarship Award, 6 Consecutive Pricipal Award in two years; [oth.writ.] "Tanchi, the Brave Warrior", "Lighter Little Please" in district wide poem book Imagine This; [pers.] You are never too young to dream and it is never too late or early to believe in yourself and make your work of art. Never lose hope; [a.] Walnut Creek, CA.

ENGLISH, ELTON
[b.] May 10, 1925, Searcy, AR; [p.] Mr. and Mrs. A. J. English; [m.] Mary A. English, February 12, 1944; [ch.] LaWana Stone and Lareece English; [ed.] Freed-Hardeman College, Harding College, and Blackstone School of Law; [occ.] Minister Church of Christ; [memb.] White County Creative Writers; [oth. writ.] Church bulletins, radio programs, sermons and articles.; [pers.] I want to exemplify a strong faith and a living hope. I have received inspiration from the poetical books of the Bible.; [a.] Searcy, AR

ERICKSON, LISA RENEE
[pen.] Lisa; [b.] July 8, 1967, Marshall, MO; [p.] William L. Erickson and Susan A. Garrett; [m.] John C. Tichenor, August 21, 1996; [ch.] Nicholas J. Elsea; [ed.] 11th grade G.E.D. Marshall High School, 1/2 yr. Missouri Valley College; [occ.] Disabled; [memb.] Henry County Writers Guild; [hon.] 1988 and 1989 Golden Poet, 1988 and 1989 Honorable Mention, 1989 inducted into The Poetry Castle Hall of Fame in Sacramento, Calif.; [oth. writ.] Book: The Fourth Voice, written by Lisa - yet to be published.; [pers.] Earliest influence: Close to me yet no shadow, before me the greatest and light. Oh my Dearest God! My Savior.; [a.] Marshall, MO

ERSKINE JR., TIMOTHY JOSEPH
[pen.] T.J.E.; [b.] November 8, 1980, Battle Creek, MI; [p.] Callie Lykins and Timothy Erskine Sr.; [ed.] Currently attending Gull Lake High School, 10th grade; [oth. writ.] All unpublished: "They Invented the Earth," "Inside a Dream," "In Death, Brings Unwanted Belief," "The Forgotten Rose," "Deep in the Weeds," "The Dark Comedy," "No Sorrow for Fate," "A Piece of Mind," and many, many more.; [pers.] We still haven't found the key to the Golden Kingdom in the clouds. Only a bond between peace and mankind will get us through the doors.; [a.] Battle Creek, MI

ESANNASON, DEBORAH
[b.] March 23, 1963, Bronx, NY; [p.] Miriam Rogers; [a.] Bronx, NY

ESPOSITO, MARY GRACE
[pen.] Mary Grace Esposito; [b.] May 15, 1956, Hollis Queens, NYC; [p.] Ralph Esposito, Marilyn Phillips; [m.] Divorced; [ed.] West Babylon High School, LI, NY; [occ.] Art Model, Housekeeper, volunteer work - route coordinator for Meals on Wheels; [memb.] Sacred Heart Church, Ladies Guild, Cor. Sec. in Ladies Guild; [hon.] 9 Editor's Choice Awards from National Library of Poetry; [oth. writ.] Other anthologies from National Library of Poetry, 3 poems at Methodist place where I live.; [pers.] Do good and it will come back to you.; [a.] Tampa, FL

ETZEL, AMANDA L.
[b.] November 30, 1982, Butler, PA; [p.] Louis and Roxanne Etzel; [ed.] Butler Catholic School; [memb.] Vice-President of Butler Catholic Student Council, Head of Butler Catholic Service Committee; [hon.] A poem published in "A Celebration of PA's Young Poets 1995."; [a.] Butler, PA

EVERLING, JACK E.
[b.] July 23, 1927, Bozeman, MT; [p.] Benedict, Florence - Deceased; [m.] Virginia (Deceased), December 3, 1952; [ch.] Michael; [ed.] 4 yr. BA Political Science and International Relations, 30 yrs. US Naval Aviator; [occ.] Real Estate Sales; [memb.] Rotary, various military; [hon.] Various military; [oth. writ.] Non-published poetry; [pers.] Poetry says more, faster and more intently than prose.; [a.] Coventry, RI

EWING, EVELYN JANE
[b.] April 19, 1961, Houston, MO; [p.] Jewel Dean and Carolyn Marie Wilson; [m.] David Ewing, May 6, 1989; [ed.] Graduate of Licking High School, Licking, MO. 35 hours completed at University of Missouri, Columbia, MO.; [occ.] Sewing Specialist and Instructor; [pers.] Writing is a great tool for survival.; [a.] Saint Louis, MO

FADELLI, NINA L.
[b.] April 10, 1965, Berkeley, CA; [p.] Andy and Patti Fadelli; [ed.] St. Mary's College, B.A. in Communications; [occ.] Graphic Artist; [memb.] Acorn Branch, Children's Hospital Oakland; [pers.] Writing for me is a journey, one that is influenced by those whose paths I cross.; [a.] El Cerrito, CA

FARNAM SR., JAMES
[pen.] J. Michael; [b.] July 5, 1961, West Palm Beach, FL; [p.] Jim Farnam and Linda Farnam; [m.] Teresa S. Farnam, February 14, 1981; [ch.] James Jr. and Melissa Rae; [ed.] Doyline High School. State Certified Class II in Water Treatment, Distribution and Production; [occ.] Maintenance Mech at Sisters of Charity, Schumpert Medical Center; [memb.] Fire District #3, Board of Directors (2 years), Volunteer Fireman (4 years), Summer Youth, Boy's Baseball Coach (5 years); [oth. writ.] Other poems, none ever submitted for publishing.; [pers.] I try to let my soul speak through life's trials, errors and accomplishments. Influenced by E.A. Poe, Wordsworth, Shakespeare, Twain and Whitman.; [a.] Dayline, LA

FAULKNER, BETHANY
[b.] March 30, 1980, Stockton, CA; [p.] Curtis and Linda Faulkner; [ed.] Manteca High School; [occ.] Student; [memb.] Member of the Church of Jesus Christ of Latter Day Saints. Varsity Softball Squad; [oth. writ.] Write for my campus newspaper. Many of my writings have been published.; [pers.] I enjoy writing about things that occur in my life. I would like others to realize that it's just not happening to them, but we all go through it.; [a.] Manteca, CA

FEATHERS, CATHERINE
[pen.] Sunshine; [b.] November 22, 1952, Darby, PA; [p.] Sarah H. Byrne; [ed.] Collingdale High School, Adelphia Business School; [memb.] International Society of Poets; [hon.] Editor's Choice Award for poems "Jesus in My Heart and Soul" in Tapestry of Thoughts, "True Love" in Moonlight and Wishes, "Trusting Jesus" in The Color of Thought, "Wisdom from Above" in The Best Poems of the 90's.; [oth. writ.] "On Stage" in In Dappled Sunlight, "Vision of Love" in Through the Looking Glass, "God's Autograph" in A Lasting Mirage, "Compassion" in Etches in Time "Prisoner of Love" in A Moment to Reflect and "Compassion and the Battle of Jesus and the Christians" in the Quill Books.; [perss.] All my inspirations and Good works come by Jesus. Thank you, Jesus.; [a.] Clifton Heights, PA

FEILER, PAULA DIANE
[pen.] Paul Feiler; [b.] July 10, 1956, Louisville, KY; [ch.] Jonathan, Ben, Danny and David; [ed.] Mercer University, B.A.; Princeton Seminary, Harvard Law School J.D.; [occ.] Attorney; [oth. writ.] Many unpublished poems and several short stories.; [pers.] I have been greatly influenced by Christian Mysticism. My writings seek to explore the "Mystery" as it is revealed in all people, religions, creatures and things.; [a.] Houston, TX

FEISTEL, VERA A.
[b.] April 10, 1981, Denver, CO; [p.] Lester and Vera M. Feistel; [ed.] Evergreen Senior High; [occ.] Currently Sophomore at Evergreen High; [memb.] Key Club, National Honor Society, Bethlehem Lutheran Church, French Club, Art Club, Science Olympiad; [hon.] Eighth Grade Valedictorian, Presidential Academic Achievement Award, First Place Poetry Interpretation at RMLSD Speech Meet, Semi-finalist in Colorado Spelling Bee; [oth. writ.] First publication.; [pers.] I believe poetry is an experience into emotion. It needs to be felt to succeed.; [a.] Evergreen, CO

FELDMAN, JACK ALLISON
[pen.] Jack A. Feldman; [b.] December 19, 1923, Amsterdam, NY; [p.] Leon Feldman and Anna Esther Olender Feldman; [m.] Margaret Waldman Feldman (Deceased), July 19, 1946; [ch.] Robert Louis and Diane Lynn; [ed.] High school and valedictorian of Electronics, Naval Air Apprentice School 1948-1952 (7588 hours), also taught math in school of study; [occ.] Retired from 35 1/2 years with Naval Air Station, Electric Engineering Tech., set-up Electronic Standards (World-Wide); [memb.] "Senior Engineering Technician" with "Institute for Certification of Engineering Technicians" by "National Society of Professional Engineers," Member of "Jewish War Veterans of America," Medic in Word War II, Platoon 7, Battalion D; [hon.] World War II, two Battle Stars, Asiatic Pacific Ribbon, American Area Ribbon, Philippine Liberation Ribbon, "Honorable Discharge," Navy. While working in Electronic Standards Laboratory, I won several money awards for inventions in calibrating electronic standards in electronics all over the world as well as the United States.; [oth. writ.] As Senior in Wilbur H. Lynch High School, Amsterdam, New York, I won First Prize in City, and Honorable Mention for State of New York and a certification for an essay titled, "How the Spanish American War Helped to Influence Our Present Latin American Policy."; [pers.] I was inspired in poetry by Robert Frost, Bliss Carmen, Henry Wadsworth Longfellow, William Shakespeare, Virgil and Homer (greek poetry). Inspired by my deceased wife, Margaret Alice Waldman Feldman, by my present wife, Shirley Elaine Gray Wachtler Feldman, and her friends as well as my friends.; [a.] Norfolk, VA

FELIX, MICHELLE LYNN
[b.] July 9, 1978, Shawnee Mission, KS; [p.] Cindy and John Felix; [ed.] Graduation from Mary D. Bradford in June 1996. Plan on attending U.W. Parkside to study in psychology, music, and English.; [occ.] Cashier at Truesdell Mini Mart; [hon.] Kiwanis Award for Music, and Who's Who of American High School Students—two years in a row; [oth. writ.] Men of Freedom, A Perfect Love So Lost, I'm Me, I Love You, A Heartless Child, Where Would I Be, My Inspiration, Open Arms, Apologies, Innocent Violence; [pers.] In 18 years I have learned that life isn't about money or success. It's about being happy, finding love, and enjoying each day, not knowing if it's your last.; [a.] Kenosha, WI

FENNEMORE, ALICIA S.
[pen.] Alicia Sara Ann; [b.] January 24, 1986, Glendale, AZ; [p.] Ron and Kathy Fennemore; [ed.] Currently attending Park Meadows School, Grade 5; [occ.] Student; [hon.] School Principal's List, Honor Roll and athletic awards; [pers.] I am 11 years old, I love writing poetry and singing. I want to become a singer.; [a.] Phoenix, AZ

FERRELL, DAVID L.
[b.] November 14, 1952, Clarksburg, WV; [p.] Helen Taylor; [ch.] David Lee, Stacie Marie, Lori Beth; [ed.] Doddridge County High School; [occ.] Truck Driver; [memb.] American Legion, Moose; [oth. writ.] Other poem titles: "Sad to Be Lonely," "Guiding Light," "The Gift of Love" and "While You Were Sleeping"; [pers.] I find great peace and tranquility in writing poems. I have written many poems inspired by my family and friends, especially the person referred to as Cinderella in "Lucky Seven".; [a.] Waldorf, MD

FIELDS, PAUL ANTHONY
[pen.] Paul A. Fields; [b.] October 1, 1958, Pensacola, FL; [p.] Charlie V. Fields Sr., Jessie M. Fields; [ed.] 12th Grade Escambia County Florida Homebound Tutoring Program; [occ.] Freelance Writer.; [hon.] I have won seven poetry awards including the Golden Poet Award for 1989, 1990 and 1991 from The World of Poetry. I also won the Editor's Choice Award for 1997 from The N.L.O.P.; [oth. writ.] I've been published ten times in books and newspapers. I've been published in two books by The N.L.O.P. in 1991 and 1997. I have a novel and a book of poetry I want to have published.; [pers.] I want to be the kind of writer that will make you smile, laugh and cry, but most of all I want to make you stop and think. I've been writing for 24 years. All of my writings are for sale.; [a.] Pensacola, FL

FIGUEROA, JULIAN
[b.] June 6, 1974, Paramount, CA; [p.] Linda Gollette; [ed.] Lyle Egan High; [occ.] Tutor; [memb.] Acjachemem-nation, Redtail Lodge; [oth. writ.] Poem accepted for future publication in a magazine called "Native California," poem published in a book called "Phoenix".; [pers.] "No matter what happens within a day, the sun continues to rise, so, so shall you . . . .."; [a.] Hawaiian Gardens, CA

FINKEL, JOEL
[b.] New York City; [occ.] New York City Elementary School Teacher; [pers.] I have been a New York City Public School Teacher for approximately 29 years. If you read carefully you will find my biography in my poetry that has been published by the National Library.; [a.] Brooklyn, NY

FISH, DOROTHY L.
[b.] September 12, 1908, Picationica, IL; [p.] Leland A. and Edna May Fiske; [m.] December 3, 1923; [ch.] Raymond A. and James A. Barnett; [ed.] High school—2 yrs. before marriage, 2 after; [occ.] Retired; [pers.] I never entered a contest before this poem was written in 1961— "Thoughts of My Spiritual Mother," I so wanted to be like her.; [a.] West Sedona, AZ

FISHBAINE, ED
[m.] Linda Kotz, 1979; [ch.] Four; [ed.] Ph.D. Psychology; [occ.] Psychologist; [a.] Forest Hills, NY

FISHER, CHAD R.
[pen.] Chad R. Fisher; [b.] June 23, 1981, Sandusky, OH; [p.] Debra Fisher, Jeff Fisher; [ed.] Bay Area Christian Academy (from grades K-8), Sandusky High School (from grades 9-12); [memb.] Northcoast Christian Center; [oth. writ.] None of my other writings have been published, however a few titles of poems that had too many lines to enter in the contest are: "Words That Wound," "Time," "Had We Only," "Believed," "The Gift Inside," "Shadow" etc.; [pers.] I have been greatly influenced by my faith in Jesus Christ. I strive to accomplish in my writings a greater depth of knowledge and understanding, which enables the reader to ascend to a higher level

by looking within himself to fully comprehend the content of the poetry, therefore setting for himself no limitations."; [a.] Sandusky, OH

FLANIGAN, TAMMY
[b.] November 19, 1971, Aransas Pass, TX; [p.] Buster and Linda Flanigan; [ed.] High school; [memb.] The International Society of Poetry; [hon.] Award for Outstanding Achievement in Poetry by the National Library of Poetry, the Editor's Choice Award; [oth. writ.] I have seven poems published in different poetry books.; [pers.] This poem is dedicated to the loving memory of my beautiful mother; she was everything to me.; [a.] Aransas Pass, TX

FLEETIN, WILLIE B.
[b.] December 9, 1927, Wetumpka, AL; [p.] Hattie M. Jackson Fleetin; [ed.] Bachelor of Science Degree in Elem. Ed.; [occ.] Retired Teacher; [memb.] N.E.A., A.E.A., O.E.S. No. 230, Fairfield AL, Metropolitan A.M.E. Zion Church, B'ham, Ala.; [oth. writ.] I have compiled 60 poems in a book entitled, "Spoken Words of God". Sample titles - 1. Enduring Faith, 2. The Wedding Vows, and 3. Envy.; [a.] Birmingham, AL

FLISSINGER, MARK
[b.] May 17, 1975, Inglewood, CA; [p.] Elsa and Eric Flissinger; [ed.] Hawthorne High, El Camino College, and a miserable life; [occ.] Data Control Lead for EDS; [oth. writ.] "Diva" which was unjustly misspelled by the National Library of Poetry. "Passing Moments" which I believe was one of my worst.; [pers.] The greatest inspirations come from our emotions, anger, love, grief, calmness and pain. My personal inspiration grows from pain.; [a.] Hawthorne, CA

FLORES, SAMUEL M.
[pen.] "Sam"; [b.] May 22, 1957, Chicago; [p.] Maria E. Flores and Felix E. Flores; [m.] Bertha Flores, December 15, 1990; [ed.] John Spry Elementary, Harrison High U of Campus, McDonalds Hamburge University, Notary Public, INS Certified "FPA"; [occ.] Owner "Servicios Flores"; [pers.] There is no better Law than Justice, there is no better justice than reason.; [a.] Chicago, IL

FLORETTA, AMY
[pen.] Flo; [b.] September 13, 1978; St. Louis, MO; [p.] Ettore and Rita Floretta; [ed.] High School, Nerinx Hall High School, College, Maryville University of St. Louis; [occ.] Student-Studio Art Major; [memb.] Musl Newsletter, Art Club, Life Club; [hon.] High School, First and Second Honors Award, Who's Who among American High School students, Art Award. College, Dean's List Art Award; [oth.writ.] Concert Reviews for Maryville University's Newsletter, (Musl); [pers.] Good oral hygfiene is important. Remember to floss daily; [a.] St. Louis, MO

FOELL, DELPHIA
[b.] August 25, 1918, Plymouth, IA; [p.] John Mullen and Flossie; [m.] Francis Foell, February 3, 1937; [ch.] Three; [ed.] 8th grade, Adult Sunday School Teacher nearly 40 years; [occ.] Widow, once was farm wife; [memb.] Body of Christ; [hon.] Many Blue Ribbons at North Iowa Fair; [oth. writ.] "Christmas Story" a tribute to "Those Daring Young Men." "This is a poem honoring airmen from the Wright Bros. to the Space Shuttle."; [a.] Rockwell, IN

FORD, TRENA ONEAL
[pen.] Trena Oneal; [b.] November 14, 1957, Chanute, KS; [p.] Leonard and Ruby Oneal; [m.] Donald Ford, February 26, 1995; [ch.] Martin, Miguel, Sarah, Jason, Douglas, Felicia, Samantha; [hon.] Being Mrs. Don Ford; [oth.

writ.] Don't Cry for Me, Tried and Convicted, I'm Afraid You'll See Me Naked, You Done Me Wrong, Low Down Uncle, Sugar Blues, Where the Hell Is You Been; [pers.] Life is a song.; [a.] Wichita, KS

FORNICOLA, PAUL L.
[pen.] Paul Louis; [b.] April 16, 1942, Bronx, NY; [p.] Paul and Amelia Fornicola; [m.] Mary Louise, May 18, 1963; [ch.] Michele, Cindy, Paul and Ted; [ed.] High school Diploma; [occ.] Owner of an insulation and dry wall business; [memb.] N. J. Shore Builders Association, Walls and Ceiling Industry; [oth. writ.] Various other poems not yet published; [pers.] I try to capture the feelings that existed and do exist in poignant moments of my life. To re-read it helps to bring back those feelings.; [a.] Wall, NJ

FORSELL, JOHN R.
[b.] August 24, 1925, Plains, PA; [p.] Enair Forsell, Clara Forsell; [m.] Alice A. Forsell, October 10, 1947; [ch.] Virginia, John, Richard, Kenneth; [ed.] 2 yrs. at Ursinus College and Wilkes University. NCO Academy 1961, numerous technical schools throughout my Navy and U.S. Air Force careers.; [occ.] U.S. Air Force and Postal Service Retiree; [memb.] Combat Aircrew-VP211 Association, Association of Air Force Missilers, ICBM—Minuteman Missile, Disabled American Veterans, American Postal Workers Union, U.S. Navy Memorial Foundation; [hon.] "Military Achievement Award" NCO Academy-1961. Air Force Outstanding Unit Award, Combat Air crew Wings and "Strategic Air Command Missilers Badge"; [oth. writ.] "The Sundown of a Dream, Wyoming Valley-2001." Poetry: "The Trial," "The Computer Operators Dilemma," "If Wishes Were Horses, Beggars Ride," "The Resume," "1929," and "Aunt Marion".; [pers.] I believe in writing as I see things happening with a flair for a vivid imagination.; [a.] Wilkes-Barre, PA

FOSTER, WARREN LOUIS
[b.] May 31, 1956; [occ.] Banker; [memb.] Global Network for Spiritual Success - Deepak Chopra; [oth. writ.] Dreams of a Child, Rain on the River, Village of New Hope, New York in the Rain; [pers.] A man kneeling, vision of a feeling, a thought in time, words on a line, a poet's rhyme.

FOUCAULT, MARY
[b.] March 23, 1951, Everett; [p.] Deceased; [ch.] Chas; [ed.] High school; [memb.] Lifetime member of Song Writers Club of America, Member of The Humane Society of the United States; [hon.] Hollywood Song Jubilee, NCA Records, Jeff Roberts Publishing Company and The National Library of Poetry; [oth. writ.] I've had other poems published in The Advocate Perkerwood, The Acorn Eagle's Flight, Nomad's Choir, Peregrine Silver Wings, Chimera, plus more, I have also sold a few.; [pers.] Hopefully my poems will bring happiness and inner peace to those who read them.; [a.] Seattle, WA

FOX, MATTHEW
[b.] June 30, 1951, Corpus Christi, TX; [p.] Wayland Fox and Ruth Fox; [m.] Lynda Carter Fox, February 1, 1997; [ch.] Ryan Matthew, William Travis and Nyl Torrey; [ed.] Beaumont High, Houston Community College; [occ.] Manager of Audio/Video publishing; [hon.] Men's Council at the Houston Area, Boy Scouts of America (Adult Leader), URBAN Harvest (Community Garden Prog.), Spring Branch Community Garden Coalition, Volunteer Shadows Elem. School - garden; [oth. writh.] Several poems published in local newsletters.; [pers.] The work of the poet is two-fold: 1. To help people connect with their inner life, 2. To go ahead of culture and come back and report the direction being taken.; [a.] Houston, TX

FRANCE, LINCOLN E.
[pen.] (Linc) France; [b.] January 30, 1921, Lewistown, MT; [p.] Fred and Stella France; [m.] Ruth France, June 18, 1947; [ch.] Five; [ed.] 9 years; [occ.] Retired; [memb.] 5 years City Council of Columbia Falls, President North Valley Sr. Citizens, 2 terms, 27 years Auto Mechanic, 4 yrs., Member of Pipe Fitter Union, 5 years; [hon.] 5 years Nominee for Senior Citizen of the Year, Certificate to Preserve Social Security and Medicare, one honor is my beautiful wife Ruth. There is not another like her.; [oth. writ.] Letters to editor of local weekly news, "Hungry Horse News," also articles in the Montana Senior Support Book that is printed and published statewide every year.; [pers.] I think there should be more interest in what goes on from day to day in our country. We need more people to do all of these things.; [a.] Columbia Falls, MT

FRANZINO, ANGELA
[b.] February 17, 1987, New York; [p.] Debra Franzino and Michael Franzino; [ed.] Howell Road School, Fourth Grade Student Top of the Class.; [occ.] Student; [hon.] Have been studying ballet, tap and jazz for 7 years. Was selected in 1995-1996 to appear in The Nutcracker as a mouse and angel in Eglevsky ballet at the Tilles Center in C.W. Post College. Has been active in Girl Scouts for the past 5 years. Presently studies the clarinet.; [a.] Elmont, NY

FRASER, HAZEL
[p.] Edward Emmanuel, Ellen Elizabeth; [ch.] Meisha, Michael, Mark; [ed.] Brooklyn Jewish Hospital, School of Radiology, Borough of Manhattan Community College; [memb.] American Registry of X-Ray Technologists, ARCC - Acts Redeeming Christian Center Women's Committee; [hon.] Phi Beta Kappa, Dean's List, Radiologic Technologist Award; [pers.] It is not what a man looks like that determines who he/she is, but what comes from the heart of man. My greatest influence is the Bible and also writings by Kahlil Gibran.; [a.] Brooklyn, NY

FRAZIER, MEGHAN K.
[b.] October 1, 1980, Ocean Spring, MS; [p.] David and Peggy Frazier; [ed.] Will begin 11th grade at Pascagoula High School in August, 1996; [occ.] Student; [memb.] Beta Club, National Honor Society, Key Club, Juniorettes; [hon.] Student Council Officer; [a.] Pascagoula, MS

FREIBERG, BEVERLY
[b.] April 1, 1959, Los Angeles, CA; [ed.] Bachelor of Science, California State University San Diego, Condoria University; [occ.] Teacher; [oth. writ.] Golden Dreams: An anthology of modern poetry 1994, best new poems - 1995.

FRENCH, SUSANN
[b.] July 7, 1948, Elk City, OK; [p.] Leo and Oneta Quigley; [m.] Divorced; [ch.] Aaron Christopher Soupiset; [ed.] High School - Elkhart, KS School of Hairdressing - Liberal, KS, Real Estate - Wichita, KS; [occ.] Hairdresser; [memb.] Roman Catholic, P.E.O. Sisterhood; [oth. writ.] Writing since 1982 - recorded in personal journal - nothing published.; [pers.] Life itself is a dream ... always moving into the unknown. Capture the positive ... learn from the negative. Think happy ... bless everyone with a smile.; [a.] Wichita, KS

FREY, TIMOTHY PHILLIP
[pen.] Timothy Phillip Frey; [b.] March 24, 1980, Greenville, NC; [p.] Rebecca and Peter Frey; [ed.] Elementary and jr. high school in Argentina. Currently studying for the GED High School Equivalency Diploma, Ft. Lauderdale, Florida; [hon.] Nominee Employee of the Month, March, 1997, Riverside Hotel, Ft. Lauderdale,

Florida; [pers.] My exposure to South American literature has shown me the importance of expressing human emotions through words.; [a.] Fort Lauderdale, FL

FRITZ, JOACHIM HEINZ ERICH
[pen.] Colonel Klink, CK; [b.] May 18, 1963, Heidelberg, Germany; [p.] Late Hans-Joachim Reinhilde Fritz (Deceased); [m.] Gracelyn Fritz (Divorced, 1997), July 6, 1993; [ed.] Johannes-Kepler Middle School, German Airforce (Marksman-medal, gold) trained, Chef, eight years in USA; [occ.] Chef, Carpenter-Framer, Evangelist, Jordan Chapel-Mayport; [oth. writ.] "One Life Is Not like Another," not published yet.; [pers.] How can you carry holy-water from one place another, if you don't know how to join your fingers and unite them as "One." You have no right to dictate your Life, but every right to be an inspiration.; [a.] Jacksonville, FL

FROLLI, ROBERT J.
[b.] August 17, 1960, Pomona, CA; [m.] Pamela A. Frolli; [ch.] Elizabeth A. Frolli; [oth. writ.] Beyond the rhyme for any reason. A book of odds and ends.; [pers.] To Pamela and Elizabeth. I'll love you both forever. And thanks to John, Mark, Cammilla, Marci, Andrea and Chris. This is one crazy life!

FRY, PHYLLIS ROBERTSON
[b.] March 29, 1924, Indiana; [p.] Lionel and Zella Spoonmore Robertson; [m.] Ray W. Fry (Deceased), May 17, 1942; [ch.] Susan, Dennis, Laurie, Jeff and Todd; [ed.] Marshall Twp. H.S., Art 7 yrs., (Private Teacher) Elective courses at Bedford College Center and Indiana University; [occ.] Retired; [memb.] American Business Women, Art Association, Altrusa International, Omega Nu Tau Sorority, Mt. Pleasant Christian Church; [hon.] Juried Art Shows, Women of the Year, National Sorority Pres. (4 yrs.); [oth. writ.] Poetry published in local newspaper, monthly church articles, articles for local newspapers. I worked for "The Courier Tribune," Bloomington, IN.; [pers.] I strive to reflect a home-spun philosophy, write about local happenings and things I have experienced. Some of my writings reflect my religious training and personal philosophy.; [a.] Springville, IN

FRY, ROBERT L.
[b.] May 7, 1950, Lima, OH; [p.] Edward and Arabell Fry; [m.] Terry Lynn Fry; [ch.] Robert, Bonnie and Andrea; [ed.] 1968 Delphos Jefferson High School, 1979 Midwestern College BRE, 1996 Midwestern College Dr; [occ.] Minister; [memb.] Church of God, Anderson Convention; [oth. writ.] Book: Sure Foundations. Poems: The Ocean, Alone, Absence, The Tongue, Don't Cry.; [pers.] Phil. 1:21, for to me to live is Christ and to die is gain.; [a.] Toledo, OH

GAGLIARDI, CORINNE
[b.] August 17, 1973, Washington, DC; [p.] Giuseppe and Africa; [ed.] George Mason University, National Institute of Children's Literature; [pers.] Writing expresses the dimensions where the mind has travelled. There is so much to say when destinations are endless. The discoveries inspire.; [a.] Vienna, VA

GAINES, SARA A.
[b.] June 4, 1987, Kansas City; [p.] Jeff and Nancy Gaines; [ed.] Fox Hill Elementary School; [occ.] Student; [memb.] Fox Trotters, and "Jumprope for Heart"; [oth. writ.] The Challenge, My Best Friend II, Happy Dog, Hearts, Clothing, Sea Adventure, School's Out, and Deep.; [pers.] "Choose an author as you choose a friend," -Wentworth Dillon (1633-1685).; [a.] Kansas City, MO

GALLOGLY, MICHAEL P.
[b.] November 5, 1978, Athens, GA; [p.] James and Janice; [ed.] Houston High School, Germantown, TN; [occ.] Student; [hon.] University of Memphis Wordsmith Award for Art; [oth. writ.] Political Cartoons published in high school paper, several poems published in school's literary magazine.; [a.] Germantown, TN

GAMBINO, RUTH
[b.] Washington, DC; [m.] Anthony Gambino; [ch.] Marina, Anthony Scott, Carollynn; [ed.] B.A. Magna Cum Laude with Honors in Education, M.S. in Education; [occ.] Teacher; [memb.] Who's Who Among Students in American Universities and Colleges, Kappa Delta Pi; [oth. writ.] Several short stories and many poems (most unpublished).; [pers.] Being a wife, mother and teacher takes most of my time. I write when I'm happy, sad or all alone. My writings are based on my experiences, beliefs and about people I know. For me, writing poetry is putting words to my thoughts and innermost feelings, then putting those feelings and thoughts on paper to look at and think about at another time. Poetry is an enjoyable way to share with others.; [a.] Brooklyn, NY

GARCIA, GEORGINA M.
[pen.] G. M. Bruce; [b.] August 18, 1967, Athens, GA; [p.] Clodualdo Garcia and Catherine Garcia; [ed.] South Windsor High, Eastern Connecticut State University; [occ.] Registrar - Office of Family Concerns - Catholic Archdiocese of Atlanta; [hon.] Sigma Delta PI, Dean's List; [oth. writ.] Dimensions Literary Magazine, Eastern Connecticut State University.; [pers.] Let go and let God.; [a.] Alpharetta, GA

GARDNER, MAUREEN E.
[b.] May 4, 1951, Ossining, NY; [p.] Deceased; [ch.] Harold and Eleanor; [occ.] Works for Data Comm. Services, Inc.; [memb.] Cest. Service Rep.; [oth. writ.] Several unpublished poems.

GARDNER, SISTINE
[pen.] S.L.G.; [b.] July 28, 1961, Detroit; [p.] Mr. and Mrs. George Landfair Sr.; [m.] Lawrence Gardner (Divorced); [ch.] Takkia, Lawrence Jr., Amber; [ed.] G.E.D., Detroit School of Cosmetology, Detroit Bus. Institute, Casinos, Wild Gaming Academy; [occ.] Mother/Student; [oth. writ.] Little Black Girl, To Go Beyond the Glass. Titles to other poems written by S.L.G.; [pers.] That diamonds and people are alike. They must be cut and polished for their true beauty to be experienced.; [a.] Detroit, MI

GARRETT, WANDA FAYE
[b.] February 25, 1948, Brownsville, TN; [p.] David Owen and Mary Owen; [m.] Tommy R. Garrett, November 25, 1984; [ch.] Dianne Mims, Wendy White and Chris Garrett; [ed.] GED, LPN; [occ.] Housewife, Home Educator, Caretaker of disabled husband.; [memb.] St. Paul Methodist Church, Memphis Home Education Association; [oth. writ.] None, I always wanted to try writing, but never had the time or education.; [pers.] I try first and foremost to live a Christian life, not an easy road, but the best one. I try to read the best of books and listen to the best in music, Classical, being first choice. This makes me happy and makes me think beautiful thoughts. I love all people and my country.; [a.] Ripley, TN

GARVEY, SUZIE
[pen.] Suzie Garvey; [b.] December 18, 1952, Chicago, IL; [p.] Joseph Campbell and Dorothy Campbell; [m.] Ken Garvey, May 4, 1974; [ch.] Genevieve Garvey, Kathleen Garvey, Amanda Garvey and Joseph Garvey; [ed.] Morton East High School, Northern Illinois University; [occ.] Wife and Mom; [memb.] Reach to

Recovery Volunteer (American Cancer Society), Race for the Cure (Susan G. Komen Foundation) Volunteer; [pers.] I enjoy writing poetry for all occasions; however, I wanted to send heartfelt feelings and wishes to those that have been touched by this deadly disease. I tried to cover all areas of life that would be affected. Finally I wanted to end on a note that we, the survivors, not the disease, will triumph.; [a.] Germantown, TN

GASSAWAY, TIMOTHY
[b.] April 5, 1967, Talladega, AL; [p.] Joe and Dixie Friday; [m.] Faye Nall Gassaway, April 8, 1991; [ed.] Graduated from Vigor High School in 1983. Served in the U.S. Navy as Electrician's Mate.; [occ.] Installer of: ceramic floor and wall tile, sub-contractor; [memb.] Member of Gulf Hills Baptist Church of Mobile, AL. Member of ABC Bowling League.; [hon.] "Best Epigram Award" in high school newspaper on another poem I wrote called, "The Thought".; [oth. writ.] I have written several other poems such as: "Images of Love," "Second Thoughts," "The American Man".; [pers.] I try to reflect in my poems truthfulness, wit and my compassion for mankind in hopes that mankind will learn to love others as he loves himself.; [a.] Chickasaw, AL

GAY, NATHAN W.
[b.] September 24, 1975, Denver, CO; [p.] Shirley and Phil Gay; [a.] Aurora, CO

GAYLE, DAMIEN L.
[pen.] Lance; [b.] August 2, 1950, New York, NY; [p.] Earl E. Gayle and Gladys D. Gayle; [m.] Vilma M. Nemrod, May 21, 1977; [ch.] Damien C. Gayle and Melisa E. Gayle; [ed.] Thomas A. Edison H.S., Foothills Technical College; [occ.] Asbestos Contractor Supervisor; [memb.] Good Shepherd Lutheran Church, National Geographic Society; [oth.] None published at this time.; [pers.] Endeavor to persevere in poetry to help others.; [a.] Brooklyn, NY

GEARHART, CRYSTAL DAWN
[b.] April 23, 1971, Ford City, PA; [p.] Patricia Warr and Glendin Gearhart, stepfather - Ronald Warr; [ed.] Elderton High and Triangle Tech; [occ.] Architectural Drafting Technician the A.G. Mauro Co., Pittsburgh, PA; [hon.] Awarded Most Artistic of my senior class, 1989 participant of the Miss Armstrong County Pageant; [pers.] My life, my family, my friends and everyday occurrences inspire and influence my stories and poems. My writing comes from somewhere within me and just happens, much like the passing of time. I do not strive for anything in particular with my writing but morals and values are strongly present and are to be taken as they will by my readers.; [a.] Ford City, PA

GEIS, ABBY
[b.] March 23, 1985, Franklin, WI; [p.] Cindy Geis and Steve Geis; [ed.] 6th Grade Okauchee Elementary School; [occ.] Student; [hon.] Several reading awards, music vocal awards and clarinet and piano; [pers.] I'd just like to say that I dedicate this poem to my cousin Tricia King.; [a.] Oconomowoc, WI

GEORGE, TARA
[b.] November 2, 1981, Texarkana, AR; [p.] Kenneth and Tina George; [ed.] College Hill Jr. High; [occ.] Student; [memb.] National Jr. Honor Society, Gifted and Talented Literature Club, Band, Newspaper, Yearbook; [hon.] Science Award, Reporter-NJHS, Drum Major Award, Straight A Honor Award, Ms. Teen of Arkansas Semi-Finalist; [pers.] Love Jesus with all your heart, and the words you write will never part.; [a.] Texarkana, AR

GERSTENBERGER, LISA A.
[pen.] Rebecca Lynn; [b.] February 8, 1964, Cocoa

Beach, Fl; [p.] Minnie and Hugh Holman; [ch.] Meghan, Danielle, Julianne Renae; [ed.] Manatee High School; [occ.] Aircraft Electrician with Raytheon Aerospace Corporation; [memb.] Women of the Moose, Naval Reserve; [hon.] Dean's List and Honor Roll; [oth.writ.] Wrote several poems and short stories while in high school. Some were published in Scholastic Periodicals; [pers.] I hope that someday my children can read my writings and identify with the things that inspired their mother; [a.] Orange Park, FL.

GETTRY, JOAN E.
[b.] Jamaica, WI; [p.] Deceased; [m.] Martin D. Gettry (Deceased); [ch.] 9 1/2 year old English Springer Spaniel dog; [ed.] La Guardia Community College; [occ.] Homemaker; [memb.] Women's Auxiliary, NY, Medical Center, International Society of Poets; [hon.] Dean's List; [oth. writ.] Recent publication of a book of poetry.; [pers.] Life is indeed a marvel, it has its ups and downs, but I've learned through experience how to ride this "see-saw" and thus, allowing me to generate my own balance.; [a.] Beechhurst, NY

GIALLORATI, MARIA R.
[b.] May 18, 1967, Detroit, MI; [p.] Rudolph and Rita Taranski; [m.] Paul Giallorati, October 25, 1996; [ed.] Fitzgerald High School; [memb.] St. Jude Children's Hospital, Cousteau Society; [pers.] My poem, "He, Whom We Loved," was written in memory of 3 extraordinary men: the grandfather of a dear friend, Mr. John Aranyos; my father-in-law, Mr. Angelo Giallorati and my grandfather, Mr. Thaddeus Poplawski.; [a.] Richmond, MI

GIBBONS, BRYAN
[b.] February 16, 1979, Middletown, CT; [p.] Jay Grieder and Laurie Grieder; [ed.] Liahona Academy; [occ.] Antique Refinisher; [oth. writ.] Several poems.; [pers.] I enjoy writing as a reflection of my thoughts and the places that I've been.; [a.] Deep River, CT

GIBBS, LAURA M.
[pen.] Chamineak; [b.] September 18, 1960, St. Louis, MO; [p.] Laverne I. McCarthy Chamineak; [ch.] Angela I. Gibbs, Grandson: Brandon M. Gibbs; [occ.] Financial Analyst; [memb.] Boystown Human Rights, PFLAG; [pers.] In memory of Marie McCarthy, my grandma and my inspiration.; [a.] Saint Louis, MO

GIDDINGS, LARRY L.
[b.] August 10, 1974, Michigan; [ed.] Petoskey High North Central, Michigan College; [occ.] Student; [pers.] I strive in my work to have people look at each other as people, not as a disabled person.; [a.] Boyne Falls, MI

GILLARD, JAMES
[b.] July 3, 1966, New York, NY; [p.] Tessie Gillard and James Gillard; [ed.] Manhattan Community College, Herbert H. Lehman College; [pers.] I write on behalf of the soul, to feed the spirit, and to nourish righteousness which lies in all of us.; [a.] New York, NY

GILLESPIE, MARLON
[b.] November 21, 1977, Flint, MI; [p.] Alma and Tom Gillespie; [ed.] Still in High School, Williow run adult education in Ypsilanti, MI; [occ.] Restaurant BW3 Grill and Pub in Ypsilanti MI., soon to be manager; [oth. writ.] None just started writing poetry last year after reading an article by Maya Angloe in titled you can be a poet just been writing for a year writing some new poems for this year '97!!!; [pers.] Only God can judge me! I'm a misunderstood black man! The mind is a seed and knowledge of self helps that seed to grow so expand and open up your mind.; [a.] Ypsilanti, MI

GIRARD, TANGUE
[b.] February 21, 1965, Harrisburg, PA; [p.] John and Anna Lehman; [ch.] Christina Girard; [occ.] Certified Psychiatric Nurse/Casemanger, Pinnacle Health Behavioral Services; [pers.] I have found a renewed sense of creativity through the support of friends and family and through my own spiritual awakening. The National Library of Poetry has given me the fuel I need to continue burning lines of passion on what once was a blank page.; [a.] Mechanicsburg, PA

GIROLAMI, LISA M.
[b.] March 12, 1972, New York; [p.] Anthony and Nadine Girolami; [m.] Anthony LaGiglia, October 4, 1997; [ed.] State University of New York at Oneonta, West Islip High School; [occ.] Public Relations Account Executive, Gothard/Greenstone Roberts, Melville, NY; [hon.] Minnie P. Olive Memorial Award for Outstanding Achievement in English, Dean's List; [a.] West Islip, NY

GITTERE, GREG
[b.] February 7, 1962, Lodi, CA; [p.] Kay King, Gordon and Joy Gittere; [m.] Debbie A. Gittere, July 17, 1993; [ch.] Jake Caeton Gittere; [ed.] Graduated Lincoln High School, Stockton, CA; [occ.] Service Rep - Anheuser Busch, Inc.; [pers.] Our first child, Jake, was stillborn 10-31-96. As I sat for hours in bewilderment I wrote "Baby Jake" as an expression of my love, pain, sorrow, and hope.; [a.] Stockton, CA

GOLDSTEIN, SHARI L.
[b.] January 9, 1963, Saint Anthony Hospital; [p.] Max and Sara Meyer; [m.] Mark Goldstein, February 26, 1983; [ch.] Christine, Nick, Tom and Ashley; [ed.] High school; [occ.] Day Care Provider and Housewife of a Dairy Farmer; [memb.] St. Anthony Church, I was in many different clubs in my school years.; [hon.] None before this. I have always enjoyed writing poems. I just write what pops into my head.; [pers.] I just right what I feel in my heart. My mom always said I had talent but I never did anything about it.; [a.] Effingham, IL

GONZALEZ, AWILDA
[pen.] Windy; [b.] March 26, 1963, NYC; [p.] Ramon Gonzalez, Milagros Colon; [ch.] Lestie, Ramon, Jose; [ed.] 11th grade and GED; [occ.] Full-time mother; [memb.] St. Joseph's School for the Deaf (Deaf child); [hon.] H.S. Silver Medal Swimming; [oth. writ.] Other writings not published; [pers.] There are 2 things God has assured: life and death. Make your life count.; [a.] Bronx, NY

GONZALEZ, YANIDMAR
[b.] October 18, 1980, Queens, NY; [p.] Yolanda and Raphael Gonzalez; [m.] February 2, 1980; [ch.] Jose Ortiz, Carlos, Marta, Nydia, Jose and Thomas; [ed.] Flushing High School; [occ.] Student; [memb.] National Junior Honor Society based on Scholarship, Leadership, Service, Character and Citizenship, Victoria Congregational Church; [hon.] Merit from the New York State Assembly, National Honor Society, Gold Honor Roll for outstanding scholastic achievement, Honor Award for Outstanding Performance of The Gondoliers, Honor Roll 1988, 1989, 1990, 1991; [oth. writ.] Poem on Marian Wright Edelman; [pers.] I thank my parents for believing me and helping me to become what I am today. I wish to reach the stars someday and succeed in all my goals.; [a.] Jamaica, Queens, NY

GOODMAN, CHARLCIE ANN MIDDLETON
[pen.] Charlcie Ann Middleton Goodman; [b.] November 3, 1947, San Antonio, TX; [p.] Casilear and Montella Winn Middleton; [m.] Enest Loren Goodman III, September 4, 1969; [ch.] Catherine Anne Goodman Noll; [ed.] Associate of Science Business Administration, Honors; [occ.] Budget

Analyst; [memb.] American Society of Military Comptrollers; [pers.] Life is not a dress rehearsal. Done in on your relationships with family and friends and love as if there was no tomorrow.; [a.] Clovis, NM

GOODMAN, VERNICE J.
[b.] June 1, 1909, Newberg, OR; [p.] James S. and Lena Herd; [m.] Elvin C. Goodman (Deceased), February 4, 1932; [ch.] Ronald-deceased, Roberts Rae Schroder; [ed.] Hillsboro, Ore. H.S., College of Ed., Ellenburg, Wash, Oregon State College, Carvallis, Oregon, College of Ed., Monmouth; [occ.] Retired (Teacher 30 yrs); [memb.] Life member National Ed. Ass. Oregon Stats Ed. Ass., Delta Kappa Gamma, Business and Professional Women, American University Women, Methodist Church; [hon.] Seaside Oregon B.P.W. Woman of Year, Distinguished Service Award senior, mayor's citation; [oth. writ.] Poems, life story (not published); [pers.] Everyone has a niche, something he can do in this life—no one is indispensable, someone can always take your place. Influenced by my early teachers.; [a.] Hillsboro, OR

GORDON, CHERILYN
[b.] October 30, 1956, Grenada; [p.] Norbert Gordon; [ch.] Kenya and Inertia Gordon; [ed.] College; [occ.] Counselor; [memb.] Secretary of 4H Club Committee which stands for head, heart, hands and health; [hon.] G.C.E., School Leaving O'levels; [oth. writ.] What's Love, Racism, A Mother's Cry; [pers.] My aim is to achieve the best and motivate others so that you always work towards higher grounds.; [a.] Brooklyn, NY

GRABOWSKI, BOBBY
[b.] November 14, 1974, Temple, TX; [p.] Lu and Jack Hubert; [ed.] I graduated from Rockdale High School in Rockdale, Texas, and attended Jr. college until now, because I'll be transferring to Texas A.M. University in summer '97; [occ.] I'm a student working at a private restaurant on Texas A.M. University campus where I manage wait staff and bartenders.; [memb.] Aggie Motorcycle Club, Weightlifting Club, local basketball team; [hon.] Other than sports this is my first honor for creativity.; [oth. writ.] My other writings deal mostly with love, and its heartaches. They have a lot to do with true love, and my doubt in it.; [pers.] I wrote "Now I Lay Me Down to Sleep" when I was 19 after my first child was never born due to circumstances out of my control.; [a.] Bryan, TX

GRAFF, JOAN T.
[pen.] Joanie; [b.] December 30, 1946, Lima, Peru, South America; [p.] Elizabeth and Everett Graff; [ed.] BA Sociology/Social Work, Washington State University, 1970; [occ.] Social Worker, County of San Mateo (California); [hon.] Nominated Girl of the Year, in high school (Spokane, Washington), Crisco Award, Outstanding Student in Home Economics (high school), college: Spurs: National Service Honorary at Eastern Washington State College, Dean's List, 20 yrs. Service Award presented by Board of Supervision, San Mateo County, Employee of the Month, Child Protective Services, Special Recognition Award for dedication to families of San Mateo County (1982 by Committee on Child Abuse).; [oth. writ.] I have written over 100 poems and stories, never published. I went to Delaware for a family reunion, and my nieces Diane encouraged me to do this.; [pers.] My writings are inspired by human suffering, my love for family, my Lord and humanity.; [a.] Palo Alto, CA

GRAND, JIM
[b.] August 30, 1931, Peninsula, OH; [p.] Edgar Grand and Elizabeth Grand; [m.] Betty Krause, June 12, 1954; [ch.] Julie Kay and Beth Ann; [ed.] Akron North High, Kent State University, B.S.,

M.S. in Ed. 1956, 1959; [occ.] Artist, Writer. Former: Teacher, School Administrator; [memb.] Ohio Education Association, National Education Association; [hon.] "American Legion School Award," "Idea Innovative Schools Award."; [oth. writ.] "Green Apple Tree," "To This Boy," "Abbie Burgess at Matinicus Rock," poems.; [pers.] My poems are an attempt to share the beauty and emotions of our time.; [a.] Massillon, OH

GRANT, KEAUNIS L.
[b.] October 24, 1983; Jackson, TN; [p.] Linda and Robert Grant; [hon.] I was awarded many trophies for Honor Roll and for my talents; [pers.] I think you must have a dream in order to succeed. Follow your dream and make it a reality; [a.] Milwaukee, WI.

GRAVES, PAULA
[b.] January 5, 1953, Logan, UT; [p.] Floyd and Myrtle Cornaby; [m.] John Wesley Graves, August 9, 1974; [ch.] Jamie Kae, Spencer Allen, Jeanette Marie, and Katie Cornaby; [ed.] Fountain Valley High School, Brigham Young University; [occ.] Sculptor, Volleyball Coach; [hon.] Most of my honors and awards have come to me because of athletic and artistic achievement. I have always, until now, kept my poetry very private.; [oth. writ.] I have written 32 poems and two short stories, all of which I have shared only with family and friends. My Mother, who was an English teacher, encouraged me to send in a poem; [pers.] My poetry is linked closely to my art work. It is an expression of what I see and feel in life. I have always been fascinated with the challenge of rhythm.; [a.] West Jordan, UT

GRAY, CECIL
[pen.] Cecil R. Gray III; [b.] September 1, 1952, Durham, NC; [p.] Cecil R. Gray Jr. and Faye Larian Gray; [m.] Divorced; [ch.] Katie Gray and Melanie Gray; [ed.] Club Blvd. Elem. Sch., Brogden Jr. High, Durham High School, Univ of N.C., Unity College ME; [occ.] Registered Maine Guide; [memb.] Professional Maine Guides Association; [hon.] Dean's List High Honors, Kennebecriver Guide of the Year; [oth. writ.] Several published poems in college annuals and newspapers.; [pers.] As all writers, I try to describe the essence of life. The pure moments are rare, and words are never really good enough, but they do a damn good job.; [a.] The Forks, ME

GREEN, DERWINN
[b.] December 22, 1976; [p.] Ralph Green and Joanna Green; [ed.] Beaufort High School, Howard University; [occ.] Student, Journalist; [memb.] Society of Professional Journalists, Palmetto Project, National Honor Society; [hon.] Most recent Howard University School of Communications Dept. of Journalism Trustee Scholarship; [oth. writ.] The Community News (staff writer), various other articles and poetry published in other compilations/newspapers or magazines.; [pers.] "Believe in yourself. We tend to neglect our personal feelings and rely heavily on those of others. Honor your dignity, spirit and singularity."; [a.] Washington, DC

GREEN, JOSEPHINE
[b.] October 17, 1974, Hartford, CT; [p.] Charles Green, Josephine P. Green; [ed.] South Windsor High School, Manchester Community - Technical College, A.S. Degree General Studies; [occ.] Customer Service Representative, JP Food Service, Hartford; [hon.] Dean's List; [pers.] In memory of Aunt Zina, whose love, courage and resilience will live forever in my heart. Special thanks to my family and friends for their encouragement and support. I love you Rhiannon!; [a.] South Windsor, CT

GREENE, KELLY
[b.] February 18, 1985, Morrisville, VT; [p.] Raymond Greene and Linda Greene; [ed.] 6th grade at Wolcott Elementary School; [a.] Wolcott, VT

GREENE, REV. DOROTHY MARIE
[b.] August 13, 1948, Columbia, SC; [p.] Aaron and Mary Caldwell (Deceased); [m.] Jimmy Greene, May 13, 1978; [ch.] Woodrow and Kevin James; [ed.] C.A. Johnson High, Columbia S.C., BS Degree Springfield College, May '89, Bethel Bible Institute, Jamaica, NY; [occ.] Customer Service Representative, Blue Cross Blue Shield of CT; [memb.] Ordained Associate Minister Liberty Christian Center New Haven, CT Chaplain Christian Women on the move for Christ; [oth. writ.] I have written several poems, songs, I play none published to date - all of which were inspired by the Holy Spirit; [pers.] I believe in the dignity and sanctity of life. That all human beings have worth and value because they are made in the image of my Heavenly Father, who is the Divine Creator.; [a.] New Haven, CT

GREENWALD, DELOME JUNE
[pen.] Delome; [b.] October 1, 1945, Milwaukee, WI; [p.] Edmund Berndt Greenwald, Flossie Louise Rice; [ed.] Menomonee Falls, H.S. (Wisconsin), B.F.A., M.S. University of Wisconsin, Ed. Specialist, University of Virginia, Doctoral candidate, University of Virginia; [occ.] Gifted and Talented Specialist at the DODDS Bamberg E.S. Theatre Director, Dancer and Choreographer, Artist, Poet; [memb.] ASCD, Phi Delta Kappa, National Ass. for Gifted Children, Animal Protection Institute, World Wildlife Fund, Smithsonian, Native Peoples, National Geographic Society, Bamberg Music Federation, Bamberg Theatre Federation; [hon.] Rotary Club Scholarship, National Honor Society, 4 DODDS (Department of Defense Dependents Schools) Outstanding Achievement Awards, University of Wisconsin - Master's Degree Scholarship funded by the U.S. Government for Inner City Education in Milwaukee, Wisconsin; [oth. writ.] Unpublished plays, poems, and children's stories; [pers.] Words are the most powerful wealth of beauty we are given besides love. I admire Schiller, Goethe, Emily Dickinson, Pound and Poe.; [a.] Bamberg, Germany

GREENWAY, DONALD C.
[pen.] Don; [b.] October 27, 1946, Shelby, NC; [p.] Jim and Hattie Greenway; [m.] Cathy Greenway, October 9, 1982; [ch.] Eric Sayne (Step-son); [ed.] High school graduate; [occ.] Self-employed; [memb.] Masonic Order, Bass Anglers Sportsman Society; [oth. writ.] Written several poems about subjects that I felt near to me. Never considered publishing them.; [pers.] I enjoy expressing myself and my feelings in poems to try and make sense out of things and situations that sometimes have no rhyme or reason.; [a.] Charlotte, NC

GREENWELL, JENNIFER L.
[pen.] Jane; [b.] March 27, 1981, Baytown, TX; [p.] Dalton and Pat Greenwell; [ed.] Attending Houston County High School; [occ.] Student; [memb.] 4-H Club, Poetry and Literature Club, Good Samaritan Club; [pers.] George Moore defined poetry best when he said, "My definition of pure poetry, something that the poet creates outside of his own personality." I believe that too, and attempt to write that way.; [a.] Erin, TN

GREGORY, GEARLDINE
[b.] July 4, 1956; [p.] Gearl and Lottie Barkley; [m.] David; [ch.] Steven and Jeremiah; [pers.] "Missing You," is for my son, Steven, who took his own life on Oct. 11, 1992. He was 20. If you know anyone suffering with depression, help them, find help. So you won't be "missing them too".; [a.] Sapulpa, OK

GREGORY, NANCY STATEN
[b.] October 16, 1942, Reno, NV; [p.] Clark and Ruth Staten; [m.] Ernest Gregory (Deceased - March 13, 1997), September 15, 1962; [ch.] Two; [ed.] High School, some college, Beauty College; [occ.] Taking care of 7 grandchildren and loving it; [oth. writ.] My Prayer, Oregon God's Country, Methinks I Saw The Face Of God, Great Reward; [pers.] Dedication: To my daughter Julie Leonard. Who had a great struggle in life because she was different. She fought and won!; [a.] Clarkston, WA

GRESHAM, BRIAN K.
[b.] September 2, 1967, Cleveland, OH; [p.] Jerry Gresham, Clarice Gresham; [ed.] Shaker Hts. High School; [occ.] Security Guard for The Cleveland Museum of Art; [oth. writ.] An article for the neighborhood.; [pers.] This is my first poetic endeavor. My poetry reflects my emotional response to situations that confront me in society and life.; [a.] Cleveland, OH

GREY, KAMALA S-T.
[b.] January 22, 1977, Jamaica, WI; [p.] Merlene Grey, Gerald Grey; [ed.] Immaculate Conception High, Queensborough Community College; [occ.] Student at Queensborough Community College; [memb.] Q.C.C. Karate Club; [hon.] Certificate of Merit from the Jamaica Chamber of Commerce for a Poster Competition Depicting Tourism; [pers.] I believe that the mind is a very powerful tool which young people should not let go to waste. It should be fed with knowledge and filled with the goodness of pure thinking. My work depicts my feelings about my physical environment and my spiritual influence is the Lord Jesus Christ.; [a.] Saint Albans, NY

GRIFFEN, AARON J.
[pen.] "Griff"; [b.] April 21, 1974, Prince George's County, MO; [p.] Carolyn Halsey; [ed.] Prairie View A&M University (English and History major), Roy Miller High School; [occ.] Student; [memb.] Sigma Tau Delta (International English Honor Society), Wisconsin Sleepers Inc., Creative Writing Club (Pres.); [hon.] Honor Roll spring '93, fall '93, spring '96; [oth. writ.] "Revolution" and "Tears of Happiness" - publication in school newspaper, "The Panther." All poems are from two personal poetry books: "The Fool's Game" and "Dark Side of the Sun"; [pers.] In my poetry I try to reflect upon and bring out the most innermost feelings, pains, thoughts, and concerns of the soul. In other words I ask and tell what one was afraid to ask and tell.; [a.] Prairie View, TX

GRIFFIN, NORMA
[pen.] Norma Griffin; [b.] September 14, 1939, Mount Airy, NC; [p.] Mr. and Mrs. S. W. Bennett (Deceased); [m.] Bobby H. Griffin, June 12, 1965; [ch.] Gina Griffin - 26 and Ginger Griffin - 24; [ed.] Taylorsville High School (N.C.), B.S., (N.C.) Pfeiffer University - Major Elem. Ed., (N.C.) Graduate Work UNCC; [occ.] Retired teacher; taught elementary school - 29 years Winston-Salem, NC and Monroe, NC; [memb.] First Baptist Church - Monroe, NC, Society of Children's Book Writers and Illustrators, NCAE and NEA (Educators Assoc.), North Carolina Writers' Network; [hon.] 1990 Teacher of Year (Local), 1991 N.C. Math Teacher Award, 1992 Outstanding Achievement (local); [oth. writ.] None published; [pers.] In my writing I hope to touch the creativity in others. Robert Frost is my favorite poet!; [a.] Monroe, NC

GROSS, DONALD RAY
[pen.] Carter Russell; [b.] November 25, 1940, Evansville, IN; [p.] Mary Evelyn Hall and William Louis Gross; [m.] Anna Karlene Gross (Fulkerson),

February 21, 1964; [ch.] Allen Lamar - Travis Jason; [ed.] Old Central High School, Evansville, Indiana - Reitz High School; [occ.] Retired—disability worked in food service - restaurant, hotel; [memb.] National Parks and Conservation, People for the Ethical Treatment of Animals - Disabled American Vets, Father Flanagans Boystown - AARP, World Wildlife Federation; [hon.] Evansville Rescue Mission Volunteer of the Year 1995, Cub Scout Master of the year 1972, Santa Ana, Calif., Management Award for Cleanliness for Captain D's Restaurants 1982 1983-1985, nominated Volunteer of the Year for Volunteer Action Center for tristate area; [oth. writ.] Nothing published as of yet but I have written a lot of poems and songs. Just never had a desire to have them published; it's science music to my soul.; [pers.] I am a member of the Nazarene Church and try to live my life as God would have me to. I try to look for the good in people and know that my purpose here on earth is to help others as Jesus did; [a.] Evansville, IN

GROSSNICKLE, NELVA
[b.] January 31, 1985, Cherry Point, NC; [p.] Nancy Grossnickle, Randy Dale Grossnickle; [ed.] 6th grade at Monocary Middle School; [occ.] Student; [memb.] YMCA, 6 years in Girl Scouts, Campfire Kids, Big Brothers and Big Sisters of Frederick; [hon.] Art, Math, Citizenship Awards; [oth. writ.] "The Ant" published in "Whispers at Dusk"; [pers.] I would like to thank my cousin, Melissa Pennington, for encouraging me in my writings and sharing all her own beautiful poems with me. "You won't know if you can do it if you don't try."; [a.] Frederick, MD

GROTH, LORI
[b.] March 11, 1958, Oakland, CA; [p.] Neil and Dorothy Gauthier; [m.] Scott Groth, September 14, 1985; [ch.] Crystal 11, Brianna 7 and Kendra 6; [ed.] High school grad; [occ.] Housewife; [pers.] "I am the Same" was written for my daughter, Brianna, who is hearing impaired. When she started school I wanted the other kids to know she was just like them. I wanted Brianna to be treated just like everyone else.; [a.] Loomis, CA

GROWER, BETTY
[b.] March 25, 1928, McKittrick, CA; [p.] Deceased; [m.] Robert Grower, December 6, 1952; [ch.] Robin and John; [ed.] Attended U.C. Berkley for 2 years.; [occ.] Retired; [memb.] Carmel Music Society, World Affairs Council, Monterey Bay Aquarium, Monterey County Symphony; [oth. writ.] None published or submitted.; [pers.] Since a child, I have always loved reading poetry, but only in the last 9 years have I tried to express my own thoughts and experiences.; [a.] Carmel, CA

GRUBBS, JULIE C.
[pen.] Diemond; [b.] December 15, 1969, Goldsboro, NC; [p.] Lowell Nelson Crawford and Rachel E. Woody; [ch.] Jerame Shane Crawford Grubbs; [ed.] Heritage High School; [occ.] United States Post Office; [oth. writ.] I have written a book of unpublished poems.; [pers.] 'Selfish and cruel, life is a tool, held in the hands of only a fool.'; [a.] Evington, VA

GUADAGNINO, CHRISTINA
[pen.] Rays; [b.] March 9, 1979, Ridgewood; [p.] Janice Guadagnino; [ed.] Senior at Toms River H.S. South. I am planning on attending either the University of New Hampshire or Johnson and Whales Univ.; [occ.] I am currently working at the Seaside Hts. Boardwalk; [memb.] Toms River South Swim Team and a Peer Advisor of Peer Leadership at T.R. South; [hon.] I am 4 year varsity swimmer for Toms River, Peer Advisor Award, and part of Who's Who Among American H.S. Students; [pers.] Something one of friends told me and I'll

never forget: "You can always judge a person by their eyes, because the eyes are the windows to the soul!"; [a.] Beachwood, NJ

GUADAGNO, MICHAEL A.
[b.] July 17, 1975, Long Island, NY; [p.] Anthony and Diane Guadagno; [ed.] Marjory Stoneman Douglas High School, pursuing a college degree at this time; [occ.] Presently serving in the USAF; [pers.] Poetry is imagination at its best.; [a.] Coral Springs, FL

GUFFEY, DOLORES K.
[b.] December 19, 1932, New Castle, IN; [p.] Mr. and Mrs. Wm. H. Shipley Straugh Ind.; [m.] Deceased, September 22, 1981; [ch.] Bobby, David and Malinda; [ed.] 10th grade; [occ.] Retired Factory; [pers.] I think this runs in the family from Abraham Lincoln on. I've been digging my family roots. Poems, and speeches.; [a.] Richmond, IN

GUIDICE, MARIE ELEANA
[pen.] Eleana Guidice; [ch.] One daughter - Melissa Jane; [ed.] Med. Tech. Degree, B.A., M.A., English Lit. and Communications; [occ.] Director, Medical Writing and Editing Dept.; [memb.] American Medical Writers Association; [hon.] Ruth Fryer Memorial Award for Excellence in Writing, 1971, Rutgers University; [oth. writ.] Published poetry, one short story; [pers.] Writing poetry or prose is for me, essentially cathartic, it keeps me balanced.; [a.] NJ

GUM, CLARENCE R.
[b.] March 8, 1918, Rocky Comfort, MO; [p.] Guy and Cleora Gum; [m.] Laura Henderson Gum, 1949; [ch.] Lawa, Guy, William and James; [ed.] Bachelor's Degree in Education and Mathematics, from Southwest Missouri University Columbia 1939, Masters Degree in Chemistry - U of Missouri Columbia 1943; [oth. writ.] Read, Roll Call, A Branch of the Gum Tree; [pers.] Clarence was hardworking and unswervingly dedicated to his life, four children and five pipe! Clarence died of a coronary on October 28, 1994, but lived the last 24 years of his life in.; [a.] Houston, TX

GVOZDAS, JAMES J.
[pen.] James J. Gvozdas; [b.] May 15, 1975, Washington, DC; [ed.] De Matha Catholic High School, University of Delaware; [memb.] The National Honor Society, (Valois Chapter); [pers.] I am currently pursuing a B.S. degree in Computer Science. I am also writing a novel.; [a.] Columbia, MD

HADDAD, SARA A.
[b.] August 12, 1953, Charleston, SC; [p.] James and Carol Haddad; [ed.] Grade 8, Glenbrook Middle School; [occ.] Student; [memb.] Longmeadow Aquatics Club, Longmeadow Soccer, First Church Youth Group, Select Choir; [oth. writ.] "Image," "KKK Poem," "Boys," a poem.; [a.] Longmeadow, MA

HA, THU
[b.] April 26, 1980, Malaysia; [p.] Dr. Hung & Dao Ha; [ed.] Junior at Ft. Smith Southside High; [memb.] Mu Alpha Theta, Thespian Society, Sail Crew; [hon.] Mu Alpha Theta, Kudos, Presidential Award; [oth. writ.] Local article writings for Times Record. [pers.] I would like to personally thank Nicholaus Kent Jones for giving me the strength to write this particular poem. I would also like to thank Susan & Jenifer Walker, and Dominic for their support; [a.] Ft. Smith, AR

HADFIELD, BOB
[pen.] Bib; [b.] November 26, 1982, Pittsburgh, PA; [p.] Robert A. Hadfield and Susan Miller Hadfield; [ed.] 8th grade, Montour School Dist. Pittsburgh, PA; [occ.] Student; [memb.] Sportsman: Soccer, Wrestling, Hunter, Fisherman,

West Park Firemen Band. "Trombone".; [a.] Pittsburgh, PA

HADFIELD, RUTH DYSON
[pers.] This silent, careless cruelty must stop in this country and people stop accepting it as normal. 'It Is Not.'

HALE, JASON
[b.] July 11, 1977, Montgomery, AL; [p.] Larry and Margaret Hale; [ed.] Valdosta High School (graduated in 1995) now attending Valdosta State Un. (Valdosta, GA); [occ.] Coordinated Services Employee; [hon.] Presidential Academic Fitness Award; [oth. writ.] Exact Interpretations (a soon-to-be-published novel); [pers.] I praise God for the blessings bestowed upon me. I would like everyone to know that I am a lover of Jesus who struggles with sin.; [a.] Valdosta, GA

HALL, ALICE
[b.] September 12, Old Town, FL; [p.] Johnny Lemon Sr. and Beulah Lemon; [m.] Ernest Hall, August 13; [ch.] Alveia Darlene, Rhonda Bertina, Anthony Tyrone and Demetria Alisa; [ed.] Booke T. Washington High School, St. Petersburg Vocational Technical Institute; [occ.] Unemployed, prays for the sick; [memb.] Church of the Living God Pillar Ground of Truth, Crystal River, Fla; [hon.] Honor Student, Several Scholastics Awards, Vocational and High School, and Elementary School; [oth. writ.] Numerous songs and poems unpublished.; [pers.] I can't do anything by myself. I am totally submitted and guided by the Holy Spirit.; [a.] Crystal River, FL

HAMBRICK, SHIRLEY
[b.] January 4, 1958, Edinburgh, Scotland; [m.] Michael Hambrick, June 9, 1986; [ch.] Keira, Kirsty, Fiona; [ed.] Portobello High School, Edinburgh, Scotland, Edinburgh College of Art, Scotland; [occ.] Artist, Home-schooler; [memb.] International Association of Scientologists, Handweavers Guild of America; [a.] Princeton, WV

HAMEN, REV. RODY
[pen.] Rody Hamen; [b.] May 18, 1945, Fremont, OH; [p.] Kathryn and Ralph Mosser; [m.] Mark L. Hamen, July 6, 1990; [ch.] Michelle, Michael and Matthew, Marlo; [ed.] St. Joseph Elementary and High School, Fremont, Ohio; [occ.] Ordained Evangelist Vocalist - Prayer Partner; [memb.] Partners in Christ Spirit filled outreach (my ministry) Tax Exemption Profit - I am inspired by The Holy Spirit in all of my poetry and it is written to glorify the Lord; [hon.] The honor of knowing and serving the Lord. To Him be given all of the glory; [oth. writ.] My Hero, Agapae Love, Amazing Indeed, It Is Finished, Great Indeed, Listen, Fear Not, The Great I Am, A Little Love, The Power Is In His Name, He Watches Me, A Mothers Love; [pers.] I have my own Sunday morning radio program - I believe with Rody - I also write music - cassette tapes - thank you Jesus and God bless America.; [a.] Rossford, OH

HAMILTON, ALICE M.
[pen.] Brink; [b.] April 17, 1927, Edenton, NC; [p.] Norman and Adell Brinkley; [m.] James N. Hamilton (Deceased), December 24, 1950; [ch.] Ronnie Lynn Watkins and Milton Hamilton; [ed.] M.A. Hampton University, Hampton, VA; [occ.] Retired English Teacher, Guidance Counselor; [memb.] Retired Teachers Assoc., Hughes Memorial United Methodist Scholarship Comm., International Training in Communication, Kappa Delta Pi, ABA Bridge Assoc., Hospice Volunteer; [hon.] Toastmaster Speech Contest Winner, ITC Council Speech Contest Winner, Article in ITC International Communicator Magazine, Outstanding Service Award for D.C. Scholarship Comm.; [oth. writ.] Winning

speech on the dandelion; [pers.] I'm fascinated by all of nature and feel that the mysteries of the universe are secreted there. My motto is to love and be loved in return.; [a.] Largo, MD

HAMILTON, SEAN K.
[b.] February 28, 1968, Hempstead, NY; [p.] Vernon Hamilton, Kerry L. Williams; [ed.] St. John's University; [pers.] My writing was the result of an internal awakening. It is inspired and dedicated to "My Lady" because with her I am complete.; [a.] Hempstead, NY

HAMLETT, JUNE N.
[b.] July 21, 1938, Brookneall, VA; [p.] Arthur J. and Mary Dalton Neighbors; [m.] Robert W., June 5, 1958; [ch.] Four Godchildren (2 boys and 2 girls); [ed.] William Campbell High School, Naruna, VA, Central Virginia Community College - Sophomore; [occ.] Retired as Sr. Employment Supervisor from a major Insurance Company; [memb.] Timberlake Baptist Church, Timbrook Woman's Club, and Rustburg VA Senior Citizens; [hon.] Godparent of 4; [oth. writ.] "First Signs of Spring" published in Whispers at Dusk, "Sisters" to be published in Best Poems of 1997, have written a collection of poems which I aspire to publish.; [pers.] Do unto others as you would have them do unto you. I was greatly influenced by my godly parents, a special aunt, and a dear older neighbor who was a role model and Sunday school teacher.; [a.] Lynchburg, VA

HANES, VICKIE R.
[b.] July 21, 1951, Portsmouth, Sciot. County, OH; [p.] Ethel (Maiden Eldridge) and Ellis Barfield; [m.] Larry E. Hanes, August 8, 1987; [ch.] 3 - Father Robert Ruggles; [ed.] Paralegal Degree Shawnee, State University; [occ.] Housewife and Student; [memb.] God's House of Prayer; [pers.] I strive to serve my Lord and Savior. This poem was a result of this and his help after the death of my beloved mother.

HANSEN, MARIA
[b.] July 11, 1953, Jersey City, NJ; [p.] John Hansen, Mary Hansen; [ed.] St. Joseph High School, Jersey City, State College, B.A. in Special Education; [occ.] Day Care Teacher; [memb.] Soka Gakkai International, an organization for world peace through enlightened education; [pers.] I chant and propagate Nam-myo-ho Renge - Kyo (the mystic law) to become happy and overcome suffering.; [a.] Winthrop, MA

HANUS, EILEEN M.
[b.] September 20, 1957, Los Angeles, CA; [p.] Frank Garcia and Olivia Garcia; [m.] Jeff Hanus, February 2, 1985; [occ.] Disabled; [pers.] I give thanks to God for inspiring me to write poetry. Thanks to my Mom who encouraged me to submit my poem. Thanks to all who had faith in me. Let it be known that it is by the grace of God that I am alive and able to share my poetry.; [a.] Bellflower, CA

HARDESTY, STEPHANIE
[pen.] Steffanie Russ; [b.] March 20, 1973, Louisville, KY; [p.] Phillip and Pam McCloud; [m.] Russell A. Hardesty II, July 27, 1991; [ch.] Steffan Russell, Rustin Michael, Allyssa Danielle; [ed.] Mary Persons High School; [memb.] Word Aflame Tabernacle; [hon.] Who's Who '89-'90, National Alpha Beta '91; [pers.] I like to turn personal experiences and feelings into written form. I have always loved to write and I want to thank those who have inspired and supported me the most.; [a.] Macon, GA

HARPER, AMANDA
[pen.] Amanda Harper; [b.] October 15, 1982, McMinnville, OR; [p.] Cynthia and Eric Harper;

[ed.] Sophomore at Michigan Center High School, Michigan Center, Michigan; [occ.] Student at Michigan Center High School; [memb.] Students Against Drunk Driving (S.A.D.D.), Peer Listening and Peer Mediator, Michigan Center Marching and Orchestra Band, and Pep Band; [hon.] Honor Roll and several academic awards; [pers.] Everyone has their own dominion, the hard part is finding it.; [a.] Jackson, MI

HARRIS, BRANDON
[b.] February 5, 1985, Thomaston, GA; [p.] David and Mary Ann Harris; [occ.] Student at Blackmon Rd Middle School; [hon.] International Media Festival Award, art award; [a.] Midland, GA

HARRISON, CATHY
[b.] July 2, 1940, Three Oaks, MI; [p.] John M and Eunice Brown; [m.] David M. Harrison, August 17, 1963; [ch.] Doreen, Kevin David, Nathan; [ed.] Bethel College and Mounds-Midway School of Nursing, St. Paul, MN; [occ.] Nurse at Erlanger Medical Center, Chattanooga, TN; [memb.] Edgewood Baptist Church, Chattanooga, TN, SHHH (Self Help for Hard of Hearing Chapter), Chattanooga, TN; [oth. writ.] Poems and short stories, The Poetry Experiment, Vol. IV Chattanooga State, 1991, Treasured Poems of America, fall 1991; [pers.] I portray God's strength in our lives and the beauties of nature.; [a.] Chattanooga, TN

HART, JONATHAN
[b.] July 28, 1970, Marietta, GA; [p.] Bettis and Donna Hart; [ed.] Georgia Institute of Technology; [occ.] Software Programmer; [a.] Atlanta, GA

HASKINS, JOSH
[b.] June 9, 1981, Scottsdale, AZ; [p.] Glenda Haskins, Pat Haskins; [ed.] Currently a sophomore at North Canyon High School; [occ.] Student; [memb.] United States Tennis Association, International Baccalaureate Program; [hon.] Dean's List, Presidential Academic Achievement Award, NCHS Academic Achievement Award, varsity letter for tennis, USTA Sportsmanship Award; [oth. writ.] Short stories and several poems published in school publications and other publications (newspapers, Merlyn's Pen, etc.); [pers.] I believe that success is a journey, not a destination.; [a.] Scottsdale, AZ

HAWTHORNE, HELEN R.
[b.] December 14, 1934, Poplar Bluff, MO; [ch.] Four daughters, 4 grand, 3 great grandchildren; [occ.] Decent Miles B. Carpenter Museum Complex; [memb.] (1) Carsley United Methodist Church, (2) Virginia Writers Club Inc. - Travelers Chapter, (3) Rusty Needle Club; [hon.] Blue Ribbon Award for poem "Touching Yesterday" from Southern Poetry Association; [pers.] My philosophy is that all mankind was created to glorify God.; [a.] Waverly, VA

HAYDEN, DON
[pen.] Dahni; [b.] December 13, 1953; Columbia, MO; [occ.] Freelance writer, Reporter Advertising Sales, Deep waters (Own Business); [oth.writ.] The Tear and The Tender-Poetry, Life's Trip-Poetry, Talons and Feathers-Poetry Various articles, present work on a screen play; [pers.] To entertain with the disire that the reader learn something than to ever try and teach anyone, anything; [a.] Rogers, AR

HAYNES, CYNTHIA
[pen.] Miss Cynt; [b.] June 22, 1944, Trinidad; [p.] Elija Charles, Garnet Charles; [m.] Lawrence Haynes, December 21, 1985; [ch.] 5; [ed.] New York City Technical College, The University of the West Indies; [occ.] Pre-school Teacher; [hon.] Adolphus Lee Poetry Award; [oth. writ.] "Lost in a Strange Land," "The Parting," "Hail to

the Steel-Pan" and "This Land"; [pers.] I use my writing to promote unity among people of all races.; [a.] Jamaica, NY

HEALY, DIANA LYN
[b.] November 25, 1973; [p.] Judy and Donald Healy; [ed.] West Islip High, Katharine Gibbs School; [memb.] World Wildlife Federation, United Way; [hon.] Dean's List; [oth. writ.] Silent Presents, The Big Red Button, Truly an Angel, Solitude; [pers.] When emotions run through my den that is where my fantasy land begins. One cannot expect the best from others if they themselves don't give their very best.; [a.] West Islip, NY

HEAPHY, ELAINE
[pen.] Rojhani Blue; [b.] July 9, 1959, Providence, RI; [p.] Dorothy Heaphy; [pers.] "Poetry: the Communicator used by the creator as well as the average Man," "Original thought."; [a.] Pawtucket, RI

HEARD, WANDA
[b.] June 15, 1957; Duluth Georgia; [p.] Rev. and Mrs. Hezekiah Bowens; [m.] Rev. Bruce Heard; August 31, 1986; [ch.] Felicia and Joche; [ed.] Graduated Duluth High School 1974; [occ.] Housewife, Mother, Prayer Partner; [memb.] Friendship Baptist Church Duluth GA; [hon.] Award for singing and for my poems; [oth.writ.] Several other poems. I Could Never Be Good Enough, and Out Of Image; [pers.] I pray that this poem may touch and save someones life. Jesus is my inspiration.

HEDRICK, KRISTA
[b.] July 25, 1980; Elkins, WV; [p.] Janie and S. Roger Hedrick; [ed.] Tucker County High School; [occ.] Student; [memb.] Hi-Y, Tri-M, Church Youth Group, Band, Band Council SAAD; [hon.] 3.5 on writers ass. test, WVU Honor Band, Marshall All-star Marching Band, Academic Honors; [oth,writ.] Stories published in the local paper- local short story writer and contest winner; [pers.] Poetry is the best way to express your innermost thoughts and emotions!; [a.] Davis, WV.

HEFLIN, NAVADA
[b.] June 11, 1942, Stonega, VA; [p.] Tony Gibson and Mary Gibson; [m.] James R. Heflin, April 18, 1962; [ch.] James Jr. and Jeffrey; [a.] Centreville, VA

HEFT, LIEUTITIA VOLENE
[pen.] "Lieu Volene"; [b.] November 28, 1924, Cimarron, KS; [p.] Vol and Mary Mills; [m.] Jimmie Harmon Heft, July 12, 1943; [ch.] Suzanne Rochelle and Desima Lynn; [ed.] High school, Dodge City Jr., College Management for Apartments, 4 years study of the Meninger Bible Class, Telephone operator, Assistant Director of the New Horizon Club at the Bank of the Southwest; [occ.] Retired; [memb.] First Christian Church, The KGS Kansas Genealogical Society, Kansas Historical Society of Topeka, Kansas, Senior Friends, RSVP, The New Horizon Club, Keenagers; [hon.] As the coach for the Bible Bowl team we won first in the nation and were honored with a free trip to Mexico City in 1975 and again won the honor of placing in 1977 first and the second trip back to Mexico City.; [oth. writ.] "J.H. and the Cook," "The Green and Fuzzy House," "The Covered Wagon Love Affair," "Reminiscing." Working on "Laughter in the Family." Writings are for family history and for my grandsons.; [pers.] I have been greatly influenced by the great storytellers in my family. I am keeping the true stories alive for the next generation. Walk and talk with the Lord and you will have the Peace that passeth all understanding. "Precious Memories" was for my mother. My mother, Mary, lived to the age of 94.; [a.] Dodge City, KS

HEGEDUS, TAMARA
[b.] June 12, 1979, Ohio; [p.] Deborah and Robert; [ed.] St. Adalbert - grade and middle school, Berea High School, Baldwin-Wallace College; [memb.] SADD, National Honor Society, Varsity Football Cheerleaders, RSVP, SIBS; [hon.] Student of the Quarter, Academic Achievement Award, All-Academic Conference Team, All-American Cheerleader; [oth. writ.] "My Mom," "East of the Sunrise" and "Of Poetry"; [pers.] I just let my heart do the talking!; [a.] Brook Park, OH

HEIDELBERG, DOROTHY L.
[pen.] Dott; [b.] August 23, 1950, Jackson, MI; [p.] Mr. Luzell, Phyllis Bullock; [ch.] Adrienne Bullock, Jeremaine, Rosie William H.; [ed.] I stayed in school, but when I passed to the 12th grade, I was in school, a couple of months, so one day, I left school and never went back.; [occ.] I am a Food Service Worker. I get my 15 year pin in June 26, 1997.; [hon.] I got an award at work for being highly successful, because my supervisors like my work. I kept my work area clean, and neat. I received money and a plaque.; [pers.] My department, is Nutrition Food Service. I work at the Biloxi V.A. I bring the patients food to their rooms. I have worked for 14 yrs.; [a.] Biloxi, MI

HEINEY, POL
[b.] October 15, 1977, Palmerton, PA; [p.] Samuel and Julianne Heiney; [ed.] Palmerton Area High School, Shippensburg University; [occ.] College student; [memb.] Game On: Improv, SUTV; [hon.] Dean's List, Honor Roll; [pers.] Thank you: Jill, Sean, Rick, Devlin, Hank.; [a.] Palmerton, PA

HELFERICH, DIANE
[pen.] Diane Balog Helferich, Annie; [b.] November 19, 1951, Chicago, IL; [p.] Olie and Phyliss Nannfeldt; [m.] Dr. Omar Keith Helferich; [ch.] Jessica Balog Combs, Jason Balog, Joshua Balog, Abby Balog; [occ.] Wife, Mother, Secretary of State, East Lansing, Michigan; [memb.] Mount Hope Church, Lansing, Mich.; [oth. writ.] I have a portfolio of unpublished poems and writings. Some of the titles are as follows: Memories, Time, Happiness, The Crocus, Our Beginning, and more.; [pers.] My pen is driven to move across the paper reflecting the feelings of the highs and lows of the life God has given me.; [a.] Haslett, MI

HELMKAY, CAROL
[b.] March 20, Bad Axe, MI; [ed.] BA Education - Arizona State University 1954; [occ.] (Retired) Substitute Teacher; [hon.] Have received several Editor's Choice Awards from The National Library of Poetry; [oth. writ.] Have had 3 other poems published.; [pers.] I began writing with the purpose of using the poem for a specific reason. I now write with more feeling and with a message in mind. I like lyric poetry and do put some of my poems to music.; [a.] Peoria, AZ

HELSTEN, HOLLY J.
[pen.] Holly J.; [b.] September 21, 1969, Ft. Worth, TX; [p.] John and Carol Gaston; [m.] Dr. Robert A. Helsten; [ch.] Julia and Adam; [pers.] Writing is so healing for the soul and mind. "Boundaries" was written in memory of my grandfather, Waymon Gaston.; [a.] Denton, TX

HENDERSON, APRIL LEE
[pen.] April Lee; [b.] September 7, 1977, Tyler, TX; [p.] Mitch Henderson and Vicki Olliff; [ed.] Pine Tree High School, Kilgore Jr. College; [occ.] Secretary and Student - Kilgore Jr. College; [memb.] National Honor Society, Precision Drill Team Alumnus, Modeling Squad, Trinity United Church of Christ; [hon.] Drill Team Dancer of the Year, All-region Band, Academic Excellence, UIL contest winner, top 5% graduate high school, Eagles Student of the Month; [oth. writ.] "Fear" and "That House"; [pers.] I hope to become a novelist. Love moves me to write.; [a.] Longview, TX

HENDERSON, BENITA
[b.] September 21, 1982; Suriname; [p.] Jonathan and Jacinta Henderson; [ed.] Attending boys and girls high school; [occ.] Student; [hon.] Honor roll, student of the month; [oth.writ.] A number of unpublished poems; [pers.] My writings reflect my feelings about life, and the people who influenced the good things I have done in my life; [a.] Brooklyn, NY.

HENRY, YUSEF LA'TEEF
[pen.] Y. L. Henry; [b.] Manhattan, NYC; [p.] Janet Henry and Albert Henry; [m.] Leah Tamiko Haynes (Fiancee); [ed.] High school diploma, 4 years military service (Army); [occ.] Club D.J., freelance writer; [pers.] As we speak there walks among us a prophet. Be he real or false is yet to be seen. Yet prophet he be!; [a.] New York City, NY

HER, BEVERLY
[pen.] Shi-Huan Her; [b.] March 13, 1983, Miaoli, Taiwan R.O.C.; [p.] Wei-Chang Ho, Ching Ying Her; [ed.] Martin Luther King Middle School (Berkeley, California); [occ.] High school student (Freshman, 1997); [hon.] I never get any writing awards, but . . . Martin Luther King Award of 1996, Honor Roll of Feb. 1996, June 1996, and Feb. 1997, Certificate of Honor of 1996. (I got these awards in middle school); [oth. writ.] "Symbols for Myself" is my first poem that I had written to be in the contest. It's also the first poem that was published in the book.; [pers.] This is my first poem that I turned in to be in the contest. I just want to try, I can't believe I have been accepted.; [a.] El Cerrito, CA

HERMAN, CONNIE L.
[b.] January 25, 1951, Mechanicsburg, PA; [p.] Scott Campbell and Neta Campbell; [m.] Terry L. Herman, April 28, 1973; [ch.] Jody Lynn and Jason Ray; [ed.] Shikellamy High School; [occ.] Stay-home wife and mother. Home based business; [memb.] Church in Christian Union Missionary Work.; [pers.] I believe it's important to listen to what people have to say, and try to put myself at their level. To hear their deepest thoughts and ideas about our world, present and past.; [a.] Sunbury, PA

HERNANDEZ, ESTEBAN
[pen.] Mr. H.; [b.] November 19, 1969, San Juan, PR; [p.] Jorge L. Hernandez and Estela I. De Jesus; [ed.] Cupcy Bajo. Second Unit High School, University of Puerto Rico, Chapman University, Monterey, CA; [occ.] Bilingual Teacher, Cesar E. Chavez Elementary School, Salinas, CA, Calisal Union School District; [memb.] CA Teachers Association, ACSD (Association for Curriculum and Staff Development), CABE (CA Bilingual Educators); [hon.] U.P.R.'s Dr. Joseph Kavetsky Award, Magna Cum Laude Education B.A., Outstanding Certificated Employee, Alisal Union School District.; [oth. writ.] Curriculum development projects for AUSD.; [pers.] I have been inspired by the beauty of nature. Life is extraordinary. We must notice the earth that surrounds us. Influenced by the art of Robert Frost.; [a.] Salinas, CA

HERRON, KELLY
[pen.] Kelly Jean; [b.] October 21, 1966, Port Huron; [p.] Katherine Johnson and Daniel Herron; [ed.] St. Clair County Community College - Major computer information systems; [occ.] Child caretaker, self employed since 1982; [memb.] Northgate Bible Church; [hon.] Honorable Mention from Eddie Lou Cole November 15, 1990 for poem "Human We Are"; [oth. writ.] Personal diary of poems. Desktop published poem in book created by Mr Kraft from P.H.H.S. 1984-85 (Port Huron High School), poem "Blinded by True Love"; [pers.] I try to relate with people heart to heart through love poems or poems of hurt, because we all feel. I've been greatly influenced by Robert Frost.; [a.] Port Huron, MI

HIGGINBOTHAM, VERNON G.
[b.] November 25, 1923, Motley Co, TX; [p.] W. E. and Mary Higginbotham; [m.] Jolene (Bloodworth) Higginbotham, June 15, 1948; [ch.] Jan McClure, Nancy Palmer and Betty Waits; [ed.] BBA, Texas Tech. University, Lubbock, TX., CPA, State of Texas; [occ.] Retired Certified Public Accountant; [memb.] Past member of various professional and civic organizations; [hon.] Various European Campaign Ribbons, World War II; [oth. writ.] Several, none of which have been offered for publication.; [pers.] Following pursuit of demanding, but gratifying profession, I enjoy the quiet time to record some of my thoughts.; [a.] Lubbock, TX

HIGGINBOTHOM, MARSHA DELAINE
[b.] June 3, 1964, Stigler, OK; [m.] Scott Higginbothom, May 26, 1989; [ch.] One boy and one girl; [occ.] Mother, Housewife; [oth. writ.] Love is beautiful, it guides the heart, fills the soul, gives us strength, and never dies.; [pers.] I am currently in the middle of writing an autobiography that I hope someday soon to have published.; [a.] Ripley, OK

HIGGINS, BILLIE
[b.] September 16, 1934, Vero Beach, FL; [p.] Robert and Lena Thompson; [m.] Matthew Higgins, October 29, 1953; [ch.] John Higgins; [ed.] Tenth grade - quit Vero Beach High School; [occ.] Retired; [memb.] Church Worship and Praise Center; [hon.] Editor's Choice Award; [oth. writ.] I write poems about doctors' and nurses' real life experiences, and also humorous little poems. I just write articles for tracts, sometimes homemade ones.; [pers.] I have never been to school to learn how to write. I just let God inspire me to write. God is my inspiration.; [a.] Okeechobee, FL

HILL, AMANDA E.
[b.] February 20, 1979, Dallas, TX; [p.] Keith and Sharon Hill; [ed.] The Colony High School; [pers.] "We take captive every thought to make it obedient to Christ," 2 Corinthians 10:5.; [a.] The Colony, TX

HILL, E. J.
[b.] October 17, 1925, Pittsburgh, PA; [p.] Deceased; [m.] Deceased; [occ.] Retired City of Pittsburgh' Detective; [oth. writ.] Poem, "The Love of Marie," "A Cop's Last Day."

HILLEY, CATHERINE MARIE
[pen.] Marie Hilley; [b.] September 18, 1961, Washington, DC; [p.] Mr. and Mrs. Dean A. Hilley Jr.; [ed.] High school diploma 1979 from Oxon Hill High School, three years of college majoring in Music and Music Education from P.G.C.C. and U.M.E.S.; [occ.] Unemployed; [memb.] I was a member of the Organization M.E.N.C. and Grace Brethren Church, plus I was a member of the Greenfelt Community Band for six years.; [hon.] Certificates of awards for performing with the Greenfelt Community Band, two of them a Certificate of Award or admission to U.M.E.S. Certificate of Award for Music Composers competitions, 3 of them and recently an Editor's Choice Award from The National Library of Poetry.; [oth. writ.] A poem recently printed and published by The National Library of Poetry and one article that was considered for publication in the M.E.N.C. Journal. I am also a songwriter.; [pers.] I like to write about subjects the way I think of them

or imagine them. My favorite poets were Robert Browning and Robert Frost. To have my writing considered for publication is an honor in itself.; [a.] Fort Washington, MD

HINES, HARRIET L.
[pen.] Sian; [b.] June 6, 1972; Brooklyn, NY; [p.] Violet R. Hines and Harry Hines; [ch.] Le Saun L. Garrido; [ed.] Public School #206, Shellbank Junior High School, Midwood H. S.; [occ.] Music Produser; [memb.] Liberty Baptist Church, Pride Block Association- Flatbush; [hon.] Shellbank J.H.S. Plaque for Character, 1986 Academic All- American Scholar Program- Volume 5, United States Achievement Academy 1986 National Awards- Volume 32; [oth.writ.] Several Poems published into musical recordings, others have been submitted as poems for obituaries; [pers.] Firstly, I'd like to thank God, for without him, none of this would be possible. To my parents, who have inspired me to get a proper education, also to my mentors Ms. Joan Pooser and Ms. Phoebe Ragin who helped develop my talents and to be all I can be; [a.] Brooklyn, NY.

HITCHCOCK, DAVID WILLIAM
[b.] January 13, 1975, Chicago, IL; [p.] Bill and Jeanie Hitchcock; [ed.] Goshen High, Scarlet Oaks Vocational; [occ.] Assistant Manager for Papa Jones Pizza, Milford, Ohio; [memb.] American Motor Owners Association, Cincinnati Nature Center; [hon.] National Vocational Technical Honor Society, several science awards; [oth. writ.] Several science fiction short stories, nothing published, several poems, nothing published except "Lost"; [pers.] My goal is to evoke emotion in people and to have them feel that they have someone that they can relate to.; [a.] Amelia, OH

HOAG, GARY THOMAS
[b.] January 30, 1972, Hackley Hospital; [p.] Steve and Caroline Hoag; [ed.] Fruitport High School and my Bible; [occ.] Looking for someone to take interest in my talents.; [memb.] Broadway Baptist Church; [hon.] Having my poem placed into this anthology is an honor to me, thank you.; [oth. writ.] The Lonely Ship, Thy Candle, Guardian, Beware - The Shadow Flags, A Thorn in My Hand, Within His Eyes, and Thy Meaning, to name a few.; [pers.] I long to make a living at something that I like to do. Also, I'm inspired by all that surrounds me, and by the one who has come into my heart.; [a.] Muskegon, MI

HOANG, LANA H.
[pen.] Micana; [p.] Dr. and Mrs. Hoang; [ed.] Currently attending Arnold and Marie Schwartz College of Pharmacy; [occ.] Student; [hon.] The "15 Elements" was published in "Spectrum 25th Anniversary Celebration Issue," Honors Program of Long Island University, Brooklyn Campus; [oth. writ.] "In the works"; [pers.] "Don't go through a day without giving a helping hand."; [a.] New York, NY

HOBBS, KIRK E.
[b.] November 14, 1954, Columbus, IN; [p.] Ken and Peggy Hobbs; [m.] Cindy, May 10, 1980; [ch.] Rachel, Kristopher and Kenton; [ed.] Columbus North H.S., DePauw University; [occ.] Manager, Integrated Community Accounts Cinergy, Cincinnati, OH; [memb.] Sigma Chi Fraternity, BPO Elks, USA United Methodist Church; [a.] West Chester, OH

HODSON, ERNEST F.
[pen.] Ernie Hodson; [b.] May 14, 1929, Detroit, MI; [p.] Francis Hodson, Agnes Hodson; [m.] Margaret D. Hodson, September 12, 1931; [ch.] Stephen, Ann, Carol, Robert, James, John, Thomas; [ed.] Stratford High School, Creative Writing: Sacred Heart University; [occ.] Commercial

Real Estate Broker, semi-retired; [oth. writ.] Several poems recently published in the Sacred Heart University Journal "Horizons"; [pers.] My poetry covers a variety of everyday subjects and situational matters wherein I attempt to express some deeper, perhaps unfelt, meaning or perspective.; [a.] Trumbull, CT

HOGAN, DEBORAH L.
[b.] February 21, 1963, Fort Worth, TX; [m.] James D. Hogan Sr., February 28, 1981; [ch.] James D. Hogan Jr. and Jason L. Hogan; [pers.] If the subject touches my heart, my pen will touch the paper.; [a.] Gorman, TX

HOLCOMB, AARON
[b.] October 21, 1971, Hartford, CT; [p.] Bruce and Pat Holcomb; [ed.] Associate Degree (General Studies), North Western Connecticut Community College, working on Bachelor's Degree at Central Connecticut State University; [occ.] Student; [oth. writ.] None on an official basis or in print currently; [pers.] I love to write fiction! Writing has always been natural to me.; [a.] Canton Center, CT

HOLLINGSWORTH, ROSE E.
[b.] March 4, 1922, Le Junior, KY; [p.] O.D. and Glenna Watson; [m.] D. R. Hollingsworth, June 12, 1943; [ch.] Donald and Gary Hollingsworth; [ed.] Evarts High School, KY, Coldiron Business College, KY; [occ.] Retired Editor, WPAFB, OH; [memb.] NARFE, Order of Eastern Star, First Baptist Church and ISP; [oth. writ.] Poems: "The Old Tree Stands," "A Moment," "Unfinished Tatting" and "Doll in the Window"; [pers.] Poetry is an expression of our inner, deeper feelings that connect us to our past, present and future: it is fulfilling.; [a.] Fairborn, OH

HOLMAN, DEANNA
[pen.] Deanna Holman; [b.] August 16, 1930, Oklahoma City, OK; [p.] F. Haywood Morris and Verne M. Griffin; [m.] Durell Holman, September 12, 1948; [ch.] Linda Holman Meadows and J.D. Holman; [ed.] Finished high school. We (my husband and myself) are cancer survivors—the most important test—knowing how great life is.; [occ.] Housewife—a job I've held nearly 49 yrs.; [hon.] Biggest honor was being grandma at 54. I could finally tell friends to be quiet and let me brag! And I did. And I do.; [oth. writ.] I have written almost 100 poems—none published. Send them to family and friends for birthdays or special times. Something I enjoy.; [pers.] In good times or not so good, I find putting my thoughts on paper has become very important—an excellent way to express one's self.; [a.] Dodge, TX

HOLMAN, DWIGHT W.
[b.] October 3, 1909, Lima, OH; [p.] Amos Holman and Martha Walls Holman; [m.] Lucile C. Schaphorst, September 11, 1930; [ch.] Franklin D. Holman; [ed.] Some college courses, high school; [occ.] Retired; [memb.] First United Methodist Church, Denton, Texas; [hon.] I was a Prudential Agent, Staff Mgr and Dist. Manager. I received many awards in my years of services.; [oth. writ.] Our Golden Wedding, Mystery of Life, God's Mercy, Master, The Rockies, Make Me Humble; [pers.] Is expressed in me, make me humble, we need to know those around us to be humble and care for others.

HOLSEY, RITA
[b.] July 13, 1968; Cleveland; [p.] Alberta and Nathaniel Holsey; [ch.] Antonio Charles Kidd; [occ.] I currently work for Nyma Inc. Subcontractor of Nasa Lewis Research Ctr. I work in the purchasing Dept. as an Office Assistant; [oth.writ.] I'm previously working on a book of short stories called "Telling it like it is"; [a.] Cleveland, OH.

HOLTHAUS, CONNIE R.
[b.] Topeka, KS; [p.] Leo and Madeleine Wyrick; [m.] Bernard P. Holthaus II; [ch.] Stacy Jay and Jeffrey Leighton; [pers.] I believe my writing ability is a gift of God to inspire others.; [a.] Topeka, KS

HOMEIER, NICOLE
[b.] August 29, 1982, Houston, TX; [p.] Angela and Robert Culpepper; [ed.] 9th Grade A.E. Beach High School, present Junior High - Tompkins Middle School, Bloomingdale Elementary; [hon.] Writing poems; [oth. writ.] Joy, Anger, Hate; [pers.] I love working with people and with my hands. I love to write poems and play with my loving dogs. I enjoy shopping with my mom and friends.; [a.] Bloomingdale, GA

HONE, DIANE
[b.] September 6, 1945; Salt Lake City, UT; [p.] Elwin and Venita Brunson; [m.] Gary M. Hone; December 22, 1963; [ch.] Lisa, Rodney, Angela, John, James; [ed.] High School; [occ.] Homemaker; [oth.writ.] Carter, Beyond The Darkness Precious Little Ones. Daddy and Me; [pers.] Many of my writings are inspired by my 5, handicapped grandsons. How special they are in family; [a.] Fillmore, UT.

HONEYCUTT, SHIRLEY ANN
[pen.] Sweet Pea Honeycutt; [b.] May 15, 1951, Tallahassee, FL; [p.] Johnnie B. Brown, Raymond Brown Sr.; [m.] Mr. Willie James Honeycutt, August 16, 1986; [ch.] Tony Jr., Ganoudis, Oliver Jordan, and Shedrick Honeycutt; [ed.] Lincoln High School, TCC Jr. College, Lively Vocational Technical Center, Commercial Artist; [occ.] Teachers Aide, Astoria Park Elementary Sch., Tallahassee, FL; [memb.] Order of Eastern Star; [pers.] I try to bring the readers of my poems and stories a personal insight into life as it is or as it was. If you can feel a part of what you read, you have been touched by true insight and life.; [a.] Tahassee, FL

HOPPE, LINDA
[b.] September 29, 1947; Slayton, MN; [p.] Floyd Gehlsen, Lorraine Gehlsen; [m.] Dennis Hoppe; October 9, 1965; [ch.] Katherine Jean, Christopher Martin; [ed.] Chandler Public School, Chandler, Minnesota; [occ.] Co-Owner Hoppe's Flying Service, Sikeston, Mo. Secretary, Kinsey's Ag. Service, Charleston, Mo; [memb.] United Church of God, AIA; [pers.] Our greatest gift we can pass on from generation to generation is the gift of love. I try very hard to pass on the love so freely given to me, by those before me; [a.] Sikeston, MO.

HORN, CHRISTINA
[b.] October 24, 1967, Huntington, WV; [p.] James and Shelia Kimball; [m.] Divorced; [ch.] Two; [ed.] Graduated from High School; [occ.] Child Care; [oth. writ.] Other poems; [a.] Chillicothe, OH

HORTON, JESSIE
[pen.] Jessie; [b.] August 18, 1983, Beckley, WV; [p.] Rob Horton and Sally Horton; [occ.] Student at Independence Jr. High; [a.] Mac Arthur, WV

HOSKINS, NANCY
[b.] January 3, 1957; Seattle, WA; [m.] Dale Hoskins; April 2, 1976; [ch.] Brooke Christine, Ryan Burt Lindsay Marie and Philip Andrew; [ed.] South High School - Salt Lake City, Utah and Utah State University - Logan, Utah; [occ.] Manager of one of Salt Lake's Largest Floral Shops; [memb.] Natl. PTA, Madd. Hillcrest High School Parents Committee for choir, Natl. Florists Assoc; [hon.] Mother of an Eagle Scout; [oth.writ.] I've written many other poems and stories... none are published at this time. but cherished by family and friends; [pers.] I find great jog and fulfillment in

capturing the beauty of the world and the sensitivity of human relationships with my pen and paper. "A moment left unshared is soon forgotten — but when expressed in writing lives forever in the heard."; [a.] Sandy, UT.

HOUIM, PENNY A.
[b.] January 3, 1964; Marengo, IL; [ch.] Amanda Marie, Sarah Ann, Christopher James; [ed.] Rugby High, Emergency Medical Tech, Certified Nurses Training; [occ.] Auxillary Pioneer and mother; [hon.] Member of the Congregation of Jehovahs Witnesses, Minot ND, member of the National Registry of E.M.Ts; [pers.] Dedicated to my God, Jehovah who sustains me and to my three children who are my inspiration every day; [a.] Max, ND.

HOUSTON, BEVERLY
[b.] January 18, 1954, Bridgeton, NJ; [p.] Josephine and Joe Burks; [m.] Elmer Houston (Deceased); [ed.] Bridgeton High, Glassboro State College, now Rowan College; [occ.] Vocalist, Recording Customer Service Rep.; [memb.] ASCAP Music, National Museum of History, Love of Jesus Church, and many other things; [hon.] CPR, Customer Service. How to start your own record company; [oth. writ.] Have other writings but Children of Innocence is my first work submitted.; [pers.] My heart cries every day for the children because there are not enough people who want to protect them from different types of abuse. I want to make people aware that children are precious to our future.; [a.] Clifton, NJ

HOWARD, ELSA LEE
[pen.] L. C. Lee; [b.] October 31, 1965, Fort Knox, KY; [p.] Karl L. Kolar and Joanne I. Trayter; [m.] David Lee Howard, March 25, 1989; [ch.] Nichole, Thomas, Meaghan and Little David; [ed.] Osceola High, Monessen Jr, Sr. High; [occ.] Housewife and Mother; [pers.] I've always believed that a good poem comes from one's heart, there is no better way to express one's feelings than with pen and paper.; [a.] Interlachen, FL

HOWARD, ROCHELLE
[b.] October 19, 1977; [p.] Ronald E. Howard Sr. and Barbara Rex; [ed.] Gettysburg Area High School, Louisiana State University; [pers.] This poem meant a lot to me. I write poetry as a hobby based on my feelings. This poem embodies the natural determination and pride I always uphold.; [a.] Gettysburg, PA

HOYT, VALERIE
[b.] September 7, 1985, Findlay, OH; [p.] Darla and Melvin Hoyt; [ed.] Going into seventh grade; [hon.] Fifth grade D.A.R.E. Essay Award winner; [pers.] My fifth grade teacher, Mrs. Shelby, got me started on writing.; [a.] Swansea, SC

HUBBARD, LOIS M.
[pen.] Lois M. Hubbard; [b.] September 11, 1943, Portland, ME; [p.] Dorothy and Robert Marshall; [m.] Harold (Ike) Hubbard, August 3, 1968; [ch.] Michael Robert Pattee; [ed.] So. Portland High School, Andover Business College, currently: student with Institute of Children's Lit, W. Redding, Ct; [occ.] Owner of "The Farm," Bakery, Jonesport, ME; [memb.] Northcoast Writers Circle, Jonesport, The Jonesport Literary Club; [oth. writ.] 2 yrs of writing weekly column for 2 local papers; [pers.] I write poetry out of the sheer joy of doing it and I hope to write books that children will want to read for the simple pleasure that reading can bring.; [a.] Jonesport, ME

HUDDLESTON, RICKY
[b.] September 10, 1982; [p.] Richard and Vanessa Huddleston; [occ.] Student; [memb.] National

Honor Roll, Society, D.A.R.E, S.T.A.R.S.; [hon.] Honor Roll, Prince pal's slistm, spelling award, English Award, Pine wood derby best of slow regional and district America's pride certificate, Pride Booster's Certificate; [pers.] If they say it can't be done, prove them wrong; [a.] Lebanon, TN.

HUDSON, TINA W.
[b.] June 4, 1966, Tallahassee, FL; [p.] Doris M. Williams and Tanny Wright Sr.; [m.] Charles A. Hudson, June 28, 1997; [ch.] Michael, MeShalle, TeMetrius and LaCharles; [ed.] Amos P. Godby High School, Talla Community College, International Career Institution, Hart School of Profession; [occ.] Customer Service Correspondence; [memb.] Greater Love COGIC, YMCA, Greater Love Gosphel Choir; [hon.] Golden Award in poetry contest; [oth. writ.] Prev. poem/writing with National Library in '89; [pers.] I pray that this poem will be used as a word of encouragement to someone who is facing battles that seem unbearable. I truly give thanks to God, who is my life and to Charles, who is my husband and best friend . . . I love you, baby.; [a.] Tallahassee, FL

HUFF, QUENTIN
[pen.] "Morgan Chamber," "Bishop"; [b.] December 25, 1974, Raleigh, NC; [p.] James and Earnestine Huff; [ed.] Wake Forest University; [occ.] Writer, tennis player, artist; [hon.] Dean's List, Wake Forest University, 1995 Scholar Athlete of the Year, ACC (Atlantic Coast Conference); [a.] Winston-Salem, NC

HUGHES, GAYE
[b.] March 18, 1928, Mount Vernon, OH; [p.] Foster Child of Clay and Vennice Scott; [m.] Divorced many years; [ch.] R. Michael and J. Brett Hughes; [ed.] Graduated from Bladensburg High School as Valedictorian, from Mt. Vernon Business School and attended Franklin University in Columbus, Ohio; [occ.] Retired Administrative Assistant, now a free-lance writer; [memb.] Christian Women's Club, Country Home Club, Grove Church of Christ, American Cancer Association; [hon.] Various poems and articles published in magazines and newspapers, several honorable mentions as a result of contributing poems to contests, wrote winning essay in Bosses Night Contest.; [oth. writ.] Two non-fiction books on the current market and one in the process of being published (fiction).; [pers.] Words of faith, love and life in self with its pain, sorrow and happiness show up in my writings. I believe that if we feel love or compassion for others we should show them by words, actions and touch.; [a.] Mount Vernon, OH

HUGHES, HOLLY
[pen.] Holly Hughes; [b.] May 18, 1986, Dallas, TX; [p.] David A. Hughes, Constance Hughes; [ed.] Country Day School of Arlington; [occ.] Actress-Student; [memb.] National Fraternity of Student Musicians, Jazz Elite Dance Company, Country Day Singers; [hon.] Principal's Honor Roll, 1st place winner Optimist Club Oratorical Contest, Miss Spirit of Arlington; [pers.] I strive to care about the earth and all nature—to help others.; [a.] Keller, TX

HUGHES, JESSIE LYNNE
[b.] October 19, 1984, Belleville, KS; [p.] Bill and Jolene Hughes; [ed.] Home school; [memb.] Lawton City Ballet; [oth. writ.] Mothers, Raking the Leaves, My Dad's Truck, God's Taste, Quilts, The Kittens; [a.] Duncan, OK

HUMPHRIES, DEVONA
[b.] April 20, 1960, Camden, AR; [p.] Bobbie and Grady Farris; [m.] Doug Humphries, December 30, 1987; [ch.] Holly Nicole; [ed.] Fairview High; [occ.] Co-owner and secretary and treas.

of Humphries Development, Inc.; [pers.] "The Last Christmas" is the first and only poem that I have ever written. This poem was based on a true story about my father and his struggle with cancer.; [a.] Kingman, AZ

HUNT, ARDIS O.
[pen.] Adris O. Hunt; [b.] 1912, Schenectady, NY; [p.] Orpha Luce Gurfer and Addison Jackson Gurfer; [m.] Ellwood M. Hunt, 1937; [ch.] Three grown, 7 grandchilren, 2 great grandchildren; [ed.] Three years College, many of study and specific reading, history, biographies, autobiographies; [occ.] Retired (writing) I am very active in my community.; [memb.] Scarsdale Congregational Church, Scarsdale Womens Club, Women Unlimited; [hon.] Published by Scarsdale Inquirer Scarsdale, NY, reflect on the beauty of the world and all of mankind's possibilities. Not pollyana, but believe in the positive power of thought and action.; [oth. writ.] Story of my life, many daily observations submitted and publish under POV. Point Of View.; [pers.] I believe as Christ said, "Even as you do unto the least of one of these, so you do unto me."; [a.] Scarsdale, NY

HUNTER, DOMINIC
[b.] August 1, 1984, Oakland, CA; [p.] Barbara Brown; [ed.] 7th grader at Claremont Middle School; [occ.] Student; [memb.] Casco Karate School, Oakland Babe Ruth Baseball, Macedonia Baptist Church; [hon.] Did a commercial for the Black Adoption Agency. 2nd place in the Oratorical Fest., 4th place in Math Olympic. 3rd place in a Karate Tournament; [oth. writ.] Poems written in class and songs written for pleasure.; [pers.] I wrote this poem this summer in summer school when we took a field trip to the cemetery. I thought it was going to be dull and dead. But, it wasn't. Different things began to happen and my mind developed pictures of different sights, and rhymes and I came up with this poem.; [a.] Oakland, CA

HYSER, DANIEL THEODORE
[b.] April 23, 1960, Hanover Hospital, PA; [p.] Benjamin and Shirley Hyser, Erma and Jonathan Ferry; [m.] Julia Ann Ferry Hyser, August 25, 1995; [ed.] Spring Grove High, Yorktowne Business Institute; [occ.] York Hospital, Safety and Security Dept.; [memb.] St. Jacob's Lutheran Church, L&M Softball Team; [hon.] Student of the Term, Dean's List, Potter County Team Marathon Trophy, York all-star Softball Player, United States Army Reserve Honorable Discharge, Runner of Year, Hanover, 1986; [oth. writ.] Majesty, Wonders, Wish, Mercy, Who Knows; [pers.] Dedicated to memory of Marshall Haugh and all glorious people caring, sharing, and exemplifying God's blessings through us for others!; [a.] York, PA

IDREES, TALHA
[b.] April 27, 1982, Adrian, MI; [p.] Zeba Idrees; [ed.] Pioneer High School Freshman; [occ.] Student; [hon.] Black Belt Tae Kwan Do certificate, 1st place tennis trophy, 1990 M.E.A.P. Award in Mathematics, story displayed in library in second grade, poem published in newsletter in 3rd grade, good behavior awards; [oth. writ.] Several, I have written a whole poetry book for myself.; [pers.] Look at your life, both inside and out.; [a.] Ann Arbor, MI

ILACQUA, ANTHONY F.
[b.] August 11, 1972, Castro Valley, CA; [pers.] It is the melody of words that gives a poem its power, not their meanings.; [a.] Denver, CO

IMERI, PAL
[pen.] P.I.; [b.] June 20, 1960, Gjakov; [p.] Nhill Imeri and Hana Imeri; [m.] Rusha Imeri, February 5, 1989; [ch.] Hana and Mhill Michael; [ed.] High school; [occ.] Elevator Operator; [oth. writ.]

Amerecord Song Writer, Journey of the Mind (poem), A Moment in Time (poem), Best Poems of 1996.; [a.] Bronx, NY

ISAKSEN, ERIK J.
[b.] July 4, 1967, Lakewood, WA; [p.] Sally and Joseph Isaksen; [ed.] Mannville High School, Mannville, AB, Canada, Washington State University, Pullman, WA; [occ.] Admin. Asst. Parent Help USA Child Abuse Prevention Center; [memb.] Orange County Cruisin' Association; [hon.] Semifinalist for National Library of Poetry contest. "Greatest Romantic Lover of the Century" plaque given by my ex-girlfriend, 1991; [oth. writ.] More poems and lyrics, none published. This was my first try.; [pers.] Don't eat yellow snow. Don't pee into the wind. Soup is good food. Celibacy is the best policy . . . or was that honesty? My influences include . . . everything!; [a.] Huntington Beach, CA

ISLER, RUBY J.
[b.] October 2, 1940, Easley, SC; [p.] Cecil Tipton and Ruby T. Richards; [m.] Lawrence C. Isler, July 5, 1962; [ch.] Mark Anthony Isler; [ed.] Easley Elementary, Easley High, S.C.; [occ.] Housewife, part-time care in helping seniors do work they can't do themselves; [memb.] Eastside Baptist Church, active in church activities, have helped in various charities and community; [oth. writ.] Have written essays in school, but nothing public as yet. Have many writings I have not yet put out.; [pers.] I enjoy being in touch with people and life. I care for others. My philosophy is that if I can't touch someone for God, then there's no reason for being.; [a.] Liberty, SC

JACKSON, ELIZABETH N.
[pen.] Lizabeth; [b.] August 11, 1981, Springfield, OH; [p.] David and Renee Jackson; [ed.] Ceredo-Kenova High School; [occ.] Student; [memb.] Civil Art Patrol, S.A.D.D., Thespians; [hon.] WV Young Writers Award, county and state level, USAA National Honor Roll Award; [pers.] A passionate soul is a precious gift, but possessing the means to express that passion is even more priceless.; [a.] Kenova, WV

JACKSON, ELSIE M.
[b.] July 14, 1947, Skidmore, MD; [p.] Howard William Jackson and Alverta Cromwell; [ch.] Rhonda Y. Cooper, LaVonia R. Jackson, Veronicia L. Jackson; [ed.] Wiley H. Bates Jr. Sr. High; [occ.] Unit Representative at Harbor Hospital Center, Baltimore, MD; [oth. writ.] Several poems published with Quill Book Company.; [pers.] I've been writing since I was 16 years of age. Poetry is a way for me to escape into far-off places. It's a way for me to express myself and hope that when people read my poetry, it will enlighten them.; [a.] Baltimore, MD

JACKSON, FREDA L.
[b.] February 26, 1916, Rockmart, GA; [p.] Robert and Lena Ogle; [m.] Frank Jackson, March 13, 1931; [ch.] Glenn and Kenneth; [ed.] College; [occ.] Retired

JACKSON, KIMBERLY ANN
[b.] June 3, 1966, Pensacola, FL; [p.] Donald Haddock, JoAnn Haddock; [m.] Daniel Jackson, September 7, 1991; [ed.] Vernon High School, Wash.-Holmes Area Vo-Tech.; [occ.] Respite caregiver, Wash. Co. Council on Aging, Chipley, FL; [memb.] Wausau Assembly of God. My husband and I are Youth Leaders of our youth at our church; [hon.] Having this poem published; [oth. writ.] This poem was my first published. It was God-inspired. I do have another private poem named "Forbidden Love". It is non-published, written many years ago.; [pers.] I only write when God inspires, so it may minister to someone else. Keep God in everything

you do, and he will always see you through.; [a.] Vernon, FL

JACKSON, VAREECE
[pen.] Pebbles; [b.] November 2, 1970, Los Angeles, CA; [p.] Dorothy Threets and Peter Jackson; [ch.] Kenyatta Demetrius Barton; [ed.] Skyline High School and The National Business Academy; [occ.] Full-time student at Chabot College, Hayward, CA; [memb.] American Heart Association; [hon.] Great Parent Award from the Grolier Corporation; [pers.] My poem is dedicated to my dearly departed mother, Dorothy R. Threets, whose memory will live on forever in my heart.; [a.] San Leandro, CA

JACKSON, YVONNE EDWINA
[pen.] Yvonne Jackson; [b.] Nashville, TN; [p.] Wilbur and Sallie Frierson [ch.] Shanee, SJ'Mone, Eve; [ed.] Glenville S. High , Bryant and Stratton Harding Bus. School; [occ.] Referral Specialist Kaiser Permanente; [memb.] Embassy of the Rock Armour Bearer's New Beginnings Radio Outreach (Pres. and Founder); [hon.] Extraordinary Customer Relations; [oth. writ.] My Journey , Sister's, I Know A Carpenter; [per.] Writing is a wonder opportunity to encourage and strengthen the reader; [a.] University Hts., OH.

JACOBS, TREVOR A.
[b.] July 25, 1976, Fremont, NE; [p.] Frank and Barb Jacobs; [pers.] I want to thank God for his love, My mom for life, my dad for my name, my grandma for being cool, and Sharon for her encouragement.; [a.] Fremont, NE

JACQUES, MYRTLE
[b.] April 28, 1921, Denver, CO; [p.] Frederick and Cora Mae Cutler; [m.] John E. Jacques, November 17, 1944; [ch.] Francine Louise, Robert Eugene and James Lee; [ed.] 12th grade; [occ.] Retired; [oth. writ.] Currently working on my autobiography for the children.; [pers.] It was quite a challenge to keep a small house and a large yard neat with two very active young sons, ages 6 and 4.; [a.] Kansas City, MO

JAMES, ALISON L.
[b.] June 28, 1954, Westcliffe-on-Sea, England; [p.] Mr. and Mrs. Stanley W. Wheal; [m.] Stephen D. James, September 14, 1980; [ed.] Linguistic and Business Studies at Bromley College, England, resides in U.S. since 1979; [oth. writ.] Writer of inspirational poetry and songs, and children's stories.; [pers.] I seek to reveal spiritual truth and lift the human spirit through all my works.; [a.] New York, NY

JAMES, STEVEN CLIFFORD
[b.] June 4, 1958, Sweetwater, TX; [p.] Ronald and Charlotte; [ch.] Ryan and Justin; [ed.] Pebblebrook High, GA State Univ.; [occ.] Chef Houlahan's, Marrieta, GA; [memb.] A.C.F. (Amer) (Cul) (Fed); [hon.] 5 time award winner pro wedding cake and sweet art; [oth. writ.] "Fallin' Friends," "Just a Thought," "Winter's Day," "Peaceful Glow," "Alive," "A Blind Man's Love Talk," "Soldier Boy," "Little Tree."; [pers.] I hope that through my writings people will see divorced dads are parents too. I love my kids, Ryan and Justin.; [a.] Smyrna, GA

JAMES, TOMEKA
[pen.] Tomeka James; [b.] November 15, 1980, Galveston, TX; [p.] Sandra James, Edward James; [ed.] La Marque High School; [occ.] In high school; [memb.] La Marque High School Choir; [hon.] V.I.L. Solo and Ensemble; [oth. writ.] I write other poems and letters for the school paper.; [pers.] I try to write my poems for younger generations, as well as my own, so they

can understand what I feel about certain subjects in life.; [a.] Texas City, TX

JARC, SAMANTHA JANE
[b.] September 26, 1979, Bangor; [p.] Helen E. Gordon and Robert A. Jarc; [ed.] Old Town High School: Freshman and Sophomore year, Nokomis Regional High: Junior and Senior year; [occ.] Student; [pers.] Poetry is my way of expressing myself.; [a.] Newport, ME

JENNINGS, ADA
[pen.] Entheos - Sadie; [b.] December 31, 1941, Salt Lake City, UT; [p.] George and Florence Catmull; [m.] JTSES, 1961, 1967, 1994; [ch.] David, Julie Barlow, Aaron/Brian Clinger; [ed.] High school, Univ./Utah 1961, Robert Steur College of Beauty 1967, Instructor License State of Utah/Mass in Cosmetology.; [occ.] Hair Stylist, Writer, Artist, Cartoonist and Teacher; [hon.] Modeling 1959-60, young timer 2 C.M.I. White Stag 1960. First Place within the class of 1965. Best Style and Student. Mother of 4 single - Grandmother/3, Vice Pres Soph. Class 1957; [oth. writ.] Outermost, More Time, The Home, A Star Through Eyes Entree, Childhood Dreams, The Voice Within the Temple, Easter Morning, Dear Mother, The Someone, How Fun It Is To Twirl.; [pers.] Birth, sound, touch, talk, reading, writing, arithmetic - Feelings, sing or dance. Do each day create yourself.; [a.] Salt Lake City, UT

JENNINGS, JOHNNY D.
[pen.] Jon P. Walker; [b.] June 30, 1948, Lafayette, AL; [p.] Morris Jennings, Minnie Jennings; [m.] Barbara J. Jennings, June 7, 1981; [ch.] Jason, Pebbles, Marcus, Jessica; [ed.] Howard High, University of Alaska of Anchorage; [occ.] Industrial/ Photographer; [oth. writ.] "Love's True Color," "Mandella (The Man)," "Play for Me a Tune"; [pers.] It is my belief that one ought to always respect the awesome power of words and use them sparingly and correctly.; [a.] Hixson, TN

JENSEN, NANCY B.
[pen.] Nancy Jensen; [b.] October 14, 1937, Montana; [p.] Mr. and Mrs. A. R. Strosky; [m.] Bill Jensen, May 18, 1970; [ch.] Michael J. Pope; [ed.] High school; [occ.] Minister (not paid), Poet, Artist; [memb.] Am Legion Aux. and VFW, The National Library of Poets, Rep. Presidential Task Force, Rep Senatorial Committee, International Poets Society; [hon.] Power of Peace, Poem read at United Nations, Republican Presidential Commission; [oth. writ.] Many poems published and in Library of Congress, over 30 poems.; [pers.] Smile and try to give credit to God and Jesus Christ and love all people.; [a.] Big Bear City, CA

JERNIGAN, C. M.
[pers.] This poem was written from the heart of a grieving mother. My son Erik died 12/25/87 in a tragic auto accident at age 19. At his wake, I realized how loved and respected he was by young and old. This poem was inspired by that respect and love.; [a.] Gastonia, NC

JOHNSON, CHRIS
[pen.] C. Jahson; [b.] March 3, 1972, Redlands, CA; [p.] Douglas Johnson and Deborah Hillock; [ed.] Bachelor of Arts in Creative Writing and History from the University of California at Riverside; [occ.] Student; [hon.] Dean's List at UCR; [pers.] "Until the philosophy which holds one race superior and another inferior is finally and permanently discredited everywhere is war."; [a.] Colton, CA

JOHNSON, JARED M.
[b.] April 4, 1991, Austin, TX; [p.] Amanda and Fred Johnson; [ed.] Kindergarten; [occ.] Student; [pers.] Jared enjoys writing about scary, creepy

things, but also likes to tell grown ups and other kids about the importance of saving the world's natural resources, plants and animals.; [a.] Austin, TX

JOHNSON, KATHERINE
[pen.] Kay Jo; [b.] July 31, 1940, Cass City, MI; [p.] Leonard and Thelma Ballentine; [ch.] 4-Dale, Shawn, Kelly, Amy; [ed.] St. Clair County Community College - Nursing Program; [occ.] LPN - Detroit Medical Center; [memb.] Life of Faith Church; [oth. writ.] Collection of "Lost Love" poems; [pers.] My writings usually reflect my own life experiences and feelings, which are shared by many.; [a.] Port Huron, MI

JOHNSON, KATRINA LYNN
[b.] July 1, 1980, Houston, TX; [p.] Willie F. Johnson and Ella F. Johnson; [ed.] Eisenhower High School, G.W. Carver Magnet School for Applied Technology, Engineering, and the Arts.; [occ.] Student; [memb.] Business Professionals of America, National Honor Society, Student Council; [hon.] National English Merit Award, National Math Award, National Honor Society, Outstanding English Student of the Year.; [pers.] I strive each day to learn about God and know God for myself. I put my trust in the Lord because I know that without him, I am nothing!; [a.] Houston, TX

JOHNSON, RACHAL
[b.] September 12, 1978, Flint, MI; [p.] Mollie and Charles Wellington; [ed.] Northern High School with a 3.0 GPA; [occ.] Going to school; [memb.] A member of the Youth Committee at New Heaven Baptist Church; [hon.] Citizenship Honor Roll, Student of the Month; [pers.] I strive to reflect the true meaning of Black Motherhood. I was influenced by my mother to write this poem.; [a.] Flint, MI

JOHNSON, RUFUS
[b.] May 1, 1911, Montgomery County, MD; [p.] Charles L. and 8Margaret (Smith) Johnson; [m.] Vaunda L. Johnson, May 29, 1971; 8[ch.] Three daughter and two sons and one adopted son; [ed.] 8Howard University, Wash. D.C. 1930-34 , A.B. Degree, commissioned 82nd Lt. ORC Army - 1934, H.U. School of Law, 1936-39, L.L.B (J.D. 8equivalent); [occ.] Lt Col USA (Ret.) Semi Retired Atty at Law; 8[memb.] Life Member: American Legion, Veterans of Foreign Wars, 8M.O.P.H., Life fellow, I.B.A. Life Patron A.B.I. Member: 8A.A.R.P., International Kempo Karate Assn., Baptist Church, 8American Judicature Society, American Law Journal, Senior 8Citizens Association; [hon.] Captain H.U. Football Team, 1933, Co 8- Champion, Pole Vault C.I.A.A. 1934 CIAA. Light heavy Weight 8Wrestling Champion, 1934, AUS, Received Purple Heart, Bronze Star 8C.I.B. Special Regimental Citation for Bravery, Expert all 8infinity Co. Combat Weapons 32nd degree Prince Hall Mason. 5th 8Degree Shorin Ryan Karate (MOP) - military order of the purple 8heart member of the Bar: US Supreme court supreme Court of the 8Republic of South Korea Dist. Court of US For DC, US Court of 8Appeal for DC. Supreme Court of California, Supreme Court of the 8State of Arkansas Federal Court of California and Arkansas.; 8[pers.] A good hearty laugh each day is better for an individual 8than any Medicine. Never go to bed with any unresolved animosity or 8anger in your heart.; [a.] Mason, TX

JOHNSON, STEVEN P.
[b.] September 14, 1967, Tacoma, WA; [p.] Merle Johnson and Bonnie Johnson; [m.] Sylvia Johnson, June 5, 1992; [occ.] U.S. Air Force; [a.] Las Vegas, NV

JOHNSON, WILLIAM C.
[pen.] Lobo; [b.] April 26, 1955; Augusta, GA; [p.] Jimmie Johnson, Joyce Prince; [m.] Divorced; April 26, 1980; Divorced Dec. 11, 1990; [ch.] Natasha Johnson, Terry Johnson; [ed.] George

P. Butler High; [occ.] Iron Worker; [pers.] My poems reflect on certain times of my life that I find hard to deal with; [a.] Augusta, GA.

JOHNSTON, JUSTINE
[b.] July 18, 1976, Hanford; [p.] Michael L. Johnston, Martha Rosas; [m.] Richard Maldonad, Jr.; [ed.] High school graduate of Hanford Adult School; [oth. writ.] I write for personal affection. I've been writing for 9 years, only to release emotions I hold in.; [pers.] It's not who you are, it's how you are and what you make of it. Set your mind to what you want and eventually you'll get it. Believe and you'll be on top.; [a.] Armona, CA

JOINER, MYRTLE
[pen.] Bic; [b.] September 9, 1941; [p.] Annimae and Floyd Adams; [m.] Harvey Joiner, December 24, 1960; [ch.] 1 son Tracy A. Joiner; [ed.] High school, vocational training; [occ.] Hair Stylist and Beauty Consultant; [memb.] Harrisonville Baptist Church, Woman's Convention Auxiliary; [a.] Batesville, MS

JONES, CANDICE
[b.] January 30, 1982, Tucson, AZ; [p.] Paul and Linda Jones; [ed.] Shepherd Jr. High, Red Mountain High; [occ.] Student - 9th grade; [memb.] School newspaper, Spanish club, after school sports, track; [hon.] Honor student, student of the month; [pers.] I guess, perhaps, most things end too quickly, and maybe nothing lasts forever, but I like to think that some things do and always will, even though we'll never know.; [a.] Mesa, AZ

JONES, IRENE
[pen.] Irene Jones; [b.] April 29, 1948, Provo, UT; [p.] J. H. Hilton and Opal M. Hilton; [m.] Wm Lynn Jones, November 11, 1966; [ch.] Deirdre, Christian, Gretchen, Parker, Taylor, Ashley, McKenzie, McGarren; [ed.] Orem High School, Snow College, University of Utah, Santa Barbara City College; [occ.] Administrative Assistant University of California Education Abroad Program, UCSB in Santa Barbara and Co-publisher of Builder/Architect Magazine, South/Central Coast edition; [hon.] Numerous awards from several journalism societies for excellence in newswriting, feature writing, and photo-feature combinations, also photography awards for color and black and white photos.; [oth. writ.] Staff writer: Provo Daily Herald, 2 yrs, Salt Lake Tribune, 6 yrs., editor and Photographer, Intermountain Contractor Magazine, 2 yrs, freelance: for Associated Press and numerous small publishers and magazines, esp. trade publications; [pers.] I try to help people find the inner selves through my poetry. My poems reflect emotional searches and expressions of eternal life and love and how to achieve these.; [a.] Santa Barbara, CA

JONES, JOSEPH ALLEN
[pen.] Joey, Joe; [b.] March 1, 1976, Gowanda, NY; [p.] Mary and Ben Jones; [ed.] High school graduate from Cassadaga High School in Stn. Clairville, NY, 3 years at the La Gudice Center in Fredonia, NY, for automechanics; [memb.] YWCA in Westfield N.Y., Patterson Free Library, Westfield; [pers.] Let your imagination run wild. You never know what you can do if you try. I always wanted to enter a poetry contest but never had the nerve to do it till now and I am glad I did.; [a.] Westfield, NY

JONES, MARVIN
[pen.] Marvin Jones; [b.] July 7, 1927, Luxora, AR; [p.] Sidney Jones, Edmon Jones; [m.] Lucille Jones; [ch.] Nine; [ed.] 10th Grade; [occ.] Farm Labor

JONES, MELINDA
[b.] June 2, 1969, Monticello, KY; [p.] Daniel and Faye Jones; [ed.] University of Kentucky Bach-

elor of Health Science May 1994; [occ.] Medical Technologist, Columbia of Georgetown Hospital, Georgetown, KY.; [pers.] If you speak what is on your mind, and write what is in your heart—something profound might come from one or the other.; [a.] Lexington, KY

JONES, WILLIAM H.
[pen.] William Henry Jones, W. H. Jones, Captain J. Bill Jones; [b.] April 1, 1924, Black Diamond, WA; [p.] Helenor Jones (Father Deceased); [m.] Barbara A. Jones, May 17, 1960; [ch.] Robert Jeffery Jones and Denise Lynn Williams; [ed.] B.A. San Diego State, Naval School of Hospital Administration; [occ.] Captain, U.S. Navy (Ret); [memb.] (1) Federal Health Care, Executives Institute Alumni Assn. (2) Fleet Reserve Association, (3) Distinguished Member, International Society of Poets; [hon.] Legion of Merit (Navy) Numerous Service Medals and awards, Graduated with honors 5 military schools, Advanced from Apprentice Seaman to Captain during Naval Career. Editor's Choice Awards (24), The International Poetry Hall of Fame; [oth. writ.] Endless Thought, Treasured Poems of America, April 1996, Am I Worthy, Treasured Poems of America, April 1996, In His Wisdom We Must Trust, Poetic Voices of America, June 1996, Garden Workshop, Poetic Voices of America, June 1996, Sequins on the Floor, Poetic Voices of America, June 1996, How Sad Memorial Day, Poetic Voices of America, February 1997, Music is a Remedy, Poetic Voices of America, February 1997, Now but Memories, Poetic Voices of America, February 1997, Precious are the Moments, Poetic Voices of America, February 1997, The Tapestry of Life, Poetic Voices of America, February 1997; [pers.] I believe in personal achievement, inspiring others to fulfill their dreams, at peace with self and others, all with a sense of humor, dedication and perspective.; [a.] Lake San Marcos, CA

JORDAN, SAMANTHA JO
[b.] September 1, 1987, Lincoln, NE; [p.] Heather J. Jordan (mother); [sib.] Has five year old brother Jordan Kemerling; [ed.] Currently attends Fredstrom Elem. School; [memb.] Chorus as well as Technology Club; [oth. writ.] Published in "The Anthology of Poetry by Young Americans" an unnamed work by Samantha J. Jordan; [a.] Lincoln, NE

JORDAN, YOLONDA
[b.] November 11, 1970, Denver, CO; [p.] Norvella Truesdale; [ch.] Tarick Brown; [ed.] High school, Mapleton H.S. (Colorado); [occ.] Cert. Nursing Assistant; [pers.] The things I write come from within me in hopes of helping others to understand and appreciate life as a whole.; [a.] Denver, CO

JOSEPH, VENOIL
[pen.] Venoil Joseph; [b.] April 15, 1954, Albu., NM; [p.] Thomas and Rosemary Joseph-Pleasant; [ed.] School of Paralegal Studies, Southern Career Institute, Certificate Paralegalist, Legal Reseacher; [occ.] Legal Aide; [memb.] Gavel Clubs, Toastmaster International; [hon.] Local essay winner for the contest held by local chapter Jaycees, Colo.; [oth. writ.] God as I Know Him; [pers.] Life is rhythm, rhythm is not without rhyme, live and let live—time is the essence of all hope, human—opportunities preserve "Eternity".; [a.] Crowley, CO

JUDNICK, ROSE
[b.] August 31, 1938, Chisholm, MN; [p.] John Strukel and Agnes Laurich Cooper; [m.] John (Deceased), September 8, 1956; [ch.] Debora, Donna, Barbara, Robert Bob and 9 grandchildren; [ed.] Mesabi CC, AAS OFC Tech, AAS Mkt. - Mgmt., BA U of M Duluth, Comm., Minor Art;

[occ.] Quality Assurance Fingerhut Eveleth, MN; [hon.] Student of Excellence UWS; [oth. writ.] "Perception," Nat'l Lib. of Poetry, "Tracing Shadows" publication; [pers.] Riches and health may leave you, but the love you have known will always be in your heart.; [a.] Eveleth, MN

KACHURA, MATTHEW TAYLOR
[b.] June 4, 1974, Easton, MD; [p.] Boris, Donna Kachura; [ed.] Arundel High School, University of Maryland College Park; [occ.] Economist, Regional Economic Studies Institute; [memb.] Economics Association of Maryland; [hon.] Omicron Delta Epsilon, Eagle Scout; [oth. writ.] Sins of the Soul (Compilation), other published poems; [pers.] Made weak by Time and Fate, but strong in Will, to Strive, to Seek, to Find, and not to Yield. Tennyson; [a.] Towson, MD

KADERKA, TRACEY
[b.] August 16, 1978, Richmond, TX; [p.] Thomas and Carol Kaderka; [ed.] Currently enrolled at Wharton County Junior College. I graduated from Needville High School.; [occ.] Filing Clerk at Polly Ryan Memorial Hospital; [hon.] I have had other poems published in your books.; [oth. writ.] I just write poems for fun.; [pers.] I just think people should follow their hearts. They should write their feelings down and let the pen flow.; [a.] Needville, TX

KANE, CAROL
[b.] October 10, 1959, Wichita, KS; [m.] Stephen Kane, September 16, 1995; [ch.] Michael; [ed.] High school; [occ.] Housewife and Private Caterer; [oth. writ.] Three romance novels, as yet unpublished; [pers.] Words are one of our most important creations. Words should be meaningful, fun, and lasting.; [a.] Longview, TX

KANE, NATALIE A.
[b.] December 25, 1971, Connecticut; [p.] James and Angela Kane; [occ.] Graduate student, Biology, University of Connecticut; [oth. writ.] "Iris" high school literary magazine, Kane, NA, CS Jones and T. Vuorisalo. 1997. "Development of galls on leaves of Alnus glutinous and Alnus incana (Betulaceae) caused by the eriophyid mite eriophyes laevis (Nalepa)" Int, J. Plant Sci. 158 (1)! 13-23.; [a.] Farmington, CT

KASHER, RONALD J.
[pen.] Kashman R.; [b.] March 15, 1934, Eveleth, MN; [p.] Molly M. and Michael J. Kasher; [m.] Nancy M. (Moats) Kasher, August 9, 1958; [ch.] Sheryl S., Ann E., Michael D.; [ed.] Pontiac Central H.S., Western Mich. Univ. (BS), Eastern Mich Univ. (MA), Michigan State Univ.; [occ.] Retired: High School Asst. Prin., Muskegon Public Schools (MHS); [memb.] Mich Ed. Ass., Co-Hco 2nd BN, 70th Inf Regt., USAR Capt., Retired North Central Educational Evaluation Team: 90, 92, 93, Muskegon Area Association of School Adm. 72-93, Mich Am Softball Ass., National Softball Ass.; [hon.] National Honor Society, Saber and Key, Scabbard and Blade State of Mich. Special Tribute 5/13/93, Educator Achievement Award for Excellence in Education 83, Meritorious Honor Award MHS 93; [oth.writ.] Ode to My Mother, Iron Mine Worker, Last Letter to Mother, My Boy Mike, Seth's Mom, Six Yrs. Old, Old Man's Lament, The Game, Fisher of Men; [pers.] If one cannot face the music, he should not expect to lead the band. Lead! Follow! Or get out of the way!; [a.] Muskegon, MI

KATIKANENI, MADHAVI
[b.] May 27, 1977, New York, NY; [occ.] Student, American University, Washington, DC; [pers.] To life's dramas, both large and small— how could I write without them?

KAUTZ, JENNIFER LYNN
[b.] September 8, 1964; Grosse Pt., MI; [p.] Terence and Joan E. Johnston (deceased); [m.] Melvin A. Kautz; May 24, 1991; [ed.] Fraser High School, Macomb Community College Assoc. Degree in Automotive Design; [occ.] Senior Automotive Designer, General Motors; [memb.] Association for Researching And Enlightenment; [oth.writ.] First published writing; [pers.] I believe we are all individual expressions of God. We are spirits in human form, with the spirit of God living within us all; [a.] Washington, MI.

KEATHLEY, BEVERLEE
[b.] June 21, 1937, New Castle, IN; [p.] Lloyd Link, Ruby Link; [m.] Wayne Keathley, February 14, 1977; [ch.] Chris, Cindy, Jeff, Melissa; [ed.] New Castle High, Ball State University; [occ.] Regional Consultant for retail stores; [memb.] Humane Society and ASPCA; [oth. writ.] I write poems every week—I have never tried to publish until now.; [pers.] I find writing poetry is a relaxing feeling that relieves everyday stress.; [a.] Mesa, AZ

KEEFFE, LAUREN
[pen.] Lauren; [b.] May 8, 1985, Somers Point, NJ; [p.] Kim and Jim Keeffe; [ed.] Sixth grade, George L. Hess Educational Complex; [pers.] "I like to write poems about things people rarely think to write about."; [a.] Mays Landing, NJ

KEELING, JAMES W.
[b.] August 22, 1944, Akron, OH; [p.] Rev. William and Guineth Keeking; [m.] Thelma (Connie) Keeling, February 15, 1965; [ch.] Jimmy, Scott, Eric/wives: Kim, Cindy, Melanie, and 4 grandchildren; [ed.] Paducah Tilgham High - Army GED, Lee's Jr. College - Gary voc. weld U.S. Steel Boilermaker Apprentice Diploma; [occ.] 32 years Boilermaker Welder, 24 years horse ranch, 16 years evangelist; [memb.] Allegre Missionary Baptist Church, Lifetime Honorary Sherrif's Posse; [hon.] Trained 8Ky state champion Appaloosa horses, received 5 singing and speaking appreciation awards, awarded Christian Development Diploma, Awarded Decision Time Counseling Diploma; [oth. writ.] "In Heaven I Ever Will Abide," "There's Gotta Be a Reason," "I'll Walk with Him," "Tomorrow's Going to Be a Brighter Day," "Alone Without Jesus" and "Did Jesus Have Blue Eyes"; [pers.] Having accepted Jesus Christ as my personal savior and being adopted into the family of God late in life, I have come to realize the importance of telling others about the "Great I Am" through song and writings, John 3:16.; [a.] Elkton, KY

KEENAN, MELISSA KUSTER
[b.] August 1, 1985, Toronto, ON, Canada; [p.] Dr. Robert Keenan and Dr. Janice Kuster Keenan; [ed.] Currently in 5th grade at Fairview Elementary School, Fox Chapel, Pittsburgh, PA; [memb.] I study voice, dance and acting at the Civic Light Opera's Academy of Music Theater. I play piano and love to write songs to express my inner feelings and to resolve conflict in my day to day life. Melissa has been in many school theatrical performances and has sung several solos at church and school. She is a member of the Killer Whales Swim Team and loves marine biology.; [pers.] Writing a journal or a poem every day allows me to express and better understand my feelings.; [a.] Pittsburgh, PA

KELLEY, RUTH
[b.] May 14, 1970; Washington CO, MD; [m.] David Kelley; September 30, 1995; [ch.] Curtis Holtzman; [ed.] Williamsport High School Hagerstown Junior College; [occ.] Sustitute Teacher; [oth.writ.] "I Wish For You" published in Treasure The Moment Quill Books; [pers.] This poem is written for my dear friend Jenny G. Thank you Jenny for your support; [a.] Hagesrtown, MD.

KELLNER, TIFFANIE NICHOLE
[b.] May 7, 1983, Vallejo, CA; [p.] Greg and Judy Kellner; [occ.] 8th gr. student; [memb.] I belong to a youth group in New Jersey called Breakaway.; [hon.] I received Student of the Month for the month of February, 1997 and November, 1995.; [pers.] I write my best poems when I am angry or sad because it helps keep me from getting angry at others. I wrote this poem because my best friend and I have gone through many things together.; [a.] Fallsington, PA

KERR, LEANDRA LEE
[b.] May 5, 1979, Indianapolis, IN; [p.] Wanda and David Kerr; [ed.] In tech. high school now; [oth. writ.] "Happiness" published in The Colors of Thought; [pers.] I write my poetry through my personal feelings, thoughts, and experiences. I hope to make a living of it.; [a.] Indianapolis, IN

KESLER, REBECCA L.
[pen.] Becky Kesler; [b.] November 21, 1962, Royston, GA; [p.] Charles Rogers and Willene Rogers; [m.] Mark R. Kesler, October 24, 1992; [ch.] Michael David and Tyler Dwayne; [ed.] Franklin County High School; [occ.] Housewife; [memb.] American Heart Assoc., New Bethel Baptist Church; [pers.] I like to express my feelings and innermost thoughts through writing.; [a.] Toccoa, GA

KESWANI, MERYL
[b.] February 7, 1927, India; [p.] George and Mavis Hiett; [m.] Deceased, December 22, 1957; [ch.] Two - daughter and son; [ed.] Matriculation (India); [occ.] Retired Homemaker; [oth. writ.] Not yet. Intending to write a book; [pers.] I'm a quiet, reserved person. Hobbies: writing poetry, doing ceramics and needle point. I like travelling in my country provinces and some in United States, New York and Montana; [a.] New York, NY

KEY, CHRISTOPHER JAMES
[b.] July 8, 1974, Brownwood, TX; [p.] Alan Clyde and Kala Rene Key; [ed.] 1 year of college at Cisco Jr. College; [occ.] Fire Control Man, Tomahawk Weapon's Systems U.S. Navy; [hon.] Two letters of commendation and a Navy and Marine Corps achievment medal in the Persian Gulf during Operation Southern Watch; [pers.] Be true to yourself, others will follow; [a.] Cross Plains, TX

KILLION, MICHAEL
[b.] October 12, 1976; Fort Stewart, GA; [p.] Nancy Napier, Mark Killion; [ed.] Richmond High School; [occ.] Warehouseman; [a.] Richmond, IN.

KILPATRICK, BERTHA M.
[pen.] The Glass Lady; [b.] May 17, 1960, Omaha, NE; [p.] Charles W. Miller Sr. and Delores Miller; [m.] Perry D. Kilpatrick, September 22, 1984; [ch.] Angela May and Michael David; [ed.] Fort Calhoun High School, Nebraska College of Business; [memb.] Girl Scouts of United States of America (GSUSA); [hon.] Editor's Choice Award, Poetry; [oth. writ.] Man In Silence Of Yesterday; [pers.] When a thought comes to my mind and it sticks inside repeating itself, I know its something I can express with others, so I always write it down and go from there.; [a.] Kansas City, MO

KIMBRELL, LOIS
[b.] August 27, 1954, Rock Hill, SC; [p.] Bob Kimbrell, Lula Kimbrell; [ed.] Indian Land, Central Piedmont Community College; [occ.] Material Handler, Stanley Tools, Charlotte, NC; [pers.] I share who I am and where I have been in hopes that someone may know that one other has been there and understands.; [a.] Fort Mill, SC

KINEMAN, LANIS E.
[pen.] Michael Starr; [b.] October 2, 1926, Massac

Co., IL; [p.] Charles and Ida Kineman; [m.] Vanda Ruth Kineman (2nd marriage), September 1, 1996; [ch.] Larry Eugene Kineman, David Paul Kineman, Kathryn Jean Ralph, Janet Ruth Windlan; [ed.] Brookport, Il, High School, A.B. Johnson Bible College, Knoxville, TN, Butler U., School of Religion-B.D.; [occ.] Minister of Seniors, Chandler Christian Church, Az. Dec.-April, Sr. Minister of Bethany Christian Church, Anderson, In. for 29 years. Retired Sept., 1991; [memb.] Anderson, In. Local Club, National Exchange Club (Past Pres.), International Disaster Emergency Service (Past Financial Sec.), Alexander Foundation, Barnabas Centers (V. Pres.), Mission Services, Trustee of Johnson Bible College (21 years), Secretary of North American Christian Convention (2 years), Arizona and Indiana State Representative for Safety Net, Second President Indiana Christian Convention; [hon.] Three awards from Bethany Christian Church, Anderson, In., four times in "Who's Who" publications, awards from In. Christian Conv. and North American Christian Convention, Award from Johnson Bible College for 21 years of service as Trustee, plaque to me and late wife, Kathryn "Distinguished Service Award" from Alumni Assoc.; [oth. writ.] Contributor of Articles to "Christian Standard" Cincinnati, Oh., Sermon Mss. to book "Ready, Set, Grow" published by Standard Publishing Co., two sermon Mss. to publisher in Nashville, TN, pamphlet on "Prayer" distributed by N.A.C.C.-"Partners in Prayer"; [pers.] I was ordained as Minister of the Christian Church in 1946. I was married to Kathryn Turnbull for forty-six years before her death in 1994. I have 10 grandchildren. Relationships both vertical and horizontal are more important to me than things. I love poetry—it communicates truths to inspire and motivate.; [a.] Anderson, IN

KING, BETTY
[b.] February 21, 1960, B.P.T., CT; [p.] Annie Nanoe - Deceased; [ch.] Londell, Faien, Larise King; [ed.] High school diploma; [occ.] Bench Machine Operator—Owens Brockway Bipit CT; [pers.] I do have other writings, I mailed two others in before this one, but did not hear anything yet; [a.] Bridgeport, CT

KING, RUBY
[b.] April 18, 1935, Greenville, SC; [p.] Fred and Nan Jones (Deceased); [m.] Percy King, April 3, 1954; [ch.] Libby, Frances, Camilla, Madding, Susan; [ed.] B.S., M.A., Ed. S. University of North Alabama; [occ.] Retired English Teacher; [memb.] Leighton United Methodist Church, Leighton Study Club; [hon.] Keller Key (highest GPA in class summer 1967 at UNA) Delta Kappa Gamma, Sigma Tau Delta; [oth. writ.] Essay in local newspaper, plus a number of poems and essays that I never have tried to publish. Basically, I write for personal expression of ideas and emotions.; [pers.] I believe that love is the necessary requirement for happiness, love for all God's creatures. Obviously the early Romantics influenced me.; [a.] Leighton, AL

KINNEY, TONIA
[pen.] Tonia Kinney; [b.] March 31, 1966, Canton, OH; [m.] Adam Kinney, August 17, 1989; [ch.] Joel Kinney; [oth. writ.] A collection of poetry combined with material from personal journals is a work in progress.; [pers.] It is my greatest wish that above what I have knowingly done in life, I will have touched someone unknowingly and mattered.; [a.] San Diego, CA

KLEIN, MAGGIE
[b.] February 20, 1986, Ann Arbor, MI; [p.] Angie Klein, David Klein; [ed.] I have gone to Burns Park Elementary School for 6 years, I am almost done with fifth grade.; [occ.] Student, babysitter; [memb.]

Ann Arbor Youth Chorale, various sports teams; [hon.] Personal Excellence from the Ann Arbor Public Schools; [oth. writ.] Other poems: Clouds, Tolerance, many short stories. I am working on a novel "Just Call It Magic".; [pers.] I wish to thank my friends, family, and teachers who have helped and encouraged my writing.; [a.] Ann Arbor, MI

KLETZKY, MICHELLE GINA
[b.] September 22, 1983, Boulder, CO; [p.] Sally and Ed Kletzky; [ed.] Eighth grade student at Southern Hills Middle School; [pers.] My dream has been to have one of my poems published and it finally happened! I include things in my poetry that mean something to me and the people who read them.; [a.] Boulder, CO

KLINE, MARY W.
[pen.] Mary Ann Wright Kline; [b.] January 18, 1929, Columbia County, PA; [p.] J. Webster and Hazel H. Wright; [m.] Milton R. Kline, December 25, 1952; [ch.] John Webster, William Herbert; [ed.] Bloomsburg High, BSTC 1952 (now Bloomsburg University) Graduate in Elementary Ed. and Speech Correction. Teacher and Tutor for Central Columbia and Bloomsburg School Districts; [occ.] Retired, but still tutoring; [memb.] Member of St. Matthew's Lutheran Church, Bloomsburg and Teacher for 37 years. Former Den Mother and 4-H leader. Member of Orangeville Civic Club and Orangeville Homemakers.; [hon.] Several Sunday School and 4-H awards for years of service. A "Good Neighbor" award in 1986 and several art awards for paintings and an award for country and western square dancing.; [oth. writ.] I have written many poems through the years. Some are: Grace, Resignation, Twilight Time, The Regulars, Recall and Desire, A Flock of Bluebirds, What Is a Treasure?, A Guiding Star, An Ode to Adrenaline - etc.; [pers.] I hope my belief that nothing is so bad that it can't be overcome, is reflected in my poetry. I have been greatly influenced by Rudyard Kipling's poem "If" and by my wonderful, poetic mother.; [a.] Orangeville, PA

KLINGENBERG JR., ROBERT
[b.] February 8, 1959, Whidbey Island, WA; [p.] Robert and Betty Klingenberg; [ch.] James David and Justine Marie; [ed.] Dublin Elementary, Amador High School; [occ.] Installer/Technician, T.C.I. Cable; [memb.] Member Victory Christian Center; [oth. writ.] Various poems and songs; [pers.] I believe we should use the gifts God gave us to help others and to do His work.; [a.] Pleasanton, CA

KNISS, SCOTT W.
[b.] February 7, 1971, New Berlin, WI; [p.] William and Marie Kniss; [ed.] Eisenhower High and Middle Schools, University of Wisconsin-Oshkosh; [oth. writ.] Various articles published in the UW-Oshkosh "Advance Titan"; [pers.] Life is a series of experiences, both good and bad, and we are meant to learn from all of them.; [a.] Appleton, WI

KOEHN, KENDRA
[b.] February 9, 1988, McPherson; [p.] Michael and LaVonia Koehn; [ed.] 3rd grade Wheatland Country School, Moundridge, Kansas; [pers.] To my sister, Fonda, who loves sunsets.; [a.] Moundridge, KS

KOMM, JENNIFER LUE
[b.] November 9, 1976, Vancouver, WA; [p.] Harold L. Komm Sr. and Sandra L. Komm; [ed.] La Center High School, La Center, WA, Eastern Washington University, Cheney, WA; [occ.] Studying Music Education and Performance; [pers.] I am who I am, I don't try to be someone I'm not. The poems I write come from me and my own feelings and emotions. That is my trademark.; [a.] Usk, WA

KOONTZ, ALICIA
[b.] May 1, 1983, Ft. Belvoire, VA; [p.] Michele Whiteley; [ed.] Jr. High, 8th Grade Rancho Starbuck Jr. High School, Whittier, CA; [occ.] Student; [memb.] La Habra Girls Softball Association; [hon.] Gate; [a.] Lahabra, CA

KORDIAK, DOROTHY
[b.] November 11, 1928, Clear Lake, WI; [p.] David and Clara Jackson; [m.] George A. Kordiak, June 10, 1947; [ch.] Eleven children; [ed.] High school; [occ.] Homemaker, wife and mother; [pers.] I was raised in a home where music, especially religious songs, were a very big part of our lives. Bible stories also played an important role. So, I've always had a special love for religious music and writings, especially the new testament. My life and that of my husband, children and families are greatly influenced by our religious beliefs and practices. My poetry reflects my love for the spiritual side of life.; [a.] Minneapolis, MN

KOWALSKI, NANCY S.
[b.] February 24, 1946, Pittsburgh, PA; [p.] Leah and John Sonnett; [m.] Don Kowalski Sr., August 2, 1969; [ch.] Donald Jr. and Shannon, Grandchild - Demetri; [ed.] Our Lady of the Sacred Heart Academy, June 1964; [occ.] Pre-School Dept. Sewickley Valley YMCA; [pers.] My hike to the bottom of the Grand Canyon was one of the most physically challenging and memorable things that I have ever done. I am proud of myself for having the courage to try it and getting it done. Everyone should.; [a.] Baden, PA

KRASSOW, SAMANTHA
[b.] June 19, 1980, Michigan City; [p.] Debe and Dale Krassow; [ed.] I am currently a junior in high school.; [occ.] Student; [memb.] I am in the JROTC (Junior Reserves Officers Training Corp.) and was recently promoted to Gunnery Sergeant.; [oth. writ.] Other poetry; [pers.] "In order to really get far in life you have to turn all your dreams into burning desires and realize it's up to oneself to make them a reality." —Quoted by Major Larry Naifen, JROTC Senior Instructor.; [a.] Trail Creek, IN

KREILING, CHRISTINA
[b.] March 30, 1974, Ontario, OR; [p.] Vernon and Marlene Reynolds; [m.] Jason E. Kreiling, June 24, 1995; [ch.] Corah Mikkaila - Jena Erianna; [ed.] Ft. Campbell High, Western Kentucky University; [occ.] Homemaker and dedicated military spouse; [memb.] Honor graduate, English and German Academic awards; [oth. writ.] Written many songs and poems. Currently writing a romance novel.; [pers.] Most of my writings are inspired by my experiences and travels. I thank God for my ability to write.; [a.] Vilseck, Germany

KRIVYAN, MICHAEL
[b.] October 23, 1985, Riga, Latvia; [p.] Olga Krivyan and Vladimir Krivyan; [occ.] A student of 6th grade I.S. 239, Brooklyn, NY; [pers.] I try to express my thoughts and feelings through the wonderful art of poetry.; [a.] Brooklyn, NY

KUMAR, ANANT
[b.] May 8, 1968, New Delhi, India; [p.] Ramesh Chandra and Suman Madhuri Gupta; [ed.] Bachelor of Technology, Electrical Eng. Indian Institute of Tech., New Delhi, India, MS Electrical Eng., Univ. of Southern Cal., Los Angeles, California; [occ.] Software Engineer; [oth. writ.] None published!; [pers.] I am constantly amazed by the creativity of man. I draw inspiration from such poets as Eliot, Brodsky, Walcott, Faiz and Ghalib. URDU Poetry is the single largest influence on my writing style.; [a.] Santa Monica, CA

LA MANNA, JAMES M.
[pen.] Jim; [b.] January 7, 1947, Bronxville, NY;

[p.] Phil and Margaret; [ed.] Eastchester High School, Bulova Watches; [occ.] Town of Eastchester Laborer; [memb.] American Legion, V.F.W. and Vietnam Vets of America Chapter 49, Westchester Co., N.Y.; [hon.] Merit award for "Islands, a Tribute to Dad." Award plaques from V.V.A. for dedication to chapter work.; [oth. writ.] "Islands," a Tribute to Dad"; [pers.] A need to succeed and not that of sadness. Poetry is my food so taste and enjoy.; [a.] Eastchester, NY

LACALAMITA, VINCENT
[b.] December 24, 1950, Brooklyn, NY; [p.] Frank LaCalamita, Dorothy LaCalamita; [m.] Patricia LaCalamita, November 6, 1982; [ch.] Michael Anthony; [ed.] Connetquet High School, N.Y., Broward Community College, FL., U.S. Air Force Aircraft Maint. School; [occ.] Inventory Services Specialist, FPL Electric Utilities; [memb.] Park Springs Presbyterian Church, member and volunteer, usher, etc.; [hon.] Honor Roll, Connetquet High School, Honor Graduate, U.S. Air Force, Aircraft Maint. School; [oth. writ.] I had a haiku published in a high school publication and wrote several others. (High school is where I started writing a few haikus); [pers.] I love writing haikus the best and would like to have more published. I thank God and nature for influencing me!; [a.] Coral Springs, FL

LACEY, DORIS J.
[b.] January 8, 1933, Burlington, NC; [p.] George and Ethel Massey; [m.] John W. Lacey, August 27, 1994; [ch.] David Maurer and Jim Maurer, (Jose, Todd, Scott - Stepsons); [ed.] Graham High School, Graham, NC, Burlington Business College, Burlington, NC; [occ.] Quit work force 2 yrs. ago - before that, a secretary.; [oth. writ.] I have written poems since my youth but none published except in school publications.; [pers.] I believe that writing brings forth our innermost feelings which might not otherwise be expressed.; [a.] Daytona Beach, FL

LACHLER, LISA
[b.] January 14, 1970, Elmhurst, Queens; [p.] Helen and Clifford Lachler; [pers.] This poem was inspired by and dedicated to Lynn Darrell. My sister, my butterfly, even death does not keep your spirit from soaring within my heart. Love for forever, Lisa.

LACHNEY, JO
[pen.] Joy N. Heart; [b.] August 9, 1942, New Orleans, LA; [p.] Norma Anderson, Earl J. Coludrovich; [m.] Divorced; [ch.] Debra Turlich, Marcella Kelly, Timothy Earl Kelly; [ed.] Warren Easton High School, Delta Business Collage, at age 23, Delgado Business Collage at age 38, LSU courses at age 54; [occ.] Purchasing Agent, plus - Accountant and Poredain Doll Maker; [memb.] Broadmore United Methodist Church; [hon.] Having this poem published because when I am gone a part of me lives on to always touch another's heart.; [oth. writ.] None published; [pers.] God gave us all many gifts, find them, use them and above all—share them. Listen to your hearts, God's love dwells there!; [a.] Baton Rouge, LA

LADSON, SHIRLEY D.
[b.] November 19, 1936; Phila., PA; [p.] John Reid and Prevelynne Reid; [m.] Albert Ladson; [ch.] Curtis, Albert Jr., Lynne, Michael and Rodney [ed.] Graduated Overbrook High School, Phila., PA, Business Management, Community Urban Action And Social Service Studies at Community College; [occ.] Former Storeown and Community Worker, Retired; [memb] Member of Mount Olivet Baptist Church, AARP, American Diabetes Association. I am now disabled and spend most time at home writing as a hobby; [oth.writ.] I have written articles in our community news letter and havee

had two poems published by the National Library Of Poetry. "I am America", in The Voice Within and "Thoughts Of Silence", Best Poems of the 90's; [pers.] I have always had interest in how we relate to each other and the spiritual side of human behavior. I write poems and essays that I hope will make people think about consideration; [a.] Phila., PA.

LAMB, EMILY E.
[b.] December 13, 1973, Cape Girardeau, MO; [p.] Charles and Elaine Wipfler; [m.] Eric L. Lamb, June 12, 1993; [ed.] St. Augustine Elementary, Scott City High School; [occ.] Customer Service, Cotton Patch Cafe, NM; [hon.] Salutatorian, Bausch and Lomb Science, State Speech Competitor, St. Augustine Yearbook Editor; [pers.] This poem is dedicated to the loving memory of my brother. May he "Rock On" for eternity.; [a.] Clovis, NM

LAMB, LORI J.
[b.] June 21, 1955, Detroit, MI; [p.] Beverly and Robert Hojnacki; [m.] Thomas E. Lamb, August 2, 1980; [ch.] Jennifer Jane, Teresa Rose; [ed.] Warren High School, Ross Business Institute; [occ.] Housewife; [memb.] Warren Assembly of God; [oth. writ.] Several poems yet to be published.; [pers.] I thank God for the gifts He has given me, without him in my life I could not accomplish anything.; [a.] Warren, MI

LAMB, TERRY
[b.] February 8, 1971, Miami, FL; [p.] Bob and Dorothy Hesse; [m.] Christopher Lamb, June 18, 1994; [ed.] Calvary Bible College, B.S. Radio Broadcasting; [hon.] Art Achievement '89 (Award), Broadcasting Dept. '95 (Award); [a.] Colorado Springs, CO

LAMPKE, JAMES DOUGLAS
[pen.] J.D.; [b.] March 3, 1986, Orange Park, FL; [p.] James E. and Frances C. Lampke; [ed.] Currently in 5th grade at Fleming Island Elementary School; [occ.] Yard Man; [memb.] National Karate Assoc., Catholic Altar Boy, Mudo College of Tai Chan Do; [hon.] Black belt in Karate and Certificate for poem, "The Ocean" presented by Fleming Island Elementary Principal Tom Ramsey 3-11-97 for Creative Expression by an Elementary Student; [oth. writ.] The Ocean, published in 1997 edition of "Anthology of Poetry" by young americans; [pers.] My goal is to be an artist and poet. I hope to go to Douglas Anderson School of the Arts in Jacksonville, FL, for middle school and high school. Special thanks to Mrs. Donna Glod for making me write poetry over Thanksgiving.; [a.] Middleburg, FL

LAMPTON, BERNICE ANNETTE
[b.] July 5, 1965, Eglin, FL; [p.] Marianne and Prof. Dr. Andor Shelby; [m.] James Daniel Lampton, May 19, 1991; [ch.] Nadine Yvette Lampton; [ed.] I received long years of wonderful lessons from the classical pianist, my Father. I studied music in Germany and Italy. I grew up in Germany.; [occ.] Pianist and piano teacher; [hon.] In September 1989 I won awards for best Interpretation in Romantic and Modern categories in an international piano competition in Ibiza (Balearic Island, Spain); [oth. writ.] I am continuing an over 100 year-old Hungarian Music tradition. My great grandfather was a conductor for Emperor Franz Josef of the Austro-Hungarian Empire. My great-grandmother was a famous violinist. My mother is German.; [pers.] I spent lots of vacations at the Mediterranean on the Spanish island, Ibiza. My love for the ocean bloomed from my early childhood in Florida to my "older" years in California. Since I was a teenager, I love to write romantic poems that mirror the atmosphere and deepness of a place or person.; [a.] Seaside, CA

LANDRY, JEFFREY P.
[pen.] Stal; [b.] August 6, 1977; [p.] Wayne and Ellen Landry; [ed.] Naugatuck High School, Johnson and Wales University 1 1/3 yr.; [occ.] Special Education Aide; [hon.] Many; [oth. writ.] Two-hundred or more, by publishing date of this, looking to be published.; [pers.] Artist, musician. Influences are James D. Morrison, T.S. Elliot, Frost, Hemingway, Kerouac, R. Hunter, K. Keesey, Grateful Dead and all the heads.; [a.] Naugatuck, CT

LANDRY-KULIKOWSKI, MIREILLE
[pen.] Benny Fits; [b.] September 18, 1946; Canada; [pers.] This is my first step in poetry; [a.] Singer Island, FL.

LANE, BARBARA A.
[b.] October 12, 1970, Chester, PA; [p.] Paulette and Freddie Fuller/Paul Lane; [ed.] Cardinal O'Hara Class of 88, Delaware County Community College 88-90, Brandywine Beauty Academy 90-91, Widener University (94-attending); [occ.] Proprietor/Stylist of Amaka for Supreme Beauty; [pers.] I thank God for granting me the gift of poetry. Because He has blessed me with many gifts, I have vowed to always share them. Trusting in Him allows me to be successful at whatever I do.; [a.] Chester, PA

LASHERAS, REJANE
[b.] February 9, 1960, Rio de Janeiro, Brazil; [p.] Gidion and Ruth Silva; [m.] Joao Lasheras, 1986; [ch.] 2 - Juan and John; [ed.] Fanelt, Rio de Janeiro, major: Educational Administration (1984); [occ.] Wife and Mother; [oth. writ.] "Journey Into My Soul" - 1995 (poem), "Destiny" - 1996 (romance); [pers.] I try to show in my writing the beauty and emotions of the human soul.; [a.] Jersey City, NJ

LATHON-WHITE, VANESSA
[p.] Vanessa Lathon; [b.] October 3, 1953; St. Louis, MO; [p.] Leroy Lathan Sr., Emma Lathon; [m.] Robert L. White Jr. (ex); [ch.] LaDonna M. White, Robert E. White; [ed.] William Beaumont High School, Columbia Community Colleges; [occ.] Lead-Analyst, Army Reserves Personnel Center; [memb.] First Missionary Baptist Church of Northwoods; [hon.] William Beaumong National Honor Society, Who's who Among High School Students. Honors Program Florrisant Valley Community College, Department of the Army Achievement Medal; [oth.wri.] Several poems in personal library, No other writings submitted for publication; [pers.] My writings reflect emotions from private moments of meditation, I write of my personal experiences as well as those of others. I am very much inspired by the works of Maya Angelou; [a.] St. Louis, MO.

LAWRENCE, LESLIE ANN
[pen.] Desire; [b.] June 25, 1967, Brooklyn; [p.] Mattie Blocker and Eugene Lewis; [m.] Walter Lawrence, November 25, 1994; [ed.] PS. 241, Jackie Robinson Prospect Heights High School; [occ.] Real Estate Agent; [memb.] Make A Wish Foundation, Feed the Children; [hon.] Million Dollar Club; [oth. writ.] Many other poems but none ever published; [pers.] I take God with me and give him all the glory, for without him I could not have survived.; [a.] Bronx, NY

LAWSON, DESSELL
[pen.] Rose Max; [b.] November 9, 1969, Brazil, IN; [p.] William DeCamp, Ruth DeCamp and Jodie; [m.] David Lawson, November 5, 1990; [ch.] David and Sara; [ed.] The School of Life; [occ.] "Mommy," Antiques Dealer, Amateur Songwriter; [hon.] Honored to sing one of my original songs at the Ryman - Nashville, 1994; [oth. writ.] Over 5 songs and poems unpublished but

cherished personally.; [pers.] The best poems ever written are the ones taken from life, that everyone can relate to and learn from.; [a.] Clay City, IN

LAWSON, SHARON
[pen.] Sherry Lawson; [b.] October 19, 1948, Illinois; [p.] Deceased; [m.] Gordon Lawson, August 27, 1995; [ch.] Jeff, Kristin, Scott and Kevin; [ed.] Northern Illinois Univ. Advertising and Graphic Communications; [occ.] Vice President of Asset Management—Hawthorne Savings; [memb.] Rotary International - President-Elect of Los Angeles International Airport Rotary Club; [hon.] Award-winning Water Colorist; [oth. writ.] Greeting cards, poems and prose; [pers.] I feel that I am here both to learn and teach, and that we all use our own talents to help each other along the way.; [a.] Thousand Oaks, CA

LAZENBERRY, LILLIAN W.
[pen.] Lil; [b.] March 10, 1928, LA; [p.] Kelly and Joanna Price Warmsley; [m.] 1st marriage, Dr. John M. Warren (Deceased), August 4, 1947 (Divorced, August 26, 1969), 2nd marriage, - LeRoy Francis Lazenberry, May, 1978; [ch.] John, Carl, Cheryl, Monica, Patricia and Todd, Stepchildren: Dennis Lazenberry and Kristie Lazenberry; [ed.] Business Adm. Major - Continuing Ed., Washington Technical High, U. of M - continued Education, Michigan State Utility Regulation, Certificate, Cornell U., Industrial Relation Certificate, and American Institute of Banking; [occ.] Freelance Writer, Consultant; [oth. writ.] Columnist - 27 yrs., Freelance Writer.; [pers.] Communication is the key to understanding.; [a.] Edina, MN

LEBLANC, BLAKE K.
[b.] June 30, 1981, New Iberia, LA; [p.] Irving and Regina LeBlanc; [ed.] Sophomore at Kempner H.S., Sugar Land, TX; [occ.] Student, Goal: Sports Medicine; [memb.] National Athletic Assoc., St. Theresa Catholic Church Youth Group, Guitar Club, (I play the bass guitar); [hon.] 2 yr. Letterman for Athletic training in 4 sports, A-B Honor Roll (high school), poetry contest winner for Kempner High School 1996-97; [oth. writ.] After You're Gone, Unsolved (K.D.C.), Can't Slow Down, Clue, Mind Games, Then and Now, Souls, Twins. None published—just write for my personal enjoyment.; [pers.] I strive to write about things that cannot be talked about with ease, such as death, suicide, etc. My inspiration comes from Edgar Allan Poe and my 9th grade English teacher, Ms. Linda Honea at Kempner High School.; [a.] Sugar Land, TX

LEE, WILLIAM JAMES EDWARDS III
[pen.] Bill Lee; [b.] July 23, 1928, Snow Hill, AL; [p.] Alberta and Arnold Lee III; [m.] 1st wife, Jacquelyn Lee (Deceased), 2nd wife, Susan Kaplan-Lee; [ch.] Five children from 1st marriage - Spike, Chris, David, Joy and Cinque, One child from 2nd marriage - Arnoldtone Kaplan Lee VI; [ed.] High School graduate at the Snow Hill Normal and Industrial Institute founded by his maternal grandfather, William James Edwards in 1947. Graduated Mocehouse College in 1951; [occ.] Jazz Musician (Bassist), Composer, Arranger, and Writer; [oth. writ.] "Mo' Betta' Quarter"; [pers.] He has performed as a Bass Violinist with all the notables in Jazz, Folk music and theatre, composer of 8 folk-jazz operas, wrote the music score for 4 major motion pictures.; [a.] Brooklyn, NY

LEEKS, VERNELL
[b.] April 21, 1947, Cleveland, OH; [p.] Ida M. Leeks/Archie Leeks; [ed.] B.A. Social Work, AAS, Mental, Health/Chemical Dependency; [occ.] Case Manager, Chemical Dependency; [memb.] Certified Chemical Dependency Counselor—Ohio, International Certified Counselor; [hon.] Military awards, Dean's List, Outstanding Volunteer, community service award; [pers.] I

reflect upon the good feelings achieved in caring for other people, the beauty of our world and I find peace in poetry about this beauty.; [a.] Cleveland, OH

LEFEVRE, WESLEY F.
[pen.] Wes Leigh; [b.] Auburn, NY; [p.] Frank LeFevre and May Smith LeFevre; [ed.] BA (Lyric Tenor Music Performance), M.S. in Education, MS - Reading, Magna Cum Laude; [occ.] Teacher - LaFargeville Central School; [memb.] Trinity Episcopal Church - Watertown, NY, member of the "Collectors of Primitive Antique Furniture and Restoration of Early Houses"; [hon.] Essay contest (American Legion Auxiliary 1990), presentation of my personal "Methods of Touching" to state Ed. Dept. in Albany 1998; [oth. writ.] Poetry: "In 25 words or less," "Imagination Is," "Love is," "Philosophy of Education."; [pers.] If you wish to learn anything that's worth anything, it must be practiced, practiced and practiced!!; [a.] Downtown Felts Mills, NY

LEISCHNER, REV. JAMES C.
[b.] April 30, 1935, Decatur, IL; [p.] Rev. James H. and Virginia Leischner; [m.] Delores L. (Hulber) Leischner, June 7, 1958; [ch.] Melody Ann, Duanna Gay and Sherman James; [ed.] Monticello High, studied at several colleges and Seminaries (no degree yet); [occ.] USN Retired (E8), Evangelist; [memb.] American Legion, Post Craig Reed 1181, Fleet Reserve Assn; [hon.] Military medals, Letters of Commendation for Service in Antarctica 1955, 56, 57, Ordained Southern Baptist Minister; [oth. writ.] None published.; [pers.] I follow the Lord Jesus Christ and praise His word. My denomination preference is Southern Baptist.; [a.] Cisco, IL

LEITERMAN, HEATHER
[pen.] Aurora Jackson; [b.] November 3, 1980, Brattleboro, VT; [p.] Lynn and Kim Leiterman; [ed.] Currently in 11th grade; [occ.] Student; [memb.] Brownville United Methodist Church, high school marching band, high school Bible Club; [oth. writ.] "The Dogwood" was published in the church bulletin for Easter Sunday.; [pers.] Tell your family you love them today, because tomorrow might be too late.; [a.] Watertown, NY

LEMEN, CHRISTEN K.
[b.] December 16, 1979, Marysville, CA; [p.] Douglas and Pamala Lemen; [ed.] Flowing Wells High School; [occ.] Student; [oth. writ.] I have a few short stories and many poems (unpub.) This poem "What do I do" was written about a friend, M.G.A.; [pers.] I show my feelings and thoughts through poetry, that I wouldn't be able to express in any other way; [a.] Tucson, AZ.

LEMIEUX, PETER
[b.] July 13, 1969, Boston, MA; [ed.] Chelmsford High, Chelmsford, MA; [occ.] Correctional Officer, State of Vermont; [pers.] May true justice reign again, overthrowing the fallacy that now stands in its place.; [a.] Lebanon, NH

LEON, JOHNNY E.
[pen.] John; [b.] Cuenca - Ecuador; [p.] Luis Leon and Guillermina Mejia; [ed.] Computer Engineer and Marital Arts Instructor; [occ.] Computer & Math Teacher and Karate Instructor; [oth. writ.] Several poems published in local newspaper and in A Student Journal for College at Old Westbury; [pers.] The pure air of the dawn is the divine glory of the feeling that inspires to express with what the heart feels. This gives light to the poet that listens inside!!! [a.] Freeport, NY

LESLIE, ALTHEA B.
[b.] March 9, 1959, Jamaica, West Indies; [p.]

Veronica L. Leslie, Lethan L. Leslie (Deceased); [ch.] E.J. Reed IV and Lavell A. Reed; [ed.] BA degree in Special Education, working toward completing MA in Special Education/Reading and Occupational Therapy; [occ.] Homebased Teacher for Child Development Council Headstart: Franklin County; [memb.] Member of Faith Ministries Church, Dr. C. Dexter Wise III, Pastor Columbus, Ohio Children's Ministry Worker, Media Worker, Women of Faith Choir Member, CATCO Volunteer; [hon.] Various educational certificates, educational scholarship award, Most Theatrical award; [oth. writ.] Son X2, Faces Without Expression, What Is Love, Who Is This Lady, Masked Depression, Broken; [pers.] To God be the glory. Thank you, Lord, for healing mercies. I was inspired to begin writing the poem: What Is a Man" while watching my oldest son EJ play basketball and completed it after a sermon, (Why Daddy Why?) by Dr. Wise.; [a.] Columbus, OH

LESSLY, CECIL
[b.] November 11, 1940; OK; [p.] Ozzie Lessly; [m.] Wilma; January 2, 1962; [ch.] David, Lisa, James, Robert; [ed.] Notus High 2 yrs. Magic Valley Christian College; [occ.] Machinist Own Welding and Machine shop; [a.] Wendell, ID.

LEVY, ENIKA
[b.] August 16, 1983, New Orleans; [p.] Edgar and Anne Levy; [ed.] James Lewis Extension Middle/High School; [memb.] Alpha Delta Zeta; [pers.] Writing is my hobby and a way to relax and gather my thoughts and feelings.; [a.] New Orleans, LA

LEWIS, SARA
[b.] June 5, 1981; Decatur, AL; [p.] Bob Lewis, Diana Lewis; [occ.] Student at Decatur High School; [memb.] Key Club, SADD Club, Interact Club, French Club; [hon.] A Honorable, A-B Honor Rol, United States Achievement Academy 1993 National Awards, Student of the Month, Academic Achievement Letter; [oth.writ.] Several unpublished poems, a few songs, and a book in process; [pers.] "Regret for the things we did can be tempered by time; it is regret for things we did not do that is inconsolable." Therefore, I live my life according to this theory: Seize the day; put no trust in the morrow (Horace); [a.] Decatur, AL.

LEWIS, SHARON
[b.] January 1942, Los Angeles, CA; [p.] Anita Thurston, Lefty Thurston; [m.] Thomas A. Lewis, July 1959; [ch.] Teresa Ann, Annette Marie, David Scott; [ed.] Gardena, CA., High; [occ.] Retired; [oth. writ.] A collection of rhymes of whimsy; [pers.] We can accomplish anything we set out to do; whatever that is depends on you. With an open heart and mind, you never know what you may find.; [a.] Lakewood, CA

LEWIS, SYLIA
[b.] June 10, 1977; East Chicago Heights, IL; [p.] Robert Lewis, Teresa Lewis; [ed.] Just graduated from Fair Field High School. And getting ready to go to College; [a.] Birmingham, AL.

LINDEN, ROBERT
[b.] September 29, 1951, New York City; [ed.] B.A., Communications Arts and Sciences, Queens College of the City, University of New York, Stuyvesant High School, New York City; [occ.] Radio Program Director and Consultant in Washington, D.C., Miami, San Diego, Seattle and elsewhere; [memb.] Progressive Animal Welfare Society, People for the Ethical Treatment of Animals, Last Chance for Animals; [hon.] Regents Scholarship award, Addy; [oth. writ.] Jazzy music scene, Soundtrack magazine; [pers.] I woke up today a pacifist-compassionist with a twist of militant vegetarianism. Therefore, I blame all of the world's ills, environmental destruction, hu-

man illness, and animal suffering on our fancy for flesh-eating, themes that sizzle in "sacred cow."; [a.] College Park, MD

LINDQUIST, ALICE M.
[b.] January 20, 1930, Clinton, IA; [p.] Alfred J. Knecht and Minnie V. Knecht; [m.] Howard Lindquist, May 20, 1949; [ch.] Steven Howard Lindquist and Joel Howard Lindquist; [ed.] High school grad, college 1 yr; [occ.] Business Owner, Home Accents and Decorating (paintings); [memb.] Rockford Literacy Council, Vesterheim Museum Deorah, Iowa Zion Lutheran Church. Rock Valley College Senior Center; [hon.] Volunteer work teaching English; [pers.] Trust in God, and believe in people.; [a.] Rockford, IL

LINN, FERNANDO
[pen.] Fernando Linn; [b.] January 12, 1976, Tucson, AZ; [p.] Darlene and Jorge Linn; [ed.] Palo Verde High School, Class of '94, Pima College, Class of '97; [occ.] Current student at the University of Arizona; [hon.] Associate Degree; [oth. writ.] Several poems, articles in local papers. I have a load of unpublished writings . . . from poems, short stories and screenplays. I'm a hopeless romantic with no life outside of writing.; [pers.] I have been influenced by mythology, religion, the Beatles, and good old fashion storytelling. Getting published is ultra cool.; [a.] Tucson, AZ

LINTHECOME, DONNELL
[b.] December 24, 1942, Cushing, TX; [m.] Genell Linthecome, October 3, 1960; [ch.] Donna A., Soncya V. and Patrick D.; [ed.] BA: University of Lavern, Lavern, CA. MBA: National University, San Diego, CA; [occ.] Revenue Agent, Internal Revenue Service; [hon.] Combat Infantry Badge, Silver Stars for Gallantry, four Bronze Stars for Heroism, and two Army Commendation Medals for Heroism. Master parachutist wing of the United States Army, holds the same from the Vietnamese Army. Cross of Gallantry with the Silver and Bronze Stars, Purple Hearts, Air Medal, and served in units that were awarded the Presidential Unit Citation for Valor.; [oth. writ.] Experience of 3 tours in Vietnam and poetry of a "Jungle Hunt."; [a.] Mesquite, TX

LITTLE, MARY SLAUGHTER
[b.] July 14, 1942, Dallas, TX; [p.] Felix Wyatt (Deceased), Essie Wyatt Hearns; [ch.] Deitra, Michelle, Wendy, Webster Jr., John and Joseph; [ed.] Franklin High, Stockton College, San Joaquin Delta College, CLC Bible College, Chapman College; [occ.] Retired Lic. Voc. Jail Nurse; [memb.] True Light Church Ministers, Food Bank, shelter feeding program, Pentecostal Assemblies of the World, Calif. State Ombudsmen, Prison Ministries; [hon.] Northern Calif. Auxi Women of the Year. Award of Service - SUSD/CSCS Teacher Corp Community Council; [oth. writ.] This was my first attempt at writing something for publication.; [pers.] I love people and am always willing to serve wherever I can. I feel there will always be a need for love to be shared.; [a.] Stockton, CA

LITTLE, NATHAN DAVID
[b.] May 8, 1986, New Britain, CT; [p.] Jonathan and Nan Little; [ed.] 5th grade student; [occ.] Kid; [memb.] Chess Club; [hon.] Appomattox Elementary Honor Roll; [oth. writ.] Golden Plain, Shadow on the Plain. (Collections of poems, my father printed); [pers.] I find writing poems to be like a puzzle and a chance to express my point of view. In my point of view I try to make people reconsider things, show them the consequences, and even scare them.; [a.] Gladstone, VA

LIVELL, MONIKA
[b.] January 4, 1957; Erlangen, West Germany; [p.] Samuel and Maria Powell; [m.] Bill Livell; April 23, 1993; [ch.] Michelle Dawn Marie Brightwell, William Michael Harry Livell, Nicholas Patrick Livell; [ed.] Hallie Turner Private High, Columbus, Georgia; [occ.] Self-employed; [pers.] "Fragile Breath of Life" poem is dedicated to Nicholas, all the NICU infants, their families, and the NICU staff (St. Louis, MO) at St. John's Mercy Medical Center, who believed and loved our children, especially offering them a life-saving home away from home; [a.] High Ridge, MO.

LLOYD, RHONDA
[b.] November 27, 1980, Houston, TX; [p.] Carole A. Lloyd and 8Richard E. Lloyd; [occ.] Full time student; [memb.] Baptist 8Worship Center; [hon.] P.A.L. - Police Athlete League of Phila. 8("Total positive you program"); [oth. writ.] "Love" that is 8published in Forever and a Day; [pers.] First I would like to 8thank God for giving me the talent. I would like to thank my 8mom, Carole, my brothers Ronald and Richard, and Godmother 8Juanita Jefferson for pushing me towards my goal and standing 8behind me 100%.

LOCKLIER, LISA E.
[pen.] Eugenia Johnston; [b.] December 27, 1966, Columbus, GA; [p.] Benjiman Eugene and Mary Jo; [ch.] Joshua Joel; [ed.] G.E.D., C.A.S.C. Clerical I.C.I. Nursing Assistant; [occ.] Homemaker; [pers.] My writings are influenced by The Holy Bible and an old copy of immortal poems, and also by everyday events that fill my heart with joy and thankfulness for being alive.; [a.] Phenix City, AL

LOGAN, BETSY
[b.] April 2, 1965; [p.] Jerry and Colleen Brown; [ch.] Jessee Kae Logan; [memb.] Member of the Eric Heintz BlackBelt Academy Tae Kwon Do. And - Juvenile Diabetes Foundation; [pers.] "Keep Looking Forward to Tomorrow."; [a.] Mitchellville, IA

LOKKER, PATRICIA E.
[p.] Patti Litton Lokker; [b.] December 16, 1948, Hammond, IN; [p.] Ralph C. Litton, Margaret A. Campbell; [ch.] Christopher Jon, Scott Edward; [ed.] Associate Degree of Arts, Associate Degree of Science (Developmental Disabilities), Donald E. Gavit Jr. - Sr. High School; [occ.] Inspirational (Christian) Writer, Photographer, Family Researcher; [memb.] Christian singles, groups, Church Tape Ministry, MS Society; [oth. writ.] Today's Prime Time Magazine, Quiet Times, Footsteps in the Sand (Poetry); various church newsletters; [pers.] My parents' Christian loving examples and the lord allowing Multiple sclerosis into my life are blessings. My greatest joy is sharing Christ and His love. [a.] Shelby Twp., MI

LONGAUER, EILEEN WILLIAM
[pen.] Eileen William Longauer; [b.] November 30, 1943, Washington, DC; [p.] Dr. and Mrs. John B. Sullivan; [m.] Dr. Earl J. Longauer, December, 1966; [ch.] Brian Joseph and Shannon Kerry; [ed.] Bishop O'Connell High School, Mary Mount University, University of Pennsylvania School of Oral Hygiene; [occ.] Office Manager, Dental Hygienist; [memb.] Northern VA and American Dental Hygienist Asso., International Society of Poets; [hon.] International Society of Poets, Editor's Choice Award, Hall of Fame of International Society of Poets; [oth. writ.] Old Fashioned Manners.; [pers.] I strive to write about people's basic feelings and emotions and to make people think through my writings.; [a.] Arlington, VA

LONGEN, WENDY J.
[b.] April 15, 1961, Robinsdale, MN; [p.] Beverly and Eugene Brickman; [m.] David R. Longen, September 10, 1984; [ch.] 3 - Trina 15, Tricia 14, Robert 12; [ed.] 11 yrs. - Osseo High School, working on GED, then plan on taking Computer Programing; [occ.] Mother, Housewife; [oth. writ.] I have written poems in the past but never had any published. This publishing is inspiring me to write more.; [pers.] I am inspired by sensitivity. I am influenced by hardship that people face from day to day and watching bad turn into good.; [a.] Fridley, MN

LOPEZ, BOBBYE
[b.] March 16, 1936, Colesburg, KY; [p.] James and Althea Wise; [m.] Rey, June 7, 1958; [ch.] Tia, Joseph, Jennifer, Fredric; [ed.] Presentation Academy, Louisville, KY; [occ.] Homemaker; [oth. writ.] Several poems a series of children's stories, in progress.; [pers.] A deep and abiding love for my family and friends prompts me to write. My desire is to share this contentment.

LOPEZ, CASSANDRA
[b.] March 2, 1986; Stony Brook Hospital, NY; [p.] Lydia Jose Lopez, Wilson Cubano; [ed.] Boyle Road Elementary School; [occ.] Student; [memb.] Student Council, Drama; [hon.] Taproot intergenerational poetry and pros first prize. Reflections 2-times firest prize, Principals Award, Pi Day 3rd place; [oth. writ.] First place in poetry several times, enter any contest I see in Pennysaver, newsday and Yankee Trader; [a.] Port Jefferson Sta., NY.

LOTT JR., Y. D.
[pen.] Bay Lott (sometimes); [b.] July 21, 1939, Mobile, AL; [p.] Y. D. Lott, Sarah Hunter Lott; [m.] Jeannie G. Lott, August 24, 1984; [ch.] Y.D. Lott III, Briar James Lott, Albert Hunter Lott, Ashleigh Blaire Lott; [ed.] B.A. University of Alabama, 1961, L.L.B., J.D., Birmingham School of Law, 1966, McGill Institute High School, 1957, St. Catherines Grade School, 1953; [occ.] Lawyer, Mediaton, Property Manager; [memb.] A.K.E. Social Fraternity, Certified Mediator and Arbitrator American Arbitration Association. Mobile and Alabama State Bar Association, numerous committees for lawyers since 1967.; [hon.] Hudson Strode Creative Writing Honors Program, Silver Poetry Award, World of Poetry, 1986, Gold Poetry Award, World of Poetry, 1988, Publications Award, University of Alabama; [oth. writ.] Author, poems, Archery of the Arts publication, "Rhyme Across Our Land," 191, Biloxi, Mississippi, author, "Why Not Mediate?" (Law Book) 1995, college newspaper and magazines; [pers.] A poet should be a walking sound bite.; [a.] Mobile, AZ

LOVERN, DAVID J.
[b.] June 30, 1972, Wichita, KS; [p.] Jerry L. Lovern; [ed.] High school 1990, Bishop Carroll Catholic High School; [occ.] NCR Inventory Support Management; [oth. writ.] Since graduating from high school I have written thousands of pages of poetry and one book still in the works; [pers.] I have had no formal schooling or training for writing. I never even read an entire book until after high school. Would like to get my B.S. in English.; [a.] Tualatin, OR

LU, KENNY
[b.] August 28, 1975, China; [p.] Hui Ling Chen Lu and Jin Han Lu; [ed.] George Washington High, San Francisco, CA, San Jose State University, San Jose, CA. (current student); [occ.] Cadet Officer for San Jose State University Police Dept; [hon.] Certificate for Bartending, Valedictorian for Cadet Class Fall '96; [pers.] "If You Drink, You Die! If You Don't Drink, You Die! So, Let's All Drink and Die!" (author unknown); [a.] San Francisco, CA

LUCAS, ROSEMARIE N.
[b.] In my 20's; [ed.] Bachelor Degree in Public Administration from Medgar Evers College; [occ.] Financial Administrator; [hon.] Received an award for art contest in JH-IS 161, 1983. Received award for "reliability" in the performance of my duties at the Haitian Community Health Project, 1994.; [pers.] Inspired by Romantic poets, Elizabeth Barrett Browning, William Shakespeare, and Adrienne Rich.; [a.] Brooklyn, NY

LUDWIG, JAMES
[b.] January 12, 1952, Pleasantville, NJ; [p.] Paul and Minnie Ludwig; [m.] Cynthia M. Heape, June 6, 1970; [ch.] James Jennifer and Jeffery Jonpaul; [ed.] Pleasantville High; [occ.] Carpenter; [oth. writ.] Novel - two love!?; [pers.] If it weren't for Detours, I would be standing still.; [a.] Northfield, NJ

LUJANO, VANESSA M.
[b.] May 20, 1984, Yuba City, CA; [ed.] Andros Karperos School, 6th Grade; [pers.] I very much like the arts, and hope to continue in this field.

LUNDGREN, PETER
[b.] May 28, 1940, Superior, WI; [p.] Clarence and Dorothy Lundgren (Deceased); [m.] Barbara McCann, July 30, 1966; [ch.] Amanda - 14, Brian - 24, Merri - 27; [ed.] BA - University of Wisconsin - Superior MS-Ed, Northern Illinois University also Real World Degree, School of Hard Knocks; [occ.] Teacher, English-German, Winter High School, Winter, WI; [memb.] Family of Humankind - since 1940; [oth. writ.] This is my first publication.; [pers.] Living is a serious business but not a solemn one. Poetry can be found in the small details of life. "We are such stuff as dreams are made on, and our little life is rounded with a sleep," —William Shakespeare.; [a.] Ladysmith, WI

LUZIER, BETTY LOU DRAWYER
[pen.] Bettylou; [b.] August 24, 1929, Columbia Falls, MT; [p.] Kenneth and Chrsitina Winebrenner; [m.] Eugene Luzier, June 10, 1967; [ch.] Shane; [ed.] High school grad., Asc. Motel Mgr. - several courses to better myself as a Sec. Was Sec. to City Mgr. and later in schools; [occ.] "Special Day Baskets" self-owned; [memb.] United Meth. Church - "Sweet Adelines"; [oth. writ.] None published . . yet. I write poems, short stories and children's stories.

LYNCH, BARBARA D.
[pen.] Imani; [b.] March 20, 1956, Carter, MS; [p.] William and Ruby Trotter; [ch.] Marcus and Jessica Lynch; [ed.] BSN Nursing from University Medical Center in 1985, Mississippi College 1974-1978, Hinds Junior College—1979 Jackson, MS; [occ.] Registered Nurse; [memb.] New Lake Church of Christ Hol., Evangelism Team, Reformed Thee Student, Mission and Counseling; [oth. writ.] "I Can Dream Again" 1/97; [pers.] I believe with all my heart in God and through Him I can overcome any struggle in my life and have victory and success.; [a.] Jackson, MS

MACAPINLAC, CARLA G.
[pen.] Carla Camins-Macapinlac; [b.] June 24, 1968, Manila, Philippines; [p.] Antonio S. Camins, Raceli T. Camins; [m.] Joseph Macapinlac Jr., April 20, 1996; [ed.] St. Scholastica's College, Ateneo de Manila University, St. Mary's College of California; [occ.] User Liaison/Quality Assurance Analyst; [memb.] Institute of Poetic Sciences; [oth. writ.] Poems published in high school paper ("The Blue Flame"); [a.] Hercules, CA

MACAULEY, CLAIRE ALRIA
[pen.] Carmen V. and Kaijie C.; [b.] January 30, 1980, West Africa; [p.] Eustace and Gloria Macauley; [ed.] Alief Elsik High School; [memb.]

S-A-D-D—Students Against Drunk Driving; [hon.] The Presidential Awards; [pers.] We all have the power to do things, but we have to take the step farther to recognize it.; [a.] Houston, TX

MACK, MADERIA
[b.] October 28, 1952; Chicago, IL; [p.] Leroy J. Morelands and Bessie Moreland; [m.] Divorced; July 9, 1971; [ch.] (son) Davor D. Mack Jr.; [ed.] Elementary St. Francis de Paula chg. Il.) Loretta Academy and Emil G. Hirsch, High Schools - Chg. Il. Locp Jr. College Chg. Il; [occ.] Aspiring Writer; [memb.] Nehemiah Urban Baptist Church; [N.E.L.) National Epilisey Foundation National Multiple Sclerosis Chicago Chapter Writers Digest Book Club; [hon.] Boy Scouts of America Camp Pendleton (chapter) Oceanside Ca.; Honored - San Diego Ca. 1982"; [oth.writ.] Poem - Sanctuary " published short story to be published soon, and other poems written; [pers.] I've always had trouble speaking every word, that may have been in my heart and mind at the same time, but I found through writing I could speak be heard and understood. I could express love and life to others; [a.] Chicago, IL.

MACNEILL, VALERIE ANN
[b.] June 23, 1983, Jamestown, NY; [p.] Bradley P. and Laurie C. MacNeill; [ed.] Currently in 8th grade of Allegany-Limestone Central School; [memb.] Drama club and art club of Allegany-Limestone Central School; [hon.] High Honor Roll, Student of the Year; [oth. writ.] Various poems in the school literary magazine; [pers.] I am a dreamer, and I dedicate my poems to all people who want to dream with me.; [a.] Allegany, NY

MAHMOOD, AFSHAN ALI
[pen.] Afshan Ali (Dora); [b.] April 28, 1966, Mexico; [ch.] Alfredo III and Alexis Salazar; [oth. writ.] My Son, Final Safe Place, Anyone Anymore; [a.] Victoria, TX

MALACHI, DOMINICK VINCENT
[pen.] D. Vincent Malachi; [b.] February 5, 1950; Indianapolis, IN; [p.] Helen Elizabeth Kelly, James Richard Lynch; [m.] divorced; [ch.] John Lamont, Danny Wayne; [ed.] High School, Doctorate of Divinity, United Christian College, Cleveland, Tennessee, P.C.D.I. School of Paralegal Studies, Deer Creek Barber School; [occ.] Barber Stylist, Correctional Industrial Facility, Pendleton, IN; [mem.] Vietnam Veterans of America, Secular Order of Discalced Carmelites; [hon.] Service connected awards and decorations; [oth.writ.] School publications, various newsletters; [pers.] My writings/poems are a reflection of my inner feelings and expressions of my circumstances and environment. My goal is to share with those who can identify with me in some way; [a.] Pendleton, IN.

MALDONADO III, BENJAMIN
[b.] December 27, 1979, Bronx, NY; [p.] Benjamin and Librada Maldonado; [ed.] The Taft School (High School) to - graduate 5/31 will be attending Middlebury College in September, 1997; [occ.] Full time student; [oth. writ.] Other unpublished poems...; [pers.] "And the truth shall set you free".; [a.] Bronx, NY

MALONE, JOSEPHINE
[pen.] Josie; [b.] March 27, 1927, Bunkie, LA; [p.] Rhoda and Joseph Johnson; [ch.] Betty, Harry, Charlene, Glenda, Patricia, Frankie, Ray, Carl; [ed.] Bunkie Elementary Carver High; [memb.] Chamber of Commerce, Edgefield Usher Board; [pers.] Do unto others as you would have them do unto you.; [a.] Cheneyville, LA

MANGINE-DESAW, NANCY
[pen.] Mani or Mangine-DeSaw; [b.] October 20, 1951, Trenton, NJ; [p.] Dominic P. and Mary A.

Mangine; [chi.] Angela Raynor and Jeremy DeSaw; [ed.] A.S. Criminal Justice - MCCC, B.S. Law and Criminal Justice Edison; [occ.] N.J. Superior Court Judiciary—Probation Investigator; [memb.] Amer. Cancer Assoc.; [hon.] Dean's List; [oth. writ.] Non-published (yet), "Wise Owl," "Mommy's Quiet Time."; [pers.] Poetry is my therapy of releasing suppressed feelings at day's end. With my job, you might say that's quite a release!; [a.] Hamilton Township, NJ

MANN, JON
[pen.] Jon Dig Mann; [b.] October 17, 1964, Boone, IA; [p.] Robert and Jean Digmann; [ed.] University of Colorado, New York University; [occ.] Artist; [hon.] Painting awards: Windsor and Newton Award for Painting Excellence, Dean's Award (NYU), Walter Read Hovey Award for Art, Liquitex Emerging Artist of the Year 1995; [oth. writ.] Jonny Foos - an autobiographical novel/ screenplay about an artist, musician, poet, fashion designer, pro football player and inventor. He uses his skills to overcome a superior adversary, fall in love, and create an enterprise.; [pers.] The poem, My Muse, is from my novel. The novel reads like poetry throughout the whole story. All the art, inventions, songs, and clothes are real and I created all of them. As of now it is unpublished.; [a.] Boone, IA

MANN, LAVONDA VINCENT
[b.] September 8, 1963, Eglin AFB, FL; [p.] Johnnie and Judy Vincent; [m.] David K. Mann, February 4, 1984; [ch.] Carley, Evan, Elliott and Drew; [ed.] Richland School 1981, Lynnville, TN, Samford University 1981-1983, 87, Birmingham, AL, Wake County Public School System S.T.E.T.S., Raleigh, NC; [occ.] Music Teacher/Substitute, Homemaker; [memb.] First Baptist Church Harlingen, TX, Sandi Jo Funk Hospice of VBMC - Volunteer, Treasure Hills Elem., P.T.A.; [oth. writ.] Long letters to friends, two of which were published in local newspapers, poem "Friends Are Forever" high school annual, 1981. Other poetry and essays not yet submitted for publication. Script and other projects in process.; [pers.] I appreciate so much the influence of the presence of so many people in my life. I am so grateful to our creator for giving me a place in life from which to observe life.; [a.] Harlingen, TX

MANNING, NANCY
[m.] David Manning; [ed.] BA in English, Secondary English Certification, MS in English; [occ.] English Teacher at Seymour High School; [pers.] Special thanks to Joanna Scott, Lisa Shea, and the gang at Bread Loaf.; [a.] Oxford, CT

MARALDO, HARRY
[pen.] Harry Marlo; [b.] Hartville, WY; [p.] Deceased; [m.] Marie; [ch.] Six; [ed.] Extensive study in Voice Anatomy, Perfect Voice Inst. Chicago, also Semantics, LA; [occ.] Actor, Narrator, Singer, when work available, and Sales and Marketing; [memb.] Screen Actors Guild, 1965 to present, resided in LA area 30 years; [oth. writ.] Newspaper and magazine articles; [pers.] With God all things are possible.; [a.] Augusta, GA

MARINELLI, JESSICA
[b.] July 6, 1985, East Meadow, NY; [p.] Barbara and Ward Marinelli; [ed.] At the present Copiague Middle School, Copiague, New York; [occ.] Student; [hon.] Presidential Award, Honor Roll Award, and P.T.A. Award; [oth. writ.] Two poems not presently published: Christmas Is, and Santa Claus.; [a.] Lindenhurst, NY

MARKOVICH, SUSAN
[b.] January 2, 1955, Hammond, IN; [p.] Thomas and Josephine Boren; [m.] Mark Markovich, January 12, 1973; [ch.] Shannon, Jenna and grandkids

- Ajuley, Aisha and Mike; [ed.] High school, modeling college, some computer - Purdue University; [occ.] Homemaker, Mom, Writer; [memb.] HSA - Catholic school, A. Av, F.O.P., Spouser Riot of Police, Veteran Organizations. Church, and school and Kids Qualities.; [hon.] Awards for computer classes, 3.95 high school completed in 3 years, Helping Jennals Schools, Girl Scout and 4-Hawalos; [oth. writ.] Poems, short stories, Noted From The Heart. I've also written a song!; [pers.] I love to write about sports, my family and serious issues to bring out my inner soul and sense of humor. I love to read.; [a.] Hammond, IN

MARRIOTT, SARA C.

[b.] September 23, 1965, Dartmouth, MA; [p.] William and Lena Cook; [m.] Bertram Marriott, 1937; [ch.] Son B. Rodney Marriott Yale 1960; [ed.] Sargent - Boston University 1926; [occ.] Writer/ Speaker, holding spiritual energy for the Nazare Center of Light in Brazil; [oth. writ.] Author of five books - published in Brazil; [pers.] The healing power of spiritual love fills my heart and mind as I give my life in service with new challenges to find!; [a.] Rye, NM

MARROQUIN, YOLANDA THERESA

[pen.] Tulsie Di-Geronimo; [b.] January 17, 1954, Corpus Christi, TX; [p.] Mr. and Mrs. Jesse Marroquin; [m.] David Di-Geronimo (Divorced), October 7, 1975; [ch.] 5 Sons, 2 beauty girls (all grown); [ed.] 2 years college still attending University of Hawaii, Santa Monica College/Chaffey College, Law student Fine Arts Music Cultural Arts; [occ.] Internet Consultant/Agent for all art mediums/music performer and dancer; [memb.] Citizens for Justice League/Americans Against Political Corruption, Dance Group for Children/ Woman's Collition to End Abuse of Children, P.SP All glories to all sincere fellow sovereigns working to unite the world under the true liberty; [hon.] Touch for Health Award, Editor of Monthly Newsletter "Sovereign Sun" in Hawaii; [oth. writ.] Semifinalist in National Poetry Contest. One published poem NLOP two hispanic history's in the works songs/in competition for Hawaiies artists of song.; [pers.] In todays renewal golden age of enlightment the common cause united under freedoms true path, the cultural arts may serve to bring this grand reality to manifestation. Indeed all humanity must now band together for the course of the world is at stake.; [a.] Honolulu, HI

MARSHALL, CALVIN L.

[b.] December 10, 1969, Terre Haute, IN; [p.] Linda and George Marshall Sr.; [ed.] North Natchez Adams High School (1989), Alcorn State University (1996), B.A. in Broadcast Communications; [occ.] Funeral Assistant, Century Funeral Home, Brookhaven, MS; [memb.] Publicity Chairperson, Alcorn State University Alumni Association - Natchez Chapter; [hon.] All-American Scholar (1991), The National Dean's List ('95-'96), an Alcorn State University Honor Student ('90, '91, '92, '93 and '94); [oth. writ.] Various poems and short stories published in "Cornucopia" the literary magazine of my former high school.; [pers.] "Writing is an everlasting challenge to the imagination." I hope to one day be recognized as one of the greatest writers to hail from the state of Mississippi.; [a.] Natchez, MS

MARSHALL JR., RAYMOND W.

[b.] July 23, 1971, San Diego, CA; [p.] Raymond and Jolene Marshall; [ed.] West High, Sioux City, IA; [occ.] Machinist; [pers.] Inspirations include the work of such greats as Edgar Allan Poe and Jim Morrison.; [a.] Grand Haven, MI

MARTIN, JIMMY

[b.] April 30, 1956, Lexington, MS; [p.] Bryan J. Martin and Jeannette Martin; [ch.] Jerry Lee, Jerry Wise, Melinda and Renee; [ed.] Major in English, Masters in Educational Administration; [occ.] Exec. Director of an institution for homeless children (Sunnybrook Children's Home); [oth. writ.] My writing is a continuous effort to keep track of my whereabouts.; [pers.] The occupation of the poet is translator. Creation's various languages are less foreign to his ear than to a generation desperate for a sense of belonging in an overwhelmingly vast universe.; [a.] Ridgeland, MS

MARTIN, PAUL E.

[pen.] Jean Glendenning; [b.] June 8, 1952, New York, NY; [p.] Anne and Paul Martin; [ch.] Kamie Marie; [ed.] Univ. of Pittsburgh - BA, Eng. Lit. BA. Theatre Arts; [occ.] Writer; [memb.] Altoona Community Theatre; [oth.writ.] All unpublished: Three shows for "Saturday Night Live" (complete), 90 min. screen-play, "M.A.S.H.," screenplay for "Magnum, P.I," two books of poetry (unedited). "Two Diaries" - Album of 11 songs, lyrics and music.; [pers.] Creation is the bridge to the future, however, "Family Trees" are more difficult to research than obtaining the feelings and thoughts recorded on paper in a poem, novel, or play, of a centuries-dead author—right?; [a.] Altoona, PA

MARTIN, VIRGINIA

[pen.] VE Martin (poetry), GEM (books); [b.] January 19, 1941, Massena, NY; [m.] Dale L. Martin, July 9, 1960; [ch.] K. Patrick; [ed.] Columbia College, Columbia, MO, continuing: Philosophy, Art, Accounting, to name a few. Education in public and private schools, church. Life experiences; [occ.] Retired; [memb.] Arts Council and Red Cross Boards; [oth. writ.] Poetry, none submitted for publication. (1) Children's book, Candy Computer, in the process of submission to publishers.; [pers.] Poetry, for me, is the medium I find most suitable for expressing life. I see one's well-being in life as a combination of physical, mental and spiritual, and through my poetry I can contribute to this well-being.; [a.] Nathrop, CO

MARTINEZ, BOB G.

[b.] June 7, 1949, New Mexico; [p.] Mary Jane Martinez; [m.] Annette Elizabeth Martinez, February 10, 1973; [ch.] Lita - 20 (2nd year college); [ed.] Completed high school in Denver's North High School; [occ.] Security Department at the Denver Merchandise Mart; [memb.] Distinguished Member of ISP-NLP - Colorado, Poetry Society, Mile High Poets of Colorado; [hon.] Elected "Best Poetic Husband and Father of the Year" by my dear wife, Annette and daughter, Lita Martinez.; [oth. writ.] My Time to Rhyme, a personal journal (1949 to 1994) in a single unbroken poem (302 pgs.) and Sidetracks, a compilation of my favorite poems.; [pers.] Happiness to some is a tough chess match . . . others prefer a waltz on the dance floor. Within the pages this book will dispatch this poet's peace in Dance Upon the Shore.; [a.] Denver, CO

MARTINEZ, DENNISTER

[b.] August 7, 1977, Lipa City, Philippines; [p.] Amado Martinez and Valerie Martinez; [ed.] Richard Gahr High School, California State University, Fullerton; [occ.] Student Assistant; [memb.] Feed the Children Foundation; [hon.] "Best Presentation" Award - 1996 USC Building Better Communities, High School Competition - 1994 Boys Varsity Cross Country Athletic Award; [oth. writ.] Several articles published in high school newspaper, The Forum.; [pers.] Spirit is a feeling of deep consciousness. It is like a ripple of water

that spreads to all facets of life. Each day, I give my thanks to the Almighty God for mine.; [a.] Norwalk, CA

MARTISIUS, TOBY

[b.] April 6, 1979, Redlands, CA; [p.] David Martisius; [ed.] Redlands High School; [occ.] Student; [memb.] Kaleidoscope Poetry Club, Van Golgh's Other Ear literary magazine; [oth. writ.] Several poems published in Van Gogh's Other Ear.; [a.] Redlands, CA

MAST, SUSAN

[b.] May 3, 1961; Buenos Aires, Argentina; [p.] Darrell Hudson, Esther Hudson; [m.] Martin Mast; April 26, 1986; [ch.] Joshua Robert, Melody Noelle, Andrew David, Sarah Grace, Matthew Phillip; [ed.] Tupelo High School, Tupelo MS, graduated from McGavock High School, Nashville TN. Attneded Belmont College and Tennessee State University (Nashville TN); BS Sociology, Austin Peay State University (Clarksville, TN); [occ.] Homemaker and Home Educator; [memb.] Priest Lake Christian Fellowship; [pers.] I hope to use my writings as a tool for the reader to see himself or herself and to lead them toward a peaceful healing of pains, and ultimately as a ministry to lead them to the Great Healer, Jesus Christ; [a.] Antioch, TN.

MATHEWS, B. J.

[pen.] B. C. Everybody; [b.] November 27, 1948, Navasota, TX; [p.] Roy Lee Mathews and Clarissa Mathews; [ed.] Dunbar High, Mexia, TX, Jarvis College, Hawkins, TX, State University at Brockport, NY, Minneapolis School of Art, MN, Texas Technical Coll. - Waco, TX, Sam Houston State University, Huntsville, TX; [occ.] GED Teacher, Torres Prison, Hondo, TX; [hon.] Salutatorian, high school class, Cum Laude, Jarvis Christian College, Who's Who Among Students in American Colleges and Universities, '71 ed.; [pers.] In my writing, I endeavor to seize the heart, since the heart can motivate the soul or mind to see, smell, touch, taste and feel both the tangible and intangible.; [a.] Hondo, TX

MATTERN, MARENE C.

[b.] April 19, 1949, Peoria, IL; [p.] Gene and Margery Clark; [m.] David William Mattern II (Deaf), May 4, 1974; [ch.] Claudia (Deaf) - 11, Jesse (Hearing) - 14; [ed.] Gallandet University (Deaf Students) Il. School f/t Deaf, Jacksonville, IL; [occ.] Educator Aide at The Il. School f/t Deaf; [memb.] Jacksonville community Center f/t Deaf - JCCD, Delta Epsilon Sorority, (Dean's List), Il. School f/t Deaf Alumni Ass'n Historian/Museum, IAD - Il. Ass'n of the Deaf, Frat/National Fraternal Ass'n of the Deaf - NFSD.; [hon.] Dean's List, twice Il. Alumni Ass'n (Il. School f/t Deaf ISDAA) Historian/Museum plaque for Dedication and Research.; [oth. writ.] A poem published in a collection. Some poems published by Gallandet University, a class in Creative Writing 1972. The Illinois Advance - ISD School issue - several poems, 1969.; [pers.] I write of those experiences which move me by heart, by spirit. My deafness opened a world I've been observing. I listen more than I speak.; [a.] Jacksonville, IL

MATTHEWS, NANCI

[b.] March 3, 1943, Denver, CO; [p.] Joseph and Marguerite Carroll; [m.] Roland Matthews, September 2, 1961; [ch.] Kevin Matthews, daughter-in-law: Sherri Matthews, grandson: Kyle Matthews; [ed.] Completed university courses developed for AT&T managers; [occ.] Retired AT&T Marketing Manager - 28 years. Retired Foundation Director/Fund Raiser; [memb.] Honorary Life Member of Glendale Kiwanis Club; [hon.] 1996 Community Service Award from County of Los Angeles, presented by Michael D. Antonovich, supvr. 5th

District, County of L.A.; Kiwanian of the Year 1996; Mayor's Commendation for '96 Community Service; Distinguished Service Award Kwanis Cal - Nev. HA Foundation '93,; Council of Leader - AT and T '86; [oth. writ.] "My Life Is Like a Rose"; [pers.] I found helping others enhances the joy of life. I always follow my heart.; [a.] Rockin, CA

MAXWELL, DENISE M.
[pers.] Written for Judi Swain on her 30th birthday—a true friendship that will never end.

MAXWELL, JESSIE ROBERTSON
[ch.] Bud, Brenda and Diane; [memb.] Clan Donnachaidh Society No. California Branch; [hon.] Diamond Homer Award for poem "Reverie"; [oth. writ.] Memorials, poems, prayers. One poem published in anthology.; [pers.] I have been writing for years for my church family and my family and friends in times of joy and crises. I would like to dedicate the poem, "Hope," to my grandchildren, Debbie, Jeff, Lissa, Carrie, Jessica and Bonnie.; [a.] Weaverville, CA

MAY, ELISA ALANE
[pen.] Elise; [b.] April 21, 1965, Denver, CO; [p.] Stanley May and Elizabeth May; [ch.] Samantha Joell May; [ed.] B.A. Psychology Univ. of Northern Colorado; [occ.] Graduate Student Psychology; [memb.] Legal Advocate for victims of family violence, Bethel Lutheran Church; [hon.] Phi Theta Kappa, Colorado Scholars Award, Aurorian Award; [pers.] My writings reflect processes of growth, healing, and survival. Through these processes comes the ultimate, freedom.; [a.] Greeley, CO

MAYLUM, MICHELLE D.
[b.] December 15, 1965, Flint, MI; [p.] Jack Bedell and Shirley Bedell; [m.] Kirk W. Maylum, August 30, 1986; [ch.] Kirk Walter II and Katelin Elizabeth Ann; [ed.] Byron High, Mott College, Howell College of Cosmetology; [occ.] Cosmetologist, General Labor; [pers.] I thank the Lord above for my ability to write, and my loving grandmother, Elizabeth Agnes Sheldon, who taught and showed me how the Almighty God is with us always. She was my best friend, my security in life and now, my angel eternal waiting to guide me home.; [a.] Byron, MI

MAYS, DEBBIE
[b.] January 22, 1954, New Orleans, LA; [p.] Stanley and Marie Lauland; [m.] Billy Mays, July 20, 1974; [ch.] Melissa Mays; [ed.] St. Julian Eymard Elementary School, Edna Karr Junior High, Behrman High, Graduate of a O'Perry Walker High School; [pers.] I try to reach the reality of true inner feelings, and knowledge of life to mankind.; [a.] New Orleans, LA

MAZURKIEWICZ, MELISSA
[b.] September 13, 1974, Reading, PA; [ed.] Reading High School, Antonelli Medical and Professional Institute, Emergency Medical Institute of Eastern PA; [occ.] Medical Assistant with HIV/Aids Clinic; [memb.] American Heart Asso., PA Emergency Medical Technician; [pers.] It is in touching another that we complete our souls.; [a.] Reading, PA

MCAREE, FRANCINE P.
[b.] October 6, 1946; [p.] Edson Brown and Frances Brown (Step Father); [m.] John McAree; [ch.] Kristin; [ed.] Woodbury High School, Woodbury, CT; [occ.] Housewife, formerly: Wolcott Bd. of Ed. Systems Accountant; [oth. writ.] Through Your Mother's Eyes (written for my daughter as a wedding gift). Dreams Are the Wings to Paradise; [pers.] I am currently taking time to pursue my interests in writing and art. I find great fulfillment and satisfaction in creating a poem other people can relate to with their own personal feelings and experiences.; [a.] Wolcott, CT

MCBRIDE, JILL
[pen.] Jill McBride; [b.] December 4, 1988, Grand Rapids, MI; [p.] Jeff and Sherry McBride; [ed.] 9th grade student at Wayland High; [occ.] High school student; [hon.] Honor Roll all of my life. Academic Achievement Award for maintaining a 3.8 or above grade point average. President's Education Award for outstanding academic achievement. English Excellence Award; [pers.] I believe we are like a rainbow, sometimes we fade in and out, but when people need us we come together to make something beautiful.; [a.] Caledonia, MI

MCBRIDE, ROBIN DOUGLASS
[pen.] Rob; [b.] June 16, 1958, Baltimore City; [p.] Robert and Jennifer McBride; [ch.] My cat; [ed.] Balto. Lutheran High School, Harford Comm. College; [occ.] Assistant Manager G.N.C. Store; [hon.] Selected by the college as "Artist of the Month" with a display of artwork done in pastels, and reception afterwards in honor of the artist and her work; [oth. writ.] Articles in the school newspaper, unpublished poems and prose; [pers.] Never lose sight of your dreams, they do have a way of coming true. Believe in yourself and in God, and always pray.; [a.] Joppa, MD

MCCANN, LINDA
[pen.] Tobye McCann; [b.] June 7, 1949, Riverside, CA; [p.] Betty and Roger Duran; [m.] Divorced, November 5, 1966; [ch.] Heidi Aldrich, Adam Brault; [ed.] Rubidoux High School, Copper Mountain Campus/College of the Desert; [occ.] Student, Mother, Homemaker; [memb.] A.R.E., The Association for Research and Enlightenment (The Edgar Cayce Foundation) and the Peale Center for Christian Living; [hon.] "Baby Queen of Pomona" Beauty Contest; [oth. writ.] Poetry (unpublished); [pers.] As I search for peace and happiness in my life, it brings me great pleasure to help bring them to others, through my poetry.; [a.] Yucca Valley, CA

MCCARLEY, BECKY
[b.] June 12, 1952, Portsmouth, VA; [p.] Dan McCarley Sr. and Dolores K. McCarley; [ed.] M.A. Psychology - West Georgia College; [occ.] Writer, Metaphysical teacher, Massage therapist; [oth. writ.] A book to be published soon, ccalled "The Seven Laws of the Universe - a handbook for Masters" (A meta-physical children's book) and 4 other manuscripts in process.; [pers.] Interested in teaching people about the location of Heaven (within) and the laws required to create the Kingdom in their lives and thus on earth.; [a.] Roswell, GA

MCCLURE, DARILYNN M.
[pen.] Dee McClure; [b.] May 6, 1954, Houston, TX; [p.] Lynn Durant, Jack D. Prindible; [m.] Deceased; [ch.] David "Eric" Youngblood; [ed.] Alvin Community College, A.A.S. degree - Legal Assistant; [occ.] Machine Operator; [memb.] Texas Motorcycle Rights Ass. (T.M.R.A.) and Houston Livestock Show and Rodeo—life-time on both. (P.T.K.) Phi Theta Kappa, Mu Upsilon and A.Q.H.A.; [hon.] PTK, J.T.P.A. (3.5 GPA or better); [oth. writ.] Several in "Texas Iron" magazine and newsletters for various associations that I belong to.; [pers.] Thanks to the cowboy who has inspired me to achieve so much and to my late husband, Joe Scheiern, who gave me wings and my mother and family for their support.; [a.] Alvin, TX

MCCOY, CYNTHIA
[pen.] CMCC; [b.] May 28, 1973, Denver, CO; [p.] Robert and Donna McCoy; [ed.] Middle Park High, Western State College of Colorado, have been accepted to the Institute of Children's Literature, Connecticut; [occ.] Catalog, Publishing Project Manager; [hon.] National Honor Society, Scholarship of Academic Leadership,

Grand Country Resources for Youth Award of Outstanding Service; [oth. writ.] Sparrowgrass Poetry Forum: "Cocoon" in Poetic Voices of America, June 1990 and "The Switch" in Treasured Poems of America, April 1990. Grand County Writers Guild: "Continuous Circle" in Mountain Echoes anthology, Winter 1988.; [pers.] The world will be in more chaos if we do not become spiritually aware and educated.; [a.] Denver, CO

MCCOY, DOROTHY F.
[pen.] Dorothy McCoy; [b.] October 8, 1911, Learned, MS; [p.] Hugh Fairchild and Ada Fairchild; [m.] Rowan McCoy (Deceased), December 26, 1944; [ed.] B.S. degree, plus many hours toward a Masters; [occ.] Retired from 32 yrs. teaching school; [memb.] Raymond Baptist Church Culture Club, Jackson, MS, Daylily Society, Bible a Month Club and others.; [oth. writ.] I am deaf and I write poems for my own amusement and I hope to influence someone to be a better person.; [pers.] I love to write about God's goodness, nature, flowers especially, and God's promise to us.; [a.] Raymond, MS

MCDONALD, DONNA
[b.] December 23, 1961, Akron, OH; [p.] Frank and Ruth Huffman; [m.] Robert McDonald, October 26, 1993; [ch.] Stephanie Michelle Huffman; [ed.] William Mason High, Hondros Career Center; [pers.] "Gloria, Gloria" is in memory of my brother David who passed away from cancer on May 25, 1996, and is dedicated to my sister Gloria, who was at his side at the time of his death.; [a.] Harrison, OH

MCELREATH, AMGIE LEIGH
[b.] March 17, 1979, Oconee County, Seneca, SC; [p.] Terry and Cathy McElreath; [ed.] South Pine Street Elementary, Walhalla Middle School, Walhalla High School, next 4 years Clemson University; [occ.] I work part-time after school at Winn-Dixie.; [memb.] Medical Explorer's Program, Teacher Cadet Program, Rocky Knoel Baptist Church; [hon.] Principal's List, Honor Roll, Gold Seal Achievement Award; [pers.] Do what you do with a will and a smile, and whatever you do will be twice as worthwhile.; [a.] Walhalla, SC

MCGRATH, SHARON
[pen.] Shar; [b.] October 2, 1952, Indianapolis, IN; [p.] Chester Williams, Betty Williams; [m.] Patrick McGrath, August 26; [ch.] Jennifer and Amy; [ed.] U.S. Army, Clark College, I.V. and University of Indianapolis; [occ.] Practicing Artist (oils - my favorite medium); [hon.] 1st Place for 33 Paintings 1 - in Animals, 1 - Coventry side, 1 - Seascapes; [oth. writ.] 5 or 6 poems published in school book in Chesterton, IN; [pers.] Each time I write my angel looks in over my shoulder, helping me to write.; [a.] Indianapolis, IN

MCGRIFF, TENIKA
[b.] May 30, 1982; Brooklyn, NY; [p.] Corijee McGriff, Richard Williams; [ed.] John D. Wells J.H.S. 50 Brooklyn NY; [hon.] Participation in a youth program, volley ball, perfect homework, student of the month, Gold Medal track running ECT; [pers.] I pray that one day (Love) conquers, all broken hearts; [a.] Brooklyn, NY.

MCHAWI, OSEYE
[b.] October 18, 1946, Newport News, VA; [p.] Gloria and James Cooley; [ch.] Kemba, Zuwena and Mandisa; [ed.] Associate Degree; [occ.] Executive Assistant, Community School Board NYC BOE; [memb.] The Yoruba Society of Brooklyn, The Egbe Omo Obatala, The Caribbean Culture Center, AARP, the YWCA, NAFE; [oth. writ.] Magazine articles, news articles in local newspapers; [pers.] As a Yoruba priestess and community activist, I am committed to the service of African people and mankind as a

whole. The key elements to my philosophy are integrity, commitment and generosity.; [a.] Brooklyn, NY

MCKAIN, CRYSTAL
[pen.] Crys; [b.] January 6, 1980; Daytona Beach, FL; [p.] Carol and David McKain; [ed.] I am a sophomore at Mainland Senior High School about to enter my Junior year; [occ.] Writter/Artist; [memb.] National Arts Honor Society and National Honor Society; [hons.] I am a Honor Roll student; [oth.writ.] Some of my other poems include "Hugs", "A Rose", "Begging to End" and "John S. Seeds". Many of these poems were published in "Whispers" and "Moonlight and Whispers"; [pers.] "Love never fails"; [a.] Ormond Beach, FL.

MCKINNEY, CHERYL DENISE
[b.] January 31, 1981, Springfield, MA; [p.] Verdell and John McKinney; [ed.] I am a junior at Cathedral High School; [memb.] I am on the Indoor and Outdoor Track team of Cathedral, Canaan Bapt. Church of Christ-Sun. School and Usher Board; [hon.] Indoor Track - "Most Valuable Performer 1996-1997", "Student Athlete of the Week" - sponsored by WGGB (channel 40); [oth. writ.] I have written other personal poems and short stories.; [pers.] I write from my heart. I try to speak to the reader and capture their attention. I like to focus my writing on a certain theme which is "Live Life to the Fullest". Life is too precious to waste.; [a.] Springfield, MA

MCLAIN, JERMEY
[b.] June 29, 1973; [p.] Gary McLain, Cathy (Stepmom) and (Step-father) Dennis, Teresa Lynch; [ed.] Crawford County Jr., Sr. High School; [occ.] Labor at Aristokraft Kitchen and Cabinets Co. from 1991-?; [pers.] The one way to express the inner soul without conflict from evil. Thank you, God!; [a.] English, IN

MCMICKENS, BETTY
[ch.] Rita, Kelly, Leslie; [ed.] Kellogg Community College, Mich. State University and University of Mich. Labor Studies Institutes; [occ.] President of GCIU local 135-C and Platemaker/Mounter; [memb.] Kellogg Community College President of Parent Advisory Board, Alumni for Socutus Technica (Engineering Club at KCC), Delegate with Southwest Mich. Labor Council, GCIU local 135-C; [hon.] Being a mother, a friend, grandmother, a sister and a daughter; [oth. writ.] Variety of poems on topics of love, sympathy, birthday, humor, Biblical comfort, sensual, nature, labor movement, people, living in today's world, encouragement, songs, holidays etc. . . unpublished originals; [pers.] I am inspired to write positively, constructively as my spirit moves me from my heart, dreams, my environment, my children, family, friends, and the joy as this is one of God's gifts that maintain my balance of inner peace.; [a.] Battle Creek, MI

MCNALLY, MARI
[pen.] Jasmine; [b.] December 23, 1961, Mercedes, TX; [p.] Gloria Rodriguez and Ramon Ortiz; [ch.] Melissa Medina and Michelle Harris; [hon.] Awarded several scholarships, achieved "Who's Who in American High School Students"; [oth. writ.] Wrote for inspirational purposes for other people!; [pers.] I write for the appreciation of what's inside me and others! Once my pen touches the paper I never know where it will take me!; [a.] South Bend, IN

MCRAE, CHRISTY
[b.] December 21, 1978, Hawaii; [p.] Mona-Lisa and Dennis McRae; [ed.] Currently attending twelfth grade at Pahoa High School, Honors Graduate; [occ.] Student; [memb.] National Piano Playing Guild, Leo Club, Photography Club, FHA,

Protestant Youth Group, Pahoa Assembly of God; [hon.] Principals Honor Roll—Wuerzburg, Germany, poetry publications in literary magazine—Georgia and Pahoa, Achievement for Artwork, won 2nd Place overall Kitzingen, Germany, honored for National Piano Playing Guild; [oth. writ.] Poems published in school literary magazines—Pahoa High School and Spencer High School; [pers.] "There are many things I have not done, many battles that have not yet begun, the call for death shall not come, till this my battle has been won."; [a.] Pahoa, HI

MEACOMES, CARRIE U.
[b.] December 4, 1900, Nash County, NC; [p.] James P. and Viola Underwood; [m.] Robert M. Meacomes (Deceased), September 11, 1919; [ch.] Louis Elton, Horace Melton and Robert Ray; [ed.] High school; [occ.] Retired; [memb.] Bailey Missionary Baptist Church, Nash County Extension Homemakers (Charter member since 1919) still active in both.; [hon.] Recognized as an Air Raid Warden during World War II; [oth. writ.] Many unpublished inspirational poems and life stories collected in a personal bound collection.; [pers.] God's Creation has been my inspiration. We have nothing but that which has been given by God.; [a.] Bailey, NC

MEDRANO, JOSE L.
[b.] April 13, 1972; [p.] Felix Medrano, Donny Salas; [ed.] Teaneck High School, Teaneck, New Jersey; [occ.] Restaurant; [memb.] Spanish Club, Music Club; [hon.] Varsity letters in football, soccer, wrestling; [oth. writ.] Several poems never published; [a.] Astoria, NY

MEIER, MELISSA
[pen.] Mellysa Meier; [b.] August 8, 1983, Salina, KS; [p.] Rod and Del Meier; [ed.] 7th grade student at South Middle School in Salina, KS; [memb.] Trinity United Method Church, Salina Track Club, basketball and volleyball teams; [hon.] Renaissance silver card holder; [oth. writ.] I have no other published poems but I have written well over 15 other poems about life as a 13 yrs. old dealing with life, death, dreams and the pressure of sex, drugs and other problems.; [pers.] God gave you a life to live not kill, so why kill it with hate and drugs. Live it. You only have one life, it's just a freckle in forever.; [a.] Salina, KS

MELENDEZ, CHRISTOPHER
[pen.] C. Robert Mendez; [b.] September 26, 1967; Manhattan; [p.] Norma Sosa-Chapman/Philip Melendez; [m.] Victoria Lynn Melendez; February 9, 1991; [ch.] Francine and Issabella Santiago Melendez; [ed.] GED Diploma, Completed Residential Electrian Trade School; [occ.] Temporary Work and Odd Jobs (Electrical/Butcher); [hon.] Basketball Championship (2) two years in a row. And (1) Baseball Championship as well as All-Star Champion; [oth.writ.] This is my first public published poem. "Journey Of The Mind"; [pers.] My inspiration is based on my surroundings, and have been influenced by poets like Edgar Allen Poe; [a.] Syracuse, NY.

MELTON, CHRISTOPHER PATRICK
[b.] March 1, 1977, Macon, GA; [p.] Lynn and Ronnie Melton; [ed.] High school graduate (West Laurens High, Class of '95; [occ.] Service Person; [memb.] Liberty Baptist Church; [hon.] Who's Who among High School Students (math); [pers.] Poetry comes to me; I find that inspiration is most elusive when sought after.; [a.] Dublin, GA

MENDEZ JR., JOSE A.
[b.] September 2, 1971, San Sebastian, PR; [p.] Jose A. Mendez Sr. and Margarita Mendez; [pers.] Poems are the words of the heart. Through my poetry, I can reach out to all my emotions. It is

a journey between the heart and the mind.; [a.] Allentown, PA

MICHAEL, YVONNE JANE
[b.] November 4, 1941, Munday, TX; [p.] J. B. and Velma Waller; [m.] Divorced; [ch.] Bill Michael and Chad Michael; [ed.] Hughson High School; [occ.] Hospital Dietary Little Sunshine Cafe; [oth. writ.] Not published; [pers.] My writing is inspired by my life and God's influence. He gives me the words, I just write them down.; [a.] Hollister, CA

MICHAELS, MARION
[b.] Black River Falls, WI; [p.] Leonard Doud and Estelle Payne; [ch.] Charles, David, Robert and Merry; [ed.] Milwaukee Institute of Technology, University of Wisconsin, Eau Claire, BS, MS; [occ.] President, Editor Michaels News; [memb.] International Platform Committee, American Association of University Women; [hon.] Who's Who in the Midwest, Phi Beta Kappa, Who's Who of American Women, Who's Who in the World, World Who's Who of Women; [oth. writ.] Columns: Report from Planet Earth, Single Parenting, Surviving Single, Surviving Sane, To Read or Not, Parenting Plus, Travel Tidbits; [pers.] Life is a walk with God, facing calamities as opportunities, and knowing that happiness is a habit.; [a.] Black River Falls, WI

MICHEL, KARA T.
[b.] September 14, 1967, Fremont, CA; [p.] Jerald D. and Alice A. Kitchel; [m.] Tim I. Michel, September 26, 1992; [ch.] (Potbellied Pig) Jimmy Dean; [ed.] California State University, Hayward, graduated in 1991 with a BA Degree in Speech Communications and an option in Public Communications; [occ.] Management (sales, collections and purchasing); [memb.] Member of the California Potbellied Pig association as well as a member of the Endometriosis Association.; [pers.] Don't just dream your dreams—live them instead.; [a.] Castro Valley, CA

MIDDLETON, JON T.
[pen.] Jon T. Middleton; [b.] October 24, 1970, San Diego, CA; [p.] John and Barbara Middleton; [ed.] AA in General Education from San Diego Mesa College, Mountain Empire High School; [occ.] Student; [memb.] First Unitarian Universalist Church; [pers.] May each of us strive for understanding of others through our open hearts and minds.; [a.] San Diego, CA

MILES JACKSON, BARBARA
[pen.] B. Miles Jackson; [b.] June 24, 1948, Fort Worth, TX; [p.] C. B. Miles and Maybell Dugen Miles; [m.] Divorced; [ch.] Tracy D. Jackson and grandchild Amber Jackson; [ed.] I.M. Terrell, Class of 1966; [occ.] Writer/poet; [memb.] Carter Metropolitan C.M.E Church; [hon.] State Employee of the Year 1990, Usher of the Year for Carter Metropolitan Church; [oth. writ.] Poetry: What Did You See? Christmas Still, Loving Intention, Chirping, God Gathers, A Sign, Silent Voices, Atmospteric Condition, Go Your Way, Acient of Days, Void of Times, Be Sure, Answer, Turn, Horse on South Crest, Times Changing Times, The Whole Truth. Verse: Death Comes at God's Will.; [pers.] In great times of sorrow and sadness—look up and know.; [a.] Arlington, TX

MILLER, ALBERTA
[pen.] Alberta (Allie); [b.] December 13, 1924, Bloomville, NY; [p.] Silas and Maude (Joslin) Cleveland; [m.] Ellsworth W. Miller (Deceased), October 27, 1949; [ed.] Graduate of: Delaware Literary Institute and Franklin Central School, Franklin, The University of the State of Ny, New York at Delhi, NY; [occ.] Retired (widow); [memb.] Christ Community Church of Carman, Schenectady, NY, American Center for Law and Justice,

National Association of Evangelical President Club, General Electric Quarter, Century Club, The Rutherford Council; [hon.] Merit Award - National Association of Evangelicals Certificate of Appreciation: Moody Bible Institute Christian Coalition, City Mission of Schenectady; [oth. writ.] Poem - "Thank You Lord" - written in 1979 - published in the May/June 1996 issue of "Peniel Trumpet Call," short story - "I Call It Faith" written in mid-40's (not published). My niece and I wrote a song in mid 40's (not published).; [pers.] I am overwhelmed that my poem was chosen. Thank you so much.; [a.] Schenectady, NY

MILLER, BEATRICE A.
[b.] October 22, 1958, Midnight, MS; [p.] James (Deceased) and Olivia Miller; [ch.] Aleasha, Tameka, William, Keishunda, Sharmelle, Larchelle; [ed.] Guggenheim Elementary, Parker High, Malcom X College, Illinois Medical Nursing School; [occ.] Certified Nursing Asst. (Somerset) Nursing Center Chicago; [memb.] Guggenheim Elementary P.T.A. Committee, "Say No to Drugs" Parent's Committee; [hon.] Won first place contest in college for poem on Father's Day: title, "I Remember My Dad," February 1984 written by me.; [oth. writ.] Have written poems for school's, special events and church socials.; [pers.] I have written poems since I was eleven years old. What really got me interested in poems is when I was a little girl my parents read them to me at my bedside as a way of putting me to sleep.; [a.] Chicago, IL

MILLER, CONNIE MAE
[b.] May 21, 1953, Pottstown, PA; [p.] Charles Beaudry, Eleanor Beaudry; [m.] William Eugene Miller, December 31, 1992; [ch.] Sherry McGlynn, Pamela Landis, Michael Lawrence; [ed.] Bachelor of Science Business/Information Systems from the University of Phoenix, November 27, 1996; [occ.] Product Support Engineering Associate; [memb.] Distinguished Member of the International Society of Poets, Charter Member of Toast Masters International— Above and Beyond; [hon.] Cum Laude, Dean's List, and Editor's Choice Award; [oth. writ.] Poems: Soul Ride and Words of Encouragement. Both published by The National Library of Poetry and Sparrowgrass; [pers.] My inspiration for writing poetry stems from the will to communicate my innermost thoughts and dreams. Encouragement from my husband and my friends to share my gift of writing shall deem to leave everlasting footprints for my grandchildren to follow.; [a.] Glendale, AZ

MILLER, DAVID
[b.] November 6, 1969, Fairview Park, OH; [p.] Kris and Reni Miller; [ch.] Anna-Maria and Michael Miller; [ed.] Bay High School, LCCC; [occ.] Material Control Supervisor, Johnson Controls/ Vintec; [memb.] Put-in-bay Yacht Club; [pers.] One's level of happiness obtainable in life is equal to one's past level of suffering . . . so take your pain and suffering with your head held high . . . Jesus did!!!; [a.] Fairview Park, OH

MILLER, ERIC M.
[pen.] E. M. Miller; [b.] October 6, 1964, Springfield, OH; [p.] Thomas L. and Sharon L.; [m.] Andrea Lee Sanderson Miller, December 19, 1989; [ed.] B.A. English, Millersville University of PA; [oth. writ.] Published in college literary annual, several works in progress.; [a.] Lancaster, PA

MILLER, MICHELE
[b.] November 28, 1961, Houston, TX; [p.] Louis McCoy and Josie McCoy; [m.] Divorced; [ch.] Tonia Miller and Melvin Patton IV; [ed.] Kashmere Senior High School, high school Diploma Barclay, Career School Medical Assistant; [occ.] Residential Child Care; [hon.] Perfect Attendance; [a.] Houston, TX

MILNER, CINDY I.
[b.] February 1, 1948, Detroit, MI; [p.] Fred and Grace Carter; [m.] Dave, May 15, 1982; [ch.] Christ and Scott; [ed.] Dominica High School - some college courses; [occ.] Secretary, Public Relations Consultant; [hon.] This is my very first award or recognition. I am thrilled.; [pers.] I give all the credit to God who enables me to touch people's hearts and souls through my writing.; [a.] Grand Rapids, MI

MINOGUE, LINDA
[b.] August 7, 1964, Bakersfield, CA; [p.] Ken and Carole Stebbing; [m.] Stuart Minogue, June 19, 1990; [ch.] Alexander and Bradley; [ed.] Mt. San Antonio College, Walnut High School; [occ.] Home and Office Management for Brighter Connection and Family; [memb.] Heir to the Kingdom of Our Lord and Savior, Jesus Christ; [pers.] My grandmother, Mildred and Morris, taught us all the importance of family and tradition. This was written after attending a family reunion at my uncle's nursery, Morris Nursery in Modesto, CA.; [a.] Everett, WA

MISRA, RUNJHUN
[b.] November 2, 1983, Jhansi, India; [p.] Shamita Misra, Madhukar Misra; [ed.] Currently in West Junior High School - grade 8, until grade 7 I was in London, England, being born in India, my elementary schooling till 2nd grade was done there.; [occ.] 8th grade student at school (West Junior High) Columbia, Missouri; [hon.] London Police Gold Medal for General Knowledge, Royal School of Music Award for Excellence in Piano; [oth. writ.] Awarded for best story writing at my previous school in London, writings being published in school magazine. Several poems awaiting consideration for publication.; [pers.] "A single drop of hope quenches the thirst of thousands of drought-shrivelled people."; [a.] Columbia, MO

MITCHELL, GERALDINE
[pen.] Gerry Mitchell; [b.] October 22, 1918, Castle, OK; [p.] Minnie Taylor Meek - John H. Meek; [m.] Deceased; [ch.] John G. Wilson, Sue Gandy; [ed.] High school, course in Child and Maternity Care, several IBM and supply schools pertaining to Army Supply; [occ.] Retired Civil Service, also military dependent; [memb.] President, Copperas Cove Garden Club, Friends of Library VFW Aux. #8577, AARP; [hon.] 7 Outstanding Performance Awards in Civil Service, 1 Outstanding Sustained Performance Award-Civil Service; [a.] Copperas Cove, TX

MITCHELL, SHARON KAY
[b.] December 23, 1956, Wheeling, WV; [p.] Ruth Hines; [m.] Delywynn B. Mitchell, February 9, 1993; [ch.] Gene, Kristina, Shelly, Kara and Paul; [ed.] Graduated Florence High - 75, 2 yrs - Central Arizona College in Computer Science, Certified Emergency Medical Tech. and Certified Nurses Assistant - 12 years; [occ.] Business Owner - RV and Auto Repairs; [memb.] National Womens Asso., N.R.A. and 2 years Committee to determine Public School Problems and work out and implement solutions.; [oth. writ.] A short story - A Christmas Wish, and approximately 60 poems.; [pers.] The deeper one must dig to find good in another creates the truest kind of friendship.; [a.] Cody, WY

MONAHAN, JON J.
[b.] January 19, 1972, Cream Ridge, NJ; [p.] Kathleen and John Monahan; [m.] Jodi Hyland, August 23, 1997; [ed.] Notre Dame High School, Seton Hall University; [occ.] Life-Skins Teacher, Princeton Child Development Institute; [hon.] Dean's List, Psi Chi; [pers.] I can only hope that my writing truly expresses what others may feel and relate to enjoy.; [a.] Ewing, NJ

MONTIHO III, AUGUSTINE
[b.] May 20, 1956, Honolulu, HI; [p.] Augustine Montiho Jr., Lurline B. Montiho; [m.] Donna F. Montiho, March 21, 1992; [ch.] Hanna, Nikki, Pualanni; [ed.] Damien Memorial High School, Hawaii - Golden West College, L.A.; [oth. writ.] Been writing for years while in Hawaii working in the tour industry. Giving to the people on my tour as a gift from Hawaii.; [pers.] I want to bring some hope, peace and a smile to people who journey in life, as we all have peaks and valleys. To relate and bring comfort as we travel the road of life.; [a.] Sacramento, CA

MOORE, ANITA DESIREE
[pen.] Anita Desiree Moore; [b.] April 3, 1957, China Lake, CA; [p.] Richard and Juanita Lewis; [m.] Jeffrey W. Moore, April 30, 1982; [ch.] Jeffrey N. (11 yrs.), Demi N. (8 yrs.); [ed.] Moreno Valley High, Calif., Riverside City College, Calif.; [occ.] Full-time Writer of Historical Romance Fiction; [memb.] Romance Writers of America since 1992, Colorado Romance Writers since 1994; [oth. writ.] Poem "The Writer's Prayer" printed in 11/96 issue of CRW newsletter, articles printed in various other romance newsletters. Short and long historical romance.; [pers.] The love of the written word inspires minds, lifts one's spirits and touches the emotions of the world. A writer's greatest reward is that of promoting literacy. I'm proud to offer my contribution.; [a.] Fort Lupton, CO

MOORE, RODERICK
[pen.] Roderick Moore; [b.] December 20, 1950, Los Angeles, CA; [p.] Grandparents Emmett and Etta Moore, Mother - Barbara Moore; [ed.] Jordan High School, LA, Calif., completed, two years of college also completed; [occ.] Lyricist, Poet, Singer; [memb.] Pathways Program, a foundation for socially correct thinking. Thereby minimizing character defective minds. Our goal: the eradication of dysfunctional behavior.; [hon.] I've been given eternal life through Jesus Christ, the most high honor or award that can be presented to humankind: this is my belief.; [oth. writ.] My first effort to be publicly noteworthy; [pers.] Past sky further, then almost limitless space our Holy God is pure, realm awaits all those patient lives ended with full faith tested for loyal service a few brief years and after it has been proven true, the sinful flesh now obedient is through, then one's sweet spirit life can start entering eternity's splendid side glorified.; [a.] Las Vegas, NV

MOOTEE, SHERRY
[pen.] Sona Singh; [b.] March 21, 1997, Guyana; [p.] Sandra and Dasraj Mootee; [ed.] In Guyana and half in America; [occ.] Student; [hon.] I get certification for good school work and excellent behaviour; [oth. writ.] I have a wonderful family which I am proud of. I came from a poor background. I like to help people.; [pers.] When I was seven years old I had a third degree burn. I came to U.S.A., September 3, 1996.; [a.] New York, NY

MORANDI, DORINHA E.
[b.] March 27, 1948, Amityville, NY; [p.] Thomas Mendes Faria and Robbie Hester Faria; [m.] Michael Morandi Jr., March 11, 1978; [ch.] John David and James Andrew; [ed.] Wyandanch H.S., Allen School for Physicians' Aides, Central Piedmont Community College; [occ.] Part-time student, unemployed; [memb.] Victory Christian Center; [hon.] Citizenship Award, Music Achievement Award; [oth. writ.] Presently writing a collection of poems dedicated to my mother. "Deliverance" and "Genocide in Heaven," published by the National Library of Poetry.; [pers.] I resemble the many flowers in God's Garden of Children. I am appalled when observing the injustice of social inequities.; [a.] Charlotte, NC

MORELAND, REBECCA
[b.] December 18, 1980, Columbus, OH; [p.] Robert Moreland, Alice Moreland; [occ.] High school Sophomore; [oth. writ.] Poetry, essays and short stories, all as yet unpublished; [pers.] My poem was inspired by Dr. Martin Luther King, Jr. and the Freedom Riders. I believe that the purpose of artistic expression is to aid the connection of souls. I hope that my art will be able to serve that purpose.; [a.] Fairfield, PA

MORENO, CLARENA
[pen.] Angel Spirit; [b.] July 18, 1970, Colombia; [p.] Alvaro and Tulia; [m.] Robertos Veldwijk, July 20, 1996; [ed.] Bachelor's degree in Occupational Therapy, Art Classes (painting, children's literature); [occ.] Occupational Therapist; [hon.] Poems have been read on the radio, written in college newspaper. Several speeches have been published in local magazines, social impact articles published in important newspapers.; [pers.] Love makes hate disappear, dreams come true, stars gleam, smiles sprout and magic float in the air.; [a.] Beverly Hills, FL

MORGAN, JAMES E.
[b.] September 3, 1919, Sedalia, MO; [p.] George E. and Mathilda; [ed.] BFA and MA, Wayne State University, Detroit Plus Post Past-Graduate; [occ.] Retired; [memb.] Honolulu Watercolor Society; [oth. writ.] Poetry and short stories. "Sad Song" Into the Unknown '97; [pers.] We are fortunate, we who witness the beauty of the universe. No one is important! We either think that we are, or others proclaim us to be. The universe will be beautiful long after homosapiens have gone the way of the dinosaurs.; [a.] Kailua-Kona, HI

MORRIS, DENIQUE J.
[b.] November 28, 1984, Spanish Town, Jamaica; [p.] Janice Morris and George Morris; [ed.] Long Beach S.D.A. School; [occ.] Student; [memb.] Pathfinder Club; [hon.] First Aid, Music, Pathfinder of the Year, Cacti, Drill and March, Scupturing, Swimming (beginning and advanced); [oth. writ.] Beyond Our Eyes, The World, Today, A Mother's Cry, 2 Best Friends, A Wonderful Gift; [a.] Artesia, CA

MORRIS, JAMES LOUIS RUDOLPH
[pen.] James R. Morris; [b.] December 18, 1902, Fort Wayne, IN; [p.] James C. and Mollie (Wenninghof) Morris; [m.] Jeanette Sigrid Berg, May 29, 1929; [ch.] Beverly Daun, Sharon Kay and Leanna Lynn; [ed.] Fort Wayne (Ind.) Trade School; [occ.] Retired Knitter and Tavern Owner (Oldest Tavern in FW, IN); [memb.] 32nd Degree Mason, Shriner, Moose, Elks, Police Assoc. Social order (Ft. Wayne), Bowlers, Assoc. Tavern Owners Assoc.; [hon.] Shriner's 50 year Award; [oth. writ.] Many poems but all unpublished; [pers.] First and foremost believe and trust in God. The bright, contagious smile you share with others makes life worthwhile. Our family that goes before and comes after us will all surely join together someday.; [a.] Evansville, IN

MORRIS, KAREN L.
[pen.] Karen Morris; [b.] March 10, 1962, Philadelphia, PA; [p.] Alfred and Barbara Morris; [ed.] Bethsaida Chevy-Chase High School, Montgomery County Communication College, MD; [occ.] Assistant Nurse; [memb.] Good Shepherd Episcopal Church, The Smithsonian Associates; [oth. writ.] Another poem published in the anthology "Of Moonlight and Wishes.; [pers.] I hope others will enjoy what I write.

MORRISON, INA
[pen.] Ina Walters Morrison; [p.] Mr and Mrs Upton Walters; [ch.] two daughters, 1 deceased, terminal illness; [occ.] School Teacher, Math

and Science for 25 years; [oth.writ.] Several magazines self published booklet 1995 "Bible Comforts for the Bereaved" personal anthology 173 poems and growing, books-"The Ladder of Grief" "Mothers Together in Crisis", When Only New Will Do" "Walk In My Shoes" etc. All unpublished; [pers.] With God all things are possible. Our children are not our own; they have been lent to us just for a while; [a.] Jamaica, NY.

MORTENSEN, AARON
[b.] June 5, 1981, Mission Viejo, CA; [p.] David and Sharon Mortensen; [ed.] Sophomore, Mission Viejo High School; [occ.] Honors Student; [memb.] Model United Nations, California Scholarship Federation, National Honor Society, Orange County Academic Decathalon; [hon.] First place in Orange County: Speech for Orange County Academic Decathalon, Mission Viejo High School Top 25, participant in the state finals of the California Geography Bee; [pers.] Man is good at heart.; [a.] Mission Viejo, CA

MOSBY, KAFI NANA
[b.] March 6, 1956, Detroit, MI; [p.] Walter D. Hackel and Hester Y. Womack; [ch.] Kadoga, Gerald, Djenaba and Aisha; [ed.] Highland Park Comm. College; [occ.] Coach Operator, City of Detroit; [hon.] Won 1st place in a modelling contest as a teenager; [oth. writ.] Not published yet. Currently putting together a book entitled Thoughts and Inspirations.; [pers.] I seek to inspire all people to find life a rich and rewarding experience. Those that have inspired me most are Albert Einstein, Henry D. Thoreau, Ralph W. Emerson, David Bohm and Alfred Lord Tennyson.; [a.] Oak Park, MI

MUCHIMILLI, RAJU
[pen.] Muchimilli; [b.] May 29, 1966, Vizag, India; [p.] Rao Ramadevi; [m.] Sailaja, September 1, 1991; [ch.] Sandya (daughter); [ed.] Masters in Finance, CPA; [occ.] Accounting Supervisor; [memb.] Peace Club; [oth. writ.] Some poems in English and Telugu (a major language in India).; [pers.] There cannot be happiness without peace, which is more than mere material comfort. Spreading peace, I believe, is a sacred duty making us truly the children of God. I was taught peace yoga by my father who founded the Peace Club.; [a.] Houston, TX

MULLINS, TOMMY
[b.] May 15, Norfolk, VA; [p.] Charles Mullins, Sarah Oleane Mullins; [ed.] RHS, Richardson, TX, South Plains College (Levelland, TX); [occ.] Musician—Band Leader—Songwriter—Poet; [oth. writ.] A few published 'How To' articles on live sound techniques, promotional bio's and advertisement script. Many song lyrics; [pers.] A good poet is someone who manages, in a lifetime of standing out in thunderstorms, to be struck by lightning five or six times.; [a.] Reisterstown, MD

MURPHY, GERI
[b.] May 5, 1954; [p.] Irene Owczarski (Deceased); [m.] Michael, March 18, 1995; [occ.] Homemaker; [pers.] My love for writing is attributed to my Mom, who had the same passion, wit and values that were lovingly passed on to me.; [a.] Sterling Heights, MI

MURPHY, PENNEY
[pen.] Penney; [b.] December 15, 1966, Kansas City, KS; [p.] Bob and Carmen Murphy; [m.] Jerry Bengston (Fiance); [ch.] Jimmy and Ashley Schwigen; [ed.] Kewanee High School; [occ.] Teleservice Operator for APAC; [pers.] I started writing poems at the age of 10. Because of the way I felt, I would like to see the world. It's always been a dream of mine, that someday the world would be a loving place to live.; [a.] Kewanee, IL

MYERS, DAN
[b.] February 7, 1948, Fort Wayne, IN; [p.] Calvin Myers and Mildred Myers; [m.] Alipia Myers, March 23, 1992; [ch.] Lisa J. and Kevin D.; [ed.] Woodlan High, Central Christian College; [occ.] Maintenance, St. Joseph School Dist., St. Joseph, MO; [memb.] Little United Nations Club Scholarship Committee; [pers.] The main focus of my writing has been to capture the humor in people, as well as their joys and sorrows. I'm wanting to explore other topics. Fiction, nature, romance, religion.; [a.] Saint Joseph, MO

NADAL II, FRANK J.
[b.] March 7, 1975, Wasco, CA; [p.] Frank Nadal, Rosemary Ibarra Nadal; [ed.] Wasco High, Bakersfield Community College; [occ.] Loading Dock, Montgomery Ward Warehouse; [memb.] National Space Society; [hon.] 1st Place Little League 1986, 1st Place Academic Triathalan 1988, Pythagoras Award 1990, 1991; [oth. writ.] Numerous, none published; [pers.] "God is Dead" - Nietzsche.; [a.] Wasco, CA

NADING, NICHOLE
[b.] April 2, 1978, Iowa; [oth. writ.] Many, none published; [pers.] I have had severe medical problems in the past 7 years of my life and nobody has influenced my life more than God. I only write what I'm feeling and sometimes it touches more than I expect. I hope this poem brings you, the reader, as much comfort as it has brought me.; [a.] Elgin, IA

NALLY, KATHERINE J.
[pen.] S/A; [b.] June 8, 1961; Chicago, IL; [p.] Louis S. Palka, Esther L. Palka; [m.] Divorced; [ch.] Ashley Lauren, Michael Jordan; [ed.] Carmel High School For Girls, Adrian College; [occ.] Customer Service Representative/Sales, Mid America Tile, Mundelein, IL; [oth.writ.] Verses on gift cards, many poems waiting to be published; [pers.] I believe that I am a child of God. He has given me the ability to write and speak. He graces my pen with his words and I leave myself open to the glory of his works; [a.] Mundelein, IL.

NEGRON, JOSLEANN
[pen.] Yene; [b.] November 20, 1983, Orlando, FL; [p.] Agustina Negron and Jose Negron; [ed.] Grade 7, Walker Memorial Junior Academy; [occ.] Student; [hon.] Singing Award at Carnegie Hall, this year so I have received two trophies (Lacross and Basketball) mainly because of my other team members.; [oth. writ.] Other poems.; [pers.] A dream is something you can make happen. I'd like to thank God and three friends of mine who really help and give me my inspiration in writing poems: Mrs. Estella Asumbardo, Melanie Tangunan and Sonrisa Garza.; [a.] Avon Park, FL

NELMS, SYBIL W.
[b.] March 6, 1945, Nanticoke, PA; [p.] Joseph Nelms and Jane Nelms (Both Deceased); [ed.] Wyoming Seminary Preparatory School, Wilkes College; [oth. writ.] Several poems published by the National Library of Poetry.; [pers.] My poetry is rather eclectic in style encompassing a wide range of emotions including pain, sorrow, happiness and joy.; [a.] Nanticoke, PA

NELSEN, NORMAN R.
[b.] December 13, 1936, Staten Island, NY; [p.] Bernhard and Gladys Nelsen; [m.] Divorced; [ch.] Ronald Keith Nelsen (Deceased) and Katherine Elizabeth Nelsen; [ed.] Princeton University - AB 1958, Woodrow Wilson School of Public and International Affairs; [occ.] Retired International Business Executive/Consultant; [memb.] The Presbyterian Church, Basking Ridge, NJ, The Historical Society of the Somerset Hills, NJ (Trustee);

[hon.] Phi Beta Kappa, Distinguished Poet, International Poets Society; [oth. writ.] All published by the National Library of Poetry "Revival" in Sea of Treasure, "Critters Who Aren't Quitters" in Spirit of the Age, "On Castle Rock Road" in Where Dawn Lingers, "A Risky Mission" in Across the Universe, "Loonacy" in Best Poems of the '90's, "The Tree Tad" in Portraits of Life, "Mass Murder in a Cathedral Town" in Daybreak on the Land: "The Word and The Spirit" in Colors of Thought, "Poetic Justice" in Of Moonlight and Wishes, "At Appomattox Court House, Virginia" in Into the Unknown, "A Bellyful of Wisdom" in Silence of Yesterday, "The Circle to Salvation" in Etches in Time, "Provident Paradise" in The Isle of View, "Fresh Growth" in Through the Looking Glass, "Monkey See, Monkey Do" and "Loonacy" in Best Poems of '97. "Recycling" in A Lasting Mirage, "We All Merit Differently" in Dance Upon the Shore; [pers.] Often I write of the Unity and Diversity of what God has created and continues to create.; [a.] Basking Ridge, NJ

NEUBER, CHRISTINE
[pen.] Daisy Neuber; [b.] September 9, 1939, Portageville, MO; [p.] Lester Pratt, Hazel Pratt; [m.] Carl W. Neuber, August 30, 1958; [ch.] Brenda Lynn, Dwayne Earl, Davonna Jane, Beverly Diane; [ed.] Brookside High, Southeast MO State University; [occ.] Registered Nurse, Dexter Memorial Hospital, Dexter, MO; [memb.] New Covenant Fellowship Church, Association for Utilization Nurses, Association for Infection Control Nurses; [hon.] Dean's List; [pers.] I try to concentrate on the positive aspects of people and the light side of life. I enjoy the romantic writings.; [a.] Dexter, MO

NEWHARD, MARTHA JACKSON
[b.] April 20, 1932, Bucyrus, OH; [p.] Frank D. Jackson, Beatrico Graham Jackson; [ch.] Jane Parks, Jennifer Masse, Christopher, Thomas and Persis Newhard; [ed.] Western Reserve University, BA Heidelberg College - Tiffin, Ohio, MS Dominican College - San Rafael, CA, Resource Specialist Credential; [occ.] Title I Reading Teacher grades 1-3, Pinewood School, Pollock Pines, CA; [memb.] International Reading Association, California Association of Resource Specialists, Delta Kappa Gamma, El Dorado Writers Guild, St. Stephen's Lutheran Church, Gold Country Reading Council; [pers.] I truly believe in the basic good of humanity. I believe that I am blessed each day by my family, dear friends, a wonderful profession and a lovely home. So, I wish to give love in turn.; [a.] Placerville, CA

NEWHOUSE, GLORIA
[b.] August 6, 1943, Ansted, WV; [p.] Herbert and Vivian Buckland; [m.] Paul, March 17, 1987; [ch.] Donna Nottingham, Brenda Jager and April Highstrom; [ed.] Marlinton High School, Marlinton, WV, Jones Real Estate College - Denver, Red Rock Community College, Lakewood, CO; [occ.] Student - Red Rocks Community College studying computers; [memb.] Grange, since 1962, U.S. Chess Federation, since 1987, Faith Lutheran Church; [oth. writ.] None published.; [a.] Lakewood, CO

NEWMAN, LOLITA
[b.] November 11, 1971; Columbus, OH; [p.] Rev. Marvin Newman, Gwendolyn Newman; [ch.] Juwan Lee-Harrison Newman; [ed.] South High School; [hon.] Music Award, my Senior year in High School for orchestra; [oth. writ.] Other poems sent in to The Natioanl Library of Poetry for competition; [pers.] I have always seen life as a basketball game. Always rebounding, taking hits, taking chances to excel; [a.] Columbus, OH.

NEWMAN, NANCY
[b.] December 20, 1952, Sterling; [p.] S. Jean and Snavely; [m.] Donal Paul Knuth Sr., June 10, 1971; [ch.] Shawn and April; [ed.] 1-8 East Coloma School, 1-4 Rockfalls High, Sauk Valley College - working toward a computer certificate; [occ.] ANTEC Corp. Irun: Comp. and etc. jobs; [memb.] Single Group of Rock Falls—we love meeting people and working together through good and bad times. (Friends); [pers.] Follow your dreams. Keep trying hard. Never give up, make it happen.; [a.] Rock Falls, IL

NEWTON, ALYSSA ANNE
[b.] June 29, 1981, Holyoke, MA; [p.] Donald G. and Edith A. Newton; [ed.] Currently a high school sophomore at Good Shepherd Academy; [occ.] Student; [memb.] AWANA Clubs International, Fellowship Baptist Church, SACHE; [hon.] Excellence, Timothy, and Meritorious Awards (from AWANA), perfect score in a AWANA Bible quiz; [oth. writ.] Nearly 200 poems and several short stories which I have never attempted to publish.; [pers.] The themes of my poetry: one, God and His creation, as well as spiritual contemplations. My stories are often allegorical and written to stimulate the reader to listen to God.; [a.] Linn Grove, IN

NEWTON II, STEVEN RAY
[pen.] Fig; [b.] April 3, 1978, Houston, TX; [p.] Dave and Mary Morris; [ed.] Nimitz High School in Irving, Texas, USAMEOS Biomed Tech. School in Aurora, CO.; [occ.] Soldier in United States Army; [oth. writ.] Collection of poems not published - "Terminal Grey"; [pers.] I feel that poetry is that perfect way to let the heart speak. Nothing is greater than words. They can become vessels containing some of the greatest substance known.; [a.] Irving, TX

NGHIEM, THIEN BAO
[b.] July 8, 1939, Vietnam; [p.] Ban Pham and Kim Thi Nghiem; [m.] Can Thi Nghiem, December 1974; [ch.] Thuy Nghiem, Janet Nghiem, Richard Nghiem, Phillip Nghiem; [ed.] BS Degree; [occ.] Pharmacist; [a.] La Mirada, CA

NGUYEN, QUYNH GIA
[pen.] "Hoa Bien" ("Sea Flower"); [b.] March 25, 1923, Vietnam; [p.] Nghiem G. Nguyen and Nguyen T. At; [m.] Lan Phuong Nguyen, August 26, 1954; [ch.] Six; [ed.] M.D.; [occ.] Principal Clinical Provider in DHS TB Clinics (County of L.A.); [memb.] The American Academy of Family Physicians, Vietnamese Medical Association USA, Vietnamese Physicians in the Free World; [hon.] Citation with Honor Medal from Vietnamese Armed Forces Health Services (July 15, 1953); [oth. writ.] Poems published in "Y.Te Phothong" Health Journal; [pers.] "I discovered in my dream a starry domain resounding musical tone of diverse poems."; [a.] Tustin, CA

NICHOLS, BRITTNEY LEE
[pen.] Brittney Lee Nichols; [b.] April 4, 1977, Tyler, TX; [p.] Robert and Donna Nichols; [ed.] Sophomore at Emerson College in Boston, MA, graduated with honors from Jacksonville High School, Jacksonville, TX; [occ.] Acting major at Emerson College; [a.] Jacksonville, TX

NICHOLS, REBECCA
[b.] March 12, 1949, Claremore, OK; [p.] Lillie Mae Robbins (nee McCary) and Tennis Robbins; [ch.] James Weihing and Brenda Sterner; [occ.] Furniture Salesperson; [memb.] Unity Church; [pers.] My own goal in life is to enjoy and appreciate my family and friends, including Richard Anderson, Cathryn West, and Pat Rogers who greatly enhance my life.; [a.] Mesa, AZ

NIEHAUS, JANET L.
[pen.] Jan Niehaus; [b.] July 9, 1932, Potsdam, NY; [p.] Gladys Westurn; [m.] Robert A. Niehaus, July 10, 1993; [ch.] Two; [ed.] Bayshore, Long Island, N.Y. High School and courses at Indiana University, Bloomington, Indiana; [occ.] Retired; [memb.] Springfield Township Golf Club, G.E. Golf Club, Heart Fund; [hon.] Dale Carn Award, Most Improved Golfer Award 1996, Heart Assoc. Award for Fund Raising; [oth. writ.] Poems not published and working on first novel.; [pers.] Inside each of us are all kinds of things that need to be shared. We should not be scared or embarrassed to release this energy and just let it flow. It's good for the soul.; [a.] Cincinnati, OH

NIPPER, STEPHANIE
[b.] November 7, 1967, Kansas; [p.] Judith Hokkanen; [m.] Thomas Nipper, September 9, 1996; [ch.] Joshua, Judith, John; [occ.] Housewife; [pers.] I have always enjoyed poetry and "Loving You" was written to reflect my feelings for my husband.; [a.] Colorado Springs, CO

NOLAN, PATRICIA P.
[b.] August 16, 1964; [p.] Joseph and Patricia Piech; [m.] Hugh G. Nolan, July 20, 1991; [ch.] Elizabeth Rose; [ed.] BA - Rider College 1986; [occ.] Lawrence Intermediate School, Teacher - Lawrence Twp. NJ; [memb.] Council of Elementary Science, NJ Science Teachers Assoc.; [hon.] Governor's Teacher Recognition Award - 1995; [oth. writ.] Several human interest stories published in The Princeton Pocket and Lawrence Ledger newspapers.; [pers.] I hope to offer my readers a deeper look within themselves. My writing is done so that others can feel better within their hearts.; [a.] Wall, NJ

NORDHUS, CONNIE
[pen.] Connie Herring; [b.] July 15, 1955, Chicago, IL; [p.] Frank A. Nordhus and Naldine Nordhus; [m.] William M. Herring, November 2, 1990; [ch.] Jennifer Cook, Jeff Herring and David Herring; [ed.] Jeff-Moore High, Waco Beauty School. Graduate of Institute of Children's Literature 1994; [occ.] Owner, manager and hairdresser of small beauty shop; [memb.] Good Sam Club, Sam's Wholesale Club; [hon.] Wrote, sang and performed Waco Jingle, "Waco on the Brazos". A 30 second musical commercial for Waco Chamber of Commerce. Aired on KXXUTU, Channel 6; [oth. writ.] "Waco on the Brazos" copyright 1993.; [pers.] What did you learn? Or you're only as good as your word. Or say what you mean. Mean what you say.; [a.] Waco, TX

NORMAN, VERA DORIS
[b.] October 13, 1919, West Virginia; [p.] Clarence and Iva Muson; [m.] Claude Dean Norman, September 23, 1953; [ch.] Two; [ed.] High School and a few College courses; [a.] Panama City, FL

NORTH, BEVERLY
[b.] April 1, 1947, Palatka, FL; [p.] Durwood and Patsy Creel; [ch.] Derrick Share North; [ed.] High school graduate; [occ.] Famrer and care-giver for elderly; [memb.] Trinity United Methodist Church, and United Methodist Women Sunday School Supt.; [pers.] I have lived in this rural, country area all my life in this small town of Seville. Working with children and the elderly has been my inspiration. I also enjoy working with farm animals and gardens.; [a.] Seville, FL

NORTHCUTT, BEATRICE
[b.] January 6, 1928, Castle, OK; [p.] Everett Wyrick, Henryetta Housewright; [m.] Billy D. Northcutt (Deceased), February 17, 1945; [ch.] Thomas Deverle, Garry Dwayne, Danny Vinson; [ed.] Okemah High School, Independence Community College - Communications II; [occ.] Re-

tired; [oth. writ.] Novel "Tomorrow Will Be Better," sequel, "What Time I Am Afraid" - (unpublished) I do devotionals for the Lakeside Church of God bulletin twice a month.; [pers.] Writing is my "calling". My desire is to please God with my writing by inspiring mankind for good.; [a.] Noble, OK

NULPH, WILLIAM TED
[pen.] Bill Nulph; [b.] September 21, 1973, Salt Lake City, UT; [ed.] Cyprus High School, Salt Lake Community College (Sociology); [a.] Magna, UT

ODULIO, YOLANDA Y.
[pen.] Yollie; [b.] May 20, 1950; Manila, Phils.; [p.] Fernando and Adela Yumang; [m.] Divorce; May 1, 1997; [ch.] (3) Yvette, Mark, Tristian; [ed.] B.S. Med. Tech., B.S. Bus. Adm. and (HRM) Hotel and Restauran Management; [memb.] BLD Covenant Community; [oth.writ.] Love sonnet, I love you; [a.] Jamaica, NY.

OGLE, JARNELL D.
[pen.] Dennis Jarrell; [b.] May 8, 1944; Vicksburg, MI; [p.] James H. Ogle, Ethel Ogle; [m.] Susan Ogle; October 7, 1967; [ch.] Cynthia Marie, William Thomas, Michael David; [ed.] BSBA Roosevelt U. (Chicago); [occ.] Disabled (unemployed); [hon.] Hallmark Art (high school); [a.] Lewisville, TX.

OKIN, JENNIFER S.
[pen.] J. S. Okin; [b.] May 9, 1965, Cleveland, OH; [p.] Ben and Sandra Okin; [ed.] Cleveland Heights High 1980-83, Hobonim-Dror Gesher Haziv, Israel Gsraeli Studies on Kibbutzim) 1983-84, Community College(s) 1984-85/1990-91; [occ.] Pasts Driver Associate with a Toyota-Volvo Dealership; [hon.] Certificate of Recognition Plaque with Library of Congress Re: "Sunset Sands".; [oth. writ.] 1st Published piece Mists of Enchantment with The National Library of Poetry and several of my writing have been copy written through Library of Congress in Wash., D.C.; [pers.] Be honest, be yourself and fulfill your destiny. This piece was about a former lover P.J. Brown who has help me find and understand myself and accept me!; [a.] Concord, CA

OLIVAS, KRISTAN K.
[pen.] Kristan K. Olivas; [b.] March 16, 1970, Portland, OR; [p.] Arlene Crist and James Rector (Both Deceased) Tomas Jankovsky (Stepfather - living); [m.] Divorced; [ch.] Tyler James; [ed.] Portland Community College, Marylhurst College (high school attended - Lake Oswego High); [occ.] Student, mother, art coordinator (PT); [memb.] Friendly House Community Center - United Way; [hon.] Dean's List 4 terms, President's List 3 terms consecutively; [pers.] Find your gifts and share them with the world! Act with grace and love instead of fear, trust yourself and know yourself.; [a.] Portland, OR

OLSON, SHERRY L.
[b.] October 11, 1980, New York; [p.] Ralph and Tammy Olson; [ed.] Tioga High School; [occ.] Sophomore in high school; [memb.] National Library of Poetry, International Society of Poets; [hon.] 2 awards "Editor's Choice," for outstanding achievement in poetry; [oth. writ.] Falling in Love, My Precious Heart, Untitled - "You Are My Love . . ." —of which, all three were published; [pers.] Don't ever let someone tell you that you can't do something when you have the courage to at least try.; [a.] Owego, NY

OLSON, STEVEN J.
[pen.] Steve Olson; [b.] March 19, 1952, St. Paul, MN; [p.] Leonard C. and Shirley B. Olson; [m.] Yolanda D. Olson, June 28, 1980; [ch.] David J. and Stephen I. Olson; [ed.] St. Marks Elementary School, Cretin High School; [occ.] Graphics Dept. Manager; [memb.] Desktop Publishers Association; [oth. writ.] Several dozen unpublished poems, one unpublished song.; [pers.] Poetry . . . ponders the wonders, reflects on realities, nourishes knowledge and loves life.; [a.] South Ozone Park, NY

OPPERMANN, REBECCA
[b.] July 12, 1971, Fort Worth, TX; [p.] Loutrisha A. Smith and Olen M. Smith Sr.; [m.] Trey Oppermann, December 20, 1991; [ch.] Amanda and Tracy Oppermann; [ed.] High school graduate - Haltom High School, Associate of Arts Degree - Tarrant County Junior College, currently attending University Texas at Arlington, Psychology Major; [occ.] Tupperware Manager and Housewife; [memb.] First Baptist Church of Everman, Board Member PTA, Public Relations Officer and Recording Secretary for Independent Order of Foresters; [hon.] Who's Who Among Students in American Junior Colleges; [oth. writ.] Three other poems published by the Texas Department of Health and Texas Association Against Sexual Assault.; [pers.] "Children Are People Too!" My writing reflects my life.; [a.] Everman, TX

ORTH, ELLA S.
[b.] May 21, 1959, Manila, Philippines; [p.] Bernabe and Maria Sajonas; [m.] David J. Orth, May 21, 1986; [ch.] Joy Maranatha Orth; [ed.] Bachelor of Science in Commerce, Major in Banking and Finance; [occ.] Property Manager; [pers.] All things work together for good to them that love God . . . Romans 8:28.; [a.] Florence, KY

ORTIZ, MRS. MAXINE
[pen.] Maxine Ortiz; [b.] December 26, 1948, Mobile, AL; [p.] Rev. Robert Lee May and Rev. Mary L. May; [m.] Mr. Franco Ortiz De Jesus, January 9, 1988; [ed.] H.S. Grad-Williamson H.S.- Mobile, Ala., Midtown School of Bus.-NYC. - Albert Merril School - Computers - NYC., University of So. Ala. - Mobile, Ala., BD. of ED. Asst. Bus Driver School - Long Island City, N.Y., L.C. Security Guard School - Bkln, N.Y. - ICS. - Scranton, PA.; [occ.] Entertainer - Writer - Singer - Serious Comic; [memb.] 33 years Membership in Organization "Galilee Baptist Church-447 Clinton Ave" Brooklyn, New York 11238; [hon.] "Gold Plaque" from Galilee Baptist Church" for "Appreciation of The Love and Devotion to God and others, in Oct. 1994 and for work as a devoted Christian; [oth. writ.] I am currenting working on 1st book entitled "The Great American Nightmare".; [pers.] Well I have 3 Philosophical Statements, 1. If you can't help someone, don't hurt them, 2. In your pursuit of happiness, take the time out just to "Be Happy", 3. My business is to mind my business and leave other people business alone because those who mind their, live longer that way". And they have a better bus. And a more successful one.; [a.] Brooklyn, NY

ORTMAN, JANIS
[b.] July 22, 1949; [p.] James and Lucille Warren; [m.] George, October 25, 1970; [ch.] Brandon and Geoffrey; [ed.] Currently attending Lincoln Land Community College; [occ.] Self-employed; [memb.] Church of Christ; [hon.] Dean's List; [oth. writ.] Articles for Compassionate Friends newsletter, poems for local newspaper, and poem published for Western Poetry Association.; [pers.] This poem was written in memory of our son Brandon. A tribute to parents everywhere who understand, because they know what it's like to have lost a child.; [a.] Taylorville, IL

OSTRANDER, MICHAEL
[b.] July 10, 1958, Cleveland, OH; [p.] Walter and Rita Ostrander; [a.] Astoria, NY

OTTENSCHOT, RUTH
[b.] September 27, 1943, Auburn, NY; [m.] John P. Ottenschot, November 27, 1981; [ch.] Lisa Marie; [ed.] Moravia High School; [occ.] Home school teacher for daughter; [oth. writ.] A soon-to-be-published poem, "The Pockets of My Mind; [pers.] I try to get the emotion of the moment across in my poems.; [a.] La Grange, GA

OUTLAW III, WILSON T.
[pen.] Trey Outlaw; [b.] May 17, 1970, Prince Geois, MD; [p.] Wilson T. Jr. and Martha C. Outlaw; [m.] Ginny Lewis Outlaw, September 25, 1993; [ed.] Batesburg- Leesville High School, Midlands Technical College; [occ.] South Carolina Department of Mental Health; [memb.] Faith United Methodist Church, Lexington, S.C. - Lexington County Leisure Center; [hon.] Track and Football High School - State 4-H Award; [pers.] The ability to express one's thoughts and feelings is a gift of God, whether through written verse or daily application to help others.; [a.] Lexington, SC

OVERSTREET, JULIE
[pen.] Jue; [b.] August 10, 1977; Pittsburg, TX; [p.] Terry and Laura Overstreet; [ed.] Klein High School, Kingwood Community College; [occ.] College Student; [memb.] National Geographic Society, Smithsonian, Planetary Society; [oth.writ.] Over 40 other poems (not published); [pers.] To push myself to the limits and explore all possibilities; [a.] Kingwood, TX.

OWENS, YOLANDA DENISE
[pen.] Yoyo; [b.] March 28, 1979, Singing River Hospital, Pascagoula; [p.] Mattie Beard and Timothy Owens; [ed.] Calling All Christian Academy 12th grade and plan to go to college for Journalism.; [memb.] I'm a member at Calling All Christian church and I'm save and love Jesus and am filled with the Holy Spirit; [hon.] NAACP Black History Month 1 won a trophy for writing an essay; [oth. writ.] Essay and other poems; [pers.] First of all I would like to give thanks to God for He is the head of my life and I would also like to thank my mother who always believes in me and the rest of my family.; [a.] Gautier, MS

PACHECO, INES
[b.] August 29, 1973, St. Miguel, Azores; [p.] Luzia and Jose Pacheco; [m.] Victor Furtado, October 12, 1997; [ed.] Cambridge Ridge and Latin High School; [oth. writ.] Never published; [pers.] As the first poem ever sent in anywhere, I'm very honored and encouraged to continue writing and exploring this artistic world of words.; [a.] Cambridge, MA

PACK, BETTY DANIEL
[b.] May 24, 1924, Waverly, OH; [p.] Charlie Daniel and Madge Ball Daniel; [m.] Laudie John Pack (Deceased December 18, 1988), April 25, 1944; [ch.] Melba McDaniel, Wanda Schubmehl, 5 grandchildren; [ed.] Through Mifflin High School, Columbus, Ohio; [occ.] Housewife; [memb.] First Church of God, Ashland, KY and Community Bible Study, Ashland, International Society of Poets; [hon.] Editor's Choice Awards; [oth. writ.] I have written numerous poems. Most are religious or about nature. I have written several short stories, both fiction and non-fiction, for my grandchildren. Presently, I am writing my autobiography.; [pers.] It is my desire that my writing be a witness. "I can do all things through Christ who strengthens me," — Philipians 4:13.; [a.] Ashland, KY

PALACIO, CLARENCE
[b.] October 18, 1944, Dangriga Town, Belize; [p.] Mrs. Escolastica Palacio and Mr. Frank Palacio; [ch.] Four children; [ed.] I attended Sacred Heart Elementary School of Belize Dangriga Town, also attended St. Michael College of Belize City; [occ.] I am a pensioner; [hon.] From Polystar Records

Grand Island, NY, Talent Searchers of New York; [oth. writ.] I continued writing my songs and poems, and in 1969 I came to New York and I went to Tractor Trailor School became a graduate. Also was a student of Jack Kahn School of Music.; [pers.] I was born in the October 18, 1944, in Belize Dangriga Town in CA. I am more than please to know, the world will get the chance to share my poetry with me.; [a.] Jamaica, NY

PALANGI, DAVID
[b.] January 8, 1981, Fredericksburg, VA; [p.] Joan Darby and Stephen Palangi; [ed.] Brooke Point High School (3 years); [memb.] Brooke Point Players; [a.] Stafford, VA

PALMS, JANNELL
[b.] September 20, 1971, Zanesville, OH; [p.] Caralee and Roger Davisson; [m.] Damian Andrew Davisson, November 23, 1994; [ch.] Derrick Andrew Palms; [occ.] Artistic Hair Designer; [pers.] My goal is to touch someone's life whether it be one person or one hundred and to give a hand on healing wounds, or changing perspectives. I want to reach the unreachable.; [a.] Kalamazoo, MI

PANGBURN, SHANE
[b.] February 15, 1983, Urbana, IL; [p.] John and Dianna Pangburn; [ed.] I attend 8th grade at East Prairie Elementary School in Tuscola, Illinois; [hon.] High Honors at East Prairie Elementary School; [a.] Tuscola, IL

PANOS, TEDDIE
[pen.] Penny James; [b.] April 25, 1941, Cheraw, SC; [p.] Kalliroi and Bill Perry; [m.] Nick Panos, February 5, 1961; [ch.] Jamey and Perry Panos; [ed.] Rivers High School, VA. Institute of Real Estate; [occ.] New Homes Sales Rep.; [pers.] Poetry should touch the soul.; [a.] Sewanee, GA

PANUNZIO, KAREN M
[b.] July 30, 1975; [ed.] Beverly high School B.S. Bridgewater State College; [occ.] Student; [memb.] Gamma Phi Beta Sorority - V.P, Circle K International; [hon.] Graduate of B.S.C. Leadership Institute Class of 1996; [oth.writ.] Several short stories in the magazine The AEGIS, a high school magazine; [a.] Beverly, MA.

PARMETER, LOSONE L.
[pen.] Lee Parmeter; [b.] August 9, 1934, Lexington, KY; [p.] Lyle and Marie (Deceased); [m.] Margie, June 9, 1994; [ch.] Michelle - 31, Lee and Elizabeth - 35; [ed.] B.S. Industrial Psy; [occ.] Retired USAF; [memb.] Capt Mississippi State Guard; [hon.] 23 years of Air Force duty resulted in many awards. Awarded Vietnamist Medal of Honor, Dec. '72; [oth. writ.] I have a book of prose and poetry yet unpublished.; [pers.] I like to write so that each poem will be transposed as the reader's private poem of love or feelings.; [a.] Biloxi, MS

PASCOCELLO, GRACE
[b.] November 13, 1925, New York City; [p.] Jennie Cali, Anthony Lupo; [m.] Sylvester, March 27, 1943; [ch.] Pascale (Dec) Francine Marino; [ed.] 2 yrs college; [occ.] School Secretary (Ret); [oth. writ.] Extensive collection of personal poetry; [pers.] My love overflowed into poetry to my loved and loving daughter and husband Chuck Marino, grandchildren Patrick and Lori. "Fill your hearts with love."; [a.] Brooklyn, NY

PASCULLO, MICHAEL
[b.] August 6, 1980, New York; [p.] Vito Pascullo and Patty Pascullo; [ed.] St. Dominic High School; [occ.] DJ; [memb.] Leadership Committee, Youth Group Leader, Student Council; [hon.] Played Varsity Soccer, Varsity Baseball, Honors Convocation, Student Council, Newspaper; [oth. writ.] Articles for school newspaper.; [pers.] Aerody-

namically the bumble bee shouldn't be able to fly, but the bumble bee doesn't know it so it goes on flying anyway. Thanks to Mom and Dad, Tricia, MKA, DC, and P. Cannon.; [a.] Syosset, NY

PATHIS,
[pen.] Brian Cowan; [b.] October 15, 1979; Birmingham, AL; [p.] Richard Cowan, Marcia Cowan; [ed.] Tullahoma High School; [occ.] Student; [memb.] Barrett Browning National Honors Society, Mu Alpha Theta; [hon.] Top 10%; [oth.writ.] Published works in newspapers and articles; personal collection of peotry-Encased Within The Twilight Frost.; [pers.] Granted of the arcane-a mystical desire of the gothic and darkness, this Passion wells as the maelstorm within. Beauty lies everywhere...; [a.] Tullahoma, TN.

PATRIKIOS, DAVID J.
[b.] February 23, 1977; Islip, NY; [memb.] The Council For a Free America, President, the Rock and Roll Temple, Polska Appreciation Committee; [pers.] Reject adulthood and remember who you are; [a.] Brooklyn, NY.

PATTERSON, DUSTIN
[pen.] Dustin; [b.] January 12, 1978, Washington, DC; [p.] Sandy Patterson; [ed.] College, TV and Radio Broadcasting; [oth. writ.] The Strangest of the Upright Walking Creatures, I Am Just a Car Salesman, Where I Left My Keys; [pers.] I specialize in the chaos of human tragedy and the triumph thereafter. I'm addicted to my sadness.; [a.] Adelphi, MD

PATTERSON-STEVENSON, PAULA
[pen.] Diane L. B.; [b.] January 25, 1951, Gowanda, NY; [p.] Sally and Robert Patterson; [m.] Terry Robert Stevenson, July 31, 1971; [ch.] Jodi Diane, Tammara Dawn and Tara Denise; [ed.] Troy Area Schools, Troy, Pennsylvania, East Forest School, Marienville, Pennsylvania, graduated May 29, 1969. Duff's Business Institute, Pittsburgh, PA, graduated April, 1969; [occ.] Clerk Typist for a Job Training Consortium/Part-time Waitress; [memb.] First Presbyterian Church, Marienville, PA, MACA (Marienville Area Civic Assoc.), Marienville, PA, Golf Membership - High level Gold Course; [hon.] Salutatorian—Class of 1969, East Forest School, Marienville, Pennsylvania; [oth. writ.] Poem published by EPA Book—"Reflections of Life," National Library of Poetry, book "Tomorrow's Dream," "Where Dawn Lingers," "Best Poems of the 90's," "The Best Poems of 1997," "Frost at Midnight," and "Dance Upon the Shore."; [pers.] My poems are written from my feelings. Also writing poetry is self-healing for me.; [a.] Marienville, PA

PAVLOCK, GLADYS F.
[pen.] Gladys Yeager Pavlock; [b.] February 3, 1933, Hastings, PA; [p.] Merle Yeager and Florence Yeager; [m.] L. James Pavlock, May 25, 1957; [ch.] James Russell and Thomas Eugene; [ed.] Mercy Hospital School of Nursing, Altoona, PA - R.N. Diploma, Indiana University of PA - B.S. degree in Education; [occ.] Retired School Nurse; [memb.] St. Timothy Roman Catholic Church, Salvation Army - Curwensville Unit; [hon.] Joseph Mattas Orthopedic Nursing Award, 1996 regional winner in the Nationwide Goebel Greeting Card Contest sponsored by the M.I. Hummel Collectors Club; [oth. writ.] "The Little Kite Girl" published in "RN" Nursing Journal in 1969.; [pers.] My maternal grandfather had a strong influence on me in my childhood and also in my decision to become a nurse. I reflect on my childhood, family and nursing career experiences in my writings.; [a.] Curwensville, PA

PEDERSEN, JENNIFER
[pen.] Jenn; [b.] November 3, 1973, New York; [p.] Alan Pedersen and Cathrine Kees; [ed.] Paramus High School, Class of "1991". And I start classes in the fall to study psychology.; [occ.] Hairdresser; [memb.] American Cancer Society, American Quarter Horse Association; [hon.] Awarded management position on Empress Cruise Lines, NAVI Scuba Diver Network; [oth. writ.] After losing a special cousin to the horrible disease, leukemia, I found that life is what you make of it, in good times and in bad times.; [pers.] My motivation for the poem, "Like a Mother," was a lady who helped me overcome a troubled youth. She gave me love, support and motherly guidance.; [a.] Paramus, NJ

PELCH, AMBER
[b.] April 16, 1983, Flint, MI; [p.] Jerry Pelch, Leasha Pelch; [ed.] 8th grader at Southwestern Academy in Flint; [occ.] Student; [hon.] A and B Honor Roll six years straight.; [a.] Flint, MI

PELT, ALAN
[b.] May 28, 1980, Alexandria, LA; [p.] Carlous and Carline Pelt; [ed.] Junior in high school; [occ.] High school student; [oth. writ.] "Death of a Child—Birth of a Man" and many unpublished poems and songs.; [pers.] "Sometimes it's not so much what others think of you, but what you think of yourself, and how you act upon your thoughts."; [a.] Simpson, LA

PENNINGTON, APRIL THOMPSON
[pen.] April Thompson Pennington; [b.] April 10, 1964, Bluefield, WV; [p.] Raynard and June Thompson; [m.] Mark W. Pennington, February 8, 1991; [ch.] Caleb Brendan Pennington; [ed.] Princeton High School, Bluefield State College; [occ.] Housewife; [memb.] Calvary Tabernacle Church, National Congress of American Indians, President Father's Rights for Men and Children, Secretarial College International; [oth. writ.] Editorials in newspapers standing for children's rights; [pers.] I intend to make the public aware of Native American's hardships of their past and present through poetry and through my writings.; [a.] Princeton, WV

PERA, NANCY LYNN
[pen.] Nancy Lynn Laauwe; [b.] December 2, 1965, Paterson; [p.] Harold and Linda Laauwe; [m.] David M. Pera, May 25, 1996; [ch.] One on the way; [ed.] Wayne Hills High School, The Berkely School, Garret Mountain Campus; [occ.] NIA Lawyers Title Agency as a Commitment Processor; [memb.] Christ Church, Pompton; [hon.] Dean's List, previous published writings, Music Award; [oth. writ.] Great Temptation, Man And Wife, Until You, Madman, Rain, etc.; [pers.] Most of my writings are about situations I have seem for others or been in the past.; [a.] Maywood, NJ

PERRIN, ADELE
[pen.] Elizabeth Hope; [p.] Barbara Perrin and Nelvin Perrin; [ed.] Fisher Middle/High School; [pers.] God is my best listener.; [a.] Lafitte, LA

PERRY, SEAN
[b.] February 22, 1971, Camden, ME; [p.] David and Lois Perry; [ch.] Mookie; [ed.] B.A. in English Literature at the University of Central Florida; [occ.] Publisher of Axis Magazine in Orlando, FL; [oth. writ.] Several published poems, frequently published sports articles on the NBA, including compilation on Anfernee Hardaway with Beckett Publishing; [pers.] Life is a series of challenges which I accept without restraint, and, of course, I enjoy the drink while never having read a lick of Hemingway.; [a.] Orlando, FL

PETERSON SR., CHARLES E.
[pen.] "The Poet"; [b.] May 9, 1950, Benton

Harbor, MI; [p.] Willie E.L.M.M. Peterson and Rosie Lee Peterson; [ch.] Anita, Tanisha, and Charles Jr (A'mmary); [occ.] "Rad Waste Handler" Nuclear Power PLT, Ex Director of "Poetry Plus Inc."; [memb.] Gospel Tabernacle Baptist Church (Deacon), V.B.U. Civic Org. (Trustee); [hon.] 2 "Editors Choice Awards" from The National Library of Poetry, Community Service Award, "Motivational Speaker" at schools, colleges, correctional facilities, civic organizations, churches with poetry as a base and format; [oth. writ.] Book - "The Poet Chasing After a Dream" and three other compilations.; [a.] Covert, MI

PHILLIPS, MARGARET
[pen.] Margaret Phillips; [b.] October 16, 1973, Kansas City, MO; [p.] Bruce and Catharine Phillips; [ed.] 1991- 7 grad. Calabasas High School in Calabasas, CA. 1991-1994 Attended Transylvania University n Lexington, KY. 1996 grad. University of Louisville with BA in English; [occ.] Cafe Worker at Hawley. Cooke Booksellers/ Student at University of Louisville in post-bac work; [memb.] Crescent Hill Masters Swim Team; [hon.] Won a creative writing scholarship at U of L for 1996-1997 and am currently enrolled as a post-bac student. Also won various awards in high school and college swimming; [oth. writ.] Published in high school literary magazine, editor of reviews section in high school newspaper.; [pers.] I enjoy writing about the natural forces that shape all of us inadvertently. I have always been inspired by undisturbed nature.; [a.] Louisville, KY

PHILLIPS, WENDELL M.
[pen.] Corky Bishop; [b.] May 26, 1918, Wichita, KS; [p.] Deceased; [m.] Deceased; [ch.] Three grown and married.; [ed.] High school (12); [occ.] Retired; [memb.] Masonic and American Legion; [pers.] I have composed/written many poems during my lifetime—fun only. This is a first (done on a dare from a friend of mine).; [a.] Wichita, KS

PHULLER, CHERECIA L.
[pen.] Cheri P; [b.] July 17, 1964; Atlanta,GA; [p.] Mr. & Mrs. James & Ruth Fuller; [ed.] A graduate of West Fulton High School, currently enrolled at Clayton College and State University, major is Computer Science; [memb.] Georgia Association for Interpreters for the deaf, Georgia Notary Association; [hon.] I received an honorary letter from the mayor in the City of Atlanta for writing him a poem; [oth.writ.] I wrote a poem and sent it to the Mayors office for the city of Atlanta. I have written several skits and had several people to act out the characters; [pers.] The mind is a very powerful tool to have. I encourage any and everyone to learn how to excercise and train their mind. Once you have learned and mastered this technique, you will see that the mind can work wonders; [a.] College Park, GA

PHUNKHANG, LANGZE PALMO
[b.] December 7, 1966, Bir, India; [p.] Jampa Phunkhang G. and Norzin; [ed.] Wynberg Allen School, India, St. Bede's College, India - Dev. Samaj College of Ed., India B-Ed. Himachal University, India - MA (English); [occ.] English Teacher; [oth. writ.] Many poems and articles published in local magazines, periodicals and educational papers in India.; [pers.] My poetry is a reflection of my deepest emotions. Being deeply sensitive, I use poetry as a comforting outlet for the outpourings of my soul.; [a.] Cambridge, MA

PILLARI, ELIZABETH FITZPATRICK
[b.] December 3, 1966, Red Bank, NJ; [m.] Louis Pillari; [ch.] Louis Peter; [ed.] The College of the Holy Cross, Red Bank Catholic High School; [occ.] New Home Sales (Real Estate), Homemaker; [oth. writ.] Numerous other poems on life—its beauty and

hardship.; [pers.] My poem is dedicated to and about my brother, Peter, who died of cancer at age of thirty-seven. His life was cut short, but in those years Peter shone like a star and brought love and laughter to all he touched.; [a.] Tinton Falls, NJ

PIROZOK, MARY L.
[b.] Lawrence, MA; [p.] John and Nora Regan; [m.] Raymond (Deceased); [ch.] Mary Elisabeth, Jerry, Tony, and Faith; [ed.] Associate Degree Clark State College, Bachelor's Degree - Antioch College; [occ.] Master's Degree - Wright State College, Associate Professor Clark State Community College; [hon.] L.I.L. Award - 1973 Springfield, Ohio, 1st Prize in Poetry; [oth. writ.] Many poems, book of fiction in progress; [pers.] My poems are reflections of my feelings.; [a.] Springfield, OH

PLYLER, VALERIE
[b.] March 30, 1947, Brookville, PA; [p.] Fred and Earlene Powell; [m.] Robert, July 21, 1979; [ch.] Nine Children; [ed.] Brookville High; [occ.] Mary Kay Consultant; [memb.] First Assemblies of God Sunday School Teacher; [pers.] Taking responsibility for our past and present actions should produce in us a desire for love, forgiveness and reconciliation. Let each of us take that first step.; [a.] Vienna, OH

POHLHAUS, JACKIE
[pen.] Jackie Neese; [b.] September 23, 1963, Canton, MS; [p.] Jack and Patricia Neese; [m.] John C. Pohlhaus Jr., March 1, 1986; [ch.] Christopher, Jessica, Trish; [ed.] Sidney Lanier High—Montgomery, AL, Catonsville College—Catonsville, MD; [occ.] Dillards Dept. Store and Sales Rep. STS; [memb.] Coordinator MS Food Network Ladies Auxiliary Leader. New Life Center of Clinton, MS; [hon.] My greatest honor and award are my three children; [oth. writ.] Write and design all-occasion poems and cards, children's stories, Bible and motivational studies and speeches; [pers.] Change must come from within. I want my writing to provoke and inspire someone to realize their potential both spiritually and physically.; [a.] Clinton, MS

POLK, MAXINE ASHNER
[b.] October 27, Alexandria, LA; [p.] Mack Ashner and Deloris Ashner; [m.] Jerry Polk Sr., October 12, 1958; [ch.] Jerry, Rodney and Kenneth Polk; [ed.] Masters and a Doctoral Equivalency in Education; [occ.] Kindergarten Teacher, Lockwood Elementary, Oakland, CA; [memb.] Faith Baptist Church and The Oakland Alliance of Black Educators; [hon.] Delta Sigma Theta Sorority; [pers.] I strive to touch someone in a special way through my writing. I have been greatly influenced by my family and friends.; [a.] Oakland, CA

POMER, SHIRLEY
[b.] February 12, 1945, Decoy, KY; [p.] George and Martha Miller; [ch.] Tim, Paul Hansen and Brenda Nunes Hansen; [ed.] Breathett Co. High Jackson, KY; [occ.] DeKalb Genetics Corporation; [pers.] I enjoyed writing this poem (Tree of Life.) Thank you, for seeing beauty in my poem. I'm proud. Dedication to: Grandchildren, Chad, Carlose, Brandon, Brandi, Randi, Tim and Jon.; [a.] Kentland, IN

PORTER, BYRON
[pen.] Byron; [b.] February 17, 1924, Pgh, PA; [p.] Byron and Elizabeth - Deceased; [m.] Gloria - Deceased, March 18, 1948; [ch.] 3 children, 8 grandchildren, 3 great grandchildren; [ed.] Graduate Brentwood High in June 1941, entered Slippery Rock University 55 years later (1996); [occ.] Retired V/P Sales/Marketing (currently student—major Eng, Writing); [memb.] Senator Student Government, Newspaper Reporter "The Rocket" campus weekly - ROTC Cadet; [hon.] Ass't Scoutmaster, Sgt WW II, Sales Mgr. Nat'l

Sales Mgr. V/P Sales/ Marketing Estate Liquidator, student—freshman; [oth. writ.] High school and university newspapers, submitted to Readers Digest poetry and stories, children's stories, series of 4 at illustrator before submitting to a publication; [pers.] I'm an avid writer. I write daily at 5:30 am poetry and prose and short stories (true and fictional). I write! It flows easily from my pen.; [a.] Slippery Rock, PA

POWELL, ALICE ANN
[ed.] Cedar Crest College 1994, Bachelor of Arts; [occ.] Social Worker; [oth. writ.] Published once in college poetry class; [pers.] Poetry heals so I can be kind to others and so I can move forward.; [a.] Bethlehem, PA

POWELL I, WENDELL J.
[b.] September 26, 1969, Neptune, NJ; [p.] Charlie W. Powell Sr. and Hattie B. Powell; [m.] Arnesia N. Powell, August 19, 1989; [ch.] A. Anthony Powell and Wendell J. Powell II; [ed.] Trenton Central High School; [pers.] When you believe in yourself, the inner spirit that resides in you will reveal the mystery. Give God the glory. Amen.; [a.] Trenton, NJ

PRECIE, RUTH
[b.] November 9, 1931, Orange, CA; [p.] Threecy and Bill Thomason; [m.] Raymond Lewis Precie, July 20, 1950; [ch.] Raymond, Richard, Russell, Renette, Art and Rosie; [ed.] San Jacinto High School, Fullerton College - Home Study Literature Writing Children's Stories, Stories - College Classes; [occ.] Retired Dairyman's Wife; [memb.] "Fairmount Park Citizens Group", "CCOP" Concerned Citizens on Patrol "Park Watch"; [hon.] High School - Student, Vice President - (Outstanding Student), Chino Ca., Dairy Group - Dairy Belles 1st Vice President - Philanthropy Chairman - Formed Teen Group of Volunteer for Exceptional Children's Bloomington, Ca.; [oth. writ.] Children's poems and stories.; [pers.] Devoted to helping children and others writings inspirational poems and stories.; [a.] Riverside, CA

PRICE, MICHELLE C.
[b.] May 21, 1977, Wilkes-Barre; [p.] Howard E. and Deborah M. Price; [ed.] Lake-Lehman High School, Luzern County Community College; [oth. writ.] "Journey," "Looking Glass," "Dust in the Wind." As a note "Undying Soul" is the first published.; [pers.] Ever since high school I have jotted down short, fragmented poems. My major influence came from my two favorite poets, W.W. and E.D.; [a.] Hunlock Creek, PA

PRINGLE, MARY KAY
[b.] April 28, 1929, Massillon; [p.] Robert and Harriet Butler Adams; [ch.] Gregory, Priscilla, Mark, Darryl, Craig and Kevin; [ed.] High School Grad.; [occ.] Retired; [memb.] Bethel AME Church; [hon.] Being a mother, grandmother, friend and confidante. Mostly being a christian and knowing God. Playing for my church; [pers.] Reason for writing this poem's watching this Dads that never wanted to be Dads while their children were small and after they get in high school and college accomplishments they decide to become Dads.; [a.] Massillon, OH

PRITCHARD, ALLYSON
[pen.] Natalie Michelle; [b.] October 22, 1982, Tacoma, WA; [p.] W. J. Pritchard and L. M. Pritchard; [ed.] I'm in 8th grade and attend Meadow Grade School.; [occ.] School; [oth. writ.] I have other poems, but they aren't published.; [pers.] I feel poetry is for everyone if only they can find their personal way to bring that out.; [a.] Brush Prairie, WA

PRITCHARD, MARY BETH
[b.] February 1, 1919, Greene Co, IA; [p.] Ora Atherton and Ethel Atherton; [m.] Max; [ch.] Four sons; [ed.] High school, on-the-job training, State of Iowa, employed 30 years for Iowa Public Employees Retirement System; [occ.] Retired; [memb.] Christ United Methodist Church, United Methodist Women's Organization; [pers.] Life is precious: happiness is an option.; [a.] Des Moines, IA

PROTO, ANDREW R.
[b.] February 2, 1980, Bronx, NY; [p.] Joseph and Geraldine Proto; [ed.] High school student; [occ.] Student; [memb.] Boy Scouts of America, Student Council; [hon.] Who's Who of American High School Students; [pers.] Every soul has two parts; we must examine them and then choose one.; [a.] Bronx, NY

PURSELL, CONNIE
[b.] June 25, 1946, Pasadena, CA; [p.] Max and Mary Ann Pursell; [ed.] BA, MA in English, CSULB, Long Beach, Calif.; [occ.] Consultant, Group Medical Claims, Managed Health Care; [oth. writ.] Several poems published in La Pierna Tierna, Shartlesville, PA. Another poem accepted for publication.; [pers.] I find poetry to be a stimulating emotional outlet. Over time, I've learned that the symbolism and brevity of poetry convey a wealth of universal feelings.; [a.] Laguna Niguel, CA

PYLE, VALERIE BORDELON
[pen.] Valerie Bordelon; [b.] May 1, 1952, Opelousas, LA; [p.] Francis and Helen Bordelon; [m.] Arthur Roland Pyle, October 9, 1993; [ed.] Academy of the Immaculate Conception High, Univ. of S.W. Louisiana, Louisiana State Univ.; [occ.] Secretary (for a public utility in Washington, D.C.), Customer Services; [hon.] National winner in "National Guild of Piano Teachers" competition.; [pers.] My writing often reflects on life's struggles. Amidst trials and adversity, "hope" becomes a constant companion when we believe we were created out of great love.; [a.] Frederick, MD

QUAY, MICHAEL
[pen.] Michael R. Quay; [b.] December 29, 1986; Schenectady, NY; [p.] Susan Elizabeth Quay; [ed.] Brown School 4 years, 6th Grade Elementary School; [memb.] Sons of American Legion; School Band, plays clarinet; Editor Brown School Bugle; Brown School Chorus, Rotterdam Boys Club; [hon.] Third Grade Art Work displayed at City Public Library, yellow belt Taekwondo, Caught Record Salmon for New York State in Lake Ontario (4-25-97) 34 in long, 24 lb, 140 z; [oth.writ] for school paper, Franken Troggle, Namy Haunting stories (abouth ghosts and monsters); [pers.] We have met the enemy and they are us.; [a.] Schenecfady, NY.

QUEENER, KELLY
[b.] March 1, 1982; Indianapolis; [p.] Steve and Sherry Queener; [ed.] Under construction; [occ.] Student; [memb.] National Honors Society; [hon.] Finalist in the annual Ananda Awards; [oth.writ.] Poems published in North Central High School publications article for school newspaper published in the Colors of Thought; [pers.] Poems are a great way to express feelings about something or someone. My poems are influence by real people, feelings, and places; [a.] Indpls., IN.

QUINLAN-WESTERMAN, NANCY
[b.] May 28, 1961, Cambridge, MA; [p.] Thomas E. Quinlan (Deceased) and Marjorie A. Quinlan; [m.] Frederick A. Westerman, January 26, 1995; [ch.] Genevieve Erica and Michael; [ed.] 1 yr. College; [occ.] Certified Home Health Aid, Certified Phlebotomist; [memb.] VFW; [oth. writ.] I have a personal collection of different things I have written; it is sort of a diary but more creative writing and poems based on happenings in my life whether good or bad.; [pers.] Poetry expresses feelings deep from my heart. I also like to paint. I inherited my painting skills from my mother's side of the family and my daughter has inherited my writing skills that I didn't know I had until now. Thank you!; [a.] Plymouth, MA

QUINTERO, JANICE
[b.] June 28, 1970; New York; [p.] Aura and Eliecer Quintero; [ed.] Newtown High School, St. John's University BS Criminal Justice with a Business Minor; [pers.] I have an identical twin sister Carol Quintero. I would like to thank my family for their encouragement and support for all these years. I love you very much; [a.] Fresh Meadows, NY.

RAAB, NATALIE ANN
[b.] May 20, 1982, Kankakee, IL; [p.] Jeffrey and Cinthy Raab; [ed.] Freshman (9th grade) Palm Beach Country School of the Arts (student there for 3 years)—(a magnet program for the arts in dance); [occ.] Student; [memb.] Columbia Palms West Hospital Volunteer with the American Red Cross, National Junior Honor Society; [hon.] Asst. Co Captain of the Center Stage Dance Company of Dance Unlimited, Asst. Editor of 6th grade newspaper (Wellington Landings newspaper), all A's Honor for first 4 years, Duke University/Tip Opportunity Recipient, Most Likely to Succeed out of 6th gr. class, accepted as a Caravan Kid in the summer of '96 Dance Caravan Convention, Best 7th gr. Journalist in Communications Dept.; [a.] West Palm Beach, FL

RAACH, RUTH A.
[pen.] Sally Raach; [b.] March 14, 1914, Cleveland, OH; [p.] Maria and Edward Aurada; [m.] Fred R. Raach, September 7, 1940; [ch.] Fred and Sally; [ed.] Shaw High School, Case Western Reserve University. Art schools in N.J., Washington, DC and Wayne, PA, NY School of Decoration; [occ.] Homemaker and Artist; [memb.] Tequesta Art Gallery, Turtle Creek Country Club, Tequesta Country Club, Wildcat Cliffs C.C. in Highlands, N. Carolina; [hon.] My rewards come from the thrill of accomplishments in my many areas of activities; [oth. writ.] Numerous poems.; [pers.] Creativity is my Tree of Life with its many branches.; [a.] Tequesta, FL

RAGONESE, KIMBERLY-ANN KATERI
[pen.] Kateri; [a.] Bayside, NY

RAINES, BRIAN
[b.] September 27, 1974, Anderson, SC; [p.] Edward and Nancy Raines; [pers.] Although "I'm a Rainbow" is written in my most common style, I have touched base on almost all styles and topics. I hope others enjoy reading my poems as much as I enjoy writing them.; [a.] Athens, GA

RALLO, CRYSTAL
[pen.] Crystal Rallo; [b.] October 25, 1981, St. Louis, MO; [p.] Sam and Tami Rallo; [ed.] Attending Mehlville High School; [occ.] School, Freshman high school; [memb.] YMCA; [hon.] 1st place Zoo Photography contest; [oth. writ.] The Perfect Proposal, Memories, Rainy Day, Dear Friend of Mine, January Snow, Our World Is in Trouble; [pers.] Don't take anger out on people if they are innocent.; [a.] Saint Louis, MO

RAMOUTAR, GAVIN
[p.] Chris Lachhu, Shireen Lachhu; [ed.] St. Stanislaus College, secondary school, John Adams High School; [occ.] Student; [memb.] Queens Borough Library; [hon.] St. Stanislaus College Speech Award and Special Honors for my 90% average at John Adams High School; [oth. writ.] Several essays for contests and a few poems for my yearbook.; [pers.] I enjoy writing and I wish to achieve many more goals in the field of writing. I owe my success to my family and my English teacher, Miss Ryan.; [a.] Queens, NY

RANDALL, MICHAEL
[pen.] Mike; [b.] March 25, 1953, Deadwood, SD; [p.] Mary Randall and Kenneth (Deceased); [m.] Dianna, May 11, 1996; [ch.] Billy, Sherri, Nancy Dean and Christopher (previous marriage); [ed.] Hettinger High, Hettinger, ND, one year at SDSU, Brookings, SD; [occ.] Rancher; [oth. writ.] Several poems not published.; [pers.] Most of my poems I write from personal experience. This poem is written in memory of my father (who died young) and his friend (who died old).; [a.] Prairie City, SD

RANDOLPH, MARY
[pen.] Linda Washington; [b.] May 5, 1962, Independence, LA; [p.] Florence and Samuel Washington; [m.] Darwin E. Randolph Sr., October 28, 1980; [ch.] Darwin Sr., Marvin, April and Sherrice; [ed.] Southeastern High; [occ.] Data Entry Operator, Automated Benefit Services; [oth. writ.] I write songs, none of which have been published.; [pers.] I try to write positive thoughts in my songs and this is from where my poem was created—Love is . . .; [a.] Detroit, MI

RAWLS, SHALONDA
[b.] January 24, 1985; [p.] Raymond and Glenda Rawls; [ed.] Jefferson M. School, sixth grade; [memb.] Member of the Rose Hill C.M.E. Church; [hon.] Have a gold belt in unified Taekwon-Do; [oth. writ.] Have written other poems; [pers.] I thank God for giving me this talent, and I hope others will see the beauty in God through my poems.; [a.] Columbia, MS

RAY, MARSHA ANN
[b.] January 11, 1979, Lawrence, KS; [p.] Rick and Betty Ray; [ed.] Lawrence High School; [occ.] Cashier at Walgreens; [hon.] 8th Grade Yearbook Medal; [pers.] I only write what I feel in my heart. I feel I can be honest in my writing.; [a.] Lawrence, KS

RAZRAN, GREGORY
[b.] August 5, 1977, St. Petersburg, Russia; [p.] Mikhail and Ninel Razran; [ed.] Sheepshead Bay High School (Grad. 1995) Suny-Binghamton (sophomore); [occ.] College Student full-time; [hon.] "Who's Who Among American High School Students" Award (1993-1994), Suny-B Dean's List (1996); [oth. writ.] Currently working on a collection of short stories and poems.; [pers.] When writing poetry, I've always spilled my guts onto the paper, but only lately have I stopped wiping them off my final drafts.; [a.] Brooklyn, NY

REDMAN-BARR, CAROLYN
[pen.] Lady Pureenbow; [b.] October 5, 1965; [p.] Ernest L. Barr; [ed.] Classified Dixlexic in 4th gr., completed 9th, GED, Cooking school; [occ.] Mother, wife and Saute Safe Cook; [memb.] North West Treak Foundation, World Wildlife Fund, National Park and Conservation Association, E.D.F., The Nature Conservancy, Natural Resources Defense Council, Cancer Research, Native American Rights Fund; [hon.] "Moasp Inspirational" Certificate and Trophy received as a teen in the Seattle Cascades Drum and Bugle Corps.; [oth. writ.] All unpublished poems and songs, kid's poems and songs. To my own self thought tones on the galore. I can not read or write music but in school choir managed A's.; [pers.] God as we understand created no weeds, everything in life has a purpose.; [a.] Auburn, WA

REILLY, KATHLEEN H.
[pen.] Kathleen H. Reilly; [b.] August 18, 1942, Payson, UT; [p.] Clarence Hill-Lenore Sterling; [m.] Thomas G. Reilly, February 14, 1993; [ch.] Sallie Deuel, Aimee Deuel, Craig Spencer; [ed.] B.S. Degree—Ele. Education, Brigham Young University; [occ.] Teach second grade Goshen School, Goshen, UT.; [memb.] Several educational organizations, Phi Delta Cultus Civic Club, Am Legion Aux.; [oth. writ.] Poems published in local newspapers, children's books in local publications; [pers.] I believe that God is the ultimate artist and we can only attempt to imitate and appreciate his creations in poetry, prose or song.; [a.] Payson, UT

REMALY, LINDA L.
[b.] September 5, 1947, Chicago; [p.] Dolores Ruffo; [m.] Divorced; [ch.] Shannon K. Fournier, Rickey D. Remaly, Colleen C. Remaly; [ed.] High school; [occ.] Administrative Asst.; [memb.] Co-Leader for Tops; [a.] Crestwood, IL

REYNOLDS, ALICE
[pen.] Alice Reynolds; [b.] November 18, 1947, Terrytown, NY; [p.] Edward Ethel Reynolds; [ch.] Bonnie Jean Tammy and Clarissa Thomas; [ed.] Pittsfield High School, Mass, Holliston Jr College, Lenox, MO; [occ.] Self-employed Housekeeper, Writer; [memb.] Rifle Ass., First Baptist Rigewood, Daytona B., Fla; [hon.] Editor's Choice Award, The National Library of Poetry 1997; [oth. writ.] Many poems written in the sixties and currently one poem in Colors of Thought; [pers.] I have been influenced by Robert Frost, Emily Dickinson and Ir.; [a.] Holly Hill, FL

RHOADES, SUSAN S.
[b.] March 11, 1949, Portsmouth, VA; [p.] Joe and Wanda Honeycutt; [m.] Darl Rhoades, February 27, 1972; [ch.] Nathan, Phillip and Jacqueline; [ed.] High school graduate; [occ.] Homemaker; [pers.] This poem was written soon after my mother's death, and is dedicated to my parents and grandparents, Mr. and Mrs. Percy Murray.; [a.] Littleton, CO

RHODES, SAMUEL L.
[b.] June 17, 1963, Easley, SC; [p.] Roosevelt Rhodes and Annette Salley; [m.] Cynthia Rhodes, October 19, 1987; [ch.] Sharon Shivers and Cassaundra Rhodes; [ed.] Graduated Easley High in Easley, SC in 1981, countless hours of Naval schooling; [occ.] D.S.R. at Office Depot; [memb.] V.F.W. Free Mason from Paul Drayton #7 Charlotte, NC, University Park Baptist Church; [hon.] Numerous military awards; [oth. writ.] "He Knelt" is the only published poem so far.; [pers.] The price of wisdom is the time you invest to receive the knowledge.; [a.] Charlotte, NC

RIBNIK, THELMA N.
[pen.] Tee Roberts, T. Ribnik; [b.] December 25, 1934, Denver, CO; [p.] Hyman and Mollie Rosenberg (Deceased); [m.] Harold Ribnik (Deceased), July 3; [ch.] Harlan, Linda and Susan; [ed.] Grad. BA Colorado Womens College with Scholarship, finished degree 1976; [occ.] Appraiser of Antiques and Jewelry. Volunteer, Giftshop, Indians Hsp., Phoenix; [memb.] AAUW Appraisers Asso. of America (Amer Assn of Univ. Women); [hon.] Many ribbons for art shows in Colorado, N.M. - Art Scholarship at C.W.C., Dean's List; [oth. writ.] Columnist for Univ. Park News Denver, short stories, poetry, articles and many stories not sold.; [pers.] I have been astounded at the changes in our world and delight to be here to be able to see them. Can't remember when I wasn't scribbling a story. Latest is story of my mother Malka at 9 years old supporting 4 siblings out of Russia and her sick, delicate mother.; [a.] Scottsdale, AZ

RICHARDSON, MARISA
[b.] May 6, 1977, Honolulu, HI; [p.] Charles and Gloria Richardson; [ed.] Student at George Mason University, studying English and Communications; [occ.] Student Assistant at GMU graduate Psychology Office; [pers.] Life is full of joys and poetry is one of them. In my poetry I strive to reveal the hidden emotions of man (people); [a.] Stafford, VA

RIES, EDNA L.
[b.] November 30, 1917, Montreal, Canada; [p.] Annie and John Pover; [m.] Stanley L. Ries, June 12, 1963; [ch.] Three daughters; [ed.] Cass Tech High - Detroit, Mich; [occ.] Housewife; [oth. writ.] Several poems published in local newspaper; [pers.] My father wrote many beautiful poems which motivated me into writing. A few of my poems are of a serious nature but most bring forth laughter.; [a.] Cicero, IL

RIGGINS, JHODI
[pen.] J.H. Riggins; [b.] January 10, 1959; Urbana, IL; [p.] Carter R. Hurd, Judythe Hurd; [m.] John H. Riggins; November 8, 1980; [ch.] Jhesika Heather Riggins; [occ.] Freelance Artist; [oth.writ.] Poems for various organizational programs and to accompany limited edition art. Articles for (local magazine) Clarksville Spotlight Entertainment Magazine; [pers.] I hope to edify those who choose not to be taught what to think, but rather choose to think about what they hear. I feel compelled to be a voice, as a watchman, on a deteriorating wall of social demoralization; [a.] Clarkville, TN.

RIGGLE, TERRY
[pen.] Wynter Bryte; [b.] November 11, 1955; Charlotte, ND; [ch.] Bradford (son); [ed.] Olympic High School, Attended CPCC and Queens College; [occ.] Insurance Company, Professional Support; [memb.] Distinguished Member of Int'l Society of Poets, United Methodist and Women's Association, Diabetic Society; [hon.] Three Editor's Choice Awards from Nat'l Library of Poetry; [oth.writ.] One Fictional Novel - Not Published; [pers.] I'm an advocate for children - A Volunteer at Family Center. Children are the most important blessing in life, Do keep them safe and give them positive support always! [a.] Charlotte, NC.

RIGGS, MRS. TERRI L.
[b.] October 6, 1958, San Jose, CA; [p.] Elsie Shaw; [m.] Richard Riggs, June 7, 1980; [ch.] Two; [ed.] De Voss Elementary, Union Jr. High, Leigh High, West Valley College, CA; [occ.] Housewife; [hon.] 2 yrs. award for working with 3rd graders in AWANA at our church.; [oth. writ.] Articles on water pollution, and upcoming Christmas play using puppets for children with severe neurological difficulties in reading and writing.; [pers.] I like to write because it brings me enjoyment and fulfillment. I would like to make reading pleasurable and healing to one's soul. Influenced by Hope and Helen Steiner Rice.; [a.] San Jose, CA

RINEHART, KAY
[b.] January 15, 1951, Brownwood, TX; [p.] Odell Wade, Nadean Wade; [m.] Joe Rinehart, March 7, 1970; [ch.] Kimberley Dawn, David Scott; [ed.] Brownwood Senior High Class of '69; [pers.] I have written several poems, but this is the first entered in a contest and first published.; [a.] Brownwood, TX

RIPPO, MICHAEL V.
[pen.] Excalibur; [b.] March 15, 1974, Camden, NJ; [p.] John J. Rippo and Lucille L. Rippo; [ed.] Bishop Eustace Preparatory High School, Drexel University; [occ.] Mechanical Engineer, General Instrument Communications, Hatboro, PA; [memb.] Society of Manufacturing Engineers; [hon.] Dean's List, Drexel University; [oth. writ.] About five to six dozen unpublished poems on love, morals, religion, and racism/war.; [pers.] I use no influence from early poets. The Lord puts the words in my mind, I put them on paper for the good of others.; [a.] Bellmawr, NJ

RISTESKA, DANA
[pen.] Dana Risteska; [b.] September 20, 1986; NY; [p.] M. Laden and Jagoda Risteska; [oth.writ.] The Forest, Spring, The City, If I Could Fly, Happy The World Would Be; [a.] Astoria, NY.

RITENOUR, LAWRENCE T.
[b.] August 12, 1952, Pittsburgh, PA; [p.] Charlie and Lucille Ritenour; [ch.] 1 Ryan Robert Ritenour I; [memb.] Star Trek Fan Club (U.S.S. Galloway NCC 1901); [a.] Pittsburgh, PA

RIVERA, PATRICIA
[pen.] Pat Rivera; [b.] August 17, 1954, Pasajic, NY; [p.] Donald and Margaret Lalonde; [m.] Peter Rivera, October 27, 1973; [ch.] Joseph - 22 and Veronica - 16; [ed.] High school diploma at Miami Carol City High School; [occ.] County Employee, part-time Clerk; [hon.] Service awards for being, Cub Scout Leader, Brownie Leader, Team Mom for Baseball and Softball at Recreation Centers in Kennesaw and Acworth, GA.; [a.] Acworth, GA

RIVERA, TERYN
[b.] September 15, 1984, Orange, CA; [p.] Martin and Vicky Rivera; [ed.] Mel Gauer Elementary, Prado View Elementary, Raney Intermediate; [occ.] Student; [memb.] California Junior Scholarship Federation; [hon.] Honor Roll; [pers.] I have always loved reading poetry and stories and that encourages me to write my own.; [a.] Corona, CA

RIVIERE, BETTY SHERMAN
[pen.] Ginger, Betty Riviere; [b.] December 7, 1944, St. Francis, Peoria, IL; [p.] Harold and Elizabeth Sherman; [m.] Larry F. Riviere (Former Spouse), September 8, 1963 (Divorced now); [ch.] Larry Dean Riviere (Dead), Jeannie Renea Riviere, Dawn Marie Riviere; [ed.] Trinity Lutheran Church Private School 1st grade, Woodrow Wilson, USA and Ill. Public School 2nd-3rd, Speech Medal and straight A one B, Richwoods High School, above middle of class 1959 - grad. 1962, Advanced classes of English, Biology and Algebra 1959, Freshman passed and four yrs. attendance, ICC College LPN Nurse course passed A+B; [occ.] Ill. Mason Shoe, Certificate and Dealer, poems, songs, advertising to attract employers and enter contests, nurse grad., childcare and cook; [memb.] Junior Achievement three years, Girl Scouts of America, Bakery Clerk's Labor Union, Helping Hand Pekin, Ill., Safe Place to Ask for Help, American Bowling Association, Girl's Athletic Association (bowling), high school Knitting Club (later learned it!), went to Bible schools (Bibles awarded); [hon.] World of Poetry—Honorable Mention! Never tried for a crime, The Poetry Guild contest entries, Coca Cola 1958 school "A" report card Peoria, Ill., awarded six packs of Coke school supplies! School (night) speech medal presentation, a few school attendance awards and proper behavior, Ill. driving safety citations - once have been insured against theft in employment, grade honor roll announcement at ICC College; [oth. writ.] Valentine: Not Accepted, "No Appeal! You're Mentally Ill" Love Lines contest, "Monetary Facts and Figures" Jan. 1977 contest entry, "Jesus' Birthday" 1996 Observer, "Magazines" Aug. 1996, "Delivery" Dec. 1996 Jan. 1, 1997, "Alex's Grandma" Jan. 14, 1997, "Blind" Feb. 1997, The National Library of Poetry 1997, "Circumstances," Carl Sandburg College contest 1996, "No Answer Here," The Poetry Guild, postcard "Shoes for Sale" Wexford Poetry publish, "Believe," "Grandma's Place", July 1996

"Prejudice," Poetry Guild contest June 1996 "Have Anything For Me," Better Homes and Gardens attempt and more poetry told thrown on.; [pers.] Unable to get an attorney, manager and/or place to live and eat in Peoria, Ill., or mail offers in non-hostile states and unable to be notified of date of hearing of petition to proceed as a poor person filled out by me to plead hostile states (as special Todd Gorscch special immigrants child convicted murderer of two) I began and continue to apply for employment and write poetry, etc.; [a.] Peoria, IL

ROACH, LYDIA M.
[pen.] Lydia M. Qualls; [b.] July 26, 1953, Huntington, WV; [p.] Darrell, Christine Qualls; [m.] Farris Roach Jr., May 27, 1994; [ch.] Justin Figgins, Nakia Roach; [ed.] Huntington High School O.I.C., Marshall Univ., Huntington Jr. Bus. College; [occ.] Special Ed. Para. Murphy-Candler Elementary School; [oth. writ.] Rainy Days, I'm My Master House, Now I'm Free (none publish); [pers.] Time effects all that you are.; [a.] Decatur, GA

ROBERSON, CAMILLA
[pen.] Lakay; [b.] July 11, 1979, Gary, IN; [p.] Ray and Nellie Roberson; [ed.] High school; [occ.] Student; [oth. writ.] Short stories on many subjects, and poetry in many styles and on many subjects.; [pers.] There are many people that believe angels are with them and there are people that don't believe in angels. I feel there are angels everywhere because if you believe, you can feel their presence.; [a.] Gary, IN

ROBERSON, KESHA
[pen.] Kesha Rena; [b.] November 16, 1974, Dallas, TX; [p.] Michelle Fowler; [ed.] Wilmer Hutchins High School, Jarvis Christian College, Medgar Evers College (Present); [occ.] Student; [memb.] First Family Church, Girl Scouts of America Co-Leader, Williamsburg Christian Church; [pers.] My poetry is based on matters of the heart. I enjoy hearing the heart beats of different people.; [a.] Brooklyn, NY

ROBERSON, KYMBERLI
[b.] November 16, 1958, Dover, NJ; [pers.] We really never know where life will lead us. Only what direction we would like to go—follow your dreams.; [a.] Las Vegas, NV

ROBERTS, BENJAMIN
[b.] June 6, 1969, The Gambia; [p.] William Roberts and Eliza Ceesay; [ed.] MWSC (Missouri Western State College); [occ.] Student (MBA August '97); [memb.] Alpha Phi Alpha Fraternity, Inc.; [hon.] Dean's List, Presidential and Edit Brown Scholar, Martin Luther King Leadership Award; [oth. writ.] College Life on a Continuum (to be published some time this year), The Final Verdict (currently under process—typing); [pers.] My mind is my limit.; [a.] Silver Spring, MD

ROBINSON, MARY LOUISE
[pen.] Mother Superior; [b.] January 17, 1997, Washington, DC; [p.] Alvin Brower, Brona Brady; [m.] Ricardo Juan Robinson, 1987; [ch.] Melvin, Marika, Mario, Koko; [ed.] High school diploma, Roosevelt High; [occ.] Potomac Hospital Detailed Environmental Specialist; [hon.] From age two, my daughter Marika, has won over 30 trophies, not only because she's beautiful to me. Also for my designs that she has worn in beauty pageants, and the songs I taught her and the speech on preserving the planet earth that I sent to you.; [oth. writ.] I am currently taking writing aptitude test, for the Institute of Children's Literature also other poems, Who I'm I, You and I, and Preserving Planet Earth, and The Day.; [pers.] Through Your Eyes Creations is the name of my designs and poems, which were influenced and motivated by my children. So much of me was in

limbo, through their eyes I am creating again, for the future of all our children.; [a.] Woodbridge, VA

ROBINSON, SHEILA K.
[b.] December 26, 1952, Port Chester, NY; [p.] James B. Foster Sr., Shirley M. Foster; [ed.] Greenwich High School, The Berkely School, Community Technical College; [occ.] Instructional Aide at Greenwich High School; [memb.] Distinguished Member of The International Society of Poets; [hon.] Editor's Choice Award for Outstanding Achievement in Poetry presented by: The National Library of Poetry 1997; [oth. writ.] Other poems I've had published: "Emerge," "A Child's Broken Promise." In Sensations, an anthology from Iliad Press.; [pers.] I never interpret my poetry, I leave that up to the reader, I truly feel, that poetry's real beauty is sharing it with others.; [a.] Greenwich, CT

RODGERS, LOIS BATSON
[pen.] Lois Batson Rodgers; [b.] February 10, 1923, Greenville, SC; [p.] Hovey and Lola Batson; [m.] James Ray Rodgers Sr., September 21, 1940; [ch.] Lola, Pat, Roddy, Michael and Robin; [ed.] Correspondence courses: (after high school) Washington School of Art, Writer's Digest, Institute of Children's Literature, Blue Ridge Community College - Cell in Art; [occ.] Instructor: "Landscape Painting" (10 years), Painting, Retired Sec.; [memb.] Greenville County Library, "Friends of the Library," International Society of Artists, past member of several art guilds, Greenville Art Museum; [hon.] All have been in art. Personal exhibits, fairs, festivals, sold many paintings to people throughout the Southeast and a few Northeast, three Church Baptistry Murals. Seldom after competitions.; [oth. writ.] Poems, stories, inspirational column for church newsletter. Nothing published except in small local newspaper, now writing personal journal of village life in the South during the Depression.; [pers.] Poetry, like a painting, should prick all our senses, increasing our awareness of those aesthetic qualities which surround us, which we so often take for granted.; [a.] Marietta, SC

ROGERS, DAWN
[pen.] DMR; [b.] September 17, 1975, Hobart; [p.] Don and Judy Rogers; [ed.] Graduated Kankakee Valley High School in 1994 and attending Purdue University for a creative writing major.; [occ.] I am currently a bank teller at Demotte State Bank; [hon.] I received a composition award in English and Writing my senior year of high school and since then I have been published four times. I also have my poetry book, "The Velvet Night," being published as we speak; [oth. writ.] I have completed one novel which has not been exposed for publication yet and two poetry books that I am working on getting published.; [pers.] Writing is my life. I am a composer of words. My inspiration comes from my best friend, poetically known, as the "Dark Angel". Without writing, I am soul-less.; [a.] Rensselaer, IN

ROLLAND, LISA MARIE
[pen.] Lisa Rolland; [b.] July 2, 1976, Interboro Hospital; [p.] Mary, Maryann Rolland; [ed.] Finish high school and looking forward to going to college; [occ.] Student; [oth. writ.] Many more, such as, Empty Love, Two Loves, and Secret Face, and so many more; [pers.] I'm very proud to hear that I'm a semi-finalist in the poetry contest, and very much looking forward to winning a prize.; [a.] Bronx, NY

ROMERO, CHRISTINA F.
[b.] June 20, 1976, Bronx, NY; [p.] Phyllis Falcone and Cesar Romero; [m.] Roger Singh; [ed.] William Howard Taft High; [memb.] Young Playwrights Association, ARISTA Honors Society;

[hon.] Dean's List, Silver Key for Literature, Victory Over Violence Award, Chancellor's Roll of Honor; [oth. writ.] Novels in progress: "Xenith" and "Runaway Junction."; [pers.] Mine are the journals of an adventurer in quest of artisian wells for our hearts and imaginations. A life well lived is a great unfolding novel and we each exist as whimsical characters in the epic lives of those who love us.; [a.] Bronx, NY

ROMERO-ARROYO, LOURDES
[pen.] Lourdes Plumey; [b.] November 28, 1961, New York; [p.] Efain Romero and Carmen Romero; [m.] Rick Arroyo, November 7, 1996; [ed.] Norwalk State Technical College, AS. Degree in Computer Data Processing, 1983, also completed various Technical/Writing courses. Soap set acting studio, Connecticut; [occ.] Employed by Mikohn World Wide, Technical Writer, Actress/Model, Licensed Community Television Producer; [hon.] National Honor Society (academic), TCI Cablevision South Central Connecticut CAPS Award Winner for Talk Show Category, State Finalist in Miss United Teenager Pagent, Creative Writing Recognition Award, Kampo Karate Yellow Belt; [oth. writ.] Has written a variety of technical manuals for the insurance industry, has written scripts for training videos and scripts for her own public access television talk show and commercials. Several short stories and poems.; [pers.] "Your mind is a canvas; paint your future on it. Step into your mural and live your creation."; [a.] North Las Vegas, NV

ROSE, CHERYL
[pen.] Redd's, Dream, Reality; [b.] February 26, 1969, Sumter, SC; [p.] Levern and Loretta Rose; [ed.] East Clarendon High School, University of South Carolina, Saint Augustine's College; [occ.] Computer Specialist, Department of Health and Human Services; [memb.] Spirit of Faith Christian Center . . . (New Believers class), Women's Council, Federal Centers Toastmasters, Soul Sisters; [hon.] Dean's List 1987-1991, Magna Cum Laude 1991, 1993 Director's Award, Director's Award 1995; [oth. writ.] Several poems published in the Toastmaster newsletter . . . (The Clarion), articles for The Clarion, poems for special banquets and other occasions.; [pers.] My poems and writings are a mirror into my life. They tell a story of things I've been through and places I wish to go. My wish is that my writings will encourage and help others grow through the course of life as different twists and turns come.; [a.] Silver Spring, MD

ROSS, KIM
[b.] December 6, Indiana; [ch.] Natalie; [ed.] Associate of Science Degree, Administration of Criminal Justice; [occ.] Law Enforcement; [hon.] Honorary Award MCSF (Music City Song Festival); [oth. writ.] Homegrown Homeless; [pers.] People who are searching for complete and total happiness usually don't find it, because happiness is searching for complete and total people.; [a.] Flagstaff, AZ

ROSS, KIMBERLY A.
[pen.] Kimberly A. Ross; [b.] November 16, 1969, Virginia; [p.] Richard A. and Diana L. Ross; [m.] Anthony D. Ross, October 31, 1991; [ed.] Carmichaels Area High School, Carmichaels, PA; [occ.] Residential Program Worker for Greene Arc, Inc.; [memb.] Greene Arc, Inc. TWHBEA (Tennessee Walking Horse Breeders and Exhibitors' Association), Harley Owners Group (HOG); [hon.] Bowling Championship 3rd place, State Finals and DAR Award for Art 2nd place; [pers.] I prefer to write profound poems that will in some aspect reflect the personal life of the reader, by using my own perception and some imagination.; [a.] Crucible, PA

ROSS, TIMOTHY P.
[b.] January 28, 1964, Miami, FL; [p.] Frances Weston, Basil and Linda Wetherington; [m.] Angela C. Ross, February 28, 1997; [ch.] Joseph J. Ross, Danielle N. Ross, Timothy P. Ross Jr., Patrick L. Ross, Cora A.I. Ross, Alexander Standard; [ed.] Richmond Heights Jr. High, Miami Southridge Sr. High; [occ.] Communications Technician; [memb.] Sports Club, Marching Band #1 in State, DECA and Chess Club; [pers.] I strive to touch the hearts of those who will open their eyes and souls to what is happening around us. Life is too short and we must not let progress or our lust for more blind us to what is really important. I dedicated my poem to the memory of Basil D. Wetherington and all the loved ones he left behind.; [a.] Tucker, GA

ROSSER, KIMBERLY WEATHERS
[pen.] Kimberly Weathers Rosser; [b.] September 9, 1959, Columbus, OH; [p.] William and Geraldine Weathers; [m.] Keith M. Rosser, August 15, 1981; [ch.] Miles, Bo and Angela Rosser; [ed.] Augusta Area Technical Institute, current student business tech. graduated Evans High; [occ.] Homemaker and artist; [memb.] Overcomer's Outreach Center, SBC; [pers.] I strive to reflect personal feelings of true experiences whether it is of joy, despair, hope or hopelessness. Reflections of feelings. I am greatly influenced by Helen Steiner Rice's poetry.; [a.] Martinez, GA

ROUSE, CHRISTINE MARIE
[b.] October 19, 1975; Deland, FL; [p.] Charlaine Vander Lugt; [ed.] A.S. Legal Assisting; [occ.] State Attorneys Office, Secretary in the Juvene Le Division; [memb.] Volusia Assoc of Legal Asst; [hon.] Dean's List 6X at Daytona Beach Comm. College; [oth.writ.] "Suicide"; [pers.] Like the Greeks said "Everything in moderation; [a.] Deland, FL.

ROWBOTHAM, HAROLD J.
[b.] June 9, 1939, Youngstown, OH; [p.] James and Leora Rowbotham; [m.] Norma, February 13, 1964; [ch.] Debbie and Amy; [ed.] Chaney High School, graduate; [occ.] Customer Engineer; [memb.] American Legion, VFW, Mensa; [a.] Indianapolis, IN

RUBALCABA, CONNIE C.
[b.] October 11, 1952, El Paso, TX; [p.] Pilar L. Solis, Margarita G. Solis; [m.] Victor M. Rubalcaba, December 21, 1974; [ch.] Joseph, Eric and Victor; [ed.] Bowie High School, El Paso Community College, University of Texas at El Paso; [occ.] Student, University of Texas at El Paso; [hon.] Dean's List at El Paso Community College; [oth. writ.] None at this time that have been published. I have other writings that I have written for English classes.; [pers.] I believe there is beauty in all of God's creations and so I write about mostly anything that catches my eye.; [a.] El Paso, TX

RUFF, STACEY
[b.] July 10, 1984, Saginaw, MI; [p.] Gary Ruff and Elizabeth Ruff; [ed.] I am in 7th grade at Our Lady of Sorrows Middle School in Farmington, Michigan; [occ.] Student; [memb.] Our Lady of Sorrows church bell and vocal choir; [hon.] First Place Winner Our Lady of Sorrows school science fairs (Life Science) 1995 and 1996 First Runner-Up in school Spelling Bee 1996-1997; [pers.] I love to read and also run track, play volleyball, and dance.; [a.] Farmington Hills, MI

RUHF, DOROTHY MARLEY
[pen.] Dorothy Marley Ruhf; [b.] July 26, 1924, Wilkesbarre, PA; [p.] Mabel and Bernard J. Marley; [m.] Carl S. Ruhf (Deceased), February 11, 1954; [ch.] Gary Lee and David Charles; [ed.] Hanover High, International Business, Machines Course, plus some college credits; [occ.] Retired Conrail;

[memb.] Bethlehem Charter Chapter, American Business Women's Association, National ABWA, past member Bethlehem Chamber of Commerce; [hon.] ABWA Woman of the Year 1971, past President and a member of the National American Business Women's Association Inner Circle, State Advisor, United States Congressional Advisory Board, Recognition from Defense Advisory Board Distinguished Security Council, Foundation Leadership award; [oth. writ.] The Secret of Romance in the 90's published in Colors of Thought, The National Library of Poetry, spent time oil painting; [pers.] I love people and strive for a better America and world peace.; [a.] Bethlehem, PA

RUIZ, EDDIE
[pen.] Eduardo Ali; [b.] January 18, 1979, Holland Hospital, Holland, MI; [p.] Ana and Marty; [ed.] Graduate - Class of '97 accepted to Liberty University in Lynchburg, Virginia, finished High School in 3-years and sophomore and Junior year in one...; [occ.] Soon to study English/Communications; [memb.] Journalism 2 - Newspaper Staff; [hon.] "Honor Roll", "Student of the Month", I was part of a getting published class in 8th grade, "Academic Appreciation Letter", Recommendation to the "Most Improved Writing Award"; [oth. writ.] Character Sketch, "A Cord Of Three Strands", "Palm Of The Wind", "Journalism Articles", "The Vitor's Flame Is Burning", "Go To The Land"; [pers.] "Observe the ground you walk upon, know your steps, know where you are going..."; [a.] Wyoming, MI

RUSSELL, BRANDY
[b.] March 10, 1980; [p.] Clark and Sandra Russell; [ed.] South Park High School, currently a Junior; [memb.] FBLA, Student Council, Art Club, Band, Choir; [hon.] Award for placing at districts in FBLA; [oth. writ.] Other poems being published in anthologies; [pers.] To T.C. who inspired the poem, I love ya man! To all my friends and family, and Jennifer aka Julia who gave me the confidence to try something new. Also Jeff the Bible Thumper.; [a.] Florissant, CO

RUTKOWSKI, STEVEN M.
[b.] October 27, 1974, Beckley, WV; [p.] Delma Rutkowski and Michael Rutkowski; [ed.] Chancellor High, Universal Technical Institute; [occ.] Electrician; [oth. writ.] Poems of love and heartache.; [pers.] I can only write what comes from my heart.; [a.] Fredericksburg, VA

SABO, VALARIE
[pen.] Val; [b.] December 16, 1981, North Huntingdon, PA; [p.] Debbie, Jean Sabo; [occ.] Still in School - 8th Grade; [memb.] Member in Narwin Middle School West Chorus, Art Club, and was a Girl Scout for 5 1/2 years.; [hon.] Member of the Honor Society; [oth. writ.] Short story titled "Blood Gusher".; [pers.] "Since you really don't know what chances or opportunities you'll have in life, try your best and one will come along".; [a.] North Huntingdon, PA

SAHMALKE, FLORENCE D.
[pen.] Flor Sahmalke; [b.] July 14, 1923, Ramey, MN; [p.] Paul and Rose Gorecki; [m.] Divorced, February, 1942; [ch.] Diane, Ray, Elaine, Patricia, Jim and David; [ed.] High school; [occ.] Cook for board and care home for retarded; [memb.] Several senior clubs; [hon.] Award for song "America is Beautiful Land of Liberty" 5-93, Certificate of Achievement song "Gentle People" 1991, KFC Billboard Song Contest; [oth. writ.] Write songs for several song companies, "Hill Top," "Majestic Records," "Nashco," "Rainbow," record.; [pers.] Love people around me, do oil painting of landscapes, write songs. Do gardening. Sing at luncheons.; [a.] Brooklyn Center, MN

SALT, ANTHONY
[b.] August 18, 1982, Minneapolis, MN; [p.] John Salt, Lori and Jim Garner; [ed.] 9th Grade Grand Rapids Middle School; [oth. writ.] Anthony had another poem published in anthology of Poetry by Young Americans. The name was "My Grandpa" written when he was 12 yrs. old.; [pers.] "Silent Footsteps" was written for my dad as a Christmas present in 1996.; [a.] Grand Rapids, MN

SAMANICA, DIANE
[pen.] Sam; [b.] June 3, 1945, New Bedford; [p.] Charles and Marie Cayer; [ch.] Two; [ed.] High school graduated - 1963; [occ.] Bus Operator for "City Transit"; [oth. writ.] I have written other poems in my spare time at home. 2) Also have written what could be used as card verses.; [pers.] I am normally intense and sensitive, and can usually put myself in the right frame of mind to be creative.; [a.] New Bedford, MN

SAMS III, CRAIG
[b.] December 20, 1982; Las Vegas; [p.] Robbin Sams; [ed.] 8th Grade Student currently; [memb.] St Louis Society Winners on Wheels Bye-Bye Birdie Musical Holman Choir; [hon.] Perfect Attendance Honor, D.A.R.E. Baseball, Wheelchair Racing; [oth.writ.] Various Poems and short stories;[pers.] It is important to know that the gift of talent isn't about how good it is or how well you use it-but about how great you feel once you've accomplished your goal; [a.] St. Ann, MO.

SANCHEZ, EVELYN
[pen.] Piranha; [b.] August 22, 1951, Leadville, CO; [p.] Alfonso Sanchez (Deceased), Ramona Sanchez; [m.] Divorced; [ch.] 3 Nickie, Jacob, Larry; [ed.] I graduated from 12th grade from Fruita Monument High School in Fruita, Colorado, 1970.; [occ.] I am disabled and unable to work; [hon.] I have an award for interior decorating, Tri-chem, and crafts.; [oth. writ.] Many poems, I am also writing a book that I one day hope to publish.; [pers.] All my poems are based on my life. I hope that by writing them for others to read I am able to help them so that they don't struggle as I did. Reality checks.; [a.] Colorado Springs, CO

SANCHEZ, LORIANN
[b.] June 11, 1979, Albuquerque, NM; [p.] Anita and Larry Sanchez; [ed.] Albuquerque High, 12th grade; [occ.] Student (major - Business); [memb.] Business Professionals of America, 3rd year; [hon.] Excel Program Award, Summer Youth Temporary Employment Program Award; [pers.] Time and thought run through my mind and soul for the good of inner peace . . . .; [a.] Albuquerque, NM

SANCHEZ SR., RAOUL G.
[pen.] Rolly; [b.] April 19, 1949, Oakland, CA; [p.] Guadalupe Sanchez and Louise Sanchez; [m.] The Former Griselda Rosales, June 3, 1975 (Divorced Nov. 2, 1995); [ch.] Raoul G. Jr., Enrique (Kiki), Monica E.; [ed.] Completed High School at Arroyo High San Lorenzo, CA, graduated BA from Univ. of Ariz. in Liberal Arts, Spanish, Spanish Literature, French; [occ.] Medically retired from Northwest Airlines; [hon.] Received my first poetry award in 1964 as freshman in Albany High School Albany, CA with a short Hai Ku poem entitled "The Fugitive" which was the highest rated TV program at the time; [oth. writ.] Short novels, essays on politics, and environmental concerns. Hispanic life and novels derived from this ethnic group.; [pers.] I grew up in a poor migrant workers family. We missed lots of school. I was exposed to both Anglo/American and Mexican/American which actually made it hard for me to assimilate. I believe in mankind. My hero, Martin Luther King Jr.; [a.] Newark, CA

SANDSTROM, CHRIS
[b.] October 4, 1978, Salt Lake City, UT; [p.] Ronald Sandstrom, Carol Sandstrom; [occ.] Student at Taylorsville High School, Salt Lake City, UT; [a.] Salt Lake City, UT

SANTIBANEZ, ESTHER
[b.] April 17, 1961, Brownfield, TX; [p.] Javier Santibanez and Francisca Santibanez; [ed.] Sir Winston Churchill, Trade School; [occ.] Legal Assistant, Law Firm Caballero, Matcham and McCarthy; [oth. writ.] Several other poems, none have been published; [pers.] Jesus lives in my heart and I want to share his joy with everyone I come across.; [a.] Greenfield, CA

SAUNDERS, ADAM
[b.] August 8, 1974; Syracuse, NY; [p.[Deborah and Ed Black; [ch.] Alex Delpriore; [ed.] Regents Liverpool, Baldwinsville, Grad. Mexico, Regents Diploma; [occ.] Classical Musician; [hon.] Music awards and martial arts; [oth.writ.] Poetry is a hobby for me, I have written several. Also several pieces of music, piano, Sonotas, string quartets, etc; [pers.] Only through suffering can one know true happiness; [a.] N. Syracuse, NY.

SCATURRO, JACK
[b.] February 24, 1979, Elizabeth, NJ; [p.] Martino Scaturro and Roseann Scaturro; [occ.] High school Senior at Roselle Catholic, Roselle, NJ; [oth. writ.] First published poem.; [a.] Elizabeth, NJ

SCHAEFFER, CARA
[b.] July 22, 1973, Superior, WI; [p.] Linda and Terry Martineay; [m.] Kris Schaeffer, June 29, 1996; [oth. writ.] Undying Soul (formerly untitled), The Devil (formerly untitled); [pers.] I admire Shakespeare and Poe greatly for their all-around writing abilities but I don't try to reproduce their style in my writing.; [a.] Saint Louis Park, MN

SCHENCK, JERRI LYNN
[pen.] Jerrilynn; [b.] December 28, 1962, Mount Home, ID; [ed.] Central Sr. High, Capitol Hts, MD American Banking Inst., Wash. DC 4 yr., honors; [occ.] Graphic Artist, Writer; [hon.] French Societe des Honores, National Honor Society; [oth. writ.] Currently working on first novel, several works published on the Web; [pers.] Poetry is a release. I take my feelings and emotions and set them to rhythm and meter, thus organizing and mastering them.; [a.] Roopville, GA

SCHERER, SALLY L.
[b.] October 3, 1949, Newark, NJ; [p.] Robert N. Scherer, Phyllis M.; [m.] Allen Scherer Adams (Divorced); [ed.] "J.F.K. Memorial HS" - Iselin, NJ (Class of '67), "Middlesex County College" - Edison, N.J. (Customer Relations Certificate); [occ.] Full-time Sr. Clk. Typist for "Woodbridge Twsp. D.P.W.," Recruiter for "Schlesinger Associates" Part-time (A Market Research Co.); [memb.] "A.F.S.C.M.E. Union," "Ladies Aux. Hopelawn V.F.W. - Post Home #1352," "National Geographic Society"; [hon.] 10 yr. pin - "Woodbridge Township," "You're Fantastic Award," - one of the "Woodbridge Township," Employee Awards for Outstanding Service; [oth. writ.] Songs/Poems "Glad Tidings" (We're Going Forward), "Devotion," "One Day" also: wrote a short article for "Statistical Research" (Westfield, NJ) that was printed in a company newsletter.; [pers.] Faith carries me through! Faith is what has kept me strong and alive! During times of hurt (physical or mental), loneliness, grief, sadness, despair—that's when I become strong!; [a.] Fords, NJ

SCHLOSSER, CORTNEY
[pen.] Cortney Broke Schlosser; [b.] March 24, 1980, New York; [p.] Karen Schlosser and Louis Schlosser; [ed.] Manalapan High School; [occ.] Student; [memb.] B'Nai Brith Youth Organization, Yearbook, Crossage, Volunteer Club, Adapt; [hon.] National Honor Society; [pers.] Hold on to your dreams, plan to succeed, and share a smile every day.; [a.] Manalapan, NJ

SCHMUTTENMAER, ANNABELL
[b.] September 7, 1928, Canton, OH; [p.] Charles and Mary Lungren; [m.] Norbert Schmuttenmaer, October 5, 1946; [ch.] Alan Joseph, Karen Joyce, Mark Marion, Paul Damien, John Gerard, Mary Agnes, Remi Robert; [ed.] Calumet High; [occ.] Retired; [memb.] Resurrection Hospital Ladies Auxiliary; [hon.] The 1987 "Heart of Gold Award" presented by the Volunteer Center, Crusade of Mercy for Outstanding Volunteer Service and the Pulitzer-Lerner newspapers "1987 Citizen of the Year" award; [pers.] To help people to the best of my ability and spread a little bit of sunshine in their lives.; [a.] Chicago, IL

SCHNEIDER, SARAH LOUISE
[pen.] Sarah Schneider; [b.] October 30, 1980, Greeley, CO; [p.] Jim and Jacque Schneider; [ed.] Attending Douglas County H.S. as a sophomore, also attended Castle Rock Middle School and Roxborough Elem. School; [occ.] Student; [memb.] Colorado Dance Center in Littleton, Co., Staff member of "Images" yearbook, Douglas County H.S.; [hon.] Poem in "The Write Issue" (H.S.), article in "Castle Chronicle," previously published in "Colors of Thought." Received Metropolitan Mayors Youth Award in 1994; [pers.] I write about things I personally see and feel that other people don't seem to take time to notice.; [a.] Littleton, CO

SCHONECHACK, JENNIFER
[pen.] J. S. Leigh; [b.] May 28, 1985, Rochester, MI; [p.] Terri Misffatt, Benjamin Schonechack, Anne Bartley (Step-Mom); [ed.] Currently St. Clair Middle School; [occ.] Student; [memb.] A member of Stand Quiz Bowl, Peer Tutoring; [hon.] An honorable mention for my poem "One Special Day" and might be a finalist in that contest.; [pers.] I love to read and I wish to be a famous writer when I get older, and maybe then I will be able to influence the lives of others.; [a.] Saint Clair, MI

SCHOOLEY, MARGIE
[b.] 1946, Zanesville, OH; [p.] Elva, Mildred Talbert; [m.] Paul Schooley, December 26, 1987; [ed.] 10th grade, working on diploma through ICS; [occ.] State Specialize, Foster Parent, Symbiont Newark, OH; [memb.] Tree of Life, Church of God, choir member; [hon.] Fountain of Tears, Award of Merit Certificate (Nov. 15, 1988), honorable mention, Everything 1988, Golden Poet Award, The Touch, Editor's Choice Award, published Into The Unknown, Life Within 1997, Semi-Finalist in North American Open Poetry Contest; [oth.writ] I am working on a poem book and would like to get it published someday. Also I have started some of my own 3 books about my life which I don't have them finished yet; [pers.] I give all the credits of my life to Jesus. Jesus is my life and through him all things are possible. My husband is a wonderful man, I love him whole heartedly, my parents, who have a lot of love and faith in me; [a.] Zanesville, OH.

SCHRIDER, FLORENCE M.
[pen.] Flossie; [b.] October 25, 1935, Ilion; [p.] Annabell and Robert Nelson; [m.] Harold H. Schrider, June 16, 1956; [ch.] Kim, Arnold, Pam, Debra; [ed.] High school diploma, 1 yr. College; [occ.] Retired—was a T-A. of Poland Central School; [memb.] Member of Presbyterian (North Cage) Church, former Poland Central Booster Club member; [hon.] Poland Central Booster Club Member of the Year, Award of Appreciation from Athletic Dept-BG. Shufelt, Award of Excellence from the Board of Education of Poland Central; [oth. writ.] The Gorge, Clouds and others, The Lord, Dreams, Grandchildren; [pers.] I love to write poems now that I'm retired. I hope to write many more.; [a.] Poland, NY

SCHULZ, STEPHEN PAUL
[pen.] Stephen Paul Schulz; [b.] June 24, 1955, Cape May, NJ; [p.] Carl Alfred and Lillian H. Schulz; [ch.] Charlene Yvette Schulz; [memb.] International Society of Poets; [oth. writ.] Books: Reflections of Pearls and Swine published 1996 by Vantage Press Inc. Le Poete ('Twixt the Laurel and Quill) - unpublished. Thrown from Within - A Battle for Possession - unpublished. Fruits of the Untangled Vine - unpublished. Anthology publishings: Mirrors of the Soul, Modern Poetry Society 1996, "The Apple." Carvings in Stone, The National Library of Poetry 1996, "The Poet (Mastery of the Troubadour)." Best Poems of the '90s, The National Library of Poetry 1996, "The Fire." The Nightfall of Diamonds, The National Library of Poetry 1997, "Wine and Roses." Etches in Time, The National Library of Poetry 1997, "A Quaint Mirage—In Blue (Crystal Beach, 1996)." Tracing Shadows, The National Library of Poetry 1997, "Criticism of a Critical Critic's Critique (Judgement Before Judgement Day)." The Best Poems of 1997, The National Library of Poetry 1997, "The Affair." A View from Afar, The National Library of Poetry 1997, "The Harvest (A Tale of Chaff and Wheat)." Dance Upon the Shore, The National Library of Poetry 1997, "Solitude."; [pers.] Influenced by Rudyard Kipling and Edgar Allan Poe.; [a.] Crystal Beach, FL

SCHULZ, SUSAN C.
[b.] April 29, 1965, Lancaster, PA; [p.] Carmella and John Ruhl; [m.] Thomas A. Schulz, October 14, 1988; [ch.] Thomas Michael and Jonathan Edward; [ed.] Lancaster Catholic High, Millersville University; [occ.] English teacher; [memb.] Chi Alpha Tau; [hon.] Dean's List, "Gift of Time" teacher Award; [oth. writ.] I enjoy writing children's stories and poetry, no other publications.; [pers.] My husband and friends are the source of my inspiration. I have been greatly influenced by Clara Peck Schultz, poet.; [a.] Mount Joy, PA

SCHWAB, JOHN A.
[b.] April 14, 1932, Indianapolis, IN; [p.] John T. Schwab, Mary L. Schwab; [m.] Mary Jo Schwab; [ed.] Arsenal Teachnical High, Indianapolis Culinary Institute; [occ.] Traffic Manager, Hirata Corp. of America; [memb.] Linwood Christian Church, Staff Appraisal Committee; [hon.] Tech Legion; [pers.] If your dreams have left a bitter taste in your mouth, maybe you didn't season them properly.; [a.] Indianapolis, IN

SCHWABENBAUER, MIKE
[b.] June 21, 1980, Portsmouth, VA; [pers.] I have a hard time expressing my feelings so I express them through poetry. All my poetry has been inspired by my beautiful girlfriend April.; [a.] Oil City, PA

SCHWEITZER, LINDA
[b.] November 2, 1953; [p.] William Schweitzer, Carolyn Flesch; [ch.] Matthew Niedfeldt, Nicholes Saraga; [ed.] St. Andrews Grade School, Lockport West H.S., Waubonsee College; [occ.] Rural Carrier; [hon.] Illinois Community College of Journalism Award; [pers.] My two sons are my greatest inspiration and much of my writing reflects them.; [a.] Oswego, IL

SCOTT, ROGER
[b.] October 10, 1972, Winslow, AZ; [p.] Charley and Marie Scott; [pers.] My thanks to family and friends . . . be cool!; [a.] Phoenix, AZ

SEARLS, STEVEN
[b.] June 28, 1981, Galion, OH; [p.] Debbie and Jerry Riley; [ed.] Currently a freshman at Col. Crawford High in North Robinson, OH.; [a.] Crestline, OH

SELLERS, SARAH ELLEN
[pen.] Sarah E. Sellers; [b.] January 24, 1986, Kansas City, MO; [p.] Jeff and Deborah Sellers; [ed.] I am in the 5th grade at Topeka Collegiate School in Topeka, Kansas; [occ.] Student; [memb.] Girl Scouts of America, YMCA, United States Swimming Suzuki Talent Education of Topeka Orchestra; [hon.] Citizenship Award at Topeka Collegiate School, Student Council Class Representative, High Honor Roll, Kansas Association of Teachers of Mathematics Topeka Regional Contest - 2nd place, art work selected for a local realtor's calendar; [oth. writ.] Monthly article in the community, Sherwood Gazette.; [pers.] The inspiration for my poem came from a sculpture of a wolf entitled "The Howl" at the University of Kansas Museum of Anthropology.; [a.] Topeka, KS

SEVERY, JANAKI
[pen.] Jenaki Severy; [b.] August 17, 1948, Portland, OR; [p.] Ada Clare McCall and Malcolm Severy; [m.] Tassio Bountalis, August 1981; [ch.] Eleni Bountalis and Alexa Bountalis; [ed.] M.Ed. Counselling and Guidance, graduate school in Special Ed., B.A. Drama; [occ.] Client Services Consultant, Right Management Consultants; [memb.] National Speakee's Association, National Education Association, Alpha Omicron Pi Sorority; [hon.] Who's Who of Emerging Leaders, Who's Who of Emerging Women; [oth. writ.] Unpublished: poems, songs, short stories. Workshops on: Communication, Stress, Relationships, Career.; [pers.] My personal mission is to support people being all they can be by helping them bridge the gap between their "dream of who they are" and their "day to day reality."; [a.] Seattle, WA

SEWELL, RUBY
[b.] October 9, 1945, Acorn, KY; [p.] Rayford and Thelma Wells Speaks; [m.] James P. Sewell, October 21, 1961; [ch.] Three; [ed.] Finished 9th grade at Shopville High in KY. Received GED in 1988 Monrovia High, In. 40 Hrs Nurse Aid Training, 2 yrs of Music; [occ.] Housewife; [memb.] Eternal Life Baptist Church; [hon.] Church pianist and for teaching Bible school; [pers.] I write my poems about true happenings that have happened in the lives of other people and try to reflect the moral side of people, places and things.; [a.] Mooresville, IN

SEWER, LAKEYA
[pen.] Kee-Kee; [b.] September 15, 1980, Bronx, NY; [p.] Eileen Betancourt, Anthony Sewer; [ed.] Rochambeau High School in White Plains, NY. I am in the 11th grade.; [occ.] Student; [oth. writ.] A poem published in the yearbook called, Mirror.; [pers.] I look up at the stars and analyze the sky. I ask myself, was I meant to be here? Why? And always be you and only you. Love yourself! Everyone is here for a purpose.; [a.] White Plains, NY

SEYMOUR, COREY V.
[b.] September 21, 1972, Rochester, NH; [p.] Suzanne Lundin, Bob Banagan; [ed.] 12 years general education, GED, New Hampshire; [occ.] Naval Reserves; [pers.] Life demands command and respect. But never let life command you for respect is lost.; [a.] Alton, NH

SHAFER, JOYCE E.
[b.] August 3, 1928, Wisner, LA; [p.] J. L. and Alva Evans; [m.] Deceased; [ch.] Charles and Albert Davis, Jolynn Wallace; [occ.] Writer; [memb.] Fuss W. Methodist Church, God's Recycled Angels, Counselor Windowed Persons Support Group, coordinate children's Bible club; [hon.] 10/01/1996 Nat'l Library of Poetry Hall of Fame, Teacher of Year 1996, First United Methodist church; [oth. writ.] Several poems published in local papers, Nat'l Library of Poetry anthologies, children's newspaper, working on children's book based on the Bible; [pers.] My goal is to reach out to children and to serve others, to be available and a good listener to those hurting. To be a good role model to youth.; [a.] Pineville, LA

SHAHBANDAR, OUBAI
[pen.] Omar Shariif; [b.] June 26, 1981, Damascus, Syria; [p.] Nabil and Shahfa Shahbandar; [ed.] High school - Desert Mountain, a Sophomore; [memb.] T.A.R.S. - a Teenage Republican Club however, still a Socialist at heart, Speech and Debate Club; [hon.] Have won previous essay contest in elementary, won a scholarship to Space Camp. An interesting footnote, ran for class president once, I actually won. Principal's List.; [oth. writ.] Have written many exceptional poems. However only a couple got published and those were in the school paper.; [pers.] I am influenced by no one and by nothing in nature save that of the emotion of frustration. My poems reflect the division and conquering of the Islamic peoples and many other peoples alike due to self-corruption and ignorance.; [a.] Scottsdale, AZ

SHAMSI, BENJAMIN
[b.] July 30, 1976, Boston, MA; [ed.] Currently a third year student at Ithaca College, major: Speech Communication, minor: Anthropology; [memb.] Seido Karate; [pers.] We can only look so far, but we should at least look, with a gentle mind.; [a.] Ithala, NY

SHAW, RUTH
[b.] October 18, 1954, Richland Center, WI; [p.] Carl and Gen Olson; [m.] Randy G. Shaw, September 13, 1975; [ed.] In progress VWC - Richland; [occ.] Assistant Director, Symous Recreation Complex; [memb.] Water Safety Director - American Red Cross Badger Chapter; [hon.] Dean's List, Phi Theta Kappa, numerous scholarships; [oth. writ.] Articles in local newspaper, two semesters - campus newspaper "The Express" twice published in Quintessence Campus publication of Outstanding College Writing.; [pers.] Through my writing, I attempt to enrich and heal my own soul—for only through growth of the individual, can there be growth of the society.; [a.] Richland Center, WI

SHEETS, SUNNI L.
[pen.] Juliette Brandon; [b.] March 27, 1979, Wellington, KS; [p.] Daryle J. and Cathy L. Sheets; [ed.] Sunshine Preschool, Hillcrest Bible Baptist Academy, South Haven Junior High, Belle Plaine High School; [occ.] Secretary at J. P. Weigand Suburban Realtors; [memb.] Yearbook Staff/Editor, First Baptist Church Belle Plaine, Foreign Language Club, SADD, Kays; [hon.] Honor Roll; [oth. writ.] I write on a daily basis. I have hundreds of poems and am always in the process of writing something. Have 2 others poems published.; [pers.] It's only through relationships and personal experience that I am able to write. My creative writing teacher, Mrs. Lynne E. Hewes, has taught me 99% of what I know about writing—she's amazing!; [a.] Belle Plaine, KS

SHELTON, CHRISTOPHER
[b.] September 14, 1970, San Jose, CA; [p.] Alice de la Torre, James Shelton; [ch.] Kyle and Sabreena Shelton; [ed.] Oak Grove High School; [occ.] Meat Cutter/Freelance Artist; [pers.] My writings consists of love and sorrow, two powerful emotions. I write from personal experiences and feelings. Without my true feelings, no words may be written down.; [a.] San Jose, CA

SHEPARD, BETTY JO
[pen.] Betty Jo Shepard; [p.] Elbert Shepard, Ruth Shepard; [ed.] Bainbridge High School, Clark College, Washington; [occ.] AVX Technology Corp. Testing Lab.; [memb.] Eastern Star Lodge 267; [a.] Vancouver, WA

SHEPHERD, JERRY G.
[pen.] Ted Bare; [b.] May 24, 1960, Falfurrias, TX; [p.] Jim and Janelle Shepherd; [m.] Peggy Shepherd; [ch.] Justin Michael, Andrew Col; [ed.] Refugio High, Texas Tech University, Texas A&I University; [occ.] Registered Professional Engineer (Texas), G&W Engrs. Port Lavaca, Texas; [memb.] Texas Municipal League; [hon.] National Honor Society, Man of the Day; [oth. writ.] Bunch more poems; [pers.] Always keep an open mind. Remember—ya snooze, ya lose!; [a.] Port Lavaca, TX

SHERROD, RONALD
[pen.] Harl Sherrah; [b.] November 16, 1947, Knoxville, TN; [p.] Harllee Sherrod and Harriet Sherrod; [m.] Sue Sherrod, July 11, 1986; [ch.] Tom, Jerry and Paul; [ed.] Central High, Wheaton College, University of Tennessee; [occ.] Soil Scientist and Professional Conversationalist; [oth. writ.] Co-author of several publications in scientific journals; [pers.] I believe that mankind, through artistic expression and goodness toward others, defies his own origin and attains a higher order of life, one which is part of, yet not of this world.; [a.] Strawberry Plains, TN

SHORTRIDGE, FRANK
[b.] March 11, 1955, Newark, NJ; [p.] Frank and Marie; [m.] Divorced; [ch.] Frank III, Vanessa, Aryn, Sarah Beth and Bryan Marcus; [ed.] Private school, (Prep), Whitehall Yearling HS, 3 years at Ohio State University, Associate of Applied Science degree at Columbus State Community College; [occ.] General Contractor; [memb.] Knights of Columbus, 12 years, Moose 1 year - Fourth Degree Knights of Columbus Profile; [hon.] Youth Director for Regional-State K of C Council 5801— 2 years in a row. Honorable Mention for 2 years; [oth. writ.] Several poems published in local newspapers, poems for special occasions; [pers.] I want to thank Susan Rysavy for recognizing a talent, taking it from under the bushel and placing it on top where its light will shine for all to enjoy.; [a.] Columbus, OH

SIBBALD, PHIL
[pen.] P.; [b.] January 29, 1962, Sault Ste Marie, MI; [p.] Richard and Margaret Rabineau; [m.] May 17, 1982, Divorced December 15, 1988; [ed.] Graduated high school in Sault Ste Marie; [occ.] Sales Rep. for a wholesale warehouse; [memb.] YMCA, Detroit Lions, Inn Club; [hon.] I've won several medals in the navy in Grenada and Lebanon; [oth. writ.] I've written hundreds, but none ever published. I started on The Ocean when I was in the navy. I've also started a book (science fiction). None of my poems have been titled.; [pers.] The sun is my god, Betty is my love, Jose is my son, my thoughts are a dove. I believe in life after death and the fact that we're not alone in the universe.; [a.] Salina, KS

SIEGEL, SUSAN A.
[pen.] Susan Van Loan; [b.] January 8, 1962, Cold Spring, NY; [p.] Ida M. Barley and Harrison Van Loan; [ch.] Rani 14, Chelsea 12, Hailey 9, Aubrie 8, Jessi 3; [ed.] Monroe-Woodbury High School,

Class of 1980; [memb.] 20th Century Limited Drum and Bugle Corps. - Contra Bass player; [pers.] To my children—I love you with all my heart and soul! Take your dreams and turn them into realities. Let nothing stand in your way! Hey everybody, "Horns up!"; [a.] Highland, NY

SIEMIENIEWICZ, MARGUERITE
[b.] March 27, 1919, Elkland, MO; [p.] Jon Earl Shanks and Gertrude Shanks; [m.] Robert Joseph Siemieniewicz; [ch.] Mary Ann, Robert Joseph, Marguerite and Martha; [memb.] Past-Pres VFW Aux, Chaplain American Legion; [pers.] "A book is a journey. Those who read need never be lonely. I have never felt the need to travel for I have been everywhere through my books."; [a.] Oregon House, CA

SIKORSKY, KENNETH
[pen.] Can'tdenyus; [b.] July 5, 1951, Flemington, NJ; [p.] Bertha and Leon Sikorsky; [m.] Elizabeth Anne Sikorsky, November 18, 1972; [ch.] Richard, Jack and Jennifer; [ed.] High school Flemington, NJ, Licensed Minister, Local Artist; [occ.] Retired; [memb.] The Body of Christ; [hon.] The Crown of Life; [oth. writ.] The Great River Journey, Gardenville, Mystery Island, Following the Creek, The Search for Peace, "The Kombucha Mushroom," and "The Search for God."; [pers.] I show the love of God to our fellow man, in my writing.; [a.] Berryville, AR

SIMPSON, CAROLYN S.
[b.] July 18, 1965, Laton, OK; [p.] Bill and Linda Stewart; [m.] David A. Simpson, April 5, 1987; [ch.] Melinda and Christy; [ed.] Newton Elementary, Utica Jr. and Sr. High and Licking County Joint Vocational School; [occ.] Homemaker; [hon.] I've won the Editor's Choice Award from The National Library of Poetry for a previous poem; [oth. writ.] Poem a "Marital Tragedy." I have also written a couple of young adult books that I have been working on getting into manuscript form to send in. I've also written a song. I am just beginning to send my stuff in.; [a.] Newark, OH

SIMPSOM, JASON
[b.] November 7, 1978; Odessa, TX; [p.] Jerell and Valerie Simpson; [occ.] Bodywise Health Manager; [memb.] Branson Arts Council; [hon.] Homecoming King; [pers.] I strive to present the truth in all things...For it is the truth that sets man free (John 8:30).

SINCLAIR, MICHELLE LYNN
[b.] December 3, 1981, Nampa, ID; [p.] Keith and Pam Sinclair; [ed.] Attending Alameda Junior High School when poem was written; [occ.] Student; [memb.] American Miss Teen Pageant; [hon.] Various art awards for drawings, Track and Field Award; [oth. writ.] Various poems written, but never published.; [pers.] I wish my grandma was here to see this, she always knew I could write. I don't want to say this is for me, it's more for my grandma.; [a.] Pocatello, ID

SINGH, DALE DARVINESH
[pen.] Daya; [b.] August 4, 1976, Sydney, Australia; [p.] Dharam Singh, Gyan W. Singh; [ed.] Ceres High, Los Angeles Valley College, Modesto Junior College; [occ.] Student; [memb.] Mecha, HYLC, Indian/Asian Club for Embitterment; [pers.] You must love God with your whole heart, soul and mind and you must love your neighbor as yourself. Aum Namash Shivaya; [a.] Modesto, CA

SINGH, KAMINA
[pen.] Kamina Singh; [b.] March 8, 1968, Guyana; [p.] Dyal Singh/Moonie Singh; [ed.] B.Sc. Finance, M.B.A. Marketing; [occ.] Subcontract Administrator; [memb.] Golden Key National Honor Society; [hon.] Golden Key, full MBA schol-

arship; [oth. writ.] Case studies for strategic management textbooks; [pers.] I believe your writing should reflect your inner being, it should come from deep within or it is without . . . .; [a.] Jamaica Estates, NY

SMITH, CAROL F.
[b.] January 6, 1949, Omaha, NE; [m.] Richard, October 18, 1969; [ch.] Shannon and Allison; [ed.] High school graduate - Kuemper High School. Nursing - St Anthony's School of Nursing; [occ.] Liscensed Practical Nurse (Manila Manor); [memb.] Vail American Legion Auxillary - Vail Trees Forever Vail Community Club - St. Ann's Altar Society; [pers.] Live every day to the fullest. Strive for perfection.; [a.] Vail, IA

SMITH, CHARLES
[b.] USA; [m.] Widower; [ch.] 4 (2 g., 2 b.); [ed.] J.D., M. Ed., A.B.; [occ.] Lawyer; [hon.] Institute of Hard Work; [oth. writ.] Poetry, history, news; [pers.] Carpe Diem, Metanoia; [a.] Holyoke, MA

SMITH, CYNTHIA
[b.] April 9, 1975, St. Charles, MO; [p.] Linda and Jim Anderson; [m.] Richard Smith, June 14, 1991; [ch.] Richard II, Mercedes and Phillip; [pers.] My poems are to help people see the ways of life in "expressions" and truth. What is loved and what is lost, what was there and now is gone.; [a.] Monterey, IN

SMITH, GARY ALLEN
[b.] September 24, 1954, Saranac Lake, NY; [p.] Stanley M. Smith and Evelyn M. Smith; [m.] Victoria Lynn Smith, May 10, 1980; [ch.] Benjamin Smith and Nathaniel Smith; [ed.] M.A.I., S.U.N.Y. - Plattsburgh; [occ.] Accounting; [memb.] Kairos, Emmaus, St. Mark's U.M.C.; [pers.] Any good you may perceive is because of what Jesus Christ has done in me.; [a.] El Paso, TX

SMITH, JEN
[pen.] Jif; [b.] April 4, 1979, Wilmington, DE; [p.] Les and Sue Smith; [occ.] Baker in hometown buffet-style restaurant; [hon.] Presidential Academic Achievement Award; [oth. writ.] Nothing published . . . yet.; [pers.] I believe the best poetry lies submerged within physical or emotional experiences. It takes a strong, imaginative mind to capture the moment and allow the reader to see it through your eyes/words . . . .; [a.] New Castle, DE

SMITH, LARZETTA J.
[b.] June 20, Miami, FL; [p.] Robert Jenkins (Deceased), Fannie Jenkins; [ch.] Gina R. Smith; [ed.] A. L. Lewis Elem., Mays High, FAMU (undergrad.); [occ.] Computer Spec. Campbell Dr Elem., Leisure City, FL; [memb.] St. Paul Missionary Baptist Church; [oth. writ.] Several unpublished poems and stories. Readings done at church and/or local oratorical contest.; [pers.] I always like to be positive or rewarding in my writings. Most of them have been about children and given to them. I aim to make you happy as a writer.; [a.] Florida City, FL

SMITH, MARSHALL N.
[b.] July 16, 1927, Rochester, NY; [p.] James and Idamay Smith; [m.] Shirley M., July 12, 1952; [ch.] Marlene, Valerie, M. Neilor, Lora, Terry; [ed.] Abellard Eynolds #42 and Charlotte High Sch. Rochester, NY. B.S. - Landscape Architect - major from Sony Col of Forestry and Envir. Sciences and Syracuse Univ, Syracuse, NY. State Teachers Cert. in Ornamental Horticulture taught Boces, Mexico, NY, Edison Tech, Rochester, NY; [occ.] Marketing Insurance Broker and Aquatic Sculpturer (waterfalls, bird baths etc); [memb.] Bastrop Co Rotary, Sec '96-97, ABC Emmaus Community - Bastrop County, Austin Pond Soci-

ety and Austin Butterfly Forum (both Austin, TX) and Bastrop Co Audubon Soc., Cedar Creek United Meth Church past lay leader, Troa, Austin, TX; [hon.] Won many civic business honors for lands care projects designed, develop, maintained by Brookside Nursery, Penfield, NY, owner 1960-1980; [oth. writ.] Newspapers - wrote nursery rhymes to promote Onion Creek LandscapeNnursery (owner plus a monthly publication church occasions, I write when an occasion moves me.; [pers.] I believe the world needs more love, humor (smiles) enthusiasm and hugs. "Always no above average."; [a.] Cedar Creek, TX

SMITH, SELENE
[pers.] I have long sought to keep the journey of life rewarding by endeavoring to "be the best I can be." Thus, it is my hope that at journey's end I will have added, through my writing, something meaningful to the lives of family, friends, and those whose lives I have touched even for only a moment. A life lived long and well, a fine reward!

SMITH, TIMOTHY
[b.] November 13, 1974, San Francisco, CA; [p.] Roger Smith and Beverly Smith; [ed.] Ainsworth Public School, Richfield Springs Central School, currently student at Suny Geneseo; [occ.] Security Officer; [memb.] Literacy Volunteers of America, Inter Varsity Christian Fellowship; [pers.] For Mom, with love.; [a.] Richfield Springs, NY

SMITH, TRACY DEAN
[pen.] Shane Tracy; [b.] September 22, 1962; Newton, IA; [p.] Harold Arthur Smith, Jeanette Rae Smith; [ch.] Taylor Dean 11 yrs, Skylar Damon 10 yrs., Shauna Kay 7 yrs; [ed.] Colfax Community High Grad "81" Iowa Transportation Institute "85"; [occ.] Professional Painter and Decorator; [memb.] N.R.A, G.A.S.S., North American Hunting Club; [hon.] Safe driving and log violation free awards with U.S. Mail Carriers; [oth. writ.] Several non-published poems such as "Her Sad Story" and "Two Dollar Knife" and "Time"; [pers.] I believe that words truly written from the Heart and Soul can have an everlasting effect on anyone's life, when read with an open mind; [a.] Colfax, IA.

SMITH, VERONICA M.
[pen.] Rain; [b.] November 24, 1967, Terrell; [p.] Margie Turner and Richard Davis; [m.] Richard A. Smith, August 14, 1991; [ch.] Alexis G. Smith and Richard A. Smith II; [ed.] Bryan Adams High School, Eastfield College; [memb.] North Lake Baptist Church, President of a gospel choir (Wake-Up) and President of a gospel group (story letters); [hon.] Was in U.S. Navy for a short period. Won first place in amateur body building and two second place trophies.; [oth. writ.] Several poems published in high school paper. Poems published in junior college paper. Poems recited on local TV station and various institutions.; [pers.] I truly believe that the inner man rules and governs the outter man. You are what you swallow spiritually and physically.; [a.] Garland, TX

SMITH, WALT
[pen.] Walt Smith; [b.] March 30, 1952, Alabama; [m.] Alieta K. Smith, August 15, 1975; [ch.] Spencer and Shaun; [memb.] Hilldale Baptist Church; [oth. writ.] In the past two years I've written over 50 poems and songs, most spiritually or biblically inspired, others on relationships and experiences. Songs by Walt Smith: Deity, 46th Psalm, John 3:16, The Last Psalm, Messiah etc...; [pers.] I believe in living one day at a time, take nothing for granted, look for the good in everyone you meet, do to others as you wish done to you and most love God first.; [a.] Birmingham, AL

SMITH, WALTER O.
[pen.] Walt Smith; [b.] March 30, 1952, Alabama; [m.] Alfeta K. Smith, August 15, 1975; [ch.] Spencer and Shaun; [memb.] Hilldale Baptist Church; [oth. writ.] In the past two years I've written over 50 years and songs, most spiritually or biblically inspired, others on relationships and experiences. Songs by Walt Smith: Deity, 46th Psalm, John 3:16, The Last Psalm, Messiah etc...; [pers.] I believe in living one day at a time, take nothing for granted, look for the good in everyone you meet, do to others as you wish done to you and most lost God first.; [a.] Birmingham, AL

SMITH-HINDS, SUSAN
[b.] October 26, 1965, Chicago, IL; [p.] Ralph H. and Constance I. Sutton; [m.] Rick Hinds, September 3, 1994; [ch.] Nathan Smith-Hinds, Kaylea Smith-Hinds; [ed.] University of Arkansas, Fayetteville, BA in French, Assoc. Degree Nursing; [occ.] RN, Northwest Medical Center, Northwest Health System, Springdale, Arkansas; [memb.] ASPAN American Society of Perianesthesia Nurses; [a.] Rogers, AR

SMOLEN, STEFANIE
[b.] December 8, 1983, New London, CT; [p.] Trina and Fred Smolen; [ed.] Tyl Middle School, Oakdale, Connecticut; [occ.] Student; [pers.] I was moved by the loss of my friend, Casey Kennedy, who died after being struck by a car, on January 13, 1997.; [a.] Oakdale, CT

SNAPP, SHANNON
[b.] July 6, 1983, Palmyra, IN; [p.] Robert and Susan Snapp; [ed.] I'm in 7th grade, North Harrison Middle School; [occ.] Student; [a.] Palmyra, IN

SNIDER, GARRY
[pen.] Garry Snider; [b.] August 9, 1962, Lancaster, PA; [p.] Jack and Nancy Snider; [m.] Cindy, September 28, 1985; [ch.] Ashlee age 6, Brock age 4; [ed.] Solanco Senior High.; [occ.] Construction; [hon.] I've had several poems published in the local newspaper, been asked to read them at retirement celebrations and several funerals.; [pers.] My family calls me "The Red Light Poet." The poems that I write seem to come to me when I'm driving or at a red light. It's not uncommon to see me alongside the road, jotting down some lines.; [a.] New Providence, PA

SNIDER, LE
[pen.] Le Snider; [b.] April 16, 1923, Welch, WV; [p.] Archie and Maude Pruett; [m.] Jack Snider, August 10, 1942; [ch.] Jackie Martin and Gary Snider; [ed.] Graduate Honor High (Ohio), earned diploma, Chicago School of Interior Decorating - worked in public service, appointed clerk - Co. Commissioners Elected Clerk, Township Trustees, Legal Secy; [occ.] Retired; [memb.] First Presbyterian Church, Presbyterian Womens Group, Church Choir, member, Windsor Singers, a performing group; [oth. writ.] Poems and letters published in local newspapers, poems presented at church functions. Co-authored a play, "Farmer's Daughter and the Pea," performed by Windsor Singers.; [pers.] Hobbies are life savers and decide early on something you like to do throughout your life, you will enjoy many happy moments and find that life is full and exciting to the very end!; [a.] Marysville, OH

SNITGEN, DALE B.
[b.] June 19, 1986, Lansing, MI; [p.] David and Jean Snitgen; [ed.] 4th Grade, St. Patricks School, Portland, MI; [memb.] Masters Club and S.W.A.T. Team in the American Taekwondo Association; [hon.] 2nd Degree Recommended Black Belt in Taekwondo, Straight "A" student; [a.] Portland, MI

SNODDY, JEANNE MICHELLE
[b.] February 25, 1981, Charlottesville; [p.] Sam and Kathy Snoddy; [hon.] Presidential Academic Award, 1993, academics and conduct awards, and Perfect Attendance. Also Gifted and Talented programs.; [pers.] What I reflect in my writings are my true thoughts and feelings.; [a.] New Canton, CA

SNODGRASS, ANNA ALICIA
[b.] May 16, 1983, Jacksonville, FL; [p.] Stanley R. and Alice A. Snodgrass; [ed.] 9th Grade; [hon.] Honor Roll, 2nd Place Spelling Bee, Dance Team Awards.; [pers.] Enjoy dancing, jazz, top, ballet, I am also on a dance team and go to competitions.; [a.] Jacksonville, FL

SNOOK, DANIEL J.
[b.] May 2, 1937, Layton, NJ; [p.] Albert and Mary; [m.] Patricia Ann, October 26, 1993; [ch.] James Jude and David John; [ed.] Newton High, NJ, North Arkansas Comm Coll, East Stroudsburg Univ. PA; [occ.] Retired; [memb.] American Hypnosis Asn, Masonic Lodge FYDM, Flying Home Club; [a.] Bushkill, PA

SOLOWAY, CHRISTOPHER M.
[b.] March 6, 1974, NH; [occ.] Student, University of Arizona; [pers.] Rise, Release; [a.] Tucson, AZ

SORIANO, MICHELLE L.
[b.] February 11, 1983, Vancouver, WA; [p.] Sandra Jackson, Valentino Soriano; [ed.] Honor Student at McLoughlin Middle School; [pers.] Life is not complete without love. One can never be happy without it.; [a.] Vancouver, WA

SOSTRE, NEITH HEREDIA
[pen.] Ned Future; [b.] August 15, 1963, Palma Soriano, Cuba; [p.] Luis Heredia Ph.D and Neda Heredia; [m.] Angel Sostre, July 26, 1986; [ch.] Christian A. Sostre; [ed.] Acctng Major, A.A. Degree Berkeley College, currently seeking BA in Special Ed; [occ.] Student, homemaker; [memb.] Cubans Liams Club; [hon.] Dean's List (3 times); [oth. writ.] Not published, include diaries of personal and biographical writings about my life.; [pers.] "Our lives are truly simple, why put barriers of metal in the way? Find a simple solution."; [a.] Jericho, NY

SPAGNOLA, CHRIS
[b.] July 5, 1970, Pittsburgh, PA; [p.] Chris and Janet Spagnola; [ch.] Corey Michael; [ed.] Edgewater High, Savannah College of Art and Design, Institute for Children's Literature; [pers.] I have been interested in writing poetry for a couple of years now, I was inspired by a very special person, Kim, whom "Wish" was written for.; [a.] Orlando, FL

SPARKS, GENEVIEVE
[b.] July 2, 1920, West Virginia; [p.] T. J. and Elizabeth Cox; [m.] Carl Sparks, December 23, 1940; [ch.] Seven; [ed.] Four yrs. John Tyler Community College on Arts and Business; [occ.] Voluntary; [hon.] In JTCC Magazine, first place in poetry two consecutive years '88-89 second place in Poetry '90 Honorable Mention of oil painting in 1991 "Sherwood Forest," arts magazine; [pers.] I strive to bring a blend of faith, grace and beauty to the mind of men in times of pain, confusion and even joy of the day.; [a.] Chester, VA

SPENCER, DAVID R.
[b.] June 25, 1956, Detroit; [p.] Dale and Donna Spencer; [m.] Janet Spencer, November 22, 1986; [ch.] Five; [ed.] High school, some college, School of Hard Knocks, Grandpa's Stories of Life; [occ.] Honey Dipper; [memb.] Wackos, Sam's Club; [hon.] A few; [oth. writ.] Hostile notes to elected local criminals (politicians); [pers.] To be a posi-

tive influence, bring a smile to someone at least once per day, to defend those who cannot or will not defend themselves, to protect our freedoms from our leftist elements of our government.; [a.] Rilex, MI

SPENCER, TANYA MARIE
[pen.] Tanya Lewis; [b.] August 15, 1964; Westerly, RI; [p.] Robert F. Lewis Sr; [ch.] P.J., Misty Amanda, Amber Nicole; [ed.] Chariho Regional High School, Community College of Rhode Island, International Correspondence School; [occ.] Student of mental Health, C.C.R.I, Hospice Care of R.I. Volunteer; [memb.] S.P.I.R.I.T., Immaculate Conception Church of Westerly, Artists Cooperative Gallery; [hon.] Phi Theta Kappa Honor Society, Dean's List; [pers.] "A single drop alone in unity, a river starts, compassion and love personified exemplary of the human heart"; [a.] Westerly, RI.

SPRINKLE, NICCI
[pen.] Angel K; [b.] June 17, 1982, Kansas City, MO; [p.] Steven Sprinkle, Teresa Sprinkle; [ed.] High school Student; [occ.] Student; [memb.] Math Team, Academic Team; [hon.] Several high honors for first and second place freshman at match contests, as well as in individual categories, and first place team at academic bowls.; [oth. writ.] Many other unpublished poems and short stories; [pers.] Always live life to the fullest, and let the people you love know how you feel. You never know how long you'll be here.; [a.] Excelsior Springs, MO

ST. LOUIS III, JOSEPH
[b.] January 9, 1970, Atlanta, GA; [p.] Joseph St. Louis Jr., MD and Josephine; [ed.] Marist High School, Berklee College of Music in Boston, Mass.; [occ.] Professional Musician; [hon.] Bachelors degree in Professional Music Program, Cum Laude; [oth. writ.] Just beginning to explore the possibilities of his future, he works at his home studio where he writes, arranges, produces and records for advertising, interactive media, film and personal performances.; [pers.] Exposed to canvas of vast artistic diversity and adventurous horizons, I continue to state in aesthetic creation deep personal experience in an intelligible and recognizable framework. I aim to project this inner vison to the world.; [a.] Atlanta, GA

STAFFORD, KARL
[b.] June 3, 1984; Orlando, FL; [p.] Patricia Stafford Hampson [ed.] Andrew Jackson Elementary School, Dupont Tyler Middle School; [occ.] Student at Dupont Tyler; [memb.] Y.M.C.A; [hon.] Reading Awards, 4-H, Speech Contest; [a.] Hendersonville, TN.

STANLEY, DIANA
[b.] February 6, 1978; Coon Rapids, MN; [p.] Richard and Daisy Stanley; [ed.] Elk River High School Mankato State University (FR); [occ.] Nursing Student; [memb.] National Honor Society Students Against Drunk Driving (SADD), Marching Band, Christian Drama Group; [hon.] Den's List, Lettering in marching band, and academics, Wind symphony, Scholastic Achievement Awards, Captain of Marching Band, Color Guard, Presidential Academic Fitness Awards. Alpha Lambada Delta Honor Society; [pers.] Inspiration for me comes form life's lessons, and influence of family and friends; [a.] Ramsey, MN.

STANTON, AUNDRE LABRON
[b.] June 19, 1971, Detroit, MI; [p.] Mrs. Essie "Pearl" Brown; [m.] Mrs. Tammy D. Stanton, August 31, 1996; [ch.] Ms. Breyanna D. Stanton; [ed.] Alabama State University; [memb.] The Church of the Living Way, Pastor: Bill Howard; [oth. writ.] Valentine, Stand!, What If?, Frozen Paradise, I Miss You, etc.; [pers.] My purpose in

my writing(s) is to uplift the spirits of both men and women, encourage those who may have encountered hard times and shed abroad the knowledge that is "with God all things are possible!"; [a.] Stone Mountain, GA

STANTON, NANCY
[b.] August 9, 1950, Deposit, NY; [p.] Robert and Marjorie Vaughn; [m.] Kenneth Stanton, August 26, 1983; [ch.] One son, one daughter, one stepson and one grandson; [ed.] In 1991 I graduated as a Licensed Practical Nurse. At the present time I am continuing with my education to become a registered nurse.; [occ.] Licensed Practical Nurse; [memb.] I am a volunteer for the respite program for Alzheimers. I talk to any interested people or groups on Alzheimers.; [pers.] I believe there is good in everyone and that everyone deserves to be loved by someone.; [a.] Deposit, NY

STAR, MORNING
[b.] October 19, 1915, Cherokee, OK; [p.] Chief Bunning Bear, Little Dove; [m.] (Widow) Albert L. Whitaker, December 11, 1957; [ed.] School 12 yrs, 2 yrs college, short story 2 yrs, Newspaper Inst. of America 4 years; [occ.] Retired; [memb.] Mohavie Search and Rescue, Desert Scribes and Dead Poets; [hon.] Golden Poet award, a novel about animals, dogs and cats; [oth. writ.] Novel of True Americans Oak Ridge, a novel Tenn., children's stories, songs—stories in newspapers "Love Made Me a Traitor"; [pers.] I believe in the great spirit. I try to forgive people who have trespassed against me.; [a.] Golden Valley, AZ

STARBUCK, MARY
[b.] August 11, 1965, South Haven, MI; [p.] Harold and Rita Starbuck; [ed.] Bangor High School, Michigan State University, Western Michigan University; [occ.] Pre-school Teacher; [memb.] Sacred Hearth Catholic Church; [hon.] Who's Who Among American High School Students (1982-1983); [pers.] My writing captures the innocence and simplicity of life as well as the power and endurance of love.; [a.] South Haven, MI

STARK, RHONDA
[b.] August 27, 1956, Hampton, IA; [p.] Max and Aletha Anderson; [m.] Mike Stark, November 6, 1982; [ch.] Daniel Lee and Bradley Alan; [ed.] North East Hamilton High School, Bernel's Beauty School; [occ.] Secretary, Co-owner of Stark's Auto Electric, Inc; [oth. writ.] A few poems for personal use.; [pers.] I enjoy sitting down and writing poems about subjects in my life.; [a.] Panora, IA

STATON, BRIAN EVERETT
[b.] January 23, 1980; Charlotte, NC; [p.] Robert L. and Lena C. Staton; [ed.] Mount Vernon Christian Academy, Atlanta, GA; [occ.] Student; [memb.] Who's Who Among America's High School Students, 1997 National Spanish Honor Society; [hon.] Deans List, Honor Roll, Baseball Most Improved Player Trophy, Coaches Award "Best All Around", Citizens Award; [pers.] My main goal in life is to do the best that I can in every area of my life, so that when I'm old people will remember me as a maximum achiever like my brother; [a.] Douglasville, GA

STATON, LENA C.
[pen.] Izufir; [b.] October 24, 1952; Peachland, NC; [p.] Mr. and Mrs. John W. Harrell, Sr; [ch.] Brian E. Staton, Steven Staton; [ed.] Forest Hills High, Beulah Heights Bible College, Atlanta, GA; CPCC College; [occ.] Public Relations Correspondent; [memb.] New Birth Missionary Baptist Church, School or the Prophets; [hon.] Voted Outstanding Senior; [oth. writ.] Poem published in local Charlotte, NC Magazine; [pers.] I write to comfort, encounrage and counsel others that they may know and love my Savior, Jesus

Christ, I have been greatly influenced by writing of prophets of the Old Testament of the Bile; [a.] Douglasville, GA

STEFKA, COURTNEY
[b.] October 23, 1981, Orlando, FL; [p.] Valerie Boman, Mike Stefka; [ed.] Currently attend Corona Del Sol High School; [memb.] Student against Drunk Driving, Speech and Debate; [pers.] God grant me the serenity to accept the things I cannot change, the courage to change the things I can, and the wisdom to know the difference.; [a.] Chandler, AZ

STEIR, DOROTHY C.
[b.] January 21, 1956; Seattle, WA; [p.] Lucille F. Moreland; [m.] D.J. Steir; April 15, 1973; [ch.] Dennis J. Steir II; [ed.] Highschool-working on a B.A. Degree in Business; [occ.] Contract Analyst; [memb.] Toastmasters 1370; [hon.] Certificate from congressman Goerge Brown for my work and public speaking geared to assist small business in the field of contracting; [oth writ.] Several other poems relating to motherhood, nature, happiness, sorrow and love; [pers.] Life is to be enjoyed, play when you can, work when you must; [a.] San Bernardino, CA

STENNETT, JEAN NORRIS
[b.] September 3, 1932, Taylorsville, MS; [p.] Olee Dewitt Norris and Gussie Powers Norris; [m.] Wendell Hobson Stennett, February 11, 1948; [ch.] Kathy, Sherry; [ed.] Taylorsville High; [occ.] Clerk; [memb.] D.A.R. Unobee Chapter First Presbyterian Church; [hon.] Honorable Mention Recognition, Famous Poets Society, D.A.R. Chapter Award-Poems Entered; [oth. writ.] Other Poems published in local newspapers, famous poets society.; [pers.] To share my inter-thoughts with humanity and to enlighten their moments of life.; [a.] Taylorsville, MS

STEPHEN, MICHAEL K.
[b.] October 14, 1973, Norwood, MA; [ed.] Graduated 1991, Foxcroft Academy, Certificate—Culinary Arts, Dexter Vocational Center, numerous certificates for completion of courses sponsored by Maine Fire Training and Education at Fire Attack Schools; [memb.] Katahdin Area Council, Boy Scouts of America, Dover-Foxcroft Fire and Rescue Squad, Dover-Foxcroft YMCA; [hon.] BSA Eagle Scout, Red Cross Certified Lifeguard; [pers.] Hope for the best—be prepared for the worst. Goals: Continue in my firefighting and rescue training and to be an accomplished author of a variety of poems, stories and books.; [a.] Dover-Foxcroft, ME

STEPHENSON, AMIE
[b.] July 2, 1974, Saint Louis, MI; [p.] Gerald Draiemann and Suzanne Oates; [m.] Christian Stephenson, November 24, 1995; [ed.] Mandarin High School, Florida Community College of Jacksonville Kent Campus; [occ.] Student; [memb.] Phi Theta Kappa; [hon.] President's List, International Honor Society; [pers.] I strive to let not only my heart, but my imagination live within the lines of my writing.; [a.] Jacksonville, FL

STERLING, SHEILA
[pen.] Shots or Agent 1; [b.] November 29, 1977, Appleton, WI; [p.] Lori Roehl; [ed.] Fox Valley Lutheran H.S. Class of 1997. I plan on going to Fox Valley Teach for Hospitality and Tourism Mngt.; [occ.] Student/Writer; [memb.] Students Take on Prevention, Fox Video School, News, National Author's Registry, International Pen Friends, and Tennis Youth Employment Service; [hon.] Honorable Mention for "Join in One." President's Award for Literary Excellence for "Ancient Trails".; [oth. writ.] I've written over 300 poems/songs, my own year books up to 194 pages or less. I write my own spy stories. I will

share any of my songs.; [pers.] All of my geography songs are dedicated to Walter E. Bock. He's my role model, and he was my geography teacher. He passed away on April 20th, 1996.; [a.] Menasha, WI

STEVICH, CHRISTY
[b.] November 6, 1973, Saint Louis, MO; [p.] Steve and Patricia Stevich; [ed.] Riverview Gardens Senior High School, and Florissant Valley Community College; [occ.] Secretary; [memb.] World Wildlife Fund, Humane Society of U.S.; [pers.] I am inspired by how life is always surprising me with new lessons. The older I get, I realize how much my elders must know . . . and anticipate how much I have yet to learn!; [a.] O'Fallon, MO

STEWART, TERRY J.
[pen.] Terry J. Stewart; [b.] October 5, 1928, Eugene, OR; [p.] James C. Stewart; [m.] Ingrid Winkelaar, 1962; [ch.] Tim Stewart, Tess, Ted; [ed.] Associate Degree Diesel Technology, Creative Writing, Hudson Bay H.S., Vancouver Wash. Clark College, Vanc. Wash.; [occ.] Self-employed/Relocation; [memb.] I belong to a large group of people who are forgiven for their sins and saved by Jesus Christ.; [hon.] H.S. Diploma, 57 extra credit at grad. Athlete of the Year 1983, Captain, Most Insp., Most Improved in Wrestling. My son, Collin Richard, is my most treasured honor.; [oth. writ.] Shoes in the Mud, Up Come Visions, Uncle, Climbing Mountains, From a Seedling, From the Sky, Element of Earth; [pers.] "People should read slower!" I try to explain my thoughts and hope you can understand.; [a.] Fountain Valley, CA

STINNETT, JENNIFER
[pen.] Zelda Castrow; [b.] September 21, 1983; Tillamook, OR; [p.] Susana V. Stinnett; [ed.] Still in Jr. High, attends Kodiak Middle School; [occ.] Babysit; [a.] Kodiak, AK.

STONER, ROLLIN
[b.] January 26, 1949, Mishawaka, IN; [p.] Art Stoner; [ch.] Brian Stoner; [ed.] B.A. Education, M.A. Counselling; [occ.] Elementary Ed. Teacher; [memb.] N.E.A.; [pers.] To write good songs as well as good readings . . . .; [a.] Phoenix, AZ

STOTLER, JOSEPHINE L.
[b.] August 31, 1956, Martinsburg, WV; [p.] Mary Lightner, Gene Lightner; [m.] Terry Parsons (Fiance); [ch.] Tracey Lynn, Timothy Wayne, Babby Lee, Grandson Zackery; [ed.] 8th grade North Middle High; [occ.] Food Service Worker; [oth. writ.] Have a few other poems none of which have been published; [pers.] I truly believe in having world peace.; [a.] Martinsburg, WV

STRAKA, DORIS
[b.] April 28, 1962, Cleveland, OH; [p.] Sally Scott, James Wallace; [ch.] Crystal Lea, Jennifer Lynn; [ed.] Lincoln West; [occ.] Sales Clerk; [memb.] Girl Scout Leader, Barbizon Modeling Graduate; [oth. writ.] Several unpublished poems but would like them to be someday.; [pers.] My poems I write are of true feelings of life.; [a.] Lakewood, OH

STRODE, DOROTHY
[b.] June 13, 1939, Wrangell, AK; [p.] Julia Lewis - Patric Moore; [m.] George Strode, November 16, 1957; [ch.] Colleen Sullivan, Michael Strode, Jeff Strode, 7 grandchildren; [ed.] Through high school Woodland, WA; [occ.] In-home business; [oth. writ.] Poems, songs, skits (Bible skits); [pers.] In a seminar I discovered I'm unique like an eagle stuffed in the stupidity of a do-do bird. "Were all stuffed; it's our choice to be free to fly.".; [a.] Woodland, WA

SULLIVAN, MEGHAN M.
[b.] August 19, 1980, Melrose, MA; [p.] Susan and

Timothy Sullivan; [ed.] Sophomore at Bridgewater-Raynham Regional High School; [occ.] Student; [memb.] Soccer, Track; [hon.] Student of the Month; [a.] Raynham, MA

SUMWALT, JULIE
[b.] February 3, 1972; [occ.] Sign Language Interpreter; [pers.] I hope the songs and stories I write bless someone.; [a.] Milwaukee, WI

SUNDBERG, CHRIS
[b.] June 17, 1986; [ed.] My life, Our life, Our life Our Universe; [occ.] Student; [memb.] Washington Street Players (Highschool Drama Group); [oth.writ.] Poems in Highschool Magazine; [pers.] Everything is possible, everything is happening, has happened, and hasn't happened yet. Everything over capps only obscured from each other by relative impossibility - in one person's opinion at any rate; [a.] Boise, ID.

SURFACE, DAVID LYNDAL
[b.] January 3, 1965, Cairo, IL; [p.] Roy and Winona Surface; [m.] Regina Marie Surface, May 24, 1992; [ch.] David Lyndal II and Hanna Marie; [ed.] Iberia High School, Iberia, MO; [occ.] Construction Ehlen Contracting, Inc., Imperial, MO; [pers.] "Shaun" a poem I wrote and dedicated for my nephew Shaun Thomas Ehlen who died from Group B Strep infection at birth. He was five days old. March 3, 1996 - March 8, 1996.; [a.] Cadet, MO

SURIANO, MILAGROS
[b.] September 22, 1968, Brooklyn, NY; [p.] Raquel Matta and Louis Matta-Rios; [ch.] Derrick, Dolores and Sarah; [ed.] F.K. Lane H.S.; [occ.] Secretary at General Board of Global Ministries—Women's Division; [memb.] Guy R. Brewer Democratic Club, U.S. Army Reserve; [pers.] In searching to find myself, I discovered poetry; in finding poetry, I've discovered myself.; [a.] Jamaica, NY

SUTTON, VALERIE
[pen.] Val; [b.] October 3, 1965; Queens, NY; [p.] Mary Daniel and Homer Sutton; [ch.] Anthony and Justin; [ed.] I'm presently attending La Guardia Community Colllege. I am pursuing an A.A.S. Degree in Accounting; [occ.] I am a student aid for the Financial Aid Dept. at above school; [memb.] I am an Evangelist at Mount Calvary Holiness church, where Elder Brenda Harris is my pastor; [hon.] I achieved a certificate of achievement from Baruch College c/o Cope program for a pre-college course. I also have a certificate of achievement from a math course I took at Borough of Manhattan Com. Coll.; [oth.writ.] I've written one short story (not published as of yet). I'm also working on my autobiography; [pers.] I just want everyone to know that we can make it. Even if you don't try. Just have a desire and it will turn to fire and cause anything to stand in your way to be burned. It's called Perseverance; [a.] New York, NY.

SWALBERG, LAUREN
[b.] March 25, 1961; Palo Alto, CA; [p.] Richard and Doris Schorse; [m.] Matthew Swalberg; January 21, 1989; [ch.] Stephanie Diane and Michael Thomas; [ed.] Fullerton High School, Fullerton Community College; [occ.] Deputy Clerk at Victorville Court, CA; [hon.] (High School Awards) Best Vocalist-Choir, 2nd place- Talent Show '79 (Singing); [oth.writ.] In progress; [pers.] I enjoy poetry writing as a hobby and am working on a fiction story for submission to a magazine; [a.] Victorville, CA.

SWARTZ, ROBERT
[b.] May 16, 1978, Denver, CO; [p.] William and Jeanie Swartz; [ed.] High school Diploma, working towards a degree at Colorado State University; [occ.] Student; [memb.] National Honor

Society, International Rifle Association; [pers.] Poetry to me means the manipulation of words to illustrate desires, remorse, sorrow, happiness or any other true feeling. It is merely a way of writing yourself onto the paper. To write poetry is to feel the poetry.; [a.] Hudson, CO

SWISZCZ, AGNIESZKA
[pen.] Aggie; [b.] January 20, 1982, Poland; [p.] Anna Swiszcz and Marian Swiszcz; [m.] Marian Swiszcz; [ed.] Richard Edwards Elementary School and I'm going to Kennedy High School; [occ.] Student; [memb.] Polish Club; [hon.] Several poems published in newspaper, 1st place in a book contest in elementary school; [oth. writ.] Short stories and poems.; [pers.] Life is hard, but my best friend, Natalie Pudzisz, gives me the strength to survive.; [a.] Chicago, IL

SY, ALFREDO
[pen.] "Thoughts"; [b.] September 17, 1980, Phillipines; [p.] Alfredo T. Sy Sr. and Gloria G. Sy; [ed.] Junior in high school, piano for 1 year; [memb.] Ruben S. Ayala High School's Vocal Ensemble and Sound Pups Quartet 1997; [hon.] Ranked "Good" on Cal State San Bernardino Solo Fest; [pers.] I love to sing and play the piano. I associate, compare and combine classical music to my writing. The mood and the power.; [a.] Chino Hills, CA

SYDEJKO, KATI
[b.] November 1, 1980; Eau Claire, WI; [p.] Donald Sydejko and Vickie Sydejko; [ed.] Regis High School @ present 10th Grader; [occ.] student; [memb.] Forensics, Pep Club, Spanish Club, Softball, Track and Field, Volleyball, Pep Band; [hon.] The noon Exchange Club Young Citizenship Award Numerous awards in Forensics and Sports; [pers.] People are open books from whom we read from day to day, but often we need to read between the lines; [a.] Eau Claire, WT.

SYKES, JESSICA
[b.] May 21, 1974, Port Huron, MI; [p.] Thomas and Elizabeth Sykes; [ed.] Miami Sunset Sr. High School, University of West Alabama; [occ.] Sports Writer, Douglas County Sentinel, Douglasville, GA; [hon.] Dean's List, International English Honors Society; [pers.] My poetry is a reflection of my heart.; [a.] Douglasville, GA

SZLAG, JENNIFER
[b.] October 7, 1982, Rochester, MI; [p.] Richard Szlag and Suzan Szlag; [ed.] Sterling Heights High School; [occ.] Student; [hon.] Honor Roll, Board of Education, Above Average in Science, high test scores, Citizenship, Principal's List, Michigan Psychiatric Association Award, Attendance Award, Band Awards, Miss American Coed Award, martial arts; [oth. writ.] Poems published in another book, 1st place winner in essay contest about "Drinking and Drugs Can Hurt Someone You Love."; [pers.] I strive to succeed in everything I do. All my poems are based on personal experiences and what other people go through.; [a.] Sterling Heights, MI

SZYMANSKI, SHELLY RAE
[b.] February 28, 1980, Detroit, MI; [p.] Regina and John Szymanski; [memb.] S.A.D.D., Lake Shore Chapter; [oth. writ.] Mother (short story), Angel on My Shoulder (poem); [pers.] A promise means nothing until it is kept.; [a.] Saint Clair Shores, MI

SZYMANSKI JR., JOHN STANLEY
[b.] August 22, 1978, St. Petersburg, FL; [p.] Nancy and John Szymanski; [oth. writ.] My first published work, found in Anthology of Poetry by Young Americans, questions the civility of modern man. I have also received word that my poem "Dotted" will be included in the 1997 edition of this anthology.; [pers.] Love. Jesus told his fol-

lowers, the most important law resides in love. Men with skill, who lack this, are noteworthy. Great men are those who endorse the "perfect law" of God's acceptance. Love: an overused cliche, but as many times as it has flown from a writer's pen or poet's heart, how often has it been understood?; [a.] Cary, NC

TABERNA, MARK C.
[pen.] Elijah Saadiq; [b.] August 16, 1977, Santa Clara, CA; [p.] Danny Taberna, Julie Taberna; [ed.] Piedmont Hills High; [occ.] United States Navy (USN); [pers.] Writing gives the writer a chance to sing and dance out caged feelings from the heart (the chance for immortality).; [a.] San Jose, CA

TAITANO, ANTHONY TAIMANGLO
[pen.] Jitahadi; [b.] December 13, 1954, Guam; [p.] Anthony and Frances; [ed.] Dominguez High; [occ.] Dealer, Atlantis Casino, Reno; [pers.] My poems were written from the heart about friends, nature, and life. I write for enjoyment and to see smiles.; [a.] Reno, NV

TAPIA, JOHN M.
[b.] May 21, 1948, Long Beach, CA; [p.] Felix S. Tapia - Mary Montizor; [m.] Carina Amante Tapia, November 7, 1987; [ed.] Banning High School, Wilmington, CA (Art Major) February 3, 1967, Kapiolani Com. College - Sheraton Waikiki Hotel, Hawaii, May 8, 1974; [occ.] Culinary (Apprentice Cook), Instructor Rio Rancho High School, Corona. Chef, Inland Valley Medical Center; [memb.] American Legion (Mayon Post 688) Wilmington, CA of fifteen years; [hon.] I was rated number one chef August 12, 1988 by the Long Beach Press-Telegram newspaper, Long Beach, California; [oth. writ.] "I Sail with the Seal" (title) Into the Unknown, The National Library of Poetry (book) 1996; [pers.] I have been greatly influenced by a golden being of light that eminent golden rings of light. Whenever I am endangered I call the golden being by name, "God" or "I".; [a.] Menifee, CA

TAPP, CARL
[oth. writ.] I hope this poem may be a spiritual awakening and blessing to others.; [pers.] I Carl Tapp wish to dedicate this poem to Carol Thacker, my dear friend, who led me to the Lord, and true salvation in Jesus Christ.

TARICCO, CATHERINE ROSE
[b.] October 23, 1983, Yolo County; [p.] Margaret Magner and Gregory Taricco; [ed.] Currently attending Christian Brothers High School; [pers.] A person harvests only what he plants— Galatians 6:7; [a.] West Sacramento, CA

TATINENI, PRASHANT
[b.] January 2, 1984, Chicago, IL; [p.] Radha and Satyam Tatineni; [ed.] 7th grade, Castle Junior High School; [hon.] Honor Student; [pers.] I love language arts, especially poetry. I begin with a theme, and the rest just flows out onto the paper.; [a.] Newburgh, IN

TAWNEY, JO ANNA
[pen.] Jo Anna Tawney; [b.] September 3, 1964, Dallas, TX; [p.] Nelda and Ben Spawn; [m.] Chas. Curtis Tawney, October 24, 1992; [ch.] Jarrod Austen; [ed.] Bonham High School, Bonham, TX; [occ.] Homemaker, Day Care Operator and Avon Rep.; [memb.] Amateur Trapshooters Association; [pers.] "Can You Believe It's Actually Been A Year" was written for my biological father whom I didn't get a chance to meet until I was grown. He passed away 3 years later.; [a.] Carrollton, TX

TAYLOR, CA'NISHA FAYE II
[pen.] Woman and Slim; [b.] May 16, 1981, Detroit, MI; [p.] Veronica Faye I Taylor and Henry

Butler; [ed.] I attend Murray - Wright High School, I teach Project Seed Algebra to elementary students and I attend Marygrove College for tutoring; [occ.] McDonald's Restaurant; [memb.] Police Explorer, Boys and Girls Club, and Christian Community Baptist Church Youth Committee; [hon.] Superior Writing Award in Narrative Contest, Spelling Bee Grade Champion ion 1991-92 and 1992-93, Honor Roll certificates from all grade levels, Principal Honor Awards, NJROTC Metals and trophies for the drill team and riffle team, Gold Medal for Best Cadet in 1995-96, Basketball Tournament Trophies, National Physical Fitness Award and trophy in 1992-93, Computer Technician Award in 1992-93, 1st place Babe's Alcohol contest in 1985-86. Award, H.O.T.S. Lab Award in 1991, several certificates (Higher Order Thinking Skills) for participating in church activities, Best Outstanding Student in 1994-95, Project Seed Algebra certificates in 1990 and 1991. And several trophies and metals for running track; [oth. writ.] I write poetry according to the state of mind I'm at the time and my surroundings. I write poems for people funerals which is located inside of the obituary. I also find interest in writing fiction stories.; [pers.] First and foremost I would like to thank my Lord Jesus Christ for blessing me with this great talent. I am highly influenced by the death of my mother. Her dream was for me to become a poet and author, and I refuse to let her dream be differed. I would like to thank my wonderful grandmother for taking years of her life to take care of me. She's always behind me 100% and since the age of six, she have encouraged me not to give up my hope and dream to become a poet. I would like to thank my Pastor Rev. Gooch and 1st Lady Sis Gooch for all their help and support through the years. I'm also influenced by my grandfather (R.I.P.) His favorite statement was "All things are possible through God in Christ." I take that statement very personal because it helps day by day. I would also like to thank my Godmother for all her advice and support. She understand my problems and situations, and with her advice, she tries to help me to the best of her ability. Last but not least, I would like to thank all my teachers, friends, and relatives who encouraged and supported me. My dream is to become the 1st young black female and author. I will strive to the best of my ability to make that dream true.

TAYLOR, CHARLENE
[b.] February 25, 1952, Gilford; [a.] Goldsboro, NC

TAYLOR, JOAN R.
[pen.] "JO"; [b.] October 21, 1935, Huntingdon, PA; [p.] Florence and William Rhodenizer; [m.] Robert C. Taylor, August 5, 1969; [ch.] Gary Middleton, Nancy Middleton Kruse, Lindy Middleton Belford; [ed.] Hunting Area High School, Professionals Academy; [occ.] Homemaker; [memb.] American Heart Association, National Right to Life; [oth. writ.] None published; write poems for special occasions—Christmas, Easter, birthdays - church bulletins; [pers.] My writing I hope reflects the love to God, family and friends. I love to express humor, compassion and inspiration in my poetry. Above all it is my hope that God's love for all of us is portrayed and that my works glorify Him.; [a.] Puyallup, WA

TAYLOR, KIMBERLY KAY
[b.] January 2, 1953, Portland, OR; [p.] Patricia Anderson and Don Jones; [m.] Edward A. Taylor, April 10, 1971; [ch.] Jennifer, Michelle, Justin and Melanie; [ed.] 12th grade; [occ.] Day Care Provider; [hon.] Presidential Award for Physical Fitness, 8th grade; [pers.] I would like to dedicate this to my loving husband and my children, for their love. May God bless all the children that have not been heard.; [a.] Concord, CA

TAYLOR, PATRICIA
[pen.] Patricia Taylor; [b.] June 19, 1929, Osceola, IA; [p.] Howard and Mildred Jones; [m.] Robert G. Taylor, December 2, 1949; [ch.] Carol, Richard and Jeffrey; [ed.] College courses, seminars, workshops with editors on writing articles and poetry, training courses on teaching Bible studies, research related to both teaching and writing material; [occ.] Writer of poetry, articles, assembling material for writing Bible courses; [memb.] Christian Women's Assoc., International Society of Poets; [oth. writ.] Bible courses, other poems, most being published with poetry companies at this time; [pers.] My endeavor and purpose, both in Bible studies and in all other writings, will always be to give inspiration and encouragement in other lives which will give more meaning, with a desire to pursue their beliefs and goals.; [a.] Falmouth, MA

TAYLOR, PATRICIA BERRY
[pen.] Pat Taylor; [b.] May 9, 1930, Hackensack, NJ; [p.] Granville Berry and Dorothy Berry; [m.] Robert Taylor, March 15, 1951; [ch.] John Robert, James Thomas and Patricia Carmen; [ed.] Houston Co. High School Extension Classes from University of TN at Martin. Classes at Murray State (KY); [occ.] Co-owner of Taylor Tire and Alignment. Also Taylor Farm; [memb.] Woman's Club, G.F.W.C., Creative Homemakers, First United Methodist Church; [oth. writ.] Poems: Apology, Realization, Little House by the Bay, Return to Northport and Mockingbird in the Cypress Tree.; [pers.] I see beauty all around and feel I couldn't write without it.; [a.] Paris, TN

TAYLOR, TERESA J.
[pen.] TC; [b.] July 7, 1948, Huntington, WV; [p.] Russell Sidebottom, Winifred Sidebottom; [m.] Charles M. Taylor, March 21, 1964; [ch.] Charles Allan, Jeffrey Loren, and Jason Michael; [memb.] First Assembly of God Church, Christian Motorcycle Association; [oth. writ.] Thus far my poems have been gifts for use in church, schools, CMA, family and friends. Eventually, I hope to go into business, concentrating solely on this effort.; [pers.] I try to put down on paper what a person cannot say vocally. I hope someday to have a poem for every thought or idea a person might have. God is my focus and my poems come from the heart.; [a.] Overland Park, KS

TERRELL, HILARY
[pen.] Nora O'Del; [b.] June 24, 1981, Atlanta, GA; [p.] Timothy and Mary Terrell; [ed.] Avondale High School (DeKalb Center for the Performing Arts), Atherton Elementary, Oak Grove Elementary; [hon.] Beta Club, Jr. Beta, Jr. National Honor Society, Math Team, Honorable Mention in poetry for the Iliad Press; [pers.] "Little Reflection," a poem about my younger sister, who is also a best friend.; [a.] Decatur, GA

THACKER, BRANDON SCOTT
[pen.] William Lowlagon; [b.] September 15, 1977; [p.] Dolphus and Cheryl Thacker; [ed.] 1-12 high school, Southern Alamo High School, 1 1/2 years college Appalachian State University; [occ.] United States Marine Corps; [hon.] Burlington Women's Club writing contest 1995 2nd place, Dean's List; [pers.] If a human spends ample time reflecting on his or her past, it can often lead to a better director, move forward future.; [a.] Graham, NC

THEOBALD, WILLIAM E.
[b.] February 19, 1930, Honesdale, PA; [p.] J. Alfred and Bertha Holl Theobald; [m.] Mary Helene Lopatofsky Theobald, November 27, 1958; [ch.] Catherine, Judith, Michele, Mary Elizabeth, William Jr. and Joseph; [ed.] High school graduate; [occ.] Barber since 1946 (our family business is 107 years old); [memb.] 29 yrs. Wayne County Planning Comm., Chairman since 1977, former member Knights of Columbus and its 4th Degree St. John/St. Mary's RC Church; [oth. writ.] Numerous 4-line poems to my wife.; [pers.] Always tried to be honest and sincere to everyone.; [a.] Honesdale, PA

THESING, CARISA
[pen.] Carisa Thesing; [b.] March 12, 1974, Grand Forks Air Force Base, ND; [p.] Sue Johnson and Rick Thesing; [ch.] David R. Evenle; [ed.] Bear Creek High School, Warren Tech. Trade School, Parks Jr. College; [occ.] Delivery/Driver; [oth. writ.] I write daily. This was the first time I've ever entered one into a contest.; [pers.] I have been writing since I was 12 years old. I write about my life experiences and the wonders of the world and the mysteries and power of the love that everyone shares and experiences.; [a.] Thornton, CO

THIBODEAUX, ERIK MICHAEL
[b.] October 12, 1979, Ely, NV; [p.] Patty Robinson; [ed.] Currently in White Pine High School; [hon.] Superintendent's Award in 1992; [oth. writ.] No other published work; [pers.] Writing gives me a chance to express my anger, sadness and elation. Blank paper can let me be free without guilt.; [a.] Ely, NV

THOMAS, ANDREA
[pen.] Andrea R. Thomas, A.R.T.; [b.] November 26, 1969, Montgomery, AL; [p.] Clinton Fred Freeman and Lillie Freeman; [m.] Manasseh Mendel Thomas, September 8, 1992; [ch.] Joshua Mendel Thomas; [ed.] 12th grade; [occ.] Clerk Steno II, State of Alabama; [memb.] ASEA (AL State Employees Association), Kingdom Hall of Jehovah's Witness; [oth. writ.] The Gift of Life, My Child, A Love Everlasting; [pers.] I have been writing poems and short stories since the age of 13 and I'm currently writing a book. Writing has always been my first love and will always be.; [a.] Montgomery, AL

THOMAS, MICHAEL
[b.] February 1, 1955, Lewisville, MS; [p.] Roy Foster Thomas and Flora Banks; [ed.] Williamson High; [occ.] Dining Room Attendant; [hon.] I received a gold watch and a plaque, for a drawing I 8did.; [oth. writ.] Mainly poems for myself, never had any published.; [pers.] I attempt to show great diversity in my writings, influences are Gene Rottenbury, Stevie Wonder, Maya Angelou.; [a.] Saint Louis, MO

THOMAS, MILLISSA DAWN
[b.] October 20, 1981, Brattleboro, VT; [p.] Leo Thomas and Diana Thomas; [ed.] Currently attending Brattleboro Union High School; [occ.] Student (full-time); [pers.] Life is full of opportunities. Take advantage of them.; [a.] Brattleboro, VT

THOMAS, TANGELICO
[pen.] Shelley; [b.] October 30, 1969, Eanmont, Baptist Hospital; [p.] Lee and Betty Williams; [m.] Lee Thomas, March 14, 1992; [ed.] Westbrook - graduated, Lamar College - Childcrea - 2 yrs. degree, 1 yr 3 months left; [occ.] Don's Seafood; [oth. writ.] To the One I Love - "Missing You," Happy Birthday - "From the Heart," "In the Mist," Happiness "Surprise!", Christmas - "What a Joy," Graduation: "Reach for Success," Funeral: "Sovilia," Elizabeth's Faith, Be Strong, "Don't Worry, Be Happy," "Me and Angel" Marriage: Coming Together; [pers.] I have always wished I could have my poems published. When I saw this contest, I could not believe it. I never thought I would have are of my poems published. I'm so glad. All the poems I write are dedicated to someone and come from the heart.; [a.] Beaumont, TX

THOMPSON SR., ROBERT CHARLES
[pen.] The Moon; [b.] December 3, 1952, L.I., NY; [p.] Ben and Maggie L. Thompson; [ch.] Robt II, Eddie D., Taketia - Nakeia, Lawanda - Jasper; [ed.] Trenton Central, Trenton State, Mercer County Comm., Rider College; [occ.] Workforce Development Clerk Dept. of Labor - State of N.J; [memb.] Beta Gamma Tu - President; [hon.] Single parent - my honor!!; [oth. writ.] Several publications locally in Trenton and New Brunswick, N.J., one completed play currently in production "In Between Time"!; [pers.] I believe everyone should try to achieve—that Hope is eternal and that all should strive and maintain their inner balance; [a.] Trenton, NJ

THORN, JOSEPH
[pen.] Get; [b.] January 20, 1970, Harrisburg, PA; [ed.] High school; [occ.] Tire Builder; [oth. writ.] I find it hard to hold on to my work, so I give it all away.; [pers.] I have been influenced by my crazy friends, Prison, Hendy Rolling and Jim.; [a.] Enola, PA

TIDD, ANDREA K.
[b.] August 16, 1981; Spokane, WA; [p.] Rick and Brenda Tidd; [ed.] Currently enrolled in High School; [occ.] Student; [memb.] Health Club; [hon.] Student of the Month; [pers.] Follow your heart and your dreams!;[a.]Vancouver, WA.

TILBE, GEORGE
[b.] December 19, 1947, Danbury, CT; [p.] George and Dolores Tilbe; [m.] Kate Tilbe, July 18, 1970; [ch.] Adam; [ed.] Danbury High School, Norwalk Community College, Associates, Western Ct University, Masters Degree; [occ.] 6th grade Teacher, Oxford, CT, Great Oak Middle School; [memb.] American Legion, Oxford Education Association, Connecticut Education Association, National Education Association, National Rifle Association; [hon.] Served in the U.S. Army in Vietnam, 1968; [pers.] "Make learning a treat not a chore."; [a.] Middlebury, CT

TILLERY, KRISTOFFER
[pen.] Lovell Payne; [b.] February 15, 1972, Brooklyn, NY; [p.] James Tillery and Betty Bethea; [ed.] North Carolina A&T State University; [occ.] Computer Analyst, First Union National Bank; [pers.] My poems reflect the ecstasy of my love and the pain that consumes me.; [a.] Charlotte, NC

TOBOLSKI, JESSICA
[b.] October 12, 1981, Chicago, IL; [p.] Cheri and Paul Tobolski; [ed.] Gloria Dei and Nathan Hale Grammar Schools. Currently attending Queen of Peace High School.; [occ.] Student; [memb.] Chorus; [hon.] Young Authors Award; [pers.] My favorite philosophical statement was the theme at Disney World when my grandma took me on a trip there: "If you can dream it, you can do it!"; [a.] Chicago, IL

TORRALBA, LEONARDO S.
[b.] November 6, 1962, Philippines; [ed.] Bachelor of Science in Nursing; [occ.] Staff Nurse (Psych ER) at Bellevue Hospital Center, NY, NY; [memb.] New York State Nurses Association; [hon.] "Artist of the Year" in college; [a.] Irvington, NJ

TORRENCE, JOI
[b.] March 30, 1980; Syracuse, NY; [p.] Robert and Margel Torrence; [ed.] Elementary School, Middle School. 3 years of High School. Junior at this tie; [California Scholarship, Federation (CSF), NAALP - Act So' [hon.] Royal Star for achievement, G.P.A. over 3.5 and involved in extra-curricular activity, Principal Honor Roll with G.P.A. of 3.8, Lamba Kappa - Sycaruse Univ. for excellence in academics. Citizenship award. [oth.writ.] Poem-

titled The Love of My Mother. [pers.] Through my writings I seek to put forth an articulate sense of understanding and feeling in words, with this I obtain inner-peace; [a.] La Verne, CA.

TRIGGS, JOHN J.
[b.] September 26, 1977, Plantation, FL; [p.] John L. and Susan E. Triggs; [ed.] Graduated from Eagles Landing High School in June 1996. Now attending Gordon Junior College; [occ.] Student; [memb.] Math Club, NJROTC, Boy Scouts; [hon.] Eagle Scout, NJROTC Color Guard and Drill Team; [oth. writ.] I have written other unpublished poems: Angels, and Driver.; [a.] McDonough, GA

TRIMMELL, JERRY L.
[b.] November 11, 1974, Frankfurt, Germany; [p.] Charged whole sound, might!; [m.] In my confront... Escort an investigate; [ch.] Bubbles... obstensibly; [ed.] (The sea around us); [occ.] Postal Service Data Conversion Operator, Coffee!; [memb.] A name of cakes, International Center of Photography, Melvins Army, Church of Satan, Dessert of the Month Club; [hon.] Taking it all the way with a pat on the shoulder and two wet fingers; [oth. writ.] "Legs up, tongue out", and the children's story "Monkey the Strong Coat" (incidentally, the poem in this anthology is meant to be read loudly); [pers.] The pain chips are kicking in - not to exceed - contact at P.O. Box 17024, Wichita, KS 67217-7024 - change the nature of strength.

TROWBRIDGE, ANGELA
[pen.] Valerie Renfro; [b.] March 30, 1984, Cadillac, MI; [p.] Melody Dollars; [ed.] Student; [occ.] School; [hon.] A, B Honor Roll, sports: soccer, volleyball, basketball, swimming and running; [pers.] The reason I wrote this poem is because of my boyfriend and his caring ways!; [a.] Sugar Grove, NC

TRUONG, DAN
[b.] February 5, 1975, Saigon, Vietnam; [p.] Huong Truong, Kien Thi Tran; [ed.] Mark Keppel High School, University of California at Davis, Reppetto Elementary School; [occ.] Network Support Administrator; [memb.] National Forensic League; [hon.] Optimist Oratorical Award; [oth. writ.] Pain comforts those who yearn to feel as does joy.; [a.] Davis, CA

TUCKER, DEARL
[pen.] Dearl Tucker; [b.] January 13, 1975, Oakland, CA; [p.] Joe Tucker and Gale Underwood; [ed.] College Park High; [occ.] Assistant Mechanic, Clerk at Northgate Exxon; [memb.] N.H.R.A.; [oth. writ.] Hundreds of poems, songs of various styles and subjects, all unpublished.; [pers.] Some of the worst times in our lives may turn out to be our most precious moments. Thank you T. M. for everything.; [a.] Walnut Creek, CA

TUCKER, LISA J.
[pen.] Lisa J. Tucker; [b.] December 17, 1964, Des Moines, IA; [p.] Marlene A. Stone and Larry D. Monroe; [m.] David D. Tucker, April 9, 1994; [ch.] Caitlin and Gabrielle; [ed.] Chariton High School, Indian Hills Community College; [occ.] Homemaker; [oth. writ.] None published.; [pers.] I am so honored to have the chance to share my spiritual feelings about my daughter Gabrielle's death. This helps my heart to continue to heal.; [a.] Albia, IA

TUCKER, ROGER D.
[b.] December 19, 1949, Pine Knot, KY; [p.] Roy and Georgia Tucker; [m.] Divorced; [ch.] Roger, Aaron and Anson; [ed.] Mt. Healthy High School, Cincinnati, OH; [occ.] Grocery Clerk, The Kroger Co., Cincinnati, OH; [memb.] Disabled American Veterans; [oth. writ.] Many others but nothing that has been published; [pers.] The poems I write

are all based on my own personal experiences. This poem is especially important to me because through God I was given a second chance.; [a.] Fairfield, OH

TURNER, JOSEPH
[pen.] Joseph Turner; [b.] February 14, 1923, Winston-Salem, NC; [p.] George L. and Ethel Turner (Deceased); [m.] Donna, December 13, 1970; [ch.] All grown and married; [ed.] High school, one yr college, Carolina, John W. Hanes High, Winston-Salem, NC, 3 yrs in US Navy in Medical (Honorable Discharge), musician/songwriter professionally; [occ.] Retired from MFRs Rep; [memb.] VFW, Am Legion, ARP, composed music; [pers.] Poetry has always fascinated me, particularly about love and family.; [a.] Charlotte, NC

TURNER, JUANITA
[pen.] From The Mind and Heart; [b.] September 30, 1973, Birmingham, AL; [p.] Mr. Paul Turner and Mrs. Lillie Turner; [ed.] P.D. Jackson-Olin Stillman College; [occ.] Cashier at McDonalds; [memb.] I.B.W. (non-greek organization); [pers.] I encourage anyone to write poetry to express their inner feelings. Writing poetry helps me to express my thoughts and emotions without talking to my friends.; [a.] Birmingham, AL

TURNEY, REGINA
[b.] February 3, 1961, Stuttgart, AR; [p.] Bobby Sanders and Mary Sanders; [ch.] Christopher Claggett; [hon.] Golden Poet Award, Silver Poet Award, Award of Merit (World of Poetry), (Sacramento, Cal); [oth. writ.] Several recording contracts offered for song publications. Life's ambition to be a songwriter.; [pers.] Portfolio: 150 poems and songs. Greatest influences in my life are my son, Christopher, Grandfather, Bud Dobson, and brother, Steve Sonders. Favorite poet is Hazel Lee Armstrong.; [a.] Humphrey, AR

TWARDESKY, LORETTA A.
[b.] November 26, 1972, Middleburg Heights, OH; [p.] Jim Twardesky and Kathy Twardesky; [ch.] Michael Allen Twardesky; [ed.] Brunswick High, currently Bryant and Stratton College; [occ.] Server; [memb.] Business Management Club, Writer for the evening school newspaper at Bryant and Stratton College; [hon.] Honor Award for 3.7 GPA for a part-time student.; [oth. writ.] Time in Amidst the Splendor.; [pers.] I wish to provide more intelligible writing to my readers.; [a.] Brunswick, OH

TWINAME, DR. B. GAYLE
[pen.] Jessie Dean; [b.] November 18, 1952, White Plains, NY; [p.] James Dean and Beatrice Denike Hunter; [ed.] Texas Woman's University, Lamar University, Medical College of Georgia, University of North Florida, Brunswick Jr. College, Briar Cliff High School; [occ.] Retired Nursing Professor; [memb.] Sigma Theta Tau International, National Rifle Association, Mensa; [hon.] Regent's Merit Award, Dean's List; [oth. writ.] Statistics chapter in Talbot, Nursing Research for Mosby Co., several professional nursing articles.; [a.] Beaumont, TX

TYLER, ERNEST
[pen.] Mr. Dynamite; [b.] September 13, 1971, Jersey City, NJ; [ed.] Snyder High School, South Robertson HS; [occ.] Rap Vocalist and songwriter; [memb.] Immortal Foundation (IMF), Slang Bang in Records; [oth. writ.] 1 Life 2 Live, several rap songs.; [pers.] I like to get to the heart of the matter using poetic expression so the world can know my deepest thoughts.; [a.] Jersey City, NY

UNGER, IRENE PERRY
[b.] August 23, 1960; Manhattan, NY; [p.] Howard J. Perry, Susan A. Perry; [ch.] Viginia Perry Unger; [ed.] Yonkers High School; [occ.] Administrative Assistant, Nynex-New York Telephone; [oth.writ.] My life's journals since 1979, My Dreams Journals poems: "Forever Sweet Places" and "I Love You Notes" published by National Library of Poetry; [pers.] My daughter is my life, an "Angel in Disguise", my teacher on Earth. From her lips to my ears and into my heart. In my dreams I have been shown. In my waking life it has been confirmed by the Lord and my angels. God bless the children and keep them safe always; [a.] Carmel, NY.

VALENTINE, CHRISTOPHER W.
[pen.] Christopher W. Valentine; [b.] June 3, 1978, Maryville, TN; [p.] Michael W. Valentine and Priscilla C. Valentine; [ed.] Currently a senior in H.S. to graduate from Victoria High School in Texas in '97. Also have attended 4 high schools all together.; [occ.] Student. Aspiring Screenwriter; [oth. writ.] Several poems, and one completed script, enjoy writing short skits and spoken word plays, I'm currently working on a script titled "Knoxville."; [pers.] "No matter what happens, the sun will always rise in the morning." "Without chaos in one's life, comes no order to." "If you dig it, do it. If you really dig it, do it twice," (about shortness of life).; [a.] Victoria, TX

VALLONE, GAIL A.
[pers.] This poem was written in memory of my loving mother, Ruth A. Gottschalk. I love you. I miss you.; [a.] Las Vegas, NV

VAN COTT, LORRI ANN
[b.] February 17, 1959, Salt Lake City, UT; [p.] Elman Bates Curts and Madalyn L. H. Curtis; [m.] Gerald Alan Van Cott, July 18, 1978; [ch.] Jason A., Tara A., Sheena L. and Miranda D. Van Cott; [ed.] High school (Highland High); [occ.] Financial Service Representative at Zions First National Bank since 8/86; [memb.] I have assisted in some activities for the Girl Scouts. Other than that I just love to teach children from ages 3-18.; [hon.] I have earned a number of awards in sales. None in the poetry area.; [oth. writ.] "Angel's Kiss," "My Guardian Angel," "The Christmas Candle," and "Autumn Time." None published as of yet, but I've yet started.; [pers.] My loving husband and my beautiful four children have helped inspire my poetry. Also my wonderful parents and my memories being raised with eight brothers and sisters.; [a.] Taylorsville, UT

VAN RIPER, BRADLEY W.
[b.] March 24, 1975, Hauppauge, NY; [p.] Milford and Elsie Van Riper; [ed.] Wellington Community High School, University of Florida - College of Pharmacy; [occ.] Pharmacy Student; [memb.] Academy of Students of Pharmacy (ASP), North Central Florida Society of Hospital Pharmacists; [hon.] Dean's List, Golden Key National Honor Society, Alpha Lambda Delta Freshmen Honor Society, Vice President of ASP; [pers.] For every goal met there is an infinite number yet to be achieved.; [a.] Gainesville, FL

VANDERWARKER, BARBARA
[b.] September 8, 1915, Brainerd, MN; [p.] Irma and James Templeton; [m.] Henry Vanderwarker, October 16, 1937; [ch.] Jim and Rob; [ed.] Grad. Washburn High Mpls, MN, University of Minnesota, Mpls., MN; [memb.] Life Center of Tacoma, WA, AAUW, Feed the Children, and Habitat for Humanity and Colonial Williamsburg; [pers.] I am an ardent supporter of animal rights, environmental issues and human welfare.; [a.] Steilacoom, WV

VASQUEZ, SARA
[b.] July 15, 1981, Kansas City, MO; [ed.] Still in school, 9th grade; [occ.] Student; [memb.] Newspaper; [hon.] Maintaining "B" average; [oth. writ.] Numerous poems and songs; [pers.] Writing brings out your inner self. Your imagination opens up doors for success.; [a.] Independence, MO

VAUGHN, MARY
[b.] April 20, 1930, Trafford, AL; [p.] Grover Webster and Vivian Lenore (Dorman) V.; [m.] James T. Lovvorn, July 4, 1951 (Deceased); [ed.] Cert., Birmingham Bus. Coll. 1949, modeling, Howard Coll. 1962, Therapeutic Activities Cert., Grossmont Adult Sch. 1975, Cert. Magmt. Success Inst. 1977, Lic. Adminstr., Calif., Cert. Notary Public, Calif.; [occ.] Convalescent Hospital Administrator Consultant, Community Activist, Pres./Treas. Balboa Manor Inc., San Diego; [memb.] Am. Assn. of Health Facilities; Calif. Assn. of Health Facilities, civic bds: Girls Club of San Diego, Southland Bus. & Profl. Women (past pres.), Women's Internat. Center (treas.), Mary Vaughn Scholarship Fund for Aging Res. (treas.); [hon.] Women's Internat. Center honoree and Living Legacy Award 1988, Congl. distinguished service award and citizen of month presented by Cong. Jim Bates (11/87), Women's Internat. Center Vol. of yYear award (March 7, 1992) and Vol. of the Decade award (March 9, 1996), City Beautiful campus beautiful vol. award (5/90), So. Dist. BPW woman of achiev. (1987, 90, 91) and nominee to Calif. State BPW Hall of Fame (3/92), First Runner Up: Business and Professional Women Hall of Fame Sacramento, California May, 1993, Lions International: Judge for student scholarship "Today's Youth-Why The Violence February 24, 1994, Women's International Center: 11th Woman Award, 1988; [a.] San Diego, CA

VEGA, CARLOS
[pen.] Sonny; [b.] December 24, 1974, Canal Zone, Panama; [p.] Carlos Vega Sr, Donna Dotson, Richard Dotson; [ed.] High school, James I. O'Neill, Associates degree in Commercial Art from Sullivan County Community College, working on my Bachelors degree in Computer Graphics from University at Buffalo; [occ.] Senior in college; [pers.] A poet you say, a poet not I. The poet is the words, I'm mearly the machine through which the poet allows you to see.; [a.] New Windsor, NY

VELASQUEZ, ANTHONY J.
[b.] August 30, 1984, Redwood City, CA; [p.] Edward and Jeannine Velasquez; [ed.] I'm a 7th grade student at Jackman Jr High in Sacramento, CA; [occ.] Student; [hon.] I have been competing in swimming for 5 years. I have won 3 gold medals, 5 silver medals, and 7 bronze medals. I was class president for two years, and an honor roll student.; [a.] Sacramento, CA

VELIKY, MICHELE A.
[b.] August 17, 1952, Plainfield, NJ; [p.] Daniel J. Sargeant Sr. and Joyce A. Sargeant; [m.] Divorced; [ch.] Tara Joyce and Ronald Joseph; [ed.] Piscataway Schools; [occ.] Child Study Team Secretary; [pers.] I write about things that happened in my life and what I feel inside.

VERDOORN, ERIC
[b.] June 4, 1981, Minneapolis, MN; [p.] Richard Verdoorn and Deborah Verdoorn; [ed.] Currently attending Irondale High School, class of 2000; [occ.] Student; [memb.] Member of the Irondale Football, Basketball, and Track Teams; [hon.] Piano Finalist in MMTA Music Contest, Irondale Honor student.; [a.] New Brighton, MN

VICARS, TINA KAY
[pen.] Ann Richard; [b.] November 27, 1961, Pratt, KS; [p.] Richard Gunter (Deceased), Jim and Betty Norrish; [m.] Chuck Vicars, July 8, 1989; [ch.] Mandy Lynn and Kevin Wayne; [ed.] Graduate of Pratt High School, graduate of Pratt Community College, student of the Institute of Children's Literature; [occ.] Typing Service Provider; [oth. writ.] Several poems written as personal gifts.; [pers.] If ever the sun sets and I've forgotten to smile, let me remember the children's laughter and gift and hugs.; [a.] Newton, KS

VICK, LINDA CHRISTINE
[pen.] Chris; [b.] August 16, 1983, Charleston; [p.] Linda A. Vick, Joseph W. Vick; [ed.] Middle school, 8th grade E, I went to James B. Edwards for elementary school; [occ.] Student; [memb.] Moultrie Middle School Patriot Council, Moultrie Symphonic Band, Moultrie Wind Ensemble Band; [hon.] Honor Roll Student, Student of the Month for February; [oth. writ.] Flowers, Dog, Bill and Jill, Like a Cat, Him, Just You, The Only One, and I Like. Not yet published these.; [pers.] I enjoy classical, country, cool rock music. Algebra and writing are the two subjects I enjoy. My favorite movie was "Dangerous Minds."; [a.] Awendaw, SC

VIERA, JOSE MANUAL
[b.] December 31, 1951, Caguas, PR; [p.] Teresa and Anthony Viera; [m.] Eileen Viera, February 13, 1973; [ch.] Joseph and Theresa; [ed.] Mercy College, Borough of Manhattan Community College; [occ.] President, Systems Programming Services Plus; [memb.] Philadelphia Writers Conference, Mt. Pocono Writers Group; [hon.] United Federation of Teachers Scholarship Award, Board of Higher Education, New York University; [oth. writ.] "The Eighth Sea," and "Writer's Quest."; [pers.] Journey we through endless voyages, may serenity engulf us as we sail smoothly.; [a.] Tobyhanna, PA

VOET, CHERYL LYNN
[b.] September 29, 1976, Vallejo, CA; [p.] Marshal Voet and Pamela Voet; [ed.] Armijo High; [occ.] Hostess, Red Lobster; [pers.] I hereby dedicate "Other Dimensions" to all those who've made grieving mistakes in their lives. For those who struggle to be freed from their chains of remorse, may this be a source of condolence and inspiration.; [a.] Fairfield, CA

VOLDEN, DANIEL M.
[b.] November 20, 1952, LA Crosse, WI; [p.] LaVern and Deloris; [m.] Dianne, February 25, 1973; [ch.] Dana, Derek, Darci; [ed.] High school; [occ.] Machinist; [a.] La Crosse, WI

VON BERMUTH, SCHELIKA
[pen.] Schelika; [b.] August 3, 1942; Columbia; [p.] Renato - Celia Alvarez; [m.] Rudy Von Vermuth; October 13, 1970; [ch.] Oscar A. Carlo P. Celia Helene; [ed.] Elementary and High School with Catholics Sister in Pamplona. After I attend National University, but not graduate; [occ.] I'm a qualified supervisor and I work for Environmental Services at N.W. HC; [oth.writ.] I used to write for my school, but as today I do not have my of those papers with. They are lost; [pers.] I speudeu the magic poet of my life overcies in cocentrip like turkey, Bangladesh, Thailand and others. Bueu Bangladesh my love one, for the tenderness and kindness of its people.; [a.] Mount Kisco, NY.

VORIES, DAWN E.
[b.] October 18, 1954, Chicago, IL; [p.] Mr. and Mrs. Franklin Murphy; [m.] Kimory C. Vories, December 23, 1977; [ch.] Emma, Angela, Joshua, Stephen; [ed.] B.S. Dietetics Wisconsin State University, Stephen's Point; [occ.] Homemaker, Home School Teacher; [oth. writ.] Poem "The Least of These," is my first publication; [pers.] I wanted to express in words the

eternal things I value and the eternal God I love to lay a meaningful way for my children.; [a.] Edwardsville, IL

VORIES, JOSHUA D.
[b.] March 8, 1984, Columbia, MO; [p.] Kim and Dawn Vories; [ed.] 6th Grade, Christian Liberty Academy; [memb.] Boy Scout Troop #31; [hon.] 1st Place Edwardsville Christmas Art Contest, 1st Place R and D Forum for song "I'm an Irishman," Johnson County, KS; [oth. writ.] "The Gift" in Into the Unknown; [pers.] A fun inspiration that came over me one morning in the shower.; [a.] Edwardsville, IL

VORVES, JAMIE
[b.] March 20, 1985, Prescott, AZ; [p.] Jim and Dianne Vorves; [ed.] Currently a 6th grader, at West Sedona School; [memb.] Sedona Swordfish Swi team; [hon.] I'm an honor roll student, and have received praise from my teachers Mrs. Yeatts, and Ms. Wyckoff, also from Hayley Allen, and Sarah Bunch; [oth. writ.] "He", and the rest of the poem "Why".; [pers.] This poem was written for and dedicated to Ben Payne or Woodrow Benson Payne. I appreciate the help from my teacher Mrs. Yeatts, and my friends Hayley Allen and Sarah Bunch.; [a.] Sedona, AZ

WADE, KARIL
[b.] Seattle, WA; [m.] Thomas Wade; [ch.] Matthew Rich; [oth. writ.] I am a yet to be published horror fiction writer with three completed manuscripts and an agent; [pers.] For me, writing is a pleasure no matter what form it takes. It's reading without the safety net.; [a.] Marcola, OR

WAGER, JOAN
[b.] August 30, 1946, Sacramento, CA; [p.] Eugene and Dollie Little; [m.] Joyce Wager, November 13, 1965; [ch.] Barbara Ann and Louis Eugene; [ed.] High school; [occ.] Farm Wife and Mother - Farm Worker - grandmother; [memb.] V.F.W. and Legion Auxiliary, United Methodist Church, Pheasant Bowling League; [hon.] Honor: Is to be the Daughter-in-Law of this wonderful woman and also my father-in-Law. Award: 1st in the adult division of real women contest for this story I wrote.; [oth. writ.] Only the paper clipping. But I love to write in school.; [pers.] I want people to know not all mother-in-laws are disliked. I was greatly influenced by my father and my mother-in-law. They both told me a lot. Go for it and you'll find out weather it's good or not. Don't ever put your work down; someone, somewhere might like it.; [a.] Gettysburg, SD

WAIBLE, KRISTINA
[b.] October 20, 1948, Evansville, IN; [m.] Gene Waible, March 19, 1968; [ch.] Cheri Kristina and Tracy Jean; [ed.] North High School; [occ.] Self-employed; [pers.] Nothing is more powerful than the written word or more moving than when it's from the depths of the soul.; [a.] Newburgh, IN

WALLACE SR., JESSE STEVE
[pen.] "Corn Bread"; [b.] July 7, 1954, MS; [p.] Jesse Lee and Verna Mae (Both Deceased); [ch.] Hank Lucas, Bo Tyler and Jesse Jr.; [ed.] 12th grade diploma; [occ.] Truck Driver for Texas Prison System - TDCJ-ID; [hon.] Greatest Dad, Everyone's Friend; [oth. writ.] Country songs: "Things That Gets me Down," "Rail Road Penny," "You Broke the Law of Love This Time," "Covered Up With Blue," "Gypsy Band."; [pers.] Visionary - peacemaker philosopher - sentimental. "May you find the light within you to guide you through the dark days of life."; [a.] Huntsville, TX

WALTERS, GLADSTONE C.
[b.] March 19, 1931, Jamaica, WI; [p.] Uriah and Abigail Walters; [m.] Deceased, July 25, 1966; [ch.] One daughter; [ed.] Elementary to 6th grade.

After leaving elementary school, I went to trade school, I became a tailor by trade. After migrated to NY 1969, I went to school to be a Nursing Assistant.; [occ.] Retired Nursing Assistant; [memb.] Of First United Methodist Church, Chairperson for Evangelism. I sometimes give recitals at church for building fund, I always use other people's poems. I love music very much, and I have the feeling about music, so this is why I send this: "I am music."; [a.] Mount Vernon, NY

WARD, HELENA C.
[b.] September 16, 1955, Saint Kitts; [p.] Mary and Jonathan Ward; [ch.] Three; [ed.] High school; [occ.] Manager of Sales; [a.] New York, NY

WARKOMSKI, ROBERT C.
[pen.] Robert C. Warkomski; [b.] Nanticoke, PA; [p.] Mr. and Mrs. Jos B. Warkomski; [m.] Frances J. Warkomski, December 5, 1975; [ch.] Megan and Kerri; [ed.] Masters Degree - Penn State University, Post Masters - Univ. of Penna; [occ.] Speech/Language Pathologist; [memb.] HEA - NEA; [hon.] Honors - Penna Spch. and Hearing Assoc. and the American Spch/Hrg. Association; [oth. writ.] Play and Say - and Speech Aid series - Play and Say Board Games. Play and Say Sports Games - many articles in the PA spch/Hrg Assoc. Journal.; [pers.] To continue to enhance the quality and performance of students in urban schools.; [a.] Harrisburg, PA

WARNER, KIM
[b.] October 30, 1982, Flint, MI; [p.] Thomas and Janice Warner; [ed.] Edgerton Elementary and Carter Middle School (both in Clio, MI); [occ.] Student; [oth. writ.] None that have been published.; [pers.] Writing is a deep and powerful pleasure of mine. When I write I put all my time and imagination, into my writings. Even though I'm young the dramatic things in my life have put my thoughts to meaning.; [a.] Clio, MI

WARWOOD, SHEREL
[b.] May 27, 1942, Tremonton, UT; [p.] Stanley L. Lawrence, Rosaleen Lawrence; [m.] Lance E. Lunger, February 3, 1961, George L. Johnson, October 30, 1964, Melvin Aafedt, April 12, 1969, Carl J. Warwood, August 27, 1976; [ch.] Max Lunger, Robert L. Johnson; [ed.] Ogden High, Bonneville High, Weber College; [occ.] Retired Computer Operator, Hill AFB Utah; [hon.] President Jimmy Carter 1979; [pers.] I was inspired by the goodness and pureness of heart of my cousin Patt Cude, in Kona Hawaii. I have been greatly influence by the unconditional love of my brothers, Jack W. Lawrence and Stanley L. Lawrence Jr.

WARWOOD, SHEREL
[b.] May 27, 1942, Tremonton, UT; [p.] Stanley L. Lawrence and Rosaleen Lawrence; [m.] Lance E. Lunger, February 3, 1961, George L. Johnson, October 30, 1964, Melvin Aafedt, April 12, 1969, Carl J. Warwood, August 27, 1976; [ch.] Max Lunger and Robert L. Johnson; [ed.] Ogden High, Bonneville High, Weber College; [occ.] Retired Computer Operator, Hill AFB Utah; [hon.] President Jimmy Carter 1979; [pers.] I was inspired by the goodness and pureness of heart of my cousin Patt, in Kona Hawaii. I have been greatly influenced by the unconditional love of my brothers, Jack W. Lawrence and Stanley L. Lawrence Jr.; [a.] Clearfield, UT

WATERHOUSE, ALBERT R.
[b.] April 2, 1935, Trenton, NJ; [p.] Albert Waterhouse and Ruth Waterhouse; [m.] Lucille Waterhouse, January 10, 1957; [ch.] Cynthia, Albert, Charles, William, Ruth and Lucille; [ed.] Princeton University (Physics), Trenton Technical Institute (Electronics), Tess, ICS, NYU, assorted studies.; [occ.] Senior Court Adjuster, New

Jersey Manufacturers Ins. Co.; [memb.] Bethany Pres., NAPI, Arur Inv., Salvation Army, N.A. Art. Museum; [hon.] Paintings, carvings, in private collections in the USA and Europe, Springfield Hist. Soc. Museum, Palace of Peace, Geneva, Switzerland, N.A. Art Historical Museum; [oth. writ.] "One Cold Night in Korea," a memory of fear and waste - 1959. "A House Without Foundation" - personal viewpoint on deterioration of american society - 1973. "Bottom of the Barrel" - viewpoint on Democratic Party - 1993.; [pers.] I was born with both character and honor, sell either one, and you lose the other, leaving you with nothing.; [a.] Toms River, NJ

WATKINS, BARBARA
[b.] August 2, 1947, Waxahachie, TX; [p.] V.R. Compton, Anita Real Compton; [m.] Michael Watkins, May 23, 1970; [ch.] Michael Travis, Allison Elizabeth; [ed.] Everman High School; [occ.] Homemaker; [memb.] Former Vice President Bosque County Child Protective Service Board, Alderman, City of Morgan - City Council, Womens Literary Club, Board of Directors Morgan Area Community Assoc., Ladies Auxillary Volunteer Fire Dept.; [hon.] Have received no award yet, but I am greatly honored by having my wonderful family, my good husband and 2 beautiful children.; [oth. writ.] Weekly columnist in Bosque County News newspaper; [pers.] I am inspired by a variety of writers, not just poets. Currently I greatly admire Frank McCourt, author of "Angela's Ashes."; [a.] Morgan, TX

WEATHERS, TERESA K.
[pen.] Terri Weathers; [b.] July 19, 1928, South Bend, IN; [p.] Martin and Theresa Kuharich; [m.] H. Carlyle Weathers, May 30, 1958; [ed.] University of Indiana and University of Chicago; [occ.] Retired, widow; [memb.] Smithsonian, National Historic Preservation, H.G.I. St. Patrick's, Marinst Mission; [hon.] Honorable - Prince Hutt Province Queensland, Australia, Chamide Legacy; [oth. writ.] Manuals, Family Historian; [pers.] To live in present, mindful of past, aware of future, living with God's guidance and respect.; [a.] Gainesville, FL

WEAVER, PEGGY LOU
[b.] September 6, 1943, Cottage Grove, OR; [p.] Luie, Clara; [m.] Howard (deceased), March 3, 1990; [ch.] two daughters; [ed.] graduate LPN, plan on going back to school; [occ.] geriatric nurse for 30 years, headstart nurse; [memb.] Jacyette NPLPN (nurse) Church activities; [hon.] Graduated in top of LPN class, always in volunteer programs, taught Sunday school, sang in the choir church in high school, Christ To Life; [oth.writ.] I have two other works you might be interested in. I wrote one after the birth of my first grand child. I have been writing since 1963; [pers.] It has always been my delight in life to uplift my fellowmen in a positive and creative manner. I strive to pass along the love that has been given to me; [a.] Lebanon, OR.

WEBER, DWAYNE
[b.] March 13, 1967, Texas; [ed.] G.E.D. (Few credit hours in small business mgt.); [occ.] Manager, Brake Specialist, Inc - Austin; [memb.] Friend of Bill W.; [hon.] "Life Today" is my first published—I thank all involved; [oth. writ.] None published; [pers.] I'm an alcoholic and a drug addict. I do not drink or use drugs anymore. The Grace of God, as I understand Him, has enabled me to walk away from the gates of death and insanity. For that, I'm truly grateful!; [a.] Austin, TX

WELEVER, DEBBIE LINN
[b.] November 9, 1965; Chickasha, OK; [p.] Delores Sims and Jesse Balke; [m.] Kenneth Welever Jr., June 5, 1993; [ch.] Brianna, Derek, Allesha, Justin, Kenna; [ed.] Amber-Pocasset High School, Okla-

homa City Community College; [occ.] Homemaker; [memb.] former ABWA, PTO; [hon.] Carrier of the month (Chickasha Daily Express Newspaper at age 12); [oth.writ.] only what I write in my diaries; [pers.] I'd like to express my love and gratitude to my husband Ken and my 5 children for without their support and love I would not be here today!; [a.] Ft. Sill, OK.

WENDT-CARINGI, HILDEGARD
[pen.] Hildegard Wendt-Caringi; [b.] September 27, 1939, Germany; [p.] Helmut Wendt and Hildegard Moller; [m.] Ernest J. Caringi Jr., April 30, 1972; [ed.] Have a degree in Business Administration and studied 5 years Medical Instruments in Germany. I studied Stage Acting in Germany and later for stage and screen in Florida, mainly Hollywood, CA.; [occ.] Drama-Coach, Actress - Freelance; [memb.] SAG (Screen Actors Guild) and AFTRA; [hon.] 1962, 63 and 64 Twist Champion, 1965 "Miss Bikini of Germany" (International Bikini Girl), 1964-65 "Number one swim suit model of Florida," 1967-68 "L.A. Press Club" (Bikini Contest), 1981 "The Bronze Halo Award" from the Southern California Motion Picture Council, 1983 "Outstanding Contribution to the Theater" (Masquer's Club, Hollyw. CA. - actors club); [oth. writ.] German and English poetry, children's stories. Full length plays as well as scenes for my acting workshops. Work the show business column for a German newspaper in the USA; [pers.] Some of my poetry still reflects my work time experience as a refugee during the 2nd W.W. as a child. We are what we think and form the world with our thoughts, born out of the deepest respect for ourself and others.; [a.] Quartz Hill, CA

WESSELMANN, SHIRLEY A.
[pen.] Sheryl West; [b.] September 26, 1937, Mascoutah, IL; [p.] Willard and Irene Erb; [m.] Ed Wesselmann, June 8, 1955; [ch.] Three; [ed.] 12 yrs., 2 yrs. college Ass. Degree; [occ.] Retired CMA; [memb.] St. Joseph Church Quilters (St. Joseph), St. Joseph Womens Club; [hon.] Certified CMA; [oth. writ.] Had one poem published (Life). Poetic Voices of America; [pers.] I write poems about things I feel about everyday events and people. I also write children's stories. (Religious and ecology).; [a.] Freeburg, IL

WEST, JESSICA LYN
[b.] March 25, 1982, Bryan, TX; [p.] Debra Barker, William West, Robert Barker, Gayla West (Step-parents); [ed.] A&M Consolidated High; [memb.] Bengal Belle Drill Team; [hon.] Received "Gymnast of the Month Award" twice. Received "Honorary Mayor of Muskogee, OK." Received "Honorary Okie from Muskogee, OK."; [oth. writ.] I have been writing poems since I was in grade school. Now I am a freshman in high school and continue to enjoy writing poems.; [pers.] I think of life as a huge puzzle. You are always trying to find the missing pieces. When you think you have found the piece to make it complete, you have to take it back out because it doesn't quite fit right.; [a.] College Station, TX

WETHERBEE JR., JOHN
[b.] March 29, 1977, Dansville, NY; [p.] John Wetherbee Sr., Candace Wetherbee; [ed.] Dansville High School, Suny Geneseo; [occ.] Full-time student, sophomore—Suny Geneseo; [hon.] National Honor Society; [oth. writ.] A few poems published in school newspapers—high school graduation speech published in local newspaper—no national publishing.; [pers.] Real men are those who are not afraid to show their sensitivity and vulnerability. I have been greatly influenced by the works of Walt Whitman and poets from the Transcendental/ Romantic era, as well as music groups Rush and Dream Theater.; [a.] Dansville, NY

WHITACRE, E. DIANE
[pen.] Diantha James, Diane Correll; [b.] August 22, 1929, Barberton, OH; [p.] Harry G. James and Grace A. James; [m.] Raymond E. Whitacre, February 15, 1986; [ch.] Jeffrey Correll, John Correll; [ed.] Lodi H.S., Naples School of Music, Wooster Art Center; [occ.] Retired Music Teacher, Artist, Writer, Church Musician; [memb.] D.A.R. Baptist Church, Art League, Poet's Corner; [hon.] Class Salutatorian, Honor Society, Golden Homer, Art awards; [oth. writ.] Several poems in newspapers/ ideals/ newspaper columns, and article. "Blue Bird Hill and Other Poems" book, self-published about 200+ other poems.; [pers.] Poetry is my means of giving expression to all the complex beauty and mystery of life and death as the words form pictures in the mind, from great sorrow to great jubilation.; [a.] Lodi, OH

WHITE, ANJULI
[b.] May 7, 1982, Mansfield, OH; [p.] Bill and Lori White; [ed.] Moon Area High School, Moon Township, PA (in process); [occ.] Student of Moon Area High School; [memb.] YMCA, West Hills Christian Church, Moon Area High School Drama Club; [hon.] Hickory Hills Middle School 8th Grade Honor Roll, 1994-995, Human Rights Day Contest (poetry and picture), Jane Reichardt Language Arts Award 1995-1996, Springfield, MO Speech Tournament 1996; [oth. writ.] Human Rights Day (1st place); [pers.] "It is so easy to get caught up in glory, forgetting where the glory and the gifts came from—God."; [a.] Moon Township, PA

WHITEHEAD, JAMES MADISON
[b.] July 16, 1929, Mobile, AL; [p.] James Manikee and Fanny (Salmon) W.; [m.] Elena Hulings, June 11, 1955; [ch.] James M. M., John Douglas, Kenneth Clark, Julia Harker; [ed.] BA, U. Chgo. 1951, JD Tulane U. 1959, MS LA State U. 1963, Ph.D U Pitts. 1981, Bar: LA 1959. Acting Head Pub. Svscs. LA State U., New Orleans 1965, Head Sci., Library U. Colo., Boulder 1965-66, Asst. Prof. Head Dept, Circulation VA Poly Inst., Blacksburg 1967-70, Administrv. Asst., VA Poly Ins. and State U., Blacksburg 1970-71, Asst. Prof., Assoc. Prof., Law Librarian Coll. William and Mary, Williamsburg, VA 1971-76, Asst. Prof Suny, Geneseo 1978-80, Atlanta U. 1980-84, Pvt. Practice Stone Mountain, GA 1984-85, Libr. IV U. GA Law Library, Athens 1985, Cons. Ultra Microfiche Adv. Group Ency, Britannica, Blacksburg, 1969; [occ.] Law Librarian; [memb.] LA Bar Assn., Masons, Beta Phi Mu, Republican Christian Scientist; [oth. writ.] Logos of Library and Information Science: Apperceptions on the Institutes of Bibematics with Commentaries on the General Humanistic Method and the Common Philosophy, 1981. Asst. Cubmaster Webelos, Leader Boy Scouts Am., Blacksburg 1969-70, patrol dad, adviser, 1970-71. Cpl., USMC, 1952-54; [a.] Watkinsville, GA

WHITMIRE, STEVE
[pen.] John Oscar Stevens; [b.] March 7, 1974, Colorado Springs, CO; [p.] Lieselotte Whitmire; [ed.] Harrison High, looking to attend the Colorado Institute of Art to further my education.; [oth. writ.] In progress.; [pers.] The stride of my walk may be slow, but I've got one foot down now and there's no telling how fast I can run. Open your eyes to peace.; [a.] Colorado Springs, CO

WICKETT, KATHRYN LINDA
[b.] November 10, 1943, El Paso, TX; [p.] Dolores Rubincam and George Harvey; [m.] Richard A. Wickett, September 3, 1966; [ch.] Dolores Kalata and Kathryn More; [ed.] B.E.D. from U. of M. (1965), MA (1974), from U. of M. Diploma in Collegiate Teaching from U. of M. (1974); [occ.] Retired Assoc. Professor, Miami-Dade Community College; [memb.] Modern Language Association, National Council of Teachers of English; [hon.] Mortar Board, President of the Women's Gov. Assoc. at the University of Miami and Woman of the Year for that organization in 1965, listed in Who's Who in American Universities and Colleges in 1965.; [oth. writ.] Have not been published but served as advisor of Miambiance, The Miami-Dade Community College, Kendall Campus, literary-art magazine for six years.; [pers.] I believe in the survival of the body's energy that is the essence or soul of the individual; the body is but a shell to be cast off at death.; [a.] Parkland, FL

WIESE, JUDITH C.
[pen.] Judy; [b.] March 2, 1934, Memphis; [p.] Rosa and John Cleghorn; [m.] George W. Wiese, June 3, 1954; [ch.] Chris, John and Virginia Wiese; [ed.] Grad. Central High—Memphis, TN, 1 yr college—Bellhaven College, Jackson, MS, 2 1/2 yrs college (total), 1 1/2 yrs Memphis State College; [occ.] Housewife and Church Secretary; [memb.] Church, ATA Sorority; [oth. writ.] Just personal things—special occasions, friends (often by request); [pers.] I am a Christian—all our family enjoys writing. Especially our children—very original.; [a.] Ellenwood, GA

WILHELM, ASHLEY
[b.] Febuary 2, 1997; [ed.] 6th grader in Whitten Middle School; [a.] Jxn, MS

WILKINSON, DAVID EMIL
[b.] September 12, 1986, Boston; [p.] Dr. Ruth Ruprecht; [ed.] I go to the Runkle School. I am in the 5th grade, and my favorite subjects are Writing and Math. Also, every Saturday I go to a German school.; [hon.] Every Tues., Thurs., and Sat. I go to gymnastics. I have competitions against many other gyms, and at the end, awards are handed out. (I have not ever gotten an award from gymnastics).; [oth. writ.] In school I write many fascinating stories and poems. This is probably the first poem that I wrote that is getting published.; [a.] Brookline, MA

WILLEY, LORRI
[b.] March 4, 1966, Stockton, CA; [ch.] Adam Lee and Anthony James Guthrie; [ed.] Franklin High, Andon College; [occ.] Student of Literature; [oth. writ.] Array of short stories, poems, and epics; [pers.] I have be a artist of life forever. The pay is my canvas and the words my colors. Everyone is an artist, looking for an inspiration.; [a.] Stockton, CA

WILLIAMS, ALBERTA
[b.] October 17, 1965, Abington, PA; [p.] Suzanne Johnson; [ch.] Tyshawn Tyre Williams-McRoy; [occ.] Making cards for special occasions, employed at Northtec Estee Lauder Company; [memb.] I am a member of Jacobs Tabernacle in Yardley Penna. My grandmother, the Reverend Francis Alberta Lee, and my lovely mother, Suzanne Johnson, father, James Williams, of N.J. I am a single parent and I am also a fashion model for an agency in Pennsylvania.; [pers.] I would like to thank God for everything he has done for me and dedicate this poem to my brothers, Paul Williams, Larry Williams, Jimmy Williams, my sister Betty Williams and to a host of nieces and nephews. And I thank God for giving me a son who's the light of my life. God bless.; [a.] Bristol, PA

WILLIAMS, ANN
[pen.] Ann Alyssa Elise; [b.] April 21, 1946, Jerome, AZ; [p.] George Stotts and Ruth Stotts; [m.] Stephen Williams, June 9, 1984; [ch.] Bill Owen III and Sean C. Owen; [ed.] Mingus High, Ajo High; [occ.] Antique sales; [memb.] American Bechet's Association, Scottsdale United Methodist Church; [pers.] I have love, excitement, re-

spect of life and all things living which reflects in my writing. I hope to leave behind a trail of compassion and tenderness that will influence others.; [a.] Scottsdale, AZ

WILLIAMS, DORA L.
[b.] May 24, 1933; Poughkeepsie; [p.] Francis I. Griffin and Dora L. Griffin; [m.] Robert M. Williams; December 3, 1957; [ch.] 5; [ed.] Chamber Street Num. 3 School Kingston, NY; [occ.] Housewife; [memb.] 4-H early 1940's Rockville, CT; [hon.] Honorable Mention 4-H Rockville, CT; (Horse Handling); [oth.writ.] Thousands (none published); [pers.] Look unto yourself and to God to achieve your personal best.; [a.] Rock Hill, NY.

WILLIAMS, J'HON C.
[pen.] J'hon; [b.] August 8, 1964, United States; [p.] Mary Brown, Kenneth Williams; [m.] X Runner up: Brenda McSally; [ed.] Emerson/Drama, Hollywood Way/Drama, L.A. Recording Workshop - Audio Screenwriting School, LA and New York, Wentworth Mst. Tech (Boston); [occ.] Development/C.E.O. Alternate Wave Productions Operations—John Hancock (Boston); [memb.] Club Passim (Cambridge MA), Amnesty International; [hon.] A few; [oth. writ.] Pretty Bartender (Boston) in catalog: Poetry for "Damoka" (China, Italy, New York). In LA, California, screenplays "One Moment" and "Time Division." Two books of poetry "Silent Rain" and "In Deep Thought." Others in progress . . . .; [pers.] My ambition is to break down the walls between humanity and communication through words of understanding and love— "Sincere Concern."; [a.] Cambridge, MA

WILLIAMS, JOHN C.
[pen.] Lewis Knowlton; [b.] June 18, 1927, Long Island, NY; [p.] J. Frank Williams, Ruth Knowlton Williams; [m.] Rosemarie Mehner Williams, June 27. 1959; [ch.] John C. Williams; [ed.] McBurney School, N.Y.C. - Adelphi University, B.S., M.A.; [occ.] Retired after a thirty-five year career in teaching; [oth. writ.] One poem, "Cape Sands," appeared in a collection of poems.; [pers.] Writing to me is like a vehicle of my inner self.; [a.] Northport, NY

WILLIAMS, LESLIE
[b.] October 27, 1943, Oakland, CA; [p.] Frank and Leila Carter; [m.] (Deceased), married 30 years; [ch.] Lisa, David, Jon, Jenny; [ed.] Lakeland High School, Polk Community College; [occ.] Registered Nurse; [memb.] Phi Beta Kappa, Woman's Aglow, Carpenter's Home Church where I am an elder; [hon.] Dean's List; [oth. writ.] First book in progress; [pers.] Started writing while at home recovering from accident. Enjoy addressing the fundamental issues of life and the love of our God.; [a.] Lakeland, FL

WILLIAMS, PAUL L.
[pen.] Paul; [b.] September 3, 1968, Macon, GA; [p.] Carlton and Sarah Williams; [ed.] High school, Air Force Tech School, Inside Wireman Electrical Apprenticeship School (IBEW LU 1316); [occ.] Apprentice Wireman; [oth. writ.] "Inside Eternity," "The Gift," "The Morning Chore" (none published).; [pers.] We are only as lonely, offended, or sad as we let ourselves be. If you don't let yourself be lonely, offended, or sad, then you never will be.; [a.] Danville, GA

WILLIAMS, RAY
[b.] August 30, 1964, Midland, TX; [p.] Bill and Jean Williams; [m.] Cindy Williams; [ch.] Richard; [ed.] Life; [pers.] My loving wife is my inspiration.; [a.] Memphis, TN

WILLIAMS, TRACY PAUL
[pen.] Paul Johnson; [b.] September 10, 1975, Tyler, TX; [p.] Brenda Lewis, Lula Williams; [m.] LaShundra Price; [ch.] LaShuntre Williams, TyRoddrick Stewart; [ed.] Robert E. Lee High; [occ.] Incarcerated writer; [hon.] Who's Who Among American High School Students/ multiple times; [oth. writ.] Presently writing an autobiography: "Blessing in Disguise." Also writing a continual journal of prison life, and I have an article called "The End Times."; [pers.] I strive to be a witness in my writings and let everyone know the truth that Jesus Christ is Lord, plus he is soon to return.; [a.] Tyler, TX

WILLIAMSON, BILLY JACK
[b.] December 17, 1950, Tuscaloosa, AL; [p.] Joseph Williamson and Viva Williamson; [ed.] Tuscaloosa County High School; [occ.] None at present; [hon.] Several military awards including the Purple Heart NDSM-VSM/1 - Vcm/60-CAR; [oth. writ.] Other poems of similar content and structure.; [pers.] Poetry is a building block and I hope I have reflected that ingredient in my poem.; [a.] Tuscaloosa, AL

WILSON, JEFFREY T.
[b.] September 9, 1953, Evansville, IN; [p.] Rufus M. and Vonda L. Wilson; [m.] Annalee C. Wilson, June 12, 1976; [ch.] Aaron M., Brandon M. and Aubrie M.; [ed.] BS-ME Rose Hulman Institute of Technology, Fort Branch High School; [occ.] Petroleum Engineer; [a.] Evansville, IN

WILSON, YANA PALAMARA
[pen.] Yana; [b.] September 11, 1944, Athens, Greece; [p.] Maria and Eleas Palamara; [ch.] Eleas Hugh Wilson; [oth. writ.] Children's stories, newspaper, philosophical and social articles; [pers.] Until we start walking backwards we should take past experience as reference for tomorrows not excuses for our actions.; [a.] Orange Park, FL

WINDER, BROOKE
[b.] February 2, 1981, Colorado; [p.] Aurena Lynn Winder; [ed.] Deer Trail High School; [occ.] Student; [hon.] Perfect attendance; [pers.] This has been a great opportunity for me, thanks to A. Winder and Edgar Allan Poe's poetry.; [a.] Deer Trail, CO

WISNER, JENNIE
[b.] August 26, 1982, Maryland; [p.] Tom and Kathie; [ed.] From Flower Hill Elementary to Igtosville Elementary and in the 8th grade at Gathersburg Middle; [occ.] Student; [pers.] With a pen and paper, I write what I feel, and I feel what I write. When I write it's my heart talking.; [a.] Igtosville, MD

WISNIACH, MICHAEL N.
[b.] August 1, 1978, Fountain Valley, CA; [p.] Joyce Wesson and Stan Wisniach; [ed.] Rancho Alamitos High School, Golden West College; [occ.] Web-Designer for the Internet; [hon.] 1995-96 Nominee "Who's Who Among American High School Students," 1996 Teen Talent Runner up - "Short Stories," 1996 Americanism Educational League Slogan Contest Winner; [oth. writ.] Few poems printed in local school magazine.; [pers.] Jesus Christ has given me writing as a gift of release. I am influenced by the writings of Dylan Thomas, e.e. Cummings and Shakespeare.; [a.] Westminster, CA

WITHERSPOON, JUDI
[b.] February 17, 1962, Detroit; [p.] June and Julian Witherspoon; [ed.] Wayne State University Psychology Student - Dean's List; [occ.] Business Owner (Co-owner), Gift Shop (Ann Arbor, MI); [memb.] Committee Member for the Lighthouse Youth Ambassadors, Member of the Women's

International League for Peace and Freedom; [hon.] Family and Friends Creative Writing Award; [oth. writ.] I am currently working on a book entitled "The Light of Soul." It is a book affirmations and poetry. (I am a children's advocate so I have dedicated a section to children).; [pers.] There is nothing more pleasurable than bonding with people through reading poetry. Bonding and poetry combined creates a spirituality which sort of lends itself to a peaceful ambiance for its reader and allows for all kinds of emotions to surface. I have found poetry to bring many of our own personal "abstracts" to light while bringing out the light in ourselves. I believe life is one big affirmation, learn from it, live it, hear it, accept it, believe in it and write about it!; [a.] Belleville, MI

WITT, JON MICHAEL
[pen.] Jon Michael Witt; [b.] January 13, 1969, La Porte, IN; [p.] James Witt (Deceased), Jennifer Witt; [m.] Sue Ellen Witt (Deceased), January 8, 1994; [ed.] La Porte High School, Vincennes University (Fine Art); [occ.] Clerk-Speedway Convenience Store; [hon.] Best of Show Award ("Flown-The Coop") (Graduating Student Art Exhibitions '89), 2nd place (Annual Art Exhibition '89), ("Rhythmic Progression") "Flown"-Ceramic/ "Rhythmic" - Figure Drawing; [oth. writ.] Few other poems (none published).; [pers.] Wrote part of "Seasons" 5th grade, improved and added a new for competition. Always felt I had a keen intellect, but never acted upon my poetry skills.; [a.] La Porte, IN

WOCHOS, JACKIE
[pen.] Rabbit ears, Wacker, Torky; [b.] November 9, 1983; Madison, W; [p.] Tom Wochos, Nancy Wochos; [ed.] Currently at Edison Middle School, Wheaton IL; [pers.] Don't wait for your dreams to happen, make them happen; [a.] Wheaton, IL.

WOLFORD, SHARON R.
[pen.] Sharon Raedelle and SRW; [b.] August 4, 1960, Warrenton, VA; [p.] Lee S. and Gloria A. Pearson; [m.] David A. Wolford, July 20, 1980; [ch.] David Adair Jr., Christopher Michael, Amanda Leigh, Rebecca Anne; [ed.] Graduate of Woodbridge Sr. High School in Woodbridge, VA in 1978; [occ.] Business owner . . . Antique/Thrift Store . . . also Notary Public; [memb.] Billy Ray Cyrus Fan Club; [hon.] 1993 GMFL Cheerleading Commissioner; [oth. writ.] Submissions to Country Beat, Country Fever, Country Spectacular and modern screen country music magazines. "The Dentist Dance," "You Make Your Own Luck."; [pers.] The poem I submitted in this book is dedicated to my sister, Candice, and in memory of her best friend, "Susie" Dixon. "Dreams come true if you believe" —Billy Ray Cyrus—and "you make your own luck . . . if you were walking down the street and saw $1,000 lying there . . . would it be luck that picks it up?" SRW; [a.] Manassas, VA

WORAM, ROSEMARIE
[pen.] Shona Woram; [b.] November 14, 1935, Roosevelt Long Island, NY; [p.] William and Marie Woram; [m.] William Kruppen Bacher; [ch.] William, Rosemarie and Frank; [ed.] Holy Redeemer Elementary School, Baldwin High School; [occ.] Publication Proofreader, Theatre Industry Manager; [pers.] I have always been deeply moved by the writings of Omar Kyyam, Khayyam.; [a.] Freeport Long Island, NY

WRIGHT, ANNE
[b.] April 5, 1969, Hayes, KS; [p.] Carl Helm, Melba Sunley and Lila Girton; [m.] Dennis Wright, July 1, 1995; [ch.] Erika Wright; [ed.] Computer Class; [occ.] Financial Worker; [oth. writ.] Self poetry; [pers.] My grandmother adopted me when I was two. My aunt Lila became my sister and "My

other Mother." I wrote this poem for her just before she died from cancer to let her know how I felt for her.; [a.] Kansas City, MO

WULLENWEBER, ANGIE
[pen.] Angelia, Owl; [b.] March 5, 1981; [p.] Ronald Wullenweber and Sheila Wullenweber; [ed.] East Central High School; [occ.] Student; [memb.] Faith Baptist Church; [oth. writ.] A few poems published in underground magazines, articles in the school yearbook.; [pers.] Much love to my friends and family. Special thanks to my aunt, Sherry Zinser, for all your love and understanding.; [a.] Guilford, IN

YANNOTTI, MONIQUE
[pen.] Monique; [b.] April 8, 1948; Furich, Switzerland; [p.] Frieda and Karl Aschwanden; [m.] Divorced; [ch.] Angelique (7) and Dean (12); [ed.] 9 years primary and secondary school, 3 years commercial school; [occ.] 3 years legal secretary, 8 years buyer for import/export company, Jewelry Designer, Jewelry Store Owner (20 Years); [oth.writ.] Currently I am working on a book about Gods love and His will in our lives; [pers.] God is the author of my poems-Jesus Christ-His son is my first love. The Bible is my daily guide (psalm 119); [a.] Mound, MN.

YEATTS, TWILA EVONNE
[b.] August 26, 1979, Lynchburg, VA; [p.] Margaret L. Yeatts, James L. Yeatts; [ed.] Christian Liberty Academy Satellite Schools; [occ.] Senior in high school; [oth. writ.] I have written several poems and psalms. Many of my psalms were inspired by the Psalms of David.; [pers.] I have been home schooled since an early age, and I give praise to God for I truly feel the home is the best environment for learning and is the most rewarding and complete form of education. I strive to bring a complete understanding of God's love for people in all my works.; [a.] Lynchburg, VA

YEE, CHRISTINE A.
[b.] June 13, 1977, Santa Monica, CA; [ed.] Currently a second year Psychobiology major at UCLA; [pers.] Although this is my first real attempt at writing poetry, I've come to realize that poetry is not merely rhyme and rhythm, it is an eloquent depiction of what the heart sees and experiences.; [a.] Palos Verdes Estates, CA

YOUNG, JOANNE M.
[b.] August 25, 1947, Minneapolis, MN; [p.] Walter Smith, Vesta Smith; [m.] John E. Young (Deceased), May 28, 1983; [oth. writ.] Book of poems currently in the publishing stage.; [pers.] My poems reflect the human soul, the journey we all must take through life.; [a.] Saint Louis Park, MN

ZACH, ROBYN LEIGH
[occ.] Elementary School Teacher; [pers.] This poem is dedicated to the loving memory of my uncle who served as a scout in the United States Army on Okinawa during World War II. His care and guidance have always inspired me.; [a.] Belmar, NJ

ZADELL, WILLIAM A.
[b.] January 2, 1977, Hatfield, PA; [p.] Bill and Janet Zadell; [ed.] Hatfield Elementary School, North Penn High School, Montgomery County Community College, Shippensburg University; [occ.] Student; [memb.] Environmental Defense Fund, National Wildlife Federation, World Wildlife Fund, Defenders of Wildlife, Natural Resources Defense Council; [hon.] Dean's List; [pers.] All steps must be taken to ensure the wildlife that is here today, will be here tomorrow. I base most of my writing on the beauty of nature around us.; [a.] Hatfield, PA

ZAMBONI, MARIA AUGUSTA
[pen.] Mimmi, Ceci; [b.] September 25, 1939, Bologna, Italy; [p.] Antonio Zamboni and Iris Martinelli Zamboni; [oth. writ.] Several poems (personal collection).; [pers.] I wish to think that in my life I make a difference at least for someone. Poetry "I experience as the immediate, powerful unison" of my whole being with God, my fellow brothers and sisters, nature, the world at large . . . a mystical experience innovating my life.; [a.] Birmingham, AL

ZAMUDIO, JUAN H.
[pen.] Jazz Logan; [b.] August 25, 1975, U.S.A.; [p.] Herminia and Juan Zamudio; [occ.] Screenwriter, Novelist, Poet; [oth. writ.] Screenplays/Novels: Terror Incorporated, The Hybrid, Chaos: The Fall and Mephisto's Creed. Poems: They, Them, and I, City Streets, Great Lost and Found, Sandman and Fear; [pers.] To the greatest guides to the realm of fantasy and imagination, Don Quixote and Sancho Panza. Thanks Mom and Dad.; [a.] West Covina, CA

ZIMMERMAN, VIRGINIA
[b.] Sacramento, CA; [oth. writ.] Articles published in magazines and newspapers.; [a.] Roseville, CA

ZIPPRICH, SUSAN R.
[b.] December 29, 1918, Springfield, IL; [p.] John, Zetta Osborn Zimmerman; [m.] Robert L. Zipprich Deceased, October 17, 1942; [ch.] Lynn, Robert Jr., John; [ed.] High school, business college; [occ.] Retired from business; [memb.] Bible Temple (home church) Women's Aglow Fellowship; [oth. writ.] I have a book entitled, His Way, with songs of praise and deliverance, in preparation for publication.; [pers.] Most of my verses are spiritual in nature and reflect my relationship with the Lord Jesus Christ.; [a.] Canby, OR

ZITLAW, AL
[b.] May 10, 1933, Chicago, IL; [m.] Jo Ann Zitlaw, January 28, 1958; [ch.] Clifford, Gregory, Carrie; [ed.] Graduate Univ. of Calif, Berkeley, BA Psychology '59; [occ.] Retired; [a.] Chico, CA

ZUCKSCHWERDT, HEIDE
[b.] August 7, 1965, Cadillac, MI; [m.] Richard Zuckschwerdt, October 8, 1988; [ch.] Joshua William - McDaniel, Latisha Nichole, Morgan Ray Shell, Sierrah Gray; [ed.] Manton High, Mercy School of Practical Nursing; [occ.] Licensed Practical Nurse; [a.] Saint Charles, MI

ZUKERMAN, LARRY BRUCE
[b.] March 12, 1968, Los Angeles, CA; [p.] Mel and Sefi Zukerman; [ed.] Some college; [occ.] I work for a non-profit organization providing people with basic necessities.; [hon.] High school literary awards; [oth. writ.] Many poems and short stories; [pers.] I write for personal pleasure when I am inspired. I try to reflect my life experiences.; [a.] Tarzana, CA

Index
of
Poets

Index

Turner, Joseph 513
Turner, Juanita 297
Turner, Tiffany 261
Turney, Regina 276
Twardesky, Loretta 19
Twarozynski, Bethany 228
Twiname, B. G. 391
Tyler, Ernest 501
Tyson, Ruby Lois 65

U

Umberger, Judith W. 427
Umphlett, Kasandra 377
Unger, Irene Perry 9
Ungureit, Christopher J. Jr. 414
Upton, Christia 93
Urquhart, Debra T. 407

V

Vaid, Niti 526
Valco, Magda E. 206
Valenti, Daniell 89
Valentine 265
Valentine, Christopher W. 461
Valley, Stephen 108
Vallo, Charles 20
Vallone, Gail 62
Van Den Berg, Jerome J. 505
Van Fleet, Heath 327
Van Hoff, Kempton 329
Van Riper, Bradley W. 266
Van Roekel, Jennifer 170
Van Stockum, Irene 85
Van Veen, Ann 503
VanAllen, Steve 472
Vancott, Lorri 320
Vandergriff, Chad 53
VanderKolk, Donald 189
Vanderwarker, Barbara Jane 370
Vanourney, Patricia L. 495
Vanover, Justin 446
VanSchoick, Sarah 448
Vario, Andrew F. 163
Vasquez, Sara 503
Vasvary, Zoltan 249
Vaughn, Mary 279
Vega, Carlos 402
Vega, Olivia 393
Velasquez, Alicia Vivian 425
Velasquez, Anthony 519
Velez, Fausto A. 99
Veliky, Michele A. 462
Venkat, Parth 348
Ventre, Lisa 345
Vera-Gil, Maria O. 240
Verador, Robert James 102
Verdin, Dana Louise Benson 360
Verdoorn, Eric 52
Verrinder, Teesha 222
Vert, Chris 424
Vick, Christine 411
Vickers, Barbara 450
Vickers, Terrell 461
Vidrine, Marilyn Y. 275
Viera, Jose M. 375
Viglione, Dawn 318
Vilassakdanont, Art 265
Vincent, Duane Maxwell 356
Vines-Scales, Patricia 177

Voet, Cheryl Lynn 247
Voland, Melanie Rae 360
Volden, Daniel M. 210
Von, Lord Feister III 91
VonBernuth, Schelika 216
Vories, Dawn E. 105
Vories, Joshua D. 38
Vorves, Jamie 315

W

Wadas, Janelle 463
Waddell, Patrick A. 171
Wade, Eric Clayton 294
Wade, Karil 531
Wager, Joan 68
Wagner, C. 91
Wagner, Jeremiah 176
Waible, Kristina 534
Waid, Roger A. Sr. 442
Wainwright, Jefferson 400
Waite, Steven 73
Wajda, Donna D. 110
Wakefield, Victor E. 332
Walker, Andrea 486
Walker, Doris 457
Walker, Jaime Marie 351
Walker, Jeff D. 438
Walker, Jennifer 137
Walker, Kayla Spears 353
Walker, Lea Anne 503
Walker, Sarah 256
Walkes, Dawn L. 473
Walkinshaw, Kerri J. Incitti 346
Wall, Robert E. Jr. 56
Wallace, Dianne 466
Wallace, Jesse Steve Sr. 105
Wallin, Andrew 424
Walsh, Dawn 313
Walsh-Lyons, RoseMarie 65
Walters, Gladstone C. 43
Wang, Alan 79
Wang, Stephanie 230
Wantland, Karen 382
Ward, Helena 522
Ward, Jennifer 531
Ward, Kristen 244
Warden, Nancy O. 110
Ware, Michelle 187
Warech, Evelyn 245
Warkomski, Robert C. 346
Warner, Kim 164
Warner, Vernon A. 505
Warren, Stefanie 355
Wartenberg, Estie 202
Warwood, Sherel 35
Wascom, Renee 100
Washington, Mary E. 366
Wasnik, Amanda 316
Waterhouse, A. R. 530
Watkins, Barbara 112
Watson, Jaclyn 517
Watson, John 419
Watt, Andrew James 524
Waugh, Linda 359
Weathers, Teresa K. 233
Weaver, Daniel B. Jr. 445
Weaver, Peggy 532
Webb, Darlene 152
Webb, Hollis 253
Weber, Dwayne 70

Weber, Helen E. 531
Weber, Ralph R. 83
Weekes, Joseph S. 3
Weekly, John David 469
Wehrley, Karol 500
Wei, Hsing-ju 512
Weigand-Buckley, Amber L. 196
Weigel, Diana J. 6
Weigert, Wendy 455
Weiner, Jessica Rose 248
Weintraub, Judith 98
Weisfield, Russell 278
Weiss, Jessica 390
Weist, David L. 212
Welch, Deanna 277
Weldon, Amelia 78
Welever, Debbie 406
Wells, Ashley S. 189
Wells, Sharon Shelya 418
Wells, Terrence 183
Wendlandt, Keturah Ruth 159
Wendt-Caringi, Hildegard 382
Wessel, Joe 507
Wesselman, Regina 72
Wesselmann, S. 80
West, Bill C. 95
West, Jessica Lyn 372
Westbrook, Raymond R. 61
Westergaard, Elizabeth 53
Westerman, David 99
Wetherbee, John 252
Wethington, Regina L. 433
Whetstone, Leanna Lynn 59
Whitaker, Chloe.Mourai 69
Whitaker, Teresa G. 14
White, Anjuli 179
White, Bonnie 287
White, Brandy N. 82
White, Sheldon S. 277
White, Tricia 318
Whitehead, J. M. 379
Whitehead, Robert W. Jr. 62
Whitelock, June 34
Whitley, Julie 227
Whitmire, Steve 311
Whitmore, Jean 414
Whitmore-Hennigh, Susan 514
Whitson, Shawnna R. 517
Whittaker, Sharon 444
Whyman, Marvin H. 506
Wickett, Kathryn Linda 488
Wiederhorn, Miriam 373
Wiegmann, Amanda 272
Wiese, Judy C. 383
Wightman, Bertha W. 237
Wilburn, Jimmy 356
Wilcove, J. 354
Wilde, Nichole 148
Wilde, Novalea S. 161
Wilde, Stacy J. 141
Wilhelm, Ashley 396
Wilkins, L. Farrell 248
Wilkinson, David 234
Wilkinson, Erin L. 179
Willey, Lorri Eve 140
Williams, Alberta 458
Williams, Alyce Trimm 4
Williams, Ann Alyssa-Elise 197
Williams, Anne S. 380
Williams, Christopher A. 156
Williams, Daniel 495

Williams, Dora L. 81
Williams, Eileen 37
Williams, Jean Shepard 372
Williams, John C. 407
Williams, Leisha 343
Williams, Leslie 328
Williams, Onika 499
Williams, Paul L. 55
Williams, Ray 49
Williams, Robert 480
Williams, Samantha 525
Williams, Tonya 527
Williams, Tracy Paul 159
Williamson, Billy Jack 62
Wilson, Amile G. C. 496
Wilson, C. L. 336
Wilson, D. Scott 430
Wilson, Dorothy-Marie 413
Wilson, Elizabeth 7
Wilson, Erin M. 318
Wilson, James Ashley 450
Wilson, Jeffrey T. 525
Wilson, Jennifer L. 204
Wilson, Mary Ann 531
Wilson, Rachel A. 492
Wilson, Rhett Ray 234
Wilson, Sara Jennifer 233
Wilson, Sophia 501
Wilson, Yoina Palameira 63
Wimmer, Richard O. 342
Winchel, Ernest E. 129
Winder, Brooke 428
Winner, C. F. 42
Winthrop, Philip J. Jr. 429
Wirt, Katie 236
Wishon, Michael 113
Wisner, Jennie 499
Wisniach, Michael 298
Withee, Maureen 291
Witherspoon, Judi 201
Witt, Jon M. 207
Wittenberg, Martin Daniel 321
Wittig, Doris Jackson 105
Wochnick, Rebecca E. 534
Wochos, Jackie 42
Wolf, Sharon L. 79
Wolfert, Sol 506
Wolfgang, William G. 30
Wolfley, Cynthia 235
Wolford, Peggy A. 22
Wolford, Sharon Raedelle 487
Wong, Jennifer 499
Wonsewith, Leo J. 162
Wood, Charlotte B. 198
Wood, David A. 354
Wood, John M. 66
Wood, Sarah A. 211
Wooderson, David R. 59
Woodhouse, Lavall V. 397
Woodlock, Shirley 135
Woodruff, Kimberly 145
Woodward, T. R. 5
Woram, Shona 525
Worley, Cynthia 55
Worrell, Jenene 215
Wray, Sandra L. 437
Wright, Anne 126
Wright, Geraldine 285
Wright, Jeff 197
Wright, Kellie J. 284
Wullenweber, Angie 245